Simon Jenkins

England's Thousand Best Houses

With photographs by
QUINTIN WRIGHT of The Times
and the National Trust Archives

ALLEN LANE
an imprint of
PENGUIN BOOKS

ALLEN LANE

Published by the Penguin Group
Penguin Books Ltd, 80 Strand, London WC2R 0RL, England
Penguin Putnam Inc., 375 Hudson Street, New York, New York 10014, USA
Penguin Books Australia Ltd, 250 Camberwell Road, Camberwell, Victoria 3124, Australia
Penguin Books Canada Ltd, 10 Alcorn Avenue, Toronto, Ontario, Canada M4V 3B2
Penguin Books India (P) Ltd, 11, Community Centre, Panchsheel Park, New Delhi – 110 017, India
Penguin Books (NZ) Ltd, Cnr Rosedale and Airborne Roads, Albany, Auckland, New Zealand
Penguin Books (South Africa) (Pty) Ltd, 24 Sturdee Avenue, Rosebank 2196, South Africa

Penguin Books Ltd, Registered Offices: 80 Strand, London WC2R 0RL, England

www.penguin.com

First published 2003
5

Copyright © Simon Jenkins, 2003

The moral right of the author has been asserted

The Photographic Acknowledgements on page 950
constitute an extension of this copyright page

Designed by Andrew Barker
Set in PostScript Adobe Minion and PostScript Monotype Perpetua
Typeset by Rowland Phototypesetting Ltd, Bury St Edmunds, Suffolk
Printed and bound in England by Butler and Tanner Ltd

A CIP catalogue record for this book is availabe from the British Library

ISBN 0-713-99596-3

Illustration on page ii: East Riding Renaissance: Burton Agnes Hall (Yorkshire)

Contents

Introduction:
The English House

'An English house – gray twilight pour'd
On dewey pastures, dewy trees,
Softer than sleep – all things in order stored,
A haunt of ancient Peace.'
                              – Tennyson

High on the hills behind Penzance in Cornwall is one of the oldest extant settlements in England, Iron Age Chysauster. It survives because the walls are built of local granite. Each house is formed of a protective enclosure round a two-chambered shelter. Inside the shelter would have been a fire, outside a conduit for water. Here ancient Britons found comfort and security. They found home.

First of all we live in houses. We also live in villages, streets, towns, cities. But in houses we are most ourselves. The Englishman's home is more than his castle. It is his face, his taste, his refuge and his family hearth.

This book tells the story not just of grand homes but of habitations of all sorts. In defining the word house, I soon found that I could not sensibly distinguish castle from palace, house from hut, roof from ruin, live from dead. My list embraces any structure in which men and women have laid their heads, provided only that they are in some degree accessible to public view.

I visited these buildings after writing a similar book on English churches and the experience was as moving as it was different. While places of worship were built according to the authority and liturgy of the Church, people built houses for themselves. A house was useful first and beautiful second. From this derives the joy of visiting English houses. They are a conversation between utility and beauty down the ages. Through them we hear the echo of our collective selves – and remember who we are.

Restoration House, Rochester (Kent)

THE MEDIEVAL HOUSE

The Roman legions withdrew from Britain in the 5th century AD. They left villas of astonishing luxury to decay and farms run to seed. Soon these villas might never have existed. The dwelling of the ancient Britons and Anglo-Saxons was a hut of stone or wood and daub, according to materials available locally. Animals and humans sheltered together. Stockaded settlements were located usually near water. Structures from these 'dark ages' have been rebuilt at Cockley Cley and West Stow in Norfolk.

The most prominent dwelling was a 'hall' for the village chief. The interior space would have enjoyed a screen for privacy at the far end from the door. From this hall evolved the earliest architectural form, the cruck or inverted V-frame composed of two upright logs, with a ridge beam and subsidiary rafters laid between them. The number of crucks was a sign of wealth and came to indicate rank. The military chevron had its origin in this inverted V. The end cruck formed a 'gavel' or gable, a word found alike in Old Norse, English, French and High German, wherever the northern climate demanded a sloping roof. The division of a wall into bays between crucks and with a gable at the end became the standard grammar of English building.

The Norman Conquest in the 11th century was characterized, above all, by the use of stone, whether for churches, castles or houses. The Norman keep is the earliest and still most spectacular residential building in England. As assertions of territorial control, the keeps of the Tower of London (London, C), Dover (Kent), Colchester (Essex) and Conisbrough (Yorks, S) would have towered over their settlements. To those used to wattle, mud and thatch, the appearance of a hall with the lord's private chamber either beside or above it must have been awesome. At Castle Hedingham in Essex such a keep is displayed virtually intact, still held in line of descent by marriage from the Norman de Veres.

As the Middle Ages progressed such fortified residences did not disappear. They lived on most prominently in the pele towers of the Border country. Almost all old houses in this region display peles, and are found as far south as Bolling Hall in Bradford (Yorks, W) and Turton outside Bolton (Lancs). But as the need for defensible space declined, architecture became domestic, based on the hall rather than the tower. Whether as the Great Hall of a peripatetic monarch or baron, or as the simple room of a local chief, hall houses were the dominant form of the English house for half a millennium after the Conquest.

The engineering of these structures paralleled that of the local church. Overhead would be a high wooden roof, its carved beams reflecting a lord's wealth and its decoration displaying his heraldry and taste. In the centre burned a constant fire, its smoke lost in the rafters or escaping through a louvre in the roof. At the formal end was a dais for the family, raised about the mud and dirt of the floor. The dais end was often ornamented by a canopy of wood or cloth and lit by a large side window, features that became more decorative over the centuries. Behind the dais the family's private rooms became progressively more comfortable. A ground floor parlour or undercroft supported an upstairs solar. This solar was extended into a wing at right angles to the hall, sometimes as a Great Chamber with moulded plaster ceiling, heraldic fireplace and tapestries on the walls.

At the other end of the hall was a screen to keep out the draught from the entrance. Above it was often a gallery for minstrels. Beyond the screens passage, a second wing contained kitchens, butteries, breweries, so-called 'offices' and servants' quarters. Given their different use, the family and service wings at opposite ends of the hall were rarely similar in appearance. Yet they led to a rough U-shape which, as porches also became elaborate, formed the familiar E-plan of Tudor architecture. At Fountains Hall (Yorks, N) we can see the effort to which Elizabethan masons went to impose symmetry on such façades. Additions to the rear of the wings produced the H-plan, and s the arms of the H were filled in with gatehouses and galleries, courtyards were formed. Usually two courtyards sufficed but at Knole (Kent) there were eventually seven.

The Great Hall was a hospitable place and the family and its dependent community ate there together. But it was also the setting for territorial authority. Here the head of the family would conduct the business of the manor in public. The hall thus perfectly embraced the public and private roles of the English landowner. Dozens of people could live beneath the same roof, yet without impinging on each other's space. The plan was supremely flexible. At Haddon Hall (Yorks, N) we can see the family chambers dividing and sub-dividing as successive Vernons changed their living requirements. At Tudor Hampton Court (London, W), privy chambers, suites, audience rooms, kitchens, barracks, courtyards and, remarkably, even a tennis court radiated outwards from the Great Hall, which still never lost its pre-eminence.

The way of life found in these halls lay at the root of English provincial power. It turned Norman settler into feudal landlord and gave medieval monarchy the security to fight foreign wars and raise levies to pay for them. Yet it subjected those monarchs to baronial consent, formalized in the Magna

Carta of 1215. Later in the Middle Ages, landowners needed royal licences to crenellate their manors, as much a matter of prestige as of defence, but once thus 'fortified', the duty of reciprocal homage was established. The unity of England was rooted in the partial autonomy of the medieval house. The Great Hall and its settlement were architecture as politics.

This gradation of public and private space around the Great Hall achieved symbolic status in the Tudor era and fascinated later revivalists, long after the hall's purpose was superseded by reception and withdrawing rooms. At Boughton (Northants), the Duke of Montagu encased his hall in later and grander work, but could not bring himself to demolish it. The designers of Longleat (Wilts) and Chatsworth (Derbys) had to eschew classical symmetry to incorporate traditional Great Halls in their plans. Nor was ritual altogether forgotten. As late as the 18th century, William Constable took pride in still dining in his Great Hall at Burton Constable (Yorks, E), with his thirty-four servants eating at his table.

The tradition of eating 'in hall' was long honoured by such conservative institutions as the monarchy, the Church and Oxford and Cambridge colleges. Jeffry Wyatville could not omit a Great Hall from George IV's new Windsor Castle (Berks). The manorial hall was revived with particular vigour by William Morris and his followers. It was well described by Henry James: 'Bright, large and high, richly decorated and freely used, full of corners and communications, it played equally the part of a place of reunion and a place of transit.'

Other examples of medieval living are sparse. In their last burst of wealth, monasteries acquired increasingly lavish residences. Abbots and priors built themselves private lodgings which often survived the Dissolution as houses for the new Tudor middle class, grandly at Lacock (Wilts) and Syon (London, W), modestly at Castle Acre in Norfolk. A number of hostels for the sick and for pilgrims remain, as at St Cross outside Winchester (Hants) and the delightful St Mary's, Chichester (Sussex).

Such was the vulnerability of town houses to fire, riot and renewal that few remain from the Middle Ages. We can see the Norman Jew's House in Lincoln, a restored merchant's home in Southampton (Hants) and a medieval shop in Tewkesbury (Gloucs). For better or worse, the most vivid relics of early domestic architecture are those rescued and reconstructed in country-side museums, examples of which may be seen at Singleton in Sussex and Ryedale in North Yorkshire. Unaltered medieval houses, still widely extant in France, are in England mostly confined to these museums, without which we should be bereft.

THE TUDOR AGE

The 16th century saw the first of three revolutions in the story of the English house, the next being in the 19th and 20th centuries. The Dissolution of the Monasteries in 1536–8 broke up the great monastic estates and dispersed wealth and property to a new class of courtiers, merchants and bureaucrats. Tithes that had gone into beautifying churches and sustaining clergy went into the aggrandizement of this new class. Monasteries were pilfered for stone to build such conveniences as fireplaces, porches and chimneys. Henry VIII's revolution not only founded the modern English state, it precipitated a burst of domestic house building.

The Tudor age, from the reign of Henry VII to that of Elizabeth I, saw the final flowering of medieval architecture. Great Halls remained to represent the family on parade even as that family retreated to chambers above and beyond. Gatehouses and courtyards became ever more flamboyant, notably those of brick at Hampton Court and Layer Marney (Essex).

Indoors, old spiral stairs were replaced by often massive works of oak carpentry as at Gainsborough Hall (Lincs). Screens and draught porches were carved with Renaissance motifs. The greatest advances were in heating. A sign of wealth was a brick flue on the exterior with fireplace and decorated chimneypiece within. Roofs erupted into forests of chimneys, nowhere more ornate than at Layer Marney and the unfinished Thornbury Castle in Gloucestershire. These chimneys were joined by gables, pinnacles, parapets and pavilions. The skyline of houses such as Burghley (Hunts) and Longleat (Wilts) look from a distance like townships in the air.

This new comfort found expression even in the smallest buildings. At the Priest's House at West Hoathly in Kent, the old screens passage was swept aside for a brick fireplace and chimney which not only warmed the hall but also a new upstairs chamber inserted above it. Across England, manorial halls were sliced horizontally. At Broughton Castle in Oxfordshire chambers of Renaissance splendour were inserted among the rafters of the Great Hall.

The chief innovation of the late-Elizabethans was the phenomenon known as the 'prodigy' house. The post-Dissolution rich expressed their pride in landed status as few had done before. Although a handful of medieval palaces, such as South Wingfield (Derbys), had been spectacular, most were fit for purpose. They were now to become fit for show. The E-plan developed grand porches crowned with elaborate frontispieces. Two storeys rose to three, often with the grandest rooms on the upper floors. Ambition now often outreached resources. Barrington Court (Somerset) was one of the first prodigy houses to bankrupt its owner, the Earl of Bridgwater, in the 1550s. At Hengrave (Suffolk), Sir Thomas Kytson, a cloth merchant, built 40 rooms round a courtyard behind a gatehouse encrusted with ornament. At Adlington, 60 panels of Cheshire heraldry cram the canopy above the Great Hall, while historic murals cover the walls.

Courtiers built houses to entertain and impress the monarch. Sir Christopher Hatton's Holdenby and Kirby in Northamptonshire were both intended for Elizabeth I, who never visited either house. Even today, mansions such as Burghley (Hunts), Longleat, Audley End (Essex) and Hatfield (Herts) seem as breathtaking in their ostentation as anything created by the Victorians. Although most still respected the plan of Great Hall and enclosure, in their scale and ornament they left the Middle Ages far behind.

A climax was reached with the first domestic architect of whom we have some concept of a corpus of work, Robert Smythson (c1535–1614). At Wollaton (Notts) and Longleat, Smythson recreated the style of the French château in an English landscape. At Hardwick Hall (Derbys), Bess of Hardwick, possibly with Smythson's help, created a show house of stupendous power. Its façades are symmetrical. Its Great Hall is turned lengthways and forms the approach to a great staircase climbing the height of the building.

These houses and especially their internal decoration are regarded as the first substantive manifestations of the Renaissance in England. They took their motifs from the pattern books of the Italian masters, Alberti, Serlio and Palladio, although most did so with Mannerist embellishment of pilasters, strapwork and classical imagery. The English Renaissance was, for the most part, exuberant, eclectic and Northern. It is illustrated in the gates of Caius College, Cambridge, the pilastered façade of Longleat and the Virgilian frieze in Buckland Abbey (Devon).

The final echo of Elizabethan England was created by Bess of Hardwick's grandson, William Cavendish, in his Little Castle at Bolsover (Derbys). Here, a courtier at the turn of the 17th century expressed in built form the romantic sensibility of Spenser and Shakespeare. Cavendish, aided by Robert Smythson's son, John (c1570–1634), depicted on walls and ceilings classical deities and senses, virtues and humours in settings from the rituals of courtly love. In Bolsover's painted chambers and knot gardens, medieval England was betrothed to the Renaissance. Here was Shakespeare's 'sceptered isle' in tune with Spenser's 'Dear country, O how dearly dear/ Ought thy remembrance and perpetual bond be to thy foster child.' At Bolsover history, aesthetics and architecture were one.

THE JACOBEAN TRADITION

The Queen's House in Greenwich (London, E) still qualifies as the most revolutionary house in England. The architect, Inigo Jones (1573–1652), brought his Palladian notebooks back from Italy in 1614 and proceeded to delight James I and his court. If England were to equal the elegance and decorative taste of continental Europe, it had to leave behind Bolsover's medieval fantasies. Jones ordered that 'Ye outward ornaments ought to be sollid, proporsionable according to the rulles, masculine and unaffected'. Inside, on the other hand, a total contrast was permitted: 'Immaginacy is set free and sumtimes liccentiously flying out as nature hirsealf doeth often time stravagantly.' Jones's houses were for the royal court and explicitly 'stravagant'.

No sooner did Jones lay down these Palladian rules than England was plunged into Civil War. Architectural style – where it could be afforded – was reflected in the struggle between the old ways and the new. Well into the mid-17th century, we see houses still with asymmetrical halls, gables and half-timbering. In the 1660s, the Vernons built an E-plan mansion at Sudbury Hall in Derbyshire that could be of a century earlier. At Astley in Lancashire, the Brookes designed a house of the roughest Mannerist exuberance, as if Jones and Palladio had never existed. In the universities of Oxford and Cambridge, Royalism and the Old Religion ensured that the many college buildings were still in the Tudor/Gothic style.

Not until the Restoration of 1660 were Jones's followers such as John Webb, Hugh May and Peter Mills able to establish a style that marked a clear break with the past. At Belton (Lincs) and Thorpe Hall (Hunts), reception rooms were arranged as a promenade round a ground floor entrance hall. At Ashdown in Berkshire in c1660, the Earl of Craven built a pavilion in the Dutch style for his adored 'Winter Queen', sister of Charles I. Its tall façades, wide eaves, sloping roof and cupola derived from continental buildings seen by the exiled Stuart court during the Commonwealth. This style was to embrace the terms Restoration, William-and-Mary and Queen Anne, and dominate English domestic architecture well into the 18th century.

Soon those most fanatical of builder-monarchs, the late Stuarts, commissioned Christopher Wren (1632–1723), Nicholas Hawksmoor (1661–1736) and John Vanbrugh (1664–1726) to plan palaces, hospitals and churches with a frenzy not seen since Henry VIII. Ambitious courtiers followed suit. England now flirted with the Baroque, a century after its appearance in southern Europe. From the sober classicism of the rebuilt sections of Hampton Court

(London, W) and Kensington Palace (London, C) emerged some of the most dramatic architectural set-pieces in England. They include Wren's Greenwich Hospital, Vanbrugh and Hawksmoor's Castle Howard (Yorks, N) and Vanbrugh's palace at Blenheim (Oxon). Inside, carving by Grinling Gibbons and murals by Verrio and Thornhill added to the splendour.

The prospect of a visit from the monarch still incurred spectacular and often ruinous expense. The Duke and Duchess of Lauderdale crammed so-called 'state rooms' into the rear of their house at Ham (London, W). William Blathwayt did likewise at Dyrham Park in Gloucestershire. When a visit from Queen Anne was mooted at Lullingstone Castle (Kent), the Harts hurriedly applied a new façade to their Elizabethan house and installed a new staircase inside. In house after house, rooms were built for ostentation and rarely used. Family life found itself consigned to closets and wings or, with the arrival of the *piano nobile*, to a basement called the 'rustic'. An 18th-century Lord Hervey described the *piano nobile* as being 'for taste, expense, state and parade', while the 'base or rustic storey was dedicated to hunters, hospitality, noise, dirt and business'. The English house became a 'stately home'.

The result was splendid. To many, including myself, the style dominant in England from the Restoration to the death of Queen Anne in 1714 was the most visually satisfying of all. Such houses as Ashdown, Belton and Uppark (Sussex) seem perfect within themselves. Their tall proportions, overhanging eaves, redbrick walls and white windows embody both the light-heartedness of Charles II and the tolerance of England after the Glorious Revolution. They have never lost what the historian of the English house, Hugh Braun, called 'the serenity which is the legacy of age, the graciousness which deepens with the patina of history'.

THE GEORGIAN HOUSE

The story of the English house was never still. No sooner had 'English Baroque' established itself than the Stuart dynasty ended and the Hanoverians saw a return to the purity of Inigo Jones and Palladianism. Although the spirit of the Italian classical tradition had never died, Lord Burlington (1694–1753) and his circle of Grand Tour 'men of taste' saw themselves as cleansing the architectural stables of the style of Wren and Vanbrugh. Burlington's cheer-leader, Alexander Pope, applauded his aversion to the Baroque: 'You show us, Rome was glorious, not profuse,/ And pompous Buildings once were things of use.' These new men did not have things all their own way. The old guard, in the form of William Hogarth, savaged them in a series of satirical prints, depicting them as effete, foreign and fastidious. The contest is well displayed at Chiswick (London, W), where Burlington's Italian pavilion sits next door to Hogarth's homely brick house. Yet it was a contest the old guard lost.

The Grand Tour now dominates the story. Entrance halls were modelled on a Roman *cortile*. Drawing rooms, saloons, dining rooms and libraries followed a series of decorative schemes laid down in the books of Jones and his apostles, James Gibbs (1682–1754), Colen Campbell (1676–1729) and William Kent (1685–1748). In Norfolk, Sir Robert Walpole at Houghton vied with his neighbour, the Earl of Leicester at Holkham, in creating lavish Italian interiors behind restrained Jonesian exteriors. In the Georgian rooms at Burghley (Hunts), half of France and Italy seems to be on display.

The resulting decoration can seem indigestibly rich. The voluptuousness of William Kent's gilt and paintwork, his gods and putti, heavy drapes and grandiloquent doorways can overwhelm an eye schooled to 20th-century minimalism. By the middle of the 18th century style was already being refined in the hands of James Paine (1717–89) and Sir William Chambers (1723–96). Gradually the Rococo asserted itself in the drawing room at Hagley (Worcs), in James Stuart's Painted Room in London's Spencer House and in the ethereal chinoiserie of Claydon (Bucks).

Then in 1758 Robert Adam (1728–92) returned from Rome enthused with the latest archaeological finds, and gave the English house another shock. At Harewood (Yorks, W), Kedleston (Derbys), Osterley and Syon (both London, W) he produced interiors of a subtlety not equalled before or since. Adam transformed English decoration as completely as his contemporary, Lancelot 'Capability' Brown (1716–83), transformed landscape gardening. Both introduced a refinement and a calm where previously there had been noise.

The outcome was exquisite in every sense. Adam struggled to secure rich clients who would not encumber him with parsimony. At Kedleston he exulted at Lord Curzon being 'resolved to spare no expense, with £10,000 a year . . . a taste for the Arts and little for game'. Curzon gave him 'the intire management of his Grounds . . . with full powers as to Temples, Bridges, Seats and Cascades'. As his lordship had opined in his youth, 'Grant me ye Gods a pleasant seat/ In attick elegance made neat/ Fine lawns, much wood and water plenty/ Of deer and herds and flocks not scanty,/ Laid out in such an uncurb'd taste/ That nature mayn't be lost but grac'd.'

Adam in turn was followed by a mild retrenchment, by the conservative, externally dull buildings of Henry Holland (1745–1806) and the Wyatt architectural dynasty*, and by the innovative interiors of Sir John Soane (1753–1837). Domestic architecture now took refuge in diversity. The 'Gothick' of Horace Walpole's Strawberry Hill (London, W) inspired the neo-medievalism of Arbury (Warks) and dozens of interiors of 'wedding cake' intricacy. It also fired the imagination of the Picturesque movement of landscape design. Yet by the end of the century, it was Greeks not Goths who were greeted as the stylists of radicalism. Greek was the preferred style of the American and French revolutions. In England the outcome was Belsay (Northumbs), The Grange (Hants) and pretty Hammerwood in Sussex, designed by Benjamin Latrobe, who went on to advise on the Capitol in Washington.

The end of the 18th century saw style fragmenting into what can seem mere picturesqueness. Houses became villas. Even the grandest of the urban townhouses had merged into terraces. Landscape was all. By 1815, Giles Worsley records architects being sternly advised 'to understand all styles and be prejudiced in favour of none'. The most prolific designers of the Regency, James Wyatt (1746–1813), his nephew Sir Jeffry Wyatville (1766–1840) and John Nash (1752–1835), were equally at home in Gothic and classical. At Longnor Hall in Shropshire, Nash outbid Humphry Repton (1752–1818) by offering to design 'in any style, Grecian, Swiss, any kind of Gothic'. In the early years of the new century, the young Robert Smirke (1780–1867) was at work on romantic medieval castles at Lowther (Cumbria) and Eastnor (Herefs). The pitch was rolled for the Victorians and the Battle of the Styles.

THE VICTORIANS AND BEYOND

The Victorian age presented the English house with its greatest challenge since the Dissolution of the Monasteries. Manufacturing and commercial wealth took rural England by storm. In *The Rise of the Nouveaux Riches*, J. Mordaunt Crook records that by the mid-1870s, half the Lancashire estates of more than 3,000 acres had been acquired in the previous hundred years. At the time of Waterloo, just 500 Britons had cash incomes of more than £5,000 a year other than from land. By 1880 the figure was estimated to be 4,000. The vast majority of these newly rich acquired country estates.

As in the 16th century, the appeal of land to the *arriviste* class was phenomenal. A rural estate offered security and repose, a continuity with

---

* Colvin lists 16 Wyatt architects in the late-Georgian and Victorian eras.

the past that could be handed over to the future, which transient commerce could not offer. The Englishman's craving to be 'large acred' became, in the Victorian and Edwardian periods, a de facto supertax on business. While German and American entrepreneurs were reinvesting their profits in their factories, their English counterparts were investing them in Sudeley (Gloucs), Cragside (Northumbs) and Somerleyton (Suffolk).

Nor was upward mobility confined to those vulgar souls satirized by Trollope's *The Way We Live Now*. The iron and coal magnate, the Earl of Dudley, built probably the most extravagant private house in Europe, Witley Court (Worcs), in the 1860s, coating his private suite in gold leaf. The lace-making Heathcotes became country squires in one generation after building Knightshayes (Devon). The Rothschilds colonized hundreds of acres for four great houses in the Vale of Aylesbury. The London grocer, Julius Drew, went to extraordinary lengths to find a country village sharing his name, Drew-stainton in Devon. He called himself Drewe and commissioned from Lutyens the romantic Castle Drogo.

To Disraeli, the evolution of a small land-owning electorate into a large property-owning democracy was the ideal path to reform. His Sir Plantagenet Pure refused all offers of a peerage as he owned land and did not 'need' one. The much-travelled Kipling (who also refused honours) knew what he meant. When he finally settled in Sussex, he declared, 'It is the most marvellous of all foreign countries that I have ever been in. It is made up of trees and green fields and mud and the Gentry: and at last I'm one of the Gentry!'

The hereditary gentry, along with the English Church, had survived the Georgian era only by the skin of its teeth. A characteristic of many great Georgian families had been truly stupefying extravagance. Three Hill heirs in a row brought Shropshire's Hawkstone estate to its knees. The builders of such titanic houses as Houghton and Holkham (Norfolk), Stowe (Bucks), Castle Howard (Yorks, N) and Ickworth (Suffolk) all died bankrupt or with their successors sorely embarrassed. The yearning to leave a monument to posterity usually meant leaving a mountain of debt.

Yet the dawn of the Victorian age saw the landed aristocracy show a sudden instinct for survival. Chastened by revolutions abroad and reform at home, an entire class of society seemed to turn over a new leaf. Younger sons revived the Church and ruled India. Elder ones took seriously their custodianship of family estates. Houses were no longer places of idle amusement, nor parks Augustan fantasies. They embraced living communities, with obligations and duties on which, also they were told, the fate of the body politic rested.

Crucial was the continuance in England, although not on the post-revolutionary Continent, of the principle of primogeniture, the inheritance of entire estates by eldest sons. This custom was introduced to England by the Normans, supplanting the Anglo-Saxon division of estates into equal parts. The purpose was to keep baronial lands intact and powerful. Later radicals regarded it as little short of barbaric. Yet it survives as a custom to this day and was undoubtedly vital to preserving estates which, abroad, have disappeared in subdivision. Primogeniture did not extend to Ireland and Wales, nor curiously was it imposed in eastern Kent, apparently as an early Norman concession to local lords. Here, partigeniture or *gavelkind* was maintained well into the 19th century, and may be the reason why no large houses are to be found in that part of the county.

Men now emerged who were the measure of this primogeniture, men such as Trevelyan of Wallington (Northumbs) and 'Great Sir Thomas' Acland of Killerton (Devon). The latter led his county in Parliament for most of Victoria's reign, championed political and agricultural reform and ruled his estate with a benign but firm hand. At Chatsworth (Derbys), the 6th Duke of Devonshire rebuilt the village of Edensor, doubled the size of his house and threw it open daily to the public. Cheshire's Lord Tollemache was a champion athlete who had twelve children and gave every one of his 250 labourers a new cottage and three acres. The only pleasure in land ownership, Tollemache wrote, 'is to witness the social improvement in the condition of those residing on it'. Such a sentiment would have been rare a century earlier.

The style of house chosen by old and new money alike was puzzling. Writing in 1859, the architect, Sir (George) Gilbert Scott (1811–78), reflected Lord Tollemache's view. The landed proprietor, he said, 'should be looked up to as a bond of union between the classes ... No false modesty should deter him from expressing this, quietly and gravely, in the character of his house.' Yet there was no agreement as to what style best reflected this character. The Georgian 'man of taste' had given way to the muscular Victorian gentleman. The former adhered for the most part to the two-centuries-old tradition of the classical revival. The latter seemed eager to break with that tradition but was unsure in which direction to turn.

Style became a matter of furious debate. To A. W. N. Pugin (1812–52) and John Ruskin a building's appearance should reflect its function and its materials should be 'honest'. Judgment was in favour of Gothic, brick and stone, and against pagan classicism and false stucco. Gothic satisfied the Pre-Raphaelites of William Morris's circle. It satisfied the Catholic sensibilities of the Earls of Shrewsbury at Alton (Staffs) and the pious Gibbs family of Tyntesfield (Somerset). Tollemache himself opted for medieval Gothic at Peckforton Castle (Cheshire).

Yet Gothic failed to satisfy the Elizabethan yearnings of Lord Carnarvon at Highclere (Hants) or the Italianate ones of the Duke of Sutherland at Cliveden (Bucks) and Trentham (Staffs). Nothing but neo-Jacobean with a touch of French Renaissance could equal the eccentricity of Gregory Gregory at Harlaxton (Lincs). Most Victorians understandably turned to architects such as Sir Charles Barry (1795–1860), Anthony Salvin (1799–1881) and Scott who were able to take down any style from the shelf of history.

The result was a dazzling confusion. The conservative Heathcotes found themselves commissioning the romantic Goth, William Burges (1827–81), at Knightshayes. They hated his work and commissioned Italianate interiors from J. D. Crace (1838–1917) instead. That prolific Victorian designer, Crace, also refashioned Longleat (Wilts), Knebworth (Herts) and Cliveden (Bucks).

The Victorian Battles of the Styles may have been no more than another swing of the pendulum, but it never came to rest. The modern eye finds it hard to comprehend how the Victorians detested the rectilinear façades of Georgian London. 'A wilderness of ugliness,' was William Morris's description of Bloomsbury's Gower Street, locked as it was 'in the cold grip of classicism'. But the next generation was equally averse to Morris's often gloomy Gothic. It craved the delights of the Queen Anne revival. In the mid-20th century, a further age hated anything Victorian and yearned for a return to the decorum of Georgian.

By the end of the 19th century, the chief Victorian contribution to the story of the English house was, ironically, conservative. While grandees imitated the great houses of earlier generations, the ideals of Morris (1834–96) and his circle encouraged a new middle class to appreciate traditional English vernacular. Art Nouveau found partial expression in the Arts and Crafts movement. But its impact was mostly limited to decoration, as in the inglenooks of Richard Norman Shaw (1831–1912). The interest in old manor houses was vigorously reactionary, echoing the archaism of previous 'medieval' revivals in the 18th and early 19th centuries. As Morris wrote of his new home at Kelmscott (Oxon), it had grown up 'out of the soil and the lives of them that lived on it . . . the gathered crumbs of happiness of the confused and turbulent past'. Such buildings, he declared, did not belong to any one person, for 'they have belonged to our forefathers, and they will belong to our descendants unless we play them false. They are not in any sense our property, to do as we like with. We are only trustees for those that come after us.'

The English vernacular revival was a reaction against everything that

Victorianism had come to represent, technology, industry and cosmopolis. Manor house restoration was pioneered by *Country Life* magazine, founded in 1897 by Edward Hudson. A group of owner-restorers brought back to life an impressive group of houses in the south and south-west, including Cothay (Somerset), Westwood (Wilts), Owlpen (Gloucs) and Great Dixter (Sussex). In 1909 a young stockbroker, Claud Biddulph, even commissioned the Arts and Crafts architect, Ernest Barnsley (1863–1926), to build him a completely new manor at Rodmarton (Gloucs). Every bit of the building was made by local craftsmen on site.

Soon Lord Curzon was restoring Montacute (Somerset), Tattershall (Lincs) and Bodiam (Sussex). The travel tycoon, Ernest Cook, was rescuing Hartwell (Bucks) and Montacute (again). In 1910, Sir Edwin Lutyens (1869–1944) designed Castle Drogo (Devon) and Lindisfarne (Northumbs) with the same revivalist gusto that Salvin had shown seventy years earlier at Harlaxton and Alnwick. The cause was taken up by often scholarly antiquarians. The wealthy Edwardian, Frank Green, virtually rebuilt the Treasurer's House in York. Baron Ash restored Packwood (Warks), fastidiously banning all mention of the source of his wealth (galvanized iron). Ralph Dutton rebuilt Hinton Ampner (Hants) in stately neo-Georgian. American money refloated Leeds Castle on its Kent lake like a scene from Arthurian legend.

These new owners were discovering what old ones had known for centuries, that an old house offered communion with the roots of England. The Great Hall represented local community. The family wing represented privacy and sanctuary. Servants lived on the premises. On Sunday all would worship together at their parish church. The dance of light on brick, wood and stone was externally reassuring. So too was the presence of an 'English garden' outside the drawing room window, merging softly across a ha-ha into the parkland beyond. This book records many families reclaiming properties sold by forebears – the Crofts of Croft Castle (Herefs), the Benthalls of Benthall (Salop) and the Bedingfelds of Oxburgh (Norfolk) – as if lineage required a continuous rural root to have meaning.

This old vision of England was not phoney. Its imagery was the collective memory of a substantial portion of the nation. Revivalism was adopted across suburban England and exported throughout the Empire and to America. It was reproduced from Melbourne to Vancouver, from Cape Town to Hong Kong. As the 20th century progressed, 'Stockbroker Tudor' vied with 'Neo-Georgian' in mass housing pattern books. It swept aside England's brief acquaintance (never a love affair) with the Interwar Modern Movement. Modernism's harsh materials of steel, glass and concrete found no response in the English climate or the English temperament. Among other defects, they did not age gracefully. Modernism was confined largely to public sector housing, where architects could build dwellings which photographed well but in which neither they nor those paying for them would have to live.

The English house could never be called Corbusier's 'machine for living in'. For five hundred years it was a shrine to household gods. In many respects it seemed a response to the philosopher Pascal's plea that 'the sole cause of man's unhappiness is that he does not know how to stay quietly in his room'. At the end of the 19th century, a diplomat in the German embassy to London, Hermann Muthesius, wrote a detailed account of the relationship between the English and their homes. 'The Englishman sees the whole of life embodied in his house,' he wrote. 'Here, in the heart of his family, self-sufficient and feeling no great urge for sociability, pursuing his own interests in virtual isolation, he finds his happiness and his real spiritual comfort.' More people in Britain live in a house rather than a flat than in any other European country. Muthesius understood why.

THE FUTURE OF THE ENGLISH HOUSE

Houses have always symbolized wealth and thus been vulnerable to poverty. Despite primogeniture, they have often ruined the families that built or lived in them. Castle Howard was left uncompleted by Lord Carlisle, and Nostell Priory by the Winns. The Temples had to flee the country for the debts of Stowe and the Verneys for the debts of Claydon. Wimpole crippled Chicheleys, Harleys and Hardwickes in quick succession. The architectural profession did more to undermine the English upper class than any war or revolution.

Yet nothing equalled the gloom that settled on these houses in the 20th century. The advent of income and inheritance tax, the loss of sons in the Great War, the cost of labour and the Depression were followed by widespread government requisition in the Second World War. The big house seemed condemned to life as a barracks, hospital or school. When the war was over and despite the threat of land nationalization, Saltram (Devon) desperately rehired a dozen of its former indoor staff, but within six years the Parker family placed it in the hands of the National Trust. In 1952 the trustees of the twenty-one-year-old 8th Marquess of Hertford advised him to demolish Ragley (Warks) at once. He refused, but when he later handed the house on to his son he called it 'a life sentence'. In 1955, the Marquess of

Lansdowne demolished Robert Adam's Bowood (Wilts) before anyone could stop him.

The notorious list produced in 1974 for the V&A's 'Destruction of the Country House' exhibition named over 600 country houses demolished since 1870, the majority immediately before and after the Second World War. The loss, especially of London mansions, was dreadful. The exhibition led to the foundation of SAVE Britain's Heritage by Marcus Binney and a group of friends skilled in public lobbying. A series of *causes célèbres* followed, including the saving of Barlaston (Staffs) from the wrecker's ball. New demolitions of grand houses all but ceased and concern was directed instead at restoration and contents, as at Calke Abbey (Derbys), Thoresby (Notts) and Tyntesfield (Somerset). By the 1980s, there was a consensus that major houses with no future in private hands should be taken over with public money.

England retains far more grand houses with contents intact and on public display than any other country in the world. This has been in part due to a force that dare not speak its name, *de facto* nationalization. Roughly half the properties in this book are in the public sector, in the form of the National Trust or the government's English Heritage. The diaries of the Trust's chief negotiator in the 1940s and 1950s, James Lees-Milne, demonstrate the delicate process by which distressed, often desperate, owners were relieved of their ancestral homes yet often allowed to stay living in them. They had to hand over large endowments to maintain them. The government's only contribution was in death duties foregone. Indeed Lees-Milne indicates that many owners released their property only because it was going not to the government but to custodians they considered not unlike themselves.

The National Trust duly took on such masterpieces as Knole (Kent), Lyme Park (Cheshire) and Hardwick Hall (Derbys), as well as smaller gems such as Baddesley Clinton (Warks) and Canons Ashby (Northants). With them came a cornucopia of paintings, furniture, books and gardens. The programme was a success beyond all prediction. By 2000, 10m people were visiting Trust houses each year, roughly equivalent to one in five of the British population. I can think of nothing that has so inexpensively benefited the public realm as the National Trust's country houses' scheme.

For those properties remaining in private hands, a portfolio of tax reliefs, charitable trusts, maintenance allowances and grants evolved with a quid pro quo of public access. Houses with land benefited greatly from cross-subsidies under the Common Agricultural Policy. A younger generation of owners with a more aggressive approach to exploiting their houses became prominent in the Historic Houses Association. Many of them I describe in this book as 'saints', families who have committed themselves to maintaining an old house for posterity, often against all common sense and professional advice. The result is often a remarkable bond between owner and public. Those arriving at Muncaster Castle (Cumbria) are told simply, 'This house lives entirely through the warmth and understanding which visitors bring'.

This relationship has opened a new dilemma that is still far from resolved. The tradition of accessibility to great houses goes back to 'time without mind'. It was rooted in the hospitality of the Great Hall and the custom of courtesy to strangers. Although these dwindled with the growth of domestic privacy, it never died. Even if Queen Elizabeth ignored the Hatton houses of Northamptonshire, they were visited by the curious. Anyone arriving at the gates of a prodigy house would usually be shown round by a proud steward. By the 18th century, the habit of house visiting became a cult. Owners who had spent their family fortunes on fine houses and Grand Tour art were keen to boast their taste, even to strangers.

In his survey of country-house visiting, Adrian Tinniswood lists as popular 18th-century resorts Houghton, Holkham, Blickling and Oxburgh in Norfolk and Chatsworth, Hardwick and Kedleston in Derbyshire. Queues formed outside Holkham from the day it was built. In the south-west, Georgian visitors with appropriate transport could choose between Stourhead, Wardour, Longleat (all Wilts), Saltram (Devon) and Mount Edgcumbe (Cornwall). Hotels were built to accommodate tourists at Kedleston and Stourhead. Records show the Meissen at Blenheim (Oxon) having to be locked away because visitors kept breaking it. By 1800, between fifteen and twenty catalogues to country houses were being published. There were frequent complaints of visitors finding houses closed to the public, indicating that this was considered abnormal.

At Chatsworth the public has been welcomed since the 17th century. In 1844 it was open every day of the year from ten in the morning until five in the afternoon. Instructions to staff were that 'the humblest individual is not only shown the whole but the Duke has expressly ordered the waterworks to be played for everyone'. In the 1850s, with the coming of the railway, the house received 80,000 visitors a year. At Strawberry Hill (London, W), Horace Walpole complained of the 'plague' of visitors and demanded each one buy an invitation signed by himself. He joked that he should marry his housekeeper on finding that she was charging a phenomenal guinea an invitation.

Many of these houses closed between the wars. The reason was partly a lack of staff and partly a withdrawal of many aristocratic owners from the public realm. To them, nobility no longer implied such obligation. Woburn (Beds), Haddon (Yorks, N) and Harewood (Yorks, W) all closed at this time and prices were set high for those staying open. After closures and army requisitions in the Second World War, houses were slow to reopen. Longleat became the first 'marketed' stately home in 1949. The guides were firmly told to tell funny anecdotes about the family since, in the view of the then Marquess of Bath, 'Frankly I don't think the Rembrandts or van Dycks interest [the public] very much.'

Longleat, closely followed by Beaulieu (Hants) and Woburn, decided on the aggressive selling of house, family and themed park as a package. The result was a success, however much it was deplored and derided by fellow grandees. 'I have seen the lions of Longleat' became a catchphrase and Britain, it was said, became a net exporter of big game. Such an approach depended on the resident families being content to be part of the 'visitor experience'. The exhibitionist Duke of Bedford even allowed tourists to pay to watch him having his lunch. The guidebooks to these houses make liberal use of the first person singular.

The National Trust and English Heritage veered to the other end of the spectrum. The houses that passed to them became the domain of conservationists and art historians. Human interest was airbrushed from the rooms. Blinds were drawn to protect fabrics from light and, consequently, from proper sight. Every chair, pot and painting was scrubbed and polished as if awaiting a government inspector. The Tudor chapel at Ightham Mote (Kent) is still covered in dust sheets when the house is closed, to prevent 'dust abrasion'. Every ceramic at Clandon (Bucks) is wrapped and put away in winter. Visitors who protest at early closing times are told that houses have used their quota of 'light hours' and 'must get their rest'. Such places can seem bloodless and uninspiring.

By the 1990s there was evidence that the presentation of old houses needed changing. Competition from other attractions and dwindling visitor figures directed custodial attention towards 'themes', and story-telling. Archaeological reconstruction as at York's Jorvik, West Stow (Suffolk) and Mountfitchet (Essex) proved immensely popular, as did the Tussauds' tableaux at Warwick Castle. Waxworks, anathema to the National Trust, were not so to the paying public. Castle Howard asked what most interested their customers and found that family photographs and stories were preferred to art and relics of yesterday. Houses moved away from entrapping visitors in lecture tours and allowed them to wander at will, even at some risk to objects. At Dennis Severs' House in Spitalfields (London, C), an entire house was recreated round a single story-line. The approach can border on parody. The National Trust 'kitchen experience' is bound to be almost identical everywhere.

Many custodians, especially private ones, still confuse the visitor as guest and as customer, often leading to misunderstanding on both sides. The opening of a house for money is a contract, not a philanthropic gesture. The right of public access has usually been purchased through government grant and tax relief. Many rural properties have received decades of farm subsidy. Big estates enjoy tax benefits beyond the dreams of urban businesses. The public is entitled to some quid pro quo for this. Where grant has been paid or contents exempted from tax, access is also a statutory requirement.

That said, the opening of a private house to the public is a unique form of contract. An owner is receiving a stranger into the intimacy of a home. The intrusion is invited and is paid for, but it is a sort of violation, especially in smaller houses. One owner told me, 'I treat the public as an untidy and disagreeable great aunt, whom I must humour for the sake of her legacy.' I visited a Suffolk house in which a grandmother had refused to leave the sitting room while the racing was on television, remaining static in her armchair as the Bank Holiday crowds walked past. She was voted the best exhibit and presumed to have been placed there on purpose.

This boundary will never be easy to define. While public sector houses need to do more to humanize their presentation, private ones derive much of their appeal from being privately occupied. As soon as I see notice boards, display cases, floor druggets, velvet ropes and 'teaching aids', a gulf opens between me and the spirit of a place. A home has become a museum.

In truth, nothing can stand proxy for family occupation. All houses, from castle keep to prison cell, are designed for habitation. They lose their character if they are put to a different purpose, as objects of general curiosity. A house, like a church, is a place of specific human ceremony. Entrances are intended for arriving, sitting rooms for sitting, bedrooms for sleeping, libraries for reading and dining rooms for eating. To see the Table Deckers' Room at Osborne (Hants) and know that this lavish apparatus will never again be used puts time out of joint. The unread volumes in the great library at The Vyne (Hants) are like the linen in Lanhydrock (Cornwall) and the bathroom soap at Kingston Lacy (Dorset), stage props. Visitors constantly ask if these things are used, and feel cheated if they are not.

If these houses are to retain their appeal to the public, those who look after them must never forget why they were built and why people visit them. They were built for people to live in and are visited for that reason, in a spirit of mild prurience. But that spirit is wider than just curiosity. The houses of

England have a special role in the theatre of our shared memory. They signify not the ambitions of State or Church. They are a narrative of the domestic lives of individuals. They signify personal identity. Marcel Proust, supremely sensitive to the genius of old places, wrote that, 'When from the long distant past nothing subsists, after the people are dead ... the smell and taste of things remain poised, like souls, ready to remind us, waiting and hoping for their moment amid the ruins.' To Proust, houses were a precious part of 'the vast structure of recollection'.

The Tudor grandee with his medieval fantasy, the Victorian magnate with his revivalist palace and today's conservationist all worship at the same shrine, that of history. They do so not to escape the present – though some may – but because the past is what gives the present light and shade, depth and meaning. In old houses we are able to roll out the carpet of memory. Without them England would not just be unimaginably dull. It would not know who it was.

When I cross the threshold of such places I sense a curtain rising. I see castles, palaces, mansions, manors, farms, cottages. Men and women have lived in them all. In them they have found security and created a private kingdom, a place to love, laugh, cry and die. I believe the houses of England are a treasure trove, a glory of humanity, a wonder of the world.

The Thousand Best

'I am closed to envy but always open to a friend' – motto, Loseley Park

The 'thousand best houses' are defined as English buildings which are or have been residential and are in some degree accessible to public view. They include castles, country houses and properties open by virtue of distinguished occupants. I have described a handful of almshouses, boarding schools, prisons and, lightheartedly, a dolls' house. The selection ranges from Buckingham Palace to a north country prisoner-of-war camp. Many early houses are now ruins but are included where they contribute to the story of domestic architecture. The same applies to ancient structures in countryside museums, now invaluable records of rare vernacular building. Included also are local museums and historic hotels converted from old houses and still recognisable as such.

Accessibility is a fluid concept and a vexed subject especially with occupied houses. I see no point in directing readers to a house which they cannot see and whose owner does not welcome visitors. I have not listed opening hours since they tend to alter by the year. They are published in Hudson's compendious *Historic Houses and Gardens*, new each year, and in handbooks issued by English Heritage and the National Trust. *Museums and Galleries*, published by Tomorrow's Guides, includes houses in local council ownership. These works cover almost all the properties in this book. Hudson's includes the official list of houses open by virtue of receiving grant.

I have given a general indication of accessibility in the form of a code after each entry. Most English Heritage (EH) sites are regularly open, except in winter, and ruins can often be seen from a public road or path. House museums (M) are likewise readily open, often all year. National Trust (NT) houses are less accessible, and sometimes prevent entry up to 45 minutes before the advertised closing time. Far too many houses in all categories are shut in winter and early spring, when tourism is now increasingly active.

Private houses (marked with a P) are different. Most are occupied by families who value their privacy. Some are open only on certain days of the week or months of the year. Grant requirements insist on 28 days minimum a year, which is hardly open at all. Other houses can be visited 'by appointment' with reasonable notice (telephone numbers in Hudson's). Owners may seek to cluster visitors on particular days. To a tourist, a house open by appointment is far more accessible than one not open until three months hence.

I have not included properties open only for weddings, corporate hospitality or coach parties, or whose rudeness to my polite request makes them a menace to English tourism. Houses demanding 'written application three months in advance' I regard as closed. Since some such houses receive public grant or tax relief, their access should be audited regularly. If owners do not play the game, some future government will end grants or relief, and all houses will be the losers.

That said, smaller private houses have a problem to which visitors must be sympathetic. They may be historic but not necessarily suited to mass tourism. Where visits are welcome but irregularly or only by reasonable appointment, I have indicated this with a suffix R. Other houses are now hotels, residential homes and apartment conversions, notably by the admirable Country Houses Association. Whatever one feels about the loss of their domestic character, all have at least been saved and are among the most accessible of properties, albeit sometimes for the price of a drink or a meal. Historic houses now hotels I have indicated with an H.

Finally, I have broken my own rule and included a handful of outstanding houses whose interiors are not open but where fine exteriors can be perambulated and appreciated by visitors to adjacent and popular gardens. They include Helmingham (Suffolk) and Hidcote (Gloucs). Such houses are indicated by P-G if private and NT-G if National Trust. Likewise, I have included a very few folly houses integral to much-visited landscapes, such as the banqueting house at Rievaulx (Yorks, N) and Stowe's Gothic Temple (Bucks), to which I feel readers would appreciate having their attention drawn.

The thousand include virtually all viewable dwellings and form, in effect, a gazetteer of England's accessible historic houses. I would be glad to know of any I have omitted. I have tried, with the help of my editors and friends, to be accurate in my attributions and dates, but sources often conflict wildly. The dating of houses built over a number of years can be moot, as can the architect chiefly responsible. Houses (unlike churches) change constantly. I can only plead that I have tried to ensure that information is correct as at the time of my visit.

More controversial is the awarding of stars. They are entirely my personal choice. They rate the overall quality of the house as presented to the public, and not gardens or other attractions. On balance I scaled down houses, however famous, for not being easily accessible or for being only partly open. The 'top hundred' more or less nominated themselves as England's houses of outstanding architectural quality and public display. Within that I chose twenty houses (the five stars) which qualify as 'international' celebrities. Three-star houses comprise the run of good historic houses well displayed and worthy of national promotion. Two- and one-star houses are of more local interest, hard to visit or with just one significant feature.

Are these really 'England's best thousand'? Very few of the nation's finest houses are, to my surprise, closed to the public and therefore not included. They embrace Badminton in Gloucestershire, Compton Wynyates in Warwickshire, Heveningham in Norfolk and Knowsley near Liverpool. I always regret that an owner does not wish to share his pride in possession with others, but that is a personal right. I believe in private property. The public has riches enough.

For me this has been a voyage of discovery through England as well as the English house. The voyage has often left strong impressions, negative as well as positive. At times I became depressed by the virtual collapse of countryside planning, with housing and industrial estates being allowed to mar the setting of the most beautiful places. In my view, the traditional English landscape has never been more comprehensively threatened as now. I have also found myself criticizing the dead hand of much modern custodianship, which seems intent on squeezing the life out of old houses and imposing a corporate identity on the resulting mausoleum. When I came to edit the entries I was reluctant to tone down all such comment.

I repeat, this is a personal list and a personal view. It is my vision of a thousand corners of England, warts and all. Houses are, or should be, living things and the manner in which we approach them is bound to be subject of debate. I welcome any correction or comment, especially from house owners, sent to me c/o the publisher.

Sources

The best guides to any house are the people who occupy it. They have felt its walls and sensed its seasons. They stand witness to its ghosts, real and imagined, and have thus become part of its history. As a substitute, guide-books vary widely from the academic to the plain childish. The best are published by English Heritage, erudite and enjoyable. National Trust guide-books are at last moving from the scholarly to the accessible, and the Trust's compendium *Guide*, by Lydia Greeves and Michael Trinick, is excellent.

My selection of a thousand properties derives from numerous sources. These include Hudson's *Historic Houses and Gardens,* supplemented by *Museums and Galleries* published by Tomorrow's Guides. The Historic Houses Association website is another invaluable source. Of recent house surveys, the best are John Julius Norwich's *Architecture of Southern England* (1985), John Martin Robinson's *Architecture of Northern England* (1986) and Hugh Montgomery-Massingberd's *Great Houses of England and Wales* (2000). Nigel Nicolson's *Great Houses of Britain* (1978) describes the most prominent. Their lists are not exhaustive and include houses not open to the public. Behind them stands Nikolaus Pevsner's massive 'Buildings of England' series, which deals with houses more generously (with plans) in the newer revised editions.

On English domestic architecture, the classics are hard to beat. They include Olive Cook's *The English House Through Seven Centuries* (1968), Alec Clifton-Taylor's *The Pattern of English Building* (1972), Hugh Braun's *Old English Houses* (1962), Sacheverell Sitwell's *British Architects and Craftsmen* (1964) and Plantagenet Somerset Fry's *Castles of Britain and Ireland* (1980).

On specific periods the best are Mark Girouard's *Robert Smythson and the English Country House* (1983), Giles Worsley's *Classical Architecture in England* (1995), Kerry Downes's *English Baroque Architecture* (1966) and Girouard's *The Victorian Country House* (1971). Joe Mordaunt Crook takes a lively look at the Victorian battle of the styles in *The Dilemma of Style* (1989). Jeremy Musson describes the manorial revival in *The English Manor House* (1999) and Gavin Stamp takes a wider look at the same period in *The English House 1860–1914* (1986). *Edwardian Architecture*, edited by Alastair Service

(1975), brings the story into the 20th century and Clive Aslet's *The Last Country Houses* (1982) almost completes it.

On social history, Girouard's *Life in the English Country House* (1978) is incomparable. *Creating Paradise* (2000) by Richard Wilson and Alan Mackley sets the house in its economic context. So does Mordaunt Crook's *The Rise of the Nouveaux Riches* (1999) and David Cannadine's *The Decline and Fall of the British Aristocracy* (1990). Adrian Tinniswood offers a fascinating insight in his *History of Country House Visiting* (1989). The desperate post-war bid to save houses is described in Marcus Binney's *Our Vanishing Heritage* (1984) and John Cornforth's *The Country Houses of England 1948–1998* (1998). Peter Mandler covers the same period in his scholarly *The Fall and Rise of the Stately Home* (1997).

Biographies of architects are too legion to list but Howard Colvin's *Biographical Dictionary of British Architects* (1978) was my bible over disputed dates and attributions. Of a more personal character is James Lees-Milne's delightful account of the National Trust's early acquisitions in *People and Places* (1992). Houses in distress are visited in John Harris's *No Voice from the Hall* (1998). *Writers and their Houses* (1993) is a first-class collection of essays, edited by Kate Marsh.

I am indebted to the many architectural commentaries in *Country Life*, champion of the historic buildings cause for over a century. I do not believe I could have found a thousand houses for my list were it not for its progenitors, Edward Hudson and Christopher Hussey, and their many successors.

Acknowledgements

This book arose from the rib of its sister volume, *England's Thousand Best Churches*. I visited the houses between 2000 and 2003. *The Times* serialized many of the entries, and I thank both Peter Stothard and Robert Thompson for their support as editors, and Jane Wheatley of the Weekend Section for publishing extracts. The book was published at Penguin by Stuart Proffitt, and designed by Andrew Barker.

Any book on houses is a partnership of words and pictures. Quintin Wright's photographs for *The Times'* series, reproduced by courtesy of that paper, superbly enhance my text. He is a master of the genre, giving houses a personality no words can truly equal. The pictures of the National Trust's properties come from its superb picture library, with thanks to Maggie Gowan and her expert staff.

I owe two further debts of gratitude. One is to Jeffrey Haworth for his painstaking reading of the text and checking dates and facts against his voluminous memory and almost as voluminous library. The other is to the editor of the text, Jenny Dereham. As she showed with *Churches*, her instinct for detail is matched only by her enthusiasm for the subject, a huge support to any writer. Given their respective talents, I hesitate over the normal disclaimer that all mistakes are entirely my own, though they are, of course, my responsibility. I also thank Valerie Scott and Lucy Denton for helping prepare the long and short lists. I am always indebted to my friend and mentor, Marcus Binney, who also read the introduction.

I visited almost all the houses as a paying member of the public, but in a few cases a special appointment was made. I cannot mention individually every owner who offered me time and hospitality over this long enterprise. I thank them all, heartened by their widespread awareness that most houses need visitors if they are to survive. My gratitude also goes to friends whose conveniently located houses I used as a base for regional visits. They include Jeffrey and Frances Jowell in Somerset, John and Sukie Hemming in Gloucestershire, Tim and Tricia Lankester in Norfolk, Mark and Gabriella Marlesford in Suffolk, Colin and Jane Renfrew in Cambridge, Miranda Seymour and Rosemary Seymour in Nottinghamshire, and Leon and Diana

Brittan in Yorkshire. Celina Fox was a stalwart companion in many tours of south-east England. My wife, Gayle Hunnicutt, travelled to every point of the compass. We together fell in love with English houses, if not with the English motorway network.

I lastly thank all those whose friendship or writings over the years have fostered my appreciation of these buildings. They have included Edward Montagu and Jenny Page at English Heritage, Jennifer Jenkins and Fiona Reynolds at the National Trust, and Bridget Cherry and John Newman of the Pevsner guides. Others not mentioned above whose inspiration I acknowledge include Clive Aslet, Dan Cruickshank, John and Eileen Harris, Gavin Stamp and Giles Worsley. By their ceaseless championing of old buildings, they too are part of the history of the English house.

The Top Hundred

FIVE STARS

Berkshire
WINDSOR CASTLE

Derbyshire
CHATSWORTH HOUSE
HADDON HALL
HARDWICK HALL

Dorset
KINGSTON LACY

Gloucestershire
BERKELEY CASTLE

Kent
KNOLE

Lancashire
SPEKE HALL

London, Central
KENSINGTON PALACE

London, West
HAMPTON COURT
SYON HOUSE

Norfolk
HOLKHAM HALL

Oxfordshire
BLENHEIM PALACE
BROUGHTON CASTLE

Sussex
BRIGHTON PAVILION
PARHAM HOUSE

Wiltshire
WILTON HOUSE

Yorkshire, East Riding
BURTON AGNES HALL

Yorkshire, North
CASTLE HOWARD

Yorkshire, West
HAREWOOD HOUSE

FOUR STARS

Bedfordshire
WOBURN ABBEY

Buckinghamshire
CLAYDON HOUSE
WADDESDON MANOR

Cambridgeshire
CAMBRIDGE
  UNIVERSITY:
  ST JOHN'S COLLEGE
  TRINITY COLLEGE

Cheshire
LYME PARK

Cornwall
LANHYDROCK

Cumbria
HUTTON-IN-THE-
  FOREST
LEVENS HALL
SIZERGH CASTLE

Derbyshire
BOLSOVER CASTLE
KEDLESTON HALL

Devon
SALTRAM HOUSE

Dorset
ATHELHAMPTON
  HOUSE
FORDE ABBEY
SHERBORNE CASTLE

Durham
RABY CASTLE

Essex
AUDLEY END

Gloucestershire
DYRHAM PARK

Hampshire
OSBORNE HOUSE
THE VYNE

Herefordshire
EASTNOR CASTLE

Hertfordshire
HATFIELD HOUSE
KNEBWORTH HOUSE

Huntingdonshire
BURGHLEY HOUSE

Kent
GODINTON PARK
HEVER CASTLE
IGHTHAM MOTE
LEEDS CASTLE
PENSHURST PLACE
ROCHESTER:
    RESTORATION
    HOUSE

Lancashire
ASTLEY HALL

Leicestershire
BELVOIR CASTLE

Lincolnshire
BELTON HOUSE
GRIMSTHORPE
    CASTLE
HARLAXTON MANOR

London, Central
DENNIS SEVERS
    HOUSE
HOME HOUSE
SPENCER HOUSE

London, East
ELTHAM PALACE

London, West
CHISWICK HOUSE
HAM HOUSE
OSTERLEY PARK

Norfolk
BLICKLING HALL
HOUGHTON HALL
OXBURGH HALL

Northamptonshire
ALTHORP
BOUGHTON HOUSE
CANONS ASHBY
DEENE PARK

Northumberland
ALNWICK CASTLE
CHILLINGHAM
    CASTLE
CRAGSIDE
WALLINGTON HALL

Nottinghamshire
NEWSTEAD ABBEY

Oxfordshire
CHASTLETON
OXFORD UNIVERSITY:
    MAGDALEN
    COLLEGE

Somerset
COTHAY MANOR
MONTACUTE HOUSE

Staffordshire
WIGHTWICK MANOR

Sussex
ARUNDEL CASTLE
BATEMAN'S
CHARLESTON
FIRLE PLACE
GOODWOOD HOUSE
PETWORTH HOUSE
UPPARK

Warwickshire
ARBURY HALL
RAGLEY HALL
WARWICK CASTLE

Wiltshire
LACOCK ABBEY
LONGLEAT

Worcestershire
HAGLEY HALL
HARVINGTON HALL
MADRESFIELD COURT

Yorkshire, East Riding
BURTON CONSTABLE
    HALL

Yorkshire, North
BENINGBROUGH HALL
NEWBY HALL
YORK: FAIRFAX
    HOUSE

Yorkshire, West
NOSTELL PRIORY

Glossary

I have tried in this book to avoid terms not familiar to the lay person. I assume that most readers of a book on houses can name their principal parts, inside and outside. However, a few common but specialist terms may have crept in for which translation may be helpful.

acanthus: pattern of exotic Mediterranean flower with large leaves used in classical decoration.

anthemion: honeysuckle flower pattern used in classical decoration.

ashlar: any block of masonry fashioned into a wall, either load-bearing or covering brick.

bailey: inner and outer: fortified enclosure, usually moated and surrounded by curtain wall, containing a motte (mound) on which stands a keep. Walls are topped by battlements, with crenellations which protect defenders from arrows, and machicolations or floor openings through which missiles can be fired down on attackers.

baluster: upright supporting handrail on stairs.

bargeboard: wooden board sheltering eaves of a roof.

bay: a space of wall between any vertical element, such as an upright beam, pillar or a division into a window or door.

bay window: window projecting from a flat wall, either canted if the sides are straight, or bowed if curved.

bolection mould: moulding concealing the join of vertical and horizontal surfaces, shaped like an S in cross-section.

Boulle: elaborate inlay work on the surface of furniture, customary in 17th- and 18th-century French work.

bow: *see* **bay window**

canted: *see* **bay window**

cartouche: frame for picture or statue, often oval and surrounded by a scroll.

caryatid: column in shape of a draped female figure.

casements: *see* **sashes**

chinoiserie: style of advanced Rococo with Chinese motifs, often associated with Gothick.

coffering: ceiling composed of beams enclosing sunken square or round panels.

collars: *see* **roof timbers**

corbel: stone or wood projection in wall to support a beam, statue or window sill.

cornice: ledge or projecting upper part of a classical entablature. Moulding at the top of a wall concealing join with the ceiling.

cottage ornée: late-Georgian/Victorian picturesque cottage, usually with thatched roof and Gothic windows.

crenellation: *see* **bailey**

cruck: simple structure of two, usually curved, trunks of wood formed into an inverted V which support the walls and roof of a medieval house.

curtain wall: *see* **bailey**

dressing: carving of stone to either a smooth or ornamental surface.

enfilade: line of rooms in sequence along one side of the house, usually with a line of interconnecting doors.

entablature: feature of classical architecture comprising everything above column height, formally composed of architrave, frieze and cornice.

flatwork: decorative plaster or woodwork in low relief.

frontispiece: decorative bay above a doorway in a Tudor or Jacobean building, customarily composed of Renaissance motifs.

gable: triangular end of double-pitched roof,

sometimes with stepped or scrolled (Dutch) sides.

garderobe: privy or lavatory, usually discharging into a ditch or moat outside a medieval house.

Great Chamber: *see* **solar**

grisaille: monochrome painting, usually a mural and in shades of grey.

grotesque: decorative wall motif of human figures, as found in Roman grottoes.

half-timbering: term for timber-framed house derived from the practice of splitting logs in half to provide beams.

hipped roof: sloping end to a roof instead of end **gable**.

Ho-Ho bird: **chinoiserie** motif associated with 18th-century Rococo style.

jetty or jettied floor: upper floor extended, or oversailed, beyond lower one, to give more space upstairs, and protect lower walls from adverse weather. Jettying also uses the downward thrust of upper walls to form a cantilever, preventing internal ceiling beams from bowing.

keep: *see* **bailey**

king post: *see* **roof timbers**

linenfold: the pattern on wall panels imitating folded linen.

louvre: covered turret above a medieval hall to allow smoke to escape.

machicolation: *see* **bailey**

mansard: a roof with two separate pitches of slope.

motte: *see* **bailey**

mullion: central divider of window, metal or stone.

oversail: *see* **jetty**

oriel: upper window projecting from a wall, sometimes (incorrectly) used to indicate tall medieval window lighting the dais end of the Great Hall.

Palladian: style of classical architecture, formal and refined outside, often lavish inside, named after Italian architect, Andrea Palladio (1508–80). Moving spirit behind most English classical designers, especially Inigo Jones and, later, Lord Burlington, William Kent and the early Georgians.

parlour: *see* **solar**

piano nobile: main ceremonial floor of classical building, sitting on basement or 'rustic' lower floor.

pier-glass: wall mirror supported by small table, bracket or console.

pilaster: flat column projecting only slightly from wall.

pointing: mortar or cement used between bricks.

porte-cochère: grand porch with driveway passing through it, allowing passengers to alight from carriages under cover.

prodigy house: large, ostentatious house of Elizabethan/Jacobean period.

queen post: *see* **roof timbers**

quoins: dressed corner stones.

rendering: covering of outside of building in stucco, cement or limewash.

Rococo: final phase of Baroque style in 18th century, typified by refined painted and plaster decoration, often asymmetrical and with figures.

roof timbers: a tie-beam runs horizontally across roof space. A king post rises vertically from it to the apex of the roof. Queen posts rise not to the apex but to subsidiary beams known as collars. Wind-braces strengthen the roof rafters.

'rustic': name given in Palladian architecture to lower floor or basement, beneath the *piano nobile*.

rustication: treatment of ashlar by deep-cutting joints so they look stronger or cruder.

sashes: windows opening by rising on sash ropes, as opposed to casements, which open on side hinges.

scagiola: composition of artificial stone that imitates appearance of grained marble.

screens passage: accessed from main door of medieval building and built into one end of Great Hall to shield it from draughts. Door or arches lead from passage into hall on one side and kitchens on other. Above is usually a minstrels' gallery.

Serlian: motifs derived from pattern books of Italian Renaissance architect, Sebastiano Serlio (1475–1554).

sgraffito: plaster decoration scratched to reveal other colour beneath.

solar: upstairs room at family end of medieval hall, originally above an undercroft or parlour. Originally accessed by ladder or spiral stairs, it was usually replaced by a Great Chamber in the Tudor era.

strapwork: strap or ribbon-like decorative scrolls found in Elizabethan and Jacobean design.

stucco: plaster, usually protective covering for brick, sometimes fashioned to imitate stone.

studding: vertical timbers laid near to each other to strengthen the wall. Close-studding tends to indicate wealth.

tie-beam: *see* **roof timbers**

vault: ceiling, usually of stone composed of arches.

Venetian window: Palladian window composed of three components, the centre one arched.

wind-braces: *see* **roof timbers**

Principal Periods of English Domestic Architecture

Dates	Periods and Styles	Principal Architects
11th–12th c.	NORMAN	
13th–15th c.	GOTHIC	
1485–c1550	TUDOR	
c1550–1603	ELIZABETHAN	Robert Smythson
1603–1649	JACOBEAN (Carolean)	Inigo Jones
1660–1688	RESTORATION	John Webb, Christopher Wren
1688–1714	WILLIAM-AND-MARY, QUEEN ANNE (English Baroque)	John Vanbrugh, Nicholas Hawksmoor, James Gibb
1714–c1740	EARLY GEORGIAN (Palladian)	Lord Burlington, William Kent, Henry Flitcroft
c1740–c1800	MID GEORGIAN (Neo-Classical, Rococo, Gothick, Picturesque)	William Chambers, Robert Adam, James Paine, James Wyatt
c1800–1837	LATE GEORGIAN (Regency, Greek Revival)	John Soane, Henry Holland, Robert Smirke, John Nash
1837–1901	VICTORIAN (Neo-Gothic, Jacobethan, Arts and Crafts)	Anthony Salvin, A. W. N. Pugin, Charles Barry, Sir Gilbert Scott, Philip Webb, Richard Norman Shaw
1901–c1914	EDWARDIAN	Edwin Lutyens
1918–1939	INTER-WAR (Art Deco, Modern Movement)	
1945–2000	MODERN	

Abbreviations used in the headings to the house entries

EH   English Heritage

NT   National Trust

NT-R National Trust with restricted opening times

NT-G National Trust house/garden

P   Privately owned

P-R   Privately owned, restricted opening times

P-G   Privately owned house/garden

M   Museum

H   Hotel

For an explanation of these abbreviations, *see* pages xxvii–xxviii.

Bedfordshire

Poor, rich little Bedfordshire. Sandwiched between the Home Counties, the Midlands and East Anglia, it owes full allegiance to none. Its landscape has been beaten into submission by acres of matchbox housing and industrial estates. Luton has been desperately abused and Bedford is little better. Yet the northern arms of the Chilterns still glide gracefully into the greensand ridges round Woburn and Ampthill and wealthier villages have been able to protect their character from encroachment.

With the exception of Henry Flitcroft's palace for the Duke of Bedford at Woburn, the county is bereft of great houses. Indeed, without the Woburn estate the county would be dull. Bushmead is a modest survivor of the Middle Ages. Houghton is a ruined exemplar of the Elizabethan Renaissance. Wrest Park, with a Thomas Archer pavilion in its formal garden, offers only a ghost of the eccentric Earl de Grey. Old Warden is stolidly late Victorian, but has a charming earlier Swiss cottage in its grounds.

My most unexpected find was the recreation of the bedroom the colourful Victorian medievalist, William Burges, designed for himself; this is in the admirable Cecil Higgins house in Bedford.

Bedford:
   Castle Close **
Bushmead Priory *
Houghton House *

Old Warden Park *
   Swiss Cottage *
Woburn Abbey ****

Wrest Park:
   House **
   Pavilion *

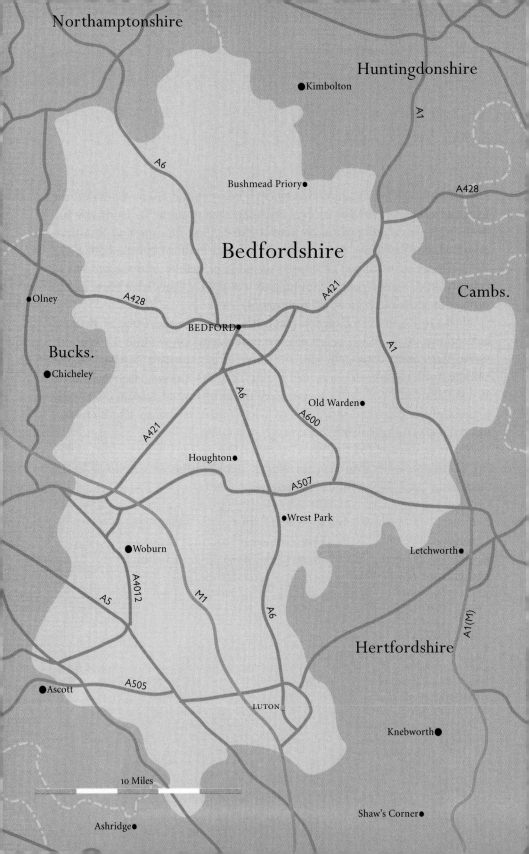

BEDFORD: CASTLE CLOSE
**

Cecil Higgins Museum, Castle Lane
Burges bedroom recreated in Victorian villa
(M)

Where would art be without younger sons? Cecil Higgins, son of the owner of a Bedfordshire brewery, went up to London and spent his inheritance on art. He eventually returned to assume control of the family firm. On his retirement he decided to bequeath his house, Castle Close, as a museum to his native town. He died in 1941.

The house was a classical villa built in the 1840s. Its trustees afforded it scant respect and pulled down some of its internal walls to create an 'open-plan' museum. When in the 1970s they extended the museum into a purpose-built gallery next door, they restored the Higgins house as a Victorian mansion. By then few of the rooms had four surviving walls. An open-plan Victorian mansion is a contradiction in terms but, as a custodian said to me, 'We were stuck with it.' Perhaps some judicious rebuilding might be in order.

That said, Castle Close is a good recreation of a late-Victorian interior. The intention is 'to give the impression that the family has just gone out for a walk and will be back any minute'. Apart from the lack of walls, this impression is spoilt only by visitors not being allowed to use the stairs, but having to return to the museum and re-enter the top floor through one of the connected galleries.

The sequence begins downstairs with the oak-panelled smoking room, with wall lights by Norman Shaw and fire irons by Charles Voysey. Beyond are the drawing room and the White Room, the latter with a rosewood cabinet by Gillow and a Tompion clock. The furniture is not uniformly Victorian. There is a Georgian satinwood writing desk and an inlaid Carolean table. But Higgins was primarily a collector of Pre-Raphaelite and Arts and Crafts work. His taste in ceramics decorates every shelf. The library bookcase is by Alfred Waterhouse.

The pride of the upstairs is a complete bedroom by the neo-Gothic architect, William Burges, including the bed he made for himself and in which he died. The room is dark yet colourful, with a superb bookcase and dressing table, both by Burges. Wardrobe panels illustrate the clothing of Adam. There are even anthropomorphic toiletries, with dancers in the form of toothbrushes and combs. The room is a delight, executed with levity and humour.

This is more than can be said for the guidebook which is saturated with political correctness. We must apparently be told that the late Victorians persecuted women and servants. A man's word was 'law'. Women were not allowed to smoke, were forced to 'love, honour and obey' and talked only of social tittle-tattle. It makes us wonder how Queen Victoria, Florence Nightingale and Sarah Bernhardt survived their long, tedious and oppressed existences.

BUSHMEAD PRIORY *

4m W of St Neot's
Ruin of priory refectory in rural setting (EH)

I include Bushmead for its setting as much as its content. The old Augustinian priory sat in a secluded valley deep in the Bedfordshire farmland. What is left sits there still, accompanied by a Georgian farmhouse next door and a half-timbered one across the valley. Bushmead is supremely peaceful in a county sadly short of that quality.

The building accessible today is the old priory refectory. It has a Gothic doorway and Tudor windows, apparently with their original wooden tracery. The roof is intact and covers a tall, single-storeyed hall with cobbled floor. This has a two-storey section beyond, presumably the prior's private rooms. This must have been a cosy, gentle retreat.

On the first floor are wall-paintings and some stained glass. They suggest that, as in other cases elsewhere after the Dissolution, new owners showed the old buildings and their decoration a measure of respect. At last, we do so too.

HOUGHTON HOUSE *

1m N of Ampthill
Ruin of innovative Jacobean mansion on hill
(EH)

Houghton is a most romantic ruin. The Middle Ages built houses in dells and by streams, with an eye to seclusion and security. The Elizabethans and Jacobeans were prepared to flaunt their wealth; if they could find a hill they would build on it. Houghton House was commissioned in 1615 by Mary, Countess of Pembroke, sister of Sir Philip Sidney, and an accomplished patron of the arts and horses. It looks out north over Bedfordshire. The scenery is now poxed with brickwork chimneys. The house, roofless but with its walls standing, lies at the end of a long, almost overgrown beech avenue. Although the brickworks have eroded its fabric, it retains its pride. It was reputedly the basis for Bunyan's 'House Beautiful' in *Pilgrim's Progress*.

The house was bought in 1738 by the Duke of Bedford for his son, the Marquis of Tavistock, but it was stripped and sold in 1794, some years after the Marquis's death. The destruction was conducted, according to one account, 'with the delight of a butcher killing sheep'. The place has been a ruin ever since, but the building remains stylistically intriguing. Houghton House is a conventional Jacobean H-plan mansion with prominent corner towers, bay windows and large gables. Yet three of the façades have, or mostly had, sophisticated Renaissance frontispieces of the sort still relatively unusual outside the court circle of Inigo Jones.

These frontispieces are barely discernible, although they are clear in the print of the old house on display on the site. One elevation retains a Tuscan loggia, with some of its metopes surviving. Other bits and pieces can be detected, a keystone here, a medallion there, all teasing ghosts of what was clearly a remarkable composition. The Victorians would have taken this building in hand and given it back its historical form. We dare do no more than stabilize it.

OLD WARDEN PARK *

6m SE of Bedford
Gaunt Jacobethan house with Victorian art collection (P-R)

Joseph Shuttleworth was a Victorian businessman from Lincolnshire eager to move up in the world. In 1872 he bought the Old Warden estate of some 4,600 acres from the family of Lord Ongley. Shuttleworth pulled down the old house and hired the London architect, Henry Clutton, to design a new one. The design he cheekily if vaguely modelled on Gawthorpe, the Lancashire house of Lord Shuttleworth, to whom he was no relation. The reaction of the Lancashire Shuttleworths is not recorded. Old Warden is far bigger than Gawthorpe, the Jacobethan style at its most grandiloquent. The house is truly a Victorian pile.

In 1940, Joseph Shuttleworth's daughter-in-law, Dorothy, decided to commemorate the death of her son in a flying accident with a trust devoted to his two interests, aviation and agriculture. The Shuttleworth Trust is now an agricultural college, while its hangars hold Britain's finest collection of antique airplanes. Dorothy Shuttleworth continued to live in the house and preside over the college, welcoming each new student personally until her death in 1968. The planes take part in regular flying displays overhead. On my last visit an 'aerial prom' was rehearsing, a falconry school was in progress and a wedding was taking place in the mansion.

The house entrance is directly into a large hall, off which lead an even grander staircase hall and formal saloon, now a banqueting hall. The ceilings are all neo-Jacobean and the fireplaces gigantic, tiled and with reliefs of hunting scenes.

Old Warden is most remarkable for its pictures, collected by the Shuttleworths with no great imagination but a fine sense of scale. It is a gallery of grandiloquent country house art. Apart from a Lawrence, the artists are Victorians only now emerging from obscurity, such as William Leader, Vicat Cole, Edwin

Long and Frank Dicksee. Their works, mostly romantic landscapes, society portraits and 'stags at bay', are on a hundred country house walls.

SWISS COTTAGE *

Old Warden Park, 6m SE of Bedford
Romantic chalet in an enchanted garden (P)

I first glimpsed the chalet on a warm summer day as a party was making its nervous way through the woods and out into a glade. Above it stood a cottage on a knoll. It was a surreal scene worthy of Tolkien.

The chalet lies at the centre of the Swiss Garden, distinguishable from an English one only by a scatter of Swiss-style buildings erected in the 1820s. Nearby is a romantic grotto, ornamental bridge and thatched canopy over a seat running round the trunk of an oak tree. The seat was reputedly where a beautiful Swiss girl caught a cold in a rainstorm and later died.

The garden was designed by Lord Ongley, then owner of Old Warden, and reflects the cottage ornée style of many of the new houses built by Ongley in the neighbouring village. The architect is believed to be J. B. Papworth of St Neot's, publisher of *Hints on Ornamental Gardening* and a promoter of the style.

The Swiss Cottage is no more than a single-room summer house, but of peculiar charm. It has a thatched conical roof and distinctive porch. A balcony runs round the outside, resting on untreated upright logs. The outside is panelled in hazel twigs and the inside is covered in fretwork. The craftsmanship is excellent. The interior has a fireplace and chimney. A fierce peacock guards the door.

WOBURN ABBEY ****

E of Woburn
Ancestral home of Bedfords, with art collection and grotto (P)

Woburn is Bedfordshire's one great house and makes the most of it. In the 1950s, the then Duke of Bedford pioneered the movement to save such mansions, in his case by opening the house fully to the public and creating a safari park and other attractions in the grounds. A true showman, he would dance the twist with the local dairy maids and lunch in the Canaletto Room while visitors walked past behind ropes. Today's Woburn is more restrained, though the personality of the family remains dominant, which is as it should be. The guidebook makes full use of the first person singular.

Nothing could be more serene than the approach. From the village of Woburn, the drive leads through an evergreen wood thick with cedar, fir, pine and yew. Suddenly it bursts out onto a Repton landscape of spacious parkland, across which deer drift like clouds. Visitors then drive round the outskirts of the U-shaped house, admiring the west front built by Henry Flitcroft in 1746–61 and south front added by Henry Holland forty years later. The north range remains mostly 17th century. Despite this variety, the house seems of a piece, stately but unostentatious.

To the rear of the Abbey are two large quadrangular courts also built by Flitcroft. They were once linked by a building containing tennis courts, a riding school, stables and ancillary offices. Since the present U-shaped main house once had a fourth side, Woburn was a very large property indeed. In 1950, decay was used to justify demolishing Flitcroft's riding school and Holland's east range, destruction unthinkable today. Yet Flitcroft's surviving quadrangles are still among the finest outbuildings of any great house.

The route through the house is not wholly satisfactory. Visitors enter from behind into the old 17th-century rooms. This means first encountering not a Great Hall but an ante-room of the sort in which a tenant might meet the Duke's agent. That said, the Book Room contains a superb collection of natural history books, some helpfully open to view. Here too is a copy of the Althorp van Dyck, of the youthful brothers-in-law, the Duke of Bedford and Earl of Bristol, who were to take opposing sides in the Civil War.

A corridor called Paternoster Row leads to Flitcroft's staircase. The walls are lined with family portraits, dominated on the stairs by a van Dyck of the 5th Countess of Bedford with a tiny dog. The rooms now become more spacious, although at Woburn never losing touch with domesticity. They are pleasantly filled with family memorabilia.

Along the Dukes' Corridor is a room dedicated to the Flying Duchess, wife of the 11th Duke. A traveller, naturalist and photographer, she was a celebrated aviator between the wars, flying both to India and to the Cape but was killed in 1937 crashing in the Fens. The Yellow Drawing Room has a spectacular Rococo ceiling and overmantel. It was decorated for the 4th Duke in the 1760s in the French style, to commemorate his ambassadorship to Paris. The so-called Racing Room was decorated by Flitcroft in the same style, and is now a shrine to the present family's enthusiasm for horse racing. The purple and white Bedford racing colours are draped over 18th-century furniture in what seems a studied anachronism. Instead of Bedford humans we now see Bedford horses and their jockeys.

Flitcroft's state rooms along the west front move up a scale in grandeur. They begin with the bedroom in which Queen Victoria stayed in 1841. The ceiling is higher, the decoration more ornate. The Queen's Dressing Room has blue walls and paintings by Jan Steen, Cuyp and van Dyck. The Blue Drawing Room claims to be where 'afternoon tea' was first celebrated in the early 19th century. A table is laid for this delicate refreshment, overlooked by Claude and Canaletto.

The state saloon, the chief reception room, rises two storeys in the centre of the west range. Its silk wall-hangings were so faded when the house was first opened to the public that they had to be removed. Rather than replace them in kind, the then Duke commissioned Roland Pym to paint scenes from Russell history as murals. They will take time to merge into the context. Beyond is the state dining room, lined with van Dycks, and at the end of the enfilade, the celebrated Canaletto room. Redecorated and with its Venetian window restored, the walls shimmer with Venetian light and colour.

The south wing by Henry Holland is privately occupied. Visitors must return down Flitcroft's Long Gallery, divided by Corinthian columns as if into three rooms. It contains a display of 16th- and 17th-century portraits. These include the Earl of Essex by Gheeraerts and the famous Armada portrait of Elizabeth I. Her hand sits proprietorially on a globe, while the Spanish fleet lies wrecked on the rocks behind her. Further Bedford treasures are now housed and displayed in secure basement vaults. They include sets of Meissen, Chelsea and Sèvres, as well as much gold and silver.

The exit is back through the 17th-century wing, including a parlour and grotto. The latter is a superb example of this genre, the gods of classical Rome turned troglodyte. The work is even attributed to Inigo Jones's protégé, Isaac de Caus, who worked for the Bedfords on their Covent Garden estate. The grotto is furnished with chairs in the form of dolphins and shells.

WREST PARK HOUSE **

1m E of Silsoe
French-style château (EH)

Terrible things were done to Wrest Park by the rerouting of the A6 round the adjacent village of Silsoe. It saved the village but spoilt the park. It reminds me of the old-fashioned obstetrician's question: 'Sir, would you like me to save the mother or the child?' At least drivers can get a glimpse of the house from behind their steering wheels.

Wrest is stylistically remarkable, indeed for its date unique in England. It was built by the Earl de Grey in the 1830s to replace what was the family's ancestral home. Unlike most English houses over the previous century, it took its cue not from Italy but from France. The Earl was an ardent francophile. The drive

The Archer pavilion at Wrest Park

from Silsoe is through grand gateposts and into Normandy.

The house lies on the right of the drive with geometric precision, simple, ashlar-faced and 13 bays long. It has deep windows, mansard roofs and corner pavilions. The model was the Hotel de Matignon in Paris. The Earl was his own architect but used the French-sounding James Cléphane as his clerk of works. Allocating responsibility between them is impossible. The Earl interfered all the time, claiming that there was not a ladder or a scaffold that he had not climbed to supervise the work.

The style of the interior is Louis XV. The central staircase hall is spectacular, richly ornamented with plaster trophies and relief panels above the doors. It is said that the Earl regarded the plasterwork females as insufficiently well endowed and 'enhanced' them with his own hands. The royal portraits, some by Kneller, are ideal to the setting. The other reception rooms face the garden beyond and form a stately enfilade. They have painted ceilings, with gold and white predominating, and fine fireplaces.

At this point interest collapses. Wrest is now owned by English Heritage but the house is occupied by the Silsoe Research Institute. The latter's outbuildings spoil the approach avenue and its abuse of the interior is dreadful. The best of the reception rooms, the library, is packed with modern bookcases and computer equipment. Other rooms are cheaply kitted out for lectures and seminars. It is like a Soviet academy of sciences camped in a St Petersburg palace.

The garden is well maintained. The Earl's French parterres lie immediately below the garden front. They have been restored as sweeping scrolls of gravel interspersed with flower beds and classical statuary. Ahead stretches the Long Water, Georgian landscaping before the era of Capability Brown,

although Brown was employed at Wrest in 1758 to make the canals curve more 'naturally'.

The grounds contain an orangery, banqueting house, Petit Trianon, temples and bridges – a rural Chiswick (London, W). At the climax of the Long Water is Thomas Archer's earlier Pavilion (below).

WREST PARK PAVILION *

4m N of Barton-le-Cley
Thomas Archer design, architectural murals
(EH)

Thomas Archer's Pavilion, designed in 1709 for Earl de Grey's predecessor, the Duke of Kent, is a virtuoso essay in English Baroque. As de Grey was later to take the Parisian *hôtel* as his model for his new Wrest Park, in whose grounds the pavilion lies, so Archer took Borromini's St Ivo's church behind Rome's Piazza Navona. It does not soar, as does Borromini. The Pavilion is closer to Wren in its English solidity. But it is a minor masterpiece, beautifully set at the end of the canal from de Grey's French château, guarded by a statue of William III in Roman dress.

The building has a large classical portal enclosing a no less grand doorway beneath a giant dome. Matching doorways guard each of the four sides. The circular interior is a superb composition, rising to a cupola. It was painted with architectural *trompe-l'œil* by Louis Hauderoy in 1712. These murals have recently been restored.

The Pavilion was more than a summerhouse. It has a series of small bedrooms, one of which has a fireplace. There are kitchens in the basement and a servant's room in the dome, reached by a concealed stair. The house was clearly intended for more than taking tea and might have been used overnight for hunting parties. There is even a two-seater privy.

Berkshire

The Royal County of Berkshire has been reorganized out of administrative existence. Yet its spirit still guards the southern bank of the Thames and embraces Slough, Windsor, Maidenhead and Reading. Its royalty is based on its one great building, Windsor Castle, so little visited by the English yet the most palatial house in England by a wide margin. Although a castle since Norman times, it is principally a monument to Restoration taste and 19th-century neo-Gothic splendour. It is also one of England's finest art galleries.

In Windsor's shadow is the old school of Eton, its core still built round its medieval collegiate courtyards. At Basildon is Carr of York's only southern house, saved by the Iliffe family. The home of Elizabeth's trusted Walsingham is at Englefield, though the building is now mostly Jacobethan. Bear Wood, built by the owner of *The Times*, is a colossal Victorian fantasmagoria.

Basildon ✳✳✳
Bear Wood ✳✳
Englefield House ✳✳
Eton ✳✳

Swallowfield ✳✳
Welford ✳
Windsor:
    The Castle ✳✳✳✳

Windsor:
    Queen Mary's Dolls'
    House ✳

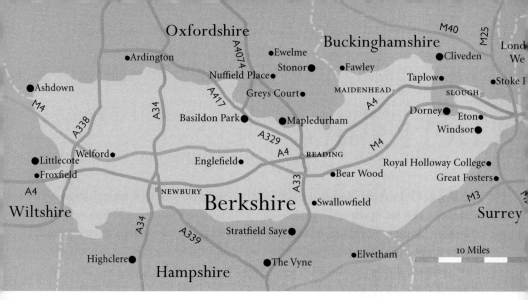

A map showing locations across Oxfordshire, Buckinghamshire, Berkshire, Wiltshire, Hampshire and Surrey, including: Ardington, Ewelme, Stonor, Fawley, Cliveden, Lond, We, Nuffield Place, Taplow, Stoke F, Ashdown, Greys Court, MAIDENHEAD, SLOUGH, Basildon Park, Mapledurham, Dorney, Eton, Windsor, Welford, Littlecote, Froxfield, Englefield, READING, Bear Wood, Royal Holloway College, Great Fosters, NEWBURY, Berkshire, Swallowfield, Wiltshire, Surrey, Stratfield Saye, Highclere, Hampshire, Elvetham, The Vyne. Roads shown: M40, M25, M4, A4074, A417, A34, A338, A329, A33, A4, M3, A339, M4. Scale: 10 Miles.

BASILDON ***

Basildon, 2m NW of Pangbourne
Carr of York's southern essay in the Adam
style (NT)

When Lady Iliffe discovered Basildon Park in 1952 there was 'no window . . . left intact, and most were repaired with cardboard or plywood; there was a large puddle on the Library floor'. She found walls still covered in Army graffiti, which the Army felt no obligation to clean when it vacated the house after occupation during the Second World War. All seemed hopeless. Yet the Iliffes cherished this place for twenty-five years and handed it beautifully restored to the National Trust. When I arrived, after trudging from the distant car park through heavy rain, I was rudely ordered to stop writing notes in the guidebook on pain of eviction. Note-taking is not allowed here. Students should stay away for fear of worse.

Basildon as left by the Iliffes is immaculate. It was built in 1776 by John Carr of York, his one building in the south, for the Indian nabob, Sir Francis Sykes. It was then sold in 1838 to a Liberal MP, James Morrison, but after his daughter died in 1910 the contents were sold and the building decayed. Some of its best plasterwork went to the Waldorf Astoria in New York (for its 'Basildon Room'). Not until the Iliffes chanced upon the house after the

war did it recover its soul. Basildon is their monument as much as Carr's.

The west façade, in honeyed Bath stone, is a harmonious composition of portico, basement and wings. It might be a town house overlooking Piccadilly. The entrance is hidden behind three arched openings, up stairs from a loggia and behind the portico. Visitors thus half-enter the building, go out onto the portico, then come into the hall through a theatrical sequence of spaces.

Carr's interiors are more refined than, for instance, in his flamboyant Fairfax House in York (Yorks, N). They closely reflect the style of Robert Adam, with whom Carr had worked at Harewood (Yorks, W). This can immediately be seen in the Etruscan ceiling panels and wall medallions of the hall. The room is as Carr left it, including the superbly crafted doors. The plasterwork is picked out in soft pastel shades of lilac, pale ochre, pink and green.

Carr's plan is based on the dramatic sequence of entrance hall leading direct into the staircase hall and then to the Octagon Saloon and its vista over the park beyond. The stair is light, cantilevered from the wall with delicate treads and iron balusters, a stair up which to glide rather than climb. The Octagon

Iliffe four-poster at Basildon

Saloon has a large Venetian window forming a proscenium to the view, hung with drapes like stage curtains. The paintings from the Iliffe collection are mostly works by Batoni, in unusual devotional vein.

The dining room is a perfect example of Carr's deference to Adam. There is a screen of columns at one end and medallions, fronds and tendrils coating every space. The room is also a triumph of meticulous restoration. In the Green Drawing Room, the ceiling takes the form of a wheel of tendrils flanked by heads of Roman emperors.

Upstairs bedrooms contain four-posters, furniture and pictures collected by Lady Iliffe at country house sales across England. She must have had fun. A side room is devoted to Graham Sutherland's cartoons for his Coventry Cathedral tapestry.

BEAR WOOD **

Sindlesham, 2m NW of Wokingham
Victorian pile in neo-Elizabethan style (P-R)

The Victorian proprietor of *The Times*, John Walter, was a very rich man. By the time he had finished the monstrously extravagant Bear Wood he was not, and *The Times* had eventually to be sold to Lord Northcliffe. Walter was an assiduous commoner. He avoided the company of aristocrats, was philanthropic, religious and refused all honours. He was also an amateur engineer, obsessed with technology. Bear Wood, begun in 1865, is Elizabethan in style, yet was packed with iron and concrete, central heating and fireproofing. It had running water, its own gasworks and five bathrooms.

The house was supposed to have been designed by William Burn, but when Walter read *The English Gentleman's House* by a self-promoting Scotsman, Robert Kerr, he cancelled Burn's contract and commissioned Kerr instead. It was a bad mistake. The building took the rest of the 1860s to complete and the cost was astronomical, some £120,000, draining the coffers of *The Times* to the fury of the staff. The house later became a Merchant Navy orphanage and is now a school dedicated to naval children. The Walter family still live on the estate, although most of their original 7,000 acres have disappeared into Wokingham suburbia.

The building is approached along a sensational avenue of Wellingtonias, one of the most dramatic I know. Driving down it on a windy day is like running the gauntlet of a regiment in fur coats. Its climax is Kerr's huge staircase tower, bristling with pinnacles. Mark Girouard comments that Bear Wood was Kerr's attempt to make Elizabethan seem as 'muscular' as Tractarian Gothic. The result is 'a sock on the jaw . . . as if Highclere had been sent on a weightlifting course'. To Pevsner, 'Bear Wood is indeed nearer to Blenheim than to our poky villas'.

The style is chaotic, an architectural doodle. A giant *porte-cochère* fronts a tower with a Belgian roof. On the right is an Elizabethan wing with large gable and projecting window bay. The answering bay on the left is interrupted by the staircase tower, its façade crammed with stepped windows and crowded pilasters. Beyond is a range culminating in the Kitchen Court, with its own gables and tower. The garden front has had the Continental 17th century thrown at it, with projecting bays, towers and Dutch gables.

The interior was one of the largest of any house of the period. The entrance is into what may be considered a screens passage, with the Great Hall to the left. The screen is neo-Jacobean and the Great Hall is coated in tooled leather. Giant arches lead to the staircase hall. This is more impressive inside than out; indeed, it ranks as a wonder of mid-Victorian architecture, now restored and brilliantly lit. The stairs rise the full height of the tower, ending in a large lantern, dark blue with stars. The balusters are of Elizabethan pillars on a scrollwork base. Stained glass fills the windows and busts the window sills.

Behind the Great Hall is a large picture gallery. The original pair of drawing rooms run the full depth of the house, divided by sliding doors. These doors are decorated with exquisite marquetry, apparently done on the estate. The panels depict musical instruments surrounded by arabesques. The Renaissance fireplaces have collage overmantels. Upstairs the Bachelors' Rooms and the Young Ladies' Rooms were separate, reached by individual staircases. So too were the Strangers' Men-servants' rooms. This fastidious arrangement is also found in Victorian Lanhydrock (Corn-wall).

ENGLEFIELD HOUSE **

Theale
Victorianized Elizabethan house with Georgian interiors (P)

Englefield was owned by Elizabeth's spy and trusty courtier, Sir Francis Walsingham, whose daughter married the doomed Earl of Essex. It passed through the Paulet family to the present owners, the Benyons. Above the front door are the armorial bearings of a young Paulet who fell in love with and married a servant girl on the estate. Since she had no heraldry of her own, he represented her on his shield in the most romantic fashion, as a simple field of pure gold. She remains thus commemorated to this day.

The house is Walsingham's Elizabethan mansion much rebuilt and reinterpreted by the Georgians, Victorians and the present day. The principal remodelling in the mid-19th century yielded the present romantic outline, a forest of turrets, spikes, cupolas and balus-trades, almost a miniature of neighbouring Highclere (Hants). Yet the house is still in form the same house as appears in the back-ground of Nathaniel Dance's portrait of Paulet Wrighte in 1775, which hangs in the house, a classic depiction of an English gentleman and his seat.

The estate is now sandwiched between the A4 and the M4, protected by a park dotted with Victorian estate buildings. The interior is full of Victorian self-confidence. The entrance hall is of two storeys, with a balcony looking down from the bedroom passage above.

A long corridor links the four main recep-tion rooms to the spacious staircase. Each is

stylistically different. The 1770s dining room is brilliant in Corinthian white on plum-coloured walls. Brackets carry the Benyon collection of porcelain beneath a ceiling of Georgian Rococo. The library is heavier, of the 1860s, with bird medallions incorporated into its ceiling. Over the fireplace is a Constable of the house, originally painted with cattle in the foreground but later overpainted with stags to give a more noble setting.

The Victorian drawing room was quietly refreshed by David Mlinaric in the 1980s. Upstairs is a restored Long Gallery, dating from the original Elizabethan house and hung with Restoration portraits. Englefield is an in-genious place, showing every age of English architecture living at ease with the 21st century.

ETON COLLEGE **

Eton
Medieval foundation with domestic courts and collegiate buildings (P)

Eton may be world famous but at its core is still a simple medieval property of gatehouse, chapel, hall and two courtyards. The old school was founded by Henry VI in 1440, to give seventy scholars a free education and display holy relics, including pieces of the True Cross and the Crown of Thorns. It was thus to be a centre of pilgrimage, with a large pilgrim-age church and community of secular priests as well as an almshouse. The original college took some eighty years to complete, by when the appeal of relics was giving way to the forces of Reformation. The scholastic role went from strength to strength.

The outer courtyard, School Yard, contains the original scholars' buildings and the great chapel, the only one of the original buildings to be of stone. The yard forms an intimate campus still with a markedly medieval atmos-phere. The range to the street was rebuilt in the 17th century because it was falling down. On the upper floor is Upper School, a Restoration classroom interior, its panelling entirely covered with boys' graffiti. To the left of School Yard is Lower School, reputedly the

oldest schoolroom in the world, in continuous use since 1443. Its heavy beams and pillars give it the appearance of a ship below decks. Again the carving of initials is much in evidence.

At the far side of School Yard is Lupton's Tower, leading to the cloisters, College Hall and Provost's Lodge. These are also shown to the public. The Hall has scissorbeams above a Victorian screen coated in Etonian heraldry. The library and the adjacent museum of Eton life are minor gems. The library was constructed when the cloisters were raised a floor in 1729, in an early Georgian style with a gallery. It comprises three interconnecting rooms beneath a rich classical ceiling. Among its treasures is a Gutenberg Bible.

SWALLOWFIELD PARK **

Swallowfield, 6m S of Reading
Talman vestibule and hidden walled garden
(P-R)

With the flight of James II from England in 1688, his closest courtiers had to make a choice. They could join him in France and hope for his early return, or they could take refuge in the countryside and watch how the wind blew. The king's brother-in-law, the 2nd Earl of Clarendon, did the latter. He had William Talman design him a mansion at Swallowfield.

In 1820 this house was sold to Sir Henry Russell, Chief Justice of Bengal, who decided he would rather have a modest Regency villa than a nabob's palace and commissioned William Atkinson accordingly. Talman's work was almost all eradicated. What survives is a pretty vestibule and a doorway from the original house re-erected as a gate to the walled garden. The Russell family held the property until 1964 when it was sold to what is now the Country Houses Association.

This serene late-Georgian house is situated at a distance from the village, with a park

Englefield's Corinthian splendour

containing Jersey cattle arranged decorously round an old bridge. The entrance is reached past picturesque outhouses and stables, their redbrick making the ochre stucco of the main front the more dignified. The interior is that of a comfortable 19th-century home. The Talman vestibule is beautiful, oval in shape with niches, statues and ceiling plasterwork with the Clarendon coat of arms. The library has what are described as 'Napoleonic' bookcases.

The chief pleasure of the house is its setting. The stables courtyard survives, and is supposedly by Talman. Its ground floor is arched, as if once surrounded by a colonnade. This enclave formed a complete estate community, including abattoir, brewhouse, stables and nursery. Beyond is a small formal garden with Talman's gate giving onto a glorious walled garden. This is not formally planted but wild with shrubs, trees and hidden corners.

WELFORD PARK *

Welford, 4m NW of Newbury
Seventeenth-century mansion much refaced
(P-R)

The house is close to its village in the French style. Outbuildings are contiguous with cottages and the church, while the entrance faces outwards towards the fields. This setting appears to date from the house's monastic origins.

Welford Park was owned by the Archer family and the building dates from the mid-17th century. The current owners, the Puxleys, are tortuously descended from the Archers and also from the Newtons of Lincolnshire. Isaac Newton, of humble origins, was keen to declare his kinship with them. Later, when he was famous, they were keen to claim kinship with him. The Newton male line died out, however, when a baby son and heir was carelessly thrown out of a window by the family monkey. All this is recorded in a fine collection of family portraits hanging in the house.

The house was designed by John Jackson of Oxford. There is much English bond brickwork on the side elevations. The history of the main elevation is vexed and has been attributed to the architect Thomas Archer, briefly married into the family, but the way the pilasters meet the corners is botched and the pediment seems unrelated. It is barely conceivable a proper architect can have been involved – or at least there must have been a fearful row.

The interior of Welford was much altered in the 1830s and remains in family use. Apart from some curious Rococo pelmets, the chief interest is a magnificent Wootton painting of a hunting scene which dominates the 17th-century staircase.

WINDSOR: THE CASTLE

*****

Windsor
Favoured home of the monarch, state rooms of all periods (M)

Overlooking the Thames at Windsor is one of the finest palaces in the world. Few English people visit Windsor Castle because they think of it as the private residence of the Queen. That indeed applies to over a third of the floor area. But this place is gigantic. Nowhere in England is as regal as Windsor, not even Hampton Court. It is the supreme expression of monarchy in architecture and art.

The castle is clearly visible from the M4 where is sits directly under the Heathrow flightpath. The castle was founded by William the Conqueror, who built the present Round Tower on the mound by the Upper Ward. Edward III built a large medieval palace round it, with the knightly precinct of the College of St George in the Lower Ward. Windsor was a Parliamentary stronghold in the Civil War.

Two great periods of expansion followed. First was under the epic builder, Charles II, for whom Hugh May constructed the state apartments in the 1670s. These interiors were decorated by Antonio Verrio and Grinling Gibbons. This range was then vastly extended by George III and George IV. Their architects were James Wyatt and his nephew, Jeffry Wyatville, designing in the Picturesque style. They gave Windsor a grand suite of neo-Gothic ceremonial and banqueting chambers, as well as semi-state entertaining rooms adjacent to the Royal Family's private quarters. They raised the Round Tower by a storey and added subsidiary towers, gates, terraces and staircases. It is principally to Wyatville that we owe the Castle's present outline.

The guidebook to Windsor is exemplary, including a plan of the furnishing and pictures in each room. The entrance to the state and semi-state rooms is from the North Terrace, leading into Wyatt's Gothic undercroft. This now houses the Dolls' House, and galleries displaying drawings by Leonardo, Michelangelo and others. It also serves as the formal entrance to the Grand Staircase and Grand Vestibule.

The staircase, further altered by Salvin, borders on the kitsch. It presents the English monarch as a figure of Arthurian, if not Wagnerian, romance. Mounted knights in armour flank the ascent. A great Gothic lantern rises overhead. The visitor emerges into a series of vestibules, all wallowing in armour, trophies, swords, guns and shields. In one is the gold tiger's head captured from the throne of the Indian Tippoo Sahib and the lead bullet which killed Nelson. The fan-vaulted Grand Vestibule is a temple to armorial glory.

Beyond is the Waterloo Chamber, intended by George IV to commemorate the final defeat of Napoleon. It is hung with the twenty portraits of allied European leaders involved in Wellington's last campaign, all by Sir Thomas Lawrence. The roof is said to have been shaped to reflect the timbers of a ship. The panels separating the portraits are salvaged work of Grinling Gibbons. This is a stupendous room.

The visitor now enters Charles II's state rooms. They are arranged as the King's and Queen's rooms, with decoration to match, and contain many of the finest pictures from the Royal Collection. The King's Drawing Room is almost all Rubens. The bed chamber is Canaletto and Gainsborough, with a magnificent French 'polonaise' bed. The dressing room has works by Steen, Rembrandt, Holbein and van Dyck. The closet has Hogarth's charming *Garrick with his Wife*.

The Queen's Drawing Room and the King's Dining Room contain Holbeins and other royal portraits. The latter carries superb carved panels by Grinling Gibbons, flanking French tapestries and a ceiling by Verrio. The Queen's Ballroom is by Wyatville, with silver furniture and massive canvasses by van Dyck. With the Queen's Audience and Presence Chambers, the visitor returns to the Restoration at its most voluptuous. No inch of wall or ceiling is without painting or tapestry, including four massive Gobelins and ceilings by Verrio.

At this point, the Queen's Guard Chamber comes as a relief, with its Wyatville Gothic vault and a return to displays of swords and muskets. Here is an exhibition of thrones, including two by Morris and Co. In the centre sits a chair of state of pure ivory; it was presented to Queen Victoria by the Maharajah of Travancore.

The tour now passes into St George's Hall, the site of Edward III's hall for the Garter Knights. The Hall was refashioned by Wyatville in 1829 and radically refashioned after the fire in 1992 which destroyed the hall and adjacent chapel and a number of the state and semi-state rooms beyond. The restoration of the hall was controversial, some critics demanding a modernist interpretation.

The chosen style – not quite a facsimile – might be termed 1990s conservator's Gothic, the latest in a long line of such fantasies at Windsor. It is a place of armoured knights and exotic lighting, with the King's Champion on a horse riding into space from the minstrel's gallery like a character from *The Lord of the Rings*. The ceiling panels are the arms of the Garter Knights, blank ones representing those who 'fell from grace'.

Beyond the hall, state rooms become semi-state ones, comprehensively and lavishly restored after the fire. The turn takes place in the Lantern Lobby, on the site of the destroyed chapel. Its ecclesiastical form was based by the architects, Sidell Gibson, on the crossing of Ely Cathedral and, so I am told, the Abbey of Batalha outside Lisbon. The semi-state rooms are open only in winter. They were designed by Wyatville for George IV and

include the Green Drawing Room and sumptuous Crimson Drawing Room. In sequence beyond is the State Dining Room, still in use, and the smaller Gothic Octagon Dining Room. The windows from here give onto the private gardens. At this point, Windsor is almost intimate.

Yet it saves its final flourish to last, the Grand Reception Room. Here the taste is French Empire for George IV. Wyatville protested at the rejection of his preferred Gothic but was overruled by the King. The panelling was brought from Paris as a backdrop to massive Gobelins tapestries. The ceiling is a post-fire reproduction. Beyond is the Garter Throne Room, where investitures take place. The exit is past the Waterloo Chamber and out into the Upper Ward quadrangle. It is a breathtaking and exhausting promenade. And this is a small part of the castle. The east and south ranges are private to the Royal Family.

WINDSOR: QUEEN MARY'S DOLLS' HOUSE *

Windsor
Meticulous recreation of royal palace by Lutyens (M)

The house was planned in 1921 as a gift to Queen Mary, to designs by Sir Edwin Lutyens. It stands (8½ft wide and 5ft tall) in a darkened chamber, the roof lifted to reveal its interior. So perfect is the miniaturization that within minutes we seem to be in a 'real' house, on a scale of 1 to 12. The eye perambulates. It wanders through halls, bedrooms, kitchens and garages alive with a 'pretend' royal family at work and play. The intention was 'to show future generations how a king and queen of England lived in the 20th century'.

The Dolls' House project involved the skills of 1,500 people. Everything works. We are told that the gramophone plays, the wine in the bottles is vintage, the lifts go up and down, the water runs, the bed linen is of the best and every light is wired with electricity. Kipling, Hardy, Graves, Belloc, Chesterton and others wrote the tiny volumes in the library. Orpen, Flint, Nicholson and Gertler contributed pictures. In the presses are 700 original drawings. It must be the world's most exquisite toy, using microscopic craftsmanship where a Russian Tsar would have lavished jewels.

The exterior is in what Lutyens called his 'Wrenaissance' style. The window sashes operate smoothly. The garden was designed by Gertrude Jekyll although the flowers are not real, a lapse. There is even a ring of toadstools, hiding a snail and butterflies. In the garage are models of the most luxurious cars of the day, including a Rolls Royce, Daimler, Lanchester and a Rudge motor cycle.

The interior is not of a palace but rather of a luxurious country house. There is no suite of state rooms or royal receiving rooms, merely a saloon, library and dining room. The Lutyens' touch is the marble front hall (with precisely crafted men in armour) and sweeping staircase. The triumph of the ground floor is the library, with books, pictures, prints, globes and even a pair of Purdey shotguns. In the dining room the ceiling pattern is repeated in the carpet. There is a real Munnings over the mantelpiece. The butler's pantry next door contains Crown Jewels in the strong-room. The saloon piano is by Broadwood and plays.

The bathrooms are astonishing: the king's bathroom is of green marble, the queen's of alabaster with silver taps. The maids' rooms are no less carefully depicted, as are the kitchen and other offices in the basement. Nothing seems to have been omitted, not even the corks in the bottles, the tiny dolls in the day nursery, the golf clubs in the bag.

To what purpose is this absurd detail, assembled at vast expense and most of it invisible to the naked eye? The answer is to excite wonder, which it does. We leave the house past a gallery of 'real' dolls with their trousseaux, given by the French government to the princesses Elizabeth and Margaret in 1938. These dolls look like giants.

Buckinghamshire

Buckinghamshire guards London from the north and west, or perhaps guards the north and west from London. It stretches from the Thames opposite Windsor to north of Milton Keynes. For part of its length, it is graced by the Chilterns and the rich Vale of Aylesbury. Its towns have been terribly abused, but its country is well protected, as are its great houses.

Of the pre-classical era Dorney still has its 15th-century hall, looking across to Eton, and Nether Winchendon and Chenies display Elizabethan remains. But it was the 18th century that took Buckinghamshire by storm. Vanbrugh gave Stowe its entrance front, followed by Kent, Leoni, Adam and others. Chicheley has an exquisite scholarly exterior by Smith of Warwick. The Dashwoods brought the Grand Tour excitingly to life at West Wycombe.

At Claydon, Lord Verney tried to outdo his rival, Lord Temple, at Stowe, producing the most exciting Chinese Rococo rooms in England. Nor were the Victorians to be outdone. Charles Barry's great house overlooking the Thames at Cliveden has been well restored. Disraeli adapted Hughenden as his country seat, and Burn rebuilt Taplow for the Grenfells. Finally, the Rothschilds arrived en masse in the Vale of Aylesbury, colonizing it as their own. They chose French château-style at Waddesdon and neo-Tudor at Ascott. At the Chiltern Museum, one of England's last prefabs is open to public view.

Ascott ✳✳✳
Bletchley Park ✳
Boarstall Tower ✳
Chalfont St Giles:
    Milton's Cottage ✳✳
Chenies ✳✳
Chicheley ✳✳✳
Chiltern Museum:
    The Amersham
        Prefab ✳✳
Chiltern Museum:
    High Wycombe Toll
    House ✳
    Leagrave Cottages ✳
Chilton ✳✳
Claydon ✳✳✳✳
Cliveden ✳✳✳
Dorney Court ✳✳✳
Fawley ✳✳
Hartwell House ✳✳✳
Hughenden ✳✳
Nether Winchendon ✳✳
Olney:
    Cowper Museum ✳
Stoke Park ✳✳
Stowe House ✳✳✳
Stowe: Gothic Temple ✳
Taplow Court ✳✳
Waddesdon ✳✳✳✳
West Wycombe ✳✳✳

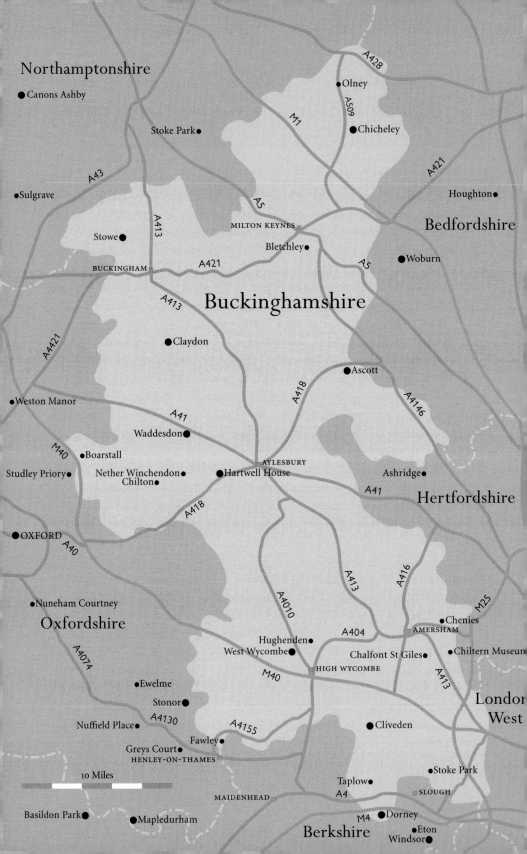

ASCOTT HOUSE ***

2m SW of Leighton Buzzard
Mock Tudor crammed with paintings and porcelain (NT)

The Rothschilds were to Buckinghamshire what the Cavendishes were to Derbyshire. Their Victorian houses at Waddesdon, Mentmore, Halton and Ascott are grouped together in the Vale of Aylesbury, as if clan proximity were as important at weekends as it was during the week in the City.

Ascott House was a small Tudor farmhouse when it was bought in 1873 as a hunting lodge by Mayer de Rothschild of neighbouring Mentmore. It was converted for Leopold de Rothschild by George Devey and extended in the 1930s for the collector, Anthony de Rothschild, who left it to the National Trust. It is now occupied by Sir Evelyn de Rothschild, and presents the antithesis of ostentatious Waddesdon.

Ascott is an overgrown cottage. It proves the appeal of Tudor to every era and condition of England. The house is a row of half-timbered, heavily gabled bays, supplemented when extra rooms were needed. Nothing is grand, except the splendour of the grounds. Yew hedges, terraces and woods slope languidly towards the distant Chilterns. On one terrace is a box and yew garden, its topiary circle spelling out 'light and shade by turn but love always'.

A fragment of the original house survives in a beam over the front door, dated 1606. Inside is a lateral corridor with the entrance hall beyond. Apart from the grand Common Room, the reception rooms are those of any comfortable country residence.

Not so the paintings. In the hall are Stubbs's *Five Mares* and pictures by Romney and Reynolds. The dining room walls, painted to imitate tiles, display Dutch Old Masters, including Cuyp's *View of Dordrecht*. In the corridor are two delightful paintings of the Rothschilds leaving Frankfurt. One shows the Elector entrusting his estate to Mayer, the other the sons taking their leave for Vienna, Naples, Paris and London. The Common Room has a frieze of Victorian maxims such as 'Waste Not Want Not', and Turner's *Cicero's Villa*. The library has a superb Gainsborough, of the red-haired Duchess of Richmond in bright turquoise against a stormy background.

The pride of Ascott is the Chinese porcelain collected by Anthony de Rothschild. I have never seen such work better displayed. It is of all periods, chiefly of the Han, T'ang and Ming dynasties. One room has the porcelain arranged by style and colour, interspersed with Chippendale chairs. From every corner, dragons and demons dart from shelves or niches. They too seem strangely comfortable in these homely surroundings.

BLETCHLEY PARK *

Bletchley
Station X of the code-busters (M)

The role of Bletchley in the Second World War is now acknowledged, but wresting it from the Ministry of Defence took as much effort as wresting Enigma from the Germans. The conversion of the house and outbuildings into a museum of wartime intelligence is not yet complete. For the time being, the place is a monument to military squalor. The epitome of British electronic genius sits in a wilderness of old huts, abandoned jeeps, concrete standings, tarmac, plastic and neon. If you are an old soldier and want all this brought back to life, Bletchley is for you.

The house was that of an eccentric millionaire named Sir Herbert Leon. He bought the estate in 1883 and built a fantasy mansion in eclectic taste. The exterior might be that of a seaside villa in Broadstairs, asymmetrical with Dutch and Tudor gables, a moorish roof and Tudor Gothic embellishments. The inside is similar. The ceilings are almost all reproduction Jacobean. The hall has marble arches and a sumptuous fireplace. The ballroom is astonishing. Linenfold panelling rises to a ceiling of deeply undercut plasterwork on a gilded background, as if pleading for a visit from Elizabeth I.

The house was sold after Lady Leon's death

in 1937 and a year later became the base for MI6's communications operation under Sir Richard Gambier-Parry. Throughout the war, it was the venue for military intercepts and codebreaking, its best-known coup being the cracking of the German Enigma codes. The work done at Bletchley by the mathematician, Alan Turing, formed the basis of electronic computing. All this is now recorded in the various displays.

Elsewhere on the site visitors can see military vehicles, a 1940s mess, wartime movies and a 'cryptology trail'. Everything is labelled Top Secret and Station X. The guides assert that 'this is where it really happened', so often as to lessen our wonder at what really did happen. The huts also encompass the Milton Keynes Model Railway Society and the Leighton Buzzard Boat Club. It is, in truth, a museum of general clutter.

BOARSTALL TOWER *

Boarstall, 8m SW of Bicester
Medieval tower with banqueting room (NT)

The story begins in the 11th century. A ferocious boar in the king's forest of Bernewood was trapped and killed by a wily forester named Nigel. The grateful Edward the Confessor gave Nigel a horn – now in the archives at Aylesbury – and land on which to build a house. Nigel's family held the house across the entire sweep of English history, until giving it to the National Trust in 1943. Even then the Aubrey-Fletchers rented it back and sublet it to the present custodians.

The old house spread round a central courtyard; this is now a garden surrounded by a moat. All that survives is a noble gatehouse in the form of a tower. This was 'improved' for use as a banqueting house at the end of the 16th century, and includes an upper chamber with windows on all four sides. In a print of 1695, the tower is seen to dominate the old house behind, set in what was then a formal

Milton's Chiltern retreat

parterre. The property passed through a succession of daughters to the Aubreys, but when a six-year-old Aubrey died of food poisoning in 1777, the grief-stricken family demolished the main house. The tower was left empty and the gardens overgrown for 150 years. Not until 1925 did an Aubrey tenant, Mrs Jennings Bramley, modernize the property and alter the old entrance to make the present dining room.

The tower is reached by a bridge over its remaining moat. The hard lines of 14th-century military architecture are softened by later parapets and oriel windows, notably over the doorway. The garden behind bears traces of a reported visit by Capability Brown. The interior has been spoilt with National Trust heating and health-and-safety regulations, but the thick walls, cosy bedrooms and glimpsed views over the surrounding landscape more than compensate.

The banqueting room above is excellently preserved, with wide windows and a large fireplace. Windows carry heraldic glass and the roof offers a view of the Chiltern escarpment.

CHALFONT ST GILES: MILTON'S COTTAGE **

21 Deanway
Poet's Chiltern refuge from the Plague (M)

The village is immaculate. Every brick is re-pointed and every hedge clipped. If you stand still too long in Chalfont St Giles, someone will paint you white. When John Milton arrived to escape the Great Plague in 1665, he had been Latin secretary to Cromwell and chief propagandist for the Commonwealth. On the Restoration, aged fifty-seven and already blind, he was evicted from his Westminster home and moved to Bunhill Fields in the City. Now the threat of disease drove him to the Puritan Chilterns. The Quakers were up the road at Jordans. The lord of Chalfont manor was Colonel George Fleetwood, one of the regicides. Milton's reader and pupil, Thomas Ellwood, lived nearby.

Ellwood found the poet a 'pretty box', the

tiniest of cottages. Milton's daughters had long exasperated him, and he had married a third time. Old friends and supporters were in prison or abroad. *Paradise Lost* was unfinished. Milton stayed at Chalfont only a year and returned to London when the plague had passed. Yet it was here that he found the peace to complete his epic, and begin *Paradise Regained*. Chalfont is full of Miltonic spirit.

The surviving cottage is a work of simple village architecture. It clings to the roadside opposite the Milton's Head pub and an Indian restaurant, and has retained its garden and adjacent meadow. The garden has a well, water butt, hand bell and 'necessarium' (latrine). The walls are of exposed timbers. Given the commercial potential of the place, the Milton Cottage Trust has kept the building in exemplary condition.

To the right of the present doorway from the garden is Milton's own study. Here Milton not only wrote but also slept, since his blindness prevented him from risking the steps to the upper floor. Here too was his small hand organ. The parlour contains a fine tall-backed chair known to have been owned by Milton, as was the writing table in the study.

The house is kept as a museum. Walls have pictures of Milton and his family, including a Kneller painted from memory shortly after the poet's death. There are first editions of most of Milton's works and, in the parlour, a case displaying them translated into foreign tongues. Despite the passing traffic, birdsong can still be heard through the window. As Wordsworth recalled of Milton at this time, 'Thy soul was like a star and dwelt apart,/ Thou hadst a voice whose sound was like the sea.'

CHENIES MANOR **

Chenies, 3m E of Amersham
Ancestral Tudor home of Russell family (P)

The Russells, Dukes of Bedford, are still buried in the church at Chenies. The family may have moved, to London, Woburn and elsewhere, but in death they return here. You can take a man from his roots, but not the roots from a man.

The manor came into the Russell family by virtue of the marriage in 1526 of John Russell to the then heiress of Chenies. John Russell came from Dorset (*see* Wolfeton) and was a rising star at court, later created Earl by Henry VIII and awarded Woburn Abbey (Beds) by Edward VI. He rebuilt the medieval hall house at Chenies with diapered brickwork and decorative chimneys. The house was used by the Russells into the 17th century, and was later occupied by their steward. It was then modernized by Edward Blore in 1829 for a younger Russell but since 1957 has been in the hands of the MacLeod Matthews family, who look after it well. The formal garden specializes in tulips, which splendidly fill every room in season.

The house is L-shaped round the front courtyard. The present entrance lies directly ahead with an octagonal staircase tower and prominent stepped gables. The original hall has been buried in later alterations, with only its solar cross-wing surviving. John Russell appears to have commenced alterations in the late 1520s. The principal downstairs room is now the Tudor parlour, with a wide fireplace arch and beamed ceiling. The coat of arms over the fire is carved of wood blown down in the gale of 1987.

Next door is an old chaplain's room, with beyond it a series of Blore interiors containing Georgian and later furniture. These are very much family living rooms. The upstairs bedrooms are effusively furnished in bright colours and four-posters. Queen Elizabeth's Room is said to be the chamber in which she worked when visiting Chenies on tour. It has a fine tapestry chair. The Pink Bedroom has a small oratory with tiny priest's hole, a charming survival.

The side wing of Chenies was the guest wing of the old Tudor house. The billiard room was once probably the Great Chamber. It is hung in William Morris wallpaper and family portraits. The attic is the most atmospheric space in the house. It was once the armoury and sleeping quarters for soldiers and servants and runs the length of the wing, full of ghosts.

CHICHELEY HALL ***

Chicheley, 2m NE of Newport Pagnell
Early Georgian mansion by Smith of
Warwick (P)

Chicheley is an architectural jewel of a house. I
once heard a lecturer devote 15 minutes to each
of its exquisitely crafted façades, defying the
distant rumble of the M1. This is one of
the least altered early-Georgian mansions in
the country. It even retains its three-sided
canal enclosing the adjacent garden.

The house was built in 1719 for Sir John
Chester and sits on the northern border of
Buckinghamshire. The family lived here until
1952, when it passed to Earl Beatty, son of the
Great War admiral, who brought to the house
his father's collection of naval memorabilia. It
is now splendidly protected and maintained by
his widow, Lady Nutting.

Chicheley's building marks the climax of
Tory Baroque at the moment of transition to
the stricter Palladian rigour of Lord Burlington
and the Hanoverians. Yet it is no less scholarly.
Every detail is from some page of a classical
textbook.

The entrance façade was attributed to
Thomas Archer but it is now awarded to Francis Smith of Warwick. Its redbrick central
bays are given Baroque thrust by the device of
raising their pilasters on a high base and
curving the cornice line upwards. The entrance
is modelled on a Bernini door in the Vatican,
with an exaggerated 'bat's wing' hood. The
windows are from Italian works by Rainaldi
and Soria. The brickwork is nip-and-tuck and
was considered by Pevsner 'among the finest of
any house of this date'. The whole composition
is superb.

With the garden front, the temperature
drops but only slightly. Here the bays are
evenly articulated by Doric pilasters rising
through the cornice to the top of the parapet,
creating a strangely unfinished effect. The
doorway is more modest, copied from Borromini. The third façade at the rear descends
another gear. The brickwork is no longer
special and pilasters are brick and Tuscan. This
architectural class system was not to every
taste. Chester's friend, Burrell Massingberd,
deplored 'such havoc made in the architecture'. The house appears to be a conversation
between two strands of early 18th-century
design, Baroque and Palladian.

The interior of Chicheley is as sumptuous
as the exterior. The hall is severely Palladian,
the 1722 work of Henry Flitcroft, a confirmed
Burlingtonian. Chester appears to have taken
Massingberd's strictures to heart. The ceiling is
even painted by Burlington's protégé, William
Kent. The hall leads through three classical
arches to the staircase, with triple balusters
to each tread and the wide low steps familiar
in Queen Anne houses, used to tiny feet and
broad dresses.

The reception rooms are original to Smith's
house. The panelled drawing room has fluted
pilasters rising from floor to ceiling. The wood
carving above doors and elsewhere harks back
to the Stuarts and Grinling Gibbons. The study
is dedicated to the memory of the first Earl
Beatty.

The old library is hidden away on the top
floor, ingeniously designed as a panelled room
in which each panel opens to reveal books
behind it. Even the door frieze is hinged to
conceal books.

The bedrooms include one with fragments
from an earlier Jacobean house on the site,
including a carved overmantel used as a bed-
head. The walls throughout are lined with
pictures of naval incidents. Upstairs they seem
curiously appropriate to the uneven floors and
creaking corridors. In parts of Chicheley on a
stormy night and with the great trees tossing
outside we might almost be at sea.

CHILTERN OPEN AIR MUSEUM

Newland Park, 2m E of Chalfont St Giles

Chiltern is a museum dedicated, like Avoncroft (Worcs) and Singleton (Sussex), to rescuing vernacular architecture and recreating it
in something like its original rural setting. This

work merits all support, since such buildings are the most vulnerable of all relics of English architecture.

CHILTERN: AMERSHAM PREFAB **

originally at Finch Lane Estate, Amersham

Working-class houses vanish faster than any other. They are the least valuable and most readily victims to the bulldozer. A few have been rescued and rebuilt, precious memorials to the early post-war way of life. We have a hundred Georgian mansions but precious few prefabs (*see also* Avoncroft/Worcs).

The term is short for 'prefabricated temporary bungalow'. Half a million were planned immediately after the Second World War, being built largely from aircraft factories no longer in use. Fewer than 160,000 were built, in part because (as with all government projects) they cost more than conventional homes supplied by the private sector. Priced at £1,300 and rented for 13 shillings a week, they compared badly even with local council houses at £450 or 5 shillings a week. Some survive in parts of South London.

The 'Universal House, Mark 3' may seem little better than a caravan without wheels to the modern eye, yet the houses were up-to-date in comparison with tenements or Victorian back-to-backs. The building consisted of two bedrooms, a living room and a kitchen, with a small bathroom and separate toilet. It was connected to electricity. Here everything is in place, except that one bedroom has sadly been replaced with an exhibition.

The house has been decorated in its original cream and green and fitted with authentic kit. The bedroom is dishevelled, apparently to appeal to children. The sitting room comes with flying ducks, sewing machine, coal stove and utility furniture. In the kitchen is a Belling cooker, washing copper, mangle and Electrolux fridge. The garden retains its rabbit hutch

Chiltern's prefab elegance

and tool-shed. I can already imagine the place as a fashion icon.

CHILTERN: HIGH WYCOMBE TOLL HOUSE *

originally at Oxford Road, High Wycombe

These houses once dotted the roadsides of England. The toll house is the exact precursor of the motorway tollbooth, and collected money from stage coaches and other road users on behalf of the 18th-century turnpike trusts which were charged with maintaining their local high roads. Toll keepers were as unpopular as traffic wardens. They were seen as tax collectors and were regularly robbed. Their houses were therefore designed as mini-fortresses. This one has iron bars and shutters on all its windows and even crenellation round its roof. The house was given to the museum in 1977 after being hit by a passing (or not-passing) lorry.

The building has been re-erected with road, gate, fence and garden. Inside is an office-cum-living room, set out to receive tolls. Behind is the bedroom with iron bedstead and patchwork quilt. Kitchen, wash house and privy are to the rear. A family of five lived here in 1841. It would not have looked so twee then. On busy days, a toll-keeper in full costume – not a waxwork – is on hand to direct visitors and lend the place authenticity.

CHILTERN: LEAGRAVE COTTAGES *

originally at Compton Avenue, Leagrave, NW of Luton

These two cottages, in effect one house, were situated by a busy road in Leagrave. The building was an early 18th-century thatched barn. This was converted into two cottages later that century by inserting partitions and a brick chimneystack. Declared unfit for human habitation in 1982, it has been reconstructed as in the 1920s. The downstairs living and eating rooms are extremely simple. A small range has a kettle, an iron and a few pots. Oil lamps hang on the walls, the floor is of scrubbed brick.

The only signs of comfort are a battered leather armchair, a pipe rack and a Bible. A row of war medals and a couple of cheap prints decorate the wall. The room looks wholly original. The privy is in the garden. The lean-to was a kitchen but Leagrave locals said it was previously a cobbler's workshop and so it has been restored as such. The garden has been planted with simple cottage flowers, some herbs and rhubarb.

CHILTON HOUSE **

Chilton, 4m N of Thame
Georgian mansion with plasterwork (P)

Chilton's façade, looking out across the fields of the Vale of Aylesbury, is supremely comforting. It is a 1740s remodelling of an earlier manor of the Croke family, itself rebuilt in 1705. The present facade is distinctly 'Queen Anne' in style. Brick walls have long pilasters and prominent windows with Gibbs surrounds, their keystones like popping eyebrows. Steps lead down to a lawned courtyard with flanking pavilions and a sumptuous wrought-iron gate.

The builder was a judge, Richard Carter, who wanted no truck with the new Whig Palladians. In those days, architecture was also politics. To the judge, certainty lay with redbrick and rustication. Architectural purists would consider them anachronisms.

The house passed to the Aubrey family (Boarstall, above) but decayed in the 19th and 20th centuries and was lucky to survive at all. It was a school during the Second World War and then a council nursing home. The current generation of Aubrey-Fletchers run it as a 'country house' convalescent home, mercifully saving a house destined for demolition.

Unlike the exterior, the interior is that of a conventional mansion of the mid-18th century. The entrance hall is decorated in soft yellows and whites. Fluted pilasters and broken pediments adorn the walls and the ceiling plasterwork is intact. The grand staircase survives beyond and the main sitting room has Rococo plasterwork. Behind lies the church and estate village.

CLAYDON HOUSE ****

Middle Claydon, 4m SW of Winslow
Georgian masterpiece of Rococo decoration (NT)

Claydon contains the most stunning interiors in England. It is a riposte to all who may find mid-Georgian houses dull. The house was built by Ralph, Earl Verney to outshine his political rival, Earl Temple, at neighbouring Stowe. The contest was to bankrupt them. They both eventually had to live abroad to escape their creditors.

In 1757 Verney commissioned as architect a carver named Luke Lightfoot, a decision he was to regret. After ten years of work, relations between them collapsed, in part on a matter of money and in part on a matter of style. The building was hugely expensive, while Verney's contemporaries did not admire Lightfoot's extravagant Rococo.

The gentleman-Palladian, Sir Thomas Robinson, was appalled at 'such a work as the world never saw', and pleaded with Verney to change course in favour of Adam's stuccoist, Joseph Rose. Eventually Verney lost his nerve and sacked Lightfoot, suing him for uncompleted decorations. The carver settled in Dulwich, and his son emigrated to Australia where Lightfoots remain to this day. I am told that they still call a son 'Verney' in each generation.

Robinson was now asked by Verney to pick up the pieces, but it was too late. Verney's flight to escape his creditors was tragic. Shortly before his death in 1791, he was found wandering through the shuttered, cobwebbed rooms of Claydon, doubtless musing on the terrors that architects hold in store for those who put their faith in them. Verney's niece demolished

Rococo joy at Claydon

two-thirds of the completed mansion, the present house being a remaining wing. But later Verneys cared for the place and passed it to the National Trust in 1956.

The original house was three times the size of the present building and must indeed have rivalled Stowe. The exterior of the present wing is modest. An elegant seven-bay west front looks out over a landscaped park with an arched central section. There are just two storeys, stone faced with side elevations of brick.

The explosion occurs inside. The North Hall was locked when I first visited Claydon but I was able to peer in. It was like Sleeping Beauty beneath a dust-sheet, light filtering through cracks in the shutters. Lightfoot worked initially with Verney's close collaboration. His sources were German Rococo pattern books, borrowing freely from Gothick and chinoiserie.

The hall is encrusted with broken pediments over doors. Mirrors and mantelpieces are festooned with swags, drapes, Ho-Ho birds, fronds and cornucopias. The Rococo shell is everywhere, defying symmetry with poise, light and joyfulness. The room transcends style, a decorative programme born of a desire solely to delight the eye. The carvings were done in Lightfoot's Southwark studio but painted *in situ*. It is said that he never saw the room complete.

The next room is the saloon, also by Lightfoot and only a little more restrained. The six doors are classical and the fireplace is surrounded by tumbling putti, supposedly illustrating the invention of the Corinthian order from an acanthus leaf. The ceiling was added by Joseph Rose under Robinson's direction after Lightfoot's dismissal. It displays exquisite geometrical detail. The deep coving is of *trompe-l'œil* rosettes.

The library ceiling is again by Rose, but extraordinary winged brackets in the frieze are by Lightfoot. The bookcases and cupboards are full of old Verney bindings, many of them dilapidated. The room is charming, as is the view through the doors of the enfilade back to the North Hall. Classicism, to the

modern eye often regarded as uniform and staid, is nowhere more variegated and alive.

Claydon's staircase is so precious that nobody is allowed to walk up it. The steps are of mahogany inlaid with box, ebony and ivory. No stair in England is its equal. The ironwork balusters are of equal delicacy, the swirling vegetation so finely wrought that it was said to 'sing' with passing movement when the stairs were in use. The dome above is a Lightfoot composition resting on Joseph Rose coving. To see these two masters of 18th-century decoration in such rivalry is a delight. In the Pink Parlour the panels tell the stories from Aesop's Fables.

All this is but an hors d'oeuvre. Upstairs is a sequence of rooms matching those downstairs. The Great Red Room is again by Lightfoot, notably the lions' heads of the window surrounds. The Paper Room contains Lightfoot's Rococo chimneypiece, composed of Chinese temples. Across a small museum is the bedroom used by Florence Nightingale, a Verney relative. Beyond is the so-called Gothic Room, so lighthearted and enjoyable as to merit the ultimate -k. Clusters of columns flank doors and windows. Even the window shutters are Gothick.

Finally we reach Lightfoot's masterpiece, among the most original works of 18th-century design anywhere. Sacheverell Sitwell awarded the Claydon Chinese Room his golden palm. Elaborate pagodas sit above the doorcases. Chinese faces peer from the woodwork. Swirling foliage interlaces scrolls, temples, bells and birds. The focus of the room is a large alcove, a grotto of fantastical woodcarving. The frame is like a proscenium revealing a divan. Inside is a relief of a Chinese tea ceremony, with two mandarins apparently waving at passers by.

None of this is kitsch, although it was seen as such by contemporaries. The design seems under control, always to a formal programme, an original work of genius. Claydon is poor in furniture and poorer in pictures, but no matter. It is a stunning monument to a master craftsman and to the waywardness of English taste.

CLIVEDEN ***

2m N of Taplow
Italianate mansion overlooking Thames (H)

Cliveden shows what money can buy. Nowhere did Old Father Thames offer a finer view on his route across England. When Garibaldi stayed at Cliveden he declared the Thames at this point comparable with the mighty river prospects of South America. It was nature's gift to architecture in the Age of Landscape.

In 1666, on this bluff above Maidenhead, the 2nd Duke of Buckingham engineered a great platform and had William Winde build him a house to capture the view. The house was handed down to various owners and architects until the 2nd Duke of Sutherland and Sir Charles Barry decided to rebuild it after a fire in 1849. Barry based his design on that of the old house, including a medieval hall off-centre to the entrance, but the outward form is of an Italianate villa. Barry incorporated earlier wings by Thomas Archer, curving round the entrance courtyard. An ostentatious clock-tower was later built by Henry Clutton.

Cliveden was the sort of house that every rich man wanted but of which they soon tired – like Moor Park in Hertfordshire. The house passed from Sutherland to the Duke of Westminster. He sold it in 1893 to the American, William Waldorf Astor, who also bought Hever Castle (Kent). The elderly Queen Victoria had enjoyed visiting the Sutherlands up river from Windsor and was mortified. She professed herself 'grieved to think of it falling into these hands'.

Fall was the wrong word. Lacking success as an American politician, Astor went to Rome as a diplomat in 1882 and acquired, said his grandson, 'a pattern of formalistic behaviour somewhere between that of a Roman emperor and his ideal of an English medieval baron'. He bought an entire balustrade from the Villa Borghese in Rome and set it beneath the house overlooking the parterre. He also bought the Rococo French dining room from the Château d'Asnières outside Paris.

In 1906, Astor went to live at Hever and gave Cliveden to his son, Waldorf, on the latter's marriage to the American beauty, Nancy Shaw. Where his father collected art, the 2nd Viscount collected people. To his weekends came Henry James, Kipling, Curzon, Balfour and Churchill. Bernard Shaw described a stay with Nancy Astor as like Sunday with a volcano. The guests later merged into the so-called Cliveden Set, advocates of the appeasement of Hitler's Germany.

Astor was an ardent conservationist, concerned to protect the rusticity of this reach of the Thames. His son, William, brought the house more notoriety when a cottage in the grounds was the setting for the Profumo affair in 1963. Shortly afterwards the house was let to Stanford University. In 1985 it reopened as a luxury hotel but remains accessible. The magnificent terraced grounds were given by the 2nd Viscount to the National Trust and are open.

The exterior is pure Barry, an Italian palace on a hill, as grand as the vanished house he designed also for the Sutherlands at Trentham (Staffs). The interiors are mostly rich 'neo-Barry', as refashioned for Astor in the 1890s. Rooms are panelled with fluted pilasters. Arches and windows are heavily draped. In the hall is a superb Italian Renaissance chimney-piece with, next to it, Singer Sargent's seductive portrait of Nancy Astor. The French Rococo dining room is as Madame de Pompadour left it and Astor acquired it. Upstairs rooms have been immaculately restored. To stay at Cliveden is expensive, but in a sense it always was.

DORNEY COURT ***

Dorney, 2m W of Eton
Tudor enclave with Great Hall and reinstated façade (P)

Dorney is an island between the Thames and the far greater torrent of the M4/A4. The enclave of hamlet with ancient church, house, lane and meadows seems impossibly fragile. But Dorney still has its family, the Palmers, who acquired the house by marriage in the

early 17th century and hold it to this day. They are tenacious.

The house is a challenge to any style historian. It is apparently a surviving late 15th-century structure. Gables sweep low over leaded windows, offset by soaring chimneys. Brick façades are carried on wooden beams, with bays thrusting and receding. Every feature of the garden is in proportion, shrub-clad walls yielding to paving and yew hedge, then to meadow and sheep. Yet Victorian prints of Dorney in the 1840s show a dull Georgian façade of three storeys with a pediment. What happened?

The answer is familiar to many old houses. A Tudor front was replaced by a Georgian façade in the 1730s which, in turn, was replaced by a Tudor one in the 1900s. How much of the garden façade of Dorney is old, how much imported and how much new is impossible to tell. The search for authenticity in the re-instatement was clearly thorough. The central gable is real Tudor from somewhere, but the overall effect more than a little 'Stockbroker Tudor'.

There is no arguing about the inside. The Tudor Great Hall survives, although much restored and magnificently displayed. A wide fireplace warms linenfold panelling. Persian rugs spread across a broad-boarded oak floor. In one corner stands a stone pineapple, in honour of the first such fruit grown in England at Dorney. Most rewarding of all are the 17th-century portraits that crowd the walls, mostly by Lely and Kneller, of thirteen generations of Palmers.

The plan of Dorney is as it always was, with service rooms and offices to one side of the Great Hall and family quarters to the other. Finest is the parlour, now drawing room, with polygonal window bays with pretty quarries in the glass. Here hangs a Jacobean needlework picture of Palmer triplets who were born on successive Sundays in 1489, and a portrait of Lady Ann Palmer on copper. Above the parlour is the Great Chamber under a barrel-vault

Dorney's Tudor jigsaw puzzle

ceiling. It contains a gigantic wooden canopied bed with posts like the legs of a Restoration courtier.

Downstairs on the other side of the hall is a small but sumptuous William-and-Mary style dining room with a painted wooden floor. It is a charming stylistic intrusion, Dutch classicism in a rough Tudor environment.

FAWLEY COURT **

1m N of Henley-on-Thames
Restoration mansion with 'Gibbons' ceiling
(M)

Fawley claims to have been designed by Sir Christopher Wren. There is no evidence for this, but the custodian assured me that Wren is 'believed to have dropped by'. Nor is the beautiful saloon by Grinling Gibbons, although perhaps he was boating on the river at the time. In matters of 17th-century style, Wren and Gibbons are still synonyms for 'good English design', which is no bad thing.

The site of the old Restoration mansion is sandwiched between the Thames and the Marlow road with a canal leading from the house to the river bank. It was built in 1684 for William Freeman, sugar merchant, and extensively redecorated by James Wyatt at the end of the 18th century. After army occupation in the Second World War, Fawley became a Polish school of the Marian Fathers. When that closed in 1986 it became a Polish museum and 'pilgrims' retreat', to offer 'a window of Polish culture onto the Western world'.

The interior is institutional but in a warm, Polish way. The hall has a black-and-white stone floor and is decorated with portraits of Polish kings. It leads directly into a double-cube saloon. This has red wallpaper and a superb Restoration ceiling. Its panels are filled with intricate naturalistic detail of birds and leaves in deep relief, as if they are about to take flight across the room. A stork holds a twig in its beak. Tiny animals run through thick vegetation. The attribution to Gibbons is understandable.

On the walls are excellent copies of Old

Masters, including a Leonardo, a Giulio Romano and a Perugino. To the right of the saloon is the museum library, by James Wyatt in classical vein, with scagliola columns and icons on the walls. The former drawing room, now a museum, is Wyatt at his most Etruscan, with a lovely Adamish ceiling. The room contains Polish national treasures, including early Bibles and sets of royal autographs. Upstairs is a chinoiserie bedroom filled with Polish weapons.

HARTWELL HOUSE ***

2m SW of Aylesbury
Restored Jacobean/Georgian mansion with Gibbs interiors (H)

Hartwell is the best that can happen to a great house if there is no family to guard it. Hotel conversion can lead to death by fire regulation. Here, as at Cliveden, the atmosphere of a country weekend has been maintained. Reception is not intrusive. Books and pictures are appropriate. Grounds are immaculately maintained.

The original house was built *c*1600 by Sir Alexander Hampden, passing to his sister-in-law's family, the Lees (*see* Ditchley/Oxon). In 1809, it won fame as home of the exiled Louis XVIII of France. A court of some 200 penniless French aristocrats descended on the place, camping in the rooms, keeping rabbits and vegetables on the roof and hanging washing everywhere. The alcoholic Queen Marie-Joséphine roamed the rooms objecting to the statuary. Louis's family stayed for five years, nearly wrecking the place, before returning to the throne in 1814 (and wrecking that).

Later members of the Lee family found Hartwell impossible to sustain. It was let to Lord Leith and a rich American wife in 1914, but sold in 1938 for his own use by the ubiquitous conservationist, Ernest Cook, grandson of Thomas Cook and saviour of Montacute (Somerset). After the war, the house became a girls' post-school academy, in which guise I recall visiting it for a dance and finding it ripe with the smell of school food and decay. Soon

afterwards the place caught fire. Cook's trustees finally leased it to the hotelier, Richard Broyd. He restored it with what *Country Life* called 'exemplary tact and sensitivity' before opening Hartwell as a Historic Houses Hotel in 1992.

The drive down to the house from the Aylesbury road is dramatic. A vista suddenly opens out onto an 18th-century landscape. On the left is a Gothic church ruin by Henry Keene of 1753, recently reroofed. It smiles as from a theatre box on the scene below. Ninety acres of avenues, lawns and architectural follies stretch to the River Thame. The lake bridge is formed from an arch of a former bridge at Kew.

The entrance front is E-plan and unmistakably Jacobean. How it survived is a mystery, since the Lees were later to employ, successively, James Gibbs, Henry Keene and James Wyatt at Hartwell. Their interiors are dazzling. In restoring the house in the 1980s, a local architect, Eric Throssell, not only put back every recorded detail but, where none survived, created fresh ones in the style of his predecessors.

The Great Hall is of original Jacobean proportions but refashioned by Gibbs with plasterwork by Giovanni Bagutti and the Artari brothers. The same team worked for Gibbs and the Lees at Ditchley. The ceiling centrepiece depicts Genius rewriting History, an alarming concept. Beyond are the three main reception rooms along the east side, designed by Keene with Rococo plasterwork by Thomas Roberts of Oxford. The latter's work is outstanding (*see* Rousham/Oxon). The staircase is a Gothick setting by Throssell for the old Jacobean stairs, adorned with statues painted to look like stone.

Beyond the staircase is a dramatic semi-circular vestibule inserted by Wyatt, rising the full height of the building. Along the south front are three new dining rooms created by Throssell. The biggest, loosely based on the dining room at 11 Downing Street, is in a Soane style. Another retains the columns of Keene's former chapel and a third is octagonal and tented. Colouring, furnishings and furniture have all been chosen in keeping with Hartwell's 18th-century period. This is a happy Renaissance.

HUGHENDEN MANOR **

1m N of High Wycombe
Disraeli's house with political mementos
(NT)

Hughenden is an ugly duckling. It was bought in haste for Benjamin Disraeli and his wife in 1848 on his selection as leader of the Conservative Party in the Commons, on the grounds that the party leader must have a country seat. The forty-four-year-old Disraeli was heavily in debt and the money was initially put up by his ally, Lord George Bentinck, and friends. Disraeli was MP for his 'beloved and beechy Bucks' and was happy to be near his father's home at Bradenham.

The house was a plain brick Georgian manor house, painted white, with a fine view south over the Hughenden valley. After twelve years of occupation, Disraeli commissioned the architect, E. B. Lamb, to embellish the outside and continue his earlier gothicizing of the interior. The redbrick refacing of the outside won the fiercest condemnation in Pevsner, 'excruciating, everything sharp, angular and aggressive . . . window-heads indescribable'. It is hard to disagree. Disraeli planted assorted evergreens on the front lawn, perhaps to conceal the modesty of his residence. The National Trust has done the same, making it look like a market garden.

The interior is more endearing, although hardly less odd. Almost everything is in a heavy-handed Victorian Gothic, enlivened only by its intimate proportion. The hall ceilings are of stone, rib-vaulted, and strangely oppressive, the wall-hangings mostly dark. The library retains some feel of the Georgian original but the drawing room is emphatically Gothic. With the adjacent dining room, it well conveys the bourgeois solidity of Disraeli's England.

Upstairs, the modesty of the house becomes even more apparent. Disraeli's study is as he

left it, a small room with desk and notepaper edged in black, used after the death of his wife, Mary Anne. Twelve years his senior, she said that 'Dizzy married me for money, but if he had the chance again he would marry me for love.' It is unpretentious in the extreme. To the rear is the Statesman's Room, recalling Disraeli's greatest foreign policy triumph, the Congress of Berlin of 1878. It displays the cherrywood fan signed by the delegates and presented to him in thanks for his diplomacy. On the staircase hangs the 'Gallery of Affection', pictures of Disraeli's political friends and associates. The house might be a cottage in the grounds of Pugin's House of Commons.

NETHER WINCHENDON HOUSE **

Nether Winchendon, 7m SW of Aylesbury
Gothicized medieval house, Henry VIII tapestry (P)

Nether Winchendon was in monastic ownership until the Dissolution, when it passed through various hands to a City merchant, William Goodwin. It has remained in that family ever since, successively as Beresfords, Bernards and Spencers. On my visit I saw the next in line wobbling on his bicycle round the kitchen garden, making it a proprietorial mess. This was strangely comforting.

The house is medieval, overlaid with Tudor, extended in Gothick and then left in peace – a typical English composition. The Tudor courtyard is fronted by an arched and battlemented screen. Two sides of the court beyond were given a Gothick front by Sir Scrope Bernard when he made the house his principal residence in the 18th century. On the far side, the house looks across lawns to the River Thame, which rises in winter to surround it with an inland sea.

The entrance leads into a Regency hall, full of dark panelling, antique swords and looming portraits. Beyond lies the original Great Hall, converted into a dining room with a ribbed Gothick ceiling. It contains a 17th-century

portrait of the Goodwin family, dominated by Lady Goodwin, her dead husbands relegated to pictures within the picture. The adjacent Justice Room replaced the old screens passage.

The glory of the house is its drawing room, a delightful work of Tudor Renaissance, c1530. The old linenfold panelling was painted white to celebrate the Restoration in 1660 and has not been stripped since. Rich carvings survive in the frieze and ceiling, dancing with arabesques, a mermaid and portraits of the owner. The windows carry armorial glass, and pictures of a butterfly and a fly.

The prize of this room is its tapestry, the only contemporary depiction of Henry VIII in this medium and said to be a close likeness. The king is flanked by Archbishop Cranmer and Lord Russell, briefly owner of the house at the time. It was probably commissioned to celebrate Russell's creation as a Knight of the Garter in 1539. Garters adorn each border. Tumbling putti celebrate the majesty of the monarch and his status as head of the new English Church.

OLNEY: COWPER MUSEUM *

Market Place
House in which the poet lived and gardened (M)

The poet and naturalist, William Cowper, occupied two adjacent Jacobean houses in Olney with his companion, a widow named Mary Unwin. Their servant occupied the other house with, so Cowper said, 'a thousand rats'. Cowper's house now has a kitchen on the ground floor with a waxwork of the servant working at her bobbins. She was paid £8 a year, considered above the local going rate. There is a rag-rug on the floor.

The rest of the house is a shrine to Cowper and his other local friend, John Newton, evangelical curate of Olney. Newton was a seafarer who was captured, enslaved and later became

Tudor-Gothic at Nether Winchendon

an anti-slavery campaigner. He and Cowper became a productive hymn-writing team in the 1770s and 1780s, their works including 'Amazing Grace' and 'How Sweet the Name of Jesus Sounds'. The house is filled with their portraits and memorabilia, including Cowper's pet hares and his smelling salts, the latter donated by Sir John Betjeman. Here too is the electric shock machine that the three residents appear to have used on each other to cure them of various ills.

The servant's house is a museum to the town's late-medieval staple, lace made by hand by refugees from the Low Countries. The garden that was such a feature of Cowper's writing has been recreated to the rear, with 18th-century plants. Its gardener corresponds on the subject of vegetables with the Gilbert White Museum (Selborne/Hants). On my visit, lavender and sunflowers were much in evidence. Also restored is the summer-house in which Cowper worked. He called it his 'verse manufactury'.

STOKE PARK **

Stoke Poges, 2m NNE of Slough
Golf club in Georgian villa surrounded by handsome park (P)

Stoke Park is astonishing. It sits on the slopes of Burnham Beeches overlooking Slough, the M4 and the Thames as if it were a country club in the American Mid-West. The American parallel is not fanciful. The house was erected by John Penn, grandson of the founder of Pennsylvania, after 1789. Penn's father had already bought and rebuilt the old Stoke manor house and commissioned Capability Brown to lay out the grounds. His son returned from America, rich on annuities, and decided he needed something grander. He built away from the manor in the centre of the park, wishing perhaps to recall his house, called Solitude, on Pennsylvania's Schuykill River.

Penn's architect in 1789 was the little-known Robert Nasmith, but after his early death the work was handed to James Wyatt in 1795. Wyatt designed corner pavilions, a dome and colonnades. This was further amended when the house was acquired by Wilberforce Bryant, of Bryant and May's matches, in the 1880s. It became a golf club in 1908. The result is a bit like a wedding cake, especially the garden side, where the dome seems especially out of place. But the ensemble is undeniably majestic, in creamy white amid its green lawns. The courtyard entrance has a glassed-in portico, flanked by niches containing classical athletes and gladiators, fit sentinels for the royal game of golf.

The house is now a series of large reception rooms. At every turn there seems to be a scagliola screen or a classical panel, some surviving from Wyatt but most introduced by a Victorian owner, Henry Labouchère. A wide staircase in the central hall rises to a lantern under Wyatt's dome. Some traces of Labouchère's obsessive classicism remain in the statues and paintings. The former dining room has romantic murals by Thorvaldsen, of Love dominating the Four Elements, perhaps another golfing reference.

I do not know how many golf courses are 'Capability Brown'. But his work has been well adapted at Stoke. Hardly a bunker or a green is noticeable from the house. Instead, sweeps of parkland are carefully interrupted by trees. Each vista offers an obelisk, a church, a manor house, a lake or a clump of rhododendron. It is space well preserved in this overcrowded corner of outer London.

STOWE HOUSE ***

3m NW of Buckingham
Classical masterpiece surviving as school
(P-R)

Stowe is a great English house in a noble landscape, symbol of the building mania that obsessed and often bankrupted the English aristocracy after the Restoration. The house and its grounds were first embellished by Richard Temple, one of Marlborough's soldiers and an ambitious Whig. He married a brewery heiress and from 1714 built in a frenzy until his death (as Lord Cobham) thirty-five

years later. In the process, he created what were declared 'the finest rooms perhaps in Europe'.

His nephew and heir, Richard Grenville, Earl Temple, was said to be the richest man in England and continued the frenzy. The Temples of Stowe built temples at Stowe until they simply ran out of money. By the 1820s, they had risen to be Dukes of Buckingham and Chandos but titles brought no money. The richest family in England soon acquired the title of 'the greatest Debtors in the World'. In 1827, the 1st Duke of Buckingham fled abroad. The 2nd Duke entertained Queen Victoria briefly and lavishly at Stowe in 1845, but with his creditors literally waiting outside for the monarch to depart. Three years later, the 'sale of the century' took forty days and scattered Stowe's contents to the winds.

For a century Stowe was on and off the market. It was sold for use as a school in the 1920s but the sheer scale of the house and grounds have remained a problem ever since. The estate is now in the hands of the National Trust. The school buildings belong to a charity which is slowly restoring them. The interiors are predictably institutional.

The house is superbly positioned, with land falling away to north and south. Both from a distance and close to, it is a work of exquisite proportion. How this came to be is a miracle. For over a hundred years from 1677, architects as diverse as Vanbrugh, Kent, Leoni, Adam and the obscure Vincenzo Valdrè all lent a hand. Somehow, the cooks did not spoil the broth.

The north entrance front is centred on a bold, four-column portico probably by Vanbrugh and flanked by long quadrants of colonnades. The wings have recently been restored in lemon-coloured render, contrasting with the rich ochre of the portico. The entrance is almost as noble as Blenheim (Oxon). The south front, the rear, is more serene, mostly by Robert Adam. Here a more elegant Corinthian portico is flanked by the main *piano nobile*, balanced by pavilions with arched windows. The wide flight of 33 steps seems to invite nature in to share the joys of architecture. From these steps the vista stretches to a distant arch and on for two miles to the outskirts of Buckingham.

The interior of Stowe is a disappointment, never having recovered from the 1840s. Stone corridors echo with the sounds of school. Floors are uncarpeted. Walls have only a scattering of Temple portraits. That said, the North Hall has a superb coved ceiling, covered in grisaille arabesques and rising to a central panel of Mars presenting a sword to Lord Cobham, painted by William Kent. Carved panels depict classical scenes. The adjacent Marble Saloon is the glory of the house. It dates from the 1770s and is based on the Pantheon, surrounded by 16 scagliola columns interspersed with niches (currently empty). Above is a plaster frieze of a sacrificial Roman procession, a Roman Elgin marbles.

The great reception rooms are blighted by decades of abuse. The dining room may again be feeding the children of the rich, but it looks and smells like an army mess hall. The reception rooms of the *piano nobile* retain their ceilings and chimneypieces – and their splendid view. On the walls are portraits by Ramsay, Beechey and John Jackson. The guidebook's pictures of these rooms in the 19th century make their appearance today the more tragic. Stowe, a monument to aristocratic hubris, is best regarded as conservation work in progress. At least it is still there.

STOWE PARK: GOTHIC TEMPLE *

3m NW of Buckingham
Architectural oddity in classical Elysium (NT)

The English landscape can offer few more blissful scenes than a summer *fête champêtre* in the grounds of Stowe. Some time before acquiring the grounds in 1989, the National Trust held such an event. The evening was warm and an orchestra played Handel on the steps of the Temple of Concord and Victory. The Grecian Valley was filled with picnickers under lighted flares, like an army encamped

before battle. It was a scene that would have gladdened the hearts of its creator, Lord Cobham.

Stowe's grounds were laid out successively by Charles Bridgeman, William Kent and Capability Brown, the latter beginning his career as head gardener here in 1741. The buildings in the grounds were by Vanbrugh and Gibbs. The Gothic Temple is the most lovable and most habitable of Stowe's twenty-five landscape structures. It is now tenanted by the Landmark Trust. It is also the only building not to reflect the prevailing classicism. Lord Cobham wrote above its door: 'I thank God that I am not a Roman'. A Whig radical, he regarded Gothic as the style of the liberal future. This 'Temple of Liberty' was to celebrate the freedoms of northern Europe against the stately tyrannies of Italy. It is ironic that by the end of the century, 'democratic' Greek, not Gothic, was the preferred style of revolution.

The Gothic Temple, built in 1741–2, sits by a clump of trees on the edge of Hawkwell Field, looking down on the Elysian Fields and on the lakes whose drainage taxed even Brown's skills. The pavilion was designed by James Gibbs and built of Midlands ironstone, a solid northern material preferred to effete southern ashlar. The building is triangular, with towers crowned by lanterns at each angle. The style is free Perpendicular, castellated but with Early English windows.

TAPLOW COURT **

Berry Hill, Taplow
Remodelled Jacobean house with Norman Hall (P-R)

Taplow's golden age was Edwardian. Its owner, William Grenfell, was an Olympic sportsman and a Mayor of Maidenhead; he was still fencing for Britain in 1906 at the age of fifty. Two years later, as Lord Desborough, he organized the first Olympic Games to be held in Britain. The outbuildings include his old gymnasium. The house also entertained the late-Victorian aesthetic set known as 'The

Souls' and was visited by Henry James, Oscar Wilde and Edith Wharton.

Tragedy soon followed. Two sons died in the Great War and a third in a car accident. The Desboroughs lived on at Taplow, housing evacuee schoolgirls during the Second World War. It then went into decline and saw decades of office use before being rescued by the present owners, a college of Buddhism, the Soka Gakkai International of the UK.

The original Jacobean house was converted by the Earls of Orkney to plans by Stiff Leadbetter in the 18th century. This house was sold in 1852 to the Grenfells, who commissioned William Burn to return it to its previous Jacobean appearance. It is Burn's house that we see today. He raised its redbrick front by one storey, undeniably Jacobean but also gaunt and Victorian. The rear is quite different, French Gothic with flamboyant window tracery and a gratuitous tower. The best feature is the roofscape, of gaily twisted and decorated chimneys.

The focus of the interior is a remarkable 'Norman Hall' inserted by the Orkney heir, Thomas Hamilton, in the 1830s, before the arrival of Burn. It is of three storeys in the centre of the house, with arches and galleries, and is said to be modelled on Kirkwall Cathedral. The doors are beautifully decorated with panels of animals and foliage and appliqué woodwork in the tympanums. The dining room, ante-room and drawing room are virtually identical, with neo-Jacobean strapwork on the ceilings and marble fireplaces.

WADDESDON MANOR ****

Waddesdon, 5m NW of Aylesbury
Rothschild mansion in style of French château, original art collection (NT)

Rothschild children were expected to marry Rothschild children. In 1865, Ferdinand de Rothschild of the Viennese branch married his cousin Evelina of the London branch. She died a year later in childbirth, but Ferdinand stayed in England and was joined as lifelong compan-

ion by his Viennese sister, Alice. In 1874 at the age of thirty-five, Ferdinand bought a large plot of hillside from the Duke of Marlborough in the Vale of Aylesbury. Here he realized what was to be his life's work, recreating in the English countryside a French Renaissance chateau, furnished in the style of Louis XIV.

Waddesdon is an acquired taste, even as now restored to its original golden state. At the time of its construction, the English rich were ordering neo-Gothic or neo-Queen Anne. Leopold de Rothschild was content with neo-Tudor at Ascott (above). But Ferdinand wanted French, a style to which Victorian England had seldom taken kindly (*see* Bowes/Durham, and Château Impney/Worcs). That is not Waddesdon's fault. The house was to a Victorian Rothschild what a Grand Tour house must have seemed to a Burlingtonian. It merely substituted France for Italy.

Ferdinand died in 1898 and his sister in 1922. The house passed to a cousin, James, who was a Liberal MP and horse racing enthusiast. When he in turn died childless, the house and his father's immense collection of French art passed to the National Trust. It is now tenanted by the 4th Lord Rothschild.

The architect used by Ferdinand de Rothschild was the Frenchman, Hyppolyte Destailleur. He intended the house to be a *coup de théâtre*. Visitors ascended a winding drive planted with chestnuts and evergreens. Suddenly they burst onto a plateau with a view across an Italian garden to a fantasy of mansard roofs, dormers, chimneys, turrets and pinnacles. It is undoubtedly a *coup*, the word appropriately French.

The interior is a museum of furnishings and fittings. Waddesdon contains one of the finest private art and furniture collections in England, yet the National Trust keeps the rooms so dark, and visitors so distant, that it is hard to see the paintings at all clearly. Many are near invisible. The collection is almost entirely French, with imported panelling, tables, chairs, tapestries, carpets and desks. Not an inch is without ornament, yet nothing is cluttered. The taste is immaculate and of a piece.

The entrance leads into the east gallery, with

two large Guardis of Venice. The chimney-piece is said to have come from a French mansion which had been turned into a post office. It must have been some post office. The breakfast room panels were from a banker's house in Paris. The dining room tapestries are 18th-century Beauvais, based on pictures by Boucher. The Sèvres table setting is so large and impressive as to defy cross-table conversation. In the Red Drawing Room are portraits by Reynolds and Gainsborough, including the latter's *Lady Sheffield*, and one of Waddesdon's many exquisite chests by the royal cabinet maker, Riesener. The Grey Drawing Room is from a house in Paris's rue de Varennes, with a Savonnerie embroidered screen.

The west gallery in the front of house is equally sumptuous, but here one needs binoculars to see paintings by Watteau and a pedestal clock by Boulle. The tapestries in the small library are designed by Boucher. Next door is Baron Ferdinand's Room, containing a desk once owned by Beaumarchais, and a Riesener secretaire with lovely marquetry. Here are more English ladies by Reynolds and Gainsborough, well poised amid so much French finery.

The west wing culminates in the morning room, said to contain Waddesdon's finest paintings. Most are by Dutch masters, including de Hooch, Ruisdael, Cuyp and Dou. The black lacquered secretaire was acquired from an English family who were short of money but ashamed to part with it. Ferdinand bought it from them in secret, paying for a copy to be left with them lest their neighbours notice the loss.

The upstairs rooms at Waddesdon have been partly restored as bedrooms, partly as exhibition space. The former are a welcome touch of domesticity in this otherwise overwhelming house. The state bedroom and dressing room are dappled with Meissen and Bouchers. The green boudoir has panelling from a Paris house, with vanishing mirrors and much lacquer and gilt. The exhibition rooms display Rothschild Sèvres, Rothschild clothes and Rothschild wine.

WEST WYCOMBE PARK ***

West Wycombe, 3m W of High Wycombe
Dashwood's raffish Grand Tour mansion (NT)

West Wycombe is the home of the Hell-Fire Club and the creation of one man, Sir Francis Dashwood. Son of a wealthy merchant, Sir Francis lived from 1708 to 1781 and contrived to be Grand Tourist, rake, dilettante, Member of Parliament and a dreadful Chancellor of the Exchequer. He was also a popular and liberal country gentleman.

Dashwood's talents as a practical joker are perhaps better known. His exploits included attending a Vatican scourging ceremony with a horse whip, and masquerading in St Petersburg as the dead Charles XII of Sweden. But it was his visits to Italy, Greece and Asia Minor that informed his conversion of the house his father had built in the 1700s. Dashwood worked on West Wycombe from 1735 until the 1770s, with architects from the Society of Dilettanti circle, first John Donowell then Nicholas Revett. Once complete, West Wycombe remained unchanged, passing to the National Trust in 1943 but with the current baronet still in residence.

The exterior is perverse. It is porticoed on three sides, each one different and each asserting primacy. The National Trust makes visitors walk round all four to find the entrance, thus affording splendid views across the valley to the church and mausoleum on the hill beyond. Beneath the hill are the Hell-Fire Caves, where Dashwood's circle would meet and indulge in rituals possibly more lurid in legend than fact. The valley is dotted with the customary features of a classical landscape – lakes, loggias, temples and lodges. The A40 and the village of West Wycombe, which cut across the scene, are remarkably invisible.

The interiors are an evocation of Dashwood's Mediterranean travels. They lack the serenity of Adam's interiors but are full of the motifs that immediately preceded him. Dashwood was mostly his own designer and the rooms are those of an eager tourist keen to show friends eye-popping pictures of his trips.

Entrance through the colonnade is directly into the hall, with its stairs screened by columns of scagliola marble. Beneath the stone floor is a hypocaust based on a Roman original found at Lincoln. The hall ceiling derives from Robert Wood's influential *Ruins of Palmyra*. The dining room beyond appears to be an extension of the hall, with the same floor and marbled walls and another 'Palmyra' ceiling. The Tapestry Room, saloon and Red Drawing Room line the main front of the house, overlooking the view. The first has Brussels tapestries after Teniers, its wooden frieze and doorcase painted in *trompe-l'œil* and its ceiling Pompeian. The adjacent saloon is more spectacular. Here the ceiling is based on Raphael's *Story of Psyche*. Statues of van Dyck and Rubens grace the mantelpiece.

Most remarkable is the adjacent Blue Drawing Room, once used for dining and decorated accordingly. Bacchic revels cascade across the ceiling in celebration of the feast below. They are from the hand of Giuseppe Borgnis, an artist brought to England by Dashwood in 1752, and are based on Carracci's mural in the Palazzo Farnese in Rome – widely popular as a Georgian decorative model (*see* Rievaulx Ionic Temple/Yorks, N). The pier-glasses carry flowers and Ho-Ho birds. To James Lees-Milne, who worked for the National Trust in the house during the war, this was one of the most enjoyable rooms of its size and period in England, a Rococo response to Adam's statuesque ante-room at Syon (London, W).

The final room, the Music Room, was intended as Dashwood's climax. The ceiling is again by Borgnis, based on Raphael's *Banquet of the Gods at the Farnesina*. Other scenes are derived from Carracci and Reni. The walls are hung with Italian paintings of humans and gods in various stages of undress. The jewel of the room is the fireplace, like those in the study and Blue Drawing Room by Henry Cheere. Venus and Cupid cavort above piers dripping with leaves and cooing birds. The doorcases and pedestals are also by Cheere, an English signature on a thoroughly Italian house.

Cambridgeshire

Just as the East Anglian Fens attracted early missionaries and stone for their ministers along their navigable waterways, so they became the outlet for medieval England's richest export, wool. The county today (excluding Huntingdon) reflects little of that wealth, concentrated as it was in great monastic houses, now dissolved, or in the ports nearer the coast. The domestic remains of the old monasteries are limited to fragments at Denny and Anglesey, while the authorities at Ely make no attempt to show their domestic architecture to the public. Parts of the old bishop's palace can be seen in a hospice.

Of later houses, only Tudor Madingley is Elizabethan in full splendour. The 18th century is better represented by Wimpole, predominantly by Gibbs and Soane and home of Harleys and Hardwickes. Of Georgian merchants' houses, Peckover survives in Wisbech, with its Rococo plasterwork. The modern age has left the eccentric galleries of Anglesey and the austere modernism of Kettle's Yard. The university buildings of Cambridge are covered at the end.

Anglesey Abbey **
Cambridge:
    Kettle's Yard **
Denny Abbey *
Ely:
    Old Palace **

Ely:
    Oliver Cromwell's
        House **
Madingley *
Stretham:
    Stoker's House *

Wimpole ***
Wisbech:
    Peckover House **

Cambridge University:
    The Colleges
    see page 54

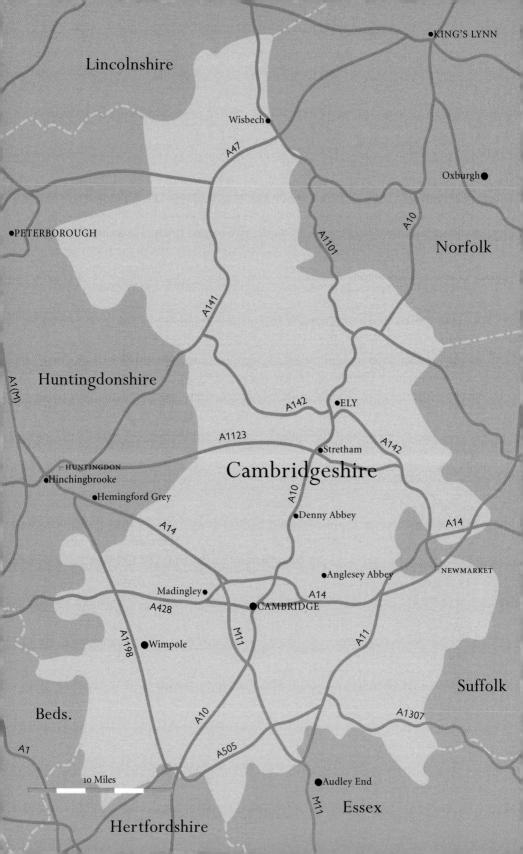

ANGLESEY ABBEY **

near Lode, 6m NE of Cambridge
Priory converted in 1920s into gallery (NT)

Huttleston Broughton purchased Anglesey Abbey in 1926 in order to be near his horses at Newmarket. He was the son of an Englishman who rejoiced in the name of Urban Broughton. Urban had gone to America to make his fortune and did so by marrying an American heiress. They returned to England and Urban became a Tory MP.

His bachelor son, Huttleston, devoted much of his time to accompanying his mother on long yachting trips. He received the posthumous barony intended for his father, as Lord Fairhaven, and when not with his mother or his horses spent his life acquiring works of art and laying out a magnificent garden in the unpromising Anglesey meadows. Here he contrived a park with the grandeur of Capability Brown. It is composed of stately avenues, woodlands and classical statuary. Its snowdrops are among the best in England and attract thousands of admirers each spring. Fairhaven bequeathed the estate to the National Trust in 1966.

The exterior of the main house is L-shaped, with the surviving medieval walls to left and right of the main entrance in the angle of the L. Although the garden front was heavily rebuilt by Fairhaven, it has the appearance of an Elizabethan mansion, with a bold oriel window, and strong chimneys. Inside, the medieval parts are confined to the monks' old parlour, now the dining room. The rest was medievalized in the 1920s to display tapestries and pictures. The designer was Sidney Parvin and the style the sort of Jacobean beloved of American subordinates. Visitors were invited to engrave their names on a window pane. In 1955 Fairhaven added a new picture gallery over a bridge from the main house; this was specifically for his strange obsession, views of Windsor Castle.

The house is the creation of an eccentric art lover and its contents must be viewed accordingly. Here is a seascape by Gainsborough, there a Constable, there two of the finest Claude Lorraine landscapes in England. In the library is a set of contemporary portraits of all the English monarchs. Apart from Windsor Castle, Fairhaven also craved the Victorian nudes of William Etty, tapestries from Bruges and Mortlake, and Ming porcelain. There are commodes and chimneypieces, writing desks, a Congreve clock and a Roentgen bureau inlaid with views of Russian cities. Nothing seems second rate. Anglesey is what English houses can always do well, offer small museums of the first rank.

CAMBRIDGE: KETTLE'S YARD **

Northampton Street
Collector's house preserved as gallery of 20th-century art (M)

In 1957, Jim and Helen Ede converted a row of cottages on the outskirts of Cambridge (once owned by a man named Kettle) into a home and gallery of contemporary art. Ede had studied at the Slade and in Newlyn and had worked at the Tate Gallery. He had a gift for befriending artists. The couple acquired works by Ben Nicholson, Christopher Wood, Brancusi, Miró, David Jones, Alfred Wallis and Henri Gaudier-Brzeska.

The Edes had specific ideas on how houses should be lit and furnished. Every item at Kettle's Yard, indeed every shaft of light, seems crafted to an aesthetic goal. Rooms should contain only 'what they absolutely need', Ede once told a radio audience. 'You will each know what is the minimum of furniture you can do with; halve that and you will still have enough to fill your room.' A row of pebbles is thus arranged to cover a table with shadow. A lemon in a painting is answered by one in a dish. Polished glass or metal is positioned to reflect and magnify some other object. The house is an artistic performance, most effective on a sunny day.

Knocked together, the cottages now comprise a long living room, bedroom and bathroom on the ground floor, with an open-plan

living-room/gallery on the first floor and attic floor. The effect is somewhat spoilt by the museum extension by Leslie Martin, opened in 1970. It elongates the cottage into an informal gallery and concert space.

At the 'house' end the fusion of modern art with vernacular architecture is perfect. The Cubism of Nicholson and Wood sits happily with the naïve St Ives school of Alfred Wallis. Chairs are to be sat in and books to be read. Most remarkable is the collection of work by the prolific Gaudier-Brzeska, who died in the Great War at just twenty-four, by when he seems to have produced a life's *oeuvre*. The entire attic is devoted to his drawings.

DENNY ABBEY *

Chittering, 3m N of Waterbeach
Fragments of nunnery surviving in Georgian farmhouse (EH)

Denny was a Benedictine monastery, then a Templar church, then a Poor Clares nunnery, then a farmhouse. It is today a memorial to the unknown archaeologist. Its interior displays scraped walls, decked floors, gaping spaces, handrails, boards, notices, guides and logos. It is a place I long to ensnare in Victorian creeper and rotting floorboards.

The site is in the Fens, north of Cambridge. During the Middle Ages, it would usually have been accessible only by boat. This was clearly a popular feature. The early Benedictine community was taken over by the Templars from the 12th to the 14th centuries, then in the 1330s by the Franciscan Poor Clares. Their abbess, the Countess of Pembroke, converted the west end of the church into her residence. It is this residence that largely survives. The charm of Denny lies in detecting the ghostly outline of the old church in the walls of what became a nun's lodging and then a substantial 18th-century farmhouse. Pembroke College, Cambridge, owned the land and gave the property to the government in 1947.

Sculptural composition at Kettle's Yard

The archaeologists then proceeded to rip out the entire farmhouse interior, the better to display the Norman and Gothic fragments, yet leaving them still roofed. In the exterior of the east wall, we can clearly see the crossing arch of the church, with the transepts on either side.

The interior displays the church's scissor-truss roof and the Norman capitals on the fragmentary arcades. In the crossing and south transept are the traces of rooms inserted into this part of the older building by the abbess. There is still a garderobe and a fireplace, as well as a mass of Norman arches, Gothic niches, carved capitals and bricked-up windows. As set out, it is all confusing but intriguing. Yet when we return outside, we appear to be looking at a smart Georgian farmhouse.

To the north lies another monastic building, the old refectory, saved as a barn. When I controlled my irritation at the over-conservation of this site, Denny grew on me.

ELY: OLD PALACE **

Palace Green
Ghostly remains of the episcopal residence in hospice (P-R)

Ely's majestic cathedral needs no mention, but visiting most of its medieval domestic buildings is near impossible (despite their having received government grants). Not so the Old Palace. It has not been the official residence of the Bishops of Ely since 1940, and the building is now a Sue Ryder hospice. Staff and patients are proud of their home and welcome occasional visitors, especially when they stop to chat to the patients. The guidebook offers recipes written by the latter. Hospital conversion for wheelchair access has done terrible damage, but at least the place has been rescued from dereliction.

Bishop Alcock (1486–1501) built the original palace and Bishop Laney (1667–75) pulled most of it down. The façade to Palace Green is a magnificent jumble of styles. Two towers guard the courtyard. That on the left is a 15th-century gatehouse with a closed entrance and pretty tripartite niche above it. Inside is the Monks' Room with lierne vault and acanthus and rose bosses. A bridge ran from here over the road into the cathedral. The tower on the right is 16th-century, with a Tudor gallery extending westwards. The courtyard beyond was rebuilt in the 17th century, when the two towers were made of equal height. The façade was given Ionic brick pilasters and a scroll canopy above the doorway.

The palace interior was comprehensively rebuilt in 1771. The large sitting room inside is Georgian, as is the staircase and most of the rooms that have not been converted beyond recognition. Most worth seeing are the bishop's private chapel with its Victorian murals and the already mentioned Monks' Room. It has a monkish ghost to whom the patients are much attached.

The murals of birds and animals in the small dining room are by a local artist, Peter Welsh. The original Long Gallery is also accessible. Although unfurnished except for a few episcopal portraits, it enjoys good views over the Green and the garden. In the latter is the palace's pride and joy, a London plane planted in 1674 and claimed as the largest in England and oldest in Europe.

ELY: OLIVER CROMWELL'S HOUSE **

29 St Mary's Street
Home of God's Englishman (M)

Cromwell moved with his family from their farm in nearby St Ives into the old tithe collector's house in Ely in 1636. It was both a post and a property inherited from his uncle, Sir Thomas Steward. Cromwell had already studied at Cambridge and the Inns of Court in London. Now aged thirty-seven and with a growing family, he became a prosperous civil servant. He stayed at the house intermittently until he moved to London in 1647, becoming Lord Protector six years later.

The house doubles as the local tourist centre and Cromwell museum. The museum is not for purists. It makes assiduous use of mobile wax effigies, plastic chickens, videos and tape machines. These are well done. The parlour has three figures in 17th-century costume, all in eerily mechanical motion, plus a baby in a crib. The panelling is original and includes a charming decorated frieze and fireplace surround. The kitchen is in the medieval part of the house. An attempt has been made to gather the herbs that Elizabeth Cromwell would have used in her cooking. The view onto Palace Green from the fireside is said to be identical to the one she would have had.

Upstairs are two rooms half-heartedly turned into a museum. An assortment of Cromwellian clothing and armour is available for children to try on in front of a mirror. Beyond are two more tableau rooms. The first depicts Cromwell hard at work in his study in London, while a recording gives a sympathetic account of his beliefs and tribulations. Next comes a recreation of the Whitehall bedroom in which he died in 1659. He is lying and breathing his last while a recording relates the fate of his remains, variously buried, exhumed, abused and dismembered. It is called the Haunted Room.

MADINGLEY HALL *

Madingley, 4m W of Cambridge
Tudor mansion in Capability Brown garden (P-R)

Madingley was hired in 1861 by Queen Victoria and Prince Albert for their son, the raffish Prince of Wales, as a residence during his brief time as a Cambridge undergraduate. The gesture was unlikely to help integrate him with his fellow students. Worse followed. A visit to the house by Albert was said to have precipitated his fatal illness. The cold East Anglian wind is notoriously bitter.

The house sits, big-boned and Tudor, at the top of a sloping lawn outside its village. It is as if part of a Cambridge college has been blown out into the country and come to rest on the

Cromwell's house in Ely

first high ground it met. In 1948, the house was bought by the University as an extramural study centre and its inside is institutionalized.

The exterior and grounds are splendid. The main façade has embedded within it the traditional hall and porch of the mid-16th-century house built by a lawyer, Sir John Hynde. It is of redbrick with diapering and stone dressings. The bay window and porch are enriched with Hynde heraldry and that of Henry VIII and his then wife, Katharine Parr. (Henry's marriages assist greatly in dating Tudor houses.) The corners are formed by towers and turrets. The north range to the right is of admirable brick, resting on what would have been an open loggia, now a basement. In front, a yew garden descends towards a lake and a modified Capability Brown landscape.

The most remarkable feature of Madingley is the Georgian arch and screen adjacent to the façade, leading to the south stables. These were built by a Hynde descendent, John Hynde Cotton, in 1758. He re-used the gateway to the Old Schools in Cambridge, dating from 1470 but gothicized during re-erection. The arch is in the form of a sweeping ogee surrounded by niches and heraldic shields. This is flanked by lesser ogee doorways and by two charming Gothick seats. It looks sophisticated next to the giant stepped gable of Hynde's south wall.

Plans are afoot to make the interior more accessible. The hall was at some point divided into a dining room below and saloon above, both with good ceilings. The staircase is 18th century. There are said to be early 17th-century murals in the attic.

STRETHAM: STOKER'S HOUSE *

5m SW of Ely
Worker's cottage, lost in the Fens (M)

Few Fenland corners are as evocative as Stretham (follow signs to Stretham Old Engine House). Here all is space, sky and the white scars of water across meadow. In the Middle Ages, this was the motorway network of the

wool trade. It then became desperately poor. The Fens were drained for farming, but were found to sink as a result, which made them even more liable to waterlogging and flooding. Ever more ingenious means were then found to drain the land, culminating in such great beam pump engines as Stretham, powered by steam coal.

The beam engine is still in being. It was built to drain the Waterbeach Level into the Old West River south of Ely. There were once sixty such engines in the area, replacing 800 smock windmills. The double-acting rotative beam engine operated from 1831 until replaced by a diesel in 1925. The pump worked until 1941. The steam engine was powered by coal, delivered by barge. Next door, in the old toll house, lived the superintendent and the stoker. It must have been a bleak existence and the farming must have been profitable to justify the expense.

What is now called the Stoker's Cottage is reputed to date back to Tudor times, although I could see no such trace. The structure appears to be early Victorian. It comprises four simple rooms with an outside lavatory, worth listing as historic. Inside is the furniture used until abandonment in 1951. Round it is a display of the work of the engine and the surrounding fen, mostly from old photographs. It is atmospheric in its scruffiness. A trust plans to refurnish this isolated place – not too much, I hope.

WIMPOLE HALL ***

8m N of Royston
Gibbs palace with Soane library (NT)

The last private owner of Wimpole Hall was Rudyard Kipling's daughter, Elsie Bambridge, who was devoted to the old house. She was a recluse and is prime candidate for the story beloved of modern country house owners. Spotting trespassers picnicking in the grounds of Wimpole, she traced their car number and

Wimpole: Georgian grandiloquence

later turned up with her chauffeur to picnic on their suburban lawn.

The tale is a far cry from Wimpole's glory days. The house was based on one completed in the 1650s by Sir Thomas Chicheley, possibly to his own designs. He lived well, too well, and had to sell his new creation. Wimpole passed through various hands before coming to the 1st Duke of Newcastle in 1710. He died within a year, leaving it and his fortune to his sole heir, Henrietta Cavendish-Holles. Three years later, in the greatest political wedding of the age, she married Edward Harley, son of the Tory Earl of Oxford. The event took place in the drawing room at Wimpole. To help pay for it, their agents set about building the Cavendish-Harley estate in Marylebone, its streets named after their country properties.

Harley commissioned James Gibbs to improve the house in the Baroque style and to accommodate his burgeoning library, already of 12,000 books. Sir James Thornhill decorated the new chapel and Charles Bridgeman laid out the gardens. By 1739, with most of the work complete, Harley went the way of Chicheley. An alcoholic, he too faced bankruptcy and sold the house on which he had expended his life and fortune. Worse, it went to a hated Whig, the Lord Chancellor, Lord Hardwicke. The contents sale in 1742 was as spectacular as it was tragic. The nation acquired 7,639 manuscript volumes and 14,000 rolls for £10,000, for the original British Museum Library.

Hardwicke now recruited the Whig architect, Henry Flitcroft, to convert parts of the house uncompleted by Gibbs. This included rebuilding the main façade with a Venetian window above the main door. Hardwicke's son then introduced Capability Brown. There followed other designers, John Soane, Humphry Repton and the Victorian, H. E. Kendall. But it takes just one bad apple to ruin the crop. In 1873, the 5th Earl of Hardwicke, the original Champagne Charlie and friend of the Prince of Wales, inherited Wimpole and 19,000 acres. Within fifteen years he owed £300,000 and Wimpole was again for sale.

The house was acquired by Lord Robartes, who was soon to inherit Lanhydrock (Cornwall), before finally coming to rest in 1938 with Captain George Bambridge and his wife, Elsie Kipling. George died in 1943 but his wife struggled for thirty years to keep the house together and recreate its collection. When Pevsner contrived an entrance to Wimpole in 1954, Mrs Bambridge declared that she had 'never been contradicted so many time in the space of ten minutes'. The house and estate passed to the National Trust on her death in 1976.

Wimpole is vast but not empty. Its shape is a long rectangle, arranged round a central hall and stairs. In the reception rooms, Mrs Bambridge and the National Trust together repaired the ravages of past sales. Flitcroft's entrance hall signals their success with a fine set of horse paintings by John Wootton. The west suite of rooms was intended by Gibbs for books but later domesticated by Mrs Bambridge. The south drawing room is in a buff colour, with imitation Georgian plasterwork, deep armchairs and Rococo pier-glasses. The Long Gallery was three Gibbs rooms made into one by Flitcroft, with a generous sweep of columns and family portraits, mostly by Hudson.

Beyond the gallery are two libraries, one by Soane leading into one by Gibbs. The first is roofed in curved Soanian arches, decorated with floral roundels. The second is a double cube completed in 1730 and intended for a collection which by then comprised 50,000 volumes. The plasterwork is assumed to be by Isaac Mansfield, working in Cambridge at the time, together with the Italian, Giovanni Bagutti. The Yellow Drawing Room, shaped as a T, is Soane's triumph. It is like a church nave with crossing and transepts, with a pier-glass mirror for a reredos. A glorious canopy of arches and fans rises to a clear-glass lantern above.

Across the saloon, the Soane library is balanced by the Great Staircase. This is by Gibbs but with Flitcroft and Soane adding their signatures. The walls are hung with Wootton landscapes of Newmarket, whose proximity was central to Wimpole's appeal to its many wealthy owners. Hunting and horse racing

Fenland Rococo at Peckover

were a 'supertax' that primed the rural economy of England for centuries.

Upstairs, pride of place goes to the state bed in the Lord Chancellor's room. It is more like a canopy over the throne of an oriental prince. At the front of the house is Mrs Bambridge's study and bedroom, kept by the National Trust as she left them. They suggest a lonely widow determined to leave her home better than she found it. From her writing table she could look down Bridgeman's great south avenue. On the wall were her favourite pictures, two by Tissot and Arthur William Devis's *Windswept Girl in a Turban Walking her Dog*.

Below stairs is Soane's plunge bath, sadly not available for use by visitors on hot days. The service rooms in the basement are in excellent order, as left by the Bambridges but eerily unused. It is as if some terrible plague had driven the servants away, never to return.

WISBECH: PECKOVER HOUSE **

North Brink
Georgian town house with Rococo plasterwork (NT)

Wisbech was once a centre of England's wool trade. Its links with the Dutch coast shows in its architecture. 'The Brink' or waterfront of the River Nene was lined with Dutch gables and steep hipped roofs beneath which sea captains and cloth merchants grew immensely rich. Among them were the Peckovers and the Gurneys, Quakers whose diligence led them to found a local bank, later taken over by

Barclays. Jonathan Peckover bought a town house on North Brink in 1794. A descendant became Lord Peckover and his last surviving relative, the Honourable Alexandrina Peckover, left it to the National Trust in 1948.

Peckover House remains a dignified mansion of 1722 in a row of such properties facing the river. Three brick storeys rise forbidding at the front, more exuberant behind. Here a classical doorway is topped by a Venetian window and wide steps lead down to an extensive garden.

The interior is familiar mid-Georgian, with a startling exception. Although the panelling and fittings of the principal rooms are restrained, the plasterwork is exceptional. That of the entrance hall is Rococo, the ceiling roundel vividly three-dimensional. This is mild compared with the drawing room overmantel. Here is a mirror frame of the richest ornamentation, crowned with a bird apparently flying free. It is attributed to craftsmen working at Walpole's Houghton (Norfolk), predating the Peckover ownership. The room contains two Chinese Chippendale tables.

A Victorian extension houses the library, of a scale more appropriate to a ballroom. In the small breakfast room is a charming collection of Norwich school watercolours, including works by Cotman and Cox.

Cambridge University: The Colleges

Cambridge is second only to Oxford – shall we say its equal – as a collection of English domestic buildings from before the Civil War. The early colleges grew either from monastic establishments or from residential halls for visiting scholars attending the 'schools'. As at Oxford, the buildings were based on a medieval town house, a defensive gatehouse leading to a courtyard round which were arranged an eating hall, chapel and master's lodging. The chief difference in both Cambridge and Oxford was that scholars tended to live one or two to a room off a private staircase rather than in a monastic dormitory. This plan held the college together as an extended fraternity while offering zones of hierarchy and privacy. It has proved astonishingly long lasting as a residential form.

The university lay along one bank of the River Cam, only straying across its 'Backs' in the 19th century. These Backs remain the city's most picturesque feature. The earliest medieval foundations, often by wealthy widows, were followed by periodic surges in building. The first came with the Dissolution of the Monasteries, leading to Jesus College and the expansion of King's, Trinity and Caius. A further surge came with the academic boom of the 17th century, with the 'transitional classicism' of Clare, Christ's and Peterhouse, typified by the work of the local Grumbold family of architect/craftsmen.

Apart from Wren's early works and the Gibbs Building at King's, Cambridge mostly slept after the Restoration, leaving a local man, James Essex to keep its chapels and halls in repair. In the 1800s it awoke with a shock, to Wilkins' Greek campus at Downing and Thomas Rickman's exercise in the Picturesque at St John's.

The Victorian period was less happy, with heavy-handed works by Waterhouse at Caius and Pembroke, Wyatville at Sydney Sussex and, less offensively, Basil Champneys at Newnham. The next burst had to await the end of the 20th century, when the Cambridge landscape was transformed, first by the stylish brutalism of Churchill, Christ's and St John's, then by the happier insertions of the 'post-modernists', at Emmanuel and Jesus. Cambridge offers a feast of modern buildings.

Christ's *	Jesus **	Robinson *
Churchill *	King's ***	St Catharine's *
Clare **	Magdalene ***	St John's ****
Corpus Christi **	Newnham **	Sidney Sussex *
Downing *	Pembroke **	Trinity ****
Emmanuel *	Peterhouse *	Trinity Hall *
Gonville and Caius **	Queens' ***	

CHRIST'S COLLEGE *

St Andrew's Street
Medieval court, early classical range

Christ's is a sister college to St John's, with a tower to match. It was built in 1505 to the glory of their shared benefactor, Lady Margaret Beaufort, mother of Henry VII and fount of Tudor legitimacy. The coat of arms is a portcullis and red Lancastrian rose, supported by two giant yales (obscure beasts with an ability to twirl their horns; *see* p. 66). The college was intended to take students from the north of England.

The ancient First Court was faced in stone in the 18th century, giving it a severe aspect, but is enlivened by the Beaufort arms repeated over the Master's Lodge. Here Lady Margaret lived while her college was being built. It has a window linked to the adjacent chapel, so Mass could be watched in private.

Christ's is an essay in Cambridge history. The Second Court behind the First comprises just the Fellows' Building, begun in 1640. It displays the hesitant Renaissance of Cambridge before the Civil War when, as in Oxford, Tudor-Gothic was considered the proper academic style. The range is adorned with a balustrade and pediments, but the classicism does not grip it in one composition. The doorways still seem entrances to individual staircases rather than part of a whole. The ground floor windows are heavily rusticated. It is attributed to Inigo Jones but is probably by the local Cambridge architect, ubiquitous at the time, Thomas Grumbold, perhaps familiar with Jones's work.

The college was clearly proud of its originality. In the 1880s, the college had J. J. Stevenson build an imitation of the Fellows' Building in the gardens beyond. When, in 1948, Albert Richardson was asked to form a Third Court, he did so in yet another variation on the same original. In 1966 the college commissioned Denys Lasdun to design one of his ziggurats at the back of its site. Its concrete surfaces are ageing badly and the basement servicing is ugly.

The Fellows' Garden contains a mulberry tree, one of many planted on the orders of James I to help the English silk trade.

CHURCHILL COLLEGE *

Madingley Road
Early Brutalist work in meadows

Churchill was the first and boldest of the post-war colleges, founded in 1958 primarily for science students. Age has not softened nor custom mellowed it. 'Remote and unfriendly', said Norman Scarfe in his *Shell Guide to Cambridge*. Designed by Sheppard, Robson Partners in the New Brutalist style, it assaults the soft contour of suburban Cambridge with an armoured concrete mixer. The senses are assailed with facts.

Yet Churchill has at least acquired a certain thuggish friendliness. The main college rooms flank a wide spine, as in an airport departure lounge. The sweep of stairs to the hall is spectacular and the hall itself is a massive space. Wooden slatted walls rise to three transverse concrete barrel vaults. Everywhere are views out into the courtyards. They look gloomy in grey weather, relieved by a scattering of Henry Moore and Barbara Hepworth.

The original plan retained some sense of collegiate intimacy. Residential blocks are based on the staircase form and set round traditional courtyards. Some brickwork is even tolerated. The newer buildings open dramatically onto spacious grounds beyond. A chapel is placed at a pagan distance on the far horizon, from where Churchill is almost picturesque.

CLARE COLLEGE **

Trinity Lane
Jacobean court with 'sinking' bridge

The original Clare College is just one court and a bridge, but what a court and what a bridge. The college was founded in 1338 by Elizabeth de Clare but completely rebuilt from 1638 onwards in the classical style probably at the hand of Thomas Grumbold, working at the same time at Christ's. Work was interrupted by the Civil War, but continued under the Restoration. The picturesque west front over the water was not completed until the 1660s.

Clare is a most enjoyable building. The gatehouse is Jacobean 'transitional', with Gothic niches and even a fan vault inside the arch. Windows have stone mullions. Its court displays the slow march of classicism through 17th-century Cambridge. On the left, south, side the Jacobean work of 1640 continues, with hipped dormer windows and a splendid rear overlooking King's College. On the hall side, the façades are clearly later, with larger windows and pediments to the dormers.

The far end of the court against the river is Clare fortissimo. Here the Restoration has arrived and the influence is clearly Wren, with giant pilasters and a Baroque frontispiece. The windows carry over-large pediments. This later façade is said to be by Grumbold's son, Robert. The bridge at its foot is by his father. This lovely work, decorated with ball finials, seems to sink slightly in the middle as if in sorrow. This feature was much admired by the novelist and lover of Cambridge, Henry James.

Clare's 20th-century expansion could only be over the Backs. The architect of the 1930s Memorial Court was Sir Giles Gilbert Scott, of Battersea Power Station fame, as is very evident. The buildings in grey stone are dignified and cold. A further extension was financed by Paul Mellon, whom the college had the good fortune to have as an alumnus.

CORPUS CHRISTI COLLEGE **

Trumpington Street
Cambridge's oldest residential court

Corpus was founded in 1352 by townsmen of the Guild of the Body of Christ, a 14th-century cult of great popularity and prestige. It was thus a work of civic rather than royal or church patronage. Its emblem was the pelican 'in her piety', symbol of Christ's sacrifice. The college has the earliest court in Cambridge, Old Court, completed in 1377. Only Mob

Corpus Christi's Old Court

Quad at Merton College, Oxford, is an older quadrangle in England.

The Old Court retains the pattern of hall and quadrangle. Its original hall is now the college kitchens and attic dormers have been added to the ranges. But the medieval windows survive, as does the form of stairs leading to study cubicles off sleeping rooms. The Elizabethan playwright, Christopher Marlowe, was a student here. An alley leads through to St Bene't's Church, where early scholars worshipped before the building of the chapel, a precious fragment of ancient townscape.

Corpus's New Court was a replacement by William Wilkins in 1823 for the previous Tudor and Jacobean ranges. This is Wilkins in institutional vein, in a rather debased Gothic. To the right is the massive outline of the Parker Library, the most precious collection of medieval books outside the British Library (closed to the public). It was gathered by an Elizabethan Master and Archbishop of Canterbury, Matthew Parker, from the wreckage of the dissolved monasteries.

DOWNING COLLEGE *

Regent Street
Greek 'campus' by Wilkins and Quinlan Terry

Downing College is the cuckoo in the Cambridge nest. Old Sir George Downing, whose ancestor built Downing Street, had been dead over fifty years when his will was finally released from grasping relatives and his desire for a new Cambridge college realized from 1807 onwards. It was the first college founded since Queen Elizabeth's reign. A proposal by the Gothic revivalist, James Wyatt, was criticized by a group of radical philhellenes, including Byron and Thomas Hope. Both Gothic and Palladian were ridiculed as archaic, and the trustees were persuaded to abandon the courtyard plan in favour of a campus of Greek temples. Greek, the style of democratic America and France, was the order of the day.

The architect, William Wilkins, was much travelled in Greece and adept at designing to his clients' preference. He proposed a series of pavilions graced with clean Ionic porticos and linked by walls set in a park. This was accepted. Downing is the first true 'college campus', predating Jefferson's University of Virginia by a decade. But while Wilkins' pavilions were built to house the hall, Master's lodgings and residences for other masters, successive Fellows had other ideas as to what should follow.

Thus the pavilions were later linked with new, heavier ranges, turning the campus into virtually a court. In 1929, Sir Herbert Baker decided he could out-Wilkins Wilkins. He filled the north side of the court with a chapel range of three storeys, wholly dominating the composition. Its second floor windows are out of sync with those below. Only the south end was left open to the paddock and ornamental trees.

More controversial still was the arrival of Quinlan Terry in the 1980s. He built to the east and west of Baker's range. Terry's classicism could hardly have been less deferential to Wilkins, although it was no less Greek in origin. The Howard Building is a rectangular essay on a series of Palladian themes, contrasting with the more formal Georgian of Howard Court behind. Terry's library is different again, a portico capped by a Tower of the Winds. Its frieze motifs symbolize the subjects of study, a Tower of Babel for modern languages, an hour-glass for history and a double helix for biology. Great fun.

EMMANUEL COLLEGE *

St Andrew's Street
Wren's early essay in classicism

Emmanuel College was a Puritan foundation of 1584 to train priests in Calvinist doctrine. Many of its graduates were later to emigrate to America, including John Harvard, who not only gave his name to his new university but set it in a place he called Cambridge in honour of the settlement's first pastor, also from Emmanuel.

The college has one architectural set-piece. In its Front Court, past a colonnade to left and right, stands the delightful chapel, designed by the young Christopher Wren in 1667. The façade is in the form of a portico that seems to grow organically out of the colonnade that runs across the court supporting the Master's Gallery on the first floor. The composition can thus be viewed either as an Italianate arcade with a portico in the middle, or as a portico with colonnaded wings. It is the sort of intellectual conceit that delighted the late 17th century. Inside the chapel is admirable Wren plasterwork and panelling. The reredos is a painting of the *Return of the Prodigal Son* by Jacopo Amigoni of 1734.

The hall ceiling has Rococo ceiling panels, by the Cambridge Georgian architect, James Essex. The right-hand side of Front Court is a Georgian range with a Baroque central section, but beyond it is a Jacobean range of 1633 in that lovably indeterminate post-Tudor style that still proliferates in both Cambridge and Oxford from that period.

The garden has a lake, known as the duck-pond, with a modern structure of exposed concrete on its far side. Matters are redeemed with the modern Queen's Building by Sir Michael Hopkins. A simple box with curved ends, like a canal barge, it is of a beautiful honeyed limestone and rests on a colonnade.

GONVILLE AND CAIUS **

Trinity Street
Renaissance gates in medieval courts

Pronounced and shortened to 'Keys', this was one of the original colleges founded in the 14th century. Gonville was a Norfolk priest who devoted his rent income to training his successors. He bought houses to form what is now Gonville Court and built a small chapel, bits of which remain. The college was refounded in 1557 and by a different personality, John Keys. He was a humanist and doctor, a graduate of both Cambridge and Padua. A man of Renaissance ideas and continental style, he was doctor to Edward VI and Mary I (both died young), and president of the College of Physicians. He latinized his surname to Caius.

The Elizabethan age was one of architectural

symbolism, reflected in such religious curiosities as Thomas Tresham's Rushton (Northants). Dr Caius applied a similarly emblematic view of a 'virtuous' education to his old college. The scholar would progress through the Gate of Humility, at the entrance on Trinity Street, across an outer court to the Gate of Virtue and then left through an inner court to the climactic Gate of Honour. This led to the Old Schools and a degree, the sequence symbolizing the student's path through the university and Renaissance man's path through life.

The Gate of Humility is now in the Master's Garden, replaced by the porter's lodge. The other gates are *in situ* and form a happy architectural progress. Tree Court carries a straight line from the entrance to the Gate of Virtue. This remarkable structure, dated 1567, is medieval in form but classical in style. Fluted pilasters flank a Roman arch with a pediment above. This is earlier than the English Renaissance of Robert Smythson and half a century before Inigo Jones brought Palladianism to Whitehall from Italy. Pevsner regarded it as one of the earliest examples of architectural, as opposed to ornamental, classicism in England.

Caius Court was left with one side open, so that air could circulate freely, a concept later adopted by other colleges. This side faces the Senate House and King's Chapel. With its final Gate of Honour, it forms one of the most picturesque compositions in Cambridge. The gate was completed a decade later than that of Virtue and is a textbook of Serlian motifs. A mini-portico rests on an arch flanked by a classical screen, the whole topped by a hexagonal cupola with sundials on its faces. The gate is set in an old rubble wall, as one might find at the bottom of a garden. This daring Renaissance import is now reduced to a quaint folly by the looming shadow of the Georgian Old Schools beyond.

If Caius was an innovator, the same cannot be said for Alfred Waterhouse. In the 19th century he constructed the new building on Tree Court, towering over King's Parade outside. The style, says John Julius Norwich, embraces every known continental château and some unknown. It is an odd replacement for a gate named Humility.

JESUS COLLEGE **

Jesus Lane
Former nunnery with cloister and Morris chapel decoration

Jesus College is on the outskirts of old Cambridge, still with the atmosphere of a college in the fens. It was based on a former nunnery, that of St Radegund, traces of which survive in the cloister. By 1496 the institution was reduced to two nuns (one of them *infamis* or guilty of some unnamed sin). Henry VII's Comptroller of Works, Bishop Alcock of Ely, anticipated the Dissolution by refounding a college under his own patronage.

The layout of the college is at first sight confusing. A jolly Tudor gatehouse is reached down a strangely unsettling straight lane between two walls, known as The Chimney. The south façade of the tower is decorated with an ogee that shoots like a rocket up all three storeys. The gate gives onto no more than an outer court, facing what would have been open fields and dating from the 16th and 17th centuries. A sense of collegiate enclosure is realized only to the right, in Cloister Court.

This is dominated by the chapel in the south-east corner. Jesus Chapel is one of the few in Cambridge with a full complement of chancel, nave and transepts. It has an Early English chancel and a fine screen by A. W. N. Pugin, but its chief glory is the 1860s restoration by G. F. Bodley, with customary assistance from William Morris and friends. Morris's heraldic ceilings are superb works, as are Edward Burne-Jones's great windows of 1873.

The cloister outside has wooden roofs installed at the time of refoundation, c1500, and contains many examples of Alcock's rebus of a cockerel. In the east range are carefully preserved fragments of the nunnery's Chapter House. The hall retains its original arch-braced roof and a fine Perpendicular oriel bay with glass by Morris.

New buildings at Jesus dribble away to the north in modern styles that are neither intimate nor spacious. They seem to apologize for intruding on the greenery. By contrast, the college's latest additions along Jesus Lane are outstanding, the best of Cambridge's 1990s architectural revival. The new library, by Evans and Shalef, is a shimmering temple of stone.

KING'S COLLEGE ***

King's Parade
Georgian and Gothic keeping watch on the great chapel

There is a problem with King's. The appearance of the college is so dominated by its chapel that the domestic buildings of the college must struggle to be seen or heard. The chapel is one of the supreme works of English Perpendicular. To sit and watch a low sun dancing refracted colours over the walls beneath the mighty fan vault is a Cambridge experience beyond compare.

The college was founded in 1441 by Henry VI for scholars from his new school at Eton. He laid out a plan for two courts. The chapel would flank a Great Court, as at Eton, while a second court would be round a cloister, again as at Eton. Almost nothing was built by his death. Henry VIII later completed the chapel, which therefore carries his heraldry, but scholars continued to be housed in makeshift buildings.

Two centuries later, the Fellows approached Christopher Wren, then Nicholas Hawksmoor, then James Gibbs for help. Hawksmoor suggested replanning the centre of Cambridge round a forum, on the plan of Rome's Piazza Navona. For better or worse, Cambridge lacked the necessary Pope. Instead Gibbs supplied his austere block as the first range of what should have been a three-sided court. It is in grey ashlar of three storeys, with only a central doorway as a Baroque flourish. Yet it has immense dignity.

The Gibbs Building set alongside King's chapel has long been a gift to dialectical metaphor. It is Gothic against classical, vertical against horizontal, licentious against restrained. Yet the contrast is entirely circumstantial. This was never meant.

The next architect to attempt a completion of Henry VIII's great scheme was William Wilkins in the 1820s. Rather than defy the chapel, as did Gibbs, he bent the knee before it. He designed a new college hall in a dutiful Gothic, though with a whimsical flourish of chimneys, turrets and louvres. Inside is a magnificent neo-Tudor roof with a forest of pendants and a Perpendicular screen. Wilkins wanted to gothicize the Gibbs Building but this was mercifully not permitted.

Wilkins' final touch was the screen to King's Parade, perhaps his masterpiece in the Gothic style. Completed in 1828, it is in the form of a low gatehouse flanked by a screen of open arches. The finials copy those of the chapel in a rhythmic sequence of spikes dancing attendance on a central cupola. They used to look oriental and faintly sinister when blackened with soot. Now cleaned, they appear to be made of sugar.

Stairs run straight to the top with no returns, and with cubicles off them. The hall is a fine survival, lit by a high bay window. Its dais end carries a large mural of the arms of Queen Anne. At the other end is a Georgian composition, unique to this college, of stairs leading to a gallery and Combination Room, or Fellows' common room. The door surround appears to incorporate earlier, Elizabethan wood carvings.

The Second Court faces the Pepys Building, containing the library and archive bequeathed to the college by the great man on his death. It was of exactly 3,000 books. Whenever Pepys received a new one over this number he disposed of an old one, an admirable practice. The building's origins can be seen round the back, a façade of the 1580s of what appears to be an H-shaped Elizabethan hall house. The front is more formal, one side of the H having been filled in with a colonnade, with pilasters and pedimented windows above. The interior is furnished with Pepys's own bookcases and writing desk, which arrived in 1724 with the books. It is a lovely room.

MAGDALENE COLLEGE ✱✱✱

Magdalene Street
Monastic courtyard with Pepys library

Magdalene College owes its isolated position to the desire of a group of Fenland monks to be kept away from sinful undergraduates. It was sponsored by the Dukes of Buckingham and was called Buckingham College until the Dissolution, when it was refounded as Magdalene. Its core was the 15th-century First Court, with monastic *camerae* as at Worcester College, Oxford, accompanied by a chapel, a prior's lodge and the hall. This simplest of collegiate forms is perfectly preserved. Post-Reformation expansion was on vacant land to the rear.

Magdalene's face to the world is much as it was when built. The First Court had its brickwork, once stuccoed and covered in creeper, scraped in the 1960s. The south range includes some of the original monks' rooms unaltered.

NEWNHAM COLLEGE ✱✱

Sidgwick Avenue
College built for women in 'Queen Anne' style

Newnham was the second women's foundation at Cambridge after Girton. It was founded in 1871 and four years later Basil Champneys began to supply his remarkable houses in the Queen Anne style. They are the finest collection of the style anywhere in England. Their façades seen from Gertrude Jekyll's garden form a gloriously variegated composition. Newnham might have been lifted from Amsterdam's Golden Bend or the Grand Place in Brussels.

Champneys wanted Newnham to be the antithesis of Girton, which was banished two miles from the city centre to be out of temptation's way. Where Girton was Gothic and austere, Newham was warm and cosy. Girls had private rooms with fireplaces, desks, flowers, patterned friezes and even day-beds.

This was to be a home, not a convent. Champneys was retained by the college as it expanded along Sidgwick Avenue for over thirty-five years. He seems to have enjoyed giving his ladies an architectural distinction absent from other Cambridge buildings at the time.

The first house was Old Hall, conventionally Dutch revival and similar to contemporary work of Norman Shaw. Then came Sidgwick Hall, with white-painted balustrades and lofty chimneys. Next was the dining hall, medieval in plan with a balcony and lantern cupola and two pronounced bow windows the size of conservatories. Next door, Clough Hall is a wonderful work, a riot of architectural festivity, with oriel windows, giant dormers, broken pediments and massive pilasters. Finally Champneys added Pfeiffer Tower to Old Hall, a bold 'Wrenaissance' pastiche of a traditional Tudor gatehouse. It contains the best gates in Cambridge, designed by Champneys himself in the Arts and Crafts style.

The college has since extended ever further along Sidgwick Avenue, the later work never achieving Champneys' charm. He believed that girls would prefer friendly corridors to staircases. The result, however, is that the houses of Newnham are now linked by reputedly the longest corridor in England.

PEMBROKE COLLEGE **

Trumpington Street
Wren's first work, in Victorian surroundings

Pembroke was founded in the 1340s by another munificent Cambridge widow, that of Aymer de Valence, Earl of Pembroke. The façade to Trumpington Street is a delicious jumble of styles: a 1690 gable end, two oriels above a medieval gatehouse, another gable end and then the tremendous flourish of Christopher Wren's first known work, Pembroke Chapel of 1663. This would all do credit to any street in Rome.

Pembroke's courts are a mess. First Court is ashlared medieval on two sides, and Wren's Chapel is too far to the right properly to enclose it. The hall ahead is 19th century and

the view leaks past it to the gardens beyond. There lurk Victorian buildings by Waterhouse which, on a dark night, can seem like asylum seekers from Transylvania.

Directly ahead and beyond the hall is Ivy Court, a place for students of 17th-century Cambridge architecture. On the left is a handsome work by Robert Grumbold, son of Thomas. On the right is the extraordinary Hitcham Building of 1659, looking as if classical features have been stuck onto an essentially Tudor façade. It shows the nervousness of the early classicists.

No such nervousness afflicted youthful Wren, designing the chapel just a few years after the Hitcham Building. It was one of the first classical churches in England since Inigo Jones's St Paul's, Covent Garden, and was based on a reconstruction drawing by Serlio of a Temple in Tivoli. The inside was altered by George Gilbert Scott the younger but retains the original Wren ceiling.

Alfred Waterhouse treated Cambridge to some of his most aggressive work. Along Trumpington Street his Red Building for the college might be a block of municipal offices. His library inside is more successful, a Flemish town hall with turrets and a clock-tower. At the far end of the college is a building by the younger Scott, facing Pembroke Street. It is Dutch Renaissance, built of stone, with Arts and Crafts decorations and a most distinguished work of Victorian architecture.

PETERHOUSE *

Trumpington Street
Medieval court with eccentric chapel

Peterhouse is the oldest Cambridge college. Founded in 1284, it was modelled on Oxford's Merton. It forms a quaint composition from the street. On the left is a gabled façade with oriel window, recalling the old student hostels that once lined the street at this point. This is balanced on the right by a sedate Palladian wing and, as if settling an argument between them, the east end of the chapel. Peterhouse has always been a place of dispute.

The original college grew round the Old Court behind. Here was the hall of 1290, with sections of medieval stonework surviving – some of the oldest in Cambridge – but comprehensively rebuilt by George Gilbert Scott the younger in 1870. Hard Victorian edges replaced soft medieval ones. William Morris decorated the fireplace, walls and windows. The rest of the court was of the Tudor period, refaced in the 18th century with ashlar. A modest pediment punctuates the west side of the court.

The chapel was begun in 1628 at the start of the transitional age of Cambridge architecture. It was completed under the Laudian Bishop John Cosin, Master after the Restoration. Cosin's work in the Durham diocese and elsewhere marked him as a master of stylistic hybridity, using both Gothic and classical motifs at will. At Durham he tended towards Gothic for the clergy and classical for the laity. Peterhouse Chapel has a colonnaded ground floor, Gothic windows and niches above, a wavy parapet and a classical square gable, all with finials. The interior is a similarly enjoyable mixture.

QUEENS' COLLEGE ***

Queens' Lane
Perfect survival of collegiate Tudor, with Pre-Raphaelite hall

Queens' is the most charming college in Cambridge, a perfect example of Tudor domestic architecture and astonishingly intact. Its ancient courts and hall, its cloister and rear to the River Cam form a complete 15th-century composition. The wall along Silver Street is a superb expanse of medieval brickwork.

The queens were two, those of Henry VI and of Edward IV, spouses of rivals in the Wars of the Roses. Queen Margaret founded it to 'laud and honour the feminine sex', her husband having founded King's. Honour was clearly from afar; it did not extend to admitting women. Edward's Queen Elizabeth sensibly decided to continue what her predecessor had

begun, aided by the college's first President, Andrew Docket, eager to protect his flank.

The college was begun in 1448 round its Front Court. A gatehouse guarded the entrance, in which Erasmus resided during his stay at Cambridge. He complained, 'I cannot go outdoors because of the plague ... I am beset with thieves and the wine is no better than vinegar.' But he was safe. The court inside claims to be the first completed with this degree of formality. The old chapel and library are to the north.

The hall at Queens' is the most spectacular in Cambridge. It is intimate and medieval in atmosphere, with a distinctively Gothic bay window which lights the High Table. The screens passage guards the rest of the hall from the entrance and the kitchens. The old louvred lantern on the roof is supplemented by a Victorian *flèche* for a bell. Credit for the present decoration must go to G. F. Bodley and William Morris, in 1861 and 1875 respectively. They used individual beams, doors and screens from the 15th century but applied to them a splendidly bold Victorian revivalism, bursting with colour. The fireplace was elaborated by Bodley, including alabaster overmantel and panels by Ford Madox Brown and other Pre-Raphaelites. Morris stencilled the walls and painted the ceiling. John Hardman supplied the stained glass.

The Cloister Court beyond contained the private quarters of the President. Built over a cloister on three sides, it has a formal façade to the north with the President's lodgings and gallery. This is a substantial Tudor building of *c*1540. It is, as Pevsner says, 'one of the most picturesque of English timber-framed structures, its beauty being one of irregularity and happy accident'. The façade to the court is a pleasant jumble of bows, oriels and stair turrets, exterior form reflecting interior purpose.

In the 20th century, Queens' architectural inspiration collapsed. For the riverside site, the Fellows sadly preferred Basil Spence to Dykes Bower. The result is like a municipal office block, although a 1964 guide to Cambridge buildings complained that 'it did not wholly escape the temptations of the picturesque'. It does for me. The new Backs buildings are reached over the wooden Mathematical Bridge of 1749. Sited on what was once a peaceful water meadow, they beggar belief.

ROBINSON COLLEGE *

Grange Road
Collegiate bastion set round lush gardens

Robinson is the most distinctive of Cambridge's late 20th-century colleges in the 'post-modern' style. It mimics medievalism, but in atmosphere rather than plan. Its flourish of gatehouse set in high redbrick walls is more that of an Italian hill town than an English courtyard house. Steep ramparts guard the inmates from life outside, while lofty galleries within look down on narrow internal lanes. There is no danger of the real world penetrating this place.

The college was founded in 1977 by a reclusive engineering millionaire, David Robinson. He paid for everything. The architects were the Scottish firm of Gillespie, Kidd and Coia. A ramp leads to a gatehouse, inside which is an enclosed court like a medieval market square. This needs more activity, perhaps vendors and street criers in ancient costume. Radiating alleys and walkways feed tiers of student rooms. Most are set along a V of corridors, with balconies looking inward over lush gardens.

The chapel is a beautiful room. A lozenge-shaped chamber is suffused with coloured light from a tall John Piper window.

ST CATHARINE'S COLLEGE *

Trumpington Street
Seventeenth-century classicism with Victorian overlay

St Catharine's runs from Trumpington Street to Queens' Lane and is, outwardly, a three-sided courtyard of dull Cambridge pink brick. The ranges appear mostly 17th century. Yet the closer one examines this court, the stranger it

seems. Indeed, to the careful eye, 'Cats' can seem surreal.

The college was founded in 1473 but was rebuilt in the 1670s, when classicism was at last taking hold at Cambridge. The far, west, range is a pure and handsome Carolean work, with a bold Baroque frontispiece. The windows are wide, without sashes, the dormers alternate triangles and segments. This is possibly the work of Robert Grumbold, working at the same time at neighbouring Clare.

Then everything starts to move. The court is not rectangular but rhomboid, the side ranges not at right angles to the far one. Each was built at a different time and to a slightly different scale. The Hall was gothicized in the 19th century, when it was felt that no self-respecting college could have a classical hall. Even a projecting bay window was added. Yet the adjacent chapel was left classical, with large windows and a fine doorcase. The chapel screen and reredos are English Baroque, with a symmetry lacking in the court outside.

ST JOHN'S COLLEGE ****

St John Street
Tudor courts with Bridge of Sighs leading to neo-Gothic on the Cam

Second only to Trinity in size, St John's College is a play of architectural splendour. Where Trinity is expansive and extrovert, St John's is enclosed and introvert. Its three courts retain their Tudor intimacy. Here is none of Trinity's windy spaces. The light of learning burns with a steadier flame.

The college was founded by Margaret of Beaufort, mother of Henry VII and basis of the Tudor claim to the throne. She also founded Christ's and was one of the many benefactresses without whom Cambridge would be a sorrier place. Building did not commence until 1511, by which time she was dead.

The gatehouse of St John's is the most magnificent in Cambridge. It might be the

Tudor ostentation at St John's

entrance to a walled city within a city. A great ogival swoop over the arch is supported by two mythical beasts, yales (with goat's head, antelope's body and elephant's tail, deriving from an Indian *yali*), the Beaufort heraldic beast. The statue above is not of Margaret, as is often supposed, but of John the Baptist, looking like a delicate maiden. He is surrounded by portcullises and Lancastrian roses. The Tudors were obsessed with their regal lineage. The heraldry was repainted by the saviour of English medieval art in the 1930s, E. W. Tristram.

The First Court suffered severely from the Victorian destruction of its north side for a new chapel. This is a big, boring work by Sir Gilbert Scott, which fails to enclose the court but instead exposes it to the north-east. The line of the original chapel can be made out in the grass. St John's should have the courage to rebuild it. The court's west range facing the gatehouse survives, containing the hall and a second gatehouse bearing a late 17th-century statue, this time of the real foundress in a Baroque pose. The hall is original, with a hammer-beam roof, crowned by two of Cambridge's loveliest cupolas.

Beyond lies the Second Court which was not begun until the end of Elizabeth's reign, the builders told to make it 'like unto the windows' of the First Court. Pretty oriels adorn the north and south ranges. On the far side is yet another, third gatehouse, this time celebrating the donor of the court, the Countess of Shrewsbury. She, too, is commemorated with a Baroque statue.

The Third Court takes us firmly into the 17th century. The library is on the right, built in 1624 but still with traceried windows in the Gothic style, ordered because 'some men of judgment . . . holding it most meet for such a building'. The rest of the court was not built until the 1670s, by when the struggle between old and new is more evident. The west range to the river is unashamedly Jacobean, with a jumbled Mannerist frontispiece above a colonnade. The link with the earlier library is a charmingly clumsy arch.

The river façade of St John's Third court is most satisfying. Brick walls fall direct into water, with swans and punts gliding past. The parapet of the library boldly carries the initials of its benefactor, John Lincoln, Keeper of the Seal (in Latin). The roofline is crowned with parapets and Dutch gables, some as late as 1671, the last flourish of the old style before the arrival of Wren at Trinity Library next door.

Regency Picturesque now takes up the St John's story. Leaping over the river is the famous Bridge of Sighs, finished in 1831 to lead to the earliest of the college developments on the far side of the Cam. New Court is a Gothic revival group designed by Thomas Rickman, the architect chiefly noted for classifying the periods of medieval architecture as Early English, Decorated and Perpendicular. Rickman's *coup de théâtre* is a screen similar to that which had just been built by Wilkins in front of King's. It has a vaulted arcade and fan vault with pendant in the middle. The main block has as its centrepiece the famous Gothic Wedding Cake, a confection of pinnacles and flying buttresses.

Transpontine St John's is controversial. New Court was the biggest building in Cambridge at the time and sorely intruded on the rurality of the Backs. Once so deep in sin, the Fellows decided in the 1960s to build on open land to the north at the junction of Bin Brook and the Cam. The Cripps Building, by Powell & Moya, is the boldest post-war building in the city. Stark white rectangles do not overwhelm the site, set on arcades with ground-level views penetrating the volumes. Grass thus survives. But as with so much architecture of the period, the massing is brutalist and the surfaces deteriorating. Beyond is a pretty Norman house known as the School of Pythagoras, c1200, much restored and now a concert hall.

SIDNEY SUSSEX COLLEGE *

Sidney Street
Ugly duckling, fine chapel woodwork

Poor Sidney Sussex. It suffered three blights: Oliver Cromwell as a past student (later a public enemy), Sir Jeffry Wyatville and Nikolaus

Pevsner, whose 'least attractive college' epithet stung. Wyatville was the worst. Best-known for changing his name from that of his architectural relatives, he was the most favoured improver of old buildings during the Regency. He took hold of the college founded in 1594 in the will of the Countess of Sussex and 'Wyatvilled' it.

The college comprised a three-sided court bounded on the street by a wall into which was set the gate. This gate, later classicized, was removed to the garden. The present entrance is into a lodge dividing the college's two courts, a visually uncomfortable arrangement.

Wyatville's refacing of Sidney Sussex in the 1820s was in the Elizabethan Gothic style. Walls were buttressed, windows tudorized and a storey added, with embattled gables. The far side of the hall range facing the garden is ugly neo-Jacobean, overhauled by one of the 19th century's normally most sensitive Gothicists, J. L. Pearson.

The best rooms in Sidney Sussex are the hall with its Georgian ceiling and the chapel. The latter was redesigned in 1912 by the Edwardian, T. H. Lyon, with pews set lengthwise. The woodwork is neo-Baroque and utterly beautiful. At the end are two elegant canopied pews. This is my favourite chapel in the whole of Cambridge.

TRINITY COLLEGE ****

Trinity Street
Biggest college with spacious court and Wren Library

Trinity can seem like one big boast. It is the largest and richest college in Cambridge. The gatehouse is the epitome of medieval ostentation. Outside stands an apple tree, cut from the one that dropped its fruit on its most glorious scholar, Isaac Newton. Great Court is the largest academic court in Cambridge (and Oxford). The library is the most sumptuous. Trinity is thoroughly grand.

The college dates back to 1337 under Edward III but it was refounded by Henry VIII in 1546. It was under Dean Nevile at the end of

Elizabeth's reign that the present Great Court was cleared and the college took on its present spacious form. The gatehouse is Gothic and richly adorned. Two gateways, one for pedestrians and one for carriages, are surmounted by traceried panels flanking the coat of arms of Edward III, English lions quartered with the fleur-de-lys of France. Above stands a rather pitiful Henry VIII, clearly past his prime, with a chair leg for a sceptre, an undergraduate prank now hallowed by history.

Inside spaciousness is all. The Great Court is of two storeys, with attics on two of the sides, forming an extended tableau as of a village street. The façades are warmly clothed in creeper. Nothing is symmetrical. The classical fountain is not in the centre, nor are the paths geometrically consistent. This is a supreme work of English townscape, the one blot being the municipalized lawns and flower beds with which the court is filled. This should be gravelled open space. Lawns have become the green tarmac of English historic spaces. Trinity athletes traditionally race round the court against the chiming of the clock, a scene depicted in the film 'Chariots of Fire'.

The chapel is 16th-century Perpendicular with, inside, an early 18th-century screen and a Baroque reredos even more ornate than on a Wren City church. The antechapel records the college's astonishing list of alumni, from Bacon and Newton through Byron and Tennyson, Wittgenstein and Betrand Russell to Nehru and Gandhi. Next door is a former gatehouse, King Edward's Tower, moved here by Nevile, with a pretty wooden lantern on top. The hall is Jacobean Tudor-Gothic of 1604, its entrance up a flowing fan of steps. The hall roof, naturally the biggest in Cambridge, is hammerbeam but with classical rather than Gothic details. The screen is a superb example of English Mannerist carving. The High Table carries just one bold painting, of Henry VIII. In the adjacent kitchens, crème brulée was invented.

The screens passage, still with its old doors, leads to Nevile's Court, completed in 1613. Here all eyes turn to Wren's Library filling the far side. This is his Cambridge masterpiece, begun in 1676. The building is set on an open colonnade, with lofty windows divided by pilasters. To fit in space for books without losing light from windows, Wren ingeniously lowered the floor to fill the tympanums of the colonnade, as if in a hidden mezzanine. Water shimmers through the openings, lifting the whole structure and making it seem to float above the Backs beyond.

The library interior is regularly and admirably open to the public. The bookcases stand at right angles to the walls, designed by Wren and decorated with dripping limewood carvings by Grinling Gibbons and Cornelius Austin. The most splendid of these are in the alcove on either side of the entrance. Above stand busts by Roubiliac and others of great writers and thinkers. This is a supreme Cambridge interior, a match for King's Chapel.

TRINITY HALL *

Trinity Lane
Elizabeth library, Henry James view

The area north of King's College Chapel is a calm retreat from the bustle of central Cambridge, a jumble of medieval façades and alleys, of colleges once surrounded by walls and secret gardens. Victorian and later expansion filled in much of the open space, but the sense of enclosure remains.

Trinity Hall is squeezed between Clare, Caius and Trinity, a small college founded for law students from Ely in 1350. The college symbol is an ermine crescent, prominently displayed on its buildings. Although the Front Court was refaced in the 18th century, a passage in the right-hand range leads to a view of its north side, of medieval windows and clunch walls.

The far corner of the court contains the hall and chapel. The former has a dignified classical fireplace, the latter a barrel vault with painted cartouches of college heraldry. The joy of Trinity Hall is its garden. Here stands the old Elizabethan library of 1600 with a stepped end gable. This is half a century later than the gates at Caius, yet it might almost be a medieval tithe barn.

Beyond is a row of inoffensive 19th- and 20th-century buildings running down towards the river. This is Cambridge still able to respect its past. Only a concrete bridge of 1960, here of all places, spoils the view. Of this spot Henry James wrote: 'If I were called upon to mention the prettiest corner of the world, I should draw a thoughtful sigh and point the way to the garden of Trinity Hall.'

Cheshire

Cheshire comes as a surprise to those ignorant of the county. Though adjacent to the depressed conurbation of the Mersey plain, it is one of the richest corners of England. A traditional farming region, it became the commuter belt for Manchester and Liverpool in the 19th century and never looked back. The north of the county is suburbanized and the eastern strip is afflicted by the M6 corridor, but parts of the county embrace the Peak District and the south and west have rolling contours and exciting rocky outcrops.

Apart from the crusader phenomenon of Beeston Castle, the earliest houses are the timbered black-and-white halls that are the signature of the North-West. There are excellent examples at Bramall and Gawsworth. The 'magpie' house Little Moreton is a feast of medieval carpentry. The hall at Adlington has unique tree-trunk pillars.

The Jacobeans produced one prodigy house at Crewe Hall, now much restored, and especially ornate Great Chambers at Combermere and Dorfold. The Georgians approached Cheshire with trumpets blaring at Leoni's Lyme Park, pianissimo at Belmont. But it was the architectural Wyatt dynasty that was most prolific, with Samuel and Lewis's masterpiece for the Egertons at Tatton Park and rooms aplenty at Dorfold, Lyme, Rode and Winnington.

The Gothic revival is displayed lightheartedly at Cholmondeley and in earnest for Lord Tollemache at Peckforton. Most remarkable in Cheshire is the new lease of life given to so many houses through commercial use. The county is exemplary in making old buildings earn their keep.

Adlington ***	Crewe Hall ***	Peover Hall ***
Arley **	Dorfold **	Quarry Bank Mill *
Beeston *	Dunham Massey ***	Rode Hall **
Belmont Hall *	Gawsworth ***	Tabley ***
Bramall ***	Highfields *	Tatton:
Capesthorne **	Little Moreton Hall ***	Old Hall *
Cholmondeley *	Lyme Park ****	Park ***
Combermere Abbey **	Peckforton **	Winnington *

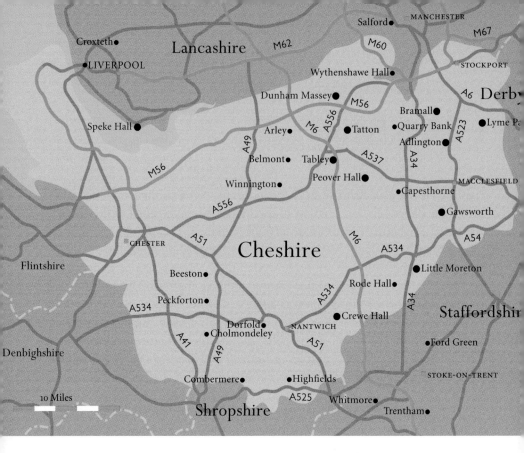

ADLINGTON ***

5m N of Macclesfield
Legh house with medieval hall and
Restoration interiors (P-R)

A Georgian stable block stands guard over its
house in a park of deepest green. Adlington is a
place of all periods and moods. It is part
Cheshire black-and-white, part Tudor brick,
part Restoration and part 18th century. The
house has been owned by a branch of the
Cheshire Legh family since the Middle Ages. In
cases of female succession, husbands have been
expected to become Leghs. The present owner,
Charles Legh, is son of Cynthia Legh and
Ralph Broughton. The house is still in part a
family home.

The core is four-sided medieval courtyard,
with a 15th-century Great Hall and surrounding wings built in the late 16th century. The
north front behind the hall was refaced and

refenestrated in brick after the Restoration, to
present a handsome gabled façade. Then, in
the 1740s and 1750s, Charles Legh decided to
demolish the two south sides of the quadrangle
and rebuild them in the Georgian style. The
exterior of this wing, formally the front of
the house, demonstrates the waywardness of
18th-century design. The portico is most odd,
apparently built for a much taller house and
heightened by elongated bases. A walk around
the outside and courtyard of Adlington is a
historical tableau of English architecture.

The old Great Hall is one of the most remarkable in England. The passage and gallery
are supported, as is the Hall, by two giant oak
trunks. They are dead but their roots are still
deep in the ground. The uprights have been
carved to octagonal shape and covered with
panels. They lean towards the hammerbeam
roof of c1480. Between the trees is a Baroque
gallery and late 17th-century organ designed by
Bernard Smith. It is one of the largest of its date

in the country and would (surely) have been played by Handel when staying at Adlington. With trumpeting cherubs in the celure above and murals of musical saints on either side, the organ marries nature and music.

The rest of the Great Hall is either window or mural. The colourful west end is formed of a huge coved canopy with 60 panels of Cheshire heraldry. Beneath is a wall painting of Hector and Andromache. Sixteenth-century murals depicting the history of Troy cover the side walls. They were hidden until 1859 when a member of the family playing shuttlecock dislodged the plaster and revealed paint beneath.

On the other side of the screens passage is a Carolean staircase, with chunky twisted balusters and pineapple finials. It leads to a suite of rooms along the 17th-century north front, all panelled and with robust Restoration furniture.

ARLEY HALL **

Arley, 7 miles N of Northwich
Jacobethan house of Victorian squire (P)

Arley has been home of the Warburtons, Viscounts Ashbrook, since the Norman Conquest. It lies in a precious enclave of green just a mile from the M6. The Georgian Sir Peter Warburton encased the medieval house in brick and stucco. His firm countenance and bushy eyebrows are captured by William Beechey in a portrait of 1811 which hangs in the house. He was of the old school and expected his house to be likewise. A footman complained that it was in such a poor state that his powdered hair was nibbled away one night by rats.

Dying without issue in 1813, Sir Peter settled his estate on his eight-year-old great-nephew, Rowland Egerton, who adopted his benefactor's name. Rowland grew to become a model Victorian squire, 'a good churchman, a good landlord, a keen sportsman and a man of literary tastes'. When at the age of twenty-six he courted and then became engaged to a local girl, Mary Brooke, she wrote that 'I am to be married to Mr Warburton! The very last person I have thought would have got so soon

into this scrape.' The couple immediately set about building a new house and garden.

Rowland Egerton-Warburton typified the change that overcame the English countryside and English taste in the 19th century. His reign at Arley lasted until 1891, his interests embracing everything from Anglo-Catholicism to the workers' cottages on his estate. Like many of his age, in selecting a design for his house, he wished to avoid the formality of classicism, preferring medieval piety with a touch of Elizabethan grandeur. And nothing should be too expensive.

George Latham, a local architect, was apparently the man. He promised a grand house for no more than £6,000. After much argument over what features were strictly 'Elizabethan', the final cost was £30,000. The outside, completed in 1841, is a dignified late Elizabethan façade of diapered brickwork, Dutch gables, stone windows and a classical porch. The interiors are variations on the same theme. Most remarkable are the ceilings, careful recreations of 16th- or 17th-century originals. Everywhere the eye is drawn upwards to what Latham assured Warburton were 'the best ceilings of their style in England'.

Arley is a place of ceilings and fireplaces. Plain panelling in the dining room sets the tone for plain early portraits. The library is more exuberant, with caryatids and niches above the fireplace and an elaborate ceiling with frieze and pendants. The gallery ceiling has been repainted in Wedgwood colours.

Arley has reputedly the earliest herbaceous garden in England, and is much loved. Gertrude Jekyll admired it as 'the best kind of English garden of the formal type'.

BEESTON CASTLE *

Beeston, 2m SW of Taporley
'Crusader' castle on Cheshire crag (EH)

Beeston and Peckforton are the twin glories of the Cheshire plain. They sit atop rocky outcrops and glare at each other. If Peckforton is a Rhineland *schloss*, Beeston is Crac de Chevaliers, a crusader fortress on a bare crag 500 ft above the plain. There are few more dramatic ruins in England.

Beeston was built by Ranulf, Earl of Chester, in 1225 after his return from the Fifth Crusade. Although his base was Chester, he wanted a fortress to display his strength elsewhere in the county. He must also have yearned for a testament of his crusader heroics, employing the new engineering seen in the Levant, cradle of castle architecture. Beeston is thus a true Levantine import, with strong baileys guarded by gatehouses and wall towers rather than a single central keep.

The outer bailey encloses much of the hillside with a series of walls and fortress towers. At the top of the hill is a dramatic ditch and bridge to the inner bailey. This appears never to have been completed as a residence, except for the rooms in the gatehouse itself. Most of the house would have been in the Outer Bailey. On Ranulf's death, the castle was taken by Henry III and used as a fort and storehouse against the Welsh. It fell into disuse but was seized, fortified and defended by the Royalists in the Civil War. After its subsequent slighting, it degenerated into a ruin until rescued as 'picturesque' by Lord Tollemache to improve his view across the valley from Peckforton.

BELMONT HALL *

Great Budworth, 4m N of Northwich
Gibbs house with original plasterwork (P-R)

There are said to be 'as many Leghs as fleas' in Cheshire. The Belmont Leighs (or Leghs) may not have been as rich as those of Lyme Park, but at least they still own the place, albeit now rented to a girls' school. The family live in the stables. The house was designed by James Gibbs c1750 for a scion of neighbouring Marbury, John Smith Barry, as a 'very Convenient Small house'. Belmont is externally plain, with pediment and bow windows.

The chief feature of the house is that Gibbs' *forte*, plasterwork. The central hall has a Rococo ceiling and a heavier Baroque fireplace. The drawing room walls, fighting against a rising tide of schoolwork, have panels draped in fronds and swags. Over the mantelpiece is the most extraordinary decoration I have encountered in any English house, a pair of knickers belonging to the singer, Cher, mounted in a frame. Are they a teaching aid?

The loveliest plasterwork is on the staircase, where there is an exquisite Rococo trophy of hunting horns below a medallion. The study has a foliage frieze looking out onto the rather bleak garden. The house is full of surprises, such as its beautifully crafted door-plates. It craves a return to family occupation.

BRAMALL HALL ***

4m S of Stockport
Partly victorianized black-and-white manor (M)

Bramall is my favourite among Cheshire's black-and-white houses, despite its burial in Stockport's stockbroker belt. The house belonged to the Davenport family from the time of its 16th-century construction until 1881. Two years later the medieval façade was 'enhanced' by a wealthy calico printer, Charles Nevill, an enthusiastic antiquarian. The encroachment of Stockport led to ever more land being sold for villas and the house eventually passed to the council in 1935. The hall is in excellent condition. Its ballroom is the most enjoyable medieval chamber in the county.

The main front of Bramall is a profusion of Cheshire fenestration. An earlier hall house was converted in the 1590s and given expanses of glass. The plan remains medieval, with an entrance to one side of the Great Hall, solar wing to the right and service quarters to the left. The new first floor is almost all window, so much so that one wonders how the roof was supported, especially as there was once a gallery on top. The present roof gables and much of the surface woodwork are late Victorian, a repeat on the entrance front of the rear façade to the garden.

The Great Hall was divided horizontally at

Ghostly murals at medieval Bramhall

the time of the 1590s modernization and has a 19th-century ceiling. It retains a Tudor pendant in its bay window. Stone felon heads on either side of the fireplace recall the Davenport sinecure of Sergeant of the Forest of Macclesfield. The banqueting room contains painted black-and-white 'timbering effect' introduced by Nevill. A huge painting of a Viking meeting a Saxon on the far wall illustrates the joint heritage of the English race. The artist is Herbert Schmaltz, whose name became a byword for such contrived sentimentality.

Above the banqueting room is the ballroom, converted from the pre-Elizabethan solar wing. The magnificent oak roof is cruck-framed with quatrefoil wind-braces. The crucks have beautifully decorated spandrels. The walls were formerly covered in paintings, long hidden behind panelling but revealed by Nevill in the 1880s. Those on the east wall depict musicians in 16th-century dress. Others are cruder, including a hunter being savaged by a boar. Behind the ballroom is Nevill's Room, Elizabethan again merging into Victorian. This is a lovely chamber, with lozenge-glazed windows filtering light over dark panelling. A billiard table waits idly at one end.

CAPESTHORNE **

5m W of Macclesfield
Ancestral Victorian pile (P-R)

Capesthorne has been the home of the Cheshire squirearchs, the Bromley-Davenports and their ancestors since the Conquest. The enormous house cuts a dash from a distance. The forest of turrets, wings, heraldry, brick and stone are the embodiment of the phrase, 'North Country pile'. Lenette Bromley-Davenport, American mother of the present owner, wrote in 1955 that Capesthorne 'can repel violently or attract irrevocably. To many the exotic towers, domes, and pinnacles are grotesque and ugly.' Yet when the light is right 'the enchantment of Eastern minarets, the tales of Arabian Nights and the romance of the Round Table trembles in the air'.

Although first built in the 18th century by the Smiths of Warwick, the house is to outward appearance mid-19th century, a ponderous neo-Jacobean work of 1837 by Edward Blore. After a fire in 1861, the more talented Anthony Salvin converted Blore's three storeys into two, raising the heights of the main rooms but making them absurdly grand. Lenette Bromley-Davenport's years of restoration in the 1950s confronted this challenge head on. She simply wallowed the rooms in colour, which is what the Jacobeans would have done. The result is an acquired taste, but successful.

Blore's entrance hall is now a vivid yellow. Its massive chimneypiece carries Flemish figures brought from the chapel. The heraldic glass is by Willement, celebrant of lineage to the Victorian aristocracy. Indeed, the halls and galleries at Capesthorne carry a quantity of family portraiture and sculpture remarkable even for an old English family. The main reception rooms are saved from elephantine tedium by Salvin's flair for decoration and by the Bromley-Davenport paintbrush. Most magnificent is Salvin's great saloon, which I saw resplendent for one of the weddings that are key to Capesthorne's financial rebirth. The squires of Capesthorne look down with approval from the walls.

An iron balustrade on the staircase has a cartoon depicting Gladstone as a felon with a rope round his neck. Bromley-Davenports were never Liberals. Upstairs, an American Room commemorates Lenette's Pennsylvania background, its contents rustic and simple compared with the bombast outside.

CHOLMONDELEY CASTLE *

4m NE of Malpas
Castellated mansion in spectacular parkland (P-G)

The 1st Marquess of Cholmondeley (pronounced Chumley) decided, in 1801, to demolish an old house by William Smith of Warwick and try to do something better himself. He also owned Houghton (Norfolk), but Cholmondeley had been the family seat (and name) since the 12th century. His self-designed neo-Gothic house was augmented in 1829 by Robert Smirke, practised supplier of castles to the discerning nobility, with examples at Eastnor (Herefs) and Lowther (Cumbria). The pile of forbidding pink-grey stone stands on an eminence overlooking its park. It has only two or three storeys, although from below it looks like ten.

Apart from a basement shop, the house is closed to the public, 'but you may get as close as you like,' said a warden, 'and stroke its very walls.' The castle, however, forms the centrepiece of one of the finest and least-known ornamental parks in the North-West. It is the work of the present Dowager Lady Cholmondeley and her late husband in half a century of labour.

Visitors drive down an avenue of chestnuts past spreading lakes to park below the house in a meadow by one of England's loveliest cricket fields. Each tree – cedar, fir, oak, weeping beech – seems to have been sited with care. Perhaps it was the sunshine on my visit, but castle, trees, grass and vista seemed in peculiar harmony. The castle is guarded by a camellia walk. The famous Cholmondeley iron gates, designed in the early 18th century by the Davies firm of Wrexham, are next to the tea-room north of the castle. In the grounds is a charming chapel with Laudian fittings.

COMBERMERE ABBEY **

8m SW of Nantwich
Gothicized house with Tudor interiors (P-R)

The abbey was a Cistercian house handed to one of Henry VIII's courtiers, Sir George Cotton, at the Dissolution. It was rebuilt as a black-and-white mansion incorporating the former abbot's hall. Cottons lived and prospered at Combermere, acquiring a viscountcy in 1827. The house was sold in 1919. The present owner, Sarah Callander Beckett, was a public relations official for Laura Ashley in New York when she discovered she had inherited the property in 1990. She thought long and hard and rose to the challenge, even asking the local public what they thought she should

do with it. The Georgian stables have been converted into holiday cottages. The garden, including reputedly the largest private lake in the country, is being restored. A fine house is returning to life.

Combermere is sited on a rise overlooking its lake. The exterior is the Gothick shell built over a medieval and Tudor interior by Sir Stapleton Cotton in 1814–21. The windows have cusped tracery and the roof is battlemented. The best work is the out-house courtyard with a clock-tower, and a game larder designed like a Temple of the Winds.

The interior is different, light hearted and domestic. The entrance, hung with Cotton big-game trophies, leads into the Porter's Hall, a gothicized version of the Abbot's Great Hall. On the stairs is a Tillemans painting of the house in its Tudor form. The upper landing is adorned with a magnificent screen, richly panelled on both sides. It appears to be a composite of woodwork from other parts of the house, installed when the hall was divided in 1563.

The upper part of the old Great Hall, now the library, is a room of great decorative force, with strapwork ceiling, heraldic frieze and carved fireplace. Shields and Tudor portraits, coats of arms and grotesques cover every inch. Filling one wall is a huge painting of Sir Stapleton Cotton, one of Wellington's generals, accepting the French defeat under the walls of Salamanca.

CREWE HALL ***

2m SE of Crewe
Ferocious Victorian interior of Jacobean prodigy house (H)

My enthusiasm for this building is partly born of relief. What was the wreck of one of the most celebrated Jacobean mansions in England has been taken in hand by a hotel company and its restoration of the Jacobethan interior is masterful. Crewe was built for lavish hospitality and that is what it now offers, although the grounds are surrounded by industrial sprawl.

Sir Randulph Crewe was Lord Chief Justice under James I and built the core of the present house between 1615 and 1639. The family continued in residence until the 1930s, when it passed to the Duchy of Lancaster who used it as a prison for 2,000 German officers during the Second World War. After service as offices, it was left empty until acquired by the hotel in 1998. The Duchy had stripped the building to its bare walls.

The old house is represented by the symmetrical brick entrance front, with Renaissance frontispiece and gabled wings. This house was gutted by fire in 1866 and rebuilt by E. M. Barry. He added a wing and lofty tower to one side. The ensemble is set on a balustraded platform adorned with heraldic beasts.

The interior is exuberant Victorian, Jacobean in inspiration and decorated by J. G. Crace at his most flamboyant. The copious stained glass is by Clayton & Bell. The style is mostly Flemish Renaissance, with flourishes of Pre-Raphaelite and Artisan Mannerist revival, a vivid hotch-potch.

The old Great Hall is to the right of the entrance, behind an overblown Mannerist screen. The large Jacobean overmantel is a relief of Plenty, a splendid, apparently 17th-century, work. Beyond, Barry converted the courtyard of the Jacobean house into a covered *cortile*, with cloister below, balcony above and hammerbeam roof on top. The whole space is richly dark, full of towering alabaster chimneypieces and mysterious corners.

The stairs to the main reception rooms pass heraldic beasts, lions, leopards and unicorns, with landings darting into stained-glass alcoves and canopies. Upstairs are the library, drawing room and Long Gallery. Carved alabaster panels depict scenes from English history. Busts portray English literary worthies. Shelves have been restocked with books and walls with paintings. Ceilings are heavy with coffering or escape into riotous strapwork.

Cusped Gothick at Combermere

Buried beneath the stairs is the Carved Room, a virtuoso Jacobean interior, apparently a facsimile of the original room on this site. Alabaster medallions in deep relief depict the Virtues of which Crewes should be proud. Over the fireplace is a relief of Father Time, with two boys portraying Industry and Idleness. Not an inch is without decoration. The restored chapel is full of coloured alabaster and marble, with Pre-Raphaelite paintings and glass. A glorious revival.

DORFOLD HALL **

Acton, 1½m W of Nantwich
Jacobean house with ornate Great Chamber
(P)

How tastes change! The present lovely lime avenue and courtyard of Dorfold Hall were designed in 1862 as a birthday surprise for the lady of the house while she was away on holiday. She was so outraged by what her husband had done that she refused to speak to him for six months. Today, Dorfold looks delightful, a vista of gables, chimneys and finials enclosed by a stone balustrade and gateposts. The brick is dark Cheshire red, with stone dressings. The flanking outhouses and the offices extended in 1824 are crowned with Dutch gables like overgrown dolls' houses.

The controversial approach and forecourt were the work of the landscape architect, William Nesfield. He was embellishing a Jacobean house built in 1616 by a junior branch of the Wilbraham family. It was sold in 1754, and the ground floor was much altered by William Baker in the 1750s and later by Samuel Wyatt. The house passed through Tollemaches (including the aggrieved wife) to the present descendants, the Roundells, who are now restoring each room in turn.

The interior reflects the familiar tension of Jacobean original and later modernization. The hall gives onto the dining room by Baker, containing some fine Morland landscapes. To the rear is a light, sunny library with a ceiling in the Adam style. The plasterwork depicts rustic themes and contains two billing and

cooing doves, said to represent a wedding.

Upstairs, Jacobean survives. A staircase with flat balusters leads to the house's centrepiece, the Great Chamber above the old hall. Its barrel-vaulted plaster ceiling, created in 1621, is one of the most intricate anywhere. The craftsmen are thought to be the same as worked in the Great Chamber at Lyme. Emblems of rose, thistle and fleur-de-lys celebrate the union of England, Scotland and (English) France. The strapwork, extended to the end walls and frieze, is of phenomenal complexity. There are Tudor pendants, as if the still-wet plaster had begun to drip and form stalactites. On the walls are 17th-century and later portraits, including bold ones of present-day Roundells by Howard Morgan.

From the windows can be seen the fields over which generations of owners indulged the Cheshire passion for hunting.

DUNHAM MASSEY ***

Dunham, 2m SW of Altrincham
Georgian house with extensive Edwardian restoration and complete service ranges (NT)

For almost two centuries Dunham Massey has clung to life, neglected by its owners and besieged by Greater Manchester. Yet it survives, protected by its park and estate. Its rooms are restored and a branch of the family who built it, the Stamfords, remain as National Trust tenants. Their standard flies from the flagpole when they are in residence (lowered only during the Falklands War because it is nearly identical to the Argentine flag).

The present house owes its existence to George Booth, 2nd Earl of Warrington. He inherited the Dunham estate at the age of nineteen in 1694, traumatized by seeing his reckless father 'aweeping for the greatness of his debts' and dying at forty-two. Booth married the daughter of a London merchant purely for her £40,000 dowry. He paid off his father's debts, rebuilt the house, produced a

Crewe's Jacobean resplendent

daughter and lived apart from his wife, his duty done. The daughter married Harry Grey, 4th Earl of Stamford. The house prospered until the gambling 7th Earl married a circus rider and was so disliked locally that they left Dunham for good.

The title and property eventually settled on a dissolute clergyman married to a Hottentot in South Africa. His possibly illegitimate son, John, claimed the Dunham estate and had to be bought off by the trustees. Great Britain was deprived of surely its only Hottentot aristocrat, who went to live in Worthing. In 1906, a Canadian clergyman arrived as 9th Earl, a liberal and enthusiastic archaeologist, only to die three years later. His son was so dominated by his mother that he refused to marry. He occupied just three rooms next to his mother's and became an active peer and model landlord. He supported the United Nations and entertained Haile Selassie, passing the property in good order to the National Trust on his death in 1976.

Family history is the most exciting thing about Dunham. The house, which the 2nd Earl of Warrington refashioned in the 1730s, is grand, beautifully displayed and a little dull. The exterior is a large redbrick box with plain stone centrepiece, enlivened only by an Edwardian alteration to the roof. The east and north fronts are plain, the former graced with a semi-circular bow on top of which the 10th Earl laid out a garden for Haile Selassie during his stay.

The entrance hall is in the south front. Until the 20th century, this was a dark passage to the courtyard, the entrance leading, medieval style, into the Great Hall on its far side. To the right of the present hall is the 20th-century Lady Stamford's suite and to the left the rooms of her son, the last Earl. Her parlour has been retained as she left it in 1959, embodying the neatness of genteel poverty that 'reuses envelopes and saves string'.

The saloon, a Georgian replacement for the old Great Parlour, is furnished as an Edwardian drawing room. The Stamford portraits are mostly by Romney. The room contains lovely satinwood bookcases, a touch of Georgian

levity amid the Edwardian solemnity. Beyond is the Great Hall; the present room is grand, with yellow walls and plasterwork in the style of Inigo Jones. What might be a cold room was turned by the Edwardian 9th Earl into a furnished and carpeted drawing room. Behind the Great Hall is a surprise, a small chapel, simple and severe as befitted the staunchly Protestant Booths. It is beautifully panelled, with 'Wren' pilasters on either side of the altar.

During the Great War, hospital operations were performed on the landing at the top of the Grand Staircase. The Earl's sister, Lady Jane Turnbull, held a torch for the surgeons. The Great Gallery beyond is hung with five paintings of the Dunham estate in the 1690s and again in the 1750s, the most remarkable topographical survey of any country house and its grounds to remain *in situ*. The long avenues are still in place, but nature has been allowed to destroy their precision and drama. In the same gallery is the Dunham Guercino, an *Allegory of Time*, and a magnificent portrait of Lord Warrington's mastiff, *Old Vertue*.

The lovely library, filled with leather-bound volumes, has over its fireplace Grinling Gibbons' early masterpiece, The Crucifixion. This was based on Tintoretto's similar work in the Scuola di San Rocco in Venice. Below is the 10th Earl's study, left full of the paperwork and clutter of a busy man of affairs. Outside rests his bicycle. The excellent service rooms are all restored and include 'one of the largest Agas ever made'.

GAWSWORTH HALL ***

3m SW of Macclesfield
Eccentric Tudor manor with tilting
ground (P)

Those despairing the fate of the English country house need look no further than Gawsworth. Since the Richards family acquired it in 1962, a family home has blos-

Magpie black-and-white at Gawsworth

somed into weddings, concerts, live theatre and opera. Talk here about the 'Glyndebourne of the North' and you receive a sniffy retort about the 'Gawsworth of the South'. Who needs National Trusts and Heritage Lotteries when there are Richardses about? But then there is money in Cheshire.

Like most black-and-white houses, Gawsworth is heavily restored. The first owners were the Fitton family, knights in the Wars of the Roses and ancestors of Mary Fitton, briefly maid of honour to Elizabeth I and mistress of the Earl of Pembroke. She was a dedicatee of Shakespeare's First Folio and a candidate for the 'dark lady'. Her father laid out gardens and built a tilting ground in the hope of a Royal visit that never came. The house was bought by the Stanhope family and tenanted for much of its life. Fittons still return from across the world for reunions.

Gawsworth's main front is much restored, but the three-sided courtyard behind is a black-and-white delight. The three-storey jettied bay on the far wing has original window leading. The interiors are warm and cluttered. The library contains bookcases by A. W. N. Pugin (from Scarisbrick) and Timothy Richards's car racing goggles (he is a Morgan enthusiast). Above the staircase hangs a Waterford crystal chandelier, apparently found in a wheelbarrow. A small chapel appears to date from 1701 but recalls chapels on this site since 1365. The Richards family has built a small ambulatory to hold a set of William Morris windows which, with other furnishings, came from a redundant church in Ipswich.

An original Great Hall, now truncated, may survive as the Green Drawing Room. Upstairs are more variations on a Tudor theme, including priest's holes dating from the late 16th century. Each bedroom seems more voluptuous than the last, with beams darting out of walls and overhangs looming above ancient panelling. More shocking is a 1950s vitriolite bathroom, apparently listed for preservation.

An RSJ has been inserted in the library ceiling to support a billiard table above. Here the

Richards's eccentricity reaches new heights. In among billiard cues and family portraits are a reclining statue of the goddess Echo and a huge devotional altarpiece. The gardens at Gawsworth embrace the remains of the tilting ground. Excavations of what may be extensive Tudor pleasure grounds are in hand.

HIGHFIELDS *

Audlem, 5m S of Nantwich
Elizabethan manor revived by Victorians
(P-R)

Highfields is a black-and-white yeoman's manor of which Cheshire must once have boasted hundreds. The house sits alone across the fields at a distance from its farm. The land was owned by the Dod family, apparently since Saxon times, and they built the present house, completing it in 1615. It passed by marriage to the architect, William Baker, in 1736 and is owned by Bakers to this day.

The exterior is remarkable for its symmetry and the generosity of its side wings, each of one bay but 13 timbers width. The porch is centred and decorated with pretty Gothic panels. The Victorians added aggressive neo-Tudor chimneys and a large drawing room at the back. They stuccoed the exterior but this has since been removed.

The interior saw the importation in the 19th century of much panelling and fireplaces, posing an impossible problem to those seeking to know what is original, imported or Victorian reproduction. It is of no consequence. Highfields is a cosy nest of vernacular carvings, portraits and horse paintings. Its passages seem redolent of dogs and huntsmen. Time and period do not matter.

All the downstairs rooms have fine fireplaces, the best in the Oak Room having cartouches and Corinthian orders. The hall fireplace is decorated with musicians. The drawing room is hung with family Knellers and Hudsons. Dods and Bakers might have been modest gentry but they visited London, sent their sons to Oxford and commissioned the best portraits. The staircase has two-strand

barley sugar balusters and an old alms chest for bread for the poor. During my visit, a hunt at full canter thundered past outside.

LITTLE MORETON HALL
***

4m S of Congleton
Definitive 'magpie' house around courtyard
(NT)

What are we to make of this place? At first sight Little Moreton is fresh from Disneyland. Neat, clean and tumbledown, it looks ready for a princess to appear from a casement, a ghost to clank from the gatehouse and a monster to rise from the moat. It seems to taunt the laws of gravity, like a pack of cards which might at any moment collapse.

Yet Little Moreton is as real as the National Trust restorers will allow. The house plan is familiar. A gatehouse gives onto an internal courtyard with the Great Hall beyond, built by Sir Richard de Moreton in about 1450. Service wings are to the left and solar and chapel to the right.

The guest chambers on the first floor of the gatehouse came later, along with lavish bay windows (1559) in the Great Hall and Old Parlour. Finally, in the 1580s, a Long Gallery was added across the top of the gatehouse wing. This is an astonishing structure, above a range that seems ill-suited to support it.

The most remarkable thing about this house is its survival. The Moretons were local magnates, challenging the Wilbrahams of Rode to 'sit first in church'. They suffered for taking the Royalist side in the Civil War and abandoned the house to tenant farmers. With the rise of the Picturesque movement in the 19th century, the house became celebrated. The watercolourist, John Sell Cotman, visited it in 1806 and found chickens in the Great Hall. Yet Moretons continued to take an interest in the house. It was inherited by a nun, Elizabeth Moreton, who was devoted to its preservation. She passed it to a cousin by marriage, Bishop Abraham of Derby, who ensured its orderly transfer to the National Trust in 1938.

Apart from its sheer quaintness, the house is chiefly of archaeological interest, a place for students of beams, trusses, braces, crown-posts and purlins. It has oversailing and coving galore. The studding is open, diagonal and quatrefoil. The inventiveness of the carpentry in a county devoid of brick and stone is seen to dazzling effect. Little Moreton was being completed by William Moreton when Hardwick (Derbys) and Wollaton (Notts) were already under construction. It was an old-fashioned house, except in its extravagant use of glass. The motifs carved into its lintels and bargeboards seem exclusively medieval.

The parlour has fragments of painted panelling, the withdrawing room a fine octagonal table. The chapel is curious, a tiny nave with a chancel that rises two storeys, facing a 'prayer room' above. Most spectacular is the Long Gallery. It is panelled but with extensive fenestration and heavy roof members to support a stone-tiled roof. At each end are primitive plaster reliefs, depicting Destiny and the Wheel of Fortune. A woman is dressed like a Botticelli angel.

The National Trust has left the interior empty. The rooms have little to distinguish them and few merit description. The guide explains that the interior has been empty for most of the past three centuries, offering an opportunity to 'appreciate its structural ingenuity'. That is fine for archaeologists, but little fun for the rest of us. In the 1940s, the then-resident custodian, Mrs Dale, dispensed scrambled eggs with scones and tea while hens scrabbled in the courtyard and cows approached from the meadow. We could do with more of that today.

LYME PARK ****

4m W of Whalley Bridge
Legh house set in ancient deer park (NT)

The noblest house in the north-west is still darkened by the tale of Lord Newton's surrender to the National Trust in 1946. James Lees-Milne wrote: 'The world is too much for him, and no wonder. He does not know what he can

do, ought to do or wants to do. He just throws up his hands in despair. The only thing he is sure about is that his descendants will never live at Lyme after an unbroken residence of 600 years.' The heartbreak was shared with a hundred owners at that time.

The family had acquired Lyme by force of arms, an ancestor being awarded a Cheshire hunting lodge for saving the Black Prince at Crécy. It was Sir Piers Legh who built the Elizabethan house and succeeding generations who added to it and altered it. Giacomo Leoni transformed the exterior and much of the interior after 1725. Here, on the flanks of the Pennines, he converted an old courtyard house into a monument to the Grand Tour. The grandest in the land danced and laughed through its halls and saloons. The park was studded with classical follies. The estate boasted its own breed of cattle and its own breed of mastiff.

Lyme then languished. It was revived by a dashing Thomas Legh in the 19th century and saw a final glow under Newton descendants in the years before the Great War. The subsequent horrors of taxation and loss of staff demoralized the family and led to the house's abrupt surrender. All was gone. Lord Newton's sister wrote that the windows were 'as blind eyes or eyes closed in sleep'.

The house today is a fine relic of Cheshire aristocracy. A sweeping drive drops down from the main road along a deep ravine. The park was a medieval deer park, enclosed c1400 but never extensively landscaped. Such architectural features as Lyme Cage 'tower' are not an integral part of a formal composition. The massive house appears round a bend in the valley as a *coup de théâtre*.

The welcoming façade is odd, composed of an earlier range with Elizabethan frontispiece of 1570. Four tiers of classical orders support a statue of Minerva. The other façades are Palladian, the orders Ionic, the stone cold and grey. The internal courtyard, however, is a total contrast, an essay in the Italian Renaissance. Rusticated colonnades support a *piano nobile*, entered by double flights of steps into a majestic doorway.

From outside, we expect Lyme's interiors to be monotonously classical. Yet enough rooms survive from the Elizabethan house to ensure that the rooms are never dull. Leoni's entrance hall is a sort of overblown drawing room, with an Edwardian Baroque overmantel and copious gilding. A frame reveals a Georgian portrait of the family's benefactor, the Black Prince, which swings out from the old Great Chamber above, thus enabling the chamber to become a gallery. The hall is hung with Mortlake tapestries. The carpet is said to be designed by A. W. N. Pugin.

Steps lead from the hall to the Great Chamber, now called the drawing room. This could not be a greater contrast from the hall. It is a room of Jacobean richness and romance. The ceiling is of delicate strapwork. Above the Renaissance fireplace is the coat of arms of Elizabeth I. Stained glass, some of it medieval, adds to the air of mystery. Beyond lies the Stag Parlour, decorated on the theme of the life of a stag. Here was plotted, and aborted, the Cheshire conspiracy in favour of the Jacobite rebellion. This dangerous moment is thought to be the origin of the Lyme tradition of men retiring from the dining room for port rather than remaining at table when the ladies have left.

The dining room was reconstructed by Lewis Wyatt in the 19th century, yet based on its 17th-century decoration, including the Gibbons-style carving for walls and fireplace. From here at breakfast Lord Newton would look out to see if the Lantern Tower on the hillside was visible. If it was, he knew he could go shooting.

Leoni's saloon is on the south front, the start of the state room sequence. The wood panelling and florid Rococo ceiling are probably original to Leoni, but it was Wyatt who inserted the Grinling Gibbons carvings from the present dining room. They are the glory of the room. Wyatt shows his respect for Gibbons by placing each composition in the centre of a panel in place of a picture, celebrating the craftsman as artist.

The staircase has been redecorated in a Victorian dark red. This is perhaps in honour of the giant moose's head that dominates the space. Upstairs is the Elizabethan Long Gallery, used by the Edwardian family for theatricals and for distributing gifts to estate staff. Two sofas are available for exhausted visitors. The ceiling is Jacobean reproduction and the pictures of worthies come from the National Portrait Gallery.

Of the bedrooms the most impressive is the Knight's Room, with a bulbous four-poster, stylish overmantel and a bold strapwork ceiling. A secret passage is said to lead from here to the Cage Tower on the hill. It was here that the 2nd Lord Newton's mother-in-law took to sleeping, convinced that the house was overrun with burglars. The gardens at Lyme are a blessed lung on the edge of the Peak District, the closest open space to the Manchester conurbation.

PECKFORTON CASTLE **

3m SW of Tarporley
Victorian castle house on a rock (H)

Peckforton crowns a rocky outcrop in the Cheshire plain. Its towers burst through a thick skirt of forest to glower across at Beeston on a neighbouring outcrop. They are like two giants preparing for combat. Whereas Beeston's towers are medieval, Peckforton's were built afresh by Anthony Salvin for Lord Tollemache in 1844.

The location reminds me of the castle of Sintra outside Lisbon. A winding track leads up through dripping woods to reach a huge gatehouse set in red stone walls. From here his lordship could command his 26,000 acres of Cheshire with the splendour of a feudal lord. Tollemache was, according to Mark Girouard, 'one of those tremendous rock-hewn Victorians who seem built on a larger scale than ordinary men'. He had twelve children and was a model landowner who rehoused all his tenants in the surrounding villages. Gladstone much admired him.

The most remarkable feature of the castle is its site. It is as if Windsor had fled north on a stormy night. The tower with its battlemented walls and lesser towers stands out from the trees as sentinels. The gatehouse gives onto a wide courtyard with the Great Hall opposite and the domestic and services ranges on either side. A tree has been left in the middle for picturesque effect.

The interiors are of cold Gothic stone, invigorating, precise and scholarly. The drama of the staircase is exceeded only by Lutyens at Castle Drogo (Devon), of which this is reminiscent.

The main rooms have rib-vaulted roofs and stone-mullioned windows. Yet their uses were those of a typical Victorian villa – dining room, drawing room, gallery and, next to the gatehouse, a small chapel. The house looks in good order and is due to re-open as a hotel at the time of writing.

PEOVER HALL ***

Over Peover, 4m S of Knutsford
Refurnished Elizabethan manor with classical stables (P-R)

The old seat of the Cheshire Mainwarings was built in 1585 and acquired by a Mancunian furniture tycoon, Harry Brooks, in 1940. Today, Peover Hall describes itself as a 'working' house. This means that the Brookses respect its history but are content to alter it to suit their needs. Wings have been demolished, rooms reordered, contemporary fittings inserted from elsewhere. Books, papers, discarded clothes and unmade beds are a feature of any visit. The place feels lived in with a vengeance.

The oddity of the house is immediately apparent outside. A range of gabled rooms is attached to a neo-Elizabethan brick façade, like a converted keep. This façade was built in the 1960s after the demolition of a Georgian wing. The resulting interior has no formal plan and is an enjoyable jumble of insertions that makes little sense and does not matter. We wander through a maze of old rooms, corridors and attics.

This is a house that draws on many houses. The Great Hall is made from old kitchens, with two large fireplaces facing each other. The walls, painted a jolly yellow, are hung with Mainwaring arms and armour. There are two magnificent dressers, one decorated with Knights of the Round Table, the other with scenes from *Pilgrim's Progress*.

The parlour and dining room have been restored with panelling from other Mainwaring properties. The parlour's overmantel has a frieze of scenes from the life of Julius Caesar and a sedan chair displaying porcelain. In the dining room, the Corinthian pilasters have been 'silver-leafed' with chocolate silver paper by members of the family over the years. It is a delightful touch that would give the National Trust apoplexy and never be permitted in any of their properties.

A Georgian staircase rises to a landing of charming pomposity, with lofty ceilings and ornate cornices, hung with portraits of Hanoverian monarchs. They include a superb George III by Lawrence. This forms an anteroom to the drawing room, with panelling and bookcases from a Mainwaring house at Oteley in Shropshire. Here hangs a copy of van Dyck's celebrated portrait of the Jacobean statesman, Wentworth, Earl of Strafford, with his secretary, a Mainwaring.

Peover has a splendid set of old bedrooms. One has a Flemish bed with unusual sliding door panels. This room offers a view over the finest feature of Peover's garden, an array of yew hedges and free-standing yew obelisks. A complex yew pattern has also been created round the swimming pool, a modernist's recreation of a medieval knot garden. The attic is a Long Gallery, with scissorbeams overhead and family junk in every alcove. Here are toy engines and yachts, chairs, pictures, rocking horses and children's books galore.

The stables at Peover are more highly 'listed' than the house. They were built in 1654 and are of a type once common but now of the greatest rarity. By coincidence, similar stables remain at another Mainwaring house, Whitmore (Staffs).

The horses are accorded classical stalls which have arches and a strapwork frieze. The ceiling is worthy of a Restoration drawing room. Sadly, there are no horses in residence.

QUARRY BANK MILL: THE APPRENTICE HOUSE *

Styal, 1½m N of Wilmslow
Grim quarters for young workers at t'mill
(NT)

Quarry Bank Mill lurks in a deep ravine in the wooded valley of the River Bollin. The spot was selected in 1783 by Samuel Greg for his water-powered spinning machine. It became one of the largest mills in the country. Here, a century and a half later in 1939, his great-great-grandson Alec imaginatively donated the still-working mill with its estate and village of Styal to the National Trust. The mill was in production until 1959. It is now fully restored, partly working and open to the public.

Above the mill buildings is the house where the apprentices lived. Such was the shortage of labour that young people were brought from workhouses and orphanages to be 'trained', which in reality meant they worked unpaid in the mill for up to seven years. Almost a third of the mill workers in the early years were children, some as young as seven. Greg was regarded as a benevolent employer but the system was hard, only a step better than the workhouse. Children received food and clothing and the rudiments of reading, writing and counting.

The Quarry Bank house could take up to 100 apprentices and was overcrowded. Visible today is the schoolroom, complete with slates, candles and admonitions to hard work. Next door is the kitchen where porridge (and little else but occasional broth) was prepared and eaten. Outside is a small garden where the children could grow vegetables to supplement their diet. Upstairs are two dormitories for girls and boys. Greg preferred the former as girls were 'less truculent' and needed less sleeping space. They slept two to a box bed on a straw mattress, replaced once a year.

The chief hazard to Quarry Bank today is the NT tour, timed and conducted with

Peover's medieval romanticism

Victorian strictness. It is aimed at primary school children and is no place for grown-ups of any age.

RODE HALL **

3m NW of Kidsgrove
Ancestral home with portraits and porcelain
(P-R)

When a woman marries a man she customarily takes his name. Not so among the English landed classes. It depends who had the bigger estate. When a Miss Wilbraham of Rode married a Mr Baker in 1872, it was he who changed his name. There had been Wilbrahams at Rode for three centuries and the lack of a male heir was neither here nor there. The house is a Wilbraham home and they 'will continue to live here for many years to come' says the present owner, Sir Richard Wilbraham.

The pleasing redbrick house looks from the drive like two houses semi-detached, one Queen Anne the other mid-Georgian. That to the right of the main door has two storeys with a cupola and Venetian windows. That to the left is of 1752, later amended with a pillared loggia in front of the entrance.

The house is chiefly of interest for the present Sir Richard's collection of china and porcelain, attracting a constant stream of admirers. Almost as impressive is the continuous line of family portraits, from Reynolds through Walter Crane to the present day. The modern works are a relief from the usual staid historical depictions.

Beyond the pillared entrance hall is a generous staircase, surviving from the 18th century, with wide treads and Rococo plasterwork. Much of the furniture is by Gillow of Lancaster, notably the superb bookcases in the library. Many of the books were those of the medical collection of the Baker family, Sir George Baker being one of the doctors attending George III in his madness. Sir George is pictured in the drawing room.

The best of the formal rooms is the dining room, designed by Lewis Wyatt in a severely classical style and with a Gillow sideboard of

1813 in an apsidal alcove. With its scagliola columns and walls in shades of green, the room on a sunny day can seem to be floating underwater.

Humphry Repton contributed a Red Book for Rode but we do not know to what effect. William Nesfield was later involved in the formal gardens. The grounds have been superbly restored by the present Wilbrahams.

TABLEY HOUSE ***

2m W of Knutsford
Georgian house with picture collection (P)

Tabley boasts itself the 'finest Palladian mansion in the North-West'. The house from the lake, with its well-formed portico and curving double staircase, is a splendid sight. The clutter of entrance, stables and service buildings round the courtyard are relegated to the rear.

Tabley was owned by the Leicester family for seven centuries. The former old hall was on an island in the lake. The new house was designed by Carr of York in 1761 and remained in the family until the last of the line died unmarried in 1975. The house was refused by the National Trust for lacking endowment and passed to the Victoria University of Manchester. It was then leased to a health care company as a nursing home, the main rooms being handed to a trust. The arrangement seems to work.

Access to the main reception rooms is from the south front, Carr's original entrance, up his magnificent sweep of steps. The rooms are chiefly of interest for the surviving paintings of the Leicester collection. Most were dispersed in a sale in 1827, after being refused by the government as the basis for a National Gallery. The drawing room offers a Dobson of the 1st Lord Byron in the Civil War and Turner's depiction of Tabley from a distance across the lake 'on a windy day'. It also displays the dramatic *Destruction of Herculaneum and*

Tabley's stately Palladian

Pompeii by John Martin, Queen Victoria's favourite historical artist.

In the Common Parlour next door is the old manorial rent table and a set of Devis pictures of the house from different angles. The parlour contains a rare 'anamorphic' picture of either Charles I or Charles II, designed for Jacobites to worship covertly on the inside of a cylinder.

The main picture gallery was created early in the 19th century from three rooms along the west front, now divided only by shallow classical arches. The furniture includes Chippendale mirrors, console tables and sofas by Gillow of Lancaster. The paintings are ghosts of the great Leicester collection, with works by Fuseli, Lawrence and Northcote. Houses with public exhibitions such as Tabley should surely be given a choice of finer works now languishing in the basements of London galleries.

TATTON OLD HALL *

Tatton Park, 2m N of Knutsford
Medieval house of the Egertons (M)

The great house of the Egerton family is unusual in retaining, half a mile across its park, the old hall which it supplanted. Hidden behind a clump of trees, alive with rooks, stands the Old Hall, like an embarrassing great-aunt who refuses to die. While crowds pack the main house, the Old Hall is neglected, possibly because of its hour-long tour.

The medieval hall was built c1520 for the Brereton family and acquired by the Egertons in 1598. It was soon leased to tenants and later divided into three farmers' cottages, the black-and-white walls encased in brick. The Great Hall is excellently displayed, with a central fire, tapestry and high table, although the display of 'medieval' catering seems earlier than the Tudor architecture. The place reeks satisfactorily of wood smoke.

The rest of the building has been restored more or less to its 19th-century form. The rear quarters are variously 17th, 19th and 20th century. Upstairs from the Hall is a bedroom of the early 17th century with hangings of the period and furniture from the original inventory. The remaining rooms are arranged as a museum, and are well done.

TATTON PARK ***

Tatton, 2m N of Knutsford
Great Regency house with original contents (NT)

Tatton is the grandest of the great Cheshire houses. When it was given to the National Trust by the 4th Baron Egerton in 1958, its rooms, furniture and art were intact. Only the 25,000 acres of Tatton land that had once rolled uninterrupted to the Derbyshire hills had gone. What remains is 2,000 acres, laid out by Repton, with avenues of limes and a deer park, a precious lung for the people of Manchester.

Tatton was first built in 1716 but rebuilt slowly after 1780 in a neo-classical style, by Samuel Wyatt and his nephew, Lewis. The house from the outside looks formal and almost modest, its garden front that of a grey Palladian villa two storeys high with portico and hipped roof. Yet this is a giant house, its rear quarters well concealed. The basement is so extensive as to have a small railway to carry coal from the back door to the main house.

The interior is mostly a gallery of pictures and Egerton furniture, the latter notably by Gillow. The entrance hall shows the Wyatts at their most Graeco-Roman, with porphyry columns and coved ceiling with classical motifs. On the wall is a painting by Henry Calvert of the Cheshire Hunt, with Egertons in the van. Here too is an exquisite Portuguese jewel cabinet from Goa, inlaid with tortoise-shell and green-stained ivory.

Four reception rooms sit round the staircase hall. The walls of the music room are hung in cherry-red silk damask. The alcove book-shelves contain leather-bound scores. Opposite hangs Guercino's *Absalom and Tamar.*

The library is the most casual of the state rooms. It contains one of the National Trust's largest collections, 8,000 volumes in this room alone. Here are globes, book presses, movable stairs, chairs for reading books of differing sizes, card tables, chess tables and writing implements galore. It is a chamber inviting scholarship, a marvellous room. Through the windows on a clear day can be seen Bosley Cloud on the Cheshire–Derbyshire border 13 miles away, once Egerton land too.

The rest of the house marks a change of key. The wide formal staircase, lit by Lewis Wyatt's lovely domes and receding arches, is crowned by ten portraits of The Cheshire Gentlemen. This is the conspiracy that gathered (at Lyme Park) to discuss whether to support the Jacobite rising of 1715, wisely deciding against.

The 'below stairs' quarters at Tatton are among the most comprehensive in any great house. They are displayed with National Trust thoroughness, with not a speck of dust and every brass pot gleaming.

WINNINGTON HALL *

Winnington, 1m NW of Northwich
Wyatt house of ICI founders (P-R)

This is for addicts. Next to the Trent and Mersey Canal and between a derelict chemical works and an ICI treatment plant is the house bought in 1872 from Lord Stanley by two immigrant engineers, Ludwig Mond and John Brunner. Here began the future ICI. The house is now a restaurant and staff club. The house would once have looked out on a wooded hillside across the fields north of Northwich.

Today the setting is undeniably sad. The mansion is of c1780 and immensely stylish, in hard blackened stone with a spattering of Adam motifs on the front and side elevations. It is by Samuel Wyatt of the architectural clan ubiquitous at this time in Cheshire. To the rear is a substantial black-and-white building, a victorianized 17th-century work now housing a series of bars. Brunner had this part while Mond took the Wyatt side. There is no doubt who had the better deal.

The Wyatt interiors are excellent. A gallery forms a corridor behind the main reception rooms, with a coved ceiling, attached columns, fans in panels and Greek medallions. It might be a miniature Tatton.

Cornwall

Cornwall is a land beyond England and feels like it. The wild north coast is open to the wind off the Atlantic, the sheltered inlets and bays of the south are almost Mediterranean. The building material is mostly granite. Cornish history was dominated by a few inter-marrying families, territorial, Catholic and Royalist, exercising quasi-feudal power over an unbiddable region. They were not unlike the Border barons. Most were rich on tin, but few survived recusancy with their wealth intact.

The peninsula lay across early trade routes between Ireland, Wales and France, its lost language reflecting those influences. England's oldest domestic structures are at Chysauster near Penzance. The Normans built the castles of Launceston and Restormel and, now much rebuilt, St Michael's Mount. Henry VIII created what was virtually a western Dover at Pendennis.

The county's chief appeal lies in the houses of its historic families: the Edgcumbes, St Aubyns, Godolphins, Prideaux, Robartes, Arundells and Carews. Almost all their houses date from the 16th century or earlier. An Elizabethan Carew could assert that every gentleman in Cornwall was his cousin. Great Halls hang with ancestral heraldry. Parlours are adorned with portraits galore, many by the 'Cornish Reynolds', John Opie. Great Chambers boast Jacobean plasterwork and tapestries. Furniture is solid oak, with thick, turned legs and muscular arms.

Of purely Georgian houses, Antony, Pencarrow and Trewithen are outstanding. Jacobean-cum-Victorian Lanhydrock is the National Trust's most visited country house. Outside these houses are their gardens, the glory of Cornwall. The county was a major participant in the exotics craze of the late-19th century. This and the mild Gulf Stream climate have made the southern coast a place of botanical resort. Rhododendrons, azaleas and camellias burst into collective song each spring. The most discordant note are the wind-power turbines and pylons now visually desecrating much of north Cornwall.

Devo[n]

A388

A30

A39

Tintagel   Cullacott●   ●LAUNCESTO[N]

A395   ●Endslei[gh]

A30

●Prideaux Place   Cornwall

WADEBRIDGE

A389   ●Pencarrow   A390   Cotehele●
A39
BODMIN●   Buckland

NEWQUAY   ●Lanhydrock   A38
Restormel●   ●Boconnoc
Trerice●   PLYMOUTH
●Boconnoc   Antony●
ST AUSTELL   Mount Edgcumbe●

A390
●Trewithen

TRURO   ●Caerhays

A30   A39

Chysauster●   ●St Mawes
Godolphin●   Pendennis●
PENZANCE   ●St Michael's Mount   FALMOUTH

A394

10 Miles

Antony ✶✶✶   Godolphin ✶✶   Restormel Castle ✶✶
Boconnoc ✶✶   Lanhydrock ✶✶✶✶   St Mawes Castle ✶
Bodmin Gaol ✶   Launceston Castle ✶   St Michael's Mount ✶✶✶
Caerhays ✶✶   Mount Edgcumbe ✶✶   Tintagel Post Office ✶✶
Chysauster ✶   Pencarrow ✶✶✶   Trerice ✶✶✶
Cotehele ✶✶✶   Pendennis ✶   Trewithen ✶✶
Cullacott ✶   Prideaux Place ✶✶✶

ANTONY HOUSE ✳✳✳

2m NW of Torpoint
18th-century Carew home with family
portraits (NT)

Life was not easy for a Cornish grandee during
the Civil War, or for his ladies. Sir Alexander
Carew agonized before deciding that he would
fight for Cromwell and Parliament, in a county
almost universally Royalist. While he was
away, the family slashed his portrait in its
frame for the shame of it. Then Carew changed
sides and decided to fight for the King, and was
executed for his treachery. For this glory, the
Carew ladies laboriously stitched the picture
back together again.

The present Carew house is a rarity in
Cornwall, a pure 18th-century mansion of
dolls' house prettiness, in silver-grey Pentewan
stone. The Carews were one of the oldest and
grandest families in the county. Cornwall's
most celebrated Elizabethan, Richard Carew,
was a lawyer, linguist and poet, remarking with
good reason that all Cornish gentlemen were
his cousins. It was later, in the reign of Queen
Anne, that Sir William Carew married the
wealthy Lady Anne Coventry, enabling him to
build a new house from scratch. The Carews
married Poles and Carew Poles occupy the
house to this day, although it is owned by the
National Trust.

Begun by an unknown architect in 1718,
Antony has a hipped roof, dormers and rusticated quoins. Humphry Repton was paid £30
for a complete Red Book scheme for the
grounds. The north front faces a long lawn of
three avenues to the River Lynher and Saltash
in the distance. The south front welcomes visitors with wings flanking a courtyard.

The interior of Antony is a sequence of
18th-century rooms round an entrance hall
and adjacent staircase, once separate but
now part of a continuous space. So dominant
is this space, rising through the heart of the
house, that the reception rooms seem almost
ante-chambers to it. Dutch oak panelling
forms a warm backdrop to regiments of Carew
portraits. There are Carews by Gheeraerts,

Huysmans, Jonson and Dahl. There is also a
late portrait of Charles I, pensive and in black
at the time of his trial. It is said to be the only
picture showing his beard turned grey.

The staircase is as grand as the hall is
intimate, the treads of 'Queen Anne' width but
with delicately turned balusters. More Carew
portraits climb the walls to the landing, here
painted by or 'after' Kneller, Lely, Hudson
and Ramsay. The family must be reminded
of its longevity and dignity even on its way
to bed.

The reception rooms, most of them oak
panelled, are crowded with more paintings,
including modern works imaginatively commissioned by the present Carews. The saloon
has two paintings by Reynolds and one of Pole
children playing cricket. The girl is seen holding the ball, and the guidebook reminds us
that girls allegedly invented overarm bowling
to avoid brushing their skirts when bowling
underarm. The Small Tapestry Room is filled
with happy, rustic pieces from the Soho workshop. The chairs are said to be covered with
fabric from papal vestments.

A few bedrooms are displayed upstairs,
hung with modern art alongside yet more
Carews, Poles, Pole Carews and even Carew
Poles. Repton's landscape is visible from most
of the rooms. The vista southwards remains
spectacular, that northwards embraces the
horrors of modern Saltash. A water sculpture
in the garden by William Pye imitates the
adjacent topiary of yews.

BOCONNOC HOUSE ✳✳

3½m E of Lostwithiel
Pitt mansion in process of urgent rescue (P-R)

Boconnoc is another house of saints. In this
case they are Anthony and Elizabeth Fortescue,
battling to rescue what was a near-derelict
family home. The great house of the Pitt family
nestles in the valley of the River Lerryn. In 1969
it was about as desperate as a house can get.
Water was pouring through the roof, beams
had decayed free of their supports and rot of
every sort was rampant. On my visit, a massive

enterprise of restoration was in full swing. Not a room was habitable, yet the roof was secure and commitment total. I could only say, good luck.

Boconnoc was a property of the Devon magnates, the Mohuns, until the death of the 4th Baron in a duel in 1712. The old house was then sold to Thomas Pitt, a Madras nabob, for the huge sum of £54,000. He raised the sum by selling the Pitt Diamond to the Regent of France for £135,000. It was later set into Napoleon's sword, a high-risk hiding place. Pitt duly erected the main, rather dull façade. In 1771–2, his grandson, Lord Camelford and a cousin of the prime minister, improved the house and added a grander gallery at right angles overlooking the valley behind.

This Pitt was a figure of some interest. He was a Grand Tourist and amateur architect who built a small house in Twickenham near Walpole's Strawberry Hill (London, W) and another for himself in Park Lane, Mayfair. In 1778 he met the young John Soane in Italy and became his patron.

In 1786 Soane carried out unspecified repairs at Boconnoc. How much of the present house may be Soane and how much Pitt himself is conjectural. Architect and client were in those days accustomed to working in collaboration. The staircase has extensive grisaille decoration, which may or may not date from this period, but is undeniably grand. The other rooms await attention but I hope a charming children's theatre in a nursery, now occupied by bats, survives.

Overlooking the house is an enclave of church, stables and other outbuildings, already restored. The Fortescues are Pitt descendants. Here is another house lucky in its ancestral owner.

BODMIN GAOL *

Berrycombe Road
Largest Victorian prison, corridors and cells intact (P)

The cliff of Bodmin Gaol still dominates the town from the north. The prison buildings were sold for demolition in 1929 and most of the roof slates removed. But lime mortar in the joints had fused the granite blocks so strongly that they were resistant even to dynamite. They appear indestructible and have defied all attempts to remove them.

This ranks among the grimmest buildings in England. An early gaol on the site dated from the 1770s. The prison reformer, John Howard, then proposed a new, purpose-built prison in place of the ancient dungeons. The new Bodmin Gaol held 13 prisoners in 1779 and 155 by 1840, from a local population which had less than doubled. Crime waves are nothing new – or at least the zest to imprison is not new. This overcrowding led to pressure for extensions, which were begun in 1855.

They were on a massive scale. The new prison of hard Cornish granite contained 200 cells, a quarter of them for women. This was a complete penal colony. There were hospital cells, laundry, exercise yard, chapel and workrooms. Floors were of slate and cells were cleaned and whitewashed regularly. A treadwheel for milling corn could take up to 32 men.

In 1887, the naval prison in Devonport was transferred to Bodmin, with 105 more cells built on four levels. This was the last Royal Navy prison in Britain, and closed in 1922 six years after the civil prison was shut.

The site was then used as a goods depot, nightclub and is now a bar. Since the gaol shut, the cells have become a tourist attraction and the civilian cells can be visited through the rear of the bar. They have been vividly equipped with tableaux, apparently depicting the crimes for which various inmates were incarcerated. Bodmin makes Madame Tussauds look tame.

The interior of the derelict naval wing can also be seen through barred windows. It stands vast, gaunt and with vegetation growing from its crevices. Mice scamper across the floor. Crows sweep ominously overhead.

As a memorial to the inhumanity of the British penal policy over the ages, Bodmin deserves more extensive access and interpretation.

CAERHAYS CASTLE **

St Michael Caerhays, 4m SE of Tregony
Nash extravaganza overlooking sea (P)

Seen from the beach, the castle seems to rise as if by magic, its battlemented blocks and towers framed by a bank of trees. It was designed by John Nash at the height of the Picturesque movement. The grounds which run down to Porthluney Cove and Veryan Bay are awash with exotic plants. The setting is among the most romantic in Cornwall.

The Trevanions held Caerhays from the 14th century. In 1801 John Trevanion, just twenty-one and rich on mining royalties, came into the inheritance and some seven years later commissioned Nash to rebuild his old family seat.

It was a disastrous decision. Nash did not come cheap and by 1824 Trevanion was bankrupt and had to flee his creditors to France. He was not the first man ruined by an architect. In 1853, the estate was bought by another mining family, the Williamses, who own it to this day. The Victorian J. C. Williams joined many Cornish landowners in importing oriental specimens for his gardens. Caerhays is now a designated home of the national magnolia collection.

The house, which is open in the spring and early summer when the garden is at its best, is a rare survivor of Nash's castellated style. The front hall is Gothick romantic, with an impressive double staircase rising to a landing. In it hangs an Opie self-portrait, a common accoutrement to most Cornish houses. Off the hall are the library and the handsome round drawing room, a dining room and billiard room.

To one side is the 'Museum' with a large painting of a dog. At the time of the Trevanion's impending bankruptcy, the house was visited by the wealthy Angela Burdett Coutts, from whom the family had been hoping for help. Their dog unfortunately bit her footman savagely and she left in high dudgeon. The dog bite was the last straw for the family's fortunes. They duly had it immortalized. A severe fire later in the century destroyed the bulk of the furniture. Most of the contents are 20th century.

CHYSAUSTER: HUT SIX *

2m N of Penzance
Excavated remains of Iron Age village (EH)

Any Chysauster hut will do, but Hut Six is the most impressive. The site is high on the hillside behind Penzance. Its view over West Penwith is superb and the climb worth this alone. Chysauster (pronounced chi-sorster) is England's most exciting Late Iron Age remain – c200 BC at its oldest – except that here it was surely 'Tin Age'.

We walk across fields for a quarter-mile from the nearest lane, praying to ancient gods for a clear day. The site must have been chosen so the inhabitants could see trouble coming, notably from the port at St Michael's Mount. If they were involved in the tin trade, they would have been known to have treasure. Others hold they were probably farmers.

The site was first excavated in the 1870s when much damage was done. But we can still make out a settlement of eight houses along a street, reputedly occupied for seven centuries. Most such ancient villages were of wood and mud. This is of granite, with the pillar stones for the roofs tooled into sockets to receive an upright. It was not a fort, which may have been elsewhere, but a series of oval enclosures about 30 ft across. The houses are of a courtyard type. Inside each enclosure are three or four rooms for living and storage. These are built into the surrounding wall, with space for animals in the centre of the yard. Some rooms survive to shoulder height.

Hut Six has the most obvious plan. One of its rooms is raised above the ground, presumably to keep food and family dry. Weather must have been a constant problem, and all the houses have tunnel entrances opening away from the prevailing south-west wind. In the courtyards are runnels for water and evidence has been found of small gardens behind each house.

COTEHELE ***

7m SW of Tavistock
Tudor house entirely hung with tapestries
(NT)

The Georgian Edgcumbes decided they could stand the damp and gloom of Cotehele no longer and made their principal dwelling Mount Edgcumbe (below), down the River Tamar overlooking Plymouth Sound. They left Cotehele alone. It was inhabited by widows, maiden aunts and spinsters. No money was spent and little was altered or rebuilt. The house fell asleep.

Yet the Edgcumbes always appreciated the place. They took Horace Walpole and many others up-river to visit it. By the 19th century, Edgcumbes were even 'adding to' its medieval aura, with tapestries and other refurbishments apparently no longer needed at Mount Edgcumbe. 'Despite the strong air of antiquity,' the guidebook concedes, 'there is little of the Tudor period left in the house and some of the 17th-century pieces were very probably introduced at a later date to enhance Cotehele's romantic appeal.'

The house was given to the National Trust in 1947 and now has a decidely 'designed' atmosphere, like a French house restored by Violet le Duc. Cotehele's guardians are obsessed with the tapestries, which are superb, but they are neither medieval nor Tudor, almost all dating from the 17th century. Conservationism also admits little natural light, making the house very much a tapestry mausoleum. But these at least recreate the appearance of an old house, a parade of fabric murals depicting everything from Romulus and Remus to Dutch children's games.

Cotehele's pink-grey stone walls lie hidden in a cleft in the Tamar valley. Dating from the late 15th century, it recalls the final flowering of domestic Gothic before the coming of Elizabethan grandiloquence. The principal access was by boat from Plymouth to a private quayside on the Tamar below. The house is arranged round two courts, the formal Hall Court and the lesser Retainers' Court.

The former leads direct to the Great Hall. There is no screens passage and no tie beams or hammerbeams to the high roof. The place is entirely medieval, with heraldic glass in the windows, linking the Edgcumbes to Cotterells, Raleghs, Tremaynes and Carews. The walls are lined with ancient weapons and armour, with the jawbone of a whale and the head of an albatross.

From the Great Hall, the visitor rises to the solar range, with the old dining room, a pretty chapel with a filigree screen and the Punch Room beyond. Here, as elsewhere, tapestries cover every inch of the walls. Age has turned the greens to blues, reds to browns and lost the yellows altogether, so one wonders why the National Trust bothers with the ubiquitous blinds.

Many fragments are cut and stitched to fit the rooms, with borders added or removed. Some of the finest needlework is on less prominent furnishings, such as the superb William-and-Mary backing to the settee in the old dining room. Upstairs are the Red Room and South Room, formed from the old Great Chamber, the former with vellum valances to its bed canopy.

Cotehele's tower was added in the 17th century, with three more floors of tapestried rooms. The White Room has Georgian crewelwork on its bed-hangings. The old drawing room retains a linenfold draught-porch and has a superb walnut cabinet carved with Adam and Eve, c1600. The top tower rooms are the loveliest, tiny chambers hung with tapestry fragments and barely enough room for their beds. Charles I supposedly slept in the larger one.

Since Cotehele was never built for entertaining or for Victorian comfort, its outbuildings are remarkably simple. The gardens are more recent, terraced down the hillside towards the river. To roam these terraces and lose oneself in the cloistered vegetation is like wandering through the tapestries inside. The interior of this house comes alive outside.

King Charles's bed, Cotehele

CULLACOTT *

4m N of Launceston
Medieval hall and parlour unaltered in
farmyard (P-R)

This is a rare medieval composition of rustic
hall, parlour and outbuilding still set round a
cobbled yard. It was manorial until the 17th
century, when it became a farmworker's cottage, later abandoned. No substantive changes
were made in the 18th, 19th or 20th centuries.
Only after storm damage in 1989 was the then
derelict building recognized for what it was,
and its murals revealed. It is rightly listed
Grade One. The group is now let as holiday
cottages by the neighbouring farm.

The hall is of whitewashed cob on granite
footings. It is dated to *c*1480 and open to a low
roof. A fireplace was inserted in the early 16th
century by new owners, the Blyghte family,
and the walls decorated with murals depicting
Tudor coats of arms of this period. The windows are original, as is the cross-wall dividing
the hall from a tiny upstairs room. In this
gallery are murals of St George, suggesting a
reasonably prosperous owner.

At the same time, in 1579, a new parlour and
upstairs bedroom were built at the upper end
of the hall, with smaller rooms projecting at an
angle, one for a garderobe. The parlour has a
large fireplace and rudimentary plasterwork.
The buildings retain original window mullions, flagstones and spiral stairs with irregular
'trip' treads to foil intruders. There is even an
heraldic settle.

GODOLPHIN HOUSE **

near Godolphin Cross, 6m NW of Helston
Medieval and Jacobean mansion in process of
restoration (P)

Godolphin lies on the side of a hill inland
from Mounts Bay. The first house was built
by the Godolphin family on the wealth of
tin in the 14th century. A more substantial
one followed in the 15th, in the conventional
Tudor style of two courtyards, a Great Hall,

Great Chamber and fine 16th-century stables.

Each generation of Godolphins carried
forward the family's fortune and status. By
the 1630s, time had clearly come for a more
imposing north front. Francis Godolphin
rebuilt the entrance front into the main court
with an extraordinary double loggia. This is of
seven bays of Tuscan columns, one loggia
facing out, the other facing in. Such loggias
were not unusual in Jacobean or even
Elizabethan buildings, but this plan of guests'
rooms over a classical cloister was a dashing
innovation in Cornwall.

More ambitious plans were not carried
out. The Civil War followed, then recession
in the tin industry and by the 19th century
general decay. The hall range was demolished,
and survives as a ruin across the courtyard.
The medieval Great Chamber survives to its
east, and is now in process of restoration. Of
the first floor rooms, the East Bedchamber
has a later Venetian window and 18th-century
furnishings. The east range of the courtyard
was plainly meant to go with the building of
the new loggia range, visible in the present
uncomfortable join between the two. Today, it
contains a breakfast room panelled in the 18th
century and a later hall, with excellent beams
and linenfold panelling, which is now the
dining room.

The house was acquired by the Schofield
family in the 1930s. They have struggled to
restore it and recapture its old glory. The
stables and outbuildings are completed and
work progresses on the main house, although
there is as yet little to be seen. The Tudor
garden is also being rediscovered. Since the
house archives were lost in a fire, this is largely
a task of archaeology.

LANHYDROCK ****

2½m S of Bodmin
'Upstairs/downstairs' Victorian mansion (NT)

Lanhydrock is always described as being 'lost
in a long Victorian afternoon'. But by the time
that particular afternoon came round, the former property had seen almost three centuries

of them. The original house was begun c1620 by Sir Richard Robartes, who spent his tin-mining royalties buying titles from James I. A barony cost him £10,000. His son married the daughter of the Earl of Warwick and became Viscount Bodmin and Earl of Radnor. Such was the wealth of tin.

The family suffered for supporting Parliament in the Civil War, in a county that was staunchly Royalist. After a series of confusing name changes and title revivals, descendants named Agar-Robartes became again Lord Robartes. In April 1881, they suffered the almost total destruction of Lanhydrock by fire. Lady Robartes, a Pole-Carew, died of shock and her husband followed within the year. Undaunted, their son proceeded to recreate a new house within the shell of the old one. Everything except the old Long Gallery which had survived the fire was new, or at least re-instated Jacobean. It was to be a house fit for the age and for the ten Robartes children. The house passed to the National Trust in 1953.

The question for the Trust was whether to treat the house as a restored Jacobean mansion or as a rich Victorian one. The decision rightly went for the latter. The house is one of the best examples in England of a late-Victorian house at work, albeit almost entirely a 1960s creation. The date of the reopening, in 1969, coincided with the popular television drama 'Upstairs, Downstairs' and Lanhydrock never looked back. It is the National Trust's most visited house in England.

The house sits in an extensive deer park stretching down to the River Fowey. All its gates and walls survive, as does the 1648 sycamore avenue leading from the gatehouse down to the Bodmin road. The sycamores were doubled with a row of beeches in 1790. In 1990, 1,100 trees were lost in a freak storm.

The approach to the house is past the charming gatehouse. This was originally flanked by the walls of an outer quadrangle, yielding the customary Elizabethan inner and outer courtyards. Today an avenue of yews leads from the gatehouse to the present entrance forming a dramatic, essentially Victorian, composition.

The interior is a warren of rooms, 50 of them open to the public. It was designed by Lord Robartes for Victorian entertaining in style, a labour-intensive activity. He ordered a new south-east wing round spacious kitchens, with male and female indoor staff carefully segregated. Men and women were to work without meeting each other, or meeting members of the family. The butler's and housekeeper's quarters are also apart. Attic bedrooms for each sex were reached by separate stairs. A prayer room was also set aside for their daily worship. The intention was 'to make them more moral and more efficient'.

Even the children and their nannies had a wing (and staircase) to themselves. There was also a separate staircase so male guests could go to bed after billiards or smoking without disturbing the rooms allocated to ladies. Even His Lordship's Bedroom with its Pugin wallpaper is in a separate suite from Her Ladyship's, although they could meet through sharing a common bathroom.

A visit to Landhydrock is a voyage through these antique arrangements. The hall, its granite fireplace a survivor from the old house, is decorated as for Christmas. The dining room with Morris wallpaper is laid ready for dinner. The table centrepiece is a spectacular sculpture of a camel and palm tree, in pure tin from the grateful miners of Redruth. The kitchen wing displays farm eggs ready to be sent by train to the house in London, where the family would eat only produce from their own estate.

The south wing comprised the smoking room and billiard room, heavy with stuffed trophies of deer, fox and moose. School photographs adorn the walls. In the adjacent steward's room stands a rabbit gun and Gladstone bag. Above is Captain Tommy's Bedroom, dedicated to the Robartes son and heir, killed at the Battle of Loos in 1915. Everything contained in his field kitbag is displayed, including rouge which he used to conceal any facial pallor of fear from the men under his command. His death devastated the family. The room was locked by his sisters and left as a shrine to his memory. Beyond is the nursery range, a row of beds

arranged like a school dormitory. The table carries much politically incorrect literature about gollywogs and foxhunting.

At every turn, one is plunged behind green baize doors to see how the house 'worked'. There are rooms full of linen, travelling trunks, bedpans and pots, trolleys and dumb waiters. Cigarettes remain in servants' ashtrays. Loofahs rest on bathtubs. All this is not Edwardian survival, it should be said, but National Trust creation on the basis of research into how such a house might have been.

The reception rooms come almost as a relief from this domesticity. The drawing room over the hall is furnished in 18th-century style, hung with family portraits by or after Reynolds, Dahl and Kneller. Beyond is Lanhydrock's one grand room, the old Long Gallery. It was saved during the fire by the neighbouring range being dynamited during the fire. The walls are panelled and hung with portraits, but all attention focuses on the barrel vault. The plasterwork is similar to that at Prideaux Place, depicting scenes from the Old Testament, surrounded by animals and birds. Executed by the ubiquitous West Country decorators, the Abbot family of Bideford, probably in the 1630s, it harks refreshingly to an era before the formality of the rest of the house.

LAUNCESTON CASTLE *

Launceston
Norman keep in old Cornish capital (EH)

There are few signs of domestic comfort left at Launceston Castle. The fortress continues to dominate the town and its surrounding valley. The motte and bailey were erected by the Normans to control the country between Bodmin and Dartmoor at the border bridge over the River Kensey. This was the seat of the Earls of Cornwall, customarily brothers of the monarch. The castle was extended by Richard of Cornwall in the 13th century but declined at the end of that century when Duchy adminis-

Bedpan room at Lanhydrock

tration was moved to Lostwithiel. Assize courts remained and the castle became a dreadful prison; demolished in favour of Bodmin (above) in 1842, it fell into disuse.

What remains is a fine gateway in the wall facing the town and, within, a sensational double keep crowning a high mound or motte. The remains of the bailey, including the site of the Great Hall, are in the park. All attention is focused on the keep. This is now an outer wall or Norman shell keep within which is a later high tower inserted in the 13th century. Although a massive pile of ruined masonry, it retains stairs and two habitable rooms, one with a fireplace.

This must have been a bleak posting. The keep was later used as the jail. From the top of the castle flutters the English Heritage flag. Surely the standard of the Duchy of Cornwall would be more appropriate.

MOUNT EDGCUMBE **

8m SE of Torpoint
Home of Edgcumbes overlooking Plymouth Sound (M)

The seat of the Edgcumbe family since the 16th century is no longer its old self. This ancient Cornish family survived all centuries until the 20th. Then, like so many families, it watched war, social upheaval and taxation drain it of the resources and the will to continue. The house is now owned jointly by the City and County of Plymouth and Cornwall, and the peninsular landscape is an ornamental park. This park, with its national collection of camellias, is nothing short of sensational in spring – like a sustained explosion of botanical fireworks overlooking Plymouth Sound.

Sir Richard Edgcumbe built the house in the 1550s to supplement his other home up the River Tamar at Cotehele (above). The house was on an unusual plan for the early-Elizabethan period. Four round towers framed symmetrical façades, with reception rooms enclosing a Great Hall in the middle. The nearest parallel is Wollaton (Notts), but that was not built until 1588. Sir Richard appears to have wanted a blast of ostentation to overlook the Royal Navy's western base.

This house is no more. It was classicized then gothicized in the 18th and 19th centuries. The towers were made octagons and the Great Hall became a two-storey classical temple. Porch and conservatories were added. Then all this vanished when a bomb, presumably aimed at Plymouth, hit the house in the Second World War. The 7th Earl of Mount Edgcumbe, though seventy-nine and with his only son and heir killed in action, determined to rebuild it.

With Adrian Scott as architect, he created a 1960s mansion inside the shell of the old house. The exterior survives as a russet sandstone mansion in the Elizabethan style of the original, with stone mullioned windows and battlemented roof. The family resumed occupation in 1964 but within a year the Earl had died and the estate was inherited by one New Zealand relative and then another, both returning dutifully to live in Cornwall. The last moved out in 1987 and house and grounds were sold jointly to the relevant local councils.

The interior is now very much a museum, furnished in what the guide calls 'a generalized 18th-century style'. There are seascapes by van der Velde and family portraits, including a Reynolds. A picture of the staff of Mount Edgcumbe at the turn of the 20th century shows 172 people, including 14 'pensioners'. It would have been much the same four centuries earlier. Such is the change a century has wrought.

PENCARROW ***

4m NW of Bodmin
Georgian house, pictures by Reynolds and Devis (P)

The house dances attendance on its family and garden. The family is that of the Molesworth-St Aubyns, whose tree since the 16th century is a spider's web of Cornish gentry. It could at one point march on 'family' land across much of the West Country. An ancestor in the 13th century accompanied Edward I to the Holy Land. The current Molesworth-St Aubyn Bt is

the 16th. A collateral line inherited St Michael's Mount (below).

Pencarrow garden, at least in April, is a stupendous display of rhododendrons, azaleas and, later, hydrangeas. The drive is like a botanical guard of honour and the house sits in a bowl of exotic flowers and trees, muting its severe classical frame. It was built in the 1760s by a young Yorkshire architect, Robert Allanson, otherwise unknown. In the 19th century, the interior received fittings from the family's seat at Tetcott in north-west Devon. The sumptuousness of the panelling matches anything in the West Country. Indeed, from its graceful Georgian exterior to its lush interiors, Pencarrow ranks with Antony as a rare example of Cornish 18th-century opulence.

The entrance doubles as a library. The room is panelled in pine, with fitted bookcases below family portraits. On show is a set of intriguing Victorian glass pens. Next door is an exquisite music room. Its furnishings imported from Tetcott include a classical alcove once filled with an organ but now containing a statue of a Grace. The room's panel decoration, ceiling plaster and even the picture frame over the fireplace are in Rococo style. Two Oswald Birley portraits depict the present owner's great-grandparents, but twenty-seven years apart. Thus the husband is a dashing young man, his wife a grey-haired elderly woman, a charming and unusual contrast.

Chairs in the drawing room are upholstered with damask, claimed, like many in Cornwall, to be from a captured Spanish galleon. The inner hall, splendidly arched, contains a curious stove whose flue goes underground. It is surrounded by a large collection of dolls and pushchairs. Pencarrow is stuffed with teddy bears. In the dining room is a great rarity, a complete set of Reynolds portraits painted at one time and of one family, the men confident, the women wistful.

The upstairs bedrooms are as rich as the reception rooms. Actresses (or their producers) who have made films in the house have been persuaded to leave dresses for exhibition, left casually as if just disrobed. The final anteroom contains Pencarrow's two treasures.

Devis's group portrait of the four Misses St Aubyn is among his masterpieces, and it is delightful to find it on this Cornish wall rather than languishing in a museum. Before it sits the Pencarrow Bowl. This was made in China for the English market, and depicts an English fox-hunting scene. The Chinese considered it bad luck to depict a fox being killed, so the animal in the centre looks distinctly like an otter.

PENDENNIS CASTLE *

Pendennis Head, Falmouth
Henrician fortress at entrance to Carrick Roads (EH)

The estuary of the River Fal, known as Carrick Roads, was the 'Key to Cornwall', the finest harbour west of Plymouth and natural objective of any invading fleet. Henry VIII fortified it in the 1540s against the French, leasing the land from the local Killigrew family, who became hereditary captains of the castle.

During the Civil War, Pendennis was held for the king by the Arundells of Trerice. Both Charles I's wife, Henrietta Maria, and their son, the future Charles II, escaped England through its gates, the queen being described as 'the most worne, weak pitifull creature in the world'. The castle then defied a five-month Parliamentarian siege from both land and sea in 1646, being surrendered to Fairfax with its colours flying.

The site is as starkly exposed today as it was then. The climb from Falmouth reaches a deep moat, a gatehouse, wall and then bare lawn with no apparent boundary but the sky and sea. Victorian and Edwardian barracks fill one side, the Tudor fortress the other. The latter is reached by a bridge into the central keep. Apart from one Georgian window, this retains the slit openings and battlements of the original fort.

Inside the fort is the governor's residence which lasted into the 18th century. The rooms were panelled for warmth and have been restored with table, chairs and even a four-poster bed. A place of war is turned into what might be a country rectory, demure china on the table and Dutch tiles on the wall. The lower gun room has thick bastions and narrow openings for guns. The upper gun room has been filled with canons, ropes, waxworks and tape recordings of explosions.

A spiral staircase leads to the roof turret, the point from which the Armada was first sighted from English soil. The vista stretches from the Lizard to Plymouth. Beneath the main fort are subsidiary defences, showing Pendennis pressed into service throughout history. It is the Dover of the west. The outer bastion was last converted as a look-out during the Second World War and contains an exhibition of its defences during that period.

PRIDEAUX PLACE ***

Padstow
Elizabethan house with Gothick interiors (P)

The Prideaux family has always backed the wrong side. Or almost always. They came over with the Conqueror and after the Dissolution acquired land on this sublime site in north Cornwall. The house sits in splendour on a hill overlooking Padstow and the sea, and is Elizabethan, Georgian and Regency Gothick in equal measure. The Elizabethan front of what was then called just Place (for palace) was built in 1592. This façade is mostly as built, warmly clad in creeper above a terrace. The remainder of the exterior was gothicized in 1810, on the garden front with full Gothick embellishments.

The porch leads into a screens passage and the Great Hall, now the dining room. This is entirely panelled in oak and has an original Great Chamber above it. The screen, probably imported in the 19th century, is no ordinary piece. Filled with superb marquetry, its panels are crowded with foliage and animals. The fireplace is flanked by a carving of Elizabeth I standing on a pig, symbol of vice. The whole composition is robust and yeoman-like.

Beyond is the family's morning room, with numerous Opies of the Prideaux-Brunes, still the present owners of the house. Here is also an

18th-century pastel of a Prideaux by the Italian portraitist, Rosalba Carriera. She allegedly fell in love with the sitter while drawing him, and wrote him a letter to that effect which she slipped into the frame, asking for his devotion in return. The letter sadly remained hidden in the frame until the picture was cleaned in 1914.

The drawing room steps abruptly forward to 1810 and Prideaux's Gothick remodelling. The room contains two exotic Rococo mirrors and looks out through the bay window onto the south lawn. Next is the Grenville Room, acquired and installed complete from another Cornish house, Stowe at Kilkhampton, in the 1720s.

The wall carvings are in the style of Grinling Gibbons and are sumptuous. Three panels by Verrio appear to have come with the room, which has been restored with green panelling and gilded picture frames.

The remarkable Gothick ceiling to the staircase is by an unknown hand, balanced by niches, iron balusters and Gothick window tracery. Upstairs is Prideaux's pride and joy, the Great Chamber over the hall. The astonishing ceiling was hidden behind another ceiling until discovered by the present owner as a small boy, when crawling across the rafters. It is a companion to the Jacobean ceiling that survived the fire at Lanhydrock and is clearly by the same hand, supposedly the Abbot family near Bideford. Scenes depict stories from the Old Testament and comprise a biblical and morality tale in one. It is possible these are themes that Catholic Cornishmen may have felt unable to display in their Reformation churches.

A divide in the stairs leads to the library, which is once again in Gothick style. The walls are green and the ceiling blue. Indeed the whole house is an exercise in the deployment of bold colour, and much the better for it. In the library is a portrait of the present owner, Peter Prideaux-Brune, in his barrister's robes, with his teddy bear mascot by his side. Prideaux specialises in cross-Channel visitors, welcomed in fluent French, echoing its Norman forebears.

RESTORMEL CASTLE **

1½m N of Lostwithiel
Duchy shell keep in Fowey valley (EH)

Edward III knew the Cornish would be trouble and ruled it through his son and heir, the Black Prince, Duke of Cornwall. Its strongholds are held by the Prince of Wales, as Duke of Cornwall, to this day.

Restormel previously belonged to the Earls of Cornwall. It was begun by the Normans and achieved its present dramatic form in the 13th century when neighbouring Lostwithiel became the base of Crown administration in Cornwall in place of Launceston. It degenerated from the 14th century onwards, a neglect that preserved its remarkably unaltered circular form.

The castle was derelict by 1610 when the historian Norden reported that 'the whole castle beginneth to mourne and to wringe out harde stones for teares'. This was an unusually evocative conservationist sentiment for that era.

Restormel Castle has a remarkable presence above the valley of the River Fowey. Apart from devastatingly intrusive modern power pylons, the view from its walls is sylvan. Shall we ever be rid of the pylons? The outer bailey and curtain wall have gone, but the inner keep with its dry ditch is remarkably intact. The crenellated wall can be walked uninterrupted. This is one of my favourite English castles.

The inner keep is technically a shell castle. The circular plan is of a palisade forming the outer wall of buildings arranged round a small inner court. Each chamber, hall, kitchen and chapel occupies a sector of this internal plan.

Only the kitchen walls stand to their original height, but all rooms are discernible. The most important are raised above extensive ground-floor storerooms. Restormel is an eerie, private place, lost with its memories. It is more evocative of the past than the scrubbed fortresses of the coast. Perhaps this is one where the authorities could allow the return of some creeper.

ST MAWES CASTLE *

St Mawes
Henrician fort overlooking Falmouth Bay
(EH)

St Mawes was the lesser of the two Fal fortresses, and gazes across the estuary to its big brother, Pendennis Castle. It overlooks the pretty resort from which it takes its name and looks as unmilitary and inoffensive as the villas that line the coast above it. Like the forts that Henry VIII built along the coast of Kent and Sussex, St Mawes is essentially a firing platform to defend the harbour, formed of a clover leaf of bastions.

These castles were also an assertion of the King's local sovereignty, hence the bold coat of arms over the gateway, with the inscription in Latin, 'Henry thy honour and praises will remain for ever'. Other mottos in praise of the king are found elsewhere in the castle. Only the most rudimentary attempt was made to defend the castle from those who might disagree. On the landward side are battlements, a ditch and gunloops.

The castle interior is divided between the domestic chambers of the governor and the gun rooms and batteries. All are well preserved and much polished by English Heritage. The central tower is of three floors, with three rooms divided by partitions and with fireplaces in all of them. Above is the barracks room and below a kitchen with a large fireplace. The roof offers a fine view over Falmouth Bay.

Below the castle on the shore is another range of positions for the mounting of artillery. This Shore Battery displays an assortment of canons from different periods of military defence.

ST MICHAEL'S MOUNT ***

off the coast at Marazion, 4m E of Penzance
Ancient monastery and castle, still home of the St Aubyn family (NT)

An offshore island, a monastery and a castle must attract mystery. St Michael's Mount sits picturesque in Mount's Bay. The causeway linking it to the mainland remains open only at low tide and on my first visit many years ago, an amphibious vehicle had to convey me to the site. Although much altered in the 18th and 19th centuries, the castle's creamy granite walls have great romantic presence, rising today above the island's subtropical gardens and the pretty harbour village below.

The Mount had been a natural refuge and centre for trade since prehistoric times, probably the ancient port of Ictis. Iron Age traces have been found on the slopes, presumably of early traders shipping tin, crossing Cornwall from the north coast and from Wales and Ireland beyond.

The rock and its church were long dedicated to St Michael, fighter of the Devil and thus blessed with churches on rocks and high places. In 1135 the Benedictine monks of Mont St Michel in Normandy were invited to establish a priory in Cornwall. Their church was destroyed by an earthquake in 1275 and never rebuilt with the splendour of its French parent. The surviving small priory was suppressed by Henry V as alien and granted to Syon Abbey by Henry VI in 1424.

The Mount was favoured as a stronghold during the Wars of the Roses and was used as a base by Perkin Warbeck during his brief rebellion against Henry VII. After the Dissolution, it was occupied by military governors and held for the King during the Civil War. With its surrender to Parliament in 1646, the captaincy passed to Colonel John St Aubyn, who later bought the Mount and adapted it as a residence in 1659. His family, now Lords St Levan, occupy an apartment in the castle to this day, albeit since 1954 as leaseholders of the National Trust.

A visit to the Mount is primarily a scenic experience. The building is an amalgam of medieval, 18th-century and Victorian work. The medieval parts are the gatehouse and hall, church, Lady Chapel and refectory, with garrison quarters underneath. The church is of the 13th century, while the monastic refectory survives as the Chevy Chase Room. This was the Tudor Great Hall and retains a magnificent arch-braced roof. It takes its name from the plaster reliefs that line its walls, depicting hunting scenes. Down the middle of the room is a massive Jacobean oak table, flanked by monastic chairs, one of them medieval from Glastonbury.

The surprise of St Michael's Mount is the Georgian conversion of the old monastic Lady Chapel. This stands detached on a platform overlooking the sea. The interior is in florid Strawberry Hill Gothick of c1750, in pale blue with white ogival arches, an ornamental ceiling and pretty oriental pediment to the overmantel. The room, in effect two rooms divided by a fireplace with chinoiserie pediment, is strongly reminiscent of Shobdon church in Herefordshire. The smaller room contains a rare landscape of the Mount, by the Cornish portraitist, John Opie. He was extravagantly acclaimed by Reynolds as 'Caravaggio and Velasquez in one'.

The rest of the castle displays the old barracks and museum rooms. Thanks to the National Trust, the island and its little port have been well conserved, a far cry from the insensitive tourist development round most of Penzance.

TINTAGEL POST OFFICE **

Fore Street
Medieval hall house (NT)

Forget King Arthur and the Round Table. The soggier side of the Victorian imagination pervades Tintagel as it does Glastonbury. There is no evidence that anyone called King Arthur came near the place. The dramatic ruins on an offshore rock are medieval. More real by far is the Old Post Office, a beguiling stone hall house dating from the 14th century.

The National Trust owns the house and has appropriated one of the precious medieval rooms as a shop as well as reinstated post office. The building crouches low and heavily buttressed on the main street, so low as if about to slink away from tourists battering on its door.

The house sags under the weight of its slate roof which, above the granite of its walls,

seems to have emerged fully formed from the ground beneath. The central chimney tapers in three steps to the top to reduce resistance to the Atlantic gales. This is a house that does not intend to be blown away.

The plan is of a medieval hall and parlour. The entrance is into a passage, with the hall open to the roof on the left. The parlour has an original slit window deep in the wall. A small spiral stair leads up to a bedroom, recently furnished in Victorian style. A gallery, probably another bedroom, overlooks the hall. Huge roof beams support the heavy Cornish slates overhead. A fire normally burns in the big fireplace below, agreeably filling the house with wood smoke. Above it is a shelf with two candles and an early gun.

TRERICE ***

3m SE of Newquay
Elizabethan gentry house with Dutch gables (NT)

Trerice, pronounced tre-rice, is a hidden Elizabethan house concealed in the hills behind Newquay. The house was finished in 1573 for Sir John Arundell and has been little altered since. The Trerice estate passed through various hands, including the Aclands in the 19th century, and went to the National Trust in 1953.

Unlike the earlier Elizabethan house of Cotehele, the façade of Trerice makes some effort at outward symmetry and display. It is an E-plan house with five wayward ornamental gables framing its attic windows, of Cornish limestone that changes colour with the light, from yellow to pink to grey. The scrolls on these gables were said to be unique at the time, comparable only to gables in the Low Countries, where Arundell had been a soldier. Two of the gables were restored in the 1950s after part of the house was thought about to collapse.

The interior remains Elizabethan. The entrance under the porch is into a screens passage to the Great Hall, with the family chambers to the south.

The hall is a fine room, its ceiling of geomet-

Gale-defying Tintagel

rical plasterwork with large pendants. Trerice's plasterwork was celebrated and much imitated elsewhere in Cornwall. The overmantel is dated 1572, its fanciful scrollwork a foretaste of Rococo. The hall is well stocked with 17th-century chairs, chests and pewter. The minstrels' gallery is enclosed, with arched openings for the music to escape.

The drawing room is adorned with paintings by Herring and Opie, including one of the many Opie self-portraits. The Great Chamber above is the glory of Trerice, the ceiling presumably by the same hand as the Great Hall, with a swaggering barrel vault. A wide bow window overlooks the garden. An Aubusson tapestry fills the end wall.

Trerice is not a big house. A gallery passes along the back of the Great Hall to what would have been the kitchen wing. This part of the house, long abandoned, was rebuilt in the 1950s, its 17th-century furniture and landscapes then introduced. This is a charming place. Here I encountered that rare sight, a National Trust guardian snoozing in a side room in the heat of a warm day. I sympathized, and tiptoed out.

TREWITHEN **

6m E of Truro
Georgian house with Rococo saloon (P)

The lawn at Trewithen glides away from the south front, divided by tapering walls of rhododendrons, magnolias and camellias. In

spring it looks like a rend in a coat of many colours. The botanical riches imported by returning British voyagers from the Orient is here on full display.

The house was begun in 1715 by Philip Hawkins. The present structure was largely the work of Philip's executors in 1738–40 for his nephew, Thomas Hawkins, who became the local MP. Thomas married Anne Heywood, daughter of a London merchant, who brought with her dowry the best of metropolitan taste. The house had to respond.

The architect is documented as Thomas Edwards, but Hawkins is believed to have employed Sir Robert Taylor for the main reception rooms along the south front. Thomas was a public-spirited figure who tried to persuade his tenants to use the new smallpox vaccine. He did so by using it on himself, the example losing some force when he died of the illness.

The house has a plain early-Georgian plan, a rectangular building with flanking pavilions. The entrance front is rendered and rather dull. Not so the interior. The house is still occupied by Hawkins descendents, a continuity reflected in the pictures, furniture, books and objects that crowd the rooms shown to visitors.

The chief room on the south front is the saloon, presumably the epitome of Anne Heywood's sophistication. It is screened at each end by pillars forming a vaulted recess. Soft green walls are offset by fine Rococo plasterwork. The fireplace is a swirling mass of curves. This must have seemed more than refreshing in a land of solid Jacobean panelling and heraldic overmantels.

The drawing room is panelled in varying shades of yellow. Here are portraits by Opie, including his favourite subject, himself. The study panelling is unpainted, with fluted pilasters, and the room has glorious views of the garden. In the rear hall is a modern mural of the Trewithen estate, now owned by the Galsworthy family. The garden was created by the Edwardian owner, George Johnstone.

Jacobean oak at Trerice

Cumbria

Cumbria was always Border country. From the Roman Conquest to the reign of James I, it was a land under threat. Its houses were either fortified or they were seized by marauding Scots. As in Northumberland, the commonest building type was thus the keep, evolving into the pele or tower house. Even when the union of the English and Scottish crowns under James I brought peace in 1603, the pele lived on, as if owners still felt in need of a place of retreat.

The county, therefore, has an exceptional stock of castles, from royal Carlisle to the curtain-walled peles of the Cliffords. Even stylish Elizabethan residences such as Sizergh, Levens and Hutton have peles at their cores. These structures complicated and often defied later attempts at Georgian symmetry. They also appealed to Victorian medieval revivalists.

The arrival of Lady Anne Clifford to take charge of her northern estates in 1649 initiated a burst of new building. She restored residential wings in her castles at Appleby, Brough and Brougham and dispensed charity in the form of churches and almshouses. Classicism ventured timidly into Cumbria in the 17th century. A new gallery and façade were added to Hutton and a new front to Appleby. With the 18th century came the cladding of Dalemain and Carr of York's embellishment of Workington, the Curwen family's once magnificent seat. The best Georgian work in the county is the lovely Cupid Room at Hutton.

The medieval revival took Cumbria to its bosom. Salvin refurbished Hutton and rebuilt Muncaster. Spectacular sites produced spectacular architecture at Smirke's Lowther Castle and Philip Wyatt's astonishing Conishead. The arrival of the Romantic poets and their followers made Cumbria a cradle of the Picturesque. Wordsworth moved from Cockermouth to Grasmere to Rydal, stopping often at the Speddings' gentle Mirehouse. He was followed by Ruskin at Brantwood and Beatrix Potter at Hill Top.

The charms of Windermere were no less appealing to the Merseyside and Mancunian plutocracy. They left houses as diverse as Storrs Hall, Wray Castle and Baillie Scott's Arts and Crafts Blackwell. Meanwhile the antiquarian, George Browne, was defying time with his remarkable carvings at Townend.

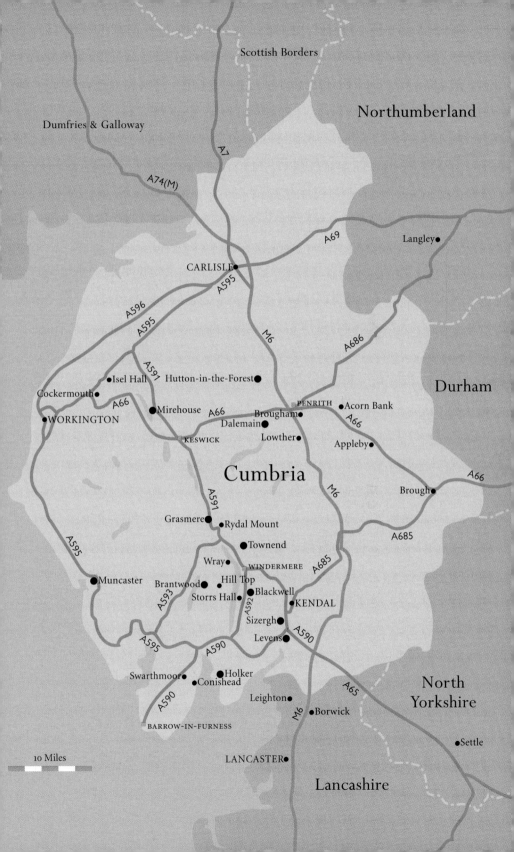

Acorn Bank *
Appleby:
  Castle **
  St Anne's Hospital *
Blackwell ***
Brantwood ***
Brough Castle *
Brougham:
  Castle *
  Hall *
Carlisle:
  Castle **
  Prior's Tower *

Cockermouth:
  Wordsworth
    House **
Conishead **
Dalemain ***
Grasmere:
  Dove Cottage ***
Hill Top **
Holker ***
Hutton-in-the-
    Forest ****
Isel Hall **

Kendal:
  Abbot Hall *
Levens ****
Lowther Castle *
Mirehouse ***
Muncaster ***
Rydal Mount **
Sizergh ****
Storrs Hall *
Swarthmoor **
Townend ***
Workington Hall *
Wray Castle *

ACORN BANK *

Temple Sowerby, 6 miles E of Penrith
Georgian front on older house with herb
garden (NT)

Acorn Bank is a leading centre for medicinal
and culinary herbs. Aconite and arnica flourish in the lee of the Pennines in a garden
created in the 1930s by the travel writer and
botanist, Dorothy Una Ratcliffe. The house is
being restored by the National Trust to allow
public access but the exterior can already be
perambulated on a visit to the garden. On an
autumn day, with the sun bright on the house
and storm clouds on the hills behind, this is a
dramatic spot.

The house has clearly been extended as
and when resources permitted. To the rear are
traces of a pele tower and much 16th- and
17th-century stonework. This façade offers a
jagged ridge of gables looking out through fine
iron gates down to a stream. From here Acorn
looks like a traditional, modified E-plan
Jacobean structure.

But that is the back. The more prominent
new entrance front is quite different. In the
1740s the ancestral owners, the Dalstons, added
a completely new façade. Apparently short of
money, they contrived little more than a stage
set. The style is Georgian, but many windows

are false and Venetian windows are scattered
almost at random. The right-hand wing is the
stable block, its windows painted on stone. The
composition looks splendid from the distant
road, which was doubtless the intention.

At Acorn Bank, the health-and-safety fanatics not only warn visitors that every step they
take is dangerous but that the smell of some
plants is poisonous. Who knows but that the
Cumbrian air is also lethal? Nothing is too
absurd for these people.

APPLEBY CASTLE **

Appleby
Norman keep and 17th-century home of Lady
Anne Clifford (P)

In 1649, the Royalist Lady Anne Clifford turned
her back on Cromwell's Commonwealth and,
at the age of sixty, went north to restore the
name and property of the Cliffords, ancient
lords of Westmorland. It was an extraordinary
chapter in the history of the North.

Clifford's building frenzy was phenomenal,
lasting over twenty-five years into her
old age. She even seized and rebuilt deserted
castles to which she had little or no claim,
feeling all castles should be used. When
Cromwell ordered her fortresses be destroyed,
she promptly rebuilt them. Not just castles but

houses, churches, hospitals and almshouses benefited from her largesse – and that of her heavily taxed tenantry.

Appleby became Lady Anne's home. She had been born in 1590, daughter of Elizabeth's glamorous favourite, the Earl of Cumberland, and spent her early life at Court. She first married Richard Sackville, Earl of Dorset, then Philip Herbert, Earl of Pembroke. Although the only surviving child of her father, as a girl of fifteen she was denied the Clifford estates on his death. They went instead to her uncle. She fought this injustice in the courts, winning the estate only when her uncle's line died out in 1643.

Lady Anne had no truck with the Renaissance. All her restorations were medieval, so much so that dating them can be hard. She charged high rents and was a stern landlord, but she spent those rents locally. Travelling on a litter with an astonishing retinue of up to fifty carts, she stayed in her properties for months at a time. Her medieval clothes were, it was said at her funeral in 1675, 'not disliked by any, but imitated by none'.

Appleby Castle's keep and fortified house within a curtain wall are superbly sited on a bluff over the River Eden. The outer gate is reached from the town centre at the top of a fine avenue of 17th- and 18th-century houses. At the time of writing the future of this fulcrum of northern history is in doubt. The interior is 'under repair' and the house is for sale. It needs another Clifford with the imagination to seize it and reassert the supremacy of northern culture.

The inner bailey has a keep to the right and the old Jacobean house to the left. The latter was extensively improved after her death by Lady Anne's son-in-law, the Earl of Thanet. Although their family origins were in Kent, the Thanets remained devoted to Appleby until its sorry sale in 1962.

The Thanets' Great Hall was erected in stone taken from the swiftly decaying Brough and Brougham castles. The façade is in a robust Northern Baroque, of which Lady Anne would not have approved. It has pilasters and dormers with both segmental and triangular pediments. Steps rise to the central door, which is crowned with a broken pediment. The hall interior carries the coats of arms of Lady Anne and the many connections of her descendants. They include Viponts, Herberts, Sackvilles, Dacres, St Johns, Russells and Ferrers, a roll call of the magnates of North and South alike. Beyond are panelled rooms and a fine staircase which leads from the rear of the hall.

Across the courtyard stands Appleby's Norman keep, called Caesar's Tower. It is in a colder, greyer stone and remains unaltered since the late 12th century, apart from a Georgianized top floor. The battlements offer a superb view of the Eden gorge below. The interior, partitioned for domestic use by Lady Anne, is rather jaded, as if eager for a new conqueror. The walls have been left to the mercy of creeper, much to their benefit.

APPLEBY: ST ANNE'S HOSPITAL *

Boroughgate
Clifford almshouse in lee of castle (P)

Lady Anne founded almshouses throughout her domain. Few are as charming as the 'hospital' she built under her own walls at Appleby. Begun in the early 1650s, the almshouses are as she left them and are still in use. They are among the most picturesque examples of this charming form of charity.

The building is formed of twelve houses round a rectangular, cobbled yard. It is of pink-grey Penrith stone, the only material to rival Somerset's Ham stone as a delight to the eye. Nowhere is it better displayed than on a warm afternoon in the inner court of St Anne's. The stone is crowned by blue-grey slates.

In one corner of the courtyard is a tiny chapel, in which services continue to be held. A fountain and small rock garden stand in the middle. Beyond is a paddock with a view of the Pennines. This is a sublime place. In matters of welfare, small is beautiful.

BLACKWELL ***

1½m S of Bowness-on-Windermere
Plutocrat's Arts and Crafts house by Baillie
Scott (M)

The saving of Blackwell in 1999 was a conservation triumph. This masterpiece of the Arts and Crafts architect, M. H. Baillie Scott, had survived the 20th century mostly unaltered, as a school and offices. The building was then acquired and restored by the Lakeland Arts Trust, under the auspices of the Abbot Hall Gallery in Kendal.

The house was designed in 1898 as a holiday home for the Manchester brewer, Sir Edward Holt. Outside and inside, it held to the vernacular manorial style espoused by William Morris. There were bold gables, round Lakeland chimneys, stone mullioned windows and a central Great Hall. The interiors, like those of Norman Shaw, were a series of variations on a theme of the hearth. 'In the house the fire is a substitute for the sun,' wrote Baillie Scott. 'The cheerfulness we experience from the fire is akin to the delight sunlight brings.' The result was rich and warm, refined Art Nouveau decoration co-existing with Holt's 17th- and 18th-century furniture.

The house and its decorative programme have been restored by the Modernist architects, Allies and Morrison. They have left it naked of any Victorian traces in their quest for 'pure Baillie Scott', which is based on early drawings for the house. The rooms seem bare. There are no curtains. The daylight is glaring and the fireplaces are reduced to mere decoration. The domestic rooms are reached through a reception area that is aggressively modern. House has surrendered to museum. Blackwell is what an Arts and Crafts house might have been like if only its architect had been Le Corbusier.

Enough carping. Blackwell sits bold on a bluff above Windermere. It contains three exquisite rooms, the dining room, hall and drawing room, representing the Indian summer of England's contribution to European Art Nouveau. It was the era of Charles Voysey, Charles Rennie Mackintosh and Baillie Scott.

The focal point of each room is the inglenook. In the dining room, this is formed by a sweeping stone arch, its benches lit by fine stained-glass windows. The fire grate is backed by Dutch tiles. Floor, ceiling, panelling and furniture are all of exposed wood. The liveliest feature is the hessian wall-hangings, of birds and flowers, 'full of still, quiet earnestness which seems to lull and soothe the spirit,' wrote Baillie Scott. Every corbel or boss or bench-end is turned into a depiction of nature, as a rowan berry, a daisy or an oak leaf. Manchester brewers on holiday were expected to celebrate nature.

The hall has heavy beams and Tudor half-timbering. Its glory is another frieze, this one depicting peacocks. More carvings fill the panels of the minstrels' gallery, a feature above the inglenook. The fire surround is a bold composition of pilasters with naturalistic capitals. The 'Manxman' piano – Scott lived for a while on the Isle of Man – is disguised as a cupboard. The room is as empty as a Shakespearean theatre without play or audience.

At the end of the downstairs passage is the White Drawing Room, with a spectacular view overlooking the lake. The decorative atmosphere shifts from warm oak to shimmering white. The chamber is serene, almost surreal. The ceiling and frieze are a forest of trees and flowers, but in white. Spindly columns round the inglenook branch out into birds and leaves. The fire-dogs become daisies and berries. An oriel window surmounts the stone fireplace with stained glass depicting swaying fronds and hidden birds. This must be one of the loveliest 20th-century rooms in England. I wish it looked as if someone lived in it.

BRANTWOOD ***

2m SE of Coniston
Ruskin's house facing Coniston Water (M)

After Wordsworth, the Lake District had no more influential sponsor than John Ruskin.

Mr Ruskin at home, Brantwood

Nowhere else in all England, he thought, could match Switzerland for scenic beauty. From here in his maturity he observed nature and the weather, honouring his dictum that 'to understand nature one must be able to see clearly what is really there'. There were, he said, hundreds who can talk for one who can think and thousands who can think for one who can see. 'To see clearly is poetry, prophecy and religion.' It was from Brantwood that he saw.

The house was Ruskin's home from 1872 until his death in 1900. He bought it sight unseen, in the sole knowledge that it faced 'five acres of rock and moor and streamlet' on the best water in Lakeland. He built a turret high on the corner of the house overlooking the lake, and this served as his study, bedroom and inspiration.

The house expanded considerably during his occupancy. It was here that he moved his art collection from Herne Hill in South London and here also that he invited his cousins, Arthur and Joan Severn, to join him. He left them his entire property, with disastrous results.

Ruskin told the Severns that he wanted the house and its collection retained as a museum, open to the public. The Severns disobeyed him and instead sold or destroyed the contents. Quantities of Ruskin papers simply disappeared, and many were later found floating on Coniston Water. Turner watercolours that famously covered the walls of the bedroom were sold, along with medieval manuscripts and paintings by Gainsborough and the Pre-Raphaelites.

Not until 1932 was John Whitehouse, MP and fanatical admirer of Ruskin, able to buy back the property and reassemble some Ruskiniana. This is now admirably displayed under the aegis of Lancaster University. It is the best of Cumbria's artistic shrines, if only because it is a little off the most beaten tracks.

The interior is furnished in Victorian style with works that would have appealed to Ruskin. The drawing room has wallpaper designed by him and contains his drawing of St Mark's, Venice. The house also has a number of copies he made of Old Masters, including a 'Botticelli' and a 'Tintoretto'. Next door is the study from which there emitted a constant stream of correspondence, books and essays. Works by Luca della Robbia and Samuel Prout remain.

The dining room was designed to admit glimpses of Coniston Water through lancet windows, as if nature were itself a picture on the wall. Ruskin's Turret Bedroom has been restored, up a small staircase from the old house.

Next door is the Turret Room, from which Ruskin would spend hours watching the lake's changing moods. In few places can man, nature and artistic inspiration be experienced in such harmony.

BROUGH CASTLE *

Brough
Clifford castle in spectacular location (EH)

Forget the sun. See Brough if possible against storm clouds rolling down from the north like invading Scotsmen. Even ruined, it is imposing, its broken walls and staring windows bravely deterring all-comers. The castle was first built as a keep by the Normans to shut out the Scots. The location was that of an old Roman fort, whose pattern can still be made out in the surrounding fields.

The keep enclosure at Brough was fortified and given a Great Hall range by Robert Clifford at the turn of the 14th century, with the Clifford Tower as his private residence. These buildings were gutted by fire in 1521 but were restored and made habitable by Robert's indomitable descendant, Lady Anne Clifford (Appleby, above), in 1663. The castle then resumed its story of decay until taken into public guardianship in 1919.

Today, Brough's appeal is mostly scenic. Clifford's Tower still stands, with the third-floor windows which Lady Anne inserted and behind which she stayed on her feudal tours. The remains of the kitchens and servants' quarters can still be seen, including the vaulted storerooms below the hall.

Most majestic is the keep, in rich red stone. Safety officials now stop people entering and climbing the steps to the upper parapet and viewing platform. When will this sort of nonsense end? A kindlier character was the pixie, Hobthrush, said to inhabit a latrine hole in the curtain wall near the keep. Each year, on receipt of nocturnal gifts, he helped gather the local harvest.

BROUGHAM CASTLE *

1½ m SE of Penrith
Clifford keep, gatehouse and hall (EH)

Brougham Castle is among the most romantic of Clifford residences. Here Wordsworth and his sister would be taken as part of their education in the Picturesque. Here they 'crept along a ridge of a fractured wall,/ Not without trembling, we in safety looked/ Forth, through some Gothic window's open space./ And gathered with one mind a rich reward/ From the far-stretching landscape.'

The castle endured the usual Border history. Founded by the Normans it was fortified by Vieuxponts (later Viponts) and then Cliffords during the 14th century. It changed hands during the Wars of the Roses but returned to the Cliffords. It was at Brougham that George Clifford, 3rd Earl of Cumberland, was born. It fell to ruin, was restored by his daughter, Lady Anne Clifford, and then fell to ruin again.

The castle remains impressive, beautifully sited on the banks of the River Eamont. The approach to the massive gatehouse, with the hall to the left and the great keep contiguous behind, is still impressive. Robert Clifford built the gatehouse at the end of the 13th century. It is, in reality, two gates divided by a court and must have challenged the most determined attacker.

The keep is in good condition. The exterior has grotesque corbel heads peering from its string courses and is covered in aubrietia. Inside stairs give access to the upper floors, including a small oratory. On the second floor is a Roman tombstone fragment built into the wall. The outer walls of the 14th-century hall and chapel remain to roof height across the courtyard.

BROUGHAM HALL *

1½ m SE of Penrith
Ruin of great house under restoration (P)

The last battle on English soil was fought in the meadows below Brougham on 18 December 1745, the climax of the '45 Rebellion. Converted by the Brougham family in the 19th century, it became known as the Windsor of the North.

In the 1960s, Brougham Hall saw another battle, to conserve what remained of the house after the neighbouring landowner, Major Carleton Cowper of Penrith, bought and demolished it in what appeared a fit of pique. He had bought it from an impoverished Clifford descendent, Lord Brougham, with whose family he had a feud. Brougham had inherited a vast estate in 1927 at the age of eighteen and had squandered every penny of it by 1934. Carleton Cowper acquired the house, stripped it of its Victorian furnishings and began demolishing the medieval pele tower and Clifford ranges. He had declared his wish to 'see an oak grow in the hall at Brougham'. Cumbrian vendettas have a savage longevity.

The building was thus left unroofed, and the site was occupied by the army during the Second World War. There followed four decades of further decay, with plans characteristic of post-war Britain to flatten the site for bungalows or a caravan park. In 1968 a businessman, Christopher Terry, came upon the ruin and determined to restore it. Terry battled builders, developers, planners, bankers and accountants through the courts for some thirty years. Since 1986, the site has been owned by Terry's charitable trust and has seen the start of a remarkable revival. This is not to 'conserve as found' but to reinstate the house's Victorian state.

The site retains the fortified walls of the original enclosure. Within the courtyard is a scatter of outbuildings surviving from Carleton

Cowper's wreckers. These have been converted for small-scale commercial activity. The ruin of the entrance is a teashop. The old Lord Chancellor's Den, which belonged in the 1830s to the reformer, Lord Brougham, can still be seen as a ruin. It will be a massive task to recreate the old house but such a dedicated owner should be given his head by all in a position to help him.

CARLISLE CASTLE **

Carlisle
Lodgings and keep within mighty fortress
(EH)

The city of Carlisle was once the graceful capital of the North. Today, it is tormented by poor redevelopment and one of the worst traffic schemes in England. A dual carriageway separates the cathedral and old quarter from the celebrated castle, leaving it isolated in a desert of English Heritage lawn.

Carlisle and Newcastle were the two great forts protecting England against Scotland throughout the Middle Ages. They hosted English kings when they came north to do battle against the foe but Carlisle was not impregnable. The walls and keep were first built by Henry I but completed by the Scots king, David, during his brief occupation of the North in the 12th century. Carlisle was captured for England by Henry II in 1157 and held even after Edward II's defeat by the Scots at Bannockburn in 1314. No English castle has seen more blood shed in anger, or more treachery. It was in the hall at Carlisle in 1323 that the loyal Earl of Carlisle was murdered 'for disloyalty' in the king's name by his rival, Anthony de Lucy.

Under the Tudors, Carlisle was a crucial bastion against the Franco-Scots alliance. It was held for the King in the Civil War and seized by Bonnie Prince Charlie in 1745, by which time the castle was vulnerable to artillery and the defenders did not bother to resist. It later became a centre of military administration and is still used by the Territorial Army today.

Two residential interiors are accessible, the Steward's rooms over the gatehouse and the early royal quarters in the keep. The gatehouse is unusual in its confined space. The hall is small and behind it is a solar. These rooms have been furnished in English Heritage's 'modern medieval' style.

The keep is reached through the Captain's Tower, past the site of the demolished Queen Mary's Tower, where Mary Queen of Scots was imprisoned in 1568. The great keep was David's palace in the 12th century and retains the proportions of an early Norman fortress, square and with massively thick walls. The round-arched entrance to the old Great Hall looks as though excavated through solid rock, as do the spiral stairs to the rooms above. The lower and upper halls were later divided into two rooms but retain their deep-splayed windows. There are storerooms and dungeons below and private chambers above. A small oratory on the second floor has been closed by a modern glass door, as has a small cell with charming carvings on the walls made by prisoners, c1480. The roof offers a fine view of present-day Carlisle.

The guidebook states that the castle today 'has a well-used look'. It does not. Every blade of grass is the statuary inch long. Not a dandelion or trace of ivy is permitted. From outside, Carlisle Castle looks almost as if it had been built by the architect of the adjacent motorway.

CARLISLE: PRIOR'S TOWER *

Cathedral Close
Painted ceiling discovered in former prior's solar (P)

The cathedral is surrounded by residential buildings, only one of which dates from its pre-Reformation days as a priory. The Prior's Tower has its origins in an ancient pele tower on the city ramparts, immediately adjacent to the cathedral itself. To this pele was added a hall to form a conventional Cumbrian residence. The hall has vanished but the tower remains, housing the prior's solar with a wide vaulted undercroft beneath it.

The solar is a gem, a small room with deep, recessed windows. Its most spectacular feature is its roof of painted oak beams. Every inch is covered in 16th-century patterns and motifs. These include popinjays, shells, heraldry and mottos. Bosses fixed to the beams depict a jester and a pelican 'in her piety'. The paintings were discovered and revealed in 1975, requiring only minimal restoration. Over the fireplace is a fragment of a carved choir screen, a maze of intricate ogival patterns.

The decoration is wonderfully colourful. It must have enlivened the droning hours of diocesan business beneath.

COCKERMOUTH:
WORDSWORTH HOUSE **

Main Street
Georgian town house and poet's birthplace
(NT)

Wordsworth's father, John, was agent to the Cumbrian magnate, Sir James (later Lord) Lowther. A solid house on Cockermouth's main street came with the job. It had been built for the Sheriff of Cumberland in 1745 but passed into Lowther hands. Here the poet was born in 1770 and found his earliest inspiration on the banks of the River Derwent that flowed past the end of the garden. The Derwent was 'the playmate whom we dearly lov'd', Wordsworth wrote. It was to him 'the fairest of all rivers' as it 'blended with his nurse's song'.

The garden was where he established his bond with his sister, Dorothy, and learned with her a love of nature. All this survives, largely thanks to the efforts of Cockermouth people who saved the house from demolition in 1937. The terrace where the children played is still in place. The Derwent still flows between grassy banks. There is still a meadow on the far bank.

The house is run by the National Trust as a Wordsworth Museum, rivalling the shrines at Dove Cottage and Rydal Mount. Of the three,

Cockermouth is at present the least evocative. It is a conventional Georgian town house with a distinguished façade to the street, declaring little more than the poet's comfortable origins. Its memorabilia collection is modest.

The interior is filled with Georgian furniture, much of it Chippendale and Hepplewhite. Parlour and dining room downstairs have good ceilings, with cabinets, clocks and displays of Staffordshire and Coalport china. Upstairs is a more remarkable room, the drawing room. This was presumably the sheriff's reception room. Scrolled pediments surmount the doorcases, one of which is an elaborate fake. Rococo console tables divide the windows. The chief interest in the house is its admirable collection of paintings, prints and drawings of the Lake District.

CONISHEAD PRIORY **

2m SE of Ulverston
Extravagant Gothic mansion now Buddhist retreat (P-R)

There is no house in England like Conishead. The priory has long gone. What we see today is a fantasy originally created by Colonel Thomas Richmond-Gale-Braddyll to a Gothick design by the little-known Philip Wyatt in 1821. The house was an exercise in pure show, set in a splendid park on the Furness peninsular. Wyatt was a wastrel who soon went to prison for debt. What he began is largely a masterpiece by the cultivated and hardworking local architect, George Webster of Kendal. But the project bankrupted Braddyll. The house changed hands many times. In the 1880s it became a luxurious 'hydropathic hotel', with resident orchestra and thousand-volume library. In the 1920s it was converted into a miners' convalescent home. By the 1970s it faced demolition.

Salvation came in the unusual form of a Mahayana Buddhist community from Tibet, who bought the building in 1976. Recruiting local volunteers, the Manjushri Centre meticulously restored the shell of the house, giving it a not implausible oriental overlay. Saffron robes glide through the trees. Bright banners deck Gothick corridors. Shrines punctuate niches and Wyatt's colossal billiard hall has become a carpeted Meditation Room, its walls lined with mandalas. A temple in the grounds contains the largest Buddha ever cast in the West. Conishead is a strange concordat between original priory, Braddyll's Gothick eccentricity, which included the hiring of a so-called 'house hermit', and the present use as a religious retreat.

The forecourt shows the building in all its eccentric glory. Wyatt designed, apparently at random, a chaotic series of gables, turrets and façades, some in brick, some in render. The entrance is between two octagonal turrets roughly based on King's College Chapel, Cambridge. The doorway leads directly into a large hall modelled on a medieval chapel, with tall stained glass windows. At right angles beyond is a corridor which is designed as a cloister, forming the spine of the building. The main reception rooms, now institutionalized, are gigantic, some of them 50 ft long.

The staircase fills an inner hall, rising and returning in two wings. The newel posts still carry the Richmond crest, which resembles a strangely upright badger. Little remains of the furnishings of the old house, but care has been taken to protect what does survive. Neo-Jacobean plasterwork has been reinstated in a number of rooms. A fine overmantel adorns the panelled Oak Room upstairs, with twisted columns and Mannerist motifs. Conishead appears to be in safe hands.

DALEMAIN ***

3½m SW of Penrith
Georgian house built onto medieval core (P)

Sir Edward Hasell bought Dalemain in 1679. His descendants have lived there ever since. The photographs in the guidebook offer a gallery of Hasell ladies down the ages. Regency Dorothea Hasell is in a flurry of muslin and ribbons, inter-war Gertrude Hasell is in pearls and fur, and post-war Sylvia Hasell poses with dogs and cut flowers. Today, however, Jane Hasell-McCosh is pictured kneeling in the garden, hard at work in dungarees and with a trowel.

Their house sits proud on a slope overlooking the north end of Ullswater. Part pele tower, part Tudor and part Georgian, it is clearly in family use. The ostensibly severe exterior was built in 1744 to enclose the old house round a courtyard. Its soft pink ashlar with grey parapet looks across a fine garden to the water in the distance.

The approach from the main road sweeps round to the back of the house as though tourists were emphatically 'trade'. But the back forms an intriguing contrast to the elegant Georgian front. It displays the house as it has evolved from the Middle Ages. Three-storey barns surround a courtyard and the remains of the ancient settlement, as it would have sheltered in the shadow of the two pele towers. Here the back of the house is 16th century and earlier. The truncated towers and linking hall range are of roughcast stone.

Dalemain's interior has not been altered since the mid-18th century. The entrance hall contains a superb shallow staircase of rich local oak. The walls are of dark crimson hung with van Dycks. Deer trophies are from the estate. The adjacent dining room, known as the Chinese Room, is a brilliant chamber. Its chinoiserie wallpaper is in excellent repair, if odd in these most English of surroundings. Pheasants and foliage swirl upwards from the floor, with birds and insects added by hand when the paper was hung. The room also has an exquisite Rococo chimneypiece by Nathaniel Hedges in 'Chinese Chippendale' style, complete with fierce dragons. Portraits are by Zoffany and Devis.

The drawing room is oak panelled, its stern family portraits contrasting with jollier modern photographs. Beyond is a passage, devoted to relics of Cumbria's early railway age, leading to Dalemain's pele tower. This once belonged to John de Morville, whose brother Hugh was one of Becket's assassins. A room is a museum

Lakeland Chinese Chippendale at Dalemain

of the Westmorland and Cumberland Yeomanry, a troop of mounted infantry led traditionally by Hasells. It was 'a force of countrymen and horsemen bound together in a rare comradeship of neighbours and friends, all from the same district'. They were mounted on bicycles in the Great War and then disbanded.

Upstairs in the pele tower is a panelled chamber with geometrical ceiling, dating from the mid-16th century. Over the Tudor fireplace is a portrait of Lady Anne Clifford (Appleby, above), looking every bit a match for Cromwell. Her secretary was a Hasell. Beyond, in the second pele tower, are nurseries and a Victorian housekeeper's room.

The Old Hall below contains a giant fireplace kept ablaze on a cold afternoon. It serves as a teashop and is an ideal refuge from the Lakeland weather.

GRASMERE: DOVE COTTAGE ***

Town End, Grasmere
Wordsworth's home as a young man (M)

Visitors to Dove Cottage must expect to share it with the world. The Wordsworth Trust, like Stratford's Shakespeare Birthplace Trust, wrestles with the task of matching overwhelming demand to miniscule supply. The cottage in which the poet and his sister and wife lived for eight years from 1799 is Lilliputian. From spring to autumn, the place is under siege. Wordsworth was surely thinking of more than daffodils when he wrote, 'A poet could not but be gay/ In such a jocund company!/ I gazed – and gazed – but little thought/ What wealth the show to me had brought.'

The cottage is in the hamlet of Town End, just outside Grasmere (not to be confused with the house of that name). It was formerly an inn, The Dove and Olive. Here, the twenty-nine-year-old Wordsworth moved with his sister, Dorothy, and a seemingly endless troop of friends, including Southey, Hazlitt, Lamb, Walter Scott and Coleridge. They passed

the cottage to Thomas de Quincy in 1809. Wordsworth moved his growing family elsewhere in the village and, in 1813, to Rydal Mount (below).

Dove Cottage has been restored as near as possible to its original appearance, although the crowds require it to be stripped of domestic clutter. The parlour, that of the old inn, has a blazing fire and rich Georgian panelling. A rag rug covers the flagstone floor. Another fire burns in the spotless kitchen, with its candle-making equipment. A spring flows under the larder floor.

The cottage was the scene of Wordsworth's most fertile inspiration. He paced its tiny garden, his 'domestic slip of mountain', and gazed out over the ruffled waters of Grasmere. Upstairs is the sitting room where Wordsworth would return from composing in the open air and write from memory. His sister wrote that he 'laboured in that one room, common to all the family, to all visitors and where the children frequently play beside him'. Its old oak floorboards are still polished by hand every day. Here are Wordsworth's skates, cuckoo clock, cameo portraits and other mementos.

Next door are the simple, and minute, bedrooms. Fire grates are still blackened, windows leaded and pots and pictures arranged. One small room to the rear has been left wallpapered for warmth with yellowed copies of *The Times*. They are dated 1800, when the Budget Statement recorded the nation's total wealth as £54,566,206/9s/4d. Another sheet has an advertisement for Wordsworth's *Lyrical Ballads*.

Wordsworth wrote of a poet's home, 'This small abiding-place of many Men/ A termination and a last retreat,/ A centre, come from whereso'er you will,/ A Whole without dependence or defect,/ Made for itself and happy in itself,/ Perfect Contentment. Unity entire.'

The garden has been restocked with wild flowers and herbs. Climbers envelop the cottage walls. The library, shop and study centre are well concealed down the road. Dove Cottage is a homage fit to the man.

HILL TOP **

Near Sawrey, 2m SE of Hawkshead
Beatrix Potter's farm and inspiration (NT)

The house owned by Beatrix Potter during her most fruitful years is now a heavily visited shrine. This is no surprise. Potter reproduced every inch of the house, garden, lane and landscape in her book illustrations. The crossroads is Pigling Bland, the front path is Tom Kitten, the farmyard is Jemima Puddleduck and the gabled porch is almost everywhere.

Potter had visited the Lake District as a girl in the 1880s with her South Kensington parents (Wray, below). After the sudden death of her fiancé, Norman Warne, in 1905 she used the profits on her first books to buy Hill Top Farm. She left the farmer in residence, building a small extension for herself in which to write, paint and observe the animals and garden. She then used every penny she earned from her books to buy and protect property in the neighbourhood. She continued to live with her parents in London until, in 1913 at the age of forty-seven, she married the local lawyer, Willie Heelis, who had handled her purchases.

Although Potter never lived permanently at Hill Top and moved elsewhere when she married, she worked at the house, showed visitors round and fashioned it as a backdrop for her stories. Well before her death in 1943, she and Hill Top were internationally famous. She did not mind. Potter capitalized on every aspect of her celebrity, one of the first writers to market and franchise products generated by her characters. She patented 'Peter Rabbit' in 1903. The house is a museum created by Potter herself. She also became an expert Lakeland farmer and breeder of Herdwick sheep. A fierce conservationist, she bought and gave to the National Trust over 4,000 acres in the area.

The house is a curiosity rather than a beauty and visitors are ruthlessly bossed by the National Trust's warders. The familiar path through the front garden leads to a simple 17th-century farmhouse. The slate porch is covered by a rambling rose. The interior is small and fragile, furnished neither as a traditional farmhouse nor quite in keeping with the Adam-style fireplace, furniture and porcelain imported by Potter. Her taste is clearly that of a London lawyer's daughter.

Downstairs are the kitchen and the parlour, kept implausibly immaculate for what was a farm. The chief pleasure lies in identifying objects with scenes in the books. The dresser is that of my favourite, *The Tailor of Gloucester*. The Georgian staircase is *Samuel Whiskers* and the bedroom *Two Bad Mice*. The most popular room is the Treasure Room, built by Potter to display her collection of Lakeland objects and of the merchandise inspired by her characters. Here too are some of her original paintings and photographs, skills at which she was proficient. Potter's books and drawings fuelled a worldwide popularity for 'English cottage' vernacular. But there is more of her spirit in the hills outside.

HOLKER HALL ***

4½m W of Grange-over-Sands
Cavendish mansion rebuilt by Paley & Austin, lavish Crace interiors (P)

One night in March 1871, Lord Frederick Cavendish, son of the 7th Duke of Devonshire, was awoken by a crash and found his house on fire. Holker was gutted, its paintings and library destroyed. Only the neo-Jacobean wing remodelled in the 1830s by George Webster of Kendal survived. True to the spirit of the age, the family promptly rebuilt on an even grander scale. They commissioned the firm of Paley & Austin, doyens of late-Victorian architecture in the North-West. The result is sumptuous.

The property was owned by Cartmel Priory and passed by descent after the Dissolution to Prestons, Lowthers and then Cavendishes, who hold it still. The exterior offers a contrast in early and late Victorian between Webster's Jacobean and Paley & Austin's adjacent exuberance. The new building includes a massive tower, apparently modelled on a

pele, and another with a copper cupola. With high chimneys, strong gables and stone-mullioned windows, the style is assertively Elizabethan. In sunlight, the sandstone walls radiate an Umbrian red-brown.

The interiors are to match. Holker (pro-nounced Hooker) is almost indigestibly rich. Warm panelling combines with stone, marble and heavy fabric, as if this were the ladies' wing of an Imperial club. For decoration, Paley & Austin employed the ubiquitous firm of J. G. Crace, without whom few Victorian houses were complete. The drawing room walls are hung with Macclesfield silk.

The billiard room is in the deepest green, described by Crace as 'hand-stencilled with eight layers of paint'. It is dominated by four huge scenes from nature by Jacques-Charles Oudry. No less confident is the red dining room, its overmantel flanked by four twisted columns carved from local oak and framing a self-portrait by van Dyck. The staircase, beyond an arch of polished local limestone, embodies Tudor solidity. It looks as if it were hacked from a block of solid oak.

The bedrooms are as richly furnished as the downstairs reception rooms. There are beds in Hepplewhite style, washstand sets by Minton and a dressing-room collection of blue-and-white Wedgwood. The Gloucester dressing room contains prints of Brighton Pavilion. Its chimneypiece is an exquisitely carved work brought by the 5th Duke from a German monastery, a common source of furnishings for Regency grandees.

HUTTON-IN-THE-FOREST
****

6m NW of Penrith
Pele house with 17th- and 18th-century rooms, victorianized by Salvin (P)

How satisfying to find a 'forest' still in place. A clearing in the thick woodland north of Penrith reveals a shimmering palace of pink

Victorian mirror at Holker

stone lying seductively across a meadow and waited on by ornamental trees. Hutton has remained in the Fletcher Vane family, now Lords Inglewood, with a hop, skip and change of name since 1605.

The original house was one pele linked to another by the customary northern device of a linking Great Hall. The house was bought in 1605 by a Jacobean knight, Sir Richard Fletcher, whose son built the Renaissance gallery and cloister that flanks the forecourt. His son, in turn, built the suave new front and entrance hall around 1685. The architect was Edward Addison. To this already remark-able building, the Fletcher Vanes in the late Georgian period had George Webster of Kendal add a great tower, pivotal in the com-position of the two principal fronts. Anthony Salvin's 1860s revisions to Hutton are among his most successful essays in medieval revival.

Entry is under the old pele tower into the original barrel-vaulted Stone Hall. Grim as any dungeon, it is hung with a fearsome variety of weapons. This medieval hall adjoins the new hall erected by the Fletchers in the 1680s: the earlier hall retains its original panelling and large fireplace.

The most prominent feature of the new hall is the bottom of the magnificent Cupid Stair-case. This dates from the 1680 remodelling and is gloriously vulgar. The putti do not merely adorn foliage or trophies in the baluster panels. They blow themselves up into grotesque nudes, completely filling the panels. I have seen nothing like them: they should have a parental guidance certificate. The staircase rises to a Mortlake tapestry and leads at right angles into the earlier Renaissance wing.

Although built in the 1640s, this gallery still has an Elizabethan air. A circular tower by the entrance looks out in contemplation over a walled garden, a wonderfully romantic spot. The south-facing windows survey the entrance court. Centuries of Fletchers gaze down from the walls. Shelves are filled with oriental porcelain. This is a superb room.

The Victorian library, created by Salvin over the hall, is lit by the five upper windows of the hall façade. It leads straight into the new wing,

built by Webster and amended by Salvin at his most light-hearted. Still Regency rather than Victorian in atmosphere, it is filled with Gillow furniture and family portraits. The windows look out over the ornamental gardens and a most satisfying fall in contour. Salvin's rear staircase is lined with tapestries and a portrait of Sir Frederick Vane's huntsman, John Peel. He set a record in his profession, a single run of 70 miles in the 1830s, celebrated in the song, 'Do y'ken John Peel'.

The Cupid Room takes its name from the exquisite ceiling supplied to Henry Fletcher in the 1740s by Robert Adam's master stuccoist, Joseph Rose the Elder. Its central roundel depicts a cupid far more demure than his fellows on the old staircase. The room is a Georgian jewel, with fine doorcases and an overmantel framing a small Hogarth.

An 18th-century bedroom has recently been decorated in a heavy Victorian style with William Morris paper and Arts and Crafts furniture. Morris wallpaper was also chosen for the dining room downstairs, graced with a modern chandelier in Art Nouveau style. The latter is decorated with cherries borrowed from the curtains and acanthus from the wallpaper.

ISEL HALL **

4½m NE of Cockermouth
Pele with Elizabethan range, painted panels
(P-R)

On its eminence above a bend in the River Dewent, Isel from a distance looks more like a fortified town than a house. Even close to, the heavy pele tower and three-storey Elizabethan range is austere. This is the ancestral home of the Leigh and Lawson families, by devious inheritance from the 14th century to the death of Margaret Austen Leigh in 1986. The house is now occupied by a distant cousin, Mary Burkett, former director of Abbot Hall, Kendal (below). She was recently introduced to the

Hutton's late-flowering Renaissance

Prince of Wales as 'the maddest woman in Cumbria'. This may apply to all those saints who devote their lives to the rescue of old houses.

The pele tower at Isel was rebuilt after a Scottish raid in 1388. It is oblong and unusually large, and has recently received a fierce pink covering in what is called lime-harling. It beams like a beacon down the valley. The main flank of the house is extraordinary. The original Great Hall, once detached from the pele, was extended in 1573 to form an extensive façade to the courtyard. It is a range of chambers just one room deep, unadorned in the rough northern style but with curious obelisks along the parapet.

The interior reflects a home much altered as succeeding generations wrestled to make an essential medieval plan conform to changing demands. The Hall, now a dining room, with its ceiling of c1520, has rich woodwork with fine linenfold panelling.

Beyond is an Oak Room with the ghostly outline of paintings on its panels. These appear mostly to represent the crests and arms of the first Lawson owner, presumably celebrating the acquisition of Isel by marriage in 1573. There are more such panels in the room above. Isel is filled with family memorabilia, warm, dark and eccentric.

KENDAL: ABBOT HALL *

Highgate
Georgian mansion, now an art gallery (M)

The mansion sits on the bank of the River Kent next to Kendal's sprawling parish church, forming rather an odd couple. The Gothic church has five wayward gables to the river, each of a different proportion. The house is Georgian and prim. Two canted bays separate three Venetian windows, all in soft ochre stone. In front is a demure lawn with municipal fencing.

The house was built for Colonel George Wilson, traditionally by Carr of York. Historians of inflation will note that it cost £8,000 to build in 1759, was sold in 1772 for £4,500, in

1788 for £2,650, in 1801 for £3,900 and in 1897 to the local council for £3,750, largely for its modest grounds. A century later that amount might buy a tenth of its garage.

The house was lucky to survive. It now houses the Abbot Hall Art Gallery which, since the 1960s, has acquired an excellent small collection of English paintings. Some effort has been made to render the downstairs rooms domestic, with furniture by Gillow of Lancaster. The main hall runs from front to back of the house, divided by handsome Doric columns. The old dining room has good plasterwork and doorcases.

These rooms contain works by William Larkin, Hogarth, Reynolds, Joseph Wright and a fine group by George Romney. The Green Room is dedicated to the memory of the 17th-century Lady Anne Clifford (Appleby, above). Two side panels of Jan van Belcamp's picture of the lady show her at the ages of fifteen and fifty-six. The main central panel is too big to exhibit, so I am told. Any public gallery that cannot display its major work should give it to someone who can. (In 2003, the panel went on loan to Tate Britain in London, sadly far from Cumbria.)

Another downstairs room contains watercolours of the Lake District, by Turner, Ruskin, Girtin and others. The upstairs rooms are a modern museum.

LEVENS HALL ****

5m S of Kendal
Elizabethan house in continuous family occupation, topiary garden (P)

Levens Hall speaks the comforts of the Elizabethan age better than any house in the north of England. The madcap guard of honour of yew trees, the medieval façade and rich Elizabethan interiors embody an architecture that has rarely been out of fashion. The house was a 13th-century pele tower and hall, converted by James Bellingham after 1580 into a gentleman's residence. Its acquisition by a member of the Howard dynasty, probably in settlement of a gambling debt, fixed Levens in

time. The hearts depicted on the rainwater heads are said to refer to it being 'won on the turn of an ace of hearts'. Howards married Grahmes who in turn married Bagots. The house remains in that family today.

What Levens lacks in grandeur it has in intimacy. The informal, rendered front reflects the architecture of the rooms inside. A four-storey pele tower stands out to the right of the entrance, with asymmetrical cross-wings on either side. The main reception rooms face the topiary garden, designed in the 1690s by Guillaume Beaumont. This is one of the oldest, oddest and most distinguished such gardens in England. Its strange, anthropomorphic shapes seem to fuse every corner of the house and people it with ghosts.

The front door opens directly onto the Great Hall, a rarity in a medieval house where entry was normally into a screens passage. The interiors at Levens seem at first overly modern. The Great Hall is carpeted, with sofas and a wood-burning stove in the fireplace. Many of the upstairs rooms were repanelled and furnished by the Howards in a neo-Jacobean style after 1818. These were depicted in the 1840s by the ubiquitous antiquarian artist, Joseph Nash, who wrote of Levens' 'genial warmth'. Yet Levens today is much as Nash saw it, the Elizabethan and neo-Elizabethan interiors barely distinguishable. This is an inhabited house, its rooms like its art adapted by families over generations.

The hall fireplace is surmounted by an excellent coat of arms of Elizabeth I, with a lion and Welsh dragon rampant. The theme of James Bellingham's loyalty to his Queen is repeated almost tediously throughout the house. When she died, a distraught Bellingham rode over to Durham to greet the new Scottish monarch, James I, on the latter's slow and celebrated progress south. He then returned to Levens and never left it for his remaining thirty-eight years.

To the left of the hall is the old Great Chamber. The original panelling is lozenge

Ghostly Levens from the gardens

patterned. Fluted pilasters mark the corners and flank the rich oak chimneypiece, heavy with coats of arms. A deep bay window looks out over the formal garden. Over one door, a statue of Bellingham appears to be holding a shield over his private parts. The walls are hung with Lelys and a fine Rubens of Anne of Hungary.

Equally fine is the adjacent Small Drawing Room, with its chimneypiece portraying the Four Seasons and Five Senses. They are accompanied by numerous American Indians, a sign of cosmopolitan sophistication in an Elizabethan house. The room contains a collection of Napoleonic memorabilia, a Bagot having married one of Wellington's favourite nieces. He gave her a number of Sèvres and Dresden depictions of the great man, and Napoleon's clasp found in his carriage after Waterloo.

The upstairs bedrooms in this wing were mostly repanelled by the Howards, although one has fine antique leather wall-hangings. The ceilings are mostly neo-Jacobean. The Redman bedroom contains Gillow furniture, the Lancaster firm also supplying an early water closet.

In the dressing room is some of the oldest English patchwork, executed by the early 18th-century Grahme daughters at 32 stitches to the inch. I wonder how many 'daughters of the house' could today achieve that output of craftsmanship.

The house now returns downstairs to the library with an overmantel composed of Elizabethan fragments. Here is a rare portrait of a child by Aelbert Cuyp. The dining room, its walls covered in embossed and painted Cordoban leather, has a set of robust Charles II chairs.

Levens is alive with family history. Every wall seems devoted to old pictures of the house, to documents, miniatures, weapons, costumes and needlework. There are paintings grand and simple, china rare and ordinary. Objects seem to have no purpose, except that a Bellingham, Howard or Bagot at some point acquired them and hoped that posterity would find them interesting.

LOWTHER CASTLE *

4m S of Penrith
Dramatic façade of Regency mansion (P-R)

Lowther Castle is open to the skies, if not as yet to the public. Its surroundings are so suborned by agribusiness as to drive any visitor west into the welcoming arms of the Lake District. At present, there are plans to restore and revive the old buildings. Ostentatiously built for show across the valley from the village of Askham, they can be admired from the road.

The original castle was begun by the 1st Viscount Lowther but burned down in 1720. It was eventually rebuilt by the young Robert Smirke in 1806, this being his first major commission on returning from a tour of classical antiquities in Italy and Greece. The drama of the setting demanded dramatic architecture, and got it. Smirke designed a medieval castle on a hillside across a sloping park, facing the old Lowther mausoleum on the edge of a ravine. He showed himself a true successor to Vanbrugh as architect of scenic theatre.

The house has a central keep, a curtain wall, turrets and angle pavilions. From a distance, the main front can be seen to rise in a series of battlemented tiers. The interior, which contained excellent plasterwork, was gutted and unroofed in 1957 and is now mostly a ruin. Even Pevsner was moved by the family's plight. While deploring its ruination, he added, 'Yet what pain must it be to the owners to live so near this memorial of past glories.' Other owners of great houses managed to keep their memorials in good repair and accessible. Lowther is now on its mettle.

MIREHOUSE ***

4m NW of Keswick
Old Lakeland manor, refuge of Romantic poets (P)

At Mirehouse, the present fights the past in amiable combat. It overlooks Bassenthwaite, a magical lake. The massive flank of Skiddaw rises to the east, Grisedale Pike to the south-west. The house sits alone in its park, attended by a stand of Scots pines. Here, the ghosts of Wordsworth, Tennyson, Carlyle and their genial hosts, the Spedding brothers, fill the rooms and pace the grounds. Every corner is occupied by anecdote, to the point where the house is in danger of being a mausoleum of poetic inspiration.

Mirehouse's charm lies in its setting and the orchards and outbuildings restored by the Speddings, who still live at Mirehouse. This setting includes a herb garden, heather maze, lovers' lane and bee garden. Everywhere offers views over the lake and mountains.

The house itself is enjoyable rather than architecturally distinguished. The modest 17th-century manor was given a more substantial rear in the 19th century. As a result, the front and back ranges are startlingly different in scale.

The interior is essentially a memorial to the Spedding brothers, James and Tom, and their friends among the Romantics of the early 19th century. The house was inherited in 1802 by their father, John, who sent the boys to study in Bury St Edmunds and Cambridge. They felt no need to 'go up to London', being content with the society and stimulus of the North. James became a scholar of Bacon and turned down an offer of the Regius Professorship of History at Cambridge. Tom wrote a book on the reform of the Poor Laws and became High Sheriff of Cumberland. They entertained writers visiting the Lake District. After the death of his friend, Arthur Hallam, Tennyson sold a poetry medal for £15 to pay for the stagecoach fare to Mirehouse in 1835.

The front rooms are those of a cultured gentleman of the early 19th century. In the smoking room is a collection of Bacon memorabilia. The library ranges wide over the interests of the Speddings, with not just poetry but philosophy, science and the classics. The drawing room is chiefly dedicated to Tennyson, including photographs of him by Julia Margaret Cameron.

The study is devoted to Wordsworth and the Lakes, with stuffed ducks and Lakeland watercolours. Everywhere are ticking clocks, letters from celebrities, drawing desks and needlepoint stools. Mirehouse is more than the sum of its parts. It is the Lake District with hand on heart.

MUNCASTER CASTLE ***

2m E of Ravenglass
Salvin recreation of ancient castle (P)

Muncaster clings to the side of the Eskdale ravine at Ravenglass like a fantasy castle on the Upper Rhine. Its 77 acres of woodland walks and gardens in spring are ablaze with rhododendrons, azaleas, magnolias, maples and camellias. The Terrace Walk is the finest scenic promenade in Lakeland.

The gardens have long been eccentric and today embrace an Owl Centre and a 'Meadow Vole Maze'. Muncaster, says its owner, 'lives entirely through the warmth and understanding which visitors bring during the summer months' – a handsome welcome which all houses might imitate.

The castle has been owned by Penningtons and their ancestors since 1208. The present owner glories in the name of Phyllida Gordon-Duff-Pennington. In 1464, Sir John Pennington sheltered the hapless Henry VI, who left his drinking bowl with a blessing that the family would prosper while it remained unbroken. Known as the Luck of Muncaster, it is wisely held in a vault, with a facsimile on display.

The present house is essentially of 1862 by Anthony Salvin, in his neo-medieval maturity. I like to think of old Salvin arriving at these northern castles and clapping his hands with delight at the opportunity they offered. His building incorporated an old pele tower in a rambling low-slung mansion of grey-pink stone.

The interior was completely rebuilt by Salvin. The Great Hall replicates the original and is filled with paintings, wood carving and heraldic windows. The guide apologizes for the family dogs lolling on chairs next to 'please do not touch' signs.

Pride of place at Muncaster goes to the

library. It dates from 1780 but was relocated by Salvin on the site of the medieval kitchen. Octagonal in shape, it rises two storeys to a Gothic vault. The oak panelling seems designed to complement the bindings of the books. From the gallery above, Penningtons gaze down in approbation, including the last Lord Muncaster who was kidnapped by brigands in Greece in 1870. He looks more like one of his captors.

The dining room has walls coated in leather embossed with gold leaf, in poor condition but apparently impossible to restore. The pictures are mostly copies, including a remarkable 'Titian' by Gainsborough.

The main staircase is adorned with a great treasure, a set of marble reliefs by Canova of ladies dancing, apparently up to bed. The bedrooms contain much old woodwork and other antique fittings gathered from elsewhere by members of the family.

Rare Elizabethan tapestry panels hang in the passage, depicting couples cavorting in a castle landscape. Here too is a portrait of Tom Skelton, the 'last Fool of Muncaster'. He gave us the word tomfoolery and looks uncannily like Tony Blair.

In total contrast is Salvin's barrel-vaulted drawing room downstairs. It is in soft blue and white. The walls comprise a fine exhibition of family portraits by or after Lely, Kneller, Reynolds and Lawrence. The finest, and most swaggering, is a de Laszlo of Lady Ramsden, the present owner's grandmother.

RYDAL MOUNT **

1½m N of Ambleside
The home of Wordsworth's maturity (M)

William and Mary Wordsworth and their three surviving children arrived at Rydal Mount with his sister, Dorothy, in 1813. They stayed until the poet's death thirty-seven years later.

Wordsworth had gained an appointment as local Distributor of Stamps. He was financially

Mirehouse and Bassenthwaite

secure and on his way to becoming Poet Laureate. More remarkable, his political opinions were turning away from the youthful radicalism of Dove Cottage. He even opposed the 1832 Reform Bill, leading a new generation of poets to pour scorn on him. It was of Wordsworth that Browning wrote, 'Just for a handful of silver he left us, just for a ribbon to pin on his coat.'

I prefer to see Rydal as Wordsworth returning to the Cockermouth background of his childhood. It is certainly not the Bohemian residence of a poor poet but the comfortable home of a public official. The house sits on a steep slope north of Ambleside. A fine 4-acre garden slopes down towards Rydal Water. The original building was a 16th-century cottage, surviving as the present dining room. It is heavily beamed and retains its spice cupboard. A mezzotint of Wordsworth's early hero, Robert Burns, has pride of place over the mantelpiece.

Of the library, Wordsworth's servant said that it was 'where he keeps his books: his study is out of doors'. The portrait of the poet in his seventies by the American artist, Henry Inman, so delighted Mary that she insisted he paint a copy. The room has since been knocked through into the drawing room, and the old cottage extended into a substantial house. The result is a sitting room so conventional in appearance that we expect to see a television in a corner. The contrast with Dove Cottage could hardly be greater.

The bedrooms upstairs contain various Wordsworth memorabilia not already claimed by rivals at Dove Cottage or Cockermouth. There are vivid pictures of Wordsworth ladies, of the 'faultless' Mary, the devoted Dorothy and the adored daughter, Dora, whose death in 1847 from tuberculosis deeply affected the poet for the rest of his life.

At the top of the house is Wordsworth's study. Display cases detract from its atmosphere. This is sad because the little window in this room has the most evocative of all Wordsworth views. It looks out through a frame of wisteria to his 'study' beyond, the mountains and lakes of Cumberland.

SIZERGH CASTLE ****

3½m S of Kendal
Massive pele tower with Elizabethan
additions (NT)

Sizergh is the ancient seat of the Stricklands,
residents since the 13th century, now as tenants
of the National Trust. Stricklands prospered
during wars against the Scots and the French.
They carried the banner of St George at
Agincourt and sided with the Yorkists in the
Wars of the Roses. Under the Tudors they
married Parrs and Nevilles and prospered
further. Only in the 17th century did Fortune
turn her back on them. Catholic marriages,
attendance on the exiled James II in France
and a genetic propensity to gambling brought
poverty if not ruin. This preserved Sizergh
from demolition or substantial alteration. It
stands with its neighbour, Levens Hall, as twin
glories of the Elizabethan North.

The core of the house is a Cumbrian
familiar: a massive pele tower with medieval
hall attached, and Elizabethan wings much
embellished over time. The wings form two
low flanks to a central courtyard, now privately
occupied. The tower itself is visible on the
right, with a Gothic coat of arms on its façade.
The old hall in the middle is concealed behind
a Georgian front. Its porch was altered by
the Victorians to bring carriages under the
house to shelter, a rare convenience in English
country houses (found also at Raby Castle/
Durham).

This entrance hall, no longer for carriages,
now contains a magnificent screen, probably
from the original Elizabethan hall overhead.
The latter had been built in the 1550s but
destroyed in 1773 to create the present Georgian drawing room overhead. A flight of stone
steps leads up to the first floor, on the landing
of which is one of Sizergh's treasures, a scagliola table made in 1708 with birds and flowers
surrounding the Strickland arms.

The medieval rooms to the left of the hall
comprise two storeys of intimate chambers.
The Stone Parlour has a Ferneley painting over
the mantelpiece and the old dining room

contains some outstanding marquetry furniture. Elizabethan bedrooms spill from one
into another. The wood panelling, much of it
moved here and there over time, is excellent,
especially the swirling overmantel in the
Boynton Room.

The Georgian drawing room comes as
something of a shock amid Sizergh's heavy
features and dark woodwork. It has sky-blue
walls, a high ceiling and tall, effete wall niches.
To make matters more fragile, it is filled with a
collection of European and Oriental ceramics,
including an exquisite pair of rustic boys in
'soft-paste' porcelain.

The old pele tower is on the right of the
hall, its once-gaunt spaces now comfortable
reception rooms. The old Great Chamber
is now the dining room, its Serlian ceiling
and carved chimneypiece similar to those at
Levens, possibly the work of the same craftsmen. Stuart portraits line the walls and the
shelves carry relics of the family's time in
Jacobite exile in Paris after 1688. Lady Strickland was governess to the future 'James III',
whose unfortunate portrait as a chubby boy
hangs in this room. He was the Old Pretender
and father of Bonnie Prince Charlie, whose
bust is also displayed. This was a house of
doomed loyalties.

The present banqueting hall was the
medieval family solar, with deep-set windows
and adze-hewn floorboards. A gallery surrounds its upper storey. Rich Elizabethan
benches at the long table are decorated with
carvings in strange imitation of hide.

Next door is Sizergh's showpiece, the Inlaid
Chamber. The plaster ceiling drips with Elizabethan pendants. There is armorial glass in
the windows and a domed internal porch.
Most glorious is the panelling, considered the
most elaborate of its Elizabethan date in any
English house. Arched panels based on Italian
Renaissance motifs are inlaid with poplar and
bog-oak to give a glimmering sheen, as if the
wood itself were impregnated with precious
metal. In the 19th century, this sumptuous
room was sold by a cash-strapped Strickland
to the V&A Museum in London for £1,000,
plus £400 for the bed. To the credit of that

The Inlaid Chamber at Sizergh

museum, the entire room has been loaned back and reinstalled.

Sizergh's garden falls away across lawns to a lake. To the north is a celebrated rock garden from which there are romantic glimpses of the house's gables and tower.

STORRS HALL *

2m S of Bowness-on-Windermere
Classical villa by lake (H)

Storrs recalls Windermere in its Victorian hey-day, with picnics on the shore and candlelit barges on the lake. In 1825, Wordsworth, Southey and Walter Scott, crowned as 'bards of the Lakes', attended such an occasion. The host was John Bolton of Storrs Hall, Liverpool plutocrat and slave-trader. By then, this was already a disreputable business.

Today, Storrs is a luxury hotel. Standing at the end of a lakeside lawn, it is a bold, almost beefy, classical villa built onto an existing early Georgian house, fragments of which survive to the rear. The architect of the new building in 1808 was J. M. Gandy, assistant to Sir John Soane.

The house is covered in bright stucco. The entrance is behind a bold Doric porch inside which a small hall gives onto a grander one. This rises two storeys on stately Ionic columns. Its staircase has been well restored, with portraits and hunting trophies gazing down from the walls. Equally fine are the main reception rooms, still with their Regency plasterwork medallions and anthemion friezes.

At the back, a conservatory looks out over

Windermere. On a bright day, the water's reflection shimmers over the grass and bounces off the stucco.

SWARTHMOOR HALL **
1m SW of Ulverston
Quaker headquarters in Jacobean house (P)

Swarthmoor was the northern home of the Quakers. Built in 1586, it later belonged to the Fell family, Judge Thomas Fell being Chancellor of the Duchy of Lancaster. One of Quakerism's founding fathers, George Fox, visited the house in 1652. Both Fell and his wife, Margaret, came under his charismatic influence. Fell continued to attend church, but when his wife held meetings in the house he sat quietly in his study, listening through an open door. Fell died in 1658 and Margaret married Fox, becoming leader of the movement in the North and serving four years in Lancaster prison for her beliefs.

The house later suffered from decay but in 1912 was bought and restored by Emma Clarke Abraham, a Fell descendant. It was sold to the Society of Friends in 1954 and is still dedicated to the 'sweet peace' of Quakerism.

The view of the front of the house from the garden is charming, with the Hall on the right and an eccentric single canted bay on the left, rising three storeys to the attic. It is all lopsided. A balcony over the door is one from which Fox is said to have preached to a crowd outside – although preaching was not a Quaker practice. The entrance leads into a screens passage and the hall. The latter is panelled and furnished as the family eating room, with stools for chairs. Beyond is Fell's study, with its door through which he listened to meetings in the hall.

The staircase is most unusual. It rises round a so-called four-post newel, probably intended to support not just the stair but the roof. Fell's bedroom has been refurnished in Elizabethan style, with Renaissance fireplace surround, carved bed-head and magnificent chest. It retains its internal porch. The bed is original to the house.

TOWNEND ***
Troutbeck, 2½m N of Windermere
Ancient yeoman's house (NT)

The house appears to be that of an unaltered Lakeland farm. Whitewashed stone walls rise past small windows to a sloping roof and round Cumberland chimneys. Opposite is a fine 17th-century barn flanking the road. The ensemble, far from the Windermere crowds below, is a Lakeland timewarp.

Yet the house is not all it seems. It was home to the Brownes since the 16th century. Though always farmers, they became prosperous professionals, notably in the law. The Victorian owner was the antiquary, George Browne, who died in 1914. He preserved the house and amassed a library of 2,000 books. A master carver, he also both collected and created the ornamental woodwork with which the interior is embellished. What is old and what is his is near impossible to tell. His daughter died in 1943, after which the property passed to the National Trust.

This is a place of Cumbrian terminology. Entry is into the 'Down House' or kitchen, where a fire burns in a range festooned with hooks and pans. A grandfather clock ticks in the background. Steps lead up to a screens passage or 'Hallan' and into the main parlour with its big fireplace, known as the 'Fire House'.

The interiors are dark and oak rich. In the Fire House, the original fireplace has gone but one can still see where there used to be a projecting hood under which the family and servants would have sat for warmth, wearing hats to protect themselves from rain-filled soot coming down the chimney. It has been replaced with a Victorian stove. A huge 'board' or table occupies the space under the mullioned window. Here every member of the farm community would have eaten. The room is now full of spinning wheels, guns, pikes, rushlights and heavy Jacobean chairs. Many carry carvings by Browne, including his bizarre emblem and 'coat of arms': he chose a Hapsburg double-headed eagle.

Behind the Fire House is the library. The

books are mostly on law, but also farming, topography and religion. It is the collection of a Lakeland yeoman, largely self-educated, well read and proud of his locality. The carpet is of Cumberland Herdwick wool, coloured with vegetable dyes. Browne bred his own upland sheep and had them painted, over and again, by the local artist, William Longmire.

The bedrooms upstairs are carefully divided between the family or 'posh' end of the house and the servants' end. The former displays Browne at his most effusive. The so-called state bedroom has panels, frames, bed-heads, chairs and cribs coated in carvings from the 17th to the 19th centuries. Browne's 'naïve' portrait is by the window.

This is the house of a comfortable Lake District family that had neither the inclination nor the money to rebuild, and who took satisfaction in the antiquity of their inheritance. Visited in solitude, Townend is the most evocative Lakeland house.

WORKINGTON HALL *

1m E of Workington
Ruin of Curwen seat (P)

Few sights so embody the poverty of the North's heritage than Workington Hall. This was among the grandest houses of Cumbria. Home of the Curwens, rivals of the Cliffords and Lonsdales, it sits on a precipice above the River Derwent on the outskirts of Workington. It is still surrounded by its old park, yet the mostly ruined house, on which public money was spent in 1970, is closed and padlocked in the care of the local council.

It is still possible to walk round the walls of the house and see through the grille into its interior. On the precipice side is an old pele tower with a flanking 14th-century range. A medieval gatehouse guards the 'inland' side of a large surviving quadrangle. This is bounded by Elizabethan wings, which were extensively remodelled by Carr of York in the 18th century. The house was sold by the Curwens to the local council after the Second World War and then left to decay.

As a result, the later work was dismantled in 1972 on government advice in order to display the earlier structure more effectively. Yet all that is visible today is the ghost of Carr's internal façade. Rooms stand open to the sky. Stairs lead nowhere. Everything is a dangerous structure, awaiting stabilization and reopening to the public. Only the park retains the dignity of a great family, foolish enough to trust their inheritance to the public sector.

WRAY CASTLE *

3m S of Ambleside
Baronial castle as belvedere folly (P)

From a distance, the castle looks like a rich man's folly – and it was. Turrets rise across a magnificent landscaped park which stretched eastwards towards Windermere. Wray was built in 1840 for a Liverpool surgeon, James Dawson, at a cost of £60,000, in the most extravagant neo-Romantic style. The architect was H. P. Horner. It was one of the few new buildings admired by Wordsworth.

The estate has long been the property of the National Trust, which at one time thought to demolish the castle and retain only the park. The castle's most prominent feature is a gigantic *porte-cochère* with battlemented turrets, arrow slits and machicolations. The outside is bleak and wholly lacking in the picture windows which might have been inserted, considering the site overlooking Windermere. Inside, a grand staircase rises from the entrance up to the central hall, which itself rises the full height of the central tower. Horner's medievalism was at least thorough.

The castle has passed through many hands, including recent use as a radar school. It is currently a training centre. The grounds are open to the public and access is permitted to the main hall and stairs. The castle's most implausible claim to fame was as inspiration for *Peter Rabbit*. The Potter family from South Kensington used to rent Wray for holidays when their daughter, Beatrix, was a young girl. It was at Wray that she fell in love with the Lake District and its fauna.

Derbyshire

Derbyshire is a prince among counties. The sweeping heights and valleys of the Peak District to the west was long a land of magnates, but even the coal country to the east saw a phalanx of stately houses which, in their day, might have rivalled the châteaux of the Loire.

As a result, Derbyshire has first-rate buildings of almost all periods. Haddon Hall is a defining house of the Middle Ages, astonishingly intact in its thickly wooded valley. The Elizabethan age is nowhere better displayed than in the works associated with Bess of Hardwick: Old Hardwick is derelict but the new hall she built next door is the most complete so-called prodigy house in England, designed in the large part by Bess herself. Her Cavendish sons developed both Bolsover and Chatsworth. The Little Castle at Bolsover is an exquisite pavilion of 'courtly love', to which the Jacobean William Cavendish added a sumptuous palace.

Later in the century, the Vernons built Sudbury, with its rich staircase carving and plasterwork. To the brief era of English Baroque can be attributed Calke, Sutton Scarsdale and most of the Chatsworth interiors. To compete with this ostentatious Whiggery, the Tory Curzons had Robert Adam design cold, magnificent Kedleston.

In the 19th century, Derbyshire did not live up to what had gone before. The 6th Duke of Devonshire brought Jeffry Wyatville to help him extend, but mercifully not transform, Chatsworth. The Sitwells extended exotic Renishaw. Since then, Derbyshire has deservedly rested on its laurels.

Barlborough **	Derby:	Melbourne ***
Bolsover ****	Pickford's House *	Renishaw ***
Calke ***	Eyam **	Sudbury ***
Carnfield Hall **	Haddon *****	Sutton Scarsdale *
Catton Hall **	Hardwick:	Tissington **
Chatsworth *****	Hall *****	Wingfield **
Chesterfield:	Old Hall *	
Revolution House *	Kedleston ****	

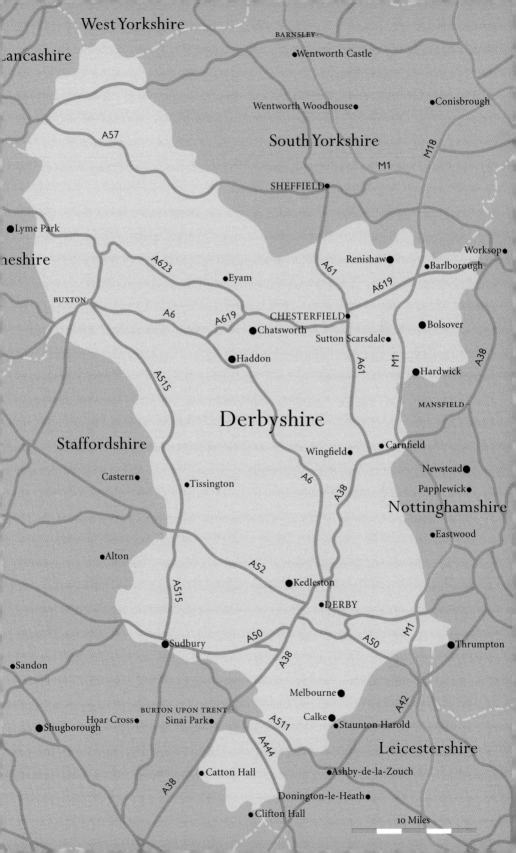

BARLBOROUGH HALL **

1m N of Barlborough, 8m W of Worksop
Elizabethan mansion by Robert Smythson
(P-R)

From a distance, Barlborough is a miniature Hardwick. Lofty towers of honeyed Derbyshire stone rise above a feast of windows. This is no rough Tudor hall. It displays the compact Renaissance symmetry of Robert Smythson. A stone's throw from the M1, Barlborough is a jewel in its landscape.

The house was built by an Elizabethan judge, Sir Francis Rodes, whose patron was Bess of Hardwick's husband, the Earl of Shrewsbury. He was thus in the Smythson orbit. The date on the outside is 1583.

The house remained in the Rodes family, later named Locker-Lampson, until the 1930s when the house was sold to the Jesuits for a prep. school which it remains today. Every stick of furniture and any removable fittings were sold, a truly tragic loss from a house of such importance. Conversion into a school has spoiled most of the interior with partitions and cheap furniture. The rooms are shown on request but the exterior of Barlborough is best.

The house sits on a high basement, with internal chimneys and corner towers, all Smythson signatures. The whole building seems to be straining after verticality. This is a wonderfully poised composition, English architecture at the moment of its emergence from the dark Middle Ages into the light of Reason.

Inside, the reception rooms are arranged round a narrow internal courtyard, now glazed. Of surviving fragments, the Great Chamber is used as a chapel and retains a 1584 overmantel. This is formal and classical, carrying the coats of arms of Rodes and his two wives. The contrast could hardly be greater with the adjacent parlour. Its overmantel of 1697 is alive with New World motifs and acanthus leaves.

Other rooms are smothered in ubiquitous school notices, pasted watercolours and other paraphernalia. In one, I glimpsed a delightful dolphin frieze.

BOLSOVER CASTLE ****

Bolsover
Pavilion of courtly love with Renaissance fireplaces (EH)

First, forget the idea of castle. Seen from the M1, Bolsover may look like a fortress but it is rather a fairytale palace on a hill. Bolsover was built on the basis of an earlier keep by Sir Charles Cavendish, son of Bess of Hardwick, whose own house stands on the same ridge four miles to the south. Working with John Smythson (son of Robert) from 1612, Cavendish intended Bolsover's Little Castle to be the embodiment of Elizabethan Renaissance romanticism and refinement continued into the reign of James I. It was a folly, a morality tale, a Shakespearean conceit, architecture as lovers' masque.

Charles Cavendish died in 1616 before the project was complete and building was resumed by his son, William. The latter entered fully into the spirit of his father's imagination, now asking Smythson for an additional palace adjacent to the Little Castle. To this, he added a Riding House round an inner courtyard. These additions, now mostly ruined, are hugely exciting works of Stuart architecture.

There are thus two separate elements to Renaissance Bolsover, the one still Elizabethan in ethos, the other Jacobean and ostentatious. To understand these two elements, one must understand William Cavendish, a man of his new age. In total contrast to his domineering, essentially medieval, grandmother, Bess of Hardwick, he displayed courtly life at its most engaging and fastidious. 'Ceremony,' he wrote, 'though it is nothing in itself, yet it does everything.' He travelled like a French courtier, his equestrian retinue trained to perfection. At soldiering, Cavendish was useless. When called on to defend the North for the King in the Civil War, he failed at Marston Moor in 1644 and fled to the Continent. For this and for his preference for 'sweet company' he was not forgiven by many Royalists, yet at the Restoration he was made Duke of Newcastle and allowed to complete his palace.

His descendants eventually moved the contents of Bolsover to their seat at Welbeck and the old castle and palace became derelict. The outer walls still stand and the Riding House, with shoeing hall and stable building, remains complete and is even used for riding lessons. The Little Castle beyond became a rectory in the 19th century before passing to the government in 1945. It has been superbly restored.

The walk through the Great Court displays these contrasting styles and uses. To the left, the spreading walls of William's palace reveal superb views over the valley below. The outside aspect of these walls is unlike anything in England: giant rusticated pilasters and pedimented windows form a façade of Baroque robustness.

The Little Castle beyond is reached through a wall to the Fountain Garden. Here a lawn, once presumably a knot garden, is overlooked by a Renaissance 'Romeo and Juliet' window. The interiors, begun by Charles and completed by William, are unequalled in England as expressions of Elizabethan romanticism. The Little Castle was built, wrote Mark Girouard, 'not for genuine barons of the Middle Ages . . . but for the half-allegorical knights and ladies of Spenser, Sidney and Ariosto, with names like Florimel, Calepine and Triamond'. The cult of the Virgin Queen gave rise to an obsession with medieval chivalry and fantastical contests of courtly love. Ceremonial tournaments were held in the yard below, albeit with few injuries.

The stone chambers of the Little Castle are part medieval, part Serlian Renaissance in style. The decorative themes are those of the literary and emotional obsession of late-Elizabethan England. To the left of the entrance is an ante-room with wall-paintings depicting the humours, melancholic, choleric and phlegmatic. The fourth, sanguinity, was represented by William himself. Next door is the hall, with a vaulted ceiling, mock Gothic fireplace and murals of the Labours of Hercules. Here William and his friends dressed in medieval costume and prepared for jousts and lovers' trysts.

The adjacent Pillar Parlour is nothing short of sensational, possibly copied by Smythson from the Great Parlour in the vanished Cecil palace of Theobalds in Hertfordshire. It has murals of the Senses and richly embossed panelling beneath classicized Gothic vaulting. It may have been here that Charles I and his Queen received their 'stupendous entertainment' in 1634. The feast reputedly cost Cavendish £15,000 and left him debt-ridden for life.

The parlour is rivalled only by the Star Chamber upstairs. The ceiling has geometrical panels painted blue and with stars. The wall-paintings represent Old Testament figures. Two smaller rooms depict Heaven and Elysium, both with ceilings of cherubs and musicians, cupids and gods. Heaven is said to be painted in shell gold, '400 times more expensive even than gold leaf'. The ceiling of Elysium, home of the gods, is copied from Fontainebleau. It was so well crafted as never to have needed substantive restoration.

In each of these rooms is a fireplace, Gothic or classical in style, idiosyncratic and symbolic of the surrounding theme. The fireplaces of Bolsover are a book in themselves. The windows look down on the garden and the Venus Fountain with its 23 statues. It carries the inscription 'All is but vanite', a sardonic postscript on the Castle of Love.

CALKE ABBEY ***

Calke, 2m S of Melbourne
Time-warp mansion with majestic bed (NT)

The picture on the cover of the guidebook says it all. Stag-head trophies lie upturned on an old bed and in an open grate. Round them are scattered birds' eggs, a broken rush chair, a dolls' house, some old prints and boxes of Hudson's Dry Soap. Every English house may have one such room. Calke is composed almost entirely of them.

I first visited Calke in 1984 when its fate hung in the balance. The last Hurpur Crewe was living there alone after inheriting the estate in 1981 from his brother, along with £8m of death duties. He had barely a penny in the world. The house lay lost in a fold of a large

deer park in the Derbyshire hills. Its stone walls were crumbling. The interior was one huge family attic, filled with paraphernalia that successive members of the family had rejected and no auctioneer would take. What was to be done?

Calke was widely described as a time warp, mainly because the arrival of a telephone and some limited electricity had to await the 1960s. To me, it was not a time warp, just a house badly in need of a visit from the dustman. Yet within a year, Calke had been saved by the National Trust with money from every quarter. The National Trust went mad. Every tonic bottle, every match box, every chipped cup and broken chair was catalogued, dusted, wrapped in plastic and stored before being put back exactly where it had been in 1984. Nothing – or rather everything – was to be disturbed. A giant pretence was that the house was asleep. Apart from one object of which more below, it now contains three centuries of what might be anyone's junk.

The house was built in 1701–3 round the courtyard of an earlier Elizabethan mansion. The architect is unknown, although Calke has features in common with houses by the Smiths of Warwick. The exterior is in warm Derbyshire stone, well proportioned and free of surrounding outbuildings. There are acres of empty grass, and then a house. A hundred years after construction, an external staircase to the present saloon was removed and a formal Ionic portico inserted. The exotic Corinthian pilasters on the corner pavilions survive.

The entrance is now into the ground or 'rustic' floor, its hall dominated by trophies of the Harpur-Crewes' prize cattle. Next door is the Caricature Room, which used to be thick with cobwebs. Georgian cartoons are pasted on the wall, some of them three layers deep.

The main saloon is English Baroque in style but dominated by glass cases of stuffed birds and animals, including a crocodile's head, set round a billiard table. The room served as a

Calke: country house as junk shop

chapel in the 19th century, when the weather was too bad for the household to get to church. The drawing room and library have more character, if only by virtue of being crammed solid with things.

Three other rooms merit particular attention. On the second floor the Bird Lobby, cleansed of all mustiness and dirt, is astonishing for the sheer weight of taxidermy. The Gardner Wilkinson Library is my favourite, a dark cell of antiquarian books given to the family by an Egyptologist of that name in the 19th century. Then there is the Calke bed.

The historian, Sir Howard Colvin, was rummaging about Calke in the early 1980s when he stumbled on some unopened packing cases. The contents are thought to be a present to Lady Caroline Manners from George II's daughter, Princess Anne, for acting as bridesmaid at her wedding in 1734. The bed-hangings of imported Chinese silk had never been unpacked. The embroidery colours were as vivid as the day they was created. The hangings (c1715), have now been put on a frame and are a unique survival of 18th-century silk embroidery in such pristine condition. Peacocks and mandarins, animals and Chinese pagodas fill every inch of the surface. The bed was displayed at the Treasures of Britain exhibition in Washington in 1985 and is now protected behind glass.

The great park at Calke is as much a survivor as the house. Acquired to protect the inhabitants from any passing intrusion, it comprises woodland largely untended over three centuries. It is an ecological paradise.

CARNFIELD HALL **

1m E of Alfreton
Atmospheric house, crammed with
curios (P-R)

Carnfield is a miniature Calke. The story of the building is common, an Elizabethan manor flanked by Jacobean extensions, then 'turned' and given a new façade in the late 17th century. It is jolly rather than grand. Owned by the Revell family, it decayed over the centuries until being bought as derelict in 1987 by the present owner, James Cartland, antiques guru, broadcaster and conservationist.

Every room is crammed from floor to ceiling with the product of a lifetime's collecting, a reminder of Dickens' Golden Dustman in *Our Mutual Friend*. Not an inch is empty of objects. It hardly matters what purpose each room once served. Everywhere is the same mix of firearms, stuffed animals, piles of crockery, paintings of former owners, archives, silhouettes, historic costumes, gems and junk. There are books everywhere, mostly dusty and leathery and looking as if they have been there since Caxton.

Some of the rooms have distinguishing features. The hall has a Jacobean overmantel. The main stairs have newel posts and balusters of yeoman robustness. The Great Chamber over the hall is panelled and has a plaster frieze. Heavy curtains keep out the light and suggest that a squadron of bats may at any moment descend from the gloom. In the many bedrooms, clothes and drapes conceal original timber and plaster partitions. Exotic feathers still adorn the four bed-posts in the master bedroom. An ante-room has been fashioned from what appears to be a minstrels' gallery. A stuffed badger guards one door, a musket another.

A visitor nurtured on Chatsworth asked Cartland, 'What is it all for, just what is it all for?' He could only shrug. Such houses are not 'for' anything at all. They are merely more precious than a dozen stately homes.

CATTON HALL **

3m SE of Barton-under-Needwood
Smith of Warwick house, original interiors (P-R)

Catton has been occupied by the same family, the Hortons then Neilsons, since the early 15th century. It was the bigamous marriage of an 18th-century Miss Horton – who had, according to Walpole, 'the most amorous eyes in the world' – to the brother of George III that reputedly led to the Royal Marriages Act. This prevented anyone in line to the throne from marrying without the Sovereign's consent.

The house has an outward plainness concealing a rich interior, a sedate lady burning with inner passion. From a distance across the park, the house looks almost modern, a redbrick box of nine bays, with windows diminishing in size on each floor and with only white keystones for adornment. The house was begun by James Gibbs but executed in 1745 by the younger Smith of Warwick, William, a new entrance being built to one side in 1829.

The finest interior is the former Great Hall, now the dining room. This has pronounced beams enriched with classical mouldings. The walls have Rococo plasterwork, musical trophies and classical doorcases. The drawing room beyond is more modest, with gilded beading to the wall panels and eagle candelabra holders. The house has fine pictures, including Stuart portraits and a Wright of Derby.

The Neilsons run the Catton estate on rigorously commercial principles, remarking that they can make more money from the house and lawn than from the whole of their farming estate. This is a stately home open for business. It is the future for many such houses.

CHATSWORTH *****

Edensor, 3m NE of Bakewell
Ducal palace in parkland setting (P)

Chatsworth is, above all, a house in a landscape. It lies on the slope of a valley against a backdrop of wooded hills. I have seen it blazing golden in an autumn sunset, or rising serene above a spring mist. Floodlit at night, it appears like a luxury liner sliding quietly down its valley. In any mood, Chatsworth is spectacular. Yet it defers to the landscape. It does not shout, like Blenheim, or roar like Castle Howard.

The house is another creation of Bess of Hardwick. It came into her ownership through her marriage to Sir William Cavendish, father

English Baroque at Chatsworth

of her only children, and has passed down the Cavendish line ever since. The house was used by Bess's last husband, the Earl of Shrewsbury, to incarcerate Mary Queen of Scots, and was then rebuilt during the 1690s. The occasion was the elevation of 1st Duke of Devonshire for his part in the Glorious Revolution. The Cavendishes have always been Whigs or Liberals (and even Social Democrats).

The house is no longer owned directly by the family. Devastating death duties in 1950 led to its transfer in perpetuity to an independent trust. But the family rent part of the house and the Duke and Duchess play a leading part in its management. Chatsworth pioneered this form of arm's-length preservation, keeping a house intact yet linked to the family. Accessibility has been traditional since the 17th century. In 1844 the house was open every day in the year, Sundays not excepted. Instructions were that 'The humblest individual is not only shown the whole but the Duke has expressly ordered the waterworks to be played for everyone.' In the 1850s, with the coming of the railway, Chatsworth received 80,000 visitors a year.

Entrance from the road is down a winding drive that displays the main façade to best advantage. This front, of 1700–3, was built after the 1st Duke had quarrelled with William Talman, who had designed the south front to the right. Talman was Christopher Wren's rival in the Office of Works. Wren was a Tory and Talman a Whig. To the purist, the exterior of Chatsworth is rough and provincial, its orders truncated and resting on a bare ground floor. The glory of its exterior derived from its scale.

This glory was enhanced with the arrival in the 1760s of Capability Brown. He landscaped the River Derwent and tamed the rough pasture and hillside. Further changes occurred in the early 19th century when the 6th 'Bachelor' Duke converted Chatsworth from great house to palace. He removed the old village of Edensor from view and had Joseph Paxton install greenhouses and a gigantic fountain beneath the great cascade behind the house. Jeffry Wyatville was commissioned to build the extensive north wing, including a belvedere, theatre, sculpture gallery and grand dining room. It is next to this wing that the public enters the house.

The hall leads into the north corridor with its coloured marble pavement, a prelude to the majestic Painted Hall. Much altered over the years, this hall is the heart of Chatsworth. It retains the ceiling painted for the original building of 1699 by Laguerre, depicting the triumphs of Julius Caesar, supposed precursor of William III as champion of English liberty. The staircase rises through a magnificent screen to a landing with metalwork balustrades by Jean Tijou. Half hidden beyond is another staircase rising to the state rooms, as if one grand stair is not enough for Chatsworth. The walls are decorated with grisaille panels and the niches filled with statues by Colley Cibber. On the landings is a set of old baby-carriages, a child's Rococo sleigh beautifully crafted.

The state rooms at Chatsworth are unusually on the second floor, behind Talman's south front. The reason for this arrangement is not clear. The family rooms are below and the assumption is that the 1st Duke decided to convert into state rooms an upper Long Gallery surviving from the earlier Tudor house. Hardwick's most formal rooms were – and are – on the top floor. The 6th Duke later referred to them as his 'dismal, ponderous range of Hampton Court-like chambers'. When the house was a girls' school during the Second World War, these rooms were dormitories, surely the most splendid in the land.

Restoration has made them less dismal. They are merely magnificent. The state dining room, in which it is said that nobody has ever dined, has a ceiling by Verrio. It includes the 1st Duke's housekeeper, Mrs Hackett, whom Verrio did not like, 'cutting the thread of life' with scissors. The sumptuous wood carving is 'school of Gibbons' and some of the furniture is by William Kent. The state drawing room contains a set of Mortlake tapestries, copied from the Raphael cartoons now in the V&A, and another ceiling by Laguerre. The state music room has a *trompe-l'œil* violin painted on its door. The stamped leather wall-hangings, introduced c1830, are anachronistic and exotic, as is the Russian malachite writing table. Viewing this room is like eating an over-rich box of chocolates. The state bedroom follows with more leather wall-hangings and ceilings by Laguerre. The furniture is by Boulle. The last in the sequence, the state dressing room, enjoys the finest views, both south and west.

The route now enters the 19th century, with corridors and stairs added to the central court-yard by Wyatville for the 6th Duke. In the Sketch Gallery are portraits of the family and more Mortlake tapestries, while the west stair-case includes paintings acquired by successive dukes, from Tintoretto to Lucien Freud.

The chapel survives from the 1st Duke's rebuild. Its superb alabaster reredos contains Verrio's *Doubting Thomas* over the altar and carvings by Gibbons and others. The eccentric Oak Room beyond was acquired by the 6th Duke from dealers who looted Continental monasteries in the 1820s and 1830s. It has twisted columns forming a sort of sanctuary in the middle and was used as a smoking room.

The route passes back through the Painted Hall and climbs to the libraries via the Oak Stairs, with its antler chandelier and Grinling Gibbons' limewood cravat. Here begins what amounts to a second Chatsworth, the Regency wing designed by Wyatville for the 6th Duke. The 1st Duke's Long Gallery was converted into the first of three libraries. It contains what is still England's finest book collection in pri-vate hands, although it is only a fragment of that owned by the family in the 19th century. Death duties saw the loss to America of the Caxtons and Shakespeare First Folios. It was perhaps a fitting transference of old wealth to new, but a great loss to Chatsworth.

The 19th-century house in no way outguns the 17th century, but it reaches a sort of climax in Wyatville's Great Dining Room. Here the Bachelor Duke came into his own, describing eating here as 'like dining in a great trunk, and you expect the lid to open'. Here are paintings by van Dyck and Mytens, and the Gains-borough of *Georgiana, Duchess of Devonshire*, acquired by Chatsworth in 1994. Beyond are more paintings and sculpture in the gallery, arranged as a homage to Canova and to Regency taste generally. It is hard to convey the sheer richness of this place. It is the National Gallery of the North and yet a home.

CHESTERFIELD: REVOLUTION HOUSE *

Old Whittington, 1m N of Chesterfield centre
Ancient cottage, scene of historic meeting (M)

Hardly a house but certainly historic, Revolu-tion House was the venue of a seminal meeting in English history. Here, in 1688, a group of men took shelter from the rain when out hunting on Whittington Moor. The hunt had an ulterior motive. The Earl of Danby, the Earl of Devonshire and John D'Arcy came to plan the overthrow of James II and the invitation to William of Orange to invade and seize the throne. They thus initiated the Glorious Revolution – and a dukedom for Devonshire. The building was then an inn, the Cock and Pynot, which later became a farmhouse.

A place of pilgrimage for those honouring Parliamentary democracy, the house stands by a green in a suburb of Chesterfield. It is a precious survivor of an ancient Derbyshire farm building. Stone walls support a thick thatch roof. A single dormer window lights a small upper chamber. There are just two rooms downstairs, with 17th-century furniture and a smattering of material about the origins of the 1688 meeting. The only intrusion is a video.

DERBY: PICKFORD'S HOUSE *

41 Friar Gate
Georgian architect's house now museum of costume (M)

Friar Gate is a precious fragment of old Derby. Its finest building is Pickford's House, built in 1769 by a local architect, Joseph Pickford. The façade is classical, pedimented and with a Doric doorcase surmounted by the tools of the architect's profession. Why cannot modern architecture use these same tools to produce streetscapes of similar grace?

The house is now a museum of mostly Regency costumes. The rooms are shuttered and lights come on when visitors enter. This is conservation gone mad, stripping the interior of all atmosphere and confining visitors to glass cages in each of the main rooms, like zoo animals.

The front hall has fine plasterwork, a sign of wealth in a town house. The main reception rooms on the ground floor are laid out by time of day. The drawing room is for tea, the dining room for dessert and the morning room 'light and airy' for the ladies, though in reality gloomy. The street outside is respectably Georgian and there is no good reason for not opening the curtains to the view.

Upstairs, the house relaxes a little. The 1930s bathroom is 'for public use', a nice touch. A bedroom is prepared for cocoa-time, with the bed linen turned down and nightshirts laid ready. The remainder of the house is an exhibition of display cases.

EYAM HALL **

Eyam, 7m N of Bakewell
Unaltered 17th-century mansion with tapestry (P)

The village of Eyam is famous for its heroism during the Plague of 1666, when the village was infected by cloth from London and sealed itself off from the world until the plague had passed. Half its people died. There are many relics of those days in the village, but not in Eyam Hall, whose story begins with its purchase and rebuilding by Thomas Wright in 1671. His descendants live in the house to this day. Eyam is a delightfully romantic place, Restoration in date but Jacobean, if not Elizabethan, in appearance. The façade, with its blank wall above the front door and austere gable ends, looks a hundred years older than its date.

The interior is a rich sequence of 17th-

century rooms, very much in family use and crammed with Wright memorabilia. A painting in the entrance hall celebrates the auspicious marriage of John Wright to the girl in the picture, Elizabeth Kniveton, a picture of Derbyshire respectability. By the hall fire are two rare 'bacon' settles, seats with cupboards in their backs for hanging hams to cure near the fire.

The main rooms are upstairs. A Tapestry Room is entirely covered in the material, cut to fit even the window openings and door surrounds as if it were wallpaper. One part is made of a valuable 15th-century piece from Flanders. The library was the old Great Chamber, a place of creaking floors and heavy bookshelves. A 17th-century 'pop-up' medical encyclopaedia is on display. Engraved in the window is a passionate love poem written by Robert Wright in the 18th century. It is dedicated to Fanny Holme of Stockport. He married twice but never to Fanny, yet the window survived.

The bedroom has a magnificent four-poster and a delightful portrait of a Wright girl in a hat. Eyam is blessed with a complete run of such pictures, none great works of art but full of local charm, one English family in continuous narrative. Many of the 17th-century works came through John Wright's marriage to Jane Farewell who brought her own collection with her. To these are added more modern photographs from the Victorian age to today.

HADDON HALL ****

2m S of Bakewell
Medieval fortified hall house round courtyard (P)

Haddon is the most perfect English house to survive from the Middle Ages. It has none of Hardwick's promiscuity or Chatsworth's bombast. It has not changed because it never needed to change. From the 15th century to today, this cluster of warm stone buildings has lain in its valley, protected by a curtain wall and surrounding forest. Those aristocratic curses of extravagance and infertility have not visited Haddon. The place is still owned by the Manners family, Dukes of Rutland. To wander up the slope to the worn gatehouse steps and enter the ancient courtyard is as agreeable an experience as England can offer.

Haddon was the seat of Sir George Vernon, 'King of the Peak', having been in his line since 1170. It passed to the Manners family in 1563 after Vernon's daughter, Dorothy, allegedly raced from her sister's wedding feast and eloped with John Manners, son of the Earl of Rutland. The houses of Belvoir and Haddon were thus united in one family and have remained so ever since. Through the 18th and 19th centuries, the Rutlands neglected Haddon in favour of their seat of Belvoir (Leics). This saved it from the drastic alterations that occurred to most houses over that period. Haddon's restoration by the 9th Duke after 1912 and recently by his grandson have been deferential.

The approach to the house is without pretension. The visitor is greeted not by a grand gateway but by an old Tudor stable block. In the adjacent garden is a topiary hedge, clipped to display a boar's head and a peacock, emblems respectively of Vernon and Manners. Up the slope to the right lies a rough medieval gatehouse with modest armorial dressings. Above it are the rooms in which the 9th Duke slept while supervising the 20th-century restoration.

The Lower Courtyard holds the essence of Haddon. It is that of a fortified house rather than castle, yet with none of the tight enclosure of Berkeley (Gloucs) or Skipton (Yorks, N). The hall, solar, chapel, kitchens and offices lie low and comfortable round an open court which for centuries echoed to the clatter of horses and the shouts of visitors.

The Great Hall at Haddon is small, almost square in plan and dated c1370. The roof is a modern restoration, but the original screens passage, minstrels' gallery, dais and panelling survive. The antlers are 17th century and the dais tapestry was reputedly given to a Manners by Henry VIII. On the screen is a manacle for those 'who did not drink fayre'. Haddon's kitchens are extensive, a warren of pantry,

buttery, bakery and courtyard. The survival of their furnishings, including salting baths, chopping boards, log boxes and baking ovens we owe to centuries of disuse.

At the other end of the Great Hall are the original family rooms, which developed round the solar. They are among the finest to survive intact from the 15th century. The original Great Chamber was divided into dining room and receiving room. The dining room has a painted ceiling depicting the Tudor rose and emblems of the Vernon and Talbot families. A frieze above the panelling continues the heraldic theme, a cartoon strip of the great figures of the day. The plan of this room is repeated in the Great Chamber above.

Next come the Earl's Apartments, domestic rooms once sub-divided for warmth and privacy. Heavy oak ceilings and floorboards are left exposed and whitewash liberally applied. The windows offer delicious glimpses of the Haddon gardens on the slopes below.

The Upper Courtyard remains mostly private to the family. Its rooms met the Elizabethan need for large entertaining spaces, before the move to Belvoir. The Long Gallery is not as spectacular as that at Hardwick. It is lit by three tiers of Elizabethan windows, the panes set at differing angles to pattern the fall of light onto the interior, a device I have seen nowhere else; it was possibly inserted during 20th-century restoration. The oak panelling celebrates the Vernon-Manners union and the reign of James I, with boars and peacocks united with roses and thistles. Over the mantelpiece is a charming Rex Whistler painting of Haddon, commissioned in honour of the 20th-century restoration.

Beyond is the state bedroom with its antechamber. Both are used to display tapestries, including the 'Sense' of smell from the Mortlake workshop. A Brussels tapestry shows a horse treading on the foot of a pike-bearer. Over the mantelpiece is a crowded tableau of Orpheus charming the beasts, with the Manners peacock taking precedence over monkeys and elephants. Haddon's state bed is sadly at Belvoir, encased in a glass box and thus a museum piece, not a bed. It should be brought back and left to fade gracefully in its proper home.

The old chapel contains Norman masonry and medieval wall paintings. Its oak pews are graded for the family and servants. The Haddon gardens are a story in themselves. They cascade down the hillside from the curtain wall towards the river, terraced by the Duchess while her husband restored the house.

HARDWICK HALL *****

7m NW of Mansfield
Greatest English prodigy house, built for Bess of Hardwick (NT)

The spectacle of Hardwick Hall, gold and shimmering in the setting sun, is one of the most splendid in English architecture. It was Bess of Hardwick's final assertion of independence from her husband, the 6th Earl of Shrewsbury (Hardwick Old Hall, below). The initials ES woven fourteen times into its parapet have even been claimed for female emancipation. The building was regarded as the highpoint of the Elizabethan 'Renaissance', yet Hardwick seems a place apart. Like Bolsover, it was built for a game of manners whose rules have largely vanished. It is now architecture as abstract sculpture, four walls of glass entombing light. Turrets, chambers, stairs and the incomparable upper gallery stand sentinel over a steep valley. Hardwick is never less than sad.

The house was begun on Shrewsbury's death in 1590 probably to designs by Robert Smythson, who was already working at Wollaton (Notts). Hardwick was the more accomplished work, both in the perfection of its proportion and in its use of the defining material of Elizabethan wealth, glass. It was the secular answer to the great Perpendicular churches of the previous century. Hardwick was for show. It was meant to make men gasp.

The celebrated entrance front is a mirror of the seasons, lowering and grim in cloud, a flickering façade of colour in sun. The walk round the outside of Hardwick shows its walls shifting and rearranging themselves before the eye. Each side seems different, each sailing in a different wind. The side elevations are tall and slender, like the prow of a galleon surging through the sea. The historian Olive Cook watched 'the immense diamond window panes flash and vibrate with a hundred molten colours'.

The house is unaltered. As at the Old Hall the Great Hall is aligned front-to-back, dividing the house into equal sides. The ground floor is for services, with pantry and kitchen on either side of the Hall. The family rooms are on the taller first floor. Taller still is the second floor, the place of entertainment and display, as if greatness lay in height and the suspense of achieving it. The exterior is fractured by six towers crowned with six pavilions, lending each floor angles of constant visual diversion. Stairs extend into towers, forming landings and private closets. On the upper floors the towers produce L-shaped, E-shaped and T-shaped chambers, all flooded with light.

Hardwick is a house of staircases, two of which thread their way through all the floors. The Great Stair rises between heavy tapestries to Bess's Low Great Chamber, linked by a bridge over the end of the hall to her withdrawing room. These chambers have glorious mantelpieces and panelling, with furniture returned over the past century from Chatsworth and elsewhere. The withdrawing room was the sitting room of the last occupant of the house, Evelyn, Duchess of Devonshire, who died in 1960. It displays Elizabethan and later embroidery, including works by Bess.

We are constantly drawn back to the stairs. The wide, flowing curve of steps to the top floor is like the approach to the chapter house at Wells. Tapestries now trumpet the approach to greatness. The High Great Chamber and Long Gallery at Hardwick are sumptuous rooms. They seem double the height of the floor below. The chamber is lined with Brussels tapestries of Ulysses beneath a coloured plaster frieze of the Hunt of Diana. They surround a Serlian fireplace of marble and

Architecture ablaze at Hardwick

alabaster. Pevsner is snooty about much of this. A visitor from Fontainebleau or Florence, he said, would have found it 'a monstrous show . . . barbaric in the extreme'. I prefer to see it as an outburst of confident northern vigour.

The withdrawing room next door contains the finest Elizabethan furniture in the house. Here stands a beautiful marquetry chest. Even Pevsner's foreigners would have admired the exquisite bas relief of Apollo and the Muses.

The Long Gallery is the apotheosis of Elizabethan architecture. The room is E-shaped, the outer wall of three bays, one shallow, two deep, filled with glass. The inner walls are lined with tapestries and 81 portraits, including one of hard-faced Bess. But this is a room not of objects but of stone framing space and light. On a sunny day it is an avenue ablaze. On a dark one it revives a belief in ghosts. After this Gallery, the remainder of Hardwick is anticlimax.

HARDWICK OLD HALL **

7m NW of Mansfield
Ruin of Bess of Hardwick's old mansion (EH)

The ghost of Elizabeth Shrewsbury haunts the hills of Derbyshire. Born in 1527, 'Bess of Hardwick' saw out the 16th century, dying in 1608 shortly after the monarch whose name she shared. She was never Good Queen Bess. She was no aristocrat, although she founded whole dynasties of them, but came of Derbyshire yeoman stock. Bess was a hard, acquisitive, upwardly mobile Elizabethan. She found wealth through her husbands, four of them. No alimony scrounger is her equal. The two houses at Hardwick are her memorial.

Bess was married at fourteen, widowed at fifteen, then married again to the wealthy Sir William Cavendish, by whom she had eight children. He died and she remarried at thirty. Widowed a third time, she then married the richest man in England, the Earl of Shrewsbury. The marriage was bitterly unhappy. The matrimonial wars of the Shrewsburys lent 'shrew' to the language. They were so ferocious that the Queen herself had to act as conciliator,

unsuccessfully. The Earl declared that 'no plague' was as evil as his wife. Even admirers found her 'of masculine understanding and conduct, proud, furious, selfish and unfeeling . . . hideous, dry, parched, narrow-minded'.

Yet Bess's lineage was to embrace the dukedoms of Devonshire, Newcastle, Portland, Kingston and Norfolk. In her own lifetime, her family houses included Chatsworth, Hardwick, Bolsover, Oldcotes, Sheffield, Welbeck and Worksop, among others. She was a fanatical architect. After Shrewsbury's death in 1590, a fortune teller (doubtless a builder) prophesied that Bess 'should not die while she was building'. She eventually died in the fierce winter of 1607–8 when cold had briefly halted work on her new hall at Hardwick.

Bess had been born in the Old Hall and it was to here that she returned after her separation from Shrewsbury in 1584. She began to extend the old house three years later, even as she was planning her new Hall opposite. The older building was thus a piecemeal structure, with ranges and grand rooms added when needed. Part was used by her favourite son, William Cavendish, for his own establishment. Between them, they had some 200 retainers. The new Hall would be for ostentation, entertainment and special guests. The Old Hall was for Bess, her family and entourage.

When the later Cavendishes rebuilt Chatsworth and made it their seat, Hardwick lost its pre-eminence. The Old Hall was partly dismantled and its fittings distributed to various family properties. It was left a ruin and by the 19th century was already the object of antiquarian interest. In 1959 it was given to the nation by the 10th Duke of Devonshire in lieu of death duties. The new Hardwick Hall opposite passed to the National Trust.

The ruin is that which Bess left, unaltered. The entrance leads into what became an 'end-on' Great Hall, running front-to-back and dividing the old service rooms to the right from the family chambers to the left. By the late 16th century, the Great Hall was no longer a dining room, more an entrance and servants' hall. Yet as Bess built, so the house divided into what was her wing on one side and her son's on the other. This produced not one but two formal suites, the Hill Great Chamber and the Forest Great Chamber. They were built high, four floors up, the extravagant stairs designed to impress visitors. The apartments were equalled in scale only by royal palaces.

Of these apartments, only fragments survive. The decoration of the Forest Chamber depicted the deer of the woods, a metaphor for Bess waiting patiently for her husband to return to her, as she wanted it thought. Off the staircase are rooms known to have been allocated to two senior servants, Mr Digby and Mr Reason, each with plaster panels. The Hill Great Chamber overlooks the valley, with windows on three sides. Its overmantel still displays reliefs of Gog and Magog, hence its nickname of the Giants' Chamber.

The Old Hall at Hardwick, although ruined, is somehow more real than the new one. It developed in response to domestic need and tells a human story. It was not just a show house but the residence of a dysfunctional family. Even centuries of decay cannot wipe the tear from its face.

KEDLESTON HALL ****

6m NW of Derby
Adam's homage to the house of Curzon and to imperial Rome (NT)

What is to be made of Kedleston? Curzons came over at the Norman Conquest and have been in residence ever since. They represented their county in Parliament and their monarch in India. Here, in the soft foothills of the Peak District, they created a house in the grandest Roman style, employing the most inventive architect of the day, Robert Adam. They preserved his masterpiece and in 1986 handed it intact to the National Trust.

Yet there is something frigid about this house. It seems to spring perfect from Adam's pattern book without human intervention. The family have lived only in the lower floor and in the north-east pavilion; the main rooms were for entertaining and showing to the public. Walking through these rooms I feel

Hogarth's longing for English roast beef. Dr Johnson wrote that it 'would do excellently for a Town Hall'. We seem to bruise Kedleston by our very presence.

The façade unfolds from the landscape like a golden summons. It was commissioned by the 5th Baronet, Sir Nathaniel Curzon (later 1st Lord Scarsdale), on his inheritance in 1758. An exquisite young man of thirty-two who had missed out on the Grand Tour, Curzon wanted a house in the height of fashion. 'Grant me, ye Gods, a pleasant seat,' he wrote, 'in Attick elegance made neat.' He tried Matthew Brettingham and James Paine, who between them built the two wing houses. But on meeting Robert Adam, recently returned from the Mediterranean, Curzon was 'struck all of a heap with wonder and amaze'. A Tory, he wanted to outdo the Whig Cavendishes at Chatsworth. The glories of ancient Rome would now be reborn on the slopes of Derbyshire. Adam was delighted to find a client 'resolved to spare no expense, with £10,000 a year . . . a taste for the Arts and little for game'.

Adam did not take over full responsibility for Kedleston until 1760. He accepted the Brettingham/Paine Palladian front but added a façade of his own to the rear, a variant on the Arch of Constantine with steps curving down to the garden. Whereas the front is severely Palladian, the rear is an echo of Vanbrugh. That was the limit of Adam's exterior alterations. Even Curzon soon ran out of money and the original plan, for four pavilions linked by curving quadrants, as at Holkham (Norfolk), was not realized.

The decoration is from Adam's sketchbooks and notebooks. No civilization has paid a greater compliment to another than was paid by Georgian England to Rome. But whereas the Palladians of the Burlington School drew on the heavier tradition of the Italian Renaissance, Adam reverted to the Roman Empire itself. His tendrils, arabesques and acanthus leaves framing classical medallions were drawn from the Emperor Diocletian's recently unearthed palace in Split. This was a lighter, more delicate, almost frivolous, revival.

The interiors at Kedleston are almost all by Adam, designed for the grandest of show. A central hall and saloon cross the centre of the building, with the family rooms to the left and state rooms to the right. They form a compact quadrilateral parade. The Marble Hall is entered directly from the flight of steps under the front portico. It is the atrium of a Roman villa, top lit and with no windows. The walls are lined with 20 columns of Derbyshire marble, behind which are statue niches with relief panels above. All depict scenes from classical antiquity. The coving of the ceiling is by Adam's plasterer, Joseph Rose. Even the iron grates and fire irons are by Adam.

The promenade begins on the left with the music room, the only ceremonial room still regularly used by the family. Beyond lies the drawing room, in part designed by Paine before Adam's arrival. Its centrepiece is a marble Venetian window balanced by marble doorcases, two of them false. The ceiling coving by Joseph Rose contains a wild naturalistic composition, like waves frothing over the frieze. The walls are lined with four superb sofas by John Linnell, glories of English 18th-century craftsmanship. The mermaids on the arms invite us to lie down and relax. (Do no such thing: this is the National Trust.)

The library beyond is a haven of sudden calm. The ceiling is patterned on geometric mosaics from Rome and Ravenna. The classical orders are no longer Corinthian but Doric, the books immaculate in their glass-fronted cases. The corner to the rear front now turns into the circular saloon. This is a sensational chamber based on the Pantheon. The ceiling is a dazzling *trompe-l'œil* of rosettes disappearing upwards to a central skylight, the niches likewise swirling to some notional vanishing point. When used as a ballroom, the effect on the dancers must have been intoxicating.

The state apartments on the other side of the hall begin with ante-rooms preparing the visitor for the state bedchamber. Its bed is not heavy like early 18th-century beds: the canopy is supported on posts carved as two slender palm trees, their roots growing from floorboards, rising up to waves of foliage. Ostrich

feathers crown the composition. Palms were illustrative of victory, ostrich feathers of power. The bed is clothed in blue brocade, a masterpiece of English Rococo.

The circuit is completed by the dining room, with an apsidal niche at the kitchen end for the display of family silver. Adam was so emphatic about how pictures were hung at Kedleston that he even designed picture frames in plaster, requiring the paintings to be hung symmetrically. Below stairs, on the ground or 'rustic' floor, is the Caesar's Hall where normal life in the house continued while the rooms upstairs were mostly covered in dust sheets. Here, too, is Curzon's Museum, installed by the Marquess in honour of his time as Viceroy of India. It includes the celebrated 'peacock dress' worn by his wife at the 1903 Coronation Durbar in Delhi.

The grounds at Kedleston are rare for an 18th-century house in *not* being by Capability Brown, but by the architect of the house, in this case Adam himself. They are in the Brown style, naturalistic but adorned with Adam pavilions and even bath-houses for the use of visiting members of the public.

MELBOURNE HALL ***

Melbourne
Jacobean and Smith of Warwick house (P)

Melbourne is a church, house, garden and one lovely room. The church was the mini-cathedral built by the Bishops of Carlisle, reluctant to stray too far north to their headquarters and the threatening Scots. The house was later leased from the bishops and then rebuilt as a private house in 1629 by Sir John Coke. He was forebear of the Lambs and then Kerrs, the present owners.

A new west wing was added early in the 18th century, forming one side of a narrow three-sided courtyard to the south of Coke's house. The Jacobean Great Hall became the new dining room. In 1744, the house was further altered when the younger Smith of Warwick, William, added a handsome wing facing the garden. It has a rusticated ground floor and decorative swags in the central pediment, forming a fine backdrop to the sweep of the garden below.

The present interior is of two parts, one of 1629 and the other Georgian. The earlier is dominated by the dining room, superbly panelled and with family portraits by Huysmans, Jansens and Lely. The colourful heraldic overmantel is an import from a Kerr estate in Hertfordshire. With its pewter and high-backed embroidered chairs, the room embodies the style and comfort of an early 17th century gentleman.

The staircase and hall are those of a conventional but not elaborate Georgian house. The stairwell has a moulded plaster ceiling. Smith's drawing room and study face the garden. All are hung with pictures tracing the ownership of the house from Cokes to Lambs, a lineage that embraced Lord Melbourne, Lady Caroline Lamb and Lord Palmerston. The Kerrs, Marquesses of Lothian, inherited the house in the 19th century. The present Lady Ralph Kerr, an artist, has added to the Melbourne collection with her own delightful paintings.

The gardens of Melbourne are not extensive but richly displayed. The main vista down to the pool is flanked by billowing waves of yew. Wooded glades are punctuated by van Nost statuary. In one glade is a charming arbour of swirling Italianate ironwork by Robert Blackwell of Derby.

RENISHAW HALL ***

2m SE of Eckington
Gothicized seat of the Sitwells (P-R)

The Derbyshire Sitwells made their money from nails and coal. Their descendants could thus afford to be 20th-century aesthetes. In the decade after the Great War, the children of Sir George Sitwell, Osbert, Edith and Sacheverell, became, in the words of their biographer Anthony Powell, 'style-setters and standard-bearers in the war against the Philistines, heroes to a new generation of dandy writers'. Their domineering father had talent and taste. Their mother, Lady Ida, was 'irresponsible,

sensual and extravagant'. To Powell they were 'tall, fair, attenuated courtiers from a medieval tapestry'. That is what nails can do for you.

Renishaw became famous and much visited by literary and artistic figures. Its ghosts were celebrated, terrifying even sceptical guests. They sometimes slapped faces and pushed people off stairs at night. The ghost of a drowned boy was said to give wet, cold kisses to sleeping ladies. There was more than a suspicion of practical joking in all this. The house is now owned by Sacheverell's son, Sir Reresby. It is as variegated and eccentric as the family's history.

Renishaw was built c1625 as a conventional Jacobean house, and gothicized at the turn of the 19th century. 'Renishaw cannot claim to be an architectural gem,' asserts the guidebook emphatically. Its exterior looks like that of an expensive prep school. The interior could not be less so. It bursts with the magpie zeal of generations of Sitwells. Two Venetian warriors in fancy dress adorn the front hall, one wearing spectacles left by a visitor in 1969 and still not reclaimed. Directly ahead is a large fireplace with an overmantel of Venice by a Renishaw regular, John Piper. Other Pipers line the walls.

The rooms adjacent to the hall retain their 17th-century proportions with Jacobean colours boldly restored. The Smoke Room is in bright red with yellow panelling. The ante-dining room is deep green, a perfect setting for the Dutch paintings. The dining room, added in 1793, is Adamish in style, soft pink in colour. It features a wide, handsome and practical apse for the sideboard and is dominated by two works, John Copley's conversation piece of the Sitwells in 1787 and a tremendous 17th-century Neapolitan cabinet, black and gold and covered in classical scenes.

The Regency wing contains the Great Drawing Room and ballroom. The atmosphere of these rooms could hardly be less Jacobean, more what Osbert Lancaster called 'Curzon Street Baroque'. They are a gallery of Sitwell acquisitions, English and Continental works tossed together in happy confusion. The floor of the drawing room was stained a discreet floral pattern in 1988. A Chippendale commode is companion to a superb piece at Harewood (Yorks, W) and was, in Sacheverell Sitwell's opinion, 'the finer of the pair'. Above it hangs a Sargent painting of the Edwardian Sitwells.

Much of the charm of Renishaw is to experience English Jacobean shifting gear into Baroque. The Brussels tapestries in the drawing room, thankfully allowed to see the light of day, gave Sacheverell his enthusiasm for the 'suavity and opulence' of the then unfashionable Baroque. So too did the sumptuous ballroom, most of its contents Italian. Two giant dolphins rest on a marble table. Near it stands the largest vase of Derbyshire Bluejohn stone extant. Dominating the space, almost as an altarpiece, is Salvator Rosa's *Belisarius in Disgrace* in a frame attributed to William Kent. Renishaw does nothing by halves.

That certainly goes for the ravishing garden, largely the brainchild of the present owner's highly eccentric grandfather. It was he who was alleged to have gazed across the crowded industrial valley of Derbyshire at Barlborough on its bluff in the distance and remarked that 'there is no one between us and the Locker-Lampsons'.

SUDBURY HALL ***

6m E of Uttoxeter
Restoration house with Baroque interiors
(NT)

The house belonged to a junior line of the Vernons of Haddon Hall. Having been abandoned by them in 1967, Sudbury passed to the National Trust with the best of intentions. The National Trust created the best of museums, a cold, rather empty place but uplifted by one of England's finest staircases.

Sudbury had been rebuilt in the 1660s after the Restoration, with a remarkably old-fashioned exterior. The north and south façades are both E-plan, with diapered brickwork and large, stone-mullioned windows with some circular tracery. The porch is even odder, with two segmental arches, one above

the other, filled with classical enrichment. The doorway in the lower arch seems to have sunk in despair below the bases of the attached columns. The composition is undeniably grand but this style was so imitated, and bloated, by 19th-century Jacobethans that it now looks rather institutional.

The inside is a different matter. The porch leads into a screens passage with a hall on the right. Over the fireplace is an uplifting Laguerre mural, Time offering a cornucopia to Industry and thorns to Idleness. But this hall is little more than an ante-chamber, giving way to Sudbury's masterpiece, the Great Staircase leading up to the promenade of Long Gallery and Queen's Room. The staircase, possibly designed by Vernon himself, is a flourish of 17th-century decoration. The carpenter was Wren's assistant, Edward Pierce. The plasterer was James Pettifer.

This is one of the great stairs of England and was, for once, by an Englishman. It rises in two shallow flights, its underside as richly decorated as its walls and ceiling. Most astonishing are Pierce's balustrade panels, in painted limewood. Voluptuous scrolls of acanthus toss and tumble down the flights. Baskets of fruit adorn the newel posts. More acanthus, now in plaster, decorates the frieze and seems to drop like ripe fruit from the ceiling. The undersides of the stairs frame paintings by Laguerre.

The stairs are now considered by the National Trust too precious to be used. When will they say this of whole houses? Instead, the downstairs rooms must be visited first and those upstairs reached from behind, an unsatisfactory arrangement. The saloon, though bare of furniture, is another virtuoso work by Pierce, with ceiling by Pettifer and his colleague, Robert Bradbury. Again, the room seems to drip with moulding and carving, palm leaves and acanthus enfolding nuts and fruit in a celebration of plenty. The wall panels frame full-length family portraits by Hudson, Dahl and others.

Restoration richness at Sudbury

The drawing room beyond has, as its overmantel, one of the earliest documented carvings by Grinling Gibbons, of a bunch of fishes. They form an intriguing comparison with Pierce's work next door, in my view superior but a close call. The remaining rooms on the ground floor are more domestic, offering views out over the lake. Their redecoration by John Fowler in the 1970s was controversial but, as he countered at the time, such decoration is always 'a striving after a sense of life and not just slavish renewal of the misguided taste of the day before yesterday'.

The reception rooms upstairs are reached by a back staircase. This means coming directly into the Long Gallery, rather than approaching it through its ante-rooms. A Long Gallery is an anachronism in a house of the 1660s, but a happy one. The ceiling plasterwork is again by Bradbury and Pettifer with the heavy richness of the late 17th century. Scallop shells and palm fronds dance along the frieze. Roman emperors gaze down from medallions. Contemporary family portraits hang along the walls beneath. In sunlight the whole room shimmers white and gold, the rush mats giving off a pleasant rustic smell.

A small library, the Talbot Room, leads to the Queen's Room. This has an ebullient alabaster mantelpiece that seems to grow in self-importance the closer it approaches the ceiling.

SUTTON SCARSDALE HALL *

Sutton Scarsdale, 4m SE of Chesterfield
Relic of a Smith of Warwick mansion (EH)

A good spot for picnics, says the English Heritage handbook. The old Earls of Scarsdale would have agreed. In 1724 they had Francis Smith of Warwick recast their mansion along the bluff from Bolsover and Hardwick. In the 1920s, their successors, the Arkwrights, stripped the house of its contents, three panelled rooms ending up in the Philadelphia Museum of Art. They thought of blowing the place up with dynamite but instead left some of the most exquisite stucco in the North to rain and ruin.

Decades later, with demolition imminent, Sacheverell Sitwell set out from neighbouring Renishaw to see what he could rescue. The reputed home of the rake in *Rake's Progress*, to Sitwell it embodied the art of the Italian revival in England. Here the *stuccadores*, Artari and Vassalli, brought the sunshine of southern Rococo to the northern uplands. Sitwell found the house already gutted. Four Venetian mantelpieces, 'all of the richest work imaginable, richer by far than anything in a Venetian palace', were still hanging in the air, coloured stucco dripping from their panels. He paid ten shillings and sent workmen and carts to remove them. They found them already fallen and smashed to pieces. But the ruin itself became Sitwell property.

Tended by English Heritage, the house is still a roofless ruin, although no more ruined than Uppark (Sussex) after its fire. An imaginative millionaire could research and restore it. Smith's design is robust Baroque, with a fine east façade gazing out over the valley.

The whole structure is in pink stone, now gnarled and weather-beaten with neglect. Inside, scraps of plasterwork, scrolls of gilding, the odd fireplace, cornices and grotesques can be made out. Mostly the walls have been stripped to their brickwork. Sutton Scarsdale is a romantic spot but eerie. It is like an old dowager who has returned from her last ball, thrown aside her clothes and stands suddenly naked.

TISSINGTON HALL **

Tissington, 4m N of Ashbourne
Jacobean house with Art Nouveau library frieze (P-R)

The hall lies in a picturesque enclave reached through park gates on the edge of the Peak District. The green, church, cottages, stables and hall seem all of a piece. The main house lies through a handsome Jacobean gate across a lawn. It is outwardly a rectangular box with none of the usual Jacobean trimmings but with round chimneys dotted along the parapet. It has belonged to FitzHerberts since the 15th century. The family valiantly maintains house and estate as a going concern.

The interior is a typically English mixture of styles. The house was built in 1609, symmetrical and with a front-to-back hall as at Hardwick. The porch leads directly into the hall, a low, warm room still with its Jacobean panelling but with 18th-century Gothick decoration. This includes a frieze of delicate ogees and a bold neo-medieval fireplace, all of 1757. The Chippendale dining chairs are also Gothick, as are the far windows, making the room an enjoyable marriage of styles.

The adjacent dining room has a panelled inglenook, possibly remaining from an old kitchen fireplace. Again like Hardwick, Tissington appears to have been planned with service rooms on the ground floor and formal rooms above. Two portraits by Ramsay, of George III and Queen Charlotte, hang over the staircase. Upstairs, the T-shaped East Drawing Room offers a light, airy alcove over the porch. It has the best panelling in the house, pilastered beneath a beautifully restored plaster cornice, and hung with family portraits by Angelica Kauffmann.

The Edwardians added a library to the rear of the house, designed by Arnold Mitchell. It is pleasantly cluttered with old books and maps and has a bold inglenook in the manner of Norman Shaw, who regarded no living room as complete without one. Its frieze depicts an Art Nouveau forest of flora and fauna.

WINGFIELD MANOR **

South Wingfield, 4m E of Alfreton
Ruin of Ralph Cromwell's palace (EH)

This was no manor, but a palace. Wingfield must rank as one of England's least-known great ruins. It leaps out of the landscape on its mound above the River Amber, a bristling rampart of 15th-century stonework. Chimneys and gables soar into the sky. The area of its courtyards is larger even than Haddon Hall.

The house was built by Ralph Lord Crom-

well, Treasurer to the hapless Henry VI and richest man in England. He began Wingfield as his principal house in the 1440s, shortly after completing Tattershall (Lincs). The house later passed to the Earl of Shrewsbury and thus fell within the panoply of Bess of Hardwick. It was one of the many prisons of Mary Queen of Scots. The house was slighted in the Civil War and, although partly restored as a formal house, became mostly a farm, as part of it still is. The ruins are approached along a muddy farm track and the area is heavy with the scent of manure.

The outer courtyard is still flanked by medieval walls, into parts of which the farmhouse has been built. The one complete building to survive, a barn near the entrance, may have been living quarters for servants or visitors. In one corner of the outer court is the High Tower, still climbable and believed to have contained chambers for important guests. The surviving ground floor chamber was a latrine, with evidence of wooden seats over discharge drains. Water cisterns are believed to have flushed them from above, allowing Wingfield to claim the title of first English loo.

Beyond the tower is the inner courtyard. It has the wall of the old guest wing on the left and ahead the customary spread of porch and Great Hall, with kitchens to the left and now vanished solar and family quarters to the right. However, here the pattern is interrupted by a Great Chamber positioned to the left of the screens passage and dividing the Great Hall from the kitchens. This is unusual. The chamber was presumably a reception room for the monarch, there being no room for one at the family end of the Hall. Either way, it is an impressive structure rising to roof height. Its end gable window is like that of a great Perpendicular church.

Although the Great Hall is mostly ruined, its undercroft survives, a magnificent Gothic storeroom with rib vaults of beautifully dressed stone. Wingfield still evokes the grandeur of medieval England. It shows that ruins need not be over-manicured or detached from rural life.

Devon

There is no county in which I would rather study English houses than Devon. Its landscape is celebrated, from the flanks of Exmoor down the valley of the Exe, with its rich iron-red soil, and from the severe granite of Dartmoor to the exotic palm trees of Torquay. Devon's principal cities, Exeter and Plymouth, were sorely bruised by war and subsequent poor planning. But its villages and coastline are as fine as any in England.

From the Middle Ages, Devon boasts two of England's most enjoyable manors, fortified Compton and domestic Bradley, and the great medieval hall of Dartington. Of the Tudor period, there is the Henrician courtyard of Cadhay and the great ruins of Berry Pomeroy. As in Cornwall, many Devon families suffered for their recusancy in the 17th and 18th centuries. There are few good houses of this period until the 1770s when John Parker was able to commission Robert Adam to decorate Saltram splendidly. The Georgian genius for landscape found ready expression, at Ugbrooke with Capability Brown and at Endsleigh with Repton. At A la Ronde, feminine enthusiasm for the Picturesque produced an architectural 'cabinet of curiosities'.

The Victorians fell in love with Devon. They expanded both Powderham and Hartland in neo-Gothic style. William Burges and J. G. Crace produced a Gothic fantasy for the Heathcoats at Knightshayes. Norman Shaw refashioned Flete and the Singer fortune created the astonishing mansion at Oldway in Louis XVI style. The 20th century is excellently represented. Lutyens built Castle Drogo for Julius Drewe. Milne, sacked from Dartington as a traditionalist, built Coleton Fishacre for D'Oyly Carte. Burgh Island is a rare memorial to English Art Deco.

A la Ronde ✳✳✳
Arlington ✳✳✳
Berry Pomeroy ✳✳
Bickleigh ✳✳
Broadclyst:
   Marker's Cottage ✳
Broomham ✳
Buckland Abbey ✳✳✳

Burgh Island ✳
Cadhay ✳✳✳
Castle Drogo ✳✳✳
Clovelly ✳
Coleton Fishacre ✳✳
Compton Castle ✳✳✳
Dartington:
   Hall ✳✳

High Cross ✳
Endsleigh ✳
Flete ✳✳
Fursdon ✳✳
Gittisham ✳
Haldon Belvedere ✳
Hartland ✳✳✳
Killerton ✳✳

A LA RONDE ***

Summer Lane, 2m N of Exmouth
Georgian ladies' 'cabinet of curiosities' (NT)

Two cousins, Jane and Mary Parminter, returned in 1798 from the Grand Tour in Italy. They were overloaded not with great art – they were not rich – but with what today would be considered up-market souvenirs.

One cousin died in 1811 and the other in 1849. They insisted in their wills that the house be kept intact for ever and inherited only by an 'unmarried kinswoman'. A clergyman descendant broke this trust in the 1890s, enlarging the drawing room and installing a central heating system. On his death, his wife then tried to sell the house (proving the old ladies' point). It was recovered by another female relative and opened to the public in 1935. The National Trust acquired it in 1991.

Partly designed by the ladies, on a plan inspired by the church of San Vitale in Ravenna, and partly by a cousin from Bath, A La Ronde is one of the most eccentric houses in England. It is sixteen-sided with a conical roof. This was originally thatched and without the present dormer windows. The result, it was said, 'would not be out of place in one of the South Sea Islands'.

A la Ronde today cuts a sad figure in suburban Exmouth. Its charm deserves better surroundings than a sea of bungalows, pubs and used-car dealers. Only from an upstairs window can one look out over the Exe to the Haldon Hills beyond and sense the Devonian grandeur sought by the two ladies as fit setting for their youthful memories.

The building's exterior is polygonal, its oddity accentuated by lozenge-shaped windows. Inside, the plan leads to awkward chambers with even more awkward alcoves between them. The rooms radiate from a central octagon, rising to a lantern lined with a collection of shells. This phenomenon is reached up a 'grotto' stair, also lined with shells and too fragile to be accessible. The ladies were shell-mad.

Yet structure at A la Ronde is subordinate to content. The interior is a shrine to the taste of a period and of the Parminter cousins. They collected mostly inconsequential oddments but were skilled craftswomen and mounted and displayed the objects with panache. They were proficient at needlework, drawing, wood-turning and collage.

Their dexterity with shells was amazing. The drawing room fireplace is a composition reminiscent of the English surrealist, Tristram Hillier. The shell gallery and its cases are a feast of scallops, conchs, quills, feathers, mica, glass, stones and bones.

The gallery and the staircase to it form the most complete example of the art of feather, shell and quillwork in England, possibly anywhere. Usually such compositions simply disintegrate. Here the pieces were fixed to card before being set in wet plaster on the walls. The shell gallery was conceived as a Gothick fantasy, with pointed arches and vaults encrusted with shells and feather, reflected in small mirrors. In the gallery itself is a clerestory of painted windows within shell-encrusted recesses. This is now so fragile that it can only be seen on a video screen downstairs.

All the rooms are crowded. There are numerous pictures of the ladies and their relatives, including a charming silhouette of them in the drawing room. This room contains a remarkable 'feather frieze', made of the plumage of native game birds and chickens. In the study is a beautifully embroidered coverlet and in the music room a piano which visitors are allowed to play. A la Ronde is a tiny jewel in the National Trust crown.

ARLINGTON COURT ***

Arlington, 7m NE of Barnstaple
Classical house with woodland garden, Edwardian lady's collection (NT)

Never did the outside of a house so belie the inside. The walk from the car park at Arlington passes a cold grey façade fronted by a semi-circular Doric portico. Ring to enter, says a forbidding notice. I felt inclined to run. Arlington's cellars are known to possess bats with the

Still life at A la Ronde

highest frequency sound pulses in Britain.

In 1820, Colonel John Chichester commissioned a Barnstaple man, Thomas Lee, to build him a villa on a wooded Exmoor hillside over the River Yeo. Lee had worked briefly in John Soane's office, an influence evident inside. Chichester's grandson was a high-living grandee who married Rosalie Chamberlayne, daughter of a yachting family. They had one child, a daughter, also Rosalie, much of whose life appears to have been spent on the family yacht, *Erminia.*

Chichester died of Maltese fever in 1881 and his wife remarried and 'went off'. The twenty-year-old Rosalie was left alone with the house, living there and caring for it for almost seventy years, latterly with her companion, Chrissy Peters. She died in 1949, when the house passed to the National Trust.

What one sees today is as it was left by Rosalie. The interior is architecturally simple, as befits a student of Soane, but decorated and furnished in *grande dame* style. At its core is a hall and spacious staircase, off which the principal rooms all lead. The three main reception rooms are divided only by screens of columns, their ceilings delicate and Soanian.

Rosalie Chichester's personality dominates every corner. She was a true lord of the manor. She regularly entertained her tenants and local schoolchildren, founded the local Primrose League, published the local newspaper, wrote for the *Daily Sketch* and, during the Second World War, ran the local Land Army. She guarded the Yeo valley with her life. It was declared a nature reserve and nobody was allowed to cut down a single tree. Birds were everywhere, including in the house, which became an informal aviary.

Above all, Chichester collected. She collected constantly, globally and indiscriminately, like the earlier Parminters of A la Ronde. She particularly liked shells and animal statues. With Chrissy Peters, she travelled the world and returned with trunk-loads of souvenirs. The two of them appear photographed in distant parts in heavy tweed skirts, sensible shoes, hat and stick. They look more than a match for any Levantine guide.

A list of these contents is near pointless. What is remarkable is the flair that Chichester brought to displaying her acquisitions. The objects are arranged in formal patterns, mostly in cases. In the morning room are ships and shells. The ante-room was for canaries, of which sadly none survive or has been replaced. The White Drawing Room has an amber elephant and a huge conch shell on which it is tempting to blow.

Beyond the reception rooms are subsidiary collections. The music room contains pots given to Chichester in appreciation of her help in funding the archaeological dig at Ur. A jigsaw puzzle is left on a table for visitors to help complete, a nice touch in an otherwise don't-touch house. The hall is filled with pictures of yachts, parrots and paintings of the house by Peters.

The upstairs bedrooms have been Trustified. Even the clutter seems to have been arranged by a committee. No speck of dust would dare show its face. But the cabinets retain their appeal: a line of elephants in descending order of magnitude, fans and baby costumes, pots and mugs, spoons and ladles, pet mice. The back rooms are even madder. One contains model boats. A cupboard is full of pewter. Shells and coral are everywhere. The visitor may wonder, why? Rosalie Chichester would shrug and say, why not?

Arlington has a spectacular collection of carriages in its stables and a tradition of modern sculpture in its garden.

BERRY POMEROY CASTLE **

2m NE of Totnes
Ruin of Elizabethan house above ravine (EH)

Berry Pomeroy is reached through dense woodland, its walls braving a ravine above the Gatcombe Brook. The castle of the Norman Pomeroys was one of many properties acquired by Edward Seymour, 1st Duke of Somerset, in 1547, at the height of his power as Protector of England under the infant Edward VI. He converted it as a local residence in Elizabethan style. After his fall, his grandson retreated to Devon and made the castle his home, rebuilding the Great Hall range, c1600, and giving it a grand Renaissance façade to the courtyard. The castle was abandoned at the end of the 17th century.

The castle enclosure is reached through a large gatehouse with polygonal turrets. This is still intact. Its upper chamber appears to have been a chapel, with arcade, small aisle and wall-paintings of the Adoration of the Three Kings. Above it are guardrooms. To the right of the gate is the surviving wall walk of the old castle, offering excellent views over the ruins of the interior, beyond which lies the spectacular ravine.

These ruins face into the courtyard. To the right is the earlier range built by Seymour senior, a sumptuous mid-16th-century house in the manner of Hardwick Old Hall (Derbys). Its walls stand three storeys high and the façade is roughly symmetrical, with a small courtyard hidden behind. The house has mullioned windows open to the sky, with fireplaces and stairs gazing out into space. It forms a ghostly tableau, as though a backdrop to an Elizabethan drama.

At right angles to this façade and backing directly onto the ravine are the footings of the younger Seymour's house. It had a loggia below and two storeys of glazed windows above. Behind would have been the Great Hall, with the kitchens and services to the left.

If Pomeroy were mine, I would be tempted to rebuild it. The property belongs to the Duke of Somerset and is displayed by English Heritage. It would make a spectacular house and a sensational hotel, with nothing to lose but a few ghosts. The Victorians missed a trick.

BICKLEIGH CASTLE **

4m S of Tiverton
Gatehouse of vanished mansion (P)

The old tower sits on the banks of the River Exe below Tiverton. The rest of the medieval Bickleigh was destroyed by Cromwell's troops on their rampage through the West Country in the 1640s, but a new wing was built, or rebuilt, shortly afterwards, yielding today's L-shaped house. Created by the Courteneys and held until 1926 by the Carews, it is now owned by Boxalls.

The gatehouse façade to the river is unusually wide, indicating what must have been a large Elizabethan house behind. The windows are mostly Tudor, earlier on the ground floor. The central arch has a fine ribbed vault. To its left is the old armoury, filled with Cromwellian weaponry and displaying a set of stone relief carvings apparently from an overmantel. They appear to show scenes from the suppression of the anti-Reformation Prayer Book Rebellion of 1549 outside Exeter; it is a work of great historical importance.

To the right of the arch are conventional Carew portraits and an extraordinary, gloomy picture of Napoleon staring into a fire in the aftermath of Waterloo. A battered old staircase leads to a Great Chamber over the gateway. This has large windows, roaring fires and two full-length Georgian portraits of John and Elizabeth Carew. In the Jacobean wing is a dining room, heavy with beams and pewter. Above is a bedroom with a chunky 17th-century four-poster.

BROADCLYST: MARKER'S COTTAGE *

Broadclyst, 4m NE of Exeter
Cob cottage with wall paintings (NT)

This pretty cottage tucked away in a back street of Broadclyst dates from the 15th century. It is outwardly a simple thatched structure, named after a Georgian owner, Sally Marker. The building has three rooms with a cross passage.

A parlour is formed by a wooden partition dividing the hall in half, apparently to exclude the smoke from a central hearth. This hearth was replaced by a fireplace in the Tudor period. A later rear stair turret led to a new upper room created in the roof, with dormer windows. All this reflects the customary modernization of medieval houses in the 16th century. The cottage belongs to the National Trust.

The delight of Marker's is the hall partition, covered on both sides by thick layers of paint. On the hall side, where the fire was located, the paintings are barely discernible but they combine abstract patterns with figures. On the parlour side is a representation of cherubs and of St Andrew with his cross and ship. It displays the sophistication achieved by artisan craftsmen in these out-of-the-way places.

There is a small chamber above the hall and an original unglazed mullioned window in the lower room, used for storage. These windows were often known as Armada windows, installed as house improvements to celebrate the end of economic uncertainty with the defeat of the Spanish fleet. The Trust has left an old 1950s fireplace, demonstrating the passage of time.

Painted screen at Broadclyst

BROOMHAM FARM *

2m NE of King's Nympton, , SW of South Molton
Derelict medieval farmhouse, re-thatched
(P-R)

When I approached this place its owner, Mr Clements, calmed his ferocious dogs and demanded of me, 'You from Devon?' When I said no, he muttered, 'A furriner!' I told him I was on my way to Cornwall, which he warned me was 'bows and arrows country'. A fine sense of territory is still alive in England.

Few readers will find this place and Mr Clements will not mind. Broomham is in a lost valley between South Molton and King's Nympton. The old buildings are part of a complete medieval group round a Devonian cruck hall, a stone and cob construction with a thatched roof, dating from the 14th century. Its discovery greatly excited English Heritage and a grant has restored the thatch but no more. The house is (or was on my visit) still semi-derelict. The upstairs rooms, last occupied half a century ago, are still filled with old bedsteads, steamer trunks, gas masks and back numbers of *Picture Post*.

The core of the farm is a hall with a later upper storey inserted. To one side is a massive fireplace. Upstairs, the crucks are evident, with plaster still clinging to them in places. The bedrooms are at the family end of the hall, the service range at the other. The latter is a tumbledown storeroom with, behind it, the old kitchen, dairy, pantry and spiral staircase to the attic, where the farmworkers would have slept. The smoking room for curing meat is intact, a great rarity.

A date of 1638 can be discerned on the front of the house, presumably the date of its last 'modernization'. Outside the wall, an old watercourse still runs past what would have been the scullery and garderobe. These are all the more remarkable for being covered in dirt and dust, frozen in time, utterly neglected. What is precious about Broomhall is not its past but its present, and that cannot last.

BUCKLAND ABBEY ***

2m W of Yelverton
Ghost of Cistercian abbey and home of
Francis Drake (NT)

The former home of Sir Francis Drake is not an abbey, a house or quite a museum. It was acquired by Drake on his return from circumnavigating the globe, a hero but still an *arriviste* in Devon circles. After the Dissolution, the old abbey had been sold to Sir Richard Grenville, whose family converted it into a substantial home. When the Grenvilles decided to sell, Drake, who disliked Grenville intensely, bought the house anonymously to spite him.

Grenvilles reacquired it after the Civil War a century later, but Drakes repossessed it and held it by descent until 1937. After a severe fire the following year, it was sold to a neighbour who gave it to the National Trust.

The Abbey was a Cistercian foundation, sited with customary seclusion in a curve of the Tavy valley. The Grenvilles did not do what most post-Dissolution occupiers did and demolish the monastery church and use the abbot's quarters as a residence. They converted the church itself. As a result, ghosts of arcade arches can be seen buried in later walls. Gothic windows are interspersed with Tudor and Georgian ones. Corbels start out of drawing room ceilings.

Tracing the original abbey plan is thus confusing. To make it even harder, parts of the abbey have been converted into private apartments. After descending the valley through charming gardens, visitors enter directly onto a Georgian staircase which rises spectacularly through four floors of the old church. It leads to exhibition galleries inserted horizontally in the volume of the old nave. The upper ones were rebuilt after the 1938 fire. Drake's coat of arms can be seen over the granite fireplace, placed within what was the old crossing arch.

Off the 'nave' galleries are the old family living rooms. The Drake Chamber and the dining room are finely furnished and hung with contemporary paintings, but they are somehow lost in the museum displays. Only the Great Hall truly holds its own, built in the 16th century into the church crossing. This was one of the earlier Grenville family's rooms, dated 1576, and has been restored as such. The plasterwork is original, a didactic display of Elizabethan imagery. Over the fireplace are the four Virtues beneath a bracket of a devilish satyr. The ceiling has geometrical tracery, but at one end a tableau depicts an old soldier retiring to cloistered Buckland and resting under a vine, a charming Virgilian vignette. The wood panelling is equally decorative, with inlaid animal masks and fertility symbols.

Beyond the Great Hall is a chapel created on the site of the Abbey high altar by a Drake descendant, Lady Seaton, in 1917. Outside the house is a knot garden, herb garden and maze of paths. Buckland's most remarkable survival is the Great Barn through which visitors pass to reach the house. This gigantic structure dates back to the Cistercian period and was reputedly bigger than the Abbey church itself.

BURGH ISLAND *

Off the coast at Bigbury-on-Sea
Art Deco pleasure palace on island (H)

Burgh Island is an acquired taste. It lies across 200 yards of open beach, requiring an amphibious vehicle to reach it at high tide. The original house was built as a hotel in 1895 by a music hall singer, George Chirgwin. In 1927 he sold it to a star-struck industrialist, Archibald Nettlefold, who had just married an opera singer.

In 1929 Nettlefold commissioned the architect, Matthew Dawson, to design what amounted to a private holiday home in which his wife and her fashionable friends might drink cocktails and dance to jazz. The house briefly fulfilled Nettlefold's dream. Visitors included Noël Coward, Agatha Christie and the Prince of Wales and Mrs Simpson. 'Harry Roy's Mayfair Four' were ferried to a diving platform off the beach to play jazz for swimming guests.

The house soon became a hotel, which it remains, much favoured by those seeking escape from prying eyes. Agatha Christie used it as setting for a number of novels, with television's Poirot following close behind. The building remains a rare example of an Art Deco residence. Its sleek white outline with small tower stands bold against the green of the island. Everything about the place, the doorways, lift, lavatories, even the menus and lettering, is Art Deco, a miniature Savoy.

Of the original rooms, the entrance to the ballroom is the most evocative. It might be the saloon of a Transatlantic liner. The bar has a skylight of stained glass fanning out into a peacock's tail. The hotel walls are decorated with Fritz Lang movie posters, photographs of inter-war movie stars and framed bathing costumes of the period. The dining room has one lapse in taste, a naval bar bought from the last sailing vessel commissioned by the Royal Navy, HMS *Ganges*, broken for scrap in 1929.

Buckland: the Georgian staircase

Below the hotel, a cluster of fishing cottages survive, together with the admirable Pilchards Inn. 'Imagine a silver shining sea of pilchards frothing to the windward,' enthuses the hotel.

CADHAY ***

1m NW of Ottery St Mary
Tudor house round Jacobean courtyard (P)

Cadhay is a Tudor house with a simple E-plan façade and inner courtyard, still in private family ownership. The house was mostly built in the 1540s in the traditional form of a hall with screens passage and service and domestic wings behind. The owner was John Haydon, a lawyer who grew rich dissolving monasteries in the West Country. His great-nephew, Robert, enclosed the three ranges with a Long Gallery, forming an inner courtyard.

This courtyard is the pride of the house. It is symmetrical, with statues of Henry VIII and his three monarch offspring, Edward, Mary and Elizabeth, adorning each façade. The stonework is laid chequerboard, of limestone interspersed with local 'chert' flint. Called the Court of Sovereigns, it is one of the treasures of Devon. The statues, erected in 1617, are wonderfully accomplished works of Jacobean Mannerism. The figures seem to burst from their niches between complex classical columns on ornamental brackets. The carver is unknown.

Cadhay was converted internally by a new owner, William Peere Williams, in 1736. Its charm now lies in the marriage of these two periods. Williams altered many of the rooms and put an upper floor in the Great Hall. The house was later rescued from agricultural use by a Cambridge academic, Dampier Whetham, who bought Cadhay in 1910 and reinstated its Tudor character in line with the Edwardian revival of interest in English vernacular. Beyond the Great Hall, where the solar range would have been, are family living rooms. The Williams-Powlett family have owned the house since 1935.

Upstairs and at the rear of the inner courtyard is the Long Gallery. The old barrel vault is

plastered and the room filled not with pictures but with odds and ends of family history. A collection of pewter finds space among bits of furniture, pistols and books about Devonian fly-fishing. The chamber above the Great Hall shows its original roof: great curved beams, braces and rafters much abused by time but the nobler for it. Cadhay has an enjoyably faded domesticity. It is warmed by oil heaters only. Cobwebs guard the rafters.

CASTLE DROGO ***

4m NW of Moretonhampstead
Truncated Lutyens castle on moor (NT)

Castle Drogo is a monument to one man's pride. Julius Drew ranked with Thomas Lipton and John Sainsbury as one of the kings of Victorian retailing. In 1883, at the age of just thirty-three, he was so rich he retired from his Home and Colonial Stores empire and set up as a country gentleman. Born of a line of merchants, he married well and bought Wadhurst Hall in Sussex. By 1900 he was a JP and appeared in *Burke's Landed Gentry* as 'Drew of Wadhurst Hall'. Neither Lipton nor Sainsbury was listed, much to his satisfaction.

Drew set about acquiring a pedigree to match his wealth, with a determination normally confined to the immigrant rich. He traced the Drew family to Devon and possibly to a Norman knight called Drogo, and added an -e to his name in the process. Land was acquired in the vicinity of the conveniently named Drewsteignton. Finally in 1910 Edwin Lutyens was commissioned to build a castle appropriate to so ancient a line. But even Drewe's reach proved more than his architect's grasp.

The moorland site was and is magnificent. It overlooks the gorge of the River Teign towards the uplands of Dartmoor. The castle was intended to be vast, with barbican, gatehouse, Great Hall and courtyards. Only a third of this was built, and that required twenty years of

Cadhay's Court of Sovereigns

effort and agony. By the time Castle Drogo was partly finished in 1925, the cost had risen three-fold. Drewe had had a stroke and lost his eldest son in the Great War. He died in 1931. Over the door, with its working portcullis, he could see the heraldic 'Drewe lion', but there was not so much as a knighthood to his name. His family passed the house to the National Trust in 1974.

Castle Drogo is a 20th-century palace piled on a rock. It is built of local granite, which is highly porous and prone to leakage. Drewe refused normal drainage pipes, sloping roofs or central heating. This was to be a medieval castle. But Castle Drogo is not a Victorian pastiche. It is unmistakably a 20th-century variation on a medieval theme, and unmistakably Lutyens.

The castle is not a lovable building. Even today, its stone oxidized and bleached with mortar, it seems spartan. Lutyens struggled to give it eccentricity and a sense of humour. The portcullis grins, the south-east tower has medieval 'beaks' or batwings to resist sappers. But the jokes are forced. It is hard to imagine a young family bouncing about the place, relaxing and cracking jokes. Dressing for dinner at Castle Drogo would imply a suit of armour.

Severity is at least relieved by furniture and fittings. Many were acquired by Drewe from a bankrupt Spanish banker, from whom he had bought Wadhurst. They are anything but 'ancestral' and give the entrance an Iberian feel. The library and billiard room contain tapestries from Wadhurst and are warmed by large Axminister carpets, something of a relief. The shelves were not fitted until 1931, the year of Drewe's death. In the library is a German table football machine of 1900. The drawing room, with its deal panelled walls and chintz chair covers, has large windows filling it with light and views.

The rest of the castle is a warren of stone corridors and barrel vaults. A staircase of spacious proportions, lit by a huge window, leads down to a modest dining room. This was Lutyens' eventual substitute for the original Great Hall and Great Chamber, intended

for this range. The room is 17th century in style, panelled and with a rich plaster ceiling. The Lutyens signature is a bare granite frieze through which water would regularly leak. Once when dining at Castle Drogo, Lutyens drew pictures on his menu card, mixing mustard and wine for ink.

Despite its structural medievalism, Castle Drogo was and is full of modern appliances. A built-in vacuum cleaning system sucked dirt from the floors into walls vents. There were 332 electric sockets and a superb and complex switchroom. The domestic wing is modest, almost comfortable. A room is kept as memorial to the young Adrian Drewe, killed at Ypres. A charming chapel was constructed in the undercroft of the south wing.

When asked about a garden, Julius Drewe told Lutyens that he wanted 'heather, bracken, broom, holly, brambles, foxgloves'. He got them. This is a Dartmoor landscape of pines and tors, rocky outcrops and sweeps of moorland. Yet a formal garden was designed out of sight of the moorland vista, to the north-west, advised by Gertrude Jekyll. It is a pleasant enclave, inappropriate to a castle.

CLOVELLY: FISHERMAN'S COTTAGE *

Clovelly, 10m SW of Westward Ho!
Cottage in picture village (M)

The former fishing village of Clovelly clinging to its cliff in North Devon is still worth a detour. I say this despite the locating of a large supermarket and visitor 'experience' on the hillside above it. This is to enable the Rous estate, owners of the village, to charge visitors for access. Most such owners might make do with a car park kiosk. As it is, the centre has stolen the village tourist trade.

The main street down to the harbour remains charming, rejoicing in the name, 'Up along down along'. The initials CH on many cottages indicate the year of their renovation

20th-century barional: Castle Drogo

under a previous benefactress, Christina Hamlyn. Behind the former house of the writer, Charles Kingsley, is a small cottage restored as that of a Victorian fisherman, although its last occupant was Mrs Webber, the village seamstress.

The conversion has been well done. Downstairs is a sitting room and kitchen-cum-bathroom. Upstairs is a single and a double bedroom, with space in the loft for drying sails, nets and other fishing paraphernalia. On the walls hang simple Biblical texts. Oilskins and old sweaters droop from pegs. Photographs convey some sense of the tight-knit community which inhabited the place from the late 1500s into the 20th century.

COLETON FISHACRE **

3m E of Kingswear
D'Oyly Carte's Art Deco holiday house (NT)

The new rich of the 20th century may have had style, but they rarely had longevity. They built their country houses as retreats, used them for a while and lost interest. Their children felt no bond with county England.

Coleton was built by Rupert D'Oyly Carte, son of the impresario of the Gilbert and Sullivan operas and proprietor of the Savoy Theatre and Hotel. A fashionable young man (his elder brother, Lucas, was said to be model for Wodehouse's Psmith), he married the daughter of the Earl of Cranbrook. He and his wife selected the site for their new country house from a yacht offshore, hardly a sign of commitment to the land.

The house was built in 1923–6 and claims to be a 'house of the jazz age'. Yet the exterior is firmly in the manorial vernacular style of the Arts and Crafts movement. It has sweeping gabled roofs, stone walls and small chimneys. The architect was Oswald Milne, who had worked in Lutyens' office and was shortly to be displaced at neighbouring Dartington for designing in an 'Early Georgian and vernacular' style that was considered 'out of keeping with [Dartington's] modern needs', as the guidebook puts it.

The site is gloriously isolated, at the end of a long lane that seems never to reach the sea. The polygonal entrance porch fills the angle of what is a 'butterfly' house, a plan favoured by early 20th-century architects. The interior is essentially a stage-set for entertaining. The entrance hall leads directly into the saloon, reached down a semi-circular flight of steps beneath an Art Deco arch. We can imagine new arrivals alighting from their Bentleys and finding themselves suddenly 'on parade' at the top of the steps. This spectacular room has a plastered ceiling, its emptiness relieved by Art Deco wall lights. The rugs are by the American designer, Marion Dorn.

The saloon is complemented by a sitting room, library and dining room, some with original fittings. Upstairs are Edward Bawden tiles in the bathrooms, honeycomb ceiling lights but as yet little furniture. Many views to the sea, such as from the dining loggia, have become obscured by trees. Such landscaping is baffling. Surely vistas intended by architects should be respected as such.

Rupert's son was killed in a car accident and his daughter Bridget sold the house in 1949. It passed to the National Trust in 1982, along with a spectacular stretch of coastline desperately in need of protection, and admirable gardens open to the public.

COMPTON CASTLE ***

Compton, 4m W of Torquay
Complete medieval fortified manor (NT)

This might be a set design for a Disney epic. Yet Compton is the real thing, a medieval fortified manor with its defences intact. The north front lies in a Devon combe beyond a long, thatched barn. Although the house belongs to the National Trust, it is still occupied and maintained by its ancestral owners, the Gilberts.

The old manor was begun in the 14th century, when a Compton married a Gilbert. A later Gilbert added the surrounding curtain wall in the 1520s, whether from genuine fear of attack or antiquarian ostentation, we do not

know. The answer by that date was almost certainly the latter.

The Gilberts abandoned Compton in the 1800s and it fell into ruin. Pictures of the house in the late 19th century show a mirage of a castle enveloped in creeper, like something from Angkor Wat. This ruin was reacquired in 1930 by the splendidly named Commander Walter Raleigh Gilbert, who restored it as a family home. This it remains.

The restored house is complete in all essentials. A high wall encloses a tight inner courtyard. The house itself is H-plan round the Great Hall, reconstructed in 1955 on archaeological evidence, with Decorated tracery in the windows. A small garden lies within the walls to the rear.

Compton is more modest than it seems from outside. On one side of the Great Hall is a solar above an old cellar, refashioned as a parlour. In front of it is a small chapel, still in use. On the other side is the steward's room, buttery, pantry, larder and kitchen. The last is a magnificent survival, with plaster crumbling over rough stone and one of the biggest fireplaces anywhere. Bedrooms were and still are confined to the five enclosing towers, a residence compact and defensible. There are even crossbow slits in the tower rooms.

The present Gilberts have refurnished the house in the Tudor style and with mementos of the family through history. Sir Walter Raleigh's mother was a Gilbert by a previous marriage, and Gilberts have long been prominent seamen. They furnished ships to fight the Armada and colonists to populate the American colonies, founding the Canadian province of Newfoundland. A Gilbert son continues the tradition by being called Walter Raleigh.

DARTINGTON HALL **

2m NW of Totnes
Restored medieval Great Hall (P)

Dartington is now the centre of a thriving arts and education foundation, embracing a summer school, crafts and training centre and organic farm. At the heart of the estate is the old medieval house, arranged round a traditional courtyard, a rare survival from the pre-Tudor era and dating from the end of the 14th century. It was one of the largest such establishments in the West Country and reflects its medieval ownership by the Earl of Huntingdon and by Margaret Beaufort, wife of Henry VI.

In 1559, Dartington was bought by the Champernownes and remained in that family until 1925, when it was sold to Leonard and Dorothy Elmhirst. Leonard was a Yorkshire squire's son and follower of the Indian poet and progressive reformer, Rabindranath Tagore. Dorothy was daughter of the American tycoon, William Whitney. With this mix of idealism and money, Dartington could not fail.

The semi-derelict medieval buildings were taken in hand and restored with more than usual rigour. The Great Hall had no roof or windows and the porch tower was about to collapse. Pevsner pondered whether the result is not 'more ideal to the American rather than the sloppier British' taste in renovation.

The courtyard is reached through a gate next to the old tithe barn. The original builder, Huntingdon, was executed in 1400, before he could build the customary ostentatious gatehouse. The main ranges are mostly of the late 14th century.

Of the heavily restored interiors only the Great Hall is accessible or of particular interest. It compares with Penshurst (Kent) among the great private halls of its time, but has none of Penshurst's atmosphere. It was restored in the 1920s by William Weir with new roof timbers from the estate. The form is hammerbeam with wind-braces. The giant window openings are worthy of a cathedral although the Gothic tracery is 18th century. The fireplace against the far wall is original. The screen is of the 1920s.

The west range of the courtyard is a rare survival of medieval guests' lodgings, in five groups with four rooms to each group. Such buildings would have housed visitors and the lord's retinue when he was in residence. The barn was converted into a theatre in 1933 by Walter Gropius.

DARTINGTON: HIGH CROSS *

2m NW of Totnes
Leading Modernist monument (M)

High Cross is one of England's few Modern Movement houses accessible to the public. The house was built in 1932 by the Dartington Hall Trust for the headmaster of its school, an American named William Curry. It expressed the latest in Modernist design. To the apostle of that age, Nikolaus Pevsner, High Cross could not have been more exciting, 'one of the first essays in the International Modern Style' in England.

The house was designed by William Lescaze, a Swiss-American whom Curry had used for a house at his previous school in Philadelphia. It showed no respect for Devon, for its materials or climate. 'Smooth-pressed steel doorcases' were imported from America. Nor did it defer to the vernacular tradition of which Dartington was an ideological offshoot, the Arts and Crafts movement. Oswald Milne, architect of traditionalist Coleton Fishacre (above), was sacked to make way for Lescaze.

The house is composed of two linked flat-topped boxes. To the road, a blank wall is relieved only by two decks of horizontal slit windows and a projecting porch. The garden front is more developed, a curved study and three-storey domestic wing. There is a roof terrace outside the master bedroom, for healthy outdoor sleeping. The windows are all metal and, where appropriate, curve round corners in the Bauhaus manner. The render is white, except the garage and guest wing where it is blue.

Curry eulogized the interiors as having 'serenity, clarity and a kind of openness', which he contrasted with houses 'crowded with furniture and knick-knacks'. Walls are white and spare, or composed of opaque glass cubes. All lighting is concealed. Fireplaces have dark tiled surrounds. Nothing is superfluous or cosy.

The house was greeted with enthusiasm by the Trust's co-founder, Dorothy Elmhirst, who found it 'stark and beautiful . . . I wonder whether in a few years we shall regard every other type of architecture stuffy, suffocating and artificial.'

Although much used for public housing projects, the style was little imitated in domestic architecture, at least when residents were allowed to choose for themselves. Cement and metal do not age or wear well. High Cross seems unable to carry its years, the exterior details shabby and the garden run to seed.

Contemplating High Cross today, we can see it only as a blind alley. Yet the house has been well restored for the Dartington archive and marks a chapter in English architectural history.

ENDSLEIGH HOUSE *

8m NW of Tavistock
Old fishing lodge above ravine landscape (P)

In a county of landscape drama, Endsleigh is supreme. On a bright April day the banks of rhododendron escort the visitor to a terraced garden and look-out over the ravine of the River Tamar far below. On every side is thick evergreen. This could be the Hudson River at the time of the early explorers. The estate was crafted by Humphry Repton in 1814 for the 6th Duke of Bedford, of whose Devonian properties Endsleigh forms part (recalled by name in his Bloomsbury streets). When Repton gave the Duke the relevant Red Book he added, 'I confess I never so well pleased myself.'

Above this setting is a Regency hunting lodge. Its site had originally appealed to the Duchess of Bedford, Georgiana, whose four sons laid the foundation stone of the house in 1810. While Repton planned the landscape, Sir Jeffry Wyatville designed a house and garden buildings. The front courtyard embraced stables and outbuildings and the main house was called Endsleigh Cottage, now House.

The house is a private fishing club and public restaurant. It is as Wyatville left it, with an entrance hall and suite of reception rooms enjoying superb views over the ravine. The house is furnished as an Edwardian sporting retreat. Old pictures are yellow with age, as is the wallpaper. Trophies peer down from dark ceilings. Battered books in sombre bookcases record sporting achievements on river and moor. The place is of a piece and should not be changed. It is for sale at the time of writing.

FLETE **

2m S of Ivybridge
Norman Shaw's house on hill for Baring tycoon (P-R)

Flete is Richard Norman Shaw's romantic evocation of a castle on a cliff. A Tudor and then Georgian building on the site had been altered in 1835 by the Bulteel family. It then witnessed a saga worthy of Trollope's *The Way We Live Now*. Left a widow in 1843, Lady Elizabeth Bulteel went to London and worked hard to marry her three daughters to rich husbands. She succeeded. One daughter went to the Prince Consort's equerry, Sir Henry Ponsonby, another to a banking Baring and another to a Baring partner, Henry Mildmay.

Lady Elizabeth's only son inherited Flete, but he was a spendthrift and eventually had to sell it. Her son-in-law, Henry Mildmay, duly bought it back in 1876 and asked Norman Shaw, architect of the Barings headquarters in Bishopsgate, to improve it. His wife insisted that the exterior appearance and floor plan be retained.

Shaw appeared to gather together all the components of old Flete and double them in size. He could always turn topography to advantage when the money was right – as at Cragside (Northumbs). Dominating the structure across the park is Shaw's great tower, of red roughcast Devon stone. It displays two niches with statues, of the Falconer and the Hunter. The rest of the exterior is a picturesque, asymmetrical jumble of façades, based on earlier houses on the site. A row of Tudor gables can be seen overlooking a rear courtyard, Shaw's bow windows glaring down at their antique impertinence.

The interior is almost all Shaw, in his grandest Jacobean style. The big-boned entrance hall is integrated with the staircase, which appears to sweep upwards round 360 degrees. The space has Piranesian drama, with massive stone arches for support and rich panelled woodwork. The main reception rooms pack the customary Shavian punch. The library has a huge inglenook with a chimneypiece worthy of Cragside. It projects on marble Ionic columns, a carved frieze carrying voluptuous putti. Inside the inglenook is a complete neo-Jacobean ceiling, a chamber within a chamber. The room's bay window has lights by William Morris.

The morning room is in the manner of a Great Hall. It has a medieval fireplace with Gothic columns and next to it a large bow window onto the rear courtyard. The drawing room has another fine alabaster fireplace. The hall of the old house became the billiard room under Shaw and is now the dining room. Reached down a flight of stairs and panelled throughout, it contains another colossal fireplace. The house, gloomy but spectacular, is owned by the Country Houses Association.

FURSDON HOUSE **

6m S of Tiverton
Waterloo hero's house with family museum (P)

The old walls of Fursdon House have sheltered twenty-three generations of Fursdons in unbroken male succession since the 13th century. Given the present family's fecundity, there seems no danger of the habit being broken. The house is beautifully positioned looking over the Exe Valley towards Dartmoor.

Fursdon was rebuilt in 1732 with a severe, rendered Georgian façade. This was amended in 1818 when George Fursdon returned a hero from the Battle of Waterloo and rewarded himself with a new ballroom and library in one, thus satisfying his twin enthusiasms for dancing and reading. He also constructed a pleasant colonnade across the front. Virginia creeper has since added a further softening touch.

Inside, the former Great Hall has had its old screen restored at one end. The parlour to the left of the entrance has Jacobean panelling, imported from elsewhere, complete with a scrollwork frieze and caryatids above the fireplace. The staircase hall is hung with pictures of Fursdons throughout history.

The family have assembled the produce of their attics into a small museum to the rear of the ground floor. This includes costumes, weapons and other family paraphernalia. It must have been as enjoyable for the family to assemble as for visitors to enjoy. It is something many houses might copy.

GITTISHAM: COMBE HOUSE *

Gittisham, 2m SW of Honiton
Jacobean house with Rococo interiors (H)

The winding drive through the woods from Gittisham gives way to parkland across which is seen a fine Jacobean façade against a backdrop of deepest green. The old house was bought in 1615 by a lawyer, Nicholas Putt, whose descendant, Thomas Putt, restored it after 1815. It is now carefully neo-Jacobean, with a picturesque flurry of gables and chimneys. The house is a discreet hotel.

The old Great Hall is still that, a high, bold chamber of the late 17th century with surprisingly grand bolection moulded panelling. Doorcases have big broken pediments and the fireplace is flanked by pilasters and carved fruit. Walls are deep crimson, adorned with stags' heads and old portraits. This room is almost ducal in scale.

Two other rooms merit attention. The dining room is decorated with recently painted rustic murals. Its neighbour, another dining room, is an amazing survival. Decorated in the 18th century, it is alive with English Rococo plasterwork. The overmantel carries fronds and Ho-Ho birds, themes repeated in high relief in the ceiling. The doorcases are likewise decorated with birds. The room is gay and lighthearted.

Combe House shows how a hotel, sensitively

handled, can bring life to an old house. There is a log fire in the grate, a burst of flowers on every plinth, a fine staircase and little sign of commercialism.

HALDON BELVEDERE *

near Dunchideock, 7m SW of Exeter
Gothick memorial tower (P)

The Haldon Hills above the Exe Valley formed a geographical barrier beyond Exeter. They forced even Brunel into a detour, taking his Great Western Railway along the coast at Teignmouth. From the top is a view to Dartmoor, Exmoor, and east to Portland Bill. Small wonder Georgian enthusiasts for the Picturesque could not resist erecting a look-out point.

Haldon Belvedere is a three-sided Gothick tower, castellated and rendered white. The tower was created in honour of the friendship of two employees of the East India Company, Stringer Lawrence and Sir Robert Palk. Lawrence was an old general who went out to India in 1747 to found the company's militia and form what became the Indian Army. Palk was the company chaplain who renounced holy orders and rose to become Governor of Madras and hugely rich. He returned to England in 1767, married and bought Haldon House (demolished in 1920) with 11,000 acres.

In 1788 Palk built the Belvedere tower as a memorial to his friendship with the general, by then deceased. He called it Lawrence Castle and set a statue of Lawrence in Roman attire in the downstairs hall. It is a Coade stone copy of one by Scheemakers in the Foreign Office in London. The tower above is remarkably handsome. Triangular in plan it has a turret at each angle. One contains a spiral staircase, reputedly the longest continuous cantilever in existence (a frequent claim). There are three floors and a roof terrace. Windows and glazing bars are Gothick. The tower has been well restored by a local trust.

The first floor is a miniature ballroom with parquet floor and Gothick plaster vault. Tripartite windows light each side. Above

is a holiday flat with kitchen and bathroom in the turrets. The views on a fine day are spectacular.

HARTLAND ABBEY ***

1m NW of Hartland
Gothick mansion with Victorian interiors (P)

Hartland Abbey seems at the end of the world. The adjacent coast was a sailor's hell, a place of wrecks, smugglers and hidden coves. The old abbey survived until the Dissolution after which it was given to Henry VIII's wine cellarer, William Abbott. It has not been sold since. In 1779 a descendant, Paul Orchard, demolished the old house and built a new one in the Gothick style. It faced inland and uphill, with a crenellated parapet and Gothick traceried windows, all in a soft grey stone.

This house was taken in hand in 1845 by another descendant, Sir George Stucley, who commissioned Sir Gilbert Scott to build a new entrance annex and outer hall. It is Sir George's alterations and decoration that give the house its present character. Hartland is a free-spirited Victorian interior, bursting with colour and pride in lineage.

Scott's entrance leads through a large trefoil arch into what is called the Alhambra Corridor, the bold spine of the otherwise modest house. Its vault was decorated by Scott in bright blue and white stencils, vaguely related to the Alhambra. The walls are hung with family portraits and pictures of the house. There is a fine G. F. Watts of a boy with a dog.

The three principal rooms are the drawing room, billiard room (now a sitting room) and dining room. The drawing room is Scott at his most inventive, ostensibly inspired by his better known work at the House of Lords. There are elongated linenfold panels and a frieze of Arthurian murals by Alfred Beer. The fireplace and doorways are effusive Jacobean revival, adorned with incised columns.

The old billiard room retains its 18th-

The Alhambra Corridor, Hartland

century decoration, in pale blue with pretty Gothick curtain pelmets. Sir George Stucley brought the fireplace back from Malta on his yacht, unloading it at Hartland Point. The dining room reverts to Scott, almost a facsimile of the drawing room. The room has an expanding round table at which the present baronet's mother used to eat in solitary splendour beneath the heraldic fireplace.

The rest is clearly a family home. The Georgian Little Dining Room contains a Kneller of an 18th-century Stucley, who saved Stonehenge from being used as a local quarry. The library is Gothick, with a charming ogival overmantel and portraits by Reynolds. In the basement is an exhibition of Hartland life in the 19th and early 20th centuries, mostly from Stucley photographs. They embrace local haymaking and war service with Kitchener at Khartoum. Nothing seems to have escaped the Stucley camera.

KILLERTON HOUSE **

6m NE of Exeter
Georgian house of Devon grandees (NT)

The Aclands can lay claim to the title of grandest of the Devonian grand, although the guide to Killerton remarks that this was 'sheer genetic luck'. First recorded in North Devon in 1155, their peculiar skill was in producing male heirs when rich heiresses happened to be available. In 1680 Sir Hugh Acland decided to move his chief home to Killerton from neighbouring Columbjohn. His son and grandson both married well and, by the end of the 18th century, Acland land straddled the county from the Exe Valley over Exmoor to Holnicote. This included the best stag-hunting country in England, much to the later embarrassment of the National Trust.

Killerton House was Elizabethan, on a rising site overlooking the River Exe, north of Exeter. By the 1770s, something nobler was required. Sir Thomas Acland asked a young gardener, Robert Veitch, to lay out a new park and James Wyatt to design a new house. As often, relations between architect and client became strained and Sir Thomas decided to rebuild his old house, engaging the little known John Johnson for the task. That house remains to this day, having proved adequate even for the Victorian 'Great Sir Thomas', a man whose territorial leadership, reformism and patronage embodied landed gentility and who straddled the Georgian and Victorian eras. He was born in 1787 and died in 1871.

Trouble was soon at hand. Four generations of Aclands were Liberal MPs before Sir Richard Acland converted to socialism between the wars. In 1942, he announced to his appalled family that he intended to sell the entire estate and give the proceeds to the Socialists. After a spectacular row, a compromise was reached and the estate was added to an earlier bequest to the National Trust (*see also* Wallington/ Northumbs). There was a gentleman's agreement that stag hunting may continue, an agreement the Trust subsequently broke.

The original Georgian house stood four square to the view but was a modest place, from the outside little more than a rectory. In the 19th and 20th centuries, alterations were made, a bay window here, a rear extension there and a new entrance to one side. But today's exterior, painted a creamy-pink and covered in creeper, looks pleasantly informal.

The interior is equally so, thanks to Acland possessions covering the walls and shelves, including a fine array of family photographs. The rooms are a contrast of Edwardian informality and some surprising Georgian or neo-Georgian grandeur, with high ceilings, scagliola and Ionic screens. The music room has an organ and a piano which visitors are invited to play.

The drawing room is severely classical, much altered in the 1900s. One picture shows Lady Harriet Acland crossing a river during the American Revolution to plead (successfully) for her wounded husband's release. The library has its shelves arranged in the collegiate style at right angles to the wall. This gives more space for books and admits more light to read them, sign of a working library. The dining room beyond has a fine plaster ceiling into which a 20th-century Acland has inserted medallions of the seasons, ploughing, sowing, hoeing and reaping.

The Edwardian main staircase gave the house some swagger. Killerton is not a great English house but is full of character. The gardens laid out by Veitch are an attraction in themselves.

KINGSTON *

1m N of Staverton, near Totnes
Georgian house with marquetry staircase and wall-paintings (H)

Visitors must travel up a lane north of Staverton, then along a farm track, then across a farmyard. Suddenly a dignified stone house comes into view with a *piano nobile* above a deep basement. The front door is at the top of a Baroque staircase. The house has a brick-walled garden and meadows to the rear and is isolated and silent, apart from the owner's giant dogs. This is surely Devon's most obscure but gracious bed-and-breakfast.

The downstairs is conventional, with reception rooms round a flag-stoned hall. The drawing room has painted panels with fluted pilasters, and a dove of peace in the ceiling roundel, indication of the Catholicism of the Rowe family, who built the house in 1743. Interest increases with the staircase at the back of the hall, with a dado crowded with fluting and inlaid with precious woods. The stair may have been an import, since it seems oddly small for its void and the join to the upstairs landing is uncomfortable.

Upstairs is Kingston's treasure. The central saloon is said to have been designed as a Catholic chapel, required to be inconspicuous in the mid-18th century. Over the fireplace is a plaster relief of the Flight into Egypt, a favourite Catholic theme. Two roundels of saints flank what would have been the east-facing altar. On the walls, religious murals are now being revealed by the house's owner beneath a thick coating of wall plaster. This could yet prove a complete and undamaged private chapel.

No less remarkable are the murals in the

three bedroom suites. These retain their four posters and original closets, some converted into bathrooms. The Blue Room has a closet decorated with lions and rustic scenery, and a bathroom with wood panelling and painted graining.

KITLEY *

1m E of Yealmpton
Neo-Tudor villa by Repton junior (H)

The house is chiefly remarkable for the name of its ancestral (and existing) owners, the Polloxfen Bastard family. The Bastards settled in Devon after the Conquest. A Regency Polloxfen (pronounced Poulson) Bastard acquired celebrity and a fortune by eloping with a local heiress, Jane Pownoll, to Gretna Green. He fended off pursuit by hiring every carriage in Devon on the night in question to ensure they could not be followed.

The sister-in-law of another Polloxfen Bastard, Sarah Martin, wrote *The Comic Adventures of Old Mother Hubbard and her Dog* in the house in 1805. It was based on the housekeeper's downstairs lair and Kitley is therefore the putative home of her celebrated cupboard. Sarah reputedly rejected the hand of the future William IV in marriage. Had she accepted, the story of Kitley would have been very different.

In 1820, Humphry Repton's son, G. S. Repton, was hired to redesign the old Tudor house and grounds. The damming of the Yealm turned a muddy creek into a freshwater lake, with the house on a slope overlooking it. This house was then remodelled in the neo-Tudor style, one of the first such examples in Devon. Salvin's Mamhead (below) did not come until 1827.

Repton's building has a façade of silver-grey granite, radiating a soft pink in sunlight. The roof is crowned with an artless forest of pinnacles and chimneys, two of them Tudor directly above the entrance. Remnants of the old house can be seen in the side basement.

Kitley's interior has two features of note.

One is the entrance hall, festooned with mock-baronial heraldic shields and banners. The other is a Georgian staircase, pre-dating Repton's work; it fills the former Great Hall and is grander than the rest of the house. On the landing is a model of HMS *Apollo*, the ship commanded by Jane Polloxfen Bastard's father. It captured the Spanish galleon that secured her fortune and trip to Gretna Green. The house is now a hotel.

KNIGHTSHAYES COURT ***

2m N of Tiverton
Victorian house by Burges and Crace (NT)

The Heathcoat family were owners of the world's largest lace business, which they moved to Devon after their factory was burned by rioters in Loughborough in 1816. Loyal workers followed them on foot to keep their jobs. A descendant, Sir John Heathcoat Amory, became a local MP and gentleman, enjoying hunting and shooting. He bought the Knightshayes estate outside Tiverton for his horses. He then hired William Burges to build him a new house on the site, on a rise overlooking the Exe Valley.

Why such a man should have hired as architect an opium-addicted bachelor Gothicist, who dressed in medieval costume, is a mystery. Burges declared that all houses he designed were 'mine' and added that rules 'are made only for incapables' and that 'money is only a secondary concern in the production of first-rate works'. It was hardly a philosophy likely to appeal to Heathcoat Amory. Burges began work on the house in 1869. Not until the family returned from a holiday in 1873 to see a volume of 57 pages of drawings of the interior did things start to go wrong. Burges declared that Knightshayes would be a 'medieval fairy-land' and hugely expensive, since 'there are no bargains in art'.

Sir John begged to differ. Burges was sacked and the decorator, J. G. Crace, put in his place. The family firm of Crace had worked at Brighton Pavilion (Sussex), Longleat (Wilts) and Knebworth (Herts), and were considered the most accomplished Victorian craftsmen. By then, the vast structure was already rising on the hill. Knightshayes was thus a marriage of Burges and Crace, the one a genius of design, the other of execution.

The house stands aggressively on a bluff. The façade is Burges at his most bold, in red and yellow stone with steep gabled roof and dormers, French Gothic in style. A giant stair tower to the rear was intended by Burges but never completed. The exterior is now softened by creeper and by the celebrated gardens fashioned by Sir John's grandson; he married the inter-war woman golfer, Joyce Wethered, who became a noted horticulturalist. The house passed to the National Trust in 1972.

The house is entered through a porch under a poem carved by Burges's sculptor, Thomas Nicholls: 'God by whose gift this worke I did begin/ Conserve this same from skaith [damage], from shame, from sin'. The plea was in vain. The Great Hall was the only work completed as Burges intended. Mighty beams hover overhead and a fireplace fills the inside wall. A screen supports a minstrels' gallery.

At one end of the Great Hall marble columns guard the staircase, carried on superb corbels depicting kings, masons, knights, animals and birds. Under the staircase is a bookcase covered in painted scenes from Christian and pagan art, by Burne-Jones and others. Beyond is a smoking room, a later addition of Sir Ernest George & Peto. Here visitors may read magazines but not smoke. It contains a charming collection of miniature elephants.

The house is a *tour de force* of Crace. His wallpapers and fabrics relieve Burges's heavy-boned proportions. Flowers and butterflies dance along corridors. Walls are hung with family prints. The main enfilade was to have been Burges's masterpiece. In Crace's hand, it remains an impressive Victorian sequence, spoilt only by the National Trust's addiction to light-reducing gloom, unkind to an already dark house.

The morning room is hung with works after van der Weyden and Rembrandt. The library has Crace decorations reminiscent of Brighton

Pavilion, with jelly moulds in the ceiling. Burges had wanted this to be even more a riot of colour, his drawing showing a monk in the corner reading a book. At the end of the range is the drawing room, deep red in colour with painted roof beams. On the walls are paintings (or copies) by Turner, Constable and Bonington. If Burges wanted more than this, small wonder the Heathcoat Amorys took fright.

On an autumn day the grounds at Knightshayes are incomparable. Lawns stretch down below the main front, with paved and topiary gardens to one side, including the famous Fox and Hounds hedge. From the surrounding woodland, the 20th-century Sir John fashioned glades, dells and an arboretum. Gardening, he said, was 'eleven months hard work and one month's acute disappointment'.

MAMHEAD *

W of Kenton, 7m S of Exeter
Late-Georgian medievalism in Brown park
(P-R)

Anthony Salvin's neo-Tudor mansion stands high on a slope with distant views of the Exe estuary. The drive down from the road arrives at a fake Norman castle. This is only the stables and laundry, splendid in themselves.

The ancestral estate of the Vaughan family, already landscaped by Capability Brown, was bought in 1822 by an Exeter merchant and local MP, Robert Newman. Five years later, he boldly offered the young Salvin one of his earliest commissions. Mamhead is innovative for its date, Tudor but still with a Georgian lightness of touch. Although recently converted into offices, it is very much Salvin's work.

The Bath stone façade rises to gables, chimneys and finials. An entrance at the side gives onto what remains of a screens passage and hall, later used as a billiard room. This archaic plan yields a chamber with openwork screen, heraldic fireplace and bold Jacobean ceiling. Many of Salvin's fittings, stained glass and wall paintings survive, visible on polite request.

The glory of the house is the Lower Gallery

running as a spine behind the main reception rooms. This is a Gothic corridor with fan vaulting, leading to an even grander sweep of staircase, apparently inspired by James Wyatt's steps to Christ Church Hall, Oxford. The rooms retain baronial fireplaces. The whole interior anticipated Newman's London 'office', the Palace of Westminster.

Mamhead was one of the earliest houses to employ figures from British history rather than classical antiquity for decorative impact. Its former life-sized statues of 'royal and noble personages c1500' were recently sold at auction in London. The stained glass displayed in windows throughout the house is by the Victorian heraldic designer, Thomas Willement.

NEWTON ABBOT: BRADLEY ***

½m SW of Newton Abbot
Intact medieval manor, wall-paintings (NT)

How fashions change! When the ancient manor of the Yardes outside Newton Abbot was offered for sale in 1841 a new owner was advised to 'distinguish his taste from that of bygone days and ... render it a suitable appendage to the magnificent Woods that adorn it'. He should build a new house and make Bradley a ruin.

The new house was duly built, and later burned down. The old manor was used for farm workers and aunts. But in 1909 it found a saviour in the egyptologist, Cecil Firth, a remote descendant of the Yardes. His family, now Woolners, occupy Bradley still, infusing the place with casual charm and guarding its every cobweb, crack and woodlouse against a possible visit from the National Trust cleanliness fanatics.

The house sits in a thick valley of trees reaching into the centre of Newton Abbot. It is superbly old. A 13th-century hall was superseded by a 15th-century one built at right angles. A banqueting hall was tacked onto one end and a chapel onto the other. The main façade, apart from some 19th-century castellation, is entirely Gothic, covered in limewashed plaster. Fifteenth-century oriel windows and deep gables enclose a passage across the façade, concealing the Great Hall behind. A tiny medieval cat-hole can be seen beside the entrance.

The interior is unusual among medieval houses in having corridors, adding to the maze-like atmosphere of rooms, alcoves, beams, changing levels and general clutter. The newer Great Hall is reached past a screens passage and has a lofty roof, giant fireplace composed of slabs of moorstone and, a concession to modernity, a modern bay window facing the back garden. A huge Elizabethan coat of arms, an assertion of loyalty to the Crown in recusant Devon, rises above the dais end of the hall. Below is a portion of a Tudor screen.

Beyond the hall at this point is the old antechapel and chapel. The latter has seen services as a chicken run, storehouse, billiard room and boot-room. It has been restored, sadly without its old wagon roof but with excellent modern bosses designed by Peter Woolner.

Upstairs at Bradley are some remarkable wall-paintings. Beyond the original hall was a Tudor banqueting hall, now divided and with portions of its walls scraped to reveal two generations of mural work. One is of fleur-de-lys, and includes a quincunx. Another is of rich Tudor decoration, now mostly vanished. I sense there is much more here to be discovered.

Nor is this all. The upper part of the early hall was redecorated in the late 17th century with Bradley's only concession to modernity, a riotous naturalistic ceiling reputedly by the Abbot family of Bideford (responsible for the earlier and very different Lanhydrock/Cornwall). It is a charming work, with scallop shells in the corners and branches, leaves and flowers dripping free along the coving. The Devon countryside might have been plucked from outside the windows and applied to the walls.

The rooms at Bradley contain nothing of value and everything of use. It is a thoroughly inhabited house. Long may it remain so.

PAIGNTON: OLDWAY MANSION **

Paignton
Versailles in a Paignton backstreet, Hall of Mirrors mural (M)

Be ready for a shock. Tucked away behind Paignton's high street is the sort of building Catherine the Great might have thrown up for a courtier outside St Petersburg. Across a gravel forecourt and parterre rises a nine-pillared loggia in shimmering white with, beyond it, a blue-grey stucco façade. It was inspired by the Palace of Versailles and looks it.

Paignton's emperor was none other than Isaac Singer in 1823, an American of Jewish and Quaker extraction who ran away from home in New York at the age of twelve. He ran all the way to France. There he was moved by how much time French women spent on needle-work, and invented a machine to save them the effort. He eventually married a French girl thirty years his junior, Isabella, whose beauty was so remarkable that she is said to have modelled the Statue of Liberty for its sculptor, Bartoldi.

The Singers settled in England and amassed a vast fortune from Isaac's sewing machines. Told to move for his health to Devon, he built himself a house which he nicknamed the Wigwam. When he died in 1875 he left his son, Paris, named after his wife's home city, the then staggering sum of £15m.

Like most sons left such fortunes, Paris was fully occupied all his life in spending it. An amateur architect, he commenced rebuilding the Wigwam in 1904 in honour of his belief that he was descended from the Bourbons. He borrowed the loggia from the Place de la Concorde, but his most sensational alterations were inside. Where his father had created a theatre, he inserted an imperial staircase modelled on Versailles' Etage de la Reine. A stupendous double flight rises to an enveloping colonnade. The floors and walls are in coloured marble while, above, Paris commissioned a ceiling copied from Lebrun's depiction of

Louis XIV as a Roman emperor in the Hall of Mirrors. The artist, a German named Carl Rossner, was sent to erect scaffolding inside the actual hall in Versailles, to make sure he matched the original colours. Rossner went on to paint murals in Buckingham Palace.

The interior is astonishing. Majestic doors are crowned with the Bourbon coat of arms. In pride of place is the upstairs ballroom, another borrowing from the Hall of Mirrors. It is 127 ft long with mirrors dripping gilt. Other rooms and corridors are equally grand, with pillars of French oak, Bourbon emblems, inlaid brass trophies and ornamental doors. As final touch of authenticity, Paris in 1898 outbid the Louvre at a Belgian auction to secure David's masterpiece, *The Coronation of Napoleon and Joséphine*. He placed it on the large wallspace overlooking the stairs.

After Paris's death, the family let the house as a country club and in 1946 the Singer family sold the David to a delighted Louvre, which sent a private train to transport it safely home. A copy can now be seen on the stairs. The house was bought as offices by the local council. It added tennis courts in the gardens and municipalized the interior fittings. With imagination it could yet be restored to its full Edwardian glory. For the time being, the Bourbon arms rise magnificent over the Mayor's Parlour.

PLYMOUTH: THE ELIZABETHAN HOUSE **

32 New Street
Restored 16th-century town house (M)

Poor Plymouth. It was badly blitzed in the Second World War and then subjected to slash and burn by its city fathers. The modern visitor will find it a maze of concrete blocks, ill-sited towers and ruthless road schemes. Most of this damage was done by one man, Patrick Abercrombie, in the 1950s. The old Barbican district would, in France or Germany, have had its façades restored or rebuilt. Here new buildings were inserted with no

feeling for the texture of the old lanes and alleys.

The cobbled area round New Street still conveys some of the atmosphere of the port from which the Mayflower departed for the New World. Most of the houses were demolished in the 20th century but one of the finest, No. 32 dating from 1580, was saved intact in 1929 and has been preserved as a museum.

The exterior displays the Elizabethan love of fenestration, with three storeys of windows above a storage basement. The upper windows rest on carved brackets and have original leading. The interiors are sparsely decorated. A passage leads from front to back of the house, partitioned from the two main ground floor rooms. In one is an old Tudor settle.

The spiral stairs are of treads slotted into a central newel, probably an old ship's mast. Upstairs is a reception and an eating room, suggesting that the ground floor was probably mercantile offices. The rooms are well furnished, the eating room having carved rush chairs. The attic contains two bedrooms, one with a delightful box bed apparently from France.

PLYMOUTH: THE MERCHANT'S HOUSE *

33 St Andrew's Street
Spectacular front to Elizabethan house (M)

The Merchant's House is not as evocative as the Elizabathan House but has a remarkable façade. The first recorded owner was a sea captain named William Parker in 1608. The front, in an area otherwise blighted with modern buildings, is of four storeys, each one jettied further into the street on bold granite corbels. Above rise two big gables. The windows stretch in continuous bands across the front.

The interior is now a museum of Plymouth history, but the feel of the old house has not been lost. To the rear of the ground floor are the big fireplaces of two generations of kitchen. The stair's pole supports appear original as is the panelling in the first-floor reception room. The second-floor fireplace is a wonderfully robust work, with caryatids holding their breasts in a suggestive fashion.

That said, it seems a pity that somewhere else could not be used for so inappropriate an exhibition as of Victorian schooling and the Blitz. Houses of Plymouth's noblest era are in short supply.

PLYMOUTH: THE PRYSTEN HOUSE **

Finewell Street
Stone house round inner courtyard (P)

The house is medieval, probably built between 1490 and 1500 for a London vintner named Thomas Yogge. We know only that he dealt here in port wine. Business must have been good. This is a substantial property built round a central courtyard. The reference to a priest's or 'prysten' house appears a later misnomer, although the building is now used by the church of St Andrew's next door.

The house lies on an incline, with its lower floor leading into the courtyard, where trade would have been done. This is now a restaurant. The upper floors were domestic and, despite their heavy-handed restoration, they remain in their original form. Windows and partitions are intact and two spiral stairs survive.

The rooms have been given ecclesiastical names, with little basis for their attribution. The main reception room, benefiting from a fine bay window, is called the Frater Room. A chair in the Bishop's Room was amalgamated by a Victorian carpenter from fragments of church pews. Upstairs is the Grammar Room where the Plymouth Tapestry is on display. This was begun in 1977 and tells the story of Plymouth in more than two million stitches.

The remaining upper chambers would have been bedrooms. They are used for exhibitions and meetings but retain the atmosphere of the old house. Many look down on the courtyard, a precious moment of urban tranquillity.

POLTIMORE HOUSE *

Poltimore, 4m NW of Exeter
Tudor mansion with Rococo saloon (P-R)

Poltimore is included here out of expectation. The old house of the Bampfylde family lies in parkland on the outskirts of Exeter, ruined and vulnerable to collapse. At the time of writing, it is in the hands of rescuers determined to convert it into an arts centre. The derelict park is no less precious. The house was a Tudor manor, its surviving ranges round an inner courtyard now encased in Georgian extensions. It was degraded as a wartime hospital and then an old people's home and has not yet recovered.

The front is that of a white stuccoed 18th-century mansion. To the rear is a gabled Tudor range with original windows and a staircase turret in the angle of the courtyard. The Tudor Great Hall was remodelled by the Georgians as a saloon, its walls covered in superb Rococo stucco-work. Much of this survives and is recoverable.

The same may be true of the early-Victorian alterations made when the Bampfyldes were raised to the peerage in 1831. A grand staircase worthy of *Gone with the Wind* was built out into the rear courtyard, facing a new entrance in the 18th-century range. The new owners want to destroy it to create an architecturally fashionable glass wall, utterly out of character with what is a remarkable composition. That such a fine building should have been brought to this pass is a poor comment on the county of Devon.

POWDERHAM CASTLE ***

Powderham, 6m SW of Exeter
Family seat on bank of Exe, with Rococo plasterwork (P)

Powderham has been the seat of the Courtenays, Earls of Devon, for six centuries and is proud of it. The guidebook folds out to reveal not a picture of the castle but a monstrous family tree. The house is still the family home and the Earl welcomes the visiting public as themselves 'making a contribution to our heritage'. He is right. This is the only way these great houses will enjoy true security.

Powderham presides over an extensive park on the banks of the River Exe. It was never a castle but a fortified manor, the old structure buried in later additions. The exterior is formed of a picturesque jumble of periods. No sooner does one guess a patch to be medieval than it appears Georgian, no sooner Georgian than Victorian and no sooner Victorian than medieval. It is a family tree in architecture.

The main front to the courtyard is mostly Victorian and was battlemented by the Exeter architect, Charles Fowler, designer of Covent Garden market in London. The great dining hall, also by Fowler, is aggressively neo-medieval. The fireplace is decked with heraldry in a sort of fairground Gothic, the panelling brilliantly coloured and restored. On the north wall is a family group of 18th-century Courtenays by Thomas Hudson.

The ante-room beyond the hall contains the castle's eccentric treasures, two giant Baroque bookcases made by J. Channon in 1740. They are on dolphin feet and inlaid with brass, crowned with stupendous broken pediments. They were given in lieu of tax to the V&A then restored by the Museum to Powderham on permanent loan, an admirable example of modern conservation finance. Beyond are two Georgian libraries with deep blue wallpaper and bright Rococo ceilings.

A large music room was added by James Wyatt in 1794. This was after the coming-of-age ball of the 3rd Viscount Courtenay, later 9th Earl of Devon, had been held in a marquee – presumably to the family's shame. It has all Wyatt's delicate sophistication. A coffered dome rises above walls of scagliola pilasters. Pipers flank the marble fireplace, above which Greek maidens play and dance. Over the mantelpiece is the Viscount in his masquerade costume. He looks like a cavalier prince. (His descendants prefer to be depicted in sweaters and corduroy.)

The staircase hall was fashioned in 1736 from the upper end of the medieval Great Hall,

clearly a massive chamber. Pevsner eulogizes the staircase as the most spectacular architecture of its date in the West Country. Three flights have three twisted balusters to each tread, with the nobility of a London palace. The stair's character is dominated by its brilliant turquoise colour, on which voluptuous Rococo fronds and trophies are picked out in cream. The plasterwork of c1755 is not by an Italian but by a local man, John Jenkins. The portraits seem overwhelmed.

A range of upstairs bedrooms displays the usual family paraphernalia, including a charming rocking-boat. A crimson and gold state bed has a sweeping tent canopy crowned with a viscount's coronet, while a small corridor is lined with Chinese wallpaper and the poles of the last Empress of China's litter. Such things do we find in English houses.

What is left of the old Great Hall survives in georgianized state, but with three medieval arches still leading to the kitchens. The room contains a magnificent long-case clock, reputedly another work by Channon. The Powderham Chapel has excellent Tudor pew ends from the old church at South Huish.

PUSLINCH **

½m W of Yealmpton
Queen Anne mansion with original interiors (P)

Puslinch lies above a creek of the River Yealm opposite Kitley. Although Georgian in date (1720), it is Queen Anne in style, standing proud against the hillside. Boundary walls flank the rear garden, beyond which meadows rise to woods. The house is privately tenanted and beautifully decorated, after having degenerated into a cat and dog home in the 1970s. On my visit the lady of the house was trying to drive a flock of vagrant sheep from the lawn.

The estate belonged to a Plymouth surgeon, James Yonge, who decided to build a new house uphill from his old Tudor property. The style is plainly old-fashioned, a mansard roof with overhanging eaves. Dormer windows have alternating triangular and segmental pediments. Inside the most remarkable feature of the interior is its completeness. The rooms are as they would have been in the 17th century, with a state bedroom on the ground floor and closets adjacent to each bedroom on the first.

The hall is a handsome chamber with tall ceiling and six doors giving access to every ground floor room. Like all the main rooms, it retains Georgian panelling, painted except in the dark oak dining room. Most of the fireplaces are identical and in local marble. The handsome staircase has three balusters to each tread and is dominated by a massive still-life in the style of Snyders.

Puslinch is crammed with paintings and prints collected by the present occupants. I know of few houses so warmed by the presence of art, both ancient and modern. Not an inch, even in closets and lavatories, is unadorned by pictures. Every shelf and mantelpiece is cluttered with sculptures and found objects. Bedrooms are all in use, one with a bed designed by Lutyens. The garden at Puslinch contains one of the largest ginkgo trees in England.

SALTRAM HOUSE ****

4m E of Plymouth
Grand mansion with Adam rooms and
'Chinese Chippendale' suite (NT)

After the Second World War, the Parker family, Earls of Morley, found their line reduced to two elderly bachelor brothers. They tried to behave as if nothing had changed and briefly restored Saltram's pre-war complement of a dozen indoor staff. But when one brother died in 1951 and incurred crippling death duties, the other gave up the struggle. House, grounds and contents came to the National Trust.

Such has been the outward spread of Plymouth that Saltram is no longer an adornment of its surrounding countryside, more a desperately precious stretch of park amid the enveloping suburb. Already the A38 has cut through its grounds and plagued them with noise.

The house was originally Tudor, but was afflicted with owners variously venal, extravagant and dedicated. The early proprietors, the Baggs, were thieves and scoundrels. A 17th-century Bagg stole £55,000 given him by the Crown to equip a fleet to attack Cadiz, sending it to sea unprovisioned and leading to the deaths of 4,000 men. The house passed to the Parkers in 1712, their extravagance matched only by their ability, like the Aclands of Killerton, to marry money at the right time.

In 1743, John Parker married well and clad the old Tudor building in a set of Palladian façades. The pediments, pavilions, canted bays, Venetian windows and urns form an amateur but engaging composition, brilliant in white render. But somehow the exterior of Saltram seems no more than a stylish box, a container for the wonders within.

In 1768, Parker proceeded to refurbish the interiors with the help of Robert Adam. They are among Adam's best later works, enhanced by fine pictures from the Parker collection. The house is today regimented by the bossiest team of National Trust wardens I have yet encountered. I thought I would be horsewhipped for retracing my steps.

The first rooms are early Georgian. The entrance hall is encrusted with plasterwork, its chimneypiece carrying a relief of Androcles and the Lion. The ceiling depicts Mercury, the god, among other things, of roads, which seems appropriate at Saltram. The adjacent morning room is hung with pictures three rows deep in 18th-century style. Italian masters are interspersed with Saltram's many excellent Reynoldses. The painter was born in the adjacent parish and often visited the house.

The Velvet Drawing Room predated the Adam rooms but begins an enfilade of which they are part. Gilded Corinthian columns frame the doorway to the saloon. Walls are heavy with Canaletto, Teniers and de Hooch. A scagliola table carries *trompe-l'œil* playing cards.

Adam's saloon was a room with 'no expense

Chinoiserie delight at Saltram

being spared'. A Venetian window lights a ceiling of fans fluttering above tropical leaves. An Axminster carpet replies with an echoing pattern. Chippendale's chairs do likewise. Over the mantelpiece hangs an early copy of Titian's *The Andrians*, once owned by Reynolds, its frame by Chippendale. In the adjacent dining room Adam adjusts his decorative programme to a smaller scale, with softly modulated colours.

The spacious staircase hall reverts to Saltram's earlier Georgian period. Its ceiling is a burst of Rococo activity while on the walls is the choice of the Saltram collection: Rubens' *Duke of Mantua*, Stubbs' *The Fall of Phaeton* and works by Angelica Kauffmann, including her portrait of Reynolds. Upstairs is a suite of Chinese Chippendale rooms. One bedroom contains wallpaper depicting scenes from Chinese daily life, said to be the most expensive of the genre. The bed is attributed to Chippendale and the walls carry Chinese painted mirrors in Rococo frames. The dressing room walls have rare 'Long Eliza' wallpapers, much coveted for depicting unusually tall women, a Chinese rarity.

Saltram ends on a pleasantly dying fall with the Georgian living rooms used by the Parkers towards the end of their occupancy. In the library, Reynolds comes not singly but in rows. The Mirror Room beyond is a Saltram favourite, darkly oriental with original wallpaper and painted mirrors, some lacquered, some with gilt Rococo frames. The reflection of the viewer is made to mingle with the work of the Chinese artist, an eerie effect.

SAND **

near Sidbury, 3m N of Sidmouth
Elizabethan hall house with alligator (P)

Sand has belonged to the Huyshe family (pronounced Hoo-ish) since the 16th century. The land has not been sold since 1584, when it was bought by a London grocer, James Huyshe, who had twenty-nine children by two wives. The old house, clad in roughcast grey stone, has defied time and economics ever since,

clinging to the edge of a steep valley above the River Sid.

Most unusually, there appear to have been two hall houses co-existing next to each other through the Middle Ages. One was detected only recently, buried within a thatched barn in an outbuilding. The façade of the main house is late Elizabethan, completed by Huyshe in 1594. The front has gables along its roofline and a two-storey porch. A conventional Great Hall is flanked on either side by family and service wings. A later Huyshe added a rear extension for more bedrooms and bathrooms. Apart from restoration after fire damage, the house is as built.

The screens passage has, looming over it, an extraordinary find in rural Devon, a huge stuffed alligator. It is believed to have been brought by a Baptist Huyshe from America in the 17th century. The inner side of the Great Hall screen has Artisan Mannerist motifs, a style repeated in the dresser on the other side of the room.

An old spiral staircase leads upstairs to the former Great Chamber, surviving from a pre-Huyshe house. It has a medieval fireplace with Gothic quatrefoils. Another staircase, with oak panelling, serves the old kitchens on the far side of the hall. This was panelled in the last century with wonderfully gnarled oak. The garden contains a thatched 17th-century summer-house looking out over terraced gardens.

SHUTE BARTON **

2m SW of Axminster
Medieval mansion with 15th-century hall (NT)

On a fine day, the drive from Axminster to Shute Barton is the essence of rural Devon. The road dives in and out of woods, with sudden views over meadows down to the River Axe. Suddenly round a bend is an old gatehouse, and beyond it a courtyard and range of medieval buildings. The house is tenanted and visits must be accompanied by a National Trust guide. Shute Barton cannot be enjoyed in peace.

The land belonged to the Bonville family, passing to the Poles under the Tudors. They demolished much of the medieval house in the 18th century to build the neighbouring Shute Hall. The old property became a farmhouse, inherited by a branch of the Carew Pole family in 1926 (*see* Antony/ Cornwall). They gave it to the National Trust in 1959 but insisted that the family remain as tenants, which they do.

Entry is into the old kitchen with reputedly the largest fireplace in England – a claim so often made that it is surely time to decide. Two oxen can apparently be roasted here at once. Most of the accessible rooms seem more domestic than medieval. The drawing room has 17th-century panelling and numerous Pole portraits. Alcove windows look out over peaceful woodland.

The most remarkable relic is the old Great Hall on the top floor, Elizabethan style, reached by a tiny spiral staircase. So magnificent is its roof as to suggest that the floor may be a later insertion dividing a chamber that once extended to the floor below. The room is *c*1450 and has a garderobe in the corner. It is wonderfully bright, lit by windows on both sides with views over lawns to woods beyond. Here one can truly sense old Devon.

Outside in the courtyard is a tiny walled garden surrounded by what appear to be fragments of the old house.

SIDMOUTH: SIDHOLME *

Elysian Fields
Ecclesiastical Earl's seaside villa (H)

In 1826, the 6th Earl of Buckingham, a clergyman, built a villa for himself and his large family. Then called Richmond Lodge, it sits on a slope above the resort of Sidmouth. The address says it all. Sidmouth was and still is a charming enclave of Victorian villas looking out over wooded glades to red cliffs and the sea.

Buckingham's villa was simple, with a carriageway where now is the entrance hall. It is said that the Countess did not get on well with the local vicar, so the Earl built an extension for use as a private chapel across the carriageway. His wife had a window inserted so that she could see who was coming and going, and this survives inside the present hall. A later owner, the Davidson family, filled in the carriageway and inserted a spectacular staircase and landing.

The main house retains its Regency bargeboards, verandas and spiral stairs, looking over gardens filled with sub-tropic vegetation. Palms mix with azaleas, cedars and sequoias, framing views of the coast below.

The best feature of the interior is the Earl's chapel, now a music room for what has become a Methodist holiday hotel. It is in the form of an irregular bow with eight windows lighting a large vaulted roof. Between the windows are Rococo mirrors beneath a star-spangled roof. A splendid organ occupies one wall. The room is still used for concerts.

TAPELEY PARK *

3m NE of Bideford
Georgian revival house in exotic garden (P)

The site of Tapeley Park is said to have been spotted from the sea by the telescope of William Clevland in 1702. He declared, 'That is the place for me.' He married a local girl and eventually acquired the property. Few Devon houses have so spectacular an outlook. Below are spread the environs of Bideford. Beyond are the sand bars of Bideford Bay with the island of Lundy and the Atlantic in the distance.

In 1855, the house passed to the Christie family when Augustus Langham Christie married Rosamond, daughter of the Earl of Portsmouth. She claimed descent from no fewer than 149 Garter Knights, 60 men 'executed by their monarch' and 11 canonized saints. Small wonder she found Tapeley 'very plain and rather dreary'. She evicted her husband from the house because of his 'childish behaviour' – allegedly, kicking the furniture with his boot to annoy her – and commissioned the neo-Baroque architect, John Belcher, to redesign the house. Her husband took his revenge by leaving the house to a Canadian cousin and then dying. Rosamond went to court to prove that he must have been insane, and won.

Her son was John Christie, founder of Glyndebourne Opera, who spent half his time in Sussex and half at Tapeley. His daughter, also Rosamond, ran the house until her death in 1988, showing visitors round with a parrot sitting on her head. Her nephew, Hector, is now in charge.

The house is to outward appearance a handsome Georgian villa, of brick with stone pilasters and entrance porch. The garden is of tropical lushness. The drive rises past pines and pampas grass to reach the Dairy Lawn. The side elevation of the house is here colonnaded. The main front beyond looks out over the Italian garden, which descends the hillside in a series of spectacular terraces. In the distance is a lake. On a hot summer's day, this might be the Ligurian riviera, with Shelley coming to tea.

TIVERTON CASTLE **

Tiverton
Tudor and later house amid medieval castle (P)

Tiverton Castle is a jolly place, although we might not think so from outside. It is approached past the medieval walls of the old fortress still standing to the north of the church in the centre of the town. Old Tivertonians recall crossing to the other side of the road in front of the house, so forbidding was its exterior.

The castle belonged to the Courtenays, medieval Earls of Devon (Powderham, above), and was built in its present form in the 14th century. The building was rectangular, with four towers defining a courtyard above the gorge of the River Exe. The gatehouse still stands facing the road to the east. The old residential quarters faced the church but these are now ruins. It is said that a network of tunnels runs from them into the town. The castle was held for the Crown in the Civil War

but the town was for Parliament, the castle being severely slighted as a result. It passed to the Carews in the 18th century and to the present owners, the Gordons, in the 20th.

Entering the courtyard from the church, the ravine of the Exe is to the left and the surviving medieval and Elizabethan ranges are to the right, hard against the wall. In the middle of the courtyard is a surprise, a pleasant villa built by the family in the 18th century, with the appearance of a country rectory rather than castle mansion. The grouping is picturesque, enhanced by a profusion of wild flowers bursting from every crevice of the old walls.

The public is usually shown only the older ranges, including the 16th- and 17th-century chambers displaying armour and historic portraits. The tower offers a good view of Tiverton and the surrounding hills. A lower room was once a surgery for a doctor who occupied the adjacent Gothick cottage outside the wall. The castle was haunted by a ghost with a bad cough. One night the doctor left out a cup of linctus which had vanished the following morning. So had the ghost.

TORQUAY: TORRE ABBEY *

The King's Drive
Georgian house now local gallery (M)

The seat of the Cary family still stands in the middle of Torquay, a relic of the pre-Dissolution Torre Abbey. Visitors are greeted by a fine medieval gatehouse with a tower and monastic range. The main house is beyond, facing the lawn, and is on the site of the abbey's refectory. It is a handsome creeper-clad Georgian rebuild. It must once have enjoyed a magnificent view out over Torbay, now interrupted by town sprawl. The Carys sold the house to the council in 1930 and it contains an excellent collection of Victorian and West Country art. A large medieval barn was used as a prison for Armada survivors.

Inside, a stone staircase leads upstairs to rooms, some furnished in Edwardian style and others more sparsely arranged as galleries. The old sitting room contains works by Burne-

Jones and William Blake, while the drawing room has, as its centrepiece, Holman Hunt's *Children's Holiday*. A Georgian oak staircase leads to the Long Gallery, with objects lent to the house by members of the Cary family.

The dining room has been refurnished, with impressive paintings of Carys in military dress at the end of the 19th century. A small study has been converted into a museum dedicated to Agatha Christie, who lived outside the town. It includes her ancient travelling typewriter. A fragment of the abbey survives at the corner of the house, with the abbot's parlour and a room converted by the Catholic Carys into a chapel following the Catholic Relief Act of 1778. This was restored in the 1980s.

UGBROOKE HOUSE **

SE of Chudleigh, 10m S of Exeter
Ghost of an Adam house, Catholic memorabilia (P)

Ugbrooke looks like an ugly duckling in a gilded nest. The house sits in a beautiful valley over the River Ug, its landscape fashioned by Capability Brown in the 1770s. The visitor is greeted with a grove of gentle oaks and a Spanish garden. The house was an early work by Robert Adam, begun in 1763 for the Catholic Cliffords. Only fragments of his work survive inside while the outside is a rare and not especially attractive Adam exercise in castellar style, with round arched windows and doors. In 1874 the walls were harshened with grey render. The entrance now looks rather like a Territorial Army barracks.

The house has been rescued from near death. The 11th Lord Clifford abandoned it before the Second World War to use as a school and hostel. It degenerated into a semi-derelict grain store, the Adam rooms filled with agricultural equipment and produce. In the 1960s, however, the present Cliffords decided to salvage it for family use, a prodigious and successful undertaking. The interiors are mostly of the 1960s, not a good time for country house restoration, but the task is done.

Adam is now encountered only in the occasional ghostly frieze or doorcase. But the dining room contains a collection of Dutch masters and the chapel wing has an intriguing museum of Catholic objects and relics. As at Coughton (Warwicks) or Stonor (Oxon), one sees at Ugbrooke a house whose faith is reflected not just in a chapel but in generations of devout acquisitions. A portrait of a Clifford cardinal hangs on the stairs. The Cardinal's Bedroom is scarlet-hung, with an ecclesiastical four-poster and lavish reliquary. The Tapestry Bedroom next door has cream wall-hangings, embroidered at each corner as if a picture frame.

The most evident Adam survival is the chapel wing itself, reached through a magnificent semi-circular library in olive and white. The chapel has a rich Victorian apse and family gallery. Next to it are two museum rooms, one of Cliffords ecclesiastical and the other of Cliffords military.

Dorset

Dorset is rich in scenery and rich in stone. It is a landscape of hills and combes that seem to roll in waves towards the sea, greeting it in giant cliffs of chalk and limestone. Dorset has one of the most diverse geologies in England, yielding hard Portland stone and Purbeck 'marble' in the south, and blue lias and Ham stone to the north and west. Its villages are universally pretty and its market towns as yet relatively unspoilt.

There are few better counties in which to study 16th- and 17th-century architecture. A 1907 guidebook said that Dorset is rich above all in the art of the old manor, 'a dewdrop from the past, pure, pellucid, peaceful . . . seeming to breathe the air of Chaucer'.

Few houses predate the Tudor era, but the 16th century offers an abundance, at Athelhampton, Mapperton, Sandford Orcas and Wolfeton, the last being a fascinating transition to English Renaissance with a 'Longleat' staircase. Elizabethan merged into Jacobean at Sherborne Castle, the home of Walter Raleigh and then the Digbys. The Prideaux alterations to Forde are a delightful shotgun marriage of classic to medieval.

The 18th century is more sparse. It is eccentrically Baroque at Chettle, Picturesque at Milton Abbey and sternly Palladian at Kingston Maurward. The Victorians were more confident. From exile, William Bankes planned his stately treasure house of Kingston Lacy in the 1840s, and Bournemouth saw the concept of the Grand Tour updated at the Russell-Cotes House. One of the last great country houses was built by Norman Shaw for Lord Portman at Bryanston.

Dorset has writers' shrines aplenty, with the Hardy houses round Dorchester and Lawrence of Arabia's eccentric Clouds Hill.

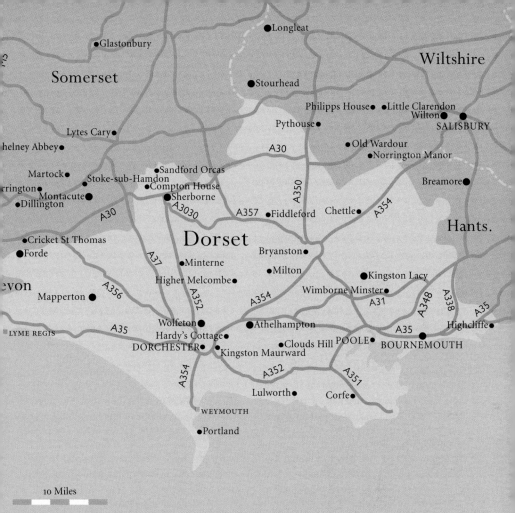

10 Miles

Athelhampton ★★★★
Bournemouth:
   Russell-Cotes
     Museum ★★★
Bryanston ★
Chettle ★★
Clouds Hill ★
Compton House ★
Corfe Castle ★
Dorchester:
   Max Gate ★

Fiddleford ★
Forde ★★★★
Hardy's Cottage ★
Highcliffe ★★
Higher Melcombe ★★
Kingston Lacy ★★★★
Kingston Maurward ★
Lulworth Castle ★★
Lulworth Castle
   House ★
Mapperton ★★★

Milton Abbey ★
Minterne ★★
Poole:
   Scaplen's Court ★
Portland Castle ★
Sandford Orcas ★★
Sherborne Castle ★★★★
Wimborne Minster:
   Priest's House ★
Wolfeton ★★★

ATHELHAMPTON HOUSE
****

near Athelhampton, 6m NE of Dorchester
Much-restored Tudor mansion with surviving
Great Hall (P)

Athelhampton is rightly celebrated as a medieval gem, glowing with promise on the main
road out of Dorchester. Its Tudor windows
and generous gables, its Ham stone walls, and
gardens like something from Alice in Wonderland suggest an age of galleons and furbelows.
Here, the past greets the present in easy
embrace.

Medieval houses bear restoration either
lightly or heavily. Athelhampton's is so light
that it is hard to know it is restored at all. Yet it
is, and drastically so. The house was built by a
wealthy merchant, William Martyn, after the
Battle of Bosworth in 1485. It was given its
generous west wing half a century later. For a
full century after that it froze, as a result of
being bequeathed in equal parts to four daughters in 1595. Each was told to occupy exactly a
quarter of the property. This version of Continental partigeniture had the effect of preventing alteration but denying maintenance.
When the desperate place was finally united in
1848, seven successive ownerships ensued.

Salvation came with a businessman, Alfred
de Lafontaine, in 1891. By then the old gatehouse had been demolished as derelict, which
opened up the forecourt to the road. Lafontaine rebuilt the south wing to the right of the
hall and laid out the garden. In 1957, the Cooke
family, whose son, Sir Robert, was an MP and
historian of the Palace of Westminster, bought
the house. The property and gardens are now
owned by his son, who clips the famous yew
pyramids himself.

Athelhampton's pride is its surviving Great
Hall, to which is attached a magnolia so large
as to make us wonder which is upholding
which. The hall roof is sensational. The beams
form giant cusps, almost clover leaves, and are
beautifully tooled and corbelled. The bay
window is worthy of a Perpendicular church,
rising almost the height of the hall. It has its

own stone vault and exterior battlements. The
screen and the linenfold panelling come from
elsewhere, courtesy of Lafontaine, and a fine
tapestry has been hung on the wall. Heraldic
glass includes the Martyn ape, the family
emblem derived from the Church's 'second
naming of animals' (the monkey was Martin
and the fox Renard).

The King's Ante-room off the bay leads
through to the Great Chamber in the west
wing, its ceiling and panelling again introduced by Lafontaine. Next door is the old wine
cellar, a little too scrubbed but a rarity in a
house of the period. Lafontaine's library above
doubles as a billiard room. Its equipment
and rules date from 1919. The scene is
adjudicated by a stern bust of Queen Victoria.

The so-called King's Room reflects the
house's status as a manorial court. Again, the
restorers have introduced linenfold and a
Gothic fireplace. Many of the recent furnishings and wallpapers at Athelhampton are
derived from A. W. N. Pugin's work at the
Palace of Westminster, of which Sir Robert
Cooke was an ardent restorer. The chairs are
Pugin designs. In the centre of the room is a
model of Big Ben. The rooms of the south
wing are either Victorian restoration or new
building. The staircase was boldly reinstated
after a bad fire in 1992.

The gardens, designed by Inigo Thomas,
were created by Lafontaine and have been
maintained ever since. The famous Great
Court is created from giant yew hedges and
peopled with pyramid yews like a guard of
honour.

BOURNEMOUTH: RUSSELL-COTES MUSEUM ***

Russell-Cotes Road
Victorian tycoon's cliff-top mansion (M)

The Victorian houses of outer Bournemouth were, to William Morris, 'blackguardly
and suitable only for ignorant purse-proud

Yew sentinels at Athelhampton

digesting machines'. This was dangerous talk, since many of their occupants were Morris's patrons. One such was the builder of East Cliff Hall, a local hotelier and mayor, Sir Merton Russell-Cotes. He presented this house to his wife, Annie, in 1901 and to the town in 1907. The architect was a local man, John Fogerty, but the inspiration throughout was Sir Merton's. He wanted the house 'to combine the Renaissance with Italian and Scottish Baronial styles'. He later declared that it was only 'after spoiling various plans my ideas were realized at last'.

The house might be in a rich enclave anywhere from Glasgow to Deauville. Its two conical towers and central pavilion gaze over the cliff to Bournemouth pier. A bold balcony below leads down to a pretty Japanese garden. The interiors are sensationally 'over the top', but executed with such bravura, and filled with such enjoyable paintings, that all can be forgiven. This is Bournemouth's Brighton Pavilion.

The house is entered from the road at the upper floor. This makes a visit seem like descending into valhalla. A huge central hall runs from top to bottom, its skylight alive with the signs of the zodiac. The house is a riot of colour. The balcony railings are in green and black. A frieze on the staircase depicts the Elgin Marbles. Every inch of wall-space has a painting, mostly of the Pre-Raphaelite and Scots Romantic period. They have such titles as *Caledonia, Stern and Wild* or Landseer's *A Flood in the Highlands*.

Since the house is now the central section of a museum and art gallery, the bedrooms are no longer displayed as such. Yet there is no museumitis. The rooms were built to display the objects brought back by the Russell-Coteses from their constant travels, many of the rooms reflecting a single visit. Some people bring back photographs. Russell-Cotes brought back roomfuls of antiques and curios.

Upstairs are the Mikado Room from Japan, a Moorish Alcove inspired by the Alhambra, and a room dedicated to the couple's friend, the actor Henry Irving, including the skull he always used in *Hamlet*. The quality of decora-tion is astonishing, with care taken over the embossing of flax wallpaper, the hanging of oriental lanterns or the arranging of Stafford-shire china in a display case. And always there is the sea below, reflecting light onto the ceilings. Here Victorian is never gloomy.

BRYANSTON SCHOOL *

2m W of Blandford Forum
Late-Victorian mansion in terraced grounds
(P-G)

The school is open only by appointment but the grounds, courtyard and terrace can be per-ambulated. Bryanston was one of the last large country mansions to be built in England. Its architect in 1889 was Richard Norman Shaw and his client the 2nd Viscount Portman, owner of much of Marylebone. The house took five years to build but was occupied by the Portmans for just thirty years before it became a school. The approach is somewhat spoiled by school buildings.

This house is Shaw in his last, most emphat-ically Queen Anne phase. It is almost a parody of Sir Christopher Wren. The best view is from the A350 across the valley to the south-east. From here the house appears to rule over the landscape like a feudal palace, secure in its plantation. Closer to, the entrance front dramatically embraces three sides of a court-yard. The façade is alive with rustication and opulence. It must be a fearsome place to arrive on a first day of school. The red bricks with white stone dressings were once black, but are now restored and sparkle in the sun.

At the rear, the garden front is no less bold. The composition appears to be of a central mansion with two lesser ones paying court on either side. The window surrounds are aggres-sively rusticated and the roof is steeply hipped, with giant chimneys. Steps descend grandly to the hillside below. The interiors have been institutionalized, though the central hall is a tremendous space, soaring to the roof.

Treasure trove at Bournemouth

CHETTLE HOUSE **

Chettle, 6m NE of Blandford Forum
English Baroque house with double
staircase (P)

Chettle sits on Cranborne Chase and was built
by the Chase warders, the Chafin family, who
had bought the estate under Elizabeth I. Their
commission was to ensure that the open moor
and woodland 'remain in a flourishing state
until the general dissolution of all things'.
They contrived to succeed in this onerous
charge until 1818. Chettle was then sold to the
Castleman family, bankers from Wimborne.
Their descendants, the Bourkes, occupy and
maintain it to this day.

The house, begun in 1710 and twenty years in
the building, is most unusual. It was attributed
to Vanbrugh until opinion settled on his assistant, the gentleman architect, Thomas Archer,
designer of St John's, Smith Square in London.
It is in a wayward English Baroque, a style
that emerged briefly under Sir Christopher
Wren and disappeared with the Hanoverian
succession and the rise of formal Palladianism.
Chettle thus represents something of a stylistic
blind alley.

The house is of redbrick with rounded
corners and a high parapet. The rounded
corners, also seen at St John's, Smith Square,
seem obsessive. The projecting centre of the
garden front has them, as does the house itself.
The entrance front is wonderfully strong, with
giant pilasters dividing each bay and deep
arched windows in the centre. Two curving
flights of steps lead up to the door, continuing
inside the entrance. They seem to draw the
visitor ever upwards. On the wall are old hats
worn by Chase warders.

Only a few rooms are open to the public.
The most magnificent is the central hall. This
has two superb oak staircases rising on
either side and coming together in a gallery, a
thrilling Baroque compositon. There are three
balusters to each step.

The drawing room was redecorated, as was
much of the house, by Alfred Stevens in the
1840s. The style is a rather fey French, quite

unlike the roast beef of Thomas Archer outside. The Bourkes are now valiantly refurbishing the rooms.

CLOUDS HILL *

4m SW of Bere Regis
T. E. Lawrence's hideout in the woods (NT)

Clouds Hill is unlike any other house in this
book. Were it not for its former owner, it
would be an insignificant two-up, two-down
cottage by a road under a hill. Yet it distils
in brick and stone all the sands of Arabia
and the romance of war. It also distils the
laceration of self-doubt and the solitude of
introversion. In May 1935, 'Aircraftman Shaw'
died in a lane nearby, thrown from his motor-
bike four months after retiring from the
services. He had swerved to avoid two cyclists.
Thus died Lawrence of Arabia.

Lawrence's exploits in the desert during the
First World War, when in his twenties, were
well recorded (by himself), including his tying
down of a huge Turkish army and his chaotic
three-day rule in Damascus. Afterwards he
went into retreat. He wrote his memoir of
the campaign, grandly called *The Seven Pillars
of Wisdom*, worked briefly in intelligence,
then vanished. He re-entered the services and
flitted from the Royal Air Force to the tank
corps and back to the air force. He did so,
said Basil Liddell Hart, 'for the same reason
that thoughtful men in the Middle Ages went
into a monastery' – or possibly to protect
his homosexuality. He demanded anonymity
and the most junior rank. He worked quietly
for thirteen years until his retirement at the age
of forty-six, shortly before his death. He was a
pioneer of flying boats.

Lawrence rented the cottage at Clouds Hill
in 1923, while serving (as 'Ross') at neighbouring Bovington Camp. He had to sleep in
barracks and used the house only for leisure. It
became his home whenever he was not on
duty, although he regarded it as 'ugly as my
sins, bleak, angular, small, unstable, very like
its owner'. There is no electricity and candles
are everywhere. The cottage is utterly simple,

its placidity spoilt only by a noisy adjacent road. Over the door is a Greek inscription, translated as 'Why worry?'

There is little to see at Clouds Hill. Downstairs is the Book Room and a small bathroom. The former contains Lawrence's divan and the steel reading desk which he designed himself. The wall-racks have books about Lawrence and copies of ones he owned, as well as photographs he took in the desert. They seem a world apart from this place.

The two rooms upstairs are the music room and a bunkroom. The first contains an old gramophone, a typewriter and second-hand Lawrence works on sale. The bunkroom was kitted out for guests as a ship's cabin, with bunk and porthole. E. M. Forster slept here. It was 'papered' in aluminium for dryness and thus used to store cheese, as it still does. Sir Alec Guinness, who played Lawrence in the eponymous film, donated an Arab robe. A habitation intended to be most ordinary is really most strange.

COMPTON HOUSE *

Over Compton, 1m E of Yeovil
Victorian Tudor house rescued for butterflies (M)

This is a remarkable work of rescue. The great house was built of Ham stone for the Goodden family in about 1839, and set about with what have grown to be giant yews and cedars. By 1976 it had become derelict, with rain pouring through the roof, floors collapsing and ceilings falling in. It was the sort of Victorian ruin that led the National Trust, English Heritage and many other enthusiasts to avert their eyes. Yet the house has been restored, at the time of writing as a butterfly museum.

Designed by John Pinch of Bath, it was clearly modelled on Barrington Court (Somerset), despite claiming Montacute (Somerset) as inspiration. The Gooddens were living at Montacute while Compton was being built, but the houses have little in common. The exterior is a feast of gables, dormers, buttresses

and finials, as if architecture were inviting that parental admonition, 'stop trying to make a show of yourself'.

The restored interior has been mostly converted for exhibition use, but fragments of the old interior are visible amid the myriad Lepidoptera. The entrance hall has a neo-Tudor fireplace, panelled ceiling and copious deer antlers. In the old dining room is another Tudor fireplace and ornate frieze. There are original bookshelves surviving in the library and the curtain pelmets have been salvaged.

CORFE CASTLE *

6m SE of Wareham
Romantic 11th-century fortress, much Civil War bravery (NT)

Corfe may be in ruins, but they are the ruins of England's most romantic house-fortress. The site is superb, guarding the road to the Isle of Purbeck. In its outer bailey, knights might joust away their fortunes. Beneath its rampart, troubadours might sing of love. This is pure Walter Scott.

The old Norman castle belonged to the Crown until awarded by Elizabeth I to her favourite, Sir Christopher Hatton (*see* Kirby/Northants). His family sold it in 1635 to the Lord Chief Justice, Sir John Bankes. It was the scene of a celebrated Civil War incident in 1643 when defended by Lady Bankes on behalf of her husband who was away fighting for the King. Lady Bankes signed a temporary peace with the surrounding Parliamentary forces, but used it to provision and refortify the castle.

The subsequent siege lasted six weeks, against over a hundred attacking troops. When the latter withdrew, Lady Bankes again refortified the castle and, with her husband now dead, faced another siege in 1645. A gallant Royalist platoon offered to rescue her but she refused. The castle finally fell to treachery, but Lady Bankes was allowed to keep the keys to Corfe in recognition of her bravery. Corfe was 'slighted' and the family later moved to Kingston Lacy (below), where the keys still hang.

The castle is easy to read, rising up the hill

from an outer gatehouse. The outer bailey's battered walls form a picturesque sequence of tumbled masonry, delighting 19th-century watercolourists. The inner bailey was first fortified in the 11th century. The principal buildings left standing are the 13th-century keep and the complex of residential chambers known as the Gloriette. The castle today is mostly of the 13th and 14th centuries, although some Gloriette windows and doorways are Tudor.

Walls and passages survive, notably between the keep and its south annex. The great Gothic windows of the Gloriette hall retain their arches. Visitors can still climb the bastions from which Lady Bankes's defenders gazed down on their besiegers below.

Protagonists in the 'scraping' debate can compare guidebook photographs of Corfe in the 1940s and 1950s, covered in ivy, trees, weeds and nature, with its present scrubbed neatness.

DORCHESTER: MAX GATE *

Alington Avenue
House designed by Hardy as his Dorchester home (NT)

Thomas Hardy was a writer by occupation but an architect by profession. Many might disregard the latter after visiting the house he built for himself and his new wife, Emma, outside Dorchester in 1885. The contrast with his boyhood home at Hardy's Cottage (below) could hardly be more stark. Max Gate is a suburban brick villa on what was an exposed site once occupied by a man named 'Mack'. Hardy phoneticized his entrance into Max Gate, and even suggested a punning 'porta maxima'.

It was here that Hardy's relations with Emma declined. Even when they moved in he was full of foreboding. 'Whether building this house at Max Gate was wise expenditure of energy is one doubt, which if resolved in the negative is depressing enough. And there are others.' Emma hated the place, complaining of its exposed location. Hardy planted 2,000 Austrian pines to shield it (they are now gone) but not surprisingly they made Emma gloomier still.

While Hardy enjoyed a social life and visited London for the 'season', Emma disliked society and preferred taking religious tracts round local village streets. She was deeply upset by her husband's overt atheism. After her death, Hardy 'fell in love with her' in remorse. His second wife and secretary, Florence, had to spend her time typing out posthumous love poems to her predecessor. It was here he wrote his later works, including *Tess, Jude* and *The Mayor of Casterbridge*.

The house is solely of interest because of Hardy. Its front was described by A. C. Benson, as 'at once mean and pretentious, with no grace of design or detail and with two hideous low-flanking turrets with point roofs', perhaps an excessively harsh judgment. The façade is asymmetrical, allowing ingeniously for a large drawing room to the right of the entrance and a smaller dining room to the left. On the wall is a sundial designed by Hardy with the motto '*Quid de nocte*': What of the night?

Hardy memorabilia have been scattered between Hardy's Cottage, Max Gate and the Hardy Museum in town. I sense Max Gate did not get the best of the deal. Some furniture has been returned to help the tenants entertain visitors. The dark Victorian interiors that oppressed Emma have been brightened and filled with Dorset landscapes. The Grand Old Man of letters brought here a remarkable galaxy of visitors – Kipling, Stevenson, Yeats, T. E. Lawrence, Shaw, Barrie, Forster, Sassoon, Wells, Galsworthy and Housman. All seemed puzzled by what Virginia Woolf called this 'ordinary, nice, conventional, never-says-a-clever-thing' Englishman. She wondered how on earth she could write his obituary. If only walls could talk.

FIDDLEFORD MANOR *

Fiddleford, 6m NW of Blandford Forum
Medieval hall house with original roof (EH)

There are many challengers for the title of 'most spectacular medieval manor house interior in Dorset' but Pevsner awarded it to

Fiddleford. The old building lies tucked away from the main road, adjoining what is now a private house. It dates from the 14th century and has been saved only by some miracle of man and agriculture.

The visible house consists of a truncated half of a hall plus a two-storey solar. The hall is open to the roof with boldly cusped braces clearly designed for decorative effect. The screens passage and solar were added in the 1550s by a Thomas White. He clearly wanted to give his house some style, including carved stone doorways behind the screen, leading to a pantry and buttery underneath the solar.

The solar's roof is c1380 and has beautifully carved members. There are fragments of wall-paintings and the ghost of a Gothic window.

FORDE ABBEY ****

4m SE of Chard
Monastic palace converted into 17th-century mansion (P)

Forde is a house far too little acknowledged. It is the best example of a historic building frozen at that exhilarating moment in English history when the Middle Ages were passing into Reformation and belated Renaissance, when monastery was becoming palace. Forde is part medieval, part modern, part ecclesiastical, part plutocratic, and still in the custodianship of a private family.

Looking down from the hillside garden, the eye takes in at one sweep the story of this transition. A rambling, asymmetrical tableau embraces medieval and Cromwellian ranges, later joined under one continuous battlement. Yet each portion is distinct and full of interest. Behind them at right angles run two medieval wings, north and east, survivors of the great storehouses of the former abbey.

The last abbot of Forde was Thomas Chard. His Great Hall and ornamented entrance tower were of such princely lavishness as to spark an entire Dissolution of the Monasteries on their own. When the moment came, Chard personally surrendered his abbey without a fight and retired to become vicar of Thorncombe. The building passed through various owners, who plundered the old abbey church for stone. Then, in 1649, the private quarters caught the eye of Cromwell's Attorney-General, Edmund Prideaux, who bought the buildings to re-fashion them as his mansion. He was said to have consulted the elderly Inigo Jones but his architect was probably Edward Carter, standing in for Jones as Surveyor of the King's Works during the Interregnum.

After Prideaux's death in 1659, his son was suspected of supporting the Monmouth rebellion. He escaped with his life and a huge fine from Judge Jeffreys, but the family fortunes never recovered. Forde went into a long decline, saving it from alteration through the 18th and 19th centuries. The house was acquired by the Evans family in 1863 who repaired it and passed it to their relations, the Ropers, who own it to this day.

Forde is entered under Abbot Chard's gatehouse porch. This is a supreme work of Tudor architecture, with friezes and window tracery of filigree delicacy. The Great Hall behind was truncated by Prideaux to create his new west wing. The hall must once have been vast. Prideaux also blocked the windows on the north side in order to insert a fireplace and staircase.

The stairs to Prideaux's state rooms are splendidly robust. A carved 'Spanish balustrade' is matched by a painted one on the wall dado. Carved wooden urns burst with flowers. The ceiling, like all Prideaux's insertions, is richly plastered, with plants intertwined with faces. This is the house of no Puritan. By the late 1650s, Cromwell's aides were clearly acquiring a taste for extravagance.

At the head of the stairs, the Grand Saloon is Forde's most sophisticated chamber. Its shallow-coffered ceiling is intricately plastered, the walls luxuriously panelled. On the walls hang a complete set of Mortlake tapestries, which were specifically ordered for this room and copied from the Raphael cartoons now in the V&A. They were confiscated by Judge Jeffreys but returned under Queen Anne.

Many Jacobean houses soon become a blur of tapestry and oak. Not so Forde. To walk

down the Tapestry Passage is like being cloaked in gorgeous fabric. The Crewel Bedroom is filled with embroidery made by Ropers in the 20th century. The old upper refectory, now a library, is a curiosity. It was built by the Cistercians for those monks who wished to eat meat, but were required to do so in a separate chamber from their vegetarian brethren. The screen is a Victorian insertion, apparently fashioned from 18th-century Breton bedsteads. The refectory chairs are covered in superb Dutch tapestry and look uncomfortable.

The enfilade of state rooms above the old cloisters is now a row of habitable bedrooms, all retaining their Prideaux ceilings. Each is furnished with some distinctive feature, doves carved in a door hood, three girls painted by Cuyp, a set of Devis watercolours, a damask bed canopy made for Queen Anne, who died before she could use it. Beyond lies the former monks' dormitory, now pristine white. The adjacent undercroft makes a fine tea-room, its vaults patterned with Ham and Portland stone.

Forde: monastery turned palace

The Old Cloister was refaced and ornamented by Chard as one of his last acts as abbot. It is virtuoso Gothic and now is home to ferns and other vegetation, like a voluptuous orangery. The grounds overlooking Forde are a tumble of terraces, water gardens, temples and borders. Go when the sun shines.

HARDY'S COTTAGE *

Higher Bockhampton, 3m NE of Dorchester
Writer's birthplace and inspiration (NT)

The point is not the cottage, nor that Thomas Hardy was born and spent his youth here. The point is the setting. The little thatched house is as Hardy would recognize it. Wild flowers abound in the garden, 'such hardy flowers as flourish best untrained'. The lane to the cottage, half a mile from the car park, is unpaved and sandy. Beyond the house is a crossroads of tracks, also unpaved, beneath a fingerpost sign – most Hardyesque. If only the distant traffic noise were reduced and the Forestry Commission induced to plant fewer conifers.

The cottage was built by Hardy's great-grandfather in 1800. It was of cob – a mix of clay, gravel, sand and chalk with straw – thatched and later strengthened with cement and faced with brick. The rooms are simple, with Hardy memorabilia downstairs and three modest bedrooms upstairs. It was in the middle one that Hardy was born in 1840. He was put aside as dead until the nurse remarked, 'Stop a minute, he's alive enough.'

At the window in the end bedroom, shared with his brother, Hardy wrote *Under the Greenwood Tree* and *Far from the Madding Crowd*, both filled with vignettes drawn from the immediate surroundings. The young Hardy wrote incessantly. When he found himself inspired and without paper, he would seize slates, strips of bark, even leaves, to capture the words.

Few writers left so many images of their childhood and few houses so evoke those images. In the poem 'Domicilium', the 16-year-old Hardy recalled how the 'Wild honeysucks/ Climb on the walls, and seem to sprout a wish . . . / To overtop the apply-trees hard by.'

The rooms are as uneventful as they always were. They have kept their cottage state, with flagstones downstairs and old bedroom furniture upstairs. Books, drawings and watercolours abound. Hardy did not leave, to marry Emma, until the age of thirty-four and still walked out here from Max Gate in Dorchester to see surviving members of his family. When the last member left in 1916, the house was tenanted until being acquired by the National Trust in 1948.

HIGHCLIFFE CASTLE **

Rothesay Drive, Highcliffe-on-Sea
Picturesque ruin with imported features (M)

Highcliffe is an architectural phenomenon on a bluff overlooking the Channel. In 1830 Lord Stuart de Rothesay, grandson of the 3rd Earl of Bute, inherited the Highcliffe estate, on which stood a cliff-edge mansion by Robert Adam. A much-travelled Regency diplomat who negotiated the end of the slave trade, Stuart decided to build himself a spectacular house in the new medieval revival style, looking out to sea and the Isle of Wight.

Antique hunters were at the time trawling the ruined medieval sites of a battered post-Napoleonic Europe to adorn English houses and churches. Few did so with the aplomb of Lord Stuart, who even insisted on putting a 'de' before his Scottish name of Rothesay. Twelve barges of Belgian stonework were duly brought to Highcliffe, most of it from the demolished Grande Maison des Andelys and the Norman abbey at Jumièges. An L-shaped house designed by John Donthorn, fearlessly inventive pupil of Jeffry Wyatville, was prepared for their reception.

The state rooms were in the south wing towards the sea, culminating in a large conservatory. The east wing was for the family. Behind was a Great Hall along the lines of the Great Western Hall at Fonthill, but filled with abbey stonework and with a sensational Gothic porch. Most magnificent were the oriel windows gracing the two towers of the rear entrance. Both are covered in Flamboyant Gothic tracery that would get Michelin stars were they on their original buildings.

All this was in good condition until 1950 when it was sold by its owners, the Stuart Wortley family. Brief use as a Catholic seminary was followed by two devastating and suspicious fires in 1967 and 1968. This left the interior of the building a ruin, from which nobody seemed keen to rescue it. The roof of the Great Hall fell as recently as 1990.

Acquisition by the local council and recent restoration is slowly bringing the building back to life, at least as a shell. Carved corbels, arches and windows adorn what remains of the Great Hall. The majestic double staircase that filled one end has sadly gone. The conservatory is in good condition. A final nonsense is that the castle has been deprived of its finest feature, its view out to sea, by a senseless bank of trees. This at least can be rectified with an axe.

HIGHER MELCOMBE **

near Melcombe Bingham, 6m N of Puddletown
Medieval manor with chapel on hilltop (P-R)

The hills and valleys of central Dorset rise and fall seductively round the Melcombes. The valleys are lush but the hills are the wild, broad-shouldered heaths of Hardy novels. Climbing up from Cross Lanes a cul-de-sac opens out onto moorland through an avenue of limes, planted to celebrate the Battle of Britain. At the top of a combe, the road peters out in a small farm and what appears to be a chapel. The land was bought in 1938 by the brewing family of Woodhouse, including the old manor. It sits looking out on the Downs, solitary and beautiful.

The house was once four ranges set round a square. Much of this was demolished in the 18th century, the stone being used to build the Ansty brewery in a local village. What remains is an L-shaped mostly 16th-century house, its old rooms gently evolving over time. The walls are banded with flints interspersed with Ham and Portland, the two finest stones in England.

The interiors are essentially atmospheric. The earlier entrance front has walls of medieval thickness and the downstairs rooms have Jacobean chimneypieces. A staircase inserted in the 18th century leads to the old Great Chamber, now a bedroom with a superb plaster ceiling of c1610. It depicts the union of the crowns of England and Scotland. Another bedroom has worm-eaten linenfold panelling.

The former chapel, now a living room, was used as a barn by various tenants until restored by the Woodhouses. It still has 13th-century windows, moved from a plague village church in the neighbouring meadow. Modern stained glass celebrates the love of nature of the present owner's grandfather. It includes the family (and brewery) emblem of a badger, also the name of its celebrated ale. The roof bosses have all been restored, including one of EII for the present Queen.

Highcliffe's Flamboyant Gothic

KINGSTON LACY *****

2m NW of Wimborne Minister
Italian palazzo housing Grand Tour collections (NT)

William Bankes was so wild, dissipated and adventurous as to shock even Byron, who called him 'my father of mischief'. Such was the scandal surrounding his life that Arthur Oswald, in his 1935 essay on the house, still dared not mention it. As a wealthy young man, Bankes travelled widely in Spain and the Middle East. He visited Mecca in disguise, returned to England and became an MP. With his new house in Dorset still a shell, however, Bankes was charged in 1841 over a homosexual incident and had to flee to Italy to escape arrest.

For the remaining fourteen years of his life he dreamed, collected, designed and directed the building of the house through his sister, Lady Falmouth. He was thought never to have returned, enjoying the house vicariously through correspondence. But family legend long held that, with Bankes's death approaching in 1854, a coach drew up one night at the gate of Kingston and a secretive figure slipped into the house to stand briefly in his beloved creation, and see the work of his mind's eye. This poignant story is now believed to be true.

The house was begun by Bankes's ancestors after their seat at Corfe Castle was destroyed in the Civil War. The architect was Roger Pratt and the present exterior is still a ghost of Pratt's work. Bankes had a vast inheritance at his disposal and wanted something grander and more in the style of Italy. In 1835, he called on Charles Barry to redesign Pratt's house as a palazzo in which a Byronic European might display the spoils of his travels. Kingston was to become not just a house but a home fit for Velasquez and Raphael, Titian and Veronese, Rubens and van Dyck.

After Bankes's death, the house seemed to sink into a lethargy of shame. It passed from one reclusive Bankes to another until, by the 1970s, its inaccessibility was the stuff of legend. Then in 1981, out of the blue, Kingston Lacy was left by Ralph Bankes, lock, stock and barrel, to the National Trust.

Everything about the house is distinctive. Although ostensibly just another grand house filled with fine furniture and pictures, it everywhere displays eccentricity and surprise. The stairs, of white Carrara marble, reach the first floor past a loggia where are set three statues by Carlo Marochetti. They are of Sir John and Lady Bankes, heroine of Corfe, and their adored king, Charles I. This staircase was built before Bankes's flight and he declared that 'there is no staircase in England to equal it in effect . . . and not many that surpass it in Italy'.

The first floor is the *piano nobile*. The library is a survivor from the 18th-century house. Over the fireplace are the keys of Corfe Castle, defended so vigorously by Lady Bankes during the Civil War. Above the bookcase is a set of family portraits by Lely and one by Batoni.

The drawing room raises the temperature. Furnished as a cluttered Edwardian sitting room, its doors are surmounted by extraordinary carved marble architraves made in Verona. The portraits are by Lawrence and van Dyck and include a set of miniatures in enamel on copper.

The dining room has boxwood doors with carved panels, copied from a Donatello altar at Padua. On the wall hangs Kingston Lacy's greatest treasure, Sebastiano del Piombo's unfinished *Judgement of Solomon*, near-ruined by restoration, and a magnificent portrait by Titian. We now enter the saloon, mostly the work of Robert Brettingham in the 18th century. It contains Bankes's most important acquisitions. These include two luxuriant Rubens portraits, of Maria Serra Pallavicino with her parrot and of Maria Grimaldi with her dwarf. Other works are by van Dyck, Rembrandt, Titian, Veronese and Gerrit Dou, some of them 'studio of'.

Beyond the saloon is the Spanish Room, clad by Barry in tooled leather from Venice and with a ceiling copied from the Ca' Pisani on the Grand Canal. The gilding reflects subdued light. The art here is Spanish and the room might be a sacristy in the Escorial.

On the walls hang Velasquez, Murillo and Zurbarán. The state bedroom beyond is grandiloquent yet not cold. The bedstead is adorned with state cupids and state bats.

The marble staircase continues to the second floor, becoming yet grander as it rises. Nude figures after Michelangelo lounge on plinths. A vast Snyders of animal violence covers the wall. The upper floors are all bedrooms, many decorated by Barry and all lavishly adorned with Kingston Lacy's store of paintings. There is a Zoffany here, a Lely or a Kneller there.

We are able to penetrate deep into this house. The attics are lit by a cupola and adorned with an apse decorated with shells. The so-called Tent Rooms were intended for bachelors and are now immaculately refurnished.

The basement holds Bankes's collection of Egyptian antiquities, many of them removed from the workmen's village in the Valley of the Kings. This would be outrageous today. Nor is that all. On a visit to Egypt, Bankes took the obelisk from Philae and spent six years wrestling it home to his park. To England's shame, it stands there eroding to this day. Its uneroded twin stands on its temple island near Aswan, bereft of its partner.

KINGSTON MAURWARD HOUSE *

2m E of Dorchester
Georgian house in Edwardian park (P-G)

The house stands handsome across the valley of the Frome. Its Portland stone façade rises glittering in the sun from a dark mass of trees. The house was built by George Pitt, cousin of the Prime Minister, c1717 and was of brick. In 1794 it fell victim to a visit from George III, who is said to have wandered round it muttering, 'too much brick, Mr Pitt'. The King's dislike for this material proved advantageous to the Portland quarries. The result is an early Georgian box, nine bays by five, with pediments and entirely clad in stone. A porch was added in the 20th century.

The house and estate were occupied by

the army in the Second World War and the building became a college, the Dorset Farm Institute. A farm exhibition forms a less than dignified approach, past rows of council houses. The main entrance hall, remodelled *c*1912, is accessible; it rises two storeys and has two giant imported fireplaces. The fine plaster ceiling, with a central oval and swirling Rococo decoration, has been picked out in bright colours.

The college has been restoring the splendid gardens over the years. Tall yew hedges and graceful terraces overlook a vista of lakes and trees, laid out in the Edwardian period. The garden contains the national collection of penstemons. There is a superb croquet lawn.

LULWORTH CASTLE **

East Lulworth, 6m SW of Wareham
Gutted ruin of Jacobean hunting lodge (P)

When the exiled King Charles X of France was lent Lulworth Castle in 1830 he is said to have exclaimed, '*Voilà, la Bastille!*' It is a good description. The castle was built 1608–10 by Viscount Bindon, a son of the Duke of Norfolk, near his seat at Bindon Abbey. With a spectacular view down to the coast, it was 'well-seated for Prospect and for Pleasure, but of little other Use'. The castle was an ostentatious hunting lodge.

In 1641, the estate was bought by Humphrey Weld whose family own it to this day. They furnished the castle and regularly modernized it, so that by the 20th century the ground floor comprised a hall, billiard room, dining room and large drawing room, with a Catholic chapel in one of the round towers. Lulworth well demonstrated the adaptability of every sort of English house.

In August 1929, a fire broke out in one of the towers. Molten lead spread across the roof which collapsed onto the floors below. The castle was completely gutted amid scenes of some drama. An ancient family ghost of a 'grey lady' was heard crying for help from a tower window and a ladder was even run up to rescue her (she, of course, had vanished).

Old Herbert Weld, shouting 'My castle, it is ruined,' had to be restrained from rushing into the inferno.

For half a century the place remained a gaunt ruin, clad in ivy and with trees growing from its walls. It was taken ferociously in hand for the owners by English Heritage, who paid for and restored the exterior and consolidated the inside.

The outside looks as if it were built yesterday, a gleaming white keep set on a billowing basement of terraces and with a fine Renaissance doorway. Four corner towers are big enough to be keeps in their own right.

The interior is controversial. English Heritage inserted new floors, ramps for the disabled, strip lighting and ubiquitous hoardings and screens. The spaces bear no relation to their origins. Overhead hang the relics of the fire. Iron beams support bare walls. Fireplaces, doorways and fragments of stairs lead nowhere. Yet there is no sense of ruination, no vegetation, bats or birds. All is sparkling clean, and is now used also for concerts and private functions. It is a modern architect's fantasy of how a ruin ought to look.

The family chapel has been reinstated in one tower. The castle basement survived the fire and the Welds have created an admirable exhibition of life 'below stairs'. This is more real than life upstairs.

LULWORTH CASTLE HOUSE *

East Lulworth, 6m SW of Wareham
Modern residence near old castle (P–R)

After the 1929 fire in the old castle (above), the elderly Herbert Weld was photographed sitting dazed among his belongings on the lawn. He had lost his wife to illness eight months earlier and had no children. Within six years he was dead and the estate passed to a cousin, Sir Joseph Weld, whose son holds it today. Sir Joseph decided that while he could not reinhabit the castle, he could live near by, and in 1971 built a new house overlooking the site. It was designed to be light, airy and servant-free. The building, rare in this book, is a post-war neo-Georgian residence open to the public.

The house exterior is dull redbrick, the garden front a rectangular façade punctuated by two spreading bow windows. The interior is more enjoyable, planned round a central hall rising two storeys and with a view to the sea framed by scagliola columns. Upstairs is a four-sided gallery with a barrel vault, hung with family portraits by Lely and others. In the dining room is an excellent tapestry based on Teniers, with his signature of a urinating peasant. It comes from a former Weld house, Ince Blundell (Lancs) where it is sorely missed.

The present owner, Wilfrid Weld, is a cricket enthusiast with an outstanding display of cricket memorabilia and commercial posters, warming the sometimes cold lines of 20th-century Georgian. Lead pipes, urns, statues and water butts retrieved from the old castle people the gardens of the new house. These merge with those of the adjacent castle. Most of the estate is open Dorset landscape, a blessed haven in the increasingly ruined Dorset coastline.

MAPPERTON ***

2m SE of Beaminster
Elizabethan house with formal gardens in valley (P)

Mapperton nestles on a flank of a private combe near the Devon border. It more than nestles, it glows, rich in Ham stone and rich in years. The years are those of a continuous line of descent from Domesday's de Moion family to the Comptons who sold the house in 1919. The present owner is the Earl of Sandwich, whose father, Lord Hinchingbrooke, bought Mapperton in 1955. Hinchingbrooke extended the formal gardens laid out in the 1920s by a previous owner, Ethel Labouchere, in memory of her husband.

The house presents a friendly face to the drive, although is easily missed on the way to the stables and outhouses. The exterior is that of an Elizabethan mansion of the 1550s, substantially extended in the 1660s and redecorated in the 18th century. A U-shaped courtyard is guarded by two splendid eagles, looking ready for take-off.

Beyond, the harmony of the lichen-clad stone and Elizabethan features is complete. To the left is the Tudor wing, with an attic gable and finials; to the right is the medieval chapel. Ahead is a porch with charming shell niches below an open balustrade. The atmosphere is intimate. Yet turn round and there is a spectacular view to open fields through symmetrical stable buildings, a surprisingly Baroque effect.

Given the simplicity of the exterior, the interior is hard to read. The cross passage, hall and dining room were reordered and given reproduction Jacobean ceilings in the 1920s. The overpowering Jacobean chimneypiece came, apparently, from another Dorset house. Old manor houses swapped and borrowed so freely that they often seem to merge into one panelled, ubiquitous, vernacular corporate design.

Abutting onto the hall is the drawing room, its original plaster ceiling rich in fleurs-de-lys. Beyond is the library, with a Rococo ceiling above a crude James I overmantel, again an import. Between the two rises the Georgian staircase, a spacious, stylish work with another Rococo ceiling. The walls are lined with Earls of Sandwich. They include the Restoration diplomat who brought back Charles II to his throne, and his descendant the 4th Earl, who invented the famous snack by demanding a slab of beef between two slices of bread when in a hurry. The present Lord Sandwich is in the same business, claiming with due authenticity to market 'the original Sandwich'. Upstairs in the old great chamber is the finest ceiling in the house.

Below are spread out the gardens, billowing down the hillside in tiers of lawn and yew, intersected by arbours and Ham stone walls. The layout is unashamedly formal, yet

Secret Mapperton above its valley

fashioned in harmony with the contours of its site. Waves of landscaping seem to disappear downhill towards the wild, as if desperate to escape.

MILTON ABBEY SCHOOL *

Milton Abbas, 8m SW of Blandford Forum
Conversion of abbey in Capability Brown valley (P-G)

Towards the end of the 18th century, the Earl of Dorchester decided to wipe out the old village of Milton Abbas round the dissolved abbey. In ardent pursuit of the Picturesque, he created a new model village a mile away. The abbey church remained as a parish church, but the monastery next door was converted into a mansion. The interior, now a school, is not normally open but the walls can be perambulated and glimpses obtained of the inner courtyard.

The house is built round this courtyard, which retains the medieval Great Hall of the monastery and fragments of its walls. The hall is a superb structure with a vast hammerbeam roof and a flourish of cusped wind-braces. The original Tudor entrance faces north up the valley.

To the west, looking across the valley, is the front built in the 1770s by Sir William Chambers and forming a delightful contrast to the abbey next door. It is intriguing that both are technically Gothic, the one true Perpendicular, the other best described as skin-deep Picturesque.

Chambers was predominantly a classical architect. The composition of his front is Palladian, a central block with two pavilion wings. The Gothic appears in nothing more than pierced parapets, pediments and finials. Except in the brightest sun, the grey Portland stone can seem cold alongside the church's honey-coloured Ham stone next door.

The architect later hated what he had done, calling Milton 'this vast ugly house in Dorset'. Historians suggest that the design was forced on him by his client. If so, it is a rare instance of an architect suffering such humiliation. The

buildings do, however, sit serene in one of Capability Brown's most beautiful landscapes. The dominant colouring of Milton Abbey is neither Portland nor Ham, but the wide torrent of green that is the valley flowing past its front.

MINTERNE **

Minterne Magna, 8m N of Dorchester
Twentieth-century Tudor in Cerne Valley (P-R)

The house at Minterne stands in a corner of paradise. The view from its terrace over the enveloping Cerne Valley is of water and park stretching towards woods and meadows. After buying the property from the Churchill family in 1768, Admiral Robert Digby would ride over to his relations at Sherborne, when Capability Brown was paying a visit there. He sought no costly commission. Digbys were their own landscape architects, but overheard ideas did not come amiss.

The present house was built in 1904 by the 10th Lord Digby. It is an accomplished Arts and Crafts work by Leonard Stokes. The design is ostensibly Elizabethan, with a modified E-plan entrance façade. Yet no sooner do we think we understand the plan than Stokes veers off into his own eclecticism. The doorway has a deeply curved hood (Queen Anne). The façades have rusticated quoins (Georgian), pedimented gables (17th century), fake castellation (Regency) and stone mullions to the windows (Tudor). There is an assertive tower, with Arts and Crafts windows (20th century).

The interior is even more eccentric. The door gives onto what appears to be a spacious screens passage and the hall with Gothic windows. But the Middle Ages come to an abrupt end when the screens passage becomes a spacious staircase up to a gallery. The hall has a classical arcade to a passage running down the middle of the house. One end of this passage is now a picture gallery of Digby portraits. Coats of arms and Digby cartouches fill the walls alongside seascapes of Digbys under sail.

The hall is the scene of Lady Digby's regular musical patronage.

The three main reception rooms face out onto the garden. The dining room is a facsimile of an earlier 17th-century room on the site. It faces east to shield the Teniers tapestries from the sun. They had been given to Charles Churchill by the Dutch after the Battle of Ramillies and 'came with the house' on its purchase by Digbys. The large drawing room is wonderfully open to the view and is Stuart in character. The smaller boudoir is in the style of Adam.

To Stokes, it seems, Minterne was a place where anything would do except, apparently, bathing. The Edwardian Lord Digby considered bathrooms 'disgusting', leaving such innovation to his successors.

POOLE: SCAPLEN'S COURT *

off The Quay
Medieval survivor behind old quayside (M)

Poole has suffered even more from bulldozers than Weymouth. An almost intact ancient harbour survived both the Victorians and wartime bombing, but it could not survive Poole's local council. It has now all but vanished, leaving a tiny enclave round the Custom House on the old quayside. Behind it is Scaplen's Court.

This was a substantial merchant's house of c1500, of the sort that still abounds in Continental ports but is virtually extinct in Britain. It is a charming corner, composed of four complete ranges round a small inner courtyard. The original hall was to the left, with a solar block at right angles and service buildings beyond. The interiors are now used as an extension of the Waterfront Museum across the road.

Scaplen's Court, at the time of writing, is remarkable in being free of museumitis. The house seems full of Tudor and later paraphernalia, with the back rooms coated in cobwebs and dust. An upper chamber has a fine restored ceiling with wind-braces. This precious house has retained at least some sense of its antiquity. I hope it remains that way. Behind is a secluded garden, planted with old Tudor flowers and herbs.

PORTLAND CASTLE *

Castletown
Intact Henrician fortress (EH)

The photographer asked by English Heritage to find a good outside view of Portland Castle has excelled himself. The castle sits in a wilderness of defence ministry barracks, offices, sheds and hangars. The Royal Navy, so glamorous at sea, espouses unsurpassed ugliness ashore.

Few of these buildings are any longer in use. Properly cleared, this could be a sublime spot, as the cleverly angled guidebook photograph indicates.

Portland is a complete Tudor fortress, built in 1539 to guard Weymouth Harbour as part of Henry VIII's south coast chain. It was reused during the Napoleonic Wars but converted in 1816 as a private house for the Reverend John Manning. His son, Captain Charles Manning became governor of Portland in 1834. It was he who promoted the building of the great breakwater, using convict labour, to link what was then an island to the mainland. The castle was reactivated by the Navy in the 20th century and used in the Second World War as an Anglo-American communications base.

The castle is most curious in shape, an outer segment of a circle. Like many of these forts, it was essentially a gunnery platform, commanding a particular field of fire. The gun room is now open to the sky, its guns never having fired in anger.

Behind it is the hall, a fine room with kitchens to one side and the gunners' living quarters the other. Upstairs are the officers' rooms, with the castle's only privy. Display panels depict scenes from the castle's history, including the Second World War. The view from the battlements is spectacular, strictly for visitors with tunnel vision, looking northwards.

SANDFORD ORCAS MANOR **

Sandford Orcas, 2m N of Sherborne
Elizabethan manor with unusual hall (P)

Sir Mervyn Medlycott Bt conducts tours of this ancient house with the air of a man baffled at anyone wanting to visit what is so patently his. Sandford has been in the family for two and half centuries. Why should others be interested? Long may the paradox continue. The house is a manor of the mid-16th century, built by Edward Knoyle sometime after he acquired the property in 1533. Its plan and interior are unusual, but beyond that there is little to say. The house makes a virtue of lacking history.

The arched gatehouse with rooms above leads into the courtyard, but no building faces it, only a gently sloping garden. The house is round to the right, as if determined to be unobtrusive. From outside it seems a curiosity. The lovely Gothic porch, intricately adorned with foliage and finials, has on its left not the customary Great Hall with solar, but rather two rooms on top of each other, both with windows running round the front and side elevations. The so-called solar is a single-storey rear structure – in effect, a closet.

Inside, the hall is divided from the door by a sedate oak screen which must be Jacobean. It contrasts with the riotous carving of a mantelpiece, also Jacobean and possibly imported. The joy of the room are its windows, both carrying heraldic glass and, as seen outside, round two sides, flooding it with light and quite unlike a traditional Great Hall.

At the far end is no grand Tudor staircase but a simple spiral stair leading to the Great Chamber above. Sandford Orcas seems to have survived in this 16th-century state, with a few Jacobean additions, and did not suffer the often drastic attention of late-Victorian manorial improvers.

Although the house is quite small, the upstairs rooms are a maze of beams, steps and levels. There are few 'important' pieces of furniture, just the accumulation of a gentry family over the centuries. Atmosphere transcends artifice. Anything as recent as the 18th century – such as a lovely Hepplewhite bed – seems impertinently modern.

SHERBORNE CASTLE ****

½m E of Sherborne
Raleigh's romantic lodge with later interiors (P)

Glamorous courtier, Sir Walter Raleigh, coveted old Sherborne Castle and in 1592 induced the elderly Elizabeth I to grant it to him. Unfortunately she soon discovered his secret marriage to one of her ladies-in-waiting and threw them both in the Tower of London.

On their release they retreated to Sherborne and began to rebuild the castle and the hunting lodge in its grounds. Raleigh's American adventures shattered his finances and James I returned him to prison in 1603 on charges of treason. By the time of his execution in 1618, the property had gone to one of the King's courtiers, Sir John Digby, later Earl of Bristol. Digbys abandoned the old castle and moved to and extended the hunting lodge. In course of time, it became Sherborne Castle.

Today, this building is one of the oddest houses in England. Raleigh's Elizabethan structure was pulled, pushed, distorted, rendered and set about with hexagonal towers. The original house was soon buried at the end of deep courtyards, while the side elevation to the park became eccentric. In the right light Sherborne is like a ghostly galleon, a Marie Celeste lost at sea.

In the middle of the building is still the ghost of Raleigh's house, with Tudor windows and a Dutch gable. This is flanked by blank walls and then two wings of classical windows that are reminiscent of a street in Florence. The building might be an architectural pattern book opened up and left in a meadow.

The interiors of Sherborne were mostly reordered by George Wingfield in 1859, when

Sherborne: the Green Drawing Room

he inherited the property at the age of sixty, at the same time adding Digby to his name. A wealthy and generous 'improver', of whom Victorian Britain had an abundance, Wingfield Digby employed P. C. Hardwick to modernize Sherborne in keeping with its Jacobean past. Hardwick was so conscientious that here is a house whose Jacobean authenticity we must take on Victorian trust.

Of the interiors, the library is not by Hardwick but 18th-century Gothick of 1757. It is a remarkable room, the bookcases alive with double-ogee arches and pierced with busts of philosophers by Henry Cheere. A copy of my childhood favourite, *Struwwelpeter*, lies casually on a table. Over the fireplace is Sir Kenelm Digby, 17th-century Royalist, Catholic, scientist and cook. Son of the Gunpowder Plot Digby and cousin of the Sherborne branch, he fell in love with the penniless Venetia Stanley and was sent to France by his mother to escape so impecunious a match. He wrote passionate letters to Venetia but these were intercepted by spies. To escape an infatuated French Queen, he feigned his own death in battle. When news of this reached Venetia, she began a stormy affair with the Earl of Dorset. Hearing of this, an enraged Digby returned and married her in secret. They lived happily with their two sons until her early death in 1633.

The solarium is Raleigh's Great Parlour, with a stupendous Victorian marble fireplace and grand paintings of Victorian Wingfield Digbys. The Red Drawing Room is mostly original to the Digby house, its ceiling a gathering together of ostriches (the Digby crest) with roses, fleurs-de-lys, flowers and monsters. At one end is a processional painting of Elizabeth I attended by her courtiers. Here too is a copy of van Dyck's picture of Sir Kenelm with Venetia and their boys. We now wander next through drawing rooms, boudoirs, bedrooms and turret rooms, each adorned with colourful fireplaces and flooded with light. They are also richly furnished. Sherborne is a treasure house of Georgian commodes, Boulle desks, lacquered cabinets and Owen Jones curtains.

A marked change in style comes with the descent to the old entrance hall and Oak Room. Suddenly we are back in Raleigh's hunting lodge. The fireplaces are rough, the arches of stone and the furniture of solid oak. The adjacent dining room retains two magnificent internal draught porches, crowned with a profusion of scrollwork. Below are Raleigh's original kitchens, hung with the usual copper but with an exhibition of curios, including Earl Digby's false teeth. They look painful.

WIMBORNE MINSTER: PRIEST'S HOUSE *

High Street
Medieval hall house with garden (M)

This was a Georgian clothier's shop that became an ironmonger's owned by the Coles family. They left it to the town in 1987. The two-storey exterior is picturesque to the street and even more attractive behind, where it is of the same banded stone-and-flint that adorn the walls of the Minster opposite.

This ancient building has been altered, bruised, extended and filled in, but it is still recognizable. From the street, the gable was once a wing of a hall recessed from the street frontage, now buried behind a later shop front. The ironmonger's store has been reconstructed behind the façade, to what it was when it closed in 1960. Behind and to the left is the old house's parlour. This is panelled and restored to its appearance when the Kings, a family of mercers, owned the house in the 18th century.

Behind the recreated shop is the medieval hall, curtailed by the insertion of a staircase and partition. It contains a set of painted linen wall-hangings depicting the story of Joseph, of the sort found in many English houses that could not afford real tapestries. These are modern copies of the rare set at Owlpen (Gloucs). Waxwork figures are discreetly arranged in these rooms – so discreetly that I could not tell them from two local ladies engaged in a lacemaking class.

Medieval grandeur at Wolfeton

WOLFETON HOUSE ✳✳✳

1m E of Charminster, N of Dorchester
Remains of Elizabethan house with
Renaissance interiors (P)

Two bastion towers flank the gatehouse like a
castle in the Dordogne. Old limestone walls
seem under perpetual siege from nature.
Inside are vaults unplastered, attics uncon-
verted and windows uncurtained. Mention to
Captain Thimbleby, the owner, that the place
might be a French château and he erupts. A
French château, he says, might be Wolfeton.

The house was home in the 15th century to
a Dorset family, the Trenchards, to whom the
Thimblebys are 'connected'. It was here in 1506
that Philip of Austria and his wife, 'mad
Joanna', were brought one night by a Trench-
ard after being driven ashore at Weymouth. A
young man called John Russell, known to
speak Spanish, was summoned from Bridport
as interpreter. He stayed with the couple on
their way to Henry VI's court at Windsor,
where he made such a mark as eventually
to become Earl of Bedford and founder of
the mighty Woburn clan. It pays to speak
Spanish.

The two round towers of the gatehouse date
from the early 16th century, one with a small
chapel inside, the other with a spiral staircase
composed of wooden blocks resting on their
own weight, without a newel post. Beyond
would once have been two courtyards, most of
which fell down in the 18th and 19th centuries.
Only the south range survives, plus an extraordinary Riding House of *c*1600, said to be the
earliest such indoor riding school surviving in
England.

The south range is a handsome composition.
Seen from the garden, the grand sequence
embraces the circular gatehouse towers, a
prominent staircase tower, the end windows
of the Great Hall, a garderobe tower and then
the three expansive 16th-century windows of
the Elizabethan house, with a Great Chamber
above. This runs the gamut from turrets, slits
and battlements to Elizabethan stateliness. The

Great Hall windows merit an essay in themselves. They are irregular and cannot all be of
the same date. What appear to be Perpendicular openings have Renaissance putti and
mullions. One of these is even stepped outwards so as to suggest perspective.

The interior is a match for the exterior.
The entrance is into a splendid passage with
linenfold panelling, classical doorways and a
17th-century plaster ceiling. The Great Hall
survives from the original building. It was
heavily victorianized but includes old panels
and a magnificent doorcase. Fragments of
Tudor carving include monkeys in human
dress and a moustachioed man.

The two most remarkable rooms run along
the Elizabethan wing. They have superb plaster
ceilings with animals, masks and Red Indians.
Even finer are the doorcases and overmantels,
apparently moved here when other parts of the
house were demolished in the 19th century.
These rise the full height of the rooms and lend
them great presence. The drawing room
doorcase is nothing less than sensational, a
giant Corinthian order framing a smaller order
round the door itself. The fireplace carries
attenuated sculpted figures in dark, rich wood
and signs of the zodiac. It had none of the
crudity of many Jacobean pieces. The dining
room beyond is less ornate, but again has an
overmantel worthy of a palace.

Behind these rooms is a stone staircase,
contemporary with the Elizabethan wing and
lavish for a house of this period. A horse
and carriage are said to have been driven up
it. At the top is the doorway to the Great
Chamber, a serenely classical work of *c*1590.
The whole space, with its wide landing and
doorway, might be in an Italian palazzo rather
than an Elizabethan manor. It is attributed
to craftsmen from Longleat (Wilts), where a
remarkably similar staircase had recently been
built. The Great Chamber itself is a large
room recently restored, with a huge fireplace
against its internal wall. This incorporates yet
more Red Indians, sign of late-Tudor cosmopolitanism. The windows look out over the
tumbled vegetation of the garden.

Durham

Durham was a handsome county of rolling hills and high moors until the coming of King Coal. Few English landscapes have been so ravaged by industrial development. Nor was any attention paid to its future appearance when that development passed. Yet Durham has its corners of delight, and its inland wilderness can be lovely.

As in Northumberland, castles predominate among the earlier buildings, with fine examples at Raby and Durham. Raby, if more were on display, would be one of the sights of the North. Both castles contain medieval rooms as fine as any in England. The Tudors left the impressive hilltop profile of Lumley Castle and its sadder neighbour, Hylton. There is little from the Georgian era apart from Croxdale and the Palladian villa at Rokeby, the latter an exquisite touch of Italy in the North.

The Gothic revival is represented by Wyatt's alterations to Auckland Castle and the refashioning of Raby and Witton. The county is excellently endowed with vernacular buildings. From medieval Crook Hall and Jacobean Washington to the admirable recreations at Beamish, Durham offers unspectacular but rewarding houses of all periods. The recently discovered German POW camp at Harperley is unique.

Barnard Castle:
  Blagraves House *
  Bowes Museum **
  Castle *
Beamish Museum:
  Dentist's House *
  Music Teacher's
    House **
  Pit Cottages *
  Pockerley Manor **

Bishop Auckland:
  Auckland Castle ***
Chester-le-Street:
  Anker's House *
Croxdale Hall **
Durham:
  Castle ***
  Crook Hall **
Finchale *
Harperley **

Headlam *
Hylton *
Lumley ***
Preston *
Raby ****
Rokeby ***
Washington Old
  Hall **
Witton *

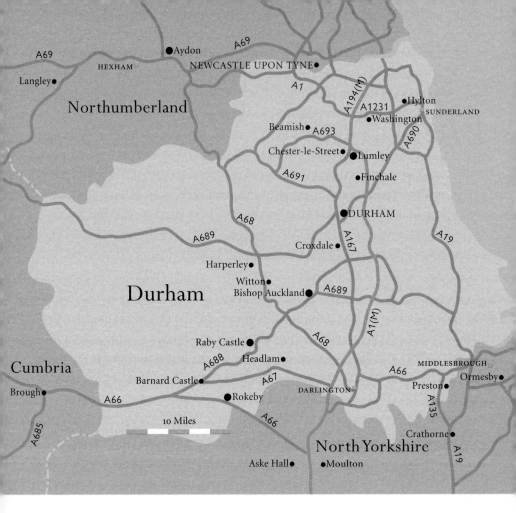

BARNARD CASTLE:
BLAGRAVES HOUSE *

30–32 The Bank
Old town house with musician adornment
(H)

Such façades would have filled the North in the 17th century. Their basements were for business and storage, with workmanlike alleys and courtyards behind. At the front entrance, steps led out of the mud to the main rooms which gasped for light and air by pushing their bay windows as far up and out over the street as money and gravity would allow. The front of Blagraves House is decorated with statues of four grotesque musicians. They were supposedly moved here, possibly from the side

wall, when the house was a local museum in the 19th century. It is now a restaurant.

The property can be traced back to the Middle Ages, when it appears to have been an inn and alehouse. The stone cellar is vaulted and might have been a brewery. The house was known as the Boar's Head in Elizabethan times, the boar being the symbol of Richard III, a hero in these parts. Tudor windows flank the door. Cromwell is said to have stayed here in 1648, consuming mulled wine and shortcake and demanding the removal of all Royalist emblems before he would go to sleep. The prominent four-storey projecting bay is also 17th century – a room carries the date of 1672 – by when the house was owned by the Blagrave family.

The main dining room has an original

plaster ceiling and fireplace. The staircase is 18th century. To the rear, across a courtyard adorned with a statue of a Stuart king, is what appears to be an ancient banqueting house, perhaps a relic of the inn, although the high windows might indicate use as a weaver's premises.

BARNARD CASTLE:
BOWES MUSEUM **

½ m E of centre of Barnard Castle
Fantastical French château housing tycoon's art collection (M)

Bowes tries to look like a French château, and succeeds. To find such a structure on the outskirts of Barnard Castle is incongruous and gloriously inappropriate. An ocean liner might as well have been towed up the Tees and left forgotten by the bank.

Bowes was begun in 1869, intended to be part house, part museum, by John Bowes, the illegitimate son of the Scottish Earl of Strathmore and a local girl. He lived most of his life in Paris, his father having settled on him his extensive Durham estates. Bowes married his mistress, an actress named Joséphine Benoîte, buying her a Paris theatre and even a title, Countess Montalbo, to conceal her origins. Barnard Castle was near his old home and was to display their vast collection of pictures, sculpture and furniture. It was never used as a house (except for top-floor apartments) and did not open to the public until 1892, by which time both Bowes and his wife were dead. They left it as a gift to the people of Co. Durham.

The museum was designed appropriately by a Frenchman, Jules Pellechet, as an exaggerated facsimile of the new town hall erected in Le Havre in 1859. A drive curves up from the road past lawns to a grand entrance terrace. The two main storeys rise above a high basement, with a generous attic above. The mansard roof is richly punctuated by dormers and chimneys. The only comparable work in this style in England at this time is Château

Impney (Worcs), designed in the same year, and the slightly later Waddesdon (Bucks).

The building and collection suffered from lack of money for maintenance, passing to Durham County Council in 1952 and now to a trust. It should be the Victoria and Albert of the North but remains instead an exotic monument to the Bowes' taste. Flocks of reluctant schoolchildren wander past lofty cases of French china and Spanish glass, beneath lowering canvasses by little-known artists. The gods of education have replaced those of showmanship. They bring more grant.

Yet the Bowes is full of delights. It has a large collection of medieval altarpieces, works by Goya and other Spanish masters and two large Canalettos. Rooms are filled with furniture and porcelain, metalwork and needlework, armour and costumes. Other rooms have been rescued from demolished houses, including one from Chesterfield House in London. In the front hall is a huge mechanical swan which periodically comes to life. Although valiant efforts are being made to revitalize the place, the museum remains a treasure trove awaiting a locksmith.

BARNARD CASTLE:
THE CASTLE *

Castle House
Tower and remains of hall on river (EH)

The castle is well sited on a bluff overlooking the River Tees. Walter Scott cried 'What prospects from his watchtower high,/ Glame gradual on the warder's eye.' It was built by Bernard, nephew of Guy de Baliol, in the 12th century and, despite subsequent ruin, still forms a magnificent pile when seen from below. The castle passed to the Beauchamp and Neville families and was held for the Crown against the 1569 anti-Reformation Rising of the North. In the 17th century, the castle was owned by Sir Henry Vane of Raby, who used its stone for his own neighbouring castle. By the 18th century it was a ruin. Vane's descendant, Lord Barnard, put it in Crown guardianship in 1952.

The castle area is divided into three sections, an outer and an inner ward, and the castle itself surrounded by an internal moat. The wards are now gardens, manicured by English Heritage within a inch of their lives and sadly divorced from the main square of this handsome town. Architecture should find ways of linking such spaces.

Of the original castle, the corner tower, Great Hall, Great Chamber and Round Tower survive, although much appears (from old prints) to have crumbled in the past two centuries. The Great Chamber's oriel window still looks out, forlorn, over the gorge. Given that so much money and effort has gone into building steps, ramps and health-and-safety contraptions, some effort could have gone into rebuilding walls and rooms.

The Round Tower was home in the 19th century to a recluse who dressed as a monk and showed visitors around the ruins. The tower retains its lower floors, which were used for storage. The ramparts offer a fine view over the valley and river below, with a picturesque bridge of 1772. Walter Scott's view must once have been spectacular. To Arthur Mee in 1953 it was still a 'glorious wooded gorge forming a lovely vista'.

The castle now faces a housing estate and young offenders' prison, both designed with complete insensitivity to the landscape.

BEAMISH MUSEUM
Beamish, 2m NE of Stanley

Beamish Hall was the seat of the coal-rich 'Bobby' Shafto family and is, at the time of writing, being converted into a hotel. The estate is more ambitious. It is the most successful 'themed' re-creation of England's industrial past. The land originally comprised the home farm, manor house and various disused drift-mine workings. All are now restored and open to the public. A complete pit village adjacent to the mine and a reconstructed North Country town centre of the turn of the 20th century (there being almost none left *in situ*) have been added to them. A light railway and a tram serve these locations from the visitor centre and car park, offering a fine view of the valley from a distance. The danger at Beamish is now of gigantism. Large display sheds are starting to appear in place of what should be a gradual organic growth. But the presentation, with lit fires and costumed attendants, is immaculate.

BEAMISH: DENTIST'S HOUSE *
originally at Ravensworth Terrace, Gateshead

The town high street is dated to 1913 and includes a sweet shop, solicitor's office, garage, bank, Co-op, newspaper office, inn and municipal park. All are refugees from various urban clearances in the North-East. At one end of the town is a row of houses built between 1830 and 1840 in Ravensworth Terrace in Gateshead. They were 'for aspiring professionals and tradesmen . . . illustrating the growing sophistication of town life available to those who could afford it'. I wonder what horror has replaced them.

The Dentist's House is the most immediate draw. Two houses, just one room wide, have been combined to form a dentist's house and surgery next door. The profession was at the time still unregulated and profit went to the brave and the well equipped. Downstairs is a waiting room and upstairs the surgery, workshop and recovery room for those given laughing gas. The operation on offer is impressively free of fastidious hygiene. The 'dentist' on duty on my visit seemed only too ready to pull out my teeth for half a crown.

The domestic rooms show the move away from Victorian gloom and clutter towards a lighter 20th-century touch. They are lit by gas and electricity. The latest Shanks plumbing is in the bathroom with a shower and Doulton Patent Flushing Toilet. A fox stole adorns the bedroom, while downstairs are prints, William Morris wallpapers and display cabinets filled with china.

BEAMISH: MUSIC TEACHER'S HOUSE **

originally at 2 Ravensworth Terrace, Gateshead

The house, also from Ravensworth Terrace in Gateshead, is infused with the personality of its supposed occupant, Florence Smith, struggling to make a living from teaching music and elocution to Gateshead young ladies at 6d a lesson. Whereas the dentist was keen on 20th-century gadgetry, Miss Smith is firmly Victorian. The house is dark and heavy and so cluttered with *objets trouvés* as to leave no inch on which to put anything down. Lighting is still by oil lamp.

The main parlour has a large fireplace with the piano beside it and an old trumpet gramophone. Sheet music is littered everywhere. China dogs adorn the mantelpiece and ornaments are kept clean inside glass domes. The kitchen at the back is exceptionally simple, with an open range and stone floor. Upstairs windows contain stained glass. The bedroom furniture is heavy mahogany. Unlike the dentist's house, there is no bathroom, only washstands and chamber pots.

The Music Teacher's House is excellently done. I can remember in the 1970s when every London restaurant aspired to such richness of period taste and decorative clutter. The essence of these re-creations is to make us aware of our own taste changing over time. How soon the once familiar comes to seem antique.

BEAMISH: PIT COTTAGES *

originally at Francis Street, Hetton-le-Hole

A lane leads from the drift-mine to a small colliery village of school, chapel and pit cottages. Each of the latter has a smallholding in front and an alley at the back, flanked by rabbit runs, chicken hutches and pigeon crees. They date from the 1860s and came from Francis Street in Hetton-le-Hole, once a terrace of twenty-seven such habitations. They are furnished as they would have been at the peak of the Durham coal boom in 1913.

Of the four cottages in the terrace, No. 1 is the colliery office, No. 2 housed an elderly Methodist couple, No. 3 an Irish Catholic family and No. 4 a miner's widow, the poorest of the row. Each of the cottages is single storey with parlour in the front, kitchen at the back and an attic bedroom. They are not spartan, the guide pointing out that miners' wages were not low and conditions considerably better than, for instance, those of farm labourers.

Thus the furnishings of No. 3 include a small pedal organ, dresser and oil-lit dining table with, in the kitchen, a grandfather clock and much decorative ornament. Furniture is solid and dignified. While the work was clearly hard and dangerous, it has none of the grimy overcrowding of the town tenements of the North. Fresh vegetables were available from the garden.

BEAMISH: POCKERLEY MANOR **

The manor house, still in its original position, stands in a copse of trees on the hillside overlooking the drift mine. Old labour looks down on new. The earliest part of the house dates from the 1440s, with a 'modern' farmhouse extension added in the 1720s. In front are a formal parterre, a kitchen garden and an orchard. The house is displayed as it would have been in 1825, a yeoman farmer's property of the sort common throughout England. This is the least 'Durham' of the Beamish properties.

The house is small, with a kitchen and back kitchen to one side of the ground floor entrance and a parlour to the other. The former is well furnished with an open fire and oven, and oak farmhouse furniture. The long-case clock has an unusual face depicting a colliery scene. The parlour is more decorous, panelled in white-painted pine and with pictures of Durham cattle on the walls. Spode china is on the table and a handsome sideboard against the wall.

The upstairs rooms are more cottage than manor, with a patchwork quilt on the four-poster bed in the master bedroom. The furnishings have been carefully chosen. There is no sense here of any old junk having been amassed to fill a 'themed' room. Even the items of food in the pantry are to a purpose. The adjacent Old House is displayed as servants' quarters, dark, medieval and poky. A sign outside warns, 'all dogs shot'. We are not sure whether it is meant.

BISHOP AUCKLAND:
AUCKLAND CASTLE ***

Bishop Auckland
Bishop's palace restored by Wyatt (P)

Auckland Castle is England's finest bishop's palace. It was seat of the one-time Prince Bishops of the Palatinate of Durham – once one of their fourteen residences. As protectors of the Border, they were granted secular as well as ecclesiastical authority under the Crown. This power was not formally rescinded until 1836, when Bishop van Mildert moved out of Durham Castle and made Auckland Castle his sole residence.

The castle lies at the edge of the town on a bluff overlooking the River Wear. The dramatic location gives it a superb park and woods. The entrance is Sir Thomas Robinson's Georgian Gothick gateway with clock-tower, built by the high-living Bishop Trevor in 1760. The drive then passes through a screen built by James Wyatt in 1796 for Bishop Shute Barrington. The medieval house was an episcopal manor with hall, domestic rooms and offices. This was gradually extended until Wyatt's arrival to impose an emphatic Gothick stamp on the palace in the 1790s. He rearranged the rooms and gave them the happily domestic touch that the late Georgians brought to much ecclesiastical building. This has recently been enhanced with pastel shades and admirable red carpeting.

Wyatt's entrance hall was the old 'Gentlemen's' or outer hall. It now opens from a pink lobby into a spreading double staircase which rises past a large picture window to a balcony with mural, a delightful sequence. The progress to the throne continues through an ante-room with its view of the Scotland wing, where the Bishops' Scots prisoners were once held. The main state or throne room lies through traceried doors and arches. It is not over-large, more a country ballroom in dimension, with the wooden throne surrounded by Gothick plasterwork, the coat of arms supported by a crook and a sword, indication of the bishops' monarchical dominion. Portraits of bishops line the walls. Wyatt's windows are tinted pink, 'to make the ladies appear less pale in sunlight'.

Beyond lies the Long Dining Room. The room was recast in 1760 by Bishop Trevor but given its oriel window by Wyatt. The walls are in a delicate turquoise. Here hangs Auckland's, indeed Durham's, pride and joy. Trevor's collection of thirteen Zurbaráns of Jacob and his Sons was brought here in 1756, part of his campaign to improve the status of Jews in English society. They stand 8 ft high and fill their canvases. *Benjamin* is an 18th-century copy, the original hanging in Grimsthorpe (Lincs). Each is dark and dramatic against a light sky, their costumes variously of 17th-century Spanish nobles, tradesmen and peasants. Painted in the 1640s, the sequence is a treasure of the North of England. At the time of writing, there is talk of putting them up for sale, a catastrophe. This is one of the first rooms in England to be designed to house a specific group of paintings, which it does to perfection.

Beyond, we enter the bishop's suite of rooms. The King Charles Room, once the king's bedroom, is now a sitting room. It has bright pink walls and Rococo ceiling. The paintings are again from Bishop Trevor's collection. The Gothick music room is now a dining room, with delicate portraits of bishops' wives on the walls. The palace chapel was formerly the bishops' banqueting hall. Though rebuilt after the Civil War by Bishop Cosin, an enthusiast for elaborate church woodwork, it retains its Gothic arches. Cosin filled the ceiling with his heraldry and the west window with his glass. To one side is Nollekens' lavish memorial to Bishop Trevor, who nonetheless preferred to be buried at his beloved Glynde (Sussex).

Zurbarán at Auckland Castle

CHESTER-LE-STREET:
ANKER'S HOUSE *

St Mary and St Cuthbert Church
Rare surviving example of church hermitage
(M)

No medieval practice is as obscure as that of
the anchorite. An extreme form of hermit,
the anchorite inhabited not a lonely cave but
a walled-up sanctuary, a preliminary tomb,
adjacent to a church. Special permission from
a bishop was needed to become an anchorite,
requiring both an endowment for sustenance
and evidence of sufficient spirituality. He or
she was, in effect, 'buried' to await eventual
death in a twilight world of intense prayer. It

was considered the most holy of vocations.
Glory would attach to any church with a resident anchorite and shame would attach to any
whose anchorite pleaded for release.

Conditions in such cells would have been
near intolerable. The only apertures were a
tiny view to the chancel itself and an opening
for food and water to be passed through over a
pit grave already dug outside. The Reformation banned anchorages as little short of
witchcraft and almost all were obliterated. The
Chester-le-Street anchorage or anker house is
a rare survivor. The chamber may have been
preserved by being attached not to the chancel
but to the tower where it gave directly onto
the street, perhaps as an example to passing
villagers. A squint enabled the anchorite
to see the sacrament on the church altar.
What appears to be the original anchorage

window, carved from a single block of stone, is preserved just inside the church.

The cell was occupied from 1383 until the Dissolution and was then converted for occupation as a small almshouse. Two extra chambers were added and four poor widows took up residence. In 1626, a curate tried to evict the ladies to make the rooms his own, even obtaining a warrant from Durham to 'duck' them. The ladies employed three strong lads of the village to bar the door and force the curate to relent.

CROXDALE HALL **

Croxdale, 5m SW of Durham
Georgian house with private chapel (P-R)

Croxdale is the seat of the Salvin family, on the old Great North Road between Darlington and Durham. Their name is derived from 'sylvan', reflecting their origins in Sherwood Forest. Croxdale was acquired by marriage in 1402 and the present family have held it through twenty generations, loyal throughout to Durham and to Catholicism. To Burke, the Salvins were 'one of those ancient houses established at the Conquest whose undeviating adhesion to the Roman Catholic faith consigned them to long and honourable retirement'. The great 19th-century architect, Anthony Salvin, was a scion of the family.

The house itself is not the prominent villa on the hill overlooking the road. That is Burn Hall, a Catholic seminary established by the Salvins on their land. Croxdale Hall lies hidden from sight, over a river and under a road and rail bridge. The drive passes through open parkland beneath thick woods. The house retains the old manorial proximity to farm and outhouses. When it was rebuilt in the mid-18th century it was on the old Jacobean and possibly Tudor plan, with two wings extending behind. The rear is, in effect, the estate farmyard and includes a row of ancient cottages. One of these is a medieval priest's house. Beyond is a magnificent 18th-century barn. The whole grouping is workmanlike.

The exterior is simple to the point of sever-ity, with yellowing stone walls, Venetian windows and a plain pediment above the south façade. Carr of York is mentioned as a possible inspiration, although the house is probably by a local builder instructed, as the guide says, by 'an intelligent client'.

The rooms are those to be expected in such a house. Finest is the entrance hall and staircase. The latter rises and divides beneath two tall windows, the walls yellow and with gloomy Salvins gazing down on their descendants below. The Rococo ceiling is virtuoso plasterwork, possibly by Cortese, with elaborate cartouches and a central goddess.

The library's mahogany bookcases were designed for the room in the 1790s, outshining the books within. The drawing room has more good plasterwork and the dining room is decorated with fluted Tuscan pilasters, lit by a generous bow window. The north wing of the house contains the family's Gothick chapel, built in 1807. The altarpiece is by Maria Cosway in what Pevsner calls the 'swoony style' of pious Catholic art.

By the rear entrance is surely the most evocative boot-room in the county, crammed to the ceiling with old hunting gear, boots, hats, capes and dust-laden trophies. The smells are of leather and canvas, wood and field. The clutter is inimitable. Such places are as precious as any drawing room.

The house is magnificently sited above evidence of an important 18th-century garden sloping down towards the river. One of these is walled and large, guarded by a crinkle-crankle wall and overlooking a lake and wooded ravine.

DURHAM: CASTLE ***

Palace Green
Norman and Gothic domestic ranges (P)

Durham Cathedral and Castle justly form a World Heritage site. They rise on their rocky peninsular over the River Wear, stupendous relics of the Norman Conquest. While the cathedral is imperious, the castle is intimate and eccentric. A gatehouse leads into a medieval courtyard overlooked by a high mound and keep. Ahead was once the Norman hall, later rebuilt as state rooms. In the 14th century, a later, Gothic, hall was built to the left, the angle between them filled with a staircase tower. The Norman hall was turned into a residence. This remarkable enclave was the headquarters of the Prince Bishops of Durham until that function was discontinued in 1836 (Bishop Auckland, above) and the castle became the new Durham University. It has been part of the university ever since.

With true Victorian confidence, the university promptly rebuilt the ruined keep as a student residence. The remaining ranges contain interiors from all periods. On the left is the Great Hall, with a porch added in the 17th century by the flamboyant Bishop Cosin. The original screens passage survives, leading on the left to a black-and-white timbered buttery. Beyond are the original medieval kitchens with giant brick fireplaces and old utensils. They are still in use after 500 years, one of the longest serving kitchens in the country.

The Great Hall is a shortened version of what must have been a gigantic chamber. Its roof beams and windows are original. The walls are hung with Cromwellian armour. Portraits of bishops gaze down on the students dining beneath. Behind the dais end of the hall is Bishop Cosin's Black Staircase of the 1660s, leading to his domestic chambers. Its wide treads and robust openwork panels were once cantilevered from the walls. Cylindrical pillar supports have since been inserted, but this is still a majestic work of carpentry, with voluptuous baluster panels.

In the 16th century, a gallery was built along the exterior of what was the original Norman hall. Even the Tudors could not bring themselves to destroy its great doorway. This survives as one of England's finest Romanesque compositions.

In place of the older hall is now a suite of state rooms, once used as Judges' Lodgings and for university guests. (I once stayed here in great splendour.) The Senate Room has a fine Jacobean fireplace and is hung with tapestries. On the floor above is the original Norman Constable's Hall, now a gallery with deep-set 12th-century windows behind double arches. Half has been converted into small rooms, surely the oldest student quarters in Europe. Laptops and film posters nestle amid Norman dogtooth and zigzag.

At the far end of this gallery, an old spiral staircase leads underground to an early Norman chapel. It was long ignored and thought to be a storeroom. When excavated in the 1950s it was found to date from the earliest post-Conquest castle of about 1080. The eerie animals that adorn its capitals speak from an older age even than the cathedral itself.

DURHAM: CROOK HALL **
Sidegate
Medieval hall, 17th-century house (P-R)

The immediate environs of Durham are as grim as the city centre is charming. Ring roads and flyovers are flanked by concrete walls and overpowering office blocks. Tucked above one such wall is a medieval hall house with traces of 13th-century walling. It sits in a small garden across a field, and is now being restored by the Bell family. They were students at the university who loved Durham so much they decided to stay, much to Crook Hall's good fortune. The place is overgrown, creeper-clad and delightful.

The core of the house is a square 14th-century hall of roughcast stone walls, inside and outside. This hall has two trefoil Gothic windows and is open to the roof. It is extraordinarily primitive in appearance, unfurnished, candle-lit and ideal as an 'historic' wedding venue. The screens passage is of stone, supporting a tiny gallery reached from what would have been the domestic wing. The kitchen, with its large fireplace, later became the main parlour. There are traces of 17th-century paintings on its beams. A fire burns in the grate and a phantom staircase of quartered logs rises into the ceiling. A new stair turret was built at the rear in the 1980s.

Linked to the old manor is a fine Georgian house facing the lane. The history of the place is a jumble but it is known to have been inhabited in the 19th century by Dr James Raine, the historian of Durham, who claimed visits from the Wordsworths, John Ruskin and numerous ghosts. The grounds are being laid out as pleasantly wild gardens overlooking the river below.

FINCHALE PRIORY *

4m N of Durham
Monastic buildings on river bank (EH)

This idyllic bend in the River Wear was a retreat for the Benedictine monks of Durham. It was founded by the flamboyant St Godric, a giant of English history. Born shortly before the Norman Conquest, Godric was an itinerant pedlar who went to Rome and graduated to Mediterranean sea captain and pirate. He visited Compostela, Jerusalem and Rome three times.

At the age of forty, Godric put all this behind him and became a hermit. He settled at Finchale and established a reputation for asceticism and sanctity until his death at the age of 105 in 1170. He wore a hair shirt and chainmail coat. His hermitage soon became a priory of Durham, founded in 1237. It was rebuilt with a 13th-century church and cloister. The full-time complement was four monks and a prior, with a further four as visitors 'on retreat'.

It must have seemed a sublime place. Although the county council has unbelievably permitted a large caravan site a hundred yards from the ruin, the slope to the river and the steep wooded bank opposite remain picturesque. Most remarkable is the survival of the refectory, undercroft and much of the prior's house. The refectory was presumably for visitors as the prior's accommodation must have been sufficient for most domestic purposes. It includes a hall and prior's chamber to the east. At the other end of the hall is a large surviving kitchen.

In the prior's study is a seat in an oriel window. It was said to be able to cure women of barrenness if they sat on it. This power was mysteriously lost after the departure of the monks at the Dissolution in 1538. It is a charmed spot indeed.

HARPERLEY CAMP **

3m W of Crook
Last surviving POW camp once lost in woods (P)

Weardale is the most exotic of the Pennine dales and nowhere more so than above Bishop Auckland. Here, hidden on the steeply wooded slopes of the dale, is an intact German prisoner-of-war camp. Although occasionally visited by trespassing German veterans, it was left derelict in the woods for half a century, partly used for farm buildings. In 2002 it was 'discovered' and listed for preservation and is now being restored by a grant-aided local farmer for public display.

Designated Camp 93, Harperley is extensive. Its fifty huts housed 1,400 inmates in 1945. The structures are of brick, wood and breeze-block with corrugated iron roofs. They stand in rows, the windows and doors broken and falling out. One was converted into a theatre, with orchestra pit and even a prompt-box. German newspaper cuttings litter the walls. Everywhere are signs of the small comforts of prison, such as fake curtains made of hardboard and canteen wall paintings of scenes of the German countryside.

The prisoners worked on farms and building-sites. They enjoyed sport and gardening in the camp grounds and made small items of souvenirs for sale. While prison is prison, those inmates who have returned to Harperley expressed some affection for the place. One prisoner settled in nearby Newton Aycliffe after the war and has been involved in the rescue.

HEADLAM HALL *

Headlam, 8m NW of Darlington
Georgianized Jacobean manor (H)

Headlam has the loveliest of approaches. It lies off the main road through whitewashed farm buildings which appear to be sheltering it from prying eyes. The house is a much-altered manorial jumble.

The front of the hous faces the garden with angular yew hedges stretching into the distance. It has five bays of sash windows. The entrance façade is manifestly 17th century, with stone mullions and an embarrassment of hipped roofs. The formal Georgian façade at the rear – which is strangely wider than the front – also has five bays of slender windows. These surround a door-way which is crowned by a single carved bracket.

The chief feature of the interior is the old hall, now a sitting room. This is graced with two bold Tuscan pillars. A Jacobean oak chimneypiece carries the coat of arms of the Birkbeck family, who built Headlam at the turn of the 17th century. The house is now a hotel owned by the Robinson family, 'who have farmed at Headlam for four generations'. They have found a new crop.

HYLTON CASTLE *

2m NW of Sunderland
Castle ruin in municipal park (M)

Hylton is for addicts of architectural heartbreak. The battered old castle is black and ruined, its windows cemented and its park lost to municipal grass, entirely surrounded by housing estates to the west of Sunderland. Nowhere is Durham's disrespect for its past so blatant as here. To add to the poignancy, Hylton gazes across the Wear valley at the great classical folly, the Penshaw Monument, on a distant hilltop. The latter was erected in memory of a Lord Durham in 1842, a Theseion in honour of this fantasy Athens of the North.

Hylton was a 15th-century tower house. It was given wings but these were later demolished. The building was acquired by William Briggs in 1869 and rigorously gothicized. This was Victorian not Georgian medievalism. The result is severe. Four towerlets rise sheer the full three storeys of the main front and continue into the sky with crenellated crowns. The roofline is battlemented all round.

Now without its roof or upper floors, the interior is hard to make out. It once included the normal arrangement of vaulted ground floor with Great Hall above and Great Chamber next to it. Ghosts of vaults, stairs and fireplaces can still be made out. With its outer walls intact, the place would be easily restorable, if anyone cared.

A few yards away is the ruin of an old chapel, apparently later converted for use as a banqueting hall. It is no less forlorn.

LUMLEY CASTLE ***

1m E of Chester-le-Street
Tudor castle, with Vanbrugh additions (H)

From the A1 heading north near Chester-le-Street, Lumley Castle rises splendid on a hill. The outward appearance is of the 14th century. Elizabethan adornments and alterations by Vanbrugh in the 18th century merely added to its majesty. Its conversion into a luxury hotel by the present Lumley, the 12th Earl of Scarborough, is firmly in the medievalist tradition of his Tudor ancestors. Everything from Vanbrugh's stylish dining room to the 'medieval' banquets in the Great Hall is done with ostentation. The bedrooms have well-stocked libraries and antique four-posters. The receptionists are in costume. Where some employ pastiche, Lumley uses panache.

The castle was built by Sir Ralph Lumley in the 1390s on a 'modern' plan of four uniform walls and corner towers round an internal court. A gatehouse punctuates one side, the raised Great Hall fills the other. The ground floor is stone-vaulted. Lumley's Tudor descendant, the 7th Lord Lumley, added shields of great northern families to the wall outside the Great Hall and surrounded the mighty fireplace inside with similar heraldry. Lumley even crammed Chester-le-Street parish church with fake medieval effigies of his supposed ancestors.

Vanbrugh arrived at Lumley in 1722 at the invitation of the 1st Earl of Scarborough and proceeded to change everything. He reversed the hall, entering it not in medieval fashion from inside the courtyard but from a new platform on the outside, facing the valley. A medieval fort was thus made a spectacular Baroque folly.

Vanbrugh is most evident in the courtyard, on whose south side he inserted a new staircase with Venetian windows. This stair serves a new range of state rooms, forming the finest of the Lumley interiors, their ceilings stuccoed by Italians some years later. Considering the battering they must get as hotel reception rooms, they are superb. Adjacent to the Great Hall, the Garter Room has fine plasterwork, deeply coved and decorated with cherubs, arabesques and foliage. Over the fireplace is a remarkable composition of cherubs building a fire. This work dates from 1745, after Vanbrugh's time.

Beyond is the panelled dining room, with more restrained Palladian decoration. The saloon is decorated in the most effete Rococo, with a large central panel of cherubs kissing. The boudoir beyond is also Rococo. Nor was this all. Vanbrugh's masterpiece at Lumley is the old library built into the medieval undercroft. This is a Piranesian chamber of groin vaults divided by heavy rusticated columns, ancient Rome come to Durham. It is now a dining room, and a superb one.

Otherwise, the present Earl's interior decorators have been at work. Vaulted passages are lined with busts. Sitting rooms are heavy with books and ornaments. Spiral staircases shoot upwards and alcoves dart off at odd angles. The restored castle is dark and mysterious and would have delighted the Elizabethans.

PRESTON HALL *

Preston-on-Tees, 2m S of Stockton-on-Tees
Victorian villa with French masterpiece (M)

When David Burton Fowler built himself a villa by the River Tees in 1825, he little knew what was to hit him. Within a year 'Locomotive No. 1' of the Stockton to Darlington Railway destroyed his silence and deposited cinders on his plantation. Within three years, Fowler was dead. The house was sold to a succession of owners, the estate finally being allocated to housing in 1944. However, wartime shortage denied it building materials and, three years later, the house and park were bought by the council and saved.

The house is of brick with extensive Victorian additions in stone. These include a porch, ballroom and conservatory looking out over the park to the banks of the Tees. The interior retains its 19th-century plan and decoration, but has been woefully restored. Someone has picked out every plasterwork detail in primary colours, so that a leaf must be green, a grape purple and a cherry red. More successful is the Victorian 'street' recreated in the service wing to the rear of the building.

Panelling has been left in place in most of the main rooms. Although the furniture has gone, the house still hangs many of its donated pictures. Among these was a recently discovered masterpiece for which alone the house merits a visit, Georges de la Tour's *The Dice Players*. Congratulations to the council for not only not selling it but for displaying it in a room of its own.

RABY CASTLE ****

1m N of Staindrop
Medieval fortress of nine towers, with Victorian interiors (P)

Raby Castle is the lion of the North, yet a lion that still sleeps. The estate is undeveloped and undisturbed. Countryside stretches to the horizon. The old castle lies along a fold in the moors, its forest of towers and battlements gaining full majesty close at hand. Legendary home of King Canute, it passed through descent and marriage to the Nevilles, Earls of Westmorland, forebears of the Plantagenet line and thus of the Royal Family. The Nevilles did not recover the inheritance when it was confiscated after the Rising of the North in 1569. In 1626, Raby was bought from the Crown by the Vanes, later Lords Barnard, who hold it to this day.

Although the medieval appearance of the

Raby of the nine towers

castle was embellished by antiquarian Barnards in the 18th and 19th centuries, Raby remains as it was, essentially a true palace of the Middle Ages. From the outside, it is immensely forbidding. This is no picturesque folly or Gothick conceit but a fortress protected by nine towers, linked by a battlemented curtain wall. They were once protected by another outer wall, now reduced to no more than a parapet surrounding the terrace. The enemies of such places today may be bureaucrats and taxmen, but even they must give a shudder as they pass beneath Raby's great gate and enter its dark court.

The exterior towers are all different and of differing periods. Clifford's Tower is massive and domineering, followed clockwise by the Kitchen Tower, Mount Raskelf, the Chapel turrets and Bulmer's Tower, the last reputedly the keep of King Canute.

The Nevill Gateway leads to an inner courtyard. This has been much remodelled but retains its medieval atmosphere. The massive keep on the left guards the old Great Hall ahead.

A serious deficiency of Raby to the visitor is that neither the keep nor the adjacent state rooms are open to the public. What can be seen is the Great Hall and the suite of family rooms inserted by James Paine and Carr of York in the 18th century, together with later work by William Burn in the 1840s. They made habitable what must have been an intolerably inconvenient place. But they are only part of what could be as rewarding as Warwick Castle.

The entrance hall was remodelled by Carr in 1787 beneath the old Great Hall. Since the courtyard was too small for 'modern' carriages to turn round, he allowed them to drive into the lowered hall and set their passengers down under cover, before leaving on the far side. The effect on visitors was dazzling, alighting beneath a great rib-vaulted Gothick ceiling to find fires blazing and steps leading up to grand chambers on either side. The columns are of ox-blood scagliola.

The rooms open to the public are mostly those of a comfortable country house, with a fine private collection of pictures and furniture. The Small Drawing Room has an 18th-century ceiling depicting musical instruments, the walls hung with sporting paintings by Herring, Marshall, Wootton and Munnings. The library, formerly a dining room, is richly panelled with, as its climax, a voluptuous Lely of the Duchess of Portsmouth. She stands above a japanned chest flanked by Chinese porcelain pagodas. The adjacent Victorian ante-library contains pictures by de Hooch and Teniers and a tortoiseshell Flemish cabinet. On the floor appears to be the skin and head of one of the Lord Barnards' pet King Charles Spaniels splayed out in front of the fire like a tiger rug.

The ante-library leads into the virtuoso room of Burn's 1840s renovation, the eclectic Octagon Drawing Room. Yellow silk, white paint and Rococo gilding rise to a sumptuous frieze of neo-Jacobean scrollwork. A giant pendant supports the chandelier. For good measure, the doors are Indian. A malachite and giltwood side table glows by the window.

The dining room, also by Burn, has rich red walls and carpet. Here are some of Raby's finest pictures, including a swirling Luca Giordano, portraits by Lely and Reynolds and an exquisite work by Cornelis de Vos, *A Gentleman and his Wife*. A few bedrooms are open upstairs, specifically the Blue Bedroom which contains a state bed; it is Regency Gothic in style with domed canopy and coronet. In contrast, a servant's bedroom is also on view.

The last room on show, the Barons' Hall, is essentially Burn's work, its floor having been raised to make space for the new entrance hall beneath. With red walls, dark beams and giant proportions, this is well suited to medieval functions. Nevilles and Vanes gaze down from the walls. At one end, five sensational Meissen birds contort themselves into noble poses. It is said that 700 knights would gather here in fealty to the Nevilles.

Here was plotted the disastrous rising of the northern earls against Elizabeth in 1569, which was to lose the Nevilles Raby for ever. The Chapel has early 20th-century decoration, with painted walls and portraits of family figures in medieval costume (*see* Madresfield/Worcs). That on the right is of the 'Rose of Raby', mother of Edward IV and Richard III.

Although Burn destroyed much of 14th-century Raby, the castle retains most of its medieval servants' quarters. The kitchen dates from 1360 and is as built. It was still in use until the 1950s, the fumes rising to a huge lantern above. Next door is the medieval servants' hall with its long battered table and dresser filled with Minton plates. But more Raby, please.

ROKEBY PARK ***

2m SE of Barnard Castle
Palladian mansion with needlework pictures (P)

Rokeby, pronounced Rookaby, will always be known for the Rokeby *Venus*, the Velasquez nude sold by the Morritt family to the National Gallery in 1906. It is sad that smaller English houses seem unable to keep hold of the greatest art. The *Venus* would make Rokeby a sensational attraction were it still there today. A good copy hangs in the saloon.

Rokeby deserves to be equally well known as an early manifestation in the North of the Palladian revival. It was built in 1725 by and for Burlington's associate, Sir Thomas Robinson, as a graceful Georgian box with recessed wings. To the rear is a more complex plan, of central bay with towers and projecting wings. It is a variation on a formal Palladian theme, the towers borrowed from Pliny's Tuscan villa and apparently unique in England. The exterior is virtually unaltered: the main block is of stone and the wings are painted a rich yellow ochre. In this rugged landscape, Rokeby is a dash of Italian refinement.

Robinson's house was bought by the Morritt family in 1769 and has been in the family ever since. Its most remarkable member was Anne Morritt, a Georgian needlewoman who specialized in recreating paintings in embroidery. The house is full of her work, including, on the stairs, a needlework copy of a portrait of her by Benjamin West. Her work is of astonishing virtuosity.

The entrance under a porch is into a stone hall on the 'rustic' ground floor. This floor contains a complete suite of domestic rooms, an 18th-century mirror for the family of the state rooms on the *piano nobile* above. The print room is a survivor of the 18th-century custom of papering rooms with prints.

Bold Doric columns screen the stairs to the rear, with copies of Roman reliefs on the walls. Busts of the family line the passage to the stairs, the walls hung with twenty-three of Anne Morritt's needlework pictures. The first floor was at some stage reversed, so that the rear saloon is now the music room, with a ceiling later painted by J. G. Crace. This gives onto the main hall, now the saloon, which rises the full two storeys of the main front. It is curious in appearing Georgian at eye level – notably the superb door to the Music Room – above which is a Victorian ceiling, again by Crace. Over the fireplace is a Reynolds and opposite hangs the ghost of the *Venus*.

The dining room fills one wing of the house and is now attributed to Carr of York. It has a Rococo plasterwork ceiling and a large apsidal alcove with small niches flanking the fireplace. Grand portraits of Hanoverian royalty adorn the walls. To one end is an unusual Venetian window – Carr, if not Palladio, at his most inventive.

WASHINGTON OLD HALL **

The Avenue, Washington Village
Putative home of the great man's ancestors
(NT)

Contest is fierce to be considered 'home' of America's first president. The rewards are great: Malden in Essex and Great Brington and Sulgrave in Northamptonshire all exploit their claims. Washington has the advantage of the name. All known Washingtons seem to have

originated from a William de Washington, alias de Wessyngton, in the 12th century. A family of that name occupied the property until the 17th century.

The old house passed to the James family, descendants of a Bishop of Durham, and was mostly rebuilt in the 1620s. It then deteriorated until declared unfit for habitation in 1932. A committee was formed with vigorous American support and the house was saved in 1951, restored and given to the National Trust in 1956. The interior has been given back its 17th-century appearance, but with an American spin. A gift shop greets visitors immediately inside the front door and the upstairs is now a museum. George Washington's links with a building which is now submerged in Washington New Town sprawl seem tenuous.

The house is impressively simple. The symmetrical E-plan exterior of honey-coloured local sandstone faces south over a sloping garden. Over the old porch is a prominent Jacobean staircase tower, with the entrance on one side of it. Inside is a Great Hall, with solar/parlour wing to the right and kitchen to the left. Two medieval arches form openings to the latter. The rest of the building appears to be a 17th-century rebuild. The parlour is the smartest room, panelled and with an imported classical fireplace decorated with scrollwork.

The rooms are furnished in the Jacobean style, with much oak, pewter, Delftware and primitive pictures. The kitchen has National Trust wax food. The house's best feature is the oak staircase, a robust work of vernacular carving apparently donated from a building in Guildford, Surrey. One bedroom has been restored upstairs.

WITTON CASTLE *

Witton-le-Wear, 4m W of Bishop Auckland
Medieval revival castle in faded grand park
(P-R)

The guide to Witton admits that the place 'seems to have a curse upon it'. War, destruction, fire and bankruptcy have followed from one generation to the next. Nor is the

present an exception. The castle is approached through a sea of caravans, uglier than any housing estate, followed by walls and gates festooned with signs ominously banning intruders and drunks. By the time I had reached the castle's outer walls, I wondered if this was a holiday camp for young offenders. Five mangy peacocks and a row of wrecked fruit machines in the yard did not restore confidence.

The Eure family built the castle in the early 1400s as a keep within an extensive curtain wall. It was partly demolished in the 17th century, rebuilt but gutted by fire in the late 18th. Eures gave way to the D'Arcys who gave way to Cuthberts who gave way to Chayters, each suffering misfortune or calamity in turn. The politician, Viscount Lambton, bought it in 1963 'for the creation of an important public amenity', apparently a euphemism for 'profit'. It is now ignominiously the clubhouse and entertainment centre for the caravan park.

Yet for all these indignities, Witton is a splendid sight. The exterior is Victorian out of Georgian romantic. A fine crenellated outer wall shields an entrance courtyard with bold *porte-cochère*. The rear façade looks out over the park to a lake. From all angles, the central block rises splendidly in a forest of turrets and towers in appropriately grim shades of grey. The gatehouse, surprisingly, is by the musician and amateur architect, Jools Holland.

Witton's interior is now institutional. A fine 18th-century Gothick ballroom can be detected on the first floor, with panelling and traceried windows. The lounge bar retains ancient panels to its window recesses, the walls here being hugely thick and presumably medieval. Of the rest I know nothing: nor did Pevsner who commented that 'The history of this building is not sufficiently known.' But what an opportunity!

Washington: Jacobean returned to life

Essex

Much of Essex is the flat alluvial estuary of the Thames. It was always the poor side of London, a place of docks, market gardens and down-at-heel resorts. Yet its sea shore is still wild and inaccessible, and inland are hills and villages of antiquity and character. Essex was home to a capital of ancient Britain at Colchester, where both Roman and Norman invaders built strongholds. Hedingham still has the best presented Norman keep in the country. Essex enjoyed a glorious Tudor era. Lacking stone, it was the pre-eminent county for brick, most notably the brick tower of Layer Marney. A more domestic Tudor can be seen at Ingatestone and Paycocke's.

The Howards' palace at Audley End is a textbook of English building, from the Jacobean era through Vanbrugh and Adam to the Victorian restorers. The late 17th century can be enjoyed at Gosfield and the Georgians, albeit piano, at Hylands. After that, Essex winds down. But it has preserved one bizarre relic of the late 20th century, Mistley Secret Bunker.

Audley End ✱✱✱✱
Belchamp Hall ✱
Coggeshall:
   Paycocke's ✱✱
Colchester:
   Castle ✱
   Tymperleys ✱

Copped Hall ✱
Down Hall ✱
Gosfield Hall ✱✱
Hedingham ✱✱
Hylands ✱✱
Ingatestone ✱✱✱
Layer Marney Tower ✱✱✱

Mistley:
   Secret Bunker ✱
Mountfitchet Castle ✱
Southend:
   Southchurch Hall ✱

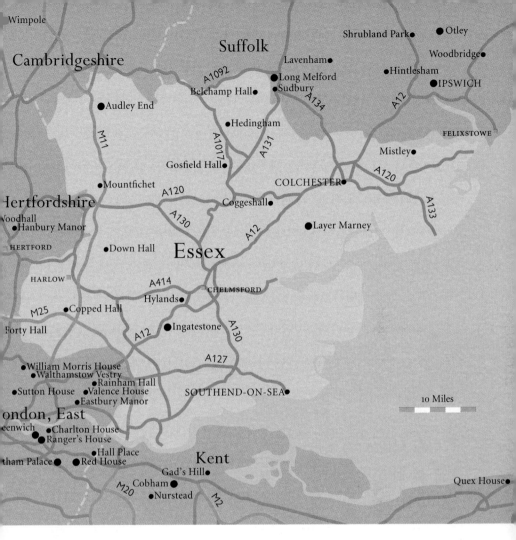

AUDLEY END ****

1m W of Saffron Walden
Jacobean prodigy house with Vanbrugh and
Adam insertions (EH)

The sudden glimpse of Audley End across its
park from the main road is so sensational that
drivers risk swerving into the river. This is
one of England's so-called prodigy houses,
built for glamour and for show, gleaming gold
in the sun, turreted, pinnacled and parapeted.
Its sheets of windows are spread like precious
metal across the façade.

Thomas Howard, Earl of Suffolk, was one of
Drake's captains. He inherited the Audley End

estate from his grandfather, Thomas Audley,
in 1582, and set about creating a house in
which a rising courtier might entertain the
monarch. The house was not completed until
1614 in the reign of James I. It was colossal,
reputedly costing £200,000, almost twenty
times that of the Cecils' Hatfield (Herts). The
layout of the original house reflected its royal
ambitions. Although Audley remains Elizabethan in style and plan, its façade is symmetrical. The Great Hall bay window is centrally
placed and the porches twinned, supposedly to
greet king and queen separately. They never
came and Howard fell from grace within four
years of the house's completion. The estate was
burdened with debt.

A sort of rescue came in 1666 when Charles II bought the palace for £50,000 to be near the racing at Newmarket. But the house, still burdened with debt, soon reverted to the Howards. They instructed Sir John Vanbrugh to demolish most of the forecourt, which then stretched down to the river's edge. Vanbrugh did this and inserted the remarkable Baroque screen to the main staircase. The house was inherited by Sir John Griffin Griffin, who recruited Capability Brown to lay out the grounds. Finally Robert Adam designed new interiors to the south wing. Somehow there was always money enough.

Audley End now passed through a maze of lateral lines, name changes and title reversions. In the 1820s and 1830s, the 3rd Lord Braybrooke decided the time had come to reinstate Audley End's Jacobean past, destroying Adam's interiors. He took the house back to its original appearance, less the courtyards. Finally in 1948 the government bought the house and, in the 1960s, reinstated the Adam rooms at public expense. The house contains the Howard/Braybrooke collection of pictures, plate and natural history. The family retain a close interest in the place and live locally.

What is seen is thus a Jacobean mansion in Victorian clothes. This is evident in the Great Hall. The Jacobean screen faces Vanbrugh's screen like two trumpeters blasting fanfares at each other from opposite ends of the room. Between the two is a virile array of banners, shields, pikes, firearms, portraits and medallions. Massive brackets hold the heraldic panels of the ceiling.

The staircase rises to the saloon, formerly the Great Chamber and sometimes called the Fish Room from the dolphins cavorting between the scrolls and pendants. The ceiling is Jacobean, the frieze Gothick, the fireplace Elizabethan. The furniture is mostly Regency. The effect is Victorian eclectic, despite it not being a Victorian room at all.

Likewise the Red Drawing Room, the two libraries and the dining room. Each contrasts Jacobean scrollwork on the ceilings with mostly Georgian walls and furnishings. The paintings in these rooms are superb. The drawing room has van Goyens and Canalettos and the dining room a rare large portrait of George II. The dining room plasterwork betrays a previous division into two rooms. All are white or cream, never gloomy. The two libraries give Audley End a studious rather than 'state room' atmosphere.

In the former second courtyard behind the Great Hall stands the picture gallery built in the 18th century. It is hung with family portraits and introduces the 4th Lord Braybrooke's collection of stuffed animals and birds, one of the largest in any English house. This continues in the gallery below, a valhalla of taxidermy.

Audley End's eccentricity now becomes prodigious. The chapel is Gothick, in white and ochre. Ribbed vaults and voluptuous fans vault the family pew. The north wing of the house, the private rooms of the Braybrookes in the 19th century, has been restored as Jacobean state rooms, with Victorian variations. The Neville Bedroom appears to have been furnished for giants. The Howard Bedroom contains a magnificent state bed, its delicate embroidery rising to a triumphal canopy crowned with a coronet.

There remains the Adam suite, reinstated in the 1960s. It comprises the ground floor rooms in the south wing where the contrast with the Jacobean suite upstairs could not be greater. The two drawing rooms, lobby and dining room were reproduced from original drawings and plans. The Little Drawing Room is among Adam's most perfect small works. Fronds wave, damsels cavort, foliage drips and loses itself in a riot of gilding. This is the effete classicism that so bored the Victorians and led them not to 'conserve as found' but to destroy it.

For once the authorities have had the courage to bring an earlier fashion back to life, even if it meant destroying its later replacement. To return from Adam's exquisite decor to the Great Hall is a shock, like going from delicate sweetmeats to a vast plate of roast beef.

Audley End: prodigious Jacobean

BELCHAMP HALL *

Belchamp Water, 6m W of Sudbury
Early Georgian house with Jacobean panelling
(P-R)

Belchamp has been owned by Raymonds since
1611 and they show no signs of giving up. On
my visit, the son of the house was making
preparations for his wedding in a marquee
on the lawn. The event was overseen by his
parents, the old church tower, the ancestral
cedars and the house that John Raymond
rebuilt in 1720. The place is beloved of film
companies and featured in the Lovejoy television series.

The nine-bay façade is a mix of dressed
bricks, with aprons beneath the windows and a
wide stone door. A later balustrade obscures
three fine dormers in the roof.

The best room inside is the dining room.
Although dating from the 18th century, it is
decorated with panelling retained from an
earlier house. Even the Georgians did 'reproduction Jacobean'. Marquetry panels flank the
fireplace and scagliola columns mark where
two rooms were combined into one. The walls
hang with Raymond portraits, including a
woman who had twenty-two children.

The other rooms are those of a conventional
18th-century country house. The drawing
room is white panelled. In the smoking room
is a small organ given to a daughter of the
family by Handel, of whom she was a pupil.
Behind is a sheltered garden with an ancient
mulberry tree. A summer house contains
windows of coloured glass depicting pastoral
scenes.

COGGESHALL: PAYCOCKE'S **

West Street
Restoration of medieval clothier's house
(NT)

Coggeshall is an Essex Lavenham, albeit more
workaday and a bit tattier at the edges. No
fewer than 97 medieval buildings in the small

town were listed by the old Royal Commission.

None is more spectacular than 15th-century
Paycocke's. To Pevsner, it merited an accolade,
'one of the most attractive half-timbered
houses of England'. But what is it? Chunks are
undoubtedly Tudor but much is Edwardian,
lovingly executed by a Buxton descendant of
the original John Paycocke. Do that to an old
house today and archaeologists would descend
on you with a ton of preservation orders.

The Paycockes were Essex wool entrepreneurs. When John Paycocke's son died in 1518
he left bequests for his shearmen, weavers,
fullers, combers, carders and spinners. The
wealth of wool was liberally spread. Nothing
that Paycocke left was more splendid than the
house he built, probably on the foundations
of an earlier one, in West Street in c1505. It
was the town house of a working merchant.
Each room had its purpose. Throughout the
building are holes for pegs on which cloth
might be hung.

The façade displays its wealth in the close-
ness of the timbering, the close-studding.
Wealth is also seen in the carving of the linenfold panelling of the carriageway doors and
in the bressumer, the long beam on which
the upper storey rests. On the latter are carved
a king and queen with, the guidebook says,
'entwined indeterminable lower parts'. The
windows are all Edwardian reproductions of
originals.

The interior comprises a simple layout of
five rooms, plus others private to the National
Trust custodian. Apart from the repositioning
of the staircase in 1905 and the uncomfortable insertion of a fireplace in the hall, the
rooms are as originally built. Students of
Tudor timbering can spend many happy hours
detecting variations in peg holes, panelling
widths and beam dressings. The ensemble is
quaint and charming. The two upstairs bedrooms have been furnished mostly by an
American donor to the National Trust. The
small sitting room downstairs contains a
display of local lace.

Linenfold serene at Paycocke's

COLCHESTER: CASTLE *

Ryegate Road
Biggest Norman keep made of Roman
fragments (M)

I visited Cochester castle as a boy and
will never forget the vast empty volume of
what is claimed as Europe's largest Norman
keep. Its walls were built of reused Roman tiles
and its rugged corner towers and bastions
looked impossibly old. Could anything be
older?

In fact, the walls and towers were re-roofed
by the Victorians to 'look Roman', and large
windows were inserted into the entrance
façade to make parts of it habitable. Since my
first visit the interior has been filled with
museum partitions, stands, placards, display
cases, reconstructions and screens. Nothing is
left to the imagination. Modern Colchester
Castle is a creation of primary education and
health-and-safety officialdom.

Yet the place still has majesty. The town of
Camulodunum was capital of the ancient
Britons in this region. It was captured by the
Romans under Claudius in AD 43 with the use
of elephants, then sacked by Boudicca in AD
60. It was recaptured by Rome, ignored by the
Saxons but refortified by the Normans. The
castle was built sometime after 1076 on the
ruined base of the Roman Temple of Claudius.
It is this that we see today – showing a building
of grand historical significance.

The keep is in the traditional early Norman
style, that is four square and massive, containing all its chambers, offices and storage within.
Added to it is a rectangular entrance wing,
grand staircase and chapel with an apsidal
east end. The plan is similar to the White
Tower in London. Health-and-safety fanatics
have closed the grand staircase but the chapel
and garderobes are still visible behind the
museum clutter. The south side was made
habitable in the 18th century and it must have
been an eerie place to live.

The museum, opened in 1992, contains
some fine objects, including the best Roman
statue in England, a bronze of Mercury, and
the Colchester Vase, depicting gladiators and
huntsmen. There is a suitably horrible prison
cell.

COLCHESTER: TYMPERLEYS *

8 Trinity Street
Surviving medieval and Tudor hall house (M)

An internal ring road cuts Colchester old town
from its suburbs as if to recreate a medieval
ghetto. Small streets and alleys lead up to the
market square and a hypermarket has destroyed countless historic buildings beneath its
footprint. But Trinity Street has kept a row
of pretty buildings. In a courtyard to its west
lies an old clock museum in a timber-framed
house.

This had been bought by a local businessman, Bernard Mason, in 1956 to house his
collection of timepieces. The structure is that
of a medieval hall house, to which an extension was added in 1580 and a staircase in 1680.
The hall has had a ceiling inserted, but its
crown-post roof may still be seen upstairs. The
two-bay windows have wooden mullions, and
there is an oversailed upper storey with attic.
The garden, now planted with historic herbs,
survives outside and across from it are the
stables, filled with more clocks.

Inside is mostly a museum, but one room
has been recreated as that belonging to a
typical 'customer', a gentleman writing at his
table with a clock ticking noisily in the background. Here too is a fireplace brought
from elsewhere in the town. The house is a
charming backwater.

COPPED HALL *

4m SW of Epping
Ruin of Georgian mansion overlooking M25
(P)

What to do with Copped Hall? The building is
an exhilarating ruin, reached by a rural drive
over the M25, which a more civilized country
would have buried at this point. Handsome

gates herald an open avenue along a ridge. At its end is the isolated mansion with views in all directions.

Copped Hall was built in 1753–8 by John Sanderson. The exterior is severely classical but with a superb façade facing the garden above curving external staircases. The house was refitted by James Wyatt and refaced in 1895 by C. E. Kempe, who added the rusticated walls and garden pavilions in the style of Inigo Jones. The house was then gutted by fire in 1917 and has lain empty ever since, a scandal. The stairs have gone, inside and out, but the pediment carvings survive and the exterior is in sound condition.

Much of this was covered in creeper and romantic gloom on my last visit. The remains of a patio and lawn could be detected leading to a platform to the west of the house. The view is still beautifully rural for this part of the Home Counties. The group aches for sensitive restoration. The walls are being stabilized and there are plans at present for open-air concerts.

DOWN HALL *

3m S of Hatfield Broad Oak
Victorian Italianate mansion built of concrete (H)

Down Hall's chief claim to fame is that it is built almost entirely of concrete. It is in High Italianate style, designed by F. P. Cockerell and covered outside in sgraffito decoration. It looks like a building in a suburb of Florence. It has no equal in England.

The previous house belonged to the 18th-century Earl of Oxford, who sold it in 1741 to a London merchant, William Selwin. Everything was demolished by Sir Henry Selwin-Ibbetson in 1871 and rebuilt with a grandeur befitting his status as local Tory MP. The concrete for the walls was poured into frames on site, with stone used for the dressings. The interior was lit by a gas works built in the grounds. The house later became a girls' school and, more recently, a hotel. It retains a celebrated hornbeam walk in the garden, a

fragment of a Georgian design by Charles Bridgeman.

The exterior and garden ornaments are liberally coated with moral sayings. One reminds us, in Latin, that 'Our God built this Place'. The rear front has two Italianate towers linked by a colonnade looking out over the garden, epitome of Victorian graciousness. The interior contains grand reception rooms arranged round a hall designed as a Pompeian atrium. This offers through access from the entrance to the garden colonnade behind. It must have been impossible to heat.

The hall columns are giants and the fireplace equally so. The latter was carved by a visiting out-of-work Italian. The bottom tier represents Youth and Age, the upper tier Time's winged chariot. The library and dining room doors have barley-sugar columns, after Bernini. The house retains a scattering of family portraits and, although a hotel, the character of the house and its former owners is respected.

GOSFIELD HALL **

Gosfield, 4m N of Braintree
Grand Tudor and 18th-century house rescued and restored (P-R)

The hall is located on a slope overlooking a mile-long lake created by its Georgian owner, Earl Nugent. It was begun in the 16th century as a courtyard house by Sir John Wentworth, whose Tudor Long Gallery survives over the entrance. This plan was altered and enhanced by later owners, each lacking enough money for a complete rebuild. The house thus comprises four ranges from different eras. It was rescued from army dereliction after the Second World War and brought back to life by the Country Houses Association as 'a magical retirement option'. It is certainly that.

The west front is still Tudor, with a central gateway and gabled bays on either side. The present entrance is on the opposite front facing the drive. It was built mostly in 1715 and looks as Wren-ish as Kensington Palace (London, C). Big windows with redbrick dressings are set into darker brick walls beneath steep pitched roofs. An ungainly neo-Tudor gallery above the door is enjoyably out of character. The garden front differs again, stuccoed and Palladian, best seen from across the lake. English architecture was never so adaptable.

The Great Hall is exceedingly grand, with a ceiling by Thornhill. Caryatid mermen embrace each other with arms and tails, most odd. The library has a plaster ceiling grained to look like wood, with giant shells as centrepieces, apparently in imitation of walnut and tulipwood. The staircase hall is so constructed as to leave the stair itself like a freestanding sculpture in its midst.

Gosfield Hall possesses a grandeur that institutional conversion has in no way diminished. The conductor Sir Adrian Boult lived here for a while after the war. It is being revived as a venue for music.

HEDINGHAM CASTLE **

Castle Hedingham
Best surviving Norman keep castle with hall intact (P)

Hedingham deserves a title for best-kept keep. It was built in 1140 by the de Veres, Earls of Oxford, grandees of Essex since the Norman Conquest. De Veres were considered so blue-blooded as to make mere monarchs seem upstarts.

They fought in every medieval war and served most kings as Chamberlain, although the 9th Earl inspired such jealousy among Richard II's courtiers that he was exiled to France where he was killed by a boar. The line went extinct in the 18th century and the castle passed by marriage to the Lindsays, who continue to live in a Georgian house within the present Outer Bailey.

Why England's Norman keeps should be better preserved than later medieval castles is a mystery. Perhaps they were better built or constituted less of a threat in the Civil War. Hedingham can be ranked with Norwich and Castle Rising (both Norfolk), Conisbrough (Yorks, S) and the Tower of London (London, C). Castle and house sit splendid on a rise from the village. The castle is virtually intact. It stands four square within its bailey, luxuriantly faced in dressed stone from Barnack. Steps lead to the original door, adorned with Norman zigzag carving. Downstairs is the dungeon; above is the garrison room.

Steps lead up to the main hall, surviving more or less as built. A single arch curves over it in a magnificent elipse. Arches to adjacent passages and windows have more zigzag. Above is a minstrels' gallery apparently tunnelled from within the walls. This runs round the room, adding to its grandeur. A Norman fireplace survives, as do the original garderobes. A further dormitory storey is on the top floor.

The hall has been furnished in a convincing medieval style and regularly echoes to the clatter of Norman reconstructions.

HYLANDS **

2m SW of Chelmsford
Classical country seat rescued at last (M)

Hylands is a great house that never recovered from being used as a hospital in the First World War and an SAS headquarters in the Second. One night, a soldier drove a jeep up the main staircase. It woke the terrified Mrs Hanbury, the last owner who, like many brave souls, had decided to remain at home during army requisition in the vain hope of diminishing the damage. The staircase did not recover, nor did the jeep. After the war, wet rot, dry rot and poverty ensued. Mrs Hanbury's death in 1962 removed what every house needs for its survival, family commitment.

Hylands had been built in c1728 by an MP, Sir John Comyns, in a sweeping park outside Chelmsford. It was extended twice, in the early and late 19th century. In the 1960s, the house passed to Chelmsford Council, which tried for many years to have it demolished. When this was rightly prevented by the government, the best was made of a now more difficult job.

The restoration of Hylands has taken half a century. The outside is resplendent, returned to the early 19th-century proportions given it by J. B. Papworth, master of dignified Grecian buildings, in creamy stucco. For the inside, great things are in store (literally) but at present the place is in the grip of council occupation. The staircase and two main reception rooms remain derelict. The Blue Room and the boudoir are tea-rooms, but other rooms are slowly returning to life.

The drawing room and library in the east wing have been reinstated to their original 1840s appearance, in the lush classicism of the early Victorians. The drawing room ceiling is thick with gilding and handpainting, restored by craftsmen from that shrine of modern conservation, Uppark. No fewer than 5,700 leaves of 23-carat gold were apparently consumed on the work. The library has its original fireplace and fragments of the old decoration are left in one corner for comparison.

The rooms are described as retaining 'an air of faded opulence'. They rather have an air of brand new conservation and desperately need furniture and clutter. But Hylands is on the road to recovery. There is an exhibition of work in progress and the public address system plays 'Land of Hope and Glory', a delightful touch.

INGATESTONE HALL ***

Ingatestone
Elizabethan home of the Petres, with priest holes (P)

The Lords Petre of Ingatestone take their name from the Latin for stone. They have lived at the hall, solid as a rock, since acquiring the property in the 1540s. They have always been true to the crown, the Old Religion and the House of Lords. On display in the gallery is the astonishingly curt letter in 1999 banishing the present Lord Petre from his hereditary seat in the House of Lords and asking him to clear his locker. Such is the style of the British constitution.

This was the family, one of whose members in the 18th century snipped a lock from the hair of a cheeky cousin, Arabella Fermor. The ensuing vendetta was defused then satirized by a family friend, Alexander Pope. His verse, 'The Rape of the Lock', ridiculed everyone involved and sold 3,000 copies in four days. It deeply embarrassed the family and made Arabella 'very troublesome and conceited'.

Not even Parliament can banish a lord from his hall. The approach from the road is under an 18th-century clock-tower above a Tudor outbuilding. Ahead lies a U-shaped house long deprived of its enclosing west wing and Great Hall. This has been replaced by a charming yard of yew hedges and pear and mulberry trees. With the hall gone, entry is now into a lobby next to the Stone Hall. Beyond it extended the chapel, which survives in the ladies lavatory. Two magnificent blue-and-white vases flank the fireplace, beneath pictures of past Petres.

The drawing room is dominated by its array of antlers from Scotland and, at each end, two superb Stubbses. The house now develops. Two wings were added to the rear at a time of Catholic persecution and the opportunity appears to have been taken to include priest holes, or at least hiding places for vestments, in the design. The Catholic Petres were enthusiasts for these holes and one is visible off the main staircase. Here too is a table that appears in the original Elizabethan inventory as an altar. The dining room has old panelling and two Mortlake tapestries.

An upstairs bedroom and dressing room are used for displays of family possessions and costumes, including a spectacular toiletry case used during the Crimean campaign. Petres fought in style. The gallery is a handsome room dating from the earliest house. It is hung with portraits and regalia, including the notorious dismissal notice from the Lords. Lord Petre writes in what is a pleasantly personal guidebook, 'I will not henceforth have the opportunity to wear these robes.'

The grounds are still recovering from the great gales of 1987 and 1989. The old stewpond is now a lake. Lord Petre recalls it being drained in the Second World War and Italian prisoners of war gathering baskets of eels from the mud. It is flanked by a pollarded lime walk.

LAYER MARNEY TOWER ***

Layer Marney, 2m NE of Tiptree
Gatehouse of great Tudor palace left
unfinished (P)

Layer Marney is the finest Tudor gatehouse
tower in England. Its turrets rise seven storeys,
and only cathedrals equal that. Nor was this all.
The tower was intended as merely the gatehouse of a palace to rival Hampton Court. Sir
Henry Marney, who lies in splendour in the
adjacent church, came of local stock. But he
rose to fame as a court official to Henry VII and
Captain of the Guard. In his dealings with
Henry's wayward successor, Henry VIII, he
was said to have 'impartially advised him of his
good, and modestly contested with him against
his harm'.

Marney attended the Anglo-French extravaganza, the Field of the Cloth of Gold, in 1520
and returned with ambitions of architectural
glory, then beginning his ostentatious building.
But by the time of his ennoblement as Lord
Marney in 1523 he was a dying man. His son
and heir died two years later. Marney's glory
was brief. The palace was never completed and
most has vanished. Only this memorial survives, looming over the Essex flatlands but it is
a proud one.

The tower form can be seen as the last throw
of the Middle Ages before English architecture
moved hesitantly towards classicism in the
Elizabethan era. There is still something raw
and northern about Tattershall (Lincs), Oxburgh (Norfolk), Hampton Court (London,
W), Eton (Berks) and St John's College,
Cambridge. They are the domestication of
the castle keep, masculine, decorative and
thoroughly English.

None is the equal of Marney. Although
the plan was medieval the decoration was
Renaissance. Brick was used for the construction, given East Anglia's lack of stone.
The battlements and window dressings are of
terracotta, a new material of Italian origin.
Dolphins cavort along the roof parapets and
window mullions have Renaissance forms.
They are possibly the work of local craftsmen
imitating the Italian decorators of Hampton
Court.

The original house would have been intended to form a square round a courtyard
covering the present approach. A model of the
likely original building is displayed in the
tower room. The best view now is not from the
courtyard but from the rear, up the steps from
the church. It is from here that Marney's full
majesty is appreciated. Above the old archway,
now filled in, was the royal apartment located
as at Oxburgh. It is adorned with the finest of
the terracotta windows. Above is a museum
room.

The most remarkable features of Marney
are the flanking towerlets. With their own
subsidiary stair turrets, they form seven floors
rising to the roof, with rooms at each stage.
Climbing to the roof we can see the Tudor
chimneys in their terracotta dress, framing
views towards the sea. In one of the towers
is an archive of the heraldry of successive
owners, beautifully drawn by a local teacher in
the 1960s. This could be more prominently
displayed.

Outhouses were mostly built by later owners. Walter de Zoete bought the house in 1904
and extensively restored it and its outbuildings. An east wing of the latter includes a
magnificent roof with pincer beams, reputedly
from the Low Countries, with wattle and daub
partitions.

The separate Long Gallery is Edwardian. In
the old barn, possibly older than the tower, are
Dexter cattle and other rare breeds collected by
the present owners, the Charringtons.

MISTLEY: SECRET BUNKER *

Furze Hill, New Mistley
Rare modern fortress on coast (M)

England has seldom needed its copious
defences against invasion. Yet still we build
them. Norman keeps and Henrician forts are

Tudor ostentation at Layer Marney

rightly celebrated, but little remains of the defences constructed after the Second World War against nuclear attack.

Although regional seats of government remain operational, a disused nuclear warning and civil defence site in Essex was released in 1993 at the end of the Cold War. It has been restored by a local trust and contains control centres, dormitories and living quarters for those who were considered 'needed' to survive a nuclear holocaust.

The bunker was first built in 1951 as part of a chain of command centres for anti-aircraft defence, fed by a chain of radar stations. Within three years, with the advent of jets, long-range radar and missile technology, this became obsolete. Defence tends to lag behind attack, and for ten years the centre lingered on as a ministry base before being sold to Essex County Council as a nuclear emergency head-quarters. All counties were required in 1963 to prepare such bases for local civil defence. They were equipped to co-ordinate the aftermath of a blast, measure radiation and help services return to normal.

The building is predictably unprepossessing. It comprises a reinforced concrete box, 2ft thick, with one floor underground. A maze of functional rooms is displayed, with a mass of interpretive gadgets, including three film rooms showing nuclear defence movies. On the top floor were four dormitories crammed with bunk beds. Staff would 'hot bed', each having six hours' sleep. Even by the standards of the Cabinet War Rooms (London, C) these are cramped. One of the dormitories has been reinstated as the old anti-aircraft operations room.

In the centre of the bunker is the main operations rooms. Round it are arranged the scientific, communications and civil defence services, all in Ministry of Defence cream and buff. There is even a decontamination room for inspectors returning from surveying the damage outside.

A startling feature of the bunker is not the antiquity of the equipment but its modernity. This was considered a vital link in the nation's defences until 1991.

MOUNTFITCHET CASTLE *

Stansted Mountfitchet

Norman settlement reconstructed on site of ancient castle (M)

Mountfitchet recalls Norman England before the extensive use of stone. The reconstructed stockade of two adjacent circles is based on archaeological evidence, although the later stone walls of Mountfitchet Castle itself are no more than strips of flint walling. The rest is recreation. The site is authentic, but since most 'historic' buildings are in varying degree fakes I cannot object to one that is at least an honest fake.

The castle was based on an earlier Iron Age fort. It belonged to Robert Gernon, a colleague of William the Conqueror, but saw its most celebrated period under Richard de Mont-fitchet, one of the twenty-five barons chosen to enforce the observance of Magna Carta in 1215. His castle was destroyed by King John and not rebuilt. The stones were taken for use by villagers and the motte was left for 700 years to decay. A commercial enterprise has since reinstated it but in its pre-castellar form. There are no surviving stone walls or keep.

Thus Mountfitchet is a rare example of the pallisaded fort that was the norm in England before building in stone. The walls are of oak stakes driven into the earth (in 1985). The inner bailey contained the Grand Hall. The outer bailey had the remaining domestic buildings, including the communal house in which most of the inhabitants slept. The hall has been reconstructed (or reinvented) as a simple chamber in which the baron ate and the populace wandered in to gain what food they might. It has a simple tower with a private baronial chamber, the only room of any privacy in the entire settlement.

The other buildings were (and are) devoted to the activities of an early Norman castle, including smithy, brewhouse, pottery, dove-cote and well. The buildings are well displayed with impedimenta of the period. My chief quarrel is that the whole place is almost ridiculously clean and tidy, detracting from its authenticity. Nor is this a place for those who dislike wax models and re-enactments of surgical operations.

SOUTHEND:
SOUTHCHURCH HALL *
York Road
Medieval farmhouse in moat garden (M)

The hall is a pleasant surprise in the eastern suburbs of Southend. After what seem interminable miles of bungalows and villas, a clump of trees and terraced gardens conceal an old hall house. Southchurch was an important medieval estate, albeit in a bleak coastal spot. It passed from the Church to the Crown at the Dissolution and became a tenant farm until bought as an amenity by the local council between the wars.

The house sits above a moat converted into lush gardens. The 13th-century Great Hall looks remarkably authentic, with a solar wing rebuilt in the 1560s and a kitchen wing, part half-timbered, part tile-hung. The Hall retains its old windows, including wooden mullions. A steep hipped roof has 17th-century (or later) dormers.

The interior has the usual contemporary clutter. The Great Hall's open roof displays cusped beams. The parlour is crowded with an Armada chest, Bible box and Jacobean glass and weapons. Upstairs, the bedroom is 'Victorian'. Southchurch has an enjoyably casual accumulation of objects, rather than the studied collections of most museums.

Gloucestershire

Gloucestershire is really two counties, the Cotswold uplands and the valley of the River Severn, with the appendix of the Forest of Dean attached to the west. The first embraces the great limestone ridge running from Wiltshire to the Warwickshire borders, a landscape of high wolds, hanging woods and sheep. Here flourish some of England's more serene towns and villages, developed on the wealth of wool and frozen in time when the cloth industry declined. Here too is Gloucestershire's glory, the malleable oolite stone that changes from Midlands rust-brown in the north, through creamy-white to golden honey-colour in the south.

A second Gloucestershire lies below, now bursting with development around Cheltenham and Gloucester. Timber and brick replace Cotswold stone, and suburb is fast replacing countryside. This is not a county of great houses, despite the magnificent presence of Berkeley and Sudeley. The Middle Ages are mostly displayed in great churches, financed by wool merchants rather than landowners. But comfortable Elizabethan houses survive at Stanway, Chavenage and Whittington. A grander property on the outskirts of Bath was the Blathwayts' great house at Dyrham, still the jewel of the county.

For eccentricity, Gloucestershire had to await the 19th century. An Indian nabob brought orientalism to Sezincote and a Catholic enthusiast planned but never completed Woodchester. At Batsford and Westonbirt, Victorian gigantism had the better of good taste.

Even more remarkable was the revival of interest in early manorial architecture, instigated by William Morris in the 1870s and *Country Life* in the 1890s. The Cotswold branch of the Arts and Crafts movement, C. R. Ashbee's Guild of Handicraft based at Chipping Campden, brought to life Owlpen, Snowshill and Hidcote, and found its modern incarnation in the Biddulphs' 20th-century Rodmarton.

Batsford *

Berkeley Castle *****

Bibury Court *

Chavenage ***

Chedworth **

Cheltenham:

   Holst's Birthplace *

Dyrham ****

Frampton:

   Court **

   Manor **

Hardwicke Court *

Hidcote *

Iron Acton:

   Acton Court *

Kiftsgate *

Littledean **

Lodge Park **

Newark Park **

Owlpen ***

Rodmarton ***

Sezincote ***

Snowshill ***

Stanway **

Sudeley ***

Tewkesbury:

   Merchant's House *

Thornbury Castle **

Wallsworth Hall *

Westbury Pavilion *

Westonbirt *

Whittington **

Wick *

Woodchester ***

BATSFORD PARK *

2m NW of Moreton-in-Marsh
Victorian house in arboretum (P-G)

Batsford stands on the slopes of the Cotswolds near Moreton-in-Marsh, visible for miles around. The home of the Wills family, the house is not open to the public but can be appreciated as centrepiece of its arboretum, which it dominates. Batsford is like an imperious great-aunt, eager to shout its presence across the whole of Gloucestershire.

The estate passed from the Freemans to the Mitfords in the 19th century, who linked their two names and later became Earls Redesdale. On inheriting in 1886, Lord Redesdale decided to pull down the old house and build a bigger one on a more prominent site. The basement of its predecessor is believed to lie beneath mounds next to the present drive. Redesdale turned to the firm of Sir Ernest George and Peto, chiefly known for its Dutch Renaissance revivalism in London's South Kensington. The Earl, who lived in J. J. Stevenson's Kensington Court (London, C), clearly liked the style.

The new Batsford dates from 1888. It is severely Elizabethan, of four storeys in golden ashlar. The central porch rises to the Great Hall above a blind basement. The plan is medieval, with a hall to the left of the entrance. The right wing contains a huge ballroom with bay window to the west. The windows are monotonous. The exterior is friendlier on the garden side, an E-plan with generous bay windows benefiting from the sweeping view. Here Peto designed a fine terrace, a stage set with the Cotswold landscape and sky as its backdrop.

Redesdale was a diplomat (and grandfather of the Mitford sisters). He served chiefly in the Far East and his arboretum is full of echoes of the Orient. It includes a Japanese rest house and a large collection of magnolias, ornamental cherries and maples. After Redesdale's death in 1916, the estate was lucky to be bought by the Wills family, with an equal enthusiasm for trees. Successive members of the family have enhanced the arboretum, now owned by a trust.

BERKELEY CASTLE *****

Berkeley, 14m SW of Gloucester
Medieval fortified keep and house with state apartments (P)

Berkeley is Britain's 'rose-red city half as old as time'. It is precious not just in its setting and antiquity but in surviving on such a scale under one family, at least since the 11th century. On my last visit, in the autumn gloaming,

Aristocratic Gothic at Berkeley

the Berkeley Hunt was returning home. From the battlements I could hear a clattering of horses and a barking of hounds from the kennels across the meadow. The scene might have been witnessed for eight centuries.

The castle's plan is unusual. It is that of a shell-keep on a mound encircling a small inner courtyard. Round it is an inner bailey with a high curtain wall which shelters the Great Hall and main domestic buildings. Beyond this wall is an outer courtyard with another gatehouse and a largely ornamental outer wall. Most such English castles are creations of the 19th-century Picturesque. Berkeley is the real thing. Its enchanted pink-grey stone can look unreal in a low sunlight, a fantasy castle, a place of theatrical invention.

The inner bailey has a remarkable medieval presence. Its walls are 14th century and earlier. Although the interiors were occasionally amended, the buildings are essentially those completed by Lord Berkeley in 1340–61. Later Berkeleys have wisely seen no need for improvement.

The keep, dating from 1117, rises to the left of the gatehouse. It was here that Edward II was imprisoned and killed, and a room is dedicated to his stay. Marlowe wrote of 'the shrieks of death through Berkeley's roof that ring,/ Shrieks of an agonizing king'. A hole in the floor of the present King's Gallery looks down into the dungeon. Here prisoners would be thrown on top of rotten animal carcasses to die of asphyxiation in the fumes. Edward apparently survived this horror only to be murdered by jailers in his bed. Nearby is the Norman chapel where his body lay before being moved to Gloucester.

The King's Gallery looks onto the keep's own inner court, with the breach in its wall caused by Cromwellian guns mounted on the church tower opposite. A law stipulated that the Royalist Berkeleys were never to repair the breach. The keep also contains a suite of rooms with furniture and tapestries belonging to Sir Francis Drake.

Outside the keep but still in the inner bailey are the domestic rooms of the present castle backing onto the curtain wall. The first is the Picture Gallery, with a fine Stubbs of *A Groom and Horses*. The dining room is hung with Lelys and Knellers, and with portraits of Berkeleys in their hunting yellow. Beyond are the 14th-century kitchens, in use until the 1950s, with a full complement of game larders, butteries and a beer cellar, still smelling of the house ale.

The Great Hall is, as it always was, the core of the castle. Built in the 14th century it has a high saddle roof. It also displays the celebrated 'Berkeley arch'. This consists of a multi-cusped arch inside a polygonal one, curved edges inside straight ones. It appears to have originated in Persia and is similar to one in the porch at St Mary Redcliffe, Bristol. One such arch graces the door to the Grand Stairs, others the window openings. The Berkeleys are the only family with an architectural motif of their own.

The Great Hall's 15th-century screen has original paintwork. It was imported from a Glamorganshire house in the 1920s and forms a theatrical palisade beneath the minstrels' gallery. Over the fireplace is a Gainsborough of Admiral Sir George Berkeley, to whose incompetence (with others) is attributed the loss of the American colonies.

The Grand Stairs lead to the state apartments. Family portraits and lacquered chests line walls heavy with embroidered tapestries. What was a chapel is now the morning room; its side ambulatory overlooks the grounds. A Gothic inscription remains along the frieze of the panelled ceiling. This was taken from a 14th-century translation of the Bible from Latin to Norman French by John Trevisa, friend of Wycliffe and chaplain at Berkeley. It displays Wycliffe's determination to make the Bible accessible, if not to English speakers at least to those who could understand French.

Beyond the chapel are the Long and Small Drawing Rooms, the last two reception rooms before the private family apartments begin. These rooms have survived four centuries of changing taste with their medieval form intact. Walls are of stone, floors of wood. Full of colour and activity, they greatly excited the Victorian neo-Goths. Everywhere are tapestries and rugs. In the Long Drawing Room is a two-storey Gothic screen, the King's Pew moved from the chapel. There should be a lutenist playing in the gallery overhead.

A Hoppner in the room depicts Mary Cole, daughter of a local tradesman whose secret marriage to the 5th Earl of Berkeley gave rise to a celebrated trial over the legitimacy of his heirs. Some were born after the secret wedding but before the 'official' one. In 1811 the House of Lords declared the earlier offspring illegitimate. The eldest could thus not inherit the earldom, but his father made sure he kept Berkeley Castle. The present head of the family, John Grantley Berkeley, may be described in *Debrett* as 'descended in direct male line from Eadnoth the Staller, nobleman at the Court of Edward the Confessor', but he rejoices in that finest of English titles, Mr.

BIBURY COURT *

½m E of Bibury
Jacobean manor, Art Deco bar (H)

Few Cotswold enclaves are as serene as Bibury – at least, out of season – nestling in a secret glade of the River Coln. Its 14th-century Arlington Row must adorn a million biscuit tins. To William Morris this was 'surely the most beautiful village in England'. The Romans built a villa here. Saxon gravestones occupy the churchyard.

The big house, Bibury Court, stands east of the village under a limb of the hill. It is reached down a drive, where cedars and beeches dance attendance across a handsome park. The building seems to grow out of the soil on which it stands.

The house was owned by the Sackvilles. It has a 16th-century north wing but the bulk of the house is Jacobean of 1633. The one nod in the direction of the Renaissance is the porch doorway with Serlian pilasters and Sackville arms in a plaque above. By this date, Great Halls were no longer dominant, serving more as entrance lobbies to the family reception rooms in the wing. The grandest room at

Bibury is thus the Grand Parlour, with large windows enjoying a view over the park.

Bibury Court was much altered in the 18th century, the hall being redecorated in 1759 with handsome doorcases. The Parlour is neo-Jacobean, with oak panelling and a bright red ceiling with geometrical mouldings. Blue-and-white china forms an attractive frieze.

The house was again altered in the 1920s, for an owner who had married a Roosevelt. This led to the insertion of astonishing Art Deco wallpaper in the bar, depicting dancing nudes. The house has been a hotel since 1968 and well respects the past.

CHAVENAGE ***

2m NW of Tetbury
Medieval manor with Cromwellian tapestry rooms (P)

Inheritance inflicts many oddities on English house-ownership. Few can have been odder than the Victorian named George who, in order to inherit Chavenage, found himself having to adopt the surname of Williams Lowsley Hoole-Lowsley-Williams. It is the only palindromic surname I know. The present owner can muster only David Lowsley-Williams. He is principal guide and anecdotalist and is bravely suffering the unavoidable commercialization of his old house. He had, on my visit, just survived Chavenage's first gay wedding and was still reeling.

The house was built after 1564 by Edward Stephens and remained in the same family until bought by the Lowsley-Williamses in the 19th century. The front is E-plan, with a date of 1576 on the porch. The Great Hall is high, though not reaching the roof, with deep windows. It retains its minstrels' gallery, a fine fireplace of c1625 and ancestral portraits.

Behind it is the Oak Room, the former parlour, with panelling of fluted and gilded pilasters. This is a wonderfully rich chamber. Parts of the fireplace appear to have come from a Gothic monastery.

The staircase leads to the house's twin treasures, the Cromwell and Ireton bedrooms.

Colonel Nathaniel Stephens was a Parliamentarian soldier and relative of Cromwell's General Ireton. In 1648 Ireton came to Chavenage to persuade Stephens, a powerful figure in the district, to support the regicides, which he reluctantly did. This led to his enraged daughter laying a curse on him. He died soon after. Legend holds that the ghost of the headless Charles I attended Stephens' funeral in a black carriage. History records that there is not a grain of truth in the story, but the house is so full of ghosts it is a wonder anyone wants to marry there.

The walls of both bedrooms are hung in Flemish and Mortlake tapestries of 1640 and contain numerous relics of the period. A third chamber, Queen Anne's Room, has a bedhead depicting the Judgment of Solomon. Flemish glass in the window shows God and the Pope presiding over the creation of Eve from Adam's rib. The house contains a contemporary copy of Lely's portrait of Cromwell and a hair of Charles I concealed in a pin.

To the rear is an extension added by the Arts and Crafts architect, John Micklethwaite, in 1904. Its spacious ballroom comes as a shock after the intimacy of the 17th-century chambers. The adjacent chapel was built onto an 18th-century folly tower and contains two delightful statues of Ceres and Hades.

CHEDWORTH ROMAN VILLA **

Yanworth, 5m SW of Northleach
Isolated Roman villa with extensive mosaics
(NT)

Chedworth is the most enjoyable Roman villa in Britain. Its location, in a hidden fold of the Cotswolds, is isolated and serene. The excavation of the ruins in the late 19th century and the stabilization of the mosaics also predated the miserable post-war practice of encasing such remains in a giant shed. We can thus see the outline, footings and mosaic remains of a villa set in the most glorious landscape. This is vastly preferable to the warehouse sheds

covering the remains of Lullingstone (Kent) and Fishbourne (Sussex).

A villa appears to have existed here from the 2nd to the late 4th centuries. The Cotswolds round the Fosse Way were an early frontier of Roman Britain and populated initially with war veterans. There are twenty-two villas within ten miles of Chedworth. Relatively protected from Saxon invasion, it may have survived in some form until the battle of Dyrham (577) when the Saxons defeated the Romano–British kings of Cirencester, Gloucester and Bath.

The subsequent collapse of the local economy, its civilization and religion was near total. To wander these ruins is to wander the Russian villas of the Caucasus or the relics of British India. They are the ghosts of a departed empire.

The site is spread out round the head of a combe leading off the valley of the River Coln. The landscape is solitary and the drive from the nearest main road forms an admirable transition from present to past time. The ruins, first discovered in 1864, are set round three sides of a courtyard, now sadly a lawn. This has been disfigured by an eccentric neo-Tudor custodian's house in the middle. Access is past a latrine block, complete with Roman guttering and sewer, to the dining and bathing range. The bath-houses of Chedworth are astonishing. They include a Turkish bath, a sauna and a cold plunge, most with surviving mosaic floors.

The heated hypocaust of the primary living room remains in place, and the complex heating system can be studied. The whole building is an exercise in the conduiting and heating of water and air. Undoubtedly the finest feature of the site are the mosaics, in the bath-houses, passages and, grandest of all, the dining room. They are like such work across the Roman Empire from Britain to Tunisia. The scenes of Bacchic revels are mostly gone, but lovely representations of Winter, Spring and Summer survive, as do extensive geometrical patterns. My favourite is Spring, scantily clad and carrying a basket of flowers and a bird.

The Chedworth mosaics have been identified to a school of mosaicists working across the West Country from the local centre of craftsmanship at Cirencester.

CHELTENHAM: HOLST'S BIRTHPLACE *

4 Clarence Road, Pittville
Composer's birthplace in Victorian terrace, now shrine (M)

Holst's great-grandfather came from Latvia. His grandfather married an Englishwoman and settled in Cheltenham, where Holst's father became a local teacher of the piano and harp.

Born in 1874, Holst went to Cheltenham Grammar School where he showed an early musical talent and found work at seventeen as organist at Wyck Rissington church. He entered the Royal College of Music in London but neuritis in his arm forced him to abandon a career as a concert pianist, instead studying composition and working as a trombonist in the theatre during the summer.

Holst eventually broke his link with Cheltenham, married and settled as a teacher at St Paul's Girls School in London and at Thaxted in Essex.

The Clarence Road house is by way of being Cheltenham's homage to its distinguished son. It dates from 1832 and is in the heart of the Regency spa quarter of Cheltenham. The neighbourhood was mostly of stuccoed brick, poor relation to Bath's stone, but it looks no less smart when painted.

The house has been furnished as a home rather than a museum. In the music room downstairs is the piano on which Holst worked, with a picture of Mozart near at hand. The first-floor sitting room is Regency in style, with a harp and a fine collection of Holst family pictures.

The bedroom in which Holst was born contains a portrait of his mother with the family characteristic of an unusually long nose. The attic has been equipped as a day nursery. The downstairs includes a kitchen, larder, servant's room and scullery.

DYRHAM PARK ****

8m N of Bath
Restoration mansion with Dutch-style interiors (NT)

William Blathwayt, creator of Dyrham, was a Restoration civil servant. He was hard working, fluent in Dutch, and secretary to the British ambassador to The Hague when relations with Holland were crucial. He rose to become clerk to the Privy Council. He was loyal to James II, yet equally loyal to William of Orange.

Two years before William's coronation in 1688, Blathwayt married the thirty-six-year-old heiress to Dyrham, Mary Wynter, and began rebuilding her Tudor house in a style commensurate with his status. The unfortunate woman died after producing five children and before the house was finished. He lost his job under Queen Anne – it is said for making a dreadful joke – and never remarried.

Blathwayt became a slave to his house. His first task was to give a new front to the Tudor building, facing west over the garden. For this he employed a Huguenot architect named Hauduroy, who produced an elongated façade of 15 bays, French in inspiration. When Blathwayt was promoted to the Board of Trade, he went for broke. He commissioned the court architect, William Talman, for a suite of state rooms on the opposite side from Hauduroy's, facing uphill to the east. Talman supplied 13 bays of golden Bath stone, with the Blathwayt eagle hovering above the parapet.

Blathwayt's descendants did not prosper. One had to sell the family Murillo. The water gardens became overgrown. Later a Hobbema was sold (to the Frick in New York) to pay for electric wiring. The house was sub-let. One tenant, the Edwardian beauty Lady Islington, altered some rooms in the 1930s. After she left sheep were seen wandering in the Great Hall. In 1961 the surviving Blathwayts transferred the house to the National Trust.

Dyrham is still as William Blathwayt built it. Seen from the hill above, the east façade is a superbly romantic composition. The interiors are in the Anglo-Dutch fashion of the late 17th century, with front and rear ranges sandwiching the old Tudor hall in between. Despite disposals, Dutch pictures and porcelain survive in abundance. Chests, vases, cases, fabrics echo the taste of the 17th-century Netherlands. Flowers, essential to a Dutch house, are still supplied in profusion to the rooms.

Entrance is through the panelled West Hall, kept full of weapons should the staff need to repel local rioters. The old Great Hall beyond has a beautifully sprung dance floor of Flemish oak and contains what survives of Blathwayt's book collection. The drawing room is the least typical of the chambers, reflecting Lady Islington's neo-Regency style as she tried to brighten what must have seemed a gloomy suite.

One of Blathwayt's many sinecures was Auditor-General for Virginia. The walnut for his Walnut Staircase came from that colony. From the landing, we enter the Balcony Room, ante-room to the Tapestry Bedchamber next door. This Blathwayt kept as a shrine to his wife after her death. Beyond are the bedrooms of the family and their servants. These rooms predated the state rooms on the east front but were clearly the formal rooms of their day. The panelling and pilasters with gold capitals are particularly rich. Two black slaves carry shells, reflecting another trade from which Blathwayt prospered. The door locks are exquisitely chased with fruit and flowers.

The Talman front comprised the later state rooms, which Blathwayt fondly hoped Queen Anne might grace with a visit but in vain. Here the staircase wood is of American cedar. On the ground floor is the library with, on its far wall, a Hoogstraeten *trompe-l'œil*, *A View down a Corridor*, imitating a series of interiors in the manner of Pieter de Hooch. In the foreground are a dog and a mop, symbols of domesticity.

The rooms along this front are a succession of Dutch interiors of exquisite design. The East Hall has embossed leather wall-hangings and still-lifes by Melchior de Hondecoeter. The vases are admirably arranged with tulips. The Diogenes Room next door contains Mortlake tapestries and two lovely blue-and-white tulip vases. Beyond is the State Bedchamber with one of England's great beds. Its Baroque canopy is almost top-heavy, hung with crimson and yellow velvet. The bed has never been used, which a footsore visitor might regard as a challenge. The closet beyond contains a picture of a Jamaican cocoa tree.

Few houses have become so identified with a film as has Dyrham with Merchant-Ivory's 'The Remains of the Day'. It beautifully evoked the house in the 1930s, its staff and hospitality still Edwardian, its atmosphere overwhelmingly sad.

FRAMPTON COURT **
Frampton-on-Severn, 10m SW of Gloucester
Baroque mansion with panelling and orangery (P)

There have been Cliffords at Frampton since the Norman Conquest. The ancient manor (below) stands by the village green. Legend holds that it was there that Jane Clifford was born, she who caught the eye of Henry II, became his mistress and thus the 'rose of the world', or Rosamunda. Allegedly accosted by Henry's Queen Eleanor, she was told to choose between death by poison or the dagger. She escaped with nothing worse than Godstow nunnery. Frampton Common is still named Rosamund Green after her.

Frampton Court, opposite the manor, was built in 1731 by a Clifford descendant who married a Clutterbuck, an official at the Bristol Customs House. The Clutterbucks, originally Cloeterbooke, came to England as Dutch wool merchants in the 16th century. The house is in a rich urban Baroque, probably designed by the Bristol architect, John Strahan. Curving steps rise to the front door, as if to a palace in the Veneto. A bold *piano nobile* sits above a cramped basement. The windows on the façade are not quite in balance and the Vanbrughian bell-towers on the wings look most odd.

The interior is superbly panelled, the carpenter anonymous. A pale pine hall, originally painted, leads into the dining room facing the park. This is in a darker wood, with fluted pilasters from floor to ceiling and stern pedimented doorcases. The staircase is beautifully carpentered and the bedrooms also have fluted panelling. Many of the rooms are hung with floral watercolours painted by Clifford ladies in the 19th century. These were celebrated in a book, *The Frampton Flora*, by Richard Mabey.

In the grounds is a canal leading to a Gothick Orangery. The windows and doors have pretty ogee hoods with hexagonal glazing bars. The building is battlemented with a cupola, like a funny hat on an oriental magician.

FRAMPTON MANOR **

Frampton-on-Severn, 10m SW of Gloucester
Medieval manor, old farm buildings (P)

The old manor of the Clifford family lies across the green from Frampton Court. Its L-shaped exterior is not easy to read since a comprehensive restoration took place in the 1920s. The oldest part, to the left of the courtyard, has timbered walls over a stone ground floor, with oversailing and many re-used beams. Windows do not match openings, stonework is clearly retooled, timber braces dart at odd angles and, to the rear, gables and roof ridges seem to have minds of their own. It is a most lovable composition. To add to the pleasure, a rear façade is covered in burgundy render.

The interior arrangement is of a 16th-century Great Hall with renewed windows. A sitting room has a Gothic fireplace, perhaps quarried from an old abbey, with a green man carving. From here a rear wing runs at right angles, with rearranged woodwork dated to the 14th century. There follows a warren of staircases, upstairs chambers, a 'snuggery' and possibly a former chapel.

A small room has been dubbed 'Rosamund's Bower', where Jane Clifford is said to have been born. It is hard to believe any part of this building is that old. It cannot date from Henry II's time.

The present Cliffords are repairing the roofs and walls with local wood, and planting a rose garden. In the farmyard is a magnificent dovecot and barn, the latter bearing every sign of ferocious, English Heritage-induced, restoration.

HARDWICKE COURT *

Hardwicke, 4m S of Gloucester
Smirke house set in park facing Cotswolds (P)

A portrait in the library at Hardwicke depicts Thomas Lloyd-Baker looking every inch the Regency gentleman. He has a dog at his feet and a gun over his arm. An ardent 'improver', he has next to him on the table his plans for a new Gloucester prison, of which he was proud patron. When his son, Barwick Baker, inherited the house in 1841 he established one of the first reformatories for young offenders here at Hardwicke. Can one imagine such a thing today?

In 1814 Lloyd-Baker met Robert Smirke, then building Gloucester Shire Hall, and commissioned him to replace his new purchase, the former house of the Earl of Hardwicke, who had become Lord Chancellor and moved to Wimpole in Cambridgeshire. Old Hardwicke Court was a rambling property riddled with dry rot. Smirke designed in its place a modest villa sitting in a spacious park, looking across the Severn valley to the Cotswold escarpment. Its smart façade is chaperoned by a huge Wellingtonia, like a good boy on his way to school.

Smirke's house is generously proportioned. The façade is of seven bays with a no-nonsense porch. External decoration is left to those twin masters of Regency Rococo, wisteria and magnolia. The interior is as stately as the exterior is plain. Nothing could be further from the florid style of Regency London than these comfortable but simple rooms, their character conveyed by furniture and paintings.

Most of the paintings came to the house through Lloyd-Baker's wife, Mary Sharp. One of these is a delightful Gainsborough of a village scene. Another is a Sharp girl in a blue-and-white dress. She was predicted by the 18th-century Irish beauty, Lady Coventry, to be 'more beautiful than anyone I have ever met, except myself'. (That lady was famed for her gaucherie, once telling George III that what she most wanted to see was a coronation.) In the dining room is a magnificent portrait of Granville Sharp, an early opponent of the slave trade. It was painted to be shipped to America but never dispatched.

HIDCOTE MANOR *

Hidcote Bartrim, 4m NW of Chipping Campden
Manorial focus for 'architectural' garden
(NT-G)

Hidcote Manor and 300 acres of land were bought in 1907 by a wealthy American, Gertrude Winthrop, for her sensitive son, Lawrence Johnston. 'The boy' was already thirty-six and had fought as a naturalized Briton in the Boer War, earning the rank of major. After that, he had led a Jamesian life, rootlessly wandering Europe with his twice-widowed mother.

Johnston now settled down and quietly turned Hidcote into one of the most influential gardens in England. Where Lutyens had pioneered the architectural garden with walls and pergolas, Johnston used hedges and lawns to the same effect. He conjured them into halls, galleries, corridors and alcoves. Hidcote was chief inspiration for Vita Sackville-West's Sissinghurst.

As the guidebook points out, we know almost nothing of Johnston. He collected books by Gertrude Jekyll and studied the work she had done with Lutyens. But he did not copy them, any more than he copied the cottagey style of the Arts and Crafts movement. The house was a traditional Cotswold manor restored and embellished by the Georgians. A new wing was erected by the Arts and Crafts architect, Norman Jewson (Owlpen, below) for Johnston's mother, Mrs Winthrop.

The front facing the road is a handsome façade with classical detailing. The present entrance is through the old courtyard, reached past noble gate piers and farm buildings. The house doorway has a remarkably elegant broken pediment. Part of the house is used as the National Trust's restaurant, the rest is tenanted. To one side is a barn reconstructed by Johnston as a Catholic chapel but no longer used as such.

The charm of the exterior lies in its relationship with its garden, the one intended as an echo of the other. The older part forms an L-shape, protected by a magnificent cedar. Unlike most of Lutyens's houses-with-gardens, Hidcote is not on an axis with the garden, which is rather a giant medieval mansion to which the house is merely one wing. Thus the Theatre Lawn is a Great Hall, culminating in a mound as dais. To the south is a maze of 'rooms', the White and Maple Gardens and the circular Bathing Pool. Along the north–south axis, the Long Walk serves as Long Gallery.

IRON ACTON: ACTON COURT *

Latteridge Road, Iron Acton
Tudor house to entertain Henry VIII (P)

Acton Court in the 1980s was a wreck in the middle of a slum. It seemed nothing more than an old farm building with a leaking roof. Yet this was a Tudor palace, that of a prominent courtier, Sir Nicholas Poyntz (Newark, below). Its east wing was built to receive Henry VIII and Anne Boleyn in 1535. English Heritage took a deep breath, excavated the footings of the courtyard, restored the building and handed it to a private trust, an admirable arrangement.

The surviving ranges are L-shaped, with a staircase turret in the angle. The walls are of rubble but the windows are stone mullioned and handsome. A passage runs beneath the main range flanked by gigantic buttresses supporting the chimneys. These are clearly structural rather than decorative, testament to the speed with which Poyntz must have extended his family's medieval house for the royal visit. The effort was clearly a success, Poyntz being knighted at the time.

The east wing apartments, now empty, include original panelling and fragments of a painted frieze. Here are some of the first traces of Renaissance decoration in any English house, robust arabesques, urns and a lady with braided hair.

These are no more than Tudor ghosts, but I would rather have ghosts than nothing. Elsewhere is a royal privy, enabling the guide to boast that 'King Henry sat here'. Acton shows what can be done with old buildings when someone decides that nothing is past saving.

KIFTSGATE COURT *

Hidcote Bartrim, 4m NW of Chipping Campden
Georgian house moved uphill, centrepiece of hillside garden (P-G)

The twin gardens of Kiftsgate and Hidcote sit opposite each other, both clinging to a northern limb of the Cotswolds as if desperate to avoid sliding downhill towards the Midlands. While Hidcote is a National Trust aristocrat, Kiftsgate is private, both in ownership and atmosphere. The house stands at the centre of a garden that looks over the Cotswold escarpment towards the Malvern Hills. Created by Heather Muir in the 1920s, it was inspired by her friend, Lawrence Johnston, at Hidcote next door.

The house is omnipresent in the garden but not open to the public. It is an architectural curiosity, having been erected on the site in 1887 by Sydney Graves Hamilton, owner of Mickleton Manor at the bottom of the adjacent hill. Mickleton had a fine Georgian front composed of a six-columned portico with a balustrade. Hamilton decided that this would look much better on the hill and, being a man of means, constructed a railway to move it lock, stock and portico, up to the new site. A sprung-floored ballroom was constructed behind the portico.

In 1918, the house was bought by the Muirs who altered the interior to provide more bedrooms. It is now the family home of their grand-daughter, Anne Chambers. The portico presides over the surrounding borders in lemon-grey North Cotswold stone. The windows have pediments but, sadly, no glazing bars.

Like Hidcote, the garden was intended to be in the formal rather than naturalistic English tradition. Its forte was colour. Early descriptions of Kiftsgate in the gardening press were of 'the finest piece of skilled colour work' and 'the colours associated with fine tapestry'.

Today, spectacular terraces lead down to a semi-circular swimming pool. Unlike Hidcote, Kiftsgate is a house and garden very much in use. Children swim in the pool and play on the tennis court.

LITTLEDEAN HALL **

Littledean, 1m SE of Cinderford
Jacobean house with earlier remains beneath (P)

The Forest of Dean is an English mystery, lost on the road to nowhere, or at least to Wales. Small former mining villages cling to wooded hills. The River Severn cuts it off from the rest of the county. Were this central Europe, a local grandee would have declared it independent and made it a tax haven.

Nothing could be more suited to such a place than Littledean. It claims to be the oldest inhabited house in England, lost in the trees near Cinderford. It is certainly old, not to mention decrepit. On my visit, the place seemed deserted but for a barking dog. Outhouses oozed damp, doors were held on with string, a cat patrolled crumbling window sills and signs were handwritten. Through a window I spied a boating cap and a top hat draped over antlers in the hall. If this house is loved, as I am told it is, the love appears unrequited.

Littledean was acquired in 1997 by John and Sheila Christopher, who hurled themselves into its preservation. One day a museum of ballooning is planned, as is the restoration

of the formal Victorian garden. For the moment, the house is a romantic shambles, to be appreciated for its atmosphere of genteel decay and for the Roman remains recently excavated in the grounds.

The antiquity of the house is justified by the claimed survival beneath its east wing of a Saxon 'hall garth', entered from one of the courtyards. This would be remarkable if, as claimed, some of the stonework is Roman and the floor above is of a Norman hall. A fire hearth has been placed in the middle, with a fake thane's seat and some shields and spears. All this seems highly questionable.

The present house is Jacobean, built for Charles Bridgeman after 1612. It is fronted by an eccentric six-gabled façade added in 1852 for the enthusiastic medievalist, Duncombe Pyrke.

What would have been the Jacobean Great Hall is now divided between an entrance hall and a dining room. The latter has dark panelling and a large dresser. A vicious skirmish took place at Littledean during the Civil War, leading to the deaths of two Cavalier officers in this room. The floorboards are said to be still stained with their blood.

The rest of the ground floor is filled with country house paraphernalia, oars, lacrosse sticks, armour and pikes. A young man in white flannels might at any moment dash in to announce a game of tennis or the outbreak of the Great War.

The library has a Flemish overmantel and collection of miniature furniture, including a tiny typewriter. In the drawing room is a primitive picture of Charles Pyrke with a black servant, reputedly from the family's estate in the West Indies. The two men had been friends, but the servant later killed Pyrke for fathering his sister's child.

In the panelled bedroom upstairs is a fourposter with an officer's uniform and an old morning suit hanging over the door. There is also a priest's hole. Long may such houses defy modern presentation.

Littledean: Charles Pyrke and servant

LODGE PARK **

3m E of Northleach
17th-century coursing lodge (NT)

Crump Dutton was a Jacobean phenomenon. A hunchback, socialite, gambler and aesthete, he lived at Sherborne House and was reputed to have recklessly wagered his entire estate on a bet. At the cry 'Sherborne is up!', his faithful butler raced forward to the table and rescued matters by bodily lifting him in his chair and carrying him from the room. Yet Dutton embodied Mark Girouard's description of a gentleman of that age, 'who went hunting with Virgil in his pocket, and could draw the Five Orders as well as a covert'.

Dutton decided in 1634 to build a grandstand on a remote and windswept part of his land. Here he and his friends would watch deer coursing and take bets on the dogs. The 'course' was a straight mile and survives to this day, alongside a side road south of the A40. Deer pursued by greyhounds were said to reach speeds in excess of 40 miles per hour. Spectators bet on the speed of the greyhounds. A ditch stopped them actually reaching the deer, unless more than £20, a huge sum, was being wagered, in which case a kill was in order.

The grandstand must be the most magnificent in England. After a remodelling involving William Kent, it fell into ruin. About 1830 the back was demolished and the front made into a small house. This became cottages, later converted as the home of Charles Dutton, 7th Lord Sherborne. He died in 1982 and left it and the estate to the National Trust; he had occasionally used the course as a landing strip for his plane. Their housekeeper, a psychic, laid a place at table each day for Crump Dutton's ghost and refused all demands to clear it away. She swore she often heard him coming down the stairs to eat.

The National Trust decided to restore the house to its 17th-century form, despite protests that 'Lordy' Sherborne's rooms were equally 'historic'. Although the house had had four different incarnations, it was decided to put the clock back to the first. Visitors can now promenade the restored race course and look out over it from the balcony and, most excitingly, from the roof.

The joy of Lodge Park is its façade. This was first attributed to Inigo Jones, in 1634 still building the Banqueting House in Whitehall. The detailing is now regarded as too crude for Jones, 'too bursting with architecture' said *Country Life*. The window pediments are jammed against each other and the balustrade seems more likely to be the work of a local mason. The 'rediscovered' downstairs hall, staircase and upstairs banqueting hall are undeniably fine but badly in need of the milling crowds for which the place was built.

An 18th-century Dutton not only hired William Kent to design the lodge's furniture – two tables and benches have been restored to the rooms for which he designed them – but also hired Charles Bridgeman to plan the surrounding estate. The work was Herculean, including the purchase of 800 willows, 4,000 hawthorns and 10,000 pines. This in large part survives. This is a splendid backwater. The noise of fashionable Gloucestershire is lost amid the bleak High Cotswold plain.

NEWARK PARK **

2m E of Wotton-under-Edge
Wyatt conversion of Tudor hunting lodge (NT)

The Cotswold escarpment above Wotton-under-Edge is cut through with hidden valleys, many inaccessible by road. The plateau is wild and open while below is thick woodland. This was (and still is) spectacular hunting country. Newark was the hunting lodge of Sir Nicholas Poyntz, diplomat and courtier, who entertained Henry VIII at Iron Acton (above). He perched his lodge on a hill overlooking Ozleworth Bottom.

The original 1550s building was symmetrical and early classical, indicating Poyntz's links with cosmopolitan court circles. It was a rectangular building, with projecting centre bay facing the present walled garden. High windows lit a banqueting hall on what is now the

second floor. This side survives, with later battlements and buttresses.

The house was extended westwards in the 17th century when a matching rear block was added by a merchant, Sir Gabriel Low. He turned the lodge into a proper home. In 1790 this was again remodelled for a Bristolian, James Clutterbuck, by James Wyatt. Instead of a lodge located to watch a hunt, the house was made a feature in a Picturesque landscape. Where the east entrance was classical, the new south entrance was Gothic. A lake was formed in the valley below and a drive uphill designed to add drama to the approach.

The house was given to the National Trust in 1949 and, after use as a nursing home, fell into near ruin. There was even talk of leaving it that way. A Texan, the late Robert Parsons, took up the challenge. He restored Wyatt's interior and what remained of the Tudor upper floors. The central hall, apsed at each end, retains Wyatt's classical screen. His plaster friezes remain in the downstairs rooms and coloured heraldic glass has been put back in the staircase oriel window. There is original William Morris wallpaper in the dining room.

The most exciting floor is the attic, where the outer wall of the old hunting lodge has been exposed, along with Poyntz's bedroom and even his garderobe. Next door is a bedroom entirely filled by Parsons with swan images. From here you can see from the Costwolds to the Mendips.

OWLPEN MANOR ***

Owlpen, 3m E of Dursley
Definitive resuscitated Cotswold manor (P)

Owlpen was to the Cotswold Arts and Crafts movement what Janey Morris was to the Pre-Raphaelites, their idol and epitome. A young architect, Norman Jewson, then living at Sapperton, first discovered it before the Great War. He declared it 'romantically situated' and full of 'symbols of the accumulated experience of the past'. The house was bought in 1925 and restored with local workmen and materials. These included handmade nails and locally wrought iron. Owlpen with its platoon of yews was depicted in an E. L. Griggs etching of 1930 as a chauvinist icon, 'a paradigm of the values of English civilization for which his generation was prepared to fight'.

The house had passed by family descent from c1100 until acquired by Jewson in 1925. In 1974 it was bought by the Mander family (of Wightwick/Staffs) and Jewson's work of restoration continued. Owlpen has the informal domesticity essential to the character of English pre-Georgian houses. Shortly before his death in 1975, Jewson was invited back by the Manders to refresh them with his vision of the house.

The plan is familiar, that of a central hall with later wings and a roof raised and emboldened in the 17th century. The house seen from the south is ungainly – James Lees-Milne called it 'illogically satisfactory' – each of its three gables being completely different in character. The right one has sashes, the centre looks medieval, the left one has a pretty canted and battlemented bay. The slope of the land, as at Snowshill (below), gives the house great presence from below.

Entry is into the kitchen wing. Polished flagstones lead into the Great Hall, its low ceiling dating from its construction in the 1540s. Jewson's Arts and Crafts touches can be detected everywhere, as in the ubiquitous plasterwork owl. A wall painting depicts the Daunts, a family of Wotton clothiers who acquired Owlpen by marrying into the 'Olepenne' family in 1462.

On one side of the hall is the Little Parlour, prettily panelled and dating from the 18th-century renovation. On the other is the Oak Parlour, a Jacobean room running front to back, its Tudor and 20th-century furnishings so intermixed that old and new are indistinguishable. It has a fine oak floor by Jewson. The upstairs solar, now a bedroom, contains a Flemish four-poster and a table by Sydney Barnsley of the Arts and Crafts workshop.

The room over the hall is the Great Chamber, now Queen Margaret's Room, said to be haunted by Henry VI's wife. She reputedly slept here before the final battle of the

Wars of the Roses at Tewkesbury. Its walls are clothed in the Owlpen's most celebrated feature, its ancient painted-cloth hangings. These were poor men's tapestries, which in most houses decayed to dust. They are of canvas painted with a water-based tempera. The hangings depict scenes from the story of Joseph and the Coat of many Colours. They are thought to be not medieval but 17th or even 18th century.

So prominent are Owlpen's yews and related topiary as to constitute architecture by other means. Vita Sackville-West wrote of them that they 'make rooms in the garden with walls taller than any rooms in the house; dark, secret rooms of yew hiding in the slope of the valley'. One of them was known as the Yew Parlour or Green Drawing Room, and dates from well before the 1920s restoration.

RODMARTON MANOR ***

Rodmarton, 4m NE of Tetbury
Arts and Crafts house, furniture and fabrics
(P)

Rodmarton is a serious enterprise. Outwardly severe, its smile is within. It was built to display the Arts and Crafts principles of pre-industrial manufacture, as interpreted by the Cotswold Guild of Handicraft. These principles were mostly applied to the restoration of existing manors for rich patrons. Rodmarton was different, a 'manor' designed from scratch.

After his marriage to Margaret Howard in 1906, an Edwardian stockbroker, Claud Biddulph, wanted a house in the style dictated by Ruskin and Morris. Three years later he commissioned a house from C. R. Ashbee's Chipping Campden follower, Ernest Barnsley, on land given him by his father. Barnsley began work in 1909 and continued until 1929.

According to William Rothenstein, everything was local. 'They employed the village blacksmith, carpenters and masons . . . stone was quarried and dressed, trees felled and adzed, while ironwork, window frames, door hinges, garden gates, fire irons – all these were given over to the Rodmarton smithy. So for years an English village carried out all that was needed for building a great country house.' The house is occupied and presented by the Biddulph family to this day.

Ideology is seldom a good basis for a home. It can lead to indulgence in the architect and cost and misery to the client. Rodmarton's exterior displays a cold neo-monasticism, partly due to the silver-grey limestone of this part of the Cotswolds. But internally the house is a delight. Everything was made by Barnsley and his colleagues in Ashbee's Guild, including Ernest Gimson and Norman Jewson. The Biddulphs entered completely into the spirit of the Guild, even devoting the central section of the house, the ballroom, for use by the local community for meetings and craft instruction.

The house plan is simple, a series of reception rooms facing out over the garden along a spinal corridor. Domestic offices are set at an angle round a courtyard beyond. In the more formal rooms is a gallery of Arts and Crafts furniture by Barnsley's friends. Almost everything is handmade of local wood and in the Cotswold style. The rooms are mostly panelled and have timbered ceilings, giving them a warm and colourful feel. These are the Chippendales and Sheratons of their day.

The entrance corridor is lined with beautiful travelling chests designed by Peter Waals. The drawing room is full of chairs, carpets, plates, lamps of the period, the walls adorned with large dishes. A teapot is designed by Grace Barnsley and a spinet decorated by Louise Powell. The drawing room and ballroom-cum-library form a Long Gallery, with large tables at each end and a seating area round the central fireplace. In the dining room beyond is a built-in dresser by Sidney Barnsley, brother of Ernest, with pottery by Alfred and Louise Powell. The style of these works is beguiling, robust Jacobean married to a light-hearted English Picturesque, and everywhere a sense of hands working wood, metal and clay.

Upstairs rooms likewise have the charm of old interiors yet are unmistakably 20th century. Elm, walnut, ebony, oak, pine and a number of (unlocal) tropical woods are pressed into use. The bedroom corridor is hung with appliqué tapestries of local scenes by the local Women's Guild. One depicts the coronation of George VI, his head adjusted at the last minute from that of Edward VIII.

The final room to be built at Rodmarton was a small chapel. It has stone arches, beamed roof and appliqué curtains, rustic, simple and serene. The family worshipped here every morning. Margaret Biddulph declared that at Rodmarton she and her husband had created 'a perfect union of good workmanship with happy thought'. In later life she converted to Roman Catholicism after what a friend called 'a terrible row with a bishop'. She also created a splendid Arts and Crafts garden, presiding over house, garden and village, in Sir John Rothenstein's words, 'like the abbess of some great medieval house'.

SEZINCOTE HOUSE ✳✳✳

2m SW of Moreton-in-Marsh
Indian extravaganza in Cotswold glade (P)

Stand across the valley from Sezincote and look towards its onion domes, and you can imagine a line of elephants slowly emerging from the woods and depositing the Kleinworts at their front door. The house is unique among English country houses in being in the Indian Moghul style. The nearest parallel is with the Royal Pavilion at Brighton (Sussex), which the Prince Regent ordered after a visit to Sezincote in 1812. The architect was Samuel Pepys Cockerell. It is a measure of his skill that such an apparition seems perfectly in place in a Cotswold landscape.

The house was commissioned in 1805 by the architect's brother, Sir Charles Cockerell, who had been in the service of the East India Company in Bengal. Another brother, John, had bought the estate in 1795 because he wished to be near Daylesford, where the Indian nabob, Warren Hasting, was also building a mansion by Cockerell. The Georgian enthusiasm for classicism was already ceding to more exotic styles, mostly neo-Gothic. Sir Charles wanted to recreate India in England, finding inspiration in the paintings and prints of Thomas and William Daniell, artists-laureate to Anglo-India. Thomas Daniell visited Sezincote to advise on the garden, most of which is attributed to Repton.

The Indian influence was mostly confined to Sezincote's exterior. The house is not big, just two rooms deep and three across the front. Though apparently two storeys, the ground floor is low and the main rooms are on a *piano nobile*. The central feature is a lantern crowned by an onion dome, as if on a mosque. Chattris or minaret-like pavilions decorate the roof corners and multi-cusped arches adorn the hooded window openings. Sezincote is a quiet Regency villa, clothed in the garb of Fatehpur Sikri. Its Costwold stone façade was stained ochre, apparently to seem more oriental.

The interior is of late-Georgian simplicity. It was enlivened in the 1960s with a drastic renovation by John Fowler, often adding orientalism where Cockerell had stuck to Regency. In the downstairs dining room, Fowler invited George Oakes to paint wallpaper of Indian scenes, a picturesque complement to the exterior. Daniell's paintings of the house are prominent on the walls. The hall leads through Gothic arches straight to the staircase. This forms a splendid central flourish, rising on cast-iron arches to the landing, with anthemion iron balusters. Semicircular windows rise to the lantern above. On the walls are Aubusson carpets.

The upstairs rooms are Moghul in scale but not in style. The former dining room is now a massive bedroom, with panels in three tones of Fowler blue. The gilded ballroom next door has curtain rails with Indian motifs, and looks out onto the formal Paradise Garden, at the end of which are two sculpted elephants. The Peacock Room has *trompe-l'œil* wallpaper and a domed four-poster. The ceiling roundel of leaves is at least a hint of Brighton's floribunda.

The main house is balanced by two curving quadrants, each culminating in a tent-like temple crowned with chattris and minarets. The one on the left houses a conservatory from which, in summer, spiky palm trees emerge to add yet more exoticism to the scene. Cockerell

even embellished the stables and farm buildings with chattris. The house was acquired by the Kleinwort family in 1944. They have been carefully restoring this most romantic English house-in-a-landscape ever since.

SNOWSHILL MANOR ***

Snowshill, 2m S of Broadway
Eccentric collection stored in old manor (NT)

Charles Paget Wade's story is a sad one. He was born in 1883, the son of a West Indian tea planter, and brought up in England by his grandmother. In her house, he recalled, there was 'seldom any laughter, and never any visitors or young folk'.

The rest of his life was spent making up for that lack. He qualified as an architect and spent the Great War on the Western Front leafing through pages of old copies of *Country Life*. Afterwards he decided to commune with the ghosts of the Cotswold Guild of Handicraft and in 1919 lighted on Snowshill. The place was tumbledown, lost in weeds and nettles on a steep hillside. Wade spent his inherited fortune filling it from top to bottom not with antiques but with curiosities, *objets trouvés* and spectacular junk.

At the age of sixty-three, Wade amazed his friends by marrying, but his wife spent most of her time in the West Indies, as eventually did he. When at Snowshill he wore his hair long, loved dressing up and staged amateur theatricals. Although a flamboyant poseur, he was also a competent architect and craftsman. He restored the pieces he acquired and left a treasure trove unique in England. It passed to the National Trust in 1951.

As a result, Snowshill is not so much a house as a psychological case study. It is a shrine to collecting mania. The rooms of the old manor contain, among many other things, a store of toy soldiers, dolls' houses, bicycles, costumes, swords and the biggest collection of Samurai body armour outside Japan. It is the fulfilment of what appears a childhood dream, a fantasy world born of some deep sadness.

The shell of the house comprises an early

Tudor hall and subordinate rooms lying, as at Owlpen, along the contour of the hill. The house had been extended by the Elizabethans, with a floor above the hall and a new stone extension to the south towards the garden. A century later, about 1712, this extension was widened 'downhill' by two bays and given a hipped roof and classical appearance.

All this is immaterial as soon as one goes inside. Wade installed old panelling and charming Arts and Crafts barrel vaults in two rooms and created a maze of passages, secret doors, corridors and spiral stairs. Soon there was no room for Wade to sleep in the house, although brave guests were offered a single guest alcove in the attic, if they dared.

The rooms are arranged with such suggestive names such as Meridian, Zenith, Dragon and Admiral. Wade took a particular interest in the Orient and in maritime objects. Thus we find Eastern shrine cabinets, masks, carpets and lanterns scattered among Tudor beams, tapestries and heraldic banners. A statue of Ignatius Loyola stares out from a Venetian lantern next to a Turkoman tent. The Green Room, housing the Samurai warriors, is lit to present them as charging towards the viewer on a dark night, terrifying adults and delighting children.

The National Trust's ideologues have appropriated one of the rooms, removing the collection of 2,000 costumes to 'environmentally controlled storage' and subjecting other objects to 'optimum levels' of fibre optic lighting. The Arts and Crafts pioneers must be turning in their graves. But Wade wins. Everywhere are toys of all sorts, their significance almost painful to observe. In the attic is a traffic jam of boneshaker bicycles, prams and pushchairs. Seventh Heaven contains Wade's own childhood toys.

Across the yard is the separate Priest's House where Wade lived. On the ground floor is a kitchen/living room arranged round a huge fireplace, still thick with tar and soot and adorned with a collection of roasting spits. The

Collecting mania at Snowshill

fire was always lit and Wade would sit in the tall porter's chair listening to the Brains Trust on the radio.

Upstairs is an attic room, with Wade's panelled box bed beneath a large crucifix which he made himself. An apology for a bathroom was installed over the landing. Below is the workshop, still crammed with tools. Wade had no sense of food. He did not cook and was brought dishes by women in the village, worried that he might starve.

The chaotic Priest's House is more evocative than Snowshill itself of this odd man. The main house has been dusted, polished and conserved beyond all necessity. Here, if anywhere, is a house that needed to be left to gather a bit of dust and decay.

The garden was fashioned from a steep hillside of nettles with help from the architect, M. H. Baillie Scott.

STANWAY HOUSE **

Stanway, 4m NE of Winchcombe
Elizabethan and Jacobean mansion,
Chippendale furniture (P)

Visitors to Stanway who complain of the mess are sent at once to the nearest National Trust property. The house has been in the hands of Tracys and their descendants since the Dissolution. It was restored in the 1900s by Lord Elcho, a member of the 'Souls', aristocratic patrons of William Morris and the Arts and Crafts movement. His daughter, Lady Cynthia Asquith, wrote of Stanway that 'I loved my home precisely as one loves a human being, loved it as I have loved very few human beings'. Love likes a measure of disarray and the present owners, Lord and Lady Neidpath, continue in that tradition.

The house from the Tewkesbury road could only be in the Cotswolds. It is guarded by an exuberant 1630s gatehouse. Three large Dutch gables crown an arch above which is a miniature Great Chamber with oriel window. The gables contain little shells. A Tracy was co-murderer of Thomas à Becket and had to do penance of pilgrimage, later using the pilgrims'

STANWAY
HOUSE

WATER
GARDEN
OPEN

shell of St James of Compostela as his crest.

Behind rise the clustered gables and chimneys of the big house in the sort of Cotswold stone that captures and radiates the evening sun. The house has various 'fronts'. The entrance is conventionally Elizabethan of *c*1590, dominated by the Great Hall window. Round the corner, the south front is of *c*1640 and sophisticated. The windows are in symmetrical bays, the roof lined with battlements and the gables with strapwork. In the centre is a classical doorway by Francis Smith of Warwick.

From here, the grounds slope steeply up the Cotswold escarpment, across which a canal and avenue have been constructed along the contour of the hill. Above is a pyramid obelisk and below it a cascade, a perspective worthy of Chatsworth.

The interior begins with the Audit Room for rent-collection, still used as such and kept in a splendid clutter. The Great Hall remains 16th century, stark and medieval, with a flagstone floor. Hatchments, antlers and tapestries gaze down from the walls and a giant oak table is laid out for shovelboard.

Beyond is the Great Parlour, now the family drawing room. It contains two unique Chippendale day beds, like palanquins with chinoiserie canopies. Family portraits adorn the walls, including one of the adventurous Lady Jane Digby with a bluebottle on her breast, symbol of dark premonition.

The principal rooms are along the south wing. They include the old library with Chinese Chippendale bookcases and, beyond, the Elcho sitting room. On either side of the fireplace are cut-out models often situated in boudoirs, or 'sulking' rooms, as silent companions. Both this room and the bedrooms upstairs are hung with Pre-Raphaelite family portraits.

No inch of the house is free of Tracys and their descendants, the Charteris and Wemyss families. Inheritance hangs heavy on some old houses, but light on Stanway.

Stanway: the Jacobean gatehouse

SUDELEY CASTLE ***

Winchcombe
Tudor palace much victorianized (P)

Every English house needs a wife of Henry VIII. Sudeley had not one but two, Jane Seymour and Katherine Parr. It makes the most of them both. The castle can be approached from the centre of Winchcombe or, more romantically, on foot down one of the many tracks off the Cotswolds. From the latter, it offers a vision of a medieval palace shimmering across the woods, a limestone jewel in an emerald sea.

This country was rich in the Saxon period and local lords, such as the Sudeleys, were often left in peace by the Normans. By the 14th century, the castle had passed from Sudeleys to Botelers but was too important a stronghold to escape the Wars of the Roses, eventually passing to the Crown. The house was taken by the dashing and reckless Thomas Seymour, brother of Jane, who proposed to Elizabeth I and married her step-mother, Katherine Parr, widowed wife of Henry VIII. He rebuilt Sudeley to accord with his wife's status. It was written that 'He spared no cost his lady to delight,/ Or to maintain her princely royalty'.

The glory was short-lived. Katherine died within a year and Seymour was executed on 33 counts of treason for plotting against his brother, Protector Somerset, guardian of the boy Edward VI. The house passed to the Brydges family, Lords Chandos, but once again suffered from the politics of its owners. Declared for the King in the Civil War, it was mostly destroyed and left a ruin for almost two centuries.

Sudeley is one of many English houses saved not by ancestral wealth but by new money. The Dent brothers, Worcestershire glovemakers, acquired the property in 1837 and infused it with antiquarian zeal. Sir Gilbert Scott was summoned to rebuild the north quadrangle, stabilize the ruins and restore parts of the south court. Rooms were filled with Gothic fittings and furnishings, including many sold from Horace Walpole's Strawberry Hill (London, W). Both Dents were bachelors and in 1855 the house passed to a nephew, John Dent.

It was John Dent's wife, Emma, who dominated the house throughout Victoria's reign. A collector, historian and eccentric, she walked with a pedometer to record her miles covered each year. She corresponded copiously with famous people, acquiring letters from Charles Darwin, Abraham Lincoln, Florence Nightingale and Sir Walter Scott. Her Jack Russell was called Busy. Like her predecessors, Emma died childless and the estate again went to a nephew, Henry Dent-Brocklehurst, whose granddaughter-in-law, Lady Ashcombe, remains in command.

The house is presented largely as it was under Emma Dent. Scott's work was so deferential to the spirit of the old palace that medieval and Victorian are near indistinguishable, although the atmosphere is very much the latter. At every turn is a surprise, a hat, a cloak, a suit of armour, a Reynolds self-portrait. By the entrance is an archive room, thick with old volumes and boxes of estate papers.

The bedroom suite is furnished by William Morris, as is much of the castle. A Gothic Miniature Room is full of fussy fretwork and offers a charming glimpse of the knot garden below. Loveliest of the rooms is the library, with a superb 16th-century fireplace and Elizabethan tapestry. On the wall is a delightful Jan Steen.

TEWKESBURY:
MERCHANT'S HOUSE *

34–48 Church Street
Restored shop in medieval row (M)

The ancient houses flanking the Abbey grounds were miraculously saved by Jeremy Benson, doyen of the Society for the Protection of Ancient Buildings, in 1965 after local trustees had tried to demolish them. The medieval row appears to have been built by the Abbey immediately before the Dissolution.

The houses, with their oversailed upper storeys, lean-tos and rear garden plots, had been derelict. They are now restored and let to tenants. One is a botanical museum, another was returned to its 15th-century state and opened to the public.

The building was that of a shopkeeper, essentially just 'one-up, two-down', fronting directly onto the street. The ground floor would have had folding shutters, open when the merchant was doing business. Behind the shop is a downstairs parlour in which a fire would have burned in an open hearth, the smoke escaping up a 'smoke void' that heated the building. The walls are wattle-and-daub. To the rear is a small kitchen and allotment.

A wood-block stair leads to the bedroom. Here a shuttered window is still unglazed and open to the street. Some rudimentary furniture has been installed, including an improbably large bed, its covers left rumpled in the latest curatorial fashion. But everything is rather too neat.

THORNBURY CASTLE **

Thornbury
Tudor ruin with chimneys restored by Salvin (H)

Thornbury was cursed. The old house was owned in the 15th century by Henry Stafford, 2nd Duke of Buckingham, but he was betrayed by a servant and executed for plotting against Richard III. His son, the 3rd Duke, had Thornbury restored to him by Henry VII and rose to be Constable of England. He began rebuilding Thornbury as a great house.

But he too was betrayed by a retainer, executed in 1521 on dubious evidence for treason against Henry VIII. The king seized the house and visited it with Anne Boleyn in 1533. The next Stafford regained it but still it remained unfinished, indeed a ruin. Not until 1850 was a wing partly completed by Anthony Salvin for a new owner, Henry Howard. It is now a hotel.

What was built is magnificent. A crenellated

wall encloses a Tudor privy garden with, beyond it, the original tower and gatehouse of 1511. These lead into the inner courtyard, complete except for the far, east, side where the missing Great Hall would have stood. The main rooms are to the right, partly ruinous and open to the sky, partly those of Salvin's restoration.

Thornbury's pride are two huge Tudor chimneys and a glorious set of windows. The chimneys soar into the sky and are among the most elaborate in England. Chimneys embodied the comfort and wealth of 16th-century home owners and were therefore made to be beautiful. Similar architecture today would boast air-conditioning ducts.

Other symbols of status were glass windows. On the garden front at Thornbury are three Tudor bays, each different and multi-tiered. The most extraordinary is to the east, of a five-lobed bow thrust into the garden and rising two storeys. It is a lovely design and, in my experience, unique.

Salvin's interiors are strangely un-grand, as if he were awaiting the commission to build something bigger next door. Three reception rooms correspond to the window bays outside. The library extends into its five-lobed bow with a view over the restored privy garden. Furniture, pictures and tapestries are all reproduction. An upstairs bedroom four-poster looks as if it is expecting Henry VIII and Anne Boleyn at any minute.

WALLSWORTH HALL *

Sandhurst, 3m N of Gloucester
Georgian house endearingly abused (M)

Wallsworth shows what happened when the Victorians became exasperated with the taste of their Georgian predecessors. The house was built in 1753, albeit in an old-fashioned Queen Anne style. The pillars flanking the doorway are heavily rusticated, a form known as an 'icicle pattern'. The builder was a West India trader, Samuel Hayward.

Wallsworth passed by inheritance to the de Wintons, who in the 1860s altered it completely with the help of an elderly 'rogue' architect and neighbouring squire, Thomas Fulljames. He added an extraordinary new top floor with a French mansard roof and off-centre Italianate tower. The attic now looks like a set for 'Psycho', concealing unmentionable secrets. The interior is a gallery for pictures and sculpture depicting 'Nature in Art'. No room survives in domestic form but many retain their fittings.

The entrance hall has a fine Rococo ceiling of *papier mâché*. A motto crowns one of the doors, proclaiming the de Winton creed, 'Look unto thyself' in what is called ancient Welsh. Behind lies a handsome Georgian staircase. The two front rooms retain their fireplaces and overmantels. The one in the left-hand room is carved of pine, with a painting of the house before its Victorian alteration. All these rooms are panelled in oak and mahogany but were later painted. They are now a backdrop for works by Audubon, Sutherland, Lalique, Moore, Dali and Shepherd, happy landing for a house with a chequered history.

WESTBURY PAVILION *

Westbury-on-Severn
William-and-Mary pavilion in formal garden (NT)

This is one of England's most serene essays in domestic architecture. The Anglo-Dutch tradition was never happier than during the reign of William and Mary. Here red-brick walls are punctuated by stone quoins. Windows and eaves are picked out in white woodwork. Pediments are decorated with colourful heraldry, roofs capped with cupolas and lanterns.

Westbury Court was built in 1696 for Maynard Colchester in celebration of all things Dutch after the accession of William of Orange. The house was demolished by a developer in 1960 but the National Trust took over the formal water gardens. They were restored as the most immaculate example of their type in England. The layout is of geometrical avenues interspersed with 'canals', everything to which Capability Brown was later to take costly exception.

At the end of the Long Canal sat the Tall Pavilion, completed in 1704 but in so fragmentary a state that the Trust decided to rebuild it from scratch. It is usually pictured reflected in the water like an English Taj Mahal. Its form is of a banqueting house raised above a pillared loggia, as if on stilts over the water. Flanking brick walls sweep upward to frame the loggia. The three-bay façade has elongated windows, the outer ones narrower than the central one. They are crowned by a pediment and coat of arms beneath the cupola.

The panelling of the Prospect Room, shown in old photographs, was stolen and was copied in 2001, vigorously grained and marbled. On all sides are clipped hedges and decorous flowerbeds. From any angle the proportion and detail of this composition seem perfect.

WESTONBIRT HOUSE *

Westonbirt, 4m SW of Tetbury
Neo-Elizabethan mammoth in arboretum (P-G)

The house is a girls' boarding school and looks it. On a dark, wet afternoon, it rises up over its park in massive Victorian gloom, enough to make any new girl clasp her mother's hand and scream for mercy. The house is occasionally open to the public by appointment but its exterior grandeur can be appreciated from the famous arboretum opposite and from the churchyard in the garden to the rear. The latter is reached through the village and golf course.

Westonbirt is classic Elizabethan revival, a monster mansion of Victorian plutocracy. In 1863 an earlier house, built as recently as 1823, was demolished by Robert Stayner Holford, whose wealth derived from the New River Company, supplier of London's water. The design was born of Wollaton (Notts) out of the Loire Valley. The architect was Louis Vulliamy, who constantly complained at Holford's wish to design the house himself. (This habit of clients has long been considered impertinent by architects.)

At the peak of the work, which continued for ten years, some 300 men were employed on the site. Holford also owned Dorchester House in London's Park Lane, which he had Vulliamy model on the Villa Farnesina in Rome.

The main front is emphatically English Renaissance in style. Pilasters rise past Tudor windows to Mannerist scrollwork and rooftop pinnacles. A giant *porte-cochère* spoils the balance of the façade but is ideal for snatching girls into its jaws from cars. The rear façade, visible from the church, is more friendly. This has high dormer windows, gables and chimneys more characteristic of old France than Olde England. It stands on a series of garden terraces surrounded by decorative pines and cedars.

Holford's declared intention was that new money could build as well and live as long as old. It rarely does. In 1876 his daughter married the 3rd Earl of Morley of Saltram (Devon). In 1926 the Morleys put the Gloucestershire and London houses up for sale, together with one of the greatest private picture collections in Britain. Saltram was old money and Westonbirt and Park Lane were not. Saltram was for ever. Dorchester House was demolished for a hotel, but at least Westonbirt was left standing. Its arboretum is a glory of the county.

WHITTINGTON COURT **

Whittington, 4m E of Cheltenham
Elizabethan manor with three-storey staircase (P)

Church, house and barn form a delightful Cotswold group as they poke their heads above rolling waves of yew. The house has an Elizabethan Great Hall at its core, with a bold Charles I wing and an equally bold staircase behind. The house has been bashed about over four centuries of occupation, but each bash seems to have enhanced its charm.

Whittington was held by the Cotton family from the 16th to the 18th centuries and entertained Queen Elizabeth on a progress in 1592. In 1663 it was inherited by the poet and

Surveyor of the King's Works, Sir John Denham. Sold *c*1748, it has had a convoluted descent down to 1985 when it was bequeathed to the family of the present occupants, the Stringers, who maintain it well.

The Great Hall has been much altered and is now a modest reception room. The adjacent library has a fine Serlian fireplace while the dining room displays the Lawrence/Washington coat of arms of stars and stripes. This reference, to a previous owner, is found in a number of English houses and naturally delights American visitors, although it has no connection with the American flag.

The most prominent feature of Whittington is its magnificent staircase. This sturdy structure of 1657 rises like a stout yeoman on broad treads the full height of the house. Thick newel posts have lost their finials, sawn off by a previous occupant to help him get sacks of grain upstairs.

The first floor landing is glorified with a sudden flourish of classical arches, with heavy 'Vanbrugh' keystones where we would expect to find wooden lintels. This self-consciously stylish gesture probably relates to the Denham occupancy. A Royal surveyor would have had access to the latest pattern books and may even have imported skilled London craftsmen. The rooms behind also have classical doorcases and one retains a rare internal draught porch.

WICK COURT *

Wick, 10m SW of Gloucester
Ancient house, part of working farm (P)

This eccentric place lies in a cul-de-sac on a peninsula created by the River Severn beneath the Forest of Dean. It is approached through a muddy farmyard packed with mahogany-coloured cows, sheep, pigs, chickens and a duckpond.

A farming and fishing settlement has existed here since the early Middle Ages, with a 14th-century hall at its centre. Onto this was added a new range in 1657, capped by five 'dragon's teeth' gables and a brick-pilastered porch. The

internal decoration of the house was never completed.

The house was unaltered for three centuries. Its last owners, the Dowdeswells, bought it in 1919 and lived there as 'poor but proud' yeoman farmers. The last of four Dowdeswell daughters died in 1985 and left it in trust 'to the public'. Unfortunately, there was no endowment and no real public for so isolated a spot. Wick Court eventually passed to a charity intended to give city children experience of a working farm. It has been drastically converted, but retains its exterior and many features inside. Cider from local apples is still made in the brewhouse and Single and Double Gloucester cheese is made in the dairy.

The house exterior has been coated in traditional pink limewash. Stone-mullioned windows lend antiquity, and dignity, to the façade. The interior has an original staircase and 17th-century ceiling plasterwork. There is a decorative fireplace surround in 'Queenie's Bedroom' and most of the bedrooms retain open beams. The attic has been converted into a classroom beneath a forest of structural woodwork. This must be a revelation for children normally cooped up in a Bristol housing estate.

WOODCHESTER ***

5m SW of Stroud
Uncompleted Victorian Gothic, quite lost (P)

When I first visited Woodchester in its secret valley I was promised mystery and magic. I made my way down past woods into a dripping vale of green. In this valley, I had read, once lived a lord who had seen his father's ghost sitting in his chair at dinner and fled the house never to return. In his place had come a pious Victorian, cursed by the deaths of his daughters and destined never to occupy his new mansion. A soaring Victorian ruin was occupied only by a rare breed of Greater Horseshoe bats.

Some of this is true. Woodchester is one of the eeriest mansions in England. The site was acquired in 1845 from the raffish Lord Ducie by

William Leigh, a 'gentleman of leisure'. Leigh was the son of a Liverpool trader, and a Catholic convert. He commissioned a new house and Catholic monastery from A. W. N. Pugin. Plans were prepared, but Leigh baulked at the effort and cost. Pugin having died in 1852, the commission for the house passed to Charles Hansom, who built the monastery in the local village, now demolished. It went in turn to Hansom's assistant, the young Benjamin Bucknall, who was much influenced by the French revivalist, Viollet-le-Duc, whose work he translated. Bucknall was eager to show that a house could be built as far as possible of stone.

Leigh was famously parsimonious, a characteristic that does not sit well with architectural novelty. Work began in 1858, with Leigh and his family living in a large house on the estate. Since they appeared happy where they were, rumour grew that the house was intended not for them but for no less a person than Pope Pius IX. Leigh had met the Pontiff on a visit to Rome, where the Pope's security was precarious. Many English Catholics offered him refuge.

The plan of the house encouraged such a rumour. Much of it was true to Pugin's original, designed round a cloister/courtyard with a large chapel and service ranges integrated into the main building. Plumbing was almost non-existent and heating confined to a few huge fireplaces, yet the craftsmanship was of the highest standard. The completed roof was vaulted in stone, as were the ceilings of the corridors, chapel and drawing room. Everything except the floors were to be of stone.

After just four years of building, work suddenly ceased with the house as yet uninhabitable. Again the rumour mill was at work. It was said that terrified workmen downed tools after a mysterious death. Ghosts had been seen. The project was vast and not sensible. The valley was damp and the building hopelessly inconvenient.

The truth was that Leigh, all but one of whose children had died before him, simply lost heart. His one son thought better of the extravagance and the house remained a roofed shell for a hundred years. Leigh's granddaughters briefly decorated the drawing room for a visit by a cardinal in 1894 and their brother lived for a while in the servants' quarters. But the house was let to a farmer and some rooms were used by a local school. Evelyn Waugh gave a lecture in the drawing room in 1938.

The site was sold many times until taken over by local bat enthusiast, Reginald Kelly, who maintained the roofs from the 1950s until the 1970s. The house was regarded as a hopeless problem, in part because of its indestructibility. In 1886 the house was taken on by the local council and passed to a trust. It has now been stabilized, at a huge cost in grants, and has become, most aptly, a centre for the study of stonemasonry. Two miles of park with five lakes were acquired by the National Trust on the eve of their being sold in small lots.

From the outside, Woodchester appears almost intact. Roofs and gables are in place, with beautifully carved gargoyles projecting rainwater away from the façades. Only inside is it clearly unfinished. In one room, the wooden builders' frames for centring the arches are still in place, as if the masons had indeed vanished overnight. The stone lierne vault in the drawing room survives, with over 50 carved bosses. So does the lovely tierceron vault in the chapel, with its large rose window.

The great staircase, fashioned of large blocks of stone, has been repaired. A rear staircase leads to a completed bathroom. Bath, taps, pipes, water tanks are all of stone. From upstairs, the entrails of a neo-Gothic house can be seen. Arches spring into nowhere. Stairs lead into nothing. Brick-and-rubble walling stands ready to take its dressing of stone. Nothing moves. Only the horseshoe bats could regard the place as home.

Woodchester: Gothic ruin in the Valley

Hampshire with Isle of Wight

Hampshire shared with Kent and Sussex the frontline against invasion across the English Channel but its wooded hinterland was harder to penetrate than points east, and the chalk uplands were less populated and less rich. Medieval kings were meeting in the Great Hall at Winchester Castle and medieval bishops at Bishop's Waltham. More extensive pre-Reformation remains can be seen at Winchester's College and St Cross Hospital, both superb examples of collegiate domestic architecture. The 16th century left two significant works, Breamore and The Vyne.

Charles II began a new palace at Winchester, and although that has been altered beyond recognition, the rooms prepared for him at Avington survive. By the 18th century, the county was in its stride. The Baroque façade of Appuldurcombe on the Isle of Wight is sadly a ruin. The dazzling Gothick interiors by John Chute have been restored at The Vyne. Hampshire has Georgian literary vernacular aplenty, from Jane Austen's House at Chawton to Gilbert White's delightful enclave at Selborne.

The 19th-century Picturesque movement is shown in its extremes, in the *cottage ornée* of Houghton and the lonely Grecian splendour of The Grange. The county moves into higher gear with Charles Barry's conversion of aristocratic Highclere, and Prince Albert's Italianate retreat at Osborne.

Avington **
Beaulieu ***
Bishop's Waltham *
Breamore ***
Bucklers Hard:
   Labourer's Cottage *
   New Inn *
   Shipwright's Cottage *
Chawton:
   Jane Austen's
    House **
Elvetham Hall **

The Grange **
Highclere ***
Hinton Ampner **
Houghton Lodge **
Hurst Castle *
Mottisfont **
Portchester *
Romsey:
   Broadlands ***
   King John's House *
Selborne: Gilbert
   White's House **

Southampton:
   Merchant's House *
   Tudor House **
Stratfield Saye ***
The Vyne ****
Winchester:
   The College **
   Great Hall **
   St Cross Hospital **

Isle of Wight *see* page
   302

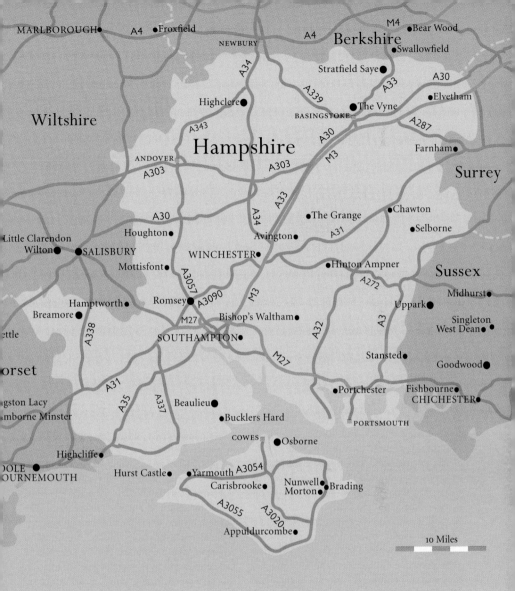

AVINGTON PARK **

Avington, 4m NE of Winchester
Charles II's retreat with painted state rooms
(P-R)

The Countess of Shrewsbury, mistress of the Duke of Buckingham, achieved notoriety by disguising herself as a groom and holding his horse while he killed her husband in a duel. She then married a prominent courtier, George Brydges. The association did Brydges no harm. He was a Groom of the Bedchamber and much involved in Charles II's frequent visits to Winchester, where the King was building yet another of his 'English Versailles'.

During one such visit, the Dean of Winchester had point blank refused to allow the King to lodge with his mistress, Nell Gwynne, in the Cathedral Close. It is possible that Brydges adapted his house up the Itchen Valley at Avington as a backstop.

Avington is the sort of English house on which Austen's Elizabeth Bennett might have gazed from afar and felt a flutter in her bosom. It is calm and magnificent, a Georgian villa set in a landscaped park. This is deceptive. Doubt surrounds the date of the impressive portico and wings but it seems probable that they date from Brydges' alterations for Charles II. The portico appears to be of stone but is of painted wood and remarkably similar to Inigo Jones's St Paul's, Covent Garden. After a colourful life, Brydges died in 1713 trying to save his dog in the lake.

The house was next taken in hand by Brydges' successor, the Duke of Chandos, in the 1760s. He embellished it inside and put three statues on the portico. He also made plans to turn the house to the side and build a new wing to link it with its old banqueting house set across a yard at the back. This wing was aborted and remains only as a wall, a colonnade and two charming greenhouses. Avington's hind quarters are pleasantly picturesque. The house was bought by the Shelley family in 1848 and sold in 1952. It was then divided into eight apartments. The main rooms remain intact and are accessible.

The house interior appears to be mostly of the Brydges period. The entrance hall has paired wooden columns, like those of the portico. The walls are later, painted to look like trellis work and the ceiling to look like sky. The artist was a Frenchman named Andien Clermont who worked in the 1780s in a festive style known as 'singeries'. The staircase has honeysuckle climbing up the balustrade. Upstairs is the ballroom decorated by Chandos and remarkably grand for a building of this size. The panels of the seasons of the year, however, are attributed to Verrio and installed earlier, by Brydges' wife. The figure of Bacchus is prominent everywhere. This must surely have been intended as the monarch's private retreat.

Beyond the ballroom is a drawing room. The walls are by Clermont but adapted, some might say defaced, in the Regency period with panels depicting the royal dynasties of England. A superb mirror is from the lost Chandos house of Cannons Park in Middlesex, and is in Grinling Gibbons style. To the rear of the house is the library with a curved wall, a charming neo-classical room.

BEAULIEU: PALACE HOUSE ***

Beaulieu, 6m NE of Lymington
Medieval and Victorian Gothic house near motor museum (P)

In 1951, the twenty-five-year old Edward Douglas-Scott-Montagu, 3rd Baron Montagu, inherited one of the many properties of the Duke of Buccleuch. A colourful man-about-town, Lord Montagu enjoyed old cars, jazz and high living. Above all, he loved Beaulieu, a house set in 7,000 acres of the New Forest. At a time when large country houses were embattling themselves against a grim future, he threw his house on the mercy of the public. Taking his cue from Longleat, he opted for showmanship. Five antique cars were dragged into the entrance hall of the house and put on show. Outside, he staged the first country-house jazz festival.

Lord Montagu's Beaulieu (pronounced Bewley) was criticized by his contemporaries but widely imitated. The adjacent National Motor Museum has never looked back. The house has been made part of the same experience. Here the English aristocrat is impresario and his family an exhibit. Hardly a caption in the guide is not in the first person singular. In his portrait by John Ward, Lord Montagu includes his two wives together with his children, horse, dogs and a 1909 Rolls-Royce Silver Ghost. Beaulieu is a rejoinder to all who find stately homes bloodless and impersonal.

The Abbey lies on a bend in the tidal Beaulieu River. The view from the south is idyllic. The site is that of a Cistercian abbey, of which the cloisters and dormitory remain. These have been carefully restored and converted as part of the museum. Palace House itself was the abbey gatehouse, where guests would be greeted and entertained. It contained a porch, hall and two first-floor chapels, and was converted into a manor house by the Wriothesleys, Earls of Southampton, after the Dissolution.

The house passed by marriage to the Dukes of Buccleuch in the 19th century and thus to the present baron's great-grandfather. It was extensively rebuilt by the Gothic revivalist, Sir Arthur Blomfield. While he retained what he could of the medieval work, the house is mostly Victorian, colourful and busy. Montagus, old and young, are everywhere. Although they live in rooms upstairs, there is no sense of this being anything but a family home.

The entrance hall contains modern portraits and a Wilton carpet designed by Lord Montagu's son, Ralph, based on an Abbey tile pattern. The original 14th-century inner hall survives as a dining room, and includes information on how medieval meals were eaten. It has a stone ribbed vault, as does the adjacent lower drawing room. This contains a large travelling medicine chest, which was used by the present Lord Montagu's asthmatic grandfather. The kitchen has been recreated in its Victorian form.

Upstairs are two former chapels, now an ante-room and an upper drawing room, where the ladies of the house would gather. The drawing room is prettily decorated with Gothick stencils, cusped tracery in its windows and a wooden beamed roof. The dining room has linenfold panelling salvaged from the old House of Commons. The guide is meticulous in describing how each of these rooms has been used by Montagus past and present.

BISHOP'S WALTHAM PALACE *

Bishop's Waltham
Ruins of great episcopal palace (EH)

The palace was reputedly the finest of the many residences of the Bishops of Winchester, outshining Wolvesey (now ruined) and Farnham Castle (Surrey). It was built by King Stephen's brother, Henry of Blois, in the 12th century and rebuilt by William of Wykeham in the late 14th. It ranked in splendour with his work at Winchester and New College, Oxford. William is known to have used his master mason, William de Wynford, at Waltham, as well as Henry Yevele and Hugh Herland, bringing together the work of the three great names of English late-Gothic architecture.

Their work embraced a new hall, tower chambers and service buildings. All survive to full height but in ruined form. The shattered windows of the outer wall indicate the scale of the work. Wykeham's successor, Cardinal Beaufort, half-brother of Henry IV, expanded and added further storeys. Here he entertained Henry VI's queen, Margaret, during the Wars of the Roses. She lay in Beaufort's 'blue bed of gold and damask … and three suits of the arras hangings', all of which he bequeathed to her in his will. Queen Mary I also stayed here as she eagerly awaiting the arrival of her husband, Philip of Spain.

The palace did not survive the Civil War, having been garrisoned by Royalists troops. The bishops concentrated their subsequent building work closer to Winchester. It is now a quiet but atmospheric spot.

BREAMORE HOUSE ***

3m N of Fordingbridge
Elizabethan house with Mexican treasures (P)

Mention the Renaissance to most country gentry of the Elizabethan period and I am sure they would have muttered against all that foreign nonsense. What was good enough for the Middle Ages was good enough for them. They preferred plain building, brick without ornament, with deep gables, tall chimneys and stone-mullioned windows.

The Breamore estate was bought by William Dodington in the 1570s and a new house completed in 1583. Dodington later committed suicide while awaiting 'a suit pending in Star Chamber', not the first to suffer that fate. His house passed by marriage to the Grevilles of Warwick Castle. In 1748, they sold it to Sir Edward Hulse whose family occupy it to this day. It remains a working rural estate, gracious and uncommercialized.

The house's façade is a conservative E-plan, its main rooms looking over the valley of the Hampshire Avon to the New Forest. The pink-red brickwork is aged with lichen and lime. The interior is late Elizabethan, much battered in a Victorian fire but well restored. The entrance is to the rear through what is now an inner hall.

The Great Hall is beyond, looking out over the view. It is a sumptuous room with geometrical plasterwork and two Mannerist chimneypieces, coated in chunky pilasters, grotesques and heraldic cartouches. The panelled walls have tapestries and paintings, including a Gheeraerts of Sir Thomas Coningsby with his dwarf. Here too is a Teniers, *The Coming Storm*, which I saw as just such a storm was gathering outside. I could imagine the same party of peasants racing for cover in Breamore yard.

The dining room contains four still-lifes by Peter Rysbrack, father of the sculptor. The Blue Drawing Room is more feminine, with white walls and 18th-century furniture, including a lovely Chinese Chippendale mirror over the fireplace. In the West Drawing Room is an early cricketing picture, *The Boy with the Bat*, of c1760. A rare early English carpet of 1614, covered in exquisite arabesques and foliage, hangs over the staircase.

On the staircase landing is a remarkable ethnographical treasure, a set of 14 paintings celebrating the mixed races of the New World. They are painted by a mixed-race Mexican, known to have been the son of Murillo by a local girl, who clearly inherited his father's talent. Next to them hangs an Indian feather fan. These works were all captured from a Spanish galleon by one of Charles I's privateers, Admiral Westrow, who gave them to his niece, wife of Edward Hulse. They lend an exotic touch to very English Breamore.

The bedrooms, restored after the Victorian fire, are furnished with four-posters, tapestries and precious hangings. In the Blue Bedroom is a set of pastels of the Hulse family by Francis Cotes, as vivid in colour as any oil. Each win-dow has a view over the lovely Hampshire landscape. There is no formal garden at Breamore, just woods and fields, calm and serene.

BUCKLERS HARD

8m NE of Lymington

Buckler's Hard is a hamlet that grew up round an 18th-century boat-building yard on the Beaulieu River. Despite being partly a museum, the houses are all occupied and shops, school, chapel and pub are still active. There are, however, no cars and no television aerials. The river front remains navigable; it was from here that Sir Francis Chichester set sail round the world in 1966.

The houses were the beginnings of a model town intended by the 2nd Duke of Montagu in the 1720s. The ambitious project collapsed after a failed venture in America. The settlement remained a centre of shipbuilding and now yachting. The paved street was replaced by a gravel drive in 1971. The enterprise is now part of the Beaulieu Estate, to whom we owe the taste with which it has been restored. Various houses come under the auspices of the Maritime Museum. The designers have sought authenticity in everything, but those averse to waxwork should stay away.

BUCKLERS HARD: LABOURER'S COTTAGE *

At the start Buckler's Hard had neither church nor school and most goods had to be fetched on foot from Beaulieu. The gulf between a skilled worker, as below at the Shipwright's Cottage, and a mere labourer was a yawning one. This is a house of utter poverty, just one bay wide. It is displayed more or less as acquired by the museum, with the most rudimentary furnishings restored in a late 18th-century setting. So cramped are the two rooms, one up, one down plus a tiny kitchen,

Spanish treasure at Breamore

that it can only be seen through holes cut in the wall of the adjacent house.

The characters depicted, James and Elizabeth Bound with their four children, lived in the house in the 18th century. The guidebook points out that others in the village might have been even poorer. This family at least had regular protein and vegetables in their diet.

Upstairs is a single bedroom with a small fireplace but no beds. On the floor are two mattresses, one for the adults and one for the children. How six people fitted in here is a mystery. A mouse eats the cheese in the kitchen.

BUCKLERS HARD: NEW INN *

The first building at the top of the street is a house and shop that became the New Inn in 1792. It has been reconstructed as it might have been in the evening, with known historical characters from the village portrayed in effigy, drinking and chatting. Even their conversation is recreated through recordings. An elderly shipwright plays cards on a settle. Joseph Wort, the landlord, is at the bar in conversation. His daughter examines the wares of a travelling tinker while the local blacksmith does a deal with a visiting iron merchant.

The recreation is vivid, portraying not just the building and decoration but clothes and everyday objects more naturally than on hangers or in cases. Anecdote is brought to life. Above all sound is welcome, a dimension absent from most English historic buildings; here it is in the form of a careful Hampshire dialect. This is an admirable tableau of working-class life.

BUCKLERS HARD: SHIPWRIGHT'S COTTAGE *

Here is a reinstatement of the cottage of a more prosperous worker, Thomas Burlance, who lived here in 1781. It comprises a sitting room, an alcove for storing apples and a small rear kitchen. In the latter, we see Burlance

coming home after work, his precious craftsman's adze over his arm. Apart from the food in the kitchen, a quantity of laundry indicates the family's comparative wealth.

Burlance's wife and daughter are sitting in the living room with their needlework. Upstairs in the bedroom a daughter looks after her baby sister. A further bedroom is on the second floor. I find the place just too spotless for comfort, Did these people really find time to scrub and whitewash their abode every week?

CHAWTON: JANE AUSTEN'S HOUSE **

Chawton, 2m S of Alton
Author's evocative family home (M)

This house might have sprung from a Jane Austen novel. The old building in friendly redbrick sits in the village centre where the old Alton–Winchester road turns a corner. Behind its rose-clad windows and wicket fence, a novelist might watch the world pass by and commit it to her notebook. The house is comfortable without ostentation, genteel but not rich. Here an Austen heroine could dream of launching herself into social orbit, yet safely retreat should she fall.

Austen lived at Chawton for the last seven years of her life, from 1809 to 1817. It saw her last masterpieces, *Mansfield Park* and *Emma*. The house had been inherited by one of her many brothers and was furnished by him for his widowed mother and sisters. They lived happily but always in straitened circumstances. After their deaths, the house became farm cottages until it was acquired by the Jane Austen Trust and opened as a museum in 1949.

Austen's work cannot be commemorated in inanimate objects. The custodians have been able to do little beyond creating a 'Jane lived here' museum. The drawing room has no armchairs and the bedrooms no beds. The collection is of Georgian antiques and Austen memorabilia, with no suggestion of the

Chawton: Austen's window on the world

busyness or clutter with which the family must have been surrounded. The most human touch is the still-squeaking door, kept that way so Jane would have time to clear away her writing materials should visitors approach.

That said, much is instructive. The drawing room contains the piano to which the Austen girls loved to dance and a Hepplewhite bureau belonging to their father. There are two topaz crosses, the booty which Jane's sailor brother, Charles, brought back from the Napoleonic wars. In the dining parlour is the table where Jane used to serve meals and settle down to write after breakfast.

The upstairs rooms are laid out as a museum, mostly with pictures and documents on the walls. In the bedroom which Jane shared with her beloved sister, Cassandra, are examples of her needlework. The Admirals' Room reflects the family's links with the sea, two brothers serving in Nelson's navy. Exhibits include an exotic bell brought back by Charles from the siege of Rangoon. At the end of the passage is a small display of Georgian ladies' costumes. To them could surely be added stills from the many period dramas inspired by the novels.

The garden is smaller than in Jane's day but still boasts the flowers that fill her books – pinks, sweet williams, columbines and peonies. The donkey cart in which she visited local friends is in the barn.

ELVETHAM HALL **

1m SE of Hartley Witney
Polychrome house with historical saga decoration (H)

The Elvetham, they call it now. If a modern conference hotel and 'advanced learning environment' is the only way to save desperate Victorian mansions, so be it. Elvetham has been transformed from wreck to splendour. Little has been altered beyond the chapel (now a squash court) and much has been revived. Twenty years ago it faced demolition.

The house is a rare domestic work of the Victorian Gothicist, S. S. Teulon. The estate had belonged to Seymours in the Tudor period and reputedly saw an evening's revelry attended by Elizabeth I, on which legend has it Shakespeare based (vaguely) *A Midsummer Night's Dream*. The oak she planted is still here.

The old house passed by marriage into the Gough family, Barons Calthorpe, and was rebuilt by Teulon for the 4th Baron in 1859. It was sold to ICI in 1953, passing through various hands until acquired and restored in its present form in 2001. The estate is still owned by the Calthorpes.

Calthorpe's building survives virtually intact. He wanted Teulon to conjure into life the antique works he had admired on his European travels, as had the Grand Tourists of old. His tour had been conducted in the company of Victoria's eldest son, the Prince of Wales. Hence the works were not of Greece and Rome but of Gothic Northern Europe. Teulon, lover of medieval polychromy, was the man to recreate them.

The exterior is (still) hard to find beautiful. The red-and-black banded and diapered brickwork is harsh on the eye. Dark turrets and towers seem grotesque in this peaceful setting. It is what Mark Girouard calls Teulon's 'belligerent chaos'.

The interiors are of a piece. The theme of medieval chivalry runs from the entrance hall through to the staircase hall and the reception rooms. Everywhere are panelled ceilings painted with medieval motifs. The drawing room illustrates Walter Scott's *Kenilworth*, cult mid-Victorian novel. The stained glass carries scenes from Arthurian legends, Elizabethan romances and local Hampshire history. The whole forms a remarkable artistic programme.

The best features of the rooms are the fireplaces. Some are decorative beyond description. Gone are the classical myths and heraldic boasts of the classicists and neo-Jacobeans. Here tales are told of noble deeds in stone and paintwork. The drawing room fireplace has Queen Elizabeth arriving at the house. The dining room portrays Raleigh and Essex declaiming to the public, either from the pulpit or the dock.

THE GRANGE **

near Northington, 3m NW of New Alresford
Classical ruin in landscape, now opera
house (EH)

I first saw this house wholly derelict. The
Barings, owners of the neighbouring Stratton
estate, were intending to dynamite it. They
had already destroyed George Dance's Stratton
Park across the lake and Norman Shaw's
Baring's Bank building in the City of London.
At The Grange, magnificent plaster ceilings
were falling to the floor and the central roof
was on the point of collapse. The place had
been maltreated by American soldiers billeted
here during the Second World War, but was
not yet a ruin. Within a few years of my visit, it
was a total loss.

The Grange has now been stabilized by
English Heritage and given a roof, but that
organization's scorched earth policy of restoration resulted in all the interiors being lost.
Since then an opera house has been added as a
succubus, tucked into the side of the hill and
penetrating the rear wall of the building.

The Grange is important both historically
and scenically. The architect, C. R. Cockerell,
who embellished the building in the 1820s,
declared that it was as good as Poussin. The
house was one of the early Greek revival set
pieces in Georgian England (with Hammer-
wood/Sussex, and Belsay/Northumbs). It was
designed in 1804 by William Wilkins who
encased an earlier 17th-century house for
the Barings' predecessors, the Drummonds.
Wilkins was already engaged in the battle of
'Romans versus Greeks' at Downing College,
Cambridge, which he won for the Greeks.
At The Grange he erected a copy of the Athens
Theseion. Six columns of mighty solidity gaze
from the portico over a sweep of parkland to
the lake.

The house cannot have seemed a friendly
place. The sides have severe pilastered walls.
The whole thing is largely for show, not
of stone but of cement render over brick. Yet
the interiors were sumptuous, some surviving
from the 17th century but most added by

Cockerell inside Wilkins's shell. Cockerell's
adjacent detached dining room is being rebuilt
and the whole place thoroughly tidied up for
opera-goers.

If The Grange must be a ruin, I preferred it
left, like the trunk of Ozymandias, splendid
and decayed amid the rooks, cedars and memories. Now it is a stage set.

HIGHCLERE CASTLE ***

Highclere, 6m S of Newbury
Italianate mansion with Egyptian collection
(P)

Highclere is the only house I know where the
client constantly protested that the architect
was not spending enough money. In 1838, Sir
Charles Barry was asked for a new house by
the 3rd Earl of Carnarvon, junior line of the
Herberts of Wilton. Barry's proposals were
twice rejected as too modest and he and
Carnarvon spent their lives in ceaseless argument. Carnarvon queried every detail, usually
for its lack of ostentation. He also disliked the
existing Capability Brown landscape, which
he victorianized with conifers, rhododendrons and follies. Highclere emerged as the
archetypal early-Victorian mansion, although
it was not completed until the Earl and Barry
were both dead.

Highclere's most celebrated occupant was
his descendant, the 5th Earl, who financed and
led Howard Carter's Tutankhamun expedition
in 1923, during which he died in Egypt,
whether of blood poisoning or of the notorious curse nobody knows. The present Earl,
who lives elsewhere on the estate, is racing
manager to the Queen. The guidebook depicts
the house like a shimmering wedding cake,
framed by a great cedar and with three horses
being led past as if to the start of a race.

The house stands alone in a sea of lawn.
Barry did not demolish the Georgian house
but encased its brick walls in stone, festooning
the roofs with Elizabethan strapwork and
finials. A large tower was added, reminiscent
of his Victoria Tower at the Palace of Westminster. The porch is guarded by two armorial

wyverns. The house is thus more a work of embellishment than original architecture, but its decorative impact is tremendous.

By the time the walls were finished, the 4th Earl had turned to Thomas Allom and others for the interiors. The result is a series of eclectic but sumptuous rooms. The entrance hall is said to be by Sir Gilbert Scott and might be the transept of a church. Its polychrome floor is by the master of Gothic colour, William Butterfield. Beyond is the heart of the house, a baronial hall rising to the roof. This is Arthurian Gothic. The space is top-lit with a balcony above heraldic panels of Herberts and Carnarvons. The lower walls are covered in tooled and gilded leather from Cordoba.

From the rooms of bishops and barons, one passes to those that might be a comfortable Pall Mall club. The library, probably by Allom, is like Barry's Reform Club, full of male opulence and the motifs of a Grecian gymnasium. The ceiling is panelled and gilded, the bookshelves likewise. The fireplace surrounds are after Grinling Gibbons.

The adjacent music room and drawing room offer a contrast, redecorated in French 18th-century style by Almina, wife of the 5th Earl and a Rothschild relation. In the drawing room are family portraits by Reynolds and Beechey, notably of children. The smoking room has a magnificent Jan Weenix still-life over the fireplace and works by Van Goyen and Wouwerman. Hidden in a space between the two rooms, a collection of Egyptian archaeological treasures was found in 1987. The 5th Earl's entire collection had supposedly been sold to New York's Metropolitan Museum in 1923 but these items had clearly been forgotten (or hidden). The surviving items are now displayed in the basement.

Highclere never takes itself too seriously. The elephantine staircase behind the hall is lightened by a sentimental Italian statue of Carnarvon children and a Reynolds of Mrs Musters as Hebe. Wherever a bit of wall is spare, someone has crammed in a Roman trophy or a heroic portrait. The downstairs dining room is a gallery of such pictures, mostly of Stuart cavaliers.

HINTON AMPNER **
8m E of Winchester
Neo-Georgian phoenix recreated after fire (NT)

In 1960 Hinter Ampner was gutted by fire. The creation of the neo-classical antiquarian, Ralph Dutton, the house was totally destroyed, along with his collection of furniture, pictures and books. So intense was the heat that antique volumes in the library calcified in their bookcases and had to be chipped out with pickaxes. Dutton seemed rejuvenated by the catastrophe. Rather than abandon the place, he set about building a new house and amassing a new collection. The present structure is essentially a monument to his determination. The renaissance is as related in his account of the work, *A Hampshire Manor*.

Hinton had been a Dutton house since its heiress married the 2nd Lord Sherborne in 1820 (*see* Lodge Park/Gloucs). It was rebuilt after 1864 in a Tudor style described by Ralph Dutton, in 1936 as of 'exceptional hideousness'. Ralph promptly remodelled it, reverting to the then fashionable neo-Georgian. What he was to reconstruct after the fire thus merits the term, neo-neo-Georgian. The outcome was regarded by another antiquarian, Sir Brinsley Ford, as 'the most beautiful neo-Georgian interior in England'. Dutton, who became the last Lord Sherborne in 1982, died in 1985 and left the house and garden to the National Trust.

The exterior is uninteresting, a conventional box of suburban 18th-century revival. The inside is more dramatic. Dutton transformed the old Tudor entrance hall from dark oak and sporting trophies into an aesthete's stage-set of marble floor, scagliola columns, giltwood and Louis XVI furniture. The other rooms he likewise georgianized, the work illustrated in before-and-after photographs in the guidebook. The furniture is predominantly French, the pictures Italian. In the drawing room, the mirrors have extravagant Rococo frames. An exquisite clock is of French porcelain. A no less exquisite carpet is c1800 from 'the collection of the Princess de Broglie, Paris'.

Echoes of Robert Adam survive in some of the rooms. Dutton made casts of ceilings and rescued fireplaces from Adam houses being demolished between the wars in London's Adelphi and Berkeley Square. The ceiling in the dining room was recreated after the fire, its Angelica Kauffmann roundels replaced by Elizabeth Biddulph.

The garden is spread along the line of hills south of Alresford. Everything about the approach is immaculate, embracing farm buildings and church. Beyond are terraces and walks leading to dells and rose gardens. Dutton remarked that 'what above all I want from a garden is tranquillity'. I fear that is the one quality that popular Hinton Ampner may now have to go without.

HOUGHTON LODGE **

Houghton, 1½m S of Stockbridge
Cottage ornée on banks of Test (P-R)

The idyllic *cottage ornée* of Houghton crowns a hillock on a bend in the River Test. It is the perfect embodiment of Georgian Picturesque. In such houses, wrote Mark Girouard, 'jaded noblemen or well-heeled city merchants could retire with a mere handful of servants to taste the delights of rustic simplicity'. In the town, their mansions created an illusion of grandeur. In the country their cottages were illusions of poverty, like Marie Antoinette on her farm.

Houghton Lodge is one of the best examples of *cottage ornée* architecture. The house is open by appointment, but can be perambulated and appreciated from outside. It is approached from the stables adjoining an impressive walled garden. The walls are of a rare chalk-cob construction, chalk and straw mixed and laid layer on layer as each dried. Greenhouses contain exotic orchids, jasmine and plumbago in profusion. Beneath it is a spectacular herbaceous border.

The main lawn spreads between the walled garden and the River Test as a green plinth to the Lodge above. Built around 1800, it has four Gothick bays to the south and a bow window and iron veranda to the east, under a conical

roof. The main roof is steep, with deep barge-boarded dormers and high neo-Tudor chimneys, bundled together as if in fear of toppling. The roof would once have been thatched but is now tiled and shingled, a solecism that might one day be corrected.

HURST CASTLE *

2m SE of Milford on Sea
Henrician castle with Victorian extensions (EH)

Whatever the weather, Hurst has drama. It stands on a shingle spit jutting out into the Solent and holding the key to its defences. Of all the Henrician coastal forts, this was the most important, recognized by its later refortification. The castle is reached either by ferry from Keyhaven or by walking a mile along the shingle spit.

The original castle was begun in 1541 as a 12-sided tower surrounded by a clover leaf of bastions, bristling with cannon and surrounded by a moat. It was unused in the 17th and 18th centuries, although Charles I was imprisoned here on his way back from the Isle of Wight in 1648. The castle was a prison under the anti-Popery acts, a priest being incarcerated here in 1700 for twenty-nine years until his death. It remained garrisoned and enjoyed a garden and even a fishermen's inn.

The castle was massively extended by the Victorians with two long bat-wing batteries and a lighthouse. Such was its importance that the defences were regularly upgraded to resist each new development of high explosive shells. The fortifications were further strengthened to take big guns in the 20th century. The castle was finally abandoned in the 1950s.

Although the Tudor tower was strengthened and extended and its moat filled, the original interiors survive. The entrance door still has its Tudor arch. The ground floor held the barracks, with more comfortable accommodation for officers on the first floor, with fireplaces and latrines. The walls are of impressive thickness. From the roof is a spectacular view of the Solent and Isle of Wight.

is no portrait of him but his effigy stands modestly in the dining room. He never married and devoted his life to the observation and recording of natural phenomena. He was fascinated by interdependence, relating bird migration to harvest and habitat. He wanted every naturalist to dissect a crow each week to examine the contents of its crop. Despite his popularity in his lifetime, he received no scientific recognition.

The core of the house was a medieval hall, The Wakes, which White incorporated into his new dwelling. White added a reception room for a view of his garden and the Downs beyond. It has Georgian furnishings, and family portraits depicting strong, simple English faces. The fire-dogs were for holding hot drinks. In this room, 'Uncle Gilbert' would entertain an array of nephews and nieces with tales of nature.

The hall of the old house became the Little Parlour and contains White's chair, possibly his desk, and various other memorabilia. White's kitchen may have been where he took his meals and where he would continue his observations. Fruit and vegetables would come in from the garden to be inspected and different preservatives tested. The room saw a constant war on cockroaches and house flies. On a shelf lies a desultory Christmas pudding. Upstairs is White's small bedroom. The hangings were stitched for him by his aunts. The table is where he wrote into the night. It is an evocative chamber.

The gardens are as curious as the house. White was clearly eager in his modest way to create a classical landscape in the style of Kent at Chiswick House (London, W). Close to the house are formal topiary, pond garden, herb garden and the 'six quarters' flower beds. A walk leads across the meadow towards the Hanger, including a quincunx of five cypresses arranged as a cross. From here one can see such oddities as a distant statue of Hercules, a barn and White's half-barrel seat in which he would sit and turn gently in the breeze.

A naturalist's bedroom at Selborne

SOUTHAMPTON: MEDIEVAL MERCHANT'S HOUSE *

58 French Street
Restored wine shop with replicas (EH)

Nowhere is the contrast between styles of conservation more glaring than in the two medieval houses in the old part of Southampton. The area was once a lively warren of streets and is now a memorial to England's loss of urban design confidence after the Second World War. While the rest of Europe restored the character of cities such as Warsaw, Hamburg and Tours, the English fled to the suburbs. Inner Southampton is what they left behind, gap-toothed walls, car parks and new buildings erected without thought.

Lost in this wilderness is a fragment of one of England's earliest surviving town houses. The Medieval Merchant's House was erected in about 1290 as house and wine shop. It later became three cottages, a lodging house and a brothel. Bomb-damaged in 1940, it was restored in 1983. The house has been returned to how it appeared in the mid-14th century by the removal of later additions. Only walls, gable timbers and floor members survived and much of this had to be replaced. Medieval furnishings were reproduced from contemporary records. My reaction in that case is why not restore the whole neighbourhood to its ancient form, known from photographs, and give it back some life?

The house plan is unusual. A passage leads past the hall to an inner room at the rear. The hall is open to the roof above while below the floor is earth. There are hangings on the walls and a trestle table. The repointed brick chimney-breast looks like suburban neo-Tudor. The inner room contains a reproduction medieval cupboard. The two upstairs bedchambers are furnished with replicas, the front room with two cosy four-posters. Beneath the house is a brick-floored undercroft where the wine was stored.

The house is a frigid academic exercise,

neither a ruin 'as found' nor recreating the atmosphere of its original. But at least it is still with us and for that we are thankful.

SOUTHAMPTON: TUDOR HOUSE **

Bugle Street
Town house with recreated Tudor garden
(M)

The house dates from the 15th century and is the best surviving medieval building in Southampton. It was the property of a wealthy citizen, Sir John Dawtrey, Controller of Customs. His widow Isobel was a merchant in her own right, dealing in building stone. She is one of the few ladies of the period of whose appearance we have a record, for she later married a Lord Chief Justice and was painted by Holbein.

The house is of close-studded timbering and wide windows. It was restored in 1895 and became a local museum in 1912. Each generation of curators has felt obliged to add his or her mark, in signs, captions, notices, warnings and educational diktats. While the Medieval Merchant's House (above) is a private conversation between archaeologists, this is a municipal memorandum. On my visit I was bidden to report any sign of 'racial harassment' in the property. There were moments in Southampton's past when that would have been a fulltime job.

Behind the bureaucracy is a fine Tudor building. Its core is a lofty hall, left in its much-altered 19th-century state, with a large Gothic window and fireplace. The screens passage and gallery appear original. A door leads into a small rear garden, delightfully recreated in Tudor style. Crammed into its tiny space are arbours, knots, squares, herb beds and even an orchard. Tudor posts carrying heraldic emblems have been erected. An old cannon points appropriately at an ugly modern hotel opposite. It should be regularly fired.

Upstairs a small writing room, properly furnished, leads into the Baltic room. Here a chest and chair are inlaid with ivory. The remaining rooms are a museum. A Georgian attic extension is filled with so much real junk as to defeat all curatorial discipline. It includes a magnificent pennyfarthing.

STRATFIELD SAYE HOUSE ***

Stratfield Saye, 8m NE of Basingstoke
Jacobean house refashioned for Duke of Wellington (P)

The Duke of Marlborough was given Blenheim. Winston Churchill bought Chartwell. The Duke of Wellington found himself somewhere in between. As his prize for victory, he chose a comfortable Carolean mansion near Basingstoke, largely for the quality of the land. He considered Uppark (Sussex) and even pondered building a palace across the River Loddon from Stratfield Saye, for which a number of architects submitted schemes. But the cost and an affection for the old house left him content. He had grandeur to spare in his London home, Apsley House (London, C). The Duke's descendants live in the house to this day.

From the outside, Stratfield Saye looks deceptively domestic. Indeed, its modesty was treated with derision by Wellington's contemporaries. The house is long and low, two storeys with dormers in the roof and Dutch gables on the wings. Painted white, it might be in Cape Town. Its builder, probably in 1635, was an early member of the Pitt dynasty. The central portion of the garden front was inserted by a later Pitt in 1740. This portion looks like a totally different mansion forcing itself to the centre of the composition like a creature from a different age.

The interior had been much altered by a later Pitt, Lord Rivers, in the mid-18th century and has a stateliness lacking in the exterior. The hall rises two storeys, with a gallery over marbled wooden columns. Paintings are of battle scenes and portraits of all the Wellingtons from the 1st Duke to the present day. Into the floor are set mosaics from the Roman town at neighbouring Silchester. Its loss is Stratfield Saye's gain.

The library is sumptuous, in the manner of William Kent. Gilded rosettes fill the ceiling and gilded foliage the cornice. The walls are lined with leather books, some of them Napoleon's. Everywhere are Wellington memorabilia. There is a lock of George Washington's hair and another of the hair of the Duke's horse, Copenhagen. This noble mount is buried in the grounds and has the entire music room as its shrine. The staircase is from the early house, heavy and friendly.

Lady Douro's Room commemorates Augusta Pierrepont, who married the Great Duke's second son and heir. Those who find Wellington names confusing (Wellesley, Douro, Mornington) should not attempt the Pierreponts, who embrace Kingstons, Manvers, Medows, Cecils and Exeters (see Holme Pierrepont/Notts). Instead, enjoy a delightful set of family portraits and a Rococo fireplace.

The print room and gallery are decorated with contemporary prints as wallpaper, a brief fashion of the 18th century and rarely in such profusion as at Stratfield Saye. The print room also has whimsical Rococo designs in the ceiling. The gallery is more majestic, its prints offset by classical busts in partly gilded bronze. France appears to have won in style what it lost in battle. The Duke spent freely in Paris to furnish both his houses.

Both the small and large drawing rooms have bright French wallpaper and Rococo decoration. In the former is a charming painting of the Great Duke in old age, surrounded by his offspring. The rooms contain pictures captured after the Battle of Vitoria during the Peninsular campaign. Like those at Apsley House, many had been stolen by the French from the Spanish royal collection and were granted to Wellington as a present by the Spanish king. Some had been used to protect pack horses from the rain. They survived remarkably well.

The grounds contain a magnificent stand of Wellingtonias, sequoias first named in honour of the Duke when they arrived in England in 1853.

THE VYNE ****

Sherborne St John, 4m N of Basingstoke
Tudor house with exquisite 18th-century insertions (NT)

The Vyne is the classic house of the English gentleman down the best of ages. Its style embraces Tudor, early Palladian, Georgian Gothick and Victorian revival. It is a model of steady stylistic accretion and the loveliest mansion in Hampshire.

The first part of the building was erected 1518–27 by William Sandys, Lord Chamberlain to Henry VIII. It was acquired in 1653 by Chaloner Chute, Speaker of the Cromwellian House of Commons. He commissioned Inigo Jones's pupil, John Webb, to classicize the façade. A century later his descendant, John Chute, came back from the Grand Tour and produced a bravura set of classical and Gothick interiors. The house then mercifully went to sleep. Later Chutes dusted its eyelids and tucked in its sheets, until they handed it to the National Trust in good order in 1956.

A walk round the exterior reveals Webb's portico of the mid-1650s, said to be the first on an English country house. To the west is a long range with the 16th-century Long Gallery above. Entry is through the Stone Gallery, created below the long gallery and filled with John Chute's Grand Tour acquisitions. A small corner room served as a classroom during The Vyne's brief time as a school in the early 20th century. It is now hung with silk. I would have preferred it left as a schoolroom.

The rooms along the portico front were mostly restored to their 17th-century appearance by a Victorian descendant, the antiquary Wiggett Chute. The drawing room has a light-hearted Rococo ceiling but faded wall-hangings and dark pictures. Beyond the vestibule is a saloon, again with dark panelling and pictures hung in tiers round a piano and harp. For the parlour, Wiggett Chute brought Tudor linenfold panels from elsewhere in the house. The restoration of these wonderfully atmospheric rooms was aided by Martha Chute's watercolours of the 1860s.

The ante-chapel and chapel date from the Tudor house but received the attention of John Chute from 1755. Here 18th-century Gothick overlays Tudor. The ante-room was fashioned from the nave of the old chapel, with lozenge fretwork panels. The chapel is of extraordinary richness; its gallery dates from Lord Sandys' time, as do the Tudor choir stalls. Most remarkable is Chute's *trompe-l'œil* Gothick vaulting of the gallery, apparently a Horace Walpole suggestion. The murals were executed in 1769 by the splendidly named artist, Spiridione Roma.

The glass in the chapel is from the best Flemish work of the early 16th century, the classical enrichment of the upper and lower lights being particularly fine. So too is the glass in the eerie Tomb Chamber next door. This was designed by John Chute himself as monument to his 17th-century ancestor, Speaker Chute. The effigy lies recumbent on a chest adorned with coats of arms and swags.

The Vyne's masterpiece is the central staircase and landing that John Chute created in place of the old Great Hall of the house. He sketched Gothick, chinoiserie and classical designs but the choice fell on classical. The stairs thus rise symmetrically through three planes to an upper landing, each volume carefully modulated. The coffered ceilings and fluted columns seem perfectly in scale. Double the proportions and this could be a Russian palace. The colours are not the rich greens and golds of the early Georgians; here all is soft blue and white, Italian serenity. We know of no designer or craftsman other than Chute himself.

Upstairs is the library and a return to Wiggett Chute's neo-Jacobean. Small plaster busts of literary luminaries stand above the bookcases, attended by portraits of 17th-century Chutes. This is a room in which one yearns to pull down a book from these enticing shelves and read. I asked if National Trust members could use these books and was told emphatically not.

Classical serenity at The Vyne

Next door are two tapestry rooms, with Indian and chinoiserie designs from the Soho workshops. They lead into the original Sandys Oak Gallery, for once untouched by any Chute hand. This is a rare pre-Elizabethan chamber. Linenfold panels of outstanding quality rise from floor to ceiling, enriched with lavish heraldry of Sandys and other Henrician courtiers. The doorcase is a study in transition, a Gothic opening carrying a royal coat of arms held by cherubs in classical poses.

Compared with the house, The Vyne's grounds are comparatively modest, befitting a Tudor rather than a Palladian mansion. The National Trust has replanted much of the area round the lake and created an Edwardian formal garden near the summer house. This dates from Chaloner Chute's day. The house takes its name from a vine which still grows by the Stone Gallery entrance.

WINCHESTER: THE COLLEGE **

73 Kingsgate Street
Medieval collegiate buildings round courtyards (P)

The college was founded by William of Wykeham in 1382, shortly after his New College at Oxford (Oxon) and built by his master-mason, William de Wynford. It was for seventy 'poor and needy scholars', and ten commoners who paid fees. The commoners now predominate.

Both colleges were the first in England to be planned as residential academic communities, yet they retained the form of a medieval town house, a walled enclave of gatehouse and utility ranges looking inwards over one or more courtyards. Grand apartments could be kept distinct from lesser ones, but within a joint defensible space.

An aerial view of Winchester College thus shows a small medieval court reached through a gatehouse from the street, then courts of increasing grandeur beyond. The gatehouse carries a lovely medieval statue of the Virgin in a niche. The outer court was for college services, the bakehouse, brewhouse, laundry, even slaughterhouse. This was the only part of the college into which women were admitted, and then only if they were 'of such an age and appearance as to give rise to no suspicion'. On the far side of the court is a middle gate leading to Chamber Court. This was the core of the medieval college, round which were the rooms of scholars, ushers, chaplains and headmaster.

On the far side of this court is the chapel and hall, back-to-back as at New College. The chapel windows are high and buttressed, its glorious vault covered in red on white Gothick decoration. The hall next door is more domestic, reached by a flight of steps. Below is a range of domestic offices, altered but still evoking the ritual of medieval hospitality. The buttery contains a much-copied painting of the *Trusty Servant* with the head of an ass. The Treasury contains plate donated to the school over the centuries.

Beyond Chamber Court, Winchester takes on a more institutional character. Cloisters extend round a delightful chantry chapel erected in memory of a college steward, John Fromond. To its right stands 'School', a magnificent Restoration hall and the first room in the college designed specifically for teaching. Legend attributes it to Christopher Wren. On the wall, a board demands '*aut disce*', an admonition either to learn or risk expulsion or a beating.

WINCHESTER: GREAT HALL **

The Castle
Medieval hall with 'King Arthur's Round Table' (M)

All that remains of the castle that William the Conqueror built and Henry III extended is its Great Hall. But what a hall! It was described in Pevsner as 'the finest medieval hall in England after Westminster Hall'. The palace was for residence as well as ceremony, a place where a king on his progress could show his face to his people, on his own territory and in his own splendour.

The outside setting is Victorian medieval, made bleak by post-war municipal tat. The interior is breathtaking. For much of the 20th century, it served as a local courtroom, but this purpose has been removed and the space restored to its former appearance. The double cube of five giant bays was completed in 1235, with aisles and plate tracery windows. The entrance is Victorian, anachronistically placed in the middle of the façade. The original door was behind a screen at the far end from the dais, its outline still visible in the stonework of the wall. The aisles are supported on clustered shafts of handsome Purbeck marble.

At the east end, an imaginative Victorian magistrate commissioned a mural with the names of all Hampshire's MPs. The other end displays the celebrated 'King Arthur's Round Table'. The magnificence of this medieval furniture is sadly diminished by its name. It has nothing to do with a putative King Arthur; the wood has been dated to the turn of the 14th century. It was probably constructed in the hall and was first hung on the wall – why? who knows – in 1348. Its decoration is Tudor, as indicated by the white rose enclosed by the red. The portrait of King Arthur is said to bear a striking resemblance to the young Henry VIII. The table was last taken down for examination in 1976.

The lighting of the hall is worthy of *son et lumière*. The statue of Queen Victoria by Sir Alfred Gilbert portrays the queen regal on her throne but lit as if in a horror movie. At the east end are steel gates of an elegant modern design, installed in 1981 to celebrate the wedding of the Prince of Wales and Lady Diana Spencer.

Behind the hall is Queen Eleanor's charming garden, based on a 13th-century illuminated manuscript. It has Gothic arches, turf seats, a herb border and an arbour. Each of the flowers had romantic or religious significance – roses, lilies, columbines and strawberries. It is a pleasant diversion from the sound and fury within.

WINCHESTER: ST CROSS HOSPITAL **

2m S of centre of Winchester
Early almshouse complex with Great Hall (P)

St Cross is one of England's oldest charitable institutions, set in the water meadows of the River Itchen outside Winchester. The hospital was founded in 1136 to support 'thirteen poor men, feeble and so reduced in strength that they can scarcely, or not at all, support themselves'. They should receive a bed, food and clothing and 'drink in sufficient quantity'. Most of the present domestic buildings date from Cardinal Beaufort in 1445.

A daily allowance was stipulated as a loaf of bread, three quarts of small beer, pottage of milk and bread, and a dish of flesh or fish according to the season. This surely must have supported more than just one person. In addition, 'one hundred other poor persons, as deserving as can be found and more indigent, shall be received at the hour of dinner'. Even they were entitled to three quarts of beer. Nor was this all. Money was allowed for a Master, steward, four chaplains, thirteen clerks, seven choristers and 'sundry servants'.

The relevant endowment to support this generosity became the cause of much mischief. St Cross became a byword for corruption, surviving the Dissolution under the patronage of the Bishops of Winchester only since it was a lay foundation. The Master appeared able to pocket much of the revenue and not even attend at all. One absentee Master, the Earl of Guildford, relative of the then Bishop of Winchester, lifted an estimated £250,000 from the accounts in the early 19th century, leading to a Parliamentary outcry. St Cross was the most plausible model (of many) for Hiram's Hospital in Trollope's *The Warden*.

The place survived and today honours its founder's charter. The brothers still wear the traditional smock and cap. The wayfarer's dole is still dispensed to passing ramblers, 'a morsel of bread and a horn of beer'. The residential buildings are similar to those at Winchester College up the road, set round an outer more public courtyard and an inner residential one. A Tudor gatehouse leads into the outer quadrangle past the site of the Hundred Men's Hall. This was for the so-called out-pensioners. On the right is the old kitchen and ahead the 15th-century Beaufort Tower and porter's lodge, where the dole was and is dispensed.

The inner quadrangle is dominated by the Norman church of St Cross towering over its south-east corner. On the north side is the 14th-century Brethren's Hall, formerly the Great Hall of the Master's House. It still has its old screen and central hearth unaltered. Here the brothers ate and gathered, as they still do for occasional feasts. The minstrels' gallery survives, as do the steps to the Master's private rooms. Was a welfare state ever as lavish as this?

On the east side is an ambulatory beneath what was the old infirmary, prettily timbered with brick facings. Opposite, on the west side, are the present brothers' dwellings, built in the 15th century and a magnificent work of medieval domestic architecture. Each staircase has four sets of three rooms, each having a bold Tudor chimney. The brothers themselves act as eloquent guides.

The surroundings of St Cross are still blessedly tranquil. A Victorian visitor rightly remarked that this 'is where a good man, might he make his choice, would wish to die'.

Isle of Wight

Appuldurcombe *   Nunwell **
Brading: Osborne House ****
   Rectory Mansion *   Osborne:
Carisbrooke **   The Swiss Cottage **
Morton *   Yarmouth Castle *

APPULDURCOMBE HOUSE *

Wroxall, 1m N of Ventnor
Ruin of the island's greatest house (EH)

Appuldurcombe is a ruin but you would not think so from a distance. The façade is of a great Baroque mansion set in a park designed by Capability Brown. Its rooms once looked out through stately cedars to the sloping hillside across the valley, as Brown intended.

Appuldurcombe (the stress is on the last syllable) was the ancestral home of the Worsleys, a branch of the family that now lives in Hovingham (Yorks, N). James Worsley was Keeper of the Wardrobe under Henry VIII and was awarded the military Captaincy of the Isle of Wight, marrying Anne Leigh, heiress of Appuldurcombe. His descendant, Sir Robert Worsley, returned from the Grand Tour in 1690, married a Thynne of Longleat, and decided to rebuild his family seat.

No sooner was the new house complete than Worsley fortunes swiftly declined. By the 19th century, the house was unoccupied except for visitors coming to see the pictures. In 1855, it was stripped and put on the market. It became successively a hotel, a school, a barracks and, after a bomb fell nearby in the Second World War, a ruin. This was stabilized in 1952 and restored to its present state in 1986. The main hall and a few downstairs rooms have been re-roofed and the façades and windows made to appear intact. That is all. It is the Isle of Wight's answer to The Grange, but with no opera.

The architect of Appuldurcombe is unknown. It was a work of metropolitan sophistication in the style of Wren. Various experts have suggested John James, under the influence of Vanbrugh. As often with a William-and-Mary house, the side pavilions project forward and the central façade recedes. The entrance doorway has no pediment and is thus weaker than the pavilions. There is a colonnade to the south elevation.

Appuldurcombe was the finest and most original house on the island. Its shell has been beautifully and expansively restored. I cannot see what purpose is served by not restoring and tenanting the interior.

BRADING: RECTORY MANSION *

Brading
Tudor house round courtyard with recreated interiors (M)

This place requires a deep breath. Buried within a brazen tourist attraction is what claims to be the only surviving Tudor building on the island. Tudor it certainly is. The Rectory Mansion and its adjacent inn sit round a picturesque courtyard, cluttered with a gallery, a well, seats, settles and Coke machines. The building must be enjoyed while we avert our eyes from a zoo of stuffed animals, Henry VIII and a corpse rising from its coffin. The Isle of Wight Waxworks Museum is way over the top and very popular.

The general horror has as its backdrop

well-reinstated Tudor interiors, filled with beams, ancient partitions and tiny windows. In the pub section, an exhausted ostler is resting his feet in water. The bedroom in which Louis de Rochefort was reputedly killed by a mysterious assassin looks much as it must have done in 1640.

The skivvy's attic bedroom recreates the cramped conditions in which servants lived in such houses. The skivvy is naked apart from one stocking, for reasons best known to the museum's marketing director. In another bedroom, 'Little Jane' is dying, surrounded by her dog, a rose, prayer book and the curate for consolation. Apparently the scene is authentic to the house.

In the attic another real incident is depicted. A chimney-sweep's boy is stuck in the chimney with no means of escape. He eventually died here. It is as realistic as it is horrific.

CARISBROOKE CASTLE **

1m SW of Newport
Remains of great fortress on hill (EH)

Few castles are more romantic than Carisbrooke. Its site dominates the centre of the island. 'He who holds Carisbrooke holds the Isle of Wight', went the saying. Given the strategic importance of the island in the Middle Ages, this was power. Elizabeth I gave the governorship to her cousin, Sir George Carey, to defend it against the Spanish. The castle was again a centre of attention in 1647–8, when it imprisoned Charles I between the Civil War and his execution.

This had been Charles's wish. Having escaped from Hampton Court he wished to remain on British soil and duly put himself under the care of the island's governor, much to the latter's embarrassment. Charles was free to ride round the island. But various hamfisted attempts at helping him escape led to his being removed to London and his eventual execution.

The place then settled into gentle decay until Queen Victoria appointed her son-in-law, Prince Henry of Battenberg, as governor. On his death, his wife, Princess Beatrice, took on the office herself and drastically restored the castle as her summer residence, living there until her death in 1944.

The building is impressive from a distance, its grey stone walls encircling the crest of a hill with land dropping steep on three sides. Entry over the moat is by a stone bridge through a battered gatehouse. Beyond lies an informal group of buildings of all periods. The interiors are disappointing, largely due to a clash between the Victorian museum installed by Princess Beatrice and English Heritage's house style.

The medieval hall still stands but was divided by the Elizabethan, George Carey, into two floors. It retains a 14th-century fireplace next to a charming window seat. Carey almost obliterated an old chapel at the far end of the hall when he inserted a floor but fragments are discernible. An 18th-century staircase occupies the chapel space. All this has been heavily modernized.

Upstairs is the constable's lodging. Only some of the rooms are accessible, but these include Princess Beatrice's bedroom and the chamber where Charles I's daughter, Elizabeth, died of a chill. The rest of the upper storey is a museum devoted to the Isle of Wight generally and Carisbrooke specifically. Outside is the old well-house, its buckets raised by a donkey treadmill, although earlier by prisoners. The well is still in working order and donkeys perform regularly in the summer. The chapel is another of Princess Beatrice's works, a lovely chamber of early 20th-century Perpendicular. The walk round the castle walls is spectacular.

MORTON MANOR *

½m S of Brading
Old manor house filled with antiques (P)

The Trzebski family open up their small estate above Brading each summer, showing off their garden and plying visitors with wine made from their own vines. Mr Trzebski was a Polish immigrant who served with the RAF and bought the manor after the war. He filled it with whatever he could find from local houses that had fallen on hard times. His taste was and is wildly eclectic, from the exquisite to the kitsch. The latter includes plaster variations on garden gnomes. I am sure that one day everything will prove of value.

The house interior is so complex as to be hard to read. A medieval core leads to a Tudor longhouse, rebuilt in the late 17th century and altered since. The drawing room has a lovely Adam-style mantelpiece. In the dining room is Jacobean panelling supposedly removed from a galleon, some of its cracks still containing nautical caulking. The pretty library has original fabric wall-hangings. Everything is dominated by the clutter of objects which fill every shelf, bracket and tabletop. Morton is an antique shop waiting to happen. But it is also a family home, and the more jolly for its eccentricity.

The gardens are arranged round the house, with formal gardens below and rhododendrons and wilderness above. A wine-making museum occupies an old storehouse on the main lawn.

NUNWELL HOUSE **

1m NW of Brading
Family house of all periods, set in coastal parkland (P)

Nunwell sits comfortably surrounded by park on a hillside overlooking the Solent. On a fine day the grandstand at Goodwood can be seen on the South Downs. Here Oglanders were granted land by William the Conqueror in the 11th century. They served king and country, sheltered Charles I and commanded the island's militia. Their tombs fill Brading church. Sir John Oglander exhorted people in the 17th century to 'fear God, as we did; marry a wife one can'st love; keep out of debt; see the grounds well-stocked; and thou mayest live as happily at Nunwell as any Prince in the World'.

A descendant lives on the estate today, having occupied the main house until 1982 when he sold it to Colonel and Mrs Aylmer, who now open it to the public.

Nunwell is a fine example of a country gentleman's house, filled not with great works of art but with family pictures and furniture acquired over generations and with taste. Most are Oglander, some are Aylmer. The outside walls look as though they were made from a selection of English biscuits, in browns, creams and ochres. Georgian symmetry faces downhill, where the walls are of grey bricks and redbrick dressings. To the rear all is different, a rubicund 17th-century façade with bold doorway and big windows flanked by heavy wings. All we know is that the house was begun in 1607 and has been growing ever since.

Access is behind a Victorian extension, which means walking through the house from the latest period and ending with the earliest, a strange sensation. The music room is Edwardian and is filled with Oglander portraits. The dining room is Victorian, with an equestrian picture of an Aylmer driving his coach in Ireland. The drawing room and library, built or rebuilt in the 1760s, face out over the terrace. Paintings include van Dyck's 'sunflower' self-portrait, showing the artist as an ardent Royalist. The library has Chippendale-style bookcases made by a local carpenter.

The entrance hall is the oldest part of the building, low, rich and Jacobean. It was reputedly here that Charles I dined on his last day of freedom before being taken to Carisbrook, imprisonment and eventual death. Upstairs is the bedroom in which he slept with the equerry's tiny room next door. It is a poignant chamber. A small military museum recalls Colonel Aylmer's regiment, the Irish Guards, and the family's distinguished record as soldiers.

Nunwell's glory is its park and woodlands. Cedars and oaks dot the landscape towards the direction of the sea. They nod their heads gently in the wind while foolish tourists ignore them and stream along the coast. This is an Isle of Wight that I feel might be a distant colony.

OSBORNE HOUSE ★★★★

1m SE of East Cowes
Victoria and Albert's summer retreat restored
as a shrine (EH)

There is no doubt where lies the emotional
heart of this remarkable house. The Queen's
massive canopied bed lies as it did on the day
of her death. On Albert's side, his portrait lies
on its pillow. Above it hangs the bag for his
watch. After his death, the Queen never slept
without them beside her. She died on the
daybed here in 1901, with her vast family round
her. The room was kept as a family shrine for
half a century.

Osborne is the most eccentric of England's
royal palaces. It was the home of only one
monarch, Victoria, and is a memorial not just
to her but to the Victorian family in general.
We see her and her husband working together,
playing together and enjoying their nine
children. We also see where, for almost forty
years, the Queen mourned her dead husband.
Osborne is England's true Victoria and Albert
Museum.

The house stands prominently in a park on
a wooded bluff overlooking the Solent. It was
designed in 1846 by Albert himself, six years
into their marriage. Albert said the setting
reminded him of the Bay of Naples. The
Queen wrote in 1852 of the 'calm deep blue sea,
the balmy air, all quite Italian'. After Albert's
early death in 1861, it became Victoria's haven.
She returned here for ever longer holidays,
sometime for three months each year. After
her death, the house was never used again
and still evokes the sadness of her old age. It is
a place of memories, through which her multi-
tudinous family might later have wandered,
recalling happy childhood incidents.

Albert designed the exterior in association
with the London builder of Belgravia, Thomas
Cubitt. Although the main villa is symmetrical
– indeed, it might be an Italianate house in
Belgrave Square – later wings sprawled over the
hillside to accommodate courtiers and staff.
After the Queen's death, these wings became a
convalescent home and naval college. Their
future remains uncertain. The main house
opened to the public in 1954.

The interiors have been restored as a
virtuoso display of Victorian taste. They were
mostly decorated, again by Albert this time
with his German art adviser, Ludwig Grüner.
Ceilings and cornices, brightly coloured, are
set above Italian and German sculpture and
furniture. Osborne is never French and rarely
English.

Entry is at the end of the Grand Corridor, a
gallery of classical sculpture, its frieze a scaled-
down copy of the Elgin Marbles. At its end are
the Council Chamber and Audience Room for
Privy Council meetings. In the corridor stands
the Marine Venus in a shell niche. It came
from the Baths of Caracalla in Rome and was
bought by Albert at the great Stowe (Bucks)
sale in 1848. Before entering the central
Pavilion, visitors are treated to a fascinating
diversion. They must dive downstairs to the
Table Deckers' Room and Servery, as if looking beneath the bonnet of a car. Here is an
underworld packed with tools of the server's
trade: crockery, cutlery, sharpeners, cloths,
sinks, china and glass galore. Is this wealth of
equipment really never used any more?

The first of the Pavilion rooms is the dining
room. The table is being laid by staff using
measuring rods to get the precise settings.
Their work is overlooked by copies of
Winterhalter's great portraits of Victoria and
her family, the embodiment of Victoriana. Yet
the rooms are not overgrand. The one drawing
room is designed with the billiard table in
one arm, so that men are not completely
segregated from ladies after dinner. Here
family and guests gathered for music, games
and conversation. Visitors often commented
on the informality, a contrast with the normal
image of Victoria's court. The rooms were
designed by Albert in an extravagant Italianate
style, the ceiling in a wild neo-Rococo.

The staircase is the one space in the Pavilion
that merits the term palatial. Opposite the
Page's Alcove, with its myriad bells, is a fresco
by Dyce of Neptune resigning his dominion
over the seas to Britannia. The landing gives
onto Albert and Victoria's bedroom suite. This

comprises their separate dressing rooms and bathrooms but joint bedroom and sitting room. Everything – toiletries, notepaper, even flushing lavatories – is still in place. In the Queen's sitting room, with sweeping views over the Solent, are the adjacent desks at which she and Albert sat next to each other, working on state papers. He was always her 'private and personal secretary'.

On the second floor are the children's rooms, permitting easy access for their parents from below. The day and night nurseries have been restored from old photographs. They include a row of cribs and cots under the command of the Superintendent of the Royal Children, Lady Lyttelton. At the age of six, each would graduate from nursery to schoolroom. Downstairs is the Horn Room, furnished almost entirely from antlers, including a set of most uncomfortable chairs. Here hangs Landseer's painting of Victoria in black on a black horse, held by her much-loved servant, John Brown. Its title is *Sorrow*, though the ladies-in-waiting look unduly relaxed.

The final Durbar Room was added in 1890, in honour of the Queen's new status as Empress of India. It gave Osborne what it lacked, a formal state dining room. The decoration is astonishing, Indian mughal in style, designed by Bhai Ram Singh and John Lockwood Kipling, father of Rudyard. Although ivory in appearance, the walls and ceilings are of plaster and papier mâché, with doors and woodwork of teak. The room is now used for an exhibition of Indian gifts, received on Queen Victoria's Golden and Diamond Jubilees, and is sadly no longer used for banquets.

Albert's terraces at Osborne are paved with 'metallic lava', a 19th-century material intended to look like real lava. The copies of Italian statues are made of cement, Albert always being economical in his materials. The original parterres have been recreated, including such fiercely coloured Victorian favourites as hyacinths and pansies.

Osborne: the adjacent desks

OSBORNE HOUSE: THE SWISS COTTAGE **

1m SE of Osborne House
Albert's folly for his children's education and enjoyment (EH)

Albert was an obsessive father. He wanted his children to grow up as normal as possible, and in 1850 he gave them a corner of Osborne for their own. Here they would cook and keep house, 'entertain' their parents and meet their friends. In the garden they grew vegetables to sell to their father at the going market rate. This was to be a citadel of childhood independence.

The cottage was built in the then fashionable Swiss style. Investigation has shown the logs to be American and joined with metal ties. The kitchen still has the range and utensils used by the children. Upstairs is the dining room furnished, as is most of the cottage, in American birch with bobbin-turned legs. Against the wall is a writing desk at which Victoria is said to have continued working even when supposedly being entertained by her children.

The adjacent sitting room is less cosy: it was originally intended to be a small museum for which Albert encouraged the children to collect specimens and works of vernacular art. So many were collected – or donated – that most have been moved to a separate museum next door. The model shop front of Spratt the Grocer is still in place, with a selection of Victorian teas and wines.

We do not know how much the cottage was really enjoyed by the children, or how far it was more the fantasy of a well-meaning Teutonic father. It certainly shows Albert as a modern parent, eager to make Osborne a family home away from the pressure of Court. He described himself at Osborne as 'part forester, part builder, part farmer and part gardener'.

Below the cottage is a hut containing Queen Victoria's bathing machine. This was once used as a chicken coop but is now restored to regal glory.

YARMOUTH CASTLE *

Quay Street
Last of Henry VIII's coastal fortresses (EH)

Yarmouth is the most personable of the coastal forts built by Henry VIII against attack from the Continent. It was completed in 1547, with a square rather than round bastion design. Its guns were trained over the Solent, flanking those of Hurst opposite. Now the best thing they can do is survey the yachts in the harbour below.

The castle today has the familiar Henrician gun platform, with a field of fire to left and right. The entrance was from the foreshore but is now down an inviting alley from the centre of the little town. This passes over the site of the moat and directly into the living quarters. These are in a tight courtyard, made smaller by the extension of the higher gun platform in the early 17th century. It all feels very Tudor.

The interior has a domesticity rare in the Henrician forts. To the left is the cellar where the gunners lived. To the right is the Master Gunner's house, with hall and parlour, well supplied with fireplaces. The kitchen is in the bastion beyond, with a bedroom upstairs. This is a proper house. A second storey, mostly a single long room, was added in the 17th century. The rooms are sadly bare.

Herefordshire

Of all the counties of England Herefordshire is the most blessed. It runs from the Malvern Hills across the Wye Valley to the Welsh border. Scarcely a prospect is not pleasing. Herefordshire has no truly ugly towns and is safely distant from commuter sprawl. Yet none of it is within a national park and all must one day be vulnerable to the press of the Severn Vale.

The county's houses suit this retiring image. They are modest, made of many-hued limestone, sometimes creamy-white, sometimes deep red-brown. Norman Goodrich is the finest of the Marcher forts extant, and appears the least visited. Hereford boasts the secluded medieval courtyard of Coningsby Hospital and the charming Old House in its main street. Of the 15th–17th centuries we have picturesque Lower Brockhampton, the robust Elizabethan ceilings of Kinnersley and the secluded, idyllic Langstone.

The grandest Restoration house is Holme Lacy with superb William-and-Mary plasterwork. The mansions at Moccas and Berrington are serene examples of late-Georgian design, with work by the rivals Robert Adam and Henry Holland respectively. They are preceded by T. F. Pritchard's charming Gothick interiors at Croft. The astonishing Norman Revival of Eastnor by the young Robert Smirke, now a model of bold restoration, overshadows all.

Berrington ∗∗∗
Burton Court ∗∗
Croft ∗∗∗
Eastnor ∗∗∗∗
Goodrich Castle ∗∗
Hampton Court ∗

Hellens ∗∗
Hereford:
    Coningsby Hospital ∗
    Old House ∗
Holme Lacy ∗∗
Kinnersley ∗∗∗

Langstone ∗∗
Lower Brockhampton ∗∗
Moccas ∗∗
Sufton Court ∗

Dudmaston●

●Walcot

Shropshire

●Clun

Stokesay●

Detton●

LUDLOW●   ●Mawley

A456

Worcestershire

A4110

Croft Castle ●   Witley Court●

A49

Berrington●

LEOMINSTER

Burton Court●

Powys   A44   A44   ●Lower Brockhampton

A4112

A49   ●Hampton Court

Herefordshire

Kinnersley●

A465

A4110

A417

Moccas●   A438

HEREFORD●   Little Malvern●

A438

Sufton Court●   LEDBURY   ●Eastnor

Holme Lacy●

Hellens●

A465   A449

A49   M50

A466

ROSS-ON-WYE

Langstone●   A4137   A40

A40

Monmouthshire   Goodrich●

Gloucestershire

Westbury●

Littledean●

Hardwicke●
●Wick Cour

Frampton●

10 Miles

Woodchester

BERRINGTON HALL ***

3m N of Leominster
Georgian mansion by Holland, Adam-style
plasterwork (NT)

Berrington looks like a Palladian doll's house
from the A49, which cuts a gash across its park
and leaves the russet-brown portico looking
deeply offended. The house was begun in 1778
by Thomas Harley, a Tory banker who made
so much money from the government that he
was able to retire to the country in his mid-
forties. His daughter married the son of
Admiral Rodney, and it was their descendants
who gambled away Harley's inheritance. In
1901 the house was bought by a Lancashire
cotton tycoon, Lord Cawley. He made his
fortune from selling patent black dye on the
death of Queen Victoria. From the Cawleys,
the house passed to the National Trust.

To build Berrington, Harley had first summoned the elderly Capability Brown. The latter approved the setting and suggested a layout
for the park, and then sent his son-in-law,
Henry Holland, with designs for the house.
Holland, just thirty-three, produced the beautifully controlled composition we see today.
The interiors are sometimes in the style of
Robert Adam, sometimes in a French style that
the guidebook refers to as effeminate.

Berrington is not big but undoubtedly
grand. The Marble Hall is classical, with a
ceiling designed to appear domed. The walls
carried trophy roundels, heavy cornices and
fine doorways. It might be the foyer of a French
mausoleum. The drawing room is the principal
reception room. Its ceiling is attributed to
Biagio Rebecca, the Italian decorative painter
who enabled Holland and James Wyatt to rival
Adam in Etruscan revivalism. The original
furniture was considered so precious that the
housekeeper would lament that 'gentlemen
sit on the chairs, tho' there are second ones
for use'.

The little boudoir is a gem, again very
Adamish. One side takes the form of a decorative alcove with fan ceiling, behind a screen of
columns of blue scagliola. On the floor is the
stain of an inkwell upset by an inter-war
burglar. A series of smaller family rooms follow, culminating in Lady Cawley's Room, the
last owner's sitting room. She remained in
residence until her death in 1978 at the age of
a hundred.

The dining room celebrates the Rodney
connection in a collection of stormy sea
paintings. The ceiling roundel is a more serene
Feast of the Gods. The library bookcases were
designed to resemble classical façades, with
ceiling cameos representing English men of
letters. One of the Rodneys sold Harley's
books to turn this into a billiard room. England's great collections are at the mercy of
such whims.

The climax of the interior is Holland's great
staircase, rising up the centre of the building
and remarkably compact despite appearing to
consume much of the interior volume. The
space is Piranesian, rising over coffered arches
supporting the landing. Above is a veritable
Roman temple of scagliola, niches, statues and
grisaille medallions. The soft white colouring
is offset by ochre, blue and grey. It is most
handsome.

The bedrooms are furnished with mild
informality. A dressing room door reveals a
collection of military uniforms – male Cawleys
were all but wiped out in the two world wars.
A fine Edwardian nursery is a museum of
every childish delight and fantasy.

The house has handsome offices and stables
round a Palladian courtyard to the rear. These
have been immaculately restored, with even
the laundries ready for action. This is the
National Trust at its most fastidious. Arrive
with a crease out of place and a housemaid will
descend on you with a steaming iron.

BURTON COURT **

Lower Burton, 5m W of Leominster
Victorian mansion overflowing with curios
(P)

Visitors to this outwardly dull house are
warned that it is a 'typical squire's house and
not a stately home'. It is neither. At Burton an

entire Victorian attic appears to have collapsed into the rooms downstairs. They are one gigantic and glorious junk-shop of costumes, curiosities and fantasmagoria. Not an inch is uncolonized. This is the home of what appears to be a family of demented magpies and hugely enjoyable.

The medieval manor was bought by the local Brewster family in the 17th century and passed to the Clowes in 1863. It was John Clowes, a local MP, who embellished a Georgian villa round the ancient Great Hall. In 1912, Colonel Clowes commissioned the young Clough Williams-Ellis to reclad the entrance and give it the present neo-Tudor façade. The style is sub-Lutyens.

The present owners, Robert Macauley Simpson and his wife, bought it in 1960 'for use as a residence and for a soft fruit growing enterprise'. On leaving, I was invited to 'pick your own' strawberries but asked not to touch the yew, which was being harvested for cancer cures.

Of the interior, the only architectural attraction is the roof of the Great Hall, a remarkable 14th-century survival. Below is a large and finely carved Cromwellian overmantel of 1654. On my visit the room contained dresses, hats, boots, a cheetah, a lady at the virginals and trophies from the Afghan wars. The dining room is High Victorian, 'the design, of course, always a matter of opinion', says the guide. It is divided from the study by a screen carved by a former Mrs Clowes.

Most of the rooms display the Burton Court collection of costumes, first formed in 1951 for showing in city department stores. Although itself of high quality, the collection's appeal is enhanced by the oddity of the setting. The Chinese costumes are in what might pass for an opium den. Every shelf, corridor, cupboard and alcove is filled to bursting with typewriters, model boats, toy roundabouts, train sets, atlases and assorted stuffed fauna. At Burton, the eye never rests.

Outside is a path to the church along which Victorian estate workers were expected to walk two abreast on Sundays. The house has an excellent teashop.

CROFT CASTLE ***
7m NW of Leominster
Gothick rooms in ancient castle (NT)

There have been Crofts on this spot on and off since Domesday. Indeed there is evidence that the Crofts were in Herefordshire well before the Conquest. They were driven out by family poverty in 1746 and the temporary owners, the Knights and Johnes, transformed the old house into a Gothick delight. But ancestral shame caused a later Croft to re-acquire the place in 1923. The family lives here still, albeit courtesy of the National Trust.

Recent excavation has revealed a tangle of early buildings on the site, but what one now sees are basically the outer walls and turrets of a Jacobean sham castle. The entrance is beside a pretty church, with informal gardens and park beyond. The latter contains lime and Spanish chestnut avenues that drift off into the landscape seemingly without purpose.

The Knights who bought Croft in 1746 were ironmasters of Coalbrookdale, and aspiring to county landed status. Richard Knight's son-in-law, Thomas Johnes, decided in the 1760s to ask the Shrewsbury architect, T. F. Pritchard, to refashion the rooms at Croft in Strawberry Hill Gothick, as on display locally at Shobdon church. They are Croft's most celebrated features. To Johnes's son, also Thomas, they evoked 'times of fairies and chivalry'. Thomas was a glittering late-Georgian figure who went on to create the Picturesque house and landscape at Hafod in Cardiganshire, wickedly dynamited for a caravan park in 1958.

The entrance hall, recast in 1913 but with earlier panelling and Jacobean furniture, is hung with pictures of Crofts and their relations, a remarkable family collection. A gallery leads along the central courtyard to the Gothick Staircase, a Pritchard confection of cusped and crocketed ogee wall panels in cream on a coffee-coloured background – and this from the designer of the robust Iron Bridge at Coalbrookdale.

Croft now jumps back and forth in time and style. The dining room is neo-Georgian of 1913, with portraits by Beechey and de Laszlo. The Oak Room is panelled and 17th century, but with a Rococo ceiling of vines and ribbons. The Blue Room panelling has *trompe-l'œil* rosettes arranged round a Rococo chimney-piece by Pritchard, the decoration described in the guide as 'probably unique'. The over-mantel frames a lovely Gainsborough of a Croft lady.

The library ante-room continues the Gothick theme. It is a serene chamber lit by three lancet windows from floor to ceiling, with tall pier-glasses and a superb Gothick chimneypiece. On the stairs are pictures of Thomas Johnes's glorious Hafod, one of the most exquisite creations of the 18th century in Wales.

EASTNOR CASTLE ****

2m E of Ledbury
Regency castle with Pugin and Italianate interiors (P)

Eastnor spent most of the 20th century being told it was too ugly, too big and too costly to survive. Demolition was debated in the 1950s, but even that was considered too expensive. Today, in the hands of the Hervey-Bathurst family, it is one of the most convincing works of grand house restoration.

The castle is set in lush countryside over-looking a tree-lined lake. It was built at one burst by John Somers Cocks, 1st Earl Somers, a legal and banking grandee who spent a phenomenal £80,000 on Eastnor. The work took almost ten years and the architect, from 1810–20, was the young Robert Smirke. He had just completed an equally ostentatious project at Lowther (Cumbria).

Like Lowther, Eastnor is symmetrical, still Regency rather than Victorian medieval revival. The labour involved was prodigious. For six years, stone was carried by mule train from Ledbury to the site. There were some concessions to the 19th century, such as a *porte-cochère* and large picture windows over-looking the lake. But the great walls are pale grey and hard, with Virginia creeper clinging

on desperately. Eastnor will take two more centuries to 'gentlify'.

After the Second World War the interior was all but ruinous and uninhabitable. Only the boldest of redesign was appropriate, and commenced in 1989 under Lord Somers's descendant, James Hervey-Bathurst, and his former wife, Sarah. The task was as Herculean as the original building. The Norman Great Hall has been reinstated as a family sitting room under the guidance of the designer, Bernard Nevill. Given that the room rises three storeys to the roof, this is no mean achieve-ment. The walls have been repainted, a fire lit in the grate, carpets laid, and portraits and suits of armour positioned to break up the space. In the adjacent Red Hall is the 3rd Earl's collection of armour, including a tremendous knight on horseback with the Visconti arms on his shield. The Earl admitted to suffering 'armouritis'.

Each of Smirke's main rooms had been designed in a different style as building progressed. This has been respected in the restoration. Outstanding is the High Gothic drawing room, redesigned by A. W. N. Pugin for the 2nd Earl in 1849 and executed by J. G. Crace. It is one of the latter's finest com-positions. Framed tapestries rise to heraldic beasts, crowned by gilded fan vaults. The fire-place is decorated by an ogee arch beneath a Tudor coat of arms, topped by a family tree. The large chandelier is by Hardmans of Birmingham. This room is as good as anything Pugin did in the House of Lords, a blaze of Gothic fantasy.

After Norman and High Gothic, the Octagon Saloon offers a restrained classicism, its corner pilasters recently marbled. Portraits by the 3rd Earl's favourite artist, G. F. Watts, hang on the walls. The Little Library, now billiard room, has a remarkable pearwood surround to the overmantel mirror. Dark-patterned wallpaper was hung here in 1990, well serving Watts's Pre-Raphaelite portrait of Virginia Pattle. It was on seeing this portrait in Watts's studio that the 3rd Earl fell instantly in love. Virginia duly became the Countess Somers.

The dining room had its Gothic arches removed in 1933. They are now reinstated as Tudor, with an heraldic ceiling. It is hung with family portraits, including a Romney of the 1st Earl, builder of Eastnor. Downstairs is the state bedroom, with Italian Renaissance pictures and an Italian bed with heavy drapes, the decoration dark yet not oppressive.

The staircase is of stone with a cast-iron balustrade. There is a chandelier from Florence, chairs from Venice and tapestries from Bruges. The once derelict bedrooms are all back in use, a remarkable testament to country house confidence in the 21st century.

GOODRICH CASTLE **

4m S of Ross-on-Wye
Marcher castle set round Norman keep (EH)

Goodrich was first built by the Normans to assert their authority along the Welsh border. In a rich ochre sandstone, it perches on a rock overlooking the River Wye, massive and surprisingly intact. Everything about Goodrich is other-worldly, including the walk through the fields from the nearest road to get to it. It must have been even more impressive when Goodrich Court still adorned the opposite bluff of the Wye. This was demolished c1950.

The Norman keep dates from the 12th century but it was enclosed by Edward I with a heavily fortified inner ward of curtain walls and corner bastions. These dominate the castle's appearance, set on a rocky outcrop and protected on its 'landward' sides by a dry moat. The Tudor ascendancy meant it was no longer required, although it was slighted after the Civil War.

The castle is immediately impressive. Most of the curtain wall stands to full height. The stone bastions are supported by battered spurs to resist undermining. A barbican with bridge over the moat offers access to the gatehouse, with a sequence of potentially lethal barriers against hostile visitors.

Pugin and Crace at Eastnor

Next to the gatehouse is a chapel, in good repair and roofed. It has a Perpendicular east window and a modern west window commemorating the wartime crash nearby of a plane testing radar. From the chapel, a wall walk leads round the extremity of the castle, from which the outline and walls of the great hall and solar wing can be seen in the inner ward below. The solar is indicated by a majestic double arch rising through two storeys.

The old Norman keep looks diminutive within all this 14th-century protection. It is a good example of its type, with stone pilaster strips and original round-headed windows. The dungeon prison is next to it. From the adjacent ramparts are splendid views over the Wye valley.

HAMPTON COURT *

Hope under Dinmore, 4m S of Leominster
Restored medieval mansion with new gardens (P-G)

Hampton adds another chapter to the story of country house rescue. The old building sits on the banks of the River Lugg beneath a sweeping gallery of wooded hills. Begun after Agincourt by Sir Rowland Leinthall, it was the home of Herefordshire's Cornewall and then Coningsby families until the early 19th century. Under Lord Coningsby, keen supporter of William and Mary, Hampton acquired the suffix 'Court', said to be in honour of their majesties' favourite palace in Middlesex.

The medieval house remained little altered until bought in 1810 by Richard Arkwright, son of the cotton entrepreneur and in his day 'the wealthiest commoner in England'. The price of the house and 6,220 acres was a then staggering £226,535 (estimated in the guidebook at £6.2m today). It must have been the most expensive house purchase in England in the 19th century.

The Arkwrights spent lavishly on both house and estate. They duly became country gentlemen, Lords Lieutenant and Members of Parliament. The house was much rebuilt, the exterior gothicized and battlemented. Relations between client and architect (Lord

Sudeley) grew ever worse until John Arkwright admitted that he 'wished he had never touched a stone' of Hampton. His son declared himself 'penniless' at the dawn of the new century, leaving it to the next generation to sell the house and its contents.

Hampton Court had a bad 20th century. The old chapel and the greenhouse built by Joseph Paxton fell into ruin. Grounds laid out over Coningsby's 17th-century Dutch parterres ran to seed. Having had just three owners in over four centuries, the house now had nine inside one. Each came, struggled and departed.

Then in 1994 an American couple, Robert and Judith Van Kampen, arrived with new money and commitment. They embarked on a full restoration of the interiors and gardens, to enhance their foundation, Sola Scriptura, dedicated to biblical scholarship. The Tudor chapel roof has been reinstated. The house is sometimes open and used for conferences and seminars. It is for sale at the time of writing.

Although the interiors are much altered, the exterior is hugely romantic, a castellated gothic castle by the river, a Herefordshire Windsor. It is surrounded by extensive public gardens, still being restored. They include an extensive walled area with kitchen and flower garden, laid out by Simon Dorrell. The displays are eccentric. A maze has been created round a Gothic tower, with the Van Kampens' initials woven into the yew pattern. Waterfalls and gazebos create a picturesque landscape. There is also a Dutch parterre. The admirable ambition is to create the finest garden in Herefordshire.

HELLENS **

Much Marcle, 4m SW of Ledbury
Jacobean house, much altered and filled with family memorabilia (P)

Hellens nestles among trees in Much Marcle, close to the church in which lies the exquisite medieval effigy of Blanche Mortimer. The house has remained in the same family since the Middle Ages, variously named Mor-

himes, Audleys, Walwyns, Whartons and now Munthes. An early Munthe, Axel, wrote the romantic bestseller, *The Story of San Michele*. Malcolm Munthe took over the Jacobean house in the 1950s and thoroughly romanticized it. The house is still a home, with a splendid collection of family portraits and tall stories, including ghostly visitations by such luminaries as the Black Prince and Bloody Mary. The exterior is Jacobean, brick and charmingly informal.

The former courtyard was converted by Munthe into a gallery, hung with 17th-century paintings, leading into the original Tudor Great Hall. Beyond the screens passage is the Jacobean house. The drawing room is panelled, with a sky-painted ceiling, with windows giving a view over Hellens' parterre and knot garden. An overmantel made from a bed-head has its pattern repeated in the knot garden outside. At every turn are family relics and mementos, not least of a Wharton who briefly became a duke.

The staircase is giant and Jacobean, with heavy balusters and an imported frieze with mythical beasts. On the stairs is Anne Boleyn's last comb, donated by a son of her sister and forerunner in Henry's favour, Mary Bullen. The bedrooms upstairs are laden with more bric-à-brac. One has Spanish leather wall-hangings, a Lely and an embroidered frieze. Another room was laid out for Bloody Mary, although she is not recorded as visiting the house. It contains a Tintoretto and a Venetian mirror.

The third room saw service as the 'prison' of Hetty Walwyn. She is said to have run off with a local boy, but soon returned on repenting her rashness and asked her father for forgiveness. He sent her up to her room and locked the door behind her, leaving it locked for thirty years. She engraved on the window pane a single pious reflection: 'It is part of virtue to abstain from what we love.'

That apart there is a relaxed atmosphere to Hellens. Like the family's other house,

Hellens: mythical beast on stairs

Southside in Wimbledon (London, W), there are no ropes, signs or instructions. If furniture is bashed, it stays bashed. If a book jacket is left lying about, it stays. This is an inhabited home, not prettified for public display. A magnificent stand of trees keeps guard outside.

HEREFORD: CONINGSBY HOSPITAL *

Widemarsh Street
Almshouse quadrangle with infirmary (M)

Outside any medieval cathedral city would be a ring of monasteries built at a safe distance from the dirt and plague 'within the walls', trusting to God for protection from bandits. A Dominican priory was located east of Widemarsh Street in Hereford, its ruins now a public park. Next door were the local headquarters of the Order of the Knights of St John.

After the Dissolution, the properties passed to the prominent Herefordshire courtier, Sir Thomas Coningsby. In 1614, he adapted the Order's old buildings as a hospital and almshouse. It was to accommodate 'a chapleyne and eleven poor ould servitors that have been soldiers, mariners or serving men'. They were charged to the honour of God for his protection, 'as also for his preservation against malice'. The present inmates still wear the original uniform on special occasions, the senior man being 'Corporal of Coningsby's Company of Servitors'.

The hospital quadrangle dates in part from the days of the Knights of St John. Built of stone and with pretty trefoil windows, it is a charming backwater. One side comprises the dining hall of the old St John's House. Above is the infirmary, from which patients could look down from a gallery onto the chapel beyond. This is a rare survivor of this medieval arrangement, giving the sick and dying the comfort of hearing Mass. A similar facility is at St Mary's Hospital, Chichester (Sussex).

The infirmary has been made into a small museum of both the hospital and the Knights of St John, with some confusion. The infirmary is so crowded with waxworks that it is hard to tell who is wax and who real. A buried skeleton is displayed in a grave downstairs. It is real.

HEREFORD: OLD HOUSE *

High Town
Black-and-white merchant's house in city centre (M)

Hereford once possessed England's finest Elizabethan town hall, three storeys of jettied and gabled decorative timber above an open arcade. The building was demolished in 1862 for 'road widening'. Other similar 'annoyances' were removed to 'add much to the ornament and convenience of the said city'. One was Butchers' Row in the middle of High Town, all of which was demolished except one property, saved by the obduracy of its occupant.

The house was built in 1621 for a butcher, who would have traded from the ground floor. Later owners were butchers, saddlers, hardware merchants and, in the 1880s, bankers. The house was given to the local council as a museum by Lloyds Bank in 1928 and is now itself an 'ornament and convenience', as would be its neighbours had they only been protected.

The exterior of the building is extraordinarily rich, given that this was a poor part of the city. The house is three storeys, one bay by three, gabled and with richly carved bargeboards. The windows are delightful oriels. A protective canopy surrounds the ground floor. Over the porch is the Butchers' Guild coat of arms.

The house interior combines original features and some imported from other demolished buildings, forming a fine museum of 17th-century domesticity. Both ground and first floors are open, crowded with dark Jacobean furniture in oak, yew and mahogany. Downstairs is a large refectory table. A Mannerist overmantel graces the first-floor parlour and a Welsh four-poster the bedroom. Upstairs is an unusual Queen Anne baby-walker designed for twins.

HOLME LACY HOUSE **

Holme Lacy, 5m SE of Hereford
Restoration mansion with ornate
plasterwork (H)

If you like to gaze at some of the finest
Restoration plasterwork in England with a pint
in one hand and the handle of a fruit machine
in the other, Holme Lacy is for you. The
great house stands proud on a hill overlooking
the River Wye, as if it knew it was once the
finest classical house west of the Severn. It was
built for the Scudamores in 1674, probably by
Hugh May.

The house passed to the Earls of Chesterfield who moved out in 1909, carrying
off Holme Lacy's celebrated state bed to
Beningborough (Yorks, N). Holme Lacy was
sold to Sir Robert Lucas-Tooth, who un-
accountably found it too small and filled in the
central courtyard with a massive ballroom
and built a new Edwardian staircase. It passed
to the NHS and is now with Warner Holidays
as a 'leisure complex'. As with that company's
other houses, the result can be unnerving
to those not warned, but the house is well
restored.

The exterior, mostly in soft red and pink
sandstone, remains supremely elegant. The
south front has a pedimented centre and projecting bays, with widely spaced windows and
hipped roofs, all William-and-Mary and
friendly. The interior has lost its furniture and
fittings, but it has not lost its plasterwork,
which alone is worth a visit and a drink.

To Pevsner, Holme Lacy's ground-floor
ceilings were among the finest in England of
their date, matching those in the royal palaces
in London. They survived the various alterations to the exterior, although the ceiling pendants were removed during the house's NHS
ownership. Health officials dumped them in a
damp heap in the cellar. The saloon still has
the finest work, deeply undercut ceiling panels
with armorial cartouches in the coving. Some
of the foliage is so realistic as to appear almost
hanging free. Bits of Holme Lacy's decorative
woodwork, probably by Grinling Gibbons, can
be seen in the Metropolitan Museum in New
York.

The grounds complement the graceful exterior, with parterres and yew walks running
down to a distant lake.

KINNERSLEY CASTLE ***

Kinnersley, 12m SW of Leominster
Elizabethan mansion with fine plasterwork
(P-R)

If corporate hospitality is one way of keeping
an old house alive, 'alternative hospitality' is
another. On my visit to Kinnersley, a promised
group of 'Georgians' turned out to be *yurt*
owners from the Caucasus. A class of art
students had just departed and a homeopathy
course was about to begin. The giant ginkgo
tree on the lawn, bigger than that at Kew, was
being used for herbal medicine and 'to ward
off fires'. The house welcomes groups committed to the arts, alternative healing, organic
gardening, woodland crafts and sustainable
energy. A washing line flutters from the battlemented tower.

The house was acquired by the Vaughans
in the late-Elizabethan period. They appear to
have built the present house but sold it
to Francis Smallman in 1618, after which it
changed hands with unusual frequency to the
present day. Occupants included the brother
of the buccaneer, Henry Morgan, the father-
in-law of George Bodley, the architect, Major
Davey, inventor of the fire escape sling, and
Lord Brocket, the pro-Nazi peer. In 1954,
Kinnersley was bought by H. Garrat-Adams
for his stamp collection, but let as an old
people's home until 1989. His family are still in
occupation.

The house is magnificent and slightly
scruffy. At its core is a medieval fortified manor
house. This was converted by the Vaughans at
the end of the 16th century into an L-shaped
mansion, with its staircase turret nestling in its
angle. Large restored gables adorn the roofline.

Every room downstairs is of interest. The
drawing room was redecorated in the 18th
century, with wood carvings in the style of

Grinling Gibbons. The Georgian door (inside) is spliced onto a Tudor door (outside). The old hall, or possibly parlour, has a neo-Jacobean ceiling inserted by Bodley. To the left of the fireplace is a treasured secret passage, hardly remarkable since the house is a warren of both secrets and passages.

Up the massive stairs is the solar, the most remarkable room in the house. The decoration honours the Vaughans and Good Queen Bess. The gilded ceiling depicts the family emblems of serpents and black dogs, while the frieze carries royalist emblems of England, Wales, Ireland and France (but not Scotland, which Elizabeth did not claim to rule). Above the fireplace is a superbly executed oak tree rising from a Tudor rose. This was a celebration of the Armada victory, said to have saved the oaks of the Vaughans' Forest of Dean from destruction. The Spaniards had threatened to burn England's oak forests to stop ship-building.

Other rooms are panelled and patched, decorated and obscured by changes of purpose. The Oak Room has an overmantel said to be by the Herefordshire carver, John Abel, of 1618. The floor beams still carry their carpenters' adze marks. A panelled Tudor room is now a dormitory. From the tower is a view over the roofs of the castle to the landscape beyond. Kinnersley is still in the process of being restored, which means still being discovered.

LANGSTONE **

Llangarron, 6m W of Ross-on-Wye
William-and-Mary house with Tudor rear (P-R)

There have been Joneses at Langstone since 1794 and they are in no mood to leave. On a warm spring day, this place is in love with its landscape. An Elizabethan manor house is fronted by a lovely William-and-Mary façade, presiding with gentle dignity over a wooded

Elizabethan gables at Kinnersley

garden sloping down to a brook. Langstone is Herefordshire at its most English.

Inside, the drawing room appears earlier than the 1690s façade. The front door leads into one side, as if into an earlier hall. The fireplace is flanked by balancing doors but the plasterwork ceiling is not symmetrical. The adjacent parlour is panelled, its 17th-century ceiling composed of large domed panels and a circular band of fruit and foliage.

The dining room was refashioned in 1825, with a bow window and two Ionic columns as a screen. Behind is a carved staircase rising the four floors to the attic. No less delightful are the Tudor rooms to the rear. Here an older staircase has a revealed cruck beam. Beyond is a small medieval room with simple ceiling plasterwork, oak table and old pewter. The present Mr Jones explains that the house is 'unspoilt because Joneses had no money'. This is a good place for house detectives.

LOWER BROCKHAMPTON **

2m NE of Bromyard
Isolated moated manor with gatehouse (NT)

The motto of Lower Brockhampton might be 'picturesque with everything'. The timbered farmhouse with its moat and gatehouse must adorn the lids of a hundred biscuit tins. It was lucky to be inaccessible when the Barneby family decided, in the 1760s, to build something grand on the neighbouring hill. The new Brockhampton House, built by T. F. Pritchard in 1765, captured the views over the Vale of Worcester and the Malverns.

The old house was left to farm use until taken in hand in the 1870s by John Barneby Lutley. He commissioned J. C. Buckler to restore the building to its medieval, manorial state, an early exercise in vernacular revival. Buckler documented his every move, calling it his 'labour of love'. The house was stripped of later wall-covering and of the ceiling which divided the Great Hall into upstairs and downstairs. Exterior timbers were exposed. The separate 1530s gatehouse, with pretty upper chamber, was restored over its small moat, which curves round the outside of the main house. The manor passed to the National Trust in 1946.

The drive to Lower Brockhampton passes round the back of Pritchard's house, and sweeps through lush woodlands to a private valley beyond. The old manor is still the centre of the estate farm, its moat alive with ducks. For all its modest size and later use as a farmhouse, this is clearly a proper manorial property.

The building is 15th century, T-shaped, with hall and solar wing at right angles. Timbered walls rest comfortably between solid brick chimneys. A possible kitchen wing on the left end of the hall has vanished. Buckler restored the interior to its pre-Tudor state. The hall roof is now exposed, its cusped braces another indication of the house's importance. The gallery over the screens passage and the stairs to it are Buckler's.

The rooms have been partly furnished to reflect the Victorian usage, with a Georgian vernacular table of no fewer than five parts. The hall was primarily used for shooting lunches from the big house. There is an enjoyable photographic exhibition of the Brockhampton estate over the years.

MOCCAS COURT **

Moccas, 12m W of Hereford
Georgian villa on river bank, with Adam drawing room (P)

Moccas is an 18th-century idyll on the banks of the River Wye. The park was designed by Capability Brown and later enlivened by touches of Repton Picturesque. The house was the product of a union between two old Herefordshire families, the Vaughans and Cornewalls, celebrated in the Norman church that guards the drive to the house. When a Cornewall heiress was courted in 1771 by Sir George Amyand, he was told that if he wanted Moccas as well he would have to take the name and arms of Cornewall. The house has remained in the same family ever since.

Sir George replaced the old house with a design by Robert Adam. He was a Whig MP and may have been competing with neighbouring Berrington, being built at the same time by Henry Holland for his Tory rival, Thomas Harley. Designs by Adam survive from 1775, but Sir George had a local architect, Anthony Keck, execute and considerably vary them.

The exterior displays late-Georgian austere simplicity. Adam's plan for an Ionic frontispiece was not executed. (Adam had bad luck with almost all his exteriors.) The interior, however, is remarkably inventive, the core of the house being three circular spaces leading from the door to the rear terrace. The porch gives immediately onto an extraordinary *coup de théâtre*, a double curve of steps up round a broken pillar. The effect is pure architectural drama, leading the eye up to the hall and across to the arched opening to the staircase hall beyond.

The staircase hall is apparently by Keck – it is not on Adam's drawing – yet it is similar to the confined staircases found in Adam's town houses. A screen of doors guards the rooms beyond, while the cantilevered stair rises in an exhilarating sweep to a first floor balcony. Beyond the staircase, a door leads into the set-piece of the house, the circular Summer Drawing Room.

The design for this room was commissioned from Adam by Cornewall in 1781. The decoration is pure Adam, apparently with its original printed French wallpaper. The condition of the paper is said to be due to the room never having been heated and never lit. The motifs are Pompeian arabesques, fronds and grotesques, also found in plaster relief on the ceiling. Only the white background has been touched up, carefully not disturbing original pattern.

The other rooms are inevitably an anticlimax, their original contents sold in 1946. Some Adam friezes and fireplaces survived, and the present Cornewall descendants, the Chester-Masters, are seeking furniture appropriate to the period. But the house glows outward from its core. The sequence from entrance to exit is still a glorious progression from countryside to countryside, as if the house were a pavilion of pleasure in a Poussin landscape.

SUFTON COURT *
Mordiford, 4m SE of Hereford
Wyatt house in Repton landscape (P-R)

The Hereford family have been at Sufton since the 12th century and the present James Hereford has archives to prove it. The older 16th-century house is tenanted, but the new one erected in the 18th century is in family occupation.

The site of the new property is spectacular, on a hill overlooking the River Wye as it departs Hereford and meanders its way to Ross. Hills enclose the view on all sides. The setting captivated Humphry Repton, who was commissioned to landscape Sufton Court park and

left a Red Book as evidence, dated 1795. A facsimile is in the house.

The building is modest, despite being designed by James Wyatt in 1788. It has a sombre visage, the lichen-clad stone looking like render and the windows made severe by the removal of glazing bars. The doorway is hidden behind a Victorian Gothic porch.

The interiors are all by Wyatt. A small hall gives onto a drawing room to the left and dining room to the right. The former was the music room, a use emphasized by the instruments depicted in the pretty plaster frieze. The room has marquetry doors, one of them a dummy. On the walls are fine landscape watercolours by a Victorian Hereford. The present library was once the dining room, Repton having apparently insisted that no two main reception rooms should have the same view from their windows. Only recently has the family dared countermand the great man's instructions.

Hertfordshire

Hertfordshire was an ideal county for aspiring 16th-century courtiers and City merchants with no landed estate and a need for a country house within a day's ride of London. This also applied to the monarch. Henry VIII kept his children out of harm's way at Hatfield Palace. This house passed from the Crown to the Earls of Salisbury in the 17th century, who built next to it a second palace, one of the great mansions of Jacobean England. Nearby were lodged other Tudor dignitaries. There was Cardinal Wolsey at Moor Park, Lord Lytton at Knebworth, Lord Egerton at Ashridge and Nicholas Bacon at Gorhambury.

Moor Park was to see a succession of aristocratic owners, both before and after its rebuilding in the early 18th century. It is now a magnificent golf club. Robert Taylor rebuilt Gorhambury for the Earl of Verulam, and James Paine designed Brocket Hall for Lord Melbourne. Ashridge was rebuilt in the most grandiloquent Gothic by the Wyatts for the Duke of Bridgewater. Knebworth was then decorated and fantasized by the romanticist, Bulwer-Lytton.

In comparison, the 20th century's contribution to Hertfordshire has been modest. Shaw brought early socialism to Shaw's Corner and the architects Parker and Unwin brought the same to Letchworth Garden City. Which did more to change the world is moot.

Ashridge *
Brocket Hall **
Gorhambury ***
Hanbury Manor *
Hatfield:
  House ****

Hatfield:
  Old Palace *
Knebworth ****
Letchworth:
  296 Norton Way
  South *

Moor Park ***
Shaw's Corner **
Woodhall Park **

ASHRIDGE *

4m N of Berkhamsted
Gothic masterpiece of Wyatt family in Repton landscape (P-G)

Ashridge lies at the centre of a large wooded estate owned by the National Trust on a limb of the Chilterns north of Berkhamsted. The house, a huge and romantic Gothic work by James Wyatt and his nephew, Sir Jeffry Wyatville, is now a management college. Neither house nor Repton's formal gardens are normally open to the public, but can be seen from the park. A guidebook can be purchased at reception, offering a discreet glimpse of the interior.

The house was an Augustinian monastery seized at the Dissolution and used, like Hatfield, for the safe keeping of royal children. It was from Ashridge that Elizabeth was sent to the Tower by her sister, Mary, in 1554. The old house passed to Elizabeth's Chancellor, Thomas Egerton, whose family were later Dukes of Bridgewater. It was they who demolished the old building and began a new one with James Wyatt in 1808. The house was created in honour of the deceased 2nd Duke, promoter of England's canal network. The house passed to the Brownlow family of Belton (Lincs), became a Conservative Party training college in the 1930s, a wartime hospital and a finishing school before its present incarnation as a business college.

The house was built for show, like James Wyatt's now vanished Fonthill in Wiltshire. The main façade is to one side overlooking the garden. Its central feature is Wyatt's chapel, the steeple making the house seem like a complete village when seen from a distance. Turrets, towers and ranges of buildings sprawl on all sides. Facing the road is the entrance front, Tudor Gothic in silvery white stone. The entrance hall has a double hammerbeam roof with, guarding the second hall within, a stone screen with triple arched gallery.

Behind is the staircase hall, a thrilling medieval-style chamber rising to a high fan vault. A decorative wind vane is embedded in its central rose. The walls carry Gothic niches with effigies of figures from the history of the old monastery. The cantilevered stairs have iron balusters. These vast, interpenetrating spaces, new to English domestic architecture, were made feasible by the great advances in heating technology.

The chapel has fan vaults and an oak organ case by Wyatville. As John Julius Norwich writes, 'architecture more unsuitable for the study of advanced business techniques could hardly be imagined'.

BROCKET HALL **

Lemsford, 1m W of Welwyn Garden City
House of the Lamb dynasty with grand saloon (H)

Brocket Hall is a monument to aristocratic misbehaviour. The lady of the house, Lady Melbourne, was a mistress of the Prince Regent, who often came here to visit her and her husband, Lord Melbourne, later Queen Victoria's prime minister. The daughter of the house was Lady Caroline Lamb, briefly mistress to Lord Byron. It was in the ball-room at Brocket that Lady Caroline is said to have been 'served up' naked in a giant tureen. Both Lord Melbourne and later Lord Palmerston lived and died at Brocket. After the current Lord Brocket fell foul of the authorities and spent some time at Her Majesty's pleasure, the house became a hotel,

although it is still owned by the Brockets.

The building lies across a generous park of cedars and willows, with a spaciousness rare in confined Hertfordshire. The drive reaches its climax when a corner is turned and the house is seen in the distance, on an elevation overlooking a lake. The positioning is superb but, as often with mid-Georgian buildings, the exterior is disappointing. The architect was James Paine in 1760 and the proportion seems lumbering and top heavy. He always preferred an arresting roofline. From a distance, Brocket Hall might be an army staff college.

The more remarkable is Paine's interior, mostly decorated for the 1st Lord Melbourne who inherited in 1768. The staircase rises between balusters of a lively honeysuckle pattern and returns to a balcony beneath an arched and panelled ceiling. It is Paine's masterpiece and has been restored with appropriate bravura. The main reception rooms retain their 18th-century decoration and some of the house's original paintings.

The saloon, now ballroom, was decorated by Paine for the 1st Lord Melbourne in a style worthy of his princely guests. It abandons all restraint, allegedly inspired by Adam's celebrated (and lost) Glass Drawing Room at Northumberland House in London. It seats fifty-four people, not including the occupant of a tureen. The coved ceiling is gilded and filled with painted panels, most by John Hamilton Mortimer. He is dismissed in the county's *Shell Guide* quaintly as 'a painter of the grotesque and horrible, dissolute, a cricketer'. On the wall is a Reynolds given to his mistress by the Prince Regent. Among the guest bedrooms are some decorated with his favourite chinoiserie.

GORHAMBURY ***

3m W of St Albans
Classical mansion, picture collection with Tudor portraits (P)

Where would the Home Counties be without the tenacity of old landowners? The first Gorhambury, now a ruin, was built by Sir

Nicholas Bacon, courtier under both Henry VIII and Elizabeth and father of Francis Bacon. The estate passed by marriage from the Bacons to the Grimstons, later Earls of Verulam, who hold it to this day. It was the 3rd Viscount who, in 1777, commissioned Sir Robert Taylor to build a new Palladian house at some distance from the old building.

The park lies sandwiched between the suburbs of St Albans and the hell of Hemel Hempstead. Taylor's house has a lofty Corinthian portico raised on a plinth, with a modest house attached behind it. This makes a tremendous show across the park, especially since its recent recladding in Portland stone. The house is mostly a casket for the family picture collection, including a so-called 'gallery of the great', of English monarchs and others. There is a run of Grimston portraits from the 15th century to the present day.

The hall's interior is a match for the portico outside. Taylor imported the floor of black-and-white tiles, together with a chimneypiece and enamelled glass window, from the old Tudor house next door. The window includes coloured quarries of New World scenes. The wall is also hung with the earliest known English pile carpet, of 1570. The gallery round the hall above was installed in the 19th century and is hung with family portraits, gazing down admiringly on their descendants below.

The dining room contains Jacobean portraits, including one by van Dyck, while the mantelpiece displays 18th-century bronzes of classical figures. In the ballroom are two startling Hilliards, one of the elderly Elizabeth I, so unappealing as to be surely a likeness. Essex is depicted in a more glamorous light. Everywhere are Bacons and Grimstons, in ruffs, doublets, ringlets, cloaks, stovepipe hats and swirling silks. The history of English costume is at Gorhambury.

The Yellow Drawing Room is dominated by a Grand Tour chimneypiece commissioned from Piranesi (another is in the library). Above it hangs a Reynolds conversation piece of the Grimston children. On the far wall is an extraordinary work, de Laszlo's portrait of the wife of the 4th Earl with her son. They are in classical pose and costume, but with unmistakably 20th-century faces.

HANBURY MANOR *

1m N of Ware

Late Victorian brewer's mansion in Jacobean style (H)

Entering Hanbury Manor is like passing into Alice's Wonderland. Either we are suddenly very small or it is very big. The old house was called Poles and was Georgian. In 1800 it passed to Sampson Hanbury, the London brewer, whose family owned it until 1884. The house was then demolished and replaced by an 'earlier' building designed in 1890 by Sir Ernest George & Peto in a Jacobethan style. It is one of that firm's most extravagant creations, a Jacobean manor blown up to twice its normal scale.

Hanbury then had a sad history. In 1913 it was sold to a businessman, Henry King, who lost a son in the Great War and a daughter at the house when her beekeeping equipment caught fire. The family could not bear to stay. From 1923 to 1986 the house was a convent school. New wings and courts were added in 1930s Tudor. The place was converted into a Marriott hotel in 1996, but no amount of corporate design can obliterate George & Peto's monumental façade and reception rooms. Outside is a fine lawn and arboretum.

The exterior combines Jacobean and Renaissance themes. Redbrick chimneys rise above gables, each different in style and each larger than life. The interior is no less monumental. The Oak Hall has long Elizabethan windows above rich panelling.

The library is panelled in mahogany and rosewood, with original bookcases and an astonishing Italian Renaissance fireplace. The dining room comes complete with barrel vault covered in the signs of the zodiac. Other rooms are equally grandiloquent. At the end of a corridor is the former convent chapel, now a banqueting room, with a stone reredos still in place.

HATFIELD HOUSE ★★★★

E of Hatfield
Palace of the Cecils, Marble Hall and portraits of Elizabeth I (P)

Hatfield is the epitome of early Stuart ostentation, a massive, overstated pile and beloved of Victorian imitators. From here, a cavalcade of Cecils has ridden forth to serve as statesmen, writers and controversialists. For four centuries, the English state has seemed unable to survive without the oversight of Cecils. Three Marquesses of Salisbury in a row were leaders of the House of Lords.

The house is next door to Henry VIII's old palace (below). The new building was created by the hunchback 1st Earl of Salisbury, after James I had exchanged Hatfield Old Palace for Salisbury's Theobalds (which stood about 10 miles away to the south-east and was demolished in 1651). Today's Hatfield is thus Jacobean and prodigiously so. It sits in its sweeping park, surrounded by parterres and avenues, lakes and woods, defying the encircling suburbia of Hertfordshire. The enclave is hugely precious.

The house was built between 1607 and 1612. The plan is certainly Elizabethan, E-plan above a Renaissance loggia with classical frontispiece and brick wings. The designer was Robert Lyminge, who also created Blickling (Norfolk), although the frontispiece is attributed to Inigo Jones. The house has lost the surrounding terraces and statuary, but remains hugely imposing in its landscape. Visitors are able to see only the state rooms and then only in one direction. The experience is not so much of a tour round a great house as of a sustained *coup de théâtre*.

The principal coup is undoubtedly the Marble Hall, a glowing edifice rising above its marble chequerboard floor. The room was completed in 1612 and has not been altered since. The tables and benches were made for it. The colossal screen and minstrels' gallery carry their original carving, of cartouches, scallops and scrollwork panels heavy with heraldry and gilding. Few screens of the period tell of such

inherited assurance. Beneath the Brussels tapestries are portraits of the Tudor dynasty on whose favour Hatfield was built, the *Ermine Portrait* of Elizabeth I by Nicholas Hilliard and a portrait of Mary Queen of Scots. The room is like a theatre perpetually awaiting an audience.

The Grand Staircase was by the same hand as the hall's screen, a craftsman called John Bucke. The newel posts carry statues and heraldry, including one of the Stuart gardener, John Tradescant. At the foot of the stair is the enigmatic *Rainbow Portrait* of Elizabeth, her dress covered in eyes and ears, her hand resting on the rainbow of peace. The white horse depicted on the wall above is reputedly the one on which Elizabeth reviewed her troops at Tilbury.

The staircase ascends on a cloud of Cecil glory to the King James Drawing Room, the former Great Chamber. The ceiling is of white and gilt panels. A painted statue of James I adorns the marble fireplace, standing lifesize but looking even larger and wonderfully pompous. The Long Gallery runs the length of the south front, its ceiling covered in gold leaf. Two great fireplaces face out across the room to gardens. These and the Long Gallery's sumptuous panels leave little room for pictures. A charming alcove, the North Gallery, looks down on the Marble Hall.

Beyond is the Winter Dining Room, fashioned from two rooms in the 19th century with a majestic Renaissance chimneypiece. On the walls are portraits of James I and Charles I by Mytens. The library completes the circuit. This is a dark room heavy with a marble fireplace. This frames an unusual mosaic portrait of the builder of the house, the 1st Earl of Salisbury, said to be a perfect likeness. The red leather furniture has been restored using dyed Nigerian goatskin.

The way out is through the Armoury, fashioned from what was once an open loggia. Polished breastplates and halberds are reflected in the shining marble floor. At one end, somewhat incongruous, is a Dutch organ supplied to the house as early as 1609. It should be playing a galliard as we depart.

HATFIELD: OLD PALACE *

E of Hatfield
Tudor royal palace, home of the young
Elizabeth (P)

There are two Hatfields, adjacent but wholly
different in history and character. The old
palace was built by the Bishop of Ely in about
1485 and seized by the Crown on the Dissolution. It was used by Henry VIII to warehouse his children well away from the danger
of court. Here the young Mary was said to
have waved to him on a visit, after he had
divorced her mother, Catherine of Aragon.
Henry cruelly turned his head away. Edward
and Elizabeth were also kept here for much of
their young lives, Elizabeth falling in love with
poor Seymour.

It was at Hatfield that Elizabeth endured
virtual imprisonment during Mary's short
reign. She enjoyed acting and singing, and
even entertained her sister when the latter
made a brief visit. It was in the park at Hatfield
that she was told that she was queen, a scene
repeated so often in films as to be beyond
authentication. 'It is the Lord's doing,' she
said, 'and it is marvellous in our eyes.' Her first
council took place in 1558 in the Great Hall of
the palace. It was here that she summoned
her closest counsellor, William Cecil, Lord
Burghley.

Elizabeth did not favour Hatfield as a palace,
perhaps for its past associations with her unhappy youth. Her successor, James I, swapped
it for the grander Theobalds, Hertfordshire
home of Burghley's son, the 1st Earl of Salisbury. Salisbury demolished most of the old
Hatfield palace when he built his own mansion
next door, but he retained the hall range as
stables.

This range now stands darkly magnificent
in the lee of the big house, gazing across at it
like a spinster aunt. It is one of the most
extravagant brick buildings to survive from the
Middle Ages. The expanse of 15th-century
brickwork, laid in English bond, must have
seemed sensationally rich when built. The
windows are set high, like a clerestory, and run

the length of the façade. The stub ends of the
demolished side wings are now gabled chambers. The central porches on both fronts carry
towers.

Inside, the hall roof now runs clear along the
entire building. It is arched and with two tiers
of wind braces. The Tudors removed the partitions from the kitchen side of the entrance to
form one massive space for horses. It is a now a
splendid venue for neo-Elizabethan banquets.
The old palace courtyard is a knot garden,
laid out with Tudor plants by Lady Salisbury
in 1984.

KNEBWORTH HOUSE ****

1m W of Knebworth
Lytton mansion with Crace interiors and
Bulwer-Lytton shrine (P)

Knebworth is a Victorian fantasy house,
creation of the eccentric novelist and statesman, Edward Bulwer-Lytton, 1st Lord Lytton.
He inherited the house in 1843 shortly after the
break-up of his disastrous marriage to an Irish
girl, Rosina Wheeler. The unhappy liaison had
led Lytton's mother to cut off his income and
force him into a voluminous writing career
and then into public life. After their separation, Lytton and Rosina fought for forty years.
He tried to incarcerate her in an asylum after
she disrupted a political meeting at which he
was speaking. She was released by public demand and wrote fierce novels and pamphlets
attacking the subjugation of women. Ostra-
cized by the family, Rosina became an icon of
the suffragette movement.

Lyttons have lived at Knebworth since the
15th century, passing so often through the
female line as to exhaust even the English
talent for deed polls and triple-barrelling.
Successive alterations to the house tended to
be made by strong-minded women, including
Bulwer-Lytton's domineering mother. Henry
Lytton Cobbold is the latest owner struggling
to keep the show on the road.

The house today is a memorial to Edward
Bulwer-Lytton, 1st Baron Lytton. It was originally a Tudor courtyard mansion, much

bashed throughout history. It became successively Jacobean, castellated Georgian and gothicized Victorian. It now looks like an oriental palace, with turrets, onion cupolas and protective griffons on pillars, a sort of Home Counties Brighton Pavilion. The building material is variously redbrick, pink wash, stone and render. Parts of the façades are well restored, parts creeper-clad and shabbily genteel, enhancing the picturesque effect.

The interior is in a rich variety of styles. It is mostly the work of the Victorian decorator, J. G. Crace, and Sir Edwin Lutyens, a Lytton relation. The entrance hall is by Lutyens, another of his whimsical variations on a classical theme. The adjacent banqueting hall has Palladian panelling attributed to Inigo Jones's pupil, John Webb. The raucous minstrels' gallery and ceiling are also Jacobean, but could hardly have less in common with Webb's classical severity. Lytton's friend, Charles Dickens, performed amateur theatricals in this room and Churchill painted it in the 1930s.

The downstairs dining parlour and library are relatively staid. The former is Jacobean in character, with 17th-century red-and-silver embroidered chairs and portraits of Lyttons, both Parliamentarian and Royalist. The library is almost demure, crowded with editions of Bulwer-Lytton's seventy published works and a treasured miniature of Mary Queen of Scots. Over Lutyens' fireplace is an intense study of Lytton by G. F. Watts.

Upstairs matters are more riotous. The staircase is heavy with Nubian slaves and suits of armour. Everywhere are pictures of Lyttons. On the landing is Daniel Maclise's 1850 study of the author at his most romantic. Next to it is a sketch of the unhappy Rosina, who has now been reinstated as a celebrated figure in the family story.

Crace's two masterpieces at Knebworth are Bulwer-Lytton's study and the state drawing room. The study is furnished as the writer left it, richly panelled although not as rich as in his day. His long pipe rests on the chair. He

Knebworth's Gothic romanticism

described the pipe as 'that great soother and pleasant comforter . . . blue devils fly before its honest breath'. Here too is the crystal ball into which he would gaze for hours in search of inspiration. The oval ante-room and state drawing room are remarkable interiors, the embodiment of Victorian Gothic romanticism. The theme of the ceiling, chimneypiece and stained glass is of the Lytton descent from the Tudors, with Henry VII in pride of place. A Maclise painting depicts Edward IV visiting Caxton's printing press, an iconic Pre-Raphaelite moment.

Knebworth has admirable bedrooms on show. Most magnificent is the Queen Elizabeth Room, supposedly slept in by the queen. The decoration is heavily Jacobean, with caryatids supporting the overmantel. On the wall is a curious picture of a nun, a monk and a baby. A painting of Diana the Huntress has been considered as possibly of the young Elizabeth.

Edward's son, Robert, rose to become Viceroy of India and 1st Earl of Lytton in the 1870s. An Indian exhibition is in the squash court. Giant rock concerts grace the grounds.

LETCHWORTH:
296 NORTON WAY SOUTH *

Garden City Heritage Museum
Shrine to the first suburban 'garden city' (M)

Letchworth Garden City was intended as a Utopian heaven. The vision was that of the planner Ebenezer Howard in his book, *Tomorrow: the Peaceful Path to Real Reform*, published in 1898. The community was a suburban idyll of health and efficiency, co-education and a 'creative' curriculum. Cottagey houses and summer schools would stimulate a world of self-help, book-binding and sandal-making. A non-alcoholic pub, the Skittles Inn, served Cydrax and Bovril and was to be used for adult education. It would also act as a 'meeting place for striking workers'. Residents did not vote to admit a real pub until 1958.

While there was nothing new in garden suburbs or model communities – from Bedford Park to Port Sunlight – the idealism of

Letchworth, founded in 1903, captured the enthusiasm of new socialist planners. It seemed a fit response to the overcrowding, smoke and disease of 19th-century inner cities and was soon imitated across the Home Counties and in France, Germany, Russia and Japan. That idealism is now dissipated in a sprawl of commercial low-density suburbs, costly in infrastructure and hard to weld into working communities.

Cut out the idealism and the early exemplars have undoubted charm. Letchworth is proud of its pioneering past. No. 296 South Norton Way is the house where the architects, Barry Parker and Raymond Unwin, first put Howard's ideals into practice. The neighbourhood has the feel of a modest American suburb. The original offices were in a tiny thatched cottage set in a generous garden. After Raymond Unwin moved to Hampstead Garden Suburb, Barry Parker stayed behind and in 1937 built a small wing onto the office as a house for his family. They are linked by a small passage. A museum building has been added on the other side. Two original rooms survive in the Arts and Crafts style of the day.

At the far end is Parker's office, with a waxwork of Parker on the telephone at his desk, every inch the Edwardian architect. The room is beautifully furnished, with stained glass quarries in the windows, Arts and Crafts chairs, chests, bookcases and a copper fireplace. The family's old drawing room has been less successfully recreated as an Ebenezer Howard exhibition. The old man sits at his desk doodling on blotting paper, surrounded by architect's drawings. The garden outside was designed on the ideal of a 'tamed wildness', attributed to Gertrude Jekell.

MOOR PARK ***

2m SE of Rickmansworth
Thornhill and Leoni mansion with enriched
Hall and murals (P)

Somewhere north of Harrow the Rickmansworth housing estates retreat amid tumbling hills and hollows. Here in the early 18th century was an ideal spot for grand villas from which their owners could keep a weather eye on London. On the corner of a road, a sign points uphill across a golf course and into the woods.

To the schoolboy question, who made the money lost on the South Sea Bubble, the answer is Benjamin Styles, stock jobber and self-made man. But like many such men, he spent as fast as he made. He blew it all on a stately home. The Moor Park estate had already been owned by Cardinal Wolsey, then by the Earl of Bedford, the Duke of Monmouth and the Duchess of Buccleuch. Styles bought it in 1720 and proceeded to rebuild.

His first architect was, strangely, the painter, Sir James Thornhill, soon dismissed as too expensive and too old-fashioned. His style was for the Baroque and for historical and military decoration. By the 1720s, fashion was becoming lighter, with myths of Greece and Rome as mural themes. Thornhill is supposed to have been succeeded as architect at Moor Park by Giacomo Leoni, builder of Lyme Park (Cheshire).

The exterior is extraordinarily impressive. Partly because Moor Park lies in a hollow, the façades seems to shoot upwards like rockets from the ground, making it one of the most exciting houses close to London. The exterior is severely classical, yet still in the pre-Burlington Baroque tradition of Wren and Hawksmoor. The portico is stately, of four Corinthian columns rising to an enriched pediment. Pilasters on high bases decorate the walls, rusticated on the ground floor. The pediment cries out for statues, as at Lyme.

Inside, we can still see fragments of Thornhill the muralist. Moor Park vies with Queen's House, Greenwich (London, E) as a display of the heroic scene painting at the end of the Baroque era. But by now, the pomp and flattery of Greenwich and Kensington Palace (London, C) were on the wane in favour of the finesse of William Kent and Giovanni Pellegrini, Thornhill's rival at

Baroque climactic at Moor Park

St Paul's Cathedral. In 1728, Thornhill suffered the humiliation of being dismissed, not just as architect but as muralist, to be replaced by Francisco Sleter and Jacopo Amigoni.

The front door gives directly onto the Great Hall, probably gutted by Styles on dismissing Thornhill. It is a giant cube rising the full height of the building, galleried, sculpted and painted throughout. The plasterwork was by Giovanni Bagutti and the Artari brothers. Huge trophies fill the wall panels. The murals here are by Amigoni, classical myths replacing Thornhill's histories. Female figures lie languidly over the door pediments. To one side is a concealed staircase with more murals, again on classical themes by Amigoni and Sleter. From the upstairs gallery the *trompe-l'œil* of the ceiling is more apparent, beneath which are grisailles of gods and plaster effigies of classical dignitaries.

Beyond the Great Hall is the saloon. This voluptuous room celebrates the god Apollo in dark greens and blues. The god himself drives his chariot across the ceiling while the seasons adorn the walls. The artist is believed to have been Verrio, dating from the pre-Thornhill house. Along one side of the building runs the dining room, once a ballroom. A later owner had the ceiling panels painted by G. B. Cipriani.

The subsequent history of Moor Park was remarkable, even for a desirable villa near London. Styles blew his fortune and was followed as owner by Admiral Lord Anson, by an army provisioner, by a rich MP, by the Grosvenors, Dukes of Westminster, and finally by Lord Leverhulme. He formed Moor Park Golf Club in 1923; it is now owned by the local council. Moor Park was headquarters of the Parachute Regiment in the Second World War and it was from here that the unhappy Battle of Arnhem was planned (but *see* Stoke Rochford/Lincs). This is commemorated by an exhibition on the first floor.

Moor Park is a major London monument and should be better known. Its entrance front is spoilt by tarmac, car parking and adjacent tennis courts. It may be a golf club, but surely golfers have taste.

SHAW'S CORNER **

Ayot St Lawrence, 3m W of Welwyn
Shaw's house, restored as shrine (NT)

'The villagers all thought he was a rum one, a very rum one.' George Bernard Shaw was forty-eight when he and his wife, Charlotte, went house hunting in the Hertfordshire countryside. They sought a place of peace and quiet, yet not too far from the bright lights. When they first saw the New Rectory in Ayot St Lawrence, they both disliked it – and therefore decided to buy it. Hating it suited Shaw's passion for work and his wife's passion for travel. Here they were happy in their celibate life together, with a staff of six and a distant relationship with the village.

Shaw would work ceaselessly in his garden retreat, dress formally for dinner and afterwards play the piano for his wife as she lay upstairs in her room. They lived here for four decades, until Charlotte died in 1943, and Shaw continued a further seven years until his own death. Shortly beforehand and aware of its likely fame, he wondered if the National Trust might be interested. He would not impose any conditions, but did not want it to be a dead museum. That is what it is. His bequest to the British Museum to reform English spelling met the same fate.

The house had been built in 1902 as a rectory but was too large for the local parson. It is an Edwardian villa set in a spacious garden and filled entirely with the belongings of the great man. The door knocker was donated by a friend with the inscription 'Man and Superman'. Inside the door is Shaw's collection of hats, including a tin miner's helmet in which he chopped wood. The decor is late Arts and Crafts, moving to inter-war chintz. The study was Shaw's room, where he could sit either in the company of his friends or at least with pictures of them. The latter include Webb, Yeats, Barrie, Wells, the boxer Gene Tunney and many versions of Shaw himself.

'Mr Shaw is not at home'

The drawing room was Charlotte's room, but there is no escape even here. There is a bust of Shaw by Rodin and his Oscar for Best Screenplay (for *Pygmalion*) in 1938. In the dining room Shaw would spend up to three hours munching his vegetarian meals, believing that digestion should begin in the mouth. He would listen to music on the wireless in the evening, regularly calling the BBC if he heard a wrong note. The bedroom upstairs is as he left it, with his clothes still in the cupboard and shoes spotlessly shined. The kitchen displays the window through which Shaw's fan mail was passed by the postman each day.

Shaw's exercise was chopping wood and walking in the garden. At the bottom of the lawn behind a clump of trees is the hut to which he retreated if unwelcome visitors were hovering, to avoid the housekeeper having to lie by saying that he was 'out'. The hut is on a swivel enabling it to be turned to get the best light. It is laid with his notebooks and typewriter.

WOODHALL PARK **

4m N of Hertford
Nabob's mansion with print room (P-R)

This is one of the sumptuous mansions built by Indian nabobs in the Home Counties, within easy reach of London. The nabob was Sir Thomas Rumbold of the East India Company. He had left for Bengal in 1777, telling Thomas Leverton, architect of Bedford Square, to build him a house and have it ready for his return.

We assume Rumbold was content. The magnificent house glows in cream-coloured brick on an eminence north of Hertford. Rumbold did not stay there long and the house passed to the Smith family (now Abel-Smith) who own it to this day. It is a prep school, accessible by appointment.

Leverton's house is firmly in the post-Adam style of Henry Holland and James Wyatt. It contains three sensational rooms, the saloon, staircase hall and print room, all somehow surviving seventy years of school use. The painting of the Etruscan saloon, now the entrance hall, is outstanding, more spare in its motifs than Adam and reminiscent of Wyatt's saloon in the style at Heaton Hall (Lancs). Palm and anthemion leaves fall from the domed ceiling. The fireplace is of exquisite refinement, its medallions painted on canvas and stuck onto the painted marble.

The staircase rises to a domed skylight past richly stuccoed walls. These become more ornamental the higher up they go, until they burst into half-moon fans at the top. The swags and drops are worthy of Joseph Rose, Adam's stuccoist, in white on sky-blue. Grisailles depict the four seasons and medallions the four continents. The staircase itself rises in a continuous sweep, with delightful iron balusters. On the first floor there are four real doors and four fake ones.

The print room of 1782 has recently been restored and is the finest of this rare genre in England. Whereas at Strafield Saye (Hants), Rokeby Park (Durham) and Calke Abbey (Derbys), the prints are treated almost as wallpaper, here they are stuck onto the wall in a careful programme. Pictures of Rome and Florence take pride of place, with lesser pictures of landscape and famous people set symmetrically round them. They are divided by imitation pilasters and even have imitation hooks and wire. The house has a plan of the arrangement and a code to the print sources. It is a precious survival.

Huntingdonshire

Huntingdon is now part of the county of Cambridge but its separate identity is fiercely defended by its inhabitants and I therefore respect it. The county possesses one gem of early vernacular building, Hemingford Grey, and just within its borders is the grandest of Elizabethan mansions, Burghley outside Stamford. It also contains the early classical Thorpe Hall, and a charming composition by Vanbrugh at Kimbolton, with work by the Venetian muralist, Pellegrini. The Gothick movement transformed Elton into a decorative treasure house.

Burghley ****
Elton ***
Godmanchester:
  Island Hall *

Hemingford
  Grey **
Hinchingbrooke *
Kimbolton ***

Peterborough:
  Longthorpe Tower *
  Thorpe Hall **

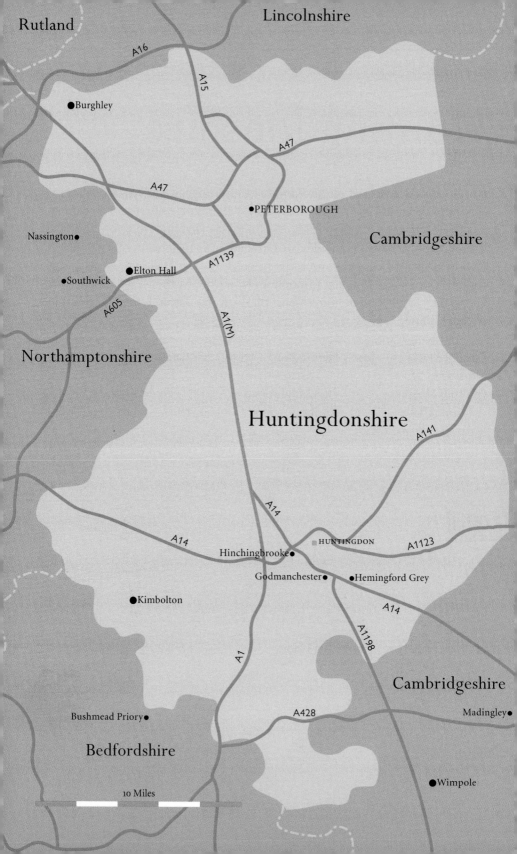

BURGHLEY HOUSE ★★★★

1m SE of Stamford
Elizabethan palace with Grand Tour collection
(P)

Burghley is the most swaggering of Elizabethan palaces. To Daniel Defoe it was 'more like a town than a house . . . the towers and pinnacles like so many distant parish churches'. Hardwick (Derbys) and Montacute (Somerset) are villas in comparison. Nothing else from the reign of Good Queen Bess equals it for splendour. Its obelisks and cupolas, billowing porches and fluttering pennants were much imitated by the Victorians. Most remarkable, the house remains much as built by that prince of courtiers, Elizabeth's faithful Burghley.

William Cecil, Lord Burghley, was the son of a Stamford man, a lawyer who rose under the Protector Somerset and survived to become the leading counsellor of Elizabeth's early years. He begat two great dynasties, the Marquessate of Exeter at Burghley and the Marquessate of Salisbury at Hatfield. The Salisburys remained politically active for centuries. The Exeters did not. The current Marquess lives abroad and his cousins, the Leathams, occupy part of the house which is owned by a preservation trust.

Burghley's exterior is a palace of silvery stone. It was designed by William Cecil himself and was built over the course of his career. The date on the great obelisk and clock-tower is 1585. Cecil died in 1598. The house is not a single block, like a Smythson house, with ornamental floor piled upon floor. The plan was medieval, of gatehouse into courtyard, with a porch on the far side giving access to a screens passage and Great Hall. But this plan was soon overwhelmed. The courtyard developed its surrounding suites of state rooms looking out over the park. Each of three façades is so splendid as to seem a palace in itself, reflecting the new symmetry of Elizabethan design. The roofs are peopled with cupolas, pavilions, belvederes and chimneys, tidied by Capability Brown who formalized Burghley's appearance after 1756.

The interiors are a parade of English taste from the Elizabethan period to the Grand Tour. Most were not decorated and furnished until a century after Burghley's death, by the Restoration 5th Earl of Exeter. The rooms are almost indigestibly rich, not unlike Blenheim (Oxon) in this respect. Visitors are regrettably not able to enter through the Renaissance porch in the courtyard. Nor do they enter, medieval style, through the Great Hall. They are admitted through the kitchen, like estate tenants begging a loan. Burghley's fusion of medieval and Renaissance, informality and dignity, is thus confused. The invisibility of the central courtyard and its clock-tower is also disappointing. I never complain at not being able to see a private house, but must point out this deficiency of a visit to Burghley, which would otherwise merit the highest ranking among European palaces.

The Tudor kitchens are sensational, with a vault carrying the smoke up to the louvres. A prominent diagonal wall is adorned with the skulls of baby turtles. Outside, the Roman Staircase rises to the principal reception floor. To be seen are seventeen rooms filled with the collection amassed over four Grand Tours by the 5th Earl and his wife, Lady Anne Cavendish, in the 1680s and 1690s. The couple acquired over 300 paintings, as well as sculptures, tapestries and furniture. They commissioned murals from Antonio Verrio and Louis Laguerre. For sustained lavishness, these rooms are equalled in my experience only by those at Windsor Castle (Berks). Like Windsor, they are essentially a museum.

First comes the ante-chapel and chapel, adorned with works by Mattia Preti and Paolo Veronese. The latter was lifted, for a price, from a church on the island of Murano near Venice. The extraordinary marble fireplace was acquired, presumably on the same basis, from Lisbon. Star of the north front is the Bow Room or state dining room. Its walls are painted by Laguerre, a grand work of *trompe-l'œil* on the theme of Antony and Cleopatra and scenes of classical mythology. On the mantelpiece is a row of Chinese porcelain figures, a charmingly modest contrast. Beyond

are the Brown Drawing Room, with portraits by Gainsborough, and the Black-and-Yellow Bedroom with a limewood overmantel of the school of Grinling Gibbons.

The west front was refashioned by the 5th Earl from Burghley's old Long Gallery. The Marquetry Room contains exquisite Dutch walnut chests and floral panels, which inspired William Morris. Queen Elizabeth's Bedroom was prepared for the Queen, but her only visit to Burghley was prevented by a local outbreak of smallpox. The tapestries are Gobelins and the bed-hangings so sumptuous as to suggest Las Vegas. In the Pagoda Room are mother-of-pearl pagodas and two Gheeraerts paintings, of Burghley and his Queen.

Burghley: Elizabethan spectacular

So far, the rooms have reflected the taste of a Restoration Grand Tourist. Turning into the south front one encounters the official state rooms, known as the George Rooms. These were furnished by the 9th Earl in honour of the first of the Hanoverians, yet deliberately respectful of the style of his ancestor, the 5th Earl. Most are painted by Verrio. They contain a fireplace by Piranesi, furniture by Boulle, busts by Nollekens and Italian Old Masters by the dozen.

Climax of this range are the two chambers known as the Heaven and Hell Rooms. The

first is a huge work of architectural *trompe-l'œil* by Verrio. He invites us into a Roman temple to consort in person with the gods. The join of walls and ceiling disappears in the sky. The second room had its floor removed in the 1780s to become a flight of stairs, giving a new depth to the torments of Hell.

The circuit ends in the Tudor Great Hall, the heart of Burghley's original house, with a steep hammerbeam roof. It is now furnished with Victorian bookcases, making it seem more a drawing room than the audience chamber of a grandee. In its midst is a Huguenot wine cistern of solid silver, said to be the largest ever made. Chairs line the walls, with jutting feet that appear to need their toenails cut.

Burghley's grounds were laid out by Capability Brown and include an imaginative modern sculpture garden, discreetly placed.

ELTON HALL ***

Elton, 8m SW of Peterborough
Gothic Revival house with art collection (P)

Elton is the epitome of early Victorian Picturesque. It demonstrates the English tradition of extend, reface, restyle and alter, anything but pull down and start again. Home of the Proby family since the 17th century, it is the county's most vigorously promoted house.

The front entrance has, on its left, a 15th-century gatehouse, belonging to an earlier mansion which lay to the north. This has small medieval windows, although the battlements are later adornments. Beyond lies what was the old chapel, its undercroft used for that purpose after the chapel was later converted as a reception room. Ahead is the family wing, converted back and forth in style since the 17th century. Its mansard roof, dormers and tall windows look faintly French. The best front is to the garden, a mix of Gothick features that might come from a Horace Walpole sketchbook. These features, added by enthusiasts in the 18th and 19th centuries, include a tower, turret, stepped gable, octagonal bay and oriel windows.

The interior is a mirror of the exterior but crammed with antiquarian surprises. The Lower Octagon Room is a small art gallery, containing Henry O'Neil's *Eastward Ho!* and a lovely Alma-Tadema. The staircase hall might be that of a French town house, cleverly inserted by Henry Ashton in the 1850s. The severe portrait of the last Countess of Carysfort is by Millais. In the Yellow Drawing Room is another Millais, of his daughter in *The Minuet*, over the fireplace.

Elton is a house in which each room seems to adopt a new style, as if to challenge the eye. The Upper Octagon Room reasserts the Gothick, as a gallery of miniatures. The scale opens out again in the main drawing room, fashioned from the former chapel. The style here is sumptuous classical revival. Heavy plaster cornices and pilasters are crowded with gilded foliage and trophies. So rich are the walls that the unpainted ceiling roundels look naked. The furniture is French and the portraits mostly by Reynolds, including one of the courtesan, Kitty Fisher. The Victorians banished this picture to the housekeeper's room, she being presumably less shockable than other ladies of the house.

Outside the dining room hangs Constable's *Dedham Vale*, while the room itself is superbly decorated in scarlet. The walls are crammed with paintings in the 18th-century manner, with Dou's *The Flute Player*, and works by Hobbema and Poussin. The two libraries are the warmest and most inviting chambers, their contents including an annotated prayer book that belonged to Henry VIII.

GODMANCHESTER: ISLAND HALL *

Post Street
Georgian house, voluptuous interiors (P-R)

Some Georgian houses are decorated in various shades of white. Others know no such nonsense. Of the latter is Island Hall, owned by the Percy family since 1804 and vigorously redecorated by the present Vane Percys. The house is outwardly a redbrick mansion in the centre of Godmanchester, backing onto what is claimed to be the largest water meadow in England. The front and back façades are the same, with bold central pedimented bays in the Baroque style of Thomas Archer.

The oddest feature of the interior is the asymmetrical hall. An off-centre arch frames a grand staircase and access to the garden. The doorways have good pediments and the walls are pale green. The panelled dining room has been boldly grained and gilded in a version of what Osbert Lancaster termed 'Curzon Street Baroque'.

The upstairs is even more bravely handled. Pillars are painted blue, anything that juts is gilded. The saloon is like a *fin de siècle* nightclub, in velvet with grained door and painted fireplace. I have seen too many boring Georgian interiors to find Island Hall anything but a delight. If a later generation dislikes it they can always repaint it.

HEMINGFORD GREY MANOR **

Norman house of *Green Knowe* (P)

During the Second World War, Lucy Boston asked the commander of the local US air base if his pilots might like to come to tea and listen to classical music on her old gramophone. The response was at first hesitant, but the invitations soon became popular. Eventually, Boston had to import old car seats for the crowds of young men eager to escape the tedium and stress of the bomber base. At the end of the war, the men inevitably returned home and Boston was left with a sad and empty room. She left it as it was. The old trumpet gramophone is still there. The patchwork wartime furnishings sit comfortably with the battered plaster of the walls.

Nor is that the only memory to haunt this magical house. Boston told the story of growing up in the house in her *Green Knowe* books. This has given it cult status among thousands of children, eager to visit the scenes imagined in the various rooms. Boston filled the house with her patchwork and also laid out its English garden. Her family maintain it, in part as a shrine to her memory. The house is very much occupied. It claims to be the oldest continuously inhabited house in England.

The manor sits on the banks of the River Ouse, a tall gabled building of two storeys. The structure is clearly Norman in part, with a Tudor lean-to on one side. Whether it was itself a hall or was the solar wing to a vanished hall is unclear. Pevsner suggests a two-storey hall house with an upstairs door leading to an adjacent church.

Following a fire in the 18th century, bits of the house were moved, patched, altered and inserted so often as to make an accurate 'reading' near impossible. No matter. Downstairs in the dining room is a fireplace and deep window splays of the Norman period. Upstairs, a Tudor or later bedroom is attached to the outside of the old house, with a Gothic window buried in the inside wall. Another bedroom has restored Norman windows.

Most evocative is the upstairs music room where the gramophone sessions took place. To one side is a Norman fireplace, again of uncertain origin, facing a large Tudor chimney flue. Overhead beams leap past round-arched windows. Ladders clamber to the attic (of *Green Knowe* fame), where there is a children's wonderland of rocking horse, toys, quilts and birdcages.

From upstairs we may look down on Boston's garden, full of secret places and paths to the river. The garden is rich in English roses and topiary, the latter including chess pieces set on black-and-white squares.

HINCHINGBROOKE *

1m W of Huntingdon

Ghost of Jacobean mansion (P-R)

This is the house in which Sir Oliver Cromwell, uncle of the Lord Protector, entertained James I in 1603 on his glittering progress south from Scotland to take up the crown. The king declared that Cromwell 'treated me better than any since Edinburgh'. That must have been some compensation since the visit bankrupted Cromwell. He had to sell his house in 1627 to the Montagus, later Earls of Sandwich, and retire to his other house at Ramsey Abbey. A passionate Royalist, he later raged against his Revolutionary nephew, who persecuted him in return.

The old house looks promising from the Huntingdon road. Turrets and gables in rich redbrick rise beyond an old wall on a mound. The Tudor gatehouse, moved from Ramsey, is ornamented with two wild men holding clubs. Beyond is a glimpse of 16th-century oriels, battlements and outbuildings. This appears to be a substantial Tudor and Jacobean house with its service quarters and grounds intact.

The chief pleasure is the exterior. The main front has not one but two bay windows to its Great Hall, richly decorated with Cromwell heraldry. Round the sides, every period seems to have its say, mostly 16th century, sometimes brick, sometime clunch stone, sometimes ashlar. The chief feature of the south front is a magnificent Jacobean bow window of 1602, perhaps built for James I and apparently moved here from the east front.

The house was built round the cloistered courtyard of a former convent. It was gutted by fire in 1830 and rebuilt by Edward Blore, one of the least inspiring mid-19th-century architects. (His front to Buckingham Palace was so dull it was covered by the present

Edwardian one.) The interiors are almost all by Blore. The house is now a school, but antiques fairs are held most weekends, offering visitors the run of the place. The library is exuberantly 'Elizabethan'.

A range of kitchens, laundry and brewery survives at the back. These are crowned with a remarkable group of gables and dormer windows behind brick battlements.

KIMBOLTON CASTLE ***

Kimbolton, 7m NW of St Neots
Stuart mansion altered by Vanbrugh,
decorated by Pellegrini (P-R)

An avenue of Wellingtonias trumpets the old drive from the main road to a distant portico. This is of just two columns screening an empty lobby. Above are battlements. Beneath spreads an apron of steps. This Baroque composition was the 'castle' of the Earls then Dukes of Manchester, rebuilt after the old house partly collapsed in 1707. The architect was Vanbrugh although the portico was by an Italian, Galilei. The Duke of Manchester sold the house in 1960 and it is now a school.

Vanbrugh's four façades are deceptive since they conceal a most exciting Tudor and Stuart courtyard within, giving access to the formal entrance to the old Great Hall. This courtyard received classical façades in the 1690s, but the Tudor house could not handle the symmetry and everything in the courtyard is endearingly askew. One side of the court has Tudor brick-work with stone mullions. The hall exterior has pilasters and scrolls above the windows. Its magnificent Baroque doorway adds a dash of Hampton Court. Oddest of all are the drain-pipes, which rise in the form of palm trees to end in acanthus leaves at the top. There is a thesis to be done on the palm in English design; they are also found on the stairs at Charlton House (London, E), the state bed at Kedleston (Derbys) and the alcove at Spencer House (London, C).

The cascading coronets of Kimbolton

The school deserves credit for displaying as much as possible of the interior. In the base-ment, Tudor corridors and Gothic windows offer echoes of the old castle. The chapel has a Vanbrugh balcony with fine murals of saints. They are by Giovanni Pellegrini, the first Venetian artist to visit England in the 18th century, in the retinue of the Earl of Man-chester. The White Hall is the former Great Hall, as transformed in the 1690s. It has pilasters and coving, but still awaits a painted ceiling. Can the benefactor not oblige?

The dining room and drawing rooms are used by the school, but retain fine pictures and wallpapers. The saloon is among Van-brugh's most sumptuous interiors, filled with gilded pillars and pilasters and hung with Lelys on dark red backgrounds. Next door is the handsome Queen's Room, where Catherine of Aragon came to die after her divorce from Henry VIII, vainly protesting her devotion and loyalty.

Kimbolton's masterpiece is Vanbrugh's staircase, squeezed into a passage in a corner of the old house and full of Baroque incident. The steps rise easily through a screen of giant fronds, and then turn back on themselves, like the hidden stair at Chatsworth (Derbys). Pellegrini covered the walls and ceilings with narrative scenes, mostly in praise of the Tri-umph of Caesar and William III, his worthy successor. One scene depicts cherubs casting aside a baron's coronet and raising up that of an earl in celebration of Manchester's elevation.

Pelligrini saved his best work for the upper landing. Here three musicians play a fanfare while a fourth leans over a *trompe-l'œil* balcony. The artist clearly loved animals.

PETERBOROUGH:
LONGTHORPE TOWER *

Longthorpe, 2m W of Peterborough
Domestic wall-paintings inside 13th-century tower (EH)

The tower is an oddity, like a pele tower in the Border country. It appears to have been added to a 13th-century hall, belonging to a steward of Peterborough Abbey who may have felt in need of some protection from the tenantry. The property later passed to the Fitzwilliams of Wentworth Woodhouse (Yorkshire, S), who gave the tower to the nation in 1947. The attached house has been changed beyond recognition. The tower now has two storeys accessible, its roof and lookout having been closed by health-and-safety.

The attraction of the tower is its wall-paintings on the walls and vaults of the first floor chamber. They are unique in England among domestic murals of this date. They were discovered in the 1940s and depict a mix of themes, part biblical, part moralistic, part domestic. A comprehensive guide is supplied inside by the mural expert, Clive Rouse, who has a remarkable ability to discern a narrative from a few twists and outlines.

Rouse thus gives us a Wheel of the Senses, a 'Three Living and Three Dead' and a collection of birds. As he says, 'We are looking at only a ghost of the original, which must have been of great richness.' The upper room is of little interest, and the tower has no remaining appeal since the view has been denied us on the idiotic grounds that the tiny staircase is suddenly dangerous.

PETERBOROUGH: THORPE HALL **

Longthorpe, 2m W of Peterborough
Early classicism with rich plasterwork (P-R)

Why should not a Sue Ryder home co-exist with a rare Commonwealth mansion? The answer can only be that the needs of the sick and elderly conflict with the splendour of great architecture. At least the Ryder homes have rescued the house, and it is occupied by people who clearly are happy to live there.

The mansion was built in 1653 by Peter Mills, a prominent follower of Inigo Jones, for Cromwell's Chief Justice, Oliver St John. It passed to the Bernard family and then became a school for sons of gentry, including those of the Dukes of Devonshire. It was in private occupation until 1937. Thorpe's fate was uncertain, indeed desperate, until in 1984 the Ryder Homes appeared on the scene. Visitors are welcome by appointment.

The exterior is typical of the earliest English classical houses, much copied by late-Victorians such as Norman Shaw (at Bryanston, Dorset). It has a steep pitched roof and spreading eaves with prominent dormers. The windows are generous and pedimented, identical front and back. The house could hardly be further in style from the conventional post-Elizabethan mansions of a few years earlier. The Venetian windows in the east façade are believed to date from the 19th century. The drive and gardens are still graced with their ornamental walls, urns and niches.

The interiors are not easy to appreciate but they display the refined 'Artisan Mannerism' of the mid-17th century more completely than in any other English house of the period. In the Great Hall, two giant putti flank the fireplace. Original plaster ceilings survive in most of the reception rooms. Upstairs in the former library, now a chapel, the ceiling seems to have taken root and flowered in abundance. The one outrage is the loss of the great panelled drawing-room to Leeds Castle (Kent). Surely this should one day return. The staircase has openwork foliage panels typical of the 17th century. Everything at Thorpe is bold and extrovert. Here one may see the beginning of a style that was to serve England well for almost 300 years.

Kent

Kent is the heel of England. It is the closest point to the continent of Europe and has long been the first line of defence against it. Whether or not for this reason, it has one of the most unsightly coastlines in the country. Yet it has three admirable physical features: the North Downs, the High Weald and the former inland sea north of Romney. History and topography have thus given Kent the most diverse gallery of historic houses in England. Remains of its Roman and medieval architecture are substantial. Its 16th- and 17th-century houses are beyond compare. The Georgians are well represented. And if later ages were of relative decline that was merciful. Much was saved.

As the chief point of entry to England from France, Kent saw a burst of Norman building after the Conquest. The castles at Dover, Rochester and Tonbridge are matched by houses at Maison Dieu, Canterbury and Old Soar. These are overshadowed by the great palace at Penshurst, its hall one of the most impressive in the land.

The Tudor and Elizabethan ages are nowhere better displayed than at Knole, joined by grand Hever and intimate Ightham. The Jacobean age created the colossus of Cobham and the eccentric delights of Godinton. Restoration House in Rochester is an immaculately restored 17th-century town mansion.

Early 18th-century Baroque is represented by Finchcocks and Queen Anne at Lullingstone. The later Georgians left Samuel Wyatt's Belmont. The Picturesque movement descended with delight on Leeds Castle, Scotney and Chiddingstone.

Nor is Kent short on celebrity shrines. Ellen Terry settled at Smallhythe and Churchill at Chartwell. Philip Sassoon brought the story full circle by recreating a Roman imperial villa at Port Lympne. Kent also hosts the smallest house in this book, the poignant hoppers' hut at Cobtree.

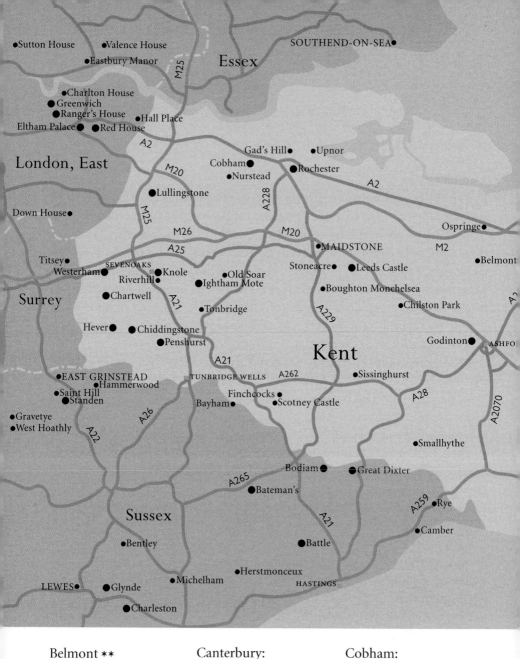

Sutton House • Valence House •
• Eastbury Manor
SOUTHEND-ON-SEA•
Essex
M25

• Charlton House
● Greenwich
● Ranger's House
• Hall Place
Eltham Palace ● ● Red House

A2

Gad's Hill • • Upnor
Cobham• Rochester
London, East
M20
• Nurstead
A2
• Lullingstone
A228
Down House•
M25
M26
M20
Ospringe•
A25
MAIDSTONE
M2
Titsey•
SEVENOAKS
Stoneacre• Leeds Castle
• Belmont
Westerham• Knole • Old Soar
Surrey
Riverhill• Ightham Mote
Boughton Monchelsea
• Chartwell
A21
Chilston Park
Hever• • Chiddingstone
Tonbridge
A229
Godinton•
ASHFO
• Penshurst
Kent
A21
EAST GRINSTEAD
TUNBRIDGE WELLS
A262
Sissinghurst
• Hammerwood
Finchcocks •
A28
• Saint Hill
Bayham• Scotney Castle
• Standen
A26
• Gravetye
• West Hoathly
A22
Smallythe
Bodiam ● ● Great Dixter
Sussex
A265
Bateman's
A259
Rye
• Bentley
Battle
• Camber
A21
• Herstmonceux
LEWES•
• Michelham
HASTINGS
Glynde
● Charleston

Belmont **   Canterbury: Cobham:
Boughton   Eastbridge   New College *
    Monchelsea **   Hospital *   Deal Castle *
Broadstairs: Chartwell ***   Dover:
    Bleak House **   Chiddingstone ***   Castle Keep **
    Dickens House   Chilston Park **   Roman Painted
        Museum *   Cobham Hall ***   House *

10 Miles

BELMONT HOUSE **

Throwley, 5m S of Faversham
Indian soldier's house with clocks (P)

In 1801, General George Harris, victor over Tippoo Sahib at Seringapatam, used his prize money of £150,000 to buy a country estate. Here, as so often, the fruits of empire were sunk in the acres of England. However great the imperial ambition, its culmination seems always to have been a plot of land back home.

Harris fastened on Belmont, completed in 1793 for a fellow soldier, Colonel John Montresor. The latter had been desperately unfortunate. He was wrongly accused of embezzling army funds and died in prison before his family won his exoneration. By then an uncharacteristically hasty War Office had already sold his property. It now holds the finest collection of clocks in private hands, amassed by the 5th Lord Harris, who died in 1984.

Montresor's architect was Samuel Wyatt, elegant and restrained member of the architectural dynasty. He supplied an understated late-Georgian building faced with pale yellow mathematical tiles, as if Harris were eager for a muted contrast to the noise and colour of the sub-continent. The main façade has semicircular pavilions with shallow domes at each end. Coade stone medallions below upper floor windows are the only decoration.

The interior is altogether grander. Wyatt built a wide corridor along the spine, with domestic rooms on one side and three reception rooms on the other, facing the park. In the centre is a dominant staircase rising the full height of the building.

The drawing room is Regency, with French Louis XV furniture and a picture of the 2nd Lord Harris pole-vaulting over a church gate, as dangerous an undertaking as anything done by his father in India. He went on to fight heroically at Waterloo, while his son became Governor of Madras and his grandson Governor of Bombay. The dining room has an Indian carpet, made for the Bombay Harris.

Wyatt's library is filled with beautifully crafted bookcases beneath a grisaille frieze of great authors. The corridor in pale blue-and-white has Soanian arches to the staircase hall. A silver and mother-of-pearl trolley and spade are displayed, as used by the 4th Lord Harris to cut the first sod of the Jamnagar railway in 1893. The place is alive with ticking and chiming, an eerie sensation when the place is empty, as if time alone survived the glory.

BOUGHTON MONCHELSEA PLACE **

5m S of Maidstone
Tudor house with Wealden view (P)

I arrived at Boughton one summer evening to see its new owners, the Kendricks, sitting peacefully on a bench gazing out over the Weald. Those who take old houses into their care must snatch their moments of calm. Their view was over a secret glade, grazed by deer, to a rolling landscape beyond. In this part of Kent, nature needs no help from Capability Brown.

The house was acquired by the Kendricks in 1997 as an oddity. It is essentially Tudor, built in the 1560s onto a medieval core. The Tudor house was of four ranges set round a central courtyard, but this was gothicized and reduced in size under the Regency. The pleasure of Boughton lies in its jumble of additions, subtractions, multiplications and divisions, not to mention relocations. The main Tudor façade has received later battlements and dormers. The porch appears to have arrived from somewhere else. The inner courtyard behind has been refashioned as the entrance to the fine walled garden.

The interior was stripped of its original furniture by a previous owner and valiant efforts are being made to replace it. The entrance hall has been gothicized, while the adjacent dining room retains its Tudor proportions and rich red walls. These two rooms would once have formed the Great Hall. Sixteenth-century quarries of stained glass have been reset in many of the windows, some of them casements replacing sashes that replaced casements.

The finest interior space is that of the staircase, dating from 1680 and generous for a house of this size. Its windows contain medieval glass from the parish church, reassembled as a kaleidoscope.

The rest of the house is a warren of chambers and corridors. We stumble on a classical doorcase, a hidden passage, a sudden view over the garden, an eerie attic. Some bedrooms have panelled walls and parquet floors, others are small and medieval. One has a closet for drying herbs. A large kitchen survives from the Tudor house.

BROADSTAIRS: BLEAK HOUSE **

Church Road
Dickens's holiday house with bric-à-brac (M)

Dickens summered frequently in Broadstairs with his young family in the 1840s. He rented Fort House, as 'Bleak House' was originally known, in 1850 and 1851 and testified often to his love of the place. He called it 'a good, bold house on the top of a cliff with the sea winds blowing through it and the gulls occasionally falling down the chimneys by mistake'.

From these windows, Dickens could watch the doings of the seaside, holidaymakers on the shore and the wrecks on Goodwin Sands. The house was then separated from the sea by a field of corn. Here Dickens wrote most of *David Copperfield* and some at least of *Bleak House*.

Today Broadstairs is the most engaging of the Kent resort towns, bustling round its scalloped bay. The town is virtually a Dickens theme park. Not a corner is without its Old Curiosity Shop, its Barnaby Rudge pub, its Betsey Trotwood café, its Peggotty's Tearoom. Of the two houses devoted to the memory of the great man, I prefer the touristy Bleak House to the pukka Dickens House.

The house was extended on the west side in 1901 and remains in part a private residence. It has a castellated roofline, in honour of its former name, and a charming garden. The interior is a pastiche of a Dickensian curiosity shop. Downstairs the drawing room has a display of shipwrecks and next door is an excellent re-creation of a Victorian dining room. Upstairs is Dickens's bedroom and the celebrated 'airy nest' of a study, with its raised dais and the desk from where he looked out to the sea. The contents of these rooms are mostly Dickensian junk. By the desk is a chair declared to be 'identical to the Empty Chair' in Luke Fildes's picture of Dickens's study after his death.

The house contains a bed in which Dickens 'would have' slept at The Bull in Rochester, and a mirror in which he 'would have seen himself'. On all sides are letters, coats, cheques, pen knives, magazines, playbills, telescopes, pots, spoons, boots, busts, pin cushions, candlesticks, lamps, prints, scraps of papers, stuffed eagles and anything that could remotely be associated with the great man.

The guidebook tries to be scrupulous in assessing the authenticity of much of this, but finds the task beyond it. Bleak House is the sort of place that would have inspired a dozen Dickens interiors. In the basement is a museum of smuggling, which seems most appropriate.

BROADSTAIRS: DICKENS HOUSE MUSEUM *

Victoria Parade
Town house 'home' of Betsey Trotwood (M)

The name is deceptive. This terraced house was lived in by a Mary Strong, who fed the young Charles Dickens on tea and cakes during his early visits to Broadstairs. She claimed the right to stop donkeys passing in front of her house, thus forming the basis of Betsey Trotwood, David Copperfield's aunt. The novel located Miss Trotwood's house in Dover but this was explained by Dickens as his wishing to avoid Miss Strong any embarrassment.

The house appears to be a combination of Tudor cottage and early 18th-century house with added Regency veranda. Downstairs is

Trotwood's parlour, Copperfield's refuge on running away from London. It is furnished on the basis of its description by Dickens's son, Charles, in the style of the period. It is delightfully evocative. The rest of the house forms a quiet and dignified museum. The contents include costumes, pictures of the town and Dickens's letters mentioning Broadstairs.

Among the memorabilia is a collection of prints of Dickens's novels by H. K. Browne or 'Phiz'.

CANTERBURY:
EASTBRIDGE HOSPITAL *

High Street
Medieval pilgrims' resting place (M)

Eastbridge Hospital of St Thomas the Martyr was one of many such institutions for pilgrims to the 12th-century shrine of Thomas à Becket. Its first master, Ralph, was said to be a nephew of Becket himself. Such 'hospitals' displayed a mix of religious, charitable and commercial motives. Their destruction during the Reformation stripped England of an extensive welfare establishment – albeit one swiftly replaced by the Tudors.

Eastbridge survived as an almshouse for ten poor people of the town, an admirable purpose it still contrives to serve. The entrance was once directly from the street, but the street has so risen that steps now lead down to the vestibule and the small chantry chapel. This is still in use.

The undercroft beyond contained sleeping quarters for pilgrims and the infirm, or those in need of shelter. Round Norman arches indicate a 12th-century date. The alcoves would have been where they slept.

Upstairs is the refectory, open to a magnificent roof. The north wall carries a remarkable 13th-century mural of Christ in Glory, a great Canterbury treasure. The long table is 18th century, the minstrels' gallery a 20th-century concoction of Tudor panels from elsewhere. The room is spoiled by being filled with exhibition boards. The bedesmen and women still live in buildings to the rear.

CHARTWELL ***

2m S of Westerham
Home and shrine to the great man (NT)

Most houses seem bigger than their owners. Chartwell seems smaller. Winston Churchill longed for a house commensurate with his fame. He hung on his study wall a painting of Blenheim Palace (Oxon), the house where he was born and which had been granted by a grateful nation to his ancestor, the Duke of Marlborough, at least until its building became too expensive. Chartwell was never the house of a political grandee, let alone of a victor in war. It is almost suburban. Churchill bought it at a low moment in his career as a retreat from London. Yet the world made it his Blenheim and his Blenheim it has remained.

Churchill fills every inch of Chartwell. This does not make life easy for its owner, the National Trust. The house had been bought by Churchill in 1922 as a dark, ivy-clad villa on a hillside overlooking the Weald. He collaborated with the young architect, Philip Tilden, to make it a cosy home, the rooms angled to benefit from the view. They were never designed for the present coach parties. The visitor centre, car park and catering buildings have been erected on the hillside at a distance from the house and visits rationed. This is discreetly handled.

The approach uphill shows what drew Churchill to the spot. Chartwell looks out over a lake and private valley, the Wealden hills rolling towards the horizon. This is very much rural Kent.

Visitors are led past a series of landscape 'incidents', such as the rock on which Churchill sketched, the fish pond where he fed the golden orfe, the brick wall he built against passing traffic and his wife, Clementine's, rose garden. A plaque lists the names of donors who bought Chartwell for the National Trust so Churchill could continue to live there in old age. His finances were always parlous and he relied heavily on friends.

The house that Tilden converted was undistinguished. Rooms were added where and when they were needed, not for aesthetic balance. Visitors pass through the front door with its much-photographed 18th-century surround, bought from an antique dealer. The drawing room and library are comfortably modest.

Apart from a Monet given him by his publisher, Churchill is the artist most represented on the walls. His Impressionist style sits well in Tilden's interiors. The corridors are pleasantly littered with memorabilia, including walking sticks, photographs of the famous, old cigars and a buddha.

The chief rooms upstairs are Churchill's study and Lady Churchill's bedroom, where she spent much of her time in her 'magnificent aerial bower' when her husband was in London during the war. The Study is the heart of the house, recalling a Tudor hall that may have been on the site. Tilden revealed old roof timbers, imported a Tudor doorway and opened up windows for the view over the valley.

This is essentially the room of Churchill the historian, especially after his retirement. Here he would work, either at a stand-up desk alone, or dictating to secretaries on call during the night. He slept in a four-poster bed from which he would continue to dictate in the morning. The room is filled with relics of the famous who came to pay him homage.

The remaining rooms, indeed much of Chartwell, are a shrine. There are exhibition rooms, uniform rooms and museum rooms. The most human corner of the house is probably the dining room, bathed in light from windows on three sides. Here Churchill showed films after dinner. A gramophone is in one corner. Furniture is by Heal's.

Visitors can also see the studio, a short walk downhill across the garden. Here Churchill painted, easel and palette as he left them. Indeed his art, full of the soft light of the Weald, can seem the most moving of the memorials in this otherwise rather ersatz place.

Churchill was lucky never to have had a Blenheim. Chartwell brought him peace. Blenheim brought Marlborough nothing but expense.

CHIDDINGSTONE CASTLE ★★★

Chiddingstone, 5m SW of Edenbridge
Gothic conversion of 17th-century house (P)

By the time of his death at Chiddingstone in 1977, the lonely and eccentric collector, Denys Bower, was reduced to escaping to the village for bacon sandwiches for his supper. Two decades earlier he had set his sights on the castle as a place to display the wonders he had gathered from across the globe. The house had suffered 20th-century abuse by educational and military occupation. It was in terrible shape, but when in 1955 Bower convinced a bank to lend him money to open it to the public, he hoped for profit. The money ran out but Bower lived on there alone. His study reputedly never saw a duster. On his death he bequeathed it, unendowed, to 'the nation'. The nation hardly noticed. Yet the house is well maintained by a local trust and Bower's collection is on display.

Chiddingstone was the 17th-century mansion of the Streatfeild family, who had owned the estate since Tudor times. In 1805 they decided to gothicize, castellate and generally romanticize the old house. The architect was William Atkinson, and the house was completed in 1838. The result appears to be two gatehouse façades, a Tudor façade, a Gothic tower and, on my visit, no obvious way in. The door is through a French window in the well tower next to the Tom Close courtyard. Visitors are made to seem not so much tradesmen as burglars. It is a good start.

Chiddingstone is as eccentric as its saviour. The exterior is surrounded by unkempt parkland, which should be allowed to go even wilder. The same applies inside. Bower's study, apparently left a complete tip, was mistakenly tidied up when he died. The room contains a portrait of Bower by Laura Knight. The reception rooms have been turned into galleries, depending on how Bower used them. The Buddhist room smells faintly of incense. The Jacobite room contains a selection

of eponymous glasses, to be smashed after Royalist toasts.

The Great Hall is a 19th-century creation, with heraldic windows, panelling and a gallery with a fierce turquoise ceiling. The print room contains a Lely of Nell Gwynne with her baby son, both depicted naked as Venus and Cupid. The drawing room beyond is classical in style, the walls hung with Stuart portraits. The remainder of the rooms contain Japanese and Egyptian art, of which Bower was particularly fond. The collection includes an exquisite set of Japanese lacquered ladies and a claimed head of Cleopatra. The charm of Chiddingstone is not knowing what to expect round the next corner.

CHILSTON PARK **

1½m S of Lenham
Antiques treasure trove with Victorian fantasy staircase (H)

Chilston is Kent's most atmospheric country house hotel. Its walls must be hung with a thousand pictures and its staircase is a set for an aristocratic murder. The grounds are still as described by John Evelyn in 1666, a 'sweetly watered place'. I am not so sure about sweetly; a monsoon accompanied my visit.

The house was a characteristic Kent manor of the Tudor period. It was remodelled in 1728 by John Hamilton, High Sheriff of Kent, and later became the seat of the Akers-Douglas family, Viscounts Chilston. The head of the family rejoiced in the Christian name of Aretas. On the death of the 3rd Viscount Chilston in 1982, the house was bought by the antiquarians, Martin and Judith Miller, who opened it as a hotel in which to display their large collection of pictures and antiques.

The exterior is that of a comfortable two-storey house of the early Georgian period, redbrick with pedimented entrance bay, hipped roofs and sprawling extensions. Traces of diapered brickwork survive in the walls. The

Gothic calm at Chiddingstone

old entrance hall is now the dining room, with a giant fireplace and scagliola columns. Behind was once an open courtyard, roofed by the Victorians for a new staircase that is now the chief feature of the interior. It is panelled with Renaissance fragments from a demolished local chapel.

Guests are escorted upstairs by the Kings of Judah and the Emblems of the Passion. Ferocious dragons guard the fireplace and stern family portraits gaze down from the walls. The bedrooms have such names as Camelot, Raj and Gothic.

The former parlours have been knocked into one long drawing room and billiard room. Every inch is covered in paintings, prints, drawings and cartoons. The room is lit by candelabra with real candles and huge log fires. It has the deep armchairs and faded cream walls of an Edwardian club.

COBHAM HALL ***

1m E of Cobham
Elizabethan mansion enhanced by Chambers, Wyatt and Repton (P-R)

Cobham Hall is one of the largest Elizabethan houses in England. The drive from the M2 interchange appears so grand that the motorway might have been built for its private convenience. Cedars and firs stand over the entrance, like bodyguards in conversation. Behind them the old building gradually reveals itself, with the familiar Elizabethan signature of redbrick gables and octagonal towers with cupolas.

The medieval Cobhams were the magnates of Kent. Embarrassed by a visit from Elizabeth I to their earlier, more modest establishment, the family began a programme of 'statelie augmentating' in the 1590s. This meant extending two long wings from the hall towards the park. This stopped abruptly when a younger Cobham conspired against James I and saw his estates sequestered. They were given to the Scottish Stuarts, Dukes of Lennox. One lady of the house so took the fancy of Charles II that he selected her as the model for

Britannia, replicated on coins and elsewhere. Paignton's Oldway House (Devon) was likewise residence of the 'Statue of Liberty'.

The house was sold in 1677 and passed to the Earls of Darnley at the turn of the 18th century. Their chief claim to fame was their sponsorship of cricket, the first recorded match, Cobham versus Addington, taking place on the local village green in 1776. The 8th Earl, with the family name of Bligh, took an English team to Australia in 1882 and brought back the small urn that contained the reputed 'ashes' of English cricket, the stumps having been burned after a previous defeat by Australia in England. The Ashes were duly lodged at Cobham, moving to their permanent home at Lord's in 1927.

In 1960 the family gave up the struggle to maintain the house and handed it over to the present girls' school. But they did not wholly abandon it. Family pictures were left on the walls and trusts left in place to manage buildings and park.

Cobham's U-shaped west front is composed of a 17th-century centre but still with the original Elizabethan wings. They are virtually houses in themselves. The north wing has a three-storey Renaissance frontispiece of 1594, probably the former entrance moved from the central range. The south wing to the knot garden, of fifteen bays, is a majestic façade, one of the grandest sweeps of Elizabethan brickwork anywhere. The corner towers rise four storeys.

The Duke of Lennox rebuilt the central range after the Restoration, designed by Peter Mills (see Thorpe Hall/Hunts). As work progressed, his wife wrote that familiar wail, 'tis the hardest thing in nature now to gitt workmen'. Mills's new hall is now the Gilt Hall, its heavy ceiling dated 1672 and dripping with gilded plaster. The walls and organ gallery were not finished until the 1770s, when Sir William Chambers added an attic to this wing.

The rest of the interior was heavily altered by James Wyatt in the late 18th century, his Gothick work sitting comfortably in these Tudor and Stuart surroundings. A delightful vestibule with Adamish plasterwork is now the head mistress's study. Most of the Tudor interiors have lost their furnishings and are dominated by the atmosphere of school, but they retain Darnley pictures on the walls and flocks of teenage girls represent, with an effort of the imagination, the Stuart beauties that once peopled the walls. At the end of one corridor is the Darnley state coach of 1715. Although fully restored it was declared not roadworthy for the coronation of Elizabeth II, a spineless decision.

Cobham also has its fireplaces. When the property was valued in the 1950s these were considered worth more than the house itself. They form an outstanding collection. The two in the picture gallery are by the Flemish craftsman, Giles de Witt, carved in the 1590s. The dining room has another de Witt fireplace. The ceiling of Queen Elizabeth's Room, which she never used, has her emblem in the elegant plasterwork.

Cobham's park was designed by Repton in the 1790s. By the 19th century it had become a celebrated excursion, by boat and train from London. The park is a miniature Stowe, with Ionic temple, grotto, aviary and mausoleum. A Dickens Chalet commemorates his many visits to the Darnleys from neighbouring Gad's Hill (below).

COBHAM: NEW COLLEGE *

Cobham
Medieval almshouses round quadrangle (P-R)

Most almshouses date from the 16th century. These are truly medieval. In the shadow of Cobham church, a member of the Cobham dynasty founded a chantry in 1362 to pray for his soul. After the Reformation and the suppression of chantries, the 10th Lord Cobham contrived to save the old buildings and reused them as a 'new college', for twenty poor men and women from local parishes. The fabric was modernized in 1598.

The new occupants were to be 'elected, relieved and maintained' by their local parsons, but also 'governed, visited, corrected and expelled' by the trustees. Thus did the Reformation welfare state, based on parish and manor, supplant that of monastery and church.

Despite the discipline, it is hard to imagine a pleasanter place to live out one's days. The college is formed of a simple ragstone and flint quadrangle. Above each door is the name of the sponsoring parish. A restored pump stands in the courtyard. Peace reigns. In the south range the old Great Hall survives, with two tall Gothic windows. It has its screens passage and a crown-post roof with wind-braces. Against the inside wall is a big 15th-century fireplace with signs of regular use. Charming 19th-century watercolours of the almshouses and their inmates decorate the wall.

Adjacent to the old buildings is a new range built in a deferential 20th-century style. The chantry kitchens survive to the south, albeit now in a ruined state.

DEAL CASTLE *
Victoria Road
Henrician firing platform on sea-front (EH)

The castle was the middle of the three intended by Henry VIII to protect The Downs anchorage inside the Goodwin Sands. It was a sophisticated structure, in effect a firing platform covering a panorama of coast. Never used in anger, it remains as built, although decorative crenellation was added in the 18th century. Even the shot furnace is retained, for heating cannon balls. The castle offers a fine vantage point for looking out to sea and is refreshingly uncluttered by development. Henry VIII would recognize the place – that is, if he ever visited it.

The castle is low lying so as not to offer an easy target to enemy ships at sea, its walls thick rather than high. The plan is of a circular keep with two concentric rings of lobes or bastions, designed so each can fire both out to sea and down into the moat.

The ground floor has been restored to portray the main living quarters of the garrison's soldiers, with bread ovens and fireplace. Up the Tudor stairs are the captain's quarters, refurbished in the 18th century. Some Tudor

panelling remains. The chapel was an innovation of a devout 20th-century captain, by then an honorary post.

DOVER: CASTLE KEEP **
Castle Hill Road
England's premier costal fortress (EH)

From the Norman Conquest to the Second World War, Dover was one of England's most crucial fortresses, standing guard over the Channel at its most vulnerable point. The profile of the Roman lighthouse, Saxon church and great keep are as symbolic of England as St Paul's Cathedral or the Tower of London. Yet the rebuilding of the town of Dover since the war devastated what bombing had left standing. The 'theming' of the castle by English Heritage has been no more kind.

A new fort was built at Dover by William the Conqueror immediately after the Battle of Hastings. The keep was built by Henry II, the cost almost equal to his annual income. By 1250, the extensive outer bailey was complete. The fortifications were later extended, most drastically in the Napoleonic era and again in the 20th century, when Dover organized the evacuation from Dunkirk and commanded the Channel defences. The castle was garrisoned until 1958.

The keep was the heart of the castle and the residence of the constable. When he moved out it became successively a prison, a barracks and a military warehouse. Two residential floors have been restored and constitute a surviving early Norman keep in something like its original form. On the first floor are the Great Hall and Great Chamber, replicated on the second floor by two more such chambers. The chief alteration since the 12th century was the insertion of fireplaces under Edward IV in the 15th century.

The survival of Norman arches and stairs, even garderobes inside the wall thicknesses, is remarkable. Two Norman chapels have been restored. Sadly, the presentation of all this is aimed exclusively at children. The two main storeys have been decorated as if in preparation for the arrival in 1539 of Henry VIII, considered the most marketable English king. Disembodied voices speak out of public address systems. Mock-medieval furniture is littered about the floors and garments spill out of trunks. Only the principal bedchamber in a wall of the second floor, cluttered with chests and fabrics, makes a passable attempt at medieval authenticity.

Round the keep is an extensive display of the military history of Dover, including most impressive tunnels and command posts dating from the Second World War.

DOVER: ROMAN PAINTED HOUSE *

New Street

Rare surviving Roman murals (M)

The Roman Painted House is a good test of aesthetic sensibility. It is the largest expanse of Roman painted plasterwork to survive in England. This was due to the later construction of part of a Roman fort on top of the house. The site, discovered in 1970, was intended for a multi-storey car park.

The Painted House now lies immaculate in its pit. Each feature is scrubbed and labelled. The paintings rise just a few feet, to the level of the later structure but still impressively coloured. The dado is green, speckled to imitate marble. Above is a series of panels separated by columns painted to convey depth and perspective. There are fragments of human figures, vines and other Bacchic motifs. This is more evocative of a Roman villa than the flat mosaics familiar elsewhere.

My reservation is the setting. The visitor looks down on the remains from a gallery that bears no relation to context. The gallery is lined with display boards and exhibitions of Roman Dover. Conservators are ideologically forbidden to reconstruct a Roman villa above the line of surviving remains, yet are not forbidden to surround it with their own clutter. These ruins now need 'excavating' from their own archaeology.

FINCHCOCKS **

6m W of Cranbrook

Baroque mansion rescued as music centre (P)

When I first visited Finchcocks it was magnificent but sad. The owners had just bought it from a ballet school but could ill afford the repairs. Changing rooms, hooks and mirrors were everywhere and a smell of school pervaded the place. The sheets on the beds were black, the hostess later explaining that this made the bedbugs less conspicuous. Above all I remember the shallowness of what seems from the outside a big house. It was just one room deep and we tried to see in how many leaps we could cross it.

Since its acquisition in 1971 by Richard and Katrina Burnett, Finchcocks has come to life as a home and centre of musical activity. The house was built in 1725 by a barrister, Edward Bathurst, a relative of the Bathursts of Cirencester. The house was to be of 'great expense and in a most stately manner', to cost the then astronomical sum of £30,000. The design has been attributed to Thomas Archer or even Vanbrugh but is more likely by a local builder using a pattern book.

What is extraordinary is the way a façade concealing a house of just twenty rooms soars upwards as if aspiring to Baroque grandeur. The central bays are thrust forward with a pediment crowning the lower two storeys and cheekily ignoring those above. A mutilated statue of Queen Anne fills the central niche, surrounded by excellently dressed brickwork. The wings project on curving walls, decorated with short pilasters. The rear elevation of the house is more conventionally Georgian.

The interior is of the 18th century untouched by the 19th. Until 1920, Finchcocks had no heating or plumbing, its lavatory an earth closet under the stairs. The hall has a fireplace that appears to be a Tudor acquisition.

The remaining reception rooms are filled with some seventy keyboard instruments. These are in working order and regularly played by visitors. Wooden floors and panelling offer an ideal acoustic. Finchcocks is a centre of the 'authentic instrument' movement. On the staircase landing is a tapestry of an 18th-century musical scene alongside a large collection of mementos.

GAD'S HILL **

Higham, 1½m NW of Rochester
House where Dickens lived and died (P-R)

If the city of Rochester was, according to Charles Dickens's biographer, the 'birthplace of his fancy', Gad's Hill was the house of his dreams. His father pointed it out to him on a walk as the goal of his endeavour. 'If you were to be very persevering and were to work very hard indeed, you may some day come to live in it.' The house reappeared as Scrooge's old school in *A Christmas Carol*. In 1856 the house came on the market and Dickens bought it for £1,770, shortly before the break-up of his marriage. It was the only house he ever owned, his 'little Kentish freehold'. He died there in 1870. On his death, the house was sold and its contents dispersed.

The building became a school, as it remains to this day. The exterior is unremarkable, a plain Georgian house of 1779 with pedimented porch and a Venetian window above. A cupola crowns the roof. The grounds have deteriorated and additions to the school are ugly. The old tunnel under the main road to Dickens's Wilderness is shut, the chalet where he worked having been moved to the Dickens Centre in Rochester.

To the right of the school entrance, the principal's study was Dickens's study. Books line the walls, including mock titles over the back of the door such as *Five Minutes in China* and *Hansard's Guide to Refreshing Sleep*. Over the mantelpiece is a print of the *Empty Chair*, Luke Fildes's painting commemorating Dickens's death. The dining room is where Dickens fell ill and died, on a sofa now at the Dickens Museum in London. The conservatory beyond was financed from the income of his last American tour.

The drawing room was extended to double its length by Dickens to enable him to practise

and perform his public readings, staple income of his later years. Like his summer house, this was lined with mirrors in which he could study his stance and appearance. He would emerge from a door beside the window and have special lighting on his face. A piano added to the effect. Dickens was never not performing.

The house is ardently supported by friends eager to make it more Dickensian. Not too much, I hope. There is a spirit to this house. The creepers and roses of the old garden cling like memories to the walls. A school filled with fantasies and fears, nervous relationships and childish dreads is a good memorial to the Dickens of *Nicholas Nickleby* and *Our Mutual Friend*. This is a museum of the Dickensian mind.

GODINTON PARK ****

2m NW of Ashford
Jacobean house built round medieval core (P)

'This house will be the death of me,' said the wife of Captain Nicholas Toke in the 1620s. It soon was. Captain Toke's house worked its way through five wives and was the death of all of them. The original 14th-century house was acquired by the Tokes – otherwise Touques, Tuke, Tooke and Tuck – in the late 15th century. Captain Toke completed the present house in 1628, filling it with the most exhilarating, indeed wayward, panelling and carving.

The house was eventually bought in 1919 by Mrs Bruce Ward, whose grandson, Alan Wyndham Green, was of a similar cut to Toke, at least in the matter of collecting. In 1995 he left it 'to the people of Ashford' with instructions that there were to be no roped-off rooms. This sadly involves that curse of country house visiting, the incessant chatter of the compulsory guided tour.

The house is not grand, despite the splendour of the park and gardens laid out by Sir Reginald Blomfield about 1902. The entrance is into the original main front of 1628, with elaborate Dutch gables. The south front is part

Jacobean, part Victorian and probably mostly both. Outside, everything seems sedate.

The interior of Godinton and especially its hall is a textbook of the Jacobean-cum-Victorian style. Anything comes and anything goes. It is near impossible to disentangle original from imported or reproduction work. The dining room had its roof raised in the 18th century and has a fireplace of Kentish Bethersden marble. The Great Hall retains the proportions of the 14th-century original, with a giant chestnut tie-beam. It is a gallery of carving. Round the fireplace is a 16th-century Flemish chimneypiece, introduced in the 1800s. Carved arcading lines the south side of the room, allowing light into the staircase behind.

Beyond the hall is a priest's room, possibly an old chapel and said to be the setting of Martineau's heart-rending painting in the Tate Gallery, *The Last Day in the Old Home*. Such emotive depictions of old England were a huge spur to the Victorian Jacobethan revival. Above the priest's room is a gallery overlooking the hall, possibly once the upper part of the chapel. It was remodelled in the 1630s and then again by Blomfield, with a fretwork screen to the hall below. The pictures here are all in needlework.

The gallery leads into Toke's astonishing Great Chamber. The pilasters are of two designs, tapering and arabesque. More extraordinary is the frieze. This is composed of panels depicting soldiers doing Dutch pike drill, as performed by Toke's soldiers in the Civil War and as still performed by the Honourable Artillery Company in the City of London. Above the frieze are finials silhouetted against the plaster, adding an oriental touch to the composition. The mantelpiece depicts Adam and Eve amid an array of field sports, including pig-sticking. The room contains Chippendale furniture and a travelling Dresden tea service, along with much Worcester and Chelsea. There is a fine Reynolds portrait of David Garrick.

Dutch musketry at Godinton

The staircase is a miniature of that at Knole. The heraldic newel posts are original to the 1630s, but with Victorian additions. Beasts, monsters and half-clothed natives from the Age of Discovery jostle for space. The stained glass is of Toke ancestors. Glorious carving in the library depicts four of the five continents, the fireplace flanked by palms. The White Drawing Room has a Jacobean revival ceiling by Blomfield, clearly not to be outgunned by the surrounding originals. On the walls are Kate Greenaway watercolours.

The old oak tree on the meadow facing the entrance split down the middle with a huge crack at 11 am on 3 September 1939, the moment when Chamberlain announced war with Germany. It died that evening.

GOODNESTONE PARK **

Goodnestone, 8m E of Canterbury
Grand Tour home with family pictures (P-R)

Norman land tenure in East Kent, unlike the rest of England, was based on partigeniture, as in France, as opposed to English primogeniture. The result is a paucity of extensive landholdings and thus of big, wealthy houses. A Grand Tour house with spacious park, in single family ownership for three centuries, is thus a rarity.

Goodnestone (pronounced Gunstone) was built by Brook Bridges in c1704 and later passed to the Plumptre and FitzWalter families. The 20th Baron FitzWalter died without heir in 1932 and the house subjected itself to the horrors of military requisition. A nephew revived the title (700 years old) in 1953, returned to the house and restored it. Given the hundreds of such houses lost in the 1950s and 1960s, every one saved is precious. Goodnestone sits content in its landscape as if the present Lord and Lady FitzWalter had been in residence for ever.

The house is not large. The 1704 building was of two storeys, nine bays wide. This was raised to three storeys probably by Robert Mylne in the 1780s. Then in the 1840s, a severe rear entrance was created, the windows surrounded with stone and the Bridges coat of arms inserted in the main pediment. The effect, when seen from the garden below, is stately and composed. Goodnestone has a fine view east, its parkland falling away between swathes of trees. This is complemented to the west by an amphitheatre of terraces, dominated by a stupendous cedar of Lebanon, a grande dame from the 17th century.

The interior is modest. The hall and staircase date from the Queen Anne house, the staircase handsome with paired balusters. Mylne would have been responsible for the pretty oval vestibule, with niches and painted walls in an Adam style. This is flanked by two reception rooms, the Green Dining Room and Blue Drawing room, each with gently bowed ends. A later Bridges was rare among Grand Tourists in being painted by both Mengs and Batoni. The two portraits still hang in the house.

HEVER CASTLE ****

2m SE of Edenbridge
Astor conversion of Boleyn house (P)

Did two less similar characters ever breathe Kent air than Anne Boleyn and William Waldorf Astor? Yet they had Hever in common. The Tudor queen spent years trying to get out of it, and the American tycoon spent years trying to get in. Both succeeded.

Hever is not so much a classic Tudor house as an American ideal of such a house, like Leeds Castle. It evokes the age of Henry James and Edith Wharton. After Astor announced in 1890 that America was 'no longer a fit place for a gentleman to live', he exported a hundred million dollars across the Atlantic to find somewhere that was. This included becoming British and buying Hever and Cliveden (Bucks). Hever passed to his second son, John Jacob, and is now owned and displayed by a private company.

The castle that Astor first saw in 1901 lay in a valley surrounded by a moat. It was first crenellated under licence in 1384 but its fame lies in its Tudor ownership by Sir Thomas

Bullen, an ambitious Tudor courtier. Bullen's two beautiful daughters, Mary and Anne, were both to catch the eye of the young Henry VIII, the first as mistress, the second as ill-fated wife. Anne was a strong-willed girl whose education at the French court frenchified her name as Boleyn. She at first refused the king's advances. But after she succumbed and failed to bear a son, she and her family were savagely treated. She and her brother were executed on trumped-up charges varying from treason to incest.

The house passed through many hands and was a virtual ruin by the time it came to Astor's attention. He had begun collecting when American Minister in Rome, acquiring an affection for all things European. At Hever, he set out to recreate the country seat of a Tudor magnate in the grounds of an Italian count. The architect was J. L. Pearson's son, Frank, and the undertaking was prodigious. Beginning in 1903 and working for just two years, he employed 800 labourers and craftsmen in an operation that rivalled Hearst's at San Simeon in California. Hever remains one of England's most prodigious works of architectural revival.

A 35-acre lake had to be excavated, roads and streams diverted, woods, avenues and loggias built. The old house was restored, repanelled and refurnished. In addition, since the house was too small for large numbers of guests, an entirely new 'Tudor Village' was built adjacent to the castle on the far side of the moat, with underground ducts, pipes and wiring needed for a modern 20th-century mansion. The effect of all this borders on the Disneyesque.

To enter Hever is to flop onto a large Tudor bed. The moat is crossed through the old defensive gatehouse into a courtyard. The gate reputedly has England's last working portcullis. The Great Hall created by Astor was previously the medieval kitchen. As throughout most of the house, the woodcarving was by Astor's master craftsman, W. S. Frith, true

Hever: drawing room marquetry

hero of Hever. Work on the plaster ceilings had to be entirely by hand, with the workmen forbidden to use rulers or set squares. Everything was measured by eye. The hall gallery was based on the screen in King's College, Cambridge. The painting of Henry VIII is after Holbein, as is the portrait of Mary Bullen, Anne's sister.

The panelling in the drawing room is Frith's masterpiece, each section inlaid with marquetry in a classical frame. This must have been of the finest 20th-century craftsmanship in England. The dining room, the original Great Hall, has rich linenfold and a huge Brussels tapestry. A door has one of Henry VIII's private locks, taken with him and fixed to every room for security. The cabinet-making of the bookcases in Frith's library is exquisite, the American sabicu wood so hard that it apparently sinks in water. It must have blunted a hundred chisels.

Upstairs, the house takes on more the character of a museum. Two rooms are dedicated to Boleyn memorabilia, including her inscribed Books of Hours. The staircase gallery is filled with Tudor portraits, including one of Anne's daughter, later Elizabeth I. The Rochford Room commemorates Anne's brother, George, who was executed on charges of incest. Beyond is the bedroom in which the monstrous Henry is said to have stayed when courting Anne. It contains a French Gothic four-poster of c1485, one of the finest of the period still extant.

From here Hever loses some of its flair. The second floor Long Gallery contains extensive waxwork displays of scenes from the life of Henry and Anne. The chandeliers are of solid silver, copied from originals at Hampton Court. Beyond are small bedrooms known as the Dog Kennels, designed by Astor daughters in the 1970s. They lead to an exhibition of Astor memorabilia and then to the old Council Chamber, where Bullens held court as local magistrates. The room contains a display of torture instruments.

The grounds at Hever are a visit in themselves and are immensely popular. They divide into the Italian Garden and maze adjacent to the castle, and the wilder surroundings of the lake and Sixteen-Acre Island. Everything was Astor's creation. The 4-acre Italian Garden is as much a work of architecture as horticulture. A 'Pompeiian Wall' is the setting for classical antiquities, with busts, vases and broken columns among the herbaceous borders.

Beyond is a loggia and piazza by the lake. From across the water and in the right light, the informal scatter of arches and colonnades shimmers like a scene from Poussin. The only solecisms at Hever are the commercial shops and cafés allowed to intrude on the slope below the car park. Astor would not have approved.

HIGHAM PARK *

3m SE of Canterbury
Restoration of Edwardian pile (P-R)

In 1995, Patricia Gibb and Amanda Harris-Deans 'amicably separated from their husbands' and pooled their money and energy in the restoration of Higham Park and garden. The task was Herculean and, given the ungainly modernity of the 20th-century house, reckless. Bless them both.

Higham's façade dates from 1904 and is strangely urban for the Kent countryside. Its high windows and corner pavilions are in the 'French Empire' style of Edwardian architecture and look as if the Champs Elysée had popped out of the Channel Tunnel and lost itself amid the apple blossom. A previous house on the site boasted visits from Mozart and Jane Austen. I am told there are eighty-seven rooms beneath its roof.

The façade and chief reception rooms were created for an American, Countess Margaret Zborowski (née Astor). Her racing-driver son, Louis, created the 'Chitty Chitty Bang Bang' cars and died in the 1924 Grand Prix at Monza. The house contains various mementos of this occupation.

The hall was comprehensively rebuilt by the next owner, a banker named Walter Whigham, in a style that might be called Twenties Totalitarian, with a nod towards Art Deco. It has scagliola columns and a marble floor. The stairs are 'Hollywood' spectacular and the front door apparently made of cast iron.

The other rooms are in process of restoration. On my visit they were in garish colours with modern reproduction paintings, as in a seaside hydro. The gardens are also being restored, their layout having been plotted from the air. The place deserves an award for effort.

IGHTHAM MOTE ****

4m S of Borough Green
Idyllic moated manor round courtyard (NT)

Ightham is a dream house. It appeared in its valley as if in a vision to a young American, Charles Robinson, on a cycling tour of Kent before the First World War. Many years later, in 1953 and in America, Robinson noticed in *Country Life* that the house was for sale. The past owners, the Colyer-Fergusson family, had sold it to a local consortium which had intended to conserve it but which had also given up the struggle.

Robinson dashed over and made an offer on the spot. Travelling home on the *Queen Mary*, he thought better of his rash decision and wrote withdrawing his offer. He forgot to post the letter and was duly informed that he was the owner. He returned, paid for the restoration and eventually left the house to the National Trust with 500 acres of farmland in 1985. His relatives still live in an adjacent cottage.

The approach to Ightham Mote down the hollow of Dinas Dene is supremely picturesque. The house emerges round a bend, floating serene on its moat as if in a Venetian lagoon. Gothic windows pierce ragstone walls. Tudor ranges are jettied over the water, once allowing guests to fish from the windows. The place is a symphony of water, stone, timbering and brick. Ightham is England at peace with nature.

The house within the moat is built round an internal courtyard. The semi-fortified gatehouse faces the Great Hall. The solar wing, chapel, crypt and other chambers are on the remaining sides. The earliest work is 14th century while the courtyard was complete by the early 16th.

The owner was Sir Richard Clement, a courtier to Henry VIII. Succeeding owners struggled to keep the place dry and habitable. Ightham was visited and admired by Burne-Jones, William Morris and Henry James. Gentle modernization took place in the 19th century under the hand of Richard Norman Shaw. More drastic work was undertaken by Robinson.

The Great Hall, under large arch braces, was once entered direct from the courtyard. The windows and fireplace are later insertions, as is Norman Shaw's screen to keep out draughts. The circuit of the house begins with the oldest part, the solars with adjacent chambers for servants. The Oriel Room was for the family, behind which are a series of small bedrooms known as the Boys' Rooms. Colyer-Fergusson grandsons offered the National Trust advice on recreating these spartan chambers, one of which includes an old rocking horse with marbles making a noise in its belly.

After the hall, pride of place goes to the chapel. The painted roof refers to the brief reign of Catherine of Aragon, with Tudor roses twined with Aragonese pomegranates. There is a smaller, earlier chapel upstairs, perhaps in use when the house was later described as 'vile and papistical'. The drawing room dates from the 1480s but has a magnificent Jacobean fireplace and 18th-century Chinese wallpaper, immaculately restored. Beneath is the billiard room, dark and Victorian but with a bizarre frieze of fifty-six assorted meat dishes.

The last reception room is the library, Charles Robinson's favourite and kept as a memorial to his occupancy. It is ceiled and painted in light colours, with a faintly American atmosphere. It might be the state room of an ocean liner, a New Englander's dream of Old England moored in a Kent moat. Outside dark lawns, fields and trees embrace the moat on three sides, with Tudor cottages looking on from beyond the water. These cottages are contemporary with the house, dated *c*1475.

KNOLE *****

South end of High Street, Sevenoaks
Medieval palace of the Sackvilles, cream of
Elizabethan and Jacobean craftsmanship (NT)

The clogged arteries of Sevenoaks suddenly recede as visitors pass through ancient gates to find themselves sharing a parkland with deer wandering ghostly through the trees. Avenues and footpaths lead to private dells. Above them lurks an old dark house, concealing a myriad courtyards and corridors, turning an aloof back on the park and the world alike. Knole is the most utterly old of English houses.

The present house dates from 1456 when Thomas Bourchier, Archbishop of Canterbury, bought himself an old manor and began rebuilding. He felt no need of exterior fortification, nor did he feel obliged to make an architectural statement. The exterior is not impressive. As Horace Walpole said, it 'has neither beauty nor prospects'. It has what a former resident, Vita Sackville-West, who was born here called the 'inward gaiety' of an ageing woman who 'has had many lovers and seen many generations come and go'. She saw its walls melting 'into the green of the garden turf . . . into the blue of the pale English sky'.

The house passed at the Reformation from the Church to the Crown. Henry VIII demanded it of Cranmer much as he had demanded Hampton Court of Wolsey. His daughter Elizabeth gave it to the Sackvilles, later Earls then Dukes of Dorset. The 1st Earl came into the freehold of the property in 1605 and immediately began rebuilding the interior. The house has remained in the family ever since (now as tenants of the National Trust). Of the 365 rooms, only eighteen are open to the public, which is sad.

The house has a classic Tudor plan, with ranges of rooms set round courtyards, of which there are seven in all, with a variety of purposes. The main façade of grey Kent ragstone has Dutch gables to each wide bay and a central gatehouse. This leads into Green Court, with a second gatehouse ahead known as Bourchier's Tower. This is flanked by grand galleries, each surmounted by a gable and the Sackville crest, a leopard rampant. The effect is of growing stateliness.

The next court is Stone Court, the chief ceremonial court fronting the Great Hall. It is surprisingly light-hearted, with a colonnade beneath whitewashed walls and Cape Dutch gables. Inside is the hall, its stupendous Jacobean screen comparable with those at Hatfield (Herts) and Audley End (Essex). Over the fireplace is a large painting by John Wootton of the Duke of Dorset at Dover Castle. The Hall leads on to Knole's first pride and joy, the Great Staircase.

This was constructed in 1605 for the 1st Earl of Dorset at the same time as the hall screen. Like Charles Cavendish's Little Castle at Bolsover (Derbys), the staircase at Knole embodies the taste of an English Renaissance man of letters. In grisaille and based on Dutch sources, the murals depict the Five Senses, the Social Virtues and the Four Ages of Man, interspersed with effusive scrollwork. The stairs rise past Doric and Ionic columns to a Corinthian climax. The whole work is exquisite.

The remainder of the accessible rooms are upstairs. Most Elizabethan houses had a single suite of state rooms culminating in a Long Gallery or promenade. Knole has many such suites, each sumptuous. It is hard for us to envisage how these astonishing chambers were used. We must imagine the difficulty of accommodating many grandees at one time, each with a large retinue and each expecting palatial chambers. The suites at Knole are in roughly ascending order of magnificence.

The first is reached down the Brown Gallery, lined with Jacobean chairs. Above them hang two tiers of prelates and kings of England. To the right are Lady Betty Germain's rooms, filled with huge Restoration armchairs, Flemish tapestries and cream silk bed-hangings. Lady Betty was a friend of the 1st Duke and Duchess, who lived here in the early 18th century. She adored pot-pourri and the rooms still

Knole's heraldic Renaissance

smell of her concoctions. Sleeping here must be like lying on a bed of forest leaves.

A second suite to the left of the Brown Gallery begins with the celebrated Spangle Bedroom. This was named after the sequins, now faded, sewn into the satin appliqué bed-hangings. The walls are covered in dark green tapestries. The suite culminates in the Venetian Ambassador's Room. This contains the state bed made for James II in 1688, with attendant chairs, stools and tapestries. Like many of the furnishings at Knole, they came to the 6th Earl as a perk of his office as Lord Chamberlain, probably from Whitehall Palace.

We return to the heart of the house down the Leicester Gallery, with its 17th-century billiard table and, at one end, the great Mytens portrait of James I in old age. He sits in a chair much like that on show beneath it. From these rooms we glimpse two private inner courtyards, the Water Court and Pheasant Court, before reaching the ballroom.

This is an astonishing chamber, coated in decoration by the 1st Earl. Rich Mannerist pilasters rise to a frieze of mermaids so deeply carved they seem ready to swim into the room below. The chimneypiece is among the finest works of Renaissance sculpture in England. It is of marble and alabaster and was carved by Cornelius Cure. The pictures are full-length Sackvilles, by Larkin, van Dyck and Kneller, in clothes of a splendour fit for the setting.

Beyond lies the grandest suite. It starts with the Reynolds Room, so named for the portraits which fill its walls, one of which is of the 3rd Duke of Dorset's Chinese page. Even the paintings are outshone by another superb chimneypiece, in delicate marble marquetry. Putti are depicted holding trophies and riding sphinxes. Beyond is the Cartoon Gallery, with copies of the Raphael cartoons in the V&A.

The King's suite begins with two closets, a lavatory or 'lieu d'aisance' (hence loo) and a dressing room of green mohair wall-hangings. Beyond is the King's Bedroom, its furnishing so precious as to be kept in exquisite gloom (for once a conservation precaution I would accept). The fabrics and furniture are seen glowing in artificial candlelight. Everything

about this room is impressive, the delicacy of the plasterwork, the silver filigree mirrors, the gold thread of the bed hangings. These hangings were believed to have been sent from France to James II, the finest such work extant. The toilet set is entirely of silver.

I can see that, to some, such richness can seem stifling. Yet Knole has its antidote ready. Outside the long shadows of the park and the silent drifts of deer offer gentle relief.

LEEDS CASTLE ✯✯✯✯

5m E of Maidstone
Re-creation of medieval castle in lake (P)

Leeds is an English Udaipur. Its walls rise direct from a shimmering lake, gold and untouchable, guarded by fierce black swans. The marriage of castle and water might be a chivalric fantasy of incarcerated maidenhood. Most of the place is 19th- and 20th-century ersatz, but Disney did nothing to match it. I have seen Leeds in all weathers and love it, the Picturesque revival in all its glory.

Leeds Castle is not without vanity. It is a conference centre that promises the promotion of art and 'the furtherance of peace'. Visitors park outside the gate and enter by bus past woods and ponds. Inside are shops, restaurants, aviaries, museums and a golf course. No event, be it balloon rally, three tenors concert or international summit, is too much trouble. Leeds is run by a charity and receives no public money.

A castle on the site was held for most of the Middle Ages by the monarch, Leeds being established by Edward I as a gift to the queen of the day. It was a useful staging post for trips to and from France. The walls imprisoned the deposed Richard II and entertained the Holy Roman Emperor, Sigismund, in 1416. Henry VIII transformed it into a palace for Catherine of Aragon, well out of sight.

In due course, the castle fell into ruin. In the 17th century, a Jacobean house was built on the

Leeds' fairy-tale Gloriette

main island but this house was demolished in the 1820s and rebuilt by new owners, the Wykeham-Martin family, in a Gothic style. They also rebuilt the Gloriette or keep on the smaller island, which had been destroyed by fire. The Martins lived at Leeds until the 1920s when death duties forced its sale. The buyer was the Anglo-American Olive Paget, later Lady Baillie, beneficiary of three husbands and the Whitney millions. She modernized the interior and left it in the immaculate condition of today.

The castle is approached from the south over the moat. Visitors pass through a gatehouse and medieval outbuildings (one contains a dog collar museum) into the outer bailey. The detached Maidens' Tower on the right is of 16th-century origin and was reputedly the home of the royal maids of honour.

Ahead lies the mock medieval New Castle. The interior was rebuilt by Lady Baillie, using a French decorator, Armand Rateau, and is of interest chiefly for its tapestries and antiques. The drawing room was removed from Thorpe Hall (Hunts) and contains sumptuous panelling. I hope it can one day be returned there since the loss from Thorpe is conspicuous.

Over the inner hall presides a superb statue of the Lumley horseman, the earliest known English equestrian statue, c1590. I hesitate to wonder if this belongs in Lumley Castle (Durham). The library is 17th-century French (of 1938), and the dining room of the same date is designed to display 18th-century Aubusson tapestries.

Behind this building and over a picturesque bridge like a relic of medieval Leeds is the Gloriette. Its internal timbered Fountain Court is memorable, says the guide, for its 'apparent historical authenticity'. The group comprises a banqueting hall, Queen's gallery, chapel, state rooms and spiral staircase, all furnished with antiques. The hall floor is of ebony.

The real pleasure of the Gloriette is to wander its corridors on a sunny day and watch the light dancing up from the lake onto walls and ceilings. One day Leeds will seem as old as it now seems new.

LULLINGSTONE CASTLE
***

½m SW of Eynsford
Tudor mansion converted to receive Queen Anne (P)

The Tudor John Peche was a City alderman and obsessive jouster. He laid out a ground in front of his gatehouse and entertained the young Henry VIII to the sport, thus becoming a favoured courtier. Peche's jousting helmet survives in the dining room at Lullingstone Castle. The present lawn was once the front courtyard of the Tudor house and parts of the old building survive to the rear. The Peches were succeeded by the Harts, loyal Jacobites and friends of Queen Anne. Harts married Dykes in the 18th century, and Hart Dykes own the house enthusiastically to this day.

The house and its enclave are now surreal. They lie at a point where the valley of the River Darent slips between sloping hills, surrounded by motorways, Eurostar routes, golf courses and suburbs. Visitors must follow a long drive over an ancient ford and past a Roman villa (*see* below). The quiet group of Tudor gatehouse, church and mansion is set round an ancient lawn, protected by giant cedars.

The building that presents itself across the lawn appears to be Queen Anne. It was indeed built in honour of a visit from the Queen, but that façade is barely one room deep. The external proportions look odd, with a two-storey central bay at a loss how to keep the larger wings from coming to blows. Only on the north side, under the cedars, do we see reality of this house, a beefy Tudor mansion with an effete façade for the Queen's benefit.

The interior seems equally rushed together, from which it derives much of its charm. The Great Hall still looks onto a Tudor inner courtyard, but with a huge Queen Anne staircase built to one side. Over the hall fireplace is a picture of the Tudor house, with two gatehouses. The dining room door carries the emblem of the Roses of York and Lancashire, later a sign of Jacobite sympathies, secrets being exchanged *sub rosa*. The room is darkly panelled and contains the jousting helmet. The library and vestibule beyond are again Queen Anne in decoration but Tudor in proportions, warm, rich and inviting.

The staircase rises behind the hall. Its shallow treads were reputedly to accommodate Queen Anne's short, fat shape, wide dresses and dainty steps. On the landing is a display of tennis equipment. The rules of lawn tennis were devised here by Sir William Hart Dyke and the Prince of Wales, later Edward VII. At the top of the stairs is the state drawing room, formerly the Tudor Great Chamber. It is a splendid room with a barrel vault covered in strapwork and Roman medallions. The Queen is honoured with rich classical panelling, a leather chest and fine portrait.

Beyond is the state bedroom with a large bed into which the tiny monarch must have completely disappeared. Next to it is a powder closet with wig stand and box for face patches.

LULLINGSTONE ROMAN VILLA *

½m SW of Eynsford
Site of early chapel and villa mosaics (EH)

Every culture has its way of handling its precursors. Pre-war Italy reconstructed the Greek temples of Sicily. Sir Arthur Evans rebuilt the ruins at Knossos. The forum in Athens was partly reinstated by the Americans. When the remains of a Roman villa were discovered on the side of the Darent valley in 1939, the excitement was therefore intense.

Excavation was delayed by the war but commenced in 1949. A cellar with wall-paintings and a virtually complete mosaic floor were revealed, the best surviving in England. But what to do with the site? Should the best parts go to a museum and the rest be left a ruin? Should everything remain *in situ*? Or might an effort be made to reconstruct what had vanished, as the Victorians would have done?

The answer is the worst of all worlds, a monstrous modern shed over the entire site and opened in 1963. This seals the villa completely

from its setting. It is today aimed exclusively at school parties. There is no attempt to evoke Roman remains, only a history class. The shed is like a municipal swimming bath with, instead of water, scrubbed rubble walls, all of the same height, amid raked sand and gravel. It needs only garden gnomes for complete absurdity. If an important building is treated so cruelly, I cannot see any argument for not rebuilding the villa complete.

The villa was built *c*AD75, and regularly rebuilt until its destruction in *c*420. Most exciting was the discovery of what appeared to be a chapel over the hypocaust to the right of the villa. This contained Chi-Rho Christian monograms, together with wall-paintings said to depict early Christians at prayer. The villa also had bath rooms, verandas, sleeping chambers and kitchens.

Most remarkable are the mosaics on the floor of the audience chamber and apse. The largest depicts Bellerophon riding Pegasus, surrounded by a geometrical pattern of squares, leaves and swastikas. The apse mosaic is of Jupiter abducting Europa, accompanied by a passage from Virgil. The artistry is not of the highest quality, compared for instance to mosaics in North Africa, but it is supremely moving to find such work so far from its Mediterranean inspiration.

MAIDSTONE: ARCHBISHOP'S PALACE *

Mill Street
Survivor of ecclesiastical mansion (M)

Maidstone once enjoyed a precious medieval enclave round the parish church and Archbishop's Palace. This has been spoiled by a one-way stream of traffic and insensitive infilling. The decision to make the ground floor of the old palace a local registry office adds insult to injury. Maidstone is strictly for Philistines.

The old palace belonged to the Archbishops of Canterbury from the 13th century, as a stopping place on their way from London to their cathedral city. Many preferred the charms of

Maidstone and stayed. After the Reformation, the palace passed to the Astley family, who rebuilt the east front in 1581. It is outwardly a fine Elizabethan work. The E-plan is symmetrical, with a central two-storey porch but two staircases leading to separate entrances in the wings. The façade has gabled dormers and a large timbered extension on either side.

The façade to the river behind is equally interesting. A wall of creamy Kentish stone rises straight from the water, with a roof of red-tiled gables. A large window lights the old solar and steps lead down to what would have been a landing stage. At the time of writing, the only interiors accessible are on the first floor, including the empty Great Hall and Great Chamber. The restorers have felt obliged to use light-coloured wood for new rafters to distinguish them from originals, a silly scheme. In the side wings are the panelled Cranmer and Wareham rooms, containing an enjoyable collection of old municipal photographs.

Across the one-way system, visitors with a death wish can reach the charming palace stables. These survive from the 1490s, with a large timbered central projection. The interior contains an impressive collection of carriages and historic vehicles.

MAIDSTONE: CHILLINGTON MANOR *

St Faith's Street
Elizabethan manor converted for local museum (M)

Chillington Manor is now Maidstone's municipal museum and is correspondingly less of a house. Buried among the display cases and garish exit signs, however, are the relics of a fine manor erected in 1561 for Nicholas Barham, the local MP. The main brick façade to the street is that of a substantial Elizabethan mansion, with two storeys and high gables, similar to those on the Archbishop's Palace by the river. A Long Gallery existed to the rear.

All this and later alterations were converted in 1858 for a town museum to house a collection left by a local doctor, Thomas Charles. What we see today is a victorianized Elizabethan house in which fragments of old and new co-exist. The interior has been institutionalized. Modern curators find it impossible to resist stamping their personality on old buildings, but Maidstone is at least a first-rate museum.

The old Great Hall and screen survive on the ground floor, with some good chests. The staircase is Jacobean, as is a fine chimneypiece in the old Great Chamber upstairs. Here a group of 17th-century waxworks figures are engaged in some obscure conspiracy. This should all be taken in hand so the 'house' rooms can speak for themselves.

MAIDSTONE: THE COBTREE MUSEUM OF KENT LIFE – HOPPERS' HUTS *

Lock Lane, Sandling
Seasonal shelter for hop pickers (M)

This is the smallest and meanest dwelling in this book. With the standardization of European beer, the market for Kent hops collapsed and with it the lifestyle of those who grew and picked the fruit. The summer migration from London to the hop-fields was a social phenomenon. For tens of thousands of families 'hopping down to Kent' in summer compensated for the seasonal lack of work for women in service and for men in the gasworks. In 1877, it was estimated that 35,000 families left on the cheap trains from London Bridge. Rural villages became homes from home. Nor was this just for Cockneys. Hopping was, said Henry Mayhew, 'the grand rendezvous for the vagrancy of England and Wales', with thousands of gypsies and Irish also flocking to the fields.

Living conditions were appalling. Many workers slept under hedges. George Orwell wrote that the people did not mind 'since the pickers saw their three weeks in Kent as a sort of holiday'. For many it was the one occasion when the whole family were together, engaged on a common task, a time recalled by them as of intense happiness. By the 20th century, efforts were being made to house the workers decently. At Cobtree, three such huts are preserved, dating from the 1930s and still in use in the 1950s.

The relocation is not ideal. The Cobtree Museum of Kent Life is squeezed onto meadows clinging to life amid a frenzy of motorways outside Maidstone. The hut roofs are of corrugated iron and the floors of concrete, an advance on the original mud. One large bed occupies half the hut, high on posts so that children could be crammed onto birch-twig mattresses beneath. Adults slept head to toe with as many as could be fitted onto the bed. With so much humanity in one tiny space, the roof was said to drip with condensation, soaking the covers.

Next to the bed a stove stands ready for making the first brew. A shelf holds a few mugs and bottles and, implausibly, a wireless and copy of the *Fireside Dickens*.

NURSTEAD COURT **

2m N of Meopham
Medieval hall buried in modern farm (P-R)

A potholed drive leads past a handwritten bed-and-breakfast sign to a rendered façade and unkempt outhouses. They are attended by an ominous group of very used cars. If this place is historic, it keeps the fact well hidden: more likely Cold Comfort Farm.

Yet this is a place full of excitement. The façade conceals two reception rooms, apparently by the Victorian architect, Edward Blore. Buried behind is half of a 14th-century aisled hall, an ancient family library and guest rooms tucked in among the struts and beams of the original roof. To stumble through Nurstead is like negotiating the decks of an East Indiaman, of the sort once commanded by a past member of the family. Headroom is limited and gusts of wind seem to emerge from unseen holes. The owner points out the 'medieval soot' in the attic. This is a place for connoisseurs of eccentricity.

The Starkadders of Nurstead are the Edmeades. There have been Edmeades here since the 16th century. They clearly had no desire, or no money, for grand building projects. Daughters kept the Edmeade name in marriage, the present incumbent being Mrs Edmeade-Stearns. The family motto is *Cave, cave*, beware. The guidebook attributes the ploughing of the old park and the B&B to 'the modern practice of confiscating inherited wealth' and 'the vagaries of the Common Agricultural Policy'.

The medieval house would have been a hall of four bays with aisles on both sides and a crown-post roof. There appears to have been a defensive tower detached at the rear corner. The two eastern bays of the hall were demolished in the 18th century when the upper level was filled in with bedrooms. The timbering remains, including a fine carved capital in the library downstairs and head-banging intrusions in the bedrooms above. The roof seems to be held on by faith.

This is a house of faded gentility. Family portraits adorn the walls, alongside old prints, stags heads and a dejected harp. Dogs tug at carpets. Books and papers are scattered on all sides and chests hint at ancient archives. In a pantry ceiling is a trapdoor through which a seagoing Edmeade raised his crippled wife to the bedroom above, as if to the crow's-nest of his ship.

OLD SOAR MANOR *

Old Soar, 2m S of Borough Green
Solar and undercroft of medieval manor (NT)

How did these places survive? The main house is a redbrick early Georgian box, covered in wisteria and guarded by a promiscuous cherry tree. Attached to it next door are the remains of a manor of c1290, apparently awaiting the return of its medieval knight on the 6.20 from Charing Cross.

The Georgian house is probably on the site of a medieval hall, so what survives is the latter's undercroft and solar apartment. The undercroft was presumably used for storage.

The latter is a comfortable room with fireplace open to the roof. It has two small chambers extending from each end. One is a small chapel, the other a large garderobe. The garderobe is surprisingly big and would also have been used for storing clothes. It was thought that moths were deterred by the smell, hence the term wardrobe. People were presumably less fastidious.

Old Soar is hard to find. It is in one of those rare corners of Kent where the sound of birdsong is not drowned by the roar of a road.

OSPRINGE: MAISON DIEU *

Ospringe, ½m SW of Faversham
Fragment of pilgrims' hospital on Watling Street (EH)

The old Watling Street was lined with pilgrim 'hospitals' on the route from London to Canterbury. Set up by religious houses to care for weary travellers and the sick, they were financed by rich benefactors. Two-thirds of all the medieval hospitals in Kent were on Watling Street. Maison Dieu would have seen Chaucer and his colleagues pass by on the road outside.

Maison Dieu, or God's House, was founded in the early 13th century. The foundation flourished, prospered, declined and was empty by 1483. The property was then ceded to the Crown and ended in the hands of a local developer. He demolished most of the buildings and used the stone elsewhere. The main part of the hospital, the hall, close, church and gatehouse were on the north side of the road. Only two lesser buildings on the other side by Water Lane survive. They were probably occupied by lay members of the order. One is now a small museum.

The house has a flint ground floor and timbered upper storey. The downstairs hall was refashioned in the 16th century. It has a fine fireplace and plaster ceiling with geometrical and floral designs. Moulded beams are interlaced with roses. Down steps is a small medieval undercroft of uncertain purpose, either for storage or perhaps for bathing. Upstairs is a Great Chamber with an open kingpost roof, retaining 16th-century windows and a later fireplace.

The house contains a museum of Roman and other finds from the vicinity of Watling Street, set out in old-fashioned display cases.

PENSHURST PLACE ****

Penshurst, 4m SW of Tonbridge
Palace with Great Hall and Elizabethan state rooms (P)

Penshurt is a picture of England and home of one of history's most glittering figures. Sir Philip Sidney blazed across the Elizabethan firmament. He was the *beau ideal* of English Renaissance gentleman: erudite, gallant, poetic, dashing and reckless. Men and women alike were infatuated by him. Elizabeth fell for his charms and, when she fell out of them, sent him to be governor of Flushing in the Netherlands. He died there on the battlefield in 1586 at the age of thirty-four. His legend and his writings lived on, as does his house.

Sidney's country mansion was already one of the grandest pre-Tudor fortified houses. It dates back to 1341 when a City merchant, John de Pulteney, won a licence to crenellate and built himself that symbol of grandeur, a Great Hall. It was, and still is, the mightiest owned by a commoner in England. Within a decade Pulteney was dead of the plague. Before the end of the 14th century his successor, Sir John Devereux, built a defensive wall round the hall, fragments of which survive in the structure of the later house.

That house passed to the Duke of Bedford, who built a second, even bigger Great Hall. Here, in 1519, a later owner, the Duke of Buckingham, entertained Henry VIII with such extravagance that Henry grew suspicious and executed him. Henry's son, Edward VI, eventually settled the house on his tutor, Sir William Sidney. It was his son, Sir Philip, who

Medieval might: Penshurst hall

converted Penshurt from baronial hall to Tudor palace, dividing the larger second hall into chambers. Another wing of private rooms was built north of the halls, with an Italian loggia.

Sidney was succeeded by his brother who became 1st Earl of Leicester. Penshurst then passed through the usual cycle of Georgian decay, 19th-century romantic revival and 20th-century crisis and eventual rescue, all under the Sidneys. Their present De L'Isle and Dudley title date from 1835.

Entrance through the rear courtyard is past the stables and outbuildings, in effect a small medieval village. Access is directly into the Great Hall, its mighty roof, arched braces and prickly Kent tracery towering overhead. Life-size figures carved on the corbels are said to be workers on the medieval estate. The screens passage is still in place, as is the old tiled floor and the octagon for an open fireplace. Only the louvre in the roof for escaping smoke has gone. This is truly a secular monument to compare with the great cathedrals of the 14th century.

Upstairs is the sequence of Tudor and Sidney's later state rooms. The first was the medieval solar, a gigantic chamber for the 14th century. It is now the state dining room, with a squint down to the Great Hall below. On the walls are Elizabethan and Stuart family portraits, including a picture of Queen Elizabeth dancing with Lord Leicester. Next comes the Queen Elizabeth Room carved from the second hall, a sumptuous chamber furnished in part with fittings rescued from the family's London house, on the site of the present Leicester Square. The walls have a panelled dado, with tapestries above. The large chairs, including a magnificent day bed, are covered with damask and silk embroidery. The adjacent Tapestry Room is similarly decorated and has a cabinet with Dutch landscape scenes painted on each drawer.

The visitor now passes out of the Buckingham Building to the Pages' Room, with a display of family china. Beyond stretches the Long Gallery, Renaissance in style with pilasters, a frieze and a rich plaster ceiling. The room is gloriously lit on three sides by windows and displays an exhibition of family costumes. At the far end is a Jacobean bedroom, curiously lost in this wing of the house, as if somewhere to sleep were beneath the dignity of such a palace. The exit is through a gallery of old arms and armour.

Garden records at Penshurst date back to the 14th century and are among the oldest in England. Poverty and decay saved the grounds from landscaping in the 18th century and left them ready for the revival of formalism, under the 2nd Lord De L'Isle, in the 19th. They have been restored to their Elizabethan splendour, a marriage of flowers to trees and topiary. They include a mile of yew hedge.

PORT LYMPNE **

Lympne, 4m W of Hythe
Edwardian villa with murals amid terraced garden (P)

To get to the house, we must brave apes and tigers lurking in the woods. A zoo was established by the late John Aspinall in the grounds of the house, designed in the Cape Dutch style by the imperial architect, Sir Herbert Baker. On a warm day we might be looking out from an East African cliff over the Indian Ocean. To arrive past wild animals seems appropriate.

The house was built in 1912 for Sir Philip Sassoon with didactic intent. The courtyards and terraces were to evoke the spirit of the Roman legions who occupied this escarpment over Romney Marsh. They then left to defend their empire elsewhere, a parallel with the British Empire that appealed to Sassoon. A Roman trophy adorns the studded entrance, in tribute to the Roman Tournay Regiment.

In the immediate aftermath of the Great War, the house enjoyed similar status to Cliveden. Sassoon, a millionaire at twenty-three and aide to Lloyd George, offered the house as a venue for various peace conferences. It contained an early 'hot line' to Paris. Here he variously entertained Charlie Chaplin, Bernard Shaw, T. E. Lawrence, Edward VIII and Winston Churchill.

Baker's exterior is designed in deference to the view. It sits above a series of steep terraces on the pattern of a Roman garden, running down to the edge of the Marsh. Two bold Dutch gables crown either side of a U-plan house. Roofed colonnades flank each wing. The interiors were refashioned after the Great War by Philip Tilden, designer of Chartwell, and retain a touch of Surrealism. They are chiefly notable for their mural paintings. The greatest of these, of elephants and exotic animals, was by the Catalan artist, José-Marie Sert, in the drawing room. It was destroyed in the Second World War and has been replaced by Arthur Spencer Roberts, showing 220 species of animal. It is bravely garish.

Across the hall is the Tent Room, decorated by Rex Whistler in 1934. The murals are a capriccio of scenes from Wren's London and 18th-century Dublin, with curtains and perspectives, all in the soft tones of English Picturesque. It is a sublime chamber, a desert canopy over a fantasy of an English town. Whistler's death on the Western Front in 1944 was particularly tragic (*see* Mottifont/Hants).

Beyond lies Tilden's Moorish courtyard, a water garden flanked by cool white arcades and sloping tiled roofs, again Roman in inspiration. The grounds of Port Lympne retain the grandeur of the Sassoon years. In the distance shimmers the Channel. 'It is so quiet at Lympne,' wrote Sassoon, 'one can hear the dogs bark at Beauvais.'

QUEX HOUSE **

Birchington, 3½m W of Margate
Victorian explorer's house and wildlife museum (P)

Quex is a monument to a lost England, that of the adventurer, wanderer and big game hunter. It was built by John Powell Powell in 1813 to designs by Thomas Hardwick. It was his descendant, Major Percy Powell-Cotton, who created what we see today. Powell-Cotton was born in 1866 and led twenty-seven expeditions to Africa and Asia, including one in search of the five-horned East African giraffe. He killed

anything that moved, collecting his trophies assiduously and with scholarship. He was once savaged by a lion. The relevant torn jacket and the dead lion are displayed in the house.

The product of this labour is the museum of some 500 specimens which Powell-Cotton established in a pavilion next to his home. The museum is still maintained by his son. The house is a perfect foil for the museum, a late-Victorian mansion to whose warm, leathery bosom the wanderer would dream of returning. The exterior is an 1880s refacing of Hardwick's façade, with iron veranda shading the ground floor rooms.

The drawing room is in a Victorian 'mughal' style, with rugs, skins and wall sconces in Kashmiri walnut. The earlier marble staircase has been replaced by one of oak. The weapons in the former armoury are now displayed in the museum. Upstairs is the Powell bedroom, boudoir and library, mostly by Hardwick; the library contains a Congreve moving ball clock.

In the grounds of Quex is the Waterloo Tower, one of the oddest follies in England. It was built by the first Powell for his ring of 12 bells, one of the few secular bell towers still in use. The cast-iron spire is modelled on that of Faversham church but is more reminiscent of the Eiffel Tower in Paris.

RIVERHILL HOUSE *

1m S of Sevenoaks
Georgian mansion with Jacobean panelling (P-R)

Riverhill is a Georgian box surrounded by a charming garden that looks out towards Ashdown Forest. Only the pounding Sevenoaks by-pass spoils its bliss. The house has been owned by the Rogers family since 1840, when a clean-limbed new wing was attached to the side of a Queen Anne façade of 1714. The composition is quaint, with a projecting porch three storeys high breaking the symmetry of the old front. Creeper is welcomed and the exterior has an air of faded gentility.

The interior is filled with Jacobean lozenge panelling, clearly earlier than the date of the house. A Victorian Mrs Rogers is said to have visited a local tenant who complained that her panelling was old and concealed rats. It was promptly removed and installed in the big house. The entrance hall doubles as a library, a cosy arrangement. The ceiling covering the hall and staircase was copied from one at neighbouring Knole.

Other rooms on show are the dining room and drawing room. Pictures depict the Rogers family's distinguished Protestant ancestry. One was burned at the stake by Mary I and another, a prominent Dissenter, was buried in Bunhill Fields north of the City of London. Their descendants have preferred soldiering, at least one of each generation being in the army. The house exhibits such military mementos as a Dragoon helmet and a 'Welcome Home' painting of Sevenoaks after the Boer War.

ROCHESTER CASTLE *

The Lodge
Grandest of Norman keeps (EH)

Rochester Castle is a thundering mass of masonry. When King John besieged the rebel barons here in 1215 it led to one of the few epic castle sieges ever staged on English soil. Five stone-throwing engines and two wooden siege castles were built. The castle gave way only when it was undermined by sappers who burned their pit-props with 'the fat of forty pigs'. A round tower replaced the corner that had collapsed, with a further drum tower beyond it.

The keep was built in 1127 by Henry I. Its walls still stand to their full height of 125 ft, with only the battlements restored. The interior lacks floors or roofs but the wall passages remain and the corner turrets are still roomed. Apart from the rebuilt round tower of c1226, everything is of 1127 – that is, within living memory of the Conquest.

The structure comprised a basement with three storeys of living rooms above, each divided in half by a cross-wall, with an arcade of Norman arches. On entering the castle,

steps and mural passages offer glimpses of openings and galleries, as in a Piranesi engraving. Rochester packs a bigger punch even than Dover or the Tower of London.

Little remains to indicate the domestic life of the castle. There is a well, some garderobes and holes for pigeons. English Heritage has mown the lawn outside and scattered sales litter everywhere, as if to bring the old warrior down a peg.

ROCHESTER: RESTORATION HOUSE ****

17–19 Crow Lane
Richly furnished house of 16th and 17th centuries (P)

There is no finer pre-Civil War town house in England. The building takes its name from Charles II's visit in 1660 on his way to claim his throne, but parts are a century older. Dickens used it as the model for Satis House in *Great Expectations*, with 'seared brick walls, blocked windows and strong ivy'. The upstairs chamber thus boasts Miss Havisham's tragic wedding feast, and her burning to death.

Restoration House takes its present character from more recent owners. The comedian, Rod Hull, devoted himself to trying to save the house. He died bankrupted by the effort, with the building unrestored, the latest in a long line of Englishmen ruined by the 'love of the house'. Since 1994 Robert Tucker and Jonathan Wilmot have restored the interior and filled it with an impressive collection of furniture, pictures and objects. No compromise has been made. This is a lived-in house of its period, still in the process of rediscovery.

The façade appears to be that of an E-plan house, with brick centre block and wings. Yet a closer view shows little symmetry. No two windows are the same. Stair turrets fill every corner and string courses vanish into earlier, or later, brickwork without explanation. One wing is hip-roofed, the other gabled. The place

Restoration House: 'Pip's' staircase

is a fascinating archaeological jigsaw puzzle.

The puzzle is even harder inside. What is ostensibly a medieval hall and solar may have been that but is now a Jacobean drawing room. The staircases are inexplicable. I counted eleven flights going in different directions from the first floor alone. With candles, pictures and pewter, each seemed to promise a different adventure. Small wonder Dickens could see poor Pip taunted by Estella at every turn.

The earliest parts of the house are the two wings. The one on the right has been dated to 1454 and on the left to 1502–22. They were then probably separate dwellings. Archaeology is continuing to uncover features of this period buried in walls, roofs and fireplaces. The two houses were united sometime after 1640 by a new hall and screens passage in the medieval style, with Great Chamber above. These now form the core of the house. In about 1670, the present façade was added to this hall and the internal space rearranged. Staircases and doorways were inserted, moved, duplicated and made gloriously chaotic.

The two principal rooms in the south wing are the Oak Saloon and the Tapestry Room, the former with an oak fireplace of 1610 with superb strapwork. The latter is hung with tapestries said to have been donated by Charles II after his 1660 visit. Upstairs, the Great Chamber is 'Miss Havisham's Room', with narrow sash windows and a ballroom floor, beautifully repainted in original pale green and black.

In the north wing is the King's Bedroom with 17th-century glass in the windows and, an anachronistic touch, Victorian murals of Tennyson's 'Idylls of the King' inserted by a Victorian owner. The chest-of-drawers has original lining paper celebrating the marriage of Charles II.

No furnishing is considered superfluous if it is of the 17th century. The eye rests on a quill pen, a tankard, a leather book, a Dutch plate. This is no museum but a house revived. The rear garden is also being restored to its original appearance, based on whatever is unearthed beneath the rubble. Never was a house so aptly titled.

SCOTNEY CASTLE **

1m E of Lamberhurst
Romantic ruin in woodland garden (NT)

Scotney is not so much a castle as a view, that of an old tower deep in a watery vale framed by rhododendrons and azaleas. The castle was once, like Bodiam (Sussex), four-square with towers at each corner. It was fortified by Roger Ashburnham in the 14th century. A new mansion was built on most of the site in the 1640s. Of the castle, only one tower was left standing, overlooking the moat. This tower was capped with a conical roof and cupola in the 18th century, rendering it more a folly than a bastion.

Scotney was bought by Edward Hussey in 1778 but the family soon moved out of the old house to St Leonard's. It was not until 1835 that Hussey's grandson, also Edward, recognized the picturesque potential of the old place and returned. He abandoned the castle site and had Anthony Salvin build a new house in the Elizabethan style on the hill overlooking it. Margaret Thatcher had a weekend retreat here.

Salvin rose to the challenge of the dramatic contour, enhancing it by quarrying stone from the slope beneath. As the old buildings declined into ruin, they grew in Hussey's romantic imagination, aided by the landscaper, William Gilpin. Hussey died in 1894 and his grandson, Christopher Hussey of *Country Life*, bequeathed it to the National Trust in 1970. The family motto, 'I scarcely call these things our own', might be the motto of every great house in this book.

This is a place to see in the spring and, to a lesser extent, the autumn. The delights are those of landscape, of the Bastion View and Quarry Garden, of vistas, contours, trees, shrubs and sudden reveals. At the centre is the moat round the site of the 17th-century house. Of this, only blank walls remain, but its earlier Tudor wing survives, as does what is known as the Ashburnham Tower.

The Tower is just a tower, but its Tudor wing contains an exhibition of Hussey relics. There is some linenfold panelling, antlers and a spinning wheel. The National Trust has also installed one of its more half-hearted historic kitchens. There is an admirable garderobe with a drop straight into the moat. The best feature is the robustly medieval staircase.

SISSINGHURST CASTLE **

3m NE of Cranbrook
Castle fragments in famous garden (NT)

What is the first thing about Sissinghurst that comes to mind? Is it a romantic tower soaring above a frothy confection of white, yellow and green, or is it the oft-told story of Harold Nicolson and Vita Sackville-West, complaining, struggling and triumphing over nature in this private corner of Kent?

I do not find Vita sympathetic, English haughtiness justified by aristocracy. Yet she was a formidable gardener. Sissinghurst, she wrote, 'broke my back, my fingernails and sometimes my heart'. It is currently the most popular garden in England.

In 1930, Vita found her own garden near Knole threatened by a chicken farm and went in search of somewhere new. She chanced on the ruins of Sissinghurst, dating from the 1490s and one of the first Kent houses to be built of brick. It had housed Napoleonic prisoners, fallen into decay and mostly vanished. Only a range of outbuildings and a gatehouse-tower survived.

Vita bought them with 400 acres of farmland and set to work. She wrote: 'One might reasonably have hoped to inherit century-old hedges of yew, some gnarled mulberries, a cedar or two, a pleached alley, flagged walks, a mound. Instead there was nothing but weed, rough grass, a shabby eyesore of a greenhouse in the wrong place, broken fencing, wired chicken runs, squalor and slovenly disorder everywhere.'

Bringing this to order was a joint effort of husband and wife. Harold planned the overall layout of walls, courts and terraces while Vita gardened. Harold's layout is in the post-Picturesque tradition, of a garden not as an imitation of nature but as imitation of a house. The thesis owed much to Lawrence Johnston's Edwardian garden at Hidcote (Gloucs), much admired by the Nicolsons. Harold described his intention to create a 'succession of privacies' from forecourt through the first arch to the main court, the lawn and finally the orchard, creating 'the impression of cumulative escape'.

This escape is over the ruins of what was an Elizabethan courtyard house. The visitor is first confronted by a long, low medieval range of brick, forming a sort of outer hall to the later house behind. This is today the Nicolsons' Long Library. Two gables flank an arch leading to the castle and garden beyond. Of the castle, all that survives is the great gatehouse tower and a fragment of the courtyard range, now South Cottage.

Although deprived of the surrounding court, the tower is a magnificent set-piece. Four storeys of brick, one room deep, are flanked by spacious stair turrets with conical roofs. Here Vita wrote her novels and gardening articles for the *Observer*, her 'sticklebacks', which she professed to hate.

Nobody but her dog was admitted here during her life nor did she ever light the fire, merely covering herself in coats. From this eyrie she could look out on her life's work and plan each season's campaign. 'From March to the end of April is youth, from May to June is middle age; after the end of July we enter the painful stage.' She died in 1962.

SMALLHYTHE PLACE **

Small Hythe, 2m S of Tenterden
Ellen Terry's cottage shrine (NT)

When James Lees-Milne first visited Smallhythe Place at the request of Ellen Terry's daughter, Edy Craig, his reaction was twofold. He had 'never walked through rooms more nostalgic of a particular owner,' he said, and he fell in love with Craig and her two lady friends. This, he later admitted, was a mistake. All subsequent dealings between them and the National Trust, who accepted the cottage unendowed in 1939, were fraught. The two

friends (Miss St John and Miss Atwood) claimed they 'do not do money', and refused point blank to try. A request for vouchers of visitor income and expenses was met with vituperative solicitors' letters. They said that they were artists and did not 'do vouchers'. Their neighbour and go-between, Vita Sackville-West, called them 'the trouts'.

Any shrine to a performer must be sad since it cannot perform. Ellen Terry was the great actress of her age and a woman of intense and unconventional vitality. She lives on at Small-hythe only in pictures, playbills, clothes and props. A theatre festival is held annually in the barn. The voice is silent, the gestures dead. But what is done is well done.

Terry was the daughter of travelling actors. She showed both talent and precocity, marry-ing the forty-six-year-old artist, G. F. Watts, in 1864 at the age of seventeen. Within four years she eloped with the architect, Edward Godwin, by whom she had two children. The relation-ship did not last and Ellen returned to the stage in 1874. For twenty-five years she domi-nated it, mostly partnering Henry Irving in Shakespeare at the Lyceum. It was in 1899, at the end of this period, and before her long decline into illness and death in 1928, that Terry bought Smallhythe. She saw it when driving round Kent with Irving, declaring on sight that this was where she would live and die. She did.

She adored the place, proud of having bought it 'with my own money'. A timbered house with overhanging first floor and ram-bling roses, Smallhythe had been the Port House for the adjacent 'hythe' on the River Rother. The outside displays close-studding and original windows. The interior has a cross passage rather than a hall, often a sign of a building not meant originally for domestic use. The rooms both upstairs and down retain their Tudor character, being dark and cosy with heavy beams and open fireplaces.

Smallhythe is overwhelmed with Terry memorabilia. The Terry Room contains

Vita's tower at Sissinghurst

sketches of her and her family, make-up boxes, stage furniture, props from her plays and a letter from Oscar Wilde. Here too is her instruction to her friends, 'No funeral gloom, my dears, when I am gone.' The adjacent dining room was once the house kitchen, but today celebrates other actors, including David Garrick and Sarah Siddons. Upstairs is mostly a museum, including a room of Terry cos-tumes and another dedicated to the Lyceum years. This includes Irving's collection of swords.

The best room is the bedroom, free of theatrical impedimenta. Here are pictures of family and friends. On her dressing table are the brushes and combs that tended her famous red locks. By the bed is her much-thumbed and annotated Shakespeare.

STONEACRE **

Otham, 4m E of Maidstone
Tudor farmhouse restored by aesthete (NT)

Stoneacre in spring is ecstatic. An old Wealden farmhouse creams through the enveloping blossom like an old ketch in mountainous seas. The village of Otham has at least four of these delicious houses hidden in its glades.

The farm was built in the 1480s and tenanted, with increasing dereliction, until the 1920s. It was then bought by the clerical aesthete and art historian, Aymer Vallance, who restored it and presented it to the National Trust in 1928. It consists of a hall house with wings, the hall having had a first floor installed in 1550. Beyond lies the solar. The kitchen wing to the right of the entrance has had to be supported on a stone foundation due to slippage.

Vallance took all this in hand. The Great Hall was reopened to the roof. Its main win-dow was restored and the magnificent crown-post revealed. A brick chimney with imported Tudor fireplace is a Vallance feature, faintly surreal. Beyond is a spiral staircase, also im-ported, with solid wood treads and Vallance's favourite decorative device, stained glass quar-ries in the window panes of the stairwell. The upstairs rooms were carefully restored to their original layout and appearance. The solar has a small crown-post roof and 17th-century furniture. The hand of the restorer is light. This is a house that its original builder would recognize.

The garden is a gem of Kentish intimacy, with secret views over the adjacent orchards. From here we can also admire Vallance's most substantial import, the close-studded exterior of the north wing, richly black-and-white and more Cheshire than Kent. Vallance's 'before and after' plans of the house, showing the stripping of the plaster, make a fascinating essay in Tudor revival taste.

TONBRIDGE CASTLE *

Castle Street
Gatehouse with medieval interiors (M)

The gatehouse at Tonbridge is every child's ideal of a castle. It is massive and completely dominates its corner of the town. The chambers are heavily populated with waxworks. There is even a soldier sitting, still armed to the teeth, on a garderobe in one of the privy towers. In my experience this is unique.

The castle was built soon after the Norman Conquest in the form of a motte and bailey, thrown up to guard a ford over the Medway. It was held by the de Clares and much patronized by monarchs on their way to Dover and France. The curtain wall and gatehouse were built c1300. The castle then passed to the Duke of Buckingham and was described, at the time of his execution in 1520, as being 'as strong a fortress as few be in England'. The castle was held by Parliament during the Civil War and later used as a local quarry. When Horace Walpole visited it a century later, he found it housing a vineyard.

Although the castle had a keep, the residential gatehouse constituted a keep in itself. There is a guard room on the ground floor, private chambers above and Great Hall on top. The basement and ground floor survive in a restored state and the roof battlements are manned by waxwork soldiers.

The basement is equipped as a storeroom, displayed with vats of salted meat, spices and rats. Beyond is the armoury. Its collection of swords, helmets and arrows is highly realistic, with no nonsense about geometrical patterns on walls. A waxwork figure is mending a knight's chainmail. In the guardroom realism frankly becomes absurd. Not only do we see the soldiers eating a meal, but are obliged to hear a tape of them cutting and chomping their food while they themselves watch a video of medieval history.

Upstairs the Great Hall is now open to the sky, its parapet offering a fine view over the Medway valley.

UPNOR CASTLE *

Upper Upnor, 2m NE of Rochester
Elizabethan castle on Medway estuary (EH)

This is a strange corner of Kent. Few visitors ever go near the mouth of the River Medway, a muddy waste of warehouses and dereliction. Yet its military importance led to its creeks and bluffs being lined with forts. From Grain to Sheerness and Queenborough, garrisons have sat out the years bleakly awaiting the enemy. It should be an exciting maritime museum.

Down the side of the Hoo peninsular is a small lane that might be in Cornwall. The village street of Upnor leads straight to the shore and a castle built by Elizabeth I to protect her ships at Chatham. The castle was built in 1559 and, unlike most British castles, saw real action. In the final moments of de Ruyter's spectacular Medway raid in 1667, the castle battery rained fire on the Dutch fleet until it ran out of ammunition. The enemy retired after firing a large number of English vessels at Chatham. The fort was later used as an ammunition store.

The path to the castle passes some 18th-century barracks, described as the earliest such buildings in England. The castle itself presents its best face to the river, and access is gained only through a modest door in the landward gatehouse. The walls are surrounded by an extraordinary wooden pallisade, designed to obstruct landing parties from disabling the guns (as the Dutch were believed to have done at Chatham).

The main building inside is guarded by two Turkey oak trees brought from the Crimea. The two side towers of the castle were originally residential with, between them, two floors of ammunition stores, one of them now manned by waxwork figures. A windlass conveyed the stores down to the Water Bastion, for ferrying to warships at anchor. From the Water Bastion one can look out over the eerily peaceful lower Medway.

WALMER CASTLE ***

Walmer, 1m S of Deal
Grace-and-favour residence in old fort (EH)

Walmer is the third in the chain of artillery forts built by Henry VIII c1539 facing the Goodwin Sands. Like Sandown and Deal, it was less a castle than a low-lying firing platform, designed to be inconspicuous from the sea. In 1708, the castle became the official residence of the Lord Warden of the Cinque Ports, a post important in the Middle Ages when the loyalty and security of the Channel harbours was crucial in fending off the French. It has long been a Crown sinecure.

Walmer is delightful, a mini-mansion fashioned within gardens inland from the beach. The gardens were laid out by Lady Hester Stanhope, niece of William Pitt the Younger when he was Lord Warden in the 1790s. The old quatrefoil buildings of four semi-circular bastions round a circular keep had been refashioned as a comfortable country house in 1730 and again in 1763. The Duke of Wellington later took pride in his wardenship and died at Walmer in 1852. Further alterations were made for Earl Granville in the 1870s. His wife was determined to regard the wardenship as a real job and the castle as a family home.

This is a place to wander at will. The inner passage gives onto the Gunners' Lodging, a weatherboarded structure inside the south bastion. This contains pleasant Georgian rooms that might be in a country rectory.

Upstairs are small museums devoted to the two most distinguished wardens, Pitt and Wellington. The Wellington Room is as it was when he died in the armchair, sitting next to his old camp bed. His celebrated boots are on display. The Pitt Museum contains Pitt's gaming chair.

The keep is bisected by a long corridor lined with prints and lit by skylights. Halfway along are two rooms occupied by Queen Victoria and Prince Albert during their visit to the elderly Duke in 1842. Their retinue was so large that the Duke had to move out to the Ship Inn at Dover. The dining and drawing rooms carry prints and portraits of the castle and its wardens. A door gives directly onto the gardens, including the Queen Mother's Garden presented to her as Lord Warden in 1997 on her 95th birthday.

WESTERHAM: QUEBEC HOUSE **

Quebec Square
James Wolfe's childhood home (NT)

I lived near Westerham as a boy and found visiting Quebec House a brush with death. James Wolfe, whose shrine it is, seemed to have done nothing but scale the Heights of Abraham and die. Since this was to stop the French getting Canada, I was not convinced the heroism was worth it. Wolfe lived in this house, then called Spiers, before his parents moved to Greenwich in 1738, when he was eleven. The house remained in obscurity until bought by a patriotic Canadian, Joseph Learmont, in 1913 and passed to the National Trust as one of its first properties.

Quebec House remains pleasantly dull. It is a redbrick building of Tudor and Jacobean origins, the gables restored in the 20th century. The rooms are those of any comfortable town house of the period, wholly dominated by the memory of Wolfe. As the guidebook remarks, 'Wolfe dies many times in Quebec House.'

He does little else. A bronze of the general stands in the parlour. Engravings of the death

scene adorn the inner hall. In the Bicentennial Room at the back is the gown in which his body was wrapped. Here too is his travelling canteen, used during the Quebec campaign. It contains everything from a frying pan to a decanter. The staircase is spacious and rises through two floors. Its walls are hung with more Wolfe pictures and a portion of the black cloth from his coffin.

The upstairs drawing room is a delightful chamber, with a Broadwood square piano. On it stands music composed in Wolfe's honour, 'Britannia or the Death of Wolfe'. The pictures are almost all variations on the same them, including a grisaille copy of Benjamin West's painting of, yes, the *Death of Wolfe*.

WESTERHAM: SQUERRYES COURT ***

½m W of Westerham
Restoration house with Grand Tour
collection (P)

Squerryes is the sort of house in front of which Georgian squires like be painted, attended by wife, family, dogs and retainers. John Warde acquired the house in 1731 and appears in just such a painting by John Wootton. The background is remarkably similar to today. His descendant of the same name lives here still.

The house, built in 1686, is typical of the Restoration. Its walls are of well-laid red bricks with a pedimented façade and dormer windows. The front lawn stretches down to a lake, beyond which lies a knoll, a pavilion and a view. The interior is classical, partly altered in the 19th century and chiefly of interest for its paintings and tapestries. In the entrance hall is a portrait of Sir Patience Warde, so named because his father was tired of having sons (he had six) and promised his wife that the next child would be called Patience. Undaunted by his name, Patience became Lord Mayor of London.

The upstairs landing is a picture gallery, displaying a small collection of Grand Tour paintings. This is a remarkable set in a relatively modest gentleman's residence, the more so as the then John Warde did not go on the Grand Tour but bought the pictures in England between 1747 and 1774. They include works by van Dyck, Rubens and Pieter de Ring. The Tapestry Room contains Squerryes' other treasures, three Soho Rococo tapestries. Acanthus scrolls embrace a charming cast of monkeys, parrots and wild flowers. Next door is a small shrine to the memory of General Wolfe, including the sword he wore during his final campaign (how did it escape Quebec House?).

The gardens were once formal but were 'naturalized' in the 18th century. The great storm of 1987 brought down 147 trees, whereupon the Wardes decided to restore the 17th-century parterres, a task now triumphantly accomplished.

Cinque Ports wardenship at Walmer

Lancashire

Lancashire lost its Lakeland beauty spots to Cumbria in the 1970s county reorganization and captured, in return, only some fragments of Yorkshire moorland. The north-east of the county remains remarkably wild and there is scenic drama in the Pennine backdrop to the old mill towns. The southern belt – reputedly the most densely inhabited region in Europe – is now almost completely de-industrialized. Built on the wealth of slaves and cotton, coal and iron, it collapsed economically in the 1960s and 1970s. Planners demolished and depopulated much of inner Liverpool and Manchester, driving people out to colonize precious countryside with suburbs and new towns. South Lancashire is not a pretty place.

Today we must pick over this wreckage to find traces of the past. There is a surprising amount. In the north of the county, medieval peles are buried in later houses at Borwick and Turton. Lancashire's medieval glory is its black-and-white 'magpie houses'; if anything, they are even more spectacular than those of Cheshire. There is nothing to match the timberwork at Smithills, or later at Speke, Rufford, Ordsall, Samlesbury and Wythenshawe. Of no less distinction are the stone courtyards of Stonyhurst and Hoghton and the compact mansion at Gawthorpe, probably by Smythson.

These houses and their successors were mostly those of a recusant gentry. As in the West Midlands and the South-West, distance from London seemed to entrench Catholicism and resistance to the Henrician Reformation. This latent hostility to the Protestant monarchy denied local grandees preferment. It held them to their land and starved them of the wealth to rebuild. Some eccentricities resulted, such as the archaic façade at Astley, contrasted with the novelty of its interior plasterwork. A modest Queen Anne front was applied to Croxteth and a fine Great Hall at Towneley. Yet the gentry recovered enough in the 18th century to go on Grand Tours and return to commission Carr's Lytham Hall and the great James Wyatt mansion at Heaton.

Given its 19th-century wealth, Lancashire is short of fine houses of the period. Its most notable product over two centuries was the furniture of the Gillow family of Lancaster, found in most grand houses of the North. It was the foundation of the London store, Waring and Gillow. Of big houses, pre-eminent is Scarisbrick, eccentric Gothic mansion of the Pugins, father and son. Most families concentrated on refurbishing the houses of their forebears. Leighton was gothicized early in the century, to be followed by Charles Barry's work at Gawthorpe, virtually a new house. The Jacobean revival restored Speke, Samlesbury and Hoghton. Of the 20th century, the best on offer are the Beatles' houses of Liverpool. Enough said.

Astley ★★★★

Borwick ★

Browsholme ★★★

Burnley:

   Towneley ★★

Croxteth ★★

Gawthorpe ★★

Haigh Hall ★

Hall i' th' Wood ★★

Heaton ★★★

Hoghton ★★★

Ince Blundell ★★

Lancaster:

   Cottage Museum ★

   Judges' Lodgings ★★

Leighton ★★

Liverpool:

   Lennon House ★

   McCartney House ★

   Sudley House ★

Lytham Hall ★★

Martholme ★

Meols Hall ★★

Rufford ★★★

Salford:

   Ordsall ★★

Samlesbury ★★

Scarisbrick ★★

Smithills ★★★

Speke ★★★★★

Stonyhurst ★★

Turton ★★

Wythenshawe Hall ★★

ASTLEY HALL ****

2m W of Chorley
Refashioned Elizabethan mansion, voluptuous stuccowork (M)

Astley Hall is the most exhilarating house in Lancashire. I last visited it on a summer afternoon when huge crowds were trooping past to the Royal Lancashire Show in the park. The house was open, free and completely empty. If we cannot promote these houses, so admirably rescued from dereliction, they will die a second time.

Astley was the house of the Charnocks of Chorley. Like most of the Lancashire gentry, they were fiercely Catholic in the 16th century and Royalist in the 17th. A Charnock was executed for seeking to dethrone Elizabeth I in the Babington Plot. Their Elizabethan house forms the core of Astley, round an inner courtyard.

In 1653, the last Charnock died without seeing the Restoration, leaving the house to his daughter and her husband, Richard Brooke. In the 1660s, they supplied the front and main reception rooms that we see today. Astley passed by descent, latterly as a preserved 'second seat', through the Brookes, Townley-Parkers and Tattons – all great Lancashire families. It was given to Chorley Council in 1922 as a memorial to the Great War and is well maintained.

The Brooke house is most unusual. It is plainly old-fashioned for its late 17th-century date. Sheets of unadorned windows rise two storeys to a huge long gallery with continuous windows and a parapet. The façade must carry the most sensational glazing of any house in England. The bold functionalism might qualify as 'Modern Movement' neo-Elizabethan. The material is pink stone and brick, now rendered. Two projecting bays flank a wayward classical doorway. Despite first appearances, this composition is not symmetrical, since one side conceals the former medieval hall. The doorway has crudely fashioned paired Ionic columns, crowned by two lions trying to look fierce. The back of the house dates from the earlier building, with a magnificent stepped chimney to the kitchen.

The door opens directly onto the Great Hall. The impact is breathtaking. Astley's hall and parlour have some of the most astonishing plasterwork in England – astonishing rather than beautiful. An apoplectic Pevsner uses the word 'barbaric' three times, as well as 'grim', 'ruthless' and 'breathtaking'. It is as if the young Brookes, loyally Catholic on the outside, decided to order something riotously novel within.

The Great Hall is the chamber of a Renaissance prince. The floor is of rough stone and the bay window is medieval in form, but the walls are lined with panels, divided by pilasters, depicting famous people, a cultured fashion said to predate the Brooke rebuilding. They include Tamerlane and his opponent, Sultan Bajazet; Scanderbeg and his opponent Mohamed II; Columbus and Magellan; Philip II and Leicester; Elizabeth I and Drake; Farnese of Lepanto and Henry IV of France; Spinola (Spanish victor over the Protestant Dutch) and the Hungarian hero, Gabor Bethlen. In other words, the list is carefully chosen to show both sides of each war. The politic Brooke later added William of Orange.

The walls are overshadowed by the ceiling. This is so enriched with undercut plaster as to defy gravity. Beams are coated with stucco. In each of the panels are wreaths containing cherubs and flowers, carved in three dimensions and some appearing to hang free of the ceiling. The frieze holds shields and cherubs cavorting amid garlands. Much of the craftsmanship is crude and some of the figures are not of plaster but of painted leather and lead. Adding to the magnificence is the staircase placed directly opposite the entrance, with thick acanthus balustrading and newel posts with vases of flowers.

Next to the Great Hall and beginning what would have been the family wing of the old house is the drawing room. Here the same plasterers have been at work and here Pevsner's word 'barbaric' has some application. The roundels are cluttered with incident and the design is never allowed to breathe. The putti

are grotesque and ferns appear as the bones of a skeleton. The effect remains sumptuous. Flemish tapestries and walnut and rosewood furniture are the icing on the cake. The Inlaid Room or library and dining room beyond were rebuilt in 1825 but in Jacobean style, re-using old panelling and family portraits.

Back on the other side of the hall is the morning room, benefiting from the left-hand bay of the façade and with further ceiling stuccowork, here more restrained. The room is furnished as a parlour but with a desk and wall safes reflecting its later use as a rent office. A carved relief of two large fish adorn the overmantel.

Upstairs, Astley has strength in depth. The Cromwell bedroom – oddly named given the allegiance of the family – has unusually enriched panelling and a plaster overmantel dating from the 16th-century house. The four-poster carries the Charnock arms. The Stucco Room is more unusual. Decorated a vivid white-and-blue, it has classical pilasters and a ribbed ceiling. By the fire is a priest's hole. In the Oak Room is 'Cromwell's bed', with the most exquisite inlay on the canopy and floral carvings on the headboard.

The top floor is occupied by a Long Gallery, three of its sides completely fenestrated and in a style that must surely predate the 1660s rebuilding. The floor and ceiling undulate gently from one end to the other like the deck of a ship. In the middle is the longest shovel-board table in existence, 23 ft long and with twenty legs.

BORWICK HALL *

Borwick, 3m NE of Carnforth
Pele tower and hall (P)

The setting of Borwick is vaguely French. Towers and gables peer over a surrounding wall in the centre of the little village rather than across a spreading estate. The pele tower had an Elizabethan house built by the Bindloss

Royalist profusion at Astley

family. The building's glory was briefly revived by *The Times*'s music critic, J. A. Fuller-Maitland, who lived there from 1911 to 1938. It then endured decades of humiliating decline until it was rehabilitated as a dwelling in the 1960s. In 1970 it became a hostel and youth activity centre, and is now institutionalized.

The building is an exciting example of that familiar northern form, a pele with Tudor additions. From the garden terrace, the grey-rendered tower rises four storeys. The Great Hall is in the centre with a three-storey porch and the family wing to the left, all of 1595, as dated by the mason, Alixander Brinsmead at the top of his staircase. He sought to unite these elements in a harmonious façade by adding a row of four pinnacled gables. The house saw a visit from Charles Stuart on his progress south, to be defeated at Worcester in 1651. Sir Robert Bindloss judiciously absented himself from the house for the occasion.

The interior is of little interest, the rich heraldic overmantels having been scattered by dealers across America. The Great Hall (renamed 'baronial') and the staircase retain echoes of more gracious times. One panelled room survives, as does the upstairs library. At the rear is a cluster of old façades, some in pink stone, with buried among them a picturesque 16th-century timber gallery. This was possibly for the use of cloth spinners.

BROWSHOLME HALL ***

5m NW of Clitheroe
Medieval moorland house with Elizabethan and Wyatt interiors (P)

The Royal Forest of Bowland, once part of the West Riding of Yorkshire, is still wild England. From Clitheroe north to Lancaster are moors and fells over which kings hunted throughout the Middle Ages. Such parks had to be policed and their ancestral keepers became powers in the land. The Parkers of Browsholme, pronounced 'brusom', go back in line to the 13th century. A Thomas Parker bought the freehold of the property in 1603.

The house's most celebrated occupant was

Thomas Lister Parker (1779–1858), antiquarian friend of Charles Towneley (Burnley: Towneley Hall, below) and patron of Turner, Opie and Northcote. He commissioned the fashionable Jeffry Wyatt (later Wyatville) to extend his old house with classical dining and drawing rooms filled with Grand Tour pictures. In the process, he went the way of many owners, overspending and declining into genteel poverty. Forced to sell the house and much of his beloved collection to a relative, he spent his life staying in the houses of friends, struggling to keep up appearances. The house, proudly maintained by the Parkers to this day, is much as Lister Parker left it.

The approach is glorious. The road rises from the Calder Valley towards the moors. The façade appears down a long, bosky vista, disappearing then reappearing close to. It is informal and plain, with a three-storeyed classical frontispiece. One gabled wing is Jacobean, the other is formed by Wyatt's 1807 dining room, with two storeys here replacing three under the same roofline.

The medieval origins of the house and of the Parkers are immediately asserted in the splendid Hall. It is exactly as one might expect of a long-serving constable of these parts. The walls are thick with antlers, boots, shields, suits of armour and old buckskin coats. Heavy beams loom overhead. Bobbin chairs flank the fireplace. Much of the furniture is pieced together by estate carpenters from ancient fragments. It is a fine muddle, marred only by being too clean.

The library was cut from part of the hall in 1754. It is dedicated to the antiquarianism of Lister Parker, with the rare diagonal panelling brought from Parkhead near Whalley in 1809 and a Towneley family overmantel. The book shelves are not flat against the walls but in low cases jutting into the room and decorated with church bench-ends. The walls display Jacobite relics and two Devis portraits. On either side of the fire are giant tusks, as if the fireplace were a walrus spoiling for an argument.

Browsholme's Parker window

Beyond the library are Wyatt's two formal rooms built in 1805–8. The style is Soanian, with sweeping arches and Regency plasterwork, although the drawing room has some neo-Jacobean stucco. The walls are crammed with family portraits and Grand Tour scenes, including works by Northcote, Romney and Batoni. The large dining room must have seemed the height of sophistication when approached from the entrance hall. Muddy boots are exchanged for dancing pumps. Parkers gaze down from every side. This was to have been Lister Parker's finest hour.

Behind these front rooms, Browsholme reverts to pre-Wyatt smaller rooms, dark corridors and vignettes. The ante-room has a magnificent Jacobean overmantel, and stained glass recording generations of Parkers and their connections. The stair window is a kaleidoscope of such glass, apparently assembled from all periods.

Upstairs, the Oak Drawing Room has richly carved panelling of c1700 in the style of Grinling Gibbons, with five distinct tiers of entablature. The bedrooms are panelled with different Bowland woods, installed over the centuries by estate carpenters with a skill that defies dating. A magical house.

BURNLEY: TOWNELEY HALL **

1½m SE of Burnley
Antiquarian's mansion with Italian plasterwork (M)

The house has seen no fewer than nine incarnations. The ancestral home of the Towneleys (or Townleys) since the 14th century today appears grey, Gothic and forbidding. Its exterior is relieved by fine creeper, a glorious scarlet in autumn. Creeper was once the adornment of every English house but is now mostly stripped by conservationists. Inside the house displays one of Lancashire's most magnificent Great Halls, evocative testament to its most celebrated occupant, the Georgian antiquarian, Charles Towneley (1737–1805).

The Towneleys shared recusancy in the 16th century with virtually all other Lancashire landowners. One member of the family had the last head to be spiked on Temple Bar, an unfortunate honour.

Later they settled for rebuilding their ancestral home to display a vast collection of works of art. Zoffany's picture of Charles Towneley and friends surrounded by his 'marbles' in a London town house became the classic depiction of Grand Tour taste. His collection of classical statuary later formed the basis of the British Museum collection. Towneley Hall is now home to Burnley's art gallery, including a large Victorian collection and the Whalley Abbey vestments, made of 14th-century cloth of gold.

The heart of the house is the Great Hall, rebuilt by Richard Towneley, grandfather of Charles, in 1725 in high English Baroque. Fluted pilasters rise to the entablature, white against deep red walls. At either end, baldacchinos in relief frame classical statues. The ceiling plasterwork is by the early Georgian master, Francesco Vassalli, stuccoist to James Gibbs and others. This gloriously assertive chamber, one of the most splendid in the north of England, is too little known.

The left-hand range is of grand reception rooms in high Regency style, designed by Jeffry Wyatt (later Wyatville). The right-hand range survives from the 17th-century house. It includes a small dining room with diagonal panelling (Browsholme, above) and more plasterwork by Vassalli.

The Long Gallery survives on the top floor above the Wyatt rooms. It is a poignant promenade, having lost almost all its frieze of paintings of Lancashire recusants, which the museum is now trying to reassemble. Small bedrooms have been refitted to display 17th-century Lancashire furniture.

Some of Towneley's exterior stonework is of rare 'watershot' masonry. This involves stones being laid on an inward slant, apparently to assist water evaporation.

High Baroque at Towneley

CROXTETH HALL **

Croxteth, 4m NE of centre of Liverpool
Sefton family house (M)

In the 1960s and 70s, the City of Liverpool fled out of town. Planners left the centre empty and blighted, and covered the precious South Lancashire countryside with suburban housing. This soon enveloped the Croxteth Park estate of the Earls of Sefton, the last of whom died in 1972. The house and park were given to the city. Croxteth is now accessible, enjoyable and well displayed, despite a bad fire in 1952 which destroyed many of the 18th-century interiors. One of the rooms has been left undecorated to show the fire damage, an unnecessary conceit.

The hall appears from the park to be of two periods. A Queen Anne range built for the Molyneux family in 1702 looks over a Baroque terrace, and a ponderous Edwardian range forms the entrance. The former is one of the finest façades of its period in Lancashire. A central doorway comprises a broken pediment above paired attached columns; a panel above contains a flamboyant trophy. The eleven-bay front is of red brick with stone dressings, most jolly. The Edwardian entrance range by J. McVicar Anderson is a joyless reproduction.

The house is laid out round a central courtyard, part of which is Elizabethan, part Queen Anne. The Molyneuxs enjoyed a surge in fortune following a lucrative marriage in 1771. Shrewdly switching from Catholic to Anglican, they were duly elevated from Viscounts Molyneux to Earls of Sefton. The house was extended in the 1870s, and in 1902 the west range was rebuilt and enlarged to accommodate the gargantuan sporting parties beloved of Seftons.

The Edwardian period is recalled in the museum presentation of the interior. This may have been the house of the mighty Seftons, but it is now in the care of left-wing Liverpool. Visitors are thus directed past McVicar Anderson's grandiloquent staircase to begin in the steward's room, servants' hall, kitchens and pantries, as if applying for the job of scullerymaid rather than visiting the family as guests – or even tourists. Downstairs takes precedence over upstairs. That said, these rooms are admirably furnished, with copious use of waxworks and ladies in period costumes. I could not easily tell them apart.

'Upstairs' takes the form of an Edwardian house party, in the manner of Warwick Castle. The use of effigies is excellent, peopling rooms that would be otherwise empty and meaningless. There are ladies at breakfast, children playing cards and men playing billiards. Lady Sefton is shown 'relaxing in her dressing room'; she is surrounded by an evocative arrangement of flowers and scents. The contrast between the 'two houses' is forceful, and it works.

GAWTHORPE HALL **

½m E of Padiham
Elizabethan mansion restored by Barry, with textile collection (NT)

The National Trust's only property in rural Lancashire is disappointing. The present house is attributed to the Elizabethan, Robert Smythson, and was the seat of the Shuttleworths, owners of Gawthorpe from the 14th to the 20th centuries. A Shuttleworth named Ughtred is recorded in 1388, another began the present house in 1600. The social reformer, Sir James Kay-Shuttleworth, restored it from near ruin in 1849 with the help of the architect of the Houses of Parliament, Sir Charles Barry.

His descendant, Lord Shuttleworth, gave it to the National Trust in 1972, to be run by Lancashire County Council. A requirement was that the first-floor rooms be a museum displaying the textile collection of Rachel Kay-Shuttleworth – known universally as 'Miss Rachel' – who died in 1967. Architectural interest is thus confined to the exterior and a handful of the rooms. The grounds are gracefully terraced down to the River Calder.

The exterior is undeniably impressive. The house was probably built round a pele, but rather than erecting a hall to one side, the Jacobeans used the tower as a staircase core,

the rooms being arranged round it. The result has a powerful, four-square compactness to which Barry was able to add dramatic embellishment, as he did on a grander scale at Highclere (Hants).

Barry rebuilt the stair tower as a strong central feature. The exterior, however, appears to be authentic Smythson, three storeys of mullioned windows with a dramatic outlook to the back over the valley.

Inside, one is immediately aware of Barry. The entrance hall is panelled, and has a church-like screen, reminiscent of a corridor in Barry's Palace of Westminster. A frieze is formed of Shuttleworth portraits. Beyond is the dining room which retains its 1605 screen and minstrels' gallery. The two openings beneath were allegedly designed for the performance of plays. The fireplace carries the Kay-Shuttleworth coat of arms and the neo-Jacobean ceiling is a copy of what was there before.

The drawing room, still on the ground floor, is the most successful room in the house. Mostly original, it is richly panelled with arabesque inlay. The plaster frieze of fruit and foliage is interrupted by free-standing plaster figurines while the ceiling is a whirl of geometry and foliage. The room's furniture boasts an octagonal table by A. W. N. Pugin and J. G. Crace, resting on ogival supports. On either side of the fireplace are two huge wooden armchairs, composed from older backs and looking most uncomfortable.

The staircase is by Barry, looking cramped in the confined space left him by Smythson. On the top floor, an old bedroom contains a 1650s bed. Its superb crewel-work Tree of Life was embroidered by Rachel Kay-Shuttleworth copying ancient motifs found throughout the house.

The Long Gallery has a Jacobean ceiling and classical frieze, its character set by Pugin's vivid wallpaper. Portraits are mostly school of Lely but include two splendid Knellers. These were lent by the National Portrait Gallery. Throughout the house are examples of the crewel-work and other embroidery collected by Miss Rachel.

HAIGH HALL *

Haigh, 2m NE of Wigan
Classical mansion in extensive park (M)

To each Lancashire town its 'hall'. Wigan's Haigh Hall was that of the ancient owners of the town, the Bradshaighs. In 1770, the line died out and the estate overlooking the town was inherited by Elizabeth Dalrymple, who married the 23rd Earl of Crawford and Balcarres. The earl was an enterprising Regency 'improver'. On his marriage, he moved south from Scotland to develop his new-found coal and iron resources of the Wigan area.

In 1827, his son, no less enterprising and an engineer, decided to rebuild the old hall with a dignity more fitting for an earl. He reputedly drew up the plans himself, lived on the site and was his own clerk of works. All the materials were produced in the Wigan area, including the hard sandstone for the walls, the ironwork and the wood. The craftsmanship is superb. The earl laid out 40 miles of walks in the grounds, employing large numbers of local workers during the cotton recession of 1861–3. Haigh Hall passed to Wigan Council in 1947 and was heavily municipalized, with too much signage and tarmac.

The exterior is logical and classical, its chief virtue being the view out over the town from the tiers of bay windows. Behind its severe Tuscan porch, the Entrance Hall has a painting of a fine stag at bay over the fireplace. To the rear and off-centre, a huge staircase fills the heart of the house and is unquestionably its finest feature. It rises to a wide domed lantern resting on sail-vaults, wide billowing arches with decorated lunettes. The plasterwork is said to be Parisian, with eagles and grotesques, griffins and acanthus. It might be a hot-air balloon, ready to rise gracefully into the sky.

Similar plasterwork adorns the main reception rooms, now run together for weddings and other 'events' but which, until 1947, housed the Lindsay Library of the 25th Earl, one of the best collections of books then in private hands. Outside in the park, all Wigan is at play. At the present rate of sprawl, these ancestral estates may yet be the only Lancashire greenery to survive. Haigh is the more precious.

HALL I' TH' WOOD **

Green Way, 2m N of Bolton
Timber-frame and stone house, home of inventor of spinning mule (M)

This is chocolate-box Elizabethan. The house with the quaint name on the outskirts of Bolton must be reached through a housing estate that shows it no respect at all. There is only an apology for a 'wood', but the glimpse of the house down a short approach is delicious. The exterior includes some of the most exotic black-and-white studding in the county, with overhanging upper floors and cusped St Andrew's crosses.

The original house was built for a clothing family, the Brownlows, who held property here in 1483, but work appears to have stopped with the Great Hall. The domestic wing extended behind rather than across the end. This wing was rebuilt in 1648 by a leading Puritan, Alexander Norris, on the doubtless considerable spoils of confiscating property from the plentiful Lancashire Royalists. He added the two-storeyed entrance porch and the flourish of finials.

The house later became the home and workplace of Samuel Crompton, inventor of the spinning mule in 1779, to whom much of the interior is now dedicated. It then degenerated into tenements and was near derelict when bought, restored and given to the local council by Lord Leverhulme, a Bolton man, in 1899. Many old features were imported and the house is afflicted by museumitis. The only guide is aimed at children. When I arrived, I was greeted with deep suspicion for not having brought a child. Such is the cult of education.

Hall i' th' Wood's exterior shows a typical Lancashire marriage of black-and-white on one side and sandstone on the other. It is as if a stern squire had gone to market and returned with a painted lady on his arm. The interior is similarly variegated. The old Great Hall has lost much of its character; the screen has gone, though the wall mortices survive. Behind, in the stone part of the house is the dining room kitted out by Leverhulme with a ceiling copied from a Bolton inn and panelling from Hertfordshire. The overmantel has caryatids with tiny breasts.

Up a fine Restoration staircase is the drawing room, again refurbished by Leverhulme in the style of the 17th-century house. Here, the caryatids' breasts are bigger. In the small study over the porch, with a view over the roofs of Bolton, Samuel Crompton worked on his 'mule', spinning thread at a fraction of the cost of hand-spinning.

The upper rooms are mostly devoted to Crompton's life and work. An artist, musician and inventor, he naturally fell foul of machine-breaking rioters and often had to hide himself and his machine in the attic at Hall i' th' Wood. In one of the rooms, the mule has been rebuilt and set as depicted in a charming portrait of Crompton, sitting by his machine playing a violin. Next door is a small exhibition of the house's benefactor, another local boy made good, William Lever, who rose to become Lord Leverhulme of Port Sunlight.

HEATON HALL ***

1m NE of Prestwich, Manchester
Egerton family seat designed by James Wyatt
(M)

The Heaton Egertons were 16th-century magnates and relatives of the Egertons of Tatton Hall (Cheshire). The discovery of coal to the north of Manchester in the 18th century brought them huge wealth. In 1772, at the age of twenty-three, Sir Thomas Egerton was able to rebuild the old family home at Heaton with the aid of the already fashionable James Wyatt, who was just twenty-six. They produced the most handsome house of its period in Lancashire, and Wyatt's finest surviving house anywhere. Egerton became Earl of Wilton but died without male heirs. The house passed to a younger line of the Grosvenor family and was sold to Manchester Corporation, minus its

principal furniture and art, in 1901. The city was acquiring much needed open space. The Corporation thought the house might be useful as a tea-room, nothing more.

Although valiant efforts have been made to restore some contents and dignity to Heaton, a century of municipal ownership has drained the house of humanity. Worse, the conservationists have drawn all the blinds. From the outside, the house looks closed even when it is open and from the inside it looks as if someone has just died. The point of Heaton's location was to look out over the Manchester skyline. On my last visit, the house seemed under a shroud.

The south front is one of Wyatt's most serene works, every bit a match for the façades of his contemporary, Robert Adam. The house is just two storeys high, a villa rather than a mansion. A three-bayed central bow is flanked by Venetian windows with, on each side, a colonnade and two pavilions also with Venetian windows.

The composition has both balance and symmetry. The entrance, to the rear, leads into a hall and staircase but these rooms are wholly subordinate to the main enfilade on the south side. In the middle is the saloon, Wyatt classicism fortissimo. The room is painted in soft blues and greens, with a frieze of harps by Joseph Rose, Adam's stuccoist. It has been filled with Wyatt furniture removed by the government from his other great interior, Heveningham Hall in Suffolk, when that was being sold to a private owner.

To one side of the saloon is the dining room, with an exquisite apsidal alcove decorated with Bacchanalian medallions. The chairs here are also from Heveningham. On the other side, the billiard room has pride of the place, the table by Gillow being one of the first installed in an English house. The room has kept its historical wall paintings, grand classical scenes by a Polish artist, Michael Novosielski, said to be his only surviving works.

Lord Wilton was an enthusiastic cellist who inaugurated the music room at Heaton with a grand concert of works by Handel and Corelli in August 1789. The following year, a Samuel

Green organ was installed, with Rococo panels painted in grisaille. The ceiling looks naked and was surely meant to be painted. Beyond is the library with bookcases by Gillow.

The staircase is Wyatt at his most grandiose. Shallow flights rise to a pillared landing running round three sides of the hall and lit by a magnificent Venetian window. Here is the finest room in the house, the Cupola Room, which is in the Etruscan style normally associated with Adam. This is one of Wyatt's few such imitations. The delicate paintings in the pilasters and ceiling panels are by Biagio Rebecca. It is a lovely room, comparable with Adam's Etruscan Room at Osterley (London, W). But, at least during opening hours, it should be allowed the light of day.

Heaton's park is a precious if municipalized lung. Manchester should perhaps admit that, unlike Leeds at Temple Newsam, it is not up to running a major historic house and should put it under a trust capable of celebrating what should be one of England's great neo-classical works of art.

HOGHTON TOWER ***

5m SW of Blackburn
Elizabethan house on a hill, Jacobean interiors (P)

The view of Hoghton painted in 1736 by Arthur Devis is one of the finest country house pictures. It shows the house exposed on a naked hill at the end of a long rising avenue, the Lancashire plain spread round it on all sides. The hill is now encased in woodland, but it is still possible on a clear day to see the Lake District and Snowdonia from the heights of Hoghton.

The estate straddling the Ribble Valley has been in the same line since the 13th century, and once totalled 40,000 acres. Albeit smaller, it is still owned by Sir Bernard de Hoghton. In the 1560s, Thomas Hoghton built himself a new house, possibly based on an old keep, round two courtyards. His intention must have been part ostentation, part defence. He was a passionate Catholic and friend of the

Jesuit Edmund Campion, eventually going into voluntary exile to Antwerp to escape Elizabethan persecution.

The Hoghtons supported all sides and none in the political turmoil of the 17th and 18th centuries. The house welcomed James I with a massive feast in 1617, its menu proudly preserved. It was here he was said to have knighted a favoured loin of beef, thus inventing 'sirloin'. Later Hoghtons married Nonconformists and defended Lancashire against the Jacobites. The family moved to Preston and the tower on the hill was abandoned to tenants, weavers and gamekeepers. Not until the antiquarian, Sir Henry Hoghton, inherited the estate in 1862 was the old seat restored. He added a medieval 'de' in his surname and employed Paley & Austin to recreate a suitably antique place. Most of the interiors are from this time.

Hoghton Tower appears well fortified from the approach up nearly a mile of avenue. The central stone gatehouse is flanked by walls and battlemented towers, leading to the first of two courtyards on the slope. Both are original to the 16th-century house, the lower one surrounded by offices and much restored. Fine iron gates lead to a second gate-tower behind which is a higher courtyard. This formed the heart of the 16th-century house.

The Great Hall is unusually on the left of the court, suggesting an earlier keep to which it might have been attached. It is at the top of an enticing flight of steps and has two tall bay windows at the dais end. The one on the far side looks out over the steepest part of the hill.

With the kitchens and offices in the outer court, family rooms could extend comfortably round the inner one. They form a remarkable sequence. Those downstairs are mostly Elizabethan or Jacobean, used by the family and for business. They include the Guinea Room, decorated with coins symbolizing the estate rents. In this room, it was said, a Hoghton baronet gambled away the entire site of the city of Liverpool.

Upstairs are the state rooms, celebrating the royal visit of 1617. The Buckingham Room

honours James's constant companion, the Duke of Buckingham. The state bedroom houses a magnificent Elizabethan bed with intricate carved panels. The ballroom contains a severe classical fireplace and an eccentric Mannerist one. All the panelling is by Gillow, as are the quite exceptional superb neo-Georgian doorways.

Across the King's Staircase is the suite in which James I himself stayed. The rooms are ancient and intimate, their windows surveying the surrounding landscape as they would have done four centuries ago. The king remained here just two days. The cost brought the Hoghtons close to ruin. They are at last able to claim some return.

INCE BLUNDELL HALL **

Ince Blundell, 5m NE of Crosby
Antiquarian's house with Crace interiors (P-R)

Those who would visit the great recusant house of Ince Blundell must brave the Canonesses of St Augustine, Nursing Sisters of the Mercy of Jesus. Their purchase of the great house of the Blundells in 1960 was, according to the Mother Superior at the time, in every sense 'an act of faith'. The act has been admirably honoured both as a religious convalescent home and as a work of architectural conservation.

The Blundells arrived at Ince in the 13th century. They were later linked by marriage to many of the great recusant families, to Tempests, Stonors and Welds. Robert Blundell began the present house, designed by the Liverpool architect, Henry Sephton, in about 1720. Blundell's son, Henry, an antiquarian with the same obsessive taste as Charles Towneley (Burnley: Towneley Hall, above), gave the hall its present character. He first built a Doric temple in the garden for his sculptures. When this was outgrown in 1802, Blundell added a large Pantheon on the far side of the garden front.

Medieval enclosure at Hoghton

The interior of the Pantheon is covered in ornamental coffering. It is heartbreaking to see photographs of it before the sale of its statues to Liverpool's Walker Gallery in 1960. These surely could be returned to help re-found what had been one of the most important Grand Tour galleries in the country.

In 1837 the house passed to Thomas Weld of Lulworth Castle (Dorset), on condition that he changed his name to Blundell. In 1847 he commissioned J. G. Crace to redecorate the dining room and picture gallery. The result is outstanding, quite unlike the rich Italianate interiors that Crace produced for Longleat (Wilts) or Knightshayes (Devon).

The wall panels of the drawing room carry delicate painted grotesques, a light-hearted Adamish design of c1750. Bunches of grapes drip from the ceiling. The smaller music room next door has a Rococo ceiling containing an eagle and gold thunderbolts. The dining room is by Crace, but the walls are embarrassingly filled with blown-up Italian photographs of woodland scenes, replacing the tapestries moved by the Welds to Lulworth. There they can be seen today in the new house, splendid but sadly removed in spirit.

The chapel walls are by Crace, with delicate Italian motifs surrounding large grisaille panels. This is now the local Catholic parish church. Meanwhile the old sitting room has been converted by the Sisters into their private chapel. It is one of the most endearing rooms in the house and also has walls by Crace. Ince Blundell may have lost its works of art, but it remains a monument to the talents of this underrated craftsman.

LANCASTER: COTTAGE MUSEUM *

15 Castle Hill
Worker's cottage saved from wreckers (M)

In 1961, the buildings facing the castle's entrance were declared unfit for human habitation. In the manner of the age, they were to be demolished. By a miracle they escaped and are now a town treasure. Nos. 15 and 17 were once a single house with the date 1739 over the door, although the interiors look older. The windows once had stone mullions. In the 19th century, the property was cut in two: half is now a private house and the other half is open to the public.

The cottage is one of the smallest I know. It consists of a single parlour downstairs with a scullery and wash-house at the back, and two tiny, sparsely-furnished bedrooms upstairs. In the parlour the family lived, fed and spun, as did most out-workers in cloth-rich Lancaster. The fireplace is still open. There are boxes to keep salt, candles and knives free from damp. On the floor are rag rugs.

The small wash-house has a stove/boiler and a cellar beneath. There is no well or privy. Both were in the garden and have long vanished. All the place needs is more junk and dirt and an aspect onto what should be the busy heart of the town.

LANCASTER: JUDGES' LODGINGS **

Church Street
17th-century town house with Gillow furniture (M)

Lancaster is a sad place, the denuded capital of a lost dukedom. The town is splendidly set on a hill but has been besieged by pylons and industrial sprawl. At its heart is not a busy market or great cathedral but, of all things, a Victorian prison still in use. In the 1960s, a disastrous decision located the new Lancaster University not in the town, which it might have regenerated, but on green-belt land outside it.

Nonetheless, an enclave of old streets and buildings survives immediately beneath the castle. These are overseen by the residence of the castle's Keeper, later the lodgings of the Circuit judges. From here, Keeper Thomas Covell hunted down the ten 'Pendle Witches' in 1612.

The house is located at the top of a flight of steps looking down Church Street. The castle is its backdrop, with the original Gillow furniture works to the left. The view to the other end of Church Street is of Pevsner's 'grandest monument in England', the Ashton Memorial on the distant hillside outside the town. It was designed by John Belcher in 1906, the last age to dare such follies in the landscape.

The house façade has the rough-and-tumble classicism of the 1670s. Seven bays of soft ochre stone rise above a jolly doorway with a colourful pediment. Its panel contains a coat of arms and the red rose of Lancaster. The house is no longer judges' lodgings and is used as a museum. Inside is an earlier entrance hall decorated with pikes, muskets and a set of stocks. On the walls are portraits, some by George Romney, of distinguished Lancaster merchants, most of them slave-traders. Off the hall is the old parlour, containing a superb desk of 1778.

The main reception rooms are upstairs and house a superb exhibition of Gillow furniture. The splendour of these rooms shows that the Court's visit was an important social event. Drawing room and dining room are beautifully furnished and enjoy views down Church Street. Opposite is an early billiard room, Gillow being the first extensive manufacturer of such tables.

The senior or 'hanging' judge's bedroom displays the wig, gown and even the black cap for passing the death sentence. The furniture is appropriately lugubrious, including a large wardrobe in Gillow's Regency style. In the massive bed, the judge slept alone (we assume) with his conscience. On the staircase is a cruel caricature of John Wesley preaching in Rochdale and other prints of legal and political Lancashire.

LEIGHTON HALL **

Yealand Conyers, 3m N of Carnforth
Gothick family house with Gillow furniture and Lakeland views (P)

The site is the finest in Lancashire, a platform in the midst of a sweeping park with the crags of Silverdale and the Lake District beyond. Although the house exterior is of no great distinction, it contrives to take on the grandeur of its surroundings.

Leighton passed through many hands until rebuilt in 1763 for the Towneleys of Towneley Hall, whose zest for property knew no bounds. In 1822, the house was sold to Richard Gillow of the Lancaster furniture firm and has remained in the same family ever since, housing a superb collection of Gillow furniture. The exterior and hall were gothicized in the 1820s, and in 1870 a three-storey billiard room wing was added by Paley & Austin. This wing now dominates the main front, rather spoiling its symmetry.

The entrance hall and staircase are Gothick and enjoyably cluttered with trophies, hats and sporting prints. Three slender arches screen an elegant staircase. Doorways all have pointed arches. The adjacent dining room is the star of the house. It has Gillow dining chairs of a sinuous solidity, offset by a massive Jacobean carver at one end. The ceiling plasterwork is an unusual lierne pattern, its central oval originally intended to light that essential of every Gillow house, a billiard table. The walls carry French pastoral paintings fixed to the panelling. The spectacular portrait of Mrs Reynolds, mother of the present owner, is by Edward Seago.

The other rooms are those of a comfortable Regency house, occupied by a family manifestly of the Catholic faith. The library leads into the drawing room, with superb views to the Lakes beyond. The furniture is various in style, Gillows being 'catholic' in taste as well as religion. A lady's workbox combines as a desk with niches for Catholic figurines. The house has an excellent collection of English landscape and genre paintings, including a Jordaens and a fine Morland. Upstairs is a tiny recusant chapel.

The music room in the Victorian wing saw the last private recital by the contralto, Kathleen Ferrier. It contains a fine picture of St Jerome, once thought to be by Domenichino. The gardens are arranged to take advantage of the site. Leighton also has a reputedly ferocious collection of birds of prey.

LIVERPOOL: LENNON HOUSE *

Mendips, Menlove Avenue, Woolton
Residence of musician in suburban street (NT)

Not content with Forthlin Road (below), the National Trust acquired in 2002 another extremely modest work of 20th-century Liverpool architecture. It is the three-bedroom semi-detached house to which the five-year-old John Lennon moved in 1945. He was brought up there by his Aunt Mimi after his parents separated, and his mother was killed by a bus in the road outside. It was in a bedroom here that the introverted youth dreamed his musical future. On the porch he played his guitar when his aunt and her other lodgers, mostly veterinary students, could stand it no more inside.

The house was donated to the National Trust by Lennon's widow, Yoko Ono, when she heard it was to become a 'Beatles themed hotel'. She told the Trust, 'He was always in his room, thinking, dreaming – he was an incredible dreamer. I particularly wanted to save his bedroom, instead of their ruining it by making it a honeymoon suite ... Once I walked in there, it was like walking into that childhood.'

The house is considerably more genteel than the McCartney house. Situated on a dual carriageway in Woolton, it has the rendered exterior, canted windows and hipped roof of tens of thousands of inter-war houses of the New Ideal Homes movement. There is a garden front and back.

The interior has been restored by the Trust in the ascetic style of the 1950s. There is a touch of Arts and Crafts in the staircase window and a touch of Art Deco in the tiled fireplaces and mirrors, but both attributions are stretching a point. Lennon's own room has been evocatively recreated. It has Bardot and Presley posters, 45 rpm records by Lonnie Donnegan and Little Richard, and coffee mugs.

Everywhere are reminders of Aunt Mimi's famous warning: 'The guitar's all very well, John, but you'll never make a living at it.'

LIVERPOOL: MCCARTNEY HOUSE *

20 Forthlin Road, Allerton
Another suburban musical echo (NT)

This is where Paul McCartney lived as a boy and where he and Lennon wrote their early songs. As McCartney writes in the guidebook: 'My Mum and Dad would have found it hard to believe that the house is now a National Trust property – you expect the National Trust to own places like Blenheim Palace, not a little terrace house like this. But they would be chuffed.' We might shared their bafflement.

Apart from assiduous rubber-neckers with a good map, the house is accessible only to National Trust coach parties. The 1950s estate house, off suburban Mather Avenue, was taken by the McCartneys in 1955 when Paul was thirteen. Designed by the City Architect, Sir Lancelot Keay, it was called 'Intermediate Type Standard Building 5'. Of two storeys, the exterior had a simple two-bay façade with Georgian-style sashes.

Is this now a style? Inside are a hall, sitting room, dining room and kitchen downstairs and three bedrooms upstairs. The roof slopes. In front is a small area surrounded by a privet hedge. To the back is a tiny garden with shed and outside WC, although there was also one upstairs. The family had a television by 1953. This was unquestionably smarter housing than would have been available at the time for working-class families in central Liverpool. Owned by the council, it cost £1,369.9s.1d to build.

Paul's mother died in 1956 but it was from here that he met George Harrison on the bus to school and John Lennon at a Woolton fete. They formed a band in 1958. By 1963 they were already history and the Forthlin Road house was uninhabitable for the crowds outside. In July the following year, Paul bought his father a large house in Heswall on the Dee estuary, moving him out at dead of night to avoid pub-

Beatles bedroom at Menlove Avenue

licity. With no respect for history, his aunts recklessly painted over the Beatles' doodled lyrics on the toilet wall. Perhaps, like medieval frescoes, they can be recovered. A later occupant, Mrs Jones, gave visiting fans snippets of the old lace curtains as mementos.

The house was bought by the National Trust in 1995. Some Fifties furniture was acquired and a selection of photos of the band by Mike McCartney, Paul's photographer brother, put on display.

LIVERPOOL: SUDLEY HOUSE *

Mossley Hill
Ship-owner's house with fine art collection (M)

The house is typical of dozens of mansions built by Liverpool shipping magnates on the slopes of Sefton Park and Mossley Hill in the mid-19th century. Visitors to Liverpool must pinch themselves to appreciate that this was once the greatest concentration of conspicuous wealth in Britain, if not the world. The Holt family built solidly and collected prodigiously. George Holt's gallery of mostly English 18th- and 19th-century works was left to the city on his daughter's death in 1944.

The house exterior is exceptionally severe, Grecian revival of *c*1830. A Doric porch is flanked by walls of Lancashire 'new red sandstone', free of decoration and relieved on the garden side only by a small conservatory. The interior is a contrast, warm and rich, dating mostly from the 1880s. It houses the Holt collection in all its glory.

The rooms are similar in their present decoration, mostly panelled and with stencilled or hand-blocked wallpaper. They are sparsely furnished but with Pre-Raphaelite tiled fireplaces. In the library is Millais' Vanessa. The Drawing Room contains a fine Gainsborough of Lady Folkestone, a Romney, a Raeburn and a Reynolds. In the dining room are Turner's *Rosenau Castle* and a large Landseer of a Scottish hunting party. The Morning Room is devoted to the Pre-Raphaelites, pride of place going to Holman Hunt's *Finding of the Saviour in the Temple*, and a Leighton of a girl reading a book. The house guide was written by the jazz singer, George Melly, who used to visit the house as a child.

LYTHAM HALL **

½m N of Lytham, 2m E of Lytham St Anne's
Carr of York house with Baroque staircase (P)

At first sight, Lytham might be a Georgian mansion in the Home Counties. Set in flat parkland near the centre of Lytham St Annes, its redbrick-and-white dressings are unusual in sandstone Lancashire. Perhaps the seaside was considered no place for stone. Or as Sacheverell Sitwell said of its creator, Carr of York, 'His buildings could stand as well in any part of England.'

As recently as the 1960s, Lytham was still owned and occupied by the Clifton family, one of the oldest landowners in the county. Their estate of 16,000 acres embraced Lytham and much of the Fylde up to Blackpool. Staunchly Catholic, they endured a terrible 17th century, four sons dying in the Civil War. Yet the family recovered sufficiently after the Restoration to pull down the old house and, in 1757, commission a new one from Carr of York.

The Cliftons' interest in the estate collapsed in the 20th century. Land was sold, the house contents dispersed and the building passed to Guardian Assurance in 1963. The company did it proud, with the possible exception of its sense of colour. The house was restored and has now passed to a local trust, which is struggling to reassemble pictures, furniture and mementos of the Clifton past.

The house is magnificent to its drive, three storeys with a rusticated ground floor and a central pediment above Ionic pilasters. The plan is conventional, the decoration not. The entrance hall has pedimented doorcases and a low-relief stucco ceiling, the roundel a swirling Rococo work. Similar stucco is found in the adjacent morning room and dining room, the latter with a wide apse in a tentative Adam style. By the time the ballroom was built, Adam's neo-classicism is firmly in the ascendant.

The staircase hall at the rear of the building is one Carr's finest works. The flights rise, divide and return to a landing. Here the lower door from the hall is answered in a Venetian screen, behind which Carr created a Baroque inner door. The order is Ionic below, Corinthian above. The whole composition is most satisfying. Nor is that all. The ceiling is a tremendous decorative flourish. The Rococo roundel contains a relief of Jupiter, decorated with facial make-up and a red staff. It looks as if medical students have been at work after a party.

In a house of fine craftsmanship little altered since it was built, the carved chimneypieces in the bedrooms take the palm. The house is filled with works collected by the trust and not yet distributed to the rooms. On a back stair I encountered a huge Gustave Doré. Near a side entrance is a Richard Westall of Cardinal Wolsey. Some rooms are now panelled and furnished. Lytham is fighting its way back to life.

MARTHOLME *

1m NE of Great Harwood
Medieval fragment with strange door (P-R)

Martholme is chiefly of archaeological interest. Thousands of such houses must have survived into the 19th century, only to fall down or be wiped out by careless owners. Martholme is at the end of a quiet lane beneath a magnificent railway viaduct. It is an attractive grouping of medieval gatehouse and fragment of a hall house, apparently its service wing. The hall has vanished but the wing has been joined by a passage to a detached timber-framed kitchen, later encased in stone.

The original house belonged to the lords of the Heskeths from 1289. The Hesketh double-headed eagle is carved into a wall. The old house is believed to have collapsed in the 17th century. The remnants were tenanted and finally sold in 1819. The building is now occupied by the Codling family, who love it dearly.

Of the original interiors, only the former buttery and pantry survive. In one wall is set a strangely wide doorway leading to what must once have been a outside passage. This looks very 'vernacular'. Across the passage is the former kitchen. This has upstairs a small Gothic window, possibly of the 14th century. Could this have been a secret chapel? Martholme should keep 'house detectives' occupied for hours.

MEOLS HALL **

Churchtown, 2m NE of Southport
Antiquarian's 1960s manor to display family pictures (P-R)

Churchtown's chief claim to fame is to have seen the first potato planted in England (from Ireland), before Raleigh's more celebrated imports from America. The property of the Catholic Heskeths once commanded much of this part of Lancashire, with the recusant Scarisbricks next door. A Hesketh was imprisoned for supporting a Jacobite rising in 1692 and there was reputedly a priest's hole in the house. It later became a farm.

Meols was comprehensively rebuilt by the late Roger Hesketh, who from 1959 began to reassemble the village and surrounding estate after disastrous property sales by his disagreeable father. He created the house to display the family's large collection of paintings. It now clings to the past amid the suburbs of Southport, Torquay of the North.

The house shines like a beacon from the 1960s in sharp contrast to the architectural dreariness of the era. The idea of the Neo-Georgian Hesketh was that the main front in Smith-of-Warwick manner should preside over the fragment of the old Meols Hall, with the service wing 'later Georgian' and the library extension 'Regency'. It was designed to the last detail by Hesketh himself. He even wrote music in the style of Haydn for Churchtown church. His passion for the patrician traditions of old Lancashire were strongly expressed in his building.

The interior of Meols (pronounced Meels) shown to the public is essentially a gallery of paintings and not much else. Yet the effect of wandering through small rooms of dusky pictures and family paraphernalia is strangely reassuring in this bleak corner of Lancashire.

The paintings are mostly family portraits but include a satisfying scatter of landscapes and devotional works. In the library is a superb James Ward of a gigantic white horse. Heskeths and related Bolds rub shoulders with French landscapes and a Brueghel of the *Sermon on the Mount*. There are prints of hare coursing on Formby sands. Meols Hall hosts the Waterloo Cup, England's premier hare coursing championship.

RUFFORD OLD HALL ***

Rufford, 6m N of Ormskirk
Great Hall with movable screen (NT)

Rufford stands with Speke as champions of Lancashire black-and-white. Its Great Hall is exhilarating and all later additions have deferred to it. The original house was built by the Hesketh family in the early 16th century, highpoint of English timber-framing. It would have been on an H-plan, with wings on either side of the hall. One wing has gone, making way for a pleasant enclosed garden. The other has been replaced by 17th-century and later buildings. The family moved into a neighbouring 'modern' house in the 18th century, but restored it in the 1820s when 'the olden times' came back into fashion. Such is taste. The Heskeths later inherited Easton Neston in Northamptonshire and in 1936 gave Rufford to the National Trust.

The approach to the house is dominated by the exterior of the Great Hall ahead. Part of this is a Victorian reconstruction, including the lantern and left-hand gabled wing, giving the outside too much the appearance of a Swiss chalet (compare Turton below). To the left and at right angles is a redbrick wing of 1662, probably built by a lessee of part of the property. It is handsome and gabled but clearly not modern enough for the Georgian

Heskeths. Behind and facing the gardens are façades of all periods, mostly Victorian.

The interior is essentially the Great Hall. The roof is of crenellated hammerbeams, enriched with angels. At the family end, the wall is coved with a gable filled with black-and-white quatrefoils above and a generous bay window to one side. Every detail is lavishly carved. The doors in the end wall would have led to private apartments, now vanished.

The other end of the hall is even more extraordinary. There is no screens passage as such, instead the wall of the former service wing, decorated with giant quatrefoils and with arches below. The latter have arches enriched with heraldry and Gothic patterns.

In front of this end stands a movable screen, the only such work to survive in England. It is of astonishing decorative force. The panels are filled with Hesketh heraldry and Gothic vine leaves. Above rise three fantastic finials, higher than the body of the screen. I have seen this work, of c1530, called barbaric, outlandish, 'medieval Baroque' and even Polynesian. It is certainly the product of a most fertile imagination, showing a decorative freedom soon to be disciplined, some might say crushed, by the Renaissance. This wonderful room embodies the splendour of Lancashire's late Middle Ages.

After this, Rufford is something of an anticlimax, although it has been well presented by the National Trust. The dining room is an 18th-century addition hung with earlier Brussels tapestries. The study, created in the 1830s, is in Jacobean style with an overmantel banged together from old fragments, and tapestries on the walls. The upstairs rooms are Victorian in decoration, enjoyably cluttered.

SALFORD: ORDSALL HALL **

Ordsall Lane
Medieval hall lost amid housing estates (M)

Poor Ordsall. One of the great timbered houses of Lancashire once lay on the fertile banks of the River Irwell, a miraculous survival against all odds. It now languishes on a side road near Salford Quays, its wretched garden enfolded in municipal housing and warehouses. It was once a home of the Radclyffes, passing through many hands before being rented by a Pre-Raphaelite painter, F. J. Shields, and then restored by the Egertons of Tatton in the 1880s. Salford Council bought the house in 1959. I hazard the suggestion, but surely the whole building might be moved from this hopeless place to greater dignity on the adjacent Salford Quays.

The house has a Victorian brick exterior to Ordsall Lane and 17th-century extensions. The one important feature is the 15th-century Hall. Outside, it has the dazzling quatrefoil studding found (probably copied) later at Samlesbury. There are not one but two window bays, both generously glazed and jutting out into the former courtyard. With their upper windows and bold gables, they are almost houses in themselves. Such lavish timbering was always a sign of a prosperous owner.

The hall's interior is sensational. It is open to the roof, with quatrefoil panels and trusses everywhere. Most extraordinary is the screen. This is not the customary, horizontal feature with minstrels' gallery but a wall of panelling with a central arch and decorative gable above it, a design more appropriate to a church chancel. The uprights are beautifully moulded and the quatrefoils on the walls have an almost jazzy effect.

At the family end, a bedroom survives with a star-patterned ceiling and simple furniture. But a huge effort of imagination is needed to recapture the aura of this house, once surrounded by fields and simple cottages over which these great windows would have glowed with wealth and welcome.

SAMLESBURY HALL **

Samlesbury, 4½m W of Blackburn
Hall house with quatrefoil timbering (M)

The seat of the Southworth family is but a fragment of its old self, but this fragment includes a dazzling display of black-and-white architecture. Samlesbury speaks broad Lancastrian. Southworths fought at Agincourt but fell foul of the Reformation and, like many Lancashire families, kept on falling. They were ruined by the 17th century, but at least collected a saint along the way. Father John Southworth was the last Englishman to be executed for his faith, at Tyburn in 1654. His remains are in Westminster Cathedral.

The hall was tenanted until the 19th century when it was partly demolished and became an inn then a girls' school. In 1924 it was about to be demolished and shipped to America, where these buildings are better appreciated, when a group of enthusiasts saved it.

The original hall was three-sided, with a Great Hall and wings. Only the Great Hall and one wing remain, coated in the most vivid black-and-white – herringbone on the 15th-century hall and thick quatrefoil on the left-hand wing. The hall bay has a delightfully romantic gabled chamber jutting above it. Although heavily restored in 1835 and again in the 1860s, the composition is picturesque. The side wing has a rear brick wall with large chimneys, said to be the oldest brick in Lancashire.

The Great Hall's interior is open to the roof, with boldly cusped wind-braces. A huge fireplace dominates one side and a bold bay window the other. The hall used to have a rare free-standing screen, usefully dated 1532, like that at Rufford, but this was dismantled and incorporated into the minstrels' gallery in the 19th century.

The restored parlour is thick with carved panels and ceiling beams. Over the doors are reliefs of Henry VIII and Catherine of Aragon, while two giant coats of arms adorn the overmantel. The entrance hall beyond is a Victorian insertion to link the hall range with the chapel at the end of the wing. This was originally built in 1420, and has Perpendicular windows and a family pew in a gallery.

Upstairs is Samlesbury's Long Gallery. The decorated oak ceiling is of 1545. The rooms are here filled with antiques for sale. They at least appear to have been chosen with some care for the period of the rooms. I would rather have this than that the house be left empty.

SCARISBRICK HALL **

Scarisbrick, 4m NW of Ormskirk
Masterpiece of Pugins, father and son (P-R)

I cannot omit Scarisbrick although, at the time of writing, its owner, Kingswood School, rarely makes it accessible. It can be seen from afar and may be discreetly perambulated with glimpses through the windows to its stupendous interiors. This is one of England's great houses. Threatened with demolition in 1962, the years have surely won it the right to greater public display.

Victorian houses usually had a more exciting birth than Georgian ones. Scarisbrick (pronounced Scasebrick) was the product of a marriage of minds between an eccentric and reclusive landowner and a twenty-five-year-old prodigy, Augustus Welby Northcote Pugin. Charles Scarisbrick's family had lived on this land since the Middle Ages. A devout Catholic, he never married but had a mistress and illegitimate family of thirty years' standing. A miser and magpie, he amassed a huge collection of antiquities from all over Europe, leaving a fortune of £3m on his death. None of it was to go to his legal heir, his sister, whom he hated so much that he ordered his death to be kept secret. She fought for and won her rights.

In 1837, Scarisbrick asked Pugin to redesign his much-altered family house on the marshland north of Liverpool. The country, as Humphry Repton had said, 'was too flat and bleak to be deemed picturesque'. What was true in 1802 is more so today. Pugin was working on a building that the Gothic scholar, Thomas Rickman, had already begun, including the new Great Hall. But work proceeded slowly and Pugin was constantly complaining of delay. Scarisbrick took to living in total seclusion, not even talking to his steward. By 1860, Pugin and Scarisbrick were both dead and the house unfinished.

The sister, Anne Scarisbrick, took matters

Overleaf: Magpie quatrefoils at Samlesbury

impressively in hand. She hired Pugin's son, the impetuous Edward Welby Pugin (*see* Carlton Towers/Yorks, N), to complete the house with a new wing and the present tower. How far the result is as the elder Pugin intended is a matter of debate. Either way, the house was finished and furnished, and gloriously so. Despite years of abuse and the stripping of most of its contents, Scarisbrick remains an awesome monument.

From a distance, only the grim, fantastic tower rises over the trees, echo of the elder Pugin's involvement in Big Ben. From the front drive, the difference between father and son is evident. To the left is the façade which the elder Pugin applied to the earlier house. A solid Gothic porch fronts the Great Hall with bay windows to its left. The Great Hall's roof is crowned by a lantern. The style is studiously Perpendicular.

To the right of the entrance is the wing and lofty tower erected by E. W. Pugin. It is as if he were eager to outgun anything his father might have achieved. A Gothic riot appears to have broken out. The architecture is now effusive, enriched with turrets, niches and statues. An octagonal stair-tower is crowned with giant birds flapping their wings as if to escape. The tower is twice the height of what the elder Pugin apparently intended.

What survives inside makes even more tragic what must have been lost in the course of the 20th century. The Great Hall is an epic of Gothic revival. Overhead are arches and wind-braces, painted and graceful. For once A. W. N. Pugin has created a roof of compelling strength and dignity.

To the left of the Great Hall is the Oak Room, its fittings too embedded to be removed by saleroom vandals. This is among the richest 19th-century rooms in England. Every inch of wall has carved panels, mostly of biblical scenes. The chamber is designed to glow with flickering medieval candlelight. Next door, the King's Room is a Tudor Gothic chamber, a foretaste of A. W. N. Pugin's Palace of Westminster. Gothic panels fill the ceiling, and kings and queens the walls, framed by Gothic pilasters.

In the Red Drawing Room is a fireplace in which Gothic merges into Renaissance. A picture appears to celebrate Charles Scarisbrick, his mistress and children in front of the house. What is imported carving and what is by the elder Pugin is hard to tell. The decorative colouring in this and most of the rooms is by J. G. Crace, the AS initials suggesting it was executed for Anne.

SMITHILLS HALL ***

Smithills Dean Road, 2m NW of Bolton
Medieval house with Victorian wing by George Devey (M)

A path from the stables leads over a ravine through thick trees to where the old house of the Radcliffe family lies along a ridge. It was here that the Protestant, George Marsh, was investigated and burned during the Marian persecution in 1554. He stamped his foot on a flagstone at the entrance to the withdrawing room to assert his faith, the imprint remaining visible to this day. In 1801, the house was acquired by a family of Bolton bleachers, the Ainsworths. They commissioned George Devey to remodel and extend the old hall house with a wing and interiors in the style of William Morris. The building is now run by a local trust. Since entry is via the institutionalized Victorian wing, visitors should ask to be guided blindfold to the old rooms.

The Great Hall is older and smaller than the Lancashire norm. Its timbers date, according to local archaeology, from before 1350. The partition between hall and service wing, with four arched openings, is a virtuoso display of local carpentry, one tier of trefoils then one of quatrefoils rising to the open roof like giant scissors. This idiosyncratic style clearly dominated Lancashire architecture for a full two centuries. At the family end the timbering is simpler but behind is a rare 'bower' or downstairs parlour, complemented by a solar upstairs. The floor of the latter is rough with adze marks. The rooms have 17th-century furnishings and are well done.

In 1537, more rooms were added to form a

new wing beyond the bower. Although much restored by the Victorians, they retain the intimate atmosphere of the 16th century. The withdrawing room has rich linenfold panelling, to Pevsner the finest in the county, and a frieze with heads facing each other in medallions. These are supposedly members of the Barton family, owners of the house at the time.

The balancing victorianized wing of Smithills contains the rooms converted and extended by Devey. They include the Green Room and the library, both darkly Jacobean. The library, with its caged books and inlaid overmantel, is strongly reminiscent of William Morris's work.

SPEKE HALL *****

Speke Airport, 6m SE of centre of Liverpool
Elizabethan mansion, restored but largely as built (NT)

Has any house suffered greater humiliation? The airport roundabout places Speke Hall as an afterthought to Arrivals and Departures. Runways thunder east and west of the old timbers. Even the River Mersey at the end of the garden seems defeated and inert. When Liverpool decided to build its airport next to the Hall – even taking its name – the temptation to move it to a more kindly spot must have been overwhelming.

Yet Speke sits defiant in incongruity, a black-and-white palace amid pleasing lawns and generous trees, shielding it from the roar of jets. The house was built by the Norris family during the 16th century, an arch declaring it finished in 1598. In 1795 it was sold to the Watt family, who restored it and rented it in 1867–77 to Frederick Leyland, Liverpool shipping tycoon and patron of Morris, Rossetti and Whistler. The house was later bequeathed back to any surviving Norris as a remarkable gesture by Adelaide Watt in 1921. Twenty years later, it passed to the National Trust, following a secondary clause in the will.

Speke is one of the most developed, and complete, examples of a moated courtyard house of its period. Four ranges sit round a small court in which stand two ancient yews, Adam and Eve. Inside the court, the four façades are remarkably consistent, of herringbone timbering set on a sandstone plinth with a dazzling display of quatrefoil above. On two of the ranges and on both floors are continuous rows of windows overlooking the court, a cloister effect that renders the house picturesque both within and without. This is English domestic architecture at the limits of its ingenuity before succumbing to the Renaissance.

Inside, the house is strongly Victorian. The Watts and their tenant, Leyland, were medieval enthusiasts, happy to combine old with 'olden'. The rooms are full of de Morgan tiles, Pre-Raphaelite pictures and Morris wallpapers. Yet it is more old than new. The desire for authenticity at Speke is palpable. To wander these corridors and chambers is to immerse oneself in a past whose moment in time seems immaterial.

Of the chief rooms, the Great Hall is the star. It is an extraordinary chamber, almost square, its main timbers felled in 1530. By that time, a hall was for display rather than for eating. It has two large bay windows flooding it with light, one with its own fireplace. Most remarkable is the Great Wainscot. Sporting carved busts, it rises to a jettied cornice crowded with black-and-gold enrichment. Nobody knows from where it came. The screens passage is no less curious, located behind a giant stone fireplace festooned with antique armour. It is a majestic space.

The Great Parlour is set at right angles to the hall and dates from the same period as the Great Hall. A later Jacobean ceiling is coated in beautiful floral plasterwork. Over the fireplace are portrayals of the Norris family, as if they were weepers on a tomb chest. The carving has the appearance of spun barley sugar. The room has been refurnished in Victorian style.

The rooms along the west side of the court all reflect Leyland's occupancy. His particular contribution was in replacing most of the fireplaces in an artistic manner. The dining room has a delightful Dutch-tiled overmantel and fire surround copied from a house demolished for the Halewood car factory. The library is

suitably cluttered with rich leather books and Morris wallpaper. Another Leyland room is beyond the hall, the charming Blue Drawing Room, its grate decorated with sunflowers.

The upper galleries at Speke would have served as Long Galleries in more compact houses. Light floods into panelled corridors, fortuitously aligned so the noise of the adjacent airport is dampened.

STONYHURST **

4m NW of Whalley
Unfinished Elizabethan house reclaimed as Catholic school (P-R)

Most great recusant houses started as Roman Catholic and became less so. Stonyhurst has become more so. One of the most splendid Elizabethan houses in the North, it is now a leading Catholic school run by the Jesuits. The building is reached along a drive that passes through the village and grows in confidence until it reaches a huge statue of the Virgin Mary. It then puffs out its chest, turns right and charges towards the massive pile on the hill. For a small boy on his first day at school, it must be terrifying.

The old house was built in 1592 by Sir Richard Shireburne, variously spelt, on land that his family had occupied since the 13th century. He clearly built to impress, but not for long. The family's Catholic and Royalist sympathies brought them scant prosperity in the 17th century. The quadrangle behind the tower gatehouse was never completed. The house passed by marriage to the Weld family of Dorset and when Thomas Weld heard that his old Jesuit school at Liège had been closed by Napoleon, he offered Stonyhurst as a refuge. It has been the headquarters of the English Jesuits ever since.

The approach up the half-mile avenue is flanked by beautifully landscaped canals. The gatehouse is adorned with cupolas added in 1712, the effect enhanced rather than dimin-

Time without moment: Speke Hall

ished by the collegiate ranges extending on both sides. The large chapel was copied from King's College, Cambridge.

Shireburne's gatehouse at Stonyhurst is one of the grandest of its period in the country, carrying a full four storeys of classical orders. Inside, the courtyard is overpoweringly medieval, almost sinister. The hall lies ahead; its entrance has gone but the three-storey bay window survives. The right range was converted, with a new doorway, by Sir Nicholas Shireburne in a short-lived burst of Catholic enthusiasm under James II. The left range is Victorian. In a gloomy northern dusk this might be a prison courtyard.

The inside is inevitably institutionalized. The Great Hall has became the school Refectory, with a thinly ribbed ceiling and modest fireplace. It is hung with pictures of Jesuit masters and old-boy VCs, heroes of mind and body. The stained glass recalls champions of money, the great Catholic dynasties educated at the school.

A series of undercrofts beneath the hall has been converted into an admirable museum of the school's history. Thomas Weld is rightly honoured along with the customary school relics, the more exotic because of its continental past. Of Sir Nicholas Shireburne's Stuart range, the Duke's Room retains an original floral frieze. The finest space is the Victorian staircase, uniting old house and later school with panache.

TURTON TOWER **

Turton, 4m N of Bolton
Pele tower with Elizabethan extensions (M)

Turton Tower is an old house run as an informal, slightly dotty museum in the care of Lancashire County Council. Such custodianship is normally a disaster. Not here. The house was inhabited by the Orrells and the Chethams before being restored 'in the olden style' by the Kay family after 1835. It was the local town hall from 1930 to 1974. From all this it has recovered. The stone is warmed by Virginia creeper. The rooms show no trace of municipalization and little museumitis. Some even contrive to look inhabited.

Turton is in the northern tradition of pele tower and Tudor additions. The difference is that here the 15th-century tower is wholly dominant, the black-and-white extensions clinging like parasites. The extensions are not all they seem. Most are a 19th-century wrapping for what was a free-standing cruck house, now encased in Jacobethan gables.

The entrance is at the foot of the battlemented tower through a two-storey porch of 1592. Beside it is a much-altered stair turret of the same date, its own porch covered in rich quatrefoils. The rest of what is visible is attractive but early Victorian, with oversailing, herringbone timbering and bargeboards, a sort of 'chalet Lancastrian'.

The rooms are greatly enhanced by being an approved outpost of both the Victoria & Albert Museum and the National Portrait Gallery. The downstairs hall thus has a lovely Gothic chest, a suit of armour and Pugin wallpaper. The adjacent dining room, in the pele tower, is a Victorian recreation of a 17th-century interior, installed by the Kays in the 19th century.

The drawing room upstairs would have been the pele tower's Great Hall and was later used as Turton District Council chamber. The room was therefore never far from the centre of local power. Panelling, ceiling and internal porch have all been restored to their 1590s state. The Tapestry Room contains the V&A's Courtenay Bed of 1593, a masterpiece of late Elizabethan design, with astonishing scrolled bases to its posts and intricate canopy carvings. It had been at Turton for much of the 19th century. In another room is a German overmantel of the *Last Supper*; the disciples are sitting round a huge chicken. Upstairs can be found a V&A wardrobe by Ashbee and a chair by Rossetti. This is where such objects should be housed.

The rooms within the cruck-framed wing remain in their 16th-century condition. The cruck uprights are visible in some of the walls. The top of the tower has been seized for a museum.

WYTHENSHAWE HALL **

Wythenshawe Park, S of Manchester
Former seat of Tattons with ornate Tudor interiors (M)

Any attempt to disentangle the relations between the Tattons (or Egertons) of Wythenshawe and the Egertons (or Tattons) of Tatton is doomed to confusion. Like the Leghs and the Davenports of Cheshire, the big families of old Lancashire inter-married and sought deed polls to protect their entails. Suffice that the first recorded Tatton was in 1290 and the last, Robert Tatton, died in 1962.

Manchester Corporation tried to buy the Wythenshawe estate compulsorily in the 1920s for housing. The family bitterly resisted, pointing out that being besieged and 'reduced' by Cromwell was surely punishment enough for their wealth. In 1926, however, the fight had gone from them and 2,500 acres were indeed sold. The house and park were bought by the Manchester tycoon and benefactor, Lord Simon, and donated to the city corporation for public use. The old family chauffeur was retained to serve teas. The two Tatton heirs died, one as a boy at Eton and the other in the Second World War. Their father died in 1962 and the line ended.

The house presents a conventional Tudor entrance front, heavily victorianized. Wings, gables and a turret have been added, making the survival of the house's medieval core the more remarkable. The Great Hall has dark red walls and is superbly panelled, with delicate Renaissance details. On the stairs is a sympathetic painting of a Commonwealth soldier being taunted by Royalist troops.

The old chapel, converted into the Chapel Bedroom, has its original coved ceiling, fireplace and Tudor bed with a charming crib beside it. Another bedroom has a bed with caryatids holding its tester and bold Renaissance panels. In the library is a painting of *The Old Squire*, symbolizing the constancy and family pride in place that sustained these houses through many centuries of change – only to be defeated by the 20th.

Leicestershire
& Rutland

Leicestershire retains fine sweeps of country and handsome market towns, and Rutland is still a peaceful rural enclave. But this is threatened England. Much of the countryside is in the process of disappearing under the great East Midlands sprawl. The county's stock of medieval buildings – Ashby, Kirby Muxloe and Donington – is modest and Leicester's castle hall is inaccessible. Rutland does better with Oakham's Great Hall and its extraordinary horseshoe collection.

Leicestershire does, however, boast two jewels, both still in their ancestral ownership. One is the immaculate William-and-Mary mansion of Stanford, masterpiece of the Smith family of architects, of Warwick. The other the late Georgian castellated extravaganza of Belvoir. The latter has been robustly restored, surrounded by an exotic sculpture garden. It dominates the Vale of Belvoir and can surely resist encroaching suburbia.

Ashby-de-la-Zouch
    Castle *
Belvoir ****
Donington-le-Heath *
Kirby Muxloe *

Leicester:
    Belgrave Hall *
    Newarke Houses *
Lyddington Bede
    House **

Oakham Castle *
Stanford ***
Stapleford **
Staunton Harold *

ASHBY-DE-LA-ZOUCH CASTLE *

South Street (Leics)
Keep and kitchen range of Roses warlord (EH)

Powerful men lived dangerously in the 15th century. William Hastings rose to be Lord Chamberlain and close favourite of the Yorkist Edward IV during the Wars of the Roses. He was duly awarded the Ashby lands of the Lancastrian Earl of Ormonde. In 1474 he applied for permission to fortify the castle and also his house at Kirby Muxloe. Though loyal to the House of York, he was suspected of treachery by Richard III and was beheaded in the Tower in 1483. Muxloe was uncompleted and remained so. Hastings' descendants were no more fortunate during the next Civil War. They held Ashby for the King and saw it slighted in 1649. The slighting can still be seen, the keep and kitchen being sapped with explosives.

Ashby Castle is impressive, as if wrecked only yesterday. The most dramatic ruin is of Hastings' ornamental 'pretend-keep', a huge structure for its day. It stands apart from the earlier medieval castle ruins. Such towers were for show, like Ralph Cromwell's Tattershall (Lincs). It stands proud, four storeys high, shorn only of its top battlements. Beneath are the remains of four floors of grand rooms with spacious windows, chopped clean in half by the slighting. One window has a charming ogee canopy. There are polygonal corner turrets with pilasters. This must have been a medieval fantasy tower of the sort the Victorians spent fortunes recreating. Why cannot we restore this original one? It is purely a matter of courage.

The spiral staircase survives and leads to the roof, unless the health-and-safety gnomes have closed it. Of the remainder of the castle, the footings of the chapel and priest's house can be seen. The best survival is, oddly, the kitchen range which predates Hastings's work. It is one of the biggest medieval kitchens extant, comparable with Glastonbury (Somerset). Inside can be seen the fireplaces with flues, spaces for cauldrons, ovens and serving hatches. Spiral staircases lead to blocked doors and upper chambers. All trace of life has gone but mystery remains.

BELVOIR CASTLE ****

Belvoir (Leics), 6m W of Grantham
Gothicized castle-palace of the Manners family (P)

If the monarch visits Belvoir, the key is handed over not by its owner, the Duke of Rutland, but by the local Staunton family, its ancestral keepers. As manorial rent to the Rutlands, the Stauntons are charged with defending the tower with their lives. Such are the privileges of dukedom.

Tradition hangs about Belvoir like the cedars and creepers that guard its scenic approach. Leather water buckets protect the inhabitants against fire, and muskets against rebellion. Yet Belvoir is not a real castle but a 19th-century fantasy. The place is faintly institutional, stacked with military regalia, ancient custodians and, on my visit, an unappetizing smell of school food. It is not so much ducal as regimental.

Belvoir (pronounced beever) has been the home of the Manners family since Tudor times. It was an ancient stronghold on a bluff, rebuilt by the Earls of Rutland in the 16th century. The castle was demolished after the Civil War and rebuilt in 1668 by John Webb. This house was in process of being altered by Matthew Wyatt when, in 1816, a fire destroyed almost all of what remained of the 17th-century building, also consuming works by Titian, van Dyck and Reynolds. What is seen today is a monument to the architectural Wyatts.

Four of the family served Belvoir, aided by two amateurs, Elizabeth, Duchess of Rutland at the time of the Regency rebuilding, and her chaplain, Sir John Thoroton. Elizabeth was an enthusiastic amateur architect.

The result is a Regency Gothic castle in the manner of Windsor or Arundel. The entry is up a long avenue which passes sweeping lawns and long views over the Vale of Belvoir below. The castle itself is massive, built in soft ochre ironstone. The exterior is composed of variations on a tower theme. One tower is square, another round, another apparently lozenge-shaped. Others are octagonal with Gothic pinnacles. Some windows are Gothic, some 17th century. Chimneys look like towerlets and vice versa. From every battlement we expect a knight to wave a banner or a lady to sob for love.

The inside is no less fantastical, a variety of Gothic, French, Italian and even Chinese. Thoroton, working possibly to Matthew Wyatt's design, produced an impressive entrance sequence of Gothic chambers with rib-vaults, stone floors, muskets, banners and fire buckets. The guardroom looks ready to explode. A troop of horse could ride upstairs, where they would be greeted with a cavalry museum and a ballroom on the landing. An eternity of Manners' faces look down from the walls.

The style now changes abruptly. The formal tour goes not into the reception rooms but into the Chinese Rooms. These are decorated with 18th-century hand-woven silk. A domed bed, drooping with fabric, might be from a Gothic romance. The chinoiserie is exquisite, the more enjoyable for being old and apparently

much in need of restoration. Opposite is another contrast, the Elizabeth Saloon by Matthew Wyatt. This is the ladies' withdrawing room, French and shimmering in reds and golds. The 5th Duchess is sculpted in marble. On the ceiling ladies play with peacocks and putti. Ebony cabinets line the walls. The panelling is from a French château. Everywhere is gilded plasterwork with crimson hangings. This is the room that the envious Gregory sought to reproduce in neighbouring Harlaxton (Lincs).

The adjacent dining room is no less grand, with a deep coffered ceiling of gilded flower patterns, each one different. Over the mantelpieces are two Manners portraits by Reynolds. The picture gallery contains the finest paintings to survive the fire, including works by Poussin, Teniers, Steen, Gainsborough and a splendid Holbein of Henry VIII. They are relics of one of England's greatest private collections. In the middle of the room, incongruously encased in glass, is the Queen Anne Bed, brought from the Rutlands' other seat, Haddon Hall (Derbys). It is of sumptuous craftsmanship, but there is something sad in an unused bed, a true sleeping beauty.

The King's Rooms, decorated for George IV, resume the chinoiserie, with yellow drapery and pretty hand-painted wallpaper. An entire wing of the castle is occupied by the Regent's Gallery, filled with pictures and furniture and with spectacular views over the Vale. Here are more Rutland treasures, the Gobelins tapestries of Don Quixote acquired by the 5th Duke in Paris in 1814. To one side is a table designed for a version of cat's cradle.

The large and small libraries were by Thoroton in Regency Gothic style. They have ecclesiastical window frames and the customary busts of emperors and philosophers. The family chapel contains paintings by Murillo and Bassano and effigies of monks. The castle grounds are occupied by often startling examples of modern sculpture, an admirable innovation.

Ancestral Gothic at Belvoir

DONINGTON-LE-HEATH MANOR HOUSE *

Donington-le-Heath (Leics), 1m SW of Coalville
Medieval hall house with formal parterre (M)

The area between Leicester and Derby is as grim as any in England, a wilderness of giant sheds and dreary estates with feel neither for history nor contour. Yet it has surprises. One is this medieval hall house, besieged with gravel and municipal lawn. It claims to be the oldest house in Leicestershire.

The building dates from c1290, when it consisted of a hall above an undercroft, with wings to the rear. These now compose a courtyard which, apart from the glazed windows, appears authentically medieval. Numerous original lancet windows survive, along with early 17th-century casements. If the exterior had not been scrubbed ferociously after being used as a pigsty in the 1950s, it would even be atmospheric.

Ryedale (Yorks, N) has shown how medieval rooms can be recreated with some truth-to-life. The sparkling white walls, polished floors and modern display cases at Donington-le-Heath are a parody of antiquity. There is some good Jacobean furniture in the hall which is open to the roof. Part of the garden has been laid out as an ancient parterre. There are strange statues in the garden and some welcome bee-hives.

KIRBY MUXLOE CASTLE *

3m W of Leicester
Unfinished castle of Hastings family (EH)

For a minute, the Leicestershire sprawl draws back and the eye blots out the estates. By blessed chance – and for how long? – a meadow supplies the backdrop to the old Hastings castle. Set on a grassy rectangle inside a restored moat, this might be the crumbled relic of an Indian Mughal fort.

The castle was begun in 1474 under licence by Lord Hastings (Ashby-de-la-Zouch, above). That was a fantasy castle, this was a fortified house. Work did not start until 1480 but, since Hastings fell from grace three years later, was never completed. Unlike Ashby, Kirby Muxloe is of brick, beautifully laid with diaper patterning and a pleasure to the eye. This was intended to be as fine as any house of its day in England.

What stands is a symmetrical gatehouse, one of the first to have gunports for firing small cannon at attackers, and a high corner tower. The gatehouse is most impressive when approached over its bridge across the moat. It has projecting bays, the gunports in them looking like drains. Since the upper floors were not completed we must assume that the upper walls would have enclosed a large chamber over the entrance. The Great Hall would have been on the far side of the courtyard. The panel over the entrance still awaits the Hastings arms, not being incised before his execution.

The corner tower has three storeys and was finished. It is battlemented and has an exciting spiral staircase of brick leading to the roof. The rooms are what would now be called en suite, with their own garderobes dropping into the basement, where the nightsoil would have been collected. Here, too, are small gunports, surely as dangerous for their users as for their victims.

LEICESTER: BELGRAVE HALL *

Belgrave, 1m N of city centre
Georgian merchant's house (M)

The enclave of Belgrave Hall on the outskirts of Leicester is precious. The old house is early Georgian begun in 1709, its façade eerily puritanical. A narrow entrance of three bays is recessed behind two wings, each with five identical windows on three floors. There are no quoins, no parapet, no adornment. The back, apart from the three gables to the third floor, is as simple. All this was built by a rich merchant in the age of Vanbrugh.

The house was the home and headquarters of the Vann family, Leicestershire hosiers. Their descendants sold it to the City Council

in 1936, from whom it passed to the county. The interior has been refurnished and is refreshingly free of museumitis. The waxworks are decorous and the rooms, if rather bare, reflect the undemonstrative comfort of a prosperous family of the period. Nothing is spectacular.

The ground floor plan is strange. The kitchen is where we might expect a drawing room, but close to the dining room across the hall. Was this meanness or did the Vanns like their food hot? The dining room has columns to the bay window, with crude Corinthian capitals. The staircase has fine twisted balusters. On the first floor are the drawing room, a bedroom, bathroom and parlour. In the last a stuffed cat plays with a ball of wool. The top floor is for the nursery and housekeeper's room. Walled gardens survive at the back.

LEICESTER: NEWARKE HOUSES *

The Newarke
Elizabethan houses backing onto castle (M)

Crouching in the backwash of a domineering Leicester gyratory traffic scheme is a fragment of the old city next to the castle and river. The castle includes reputedly the longest Great Hall in England, that of the Earl of Leicester's 1351 hospital. It is not regularly open to the public, unimaginable in any other city in Europe. Instead, we are allowed to see two town houses in The Newarke outside. A fragment of medieval wall survives in their garden.

The two houses were once Skeffington House and Wyggeston's Chantry. They are both Elizabethan or older in origin and traces of this can be seen on the exterior, in gables with ball finials and a few old windows. The insides have been so altered over the years and recently knocked about by the museum as to be barely 'old'. Yet there are three fine panelled rooms, one of them spectacularly rich, with lozenge panels and pilasters and appropriate furniture. The staircase is 18th century and has portraits of the period on the walls. In the upstairs Long Room is a charming overmantel of 1631. This was rescued from Ragdale Old Hall, a Leicestershire Tudor mansion scandalously demolished in 1958 at the time when English houses suffered the equivalent of the Black Death.

As a museum, the Newarke Houses are full of oddities. There are dozens of clocks, including a display of how they were made. There is also an excellent fake street to the rear and a museum of one of Leicester's favourite sons, Daniel Lambert. At 53 stone, he is still unbeaten as 'the fattest man in England'. He was keeper of the local jail in the 18th century.

LYDDINGTON BEDE HOUSE **

Lyddington (Rutland), 6m N of Corby
Fragment of palace later used as almshouse (EH)

The house was once part of a summer palace of the Bishops of Lincoln. The range was built in the mid-15th century and passed at the Dissolution to Lord Burghley, who converted it to almshouses in c1600. That use survived until the 1930s. It seems a pity that it cannot still serve that purpose, at least in part.

The Bede House sits next to the church, built of the same astonishingly rich, honey-coloured ironstone in which this part of England abounds. The grey ashlar dressings and buttresses seem an impertinence to this superb material.

At the time of conversion in the 16th century, Tudor windows were inserted into the main walls upstairs while smaller windows light the bedesmen's cells downstairs. Tall chimneys indicate creature comforts. Along the north side is a wooden pentice, a walkway for sheltered promenading which was much favoured by Tudor almshouses (*see* Abingdon, Oxon).

The bedesmen's cells are in what would have been an open undercroft beneath the Great Chamber. They offer a fascinating relic of an ancient old people's home, tiny but neat, warm and secure. They must have seemed luxurious to those whose lives had been spent in the fields and hovels of the village. Above is the Bishops' Presence Chamber, survivor of the old palace, and a smaller private room. This is where the bishop would have received petitioners and conducted local business on his visits. It is ceiled with wood and has unusual coving carved in imitation of fan vaulting. There is painted glass in the windows.

OAKHAM CASTLE *

Catmos Street (Rutland)
Norman hall with Romanesque carvings and horseshoe collection (M)

All that survives of the royal castle of Oakham is its Great Hall. The rest is a series of lumps, dips and mounds in the park, precious to archaeologists and children but no one else. The hall is reached down a charming alleyway from the market square and is one of the most spectacular domestic interiors to survive anywhere from the Norman era.

From the outside, one might be looking at a conventional church hall, with aisles and dormer windows above walls cruelly set in tarmac. Inside, an aisled hall rises to a king-post roof. The arches on each side are divided by piers, with superb Norman sculptures for capitals. These would be remarkable in a church and are exceptionally rare in a secular building. We see the heads of kings and queens, animals and musicians, some with their instruments still discernible. The carving has been related to 12th-century work at Canterbury Cathedral and indicates the early prominence of Oakham on the route north.

A quite different matter is the astonishing decoration, of horseshoes covering every inch of the walls. They look at first like the collection of some obsessive schoolboy. The horseshoes are of differing size and materials. All are hung upside down, despite the tradition that horseshoes should be kept upright to prevent the luck falling out. Some are gigantic, a yard across.

The horseshoes carry the names and arms of

visiting peers and royalty who were required to donate a horseshoe or its monetary equivalent to the lord of the Manor of Oakham. The custom is first mentioned in the 16th century, although the oldest is claimed to date from 1470. There are some 200 in all, many more having been thrown out by the Victorians, and lost.

STANFORD HALL ***

Stanford on Avon (Leics), 5m SE of Lutterworth
Smith of Warwick house with Baroque ballroom (P)

Stanford is the perfect William-and-Mary house. When seen from the road, the south front floats like a palace of romance across a distant meadow. Two tiers of windows are set in pale stone walls beneath a protective hipped roof.

The property has belonged since 1430 to the Cave family, now represented by Lady Braye, a lineage celebrated in the superb memorial in the local church. The architect of the present house was William Smith, the older Smith of Warwick, in that most exquisite of decades, the 1690s. Younger members of his family georgianized the east front, making it the entrance, and built the stables.

Inside, each room is a gem, enhanced by evidence of continuous family occupation. Everything seems in regular use and not merely 'on display'. The front entrance leads not into a hall but unusually into one end of a long passage. This is the result of the original entrance hall having been made into the ballroom in 1745.

Immediately to the left is the panelled library, displaying historical documents and accounts for the original building. A family Bible was embroidered in silk in 1629 by a Cave daughter in thanks for having survived the lustful advances of the Pasha on a visit to Turkey. A silhouette depicts a Georgian family playing a quintet. How many families could do that now?

The ballroom was created by the younger Smith with a flamboyance worthy of a Viennese palace. The deeply coved ceiling has giant *trompe-l'œil* scallops in each corner while the central roundel depicts Apollo in a sunburst. It is a sensational composition. Doorway and overmantel are sumptuous, bold pink with heavy gilding. Most of the paintings are of the Stuarts, their Pretenders and courtiers, acquired as a lot by Lady Braye in Rome in 1842 during a burst of Stuart revivalist fervour. They include a rare portrait of Bonnie Prince Charlie in exile at the age of fifty.

The Green and Grey Drawing Rooms have more paintings of Stuarts. In the former is a magnificent black cat of Staffordshire pottery and an unusual German cabinet inlaid with Persian hunting scenes. Over the Grey Drawing Room mantelpiece is a masterful flower painting by Bosschaert. It outshines a copy of van Dyck's royal children on the adjacent wall. The Old Dining Room is hung with Tudor and other portraits set amid the most brilliant crimson damask wall-hangings.

A spacious Georgian staircase hall fills the core of the house. It has triple balusters and is hung with Cave portraits of all periods. The upstairs bedrooms are admirably cluttered. In the Bachelor's Room – so called for being 'too dark for a lady' – is a pleasing contrast of fabrics. A Flemish tapestry covers a wall, the four-poster has a 19th-century pelmet and the bed an American quilt. Stanford is in good hands.

STAPLEFORD PARK **

Stapleford (Leics), 4m E of Melton Mowbray
Much-altered mansion with early Jacobean wing (H)

The first owners of Stapleford were old money, the Earls of Harborough. They held it for four centuries. The next owners were new money, the brewing Grettons, who held it for one century. Since 1982 it has changed hands repeatedly and is now a luxury hotel. Novelty is regularly proclaimed, the latest being 'an

Staunton Harold: English epitome

executive chef who is spiking his cuisine with light fresh flavours'.

Stapleford was acquired by the Sherard family, Earls of Harborough, in 1402 and a new house built by 1500. One wing of this survives and holds the chief architectural interest of the building. It was embellished by Lady Abigail Sherard in 1633 with extravagant Dutch gables and Gothic niches, considered early examples of Gothic revivalism. In its appearance it is 'reminiscent of Flemish town halls', said Pevsner. Six of the twelve niches purport to show Sherard ancestors, making it more likely that this was calculated antiquarianism, like Lady Anne Clifford's work in the Borders at the same time.

The rest of the present house was built in a U-shape onto the back of the old house, facing the park. It is of the late 17th century, of two storeys with a boldly hipped roof. The present hotel entrance front is of this date, but on the far side we can see that the house was drastically altered by the Grettons at the end of the 19th century. A modern, neo-Elizabethan block was crudely inserted between the two arms of the U. The result looks like an Edwardian swell with a lady on each arm.

As a result it is near impossible to date the interior. The entrance leads to a Victorian hall with a bold stone balcony, heavily decorated with trophies and paintings of stags. Many of the reception rooms retain 17th-century ceilings and fittings, notably the 'Grinling Gibbons' overmantel and doorcases in the dining room, moved from the original saloon upstairs. Lord Gretton allegedly rebuilt the house to advance his social position in the county. He should have let the 17th century do it unaided.

STAUNTON HAROLD HALL

*

5m NE of Ashby-de-la-Zouch (Leics)
Mansion and church in park setting (P-R)

Glimpsed amid thick woods from the Ashby to Melbourne road is the epitome of old England. Lying in the valley below is a curving lake with, amid cedars, an old mansion, church, stables and outbuildings, arrayed as if for a chocolate box. This was the seat of the Shirleys, later Earls Ferrers. The church, now owned by the National Trust, was built during the Commonwealth and its defiant Shirley builder eventually died in the Tower of London.

By the 1950s the Ferrers could not manage the building and it fell into disrepair. It became a Cheshire Home, and sadly institutionalized. Rubbish, car parking and tarmac greet the visitor. At the time of writing the house has been sold to the Blount family (*see* Clifton/Staffs) as a residence with the intention of re-opening it to the public. The grounds, the church, stables, kitchen garden and former library are already accessible. There must be as many gardeners, artisans and craftsmen busying themselves in Staunton's crafts centre as during its heyday.

The exterior of the hall is serenely Palladian, built piecemeal over the 18th century, with a north front of c1700 and a formal east front looking out over the park. Its façade was designed by the 5th Earl in 1763. There are just two storeys. The three central bays are of stone, the rest of beautifully laid red brick. The nether regions of the house are a warren of rooms, passages and courtyards. I am sure that one day Staunton will be again resplendent.

Lincolnshire

Lincolnshire is one of England's biggest and least known counties. Medieval wool wealth left it rich in churches but, when that passed, its damp fens and infertile uplands left it poor in houses. From the early Middle Ages is the Jew's House in Lincoln and, from the 15th century, Tattershall, the finest early brick tower in England. Gainsborough's Old Hall is a little-known but spectacular medieval group. Doddington's prodigy house by Robert Smythson stands guard over Lincoln from the adjacent plain.

The Restoration is superbly represented at Lord Brownlow's Belton House. Vanbrugh's Grimsthorpe is one of his most theatrical stage sets, containing a Great Hall to rival Blenheim's. The Georgians are displayed chiefly in the Wyatts' work at Belton. The 19th century left Gregory's astonishing creation by Salvin and Burn at Harlaxton, a revivalist house of a quality unique in England.

Aubourn *
Belton House ****
Doddington ***
Epworth:
   The Old Rectory **
Gainsborough Old
     Hall **

Grimsthorpe ****
Gunby ***
Harlaxton ****
Lincoln:
   Jew's House *
Marston *
Normanby **

Spalding:
   Ayscoughfee Hall *
Stoke Rochford **
Tattershall **
Woolsthorpe *

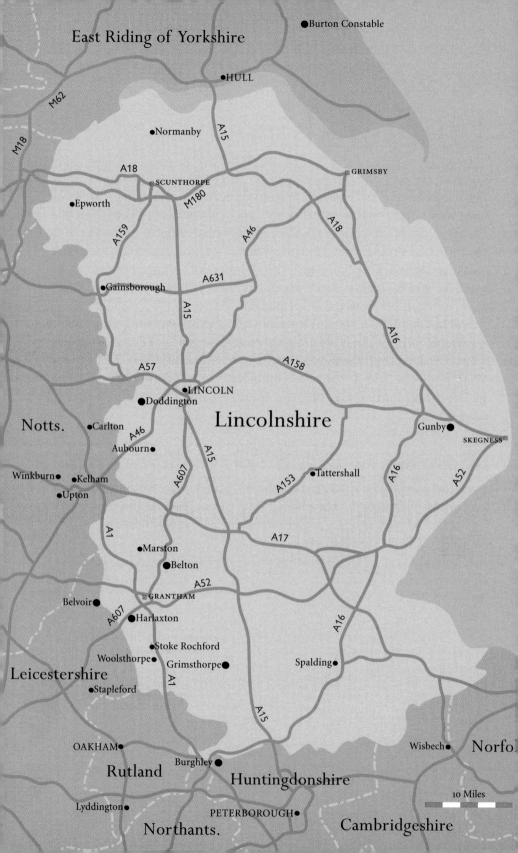

AUBOURN HALL *

Aubourn, 6m S of Lincoln
Possible John Smythson house with fine
Jacobean staircase (P-R)

Aubourn is an odd Elizabethan house of
brick, very tall and said to be influenced by
John Smythson, son of Robert. The Neviles,
who still live here, employed Smythson junior
in Nottinghamshire and Robert's biographer,
Mark Girouard, remarks that 'this attractive
but puzzling house or fragment of a house'
seems to show Smythson influence. It sits
quietly in a pleasant garden outside Lincoln,
with the River Witham for company.

The front is high and asymmetrical with
almost square windows, distinctly Elizabethan.
The doorway is Jacobean and the inside offers
Elizabethan and Jacobean in confusing profusion. The study chimneypiece, of tiered
pilasters, is Elizabethan Renaissance. The staircase, pride of the house, is clearly later. It has
elongated newel posts and pendants, each
fashioned from a single piece of wood. The
serpents and foliage are what Pevsner calls
'Gothic-Viking' in style.

The baluster panels are of flat geometrical
strapwork, plain yet handsome. The stairs rise
two storeys to the top of the house, indicating
the increased importance of upper chambers,
whether for guests or servants, in the 17th century. At the foot is a superb carved wooden
gate to keep dogs, or possibly children, from
going upstairs.

BELTON HOUSE ****

3m N of Grantham
Carolean mansion altered by Wyatts in 18th
century. (NT)

Belton is the perfect Restoration house, well
mannered yet a little frigid. The ancestral
owners, the Brownlows, were Elizabethan
lawyers who always did the right thing but
never set the Thames on fire. I cannot imagine
a Brownlow galloping into the Saloon at
Belton and decapitating the porcelain. Inter-
war Brownlows were friends of Edward VIII
during the Abdication crisis. The King had
stayed at Belton with Mrs Simpson and it was a
Lord Brownlow who persuaded her, in a letter
from France, to renounce him and let him
remain king. The letter arrived too late.

The exterior of 1684 was once believed to
be by Christopher Wren. It has a deep-pitched
roof, dormer windows and white-painted
balustrade with cupola, typical of Wren's work.
The building material is a rich, honeyed limestone. Belton is now attributed to William
Winde, architect of Ashdown (Oxon), but
most of the interiors were altered in the late-
Georgian era by various Wyatts. The pleasure
of the house thus lies in distinguishing the
robust 17th century from the more effete 18th.

The Marble Hall is early, balancing the
saloon behind. The two rooms almost cheat
the eye, offering vistas through from the formal
garden on one side to the landscaped park on
the other. The hall has stone floors and limewood carving, some of it attributed to Grinling Gibbons. Paintings and porcelain here, as
throughout the house, are superlative. The former include Lelys, Reynolds and Romneys of
the Brownlow and related Cust families.

The saloon is more ornamental. Here boots
are metaphorically removed and Aubusson
covers the floor. The style is still 17th century,
with heavy doorcases and ornate plaster ceiling. Again some carvings are probably by
Gibbons. The overmantel surround has so
many birds it looks as if it might take flight.
Next door is the Tyrconnel Room, with a
painted floor and carved frieze panel not by
Gibbons but by his contemporary, Edmund
Carpenter.

The east wing of the house comprises a
chapel, complete with family gallery and withdrawing room, surviving from the original
house. The guide says the chapel is here
'a quasi-public room of state', its opulence
'arising much from the desire to express status
as from more spiritual motives'. Its Baroque
reredos is worthy of a City of London
church. Exquisite limewood carving surrounds
a Flemish Madonna in the chapel gallery.

The remainder of Belton is immaculately

displayed. The bed in the Blue Bedroom downstairs has a backing like a majestic organ case. The staircase has wall panels by Jeffry Wyatville and ceilings by Edward Goudge. Lord Leighton's sublime portrait of Lady Brownlow gazes down from on high.

The upstairs bedrooms have canopied beds, with hand-painted wallpaper in the Chinese Room. The birds and butterflies are cut-outs added by hand. Pride of place on the first floor goes to the library and ante-library. The latter contains a collection of mostly blue-and-white Chinese porcelain. In the library is a quaint exercise chair on which the user was expected to bounce. The adjacent boudoir has the finest of the James Wyatt ceilings, every bit the measure of his rival, Robert Adam. Next door is the Windsor Bedroom, in which 'they' presumably stayed. It displays photographs of the couple and a flurry of Cust portraits.

Belton is left through the Tapestry Room, designed to display four Mortlake tapestries depicting the story of Diogenes. The room appears 17th century but is a Victorian re-creation of that period. In a corner of the ground floor is the Hondecoeter Room, designed by Wyatville to take three large paintings by the Dutch decorative artist. They bring indoors the rural scenery which 17th-century landowners across Northern Europe were seeking to create outside, packed with flora and exotic fauna drawn from the new continents of Dutch colonization.

DODDINGTON HALL ***

Doddington, 6m W of Lincoln
Elizabethan mansion converted in 18th century (P)

There are really two Doddingtons. The house appears from the road as an Elizabethan prodigy mansion. Its romantic exterior has three belvedere cupolas, large and serene when seen across a lawn beyond a gatehouse. The tableau is immaculate. The inside is quite

Gibbons profusion at Belton

different, a Georgian house conversion of 1760.

The Hall was built c1600 by Thomas Tailor, Registrar to the Diocese of Lincoln, which then stretched from here to the Thames. Tailor was a lawyer and therefore rich. From the roof of the house, the towers of Lincoln Cathedral are proprietorially visible. Despite a lack of documentary evidence, the house is attributed to Robert Smythson.

It passed down the generations to the Hussey and Delaval families, whose misbehaviour (*see* Seaton Delaval/Northumbs) led to a curse that they would have no male heirs. Such curses tend to be remembered only when they turn out to be true. When Sarah Hussey's daughter and heir married a Delaval in 1724, she entailed the estate never to be joined to Seaton Delaval. Her Delaval grandson, Sir John, added Hussey to his name. The house passed to George Jarvis, whose descendants live there to this day.

The exterior is symmetrical and finely proportioned, three storeys of brick with stone quoins. Two wings embrace a façade punctuated by three projecting towers, one for the porch, the others occupying the angles of the wings. Above are hexagonal belvederes with cupolas. The only classical detail is the doorway, topped by Jacobean scrollwork. Despite its impressive façade, Doddington is only one room deep.

The interior can seem a disappointment. Smythson's large rooms – the house had only nine bedrooms – invited modernization rather than demolition when Sir John Hussey Delaval restored the interiors in the 1760s. The Great Hall has lost its screens passage but still extends, medieval fashion, to one side of the porch. The broken pediments of its panelling are adorned with blue-and-white china. Portraits chart the story of the Hussey, Delaval and Jarvis families.

The house's plan has the kitchens and offices to one side of the entrance and the family wing to the other. The latter contains just two rooms on each floor. The library and parlour downstairs are crowded with portraits and china and are in regular family use. They are divided by a grand staircase, beautifully

carpentered but rather dull. At its foot is a Reynolds of a glamorous Delaval who raided St Malo in 1758. He swam ashore ahead of his ship and completed the 'conquest' of the undefended port by getting drunk in a bar.

One of the first floor bedrooms, the Tiger Room, has a bed from Seaton Delaval in which the 'Butcher' Duke of Cumberland slept on his way to the Battle of Culloden. He was apparently 5 feet tall but 23 stone in weight, near incredible proportions. Hence the bed steps. The drawing room, formerly the Great Chamber over the Great Hall, has more Delavals and more china, a speciality of Doddington. The chess set was carved from mutton bones by Napoleonic prisoners in the care of a Jarvis ancestor commanding Dover Castle.

The upper floor comprises a Long Gallery running the length of the house. It once had windows on both sides, now bricked up to give more space for hanging pictures. Although the paintings generally are of no great quality, a superb Reynolds fills an end wall. It was sold to the nation in lieu of tax and allowed to remain here 'on loan' provided there is public access, an admirable system.

EPWORTH: THE OLD RECTORY **

Epworth, 11m SW of Scunthorpe
Childhood home of John Wesley (M)

The Reverend Samuel Wesley arrived as Rector of Epworth in 1697. It was a time when Baptists were rioting and threatening all manifestations of the Established church. Wesley was a High Churchman and Royalist, immediately in conflict with the Nonconformist temper of his parish. In 1702 the Rectory was damaged by fire and in 1709 was burnt to the ground. The family of eight children were in bed, but escaped before the roof collapsed.

The last to be rescued from an upstairs window was the six-year-old John, his mother regarding his salvation as being by the hand

Doddington: pavilions of splendour

of God. He was 'a brand plucked from the burning'. That brand, John Wesley, came near to destroying the same Church of England that his father had so bravely upheld. When old Wesley died, his epitaph stated that 'as he lived, so he died in the true Catholic faith'. The young Wesley never rejected that faith and always maintained that his was the true Reformation Anglicanism. This was not how his followers saw it.

Epworth Rectory was rebuilt and often visited by John Wesley during his travels. By the 1950s it was decrepit, and was offered by the diocese to the World Methodist Council. It was opened as a museum in 1957 and is now a Wesleyan shrine. The depiction of young John Wesley's rescue from the fire became one of the most popular of all Victorian engravings.

The rectory is still recognizably the Queen Anne house in which the Wesleys lived. It is a genial box of seven bays by four, the roof gabled at one end and hipped at the other. The interior is simple but not poor. In the entrance stands a Jacobean sideboard and furniture more Methodist than 'High Church' in taste. There is a schoolroom in which 'the incomparable Susanna' Wesley taught her ten surviving children, including John and his young follower, Charles. She determined to 'take such a proportion of time as I can spare every night, to discourse with each child apart'. John had Thursday, Charles Saturday. The girls had to share. On the Queen Anne staircase is the picture of the fire. The attic contains an exhibition of Wesleyana, with much commemorative Staffordshire pottery.

GAINSBOROUGH OLD HALL **

Parnell Street
Complete medieval and Tudor hall house (EH)

For once the hyperbole is justified. 'One of the country's best preserved medieval manors', says the guidebook. Gainsborough Old Hall is set on a lawn in a back street behind a dull town centre. It comprises a 15th-century manor with tower, Great Hall, kitchen range, solar and extensive suite of state rooms. Anywhere but in Lincolnshire, the place would be famous.

The house was reputedly rebuilt by Sir Thomas Burgh after a fire, to entertain Richard III in 1484. The property passed to the Hickman family, under whom it became a factory, Congregational chapel, ballroom and auction house, each use saving it from destruction. The Old Hall was given to the nation in 1970.

The building is a textbook of medieval architecture. The Great Hall fills the centre of an H-plan. The hall range is timbered, with lath and plaster, except for a church-like stone projection for the bay window, with traceried openings. The wings are of brick, enclosing a three-sided courtyard to the south.

The interior is remarkably intact, its sensational Great Hall open to a roof of sweeping trusses. There is no chimney and the lantern remains above what would have been a smoke louvre. At one end are the kitchens which have huge fireplaces, and a complete suite of pantry, buttery, bakery and, up ladders, the servants' quarters.

The other end of the Great Hall leads to a Tudor staircase built round a massive newel post. This rises to a gallery and the surviving solar chamber. Beyond in the east wing are the state rooms prepared to welcome the monarch. These include an Upper Great Chamber, with bedrooms on either side. They contain original fireplaces and furniture gathered from the Tudor period, although the ceiling was raised to form a Victorian ballroom. A bedroom in the tower has been restored with wall-hangings. What a survival!

GRIMSTHORPE CASTLE
****

Grimsthorpe, 5m NW of Bourne
Vanbrugh façade and Great Hall fronting Tudor house with Georgian interiors (P)

Grim by name but not by nature. Grimsthorpe is one of the great houses of England. To the approaching visitor, it offers Vanbrugh's last masterpiece, a true northern Blenheim. The

rear elevation, however, is wholly different, a delightful jumble of earlier towers, gables and chimney flues, no two bays the same.

The house has belonged to the Willoughby de Eresby family from the 16th century to the present day. Its architectural history reflects their fluctuating fortunes, as variously Barons, Earls and even Dukes (of Ancaster). The original barony was one of the few that could descend through the female line, greatly simplifying the genealogy. The house, now owned by a charitable trust, is occupied by the 27th Baroness Willoughby de Eresby.

Vanbrugh's front elevation, when seen from a distance, seems weak, its recessed centre flanked by pavilions. It might be a child hiding between the skirts of two governesses. Yet the façade grows in potency on closer view, eventually displaying true Vanbrughian energy. The seven centre bays have uniformly arched windows, framed by paired rusticated columns and a strong entablature. The parapet carries plinths and triumphal statues, glorifying what was the newly ducal house of Willoughby. This is a true architectural calling card.

The Great Hall interior is to Pevsner 'unquestionably Vanbrugh's finest room'. It has the scale of a Tudor great hall but the perspective of a Roman palace. The walls are composed of two storeys of restless arcades, some open, some blind. One upper tier contains grisailles of English kings. The chimneypiece is thought to be by Hawksmoor. The arms are those of George I, who gave Willoughby his dukedom. Behind arched screens on either side of the Great Hall are double flights of stairs, rising theatrically as if the foyers of an opera house. An arched door beneath each landing leads to Vanbrugh's Piranesian undercroft. The doorcases to the floors above are Michelangelesque.

Some of the upstairs rooms are original to the earlier house, some were inserted by Vanbrugh and some later. The state dining room is original but redecorated and has a Rococo chimneypiece by Henry Cheere. At the end of the room is the Coronation Banquet throne used by George IV, presumably designed to accommodate his girth. The east range contains state rooms inserted in the 18th century, some making use of Tudor oriels, others with new bow windows.

The King James Room has fluted gilt pilasters and a full-length portait of James I. The state drawing room moves forward to Charles I and his family, in a group of portraits 'derived from' Mytens and van Dyck. The Tapestry Room reverts to the earliest part of the house, with a lower ceiling. The tapestries are from the Soho workshop and the wall mirrors are, for some reason, from the Danieli Hotel in Venice. The diversity of Grimsthorpe's furniture derives from the need to restock it after a disastrous sale of contents in 1828.

Along the back of the central courtyard is a corridor hung with Willoughbys galore. The family served as hereditary Lord Great Chamberlain, the perk taking the strange form of regular gifts of royal chairs, now scattered throughout the house. The Gothic bedroom has a canopy tester from the House of Lords, en suite with the royal throne now in the dining room. The Tapestry Bedroom contains a Gothick bed with crockets climbing the frame like snails.

At the end of the upper corridor is the chapel gallery. Here, almost hidden, is a great treasure, Zurbarán's *Benjamin* missing from the set now at Bishop Auckland (Durham). Delightful though it is, he seems orphaned from the rest of his family. Some deal could surely be done to make the set complete. The chapel itself is a superlative work, by Vanbrugh or Hawksmoor in full mastery of the classical language. A giant Venetian window lights serene pews and a lofty pulpit.

Next door is the sort of contrast in which English houses excel. Baroque trumpets give way to delicate minuets. The Chinese Drawing Room at Grimsthorpe is one of the finest of the genre. Each ceiling panel carries a different pattern. Yellow and black pilasters frame the Gothick fan vault in the bow window. Lacquered cabinets sit against a wall. The wallhangings are Chinese paper of delicate trees and fronds against a soft blue background. Coloured birds seem to dance across the walls. This is an exquisite chamber.

GUNBY HALL ***

Gunby, 7m W of Skegness
Squirearch's atmospheric house on edge of Wolds (NT)

Gunby sits comfortably above a fold in the Wolds. Below lie the flatlands of the Lincolnshire fens, than which nothing is flatter. The house is reputedly Tennyson's model for an English house 'Softer than sleep – all things in order stored,/ A haunt of ancient peace.'

The home of Massingberds since the 15th century, Gunby was threatened by an airfield in the last war. It was saved by the intervention of the owner, Field-Marshal Sir Archibald Montgomery-Massingberd, whose name alone must have daunted the Air Ministry. The house passed to the National Trust in 1944 and is tenanted. Hugh Montgomery-Massingberd's excellent country house books on display.

The exterior is a sophisticated William-and-Mary façade of 1700, redbrick with stone dressings beneath a severe brick parapet. The interiors are domestic and unspectacular. The drawing room contains portraits by Reynolds of Bennet Langton and his wife, friends of Dr Johnson. Langton so admired Johnson that he would read the latter's dictionary to his family at meals, while his valet combed his hair.

In the ante-room are Victorian watercolours and a model of a Napoleonic battleship. The latter is made of mutton bones gnawed into shape by prisoners of war. The dining room is prettily divided by a screen with barley-sugar balusters. On the wall hangs an Arthur Hughes portrait of Margaret Massingberd in rustic pose with a basket of flowers and doves overhead. The generous staircase has three balusters to each tread and a fine plaster ceiling.

The library was recently restored with a bequest from James Lees-Milne, long a lover of this place. He did more than anyone to ease the passage of fine houses into National Trust ownership in the middle years of the 20th century. His description of Gunby as 'an Augustan squire's domain, robust, unostentatious, dignified and a trifle prim' is the happiest of many in his memoirs.

HARLAXTON MANOR ★★★★

Harlaxton, 3m SW of Grantham
Victorian fantasy mansion with Elizabethan
and French revival interiors (P-R)

When Victorian architecture is as valued as
Georgian, Harlaxton will be honoured as a
masterpiece. Why classical revivalism should
be regarded as 'pure' and other revivals as
ersatz is a mystery of art history. Either way,
the extraordinary Gregory Gregory, builder
of Harlaxton, ranks with the Scarisbricks of
Lancashire and the Shrewsburys of Staffordshire as English precursors of Ludwig of
Bavaria. Gregory's inspiration appears to have
been Walter Scott and perhaps Byron.

The house clings to the edge of a hill overlooking the Vale of Belvoir, with the Duke of
Rutland's castle in the distance. Gregory was
determined to outdo his aristocratic neighbour. Modestly rich, he was born in 1786 and
remained a bachelor, devoting his life to
researching and building his palace. In 1832, he
began work with Anthony Salvin on what was
then a purely Elizabethan mansion. Soon
afterwards he dispensed with Salvin and hired
William Burn, the house interior moving
towards Jacobean and, in the astonishing staircase, to Baroque. The reclusive Gregory died
in 1854. Although he lived in the house, like
many over-ambitious Victorians, he never
saw it complete. He designed a family wing but
it lay empty. He had a modest staff of only
fourteen.

Harlaxton passed through various Gregory
descendants until, in 1937, it was on the point
of demolition. It was saved by Violet Van de
Elst, an eccentric cosmetic tycoon. Offspring
of a coal porter and a washerwoman, she
invented brushless shaving cream. On the
strength of this fortune, she bought Harlaxton,
held séances in the library, fought against
capital punishment and blew every penny on
obsessive litigation. She sold the house to the
Jesuits, who passed it to Stanford University
and eventually to Indiana's University of
Evansville, now its admirable custodian.

The excitement of Harlaxton lies in the
interplay of fantasy medieval exterior and
eclectic interior. Its silver-gold towers, chimneys and gables rise like a fairy castle at the end
of a mile-long drive. Close to, the front is
a restless façade of projecting and receding
windows, as if Salvin could not bear flatness.
The roofline is festooned with scrollwork parapets and stone carvings. Massive lions languish
on plinths. Putti grasp at grapes. Walls, pavilions, steps and balustrades are as inventive as
in any Austrian belvedere.

Little is known of the genesis of the interiors, except that Gregory himself played a large
part in their selection. While the dominant
style is Baroque, of the heaviest and most
Germanic sort, diversions are made into Elizabethan, Louis XIV and Rococo. The quality of
recent restoration is admirable. Stuccowork,
gilding, woodwork, even door-plates are
alive and colourful. Only furniture is missing,
a serious loss.

The entrance hall is dominated by a screen
as brutal as a Baroque thug spoiling for a fight.
Rusticated arches rise to an urn and stairs
beyond. They are covered in studs. Baroque
scrolls are hung with curved trophies. The
door-plates are of etched bronze. The stairs
rise to the state dining room with a grand view
down the main drive. Here we are still with
Salvin. The ceiling is in the richest Elizabethan
stucco with heavy pendants, the chimneypiece
of stately marble. The room has the two
biggest 'secret doors' I have seen, taking two
men to open them.

Beyond is the Great Hall, with a massive
Jacobean fireplace rising to huge wooden
brackets under the roof. Screen and panels
burst with Mannerist detail. The bay window
has heraldic glass by Willement. The ante-
room next door is a complete contrast. It is
serenely Italian, in white and green, with
panels of foxes and pheasants playing round
Rococo trophies. The Long Gallery fills the east
wing of the house. As in the ante-room,
Gregory here used French rather than English
themes. The ceiling is a startling blue sky,

High Baroque at Harlaxton

one of the earliest brick structures in England. Ralph, Lord Cromwell fought at Agincourt in 1415 and became King's Treasurer in 1433, a post with opportunities for personal enrichment that he exploited to the full. He was among the wealthiest men in Henry VI's unhappy kingdom, living and travelling with a retinue of over 100 liveried men, not including servants. Regular decrees were passed forbidding such magnates to bring their retinues to London, but Cromwell was in the habit of going to town with 120 horsemen.

Tattershall Tower was built at the height of Cromwell's wealth (see Wingfield/Derbys). The tower was added to a hall and other buildings of what was already a substantial castle. Brick was newly fashionable and in this material Tattershall was equalled at the time only by Herstmonceux (Sussex). It is in reality a glorified solar wing, dressed up in military guise. The castle has gone but the tower is still approached across the remains of its moat and outer ward. It stands stark and lonely.

The four storeys of grand rooms are a palace in the sky. The corner turrets were once capped with spirelets. The interiors have no dining room or kitchen, functions performed in the now vanished hall. The building was essential for privacy, each bedroom being surrounded by lesser rooms buried in corner towers and walls. The tower thus has forty-eight distinct chambers, with latrines on each floor.

None of the rooms is approached directly from the spiral stairs but always through some device or ante-chamber. Some of these, notably the entry to the Audience Chamber on the second floor, is in the form of a brick-vaulted passage, virtually a gallery. The chimneypieces have Cromwell's fat purse as emblems.

If Lord Curzon could save and restore the upper storeys and replace the floors, the National Trust could surely refurnish the interiors. Medieval need not mean empty.

WOOLSTHORPE MANOR *

Woolsthorpe-by-Colsterworth, 8m S of Grantham
Farmhouse where Newton first 'saw light' (NT)

Isaac Newton was born in the same year, 1642, that Galileo died. He was brought up in a simple cottage south of Lincoln, the son of an illiterate farmer. He left home at twelve and went on to Grantham Grammar School and Cambridge, returning only in 1665 to escape the plague in Cambridge. It is said that it was here that he invented differential calculus and conducted his celebrated experiments with prisms. He must have been inspired by the soft Lincolnshire rain. The house remained a farmhouse but was acquired by the Royal Society in 1942 and opened to the public.

The house is secluded, still with its old farmyard, on a sloping hillside outside the village of Woolsthorpe. Creamy stone walls support a tiled roof. The entrance is reached past a small orchard in which, so legend claims, is a sapling of the apple tree under which the great man sat and felt the force of gravitation. The orchard is unchanged.

The interior of the house could hardly be more simple, nothing but a farmhouse. On the ground floor is the parlour and the kitchen, with 17th-century furniture. There are signs of graffiti said to be those of young Newton unable to find paper and frantically using the walls for his calculations. Experts conclude only that they 'may' have been by Newton.

In the bedroom upstairs is displayed Pope's celebrated epitaph on Newton's birthday: 'Nature and Nature's laws lay hid in night:/ God said, Let Newton Be! and there was light.' The other room is reputedly Newton's study, although he rarely visited his mother in adulthood. In the closet is a reconstruction of his prism experiment.

London, Central

The houses of central London were first dominated by the palaces of the Crown, then of the aristocracy, then of the plutocracy. Only later do we encounter town houses of the middle class, accessible usually because a famous resident merits commemoration. Ancient buildings are more plentiful than is commonly supposed. The City of London has no domestic houses open to the public, but on its border is the medieval enclave of the Tower of London, with the remains of a castle, royal palace and early street. Medieval work also survives in the hinterland of the old abbey at Westminster and as part of Lambeth Palace south of the river.

West of the City, the Crown holds sway. One fragment alone remains of Whitehall Palace, Inigo Jones's Banqueting House. St James's Palace and its adjacent mansions of London's *quartier royal* remain sadly shut for the time being. But Nash's Buckingham Palace and Wren's Kensington Palace are both now accessible and palatial. Kensington, in particular, is an underappreciated gem.

Most of the large aristocratic palaces of the West End have disappeared but the best are now on display, Spencer House overlooking Green Park and Apsley House at Hyde Park Corner. Robert Adam's Home House in Portman Square is supreme among terrace properties. On a smaller scale is the eccentric residence built by Sir John Soane in Lincoln's Inn Fields.

A selection of 18th-century properties includes the houses of John Wesley in the City, Dr Johnson in Fleet Street, Dickens in Holborn and Handel in Mayfair. Carlyle's House survives, rather gloomily, in Chelsea. The most successful re-creation of domestic London in the 18th century is Dennis Severs House in Spitalfields.

Dartmouth House and Kensington Court represent opulent Victorian properties, in the French and Dutch traditions respectively. The residences of Lord Leighton and Linley Sambourne are memorials to two Victorian artists.

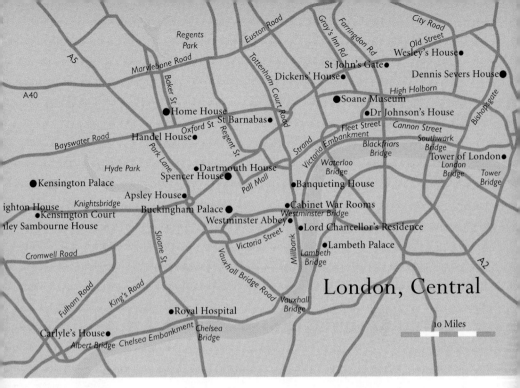

London, Central

10 Miles

Apsley House ✷✷
Banqueting House ✷✷
Buckingham Palace ✷✷✷
Cabinet War Rooms ✷
Carlyle's House ✷✷
Dartmouth House ✷
Dennis Severs
   House ✷✷✷✷
Dickens' House ✷✷
Handel House ✷
Home House ✷✷✷✷

Dr Johnson's House ✷✷
Kensington Court ✷
Kensington Palace ✷✷✷✷✷
Lambeth Palace ✷✷
Leighton House ✷✷✷
Linley Sambourne
   House ✷✷
Lord Chancellor's
   Residence ✷
Royal Hospital,
   Chelsea ✷✷

St Barnabas ✷
St John's Gate ✷
Soane Museum ✷✷✷
Spencer House ✷✷✷✷
Tower of London:
   Bloody Tower ✷
   Medieval Palace ✷
   White Tower ✷✷
Wesley's House ✷✷
Westminster Abbey:
   Little Cloister ✷✷

APSLEY HOUSE **

Hyde Park Corner, w1
Wellington's London home, Napoleonic
trophies (M)

Each year after the Battle of Waterloo, Wellington would hold a banquet in his London
house for his surviving officers. On the walls
hung masterpieces which the French had
looted from Madrid and which Wellington
had recaptured and been given in thanks by
the King of Spain. Down the centre of the
dining table ran the stupendous silver service
of 1,000 pieces which Wellington had also

Wellingtonian grandeur at Hyde Park Corner

been given as a thank-you by the Portuguese.
Its centrepiece shows four continents dancing
in joy round fasces representing the allies. This
annual reminder of England's past glory drew
huge crowds to Hyde Park Corner to witness
the heroes arriving in their carriages.

The house was known (and still is to taxi
drivers) as Number One, London. It had been
built in 1771 by Robert Adam for Baron Apsley,
Lord Chancellor and later 2nd Earl Bathurst.
In 1807, the 3rd Earl sold the house to the
Marquess Wellesley, who in 1817 sold it to his
brother, Wellington. At that time, Wellington

was launching himself on a political career. He had Benjamin Dean Wyatt turn the Adam town house into a Regency palace. Grandeur took the place of domesticity, neo-classical coldness for Adam warmth. Wyatt added gates, a portico and galleries. The impact of this work was ruined in the 1960s, with the demolition of houses to the east and the building of a dual carriageway and modern hotel in their place. The building now stands isolated, classical and rather sombre.

Apsley House was given to the nation in 1947. While the family retained the upper floor, the *piano nobile* has become little more than an art gallery. Moves are afoot to give the main rooms more the feel of a house, although Apsley House was always essentially for show. The Wellington memorabilia complements the collections at Stratfield Saye (Hants) and Walmer Castle (Kent), where the Duke died.

The downstairs rooms are crammed with statues, busts, plate and porcelain, including the great Wellington Shield. A pictorial reconstruction of Waterloo by Felix Philipotteaux well illustrates 'the fog of battle'. In the stairwell stands a bizarre statue of Napolean as a Greek athlete, naked but for a figleaf. Although by Canova, Napoleon disliked it for lacking his 'calm dignity'. It was bought by the British government and presented to the Duke.

The upstairs rooms form a grand circuit. The Piccadilly Drawing Room survives from the Adam house, with an apse at one end and Adam's ceiling decoration in white and gold. The paintings are mostly Dutch genre, including a de Hooch and works by Teniers. Also by Adam is the Portico Drawing Room, once completing the west side of the house.

Apsley House now changes from West End town house to latter day Blenheim. The Waterloo Gallery was added by Wyatt in triumphal style. Windows, cornices and ceiling panels are heavy and ornate, coated in gold leaf and with rich red hangings. The pictures, from the Spanish prize, include Velasquez's *Waterseller* and works by van Dyck and Rubens.

The remainder of the Adam rooms were altered beyond recognition by Wyatt. The Yellow and Striped Drawing Rooms were converted from Adam's Etruscan Room and state bedroom, a sad loss. The latter contains a flourish of military portraits and landscapes. The final room is the dining room, the setting for the Waterloo Banquets. It is eerily empty without its heroes.

BANQUETING HOUSE **

Whitehall, sw1
Survivor of Whitehall Palace, Rubens ceiling (M)

The Banqueting House was the London stage on which the Stuart dynasty acted out the 17th century. Created by James I, it witnessed the death of his son, the Restoration of one grandson, the usurpation of another, James II, and the formal offer of the Crown by Parliament to his granddaughter, Mary. Today, it is the only fragment of what was once the grandest and most important of London's royal palaces. The former York Place was the home of Cardinal Wolsey, from whom it was seized along with Hampton Court by Henry VIII. It succeeded the old Palace of Westminster as chief residence of the Tudor and Stuart monarchs and was, to Macaulay, 'the most celebrated palace in which the sovereigns of England have ever dwelt'.

In reality, Whitehall was a jumble of buildings erected as and when money was available. The mostly Tudor reception rooms could not handle large occasions, which therefore called for separate premises. Elizabeth erected temporary pavilions for entertainment and it was one of these that James I rebuilt to a new 'Italian' design by Inigo Jones in 1619. The building was studiously Palladian, a double cube with a ceiling painted by Rubens, and was Jones's second work in this style after the Queen's House in Greenwich (London, E).

The splendour of the Banqueting House stimulated Charles I to plan a new riverside palace to rival the Louvre, a fantasy that was to consume the ambition of his son. Plans were prepared by Jones and his pupil, John Webb, but curtailed by the Civil War. In 1649, the

Banqueting House saw its most celebrated moment in the trial of Charles himself and his execution outside. Under the Commonwealth, Whitehall Palace fell into decay and its treasures were dispersed. The Banqueting House narrowly escaped destruction.

The palace plan was revived by Charles II and put in hand by Sir Christopher Wren. But the King was building palaces across England and this work was not commenced. Two fires, in 1691 and 1698, consumed most of the old buildings and the Court moved to St James's Palace, never to return. The Banqueting House survived and was left alone, towering over Whitehall in paintings of the period like a magnificent ship beached on the banks of the river. It became a Chapel Royal and then a military museum.

The Banqueting House is now overshadowed by the 20th-century Ministry of Defence while the radicalism of Jones's design is diluted by the monumental buildings of Whitehall. Its Italian Palladianism is no longer an exception in overwhelmingly classical Westminster.

The façade to Whitehall is of seven bays, the centre three divided by attached columns, the outer ones by pilasters. Two equal storeys of windows light what is just one chamber inside. The entablatures, enriched with swags, are complex and Baroque. It is all a beautifully controlled composition, having what Pevsner called 'sobriety, gravity and learning'. But so subsequently has most of Whitehall.

The Great Hall inside is reached up a new staircase added to the north end by James Wyatt in 1809. It is a vast, empty chamber, the two storeys of windows divided by a sumptuous balcony running round the room. There would have been no furniture, the room being filled with people, but the walls were once adorned with the Royal collection of tapestries. Today, all eyes turn to Rubens' ceiling installed in 1635, on the theme of the Apotheosis of James I. It promotes the divinity of kings and depicts the monarch commanding, variously, Justice, Zeal, Religion, Honour, Peace, Plenty, Rebellion, Greed and Lust. There is no Jonesian sobriety or gravity here, only Baroque exuberance and boasting.

BUCKINGHAM PALACE ***
The Mall, sw1
Regency interiors with royal picture collection (P)

The fire that broke out in Windsor Castle in October 1992 had a silver lining. For decades, Buckingham Palace had resisted all requests to admit the public. Now, to help pay for repairs to Windsor, doors were thrown open. Tours were allowed of the Regency state rooms and England's most famous house was accessible at last.

The palace has never enjoyed public affection, regularly appearing in 'least-loved building' league tables. The early 20th-century façade is dull, while the Palladian front to the garden is hidden by walls festooned with security devices. Yet 'The Palace' symbolizes the British monarchy, as 'Downing Street' symbolizes government. The approach down The Mall to the Victoria Memorial is London's one flourish of imperial grandeur. The celebrated railings and the Changing of the Guard are steeped in British history.

While the palace does not equal Windsor or Hampton Court in grandeur, its interiors designed by John Nash for George IV are the most opulent in London. They also contain some of the monarch's most spectacular paintings, rotated with those displayed in the new Queen's Gallery off Buckingham Palace Road. No private apartments are seen. A visit is like a peep into a museum of royalty. We see a throne but no bed.

The former house on the site was built by, and named after, the Dukes of Buckingham in the early 18th century. It was bought in 1760 by George III as a semi-rural retreat from the court ceremonial of adjacent St James's Palace, to which foreign ambassadors are still accredited. George IV commissioned Nash to rebuild Buckingham House, intending to move the entire court from St James's, but he never lived to occupy it.

Nash had a terrible time with Buckingham Palace. There was never enough money and Parliament baulked at the expense of what the

King was demanding. Nash decided to keep the old house as a core and attached new reception rooms when money allowed. He added flanking wings for private apartments and enclosed the courtyard with Marble Arch. This was moved to the north-east corner of Hyde Park by the Victorians, who replaced it with an extra range of guestrooms, regrettably enclosing the entrance courtyard. This Victorian wing, by Edward Blore, was given a Portland stone façade by Sir Aston Webb in 1913, completed while George V was away on holiday. It complemented Webb's Admiralty Arch at the other end of The Mall.

Nash's palace behind is in warm Bath stone, entered under a *porte-cochère* into the 'rustic' floor of the former house. Nash capitalized brilliantly on this modesty by making the staircase rise to his *piano nobile*, as if from the underworld up to Heaven. This staircase is the best thing in the Palace. It forms a Baroque curve with gilded bronze balusters sweeping upwards beneath portraits by Lawrence, Beechey and Wilkie. From here sheer opulence takes over. Only state rooms are on show, their style reflecting George's love of 'French Empire'. Occasionally, frigid classicism is warmed by an abundance of regal red. Everything is lavishly decorated, sometimes indigestibly so.

Thus the ceiling of the Green Drawing Room is a swirl of circles above coving that drips with gilt. The Throne Room has a proscenium backed by red silk walls and a canopy over the state chairs, a scene more appropriate for an oriental potentate. Down the spine of the building is the Picture Gallery (described in the palace guide as being like an ocean liner). Here the stars are the pictures, works by van Dyck, Rembrandt, Rubens, Guercino, Poussin, Canaletto and the Queen's lovely Vermeer of *A Lady at the Virginals*. There is something calming in Vermeer's domestic allegory amid all this ceremony of state.

The sequence of reception rooms loses a sense of crescendo because visitors cannot view them as intended, leading to the (inaccessible) Great Ballroom. Each is best regarded as an individual explosion of Nash extravagance. The state dining room is a voluptuous display of red and gilt with Nash's ceiling imitating the Brighton Pavilion. Three grand reception rooms overlook the garden, all with astonishing ceilings. The Blue Drawing Room is filled with scagliola columns rising to giant brackets, while the ceiling rains gilt on guests below. High up are plaster reliefs of Shakespeare, Milton and Spenser. In the middle of the enfilade is the bow-windowed Music Room. It is a charming pavilion, with domed ceiling and lapis lazuli scagliola columns. This is where royal babies are traditionally baptized. The White Drawing Room beyond is more feminine. White walls rise through giant pilasters to a gilded tent-like ceiling. A superb Riesener roll-top desk sits quietly in a corner.

Visitors are ushered out down the Ministers' Staircase and into the garden through the Oval Room, conduit for guests heading for Palace garden parties. Here are two charming portraits of the young Victoria and Albert by Winterhalter. From the garden, the view of Buckingham Palace is almost a shock, so unlike the stately Mall façade. It is that of a comfortable, rather unpretentious, country home, which is what that decent man, George III, had intended before his son began spending so much money.

CABINET WAR ROOMS *

Clive Steps, King Charles Street, SW1
Churchill's wartime command centre (M)

'This is the room from which I will direct the war,' said Churchill in 1940 as he inspected the basement under the New Public Offices in Whitehall. The rooms had been shielded from bomb attack by a thick membrane of concrete, still visible in the wall facing St James's Park. When the war was over, someone turned off the lights and the entire area was left undisturbed, as if awaiting another war. Only in 1981 did Margaret Thatcher decree that it be opened as a museum.

The basement is now run by the Imperial War Museum but only a third of the operational area is open to the public, the rest being prepared for later opening. The accessible rooms are along the War Cabinet corridor, much like the passage of a submarine. Everything is strictly functional, with pipes and wires exposed and frequent bossy notices. Museumitis deprives the rooms of much of their period atmosphere, as does the tendency to turn any 1940s display into one of Churchilliana. But the fittings and furnishings are authentic, peopled occasionally with wax effigies.

Apart from the large Map Room and the War Cabinet Room, the exhibition is essentially about the maintenance of normality. The rooms were completely self-contained and in use round the clock. A sign even tells the staff whether it is sun or rain outside. This is mostly a habitation of secretaries and clerks. Their camp beds and typewriters remain in place. One wrote that 'even in this revolting place called "the dock", one could get a good night's sleep because you didn't hear the bombs raining down'.

Churchill at first rarely used his bedroom, preferring to risk Downing Street. Yet by 1941 he was persuaded to stay under ground during air raids. His own room is spartan. His pyjamas are folded on the pillow and a chamber pot sits at the foot of the bed. The desk dominates the room, covered in phones in a multitude of colours. Microphones were linked to the BBC and the walls are papered with maps. Never was the maxim more evident, that 'war is primarily about maps'.

CARLYLE'S HOUSE **

24 Cheyne Row, sw3
Chelsea home of Victorian sage (NT)

Why Carlyle's Chelsea home should have been so venerated is something of a mystery. He was chiefly known for two biographies of then unfashionable figures, Cromwell and Frederick the Great, and for his publicly unsociable marriage, revealed in his wife, Jane's, correspondence. Yet as the guidebook says, 'Soon after his arrival in London he became and remained an object of social curiosity. His venerable appearance, his utter independence, his doom-laden view of the folly and triviality of the world, his powerful and idiosyncratic command of language and his renowned ability to speak for hours at a time were all manifestations of genius to which the Victorian imagination readily responded.' Perhaps his unhappy marriage added an element of spice. It was exacerbated, according to a contemporary, 'by the exceptional intellect and character of the persons involved'.

The house had been built in 1708 on land running south from the banks of the Thames. The Carlyles arrived from Scotland in 1834. Chelsea was not then a smart suburb and the house was by Victorian standards modest. Jane Carlyle was intelligent, sociable and a talented correspondent. The couple lived here for thirty-two years. A painting in the house, *A Chelsea Interior* by Robert Tait, shows the couple at home in an attitude of frozen domestic hostility.

Jane died in 1866 and Thomas in 1881. A public subscription was at once launched to purchase the house as a museum, now run by the National Trust. Since London is short of terrace houses open to the public this is a blessing. The exterior is that of a typical Queen Anne terraced house, of three main floors plus attic and basement, with cheery white woodwork. The interior is said to be as the couple left it, overwhelmingly brown and rather lugubrious, perhaps reflecting Carlyle's view of the world.

The ground floor parlour was often used by Carlyle as a study. Its redecoration caused the last of his 'domestic earthquakes' with Jane shortly before her death. Downstairs is the kitchen, with the maid's cot by the stove. Upstairs is the library, with Carlyle's chair and bookcase and Morris willow-pattern wallpaper. To the rear is Jane's bedroom, a poignant chamber with a small dressing room beyond. Here we read of her suffering 'more sorrows than are common' and of a marriage afflicted by 'irritation, frustration, resentment and jealousy'.

The attic was Carlyle's study until he was too distracted by noise from the river. It is now a museum of memorabilia, every wall covered

Domestic bliss, Carlyle style

in pictures, prints and austere photographs of the pair. The house is still blessed with its garden. This overlooked meadows when the Carlyles arrived, with the Tudor wall of old Shrewsbury House as the boundary. Here Carlyle wrote that he could 'wander about in dressing-gown and straw hat, as of old, and take my pipe in peace in it'. He could do so today.

DARTMOUTH HOUSE *

37 Charles Street, W1
Aristocratic Mayfair house in the French style
(P-R)

Squeezed behind two Georgian façades is a house rebuilt in 1890 for the banker, Edward Baring, 1st Lord Revelstoke. It is a *fin de siècle* West End house in the French manner, designed to seem grander than its proportions suggest. Subsequently acquired by the 6th Earl of Dartmouth, it is now the English Speaking Union club, viewable on polite application.

The architect was W. Allwright, who gave the exterior a Baroque overlay of wayward pediments and florid ironwork. The interiors were primarily designed to show off Baring's French furniture. The entrance and main reception room are in Louis XIV style, with a Wedgwood Room to the right. This is blue and white with highly decorated panels and cherubic overmantels after designs by Boucher.

The staircase might be that of an *hôtel* on a Paris *grand boulevard*. Marble treads rise between voluptuous iron and bronze balusters past a large Venetian window. The walls are decorated with Baroque plasterwork and the ceiling is what Pevsner called 'chocolate-box Tiepolo'. The walnut-lined ballroom up-stairs is particularly extrovert, its panelling a

1740s import from elsewhere. The fireplace came from Robert Adam's Derby House in Grosvenor Square.

DENNIS SEVERS HOUSE
****

18 Folgate Street, E1
Fantasy recreation of 1720s Spitalfields interior (P)

I approach this house with trepidation. It stands in a surreal, 18th-century enclave under the looming cliffs of Bishopsgate, and might be the back lot of a film studio. No. 18 Folgate Street is a simple three-bay town house of *c*1724, built of stock bricks with brightly painted ground-floor shutters. It was acquired by an American collector, Dennis Severs, in 1979. He lived in it and filled it with mostly contemporary fittings and antiques, showing them to the public in a strictly controlled fashion. On his death in 1999 he left the house and collection to a local trust.

Severs was more than an eccentric. He presented the house as, variously, an Old Master painting, a still-life drama, an experience, an opera and a peep show. It was not for children, tourists, 'bored wives of company directors', or those who needed guiding or wanted to talk. Visits were and are conducted in silence. The house is also said to be 'post-materialist', Another Time, a spell and a soul.

Strip away the mumbo-jumbo and what do we have? The answer is what almost every house-museum in England is trying to be, while often pretending not to be. Folgate Street seeks to embalm the atmosphere as well as the physical presence of a historic building. Since all such exercises are ersatz, Severs argued, at least do them well.

Everything apart from the walls and roof has been imported as appropriate for an early-Georgian residence, including furniture, fittings, doors, even plasterwork. For authenticity, Severs stripped out a bathroom and an upstairs kitchen and ripped away all wiring. Light and heat come from candles and fireplaces. He then invented a silk-weaving couple, the Jervises, with their lodgers and servant, and equipped the house on the basis of his research into how they would have lived.

As well as a house and its people, Severs then created a moment in time, with the visitor as silent spy. The Jervises have just stepped out of the front door, leaving their wine unfinished, their tea cups a mess, cigar smoke in the air and chamber pots unemptied. Rubbish is dumped, as would have been the case, in fireplaces. Candles gutter in the draught. Wigs lie awry. The kitchen is filthy. In Severs's day, a scruffy lodger in 18th-century dress might at any moment clatter down stairs and go out of the door.

The rest is all impressions. On the ground floor, a canary cheeps in the dining room. The walls are hung with clay pipes, shell sconces and (real) game. Memos in the form of scraps of paper are everywhere. The upstairs smoking room is arranged in imitation of the picture over the fireplace. The well-appointed drawing room in front, with pilasters and panelled ceiling, has walnut shells for garlands and silhouettes against the window screens. The second floor has a boudoir, perfumed and with napkins left littering the chairs. In the bedroom, porcelain crowds the walls. The unmade bed still has the indentation of two heads on the pillows, lovingly close. The chamber pot stinks.

The masterpiece is the top floor. The family, clearly on hard times, has taken in two lodgers. The resulting garret is the best evocation of London poverty I know. Grey washing is draped from ropes over the stairs. Walls are peeling, the ceilings falling. Everything is covered in dust, top hats, clothes, books, chairs. Cobwebs decorate corners and windows. The curtains and bed-hangings are so ragged they are falling to the floor. In a corner are the desk and quills of an impecunious clerk.

These rooms smell of damp and desolation. There are gentle sound effects, as of a bird outside or the bells of Spitalfields church. Some visitors leave the room, I am told, in tears.

Poverty ungenteel: Severs House

Since the Spitalfields Historic Buildings Trust insists the house be lived in still, 'to provide noises on the stairs', an occupant sleeps in one of the pauper's beds in the rear room, in conditions of candlelit squalor. Where he bathes is a mystery.

The only lapse is back downstairs where Severs created a crowded Victorian parlour, an uncomfortable anachronism apparently because he had also acquired Victoriana in his travels. But Folgate Street is mostly of a piece. Its truth to life defies the scrubbed artificiality of National Trust and English Heritage 'time warps'. It may not be for copying, but there is not a house custodian in England who would not benefit from a visit.

DICKENS' HOUSE **

48 Doughty St, WC1
Dickens' early home converted into a shrine (M)

When the young Charles Dickens moved his family to Doughty Street in 1837 he was elated by the success of the first parts of *Pickwick Papers*. Doughty Street was respectability at last, with gates and liveried gate-keepers to keep out undesirables. The terrace house of the standard London three storeys, with attic and basement, was built in 1807–9. The ground floor windows have shutters, the front door a fanlight. It was a big step up from the cramped quarters off Fleet Street where he had lived as a journalist. He moved in with his wife, Catherine, his son Charley, his brother Fred and Catherine's sister, Mary.

For Dickens, Doughty Street was a period of intense, if brief, marital happiness. He stayed here just two years until the growing family forced a move to Regent's Park (the vanished Devonshire Terrace). The house saw the completion of *Pickwick* and the writing of *Oliver Twist* and *Nicholas Nickleby*. Soon after his arrival, Dickens witnessed the sudden death of his adored sister-in-law, Mary, at the age of seventeen. The experience shattered him. Mary's poignant death was to recur in many of his novels, notably that of Little Nell in *The Old Curiosity Shop* also written around this time.

The house was threatened with demolition in 1923 but saved by the Dickens Fellowship and reopened as a museum. Hagiography hangs heavy on the interior. No attempt is made to evoke the hyperactive Dickens, rushing from pillar to post, entertaining his publisher, Bentley, with singing and dramatic imitations. The one half-restored room, the drawing room on the first floor, is protected by an ugly glass screen. The place is a mass of memorabilia, mostly of Dickens' novels and the characters in them.

Upstairs can be seen Dickens' study desk and a copy of *The Empty Chair*, the original painting being at Gad's Hill (Kent). The top rooms are used for exhibitions of Dickensiana. Mary Hogarth lived her brief life in the room at the back. The basement kitchen has become a library and meeting room for the Dickens Fellowship, a suitably Pickwickian use.

This is not so much Dickens' House as a house out of Dickens, a musty shrine where the visitor is asked to wander amid the shades of the departed master and touch the odd stick, hat and newspaper clipping. It badly needs the man himself to burst in and roar the place to life – or even the chaos of his Bleak House in Broadstairs (Kent).

HANDEL HOUSE MUSEUM *

25 Brook Street, W1
Upper floors of composer's house (M)

George Frederic Handel lived in Brook Street for thirty-six of his fifty years in London and died here in 1759. In this simple Georgian terrace town house he composed *The Messiah*, rehearsed, entertained, sold music and concert tickets and led a gregarious, chaotic bachelor existence. He ate gargantuan meals and was the rumbustious life and soul of musical London.

For years the house was occupied by a variety of tenants. Then, rescued in the 1990s, it was opened as a museum in 2001. The custodians ask us to see it as 'not glamorous but a good, honest middle-class home'. Large sums have been spent on research, documentation, lifts, disabled access, metal back stairs, audio-visual aids, video rooms, fancy lighting and everything that health-and-safety regulations could do to eliminate the atmosphere of an old building. I am afraid that Handel's 'home' this is not.

Since the trust was outrageously denied occupation of the ground floor, Handel's 'shop', visitors must go upstairs and start their tour at the top, through an audio-visual display room. This leads into a gallery devoted to Handel's contemporaries and then to his bedroom, stark with a reproduction canopied bed and copy of Hudson's portrait of the composer. Downstairs is the rehearsal room, where students play Handel on a harpsichord.

The museum is clearly struggling to do well by the great man and is seeking more furniture. But if it could defer to the gods of conservation in 'chemically testing the paint' and filling the bed with 'authentic horse hair and feathers', it might have paid a short visit to Dennis Severs House in Spitalfields (above) to find cheaper paths to authenticity. Next door was Jimi Hendrix's house, offering a glorious challenge in London musical contrast.

HOME HOUSE ****

20 Portman Square, w1
Adam's London showcase, fully restored
(P-R)

Nowhere in London conveys the splendour of a first-rate Georgian town house as does 20 Portman Square. It is Robert Adam's urban masterpiece. That West London once had dozens of properties of comparable quality, almost all gone, is heart-breaking. The rescue of Home House after its dereliction at the hands of London University's Courtauld Institute of Art was long and painful. It is now a private club, with a big-screen television in the bar and piped pop music in the music room. But the restoration has been immaculate. Open by appointment, Home House is still a London wonder, an echo of the old West End.

The house was begun in 1772 for the widowed Elizabeth, Countess of Home, rich on the Jamaica trade and disreputable with it. Lady Montagu, her neighbour, referred to her as 'Queen of Hell'. The first designs were by James Wyatt but when he became dilatory, his rival, Robert Adam, was summoned. The latter completely overlaid the former's work, eager to outstrip his competitor in every way. Each room is a variation on a Roman theme. The Adam team of Joseph Rose, Angelica Kauffmann and Antonio Zucchi adorned the interiors. With demolished Derby House, this was to be Adam's London showpiece and advertisement.

The exterior of London's terrace houses in the 18th century display their wealth only in the width of their facades and grandeur of their doorcases. Home House was on a site five bays wide. This gave Adam three bays for the reception rooms and a full two for an entrance hall with a circular stair rising the height of the building. Though outwardly a simple brick terrace, the interior has the scale of a country house turned sideways and slotting into the square.

The ground floor is of rooms mostly by Wyatt but redecorated by Adam. They had been near-wrecked by the Courtauld, with shelves clambering up the walls and pipes and wiring everywhere (in an institute dedicated to art!). All is now well. The front room has its fireplace, walls and ceiling reunited. Red scagliola columns fill the corners and lend an illusion of length.

Large doors open to reveal the dining room to the rear, again showing Adam's genius at making modest shapes seem grand. An apse is inserted at one end while enriched pilasters run from floor almost to ceiling to increase the impression of height. The ceiling, Adam at his most effortless, adds width, decorated by Zucchi's medallions. Beyond is the Countess's private drawing room, again by the remarkable Zucchi.

These rooms were for domestic use. Upstairs is the *piano nobile* reached by one of the finest staircases in London. From the relative gloom of the lobby, it swirls upwards towards the light. One flight divides into two, then turns back onto the landing, a contained architectural explosion. The walls are adorned with Rose's plaster trophies and Zucchi's grisaille paintings. Above is the rotunda of a miniature pantheon.

At the top of the stairs, the visitor must turn left and enter an ante-room before beginning the formal parade. This room, with a Raeburn over the mantelpiece, was the office of the spy-historian, Anthony Blunt, when director of the Courtauld.

The music room ceiling teases the eye with circles gently bumping into one another. Here Zucchi's paintings are musical. Adam's fitted organ has been recreated against the side wall, but modern clubroom armchairs jar with the decoration.

The adjacent drawing room doors, fireplace and ceiling are Adam originals, richer and more colourful than in the music room. Eileen Harris, in her essay on the house, describes the frieze as of 'laurel arches springing from baskets of anthemia, and standing nymphs supporting *tazze* draped with husk chains'. The ceiling depicts Venus reading the *Aeneid* to Augustus Caesar. The decoration is the epitome of Roman virtue. Can this have been the choice of the 'Queen of Hell'?

We pass through what was Lady Home's dressing room but became a belvedere over the garden, looking over the Marylebone fields to the north. The room is circular, with curved cupboards and fireplace, an hors d'oeuvre to the Etruscan Room beyond. Here, as at Osterley (London, W), Adam displays ancient Roman motifs to 'differ from anything hitherto practised in Europe'. The walls had been destroyed and were reproduced from drawings in the Soane Museum. They drip with fronds, popinjays and grotesques. Here are Zucchi cameos everywhere, delicate on white backgrounds.

Home House was leased by Stephen and Virginia Courtauld in 1926. They not only restored the Adam rooms but created sumptuous bedrooms on the upper floor by the

same fashionable Art Deco stylist, Peter Malacrida, they used at Eltham Palace (London, E). *Country Life* called the resulting style 'Georgian Art Deco Alma Tadema, and sheer smartness'.

The rooms (which can be hired) show a liberal use of marble, black glass, aluminium leaf and ebonized woodwork. The glorious Chinese Room has 18th-century wallpaper and an astonishing Gaudi-esque fireplace. The bathroom is one of the best Art Deco rooms in London.

DR JOHNSON'S HOUSE **

17 Gough Square, EC4
Georgian residence of greatest Londoner (M)

No house can properly evoke Samuel Johnson. His personality requires people, conversation, a dinner table, an inn, a clubhouse, not bricks and mortar. It is perhaps as well that Dr Johnson's House does not try. He arrived in London from Lichfield in 1737 and was to live in a variety of rented lodgings round Fleet Street while he tried to support himself by writing. Boswell lists seventeen residences over the course of Johnson's London career.

The house in Gough Square was his home for ten years from 1748, roughly the period of his work on the *Rambler* periodical and the *Dictionary*. The latter's supposed patronage by Lord Chesterfield was meant to pay the rent, but this was not forthcoming. Small wonder he was so rude about Chesterfield's patronage and his letters (*see* Ranger's House, London, E).

Johnson at this time was perpetually destitute. Visitors were coming and going from the house, his assistants worked for a pittance in the attic and he himself was constantly vanishing to inns, chop houses and clubs. He was as desperate for company as he was for money.

The Gough Square years saw Johnson in his forties, unhappy, overworked and poor. He had not yet won his celebrated pension, nor met his companion, Boswell. It was here that his beloved wife, Tetty, died in 1752, leaving him utterly bereft. In 1759 he moved to smaller and cheaper lodgings in Staple Inn.

After Johnson's departure, the house was sub-let as rooms and became a hotel. It was near derelict in 1911 when Cecil Harmsworth, brother of Lords Northcliffe and Rothermere, bought and restored it. He erected a tiny cottage across the courtyard for a custodian. Although bombed in the war and often on hard times, the house is maintained by the Harmsworth trustees and the City of London.

The building itself is a conventional William-and-Mary town house, first known to have been owned by a City merchant named Gough in 1700. It is of four storeys with a handsome front door up a flight of steps. Exposed window woodwork predates the anti-fire building acts.

There is little Johnson aura about the interior, compared with his birthplace house in Lichfield (Staffs). There, the effigies of his father at his labours and the young Samuel reading *Hamlet* by the kitchen fire are truly moving. Gough Square might be the house of a tidy-minded Fleet Street lawyer.

The basement, where Johnson endured such food as he could afford and drank his eternal cups of tea, displays watercolours. In the parlour are portraits of his associates, including Frank Barber, the negro servant who lived with Johnson after his wife's death, on and off until the end. The childless Johnson made him his heir. Here too stayed Anna Williams, a Welsh poetess and friend of Tetty, whom Johnson also took into his company. Johnson found tea with Anna a constant comfort in adversity.

The rooms on the first and second floors are a museum of Johnsoniana. Even the garret, restored after being gutted in the war, might be awaiting a genteel society meeting. The lights are neon.

I long for some of the chaos and clutter of an 18th-century lexicographer's studio, with assistants beavering over the stacks of manuscript slips. 'We extend our knowledge of a person when we look at his home,' wrote Kate Marsh of writers' houses. This one needs more of that 'home'.

NOS. 1 & 2 KENSINGTON COURT *

Kensington, w8
Queen Anne and Gothic revival for plutocrats' houses (H)

Kensington Court was a Restoration mansion lying to the south of Kensington Palace. The old house fell on hard times, became a school then a lunatic asylum and was replaced in the 1880s by a development of the same name. The developer was Jonathan Carr, fresh from building Bedford Park in Chiswick. Here he employed the same Queen Anne Revival but on a denser, more urban plan. The east side of Kensington Court is, in my view, the most handsome group of town houses in London, of dressed red brick and terracotta with white porches and balconies on ornamental brackets. The architect was J. J. Stevenson.

The old house itself was replaced by two houses facing Kensington Gardens, Nos. 1 and 2, now forming the Milestone Hotel. The milestone itself is concealed behind the railings. No. 1 is by Stevenson, with two Dutch gables and a corner turret. Its owner was Lord Redesdale, grandfather of the Mitford sisters, who built Batsford Park (Gloucs) in a similar style.

The corner house, No. 2, is more eccentric. It is the only London building by the flamboyant Oxford revivalist, T. G. Jackson, designer of Hertford College (Oxon). It is in wild Franco-Flemish Gothic coated with early Renaissance motifs and might be nestling beside a canal in Bruges. Tall strip pilasters rise the height of the façade. A recessed side entrance is topped by an aggressive balcony. The windows, some with Gothic tracery, have beautifully dressed surrounds. Dolphins cavort above a bold oriel window. The owner was a tycoon called Athelstan Riley whose initials are on the dressings.

The houses became a hotel in the 1920s but fell derelict after a suspicious fire in 1986. Not until 1991 was the hotel restored and reopened. The main entrance lobby had been altered, but the Jackson interiors appear to survive. The sitting room is neo-Jacobean with panelling and an alcove overlooking the park. The dining room is equally so, with heavy Tudor pendants to its ceiling. The main first floor suite claims to be the most sumptuous in any London hotel.

KENSINGTON PALACE *****

Kensington Road, w8
Wren palace, Kent state rooms, Mary II's
domestic apartments (M)

Kensington is London's most unobtrusive royal palace, yet also its most satisfying. The original house on the site was a comfortable country seat that had appealed to William of Orange, newly arrived from Holland in 1688. He suffered from asthma and his queen, Mary, hated the dampness of Whitehall, 'nothing but water and wall'. They were already rebuilding Hampton Court up river, but needed a place nearer Westminster in the meantime. The Earl of Nottingham's house in Kensington suited them well and was bought in 1689 for £20,000.

The small Jacobean building was speedily extended by Wren, with four pavilions added to the corners of the old house within six months of purchase. The house grew steadily under Wren's assistant, Nicholas Hawksmoor, to its present formlessness. What was left of the old house then vanished completely under George I, with alterations by Colen Campbell and William Kent.

At its peak of popularity under the Hanoverians, Kensington accommodated a Court of 600 people. The Royal Family moved to Buckingham House in 1760 and Kensington later became the residence of the King's son, the Duke of Kent. It was the birthplace of Princess Victoria in 1819. It was she who ordered its rescue from dereliction and opening to the public in 1899.

Most of Kensington is still a residence for 'lesser Royals'. Their apartments include the west range and principal entrance, set round three courtyards not yet on public view. At the time of writing, visitors to the state rooms must make a furtive 'tradesman's entrance' from the north. Since the state rooms cannot be approached as intended, their layout is confusing. Visitors first see a downstairs museum of royal costumes, such as a selection of the Queen's hats or a fine display of clothes worn by Diana, Princess of Wales, one-time resident. The adjacent Red Saloon is where the eighteen-year-old Queen Victoria held her first Privy Council on inheriting the throne in 1837.

The pleasure of what is visible at Kensington lies (as at Hampton Court/London, W) in the contrast between the Anglo-Dutch domesticity of the Royal Family's private quarters and the grandeur of the state rooms. The latter are reached first up the King's Grand Staircase. This is one of the finest in London, of marble and painted by William Kent. Even Horace Walpole, no fan of Kent, admitted it was 'the least defective work of his pencil'.

The space is dominated by a vast *trompe-l'œil* mural filling the upper storey and depicting members of George I's court crowding an arcade overlooking the stairs. Among their number is the 'wild boy' found in the German woods on all fours and widely exhibited as a Court curiosity. The illusion continues in the ceiling, painted to look like a dome beneath which more courtiers gaze down on the unreal crowd below.

There now begins a circuit of reception rooms built by Wren round the White Court. The Presence Chamber has Kent's ceiling of a red cross on a white background. The mantelpiece is of Grinling Gibbons carving, the walls covered with Italian embroideries. Beyond is the Privy Chamber, hung with Mortlake tapestries and filled with busts of English scientists and philosophers. Here Kent's ceiling depicts Mars and Minerva as George I and his Queen, surrounded by the arts and sciences in a state of luxury they rarely enjoy today.

The exquisite Cupola Room is again by Kent, and a dramatic change from his previous chambers. This is of Roman grandeur, fluted pilasters rising to a huge coffered ceiling, painted with *trompe-l'œil* to give added height. Round the walls are statues of Roman gods, gilded and in niches. In the centre of the room is one of Kensington's most treasured objects, Roubiliac's clock of the four monarchies of antiquity, Rome, Persia, Macedonia and Chaldea. It once played tunes by Handel and Corelli.

The east range of the circuit begins with the King's Drawing Room, its Kent chimneypiece and ceiling now restored. On a wall is George II's 'fat Venus' by Vasari, with lesser Old Masters from the Royal Collection. The King's suite was converted for Princess Victoria before her accession and has been restored to that period.

It was in the bedroom here that the Princess was awakened to be told of her accession. The rooms seem happy, sunny chambers, with views over Kensington Gardens. Filled with pictures of the Princess and young Queen, they contrast with the busy mother or gloomy old lady so often depicted later in her reign. These are the rooms of a truly 'Victorian' teenager.

The Queen's rooms were those built earlier, for Mary II, and are quite different. They suggest the domestic interiors of a comfortable house in The Hague. The walls are panelled or papered, the floors are of oak and the furnishings cosy. Fireplaces have been restored with their brick backings. There are many paintings by Kneller and some of the Queen's avidly collected Chinese porcelain.

The Queen's Gallery has a fine barrel-vaulted ceiling and Gibbons's work on the overmantels. Here she would meet with her ladies-in-waiting, sitting with their embroidery whilst being read to beneath portraits of monarchs overhead.

Little of the formal gardens left by Queen Mary and her sister, Queen Anne, survive at Kensington, although we still have Queen Anne's beautifully proportioned Orangery by Hawksmoor. The 18th-century love of naturalism swept them away in favour of lawn. But the parkland of today's Kensington Gardens would doubtless be a housing estate in the manner of Bayswater but for William's urgent need to escape Whitehall. His asthma was London's most lucky circumstance.

LAMBETH PALACE **

Lambeth Palace Road, SE1
Archbishop's Victorian home with 17th-century Great Hall (P)

Lambeth Palace, the London home of the Archbishops of Canterbury, was until recently closed to the public. Its austere gatehouse and high walls along the Embankment seemed to bespeak archiepiscopal aloofness. The palace might be that of the Church at bay, facing the Crown and Parliament across the river, not to mention the old Abbot of Westminster. It was opened to the public by Archbishop Carey in 2000.

The present residence and offices are to the rear, in a Victorian range by Edward Blore, facing a spacious courtyard and gardens. Blore swept away half of the medieval palace in favour of his own version of medieval, a style reminiscent of an overblown country rectory. The interiors of Blore's palace are institutional but colourful. A sequence of reception rooms runs to the left of the entrance stairs, joining the surviving older building at the end of a long corridor. The latter begins with the rebuilt Guard Room, by Blore but with old roof timbers, and hung with portraits of past archbishops. Beyond are the remains of the palace cloisters.

The oldest surviving buildings are visible along the river. Lambeth's magnificent Great Hall is now the palace library. It was comprehensively restored after severe bomb damage and has a hammerbeam roof to rival Westminster's. This was an architectural curiosity, erected after the Restoration in 1660 but, like halls in Oxford and Cambridge colleges, a deliberate reversion to the Gothic of the 'old religion'. Even so, the exterior carries classical features, including ball finials and a pediment over the oriel windows. Inside, the form of a Gothic hall again 'crosses over' into classical alcoves and doorways.

The other principal room on display is the lovely Early English Chapel. This has lancet windows with Purbeck shafts and ribbed vaults. Severely damaged in the war, it was ferociously repainted in 1988 by Leonard Rosoman in a style I would call Byzantine Primitive. Beneath is a Gothic undercroft.

LEIGHTON HOUSE ***

12 Holland Park Road, w14
Artist's residence with Arab Hall and picture collection (M)

Leighton House is the 'unique expression of the taste and sensibility of one man', says its guide. The man was Frederic Leighton, aesthete, artist and collector. The house was built in 1864, near that of his friend G. F. Watts, on the Holland Estate, an enclave of artists' houses encouraged by the 'aesthetic' Lady Holland of the adjacent Holland House.

These artists were by no means Bohemiam. Leighton had just sold his painting, *Dante in Exile*, for the huge sum of £1,000. He was a wealthy young man whose talent was fuelled by years spent with his parents in Italy and France. His portraiture in the Pre-Raphaelite tradition was accomplished and his social celebrity no less so. He was the only artist of his generation to be made a peer, albeit on his deathbed.

The house, designed by Leighton with George Aitchison, was originally a symmetrical building in red brick. There was a reception room downstairs and a bedroom and large studio upstairs. Leighton did not intend to marry or have guests to stay. This was a house for work and for show. Over the next thirty years, it grew to reflect Leighton's changing taste, especially for Arab art, becoming what he called his 'autobiography'. Now owned by the local council, the impact of Leighton House is diluted by the difficulty such owners have in breathing life into old buildings. Entry is through a shop.

On the ground floor is a sequence of hall, ante-room and Arab Hall, the last being Aitchison's extension of 1877. The Arab Hall was based on the banqueting hall of a Moorish palace in Palermo. A black marble pool with fountain forms the centrepiece, while tiled walls rise to a high dome above. Leighton had

friends, including Walter Crane and Randolph Caldecott, design the frieze and column capitals.

The Arab Hall is dominated by Leighton's collection of 16th- and 17th-century tiles from the Middle East. They are mostly blue-and-white with arabesques, Arabic script, flowers and exquisite birds, their throats 'slit' so as not to represent 'living creatures'. Looking down from above is a *zenana*, or screened balcony.

The Arab Hall appears to have been entirely for show. Guests would admire it and pass through to the drawing room. This looks out onto the garden, its walls described by Leighton as 'the colour of the tobacco of a good cigar'. Ebony door surrounds imitate picture frames. The same doors appear in the dining room. Both rooms are hung with pictures by Leighton and his contemporaries, notably Burne-Jones. These shine radiantly from dark wallpaper backgrounds, full of the light and colour of southern Europe.

The staircase has a stuffed peacock perched on a newel post. Upstairs is a smaller hall or Silk Room hung with more paintings. They include Millais' delightful *Shelling Peas*. The biggest room upstairs is Leighton's studio, grandly lit by north facing windows overlooking the garden. It is used for concerts but is still hung with pictures, including Leighton's *Death of Brunelleschi* and *Corinna of Tanagra*. Here too is Burne-Jones's *Uninterpreted Dream*. It cries out for the clutter of an artist's studio.

LINLEY SAMBOURNE HOUSE **

18 Stafford Terrace, w8
Victorian time capsule in elegant Kensington street (M)

The stuccoed Italianate exteriors of the Phillimore Estate in Kensington was old-fashioned by the time No. 18 was completed in the 1870s. Its purchaser more than made up for that. The *Punch* cartoonist, Edward Linley Sambourne, crammed it with artistic paraphernalia, which was left untouched by his son, Roy, and daughter, Maud. The latter's daughter, the Countess of Rosse, passed the house in 1989 to Kensington and Chelsea Council, who display it in tandem with Leighton House (above). The Victorian Society was founded here in 1958.

The interior has been restored as the epitome of late-Victorian 'artistic' taste. In contrast to Leighton House, it is gloriously crammed with contents of the period. The first impression is of gloom. This is not Gilbert and Sullivan's greenery-yallery but greenery-brownery. Almost all the walls and ceilings are either early William Morris or covered in Sambourne's fake embossed leather patches. Windows are darkened by stained glass. Carpets are dingy. Even the lights are covered in shrouds. The place is deliciously swamped by dark tones.

Yet the house is full of colour. Barely an inch is without a picture, fabric or display of blue-and-white china. The Sambournes were not rich collectors, more Victorian 'car-boot sale' addicts. Sambourne photographed masterpieces and framed the prints for his walls. He photographed models and did likewise. Such reproductions coat every room, the frames often fitted like a jigsaw puzzle to leave no wall visible.

Since the rooms survived the 20th century and were regularly photographed, the work of displaying the house as the Sambournes left it has been easy. Downstairs are the dining room and morning room. The first floor is entirely one drawing room, the rear of which was for a time Sambourne's studio. Everywhere are prints, ceramics, statues and books.

Even the bedrooms are as left by the family. Roy Sambourne's bedroom is stacked with signed photographs of actresses whom he escorted, with apparent increasing desperation, in his otherwise indolent youth. He never married but pined over those pictures in solitary old age.

The top floor contains Linley's photographic studio, stacked with nude photographs. This is Victoriana as you will never see it at the V&A but beware of the guided tour.

LORD CHANCELLOR'S RESIDENCE *

Palace of Westminster, sw1
Reproduction Pugin interiors in Palace apartment (P-R)

When the newly appointed Labour Lord Chancellor, Lord Irvine, decided in 1997 to restore his official apartment in the Palace of Westminster there was an explosion of protest. He wanted to install wallpaper and furniture copied from Pugin originals, costing hundreds of thousands of pounds. Wallpaper ran to £300 a roll. The lights cost £56,000. The Pugin-style oak bed cost £16,000. Nor was the result well received. Pugin never designed these rooms as apartments and critics regarded the reproduction interiors as garish and inappropriate. His lordship wisely responded by opening the apartment by appointment.

The original Palace of Westminster was among the oldest royal palaces. Its Great Hall was first built by William Rufus and remained throughout the Middle Ages possibly the biggest assembly hall in Europe. Following a great fire in 1834, the palace was rebuilt by Sir Charles Barry and A. W. N. Pugin, only Westminster Hall having survived the conflagration.

The new palace contained only one formal residence, that of the Speaker, a magnificent sequence of state rooms, theoretically to receive the Monarch. These are not open to the public. In 1923 a flat was also fashioned for the Lord Chancellor in a far corner behind Victoria Tower, composed of apartments previously occupied by Black Rod and the Lords' Librarian.

The residence is very much an apartment composed of a single L-shaped corridor, with bedroom, dining room, sitting room and River Room. The chambers seem heavy and dark in their garb of panelling, curtains and carpets. The wallpapers were all made from Pugin's original pearwood blocks and handprinted, as in his day. Age is mellowing the new rather fierce colours, and the furnishings are enlivened by Pugin's mastery of pattern.

The family rooms constitute an exhibition

of Victorian reproduction furniture and fittings, with mirrors, sideboards and carpets all in Pugin revival style. Largest and most formal is the River Room with spectacular views up and down the river. The fireplace is of Purbeck marble. Classical marble statues stand ponderously on plinths. The windows contain armorial shields of former Lord Chancellors by Lady Elwyn-Jones, wife of a previous incumbent. The walls are hung with a fine collection of paintings displayed on rotation from public collections.

ROYAL HOSPITAL, CHELSEA **

Royal Hospital Road, sw3
Wren's home for heroes (P)

The Royal Hospital in Chelsea is little known because it is still in use, and will be for as long as there is a British army. In 2001, I attended a reception to celebrate two inmates who had fought at the Battle of the Somme (1916). Visitors may walk through the courts and chat with the veterans on seats against sun-soaked walls. Wren's Great Hall and chapel are open to the public but the wards, now divided into private rooms, are inaccessible.

The hospital was planned by Charles II in direct emulation of the Hôtel des Invalides in Paris. It was begun in 1682 and the first 476 non-commissioned officers and men moved in seven years later. Despite the grandeur of the plan, spread along the banks of the Thames, it has none of the spacious ostentation of its Parisian counterpart. After passing it daily and hardly noticing it, Carlyle remarked that it was 'quiet, dignified and the work of a gentleman'.

The hospital is still big. It is set round three spacious courtyards, two open to each side and one to the river. The façade to Chelsea is severe, a central portico with attached columns flanked on either side by the high windows of the hall and chapel. Above is a strangely elongated cupola that might have strayed from St Paul's Cathedral. A much finer portico, its columns here detached, adorns the river front.

This is London's best place to bask in pure Wren.

The chapel is large, tunnel-vaulted with modest plasterwork. The seats are arranged lengthwise. Over the apsed chancel is a painting by Sebastiano Ricci. The hall is no more decorative, here with a flat ceiling. Not for old soldiers the enrichment that was later to greet old sailors at Greenwich, but at least the soldiers are still here. At 12 o'clock the public is ushered out and the inmates troop in for lunch.

ST BARNABAS *

1 Greek Street, w1
Soho town house, Rococo plasterwork (P)

Most people assume Greek Street has something to do with Greeks. It does not. It was developed in the 1680s by a speculator, Gregory King, who gave the street his name, Greg Street, later altered to Greek. Set on its corner with Soho Square is the House of St Barnabas, built in 1746 and sold to Richard Beckford, brother of the Lord Mayor. In 1861, it became a charitable home for 'distressed ladies', a function it has performed ever since. It was here that Gladstone brought his celebrated vagrant prostitutes to be saved.

So few ordinary Georgian houses are accessible to public view in London that this example is precious, if slightly institutionalized. The house has a calm and stately exterior, its door marked by two obelisks.

Downstairs are offices but the upstairs rooms are decorated with remarkable Rococo plasterwork. The landing is adorned with barebreasted women, perhaps fortunate to survive the house's altered purpose. The saloon has the best stucco work, notably round the fireplace.

Two further rooms are less ornate although retaining Rococo ceilings. To look out from here onto the bustle of Soho Square on a summer evening is to imagine a long lost city. Behind the house is a small chapel for the women inmates, designed in 1862.

ST JOHN'S GATE *

St John's Lane, EC1
Remaining ceremonial rooms of the Knights
Hospitallers' headquarters (M)

The old gatehouse is, as they say, steeped in
history. Here lived Hogarth's father, who ran
a coffee house over the arch. Then it was
occupied by Dr Johnson while he worked on
the *Gentlemen's Magazine*. Then it became a
tavern. Sorely battered in the war, it was none
the less restored to its ancient purpose, as the
headquarters of the British Order of St John,
which succeeded the Knights Hospitallers of
St John of Jerusalem. The latter's base was here
in Clerkenwell from 1140 until its suppression
by Henry VIII. It was later revived as the Order
of St John and became much involved in
ambulances.

The original establishment extended across
the Clerkenwell Road, with properties covering the area down to Clerkenwell Green. All
has gone, except the chapel and crypt. But the
area round the gate was retained and comprehensively rebuilt by the Victorians. It now
yields a fine panelled Chapter Hall, built in
the medieval manner by Oldrid Scott in 1902,
with a Tudor fireplace and much heraldry.

Beyond are two greatly restored Tudor
rooms, the Old Chancery and the Council
Chamber over the arch. The walls are rich in
panelling and portraits of the Order's various
royal sponsors. In the Chancery is a display of
the Order's silver, once used to serve the food
in its hospitals as symbol of the knight's duty
'to serve our Lords, the sick'. The group forms
a charming London survival.

SOANE MUSEUM ***

12–14 Lincoln's Inn Fields, WC2
Georgian architect's exotic shrine (M)

This is the most eccentric home in London. An
earlier house on the site was rebuilt by the
architect, Sir John Soane, for his family and for
offices in 1792. Today, it embodies the mania
for 'curiosity' collecting that reached a zenith
in the late 18th century. The dilettantism of
the Grand Tour, focused chiefly on paintings
and sculpture, had become obsessive souvenir
hunting (*see* A la Ronde/Devon). Soane was
a scholar, fascinated by ruins, beauty, decay,
temples and mausoleums. He inhabited them
in his mind and recreated them as buildings
for any client he could persuade to pay.

Soane rebuilt No. 12 and a year later moved
into No. 13, which he also rebuilt as a house
and to display his collection. To the conventional Georgian exterior of No. 13, he applied
what was originally an open loggia of stone
arches, now glazed. These are covered in
motifs of Soane's free-style classicism, decorated with caryatids and ornamental brackets
from the outside of Westminster Hall. Soane
then bought No. 14, renting out the house but
colonizing the yard at the back. By the time
of his death in 1837, he had turned the rear of
the three properties into a warren of alcoves,
passages, light wells and caves. Every inch
he crammed with sculptural fragments, with
plaster casts, niches, mirrors and display
cabinets of objects. Soane was supremely sensitive to architectural drama. There is not a dull
corner in the Soane Museum, and certainly
not an empty one, except on the upstairs floors
which are set aside for study.

A pleasantly scruffy entrance corridor gives
onto the main dining room and library. The
wall colours here are allegedly based on scraps
of paint from a wall in Pompeii. The room is
ingeniously framed by giant pendants over its
alcoves and is heavy with bookcases. On the
wall is a portrait of Soane by Lawrence as an
ageing romantic. He was mortified in later life
by the refusal of either of his wayward sons,
pictured upstairs, to follow in his profession.
One devastated him by writing a savage,
initially anonymous, critique of his architectural style.

The study and dressing room behind were
offices but hardly seem so. They are a classical
doodle in three dimensions. Soane wanted
students to roam these galleries, sketching
and seeking inspiration. Here he arranged his
fragments of ancient Rome and fashioned
alcoves into light-hearted conceits. He paro-

died the Gothick revival with a 'Monk's parlour', containing the grave of Fanny, his wife's dog. He designed a crypt, a dome and a catacomb and displayed many carvings salvaged from old Palace of Westminster.

In the centre of the mausoleum is a giant sarcophagus of Seti I (which should never have left Egypt). This spot, wrote Soane, calls back 'so powerfully the recollections of past times that we almost believe we are conversing with our departed friends who now sleep in their silent tombs'. The artist, Benjamin Haydon, claimed to have emerged from this valhalla 'with an expression of delighted relief at finding ourselves again among the living, and with coffee and cake'.

In the picture gallery hang two Hogarth epics, *The Election* and *The Rake's Progress*, alive with pathos and wit. They are cleverly arranged on a series of sliding and folding doors, quaint but not easy to appreciate. Another gallery displays works by Canaletto.

The two most idiosyncratic Soane interiors are the two breakfast rooms, similar to his interiors at Pitshanger (London, W). Both display his characteristic shallow arch and flat-domed ceiling. No. 12 offers a 'starfish' vault and trelliswork pattern, decorated with leaves as if in a garden pergola. The other breakfast room, in No. 13, also has a shallow domed roof. It is offset by concealed light wells, softly decorated in ochre and yellow and shimmering with mirrors. Pictures depict buildings and figures, in classical poses.

The museum has recently bought the whole of No. 14 and intends to expand its displays into that building as well.

SPENCER HOUSE ★★★★

27 St James's Place, sw1
Palladian palace overlooking park (P-R)

On 20 December 1755, the 1st Earl Spencer secretly married his childhood sweetheart, Georgiana Poyntz, during his 21st birthday ball

Soane: 'conversing with friends'

at Althorp (Northants). He had already inherited both the Sunderland and Marlborough fortunes and was rich beyond dreams. The buckles on his honeymoon shoes, made of clusters of diamonds, were alone valued at £30,000.

Spencer duly planned a new London home. The architect of the exterior was John Vardy, pupil of William Kent, but he was superseded inside by James 'Athenian' Stuart. The interiors are Stuart's great work, the apogee of mid-Georgian taste, a temple to the arts and to the Spencers' youthful love. The family continued to use the house until the 1920s. Unlike most of their aristocratic contemporaries they did not yield to developer greed, although they removed fittings to Althorp and rented the building to a club and various corporate tenants.

In 1985 the house was taken over by Lord Rothschild and magnificently restored. It is not only a rare survivor of a St James's mansion, it is also the finest. Its plan and scale are those of a country mansion, a full seven bays with porticoed centre beaming out over the park. The rooms have been refurnished with paintings and furniture contemporary with its construction.

The house is now entered from St James's Place. The pleasure of the interior lies in the delicacy of its decoration and the quality of the furnishings. One passes from a 'Roman' entrance hall, heavy with busts and friezes, to a pleasant morning room and ante-room, with an apse with *trompe-l'œil* ceiling. The library beyond might be that of a comfortable town house, with prints depicting the expansion of the Christian church.

The dining room is more grand. It was redesigned by Henry Holland in 1785, with scagliola columns at either end and a Carrara marble fireplace copied from one at Althorp. The curtains are of 'French mohair cut velvet'. On the walls are three Benjamin Wests on loan from the Royal Collection. Behind is the first of the house's sensations, the Palm Room. This is composed of a wall of giant fronds exploding upwards from gilt-barked trunks, from which Corinthian columns rise like

unpeeled bananas. Palms also decorate the domed alcove beyond. Olive green walls drip with gold. It is an astonishing chamber. Palm trees were within the Palladian canon, symbolizing architectural and marital fecundity, but rarely displayed with such bravura.

Thé upstairs is even grander. The Great Room at Spencer House is that of a palace. Its walls are covered in Grand Tour paintings but its most majestic feature is its coved ceiling. This carries large medallions of Bacchus, Apollo and Venus, with coffering from Roman and Greek originals and with Pannini landscapes.

Spencer House: country in town

The house saves its jewel for last. James Stuart's Painted Room corresponds to the Palm Room below. It boasts 'one of the most famous 18th-century interiors in England'. The form is of a small rectangle with a large apsidal bow window with a screen of fluted and gilded Corinthian columns. The green walls are covered in painted garlands and fronds, as are the pilasters, friezes, medallions and chimneypieces. By daylight or at night, the decoration seems to shimmer in green and gold. The date of the design is c1759 and must qualify as a masterpiece of mid-Georgian design. Architecture has finally shaken off the age of Wren and awaits the arrival of Robert Adam. Here it has no need of him.

THE TOWER OF LONDON
Tower Hill, E1 (M)

The Tower of London, like Windsor Castle, is dominated by tourism, but not spoilt by it. Its medieval enclave round Water Lane has been well restored and sits at the foot of the Norman tower. Three of the accessible buildings within the enclave qualify as one-time residences, the White Tower itself, the 13th-century palace built by Henry III and Edward I, and the notorious Bloody Tower.

THE BLOODY TOWER *
Tower Green lies to the west of the White Tower amid a casual group of medieval, Tudor and Georgian buildings. The half-timbered Queen's House was where distinguished prisoners were held, usually in some comfort. Here lodged Anne Boleyn and the future Elizabeth I, as well as Guy Fawkes and the Nazi, Rudolf Hess. Tower officials had to be careful of their charges, never sure which were to die and which return to power.

Facing the Green from the south is the Bloody Tower, originally one of the water towers controlling the river entrance to the castle. Its portcullis survives on the ground floor. The tower was for the most important prisoners, including the two sons of Edward IV, the 'Princes in the Tower' who may or may not have been murdered by Richard III.

The Bloody Tower was built as the residence of the Constable of the Tower in c1225 and extended in c1280. But it was heightened for the occupancy of Raleigh and his family, from 1603, surely the only death cell to have been so lavishly improved for one inmate. It is displayed as during Raleigh's time. The lower chamber is his rush-matted study, with desk,

quill pens and books. The upper storey is his bedroom, with a four-poster and chamber pot. Raleigh lived here for thirteen years on a charge of high treason against James I. He went to the scaffold in 1616.

THE MEDIEVAL PALACE *
The residential buildings erected by Henry III and Edward I in the course of the 13th century were restored in the 1990s to how they were when the Tower was the monarch's chief residence in the City. Overlooking the Thames, they straddle Water Lane in the Inner Ward and comprise St Thomas's Tower and Wakefield Tower above Traitor's Gate. The composition is now more picturesque than grim, especially as previously restored by Antony Salvin in the 1860s.

The 13th-century King's Great Chamber has been left 'as found', that is as found by the archaeologists. Wall materials show through and fireplaces have been left ruined. Next door is the King's private room, properly restored with decorated fireplace hood, painted walls and furniture. A small oratory to one side looks out over the river. On a misty afternoon, this little alcove is my London secret.

A bridge leads to Wakefield Tower containing a conjectural reconstruction of Edward's throne room, the throne itself copied from that in Westminster Abbey. Other furnishings, including a candelabra and chapel screen, are also copies, but the effect is suitably grand.

THE WHITE TOWER **
The scale of William I's keep is impressive, still defying the fortresses of commerce investing it on all sides. This is the largest and most complete Norman castle of its type in England. It was built as a fort and a palace c1078, of ragstone originally whitewashed, hence the name. A sign of its palatial purpose is both the scale of the main rooms and the presence of a chapel, its apsidal east end pushing out through the keep wall.

Much has changed over the years. Medieval additions have been removed, windows altered and stone replaced. The fussy caps on the corner towers are 17th century. The removal of the surrounding clutter, mostly by the Victorians, has returned the tower to its Norman form. It is now an armoury museum, honouring its use from medieval times as the chief Royal Arsenal. It could do with some corner of its Norman domesticity restored.

The interior is divided down the middle by a huge wall, splitting each of the three floors into two chambers. The ground floor rooms would have belonged originally to the Constable of the Tower and retain their massive ceiling beams, deep window openings and Norman fireplaces. The first floor was the main ceremonial floor, one side acting as a Great Hall and the other as a Great Chamber. This originally rose the full height of the rest of the tower. Garderobes flank the side passages. Here too is the Chapel of St John, a rare unaltered Norman chapel, two-storey and unadorned apart from the carvings of the pier capitals. It was here that Mary I was betrothed 'by proxy' to Philip of Spain in 1554, the most perilous marriage in English history.

The upper storey, which has neither garderobes nor fireplaces, was probably a later insertion, perhaps when the tower was superseded by Henry III's new palace by the river. It housed important political prisoners but was later converted for storage. By Elizabeth I's reign it was an armoury. This, in varying forms, it has been ever since.

WESLEY'S HOUSE **

47 City Road, EC1
Georgian house of celebrated preacher (M)

John Wesley and his brother Charles set up their first society in the old Foundery on Aldersgate in 1740. Although the Methodists did not split from the Church of England until 1791, they were denied worship in Anglican churches. They held 'meetings' at first in the open air, then in chapels. The Wesleys lived in or near the Foundery premises from the start.

The house is exceptionally simple, although this may be because of the paucity of the present furnishings. The Wesleys were not poor. There is a kitchen and associated offices downstairs. The ground floor drawing room looks out peacefully over a small garden, across the City Road to Bunhill Fields. It is a sylvan moment in central London. Wesley's exercise horse stands by the wall with an electric shock machine for treating his ailments.

Upstairs is the great preacher's study and library, still with his annotated books in the bookcase. Behind is the bedroom and bed in which he died in 1791. A small room beyond was his private prayer room, his Bible open at The Psalms.

WESTMINSTER ABBEY: LITTLE CLOISTER **

Dean's Yard
Medieval buildings round Abbey cloisters (P)

Few visitors to Westminster Abbey penetrate to the glories hidden behind. Here in the remains of the old monastery are two cloisters housing Abbey officials and extending to the adjacent buildings occupied by Westminster School. Alleys and cloisters are open to the public and more of pre-Reformation London can be seen in these courts than anywhere else. The enclave is a quiet retreat in the heart of the capital. The Little Cloister is such a favourite that I hesitate even to mention it.

The entrance to the former monastic buildings is either through the Abbey or through Dean's Yard. The East Cloister embraces the great Chapter House, Pyx Chamber and various undercrofts and museums. From here, an ancient and mysterious medieval vaulted passage leads to the Little Cloister, formerly known as Farmery Court, on the site of the old Infirmary. Although damaged in the Second World War and with a 17th-century arched arcade, it retains its medieval aura. Walls, windows and doors seem to have been gathered from all ages. A fountain plays in the middle. On a warm summer day, it might be a courtyard of an almshouse in old Seville.

London, East

Downstream is the business end of any maritime city. London's eastern suburbs have always been its poor relation. Upstream is away from the docks and usually offers higher ground and proximity to countryside. The best land in the East End has therefore been Greenwich, Eltham and Woodford and it is here that we find the finest houses.

The most notable monument is the group of royal foundations on rising land overlooking the Thames at Greenwich. In place of Henry VIII's palace of Placentia rose James I's Queen's House and then Charles II's Greenwich Palace, later the Royal Naval Hospital. On the hill behind, Wren built an observatory, Flamsteed House. The group of buildings now forms one of the best architectural set pieces in England.

Otherwise, the better houses were built in what was then countryside, in adjacent Essex and Kent. Eastbury Manor House and Hall Place are notable Elizabethan mansions. Charlton House is, or could be, one of the best Jacobean houses in the capital. Hugh May's Eltham Lodge, now the Royal Blackheath Golf Club, is a vigorous Restoration composition.

Eighteenth-century houses are sparse in East London. Rainham Hall is a beacon of civility on the Essex marshes. The Walthamstow house to which William Morris moved as a boy survives, as does his first family house, Philip Webb's Red House in Bexleyheath. More dramatic are the dazzling alterations and additions made by the Courtaulds to Eltham Palace in the 1930s, England's best surviving interiors of the Art Deco era.

Charlton House ** \
Down House ** \
Eastbury Manor House * \
Eltham Lodge ** \
Eltham Palace **** \
Forty Hall **

Greenwich: \
Flamsteed House ** \
Queen's House *** \
Royal Naval Hospital ** \
Hall Place * \
Rainham Hall **

Ranger's House *** \
Red House *** \
Sutton House * \
Valence House * \
Walthamstow Vestry House * \
William Morris House *

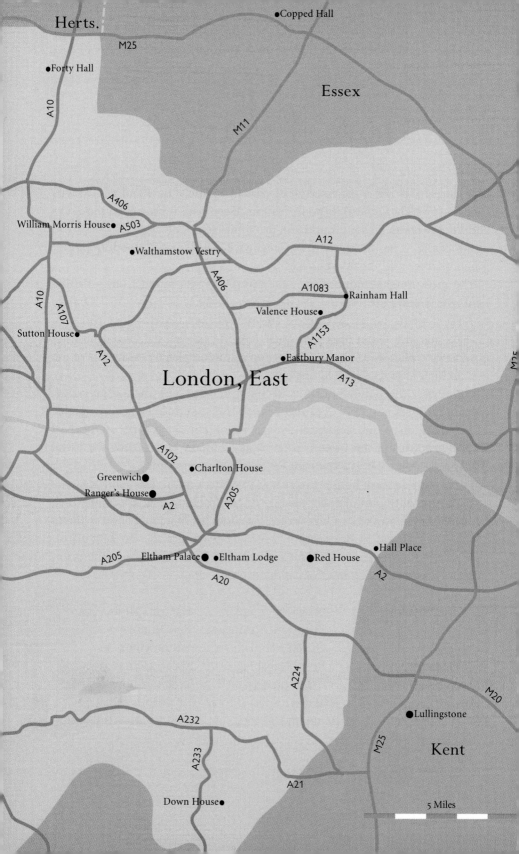

CHARLTON HOUSE **

Charlton Road, SE7
Jacobean frontispiece, palm staircase (M)

All my Victorian guidebooks to London assert, in a burst of antiquarian zeal, that 'Inigo Jones was the architect of Charlton'. Sadly, there is no evidence for this, and little likelihood. Today, East London's premier 17th-century mansion (after Greenwich) cuts a sorry spectacle. Birmingham honours its Aston (Warwks) and Leeds its Temple Newsam (Yorkshire, West). Charlton has been owned by Greenwich council since 1925 and is now a public library, municipal offices and meeting rooms. The grounds are divided into playing fields. The approach is covered in tarmac. Surely Greenwich can do better.

Charlton is an intact E-plan house built for Sir Adam Newton, tutor to James I's son, Henry, between 1607 and 1612. The house was bought in the 18th century by the Maryon Wilson family, lords of the manor of Hampstead, but was usually tenanted. Norman Shaw added a wing in 1877. Most of the original ceilings, staircases and fireplaces survive. Restored and refurnished it would be a glorious addition to the sparse attractions of south-east London. Today we can only wander empty rooms and dream.

The exterior of Charlton is tremendous. The main front carries a supremely ornamental frontispiece, the sort of Mannerist Renaissance composition one might find on a merchant's town house in Germany or the Low Countries. Pevsner called it 'the most exuberant and undisciplined ornament in all England'. Paired columns either side of the door rise to niches, consoles and brackets coated with strapwork. The whole front is united by a pierced balustrade. There is nothing like it in London, although the style was to be revived in late-Victorian developments such as Kensington Court (London, C).

The house has a two-storey Great Hall running from front to back of the building, similar to Hardwick (Derbys). As at Hardwick, the grandest rooms are on the top floor. The stair-case is remarkable, rising through three storeys with a different order of balusters on each floor. The supports are extraordinary, carved as palm tree trunks rising from vases. Red Indian headdresses, a favourite motif of the period, peer at us from the gloom. This is most exotic.

The rooms retain a wealth of Jacobean plasterwork but otherwise are without any of the character suggested by old *County Life* photographs of the house. The overmantels merit a gallery to themselves. Some are wildly Mannerist, some restrained classical, some black marble, some soft plaster relief. That in the saloon is attributed to Nicholas Stone. These overmantels represent the height of Jacobean taste in early 17th century London. In the black polished surface of one fireplace a former resident is said to have seen reflected a murder being committed on the heath outside.

DOWN HOUSE **

Downe, 6m SE of Bromley
Darwin shrine, study and exhibition (EH)

Charles Darwin brought his growing family to this Kent village in 1842, six years after returning aboard the *Beagle*. He was to spend fifteen years bringing his *On the Origin of Species* to publication, tortured by doubt over its possible reception. Recurring illness bordering on hypochondria was relieved by wandering the fields behind the house. Not until a colleague was on the brink of publishing ideas similar to his own in 1859 did he rush his book to print. He became an instant celebrity. Yet he stayed at Down until his death forty years later, surrounded by eight children, fame and contentment.

After Darwin's death, the family moved away and the house was taken over by Downe House, a school for girls (the -e was an affectation). When this moved to bigger premises, it kept the name. Down House was opened as a museum in 1929 under the aegis of the British Association for the Advancement of Science. Not until 1996 was a full restoration undertaken by English Heritage. The first floor is a museum to Darwin's life and work, mostly audio-visual displays. The ground floor has been reinstated as it was in his later years.

Down House lies in a precious fragment of countryside within the boundaries of Greater London. Here woods, fields and villages south of Orpington are so vulnerable that a finger-post sign is treated as a historic building. The house itself is a conventional Victorian villa set in spacious grounds whose appeal lies chiefly in the ghost of the great man wandering their borders, collecting beetles and leaves and watching the seasons reveal the mysteries of nature.

The heart of the house is the study located in the middle of the ground floor. Darwin enjoyed his children roaming in and out. Here, he said, 'my life goes on like clockwork'. A daughter wrote, 'He always made us feel that we were each of us creatures whose opinions and thoughts were valuable to him, so that whatever there was best in us came out in the sunshine of his presence.'

The room has been recreated as Darwin left it, which means in rather a mess. His wife, Emma, was known as 'Miss Slip-slop'. She had liked the young Darwin for 'not being fastidious' about tidiness. The room is a clutter of rocks, phials, skeletons, notebooks and spiked scraps of paper. Books are scattered everywhere. In one corner a screen hides Darwin's privy.

The other rooms are also disordered. In the drawing room, books are left open on chairs. Croquet mallets litter the hall. Coats hang at random. A Victorian family has gone out for a walk and will be back soon.

EASTBURY MANOR HOUSE *

Eastbury Square, Barking
Tudor mansion with painted chamber (M)

The old manor of Barking Abbey towers over the surrounding bog of semi-detached suburb, as if pleading for rescue. It was built by a City merchant, Clement Sysley, in the 1550s and little altered, though often decayed, since then. Used as a farmhouse, it was close to ruin

when, in 1918, the Society for the Protection of Ancient Buildings galloped over the horizon and forced it on the National Trust. Eastbury is now run by Barking's leisure department, well maintained if mostly empty.

The house from the outside is tall and distinguished, retaining a respectable skirt of garden. This is no manorial farm house, as might at first appear, but a serious, three-storeyed mansion. The brick exterior is unusually rich. While the east elevation is symmetrical, the north has its balance interrupted by a porch bay surmounted by a pediment. The roof is finely finished, with deep gables, lofty chimneys and a belvedere turret.

The interior has a Great Hall and Great Chamber upstairs, with parlours in the wings. Few fittings survive apart from some panelling but the Great Chamber contains exceptionally good wall paintings. These depict fishing scenes in ornate *trompe-l'œil* frames. The Long Gallery retains its Tudor fireplace. Eastbury should be refurnished as a major London house of the Tudor age.

ELTHAM LODGE **

Royal Blackheath Golf Club, Court Road, SE9
Restoration mansion with original staircase (P-R)

The rear wall of Eltham Lodge is the boundary of the 18th green of the Royal Blackheath Golf Club. This has required shatterproof glass to be installed in its windows. One wonders what happened before its invention. The Royal Blackheath claims to be the oldest club in England, instituted by Scottish golfers travelling south for the coronation of James I in 1603. Having played for centuries on the heath itself, members found driving balls across the main London road increasingly hazardous, and merged with the Eltham Club in 1923. Although private, the club welcomes visitors by appointment, and is proud of its small golf museum.

The house exterior is a gem of Restoration architecture. Eltham Palace and its estate were leased from the Crown by Charles II's banker,

Sir John Shaw. He let the palace as a farm and in 1664 commissioned Hugh May to build a new mansion a mile to the east. May had been much influenced by Dutch architecture during his exile under the Commonwealth. Tall windows on ground and first floors rise to bold eaves and a sweeping hipped roof. The present garden front, facing the green, has a beautiful pilastered centrepiece with decorative pediment, a style that was to typify English buildings for the best part of a hundred years.

Chief feature of the interior is a superb staircase. This has heavily sculpted relief panels, much painted, rising to a landing and ceiling with an oval garland. Although the rooms are institutionalized and lack period furniture, they have good original ceilings and fireplaces. Paintings of Royal Blackheath officials in traditional red coats take the place of ancestral portraits on the walls.

ELTHAM PALACE ****

Court Yard, SE9
Art Deco house in bailey of medieval palace
(EH)

The Eltham mansion of Stephen Courtauld and his wife, Virginia, contains the epitome of lavish inter-war Art Deco. Designed by a talented Italian playboy, Peter Malacrida, it had exotic blackbeam veneers, gold-plated taps and bathrooms smelling of gardenia. There was piped music and a telephone exchange. Virginia had a snake tattooed on her ankle. Stephen owned a rare Burney Streamline car. A pet lemur, Mah-Jongg, enjoyed a cage with bamboo murals and a ladder to help it to bed, all of which was featured in *Country Life*. The glorious dazzle ended with a bang in 1944 when the Courtaulds emigrated to Rhodesia and the house passed to the Army Education Corps.

The restoration of Eltham by English Heritage in 1999 reinstated what is now the finest Art Deco interior in England. The house was based on an important medieval palace, its Great Hall built by Edward IV at the end of the 15th century. By the early 17th century, it was decaying and from the 18th onwards the palace

ruins were solely of antiquarian interest. Jeffry Wyatville in 1827 wanted to demolish the roof and re-erect it at Windsor Castle (Berks) where it would have been lost in the 1992 fire. Eventually the Office of Works took over and repaired the hall, but an offer from the Courtaulds in 1933 came as a blessing. They wanted a house near London but sufficiently far, they hoped, to be free of suburbs.

Having taken a lease from the Crown, the Courtaulds had to fight objections to building over the ruins. Yet the architects, Seely & Paget, were respectful of the site. The Great Hall was restored as 'Hollywood medieval', with tapestries, antique furniture and an inserted gallery for minstrels. Next to the hall are two new ranges in a self-consciously 'Wrennaissance' style, above a landscaped moat and sunken garden. (*The Times* was unimpressed, calling the place 'an unfortunately sited cigarette factory'.)

Inside, Seely & Paget went for Art Deco. Money was clearly no object. The entrance hall might be the foyer of an inter-war liner, with a marquetry mural of a Viking and a Roman warrior and scenes from European cities. Stairs with blackbeam veneer sweep up to bizarre portholes round the gallery.

Everything in the house was intended to be 'the latest'. The hall has a coin-box telephone. Fixtures in the walls link hoses to a central vacuum cleaner. Themes from art and literature abound in the reception room decoration. Since the Courtauld collection of paintings was later dispersed (now mostly in Somerset House), English Heritage boldly decided to copy some of them. This works.

Upstairs, Stephen Courtauld's rooms are relatively modest, the wallpaper from Sandersons depicting Kew Gardens. His wife's suite by Malacrida is sumptuous, similar to those he designed for their Art Deco suites at Home House (London, C). Pilasters are of sycamore on maple 'flexwood' walls. Art Deco fabric covers the chairs and Brueghel copies hang on curved walls.

The principal guest bedroom is decorated with yellow Venetian panelling and fake books. The remaining rooms are in conventional

'Moderne' style. The dining room overlooking the gardens has doors inlaid with exotic animals and excellent copies of missing furnishings. Eltham conveys a sense of English design at its zenith of self-confidence. Nothing since achieved such novelty or conveys such pleasure. This is interior decoration as theatrical performance.

FORTY HALL **

Forty Hill, Enfield
Classical mansion with Jacobean interior (M)

The house sits on the fringe of the metropolis, where Enfield marches with Hertfordshire and rich men's houses were once two a penny. Nearby the 17th-century New River began its refreshing course from Hertfordshire to Islington and down to the taps of London. Forty Hall was begun in 1629 for London merchant and Lord Mayor, Sir Nicholas Raynton. It passed through many families, the last being the Parker Bowles, who sold the house to Enfield Council in 1951.

The house is architecturally odd. The outside appears to be early 17th century, with no basement but with ground and first floors of equal height below a boldly hipped roof. Although much of this façade is of a later date, it is regarded by experts as a rare classical front of the 1620s, and customarily attributed to Inigo Jones. Giles Worsley, historian of English classicism, remarks that 'it is hard to believe there was no link with Jones and it may be that he provided guidance for the architect'.

No less extraordinary is the floor plan. Inside was a traditional layout of screens passage with Great Hall to the left and steward's offices to the right. It is as if Raynton wished to display novelty outside but antiquity within.

All this must now be set aside, since a new entrance hall was inserted in the 18th century, small but astonishingly rich in plasterwork.

Radiant Art Deco at Eltham

A pillared screen, perhaps needed to support the upper floor, is meticulously decorated. The walls carry beautiful panels of musical instruments and acting masks.

The earlier screen to the Great Hall is cruder. On the inside, facing the hall, it has chunky pilasters, grotesques and a giant scallop over the door. The walls are panelled and the ceiling is a mass of geometrical scrolls, all traditional Jacobean.

The rest of Forty Hall suffers acute museumitis, with a rash of harsh lighting, lino and council art. The guidebook has the effrontery to dismiss the foliage round the Raynton Room fireplace as 'undistinguished'. Original ceilings and fireplaces survive throughout the house, needing only the touch of a wand to bring them alive. A glorious cedar of Lebanon in the grounds patiently awaits the day.

GREENWICH: FLAMSTEED HOUSE **

Greenwich Park, SE10
Wren's house for Astronomer Royal (M)

When Charles II asked the astronomer, John Flamsteed, for his opinion on how to calculate longitude, the great man, in true scholarly fashion, said the question needed more research. The King duly ordered an Observatory on the site of the old fort on the hill behind Greenwich Palace. It should, he said, cost no more than £500. It cost £520. Flamsteed took up residence in 1676 on an 'incompetent allowance' of £100 a year, from which he had to pay his 'surly, silly' assistant. From here he waged continual war on his rival, Sir Isaac Newton, calling him a robber, thief and puppy at meetings of the Royal Society.

Wren was the designer of this cheap operation and the plan could hardly have been more ascetic. It comprised a basement storehouse, four living rooms for Flamsteed and his family above and the Octagon Room for the telescopes on top. Wren described it as 'for the Observator's habitation and a little for Pompe'. Its style was in part that of the old fort, like a sham castle. Wren even built turrets on the roof. Windows are dressed with wood to look like stone.

Given that this is Britain's precursor of the Houston Space Center, its survival is remarkable. The old house is surrounded by the later Observatory complex, extended as larger telescopes arrived. These are still used for education and exhibition, one containing the famous 'line' across which visitors are able to stand in two hemispheres at once. Pollution has long since driven the astronomers to purer skies elsewhere.

The building is picturesquely sited atop the Greenwich slope. On the roof is still the red ball, raised at 12.55 pm and dropped at 1 pm, enabling shipmasters in the Docks to set their chronometers before setting sail. It now signals lunchtime to office workers in Canary Wharf to the north. The old house has been kept as in Flamsteed's day. The downstairs rooms were the official residence of the Astronomer Royal until 1948. They are restored as the chambers of a 17th-century man of letters, with high-backed chairs, dressers, canopied bed and quill pen.

The Octagon Room is a delightful chamber, built high to house the elongated telescopes required by the lenses of the day. The wall panelling is original, as are most of the telescopes and Tompion clocks. Gazing down on the scene are portraits of the early patrons, Charles II and James II. East London is spread out below.

GREENWICH: QUEEN'S HOUSE ***

Greenwich Park, SE10
Inigo Jones's Stuart pleasure house (M)

Greenwich is one of the set pieces of English architecture, best appreciated from the Isle of Dogs opposite. The scene is dominated by Wren's pavilions, rising on their great colonnades as if in homage to the delicate Queen's House sandwiched between and behind them. This house, England's first Palladian building, lies against the steep green of Greenwich Park,

with Wren's Observatory (above) set cheekily at an angle on the hill.

The queen was Anne of Denmark, much-tried consort of James I. The house was designed by Inigo Jones on his return from his second visit to Italy, inspired by the light and poise of the south. His villa on the hillside behind the old Tudor palace was to be a dazzling cosmopolitan contrast to the dark and dingy brick palace below. The house was begun in 1616 but unfinished on Anne's death three years later.

Work resumed for Charles I's queen, Henrietta Maria, but still proceeded slowly. The royal couple were able to use it for just four years before the Civil War. They spent their last night together here in February 1642, Henrietta leaving for the Continent and the King for the battlefields. The King never returned. The Queen visited Greenwich in 1662 after the Restoration, but by then the old palace by the river was being demolished and the site must have been sad.

The building's exterior, displaying Palladio's precise geometry, is unadorned to the point of severity. 'Ye outward ornaments,' wrote Jones, 'ought to be sollid, proporsionable according to the rulles, masculine and unaffected.' A contemporary account called it 'so finished and furnished that it far surpasseth all others of that kind in England'. In the middle of the north façade are two curving flights of steps, a final Baroque flourish. The steps appear from a distance like two tears running down the face of Stuart England.

Jones's original house was in two separate halves, one either side of the old Dover Road which was crossed with small bridges. A loggia at the back was for looking out over Greenwich Park. These bridges were later replaced with east and west ranges completing a building square in plan. If the exterior is chaste, the interior contains the most exquisite Italian and French decoration. The main hall, or Cube Room, must have seemed sensational to visitors used to dark Jacobean halls. The stone

Queen's House: the Tulip Staircase

floor, by Nicholas Stone, swirls outwards in restless *trompe-l'œil*. To one side rises the cantilevered Tulip Staircase, decorated with a balustrade whose pattern reflected the 17th century's love of these flowers. The stairs enclose what Jones called 'ye vacuum in ye middell', yielding the same giddy effect as Stone's floor pattern below.

Upstairs are a series of sumptuous reception rooms, recently restored and hung with some of the best of the Maritime Museum's admirable picture collection. There are portraits of early Stuarts by Lely, Hogarth, Reynolds and Canaletto. Doors and mantelpieces are decorated with the motifs that crammed Jones's Italian notebooks. Above one door is a theatrical mask, reminding us that architecture is at least in part a show.

GREENWICH: ROYAL NAVAL HOSPITAL **

Greenwich Park, SE10
Painted Hall and chapel of palace-turned-hospital (M)

The old Tudor palace of Placentia was a favourite of Henry VIII. Perhaps for that reason it was not a favourite of his daughter, Elizabeth I. It recovered some life when James I planned the Queen's House in its grounds, designed by Inigo Jones, but soon relapsed as a naval biscuit factory under Cromwell. Greenwich's revival had to await the demolition of the old palace and Charles II's ambition for a rival to Versailles at the seaward gateway to London.

The foundation stone for Charles's palace was laid in 1664 with John Webb, Inigo Jones's pupil, as architect. It was to take the form of three ranges enclosing a square open to the river. The Queen's House would thus have been left obscured, a mere garden villa. Only one range of this ambitious project, the western arm, was finished at Charles's death. With the advent of William and Mary, the palace project was converted into one for a naval hospital, with Hawksmoor designing the eastern block to balance that by Webb.

Christopher Wren next put forward plans to replace the proposed third central range with twin pavilions and domes framing the view of the Queen's House behind. This recasting of Webb's Palladianism as English Baroque has long been controversial. Was it a masterstroke, to keep open the view of Jones's house, or a bruising insult to the original concept? The answer is probably both.

Wren's domes are set on rotundas above colonnades. Each hides the entrance to the two great chambers of the hospital, the Painted Hall to the west and chapel to the east. Beyond stretch Wren's own buildings, the Queen Mary and King William courts, in dazzling Portland stone. The first pensioners arrived in in 1705.

After seeing service as the navy's answer to Wren's Chelsea Hospital, Greenwich became in 1873 the home of the Royal Naval College. It is now Greenwich University and Trinity College of Music. Little remains of its palatial character apart from the Painted Hall and chapel, both open to the public. There are also plans to display some of the old wards for public view.

The Painted Hall is one of England's great chambers. It is in three parts, rising towards the upper hall under arches and gilded pilasters, the ceilings dripping with portrayals of the achievements of William and Mary, Queen Anne and George I. Whatever the politico-religious significance of the Glorious Revolution of 1688, it in no way dimmed the enthusiasm of Stuart and Hanoverian monarchs for depicting their supposed place among the gods on high.

The paintings are by Sir James Thornhill and are his masterpiece. The main ceiling depicts William and Mary, with Louis XIV of France shown as Arbitrary Power, crouching at their feet. The upper hall celebrates the Protestant succession, with William and then George I landing on British soil to keep the wayward British on the path of Reformation virtue. Astronomers describe eclipses. Rivers offer up treasures. Everywhere are symbols of maritime might, reminding English sailors of their deserved glory.

The chapel is restrained in comparison,

largely because the original was burned in 1779 and replaced by James 'Athenian' Stuart in the style now associated with Robert Adam. The tiled floor is patterned on ships' cables. The ceiling is that of a drawing room, with *trompe-l'œil* domes and panels filled with leaves. Above the altar is Benjamin West's *Shipwreck of St Paul*. It was here that the survivors of Trafalgar came to give thanks.

HALL PLACE *

Bourne Road, Bexley
Medieval house with topiary garden (M)

Nestling beneath a roundabout off the noisy A2 appears a mirage. A flint mansion, apparently medieval, sits in a yew garden by a stream. Although overwhelmed by an adjacent leisure centre, Hall Place is real, desperate for a more sensitive reincarnation than as a local art centre.

The house was typical of many in the London suburbs. It was built c1537 by a City merchant and Lord Mayor, Sir John Champneys, and consisted of a Great Hall with wings, built of grey-and-white stone and flint in a chequerboard pattern. The hall façade was later altered to make it symmetrical, with a central doorway and a second bay window to balance the original one.

This house was sold in 1649 to another City merchant, Robert Austen, who built a jolly Restoration courtyard onto the back of the old house. This has a pitched roof, redbrick walls and plentiful windows. The join between the old and new house is uncompromising, marked on the garden side by a garderobe tower. The inner courtyard once had open arcades.

After occupation by the Dashwoods of West Wycombe (Bucks) and use as a boys' school, Hall Place was acquired in the early 20th century by the Countess of Limerick. Having lost her children in the Great War she discarded her husband and lived in the house with a lady companion until her death in 1943. She was a considerable bulwark of Bromley society, but the house, which passed to the local council at her death, sadly shows no trace of her occupation. The interior is thoroughly municipalized, the floors aggressively ramped. A smell of school food pervades the place.

What can be seen is the coved ceiling of the Great Hall, with carved bosses and an organ. In the former solar wing is a parlour and Great Chamber. The former has an excellent ceiling with enriched plasterwork, wreaths and fantastic creatures. The gallery above has a barrel vault with more plasterwork and pretty classical window surrounds.

The grounds include a sunken garden, a herb garden and a set of topiary animals.

RAINHAM HALL **

The Broadway, Rainham
Georgian merchant's house with original panelling (NT)

The hall stands beside a churchyard overlooking bleak Rainham Marshes. These downriver reaches were used to unload heavy cargoes to avoid the journey upstream. Captain John Harle dredged the Ingrebourne inlet and built a wharf to receive coal, marble, timber and Delft tiles. On the proceeds, he built himself this house and a small garden, now owned by the National Trust. They are an adornment of London's otherwise dreary eastern flank.

The house was completed in 1729 in a style still reminiscent of Queen Anne. It is remarkably big, of three storeys with an attic, each storey with arched windows. The front door has a lovely curved canopy with a scrolly pediment. The interior was given a facelift in the 1960s, with fake marble and a touch of Baroque added to the entrance hall. The main reception rooms, still in family use, retain their original panelling and fireplaces. They were clearly fitted out with the products of Harle's business in marble, wood and tiles.

The staircase is excellent. Its original *trompe-l'œil* paintings on either side of the oak leaf swags have been restored. The balusters are of mahogany. I cannot bear to think how many dozens of such houses must have vanished from East London over the past century.

RANGER'S HOUSE ***

Chesterfield Walk, SE10
Lord Chesterfield's retreat, now art and
jewellery exhibition (EH)

Ranger's House was built by an admiral,
Francis Hosier, on the hill behind Greenwich,
from where he planned to watch ships on the
river and dream of the sea. He died in 1727 in
the West Indies before he could enjoy this
idyll. The house passed to another dreamer,
Lord Chesterfield, politician, wit and writer
of Polonius-like letters to his illegitimate son,
Philip.

Chesterfield's letters were on every topic
from politics to food, wine, women, art and
table manners. When published, they became
hugely popular, although derided by Dr
Johnson as 'teaching the morals of a whore and
the manners of a dancing master'. Chesterfield
protested that he merely wanted his illegitimate boy, who would have no place in society,
as to be 'as near perfection as possible'.

At the time of Chesterfield's occupation, the
Hanoverian court was moving upstream to
Richmond. He admitted 'that I like the country up, much better than down, the river' and
Blackheath was so dangerous that he had to
keep a mastiff for protection. Yet he adored the
house, spending his summers here from 1748
to 1773 and erecting the present gallery for his
art collection. On his death the house passed to
a rakish cousin, who married 'beneath him
and in secret'. He sold Chesterfield's pictures
and then his lease to pay his drinking debts.
The house passed to the Crown and was used
to house junior members of the Royal Family
throughout the 19th century.

The house was purchased by London
County Council in 1902, for sporting facilities
and a teashop. Its fate was transformed in 1974
when the Suffolk family gave the LCC the
family collection of Jacobean portraits from
Charlton Park in Wiltshire. The house was
restored by English Heritage and further
enhanced with another donation, of some 600
works of art from the Luton Hoo collection of
the South African mining magnate, Sir Julius

Wernher. The Suffolk pictures have been
moved to Kenwood, and Ranger's House has
now surpassed its former opulence.

The house exterior is clearly a marriage
of a William-and-Mary centre with Georgian
wings. Inside, the downstairs rooms have been
decorated to reflect those of the Wernhers'
Bath House in Mayfair. The Pink Room
has French furniture and porcelain, and Reynolds's portrait of Mrs Uvedale Price. The
gallery is hung with Beauvais tapestries and
displays one of London's most erotic statutes,
Bergonzoli's *Cupid and Psyche*. Objects are
arranged, for the most part, as in Bath House.

Upstairs is an exhibition of Wernher's
promiscuous collecting mania, in the style of
the Rothschilds of Waddesdon (Bucks). He
specialized in the French and Italian Renaissance, especially miniatures and jewellery.
There are works by Memling and Filippino
Lippi, Renaissance clasps and pendants,
Limoges enamels, medieval icons, devotional
sculpture and exquisite carved ivory. It is one
of London's richest small galleries, woefully
under-visited.

RED HOUSE ***

Upton Road, Bexleyheath
Morris's first family home, Pre-Raphaelite
decor (NT)

The arrival of Red House in the National Trust
portfolio in 2003 was just cause for celebration.
It was designed by Philip Webb in 1859 for the
young William Morris and his new wife, Janey.
It was to be an enchanted medieval residence,
'a poem of a house', for a community of
like-minded artists in orchards well away from
the city.

The Morrises lived here for just six happy
years, from 1859 to 1865. Like the Wordsworths' Dove Cottage (Cumbria), Red House
was the architectural embodiment of an
aesthetic ideal. Webb was obsessed with brick,
an 'honest' material to challenge the pseudo-
stone of stucco London. In Morris's words,
Red House would be 'a joyful nook of heaven
in an unheavenly world'.

Stately Restoration: Ranger's House

The L-shaped building betrays few of the later Arts and Crafts features associated with the Morris group. It is closer to the ecclesiastical tradition of Webb's mentors, Butterfield, Street and Pugin. It is more a vicarage than a 'palace of art', and a surprisingly small one. The hipped roof is pitched and tiled, with precipitous gables and lancet windows. The porch has a Gothic arch. The material is red brick, hence the name.

The house was to be decorated by Morris and his friends, Burne-Jones, Madox Brown, Rossetti and Webb, an intention only partly realised. The windows are not generous, but Webb provided abundant light over the stairs and in the studio. The staircase is in simple wood with panelled balusters and newel posts, like those of a Puritan chapel, yet flanked by richly patterned tiles. In the roof above is a glorious stencilled lantern. The upper walls were planned to be covered with murals depicting the Siege of Troy, a strange theme for a Kentish village. These were not executed.

The hall was intended by Morris to be the climax of 'the beautifullest place on earth'. Unfinished murals by Burne-Jones are based on a Froissart romance, including Morris as king with Janey in a wimple. Here is Webb's eccentric settle, depicting Malory's *Garden of Delight*. It is crowned by a parapet and stairs leading to a diminutive minstrels' gallery. The large brick fireplace is self-consciously medieval. The ceiling has a barrel vault.

Most of the furniture is by Webb. Rubbed-brick fireplaces carry medieval mottos, such as 'Our content is our best having' and 'Ars Longa Vita Brevis'. Morris's own motto, 'If I can' was stitched by Janey into embroidery, which it was hoped might cover the walls of the house (but never did). The garden, where no tree was to be chopped down, yielded the plants that inspired the early fabrics. Morris's Daisy pattern became a favourite for girls' rooms into the 20th century.

The interior of Red House was later raided for Kelmscott (Oxon) and other Morris museums and private collections, but sufficient remains to evoke the spirit of the place. The house is like Bloomsbury's Charleston (Sussex), embodying the collective inspiration of young artists in their prime. It was always crowded with friends playing practical jokes on the corpulent Morris, engaging in apple fights, musical evenings and long drives in the country. Webb even designed the wagon that would be sent to greet them from the station.

It did not last. By 1866, Morris's business was flourishing in Red Lion Square but his private income was waning and he hated commuting. He moved Janey and their two girls to London and never returned to Red House. Marital bliss faded and Janey briefly set up home with Rossetti at Kelmscott. No more glad, confident Bexley mornings again.

SUTTON HOUSE *

2–4 Homerton High Street, Hackney, e9
Tudor mansion restored as local art centre (NT)

Here lies the ghost of old Hackney village. The house was a suburban mansion dating from the 1530s, built by a courtier of Henry VIII, Sir Ralph Sadleir. The substantial three-storey building was gabled, with a Great Hall, mullioned windows and diaper brickwork. What a battering it has taken since then.

Sutton House, named after its later Jacobean owner, was altered in the 18th century, when the Great Hall was divided and the staircase moved. Owners and tenants came and went, including a school, a trades union and a squat. The house passed to the National Trust in 1938 but was scandalously allowed to fall into dereliction. Only in 1990 was it restored and reopened as a local 'resource centre'.

The National Trust could rescue Sutton House's body but not its soul. Linenfold has been restored in the parlour and is some of the finest in London, divided by handsome fluted pilasters. Fragments of 17th-century painting survive on the upstairs walls and more panelling has been restored in the Little and Great Chambers. But shorn of furniture or pictures and filled with municipal chairs, the rooms lack atmosphere. Some effort in this direction is made in the Victorian study and Georgian parlour beyond the Great Chamber.

Everything else is fighting the twin gods of exhibition and education. The most charming part of Sutton House is the Tudor courtyard to the rear, with an arcade and view of the Edwardian 'barn' beyond.

VALENCE HOUSE *

Becontree Avenue, Dagenham
Manor house set amid Becontree Estate (M)

Some old manor houses still cling to the wreckage in the ocean of estates that covers eastern London. This part of Essex was acquired by the London County Council in the 1920s for 'homes fit for heroes'. Becontree was to become the largest council estate in England, possibly in the world at that time. On a monotonous circular plan, its terraces and cottages spread as far as any eye could see. Privatization has led owners to reface their premises with pebbledash, neo-Tudor or neo-Georgian, depriving them even of their historical curiosity. I wonder if working-class Becontree will ever be as valued as now is working-class Islington.

Even the LCC did not have the nerve to demolish the moated manor of Valence itself. The house had been owned in the 13th century by Agnes de Valence. Although 15th-century fragments remain, this is essentially a 17th-century building. Two sides of the moat survive. Subsequent use as council offices and library has spoiled the environs but the old whitewashed walls survive, with hipped roofs and dormer windows. Here Thomas May, formerly a Devon farmer, raised a stud of horses that were requisitioned for use in the Great War. The Mays lived here until the 1920s.

Downstairs is the old dining room, now with portraits left to the borough by Captain Fanshaw RN in 1963. They are a remarkable find, works by Lely, Kneller, Dobson and Gheeraerts crowded into a suddenly welcoming, warm panelled room. A rear parlour depicts a Victorian maid preparing a meal. The original staircase, with barley-sugar balusters,

Sutton House: linenfold warmth

leads to another panelled room upstairs. Its period furniture includes a baby's cradle and spinning wheel.

Elsewhere is an exhibition on the development of the Becontree Estate and other memorabilia of Dagenham's history. One room displays the fittings of a 1940s council house. A herb garden has been recreated in the grounds.

WALTHAMSTOW VESTRY HOUSE *

Vestry Road, Church End, E17
Workhouse in village enclave (M)

Church End is a London secret, a village centre lost amid the railway cuttings and terraced grids of late-Victorian Walthamstow. Here is a church, medieval house, almshouses, school and cluster of cottages on the side of a hill towards Epping Forest. In its midst is a bizarre Ionic capital, brought from the demolished General Post Office in the City of London and deposited on the green.

Next to it is a Georgian building of dark brick with white windows. Erected in 1730, it has served in its time as the old workhouse, watch house and vestry meeting room. A 'cage' for keeping troublesome prisoners overnight was added to the outside of the building in 1765. A later use was as a volunteers' exercise hall and armoury. In other words, this building, with its adjacent school and almshouse, was a complete 'one-stop shop' welfare state.

As the population grew and bureaucracy centralized, these functions were all found separate buildings elsewhere. A poorhouse was built. The Metropolitan Police stayed until 1870, installing two prison cells, one of which survives. By the 1880s, even these shreds of local government had departed the village, leaving only a literary and scientific institute and, finally, private tenants. The house became a museum in the 1930s.

Inside, the police cell is still in place and the former armoury has been furnished with panelling and a fireplace from a demolished local manor, Essex Hall. Upstairs are the usual reconstructed rooms of local history. To the rear is a vegetable and fruit garden cultivated by the paupers for their own consumption.

WILLIAM MORRIS HOUSE *

Lloyd Park, Forest Road, E17
Morris's childhood home and inspiration (M)

William Morris, who lived here as a boy, wrote of this corner of Walthamstow, 'Hark, the wind in the elm boughs! From London it bloweth/ And telling of gold and of hope and unrest.' He later deplored what had become of the Walthamstow of his youth, 'terribly cockneyfied'. Just as his banker father's speculations had fuelled Morris's socialism, so his witness of the suburbanization of London's environs fuelled his conservationism.

Morris's mother moved to the house in Walthamstow called Water House with her family in 1847 after the unexpected death of her husband at the age of fifty. Morris was thirteen at the time. The family had lived in considerable style in Woodford Hall near Epping Forest, and the move was downhill in every sense.

That said, Water House is hardly modest. It is a big Georgian mansion of 1762 and William himself was left with a legacy sufficient to see him through Oxford and into marriage and business. The façade has two large bows flanking a three-bay centre with classical doorway up a flight of steps. Behind was a large garden with a lake in which the Morris boys fished.

The interior has a large hall running from front to back, where a spacious staircase rises to a no less spacious landing. Here the young Morris would sit for hours, reading or gazing into the garden. The rest of the house is now a gallery filled with a collection of paintings and other works by Burne-Jones, Rossetti, Alma-Tadema and others.

The house would benefit from more of a sense of the domestic. This was, after all, where Morris wrote, 'One looks up and down the field . . . and I can't help thinking of tales going on among it all, and long so much for more and more books.' It needs more books.

London, West

The story of the houses of London is of a steady westward spread across the Middlesex plain. This was led by the Court but followed by wealth. It produced one of the finest concentrations of domestic architecture in England. In the lead were Wolsey and Henry VIII, together creating the great palace at Hampton Court. Money soon followed. The Greshams rebuilt Osterley and the Percys rebuilt Syon. A neglected house of the same period is the Bishop of London's former palace in Fulham, still awaiting renaissance.

The 17th century brought more adventurous architecture. Dutch classicism came to Kew Palace while the Restoration turned Hampton Court into one of the most entrancing royal palaces in Europe. The late-Stuart court produced the Duchess of Lauderdale's state rooms at Ham, and the early Hanoverians the Earl of Burlington's Chiswick House, mimicking the Veneto on the Thames.

The Georgian colonization of Richmond briefly turned the Thames bank into an Augustan Elysium. George II's mistress, Lady Suffolk, built Marble Hill. Upstream, Horace Walpole created his Gothick import at Strawberry Hill. Then in the 1760s, Robert Adam arrived in triumph, giving Syon and Osterley some of his finest interiors.

The north-western heights of the capital saw a more modest colonization. Adam's house at Kenwood for Lord Mansfield is one of his lesser works. Across the Heath is the Hampstead villa where Keats endured his brief love affair with Fanny Brawne, and the Victorian property acquired by Sigmund Freud on his escape from Vienna. W. S. Gilbert took over Norman Shaw's Grim's Dyke above Stanmore. A curious public can even visit a Modern Movement icon, the late Ernö Goldfinger's house in Willow Road.

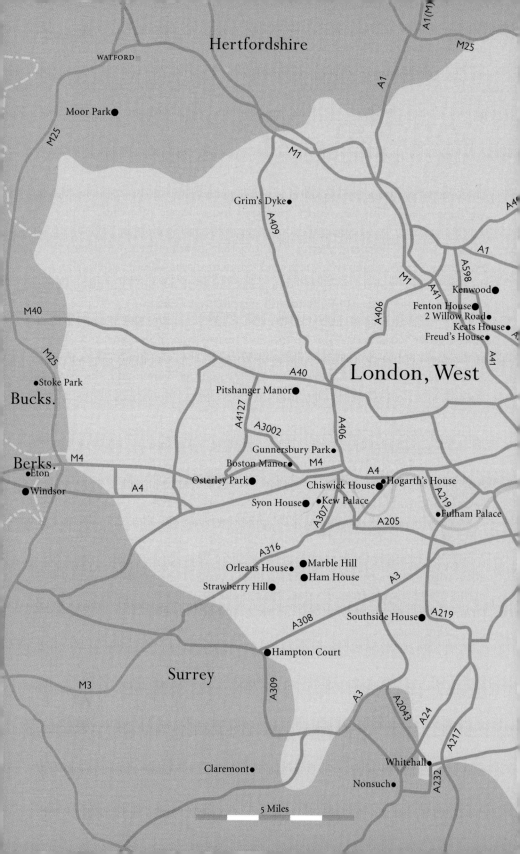

Boston Manor **

Chiswick:

 Chiswick House ****

 Hogarth's House *

Fenton House ***

Freud's House **

Fulham Palace **

Grim's Dyke **

Gunnersbury Park *

Ham House ****

Hampton Court *****

Keats House **

Kenwood House ***

Kew Palace **

Marble Hill House ***

Orleans House

 Octagon *

Osterley Park ****

Pitshanger Manor ***

Southside House ***

Strawberry Hill ***

Syon House *****

Whitehall *

2 Willow Road *

BOSTON MANOR **

Boston Manor Road, Brentford
Jacobean house with carved ceilings and overmantels (M)

Boston Manor survives. This in itself is remarkable, cowering as it does barely 400 yards from the elevated section of the M4. Traffic thunders past exquisite ceilings and radiant overmantels, protected only by thin walls and a grove of cedars.

Boston came to the public in good order. The Clitherow family, owners since 1670, sold it and its park to the Borough of Brentford in 1923. The manor was a modest Jacobean structure first built by Lady Reade in 1623. This original house appears to have been refaced with classical vigour probably by James Clitherow, a City merchant, who bought it in 1670. The building is of redbrick with bold classical window surrounds and a heavy cornice line. This makes Boston another Carolean mansion, like Forty Hall (London, E), displaying the influence of Inigo Jones, with whose classical imports its anonymous architect must have been familiar.

The entrance hall, behind an ugly Victorian porch, is dominated by a neo-Jacobean screen to the staircase, all bulbous pilasters and grotesques. To the left is a dining room filled with pictures of old Brentford. The library behind has a frame over the fireplace in the style of Grinling Gibbons and a fine early-Victorian border to its ceiling carrying the Clitherow motto, 'Loyal yet Free'.

Boston's punch is upstairs in the state drawing room. This is one of the most remarkable chambers in London. Its ceiling dates from the original house in 1623 and is a work of the most delicate Jacobean strapwork, panels and roundels, all in low relief. Its creator is believed to be Edward Stanyon, author of a similar work at Blickling (Norfolk). The roundels depict the Senses and the Virtues, complemented by a huge chimneypiece, rising through the cornice to the ceiling. The overmantel, set in a swirling field of blue, white and gold, depicts Abraham and Isaac. The room is sadly devoid of furniture.

An equally enjoyable ceiling is next door in the bedroom. Here the strapwork pays homage to Hope in the central roundel. Over the fireplace is a portrait of an 18th-century Clitherow by Kneller. The stairs have original Jacobean balusters, repeated in paint on the walls. On the upper flights are remarkable 18th-century wallpapers depicting classical ruins.

CHISWICK: CHISWICK HOUSE ****

Burlington Lane, w4
Burlington's Palladian pavilion in Kent's garden (EH)

To most Londoners, Chiswick is a place of traffic jams on the way from the west and Heathrow Airport into London proper. It is a shame that Chiswick House cannot be part of the welcome. The house is the showpiece of the 18th-century Palladian revival, a dash of the Veneto in the valley of the shadow of Heathrow.

Like Inigo Jones's exemplary Queen's House at Greenwich of a century before, Chiswick was primarily for show. Begun c1725, it was a pavilion for old Chiswick House to its east, owned by the 3rd Earl of Burlington. The Earl had already established himself as the doyen of Grand Tour taste for the incoming Hanoverian Court, eager to restore the principles of Palladian design imported by Jones, and to rebut what he saw as the degenerate Baroque of Wren and Vanbrugh.

Burlington was a rigorous antiquarian and copious collector of books and drawings. He saw himself not as a radical innovator but a purist, returning architecture to the classical principles from which the school of Wren had departed. It was a battle in which Burlington was fiercely opposed, and ridiculed, by William Hogarth, who depicted him as a Continental fop undermining the roast beef of Old England. But Burlington was new, rich and Whig. Hogarth was Tory and poor. Burlington won and Hogarth lost.

Much debate has surrounded Burlington's sources for Chiswick. They include two Palladio villas in the Veneto, a masonic temple, Inigo Jones's drawings and the works of Vitruvius, Serlio and other Renaissance authors. The entrance is graced with a portico, dome and obelisks to conceal the chimney flues. The proportions are balanced, the elevations discreet and the walls a dazzling white stucco. External embellishment is confined to a beautiful grouping of steps up to the first floor.

Access is from the basement level, its service rooms now used for museum display. Upstairs is the heart of the composition, a domed octagonal saloon, with a ceiling whose panels diminish in size towards the centre, giving an illusion of height. The walls are decorated with classical busts and Old Master paintings. To Palladio such a room was for 'feast, entertainments, decorations, comedies, weddings and such like recreations'.

Round this saloon are chambers square, rec-

tangular and octagonal. They are decorated by William Kent, the Yorkshire-born artist, architectural draughtsman and designer whom Burlington met in Italy in 1715 and brought back to London as his protégé. Burlington succeeded in getting Kent, nicknamed 'il Signior', to supplant Hogarth's father-in-law, Sir James Thornhill, at Kensington Palace (London, C). This further fuelled Hogarth's hatred.

Each of Kent's rooms at Chiswick displays his eclectic virtuosity. The Red, Blue and Green Velvet Rooms have had their original wall coverings restored, albeit in wallpaper. The ceiling of the Red Velvet Room depicts the Triumph of the Arts. The Blue Room, based on a study in the Duke of Mantua's palace, is crowned with huge console brackets and an allegorical depiction of Architecture.

At the far end of the interior is the gallery, intended not just as a museum of Italian architecture but also as an exposition of its genesis. Here the eternal verities of European civilization were to be explained, with their attendant gods and muses in harmony with Nature. Northern heaviness was rejected in favour of Mediterranean refinement, that of the well-travelled Renaissance gentleman. The order is Corinthian, most developed of the classical orders and here attributed to the baskets of foliage carried on the heads of the gods.

Chiswick later passed to the Cavendish family, who demolished the old house next door and added two wings to the pavilion in the 1780s to extend the new house. When Walter Scott visited it in 1828 he found a garden party 'resembling a picture by Watteau' taking place. It was attended by a giant elephant. Chiswick House began a long decline, eventually serving as a lunatic asylum. It passed to the local council in 1928, and then to English Heritage. It has been meticulously restored and filled with many of Burlington's original pictures, including works by Ricci, Mytens and Guido Reni.

The gardens created by William Kent and Burlington were on the formal lines of classical

Chiswick House: classicism reborn

landscape, based on a *patte d'oie* or goose foot of avenues radiating from a *rond point*. Each avenue had an architectural feature at its end. Nature was here fashioned into straight lines, a tradition with which Capability Brown was to break dramatically later in the century.

CHISWICK: HOGARTH'S HOUSE *

Hogarth Lane, w4
Artist's country house, display of prints (M)

Hogarth so detested Lord Burlington that it seems perverse of him in 1749 to buy a house next to Burlington's pavilion at Chiswick. Burlington was everything Hogarth was not, rich, stylish, influential and a commander of cultural fashion. Hogarth's print, *The Man of Taste*, depicted Burlington as foreign and immoral. Hogarth had no time for Whig dandies with Italian habits. In her biography of Hogarth, Jenny Uglow suggests the move to Chiswick was 'as if he were both laying claim to the territory, like an invader, and making peace after Kent's death the year before'. Kent had been his real *bête noire*.

Fashion sided with Burlington, and so has history. While Chiswick House (above) drips with English Heritage gold, Hogarth's House is neglected. The old lane has been wiped out by the Great West Road. The approach to the M4 passes roughly six feet from Hogarth's bedroom. An old mulberry tree, blasted by a wartime bomb, clings desperately to life. I expect one day to drive past and see the old place sighing and collapsing to the ground.

The redbrick building was little more than two rooms upstairs and two down. Hogarth installed a Venetian oriel window, the only feature to survive dereliction in the 19th century. Not until 1904 was the house rescued by the local council and reopened as a museum. The interiors have been restored with Georgian panelling but little else. No attempt is made to recreate the house as Hogarth would have known it.

The rooms are galleries of Hogarth prints, interspersed with illustrated boards about his life and work, excellently done if overly didactic. The final print is *Bathos – Old Man Time*, dying at the World's end with wreckage all round him. Hogarth might have offered it as comment on the turmoil outside.

FENTON HOUSE ***

Windmill Hill, nw3
Merchant's house with keyboard collection (NT)

The enclave round Fenton House is a Hampstead haven. Modern flats retreat, ancient walls and trees step forward and grass verges keep cars at bay. To the east of Fenton House, there is a tiny path through the trees, hiding a dogs' graveyard. We might be in deep countryside.

The house was built by 1693, the date on a chimneystack, and is a compact William-and-Mary residence surprisingly little altered over the years. Its name derives from Philip Fenton, a Baltic merchant, who bought it in 1793. His son, James, was an early champion of 'not in my backyard', convening a meeting in the Hollybush Tavern in 1829 to fight successfully against any further development of adjacent Hampstead Heath.

The house was bequeathed to the National Trust in 1952 by the then owner, Lady Binning. The gift came with her furniture and collection of porcelain, and was merged with the Benton Fletcher collection of musical instruments. These were given to the Trust in 1937 by an army major who held that music should always be played on contemporary instruments. The porcelain and the instruments charmingly co-exist to form the house's personality.

The roofs are steep-pitched with a balcony, a design so common in the neighbourhood as to merit the term 'Hampstead balcony'. The old entrance faced south, as is clear from the approach through superb gates by Jean Tijou. The façade here is of seven bays but with odd narrow windows in the outer bays, a 17th-century device to light the smaller closets beyond the bedrooms. The entrance was moved to face the road after 1800 and given a cheerful colonnade.

The interior remains as in the Fenton era, a friendly pile of twisted balusters, crowded alcoves and warm panelling, all redecorated in the 1970s by John Fowler. Each vista seems blessed with a harpsichord, spinet or virginals, often with a student practising. Similar sounds should be compulsory in all such properties, for a Georgian house would seldom have lacked for music. Fenton House is a place of bustles and bonnets, tripping feet and twittering voices, pride and prejudice.

The main dining room is now used for concerts, and contains the biggest harpsichord built in England, a Burckhardt Shudi of 1770. Other rooms are devoted to the porcelain collection. On the first floor is a rare gem, a London drawing room still with its 18th-century appearance. It has satinwood furniture, embroidered firescreens, needlework and Worcester. The former Blue Porcelain Room is now furnished as Lady Binning's bedroom, excellently displaying yet more of her needlework and porcelain.

Even better, Fenton House has its attics open to the public, from which there are marvellous views over London. Few visitors penetrate these rooms. To look out from them with the sound of music filtering up from below is to enjoy a moment's private communion with the city beneath. More could be made of the garden, especially given its inheritance of terrace walk and sunken rose garden.

FREUD'S HOUSE **

20 Maresfield Gardens, NW3
Hampstead retreat for Viennese refugee (M)

When Sigmund Freud escaped Nazi Vienna for London in 1938 it led the news. He was Austria's most famous expatriate and he rightly chose Hampstead. 'Freud flees to Knightsbridge' would have been incongruous. He was by now an old man and his family, already in Britain, sought a bright, happy house in which he might continue his work. Maresfield Gardens was sunny, 'far too beauti-

ful for us,' he said. He brought with him much of his furniture and books, as well as his treasured collection of antiquities. Sadly he had just one year to live.

Freud's family left the house untouched, a decision diluted by their also making it into a centre of Freud studies. The guidebook calls it 'a cult site, a place of mythic memory . . . which continues to pulse to a lively current of problems and challenges'. This has laid the heavy hand of education on the place. Two upstairs rooms are used for videos, art exhibitions and lectures.

The house is an inter-war redbrick building in a most un-Viennese Queen Anne style. Only two rooms evoke the master's presence, the study/library on the ground floor and his daughter Anna's room on the first floor.

The study is as he left it, lined with books and display cases, heavy with Biedermeier furniture and the trappings of a 19th-century intellectual. Spectacles remain on the desk. That favourite Proustian relic of shrine custodians, an unfinished cigar, remains in an ashtray. The couch, claimed as 'the most famous piece of furniture in the world', awaits another patient, covered with cushions and carpets. At right angles to it stands the almost as famous chair. Everywhere are statues, masks, busts and cases of figurines.

Freud's eagerness to collect significant objects caused him much concern. 'The core of paranoia,' he wrote, 'is the detachment of the libido from objects. A reverse course is taken by the collector who directs his surplus libido on to an inanimate object: a love of things.' Things were less fickle in their love than people. Freud compared his objects with a placid dog.

The work of Freud's daughter, Anna, on child analysis spread into other houses in the neighbourhood, but she kept Maresfield Gardens as a memorial to her father, transferring it to a charity before her death in 1982. Her room upstairs has her desk and bookshelves, as well as her beloved weaving loom. The room also contains painted chests and cupboards, as if from the Austrian countryside. The mix of Biedermeier and simple

Austrian vernacular is one of the charms of the house. On shelves everywhere are notices relating dreams familiar to Freud scholars, complete with context and interpretation. Hence we are given the sibling rivalry dream, the cupboard dream, the wild beast dream and the weaving dream. They are strangely discomforting. I take that to be the point.

FULHAM PALACE **

Bishops Avenue, sw6
Ghost of the Bishop's Thames-side palace (M)

Palace by name but municipal events facility by nature. Fulham Palace is a London shocker. The former country seat of the Bishops of London, easily accessible by water to Lambeth and Westminster, saw its first building in the 12th century. It remains one of the capital's most important surviving medieval groupings. At the time of writing, parts appear semi-derelict.

The bishop's estate was once big. Its moat was a mile long, the longest in England, enclosing 36 acres of ornamental and kitchen gardens. This moat was filled in with rubble in the 1920s and should be reinstated. The bishop did not move out until 1973, although by then he occupied only a flat in what was a fast decaying establishment. The estate still runs from the old church near Putney Bridge to the Fulham Football Ground at Craven Cottage. A lease was granted to Hammersmith and Fulham Council, which clearly does not know what to do with it.

The palace is two linked buildings, one early Tudor, the other mid-Georgian, arranged round two courtyards. The most interesting is the Tudor one, essentially that of a 15th-century house with gatehouse, courtyard, porch and Great Hall. There is a delightful fountain in the middle. Each of the ranges defies dating, the guidebook listing six different building periods for the entrance range alone.

The Great Hall is originally of 1480, but became a Georgian drawing room and a chapel, before reverting to serve as a hall in the 19th century. Its classical screen with open pediment comes from a demolished building in the City. Beyond are corridors and the suite of large reception rooms added in the 18th century. Some have Rococo plasterwork ceilings but little else beyond a view over the gardens.

This Georgian wing (which includes a small local museum) is best viewed from the garden and is now open to the public. The Gothick north façade retains pretty traceried windows, recalling the rebuilding of this part of the palace by Stiff Leadbetter in 1764. The elevations were given a further, classical, dressing by S. P. Cockerell in 1814, sedate and dull.

The formal grounds were among the most extensive and exotic in London but were mostly destroyed in the landscaping of the 1760s. The Tudor walled garden survives, with a superb wisteria, as do fine trees planted by generations of bishops. The ghosts of episcopal grandeur still haunt this remarkable place. But if the council cannot handle it, perhaps it should be sold and become a country house hotel.

GRIM'S DYKE **

Old Redding, Harrow
Artist's Norman Shaw house, adapted by W. S. Gilbert (H)

Frederick Goodall, the landscape painter, bought this spectacular site high on the Harrow Weald from the pickle magnate, Charles Blackwell, in 1856. He waited fourteen years before starting work on a romantic neo-Tudor house amid woods of pine and birch. Goodall's architect was Richard Norman Shaw, who insisted on changing the name to 'Graeme's Dyke', averse to the word 'grim' being attached to his cheerful style of architecture. He would have been appalled to learn that it was later chosen as a film venue for Vincent Price's 'The Cry of the Banshee' and Boris Karloff's 'The Curse of the Crimson Altar'.

In 1880 Goodall sold the house, which was bought in 1890 by W. S. Gilbert (of Gilbert and Sullivan). Gilbert changed the name back to Grim and commissioned the firm of Ernest

George & Peto to make alterations. Gilbert came to love the place, filling it with friends and a menagerie of animals. He died after a swimming accident in the lake in 1911. The house is now a hotel, vigorously committed to keeping Gilbert's memory alive.

To Shaw's biographer, Andrew Saint, Grim's Dyke is a perfect example of a suave and approachable country house, 'like some Victorian fruit cake, full of rich and diverse ingredients ... perfect for the afternoon of British bourgeois civilization'. Sweeping roofs crown rich half-timbered walls. Mullioned windows soar through two storeys and rolling lawns stretch to meet enveloping woods. The style was to be repeated on a lesser scale in a thousand north-west London semis, and across the burgeoning suburbs of the English-speaking world.

The house interiors are surprisingly domes-tic. The entrance lobby is that of a suburban villa. Off the hall is a dining room with inglenook, and a drawing room and library with spacious windows overlooking the lawn. The stairs are a feature in themselves, a mass of neo-Jacobean timbering, with split-level land-ings for Shaw's favourite conceit, the 'staircase greeting'.

The chief chamber of Goodall's house was his studio, in the form of a medieval 'Great Hall' elevated to the mezzanine level and turned on the house's axis for north–south light. Shaw designed it with a wagon roof and minstrels' gallery. Gilbert converted it to a grand reception room with a massive neo-Flemish alabaster fireplace. Photographs of the room at the time show it cluttered with heavy curtains, chandeliers and a forest of drooping palms. Today the room is a restaurant, the walls lined with pictures of G&S productions, some of hilarious campness. Off to one side is Gilbert's rehearsal room, what he called his 'flirtarium'.

Grim's Dyke was a favourite haunt of Sir John Betjeman, the Bard of Metroland, as this part of London was once known. I once caught him here, besieged by a lunch party of elderly ladies, beaming with pleasure under the roof of one of his favourite architects.

GUNNERSBURY PARK *

Pope's Lane, w3
Rothschild mansion fallen on hard times (M)

If Fulham Palace is sad, Gunnersbury is sadder. The former Rothschild mansion, sand-wiched between the North Circular and the M4 at Brentford, should be as dignified and well appointed as that family's other seats in Buckinghamshire. At the very least, it should be a decent hotel.

Today, the park is well tended but the house is a poverty-stricken museum and education centre. Terraces along which Victorian guests glided past Georgian temples and looked out towards the hills of Surrey weep with neg-lect. The windows are blind with shutters. The grand rooms are boxed in with display cases.

The original 17th-century house was built by John Webb for a prominent Stuart lawyer, Sir John Maynard, and later taken by Princess Amelia, daughter of George II. The grounds were laid out in the 18th century but the main house was demolished in 1801 and two adja-cent mansions built in its place. The larger house, Gunnersbury Park, was bought by Nathan Rothschild in 1835 and passed to his son, Lionel, Britain's first Jewish MP. The architect, Sydney Smirke, added a series of reception rooms along the south side of the house overlooking the park. The second house, known as Gunnersbury House, was bought in 1889 for the use of guests.

The two houses reached their apotheosis in the late-Victorian period, but even the Rothschilds had too many properties and sold the entire estate to the local council in 1917, in whose hands it remains.

The exterior of the house remains im-pressive, at least from the south, with a two-storeyed stucco façade and a central colonnade. Inside, Smirke's three reception rooms survive, adorned with scagliola columns and heavy classical ceilings. The central drawing room has a painted central panel. A collection of Rothschild carriages incongruously fills the music room.

HAM HOUSE ✳✳✳✳

Ham Street, Richmond
Restoration mansion with early state rooms
(NT)

Elizabeth Murray was larger than life. She was daughter of William Murray, Earl of Dysart and whipping boy to Charles I. A contemporary account describes her as 'of great beauty but of far greater parts, a wonderful quickness of apprehension and an amazing vivacity in conversation'. But there was a sting in the tail, 'what ruined these accomplishments, she was restless in her ambition, profuse in her expense and of a most ravenous covetousness'.

Elizabeth married a Tollemache and, on his death, married the Earl of Lauderdale, reputedly saving his life during the Civil War by flirting with Cromwell. She dominated both her husbands. Lauderdale rose to a dukedom, shining briefly as the L of the Restoration Cabal. To Bishop Burnet, he had a 'tongue too big for his mouth and his whole manner rough and boisterous, and very unfit for Court'. He died in disgrace in 1682. Lely's portrait of the couple in the house cannot avoid showing him arrogant and ugly and her wilful and calculating.

Ham was the house, first built in 1610, which Elizabeth inherited from her father and which she and Lauderdale struggled to convert into a place worthy of a courtier. Altered and extended by William Samwell in 1672, it was to be one of the first houses with a 'modern' promenade of so-called state rooms on the first floor. There was a matching family set on the ground floor. After Elizabeth's death, her Tollemache descendants did not alter or embellish her work. What we see is mostly still hers.

Today, no London house so embodies the transience of greatness. Mighty oaks and attendant crows still guard the shades of the departed Duchess on her foggy Thames bank. The building sits well back from the river within its gardens and grounds. No suburban estate presses close. The earlier house had been an E-plan, with a tower over the porch and projecting turrets. The Lauderdales removed the tower and turrets and adorned the entrance façade with a row of classical busts in niches. They decided not to alter the off-centre location of the hall, but added their new state rooms overlooking the garden to the rear.

The contrast between the intimacy of the ground floor and the grandeur of the first is the charm of Ham. Downstairs, one might be tiptoeing through a de Hooch painting, the atmosphere strongly Dutch. Sun streams past warm oak onto black-and-white tiles. On the walls of the Duchess's rooms are seascapes by the younger van de Velde. The Duke's Room is hung with black and gold damask. In the White Closet is a Danckerts of them both receiving guests in the ostentatious presence of classical statues. Everywhere is Dutch pottery, Dutch tulip vases and wood from the Dutch East Indies.

The first floor is reached by Murray's old staircase, its balustrade panels of 1637 still portraying not classical scenes but battle trophies. Beneath is a small family chapel. At the top of the stairs a picture gallery overlooks the hall below. Here hangs the Lely of the Lauderdales and, for contrast, one of Elizabeth as a demure young lady.

The North Drawing Room dates from Murray's house, big-boned and Carolean. It has a heavy coffered ceiling and a Berniniesque fireplace surround with massive twisted pilasters. The room is hung with Mortlake tapestries. Beyond is a dark, green closet, fashioned into a Cabinet of Miniatures or small museum.

The Long Gallery also survives from Murray's house. It is splendidly dark, filled with 22 Stuart portraits flanked by giant pilasters. Beyond is Lauderdale's library of 1674, said to be the earliest private house library extant in England, once including books by Caxton. It is a most scholarly room. The man cannot have been all vulgarity.

Along the south front of the house run the Lauderdales' state rooms. The sequence is of ante-chamber, Queen's Bedchamber and the beautiful Queen's Closet. The last is the jewel of Ham, with a Verrio ceiling and scagliola fireplace surround. An arch thick with acanthus frames a dais and 'sleeping chair'. These rooms were prepared for a visit from Charles II's queen, Catherine, which is believed never to have happened.

The National Trust has been good to Ham, although it needs a family in residence. Can some modern Tollemaches not be summoned to reoccupy the upper floors? As Queen Charlotte wrote on a visit in 1809, the place is 'beautiful and magnificent both within and without, but truly melancholy'.

HAMPTON COURT PALACE
★★★★★

Hampton Court Road, Kingston-on-Thames
Palace of Wolsey and Henry VIII, converted by Wren, Vanbrugh and Kent (M)

If Windsor is the grandest of England's royal houses, Hampton Court is the most seductive. Its Tudor profile, its forest of chimneys, its mix of intimate chambers and grand state rooms answer to every emotion. Whether shimmering above the river in summer or set about with winter snow, its entrance is the epitome of the flamboyant and tyrannical Henry VIII. To the rear is a jolly William-and-Mary building crammed with chambers in the Dutch style. Hampton Court has something for every taste.

The great palace, built on the site of a manor owned by the Hospitallers of St John, was begun in 1515 when the forty-year-old Wolsey was already Lord Chancellor. The centre of his house was set round Clock Court. Hampton Court was one of the largest houses in northern Europe in its day, based on a layout approved for cardinals. It is still one of England's most complete Tudor 'townships', more extensive even than Knole (Kent). The courts alone include Master Carpenter's Court, Lord Chamberlain's Court, Fish Court, Chapel Court and Round Kitchen Court. The palace could house a retinue of 500. Shortly before his demise, Wolsey entertained '14 score beds provided and furnished'.

Hampton Court was handed over to Henry VIII in 1528 by Wolsey after his fall from grace for failing to secure Henry's divorce from Catherine of Aragon. Henry continued to extend and embellish it, but after his death, the palace was then neglected for over a century until it caught the imagination of William III and Queen Mary, who had Wren plan its rebuilding. They ran out of time and money but the palace was occupied by Queen Anne and extended by George II. No monarch has lived at Hampton since. Although it was accessible via a (well-tipped) house-keeper, the palace was opened free of charge by Queen Victoria in 1838. By 1850 200,000 people a year were going to see it.

Henry left Wolsey's famous entrance façade and gatehouse, with Giovanni da Maiano's medallions of Roman emperors, but rebuilt the Great Hall and the chapel, to the left of the inner Clock Court. The hall is still the largest room in the palace, its massive hammerbeam roof crowded with carvings and pendants. The tapestries, regarded as the finest of the 16th century in England, were woven in Brussels of gold and silver thread.

Adjacent to the hall is the Great Watching Chamber, where retainers slept and ate. The Haunted Gallery beyond is said to echo with the screams of Catherine Howard, searching vainly for her husband to protest her innocence of adultery. Her execution was Henry's ugliest act, unredeemed by a portrait in the gallery of Henry as a Renaissance prince.

The Chapel Royal is a spectacular room, with Henry's Tudor ceiling rich in ribs and pendants, looking down on Wren's reredos carved by Grinling Gibbons. Next to the chapel is the Chapel Court, site of Henry's tennis court. These are the oldest parts of the palace, worth seeking out away from the tourist crush. They include secret courts and yards, breweries, kitchens and cellars, now crammed with ancient cooking utensils and fake game.

From here we burrow deeper into the palace and find the other Hampton Court, that of Wren and his successors. Fountain Court is a Baroque work reflecting William's desire for a memory of his palace of Het Loo in Holland.

Wren was so criticized for the court's small-ness that William had to take the blame himself. The court is surrounded by not one set of state rooms but two, an expense neces-sitated by William and Mary being joint monarchs and thus requiring separate and equal 'precedence'. The palace has not one but two royal staircases, two guard chambers, presence chambers, bedchambers, withdraw-ing chambers and closets.

The King's apartments are the grander, approached under Wren's screen in Clock Court, classical pomp inserted beneath a flurry of Tudor chimneys. The staircase is pure monarchical glorification, England's answer to Bernini's Scala Regia at the Vatican. It is entirely covered in murals by Antonio Verrio, depicting William as Alexander the Great, worshipped by the gods of Plenty. (This for a man who owed his throne to rejecting James II's divine right of kings!)

The landing commences the enfilade of the King's state rooms, three throne rooms fol-lowed by two bedrooms, all hung with massive tapestries. The state bed is so big that the king apparently used the smaller one next door in which to sleep. In this he was assisted by exqui-site works of Chinese and Japanese porcelain and a Verrio ceiling of Mars in the lap of Venus. The rooms were restored facsimile after a fire in 1986, defying misguided pleas from the Royal Institute of British Architects to rebuild 'in the style of our time'.

A flight of stairs leads down to the ground floor and a series of furnished closets beneath. The contrast with upstairs is total. This is where the king lived day to day. These might be the rooms of any late 17th-century country house, except that each has a surprise, a Gibbons overmantel, a Bassano, a van Dyck or lavish gold tableware.

The Queen's state apartments are margin-ally less grand than the King's, as completed by Queen Anne and then George II. Her staircase was painted by William Kent, the state rooms designed by Vanbrugh. The first of these, the Guard Chamber, has an extraordinary fire-place by Gibbons, the overmantel supported by two giant Yeomen of the Guard. The Queen's state bedchamber has its original Georgian bed.

Like the King, the Queen also enjoyed a suite of non-state rooms, here overlooking Fountain Court. They were built for her by Wren but not fitted out until 1716, for the future George II and his wife, Caroline. They are the most intimate and enjoyable chambers in the palace. Her bedroom appears to be the only one in the place where king and queen could sleep together in private (producing ten children). Here the queen performed her toilet, took tea with friends and prayed in her private oratory.

To reach these rooms, the visitor must pass along the so-called Communication Gallery – built to enable William and Mary eventually to reach each other – and the Cartoon Gallery. The one is now hung with Lelys of court beauties, the other with copies of the Raphael cartoons now at the V&A.

Beyond lies what can seem an exhausting new element in the palace, the range of so-called Georgian Rooms. These were converted by William Kent for George II's son, the Duke of Cumberland, on his reaching the diminu-tive age of ten. His bedroom has a columned alcove for a small bed, flanked by doors lead-ing to closets.

Behind these quarters, we can also see another fragment of Wolsey's palace, the tiny Wolsey Closet with an exquisite Tudor ceiling and murals of the Passion of Christ. It is a gem of the early English Renaissance.

Hampton Court is truly vast. Back in the Clock Court is the entrance to more of Wolsey's palace, converted into a series of gal-leries of the Royal Collection's Renaissance paintings. Outside in the Orangery is Man-tegna's epic, *The Triumphs of Caesar*, bought from the Gonzagas by Charles I and kept at Hampton Court ever since. William's Banqueting House in the Privy Garden is painted throughout by Verrio. The Great Vine still grows in the greenhouse and the parterres are restored.

Keats House: poetic retreat

After visiting the house, there is nothing more restful than to walk by the river and to lose oneself in the great park to the east.

KEATS HOUSE **

10 Keats Grove, NW3
Poet's home next to Fanny Brawne (M)

Does a happier house tell a sadder tale? In 1818, the twenty-three-year-old John Keats came to live in half the home that his friend, Charles Brown, had built on the southern slopes of Hampstead. Here he could commune with nature and visit Leigh Hunt and his friends in the Vale of Health. 'To one who has been long in city pent,' he wrote, ''Tis very sweet to look into the fair/ And open face of heaven.'

During his tenure of what was called Wentworth House, the other half of the 'semi' was rented by a young widow, Mrs Brawne, and her three children. Keats was soon infatuated with one of them, Fanny Brawne, and the couple became engaged in the autumn of 1819. It was a brief romance. Next year, Keats was ill with consumption and, despite the Brawnes' nursing, left for Rome and death in 1821. In her essay on the house, Margaret Drabble gives it 'a tragic lightness, a playful brittle terror'.

The small Regency building is still as Keats would have known it, although the garden is now surrounded by development. How Keats and Brown contrived to live cheek by jowl with the Brawnes, yet apart from them, is hard to envisage, especially before a Victorian extension was added to the east. Each household had just four rooms, two living rooms downstairs and two bedrooms upstairs. Keats's rooms are furnished more or less as he left them.

Upstairs is the tiny bedroom with the tented bed on whose pillow Keats noted the spots of coughed blood that, as a former medical student, he knew to be his 'death warrant'. In his sitting room downstairs he spent his final days in Hampstead, writing to Fanny next door and watching her walk in the garden. Outside is the tree under which, in 1819, he is said to have composed the 'Ode to a Nightingale'.

Few London houses so well encapsulate the contrast of city enclosure and open space. By the time Thomas Hardy visited the house, 'Streets have stolen up all around,/ And never a nightingale pours one/ Full-throated sound.' Today the place is a shrine. In one room is a small collection of memorabilia, including a copy of the sentimental picture (in the National Portrait Gallery) of Keats by Joseph Severn. The nightingale is supposedly somewhere in the background. Here too is a lock of Keats's hair. The house was rescued from demolition by American subscriptions and is now well guarded by the City Corporation.

KENWOOD HOUSE ***

Hampstead Lane, NW3
Hilltop Adam mansion with art collection (EH)

Kenwood spreads itself generously across the heights of Hampstead Heath, as if to separate the quarrelling sisters of Hampstead and Highgate. I have known the house all my life and still find thrilling its sudden appearance on its hill from the woods beneath. This is London's most smiling mansion.

Kenwood was owned by a succession of Scottish noblemen until acquired by the Lord Chief Justice, the 1st Earl of Mansfield, in 1754, and remodelled ten years later by Robert Adam. He added a portico to the entrance and an exquisite library. Two later wings enclosed the entrance courtyard. Most of the furniture was sold in 1922 and the house was saved from demolition only by the Guinness magnate, Lord Iveagh, who bought it in 1925 and left it to the nation with his magnificent art collection in 1927. The park was incorporated into Hampstead Heath, a blessing beyond price. The house is now run by English Heritage, which is struggling to recover much that was sold in 1922.

Robert Adam, with Syon House and Osterley Park already built, had difficulties

Adam exhuberant at Kenwood

with Kenwood. To the south the sloping site forbad a proper portico and yielded a weak composition. The only enrichment is ten pilasters and a modest pediment, unbalanced by the two wings but cheered by being coated in creamy stucco. The park is by Repton, with a lake and Adam bridge, leading to a diminutive modern concert stage.

The interior of Kenwood is gradually returning from art gallery to house. As yet, only the front hall and library vibrate with Adam exuberance. The latter is one of his richest interiors. The bays are filled with mirrors. Apses at each end are divided by screens of columns. 'Nothing can be more noble and striking when properly applied than a fine order of columns,' wrote Adam, yet nothing was 'more sterile and disgustful than to see for ever the dull repetition of Dorick, Ionick and Corinthian entablatures.' The ceilings are by Antonio Zucchi. It was at Kenwood, while painting the *Rape of Europa*, that tradition claims Zucchi fell in love with Angelica Kauffmann before carrying her off to Rome.

A lovely 1811 harp has been returned to the music room and a sideboard has been found in America and returned to the breakfast room. Adam's 'Chinese' chimneypiece in the Upper Hall is an astonishing work, architecturally plain but encrusted with mermen, gryphons and cherubs. In the rest of the house, screens, fireplaces and ceilings mainly inserted after Adam had departed must serve to decorate mostly empty rooms.

Besides that are the pictures. Kenwood contains one of the most enjoyable small collections in London, recently enhanced with the addition of the Suffolk collection of 16th-century court portraits from Ranger's House (London, E). In the music room are English women, including Reynolds's *Mrs Masters as Hebe*, apparently intended 'to comfort her jealous husband'. Romney's Emma Hamilton is depicted as a saint. Gainsborough is represented by Lady Brisco, her hair about to take flight, and Mary, Countess Howe, an aristocrat in a whirlwind of pink satin and lace against a stormy background.

The dining room contains major Dutch works by van Dyck, Hals, Cuyp and a Rembrandt self-portrait. Here too is Vermeer's haunting *Guitar Player*, a caged bird apparently singing to a lover listening in the woods outside.

KEW PALACE **

Kew Gardens, Kew
Merchant's mansion turned royal palace (M)

This must be the most domestic 'palace' in London. Buried inside Kew Gardens and still awaiting reopening at the time of writing, Kew Palace is a poignant place. It was here that the ailing George III retreated with his wife, Charlotte, as madness approached and before his removal to Windsor in 1805.

Queen Charlotte lived on in the house after his death and two of the royal sons were married in its front parlour. The King and Queen had bought the house as an annexe to neighbouring Kew House (marked now by only a sundial) for use by their fifteen children. After the Queen's death, it was shut up for almost a century until being merged with Kew Gardens.

The house, on the bank of the Thames, was originally built by a merchant, Samuel Fortrey, in 1631. The style was emphatically Dutch, much favoured in the City of London in contrast to the Court preference for the southern Renaissance of Inigo Jones. Here the classicism is expressed in carved brick. The façade might be on a canal in Amsterdam, with double-curved gables and rusticated brick surrounds to the windows.

The interior is unpalatial. A cross-passage runs from front to back, with two rooms on either side. The rooms are as decorated in the 18th century, with Hanoverian bric-à-brac, toys and snuffboxes. A fine staircase leads to the Queen's boudoir on the first floor, with original plasterwork ceiling. The house is understated, like the monarch to whom it so appealed. The gardens towards the river have been restored to their presumed 17th-century style. This is a house, currently being restored, in which someone should be living.

MARBLE HILL HOUSE ***

Richmond Road, Twickenham
Palladian box for Hanoverian mistress (EH)

Henrietta Hobart was the orphaned daughter of Sir Henry Hobart of Blickling (Norfolk). She was married in 1706 to an improvident younger son of the Earl of Suffolk, then in the Dragoon Guards. The couple were always in debt and fled, like many adventurers, to Hanover to attach themselves to the court of the future George I.

With the Hanoverian succession in 1714, they returned to England in the royal retinue. Howard was attached to the King, Henrietta to the Prince and Princess of Wales. This involved her moving to Richmond following the Prince's estrangement from his father, George I, and 'exiled' up-river.

By 1720, the Prince was said to be going every evening to the thirty-two-year-old Mrs Howard's lodgings. Yet all gossip admitted that he regarded the lady 'rather as a necessary appurtenance to his grandeur as a Prince than an addition to his pleasures as a man'. There is no evidence of a physical relationship between them, indeed everyone, including the Prince's wife, seems to have approved of Henrietta. Walpole described her as being 'sensible, artful, agreeable but with neither sense nor art enough to make the king think her more agreeable than his wife'.

Separated from her husband and eager for a house of her own near Richmond, Henrietta persuaded George in 1724 to give her £11,500 for a building and furniture. He appointed trustees from his circle to select a site and supervise the design, including Lord Herbert and Lord Ilay. Also consulted were Colen Campbell and Roger Morris; Charles Bridgeman designed the gardens. Seldom has so much talent been expended on so modest a property.

This may explain why the house took five years to build. Meanwhile, Henrietta's husband succeeded, by virtue of a lucky series of deaths of his brothers, to the Suffolk earldom and conveniently died. Henrietta, now a widowed countess, retired from Court, married George Berkeley and lived happily at Marble Hill until her death in 1767.

Today, Marble Hill peeps through the trees in the many views painted of the Thames upstream from Richmond Hill. It recalls the great days of Georgian Twickenham, with Augustan villas set in a rustic landscape with Walpole, Pope and the Hanoverian court gossips gliding by on barges. It is a handsome if plain box of white stucco.

The interior is planned round the Great Room, the reception room on the first floor. Visitors were intended to enter from an outside staircase in the manner of Chiswick House (above), but this was never built. Instead they entered into the 'rustic', through a lower hall round which are arranged the dining and breakfast rooms.

The Great Room was where the Countess would have received her guests, in a style that suggested a much bigger mansion. Lord Herbert, as his contribution to the design, appears to have intended the room to have the proportions of Inigo Jones's Single Cube Room at his seat at Wilton (Wilts). Its grand ceiling rises through the upper two storeys of the house.

The walls are lined with fine side tables, rediscovered in Australia in 1987. Robust gilded putti adorn the mantelpiece. Paintings of ancient Rome by Pannini have also been restored to their frames over the doors. The Countess's bedroom has recently been rehung with green damask and refurnished, and the second floor gallery restored. Now, it all needs more pictures.

In 1901, the shipping tycoon, William Cunard, tried to demolish Marble Hill for housing. After a public outcry, he sold it instead to the London County Council, who merely neglected it. Restoration by English Heritage has restored its dignity, if not its vitality.

The grounds are used as local sports fields, but come to life with a concert programme each summer. The garden claims the tallest black walnut, bay willow and Italian alder in England.

ORLEANS HOUSE
OCTAGON *

Riverside, Twickenham
Gibbs pavilion of lost Thames-side mansion
(M)

Orleans House was erected by the Thames
in 1710 by James Johnston, Secretary of State
for Scotland and immensely rich. Johnston's
gardens were once reputed to yield 'the best
collection of fruits of any gentleman in England'. In 1720 he added a pavilion by James
Gibbs, reputedly to receive the then Princess of
Wales. In 1815, the house was let to the exiled
Duc d'Orleans, later King Louis Philippe, a
distinction reflected in the house's name.

The shipping magnate, William Cunard,
bought Orleans House and the adjacent
Marble Hill in 1882, living in the former and
later trying to demolish the latter for development. In 1926, his executors sold Orleans
House to a gravel company for excavation.
They pulled down the great house but found
no gravel.

A local conservationist, Mrs Ionides, daughter of the founder of Shell, bought Gibbs's
pavilion to save that too from destruction and
to protect the sylvan view from Richmond
Hill. She bequeathed it to the local council and
it remains a delightful survivor in this sorely
tried landscape.

The Octagon is a gem of early Georgian
design, a single chamber with large windows
on five sides and a fireplace and two doors
on three. The doors are magnificent, worthy
of the most sumptuous town house. Reclining figures and putti adorn the pediments.
Medallions depict the then Prince and Princess
of Wales. Graceful Corinthian pilasters mask
the angles.

The ceiling is by Gibbs's stuccoists,
Guiseppe Artari and Giovanni Bagutti, then
working for him at St Martin-in-the-Fields.
The dome carries exquisite Baroque decoration. It is a room of superb poise but in need of
further restoration. To have contemplated
destroying it is astonishing. Finding a new use
for it is a challenge.

OSTERLEY PARK ****

Jersey Road, Isleworth
Elizabethan house decorated by Robert Adam
(NT)

In 1576 Elizabeth I was being entertained
at Osterley by its owner, London's premier
merchant prince, Sir Thomas Gresham,
founder of the Royal Exchange. She suggested
in the course of the evening that his central
courtyard would 'appear more handsome'
with a wall across it. Between her going to bed
and awakening next morning, Gresham's
workmen built just that. Cynical contemporaries remarked that it was not the Queen, but
'money commandeth all things'.

The wall did not survive, nor did the house
stay in the Gresham family for long. It passed
to the London developer, Nicholas Barbon,
and in 1713 to the banker, Francis Child. It
was Child's descendants who remodelled the
Elizabethan house, first using local craftsmen
and then, in 1761, Robert Adam. The family
insisted, like the Duke of Northumberland at
Syon, that Adam merely remodel their old
house and confine his talents to the interior.
Adam's masterstroke was to enclose the courtyard with a pedimented loggia linking the
north and south wings. The result enhances
the serene symmetry of the redbrick exterior,
which now floats like a ship on a sea of grass.

Of Adam's interior, Horace Walpole wrote
from neighbouring Twickenham that it was 'so
improved and enriched that all the Percies and
Seymours of Sion must die of envy'. It is now
a museum of Adam decoration, with some
of the original furniture still in place. When
Child's descendant, the 9th Earl of Jersey, gave
the house to the National Trust in 1949 and
fled into tax exile, he took the best pictures
with him, works by Poussin, Rubens, Lorraine,
van Dyck and Salvator Rosa. They were lost in
a warehouse fire. Osterley's present paintings
are on loan from the V&A.

Unlike its Adam cousins, Syon and
Kenwood, the house remains at the centre
of its original farming estate, with meadows
and livestock as well as a lake and park. This

Boucher and Gobelins at Osterley

fragment of rural Middlesex survives, incredibly, sandwiched between the Great West Road and the M4. Jets rumble low overhead on the flight-path into adjacent Heathrow. It is surreal.

Perhaps for that reason, Osterley is neglected. I have never seen it crowded and it is often empty. It is also one of the National Trust's most bloodless properties, victim of capture by earnest conservationists. Its blinds are drawn and rooms are in perpetual gloom. If something is not done to bring it to life, some future government will turn it into a First Class Terminal for Heathrow.

The plan is simple. A Roman entrance hall leads into a Long Gallery beyond, the main reception rooms running down each side. Completed over the course of the 1760s and 1770s, they display the evolution of Adam's style so vividly that his biographer, Eileen Harris, recommends that they be viewed in chronological rather than architectural order. The Trust's one-way traffic flow makes this impossible.

The hall is a glorious composition of white and pale blue, its walls crowded with giant trophies and its ceiling reflected in the floor beneath. Visitors are next ordered into a side wing to see the library. The bookcases here are boldly architectural, their leather bindings almost part of the decoration. The ceiling used to be painted in bright colours from pattern books found in the Soane Museum. Now it is white, current victor in the 'colour wars' fought by Adam experts. Over a mantelpiece is a picture by Antonio Zucchi of Catullus writing an *Epitaph on the Death of his Mistress's Bird*. I wonder how many bankers would commission that subject today.

The adjacent staircase had to be squeezed into a wing of the Tudor house, a constraint turned by Adam to brilliant effect. The stair rises to the landing past a tall Corinthian screen with honeysuckle balusters. The ceiling was filled with a canvas by Rubens, removed by Jersey and lost in the fire. The present version is a copy. The upstairs rooms include a fine Adam bed with taffeta hangings. In Mrs Child's dressing room is a Rococo chimney-piece displaying porcelain, its oval frame dipping into the mantelpiece below.

Adam was attentive to the social behaviour of the English house. He lavished attention on dining rooms and libraries, holding that the former should have neither panelling nor fabric, which would retain the smell of food. Libraries should have no carpets, since dust would spoil the books.

The Long Gallery has been refilled, thanks to the V&A, with Poussin, Cuyp, Sebastiano Ricci and others. The insistence on keeping the blinds drawn makes picture-gazing here seem like swimming underwater. The swimmer must continue down the finest Adam rooms in the south wing. His early drawing room is in deep green and gold, its ceiling roundel a burst of ostrich feathers. The furniture, the carpet, even the fire grate are all by Adam. I used to visit this room and think how well it responded to great trees waving outside. When I asked if the blind might rise to recapture this effect, I was sent on my way.

Darkness is more tolerable in the Tapestry Room next door, with its made-to-measure Gobelins to designs by Boucher. They are lit by imitation candles. Adam's exquisite ceiling, all but invisible, is reflected in the carpet, which also repeats Boucher's bunches of flowers. The bedroom beyond is dominated by a bed topped by a dome as of a Temple of Venus. It is one of Adam's most elaborate furnishings, supremely theatrical, surrounded by walls of pleated silk.

The Etruscan Dressing Room is Osterley's masterpiece, a calm celebration of the gods of love. Roman characters dance along dados, recline on platforms and lose themselves amid swirling fronds and foliage. Although Adam used the style frequently it was imitated only rarely by his contemporaries (such as Wyatt

at Heaton Hall/Lancs). Walpole regarded it as a foible, 'pure harlequinade, gingerbread and snippets of embroidery'. Today it appears serene, like a light flute playing softly. And all within a mile of Heathrow.

PITSHANGER MANOR ***

Walpole Park, Ealing
Soane's weekend retreat with original interiors (M)

The old house at Pitshanger was selected by Sir John Soane in 1800 as a summer retreat from his new family home in Lincoln's Inn Fields (Soane Museum/London, C). He also hoped that his rebuilding of it would encourage his sons to follow in his own profession. In the latter he failed. Soane never spent a night in the house, using it only for day trips out of London. He sold it within a decade.

The manor had been owned by the Gurnell family, who added a wing by the Georgian architect, George Dance. Soane demolished all except the Dance wing and rebuilt it as a variant on a classical temple. After being sold in 1810, the house was later occupied by the unmarried daughters of the murdered prime minister, Spencer Perceval, and passed to Ealing Council in 1900, reopening as a library two years later. Though immaculately restored, Pitshanger's present use as a municipal art gallery is a travesty of what it should and could be.

The front exterior has detached Ionic columns crowned by statues fronting a three-bay box. This composition is repeated pianissimo on the far side overlooking the park with pilasters similar to those on his Lincoln's Inn Fields house. The walls are in pale grey brick, lending the structure an ethereal lightness. This is a charming classical box. Dance's Georgian wing and later additions seem rather plodding next door.

The vestibule has all Soane's inventiveness. Although tiny in floor area, it soars upwards to disappear in tunnel vaults and starbursts. Medallion reliefs show the sun and moon. At the end of the vestibule, a small drawing room is on the left and the library and breakfast room run from the front to the back of the house on the right. The latter two rooms are among the most refined of their period. The library has Soane's characteristic shallow, groined-vault ceiling with coffered arches and statue niches. The ceiling has been restored with a trellis pattern .

The breakfast room is a superbly original creation. A shallow dome with clouds painted across its centre is supported by caryatid pilasters in the four corners. Walls are blue-grey and doors are inlaid with black lines, sleek and smart, like an Art Deco dressing room. These remarkable interiors come just thirty years after Adam's work and precede the voluptuous French interiors of the palaces of the Regency Court. Soane's was a stylistic blind alley, but a sensational one.

The rest of Pitshanger is anticlimax. The Dance extension, rightly respected by Soane, has a bold blue and white ceiling to its ground-floor dining room. The ceiling of the upstairs drawing room is of swirling Rococo arabesques above clashing Chinese wallpaper.

SOUTHSIDE HOUSE ***

3 Woodhayes Road, Wimbledon
Wayward 17th-century house, much
refashioned (P)

Southside is a rambling, patched and thoroughly eccentric mansion with cobwebs hanging from the ceiling and candlelit faces staring from tapestry-hung walls. The owners are the Pennington Mellor Munthes, who are owners of the equally eccentric Hellens (Herefs).

The story of the present house begins with the falling of two bombs, front and back, during the Second World War. They destroyed the front hall and the rear dining room with the lady of the house, Hilda Pennington Mellor, wife of the author Axel Munthe, sheltering in the basement below. She decided to leave for Herefordshire but had no petrol or car big enough for her goods. She fled with her maid in a 100-year-old horse-drawn wagon, only to find bombs also landing on her country house.

After the war, she returned to restore the building to its ancient state. Artist members of the family turned their hand to anything from a cement Baroque overmantel to ceiling murals and mock tapestries on canvas. Southside is not a work of art but something more precious, a house created and adorned by those who inhabit it.

The main front is a jumble of amendments to a Restoration core. Access is from the rear garden through a handsome Georgian doorway. Everything inside is clearly in use, although whether by a Jane Austen heroine or a Hobbit is never quite clear. Nothing quite matches anything else. An enfilade runs along the main front of the house, where everything is kept dark and candlelit. The restored dining room rises to a pointed roof, painted sky blue. It has a Jacobean mantelpiece and is hung with 34, mostly Stuart, portraits. They include van Dycks, a Hogarth and a Burne-Jones.

The galleried entrance hall was reconstructed and repainted after the bombing. On my visit, its massive fireplace contained a huge smouldering log which filled the house with smoke and contributed further to the darkening of its surfaces. The Tapestry Room is hung with painted canvases, from which a small door gives access to a surviving powder closet. Here visitors would have their wigs re-powdered after driving across windy Wimbledon Common.

Behind is a sudden shift from Stuart dark to Georgian light. A large 18th-century music room overlooks the garden, with a screen of fluted columns and classical statues in niches. On the walls are paintings by Raeburn and Romney while against the walls are piles of old sheet music. Concerts are still held in this room, lit by candle chandeliers. Two large Chinese vases adorn one end, two of four sent by the Emperor of China to a 17th-century tsar. They 'went astray' on their journey through Asia and were acquired by a previous owner in Paris. The other two are apparently in the Kremlin.

Upstairs, the house goes delightfully haywire. A library has sculpted heads of family members round the bookcases. The Prince of

Wales's Room next door is the formal guest room, with a huge four-poster under a canopy and with yellow brocade wall-hangings. In this room is displayed the necklace worn by Marie Antoinette at her execution. It was removed from the scaffold and came into the possession of the young John Pennington, then serving in the British Embassy in Paris. Also upstairs is a tiny chapel, surely the smallest in London, still consecrated.

STRAWBERRY HILL ***

Waldegrave Road, Twickenham
Walpole's Gothick fantasy (P-R)

Horace Walpole was the younger son of England's first 'prime minister' (*see* Houghton/ Norfolk) and destined for a career in politics. From the moment he returned from the Grand Tour, he thought this an appalling idea and devoted his life to art. Apart from his diaries and letters, his one literary work was a Gothick novel, *The Castle of Otranto*. In 1747, he acquired Chopped Straw Hall upstream of the Hanoverian court at Richmond and rebuilt and renamed it Strawberry Hill.

Walpole's architectural fantasmagoria is now all but submerged by the adjacent St Mary's College. Whether his house is a masterpiece or merely a curiosity is a matter of opinion. In his own lifetime, it became so popular that he suggested he should marry his housekeeper, so much money was she making by charging an exorbitant guinea a visit.

Work on the new house began in 1749, with Walpole forming a Committee of Taste to assist him. Chief members were his friends Richard Bentley and John Chute (*see* The Vyne/Hants). Walpole held court in velvet and silk, with kittens and poodles littered about his feet. Friends were summoned and dismissed at will. But the outcome was the first systematic programme of Gothic Revival in England, later dubbed with a suffix -k.

The house began with the conversion of the

The Music Room at Southside

old farm house, set on a site sloping down to the bank of the Thames. Walpole gothicized and battlemented the farm and then extended it round the garden, with a new gallery culminating in a round tower. The house remained small. To Beckford, builder of the gigantic Fonthill in Wiltshire, it was 'a Gothic mousetrap'. Even Walpole himself called it 'a little plaything house'.

The house is best entered, if possible, from the front or back door, not along the lengthy corridor from St Mary's College. The earliest rooms on either side of the entrance are cottagey, their fireplaces mostly copied from ecclesiastical tombs. Although the furniture and artefacts were dispersed after Walpole's death, efforts have been made to refurnish the rooms in his style.

The staircase was designed by Bentley after one in Rouen Cathedral. It rises to an armoury and a memorial to Walpole's much-researched but probably fake Crusader ancestor, Sir Terry Robsart. The breakfast room is like a boudoir, once containing 'a thousand plump chairs, couches and luxurious settees'. The doors and panelling are Moorish, the (later) ceiling is a fabric tent. Most successful of the earlier rooms is the library, designed by Chute. Decorated Gothick bookcases leap round the walls, culminating in a great canopy over the fireplace, copied from John of Eltham's tomb in Westminster Abbey.

Strawberry Hill now gains in confidence. The adjacent Holbein Chamber is where Walpole claimed to have had the nightmare that inspired *Otranto*. It contains Bentley's pierced screen, pinnacled fireplace and intricate ceiling, a Gothick delight by day but certainly a horror by night.

Walpole's Long Gallery is in the form of an internal cloister beneath a *papier mâché* fan vault. This was designed by Chute, Bentley having now been discarded because his wife was judged unable to behave 'with people of the first rank'. The gallery is flanked by Gothick canopies hiding vaulted alcoves and mirrors. I encountered an American lady photographing them in minute detail, 'to give to my interior decorator back home'.

Of the remaining rooms, the Tribune copies its roof from the Chapter House at York, its ribs and vaults like swirling flames. The Round Room (designed by Robert Adam no less) takes its chimneypiece from Edward the Confessor's tomb at Westminster. The ceiling is based on the rose window in Old St Paul's. A frieze of tiny acanthus leaves is Adam's only apparent signature.

SYON HOUSE *****

Brentford
Adam's greatest interiors in Thames-side mansion (P)

Syon House is phenomenal, an aristocratic seat complete with private estate, park and river frontage inside the boundaries of London. The family is the Percys, Earls then Dukes of Northumberland, to whom the former monastic property of Syon passed in 1597. The Percys were architecturally conservative. They never replaced the old house, rather converting it gradually over the generations.

Adam's work at Syon dates from 1761, three years after his return from Italy and already fiercely ambitious. The Northumberland commission was a valuable catch. The Percy heiress, Elizabeth Seymour, had married the progressive and energetic Sir Hugh Smithson who, in 1750 became Earl, later 1st Duke, of Northumberland. He told Adam to leave the exterior alone. Adam duly treated the castellated exterior as a disguise for the splendours within. Only two pavilions in the grounds and the Adam gate on the main road suggest this is a house of the 18th century. The latter carries the Percy lion, moved from the demolished Northumberland House in London's Strand.

The front door opens directly on the Great Hall. This serene chamber is the Georgian ideal of a Roman senate house. The cross-beams of the ceiling, coated in plaster anthemions, are reflected in the chequered marble floor. Figures of Greek and Roman dignitaries line the walls. Screens at each end flank steps to the reception rooms beyond. In front of these screens are copies of two famous statues of antiquity, the *Dying Gaul* and the *Belvedere Apollo*.

Next comes the ante-room, among the most sumptuous classical chambers in England. Adam turned a simple cube into a temple of marble and gold. To Sacheverell Sitwell it was 'as superb as any Roman interior in the palace of the Caesars'. Twelve columns allegedly dredged from the bed of the Tiber were acquired for £1,000 apiece and coated in scagliola. Their entablature occupies the entire top third of the room. Gilded statues from antiquity are interspersed with panels of gold on green. Ceiling echoes floor and floor ceiling.

The ante-room turns the corner of the house to be followed by the quieter dining room. Here is another demonstration of Adam's skill at expanding a small space to create a big one, by means of niches, screens, apses and perspective. The chimneypiece is by Joseph Rose and depicts the *Three Graces*. Rose also executed the abstract pattern of the ceiling.

After the relative calm of the dining room, the Red Drawing Room returns to full throttle. Walls are hung with faded crimson silk, offsetting the brilliant gold of the ceiling, where a kaleidoscope of classical medallions by Cipriani coats the surface. The doorcases are of gold leaf on ivory. The room has tables of mosaic, one with a top from the Baths of Titus, and a Georgian cylinder bureau covered in marquetry. On the walls are Stuart portraits, including Lely's Charles I with his son, James, and a van Dyck of Queen Henrietta Maria.

Adam planned the Long Gallery as a drawing room for ladies, to separate them from the male noise of the dining room. He took the Elizabethan gallery, which would have been a long, monotonous chamber, and gave rhythm to its walls and ceiling. Pilasters are spaced to make it seem both longer and wider. Doors, fireplaces and niches are all pressed to this purpose, as are the diagonal patterns in the ceiling. The room is decorated in pinks and mauves, softening the gilding and making the books and Percy medallions seem like precious objects attached to the walls.

The room culminates in a tiny pink-and-blue domed closet, a conversation piece in which a mechanical bird is invited to join. From the windows the view is completely rural, over the water meadows to the banks of the Thames and the great trees of Kew.

After these rooms, Syon becomes just another country house. Rooms are enlivened by Adam fittings imported from Northumberland House. Syon's gardens are partly private, but the great conservatory and arboretum are accessible.

WHITEHALL *

1 Malden Road, Cheam
Hall house with original interior (M)

If someone had the courage to grab the centre of Cheam by the throat, demolish what is ugly and fill in the gaps, it would be a jewel of South London. A scatter of old houses survives across Malden Road to the west of the church, clapboarded and painted like a New England township. Pride of place goes to Whitehall. Begun c1500 and immaculately restored by Sutton Council, the only sadness is that its two chief rooms, the hall and parlour, are shops.

The exterior is charming. White clapboards cover a timber frame, parts of which can still be seen in the wall of the rear kitchen. The door has a porch tower over it, while the wings are jettied both front and back. The old hall was not open to its roof but two-storeyed and chimneyed from the start, a thoroughly modern Tudor property. The house belonged in the 17th century to a local clergyman, who added a wing to the back. It was bought by the Killick family in the 18th century, who sold it to the local council in 1963.

The interiors suffer museumitis, but fireplaces and beams remain and the floors retain a satisfactory creak. A Cheam schoolmaster's study bedroom has been recreated in the attic, in all its cluttered asceticism. Three masters once lived here. To the rear an early garden has been recreated.

2 WILLOW ROAD *

Hampstead, NW3
Modern Movement shrine (NT)

Ask not the reason why. After the death in 1987 of the Austrian-Hungarian architect, Ernö Goldfinger, his acolytes pleaded for the National Trust to buy and preserve his house and its contents. This was done in 1994. The property is outwardly (and inwardly) unremarkable, a rectangular box of three small houses built by Goldfinger after coming to London in 1934. He occupied the largest, middle one. Here, at least, was a Modern Movement house in which its architect lived.

The building attracted outrage when constructed in 1937. Pevsner had to defend it vigorously as 'the contemporary style in an uncompromising form', that is of three storeys 'of reinforced concrete, with columns exposed on the ground floor, and with concrete used also for framing the openings in the brick-faced walls'. The brick facing makes it early Goldfinger. Later it would have been all concrete.

The guidebook says that Goldfinger was eager to display his talents to his new English parents-in-law, who were heirs to the Crosse and Blackwell fortune. The house is small but was given 'servants' quarters' in the basement and garaging for two cars, one with an inspection pit. The interior is consistent with the exterior. The entrance lobby, cramped by the garage, leads up a spindly spiral staircase to a living, dining and study floor, more or less open plan. Furnishings are spare and vaguely Scandinavian. There is little sense of privacy. The first floor is an uninterrupted expanse of glass, front and back, offering fine views of Hampstead Heath.

The one relief is the warm parquet flooring and liberal use of panelling. Shelves, dividers, chairs and tables are mostly by Goldfinger. The dining table is topped in lino, chairs are made of plywood and such materials as tubular steel and Bakelite are much in evidence. Anatomical studies by Goldfinger's wife, Ursula, decorate the walls, alongside works by Max Ernst, Bridget Riley and Henry Moore.

Norfolk

Norfolk has always seemed a county detached. It is bounded on two sides by sea, on a third by the Fens. Like all flatlands, it has long seemed a distant, introverted region and one with little respect for its towns. King's Lynn, Great Yarmouth and much of Norwich have been mistreated by planners, yet Norfolk's villages are like its churches, supreme, with cottages of flint and thatch, manors of brick and tile, great houses of imported stone.

Medieval architecture can be seen in the Norman castles of Norwich and Castle Rising, two of the best of their period in England. Tudor domestic building is exemplified in two surviving town houses in Norwich. Of the same period is the royal suite at Oxburgh, one of the great brick houses of England, still with its gatehouse and moat.

By the 17th century the county was building in earnest. Blickling and Felbrigg are Jacobean mansions of the first rank, albeit much altered by the Georgians and Victorians. Norfolk is blessed by two Palladian spectaculars, products of the Walpole and Coke rivalry, Houghton and Holkham. Like the hare and the tortoise, Houghton began the fastest, but Holkham comes through the winner. Later Walpoles could not decide between medieval Mannington and Georgian Wolterton, finally opting for both.

The Victorians confined their work chiefly to alteration and improvement, notably at Oxburgh, Felbrigg and the Long Gallery at Blickling. The century culminated in the Royal Family's development of Sandringham, today the most intimate of accessible royal dwellings.

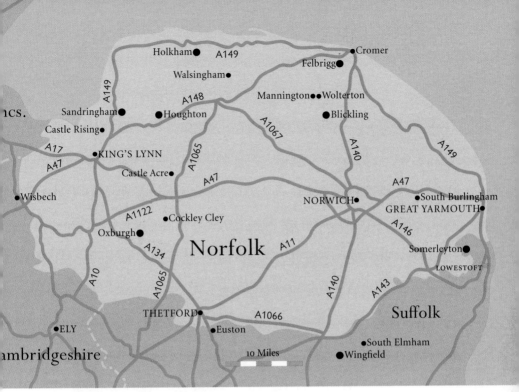

Blickling ✳✳✳✳
Castle Acre Priory ✳
Castle Rising:
    Castle ✳✳
    Trinity Hospital ✳
Cockley Cley:
    Iceni House ✳
    Old Cottage ✳
Cromer:
    Fisherman's
        Cottage ✳
Felbrigg ✳✳✳

Great Yarmouth:
    Elizabethan House ✳✳
    Row 111 ✳
    Row 113 ✳
Holkham ✳✳✳✳✳
Houghton ✳✳✳✳
King's Lynn:
    Clifton House ✳✳
    Old Gaol ✳
Mannington Hall ✳✳
Norwich:
    Castle ✳

Norwich:
    Dragon Hall ✳
    Strangers' Hall ✳✳
Oxburgh ✳✳✳✳
Sandringham ✳✳✳
South Burlingham:
    Old Hall ✳✳
Thetford:
    Ancient House ✳
Walsingham:
    House of Correction ✳
Wolterton Hall ✳✳

BLICKLING HALL ****

Blickling, 1½m NW of Aylsham
Jacobean mansion adapted in 18th century
(NT)

'The more I gazed, the more I was impressed by the dowagerial majesty of this ancient pile,' wrote James Lees-Milne when negotiating Blickling's transfer to the National Trust. 'The tight regimented façade seemed to be advancing aggressively, enticed forward by detached projecting wings and then by elephantine yew hedges in the vanguard.' Blickling is a Jacobean palace. The south front with its turrets and cupolas is approached from the road as if in a royal progress to the throne.

These houses have never lost their appeal. The Jacobeans bankrupted themselves erecting them, the Victorians recreating them and the 20th century rescuing them. Blickling's former owner, the Marquess of Lothian, was a National Trust stalwart and his endowed bequest in 1940 was a prototype of later Trust acquisition schemes. This did more to rescue the architecture and art of Britain than any other single act.

An older house was acquired by Lothian's forebear, a rich lawyer, Sir Henry Hobart, in 1616. He rose to become Lord Chief Justice under James I. Blickling appealed to him as the reputed birthplace of Anne Boleyn and home of Sir John Fastolfe, original of Shakespeare's comic creation. It dates from the highpoint of Jacobean building, the era of Hatfield House (Herts), Crewe Hall (Cheshire) and Audley End (Essex), and was commissioned in 1619 from the architect of Hatfield, Robert Lyminge. Building progressed slowly, complicated by the narrowness of the site. Lyminge's answer was radical, a thin elongated house of two internal courtyards, with the service ranges thrust forward as two arms. Dutch gables on these ranges answer respectively to those on the big house itself.

The entrance is through the gatehouse and

Blickling: Jacobean weds Victorian

into the first courtyard, in the medieval style. But just when we might expect a screens passage and off-centre Great Hall, the chief later alteration to Blickling makes its impact. This was the 1760s insertion of a 1620s staircase into the Great Hall, converting a medieval chamber into a Renaissance hall. The stairs are adorned with Jacobean and later figures, including a cossack. They are gloriously theatrical, dark with Flemish glass.

Of the downstairs rooms, the Brown Drawing Room, has a fireplace from Sir John Fastolfe's Caister Castle. This is medieval heraldry fashioned into an 18th-century setting. The dining room has a 10-fold oriental screen and rich Jacobean overmantel of 1627. The stern William-and-Mary chairs seem designed to improve posture.

Blickling's principal rooms are on the first floor, Elizabethan style. Stairs lead up to the 'Lothian Row' of bedrooms, each named after a letter of the Marquess's name, 'L', 'O' and so on. The print room has engravings by Piranesi and copies of Old Masters as wallpaper. The West Turret Bedroom retains a Jacobean ceiling and a Canaletto. The Chinese Bedroom has chinoiserie wallpaper and an exquisite carved ivory pagoda. The old Great Chamber has a ceiling with pendants, and a superb classical fireplace designed by Lyminge himself. But all this is a prelude.

Blickling's Long Gallery is one of the grandest of its period in England. Everything is in rich Jacobean ornament enhanced by deferential Victoriana. The plaster ceiling is original, by Edward Stanyon, its panels depicting the Senses and Learning, similar to ones at Boston Manor (London, W). The frieze is Victorian neo-Jacobean, by J. Hungerford Pollen, as are the floridly ornamental steel fire-dogs. The tapestry is 17th-century Belgian and the stained glass Victorian. The books survive more or less intact from the house's 18th-century collection.

Beyond the gallery is the Peter the Great Room, the most severely classical of the 18th-century alterations, with a ceiling in the style of Adam. The name derives from a large tapestry depicting Peter triumphing over the Swedes. It was given by Catherine the Great to John Hobart, 2nd Earl of Buckinghamshire and ambassador to her court, whose daughter took Blickling into the Lothian family by marriage.

This upward mobility is reflected in the last room. The State Bedroom is adorned with the coat of arms of George II, Buckinghamshire's benefactor. The bed appears more like a restless royal throne.

CASTLE ACRE PRIORY *

Castle Acre, 4m N of Swaffham
Surviving portion of monastic prior's house (EH)

England has little space for such luxuries as ghosts towns. Yet Castle Acre is one. It was a fortified settlement based on a large Cluniac priory, embracing a castle, walls, gateway and church as well as a priory. Of all this, only fragments remain. The most prominent is the 16th-century priory porch and roofed Prior's House.

The house was remodelled at the end of the 14th century and again later. Such premises often survived the Dissolution because the purchaser was reluctant to destroy a well-built, often luxurious, private residence just because it had once housed a monk. The property was held by the Duke of Norfolk and others until passing, in 1615, to Sir Edward Coke, whose family still own it as Earls of Leicester. It has been in the care of the government (and now English Heritage) since 1927.

On the ground floor is a rib-vaulted chamber, probably for receiving guests and conducting priory business. Beyond is an outer parlour, decorated with a frieze and giving onto the interior cloister. Upstairs is the Prior's Chamber with scissor-braced roof. The last pre-Dissolution prior, Prior Winchelsea, inserted the fireplace and painted the ceiling beams with red and white roses, celebrating the final union of the Houses of Lancaster and York (a union that was to lead to his downfall). The room was also given two pretty oriel windows.

The adjacent chapel also has a fireplace and painted beams, with traces of earlier wall paintings. This was much altered before and after the Dissolution but remained in use as a house into the 17th century.

Like the even grander prior's house at Muchelney (Somerset), Castle Acre recalls English monasticism in its final flowering before the collapse. The whole place has been scrubbed by English Heritage but the presentation of the site is excellent.

CASTLE RISING:
THE CASTLE **

Castle Rising, 5m NE of King's Lynn
Norman keep with earthwork and Romanesque arch (EH)

If only the Victorians had the courage of their convictions, Castle Rising might be today one of the most magnificent Norman keeps in England. It is still among the most decorative. Belonging to a junior branch of the Howard family, it remains in Howard ownership, although run by English Heritage. The Howard standard flies from its mast.

The castle peers over the top of a massive enclosing earthwork that must have predated the invention of artillery. Although a keep in form, the structure is internally complex, like Norwich Castle (below) or London's White Tower (Tower of London/London, C). The Great Hall lies alongside the Great Chamber. The forebuilding, or entrance stairway, is intact. Its decorative Norman arcading is outstanding, of a quality normally found only on churches.

The stairway is ceremonial, its wide entrance not defensive in design. It rises past scalloped capitals to a vestibule with a vaulted roof, sheltering the old door into the Great Hall. This is now blocked but has a Romanesque arch with chevron decoration. The vestibule has another roofed room above it, with plaster on its walls and a later, possibly Georgian, fireplace.

The stairs lead into the unroofed Great Hall,

relic of a splendid chamber. There is no fireplace, nor does there appear to be one in the adjacent private chamber, although the latter has garderobes. The walls are honeycombed with mural corridors and closets.

The guidebook is wrong to suggest that we cannot imagine how this place might have looked when inhabited. We can go to Hedingham Castle (Essex) with its admirable re-creation.

CASTLE RISING: TRINITY HOSPITAL *

Castle Rising, 5m NE of King's Lynn
Howard foundation in shadow of Castle Rising (P-R)

Henry Howard, 17th-century Earl of Northampton, was said to be 'treacherous, unscrupulous, learned, artistic and charitable', an awesome combination. He founded three almshouses in 1614, at Clun (Salop), Greenwich and Castle Rising. This one cost £450. Here, twenty spinsters, unlike their patron, had to be of 'honest life and conversation, religious, grave, discreet . . . single, 56 at least, no common beggar, harlot, scold, drunkard or haunter of taverns'. We assume there were enough applicants to qualify – and still are, for the building remains in use, like dozens of such excellent establishments.

The enclave is a miniature Oxford college. It has chapel, hall and warden's lodgings on the far side of the courtyard from the gatehouse. An entrance gable between two turrets and the looming presence of the castle recall the benefactor. Steep roofs slope down to a charming redbrick courtyard round which nine units are grouped. They must have been comfortable dwellings for their day and retain their original Jacobean furniture.

In the hall are portraits of past wardens and the red cloaks still worn by the inhabitants on their way to church. On the old Jacobean table I noticed a copy of *Hello* magazine. Behind is a small meadow, a charming spot and always to be preserved.

COCKLEY CLEY: ICENI HOUSE *

Cockley Cley Museum, 4m SW of Swaffham
Early British settlement in meadow (M)

We know little about the Iceni, beyond that they were among the first inhabitants of Britain in historical times. Based in East Anglia, they gave the Romans much trouble. Queen Boudicca became the first nationalist heroine, rising against the occupiers in AD60 and laying waste the settlements at Colchester and London, before being defeated and taking poison.

I doubt if there is much to choose between an Iceni hut, a Welsh one, a Pictish one and a Saxon one. The Iceni village reconstructed at Cockley Cley on an excavated site by a stream next to the Roman Icknield Way is a ghost of what was 'probably' here. The camp lies across a field and consists of just four huts within a stockade, one gate of which is drenched in blood and another has a primitive drawbridge with heads of enemies stuck on top.

Apart from covering the walls of some of the huts in pine strips rather than oak, the huts look realistic. Inside, the furnishings and utensils are simple, with stone hearths, clay pots and dyed garments. Only the waxwork models ring untrue, especially their hairpieces. They are surrounded by the desperate attempts at domestic comfort. Places such as this may seem ersatz, but isolated and amid natural surroundings, they are more authentic than a museum or television studio.

COCKLEY CLEY: OLD COTTAGE *

Cockley Cley Museum, 4m SW of Swaffham
Restoration of yeoman's house in wood (M)

The owner of Cockley Cley Hall, the late Sir Peter Roberts, decided not to demolish or convert a scatter of buildings on his estate but leave them intact for later generations. Would that all landowners were so enlightened. A

small group is clustered round an old Saxon/Norman church, later converted into a cottage, now once again a chapel. An avenue from the church leads to a 17th-century cottage restored to its former appearance.

The cottage would have been a substantial house when built in the 1640s. Downstairs is the kitchen hung with game, and behind it the parlour. In the latter, the master of the house sits penning a letter with a quill, not a labourer's pursuit. There is a picture on the wall, pewter and a wine barrel. Upstairs is a sleeping chamber with a four-poster and a truckle bed. In the adjacent loft are girls playing skittles alongside their mattresses.

The cottage was later divided into a house and forge and occupied as such into the 1950s. Instructional notices in the house seem aimed exclusively at children, a pity since adults also enjoy houses.

CROMER: FISHERMAN'S COTTAGE *

Cromer Museum, Churchyard of
St Peter & St Paul
Relic of Cromer before growth of the resort
(M)

When tourism overtook fishing as the economic staple of the East Anglian coast, the old houses went too. Cottages were swept aside for hotels and boarding houses. Fishwives retrained as hotel staff. Even where the cottages survived, their occupants were driven out in summer months to camp with relatives, so holiday visitors could sleep in their fishy beds.

Facing the east end of Cromer parish church is a group of such cottages. Through a wall and across a courtyard is a 19th-century fishermen's terrace, presumably on the site of an earlier row. The cottages were tiny, just one room up and one down, with water and sanitation in the yard outside. Only at one end was there a 'luxury' two-up, two-down with

Suffolk vernacular: Cockley Cley's Old Cottage

scullery extension. This would have been for a more prosperous seafarer. It has been restored to its Victorian appearance, complete with waxwork effigies.

The downstairs parlour with stove is furnished and cluttered with familiar objects. On the door hang an oilskin and boots. The walls display a lifeboat medal and religious mottoes. The floor is warmed by rag rugs. Upstairs, a child lies reading a book in bed. The scene is simple but moving.

FELBRIGG HALL ***

Felbrigg, 2m SW of Cromer
Jacobean exterior and 'Grand Tour' interior
(NT)

The last private owner of Felbrigg, Squire Robert Wyndham Ketton-Cremer, wrote a wistful farewell in a book, *The Story of a House* (1962). Such places, he declared, were finished. He told all enquirers that the house would be left 'to a cats' home'. Mercifully, he left it instead to the National Trust on his death in 1969.

Felbrigg is a house of character. It sits alone in an expansive park of oak, beech and chestnut. Both church and village seem to have wandered off and left the house behind, like an embarrassing relative. 'GLORIA DEO IN EXCELSIS' declares the south front parapet, but nobody is around to hear.

The house belonged to the Windham family from the 15th century. In 1620, Thomas Windham decided to rebuild the old medieval house along similar lines to neighbouring Blickling. As with many Jacobean houses, the former plan of porch, screens passage and hall was remodelled to yield a symmetrical E-plan. The surface displays many materials, stone, flint, render and brick, oft repaired and looking in places as if attacked by a scabrous disease. Round the west corner is a later extension designed by William Samwell and built in the 1680s. It now has later white-painted sash windows and a wooden cornice with dormers. Felbrigg is a good textbook for students of 17th-century architecture.

If the exterior of Felbrigg is robust squirearchy, the dominant character of the interior is effete Grand Tour. The Great Hall is to the left of the screens passage, its character now wholly Victorian. The doorcases and ceiling pendants are ferociously 'neo'. A visitor in 1953 recalled that in winter the family spent its entire day in this room, squatting 'on the few chairs that were not piled high with books'. The windows contain Windham/Wyndham heraldic and continental glass, some dating from the 16th century, which is when the name changed its spelling. Lelys and Knellers adorn the walls.

Beyond the Jacobean wing is the Restoration wing, redecorated inside by James Paine in 1752. The style of the dining room is heavy Rococo, notably in the plasterwork and picture surrounds. A stern eagle peers down from the ceiling centrepiece. A dying Gaul adorns the overmantel. The drawing room retains its ceiling of 1687. Eulogized by the guide as 'one of the finest ceilings of its period', its plasterwork is of fruit and game festooning every panel. Pheasants, mallard, woodcock and plovers may all be detected. The craftsman is believed to have been Edward Goudge. On the walls are sea paintings by both the van der Veldes.

The Cabinet is a rare survival of a Grand Tour gallery of the 1740s, displayed exactly as intended by the owner. The pictures, of classical sites, are by lesser Continental artists, each one specified by William Windham for a particular wall. Pride of place goes to 6 oils and 26 gouaches of Rome by a Windham favourite, Giovanni Battista Busiri. The staircase hall was the centrepiece of Paine's Georgian work, hung with more Grand Tour pictures and classical busts.

The finest room upstairs is the library, the Great Chamber over the Great Hall of the Jacobean mansion. Paine's Gothick bookcases have pointed finials and the room contains a pleasant scatter of leather-bound volumes, ladders and globes. In the centre stands a sturdy and richly carved table. Ketton-Cremer recalls the library in the 1920s, the sun cracking the book bindings and flies buzzing against the

windows, 'the only sound in the silence of the room.'

The bedrooms upstairs in the Restoration wing are mostly Georgian. The Rose Bedroom has two Rococo mirrors. The Chinese Bedroom wallpaper is as good as any of the genre. Hanging it was exceptionally difficult and the Windham of the day was furious at a specialist being brought from outside to undertake the work. Felbrigg has a complete set of servants' quarters on display.

The handsome Orangery dates from 1707. It is a serene miniature of its contemporary, the Great Orangery, by Hawksmoor at Kensington Palace (London, C).

GREAT YARMOUTH: ELIZABETHAN HOUSE **

4 South Quay
Town house with Cromwell room (M)

South Quay was, to Defoe, 'the finest quay in England and not inferior to Marseilles . . . the houses little palaces'. No. 4 was built in c1596 by a merchant named Cowper and managed to survive the regular fires that blighted the old town. Clearly prosperous, Cowper was granted licences to build over the adjacent rows and extend an old one-room frontage both sideways along the quay and back round a courtyard.

The exterior is 18th century and nothing inside seems to predate the 17th, so 'Elizabethan House' is pushing things. Yet it is a jolly place. In the parlour is depicted a Victorian lady in mourning. It has an electric shock machine for the relief of stress caused by bereavement. The dining room has a fine Renaissance overmantel and the reproduction food is well presented, including nuts, bread, bones and apple cores. The kitchen is in 19th-century mode. The staircase has a window of 16th- and 17th-century stained glass.

Upstairs is the Conspiracy Room where Oliver Cromwell is said to have plotted the execution of Charles I. Whether this is really where he met his officers is unclear, but he certainly was in the vicinity in 1648. The two characters depicted are the owner of the house, John Carter, and the MP, Miles Corbet, who was to vote for the king's execution and sign his death warrant. He was hanged, drawn and quartered at the Restoration. Given how others survived, this seems bad luck.

The bedroom shows the great bed prepared for the wife of the house to give birth in 1590. It displays the entire works, from midwifery equipment to layettes and teddy bears. Why an unmade bed should be considered politically correct by modern custodians is a mystery to me.

GREAT YARMOUTH: ROW HOUSES

Great Yarmouth
Ancient houses that survived the Blitz and planning (EH)

The Row Houses on the spit of land between the sea and harbour of 17th-century Great Yarmouth were architectural originals. After the Blitz, their reconstruction, in the manner of Warsaw or Tours, was rejected by the council. Instead, all but a couple of houses were destroyed for insipid council properties. Yarmouth thus wiped itself off the map as a venue for serious tourism.

There is no doubt that, at the time, these houses were slums. By the mid-20th century, old Yarmouth had the most overcrowded streets in England. The Row Houses were jammed into 156 tiny alleys, some no more than a yard wide, then subdivided. Water and sanitation were almost non-existent. They housed workers in the fishing and salting industries, many of them migratory 'herring girls' down from Scotland.

This part of the town demands comprehensive and imaginative rethinking. Still-empty sites offer the chance to build a new generation of Row Houses, perhaps even of architectural distinction as in Glasgow's Glasgow Green development. This would restore the crowded, friendly atmosphere of the old quayside.

GREAT YARMOUTH: ROW 111 *

South Quay

One survivor off South Quay is now a museum owned by English Heritage and exhibited with the nearby Old Merchant's House (Row 113 below). Row 111 was a simple early 17th-century house with two large rooms up and down. It has a remarkably fine façade to the alley. This is part 17th-century, part 18th. By the 1930s, it held three families, the Rayners, Hooks and Lees. Mrs Lee's 'cottage' of three single rooms stacked above each other somehow managed to sleep a family of eight.

Tiny spiral staircases lead upstairs and a giant chimney flue warmed the interior. Ghosts of the old house remain, such as a salt cupboard, but most of it is a museum of life in the 1940s. We see Mrs Lee peeling carrots and, in the attic, a herring girl's bedroom with the walls covered in newspaper to absorb the smell of fish.

GREAT YARMOUTH: ROW 113 *

South Quay

If Row 111 (above) was working class, Row 113 (known as the Old Merchant's House) was middle class. Also built in the 17th century but with Georgian sashes, it had two rooms on each floor before subdivision. The ceiling of the dining room is a surprise, a swirl of plasterwork of 1603, with floral patterns in a geometrical field. In its centre is a huge pendant depicting female figures. A ceiling of similar quality is in the room above. Walls are panelled, some with pilasters.

The rooms display architectural fragments that were collected from bombsites during the war by a Mr Rosie in his cart. They are arranged as if in a furniture showroom. The rooms also contain historical tableaux. The best is of a Mr Rope sitting over his wartime dinner. Next door is the Atkins family, with seven children crammed into a tiny space. Above, the steeply pitched Dutch-style attic exhibits anchors fixed to the wall.

HOLKHAM HALL *****

Holkham, 2m W of Wells-next-the-Sea
Masterpiece of Palladian revival, with original decoration (P)

Holkham and Houghton have always been rivals in celebrity. Like Penshurst and Knole (Kent), Chatsworth and Bolsover (Derbys), Levens and Sizergh (Cumbria), England's great houses seem to go in pairs. The Norfolk pair contrast the metropolitan flamboyance of the political Walpoles with the Cokes of Holkham, rich country squires. The houses also offer contrasting forms of the Palladianism of the 1720s and 1730s as it emerged from the Baroque of Queen Anne under the influence of the Burlington School.

The first Coke was a lawyer and Chief Justice to James I, credited with the maxim that 'an Englishman's home is his castle'. His descendant, Thomas, spent a full six years on his Grand Tour and returned in 1718 with numerous antiquities and the friendship of William Kent and Lord Burlington. During the 1720s, as Coke watched the building of neighbouring Houghton, he refined his design for his own new house at Holkham. The form is of a serene, almost severe, Roman villa of a single principal storey, with four corner pavilions. It is the antithesis of the vertical Houghton. Holkham's shallow gables, Venetian windows and immaculate parterres and vistas form the most Italian house in England.

Coke designed the house himself, with advice from Kent and his assistant, Matthew Brettingham. Most of the interiors were by Kent. Holkham was to consume the rest of Coke's life as such houses did many English magnates (*see* Lord Carlisle at Castle Howard/ Yorks, N). It was unfinished on his death, indeed it was not complete until 1762, saddled with a massive £90,000 debt. The Cokes were lucky in their descendants. One was the farm innovator and progressive Whig, 'Coke of Norfolk', 1st Earl of Leicester of the 2nd creation. He was an ardent supporter of the American Revolution. Another Coke's signature of the Great Reform Bill is celebrated in a panel in the hall.

The present Earl of Leicester is a champion of great house survival. The estate has over 300 houses, many lived in by its staff, sustaining school, pub, cricket team and the social fabric of a complete community. The earl is depicted with his estate staff in a series of portraits in the old kitchens. When I last visited the house, the county show was spread magnificently across its park, a medieval carpet of tents, banners, horses, riders and marching bands. The shires were being summoned to arms in defence of tradition against the banning of hunting.

Every viewpoint in Holkham park focuses on the house. It lies sleek along its contour in pale yellow brick, each bay a different plane and outline. The central rectangle contains the state rooms and is palatial, sitting above its 'rustic' or ground floor. The illusion is of space and ease. The central portico, front and back, is never overpowering. The corner pavilions were designed respectively for the family, for 'strangers', for kitchens and for a chapel.

The entrance into the Marble Hall is a tremendous *coup de théâtre*. The space is on two levels, with steps sweeping from the ground floor up to the doors of the saloon. The design is after Palladio's for a Temple of Justice. The columns flanking the walls are of brown-and-white grained Derbyshire alabaster. Behind them are classical niches and reliefs. On a wall hang Francis Chantrey's marble woodcocks, portraying two killed with one shot in 1829. The astonishing ceiling is coved upwards to deeply incised panels, the coffering distorted to give a heightened effect. Apses, dados, friezes and cornice lines are encrusted with classical motifs. The room seems in perpetual movement. It is one of the great chambers of England.

The plan of the rooms at Holkham is

Holkham: Norfolk Italian-style

unaltered since built, their decoration a monument to Kent's talent. Each feature reflects an idea perfectly understood. The North Dining Room has two marble fireplaces crowned with panels depicting Aesop's fables. The sideboard alcove is like the apse of a Roman basilica, as if food were itself a sacrament. The Axminster carpet reflects the ceiling above.

The tribunes and West Gallery were built for Coke's Grand Tour collection of statuary, still in place and undiminished by sales. The statues stand on plinths in niches, punctuated by rich Venetian windows. In an evening sun, these rooms radiate with light and depth.

The south range of state rooms commences with a library tribune, one of a series of libraries extending into the family wing. The bookcases here are for large folio volumes. The walls of the drawing room are covered in deep crimson velvet, with paintings by Poussin, Claude and a Gheeraerts of the founder of the family fortune, Chief Justice Coke. The saloon is also crimson, with an even more magnificent hang of Old Masters. They are by Rubens and van Dyck, the garments worn by each sitter reflecting the red and blue of the Virgin's robes in Rubens's *Return of the Holy Family*. Through the doors and windows is a vista across the house's north–south axis, out to distant obelisks. Geometry binds house and park together as one.

Beyond the saloon is the South Dining Room. Its two great portraits epitomize the English nobleman in the 18th century. Both are of 'Coke of Norfolk', but have nothing else in common. One is of Coke in Grand Tour masquerade costume by Batoni, looking every inch the Italian fop. The other is Gainsborough's last great painting, of the same man as an English country gentleman, cleaning his gun with his dogs at his feet. The Landscape Room has been hung in the 18th-century style from floor to ceiling, with scenes mostly by Poussin and Claude. It is a display without equal in an English house.

The final side of the *piano nobile* comprises

Houghton: statesmen on parade

the state bedroom suite. In the bedroom are Brussels and Mortlake tapestries depicting the four continents. The embroidery hangings are indigestibly rich. The dressing rooms are walled in green damask. In one is Sangallo's copy of Michelangelo's cartoon for the Palazzo Vecchio in Florence, a remarkable essay in anatomical poses. The state sitting room is hung with more tapestries and furnished with voluptuous Kent chairs. To Pevsner, 'Kent's patterns of the ceilings deserve study'. They rather deserve awe.

The grounds of Holkham comprise 3,000 acres, stretching down to pinewoods on reclaimed coastal marsh. This wild shoreline is threatened with development.

HOUGHTON HALL ****

10m W of Fakenham
Sir Robert Walpole's palace by Gibbs and Kent (P)

How can we not compare? Holkham and Houghton are near neighbours and each has its adherents. While Holkham was essentially the work of a dilettante and enthusiast, Houghton was built by the most powerful statesman of his day, Sir Robert Walpole.

The inspiration for both men was the same, to recreate the Palladian message in the English landscape, to bring to northern Europe the classical taste and gentility of the south. Houghton was begun earlier than Holkham and the ambition of its creator was grander. Walpole regarded himself as in line of descent from the clients of Vanbrugh, Talman and the English Baroque. Houghton is brass, playing fortissimo, while Holkham is quieter strings.

Walpole's building of Houghton preoccupied even his public life between 1722 and 1735. It was said that each morning at the office he opened letters from his Houghton agent before any State papers. His principal architects were James Gibbs, Colen Campbell and William Kent. The cost was reputedly over £200,000, almost as expensive as Blenheim. On his death in 1745, Walpole left the estate so crippled with debt that his picture collection had to be sold (in 1779) to Catherine the Great of Russia, to become part of the Hermitage collection.

His son, Horace Walpole, was mortified in later life to find his family seat reduced to a place of 'destruction and desolation'. It was a classic case of ambition outstripping wealth. The house passed to Walpole's great-grandson, the 1st Marquess of Cholmondeley, but the family preferred to live at their northern seat, Cholmondeley Castle (Cheshire). Not until 1919 was Houghton rescued by the 5th Marquess and his wife, Sybil. Their work is being completed by their grandson, the 7th Marquess.

The house is reached across a park alive with drifts of white deer. William Kent's stables come first into view, a curious combination of ochre carstone and redbrick. The house beyond is odd. The first design was by James Gibbs in 1722. Colen Campbell took over but Walpole decided to retain Gibbs's Baroque domes. The result is incongruous, a formal Palladian building but with a vaguely French roofline.

Entry to the house is into the 'rustic'. Visitors are made to feel as if they have come to pay the rent, as at Woburn (Beds). They see only part of the house and in the reverse sequence to that suggested by the architecture. That said, the access staircase from the ground floor is extraordinary. It is filled by a bronze of a gladiator by Hubert Le Sueur, visible only on the first floor. The mahogany balusters are chunky and dark, offsetting Kent's grisaille paintings on the walls. The tour next visits a small Common Parlour, with family portraits and an overmantel in the style of Grinling Gibbons.

The Stone Hall on the *piano nobile* is the showpiece of Houghton, more cold and ponderous than that at Holkham, but undeniably magnificent. It is in the form of a giant cube, like Inigo Jones's hall at Queen's House in Greenwich (London, E), with a deep gallery on ornate brackets. Chimneypieces and overdoor panels are by Rysbrack, with his bust of Walpole over a fireplace. The ceiling is by Giuseppe Artari, master stuccoist to the Burlingtonians.

His putti prance along the coving, occasionally dropped a teasing leg over the moulding below. In the centre of the ceiling is Walpole's coat of arms. This is truly the ante-chamber of a statesman. Trumpeters should be on duty overhead.

The remainder of Houghton is a feast of decorative richness. The Marble Parlour, designed by Gibbs and decorated by Kent, is unforgettable. Two alcoves contain marble sideboards, flanking a shimmering marble chimneypiece with overmantel by Rysbrack. A gilded ceiling glows overhead. Everything, chairs, doorcases, even the Turkish carpet, are to excess. Here Walpole is said to have consumed Margaux and Lafite 'by the hogshead'.

The small Cabinet Room is hung with blue chinoiserie wallpaper. It contains lacquer cabinets of porcelain and a Rococo mirror. The state bedroom suite comes next, the lesser bedroom first, followed by the principal dressing room and sitting room and then the Green Velvet Bedchamber. These rooms are the apogee of Kentian lavishness, although their gilded or painted ceilings do not always marry with the furnishings.

In the Tapestry Dressing Room are two Pugin thrones from the House of Lords beneath Stuart tapestry portraits after van Dyck. Kent's state bed, hung in green velvet, is an exquisite piece, the canopy embroidered architecture, the headboard a giant scallop shell enfolding the sleeper in a dream of sea. The trimmings alone cost £1,219 in 1732.

The White Drawing Room is a shimmering casket of white and gold. The Rococo wall hangings were a gift to Houghton by that enthusiastic donor of country house furnishings, the Prince of Wales, in 1797. Over the chimneypiece is a Hoppner of the Marchioness of the day. The last room is the saloon, which even the guidebook admits 'should be the first of the parade after the Stone Hall'. It is heavy with crimson hangings above crimson chairs and stools by Kent. The frieze depicts scenes from the hunting field, the ceiling from Greek mythology. The whole composition drips with expense.

Nothing in Houghton is finer than the saloon doors and window surrounds. These are in mahogany with Corinthian orders, each architectural detail picked out in gold. The door to the hall is a masterpiece, a triumphal arch befitting the nation's first so-called prime minister. At this point, the tour abruptly ends, with visitors suddenly tipped out onto the lawn. They may recover from the shock if they track down the superb apple-and-plum pie in the stables tea-room.

KING'S LYNN: CLIFTON HOUSE **

17 Queen Street
Restored merchant's house with look-out tower (P)

A tiny enclave of urbanity survives in central King's Lynn between St Margaret's Church and the River Ouse quays. Suddenly the town's commercialized outskirts and retail zone withdraw and a handful of streets convey some sense of the old town. Houses have been restored and gaps respectfully infilled. Clifton House is the most impressive of these town houses. Its fabric dates from the 14th to the 18th century. At the time of writing, its interior is being restored for public opening by an admirable local trust.

The 1708 façade to Queen Street is handsome if conventional. Constructed of brick and of seven bays beneath a deep cornice, it has spacious windows turning the corner into King's Staithe Lane. Most remarkable is the doorway and porch, recessed deep into the wall by the narrowness of the street. It is flanked by two generous barley-sugar columns, a rare exterior motif in England and perhaps borrowed from the Continent.

This door is in a façade built for a merchant named Samuel Taylor, possibly by a local architect, Henry Bell. As in seafaring Hull, mercantile salesmanship required a prominent front to the street even if nothing better could be afforded behind. The door thus leads not into a hall but into the passage of an Elizabethan house, its basement dating back to the 14th century.

Attached to the rear of the building and visible from the car park in King's Staithe Lane is a delight, a Tudor tower house of five storeys. This is the last of the look-out towers of medieval King's Lynn. Though not defensive, as in Siena, they served as residences and belvederes from which merchants could live away from the quayside smells and yet see their ships on the river. This is a fine structure, with a canted bay for its staircase, pedimented windows to all five storeys and wall paintings in an upper room.

KING'S LYNN: OLD GAOL HOUSE *

Saturday Market
Old town prison with realistic re-creations (M)

The group of civic buildings in Saturday Market next to St Margaret's Church includes the old town hall and guildhall. The former gaol was rebuilt in 1784 with a handsome façade, said to be based on George Dance's Newgate in London. Inside are cells dating back to the 18th century, built on lines suggested by the prison reformer, John Howard (Walsingham, below). On show now are the old charge room and a gruesome array of chambers depicting various forms of punishment, corporal and capital, much appreciated by tourists.

The rooms come complete with waxworks, screams and other sound effects of variable plausibility. There is a hanging room, a witch's bonfire and a set of stocks.

The old cells remaining in their original state are most evocative. They are unpleasant and claustrophobic, although they seem less isolated than modern formal prisons since the community is all round them. The cells have no external windows and each has a huge iron door.

Some are occupied by realistic effigies. One is of a pathetic boy writing his will, another cell is well stocked with rats (stuffed). My favourite reputedly displays its last occupants, a Teddy

Boy with black eye and cut lip, jailed as 'drunk and disorderly' in the 1960s. The whole place stinks of urine and carbolic soap, which I am sure is as it should be.

MANNINGTON HALL **

7m SE of Holt
Restored moated medieval hall (P-R)

Mannington was acquired by Horatio Walpole of Wolterton Hall, brother of the statesman, in the 1720s. The family is of old East Anglian stock. The medieval house with its fine moat had been built in 1460 and was intended as a dower house. It was a tumbledown place and had to await the Picturesque movement for its revival. It was not occupied by a Walpole until 1860 when Horatio's descendant, the antiquarian 4th Earl of Orford, restored it and added a Victorian wing. The house was let, but was reoccupied by the present Lord Walpole in 1969. He found it a friendlier and more manageable place than adjacent Wolterton.

The three-storey moated house is beautifully set amid stewponds and rose gardens. Water flickers onto walls of flint and sandstone. The drawbridge is in working order. Evergreens and herbaceous borders divide the garden within the moat into 'rooms'. A scented garden is laid out on the pattern of the drawing room ceiling. The moat is alive with climbing plants and water lilies.

The interior of the house combines the medievalism of the 4th Earl and the modest Bohemianism of the Walpoles of today. Medieval bits and pieces fill the rooms, some brought from Walpole properties elsewhere. The panelled hall has pilasters, carved figures and a lovely cradle. On the first floor the huge beams of the former Great Hall below reveal themselves.

To the rear, the 19th-century additions appear large and rather gloomy. Visitors are shown the 4th Earl's misogynist mottos: 'Trust your bark to the winds. Do not trust your heart to girls. The wave is safer than a woman's faith . . .' and worse.

NORWICH: CASTLE *

Castle Meadow
Keep of Norman castle, much restored (M)

Do not be deterred by Anthony Salvin's ruthless refacing of Norwich Castle with Bath stone in 1833. The neo-medievalists were studious archaeologists but showed scant respect for original materials. From the outside, the keep looks like a bad movie set, although its size and eminence remain magnificent and more than a match for the dreadful hypermarket which lays siege to it on two sides. Norwich was William the Conqueror's East Anglian base. It rivalled his White Tower in London.

The walls are adorned with wide, flat buttresses, in effect pilasters, evenly spaced on all sides. They are interspersed with Norman blind arcading. This was a building for show as well as defence. The old doorway at the top of the entrance stairs is as fine as in a cathedral. It remains in blackened Caen stone, with carvings of soldiers and animals still discernible in its surround.

The interior was also heavily treated by Salvin. The customary bipartite plan of hall and adjacent chamber remains, but the floor has been pushed down into the basement and the upper floor opened to the roof, remaining only as a gallery.

The interior is an excellent local museum, but the Norman context is treated merely as a frame. Fragments of old walling, arcading, passages and vaults start out into the exposed volume. To one side hangs the glorious *Adoration of the Magi* tapestry by Burne-Jones and Morris.

NORWICH: DRAGON HALL *

115–23 King Street
Medieval cloth merchant's hall, heavily restored (M)

The house overlooks a busy road by the river, separated from the city centre by a supermarket, the castle and a housing estate.

The exterior reminds us how all Norwich must once have looked, half-timbered, with a brick or stone ground floor. Above is close-studded timbering with plaster or brick nogging. Frequent alterations have yielded a delightful street frontage, with traces of at least six distinct entrances.

The interior is claimed as unique. The building was erected in the Middle Ages on the foundations of a Saxon house, a most rare survival. At some stage, it became a cloth merchant's hall for the display and sale of wares. While such large halls were common for guilds, this was a private enterprise for a 15th-century merchant, Robert Toppes, of whom we know little. He was mayor of Norwich in 1430 at the age of twenty-five, and called himself a citizen of Norwich and London, as did many East Anglian cloth tycoons (and some modern second-homers). He left money in his will to maintain the Norwich to London road, a generosity some might copy today.

The house is the measure of the man, probably the largest private merchant's premises of its date in England. At one end of the ground floor is a spacious undercroft and storage area, with the post-holes of the Saxon structure excavated and displayed.

The Great Hall above has only recently had its later partitions removed. It is now a gloriously open chamber, its seven bays broken in places by later sash windows. Its roof is particularly magnificent, with moulded crown-posts marching its entire length and its beams close-spaced. One of the purlins contains a carved dragon, still showing signs of its original paint.

With total insensitivity, health-and-safety teams have insisted on ruthlessly inappropriate stairs. If such liberties are to be taken, why not at least replace the sashes with casements and restore some of the atmosphere stripped out by the regulators?

A brick and timber domestic range runs at right angles to the main building behind, and is now mostly a gift shop. Gothic arches in the screens passage mark the divide between the domestic and the commercial property.

NORWICH: STRANGERS' HALL **

Charing Cross
Complete medieval town house set round two courts (M)

The post-war devastation visited on cities such as Norwich does not bear contemplating. Strangers' Hall must have been one of dozens of merchants' houses to have survived more than four centuries only to be wiped out in the two post-war decades. Yet here it is. The hall was named after foreign merchants who took up residence in the city in the late Middle Ages. It was rescued by Leonard Bolingbroke in 1899 and is now a museum in the heart of the old city.

The façade to the street is inconsequential. Not so the court inside, a yard enclosed by hall, solar wing and domestic ranges. A further stable courtyard lies to the west, surrounded by kitchens and outbuildings. The house was occupied by various merchants, including William Barley in the 15th century, Nicholas Sotherton in the 16th, and a mayor, Francis Cock, in the 17th. Each left his imprint.

The 15th-century Great Hall remains at the core of the house, stone-tiled and with crown-posts in the roof. It is reached up steps into a porch, signifying a dwelling of substance. Separate stairs installed a century later lead to the family end of the house. Beneath is a 14th-century undercroft and storage cellar, indicating the antiquity of the site's occupancy. On the landing is a framed carpet once used as a table covering.

The upstairs rooms display furniture of the period. The Walnut Room has fluted pilasters and an oyster inlaid table. The bedroom retains paint on its Tudor fireplace surround. Domestic odds and ends litter the rooms in a relaxed fashion, including a bed warmer and ancient painting of a child in a baby-walker. Downstairs is a fine Georgian dining room, panelled and with an overmantel of an appropriately mercantile scene. The house retains its kitchens, servants' halls and pantries.

This is Norwich's best historic building, a

an old leper hospital outside the abbey walls. It was originally intended to train vagrants in useful trades. Hence the word 'correction', a concept all but defunct in modern prisons. It later became a common prison.

Walsingham was visited in 1779 by the prison reformer, John Howard, who wrote a stern report on the 'two dark lodging rooms about 7 feet square and straw on the brick floors. The walls are not secure. Prisoners in irons.' The house was rebuilt on Howard's recommendation in 1787 with eight cells, an infirmary and a chapel. In 1822 this was extended with a further sixteen cells and a treadmill for grinding corn. Whatever else the prison was, it was clearly no deterrent to crime. By the 19th century, seventy prisoners were crammed into the place.

The building is now in bad repair and the adjacent mill is a warehouse. But this is no themed museum. It is a ghostly place in which we can wander back through time and see man's inhumanity to man (and woman). The cells are left open, with massive doors and dank interiors. A notice reports that in 1833 Mary Bunting was sentenced for three months for stealing turkeys, ducks and hens. Other offences were singing, talking, whistling or looking backwards on the treadmill. And this was a 'good' prison.

WOLTERTON HALL **

4m N of Aylsham
Lesser Walpole house with state rooms (P)

Do not ask the custodian of Wolterton, 'Does nobody live here any more?' He will reply curtly that while the Walpole family may have moved to Mannington, *he* certainly lives here. The hall was built by Sir Robert Walpole's brother, Horatio, in the 1720s on the site of an earlier settlement now vanished. The contrast with the present Lord Walpole's Mannington could hardly be greater. Where Mannington is medieval, intimate and wel-

South Burlingham: hunting dogs in attic

coming, Walterton is classical and austere, standing aloof across a wide park. The best view is from the lake. From there, the stone terrace breaks and spreads the house façade between a frame of trees.

The house suffered in the 19th century when the 4th Earl of Orford moved out. It was rescued in 1905 when his son and an American wife returned and brought it back to Edwardian life. Wolterton was again blighted by military occupation, a fire and a sale of contents. Only recently has the present Lord Walpole taken the house and grounds in hand, impressively determined to restore both to their former splendour.

The architect of Wolterton was Thomas Ripley, superintendent at Robert Walpole's Houghton. This is his only surviving major work. In Pevsner's words, 'the interiors are more rewarding than the exterior'. The latter is advanced for its date of 1720, a plain pedimented redbrick block above a rusticated stone basement. The only flourish is the coat of arms in the pediment. Inside, the rooms are arranged round a spacious stairwell rising the full height of the house. This is an extraordinary space, like a roofed courtyard. There are handsome door frames, cornice lines and internal windows. The iron balusters are excellent.

The domestic rooms, including the library, are on the ground floor. On the *piano nobile* is a full suite of state rooms. They are adorned mostly with Walpole portraits although the Marble Hall has a good picture of Cromwell. The dining room displays pictures of Horatio Walpole and his wife. The state dressing room and bedroom have good fireplaces and 20th-century portraits. A view from the saloon's window drifts away to the lake and into the distance.

Much of the building is used for estate offices. Lord Walpole claims that the present contents of 'vacuum cleaners, word processors, fax machines and the inevitable modern alarm systems, rather than more elegant furnishings of earlier periods, are nonetheless a real continuation of the changing life of this house'. It is a point of view.

Northamptonshire

Northamptonshire straddles middle England, with little by way of topography and a sad county town in Northampton. The county's most distinctive feature is the gloriously rich ironstone of its uplands, yielding houses and villages that look as if made of gingerbread. From the Middle Ages, there is only Rockingham Castle on its bluff and fragments at Nassington and Southwick, but the county is rich in Tudor and Elizabethan survivals. Elizabeth's favourite, Christopher Hatton, built not one but two palaces, Kirby and Holdenby, in the hope of receiving her. The former is still an exquisite example of early English Renaissance.

The county contains England's most eccentric recusancy designs, Sir Thomas Tresham's pavilions at Rushton and Lyveden. More conventional 16th-century mansions are at Fawsley and Deene, the former now a hotel, the latter a shrine to the Charge of the Light Brigade and still owned by the Brudenells.

The 17th century was Northamptonshire's finest hour. It saw one of England's earliest classical mansions at Stoke Park, possibly by Inigo Jones. In the 1630s, the Drydens built their Jacobean range and astonishing ceiling at Canons Ashby. John Webb supplied the Ishams with a classical wing at Lamport and the Spencers inserted the saloon and grand staircase at Althorp. Finally, the 1st Duke of Montagu returned from Paris to replicate a French château at Boughton, laying out miles of formal avenues which somehow survived the Capability Brown era of the 18th century.

James Gibbs built the Great Hall of Kelmarsh, and Smith of Warwick the charming front of Cottesbrooke. At the end of the century, the self-effacing Henry Holland put a new front on Althorp, now revived as a shrine to Diana, Princess of Wales.

Althorp ★★★★
Aynhoe ★
Boughton ★★★★
Canons Ashby ★★★★
Cottesbrooke ★★★
Deene Park ★★★★
Fawsley Hall ★
Holdenby ★★

Kelmarsh ★★
Kirby Hall ★★
Lamport ★★★
Lyveden New Bield ★
Nassington:
    Prebendal Manor ★
Northampton:
    Abington Hall ★

Rockingham Castle ★★★
Rushton Triangular
    Lodge ★★
Southwick ★★
Stoke Park ★
Sulgrave ★★

ALTHORP ★★★★

6m NW of Northampton
Palace of the Spencers with family picture gallery (P)

Which lasts longer, a house or a family? The answer is usually a house. But at Althorp the family demands attention. The childhood home of Diana, Princess of Wales, was turned after her death into a shrine by her brother, the 9th Earl Spencer. An 'event' is staged each year on its annual reopening, as if on a saint's day. The Diana museum is restrained and tasteful.

The Spencers were sheep farmers from Warwickshire when sheep was England's oil. They acquired the estate of Althorp (pronounced Oltrup) in 1508 and by the end of the century had built the house with courtyard and projecting wings. That plan survives, albeit altered beyond recognition. The exterior was remodelled in the 1660s, when the central court was filled with the present grand staircase.

It was remodelled again in 1787 by Henry Holland for the 2nd Earl Spencer, who amassed at Althorp the greatest private library in the world, including 58 works by Caxton. The new façade was in white brick and mathematical tiling. Unlike English limestone, these materials do not warm with age or sun. To the modern eye, they plead for stucco or the removal of the tiles to reveal the brick beneath. Althorp's exterior is frankly dull. Sacheverell Sitwell remarked that here 'we may feel that architecture is nearly at an end. So little less and it will have gone.'

Interiors were a different matter. The entrance hall is a majestic room, probably designed by Roger Morris by 1733 and rising two storeys to a great coffered ceiling. It is dominated by canvases of Spencers riding to hounds by John Wootton. Even the plasterwork depicts foxes and hounds. The floor is chequerboard. The room evokes the tastes and leisure habits of the landed gentry.

Althorp's furnishings benefited greatly from the family's abandonment in the 20th century of Spencer House in Green Park (London, C). Downstairs rooms were designed by Holland but remodelled by the ponderous Victorian, MacVicar Anderson. The billiard room leads into the library, once one of the finest in private hands in England, now moved to the John Rylands Library in Manchester. Here hangs a Reynolds of a four-year-old Viscount Althorp.

The Restoration staircase at Althorp is a marvellous set piece. It uses the entire two-storeyed saloon as its setting, rising in a single flight to the gallery. It might be the entrance to the grand circle of an opera house, with the picture gallery above as chorus, and van Dyck as soloist.

The saloon walls, below and on the landing above, are hung almost entirely with portraits of Spencers and their relatives. Artists include Kneller, van Loo, Orpen and Augustus John. In pride of place at the head of the landing, the present Earl has shamelessly placed himself and his late sister, Diana, an egotistical gesture of which his Restoration ancestors would have approved.

Family as theatre: the staircase at Althorp

The picture gallery was converted from that of the Elizabethan house. A collection of Lely 'court beauties' all bear a notable resemblance to Nell Gwynn, but are splendid when shown en masse. At the end of the gallery is van Dyck's *War and Peace*. It shows the two young aristocrats, the 2nd Earl of Bristol and 1st Duke of Bedford, brothers-in-law who were to fight on opposing sides in the Civil War. The painting became a metaphor for the divisions of loyalty caused by that tragic conflict. Bedford, in flaming red attire, looks by far the more 'cavalier' of the two yet he is the one who fought for Parliament.

The stables, flanking the entrance drive, are a superb composition of 1732 by Roger Morris. Their portico is a copy of St Paul's, Covent Garden, by Inigo Jones, to whom the building is a clear act of homage. Homage of a different sort is paid to Diana, Princess of Wales, in the exhibition within.

AYNHOE PARK *

Aynho, 9m NW of Bicester
Archer house overlooking River Cherwell (P-R)

On the 31 March 1954, the Cartwright squire and his son were driving back from Eton when they hit a truck parked on a corner. The accident incurred double death duties and spelled the end of the Cartwrights at Aynhoe. They had lived there since 1616. The house was sold and converted into apartments by the Country Houses Association.

The family had already suffered for their Parliamentary sympathies in the Civil War, a Cartwright having married a Fairfax. Royalist troops destroyed the old house but it was rebuilt in 1662 and remodelled by Thomas Archer after 1707. The entrance façade has Archer's signature of tallness of proportion, with a rusticated door and handsome side wings. These are linked by small triumphal arches and have Baroque surrounds to their central windows. The garden façade has a fine classical frontispiece.

Of the inside, only the entrance hall and main staircase survive from the Archer period. The latter is of wood with twisted balusters. A century later, the Cartwrights commissioned Sir John Soane to modernize the main reception rooms. The saloon and other rooms have shallow vaulted ceilings in the Soanian manner. Tiny fan vaults decorate the library walls. Everywhere are Ionic pillars, painted white. The main rooms offer a splendid view across Capability Brown's park to the rolling valley of the River Cherwell.

BOUGHTON HOUSE ****

3m NE of Kettering
French palace built onto Elizabethan mansion, ducal art collection (P)

The sight of Boughton across the park from the main road might be of a château in the Ile de France. The creamy limestone, the tall first-floor windows, the mansard roof and prominent dormers all speak French. French too is the rusticated entrance loggia. Even the stables look French, as if horses outranked servants. Yet this is a seat of the mighty Dukes of Buccleuch, than which nothing is more English – or Scottish.

The main entrance front of the house was built in the French style by the 1st Duke of Montagu after completing service as British ambassador to the court of Louis XIV in 1678. Any man returning from such a post would have his head abuzz with architecture. Petworth (Sussex) of the same period demonstrates similar influences. Yet Boughton's front is only a front. The house was a Tudor manor set round a series of courtyards that survive behind the 1st Duke's cold Continental façade. They give Boughton a welcome variety.

This is immediately evident when we turn the corner from the main front towards the garden. Here the mood changes. This façade is of refaced Tudor rooms, their roofs betraying various periods of construction. Further to the right is a hinterland of 16th- and 17th-century buildings, leading to the Georgian dower house. This makes Boughton not so much a house as a hamlet, still set in its park and completely rural. Beyond stretch six avenues of limes and oaks beyond lakes and canals, their formality predating the naturalism of Capability Brown.

Boughton's interiors are those of two houses, a grand palace attached to an earlier and more intimate predecessor. The entrance is attributed to a Frenchman named Pierre Pouget who also worked on Montagu's London house (now the site of the British Museum). Entry is directly up the main staircase from the side of the loggia, another Continental feature. A giant ceiling depicts Discord throwing the Apple amongst the Gods. The balustrade is of iron.

To the right of the stairs are the Low and High Pavilion ante-rooms, containing masterpieces from the extensive Buccleuch art collection. Here hang works by El Greco, Murillo and a portrait of the 1st Duke by Michael Dahl. The rooms have the demure panelling favoured by the 17th-century Stuart diaspora in France and the Low Countries.

Above the loggia runs Montagu's enfilade of state rooms completed in 1695, a miniature of the enfilade at Hampton Court. Montagu owned the Mortlake tapestry workshop and clearly had the pick of its output. Room after room is hung with the Acts of the Apostles and other biblical themes, interspersed with family portraits by van Dyck and cabinets by Boulle. The final room, formerly the state bedroom, has a nude on the ceiling whose *trompe-l'œil* trick is to rise from her reclining position as the viewer passes beneath her.

Beyond all this lies the earlier house. Directly behind the loggia is the Great Hall, rudely shorn of its entrance status. The 1st Duke 'modernized' the room by inserting a ceiling by the French artist, Louis Chéron. Gainsboroughs adorn the walls beneath more Mortlake tapestries. Gheeraerts depicts Elizabeth I as a mature and stately woman. By the window is an exquisite Boulle 'marriage coffer'.

Beyond the Great Hall is the Little Hall, with another Chéron ceiling. This would have been the parlour and family room of the Tudor house. Portraits here are by Kneller, Hogarth

and Mengs. A heraldic overmantel depicts the antecedents of the 1st Duke back to the Conquest. Beyond is the drawing room, with an Elizabethan Renaissance fireplace. Its walls are hung with 37 grisailles by van Dyck acquired by the 1st Duke from Lely's estate. They include a rare portrait of van Dyck's contemporary, Rubens.

The rooms now change in key and become more modest, although not in content. The morning room and Rainbow Room continue to prefer Mortlake to wallpaper. In one is a set of Meissen swans made for Madame de Pompadour. Corridors are lined with paintings by Ruisdael, van de Velde and Samuel Scott, looking inwards onto the charming Fish Court of the old Tudor house. They culminate in the old Audit Room, a gallery of Kneller, Lely and Hudson round a long shovelboard table. Against the walls are cases of Sèvres and Meissen.

Boughton goes on and on. Passages and corridors open into halls, armouries and outhouses. This is a true ducal palace. One wing of the new house was never furnished. As if exhausted by the task of filling so much space, the family left it a shell. It now houses a Chinese Pavilion, a picnic tent of brilliant painted oilskin. This looks rather sad in its derelict chamber, as if a garden party had suddenly rushed inside out of the rain. The stables contain the Duke's coach, painted a magnificent black and yellow, colours in which his more modest car is still painted.

CANONS ASHBY ****

Canons Ashby, 8m S of Daventry
16th-century manor with domed drawing room (NT)

In 1551, John Dryden married Elizabeth Cope of Canons Ashby, and felt he needed to upgrade the old house to his new status. Yet despite the Drydens' grocery business in London, which later enabled the purchase of a baronetcy, the family were never rich. The new house grew as and when money was available. It was never an aristocratic place, but rather the perfect evocation of a home of the 'middling gentry'. In 1921, *Country Life* described it as 'not calling for admiration . . . but quietly compelling it'.

The Drydens became devoted to old Canons Ashby. After a remodelling in the 17th century and, more gently, in the 18th, the house entered a long and merciful slumber. This culminated with Sir Henry Dryden, 'the Antiquary', who lived here from 1818 to 1899 and protected it from all change. Sometimes taken for a tramp, he devoted himself completely to his estate.

The house had no heating or plumbing, just a single tap and a four-seater earth closet in the courtyard. On the birth of his one child, a girl who suffered from polio, he complained that there were already too many women in the house. The daughter became an accomplished photographer.

Queen Mary visited Canons Ashby in 1937 and found it still had neither water nor electricity. Matters then fast degenerated. By 1980 the house was riddled with rot and damp and the garden front threatened to collapse. After a national campaign to raise an endowment, the National Trust accepted ownership and restoration. The remaining Drydens were allocated rooms on the first floor.

The house plan is medieval, grouped round a courtyard of roughly patched stone walls. The entrance is in the courtyard, reached under an arch past the brewhouse. Stone steps rise to a modest door into the Great Hall. This Hall is pleasantly dull, with the customary scatter of antlers and coats of arms. The overmantel of war trophies is probably by the 18th-century artist, Elizabeth Creed, an enthusiastic painter of Baroque monuments.

To its right are the service rooms, principally the kitchen and dairy. Next door is a Winter Parlour into which the family would retreat for warmth. Until well into the 1930s, the impecunious Drydens sought to live off whatever the estate could supply, from venison to vegetables. The parlour has walnut panelling of the 1590s, decorated with cartouches of Dryden heraldry beneath pious Puritan mottoes. The room is well stocked with pewter.

On the other side of the Great Hall is the Elizabethan south range. The dining room was repanelled about 1710 and hung with family portraits. Next door is Sir Henry's beloved book room. He refused to call it a library, a term he used for a room from which books were taken elsewhere. This was for books to be read *in situ*. Below the shelves are cupboards for tools, since guests were expected to help in the garden during their visit.

The room leads into the Painted Parlour, decorated in architectural *trompe-l'œil* by Elizabeth Creed and furnished solely and simply with high-backed walnut chairs. For once an empty room is the more serene.

The visitor now ascends the early 17th-century staircase to the jewel of Canons Ashby, its drawing room. This was added to the original house by Erasmus Dryden in the 1590s, but of this only the elaborate chimney-piece survives. The room was given an astonishing domed ceiling by his son, John, in the 1630s.

So overpowering is the steep coving and giant central pendant of the ceiling that the walls had to be thickened to sustain them. The panels are covered in leaves, pomegranates and Red Indian princesses, a common Elizabethan motif. The pendant is decorated with women in the form of ships' figureheads. The Dryden arms are picked out in vivid colours above the fireplace.

Beyond the drawing room is Spenser's Room, occupied by the poet on his many visits to the house. (The poet, John Dryden, was a cousin of the owners.) On the walls are recently uncovered 16th-century grisaille murals of the Old Testament. They depict the Puritan theme of the perils of worshipping false gods. The Georgian ceiling is of Rococo *papier mâché*. Back beyond the stairs is the Tapestry Room, reordered in the 18th century. The Flemish hangings have been restored, although a previous tenant used parts of them as bedding for his dogs.

The gardens have been given back their 18th-century formality, with lawns and terraces falling away down the contours to gentle Northamptonshire meadows.

COTTESBROOKE HALL ***

Cottesbrooke, 8m N of Northampton
Smith of Warwick house, with horse paintings
(P)

Cottesbrooke is horses. It is home to the kennels of the Pytchley Hunt and home also to the finest collection of equestrian paintings in England. This is hunting county and horse society. It may, as is often claimed, or may not have been the model for Jane Austen's *Mansfield Park*.

Cottesbrooke was begun in 1702 for Sir John Langham by Francis Smith of Warwick. It was aligned on the tower of Brixworth's Saxon church in the distance. The house is now owned by the Macdonald-Buchanan family, who acquired their equestrian pictures between the wars.

I am not normally a fan of horse paintings, but to wander round Cottesbrooke and see these glorious creatures stabled in such stately frames is to be converted. Ferneley, Marshall, Stubbs and Munnings are all present and correct. Few of their subjects ever seem to rear or gallop. They just stand, their decorum fitting their setting.

The exterior of the house is as Smith designed it, a work of stately English Baroque. The façade is chaperoned by a great-aunt of a cedar to its left. The main block is balanced by two pavilions and a linking passage. The house sits in one of the finest gardens in Northamptonshire, with such enticing 'rooms' as the Philosopher's Garden, the Monkey Pond, the Gladiator Garden and the Dilemma Garden, the latter with its two 'horns'.

The interior is country-house Georgian, dominated by paintings and porcelain. The decorative scheme is mostly that of Robert Mitchell who redesigned the rooms in an Adam manner in the 1780s. Two corridors, on the ground and first floors, are formed into galleries. The Pine Room was the original hall and contains pre-Mitchell panelling. It has Baroque scroll sconces and the view towards Brixworth. The staircase hall is in blue with the richest of *papier mâché* Rococo decoration.

There is no room on these walls for horse pictures.

The dining room is home to the great Stubbs painting of Gimcrack, identical to one at Newmarket. It is a surreal depiction of sky and heath, as if horses and jockeys were mere extras. The drawing room, in blue with a red Aubusson carpet, is more delicate, with Zoffany and Devis and a Flemish *trompe-l'œil* cabinet.

DEENE PARK ****

Deene, 6m NE of Corby
Tudor mansion, Balaclava memorabilia (P)

There is no escaping Lord Cardigan at Deene. The hero of the Charge of the Light Brigade can be imagined leaping on his horse in the courtyard, commanding the great gates to be swung open and trotting out to inspect his private regiment on parade.

He was the only son among seven daughters of the 6th Earl Cardigan and he was spoilt rotten. Yet he was a dashing figure, who charged to what seemed certain death at Balaclava. His survival, as commander, was incredible luck. The house is full of his mementoes, including a painting of him describing the charge to Prince Albert and the royal children. Legend has it that Queen Victoria demanded to be removed from the painting when details of Cardigan's colourful private life later emerged.

The details concerned one Adeline Horsey de Horsey. After serving as Cardigan's long-standing mistress, she and he married secretly in Gibraltar two months after the first Lady Cardigan's death in 1858. Society was scandalized. The couple were twenty-seven years apart in age but were happy throughout their marriage. After Cardigan's death, Adeline flirted with Disraeli, briefly married a Portuguese count, travelled widely, hunted and lived at Deene until her death in 1915. Towards the end of her life she wore thick make-up and a blonde wig, and dressed in her husband's Light Brigade uniform. Her shocking and inaccurate *Recollections* are said to be irresistible.

The house is as flamboyant as the family that has occupied it for almost 500 years. Its origins are 14th century, fragments of which survive in the inner court. Mostly this is a mansion of *c*1570. The gatehouse gives onto an enclosed court at the far side of which is the Great Hall, with a Renaissance porch and classical frieze.

Inside, the Great Hall has chestnut hammerbeams with carved pendants. The dais end forms a family reredos. Heraldic stained glass in the windows honours the Cardigan family, the Brudenells, and their spouses down the ages. This glass was inconsiderately damaged by an American bomber crashing nearby during the Second World War but is restored. Brudenells gaze down from all sides. Beyond in the billiard room are fragments of the earlier Great Hall.

Deene is a house of passages and alcoves, treasures and surprises. From the outside it is a mixture of façades, some united by Victorian battlements and neo-Tudor windows. Inside, Jacobean merges into Georgian into Victorian in a decorative continuum. The Oak Staircase with pierced panels in its balustrade leads to a landing overlooking the chapel. This must be the jolliest private chapel in England, with bright crimson walls and cushions. The old Great Chamber is now a tapestry room. Its late-Elizabethan ceiling is taken from Serlio, a rich swirl of patterns as if made of icing sugar.

A series of restored Elizabethan chambers faces out over the garden. King Henry VII's Room reputedly recalls a visit from that monarch to the earlier house. Sir Edmund's Room has exposed timber and plaster walls, while a sitting room is filled with charming monochrome portraits of staff on the estate.

Grander chambers were added in the 18th and 19th centuries. The Bow Room contains books from a 17th-century Lord Cardigan's library, a Reynolds of the 4th Earl's wife and a fine Gainsborough. Over the dining room fireplace is a dramatic depiction of the 7th Earl leading the famous Charge. What is left of his horse, now just the head, is displayed in the White Hall.

FAWSLEY HALL *

4m S of Daventry
Tudor house in park with restored Great Hall (H)

Fawsley is a battle-scarred survivor of the 20th century's country-house wars, now put out to grass. It sits in a wide deer park, surrounded by a lake, woods and deferential ducks. The house looks and mostly is Elizabethan. The land belonged to the Knightleys from the early 16th century, they having prospered as promoters of sheep farming in Staffordshire. They cleared two ancient villages at Fawsley to make way for a sheep run.

Knightleys entertained Elizabeth I and sided with Cromwell. In the 18th century they began rebuilding their medieval house but not drastically. In 1869 Anthony Salvin added a wing. The last Lady Knightley befriended John Merrick, the deformed 'Elephant Man', and gave him a cottage on the estate. She died in 1913.

Disaster ensued for Fawsley. The house was occupied by the Ministry of Defence, worst wrecker of country houses since Cromwell. The house did not recover. It became a timber works in the 1960s and, when Pevsner visited it in 1972, was derelict. New money then came over the horizon. The Saunders family bought the old place and restored it as a hotel. Today, it is again a grand house, quietly awaiting guests each weekend. The butler receives visitors at the door, including any just wanting to see round.

Fawsley's pride is still its Great Hall of 1537. This is a huge room with a dramatic projecting bay window. The roof had been removed in the 1960s but has since been reinstated on the basis of a few surviving beams and illustrations. The bay has a fan vault and secret room above it. The shield in the hall has the 334 quarterings of Knightley marriages over the centuries. The medieval wing and courtyard are now the bar and restaurant. The Salvin wing with its Gothic gables and finials contains the main reception rooms. A fire blazes in the fireplace. This is a happy restoration.

HOLDENBY HOUSE **

Holdenby, 6m NW of Northampton
Ghost of Elizabethan mansion, now
Jacobethan (P)

Holdenby was begun in 1571 by Sir Christopher
Hatton, local man and glamorous Elizabethan
courtier. Born in 1540, he was a 'gentleman
pensioner' at twenty-four, vice-chamberlain
at thirty-seven and Lord Chancellor at forty-
seven. His nickname was 'the dancing chancellor'. Witty, clever and arrogant, he evicted the
Bishops of Ely from their London palace, Ely
Place, and gave his name to Hatton Garden
behind.

In Northamptonshire, Hatton built what
was in its day one of the largest houses in
England, intended to entertain and impress
his Queen. He was explicit, remarking in 1580
that he meant to leave this 'shrine, I mean
Holdenby, still unseen until that holy saint
may sit in it, to whom it is dedicated'.

She never came. But others arrived to
marvel at the place and be entertained by
Hatton's agents. Hatton died in 1591, in debt
and dismissed as 'a vegetable of the court that
sprung up at night and sank again at his noon'.
The giant house was used as prison for Charles
I after the Civil War and was then mostly
demolished for its stone.

What we see today is what took its place in
1873 at the height of the Elizabethan revival.
The new owners, Lord and Lady Clifden,
created a long entrance range with an Elizabethan porch, pedimented dormer windows
and tall chimneys, all in grey-gold local stone.
The windows are stone mullioned and the
chimneys capped by odd classical entablatures.
The building incorporates Hatton's surviving
kitchen wing. The old gate arches stand like
silent sentinels in the gardens. Clifden descendants, the Lowthers, still occupy the house.

The interiors are solid Elizabethan revival. A
comfortable panelled entrance hall is dominated by a portrait of Louis III of France. The
old billiard room is a music museum. Apart
from keyboard instruments, it displays such
curios as a rain stick and a didgeridoo. The
more obviously Victorian dining room has silk
wall-hangings and sombre portraits of Stuart
courtiers and racehorses. Today the grounds
are being restored as a Tudor garden with
antique names and Rosemary Verey's 'too-too
fragrant border'.

KELMARSH HALL **

Kelmarsh, 4m S of Market Harborough
Gibbs house restored by Nancy Lancaster (P)

Kelmarsh was bought by a Wigan tycoon,
George Lancaster, in 1902 and twenty-six years
later it was leased to an upwardly mobile
American couple, Ronald and Nancy Tree.
Ronald had become the first American Master
of the Pytchley Hunt and used this eminence
to secure the local seat in Parliament. The
Trees then moved to Ditchley (Oxon) but
separated in 1947. Nancy returned to marry
George's son and her former landlord at
Kelmarsh, Claude Lancaster. She imported the
young John Fowler as decorator and the present house is very much their creation. Claude's
sister lived at Kelmarsh until it passed to a
trust committed to its preservation.

The house is in something of a limbo. It was
built by Smith of Warwick to a Palladian
design by James Gibbs c1730–6. It has no
portico, just a brick pediment. The outside is
serene and symmetrical, overlooking gardens
laid out in part by Geoffrey Jellicoe. The interior was fitted out by Smith, with plasterwork
by the Artaris, and later by James Wyatt. Its
glory is Smith's hall. This has plasterwork
in full 1730s flow, with flowers above the
doors and a balcony over a colonnade. The
Victorians filled it with antlers and 22 pieces of
oriental armour. It is now rather bare.

Behind the hall is the saloon, later in style
and possibly by James Wyatt. Here the plaster
is more restrained and Adamish, the colour a
mid-Georgian blue. Most of the remaining
reception rooms are in John Fowler's post-war
'Country House' style, of strong colours and
sedate furnishings. The dining room contains
American chairs, with handles on their backs
presumably for helping ladies to sit down. The

Chinese Room has 18th-century wallpaper depicting not just landscape and flora but people and animals, a rarity. In the corridor is a map of the Pytchley country.

Nancy Lancaster liked to fill the hall 'with the three things that were essential to me in any room; real candlelight, wood fires and lovely flowers'. All are needed.

KIRBY HALL **

5m NE of Corby
Ruin of mighty Elizabethan house (EH)

Kirby, like Holdenby (above), belonged to Sir Christopher Hatton. It was begun in 1570 for Sir Humphrey Stafford, Sheriff of Northamptonshire, but on his death five years later was sold to Hatton, whose Holdenby was not yet ready to receive his 'holy saint', should she grace him with a visit. Hatton worked on Kirby alongside Holdenby, as if to offer the Queen which ever was ready first.

She visited neither. James I came to Kirby four times, to visit a distant relative of Hatton's who inherited the house. The state rooms were opened only for that purpose. England was dotted with these royal suites, maintained at vast expense. By 1654, John Evelyn was already finding Kirby a 'seat naked'.

Sales of contents were held in 1772 and again in 1824, by when it was 'going fast to decay'. Estate staff were living in its rooms: a labourer in the library and dogs in the drawing rooms. Stucco ceilings were yielding to 'the vampire ivy'. A Victorian owner, the Earl of Winchelsea, preserved the ruins as picturesque but they passed to the government in 1930, a shepherd being left as custodian.

By the time money was available for restoration, the philosophy was 'conserve as found'. Today, Kirby is part ruin but with its main rooms reinserted. The place seems cold and loveless. Nowhere does the word nationalization stick so emphatically to a building, as if house and park had been weeded, gravelled,

Awaiting their Queen: Holdenby's gates

manicured and rendered fit for regimental inspection.

Nonetheless, Kirby remains an important work of architecture. The plan of the house is traditional Elizabethan, a forecourt, gateway and inner Great Court, with its hall lying on the far side. The state rooms lead off the family chambers to the right. Outstanding is the frontispiece of the entrance façade. This was built by Nicholas Stone in the 1630s, apparently as a homage to his master, Inigo Jones. This homage is repeated on the reverse side of the façade in the courtyard. Here giant pilasters rise above a loggia with a central window and balcony, like a house in Paris. Yet when this was erected, Kirby's greatness was already past.

On the far side of the Great Court, Hatton's old house remains. The façade here is transitional, a medieval plan of hall and service rooms, yet symmetrical in outward appearance and covered in Renaissance ornament. The porch, with a window later inserted by Stone, is of the 1570s. It is an English Renaissance masterpiece with three storeys of pilasters, the uppermost with seven attached columns beneath a sumptuous Dutch gable.

The interiors are either ruined or dull. Hall, gallery, Great Chamber and subsidiary rooms were refurnished for the filming of *Mansfield Park*, but then sadly emptied again. The guidebook can only resort to artists' impressions and pictures of other houses of the period. The finest rooms, the Great Withdrawing Chamber and Best Bedchamber, were those used by James I. They have superb bow windows looking out over the gardens. Sitwell described them as 'like two huge galleons tied up at anchor ... the poops of two stone ships, never meant to sail, but only to catch the sunlight'. But he saw them in a sea of glorious weeds.

The grounds have been excavated, restored and replanted in their original parterres. This has been well done. A History in Action festival takes place here each year, with jousting, quaffing, wenching and other adventures. If such 'reinstatement' is allowed outside, why not inside? Kirby would have more life as a luxury hotel.

LAMPORT HALL ***

9m N of Northampton
Webb house with garden gnome (P)

Sir Gyles Isham, 12th baronet and Hollywood actor (opposite Garbo in *Anna Karenina*), died a bachelor in 1976. The house occupied by Ishams since the 16th century was suddenly up for sale. It was 'not good enough' for the National Trust but ideal for dry rot. The prospect was for a hotel, flats, conference centre, county museum or miserable decay. Thanks to tax reform, a sort of salvation has arrived. The house passed to trustees, as Sir Gyles hoped, and a new generation has been given the task of keeping the place together.

Lamport Hall stands on a slope with cypresses joining more wayward cedars in keeping guard. The oddest feature of the exterior is a portico trying to show its face above the parapet of the garden front, not what Francis Smith had in mind in his original design. Beneath is the motto of every great house, 'In things transitory resteth no glory'.

The villa-like extension was built in 1654 for Sir Justinian Isham by John Webb, pupil of Inigo Jones. It was just five bays wide and sits in the middle of the present garden front. Inside was to be a 'high Roome' in which Isham intended to receives *des personnes d'honneur*. In the 18th century, this villa was flanked by longer wings by the Smiths, beginning in 1732. Later generations added fronts to other sides, greatly extending the size of the house and the burden on the present trustees.

The interior is laid out round the High Room. This is half a cube but with only the mantelpiece and doorways still by Webb. It is a fine work with heavy swags and broken pediment. Two delightful swans, the Isham crest, are in attendance. The upper walls are of the Smith period, a century later. Cameos of kings fill the panels beneath the coving.

The library is a warm, pleasant room filled with Regency bookshelves topped by busts of

Renaissance frontispiece at Kirby

worthies. The Oak Room next door, part of the Webb house, has been re-panelled in the Jacobean style and filled with pewter. Behind is a graceful Georgian staircase brought here in the 19th century. Its delicate 18th-century balusters give way to much heavier Webb ones on the landing above.

Beyond in the China Passage is England's first garden gnome, imported from Nuremberg by the Victorian Sir Charles Isham. These gnomes were originally carried as good luck tokens by German miners. Isham used them to hold place names at table, but later populated his garden with them. Few country house fads have proved so influential. Copies are available in the shop.

The Cabinet Room beyond, once used as a chapel, has the finest Lamport pictures, including works by Sebastiano Ricci, Reni and van Dyck, as well as Italian and Flemish cabinets. But why no video of Gyles Isham's performance with Garbo?

LYVEDEN NEW BIELD *

5m SW of Oundle
Tresham folly on hillside (NT)

Tudor England seems so familiar that we easily forget the outlook and loyalties of people still within living memory of the Middle Ages. The Henrician Reformation divided England into the Old and New Religions and his daughter, Mary I, came close to delivering it to Spain. Until the Toleration Acts of the 1680s, counties divided and families fought.

The two great dynasties of Northamptonshire were the Ishams (of Lamport) and the Treshams. Sir Thomas Tresham was born a Protestant, succeeded to his inheritance in 1559 and was knighted by Elizabeth I at Kenilworth. Twenty years later, he met the charismatic Jesuit, Robert Parsons, and became a Roman Catholic. The remainder of his life was spent in and out of prison, however much he protested his loyalty to the Crown and vowed to fight for Elizabeth should 'the Spaniard' land.

Tresham sought to express his faith in more than just his church. He expressed it in domestic architecture. At Lyveden and Rushton (below), he created icons in stone. Lyveden, built towards the end of his life, was ostensibly a hunting and banqueting lodge. It was unfinished at his death in 1605 and remains unfinished today.

New Bield is distinct from Sir Thomas's former house at the foot of the slope. It stands isolated on a hill well away from a side road, looking as if a storm has sliced off its roof. The plan is that of a Greek cross. Two wings have large bay windows in the contemporary Elizabethan style. Although the house is open to the sky, the rooms are clearly delineated, with a Great Hall and Great Chamber in one wing and kitchens in another. Near the kitchens are bread ovens and an alcove for a boiler. There are parlours and bedrooms. The house was planned to have another storey, with a lantern giving a panorama over the surrounding Tresham land.

The outer walls of the house are coated with religious symbolism, the emblems of Christ's Passion beautifully cut into stone panels and set in a symbolic landscape of mounds, canals and vistas. Here are the purse, torch, spear, sword, cross, ladder, hammer, nails, garment, dice, scourge and crowing cock. Round the basement are shields for Tresham's own heraldry, never carved. They form a melancholy parade of weepers round this strange folly. The formal gardens running down the hill to the Old Bield are now emerging from the undergrowth, a most exciting work of garden archaeology.

NASSINGTON: PREBENDAL MANOR HOUSE *

Nassington, 6m NW of Oundle
Medieval hall with garden (P)

Where would England's old houses be without the toil, sweat and tears of the saints who care for them? The Prebendal Manor House at Nassington has been nursed back to life by the present owner, Jane Baile, with a tithe barn and medieval garden by way of support.

The house is old indeed. It is claimed as the site of one of King Canute's manors and to have been visited by him in person. The Great Hall may well be 13th century, with round-arched doors to the screens passage. Two Perpendicular Gothic windows have been reinstated in one wall and large, later, fireplaces opened up. A flue rises impressively to the open-timbered roof. The Hall bay window is buried by later building but, apart from this offence, a modern mezzanine leaves most of the structure open to view. A framed copy of *The Times* for 1966, the last with advertisements on the front page, hangs on the wall, looking almost as ancient as an adjacent patch of wall-painting.

Across from the house are a dovecote and the barn. Nassington is still private. I find these informal custodians of the past preferable to the stripped-down whitewash jobs of the state sector.

NORTHAMPTON: ABINGTON HALL *

Abington Park, E of Northampton
Tudor house in suburban park (M)

There are few sadder sights than a historic house trapped by suburbia, like a vintage Rolls stuck in a bypass traffic jam. Abington Hall, with its Shakespeare association, has only its old park to guard its dignity. It is home to yet another didactic lifestyle museum aimed at local primary schools.

The house belonged to a family of London merchants named Bernard, who rebuilt it at the end of the 15th century. To this house came Elizabeth Nash in 1649 to marry John Bernard. She was the widowed granddaughter of William Shakespeare (*see* Nash's House, Stratford-upon-Avon/Warks) and his sole executor. Rumours abounded of papers and lost plays hidden about the house. The entrance façade was remodelled, reputedly by Smith of Warwick, between 1738 and 1743 in a rich Northamptonshire ironstone.

The Great Hall is medieval but has replacement hammerbeams. The panelling in the adjacent Oak Room was moved there from the Hall and is excellent, with delicate linenfold sections from floor to ceiling. This room has a 17th-century refectory table, benches, carpet and a dresser. A Tudor staircase appears to have been brought from elsewhere.

ROCKINGHAM CASTLE ***

3m NW of Corby
Medieval castle on bluff (P)

Rockingham dances on its bluff over the River Welland, protesting the horrors of Corby to its rear. A castle has stood here since the dawn of history. When no longer serving a military purpose, it was adapted as a home by generations of Watsons. The subsequent house displays the English genius for marrying history to convenience.

The old castle, a royal residence fallen to ruin, was acquired from the Crown by Edward Watson in 1544. It has remained in the same family ever since. Watsons rose to be Earls then Marquesses of Rockingham, allied by marriage to Rutlands, Straffords, Monsons and Sondes. The castle passed through daughters, younger sons and nephews to the present Saunders family. They added the name of Watson as badge of pride in the castle's custodianship.

Behind its massive gatehouse, Rockingham has the familiar medieval form of a hall with outbuildings within the bailey of an old Norman keep. The Tudors divided the hall both vertically and horizontally and built wings on both ends to form an H-plan. The house remained thus until the 19th century when Anthony Salvin was asked to extend it and revive its medieval past. He crenellated the old gatehouse, put a flag tower on the façade, cleared up the service wings and built a new residential tower to the rear. As usual with Salvin, the work was deferential and sensitive.

The castle is entered through the gatehouse in the old wall, an approach much loved by film producers. An inner courtyard looks over the Welland Valley to Leicestershire. The house lies to the left, the gap between it and the old curtain wall being filled with outbuildings forming what is called 'The Street'. At its top is a gabled laundry near the old keep. In The Street were the bakehouse, brewery, larders and dairies, with scullery and kitchen adjacent to the old hall. This is a remarkable relic of medieval self-sufficiency.

The present subdivided Great Hall is pleasantly domestic but still has the fireplace of the larger hall. On a beam is the Tudor inscription: 'The howse shal be preserved and never will decaye wheare the almightie God is honored and served daye by daye'. The lobby and staircase are Salvin insertions. Beyond is the Panel Room, with coats of arms of families joined with Watsons. This room, like many in the castle, contains 20th-century paintings collected by the present owner's forebear, Sir Michael Culme-Seymour. They include works by Augustus John, Spencer, Sickert and Hepworth.

The Tudor wing occupies the right-hand side of the courtyard. The Long Gallery contains family portraits by Reynolds and van Dyck and a Zoffany of the Sondes children playing cricket. At one end is a picture by Ben Marshall of brothers out hunting. Rockingham is one of many houses claiming inspiration for Dickens's Chesney Wold in *Bleak House*. The author visited the house at the time and the Armoury in the flag tower is duly named 'Mr Tulkinghorn's Chamber'.

The gardens are dominated by the yew walk, shaped like a herd of elephants about to stampede across the lawn. This hedge is the most warlike feature of modern Rockingham.

RUSHTON TRIANGULAR LODGE **

1m W of Rushton, 2m E of Desborough
Grandee's piety in stone (EH)

To call the Triangular Lodge a folly might seem disrespectful of Sir Thomas Tresham's religious belief. His story is told above, under Lyveden New Bield. Whereas Lyveden depicts a Greek Cross and is decorated with the Instruments of the Passion, the lodge represents the Trinity of biblical witnesses, the Father, the Word (or the Son) and the Holy Ghost. It also embraces numerous puns on Tresham's name. It is three-sided, three-storeyed, with three bays and three gables to each side, each being 33⅓ ft long. The windows are trefoils, filled with triangular tracery. The chimney is triangular. Even Tresham's wife entered into the trinitarian spirit, calling him 'Good Tres'.

The building was completed in 1597 and is adorned with symbols of the Trinity. Mottoes and texts were painstakingly worked out by Tresham during his period in prison. They have been the subject of laborious analysis (in the guidebook) and form a creed in stone. For all that, the building can be appreciated as a delightful structure built for a purpose, albeit later inhabited by the estate warriner or rabbit breeder. Rabbits, like doves, were protected game for manorial lords, to the fury of their tenants.

The interior comprises three storeys of hexagonal rooms, the corner triangles containing a stair, a chimney and a recess. The windows are small and dark. The house stands in a small enclosure near the main road, guarded by evergreens and looking out over fields and hedges.

SOUTHWICK HALL **

Southwick, 2m N of Oundle
Medieval towers with Georgian extensions (P-R)

The medieval house was built by the Knyvetts, one of whom was Lord Chancellor to Edward III. It has been restored by the Caprons, one of whom was a BBC editor, which brings things a sort of full circle. It was to Southwick that the BBC brought Alexander Solzhenitsyn in total secrecy for interview after he had left Russia. The house is suitably isolated on the steppes of Rockingham Forest.

Two towers of an old 14th-century house survive at either end of an Elizabethan hall,

with an 18th-century extension to one side. The entrance is into one of the towers, a rib-vaulted undercroft which was beneath what was probably the chapel. This appears to have been an addition of c1320 to an earlier hall house, forming a curious and picturesque accumulation of ancient rooms. The great Hall became a drawing room in the 16th century, its Tudor fireplace still in place.

The most entertaining part of the house is the unaltered medieval chambers upstairs. These include a priest's room of the 1350s and a Gothic room which may have been the chapel. Two old bedrooms inserted above the original hall have unusual barrel roofs, one of them with fine panelling.

A member of the estate staff has collected tools and implements found over the years on the estate, and displayed them in one of the barns. This is a true manorial museum.

STOKE PARK *

S of Stoke Bruerne, 7m S of Northampton
Two 'Inigo Jones' pavilions (P-R)

The great house was reputedly the first Palladian mansion to be built in England, in 1629 for Sir Francis Crane, director of the famous Mortlake Tapestry Works. The mansion is no more, but its pavilions survive as eerie architectural icons. Like the house to which they were linked by a quadrant colonnade, they are in the early classical style already seen at the Whitehall Banqueting House (London, C) and the Queen's House (London, E). Although the designs were said to have been brought by Crane from Italy, Inigo Jones is generally associated with the project. Either way, two classical pavilions of such an early date merit attention, even if the main house was burned down in 1886. The neo-Jacobean house which replaced it has also gone, replaced by a farmhouse. Stoke is now a place of ghosts, terraces, choked ponds and empty colonnades – and two proud pavilions.

Washington ghosts at Sulgrave Manor

The pavilions have been restored using a bold local ironstone for their giant pilasters. This makes them colourful, almost jazzy. Each is one and a half storeys high with a three-bay façade to the front and a side projection to pick up the surviving colonnades. Such a plan, borrowed from Palladio, was unknown in England at this early date. The hipped roofs are later, as is the Venetian window in the left-hand pavilion, as seen from the park. Both look out over a Victorian terrace flanking a small lake.

The right-hand pavilion was originally the chapel of the big house and is now a private house but the left-hand one, formerly the library, became a ballroom and is accessible to the public. At the end of a mile-long drive from the main road, these stranded monuments have an Ozymandias splendour.

SULGRAVE MANOR **

Sulgrave, 6m N of Brackley
Washington shrine in Tudor manor (M)

Some houses expect you to pay your money and take your choice. The Lottery gave Sulgrave a million pounds to turn itself into a George Washington theme park. The money was spent with panache but not to every taste. The visitor centre, lecture hall and exhibition rooms are brand new. The garden is immaculate and actors in Tudor dress say things like, 'Pray come hither, sire', and 'Enter not'. Americans love it.

Sulgrave was the Tudor manor house built by the Washington family of Durham in the 16th century and vacated by them in 1610. This was some time before the birth of John Washington, who emigrated to Virginia in 1656 and was great-grandfather of the first president. But the name is the thing. We could be forgiven for thinking that George himself drank ale by the smoking kitchen fire and galloped his horse across the lawn. When the last owners sold the house in 1914, money was raised for its restoration as a museum, with considerable help from the Colonial Dames of America.

The house is a simple Tudor hall house, restored with great attention to authenticity. The apparent symmetry is deceptive, since the left-hand side of the main porch was rebuilt in the 1920s and the rear wing in the 18th century. Nonetheless, Elizabethan coats of arms crown the porch itself and the old Great Hall remains. The rooms all contain Elizabethan furnishings and paraphernalia. In the window glass is depicted the stars and stripes of the Washington arms (unrelated to the American flag). There are actors in each room – including a lady writing a letter with a quill pen in the Hall.

The 18th-century wing running at right angles to the Hall begins with the Oak Parlour, clad in panelling of about 1700. The kitchen has been furnished from an old manor in Hampshire. On my visit it was in use by two wenches making breadcrumbs. Their fire was so fierce as to fill the upstairs rooms with thoroughly real smoke. Three bedrooms are admirably fitted out, with special attention to fabrics and embroidery. In the Great Chamber was a complicated display of spinning, with much 'Come hither and witness'.

Northumberland

Northumberland contains England's finest unknown scenery. Like Cornwall it is an extremity that craves autonomy. Despite its metropolis of Newcastle upon Tyne, it is a wild and little-visited place, emphatically Border country.

This status is evident in almost all its houses. Historians have recorded some 500 fortified buildings, castles and pele towers in Northumberland. The Crown tended to leave local clans to police the Marches in their own way, which meant violently. They became renowned for their feuding and unreliability. The Percys, Greys, Fenwicks, Herons and Forsters ruled what were, in effect, buffer statelets. The Percys became powerful enough to challenge the Crown.

As in Cumbria, almost all Northumberland houses contain fragments of defensive pele towers. The form can be seen at its purest at Chipchase and Langley: a square keep with a room for stores and animals on the ground floor, a hall above and a family solar on top. So strong were these keeps that few bothered with an outer wall. At the Percys' Warkworth, the pele became a full palace-keep. Fortified manors such as Aydon made do with a battlemented enclosure.

The county is almost bereft of great Tudor houses. Not until the union of the English and Scottish crowns in 1603 did owners feel secure enough to build conventional mansions. James I's progress south was greeted with Great Halls and new state rooms, most splendidly at Chillingham. The old families began to fade away. Though the Delavals brought Vanbrugh to Seaton and the Percys brought Adam to Alnwick, it was new money that rebuilt the county in the 18th century.

The result was the Georgian rooms at Wallington and Charles Monck's essay in Greek revival at Belsay. Salvin and his Italian craftsmen redecorated Alnwick for the Percys, resulting in some of the finest Victorian interiors in England. Norman Shaw produced his best house, at Cragside for Lord Armstrong. The latter also rebuilt the spectacular fortress at Bamburgh. Finally, Lutyens came north to convert Lindisfarne into an eccentric holiday home.

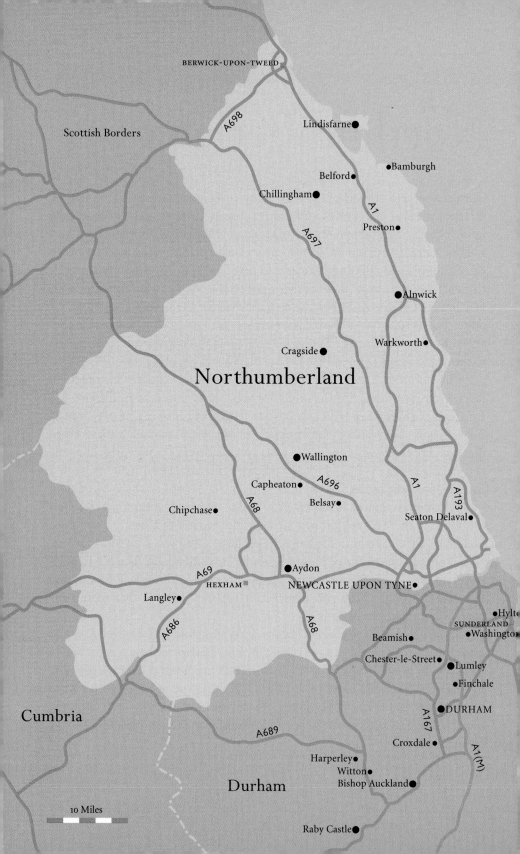

BERWICK-UPON-TWEED

Scottish Borders

A698

Lindisfarne●

●Bamburgh

Belford●

A1

Chillingham●

Preston●

A697

Alnwick●

Warkworth●

Cragside●

Northumberland

●Wallington

A696

Capheaton●

Belsay●

Chipchase●

A68

Seaton Delaval●

A1

A193

●Aydon

A69

HEXHAM

NEWCASTLE UPON TYNE●

A68

Langley●

●Hylt[o]

SUNDERLAND

Beamish●

●Washington

A686

Chester-le-Street●

●Lumley

●Finchale

Cumbria

A167

●DURHAM

A689

Croxdale●

A1(M)

Harperley●

Witton●

Durham

Bishop Auckland●

10 Miles

Raby Castle●

Alnwick ✳✳✳✳
Aydon ✳✳✳
Bamburgh ✳✳
Belford ✳
Belsay:
  Castle ✳
  Hall ✳✳
Capheaton ✳

Chillingham ✳✳✳✳
Chipchase ✳✳
Cragside ✳✳✳✳
Langley ✳✳
Lindisfarne ✳✳✳
Newcastle upon Tyne:
  Bessie Surtees
  House ✳

Newcastle upon Tyne:
  Castle ✳✳
Preston ✳
Seaton Delaval ✳✳
Wallington ✳✳✳✳
Warkworth:
  Castle ✳✳
  Hermitage ✳

ALNWICK CASTLE ✳✳✳✳

Alnwick
Ducal fortress restored by Salvin (P)

Alnwick was and is the seat of the Percys, Dukes of Northumberland, 'a family nobler than kings'. The line traces its descent from a great-grandmother of Charlemagne. Through most of the Middle Ages, Percys were virtual rulers of Northumbria, from Durham to the Border. The castle came to Henry de Percy in 1309 and, except when ceded to the Crown for rebellion, has remained in the family ever since. Even rebellion had to be forgiven the Percys.

After its military importance declined, Alnwick became the headquarters of the vast Percy estate. It was comprehensively restored, first by Robert Adam and later during the Victorian medieval revival. Today, it is one of the leading tourist attractions of the North. The current Duchess's 12-acre garden round a grand cascade, still in the course of construction, is intended to turn the grounds into 'Britain's answer to Versailles'.

The castle now has the form of an outer bailey punctuated with gates, barbicans and posterns, enclosing a massive shell keep within. The latter is a cluster of towers round an inner courtyard and contains the main domestic rooms. Although the outward appearance and plan of the building has not altered much over time, that is not true of the interior. It was gothicized by Robert Adam in the 1760s and transformed by the 4th Duke during the 1850s and 60s. The state rooms had been in later buildings elsewhere in the outer bailey. The

Duke now imported them into the keep His architect in this medievalist venture was Anthony Salvin, with Italian craftsmen working on the interiors. It is their creation that is the glory of the castle today. Like its fellow ducal residence in the south at Arundel (Sussex), Alnwick is a monument to Victorian taste as much as aristocratic power.

The approach either from the town or from across the park is awe-inspiring. The castle sits above a steep slope landscaped by Capability Brown. Entry to the keep is Wagnerian, through two gates and across Salvin's rebuilt inner court. The first room inside, the lower guard chamber, is filled with the weaponry of the Percy Tenantry Volunteers. This semi-feudal territorial regiment survived until Waterloo.

A grand staircase now leads to the state rooms. Their character needs explanation. While Salvin was responsible for the architecture, for decoration the 4th Duke imported the Italian architect and archaeologist, Luigi Canina, and his right-hand man, Giovanni Montiroli, from Rome. Italian craftsmen also came over but the brilliant Florentine carver, Anton Bulletti, was engaged to train twenty-seven men mostly from Glasgow and Newcastle.

This remarkable operation yielded what became known as the Alnwick School of craftsmanship. The state rooms are its memorial. The attention to detail, to cornices, picture frames, shelves and furniture was phenomenal. These are among the finest Victorian rooms in England, their quality compensating in part for the Duke's destruction of the earlier Adam interiors.

The upper guard chamber is chastely classical, with a Venetian marble floor. On the walls hang Canalettos, a van Dyck and a de Laszlo of the wife of the 8th Duke, painted in 1916. The small ante-library follows, with paintings by Titian, Palma Vecchio and Sebastiano del Piombo. Beyond is the library, a gallery with an upper balcony, its shelves of oak inlaid with sycamore. Busts of Bacon, Newton and Shakespeare are overlooked by emblems of arts and science.

The climax of the state rooms promenade is the saloon and drawing room, two rooms formed into one as they turn the corner and designed by Montiroli to complement each other. The fireplaces were imported from Italy, and are flanked by Dacian slaves in the saloon and caryatids in the drawing room. The ceilings of the two rooms are of the most intricate geometry; that in the saloon turns the corner under one of the towers with a brilliant flourish of coffering.

Over the drawing room fireplace is a huge mirror, its frame an explosion of gilded foliage. On either side are two majestic Italian *pietra dura* cabinets. The paintings in these rooms include works by Reni, Dobson, Lely, van Dyck and Turner. Everything is of outstanding quality. My only quarrel is with the faux artfulness that leaves a glass of brandy and a cigar stub in an ashtray.

The last of the state rooms is the dining room, with portraits of the 1st Duke and Duchess gazing out over an Italian fireplace and beneath an Italian ceiling. In a cabinet is an extensive Meissen dinner service. Salvin's picture gallery beyond begins a sequence of museum rooms that detract from the studied domesticity of the state rooms. They contain the family's second division pictures and works of art.

Raphael's superb *Madonna of the Pinks* has been removed to the National Gallery in London, another sad case of great houses unable to retain the finest treasures, passing them to national or regional collections.

Mighty Alnwick: the Percy lion

AYDON CASTLE ***

2m NE of Corbridge
Early medieval hall in fortified enclosure (EH)

Aydon claims to be the most complete 13th-century manor house in the North. It sits isolated in rolling hills above the ravine of the Cor Burn, between Corbridge and Hadrian's Wall. It seems gloriously lost in an antique world of its own.

The castle has, as its core, a fortified hall house, built largely in the late 13th century and fortified in 1305. The house was under constant threat from Scottish raiders although the owners, the de Reymes family of Suffolk, were able to do no more than build a wall and gatehouse round what was the old farmyard. The house was tenanted and refashioned in the 16th century. Kept in repair as a farm from the 18th century, the house was unaltered for 400 years until entrusted to the government in 1966.

As a result, Aydon is spartan and unfurnished, yet it remains a remarkable survival. The outer courtyard, grassed by English Heritage like a municipal garden, leads to an inner yard with the old kitchen and byre to the right. The Great Hall is ahead and the solar wing to the left. The house rises two storeys, with ancient lancet windows and external stair to the hall. On the far side, where the house overlooks the ravine, can be seen Aydon's celebrated chimney flue, built out from the wall and rising to a conical cap.

The finest of the interiors is the Great Chamber. This has Gothic windows and a carved fireplace, possibly moved from elsewhere. More unusual is the even grander fireplace in the room beneath, a room normally occupied by servants, which is decorated with face masks. This must either have been intended also as a family room, or be a sign of an owner concerned for his servants' comfort.

Both solar chambers have rear latrine extensions of considerable size, possibly used as both garderobes and closets. (Garderobe smells were believed to keep cloth free of lice and moths, from which the word wardrobe is derived.) These rooms are like those at the similar Stokesay (Salop), desperately in need of a breath of life.

BAMBURGH CASTLE **

Bamburgh, 14m E of Wooler
Coastal fortress much rebuilt by Victorians
(P)

I wish at least some English castles could be left looking as they did in old prints, if only from the outside. Bamburgh is the definitive Northumbrian fort. It stands on a rocky outcrop, 150 ft above the beach, surrounded by marsh and sea and visible for miles around. From the land side, it looks as massive as Edinburgh or Windsor, intended to be rough, tough and awe-inspiring. Yet its stone is today neatly tooled. Its bollards are brightly painted and acres of lawn are trimmed and immaculate. All castles are modern 'interpretations', but Bamburgh has lost its age.

The castle was a royal base from Saxon times through most of the Middle Ages, being regarded as impregnable and too important to be left even to the Percys. Built by King Ida in 547, it finally fell to the Earl of Warwick's cannon when defended by the Lancastrians during the Wars of the Roses. It was thus the first English castle to fall to gunfire. Three great guns, named Newcastle, Dijon and London, blasted its walls and, in doing so, signalled the end of medieval fortification.

In the 17th century the castle fell into ruin under the ownership of the Forster family, who had been appointed Constables of Bamburgh. The castle was later used as a school, charity home and military base before being sold in 1893 to the Tyneside arms magnate, Lord Armstrong. He intended it as a nursing home but it became his family's second seat. It is now held by a family trust and much of the castle is a museum of Lord Armstrong's life and work.

The public rooms are mostly late Victorian, by L. J. Ferguson of Carlisle, better known as an ecclesiastical architect. We might expect archaeological reconstruction, but so little

survived that what we see is mostly Ferguson.

The Great Hall was rebuilt at least on the site of the medieval original. It has a magnificent false hammerbeam roof rising above stone walls and panelling. Display cases contain loans from the Royal Armouries as well as family memorabilia, notably gifts from grateful foreign potentates who bought Armstrong warships and weaponry. The Cross Hall has flamboyant blind tracery over the fireplace and beautifully mounted Flemish tapestries. The Faire Chamber contains a rustic scene by Jan Brueghel the Younger and a set of Dresden china.

The keep includes the old court room and various ghosts of the Norman interior, including a kitchen with giant fireplaces. So much has been altered, rebuilt and built afresh that it is impossible to know what is medieval and what new. Bamburgh is essentially a Victorian magnate's idea of how a medieval magnate might have lived on this magnificent seaside rock.

BELFORD HALL *

Belford, 9m E of Wooler
Paine's Palladian villa on a bluff (P-R)

In a land of pele towers and castles, Belford looks defenceless and effete. Until recently, it was near derelict, next to a scrap-yard. In 1988 *Country Life* wrote that 'one more winter, and the roof would have fallen in and it might never have been saved'. The roof was rotten, the hall ceiling had fallen and wet and dry rot were rampant. Almost all the plasterwork was unsalvageable.

The story of Belford is that of English upward mobility. Abraham Dixon was bequeathed the Belford estate in 1743 by his father, a Newcastle master mariner, in the hope that he would become a country gentleman. He fulfilled his father's ambition. The estate was a wretched place, 'the most miserable, beggarly sodden town', but Abraham tackled its

Royal Bamburgh on its rock

restoration with gusto. He drained the land, planted vegetables, built a tannery and a mill, mined coal and established an inn. In 1756, on the adjacent hillside, he built a house designed by the first-rate neo-Palladian architect, James Paine. Three years later he was High Sheriff of Northumberland.

Dixon did not establish longevity. The house was sold to William Clark during the Regency and given a new rear entrance by the Newcastle architect, John Dobson, in 1817. By the mid-20th century it was abandoned. Its subsequent rescue by the Northern Heritage Trust was a triumph. The interior had to be rebuilt but the exterior was as designed by Paine and Dobson. The interior is now divided into apartments, but the hall and garden are open to the public.

Paine's Palladian villa looks serene on its hill looking out towards Bamburgh. The main building is of just five bays, the central three with a pediment and attached columns. It is, says Paine's biographer, 'a wonderfully complete and subtle essay in movement'. Bold steps lead up to the former entrance above a rusticated basement. The small entrance hall contains a discreet row of columns. Dobson's graceful staircase has been rebuilt and Paine's hall reinstated, with a frieze, fireplace and Georgian doorcases.

BELSAY CASTLE *

Belsay, 7m NW of Ponteland
Pele with adjacent Jacobean hall (EH)

There are two Belsays. They are like sisters not on speaking terms who have vanished to opposite ends of the park. The castle is old-fashioned, the hall desperate to seem modern. The castle was the seat of the Middleton family from the 15th century. When Sir Charles Monck (formerly Middleton) built a new classical hall in the early 19th century, he clearly intended the old castle to remain as a ruin. This was a common device of the Picturesque movement, as at Old Wardour (Wilts) and Scotney (Kent).

The old castle is reached from Belsay Hall along a rhododendron walk, through a dell

and a romantic quarry, all carefully contrived. Even in its ruined state, Belsay Castle is majestic. The original structure was a fortified pele, erected by the start of the 15th century and still standing today. This has an oblong hall on the first floor, with adjacent private closet. The hall is impressive, with Gothic windows and window seats and heavy corbels to support the solar above. Fragments of heraldic painting survive in the plasterwork. Spiral stairs lead onto the roof, from which the battlements and surrounding country can be viewed.

Adjacent to the old tower are the remains of a Jacobean house, from which the Middletons moved into the new Belsay Hall on Christmas Day 1817. Of these remains little survives beyond the outer walls but the Jacobean façade of 1614 has a handsome entrance bay with paired columns. It looks diminutive against the massive masonry of the medieval tower next door. A subsequent Georgian wing was reduced to the ground floor. Only the Middle Ages seemed able to produce truly undestructible architecture.

BELSAY HALL **

Belsay, 7m NW of Ponteland
Empty Grecian mansion with pillared hall (EH)

The eccentric Sir Charles Monck succeeded to Belsay Castle at the age of sixteen in 1795, changing his name from Middleton to succeed to an inheritance. He promptly extended his father's park, demolished the estate village and built a new village, to his own design, by the adjacent turnpike. He then proceeded with his great work, the erection of a hall at some distance from the castle. It was designed when he came back from his eighteen-month honeymoon tour of Berlin, Dresden, Prague, Vienna, Venice and Greece in 1804–6. Greece was plainly the enduring influence. He made some 300 architectural drawings for his new home. It took over ten years to build. Monck and his wife did not move into the still uncompleted house until 1817.

To say that Belsay Hall is 'severely' Greek is an understatement. It was modelled on the Theseion at Athens. Most houses at this time were still in the Roman style favoured by Soane and the Wyatt family. Greek was almost unknown, being employed in this archaeological purity only by William Wilkins at The Grange (Hants) and Downing College (Cambs). The exterior is two storeys of warm sandstone, with a shallow roof and two Doric columns on the entrance front. Belsay is the most refined classical work of the Regency period.

The interior is even more severe than the outside although, to be fair to Monck, this severity is partly the result of the rooms being stripped bare. English Heritage was required to leave them thus under the will of the last occupant, who insisted that no refurnishing take place. The central hall is one of the purest Grecian rooms in England. Two storeys of columns round four sides of the hall rise to a lantern, flooding the space with light. The columns are fluted, Ionic on the ground floor and Doric above, creating a four-sided colonnade on both floors. Each column was said to have been carved by a different mason. It is like a temple ambulatory with reception rooms as shrines. The material is entirely stone. The only adornment is the ornamental brass balusters.

Belsay is now empty and used for special exhibitions. On my last visit, each room was filled with seats 'as modern sculpture'. The alien aesthetic seemed an abuse of the stately dignity of Monck's rooms, which one day must surely be refurnished. The upstairs rooms retain some wallpaper but otherwise the house is bleak.

CAPHEATON HALL *

Capheaton, 10m NW of Ponteland
Wayward 17th-century façade with Georgian rear (P-R)

The house seems modest enough on first approach, a courtyard enclosed by an understated late Georgian house. This front was built in 1789 when the house was 'turned' to face away from its garden, as were many houses at this time. The earlier garden front is what merits a visit. This remarkable work was built in the mid-17th century in a style that historians call Artisan Mannerist. The two fronts of Capheaton are like a reversible theatrical mask, stern on one side and laughing on the other.

The earlier house was built for Sir John Swinburne in 1667 by a Newcastle architect, Robert Trollope. He appears to be an architect unconcerned by formal Italian precedents, or was at least content to leave local masons to decorate the façade as they chose. It is of two storeys and is dominated by its pilasters. I cannot better Pevsner's account of these pilasters: 'flatly rusticated at the bottom, with banded intermittent rustication higher up and with thick, bulgy rock-like rustication at the first floor level'. The attached pillars on either side of the door are also adorned with climbing vines. The façade is further decorated with bunches of flowers in relief and by two sundials. The window surrounds carry fishscales. The whole work is hugely enjoyable. The only sadness is that the original overhanging roof is now a recessed Georgian one.

At the time of the 18th-century alterations, Sir Edward Swinburne demolished the original Capheaton village which lay between the present gates and the house, and built a new one. He was great-grandfather of the poet, Algernon Swinburne. The family still occupy the house.

CHILLINGHAM CASTLE
****

Chillingham, 6m SE of Wooler
Restored medieval castle with Jacobean insertions (P)

The castle stands four-square in the heart of Northumberland, a landscape so deserted and dramatic as to seem like Tolkien's Middle Earth. Chillingham has long been famous for its breed of white upland cattle, threatened by European legislation. It is equally notable for its obsessive restoration over twenty years. The

castle was bought in 1981 by Sir Humphry Wakefield, husband of Kate Grey, whose family were ancestral holders of the castle since the 13th century. The place was, he says in the guidebook, 'a roofless, floorless wreck of a castle with *jungle* having taken over the gardens and grounds'.

The building is at the end of a long drive, a pile of grey walls battlemented and with narrow stone windows. The original pele tower stands to the left of the entrance, with the old hall and second tower running at right angles behind it. A Jacobean entrance was then sandwiched across the front, probably to welcome James VI of Scotland on his way south in 1603. This progress was a huge event in the social and architectural life of the North, signalling as it did the onset of (relative) peace along the Border.

Through the entrance is a tall and impressive medieval courtyard of hard grey stone. On the far side rises the new Great Hall built in 1588. It is fronted by a Jacobean arcade above what appears to be a cloister, again probably a Jacobean addition. The far side of this range facing the garden has 18th-century windows. With battlemented towers on all four corners, the castle is hugely imposing.

The Great Hall has been stripped of later plaster and is displayed inside in medieval roughcast stone, festooned with pikes, antlers and elephant armour. Wakefield's magpie acquisition of anything he can find to fill his castle is eccentric. It includes Antarctic sledges. Yet his rescue has been thorough, Wakefield fighting the purists of English Heritage from room to room like a Hollywood musketeer.

The castle divides into the medieval chambers and the Jacobean state rooms. The former include a room used by Edward I in 1298 on his northern campaign. An eating room and chapel have been restored in the pele tower. The original 'minstrels' hall', now the restaurant, is presided over by what is alleged to be the world's biggest elk head. Dungeons have re-emerged beneath turrets. Secret chambers

Jacobean welcome at Chillingham

have been opened onto roofs. There are fragments of medieval carving and dead bats everywhere.

The three rooms built for James I's visit have been admirably restored. The ceiling of the saloon has geometrical patterning with pendants in rich cream and gold. The library overmantel is a superb example of 17th-century strapwork, framing the Grey coat of arms. Rich antique and reproduction furnishings and tapestries combine with roughcast stone walls, an authentic effect. Wakefield's hang of pictures is pleasantly idiosyncratic, with large white cows jostling Augustus John nudes.

The grounds have been restored in part as formal Italian parterres, in part as wild English garden. Like the house, the presence of a guiding spirit is everywhere. Chillingham is a case of house rescue as personal statement. It is most encouraging.

CHIPCHASE CASTLE **

7m SE of Bellingham
Pele tower with Jacobean house (P)

Chipchase was the ancient seat of the Herons, lords of Tyndale and the Middle Marches. A hot-blooded family, their ambivalent relationship with both the Crown and the Scots made them rightly mistrusted. Their pele tower garrisoned fifty horsemen in time of war. Herons feuded both with their neighbours and with the Scots and their alliances were unreliable, perhaps understandable given their Border location. They did not long survive the modern age. The last Heron died penniless in a Marylebone garret in 1749. The house passed to a merchant, John Reed, and in 1862 to the Taylor family, whose descendants, the Tordays, maintain it to this day.

Chipchase overlooks the North Tyne in wild country on the edge of Wark Forest. From the south, we see the L-shaped Jacobean mansion with porch built on the site of an earlier house by Cuthbert Heron in 1621. With the coming of peace the Herons, like the Greys of Chillingham, gave their house a pacific face. In 1784 the Reeds georgianized the exterior and interior, inserting sashes in the side range and even the pele tower. The building, all of soft grey stone, is thus a delightful puzzle, of different periods yet all of a piece.

The post-medieval interiors are those of a comfortable mansion. The hall is now a sitting room with a remarkable set of cupboards for fishing tackle. A fine plaster ceiling survives in the drawing room. Most remarkable is the billiard room. The ceiling is vaguely Rococo but the chief glory is an imported Flemish overmantel depicting the March of Time: a chariot with winged horses carries the world forward, surrounded by continents and biblical scenes.

The pele tower is reached from outside. The roofline is unmistakably medieval, with heavy machicolations and corner turrets. Inside is the familiar tower arrangement, with vaulted ground floor and three storeys above, of increasing security and thus importance. A lower hall, above the basement, was for the servants and soldiers. An upper hall, much grander, was for the family. It has sleeping chambers and garderobes in the corners. An oratory was also created within the wall's thickness. The tower is a fine survival, with its roof of stone slabs intact and its fortifications still trumpeting defiance of the Scots.

CRAGSIDE ****

1m NE of Rothbury
Norman Shaw's romantic masterpiece for Lord Armstrong (NT)

Cragside is the creation of arms and the man. The arms were those of the Tyneside manufacturer, William Armstrong. The man was his architect, Richard Norman Shaw. The house they built on the wooded slopes overlooking Coquetdale embodied the mid-Victorian romantic ideal. Here were Gothic, baronial, Tudor and Jacobean fused into one. The mixture was to become familiar from the heights of Simla to the suburbs of Melbourne.

Armstrong was a titan of Tyneside industry. A local man, he trained as a mechanic and a lawyer. Throughout his life he 'swung like an erratic pendulum between the law office and the lathe'. He made waterworks, cranes, engines, guns and finally warships. In his old age he bought Bamburgh Castle for a nursing home, although this never materialized and the castle passed to a distant cousin adopted as his heir, as did Cragside on Armstrong's death in 1900. Within a decade, his heir had succeeded in dissipating the £1.4m Armstrong fortune and had to sell the most valuable works of art. The house passed to the National Trust in 1977. It is set in a magnificent 1,700 acres of forests, drives and glades. The Douglas Firs in front of the house include the highest tree in England.

Cragside had been built modestly in 1863, as Armstrong's weekend retreat, in countryside that he had known as a boy. In 1869, he asked Norman Shaw to expand it from lodge to mansion. The job took fifteen years, with Armstrong always at Shaw's elbow. They made Cragside a citadel of domestic technology. It was the first house to have hydraulic electric power and, in 1880, the first to have installed electric filament lamps. As at other houses with such lamps, guests were given cushions at dinner with which to smother flash fires.

The original house was steeply gabled on a bare hillside. Shaw added wings, drawing rooms, towers as and when Armstrong decided. The walls are of creamy stone with Elizabethan mullioned windows. The upper floors are timbered and gabled. The result is a romantic woodland folly, as if Ludwig of Bavaria had opted for Tudorbethan rather than German Gothic. Armstrong's customers were ferried up from Newcastle at weekends. Japanese, Persian, Siamese and German dignitaries paid court to the man who equipped their armies and built their navies. They left an astonishing assortment of gifts now shared with Bamburgh.

The plan of the house is simpler than the exterior suggests. It is of reception rooms on the ground floor with kitchens and services closely adjacent. Bedrooms and 'day rooms' are above. A later addition was the astonishing suite of rooms across the arch in the courtyard, containing surely the world's biggest inglenook. Rooms are richly Victorian, mostly with panelled walls and ceilings and heavily curtained. This makes the house dark, exaggerated by enveloping evergreens and by conservators keeping blinds drawn. Add in the Northumbrian weather and we have a citadel of gloom, not at all Shaw's intention.

The chief receptions rooms on the ground floor are the library and dining room. The library has glorious views over the ravine and is strongly Pre-Raphaelite in character, with Burne-Jones and Ford Maddox Brown windows, de Morgan tiles and paintings by Spencer-Stanhope. The onyx fire surround was acquired on a sales trip to Egypt. The dining room contains a Gothic inglenook, with stained glass, deep settles and magnificent brass fire irons. Emmerson's portrait of Armstrong relaxing on one of these settles embodies modest Victorian plutocracy. He is in slippers and reading a paper, his dogs sitting content beneath Burne-Jones's ladies. 'East or West, Hame's Best' says the mantelpiece.

The National Trust has restored the Cragside kitchens and plunge baths, leaving us sorry that neither is in use. A narrow wooden staircase with heraldic beasts leads to an upstairs passage with the principal bedrooms and sitting rooms. These have been furnished in the Trust's most assiduous style, making Cragside a northern Lanhydrock (Cornwall). However, the celebrated view from the morning room over the ravine is not permitted for fear of fading the fabrics. Oh dear. The Bamboo Room has Morris's 'Willow' design throughout.

An additional tower suite of bedrooms was added in the 1870s for special guests. The sumptuous Owl Rooms are an up-market garret, panelled in American black walnut with coved ceilings and Shaw's great owl bed. It was here that the then Prince and Princess of Wales stayed in 1884, a scene much recorded in the house.

The gallery forms a corridor to the later drawing room wing added by Shaw in 1883. It is sadly denuded of Armstrong's Victorian pictures, and now contains mostly lesser works. The drawing room, however, is sensa-tional, top-lit with a coved ceiling of ornate neo-Jacobean plasterwork. The chimneypiece of the inglenook is grander than anything of its sort in England, although it compares with a smaller one also by Shaw at Flete (Devon). It is a room within a room, made entirely of marble and encrusted with Elizabethan relief statuary, swirls and motifs. It is the work of Shaw's assistant, the Arts and Crafts designer, W. R. Lethaby. The interior is lined in marble and the fireplace was designed to burn peat, the smoke escaping underground.

On the walls are surviving pictures from the Armstrong collection, most of them concerned with mortality. The theme seems fitting for a man whose works caused so much death and destruction.

LANGLEY CASTLE **

2m SW of Haydon Bridge
Restored 14th-century fortified tower (H)

The castle lies hidden in a forest like something from an Arthurian romance. Langley is a hall keep, fortified by the de Lucy family in 1365, burnt out in the 15th century but well restored by the Northumberland antiquarian, Cadwallader Bates, in 1882. He moved there in 1897. Northumberland's Victorian historian, J. Hodgson, enthused that Langley 'bids stern defiance to the attacks of time, as if determined once again to resume its roof and hang out over its battlements its blue flag and pillared canopy of morning smoke, as emblems of joy and high-minded hospitality'. Langley is now a luxury hotel.

The rectangular keep is massive yet consists of just one large chamber on each floor. The corner towers contain extensive stairs and chambers. The garderobes are considered the finest anywhere. The original entrance, designed for security, is in the wall facing the garden, through a small door leading to a spiral staircase. The present Victorian stair is in the garderobe tower, its windows formed from the old latrine cubicles. The battlements and most of the Gothic windows are 19th century.

The old basement is now a low-ceilinged dining room. The first floor hall, now the drawing room, has a massive fireplace and some medieval slit windows. The second floor has been divided into bedrooms and the third is a function room. When Bates restored the house, he burned fires in every medieval hearth, but still found the place cold and damp.

The view from the roof is over woods and fields to Hadrian's Wall. The south-east turret is believed to have contained a chapel. This was restored in Bates's memory by his widow.

LINDISFARNE CASTLE ✱✱✱

Holy Island
Lutyens' refashioning of Tudor castle (NT)

Lindisfarne is a castle-lover's castle, albeit born of a 20th-century sense of the picturesque. The neighbouring priory, founded by St Aidan in 635, ranks among the most historic sites of Christianity. Its ruin lies adjacent to the village of Holy Island on a sandy spit off the Northumberland coast. The island is inaccessible at high tide.

The castle lies on the tip of the island, a mile beyond the priory. Here Elizabeth I built a fortress in 1570, whose ruin appealed to Edward Hudson, the founder of *Country Life*. In 1902, he took a lease from the Crown and commissioned his friend and protégé, Edwin Lutyens, to rebuild it. Like Castle Drogo (Devon), Lindisfarne displays Lutyens' talent at turning medieval forms to the needs of Edwardian comfort. The castle was never more than a holiday home and Hudson sold it in 1921. It passed to the National Trust in 1944.

Even modernized, Lindisfarne was to be emphatically medieval. There was just one bathroom, open fires for heat and candles for light. There was none of Norman Shaw's Cragside mod cons. Yet, like Drogo, this remains a house. There are no battlements and the outline from most angles is stark, almost Modernist. Access is by a ramp from the seaward side.

The entrance hall is 'Norman', with thickset arches and a wide fireplace. A large wind indicator is decorated by the Arts and Crafts artist, Macdonald Gill (brother of Eric), with scenes from the Armada. The dining room and Ship Room, the two principal rooms on the lower battery floor, retain the vaulting of the old castle. Thick stone walls turn into barrel vaults, stained, calcified and rugged. The Ship Room was made from the old gunpowder store and contains a charming Dutch Rococo china cabinet. The stone-vaulted roof is almost claustrophobic.

The upper battery floor is now a Long Gallery, with bedrooms leading off it. These have been furnished with vernacular pieces and whitewashed, monastery style. Bold Lutyens arches divide up the spaces. Steps lead from the gallery to the upper gallery, together forming the main reception space of the castle. The floors are carpeted and fireplaces are everywhere. In the upper gallery, Hudson's friend, Mme Guilhermina Suggia, would play Bach on the cello, as dramatically depicted by Augustus John in his Tate Britain portrait of her.

The deep windows look out, most days, onto a bleak grey North Sea. Many visitors, including Lutyens' wife, found Lindisfarne a miserable, smoky place. Yet it is one of Lutyens' most successful small works, quirkily medieval. His friend, Gertrude Jekyll, paid a visit to Lindisfarne in 1906, accompanied by a raven and a bag of bull's-eyes, to suggest the planting of a Walled Garden. It was a brave project for such a site but her flowers survive to this day.

NEWCASTLE UPON TYNE: BESSIE SURTEES HOUSE ✱

41–44 Sandhill
Rare group of 17th-century town houses (EH)

Given the devastation visited on much of Newcastle by Victorian and late 20th-century development, the survival of a group of houses on the quayside is remarkable. They are sandwiched between the Tyne Bridge, Swing Bridge and High Level Bridge, beneath the castle. Nos. 41–44 are owned by English Heritage and house its northern headquarters. The left-hand house has a Georgian brick front and 17th-century interior much rebuilt and redecorated. The other two houses retain their timbered façades. No. 41 is Bessie Surtees House.

It is named after the daughter of the owner in the 18th century, who eloped with a coal merchant's son, John Scott. The young man later rose to become the celebrated Lord Chancellor, Lord Eldon. All were later reconciled. The house rises through five storeys. Later shop-fronts form the ground floor. Above are three storeys of continuous fenestration. Fluted pilasters, forming a smart 'curtain wall' above the jutting ends of the floor joists, divide the window frames.

The three houses were vigorously restored by Lord Gort in the 1930s. His wife was a Surtees and he was eager to preserve a corner of old Newcastle in her name. Most of the interiors are now offices, but two superb 17th-century rooms survive. That on the first floor has fluted classical pilasters and ornate panelling over its fireplace, with an accomplished plasterwork ceiling. It was from this room that Bessie is said to have eloped, presumably via the window.

NEWCASTLE UPON TYNE CASTLE **

Castle Garth
Substantial Norman keep with interior intact (M)

Newcastle keep is the principal relic of one of the finest Norman castles in England, comparable in its completeness with Dover (Kent) and Hedingham (Essex). It rises mighty and black in early pictures of the city. Today, it sits rather pathetically next to a railway bridge, surrounded by the detritus of the inner city. The keep is now split from its protective Black Gate but survives intact.

The 'new castle' was built on the foundations of the old Roman fort by William the Conqueror's son, Robert, in 1080. The rebuilding was begun by Henry II in 1168 and maintained throughout the Middle Ages. The keep was fortified in the Civil War and restored in the 19th century, when the battlements were added. Much masonry has been replaced, but the form of a royal palace-fort survives, with its forebuilding and steps up to the Great Hall.

At the bottom are the customary dungeons and storerooms. Beneath the entrance stairs is a chapel, with Norman dogtooth decoration on its vault ribs. Next door is a vaulted garrison room, surrounded by walls of massive thickness. Above are two storeys of residential chambers, the lower for the constable, the other the Great Hall. Both have private solars built into the thickness of their flanking walls, along with garderobes and window slits. The Great Hall has been spoilt with modern display cases, but the King's Chamber off it remains plain, with stone floor and walls and a dogtooth arch to its fireplace.

As at Dover, the Great Hall has a gallery cut into the wall above it, from which retainers and others could watch the proceedings below. A maze of stairs, some straight, some spiral, fill the wall spaces, and seems to have been hewn from within the walls. One rises to the roof, from which there is an excellent view of central Newcastle and its celebrated bridges.

PRESTON TOWER *

9m N of Alnwick
Half a pele tower with Flodden exhibition (P)

Preston is a curiosity. It was a sizeable fortified pele or hall keep, built in 1392. After the passing of the Scottish threat in 1603, the tower was vertically sliced in half and the materials used to build an abutting farmstead. In the 19th century this farm was removed and replaced by buttresses and a belltower. The result is half a keep and two of the original corner towers.

The tower is exhibited with panache by the owner of the adjacent manor. The ground floor has a guardroom and prison cell. A narrow ladder leads to a fragment of the old Hall, with two tower rooms off it. One has been recreated as a medieval bedroom, the other as a living room. They admirably recreate their medieval appearance. Above is a small exhibition of the Battle of Flodden Field of 1513.

There is a fine, wild view from the roof over the Northumbrian plain to Bamburgh on the coast – England still unspoilt.

SEATON DELAVAL HALL **

1½m NE of Seaton Delaval
Ruin of Vanbrugh's mighty mansion (P)

What a sad place! Having crossed miles of outer Tyneside, the road reaches the coast and a vista of power stations and wind turbines. Unlike Preston (above) this is England raped by the 20th century. Yet it was not always so. Seaton Delaval was a mansion built for Admiral George Delaval in 1718. Members of the family were notorious for their beauty, debauchery and violence, all of which seem to have been genetic. Sacheverell Sitwell remarked that the women were all lovely, while 'the males of the family drank to excess and fell down dead, never in their beds'.

In honour of these traits, John Vanbrugh gave Delaval one of his most powerful and original designs. The house was gutted in 1822, when a jackdaws' nest in an uncleaned chimney caught fire. It was never restored. Though re-roofed, its blackened façade still gazes bleakly out towards the shore. Lord and Lady Hastings, Delaval's (thoroughly sober) descendants, inhabit one flanking wing. The other is occupied by Vanbrugh's magnificent stables, among the finest in the country. Each horse had its own stall, with a classical niche for its hay and its name above.

The house can be appreciated from outside even on days when it is not formally open. The front and back façades are composed of thrusting and receding bays, breaking the normal classical façade into what appears an operatic stage set. Three pavilions crown the roof on either side. A wide flight of steps leads up to the entrance, flanked by two massive attached columns. The sight through the front door into the main hall is surreal, offering a clear view to the back door, daylight and a distant obelisk beyond.

This is an eerie place, as if the fire were only yesterday. The stone walls of the Great Hall are still scorched pink, the fireplaces empty and the decorative statues broken and ragged. To the rear is the saloon, with fluted pilasters and the ghosts of Delaval beauties gliding overhead. On each side, Vanbrugh's cantilevered staircases rise to balconies overlooking the Hall.

The vaulted basements are green, damp and mysterious. The upper floors are mostly derelict, though one room has been restored as a 'tapestry room' with wall-hangings and faded pictures. A 'mahogany room' on the ground floor displays old photographs of the house in happier times, and of the Hastings family's other seat at Melton Constable in Norfolk. Seaton Delaval is used for concerts, but surely merits restoration and a grander role in Northumberland's revival.

WALLINGTON HALL ****

12m W of Morpeth
Trevelyan house with Georgian Rococo interiors (NT)

Wallington is more than the sum of its parts. Ostensibly an 18th-century mansion with dignified Georgian rooms, it was for a century and a half the home of the liberal-minded Trevelyans. Before them, it belonged to the Newcastle tycoons, the Blacketts, and before them the Fenwicks, pugnacious grandees of Northumberland since the Middle Ages. Sir William Blackett, who bought Wallington from the last Fenwick in 1688, demolished it and built what amounted to a shooting box. Such was the scale of Blackett's entertainment that six servants were retained specifically to carry drunken guests upstairs to their chambers.

It was Blackett's grandson, Walter, who remodelled the old house in a Palladian style in the years following 1738 and imported 'a colony' of Italian plasterers to decorate the

Glory ruined: Seaton Delaval

interior. Sir Walter epitomized the Georgian gentleman who 'kept many thousand hands in motion'. On his death, the estate passed to his nephew, one of the Cornwall Trevelyans, a family celebrated for the length of their noses and the breadth of their opinions.

Modern Wallington is essentially the house of the Trevelyans. The young Sir John Trevelyan was an early aesthete and enthusiast of the French Revolution. He and his clever wife, Maria, turned Wallington into a place of art and science. Their son, Walter, was a serious-minded polymath and ardent tee-totaller. He ordered the Wallington cellars to be locked throughout his life. He bequeathed what was by then one of England's great wine collections to a local vicar, to be used 'for scientific purposes'. It included port laid down for a visit of the Duke of Cumberland in 1745. Walter's wife, Pauline, was a friend of Ruskin, Millais and the Carlyles and a patron of the Pre-Raphaelites.

Walter left Wallington not to his heir but to a cousin whose radical politics he favoured. A grandson of that cousin, the Socialist MP Sir Charles Trevelyan, inherited in 1928. Distinguished Labour figures flocked to the Trevelyan table. It became the custom for Party grandees such as Attlee, Cripps, Bevan and Gaitskell to stay at Wallington rather than at a Durham boarding-house during their ritual attendance at the annual Miners' Gala. Sir Charles became the first landed aristocrat to give his entire estate to the National Trust, in 1937. His family were appalled and enraged. He pointed out that they were more likely to keep hold of the place with an assured tenancy than if the house were dissipated like many others by death duties. They in turn charged that he was a hypocrite, making his donation active only after his own death. The Trevelyan family still have a flat in the building.

The house is infused with the aura of a great Victorian family, dominated by the great central hall master-minded by Pauline Trevelyan. This was the old open courtyard, created as a roofed Italian *cortile* on the suggestion of John Ruskin in 1853. It is by the Newcastle architect, John Dobson.

The walls are painted with murals of Northumbrian scenes by William Bell Scott, a pupil of Rossetti. These include the *Arrival of the Danes*, the *Heroism of Grace Darling* and the *Triumph of Iron and Coal*. The panels are interspersed with native flora on the pillars. Two sculptures in the central hall, Thomas Woolner's *The Lords' Prayer* and Alexander Munro's *Paolo and Francesca*, became Pre-Raphaelite icons.

After this, it is hard to adjust to the Blacketts' surrounding Rococo reception rooms, which the Trevelyans must have found intolerably old-fashioned. The dining room and saloon were decorated by Pietro La Franchini, though the more recent colours are those of John Fowler. The rooms are filled with family portraits by Romney, Reynolds and Gainsborough, far distant in time and mood from the Trevelyans out in the Central Hall.

The library and study bring us back to the 19th century, with walls of heavy leather books and a National Trust 'random scatter' of newspapers and reading glasses. The remainder of the house is an engaging clutter: a corridor is lined with model soldiers, the nurseries upstairs are full of rocking horses, a needlework room is lined with examples of 18th-century embroidery in Rococo frames. A 'cabinet of curiosities' gathered by Maria Trevelyan's mother is just that, including a ferocious porcupine fish. This is more than a historic house. It is a place to inflame the imagination, a country house still with its genius loci.

Wallington came to the National Trust with 13,000 acres of precious countryside.

WARKWORTH CASTLE **

Warkworth, 7m S of Alnwick
Ancient Percy seat with residential rooms in Tudor keep (EH)

The castle, guarding a loop in the River Coquet, towers over its adjacent village. This is

Northumbrian glory: Wallington Hall

the angle from which it should be approached, since miserable housing estates picket the southern gate. Warkworth came to the Percys in 1332 and they turned it into one of the most sophisticated palace-keeps in England. Like other Percy properties, it was often confiscated but always returned. No king could rule the North without the Percys. It became derelict in the 16th century, when Shakespeare in *Henry IV* referred to the haunt of Harry Hotspur as 'this worm-eaten hold of ragged stone'.

The castle still formally belongs to the Duke of Northumberland. The 4th Duke had Anthony Salvin partly restore it in the 19th century. He re-roofed the keep and even furnished rooms in one of its towers, hoping to hold manorial courts in the keep hall. The plan came to nothing. Devoted to restoring Alnwick, the family has put Warkworth in English Heritage guardianship.

The castle has a curtain wall, gatehouse, separate Great Hall range and a keep shaped like a Maltese cross. This last rises magnificently over the town, complete to its roof and with its polygonal walls and unusual cruciform wings intact. The castle's outer bailey is entered through the gatehouse over a moat on its uphill side. On the left is the old Great Hall, a strangely gaunt ruin with a corner rising to a pinnacled tower. The ceremonial entrance survives, over which an eroded Percy lion stares defiant from its panel.

The keep is at the town end of the site. This was built for the 1st Earl of Northumberland on a single plan in the 1380s. It is of traditional keep form, with rooms stacked above each other on three floors. This plan is given the greatest elaboration. The central core has complex early plumbing. Tall ventilation shafts combine with a complex system of channels for collecting rainwater to clean floors and flush garderobes. Much of this survives, as does the suite of rooms restored by Salvin.

The ground floor is a warren of vaulted stone passages, cellars and service rooms, all carefully labelled. The main staircase is grand for a castle, indicating Warkworth's role as a palace. It rises past a delightful lobby, with stone seats and views over the town, to its internal hall. This has an oriel window and fireplace, with a large kitchen and buttery to one side. Next door is a chapel and the Great Chamber, with private chambers leading from it. Above is the solar with its own garderobe. The medieval corridors, tunnels and chambers of Warkworth, bare and ruined though they are, well recapture the proportions of a medieval interior.

WARKWORTH HERMITAGE *

Warkworth
Rare surviving hermitage carved from rock
(EH)

I must include one hermitage in this book, and none merits inclusion better than Warkworth. The house, if so it can be called, lies embedded in the bank of the River Coquet outside the village, half a mile along the river. The site is reached from the castle by footpath and then boat, apparently inaccessible any other way. With its rocky foundation and canopy of trees, it might be in an oriental jungle.

The structure consists of the remains of a hall with small fireplace, kitchen and latrine. There is another chamber above and a substantial chapel and sacristy, all apparently carved from the rockface. The chapel is a most remarkable survival, with ribbed vaulting and eroded Gothic windows. It has an altar and squint from the sacristy, suggesting that the chapel was not solely for the hermit's use. A carved depiction of the Nativity is just discernible in the window frame, and dates from the 14th century.

The earliest Warkworth hermits are not recorded, but one was well established by the 15th century, with a yearly stipend from the Percys of 66 shillings. A century later, the hermit was doubling as the Percy's Warkworth agent, with a salary of £13 and grazing rights in neighbouring fields. The hermitage was clearly a form of 'tied cottage'. The post did not survive the Reformation.

Warkworth Castle: medieval domesticity

Nottinghamshire

Nottinghamshire's image is of coal, D. H. Lawrence and the industrial valley of the River Trent. It seems a county lost along the Great North Road between the Midlands and the North. For houses, it is most celebrated for the great ducal estates laid out in the 18th century, mostly by descendants of Bess of Hardwick. Apart from as yet inaccessible Welbeck and Thoresby, now a hotel, these 'Dukeries' have gone.

Yet fragments of Nottinghamshire's past survive. Holme Pierrepont remains by the Trent, as does the exterior of Smythson's great showpiece, Wollaton Hall. Handsome gentry houses can be seen at Thrumpton, Papplewick and Winkburn, the last with unique Georgian relief carvings. Newstead displays the eccentric occupancy of Lord Byron as well as of his respectable Victorian successors.

Nottinghamshire is rich in vernacular buildings. The troglodyte caves of Nottingham's sandstone cliffs are rarities. A time warp surrounds the miner's cottage at Eastwood where Lawrence was born, and Mr Straw's House at Worksop. The latter is a brilliant evocation of early 20th-century life in an English market town.

Carlton *
Eastwood:
  Lawrence House *
Holme Pierrepont ***
Kelham **
Newark-on-Trent:
  Castle *

Newstead Abbey ****
Nottingham:
  Brewhouse Yard *
  51 Castle Gate *
  Wollaton **
  Ye Olde Salutation *
Papplewick **

Southwell:
  Workhouse *
Thoresby Hall **
Thrumpton ***
Upton *
Winkburn **
Worksop:
  Mr Straw's House **

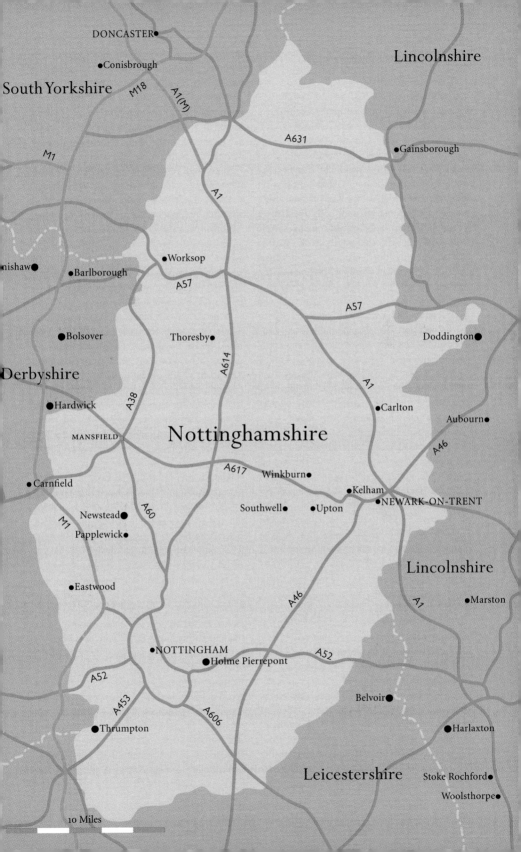

CARLTON HALL *

Carlton-on-Trent, 7m N of Newark-on-Trent
Georgian mansion with sumptuous drawing
room (P-R)

An emphatic redbrick wall surrounds Carlton
Hall. The Great North Road once ran in front
of the house, then behind it, then by-passed it
altogether. The hall was built in the 1760s for a
Newark banker and amateur architect, Joseph
Pocklington. From the outside it is a simple
brick building with pediments to the garden
and pediments within pediments on the wings.
Pocklington clearly thought pediments the
coming thing. The exterior has an endearing
shabbiness, while its Victorian paint is allowed
to peel off on its own.

The interior contains many Grand Tour
furnishings and one superb room. The staircase has rare iron 'crinoline' balusters, kinked
to help ladies descend in wide dresses. The
reception rooms retain Georgian fittings and
portraits of the Vere-Laurie family, owners
since 1832 and still in occupation today.

One room is in a class of its own. The drawing room was clearly intended by the family to
cut a dash. It is mid-Georgian in the richest
Adam style. Putti in the frieze hold garlands of
acanthus. Grapes cascade over the chimneypiece. The craftsmanship of the doors and wall
panels are identical to those in Newark Town
Hall, designed by Carr of York. His colleague
there, John Johnson, may have done work at
Carlton.

EASTWOOD:
D. H. LAWRENCE HOUSE *

8a Victoria Street
Birthplace of writer, recreated to its 1890s
state (M)

Do restored working-class cottages really tell us
anything about those born there? Richard
Hoggart, in his essay on D. H. Lawrence's
birthplace, tries hard. He points out that
Lawrence was an evoker of landscapes, notably
those of Sicily, New Mexico and Australia. His
home in this mining village, the setting of
much of his early imagery, 'reminds us also
that properly seen, inwardly seen; no landscape
is in itself uninteresting, dull'. As Lawrence
wrote in 'Piano', 'Softly, in the dusk, a woman
is singing to me;/ Taking me back down the
vista of the years.'

Eastwood certainly does Lawrence proud.
The village's old library has various mementoes and the three houses where his parents
lived have plaques. That in Victoria Street was
his birthplace and home until he was just two.
It is a tiny house on the side of a hill from
which most of the original miners' cottages
have vanished. The row is thus valuable if only
as a relic of such houses. The adjacent corner
house is a shop and visitor centre.

Number 8a is a small two-up, two-down.
The Lawrences were poor but not destitute.
Mrs Lawrence was an educated woman and a
schoolteacher and kept souvenirs of her past.
The front room of the house opens directly
onto the street but is not mean. There is a
lace tablecloth, china dogs, a few prints and
'Men of Harlech' on the piano. The front
of the room has a large window, where Mrs
Lawrence displayed linen and baby clothes
for sale.

The kitchen behind is laid out for a meal,
the range is lit and there is a sign that says simply 'Watch and Pray'. The carpet is a rag rug.
On the stairs is the miner's helmet worn by
Lawrence's father. The front bedroom upstairs
has touches of gentility, a bowler hat, books,
Bibles and rose-patterned wallpaper.

HOLME PIERREPONT ***

Holme Pierrepont, 4m E of Nottingham
Ancient family home with Tudor and later
wings (P)

Visiting Holme Pierrepont is not for the
genealogically ignorant. Over the centuries,
Pierreponts have been elevated, relegated and
renamed. They have been earls, marquesses
and dukes, Kingstons, Manvers, Newarks,
Dorchesters and Brackenburys. Their names
and titles are as confusing as the eras of archi-

tecture that jump out of the walls. At Holme Pierrepont, one can only relax and think of England, for this is a most English house.

What remains the home of a Pierrepont lies on the banks of the River Trent, approached down a track across a marshy meadow. The main entrance façade is that of a Tudor courtyard house. Once there were many courtyards, now just one.

The façade is of early brick, c1500, possibly from the King's Lynn area. It is a pleasant orange-red. The entrance range has two towers with ornamental battlements and strange alcoves on the outside. These could have been shelters for field workers since they back onto fireplaces inside. The range provided lodgings for visitors. The two ground floor rooms are divided by staircases, as in an Oxford college, and have generous fireplaces. Such early Tudor chambers still with their garderobes, doorcases, floors and fireplaces are rare.

The upstairs room at the west end has close-studded partitions and is open to the roof. This has cusped wind-braces and is a fine work of late-medieval carpentry. Victorian costumes are on display. The dressing room has drapes by William Morris.

Beyond is the one remaining courtyard, only three sides of which survive. The original Great Hall would have been on the far side, and has been replaced by the present Victorian range. The court contains a knot garden, surrounded by a conservatory in the manner of a cloister. Its walls are a mix of plaster, exposed brick, clematis and rose, charmingly informal and picturesque.

The east range of the court is an architectural jumble. Surviving medieval and Tudor fragments emerge in the form of door lintels and fireplaces, notably in the splendid Long Gallery. Pierrepont portraits are everywhere, taking us back and forth over history. In the middle of the range is a sumptuous Restoration staircase with openwork balustrading, as at Thrumpton (below). (A Thrumpton owner is said to have let out a cry of joy on first seeing this stair, finding it inferior to his own.) Overlooking the staircase are two magnificent 1850s portraits of the 3rd Earl Manvers and his

French wife. They once hung at Thoresby. Banished from the mammoth house which they created, they must hang in more modest splendour.

The reception rooms beyond have been restored by the present Pierrepont, Mrs Brackenbury, who has commissioned an admirable series of paintings depicting the house at various stages of its development.

KELHAM HALL **

Kelham, 2m NW of Newark-on-Trent
Gothic mansion by Scott with surviving interiors (P-R)

Kelham is a massive building on the outskirts of Newark, built mostly by Sir Gilbert Scott in his 'St Pancras' style. The house was begun by Scott in 1858 for the local MP, Sir John Manners-Sutton, but never finished. It became a religious retreat in 1903 and was extended in the 1920s with a new quadrangle and neo-Byzantine brick chapel. The older house contains the offices of the local council, but Scott's main rooms have been restored and, on wedding days, can even look magnificent.

The exterior displays Scott's love of Puginian Gothic. On reading Pugin, he said, 'Old things passed away and behold all things had become new; or rather modernism had passed away from me and every aspiration of my heart had become medieval.' This is what the anti-Goths most disliked about the Goths. Yet Kelham does not look medieval. Its harsh outline and even harsher materials came to epitomize municipal Victorianism, expensive but unforgiving.

The house is boldly asymmetrical, both in its plan and in its exterior details. The windows are extraordinary, with Scott trying out every conceivable variant of a Gothic opening. There are thirty-two different windows on the main façades. The interior, when it can be seen, is still in good shape. The original entrance is hidden behind a covered courtyard now used as a canteen. This has an Italian Gothic arcade round the sides, brick with banded arches and stiff-leaf pier capitals. The chapel is the council chamber. The drawing room is sumptuously neo-Gothic, with painted rib vaults rising from a central marble pier, gilded on a chocolate background. The ceiling has excellent floral stencilling.

All the main rooms are vaulted, as if Scott could not decide whether to build a house, church, museum or station foyer. Grandest is the music room, representing the Great Hall. It has a gigantic fireplace on one side, facing an arcade and gallery on the other. The vaulting is coloured and gilded, the capitals beautiful compositions from nature. This is Scott at his best.

NEWARK-ON-TRENT: CASTLE *

Castle Gate
Norman gatehouse overlooking River Trent (M)

The revival of Newark's riverside has refocused the town from the market towards the site of the Bishop of Lincoln's 'fishing chalet' on the Trent. He was allowed to fortify it in the 12th century and build a tollbridge as source of revenue. The castle came to control this important river crossing, which was why it was destroyed late in the Civil War. The townspeople of Newark were allowed to use it as a quarry to repair their homes.

What remains prominent is the old gatehouse, among the largest in England from the Norman period. Although partly ruined, it towers over the approach to the town from the bridge, still with an undercroft and two intact floors. On the lower was a hall, later a chapel, with a study next to it. On the upper was probably the chaplain's chamber. The rooms still have Norman fenestration.

The courtyard beyond retains a magnificent curtain wall overlooking the river. This includes the outer wall of the castle's Great Hall. A pretty Gothic oriel survives, which must have given guests a splendid view over the valley beyond.

The remainder of the castle has been 'stabilized' as a municipal garden. It looked far more antique when covered with ivy, as shown in Victorian photographs.

NEWSTEAD ABBEY ****

5m S of Mansfield
Late-Georgian medieval fantasy house, home of Byron (M)

Newstead was the home for six years of the poet, Lord Byron. It was, he wrote, a 'Gothic Babel of a thousand years ... old monastery once, and now/ Still older mansion of a rich and rare Mix'd Gothic'. Like Don Juan's fantasy pile it comprised 'Huge halls, long galleries, spacious chambers, join'd/ By no quite lawful marriage of the arts'.

The abbey is today a picturesque ruin attached to an impressive Victorian house. It lies in the centre of a large park with lake and formal garden. The old priory was acquired by the Byrons at the Dissolution. They decided to retain rather than demolish the cloister and domestic quarters.

Subsequent profligacy and decay drove the house to near ruin by the time Lord Byron inherited it in 1798. He used the building only occasionally. He practised shooting in the Great Hall and had a bear and a wolf roaming free round the rooms. Servants had to be beautiful, all ugly ones being dismissed. When bankruptcy again threatened in 1817, Byron sold the house to his friend the Jamaican plantation owner, Thomas Wildman.

It is mostly Wildman's house we see today, as remodelled by the neo-Gothic architect John Shaw. Such was the expense of the conversion that, once again, ruination beckoned and Newstead was sold by Wildman's widow in 1861 to William Webb, a big game hunter and friend of Dr Livingstone. By the time he gave the house to Nottingham City in 1931, it had become a conventional Edwardian mansion.

It is now well maintained and the grounds are immaculate. The lake is as it was when earlier Byrons had their servants fight across

Newstead: Byronic ghost

it in miniature battleships, with live ammunition. The Byrons were plainly intolerable employers.

Shaw's main façade defers to the Gothic west front of the old priory church next door. The latter's blind arcading is balanced by the three tall bay windows of the Great Hall. Entry is into the undercroft, which rises to the Hall up a large neo-Gothic staircase. This Hall was once festooned with Webb's hunting trophies, its floor covered in lion and tiger skins. It retains a magnificent Victorian screen.

Beyond the Hall is Byron's dining room, oak-panelled and with a dazzling heraldic overmantel brought from a neighbouring Byron property, Colwick Hall outside Nottingham. It is like a hand of playing cards, heraldry surrounded with figures in frames. The furniture is Hepplewhite.

The West Gallery was installed by earlier Byrons over the monastic cloisters and looks down on the peaceful cloister garth. It leads to the tower in which Byron himself slept. This has been recreated with Byron's own bed, decorated with reproductions of its drapes and coronets. The surrounding galleries and bedrooms were his friend Wildman's ideal of country house romanticism. They are named and 'themed' after English kings and queens, heavily panelled and with sumptuous overmantels.

The climax is the Great Drawing Room, converted from the monastery's refectory, now called the music room. It has been restored according to its layout in 1840, with an original ceiling of 1631, and wallpaper by the heraldic designer, Thomas Willement. The room is dominated by a large portrait of an 18th-century Duke of Sussex. He has the face of a country solicitor and a costume out of Gilbert and Sullivan.

To the rear is a wing built in the 18th century on the site of the monastery reredorter or latrine. These smaller domestic rooms are decorated in 19th-century Gothic style. They include Byron's study with mementoes of his days at Cambridge. On the ground floor is a colourful chapel fashioned from the old chapter house.

From here on, medieval, Gothick and 19th-century Newstead merge into one continuous act of deference to the Middle Ages, as if to atone for its original monastic Dissolution.

NOTTINGHAM: BREWHOUSE YARD *

Castle Boulevard
Row of houses converted into museum with caves behind (M)

Words fail me about Notttingham. In the years since the Second World War, this once-handsome hillside city has been variously punched, kicked and abused by its citizens. The new Nottingham is like a flayed skeleton to which patches of raw flesh cling bloodily in desperation.

One such is immediately below the castle rock, a row of 17th-century houses next to the Trip to Jerusalem inn. They belonged to the castle brewers, although they may have been built by clothiers using the river that once passed at the foot of the cliff.

The exterior of the row, dating from the 1680s, is of well-laid red bricks with projecting keystones. An arch is visible above the present entrance, presumably so a horse and cart could pass below. Like many of Nottingham's old buildings, the row has been seized by the council as a museum in penance for what is lost.

The museum vividly conveys the Nottingham that once occupied these houses. Living, sleeping and cooking areas are recreated, including an evocative bedroom. A series of workshops, such as for cobblers and barbers, are portrayed upstairs.

Typical of many early Nottingham houses are the service quarters at the back, cut out of the sandstone rock. Occupants during the war recall having to cover the cooking pots to keep out sand falling from the cave roof. A chimney rises from one of the caves to the castle above.

NOTTINGHAM: 51 CASTLE GATE *

Nottingham
Georgian house now costume museum (M)

In 1970, Nottingham City's architects department took over four Georgian houses in once-fashionable Castle Gate, from where to plan the destruction of the city. They gutted two of the houses for a 'neo-old' composition of open workshops. The other two houses were retained with some of their rooms intact. These are now Nottingham's Museum of Costume and Textiles.

The purpose is to display the city's reputation for fine cloth, especially lace, in settings of the period during which the houses were created. Five rooms have been refashioned: a 1790s dining room, an 1830s parlour, an 1860s drawing room, a 1910 boudoir and a 1935 sitting room. Costumes, accessories, wallpaper, even the pictures on the walls are contemporary. The uses are those recorded in the original houses. The displays are admirable and the lacework a delight.

The trouble is that, suddenly, conservationists who had slept so long during the loss of Nottingham's streetscape have gone berserk. Fabrics and furnishings have to be protected, so they claim, from daylight and human exhalations. They are therefore cased and shrouded like crown jewels, heavily detracting from their authenticity. Signs cover railings and walls.

The politically correct guidebook is worse. We apparently need to be told that 'the majority of costume is middle class' on the grounds that 'the middle class save their clothes . . . the working class wear them out'. The same city's leisure department displays (un-worn-out) working-class costumes in Brewhouse Yard (above). What a strange place is Nottingham.

NOTTINGHAM: WOLLATON HALL **

3m W of Nottingham
Spectacular Smythson mansion now much reduced (M)

What to say of Wollaton? It was the architectural sensation of its age, an Elizabethan house designed by Robert Smythson, creator of Longleat (Wilts) and Hardwick Hall (Derbys). Ostentatious in intent and cosmopolitan in decoration, Wollaton showed late Tudor England open to the Renaissance. Jan Sieberechts' painting shows a glittering palace, with parterres and terraces, worthy of a Loire château. It is now fearfully abused.

Wollaton Hall was completed in 1588 for Sir Francis Willoughby, a fussy, learned and increasingly demented tycoon who had made his fortune from Nottinghamshire coal. He paid his workmen in carts of the stuff. What role Willoughby played in the house's design is not known. His ancestral home was at the foot of the hill and he clearly sought to overshadow it with a gigantic belvedere, rather as did Bess at Hardwick. According to his contemporary, William Camden, Wollaton stood 'bleakly but offering a goodlie prospect to beholders far and near'. Even today, surrounded by Nottingham suburbs, the house is startlingly bold.

The façade to the park is one of the most dramatic of any Elizabethan house in England. The central hall is embraced by suites of rooms and rises to a glass-sided gallery. Four towers guard each corner. What at Hardwick is a simple box of windows is here a restless and complex series of planes. The belvedere is like a look-out lantern above a galleon. Pilasters divide mullioned windows, dressed with cartouches of classical characters. The towers tumble with gables and strapwork, each a pavilion in its own right. The effect is both Renaissance and medieval.

Smythson is known to have drawn on Dutch and German pattern books, so much so that Sacheverell Sitwell found Wollaton 'like the worst excesses of the German Renaissance ... the strapwork ornament meaningless'.

Smythson's biographer, Mark Girouard, sees Willoughby as a tragic and extravagant innovator, with an architect whose 'excitement went to his head'. The outcome was a sort of monster. Elizabethan guests driving across the park and rounding a corner of the terrace would have been 'amazed and excited but also appalled by the basilisk stare, the crash and glitter of that fantastic façade'. Yet the 16th century was the age of experiment. Nothing like Wollaton was to be attempted until Vanbrugh's essays in the Baroque more than a century later.

Wollaton suffered a fire in the early 17th century. The house passed to Lord Middleton who had the interior restored by Wyatville in 1801 in his Windsor Castle style. Wyatville even ripped out the panelling as a fire hazard in the event of an attack by a revolutionary mob, such being the temper of the times. His central hall survives with its fake hammerbeam roof and classical stone screen. Beyond is one remaining room that has been restored to the Wyatville period. The staircase also survives, with paintings said to be by Thornhill and Laguerre.

Wollaton was sold to Nottingham Council in 1924 and is now a natural history museum. At the top of Smythson's great entrance staircase, a cardboard baboon directs visitors inside. Stuffed animals jostle with ornaments. Display cases are crammed anywhere. The presentation is aimed at infants. No member of staff on my last visit could offer any guide to the building, except to assure me that the belvedere, the essence of the work, was inaccessible. There are baboons everywhere in Nottingham.

NOTTINGHAM: YE OLDE SALUTATION *

Maid Marion Way
Ancient inn with troglodyte dwelling (H)

There is a certain rivalry between Nottingham's two oldest pubs, the Salutation and the Trip to Jerusalem, both dating from the late 12th century. Despite the latter's pilgrim origins, the Salutation is the older building. It sits alone on the hideously modern Maid Marion Way with a restored Tudor exterior and timbered walls. The name derives from the Angel Gabriel's greeting to Mary. The Puritans wiped both Gabriel and Mary from the inn sign, leaving two surreal hands shaking.

What is unusual about the inn is that beneath it lies some of the most evocative troglodyte dwellings in England. These are considered too delicate for pub use. Three levels of caves extend below the main bar, the lowest with a long open room with seating. The date of these caves is unknown, but they may go back to ancient Britons. They were later used for storage and brewing.

Off one of the passages is a surviving well and what is believed to have been a cockfighting pit, favoured sport of early gamblers. Nottingham is full of these ancient lodgings, none as yet reinstated to its possible ancient appearance.

PAPPLEWICK HALL **

Papplewick, 7m N of Nottingham
Georgian house with fine staircase and plasterwork (P-R)

The late Georgians liked their exteriors dull and their interiors exuberant. Papplewick dates from 1787. From the road, it is a severe box in grey stone with Ionic pilasters, handsome but restrained to a fault. The interior could hardly be more of a contrast, a decorative scheme by an unknown hand but clearly school of Adam. The owner was Frederick Montagu, a bachelor politician who inherited the property in 1770 and decided to build in the latest fashion. He also built a Gothick church as a landscape feature.

A descendant lost the house in a gambling debt in 1910. A decade later the suffragettes targeted Papplewick for arson in a bid for publicity, but succeeded only in scorching the floorboards. The house was later bought by the Godwin-Austen family and admirably restored. The best feature of the interior is the staircase fitted into an asymmetrical hall. One side is squared but the other rises in a fine curving sweep of stairs to a landing. With no children, Montagu commissioned only three bedrooms.

Papplewick's plasterwork is excellent, attributed to Adam's craftsman, Joseph Rose. It has been restored to what are said to be the original colours. The dining room ceiling has grapes and vine garlands in purple and green. The drawing room, in contrast, has had its plasterwork left not only unrestored but uncleaned. It looks more authentic but shows only that old plasterwork tends to get dirty. The walls are hung with local landscapes.

The last of the reception rooms is the library, painted turquoise with anthemions and classical medallions picked out in white. The bookcases are in exquisite Adam style.

SOUTHWELL: WORKHOUSE *

Upton Road, Southwell
Rare surviving Poor Law relic, fully restored (NT)

Staff at the National Trust's 'not a stately home' project are emphatic that workhouses were not citadels of ghastly grim. They were, the Trust says, decent places to house the poor of the local community. As one inmate in the 1930s, May Croucher, recalls in the exhibition, her five years of childhood in the workhouse were a period of 'only happy memories'. This may explain why they have restored the interiors to look as if a modern architectural practice is about to move in.

Southwell Workhouse was regarded as the 'best preserved 19th-century workhouse in England' when it was bought by the National Trust in 1997. It had been built in 1824 by a local social reformer, the Reverend John Becher, to centralize the poor of forty-nine surrounding parishes, thus reducing the overall poor rate. It was widely influential.

Becher's concept was of humane accommodation but severe enough to be a stigma and deterrent to pauperism. It thus distinguished the Blameless and Deserving Poor, mostly the old and sick, from the Idle and Profligate Poor. Men, women and children slept apart. The work was menial, even humiliating. The old and infirm would be housed separately, as would overnight vagrants. Southwell would today be called a welfare 'one-stop shop'.

Becher's building was impressive. It is in pink brick overlooking the fields outside the town, with the towers of Southwell Minster in the background. Behind is a courtyard with washrooms and workshops. The old latrines have been excavated. The laundry has been attractively refurbished with silhouettes of inmates on the walls.

The building interiors are little more than a backdrop for an audio-presentation. Only one room is restored with bed and clothing and another is left as it was in the 1970s, when used as an extension of the local old people's home. Most of the rooms are sparkling white and empty.

I cannot see the conservation ideology that forbids the refurnishing of these places yet fills them with modern equipment. Modern curatorship shouts louder at Southwell than do the Victorian poor.

THORESBY HALL **

4m NW of Ollerton
Salvin's Jacobethan house savagely
transformed (H)

How are the mighty fallen. Thoresby was one of the great Dukeries estates. Here rose first a possible Talman mansion, then a Carr of York mansion. Then in 1864 the 3rd Earl Manvers and his French wife, Georgine, commissioned the elderly Anthony Salvin for an extravagant Jacobethan creation, fitted out in a riotously eclectic style. The eventual cost was £171,000, a stupefying sum for its day.

The house was occupied until the 1960s, then remained empty until 1980 when it was bought by the Coal Board for 'mining purposes'. These evaporated and Thoresby's fate became a *cause célèbre*. Eventually its contents were dispersed and the house sold for a time-share estate and Warner Holidays

hotel. There are now fruit machines in the bar, photographic paintings on the walls and, on my last visit, transvestite entertainers promenading in the drawing room.

Thoresby was not an outstanding Victorian house. Compared with Salvin's Harlaxton (Lincs) of thirty years earlier, Mark Girouard found it 'a depressing decline . . . a cold house, dead in its handling and dead in its detail'. It was essentially a gigantic guesthouse, sadly stripped of its original contents.

The house is at least filled again with guests. The gardens bustle with people. On my last visit there was tennis on the tennis courts and cricket in progress beneath the south terrace. The hotel additions are awful, sub-Marbella, but at least Thoresby is still with us, unlike its Dukeries neighbour, Clumber. Let us make the best of what we have.

The exterior is a Victorian evocation of Hatfield (Herts). Turrets and pinnacles rise over canted bay windows. The iron gates to the entrance courtyard form a neo-Baroque screen. It is through these that one should enter, rather than along modern corridors from the hotel reception. Stone steps lead from below to the Great Hall.

This is still the most spectacular feature of the house. Although it has lost its armour, weapons and grand paintings, the Hall retains its hammerbeam roof and an immense chimneypiece surmounted by the Manvers arms. At the far end, a hidden staircase rises behind a stone screen to twin balconies, like opera boxes. The hotel has done its best to recreate a sense of Victorian clutter. There are antlers, candelabra, stained glass, tapestries and an old trumpet gramophone.

Of the stately enfilade of reception rooms facing the terrace only ghosts remain. French period ceilings survive in the Blue Drawing Room, complementing the Rococo wall-panels brought from Georgine's Château de Coigny in France.

In the old library is an overmantel by Gerrard Robinson, depicting Robin Hood and Little John beneath a giant tableau of the Major Oak in Sherwood Forest. For this alone, Thoresby is worth a visit.

THRUMPTON HALL ***

Thrumpton, 4m NE of Kegworth
Secluded Jacobean mansion with Restoration
staircase (P-R)

The house is in an isolated enclave by the
Trent, guarded by the cooling towers of the
mighty Ratcliffe Power Station. A few hundred
yards from the main road is an estate village,
church, cricket field and moist riverside meadows. Thrumpton sits in eerie solitude under
the lee of a protective escarpment. The house
is still owned by Seymours, in line of succession from the Byrons of Newstead. It is a
precious survival.

An old Tudor house was rebuilt by Gervase
Pigot after 1607. His son enlarged and embellished it in the 1660s, with scalloped gables on
the exterior and a new staircase and saloon
inside. The latter, probably built to celebrate
the Restoration, are exhuberant works, more
than a cut above the rest of the house.

The south entrance facing the hillside was
reversed in the 19th century and the old forecourt laid out as an ornamental garden, now a
blaze of roses. Access to the present entrance is
through a dramatic series of brick arches. The
outside of the house displays a feast of wavy
gables, red brick and stone dressings.

The entrance is into the remains of the former Great Hall, which may once have spanned
the entire cross wing of an H-plan. The old
staircase by the kitchens would thus have risen
from behind the screens passage. The house
now is two rooms deep, with wings. The present hall is dark, as a hall should be, and the
library behind, fashioned from the old
entrance colonnade, is light as a library should
be. It is a happy arrangement.

At the west end of the building rises the
younger Pigot's sumptuous Restoration staircase. The proportions are of farthingale width,
the balustrade of giant acanthus leaves
embracing deer and heraldry. The staircase is
of two storeys and a superb example of its
period. The landing leads, somewhat unex-
pectedly, into the saloon. This is a serene and
beautifully panelled room, classical in decoration and hung with family portraits, looking
out over the garden.

Thrumpton has enjoyable roof leads. From
here the crowded 17th-century gables, chimneys, dormers and gulleys merge into a magic
forest with the hillside beyond. Attached to the
house are 19th-century outbuildings admirably
deferential to the style of the house.

UPTON HALL *

Upton, 3m E of Southwell
Regency villa converted into home of a
thousand clocks (M)

Upton Hall is a Regency villa of c1830 surrounded by cedars and lawns. It looks down
at heel. The outbuildings are ramshackle and
a greenhouse is home only to gargantuan
weeds. Visitors take a perilous path to the back
door and press an inconspicuous bell marked
British Horological Institute. The door opens
and reveals a wall of sound, that of a thousand
clocks.

Upton is the only house in this book worth
visiting for its noise alone. The exterior has a
seemly portico. The interiors include a fine
staircase hall, drawing room and ballroom.
The hall rises the full height of the building
into a dome and is magnificent, with a pedimented chimneypiece and acanthus frieze. All
this is mere backdrop.

No inch of space is without a clock, every
one wound up and in working order. The
place is a pandemonium of ticking, whirring,
bonging, burping and chiming. On the hour,
all hell breaks loose. The clocks include grandfather, grandmother, pendulum, carriage, railway, alarm, wrist, quartz, talking, digital and
doubtless others.

There is a Chinese dragon clock, a Congreve
rolling ball clock, and a clock made entirely
of wood. There is a counterfeit clock and a set
of clock cigarette papers. On leaving, I heard
the only sound I had missed within, that of
a cuckoo.

Restoration triumphant at Thrumpton

WINKBURN HALL **

Winkburn, 4m N of Southwell
Restored William-and-Mary mansion, Rococo
carved door panels (P)

'Left empty to decay at time of writing,' it says
in Pevsner. Not any more. Winkburn is
another modest English house taken in hand
by a sainted descendant. It lies secluded from
its village, the approach guarded by an old
sycamore, stables and a small church. The view
from the garden is so rural it might be a landscape by Stubbs. Inside are some of the most
charming vernacular sculptures to survive
from the 18th century.

Winkburn's Rococo exotica

The property had been granted by Henry
VIII to his auditor, William Burnell, after the
Dissolution and passed by descent to the
Craven-Smith-Milnes family. The new house,
attributed to William Smith of Warwick, was
built around 1695, sold by the family in 1934
but reacquired as derelict in 1980. The 16th
member of the family to live there has now
restored it, with Mrs Craven-Smith-Milnes
personally attending to the plasterwork.

The exterior is William-and-Mary, with
generous sash windows and a much later top
floor. The entrance is directly into the hall

beneath the staircase, sign that the original entrance was on the other side. The stairs are Restoration in style, with whorls of acanthus filling the panels, except that they are of iron, made in 1837. The ceiling carries a burst of Rococo plasterwork.

The main rooms have all had their plasterwork restored, the grandest being in the central dining room, previously the hall. The drawing room has an 18th-century stencilled ceiling. Many of the pictures have been generously lent from Welbeck as a boost to the restoration effort. Those in the stairwell are of the Stuart royal family, painted at the time of the house's rebuilding.

Winkburn's most remarkable possession is a charming set of carved relief panels, set above the doors in almost all the reception rooms. These are wood and of unknown origin, portraying domestic and architectural scenes. A man walks his horse home from work. Peasants besport themselves before Gothic ruins. In the library is a group of natives outside a wigwam near a grove of totem poles, a barque anchored in the bay. This may depict Captain Cook's voyages in the Pacific, widely publicized in the mid-1770s. Each panel is different. They are stylish, confident works, reminiscent of Lightfoot's work at Claydon (Bucks). They are a delight to find in so unobtrusive a house.

WORKSOP: MR STRAW'S HOUSE **

7 Blyth Grove
Time-warp house of 1920s shop-keeper (NT)

This is a semi-detached tradesman's house in a Worksop suburb, of no distinction but absorbing interest. It is the sort of 'social museum' that will seem more plausible with the passage of time. The house was left to the National Trust by William Straw on his death, aged ninety-two, in 1990. It had been untouched since the 1920s, and remains today a 'time warp' of provincial England in the first quarter of the 20th century.

William Straw's parents were craftsmen turned shopkeepers. They ran a grocery business in Worksop High Street, prospering sufficiently to move from rooms over the shop into this house in Blyth Grove in 1923. It cost £767. The Straws' two surviving sons were well educated. One ran the business on their father's death in 1932 and the other, William, became a teacher. He did not marry, lived conservatively and put his savings into Marks & Spencer shares, leaving a small fortune of £150,000 on his death in 1990. He kept everything in the house as it was when his parents redecorated it in 1923. The National Trust have kept it that way.

The style is not, in truth, that of 1920s England but rather late Victorian. The wallpaper is mostly dark and the dominant colour of the interior is brown. In the front dining room, a local newspaper rests on the table. The light bulb that fell on William's plate during dinner was not replaced. It is still not replaced. The calendar stops at 1932, the year of Mr Straw senior's death.

The remaining rooms just 'remain'. Stacks of letters and old books fill the sitting room. Cupboards are filled with (non-perishable) food. Plates, sacks and boxes remain open. The store room is a complete mess. A Tutankhamun patterned carpet leads upstairs to bedrooms more cream than brown. A bed is covered in newspapers to stop it getting dusty. Clothes remain beneath mattresses to stop them creasing. Pictures and even toothbrushes are in place. It is all odd and endearing.

Overleaf: Time stood still at Worksop

Oxfordshire

Oxfordshire is the upper Thames Valley from the Chilterns to the Cotswolds. It lies on a bed of clay in a basin of chalk, limestone and ironstone. In addition to the architectual treasure house of Oxford, the area was always a rich, medieval conduit between the wool uplands of Gloucestershire to the port of London. It is rich, too, in early houses. The Middle Ages left Minster Lovell, Stanton Harcourt and the almshouses at Ewelme. The Elizabethans produced the splendid chambers of Broughton and the lovely Thamesside mansion of Mapledurham.

The county holds two 17th-century gems. Few English houses so typify the Jacobean era as Chastleton, its ancient furniture and tapestries frozen in time. After the Restoration, Lord Craven celebrated his love for the 'Winter Queen' at Ashdown. The 18th century began with Vanbrugh's great trumpet blast at Blenheim, later to be set in one of Capability Brown's most stylish parks. James Gibbs built Ditchley for the Lee family with interiors by Kent and Flitcroft. Kent also converted Rousham in the Gothick style, its landscape still extant.

Of the past two centuries, the story is more one of restoration and rescue. Kelmscott took the fancy of William Morris, inspiring the manorial revival across the Cotswolds and West Country. Another William Morris, maker of cars, left the county's most curious relic at Nuffield Place, filled with his inventive ingenuity.

NORTHAMPTON●

Charlecote●
●STRATFORD-UPON-AVON

Warwickshire

Ettington●   Farnborough●   Northamptonshire   ●Fawley

Upton●   ●Canons Ashby   Stoke Park●

Kiftsgate●   Honington●   ●Sulgrave
●Hidcote

BANBURY   ●Stowe

Broughton●

A44 ●Batsford   ●Aynhoe

●Sezincote

●Chastleton   ●Claydon

CHIPPING NORTON   BICESTER   Buckinghamshire

Gloucs.   ●Rousham

Ditchley●   Weston Manor●   Waddesdon●

●Shipton-under-Wychwood

Blenheim●   ●Boarstall   Hartwell House
                            Studley Priory● Nether Winchendon●
●Minster Lovell   Chilton●
A40 ●Cogges

Stanton Harcourt●   OXFORD●

Oxfordshire   A418

Kelmscott●
●Buscot Old Parsonage   ●Nuneham Courtenay
Buscot Park● Kingston Bagpuize●   ●ABINGDON

                                              ●Ewelme
SWINDON●   Milton Manor●   ●Stonor
                                          Nuffield Place●   Fawley●
●Ashdown   Ardington●   Greys Court●
                                              HENLEY-ON-THAMES
Wiltshire   Berkshire   Basildon Park●
                                              ●Mapledurham

10 Miles   Welford●   READING
                              Englefield●

                                        Bear Wood●

Abingdon:
  Long Alley
   Almshouses *
   Merchant's House *
Ardington *
Ashdown House ***
Blenheim *****
Broughton *****
Buscot:
  Old Parsonage *
  Park ***
Chastleton ****

Cogges Manor *
Ditchley ***
Ewelme Almshouses *
Greys Court **
Kelmscott ***
Kingston Bagpuize **
Mapledurham ***
Milton Manor **
Minster Lovell *
Nuffield Place **
Nuneham Courtenay **
Rousham ***

Shipton-under-
  Wychwood:
   Shaven Crown *
Stanton Harcourt **
Stonor ***
Studley Priory *
Weston Manor *

Oxford University,
The Colleges
see page 614

ABINGDON: LONG ALLEY ALMSHOUSES *

St Helen's Churchyard
Ancient charity house (P-R)

Almshouses are today among the oldest inhabited buildings in England, almost all still in use for their original purpose. They offer 'sheltered' homes in the midst of their communities and are universally attractive. Of none is this truer than the enclave round St Helen's Church in Abingdon. Three sides of the churchyard are flanked by almshouses, turning what is often a bleak civic space into a place of delight. There is hardly a churchyard in England that could not be improved by some discreet building in this way.

The citizens of 17th-century Abingdon seem to have enjoyed a burst of competitive welfare. This group comprises Long Alley, Twitty's, Brick Alley and, at some distance, Tomkin's Almshouses. Each dates from the 17th and early 18th centuries. The oldest and most remarkable is Long Alley. It was founded as St Helen's Hospital in 1446 but was suppressed in 1546. Like many such charitable institutions it was swiftly refounded as Christ's Hospital in 1553. It had thirteen occupants and is still in use.

The dominant feature of Long Alley is its length. An immense tiled roof conceals a pentice or cloister beneath, sheltered by a continuous wood-mullioned screen. This is punctuated by a central porch and two lesser porches of 1605. The walls between the rooms' doors carry admonitory biblical texts. There is nothing else like this in England. A charming William-and-Mary lantern rises above the central hall.

When inaccessible, the hall can be glimpsed through its rear windows. It is an antique chamber full of ancient desks and tables, still furnished with quill pens. Dark portraits of early patrons gaze down from the walls. There is more comfort in these places than in a hundred National Health homes.

ABINGDON: MERCHANT'S HOUSE *

26/26A East St Helens Street
Medieval town house with Tudor murals (P-R)

East St Helens leads from Abingdon Market to the parish church in a graceful curve, each façade an instrument in the urban orchestra. Streets of such completeness are rare in England. The whole is so enjoyable that a casual visitor might miss Nos. 26 and 26A, owned by the Oxfordshire Preservation Trust. They are formed from the ghost of a merchant's hall house of c1430. Two cross-wings with gables to the street flank a central hall, of which the lower part was wrecked when the Victorians drove a carriageway through it.

What survives are two houses and a bridge. The left-hand wing is slightly grander, presumably the old solar wing, and is private. The right-hand wing was converted into living rooms in the 16th century and is open by appointment. Either side of its gable is a trefoiled window. The windows on the ground floor are shuttered and picturesque.

The chief feature of the house is its interior decoration. In the downstairs parlour is a fireplace with medieval quatrefoils, while upstairs is another with a Gothic frieze of trefoils. These fireplaces were possibly imported from a dissolved monastery, as found in houses all over England in the 16th century. They made chimneys available to people other than the rich.

More extraordinary are the painted walls, mostly on the stairwell. Dating from the mid-16th century, these take the form of vertical bands of red and white, entirely covered in semi-abstract fronds and flowers. An identical pattern is repeated on walls and beams throughout the house, as if in mass production. A Jacobean doublet found during restoration is on view in a case downstairs.

ARDINGTON *

Ardington, 3m E of Wantage
Georgian house, erotic staircase (P)

The house lies on the edge of a formerly Berkshire village overlooking a park and lake. It is described in Pevsner as a 'swagger' house and even Vanbrughian. The property, owned by the Baring family, was built in 1720 when English Baroque was still in vogue. It is solid and rectangular, with sheltering cedars and a pretty pavilion to one side.

Both front and rear elevations have pedimented centre bays. In the pediments are effusive carvings round coats of arms. The door frames are rusticated. The materials add to the artfulness of the façade, pale grey bricks with red bricks for the window dressings.

Ardington is a serious work of architecture, a memory of the era of Wren.

The interior is unexciting apart from the hall. This leads enticingly towards the double staircase which fills its far end, an extravagant use of space. The two arms rise separately, then turn to rush towards each other and meet out of sight. The effect is strangely erotic.

The dining room is finely panelled with fluted pilasters and Rococo ceiling plasterwork. This has been crudely picked out in white on a black background, as in a night club. On the walls are generations of Barings.

ASHDOWN HOUSE ***

4m NW of Lambourn
Restoration retreat for Winter Queen (NT)

Sacheverell Sitwell gazed on Ashdown and declared it a Danish *slott*. It should be a backdrop for 'Swan Lake', he said, with cygnets dancing across its façade on stage machinery. The house is the jewel of the Vale of the White Horse, standing alone and beautiful in a fold of the Downs above Lambourn.

The Restoration 1st Earl of Craven was a devoted admirer of Charles I's sister, Elizabeth, wife of the Elector Palatine. She was married in 1613 and became Queen of Bohemia for one winter in 1619, before her husband's defeat in war. She was known ever after as the Winter Queen. Craven was an infatuated soldier of fortune who followed the Queen and her cause round Europe, financing her family squabbles and rescuing her from debt during the English Civil War. His letters to her contain no word of love, only utter devotion. Her letters to him are to 'my little mad mylord'. He won none of the jovial affection she bestowed, for instance, on another admirer, Lord Carlisle. He was greeted with, 'thou ugly, filthy camel's face'.

Craven worshiped the Queen all her life. He is said to have built, or converted, both Hamstead Marshall (demolished) in Berkshire and Combe Abbey (Warwicks) for her use. Ashdown House was offered to her as a refuge from the Plague. She never came, ironically dying of the disease in 1662. She left Craven only a collection of portraits and some antlers. He never married and lived with these mementoes for another 35 years.

The house, empty and semi-derelict after wartime military abuse, was handed to the National Trust by Cornelia, Lady Craven in 1956. It stands, a perfect cube, beneath a steep roof with dormers. On top of the roof is a belvedere platform with balustrade. Each façade is the same. The walls are of chalk dressed with stone, shimmering silver in a low sunlight. In front of the house stand two detached pavilions with double-storey dormers. Round them roll meadows and hills, a superb setting.

Ashdown is attributed to the group of Restoration architects associated with Roger Pratt. William Winde, who worked for Craven elsewhere, is personally credited with Ashdown. There are traces of Dutch and French influence, characteristic of the Restoration. This must be appreciated outside.

The interior is not grand and the principal rooms are tenanted. Visitors see only the dramatic staircase leading to the belvedere on the roof. Its bulbous balusters rise on massive newel posts the full height of the house. Ashdown's treasures line the walls, the 17th-century portraits bequeathed to Craven by the Winter Queen. They are by Dobson, Miereveldt and van Honthorst and form a splendid progression, in tune with the spirit of the place.

BLENHEIM PALACE *****

Woodstock
Vanbrugh's monument to Marlborough and England (P)

Blenheim brooks no argument. It was primarily intended not as a home but as a monument, symbol of British pride at stemming French expansion in Europe. The moment of victory was the Battle of Blenheim in 1704. The glory was thus awarded to the nation and Queen Anne, as well as Marlborough. Vanbrugh was chosen as its architect in preference to Wren. Vanbrugh designed a

building to shout. Blenheim is an army lined up for battle. It is most un-English.

More English were the horrors of its construction. The manor of Woodstock was granted to Marlborough by Queen Anne at a time when she and his Duchess were intimates. Building began in 1705 with a labour force of 1,500, the bills met by the Treasury against a massive budget of £240,000. By 1710, the friendship of the Queen and Sarah, Duchess of Marlborough, had collapsed and Marlborough was out of favour. Building at Blenheim ceased. The grant was almost spent but work was anything but finished.

Six years later, the Duke resumed Blenheim at his own expense. Vanbrugh stormed off after a row with the Duchess, and Grinling Gibbons left as well. Vanbrugh's assistant, Hawksmoor, also departed, leaving local masons in charge. The place was not habitable until 1719, by when the miserable Duchess was dubbing it the nation's 'monument of ingratitude'. When Vanbrugh tried to see his handiwork later in life, the gatekeeper was told to refuse him entry.

Blenheim has always been as a giant among buildings, a true palace. George III admitted on seeing it that 'we have nothing to equal this'. The place is no less grand today. The grounds are the masterpiece of Capability Brown in the 1760s, long after both Vanbrugh and the Duke had departed. The drive from Woodstock to the side entrance and the axis from the forecourt out across the lake seem integral to the genius of the place. They are creations of Brown not Vanbrugh. Yet from every angle, Vanbrugh's great façade dominates the scene. It is a structure of receding planes, colonnades, towers and finials, seeming to sprout from its plateau. It is the truest manifestation of English Baroque.

Entrance is through the stables courtyard. Mighty gates reveal range upon range of offices and apartments. The main front is thus approached from the side, also a Baroque effect. Statues and trophies crowd the roofline.

Overleaf: Baroque triumphal at Blenheim

A flight of steps leads to the central portico. Visitors should ideally arrive by chariot.

The Great Hall maintains the splendour of the façade. Clad entirely of stone, it rises the full height of the central block to a lantern painted by Thornhill. A giant arch containing a balcony frames the entrance to the saloon behind. The coat of arms over the door is by Gibbons. Busts, trophies, banners, everything declares the splendour of the Marlboroughs. Even the brass locks to the front door are copies of those on 'the gates of Warsaw'.

From this point onwards, I find Blenheim starts to deflate. Visitors are required to pass through a tired Winston Churchill exhibition – he was born in the house – before seeing the house. The public rooms run along the rear of the building in a continuous, frankly tedious enfilade. Three drawing rooms culminate in the saloon, followed by three state rooms. They seem interchangeable, hung with Brussels tapestries depicting scenes from Marlborough's campaigns, or with portraits of contemporary dignitaries. The saloon is entirely painted by Laguerre in *trompe-l'œil*, the only decoration in the room.

More delightful are the surprises. These include a charming Reynolds in the Green Drawing Room of the 4th Duchess dandling a baby; a Sargent in the Red Drawing Room of the 9th Duke and his Vanderbilt wife, epitome of Edwardian swagger; and Boulle chests in the Third State Room. The three great doorways in the saloon were undertaken by Gibbons before he walked away from the job. The two-headed eagles were granted to Marlborough as a prince of the Holy Roman Empire.

At the end of the enfilade one can turn and wonder at its sheer scale. The doors are so perfectly aligned that it is said daylight can be seen through all the keyholes. The Long Library is by Vanbrugh, but its remarkable central doorway, an arch beneath a scroll flanked by columns, is by Hawksmoor. The present Duke and his family still occupy apartments at

Puritan opulence: Oak Room at Broughton

the rear of the building. Blenheim is probably more manageable today than ever in its troubled history.

BROUGHTON CASTLE *****

4m SW of Banbury
Elizabethan opulence round medieval core (P)

Broughton is Hogarth's 'The Roast Beef of Olde England' in architectural form. It survives from the Middle Ages and is still inhabited by its founding family. In 1448, William Fiennes, 2nd Baron Saye and Sele, married a descendant of the owner, William of Wykeham. A century later, under Elizabeth I, the Fiennes family modernized Wykeham's house. They patted the last stone into place, pronounced it magnificent and have seen no reason to alter it since. Broughton is the English house at its first apogee in the late 16th century, a place of great chambers and cosy parlours, attics and knot gardens.

The Fiennes were comfortable but never rich. They seem to have treated politics as a distant evil and the Renaissance as a passing fad. The upstart 18th and 19th centuries were virtually ignored at Broughton. Lord and Lady Saye and Sele remain hugely proud of their house and display it with panache. Unable to afford a new standard, they repaint the old flag each summer. His lordship was asked by an awestruck Arab, 'You must need many wives to run this place.' He shamefacedly admitted to 'three in one'.

When built at the start of the 14th century, Broughton consisted of a Great Hall and chapel, with medieval solar and undercroft added later. These remain its core today. The house sits at the far side of a walled enclosure with a moat, and is reached through a gatehouse over a bridge. It was a defended manor rather than a castle, a Great Hall with Tudor chambers extending in a series of wings and towers to the sides and rear.

Despite its Elizabethan façade, the Great Hall is a bare, medieval chamber lined with weapons and armour. The big windows, fireplace and 18th-century ceiling are later insertions. Those confused by the complexities of the Twistleton, Wykeham and Fiennes families can view them artistically set out in a family tree on the wall. There was no Cavalier romance to Broughton. The Fiennes were Parliamentarians and proud of it.

The medieval house is to the left of the Great Hall. Passages with groined vaults lead to an undercroft. The vaults carry carved corbel heads, including green men, rare in domestic architecture at this date. The undercroft is now a dining room, with 'stitched' double linenfold panelling. An early depiction of the house has been carved in one corner. The house retains its 14th-century chapel.

Upstairs, cold medieval stone changes to Elizabethan warmth. A classical portal to the upper gallery announces Broughton's brief recognition of the 18th century. The gallery was inserted above the Great Hall by the Elizabethans, and decorated with thin Gothick pilasters in the 1760s. The wallpaper is modern, a bold flaming orange. Busts by Rysbrack of Ben Jonson and Inigo Jones stand at either end. The gallery has a portrait of the 17th-century William Fiennes, who fought for Parliament, opposed Charles I's execution and was duly pardoned by Charles II. His apt nickname was 'Old Subtlety'.

Two bedrooms lead off the gallery, both with remarkable fittings. Queen Anne's Room, named after Anne of Denmark, has a classical fireplace of the 1550s, with Artisan Mannerist capitals and entablature. The chimneypiece in the adjacent King's Chamber is a work of national importance. The plaster overmantel is attributed to Italian craftsmen copying work at Fontainebleau. Dryads dance round a sacred oak in a scene from Ovid. They are held in a roundel by two naked boys, framed by a Roman soldier to one side and a female figure the other. The work is Continental and sophisticated, strangely out of place in beefy Broughton. The walls of the King's Chamber have Chinese paper and a bold modern bed in oriental style.

At the west end of this range is the Great Parlour, completed as the climax of the Elizabethan rebuilding in 1599. The ceiling is of intricate geometrical plasterwork, its outline decorated with leaves and birds and with pendants adorned with cherubs. Panels carry the family coat of arms. The wallpaper is Victorian. In an upstairs tower is the so-called Council Chamber, where Parliamentarian plotters, including Pym, Vane and Hampden, gathered under cover of the Providence Island Company in a 'room with no ears'. It has windows on all sides.

Beneath the Great Parlour is the Oak Room, once the dining room and now the most opulent of Broughton's reception rooms. The panelling is superb, divided by gentle fluted pilasters. High alcoves with bay windows look out over the garden. A magnificent internal porch shields the main door. Its Latin inscription proclaims that the past is best forgotten, a maxim much favoured by former Parliamentarians at the Restoration. The theme is repeated in a picture over the mantelpiece celebrating Charles II embarking for England from Holland. 'Old Subtlety' was still at work.

BUSCOT OLD PARSONAGE *

2m SE of Lechlade

William-and-Mary house by Thames (NT-R)

The group of Buscot church and parsonage is the Thames-side dream of every American visitor. The last Stewkley owner was a bachelor who disliked his family and wanted at all costs to stop any relative inheriting the property. On his death in the 1960s, he left it to the National Trust requiring it to be tenanted only by an American artist or writer. This did not happen at first, the house going to an English woman, Diana Phipps. It has since passed to an American with an artist wife. The house is crammed with pictures and furniture in a delightful Anglo-American jumble of styles.

The exterior is unaltered William-and-Mary of 1701. A simple stone box of three bays by five is enlivened by a steep hipped roof, generous windows and Cotswold tiles. A massive wisteria gives it a warm cloak. The front door is at the top of a Baroque flourish of steps and the rear opens onto an extensive garden of walls and lawns, merging into the surrounding Thames water meadow.

The interior has taken on the character of its tenants. The small entrance hall is entirely decorated with wild flowers painted onto the wood panelling. Twentieth-century ingenuity creates the effect of 18th-century gentility. One of the reception rooms is adorned with Diana Phipps's batik wall hangings. The upstairs dining room has a Chinese canopy hanging above the table. The wall colours were carefully chosen from 18th-century paint samples obtained from colonial Williamsburg, a fitting compliment from the New World to the old.

BUSCOT PARK ***

4m SE of Lechlade
Private art gallery in 18th-century house (NT)

The star of Buscot Park shines in its saloon, Burne-Jones' exquisite paintings of the *Legend of the Briar Rose*. When first exhibited at Agnews in 1890, the series caused a public sensation. Crowds packed Bond Street and 'enthusiasm amounted to ecstasy,' said one reviewer. The work was bought by Lord Faringdon who asked the artist to design a gilt surround as a setting. The result is one of the finest Pre-Raphaelite rooms in England. On a summer's day with the scent of flowers in the air, these languid sleepers amid so much green and gold act are truly soporific.

Buscot is a classic Georgian house enlivened by the eccentricity of its owners. Built in the 1780s, it was bought in 1889 by a City financier, Alexander Henderson, later Lord Faringdon, and filled with his collection of Old Masters. His grandson, Gavin Henderson, was of a different cloth. A pacifist and London County Councillor, he turned post-war Buscot into a Socialist salon, adding works by contemporary painters. The house was one of several bought after the Second World War for the National Trust by Ernest Cook (*see* Montacute/Somerset) and then leased back to the original

owners. The present Lord Faringdon maintains the house and its collecting tradition today.

Buscot is reached from the Faringdon road through a stately copse of limes. The drive passes a lake, stables and formal gardens, stretched out like an apron in front of the house. These were designed by the Edwardian firm of Sir Ernest George & Peto. The house exterior is rectangular and of little interest, although Felix Kelly's depiction in the guidebook gives it a mystic charm. The architect was James Darley, the work much altered in the 20th century.

The appeal of Buscot lies in its pictures and their often idiosyncratic settings. The hall is an immediate surprise, like the entrance to a mansion in a Parisian boulevard. A suite of Regency neo-Egyptian furniture is overlooked by a della Robbia panel. Behind are two scagliola columns backed by *trompe-l'œil* trophies and French Empire furniture. Having begun thus, Buscot proceeds from surprise to delight.

Buscot's character lies in its paintings not being inherited and left to hang where they 'always were' but in being bought to decorate a room. The room was then designed round them. The morning room is Dutch, with Rembrandt's *Pieter Six*, and other pictures by Rubens and van Dyck. Two tortoiseshell cabinets date from the same period. The dining room is bright red, inflaming landscapes by Wilson and Ibbetson and a picture composed of kingfisher feathers.

The saloon ceiling was reputedly by Adam's stuccoist, Joseph Rose, fit setting for Burne-Jones. Beyond is the 'Raphaelite' drawing room, bright yellow and hung with Italian Renaissance works, including Palma Vecchio and two tondos after Leonardo and Botticelli. Pictures follow fast and furious. Old Masters, drawings, sculptures peer down from the walls. A Rossetti of William Morris's wife, Janey, as Pandora gazes wistfully from a mantelpiece. A huge state bed looms behind a door. The sitting room is filled with pleasantly sentimental works by Reynolds.

The tradition of patronage continues in the

garden, where frescos adorn summer-houses and swimming pools. A ferocious modern mural of the Faringdon family is in the tea-room.

CHASTLETON HOUSE ★★★★

Chastleton, 4m SE of Moreton-in-Marsh
Jacobean mansion with contents and atmosphere intact (NT)

Chastleton could be nowhere but in the heart of England, and dating from the heart of English history, the 17th century. When, in 1936, the estate farm had to be sold, the owner apologized to the staff, explaining that the family had 'lost all our money in the war'. She meant the Civil War.

The house lies in a fold of the Cotswolds, its sandstone walls glowing with lichen and turning from crimson to ochre to grey depending on the light. Its builder in 1609 was a Welsh wool merchant turned lawyer, Walter Jones, with no great fortune or family connection. The Joneses were Royalist and remained Jacobite into the next century. It did them neither harm nor good. Nothing interesting happened here, except the invention of the rules of croquet (in 1868).

When I first visited Chastleton before its acquisition by the National Trust, its condition was as romantic as it was desperate. Damp dripped from walls. Dust lay thick beneath the cobwebs, birds occupied the attics and the garden was a jungle. Not until 1991 did Jones's descendants give up the ghost. Mrs Clutton-Brock, the last owner, excused the dust and cobwebs as 'accentuating the contours of the furniture'. She said the cobwebs should always be retained as 'they hold the place together'.

Apart from the cobwebs, the Trust decided to 'conserve as found'. For once the policy did not seem pedantic. Nothing was altered, from the broken badminton racket inside the front door to the servants' bath in the rafters. Symbolic of revival, the topiary hedge, twice replanted, is being coaxed back to life. It is an astonishing creation. A galleon, a cat, a horse, a squirrel and other animals are just recogniz-able. In an autumn mist, these shapes rise and wander down the ages, like the house itself. A King Charles Oak and Jacobite Scots pine stand in the adjacent meadow, emblems of Jones's loyalty.

The exterior of Chastleton is old-fashioned. Jones wanted a symmetrical design with pedimented gables, yet in a style suggesting ancient occupation. The plan is still 16th-century, with stair towers at each side, tall mullioned windows and a Great Hall with screens passage. The entrance had to be tucked uncomfortably into the side of the projecting porch. This feature is shared with Smythson's Burton Agnes (Yorkshire, E). There may even have been a Smythson involvement at Chastleton.

The house interior honours Jones's desire to infuse his name with antiquity, architecture standing proxy for ancestry. The rooms are arranged on three floors round a central well. The hall is medieval in plan, its long oak table constructed *in situ*. Beyond are the formal reception rooms, the White Parlour and Great Parlour, both with rich plasterwork and chunky Jacobean friezes. The latter has a French tapestry depicting not the usual military or mythical scenes but a music party in a garden.

The east staircase with obelisk finials rises to the Great Chamber and the more important bedrooms. The grandest of these, the Fettiplace Room, was named after the Oxfordshire family into which Jones proudly married his son, Henry. The entire room is clothed, with carpets, curtains, bed covers and tapestries. The closet beyond has flame-stitch fabric as old as the house. At the rear of this range is the Great Chamber, used to receive special guests or, in the 20th century, for giving Christmas presents to the estate staff. The topiary garden was designed to be seen from these windows.

The rest of the house is a quiet meander through time. Pictures, tapestries and furniture are not grand, the more precious for being of the period and continuously in the rooms.

Chastleton: Jacobean afterglow

The Cavalier Room claims a priest's hole. The Sheldon Room has a classical fireplace. The library has a rare King Charles Bible, believed to have been present with him on his scaffold and thus a precious heirloom.

The Long Gallery fills the rear of the second floor and is a superb example of the form. The barrel vault carries Jacobean scrollwork. Here the family would have promenaded on rainy days and enjoyed music and entertainment. The guidebook suggests that it is 'best in stormy conditions when the rain beats against the casements and the floor creaks underfoot like the deck of a ship in heavy seas'. Next door are the attics, including bleak servants' quarters buried among the family memorabilia.

The basements contain pantries, sculleries and kitchens, all left in some undefinably antique state. The Victorian range with its pots and pans were still in use in the 1950s. In the beer cellar is the celebrated Chastleton ladder, a battered giant once used to clear gutters at the highest point of the house. It would give modern health-and-safety officials a fit.

COGGES MANOR *

Cogges, Witney
Manorial farmhouse restored to Victorian period (M)

Suburban Witney presses hard round the old manorial settlement at Cogges. The model farm is for children, the pigs and cows kept like creatures in a zoo. But the old manor survives, reflecting the changing fortunes of big houses near manufacturing towns. The building, still in part medieval, was a farmhouse, then home to a Witney woollen draper, boarding school and, finally at the turn of the 20th century, back to farm again. The museum decided to 'stop the clock' with this last use.

The interior is that of the Mawles family, the figures portrayed in straitened times at the end of the agricultural depression. The parlour is furnished with the familiar clutter of a Victorian drawing room. The dining room is panelled, with a sideboard decorated with

Staffordshire pottery. Games are laid out on the table.

Cogges has well-furnished kitchens and pantries, with a lit fire in the former. Upstairs the bedrooms are shabbily genteel. There is one oddity, a panelled 17th-century study in which a waxwork Mr Blake, the Witney draper, is lost in thought. He must be wondering at his anachronistic survival in a house dedicated to Victoriana.

DITCHLEY PARK ***

6m NW of Woodstock
Gibbs house with Kent interiors (P-R)

Ditchley is a magnificent if rather bloodless mansion. It is now a conference centre dedicated to the cause of Anglo-American relations and is kept as immaculate as that implies. The house was built in 1720–6 for George Lee, 2nd Earl of Litchfield, whose father at the age of eleven had married Charlotte Fitzroy, illegitimate daughter of Charles II by Barbara Villiers. The architect was Francis Smith of Warwick, his design modified by James Gibbs. Also involved were William Kent and Henry Flitcroft.

Ditchley was sold by the Lee-Dillon family in 1933 to an anglicized American couple, Ronald and Nancy Tree, who were already tenants of Gibbs's Kelmarsh (Northants). They were lavish entertainers and offered the house to Churchill for occasional weekends during the Second World War when Chequers was considered unsafe. In 1947 Nancy and Ronald parted, she to marry the owner of Kelmarsh. In 1953, the house was bought by the Wills family who established the present trust.

The exterior of Ditchley is the epitome of early Georgian restraint. Gibbs wrote that grace and beauty in a building lie not in 'the Bulk of Fabrick, the Richness and Quality of the Materials, the Multiplicity of Lines, nor the Gaudiness of the Finishing ... but in the Proportion of the Parts to one another and to the whole'.

The entrance façade is a seemly rectangle, balanced by flanking pavilions reached by quadrant colonnades. The only sign of frivolity on the exterior are the lead figures that adorn the roof. They look as if lost on their way to Blenheim.

The interior is wholly different in temperament, a riot of plasterwork and ornament. Ditchley is exceptional among early Georgian houses in its lack of Victorian alteration. The hall of 1724–5 is supremely lovely, a masterpiece by William Kent and not overstated. The marble floor offsets the chimneypiece and the majestic doorcase to the saloon. Both support reclining figures of the arts and sciences. At modern Ditchley, such figures would need to depict politics, economics and international relations.

Ditchley's hall is complemented by its saloon, one of the finest such 'double acts' in early Georgian design. While the hall has the relative simplicity of an atrium, its walls imitating an exterior, the saloon is all interior. Ionic pilasters uphold a deep frieze and rich ceiling. The craftsmen were Vassalli and the Artari brothers.

In the saloon overmantels of the doors and niches are of Baroque fecundity and a complete contrast with the sedate hall. Antlers are mounted on the wall, reputedly surviving from an earlier Lee house on the site and recalling its early use as a hunting lodge. They seem a deliberate anachronism, as if determined to mock the Artaris' subtle harmonies, like bagpipes intruding on a minuet. Large windows offer a vista of sky and meadows falling away to a lake surrounded by temples in the distance.

The entire ground floor at Ditchley is composed of reception rooms, their decoration rich and most distracting to bored conferees. The Velvet Room was once the state bedroom, with a painting of Rome by Pannini and Indian satin wall-hangings. The White Drawing Room is a controlled burst of gilded plasterwork on white background, almost as exuberant as the saloon. The pictures are by Lely and Kneller of the Earl's grandparents, Charles II and the Duchess of Cleveland. In keeping with the modernity of the theme, Ditchley might perhaps dip a toe into more contemporary works of art.

EWELME ALMSHOUSES *

Ewelme, 4m E of Wallingford
Oldest church school and quadrangle (P)

When southern England is all suburb, there will still be Ewelme. It is hidden in a fold on the edge of the Chilterns, surrounded by hills and fields, a beautiful grouping of big house, farm, school and church. At its heart is a quadrangle of redbrick almshouses.

They were built by William de la Pole, Duke of Suffolk, and his wife Alice Chaucer, granddaughter of the poet. The year was 1437 in the troubled reign of Henry VI. Ewelme school was founded at the same time as the king was founding its more famous contemporary at Eton. It now claims to be the oldest church school in the country. The buildings were of brick, in a chalk landscape where timber and daub were the usual material. The masons probably came from Suffolk's East Anglian estates.

The almshouses lie down a covered way from the west door of the church. The doors are panelled and guarded by angels with extravagant head-dresses. The thirteen cottages flank a quadrangle, no longer thatched but with tiled roofs swooping over the cloistered walks. Gabled dormers on each side have pretty bargeboards. The cobbled quadrangle contains a well and, with its geraniums, is most picturesque.

The almshouses are still occupied by almsmen who say daily prayers for their founders' souls, in accordance with the statutes. The Master's House is occupied by the head of the local primary school, again, as always. This is a village welfare state as it should – and could – be across much of rural England.

GREYS COURT **

2½m W of Henley
Elizabethan fragment in Chiltern vale (NT)

I cannot rid my mind of Greys Court being once occupied by William Knollys, said to be origin of Shakespeare's Malvolio. Was it in this hall that he received his fake letter of love? Was it in this ancient tower that he was humiliated? The big house has mostly gone and Malvolio's ghost, if here it be, must be wandering this lovely Chiltern combe a sad-faced vagrant.

The true heroes of Greys Court were quite different. They were the Brunners. Sir John Brunner and his business partner, Ludwig Mond, were Victorian immigrants who together founded ICI at Winnington (Cheshire) in the 1870s. In 1937, Sir John's grandson, Sir Felix Brunner, acquired the remains of Elizabethan Greys outside Henley and set to work on their rescue. These comprised a picturesque set of brick and flint buildings round the old courtyard, including a 14th-century tower at one corner and two octagonal Tudor ones at another.

The present house is a fragment of a wing of the old mansion. It has a triple-gabled façade and is built in a warm mixture of brick and flint. A side entrance is overlooked by a pretty brick oriel window of c1570, next to a wall carrying four statues of naked cherubs with helmets. On the other side is an 18th-century extension, a modestly grand work with a bow window in rusticated stone. The architect was possibly Henry Keene.

The house interior is simple, with one exception. The entrance hall is stone-floored with niches filled with porcelain. A square table is Swiss, from the Brunners' homeland, dated 1584 and with a German inscription recording its commissioning by an earlier Felix Brunner. Behind are the 16th-century kitchens.

The most spectacular room is the 18th-century drawing room to the right of the hall. The walls and ceiling are superbly decorated by Roberts of Oxford, whose robust English Rococo can also be seen at Rousham (below). Similar plasterwork adorns the old dining room, later converted as a family schoolroom behind.

The charming outbuildings include a donkey wheel for drawing water from the old well. It was in use until 1914. Greys has grounds covering the surrounding slopes, punctuated by pines and beeches that gloriously clothe these flanks of the Chilterns.

KELMSCOTT MANOR ***
Kelmscott, 3m E of Lechlade
Morris's country house, furnished appropriately (P)

In 1871, William Morris's beautiful wife, Janey, was embroiled in a love affair with his friend, Dante Gabriel Rossetti. The tolerant Morris decided to move her with their two daughters and Rossetti away from the noise, dirt and scandal of London (*see* Red House/London, E). He found them a secluded farmhouse in Oxfordshire. 'Please, dear Janey, be happy,' he said and vanished on a walking tour of Iceland.

The house was as inconspicuous as could be imagined, in a hamlet by the 'stripling Thames'. The manor stood next to a farm and a garden stretched down to the river. The Cotswold stone was grey-green. The buildings, said Janey, were in a 'purring state of comfort . . . if you were to stroke them they would move'. Here Janey and Rossetti were briefly happy. Morris was not. He wrote to a friend that 'Rossetti has set himself down at Kelmscott as if he never meant to go away . . . he has all sorts of ways so unsympathetic with the sweet simple old place that I feel his presence a kind of slur.'

Rossetti's mental collapse and departure three years later meant that Morris was able to repossess Kelmscott until he died. It was his country idyll. Its antiquity, seclusion and introversion fitted his anti-industrial idealism. Here it was safe to be socialist and easy to be medieval. At Kelmscott, one can sense Morris's romance with nature and with the texture of man-made things. He used it as the frontispiece of his utopian novel, *News from Nowhere, an Epoch of Rest*.

Morris's daughter, May, lived at Kelmscott with her friend, Frances Lobb, until her death in 1938, leaving it as memorial to her father. Many of the furnishings were brought from Morris's London home at Hammersmith. The house is a 16th-century farm, with parlour

William Morris in his Kelmscott idyll

rather than Great Hall, a screens passage and two extended wings. One of these was added in 1670 with big gables and tiny pediments over the attic windows. The interior is Morrisonian Tudor. Every inch is hung with Morris fabrics and paper. Yet the dominant personality is Janey. Pictures of her by Rossetti and Burne-Jones seem to start from every wall, her beauty retained even in old age. Her needlework is very evident. On a corner of an embroidered counterpane she depicted Kelmscott, as in an act of private homage.

The parlour has a wide fireplace and simple country furniture. The chintz hangings are Morris's popular 'Strawberry thief': the theme of a thrush taking a strawberry was said to have been witnessed by Morris in the Kelmscott garden. Beyond is the garden hall with a large unfinished embroidery showing Janey as Queen Guinevere, a Pre-Raphaelite icon. Another tapestry was woven entirely by Morris in 1879, suggesting extraordinary industry for such a busy man. The room contains a settle designed by Philip Webb with a decorated hood.

The panelled room beyond is 17th century, with pilasters and a rustic Brueghel above the fireplace. Here hangs Rossetti's exquisite portrait of Janey in a blue silk dress. The Green Room displays Morris's own first embroidery of 1857. It is in rough simple stitches, with his enigmatic motto borrowed from van Eyck, 'If I can'.

Upstairs is Mrs Morris's Bedroom hung with Willow Bough wallpaper. Across the landing is Morris's bedroom, where he was to die. The bed is hung with a pelmet embroidered by May Morris with a poem in medieval script, the coverlet embroidered by Janey. It is a room full of colour and peace.

When Morris took the house it contained tapestries depicting the story of Samson. Morris loved their faded state, their brightness lost and 'nothing left but the indigo blues, the greys and warm yellow browns'. It gave 'an air of romance that nothing else would quite do'. In the tapestry room is a photograph of Janey, still beautiful at seventy.

The house needs more of Morris's 'faded-ness'. In the attics he had loved 'the great timbers of the roof, where of old time the tillers and herdsmen of the manor slept'. In his day they were still filled with 'the litter of useless and disregarded matters – bunches of dying flowers, feathers of birds, shells of starlings' eggs, caddis worms in mugs, and the like'. The attics are now filled with pristine fabric displays.

KINGSTON BAGPUIZE HOUSE **

Kingston Bagpuize, 6m W of Abingdon
Georgian house with Baroque staircase (P)

The house belonged to the ubiquitous Thames valley grandees, the Fettiplaces, into whose family Walter Jones of Chastleton was so eager for his son to marry. Edmund Fettiplace acquired it in the 1670s and his descendants remained here until 1917. Since then Kingston Bagpuize has passed through many hands and is now owned and well maintained by the Grants. The house was rebuilt in the 1720s, probably by one of the Townesend family of builders from Oxford.

Seen from the main road, the house has a guard of honour of beeches, commanded by two giant Wellingtonias. The style is early Georgian, front and back almost identical, as are the two sides. The exterior is mildly Baroque, each elevation pedimented and with decorative urns. The walls are of redbrick with stone quoins and elegant surrounds to the windows and doors.

The old entrance hall in the middle of the main façade is now the drawing room. As often with Georgian buildings, the house was later 'reversed'. Entry is now from a new drive at the back. The door is placed uncomfortably beneath the main staircase.

This staircase is Kingston Bagpuize's best feature. It is of pine and oak rising in light-hearted skips past swirling wainscoting to a shell-capped niche on the landing. The walls are hung with hand-painted Chinese paper, installed in the 1950s and not quite fitting. The whole composition is Rococo and fun. The library is charmingly hung with pictures of the children of the house over the years. A smaller sitting room has curious floating pediments over the doors, a 20th-century conceit.

MAPLEDURHAM HOUSE ***

Mapledurham, 4m NW of Reading
Elizabethan mansion in medieval enclave (P)

Alexander Pope, the poet, was a lifelong friend of a daughter of Mapledurham, Teresa Blount. When she fell ill with smallpox and could not go to George I's coronation, he wrote commiserating with her. She was condemned to 'plain-work, and to purling brooks,/ Old-fashion'd halls, dull aunts and croaking rooks.' Pope well describes this ancient mansion on the banks of the Thames opposite Reading.

The best view of Mapledurham is from the approach past the church. A relic of the original manor fills the foreground while the chimneys and dormers of the great house rise behind. The Middle Ages are thus seen against an Elizabethan backdrop, the latter of 1588. The Blount family have lived on this spot since 1490. It is still occupied by their descendants, now Eystons.

The house and its settlement are as rural now as it would have been when, in 1828, Michael Blount decided on drastic modernization. He stripped out most of the ancient interior yet restored the ancient exterior. He kept the old stables, church and almshouses lining the road and left the house itself ostensibly late 16th century. Like many formerly recusant Catholics, he found in old architecture the comfort of the old religion.

The house is H-plan, its wings flanking a shallow courtyard, with porch and symmetrical façade. By the 1580s, Great Halls had already shrunk to entrance halls, with reception rooms above. In this hall, a sinister Dobson portrait of the Royalist, Sir Charles Blount, hangs over the mantelpiece. On the walls are carved animal heads, including a 'wolf in sheep's clothing'. The adjacent library has a collection of recusant books and numerous Blount portraits.

To the rear of the hall is the family chapel, built after the Catholic Emancipation Act of 1791. The interior is Gothick, like that at Milton (below), the passage outside lined with drawings of Sir Thomas More and his family. The staircase to the first floor is Elizabethan, of dark oak, cantilevered and not supported on newel posts. The upstairs saloon runs the width of the house, its former rear windows blocked off. It has a fine strapwork ceiling, with Blount portraits on pale green walls and views over the park from the remaining windows.

The dining room downstairs contains an exquisite painting by William Larkin of *Lady St John of Bletso*, c1615. Its detailed sylvan background is said to qualify it as one of the earliest English landscapes.

MILTON MANOR HOUSE **

Milton, 2m NW of Didcot
Restoration mansion with Gothick interiors (P)

Few houses cling more desperately to their dignity than Milton. This faded Restoration mansion hangs on to life between the roaring A34 and the sprawl of Didcot, its grounds unkempt and cement filling the gaps in its pilasters and quoins. The house was built sometime after 1663, Dutch and wayward. It was sold to the Barrett family, City lacemakers and devout Catholics who, in 1764, added wings with Gothick interiors. The Mockler-Barrett family own it to this day, one of that band of saints who uphold great houses in defiance of financial gravity.

The façades to back and front are monumentally grand beneath a pitched roof with deep overhanging eaves. The entrance front has thin pilasters with Ionic capitals rising the full height of the wall. They are adorned with unusual garters of fleur-de-lys 'jewels' and have been crudely restored. They need attention when money can be found.

Of the downstairs rooms, the hall fireplace is a florid 17th-century work with rustic maidens lolling above a painting of exotic birds. Milton's masterpiece is its Gothick library, designed in the 1760s by Stephen Wright. Windows and bookcases are crowned with ogival decoration, encrusted with crockets and trefoils. Display cases also contain teapots collected by successive Mocklers. A set of Pinxton china was made especially for Milton in the 1790s, with a picture of the house on every piece. A cup and a saucer went to the 'Treasure Houses of Britain' exhibition in Washington in 1985.

The house interior is dominated by a 17th-century oak staircase from ground floor to attic. Its handrails have chunky balusters and massive newel posts. Yet at each landing the 18th century takes over, with delicate arches to the passages. One leads to the Barretts' private Roman Catholic chapel. The ceiling has pendants and the walls are decorated with blind arcading and ogee window arches. The 'wedding cake' effect is similar to that of Shobdon church in Herefordshire. Valuable medieval and 16th-century glass has been imported for the windows. The chapel is still in use. The chinoiserie bedroom next door has beautiful hand-painted wallpaper and marquetry furniture.

MINSTER LOVELL HALL *

Minster Lovell, 3m W of Witney
Remains of great house by river (EH)

Minster Lovell was home to one of England's great families, the Lovells, who lived adjacent to the old monastery from the 12th century. The present building was erected in the 1430s when the Lovells were a power in the land, but they never recovered from their loyalty to Richard III at Bosworth. The house passed to the Crown and was bought by the Cokes of Holkham in Norfolk in 1602. They dismantled much of the old house in the 18th century. Its ruins stand amid trees on the banks of the River Windrush, with the minster church, manor and dovecote close by. The outline of the original courtyard can clearly be seen in the grass.

A cobbled pathway leads across what would have been an outer court to the main gate and Great Hall. The porch has a complex ribbed vault inside. The hall itself is astonishingly high, lit by two lofty windows on one side and smaller ones on top of the chapel on the other. Traces of wall plaster survive. This must have been an awesome chamber. Beyond it is the solar, still with its fireplace, and a Great Chamber with traceried windows. Also surviving is a south-west tower by the river, with an impressive chimney and fragments of a spiral staircase. This was built after the main house, presumably for private apartments.

The joy of Minster Lovell is the serenity of its setting. It is easy in such places for the mind's eye to bring a ruin back to life.

NUFFIELD PLACE **

Nuffield, 7m NW of Henley-on-Thames
Thirties-style home of car tycoon (P)

Nuffield was for thirty years home to the richest man in England, William Morris. He was founder of Morris Motors in Oxford, and later became Lord Nuffield. Built in 1914, the house was bought in 1933 and extended by Morris and his wife. It survives as a fully furnished work of the mid-twentieth century and a memorial to a most unostentatious tycoon and philanthropist.

Morris was born in 1877 and left school at fifteen. A youthful cycling champion, he set up a bicycle repair business in Oxford with £4 of capital. He went on to build motorbikes and then cars, making 400 Morris cars at his Cowley works in 1919. Six years later his annual output was 56,000. With no children, he gave away all the money he made, mostly to medicine and education. The Nuffield Foundation was and still is one of the wealthiest charities in England. The house is held in trust by Nuffield College, Oxford.

Lord Nuffield's bedroom tool cupboard

The architect was Oswald Milne (*see* Coleton Fishacre/Devon), a pupil of Lutyens and in his master's 'Queen Anne' style. Nuffield was conservative, indeed Edwardian, in taste. The rooms might be those of any comfortable suburban villa, the furniture mostly reproduction pieces from the Oxford firm of Cecil Halliday. The general effect can seem charmless but the interior is uplifted by mementoes of Nuffield's various interests, notably his love of gadgets, and his lifelong passion for smoking and golf. The house is exactly as he left it, apart from an apparent lightening of the paint schemes.

The hall is filled with long-case clocks, which Nuffield tended and repaired himself. In the drawing room are Lalique lamps, a radiogram and an ingenious 'self-lighting match dispenser'. The sitting room contains an HMV television, costing £110 in 1955. Everywhere are models of cars. The upstairs bedrooms are simple for so rich a man. Lalique appears as the one extravagance. Lady Nuffield's bed is turned at an angle to give her a view of the garden.

Lord Nuffield's bedroom is the star of the house. It is starkly plain, as if harking back to his simple boyhood in the backstreets of Oxford. The carpet is said to be patched from the floorings of his cars and certainly looks it. A suite of cupboards is devoted not to clothes but to a miniature workshop, crammed with do-it-yourself tools, which he used when he could not sleep. Nuffield even mended his own shoes. He took a tool kit with him wherever he went, including on sea voyages. His Heath-Robinson lighting system survives over the bed.

So simple are these rooms that the Coronation robes on display in the dressing room come as a shock. Would Nuffield have permitted this ostentation?

Downstairs is his exercise horse and an iron lung, a machine of which he was an early sponsor. He also sponsored Borstal institutions for young offenders but was appalled when the Home Office opened one next door to his house. Lady Nuffield never quite recovered from the shock.

NUNEHAM COURTENAY **

SW of Nuneham Courtenay, 5m S of Oxford
Palladian villa, now much altered, with
Capability Brown grounds (P-R)

Have you come for enlightenment, I was asked at Nuneham. I had indeed, although not the enlightenment offered by the 'global retreat of the Brahma Kumaris World Spiritual University'. The walls are festooned with mandalas and diagrams of the Path to Knowledge. Carpets are deep and rooms are set aside for meditation. Eager students in tennis shoes and white-garmented teachers float silently through the building. The mansion of the Harcourts has, since the Second World War, been a college of education and a Rothmans International conference centre. Its new incarnation came as a shock, but the house is in good, and welcoming, hands.

The site was chosen in 1755 by the 1st Earl Harcourt of Stanton Harcourt as the spot for his new Palladian villa in an Arcadian landscape. The old riverside village was demolished and a new one built along the Oxford road, a mile to the east. This apparent outrage gave rise to Goldsmith's celebrated poem, 'The Deserted Village', deploring the removal of ancient settlements for aristocratic pleasure parks. 'Thus fares the land by luxury betrayed . . . The country blooms – a garden and a grave'.

The ground for the house ran down to the Thames, with the spires of Oxford visible in the distance. The architect was Stiff Leadbetter and a shortage of stone meant the old house at Stanton Harcourt (below) had to be demolished and its blocks floated down the Thames on barges. Nuneham was not intended as a great mansion. It embodied the new mid-Georgian fashion for the villa as the suitable form for a nobleman's country seat.

Nemesis for the removal of the village was at hand. The 1st Earl had not been long in his new home when, in 1777, he died when rescuing his dog from a well. His son was a rebellious follower of Rousseau, and remarked that he could wish only his worst enemy 'a title, a large acquaintance and a place in the country'. They were, he said, incitements to flattery and cheating. The young man disposed of all royal portraits in the house and prepared the tenantry for republican citizenship. Yet he was soon converted by the favour of George III and he and his wife became courtiers. Capability Brown arrived, the house was extended and the grounds 'improved'. Work continued with Henry Holland and later Sir Robert Smirke.

Despite heavy wings and extensions, Nuneham is still at heart a quiet Palladian villa. Especially dignified is the garden façade, with canted central bay and Venetian windows to take advantage of the view. Of the much-altered interiors, Brown's staircase with iron balusters survives, rising to an oval skylight.

On the first floor, the Octagon Room has Rococo plasterwork and a magnificent floral roundel installed by Holland. The drawing room and dining room retain their fireplaces, ceilings and Venetian window. The gilding in the former goes well with the Hindu decor. The dining room chimneypiece is by Athenian Stuart.

Horace Walpole thought the grounds at Nuneham the most beautiful in England. They are still well tended but lack their original panache and the vista to Oxford.

ROUSHAM PARK ***

Rousham, 4m N of Woodstock
Jacobean house enriched and landscaped by Kent (P)

Rousham was meant to be a rural Chiswick (London, W). But here there is no National Trust or English Heritage to discipline nature. The Augustan vista is mildly overgrown and the genius of the place has aged with dignity. The landscape is the work of William Kent. It still shows the Eyecatcher ruin, the Temple, the Venus Vale, the arched Praeneste, the Cascade and even the long-horned cattle. Everything suggests antiquity.

Rousham was built *c*1635 for the Dormer family, whose descendants still occupy it. The Dormers were staunch Royalists, 'as we still are,' says the lady of the house. The manor

suffered in the Civil War but the family fortunes recovered sufficiently for General Dormer in 1738 to commission William Kent to remodel the house and grounds. Horace Walpole called the result 'Kentissimo'.

The exterior is now 18th-century Gothic revival, retaining the Jacobean E-plan but marred by plate glass windows. The best feature of the entrance hall is its front door, surviving from the old house and with musket holes through which guns could be trained on attackers. The walls are lined with Dormer portraits by Lely, Johnson, Kneller and others.

The finest room at Rousham is Kent's eccentric Painted Parlour, fashioned from the former kitchens. It is as handsome as anything at Chiswick, but in miniature and thus habitable. The decoration is a *tour de force* of classical motifs. Vitruvian curves and scrolls tumble over every surface in wavelets. Brackets support bronze statues. The overmantel rises past griffins to erupt in a broken pediment. Overhead is Kent's ceiling, painted on canvas in a pattern that looks forward to the Diocletan designs of Robert Adam. The panelling has been painted olive green.

The Great Parlour is also by Kent but refashioned in 1764 by Thomas Roberts of Oxford, an admirable provincial stuccoist who also worked at Greys Court. To him we owe the Rococo picture frames, dripping with plaster swags and Ho-Ho birds. The room contains an outstanding full-length portrait of Elizabeth I. A range of rooms along the garden front was added in the 1860s. Its dining room contains pictures of Civil War Dormers and the music room has much family paraphernalia, including a model of an old galleon.

SHIPTON-UNDER-WYCHWOOD: SHAVEN CROWN *

6m S of Chipping Norton
Monastic guest house with Great Hall (H)

The name refers to the monks who built the old house for visitors in the 15th century. It became an Elizabethan hunting lodge, as did many former monastic hostels, before reverting to do service as an inn, now a small hotel. The only reference to hunting in its current literature is to 'antique-hunting'.

The main entrance arch has a square hood. The original hall survives to the left, with two strong gabled wings on either side projecting towards the road. They have stone-mullioned windows. The hall doubles as sitting room and hotel reception area and is still open to the roof, with complex wind-braces. Its window has Perpendicular tracery. Later stairs rise to what appears to be a minstrels' gallery with a fine battered fascia. The old parlour is now the restaurant.

The original courtyard survives to the rear, the ranges dating from the 16th and 17th centuries. The bar has a fire blazing in its ancient grate, as it must have done to welcome travellers for 500 years. The hotel entrance is marred by two gratuitous glass doors which should be removed.

STANTON HARCOURT MANOR **

Stanton Harcourt, 6m SW of Witney
Victorian house with medieval kitchen (P)

In 1755 the 1st Earl Harcourt decided to abandon his home at Stanton Harcourt and move down river to Nuneham outside Oxford (above). There he built himself a stately villa more in tune with the Palladian spirit of the age. He was so short of stone that the old house was demolished and loaded onto barges for shipping down the Thames. Not much was left behind, although the Harcourts at least did not commit the sacrilege of disposing of the ancestral acres themselves.

The manor's lineage is simple. It was given by Henry I's Queen Adela to a relative by marriage of Richard de Harcourt. The same family own it this day, in the name of Gascoigne. After two centuries of tenanting the property, the Gascoignes returned to Stanton in 1953, to occupy a Victorian conversion of the old gatehouse range, set in a fine garden. Two other old buildings also survive, the medieval kitchen and a private chapel beneath a residential tower of c1460.

The victorianized gatehouse range includes the dining room, hung with family portraits by Lely and Reynolds. In the library are works by Ruysdael, van der Welde and a superb Larkin of an open-bosomed lady. Across the lawn is the medieval tower. It is known as Pope's Tower from the poet's stay with Lord Harcourt in the summers of 1717 and 1718 when he completed his translation of the *Iliad*. The rooms over the chapel, including the domestic chaplain's lodging, have Jacobean or later panelling. We can understand why the Harcourts might have hankered after the spacious chambers of Nuneham.

The kitchen ranks with that of Glastonbury (Somerset) as a monument to medieval catering. Dating from the 14th century, it has a conical roof said to date from 1485. There are copious fireplaces and ovens against the wall. A fire was blazing on my last visit. There is no chimney, just a maze of louvres beneath a web of trusses, through which the smoke escapes as best it may. Of this kitchen, Pope wrote that 'the horror of it has made such an impression upon the country people, that they believe the witches keep their Sabbath here, and that once a year the Devil treats them with infernal venison, viz. a toasted tiger stuffed with tenpenny nails'.

STONOR ***

4m N of Henley
Recusant family home hidden in the Chilterns (P)

Stonor lies in a fold of the Chilterns, utterly on its own. The Stonors, Lords Camoys, were and are resolute Roman Catholics and the house might be a monastery of ascetics concealed from the world. On its walls hang pictures of saints and bishops where would normally be ancestors. The library has one of the finest collections of recusant literature in England.

Stonors have lived on this spot for eight and a half centuries, defying Reformation and

Tudor revivalism. Oxford, like Cambridg~~e~~
~~uni~~versity expansion of the 1970s and 1980s.
~~The~~ most recent, notably by Richard MacCor~~mac~~
~~at~~ John's. Colleges vary widely, and irritating~~ly~~

All Souls ✶✶   Keble ✶
Balliol ✶   Lincoln ✶
Brasenose ✶   Magdalen ✶✶✶✶
Christ Church ✶✶✶   Merton ✶✶✶
Corpus Christi ✶✶   New College ✶✶
Exeter ✶   Nuffield ✶
Hertford ✶   Oriel ✶✶
Jesus ✶   Pembroke ✶

ALL SOULS COLLEGE ✶✶

High Street
Medieval quad with set-piece by Hawksmoor

All Souls was founded in 1438 by the Archbishop of Canterbury, Henry Chichele, to
educate priests and lawyers and to pray for the
souls of all who fell in the French wars. It is
exclusively for 'fellows' engaged in their own
research or in public life, and has no undergraduates. Its buildings of 1441 along the
High are equally unchanged, unexciting but
medieval.

The entrance gatehouse faces the chapel on
the far side of the quad. Although heavily
restored by Sir Gilbert Scott, the great stone
reredos survives, only the carved statues in
the niches replacing those smashed by
Reformation iconoclasts.

The style of the college now transforms itself
from 15th to 18th century. The Great Quad at
All Souls was debated by the fellows, in true
Oxford style, for the best part of a century. The
burning question of Gothic or classical was
never resolved until Hawksmoor took the bull
by the horns. The result, commenced in 1715, is
Oxford's most picturesque setting. The quad
was described by critics as for lay fellows 'of
great fortune and high birth, and of little
morals and less learning'. Plans presented by

revolution. Mass has always been celebrated
in this place. Not until 1975 did catastrophe
threaten. The 6th Lord Camoys was so enraged by Labour's capital taxation that he
sold the house and its contents and departed.
Like the Bedingfelds of Oxburgh (Norfolk),
the family decided to buy it back. His son, the
present Lord Camoys, then commenced a
long campaign of restoration and refurnishing, assisted by other Stonors sending or
lending family heirlooms. The rescue has been
a total success.

The house is not grand. It is spread along
the contour of the valley, with flanking ranges
containing a 13th-century hall and solar. A new
hall was added in the 14th century, producing
an E-plan with Tudor forecourt two centuries
later. Since the family were impoverished
throughout the recusancy period, no rebuilding took place. Everything was adapted and
squeezed to fit the narrow valley site, with
the Chiltern hillside piling up behind. In the
18th century, the house received a redbrick
Georgian façade and Gothick frontispiece with
Elizabethan statues.

Almost all Stonor's interiors are newly
decorated and furnished with works acquired,
or re-acquired, by the present generation. Each
room thus has a character of its own, designed
by Lady Camoys in vivid colours. The principal rooms are along the main façade. The
dining room is hung with French wallpaper
of c1815, depicting Paris from the Seine. Lord
Camoys' adjacent study has Old Master drawings by Tiepolo and Carracci, and Venetian
globes of 1699. The staircase to the bedroom
floor is lined with a collection of silhouettes.

The first of the bedrooms has one of the
most extraordinary beds I have seen. It is in the
form of a shell floating on a sea of dolphins,
surrounded by chairs shaped like oysters. The
Walrus and the Carpenter seem about to dine.
The library commemorates recusancy down
the ages. It is filled with ancient missals, prayer
books and Bibles, its ledges peopled not with
classical worthies but with Baroque saints. A
small exhibition celebrates St Edmund Campion who took refuge here during the Reformation. The Long Gallery to the rear contains

three fine tapestries, one of them 17th-century
Flemish, and a collection of modern ceramics
from the Far East.

The family chapel is mostly a 1796 refit in
the fashionable Gothick also employed in
Catholic chapels at Mapledurham and Milton
(above). It was repainted in mauve and pink
by Osbert Lancaster and John Piper, with
ogival doors and Catholic sculpture donated
by Graham Greene.

STUDLEY PRIORY ✶

Horton-cum-Studley, 6m NE of Oxford
Medieval priory turned Tudor manor (H)

The façade of Studley Priory appears much as
it did in a print of 1640. The rambling medieval nunnery was acquired by John Croke at
the Dissolution and added to the Croke family
property at Chilton (Bucks). The house was
altered and extended in the 16th and 17th centuries but subsequently remained unchanged
until the family sold the estate in 1877. It was
used by the BBC during the Second World
War and has subsequently become a hotel.

The plan is medieval, with porch leading
to Great Hall and reception rooms beyond.
To the left is a chapel wing with sanctus bell,
added in the 17th century. At some point,
stone-mullioned windows of a uniform pattern were inserted. The two-storey porch is
prettily Renaissance, with fluted pilasters and a
gable enclosing a pediment. The Croke arms
are above the entrance with a date of 1587.

The hall had its ceiling raised and gothicized
by Sir Alexander Croke c1820, with family
heraldry inserted along the cornice and in the
stained glass. The present bar was the withdrawing room, with Victorian glass and
Jacobean panelling. To the rear is a winding
staircase rising the full height of the house,
with surviving Tudor balusters. A Winter Parlour has Elizabethan panelling, as do some
of the bedrooms. The rear of the house is
still delightfully antique and the view towards
Beckley with Otmoor beyond is a blessed
corner of peace in ever more suburban
Oxfordshire.

WESTON MANOR *

Weston-on-the-Green, 8m N of Oxford
Medieval manor within yew garden (H)

The 16th-century manor belonged to the Norreys, Earls of Berkshire, then the Berties, Earls of Abingdon, who held it until 1917. It then passed through the Greville family, enduring many tribulations before becoming a luxury hotel in 1983.

Weston was lucky to have a 'good' 19th-century, when the stone façade was restored in neo-Jacobean style. Its entrance hall was given a ceiling with vigorous bosses in the 1920s. Behind is the old Tudor courtyard. This has been left crumbling and atmospheric and

Oxford University: T

The City of Oxford contains the m pre-Georgian buildings in England. lived mostly in residential halls. T some monastic, some independent f Dissolution, were considered inviola religious foundations be exempt from is better bestowed than that which is maintenance our Realm shall be well

The earliest colleges, University, arrival of scholars from Paris in 1229. of Merton, which might be of a p date from 1304. Not until after the Bl collegiate endowment, culminating in of Wykeham (New), Henry Chiche (Magdalen). All later foundations too gatehouse, hall, chapel and chambers

The next burst of building took pl of well-heeled 'gentlemen commoner enter the Church. This meant providir and status of these new undergraduat Wren and others. As at Cambridge,

BALLIOL COLLEGE *

Broad Street
Butterfield and Waterhouse rebuilding of medieval foundation

Balliol claims to be the oldest scholarly community in Oxford, founded as a penance demanded of a 13th-century northerner, John de Balliol, for kidnapping a bishop. He was ordered to support 'sixteen poor scholars' at the then fledgling university at Oxford. British penal policy has gone downhill ever since. Balliol's widow, named Dervorguilla, founded the college in 1282, outside the city wall and beyond what is now the Broad.

The present buildings are of interest for their 19th-century rebuilding by two masters of the Gothic revival, William Butterfield and Alfred Waterhouse. They were commissioned by Balliol's celebrated Victorian Masters, Richard Jenkyns and Benjamin Jowett. Of Jowett, it was said (by him) that 'what I don't know isn't knowledge'. The Front Quad entrance and façade are by Waterhouse, in a tedious Gothic revival. Waterhouse was said to have based his entrance on a design by A. W. N. Pugin, rejected as excessively zealous. Pugin had intended the rooms to have prayer alcoves with religious texts on the walls. In the road opposite, Cranmer, Latymer and Ridley were burned at the stake during the Marian Counter-Reformation. (In my day a then down-market Randolph Hotel was offering steaks 'cooked Cranmer, Latymer or Ridley?')

Inside, Waterhouse's entrance clashes with Butterfield's chapel across the Front Quad. The chapel has Butterfield's characteristic polychrome-banded stonework. The building was so hated by the Edwardians that it was almost demolished in 1912. Next to it lies what remains of the medieval college, the old library of 1431.

The Garden Quad beyond is formed of a series of mostly Victorian buildings backing onto St Giles. In the middle is Waterhouse's hall, more successful than his Front Quad building. The style is medieval, with bold buttresses and steep-pitched roof. Its stern

gothicism was long the butt of high-living Trinity undergraduates next door, who would regularly festoon the roof with paint, obscene objects and, once, even a motor car. In the 1960s, the college Fellows upstaged them by commissioning the Oxford Architects Partnership to design Brutalist lodgings and a senior common room on either side of the hall. In their case, the offence is more permanent.

BRASENOSE COLLEGE *

Radcliffe Square
Tudor college with hybrid chapel

Brasenose was, like Queen's, a North Country college. It took its name from the old Brasenose Hall, which had a medieval knocker of a 'brazen nose'. The knocker now resides in the hall, having been retrieved from Stamford in Lincolnshire where it was taken by northern scholars in 1330, following their persecution by Oxford's southerners. The knocker was re-acquired in 1890 by buying the property to which it was attached. There are still Brasenose street names in Stamford.

The college is overshadowed by St Mary's Church, the Radcliffe Camera and the towers of All Souls. Its exterior presents itself to the square in the most delightful way. The college wall breaks step when it reaches the chapel window, where the crenellation is interrupted by a classical panel, a Gothic window surmount and a broken pediment. This mix of Gothic and classical motifs well reflects Oxford's architectural confusion in the 17th century – as with Hawksmoor's All Souls screen opposite.

The Old Quad was begun in 1509, with assertive neo-Tudor dormers added in the 17th century. The more intriguing part of the college lies to the south, the Chapel Quad with, buried on one side the medieval kitchens of the old Brasenose Hall. The chapel was begun under Cromwell and, like its exterior to the square, is a stylistic hybrid. Everywhere here

Henrician gothic: Brasenose gatehouse

one sees Gothic tracery and classical keystones and pilasters. The chapel has a conventional Oxford T-plan, but with an extraordinary roof, of hammerbeams supporting fan vaults, vividly painted in medieval colours, rising above a classical screen and organ loft. It is dated 1665, when Charles II came to Oxford to escape the plague.

To the south is New Quad, designed in 1887 by the Oxford revivalist T. G. Jackson in a neo-Jacobean style. A less conspicuous impact is made by the early Modernists, Powell & Moya, in their 1960 Platnauer Building, widely regarded as Oxford's best early post-war work. It now looks bleak in its tiny alley west of New Quad.

CHRIST CHURCH ***

St Aldate's Street
Tom Tower, Great Hall and Palladian quads

Christ Church is the grandest of the Oxford colleges. Wren's Tom Tower vies with Magadalen as symbol of Oxford University as a whole. Tom Quad is the biggest quad and Peckwater the most aristocratic. The hall staircase is the most regal and the art gallery the richest.

The college's founder was Cardinal Wolsey. The Augustinian priory of St Frideswide, dissolved in 1527, was reborn as Cardinal College, with 60 canons, 40 scholars, associated chaplains and servants. With the fall of Wolsey in 1529, Henry VIII retained the foundation as the base for his new Oxford Cathedral. The Latin for Christ Church, *aedes Christi*, gave it the nickname 'the House'.

Christ Church was staunchly Stuart. Charles I made it his Oxford headquarters, indeed his palace, during the Civil War and Tom Quad was his parade ground. Samuel Fell and his son John dominated the college under both Charleses, the latter expelling John Locke for absenteeism and William Penn for lack of orthodoxy. The college survived, recruiting well-born undergraduates and producing more prime ministers than any other institution. As late as the 1960s, rooms in its

Canterbury Quad were reserved for those with titles.

Any view of Christ Church starts with Tom Tower, gatehouse of Wolsey's college and like its bell and quad, named after him. Its outside wall to St Aldate's is confident and urban, the tower balanced by others on the north and south corners. This assertion of princely supremacy can, on a grey and foggy night, be reminiscent of the Kremlin.

By the time of his fall, Wolsey had built only three sides of Tom Quad. Even Tom Tower was not completed until the Restoration, when Wren designed its upper storey. He warned the Fellows that he would adhere to Gothic, 'to agree with the Founder's work' and to avoid an 'unhandsome medley', but the result 'will necessarily fall short of the beauty of the other way'. Wolsey's original turrets are thus given vertical shafts culminating in ogee caps. Like Hawksmoor's All Souls, Tom Tower appears to be an exercise is stylistic humour.

Tom Quad is clearly unfinished. It was meant to have a cloister, the ghost of the vault forming arches along the façades. Were it not for the Victorian additions of Fell Tower and Bell Tower, the space would seem rather featureless. The Mercury fountain in the middle is a copy of one by Giovanni da Bologna, on a base by Lutyens. Here loutish blue-bloods would soak college weaklings after dinner, to be fined money they could well afford by ever indulgent dons.

To the east of Tom Quad is the cathedral and cloister, a charming backwater that seems detached from college and city alike. On the south side is Wolsey's Great Hall approached by a majestic staircase popularly supposed to be medieval. It is not. The fan vault is of 1640, another Oxford archaism, and the staircase even later, by James Wyatt of 1805. The hall is the largest in Oxford and mostly original, with a hammerbeam roof but later panelling. Its pendants are emphatically Wolsey, as is much of the heraldry, left in place by an apparently tolerant Henry.

There remains Georgian and modern Christ Church. Peckwater Quad was designed in 1705 by the Dean, Henry Aldrich, round three symmetrical sides, beautifully proportioned and with central pediments. It was to house the new breed of Oxford commoners, said to be accustomed to such grand architecture in their own homes.

The fourth side was completed by another amateur, George Clarke of All Souls, to house the library. This is more in the Baroque tradition, its attached Corinthian columns rising directly from the ground, past boldly pedimented first floor windows to a heavy entablature. The library interior might be the ballroom of a Roman palazzo, with high classical balconies and a delightful Rococo ceiling, including a composition of musical instruments. By the 1960s the library exterior was an astonishing sight, crumbling so badly that chunks of masonry could be removed by hand. It had to be completely refaced.

To the left of the library is the aristocratic seclusion of Canterbury Quad, with a triumphal gate onto Merton Street. Behind is the new Christ Church art gallery by Powell & Moya in 1967, low, minimalist and refreshingly inconspicuous.

CORPUS CHRISTI **

Merton Street
Medieval quad with Georgian additions

The college is one of Oxford's smallest and most charming. It was founded at the end of the medieval era in 1517 by Henry VII's Bishop of Winchester, Richard Foxe. It soon became secular under the influence of Foxe's contemporary Bishop of Exeter, Hugh Oldham, who presciently asked, 'Shall we build houses and provide livelihoods for a company of bussing monks, whose end and fall we may ourselves live to see?' Despite its dedication to the late-medieval cult of transubstantiation, the college was a centre of Renaissance education. It taught Greek and its first President, John Claymond, had previously entertained Erasmus when President of Magadalen, and instituted the teaching of ancient Greek at the university.

The Front Quad on Merton Street was built on the site of five old halls. The President lived above the gatehouse, set off-centre next to the hall. The room has a 16th-century heraldic ceiling. The hall retains its hammerbeam roof with carved pendants, designed by Humphrey Coke, Henry VII's master carpenter. Its elaborate panelling, fireplace and William-and-Mary screen were installed by a wealthy President and college benefactor, Edward Turner, after 1700. In the centre of the quad is a pretty sundial with astronomical signs, bequeathed by Charles Turnbull in 1581. The foundation emblem, a pelican in her piety, crowns the obelisk.

The library is essentially Jacobean and, like many in Oxford, retains its early bookshelves. It still possesses 310 of the 371 medieval books catalogued in Elizabeth I's day. Corpus succeeded in hiding its plate during the Civil War, when such wealth was being confiscated by King Charles to pay his troops.

In addition to his work on the hall, Turner had the Oxford master mason, William Townesend, build a new cloister and Fellows' Building beyond the chapel. This charming backwater might be the courtyard of a Palladian house in Venice. The loggia faces a graceful three-storey building, whose outer façade looks out towards Christchurch Meadow.

A small building in the alley between Corpus and Christ Church culminates in the former President's Lodgings, by Michael Powers in 1957. It claims the title of first Modernist building in Oxford.

EXETER COLLEGE *

Turl Street
Jacobean college with Gothic chapel by Scott

Most colleges have some historical link to parts of Britain, now sadly eroded by political correctness. Exeter was for students from Devon and Cornwall, founded in 1314 by the Bishop of Exeter, Walter de Stapledon. The endowment was enhanced by another west countryman, Sir William Petre, in the 16th century.

Like most of the inner colleges based on medieval halls, Exeter rebuilt itself in the Stuart boom of the early 17th century. Only Palmer's Tower in a corner of the front quad survives of the medieval buildings. In 1618 rebuilding began with an entrance on the Turl, not completed until the end of the century. The hall has a magnificent Jacobean screen, the top part salvaged from the old chapel, and fine beams in its open roof.

Exeter's most celebrated building fills the north side of the quad and is unmissable. This is Sir Gilbert Scott's Chapel. The exterior is of banded stone with a lofty flèche turret. Based on the Sainte-Chapelle in Paris, it is a single vaulted chamber, immensely high, with delicate tierceron ribs and Decorated window tracery, Gothic truly 'reaching for Heaven'. A tapestry by Morris and Burne-Jones hangs in a side chapel. This is one of Oxford's best Victorian buildings and makes the surrounding Tudor-Gothic seem tame.

HERTFORD COLLEGE *

Catte Street
Jackson's stylistic mix-and-match, with Bridge of Sighs

The history of Hertford is typical of many lesser colleges. It is of inadequate endowment and inept leadership. After a false start in the 18th century, Hertford was refounded in 1874 on the site of Hart Hall by a member of the Baring banking family. The architect was the ubiquitous T. G. Jackson. Hertford is his last and most notable achievement, a display of eccentricity and humour.

Hertford is best known for the Venetian 'Bridge of Sighs' over New College Lane. By then Jackson had already composed the college entrance facing the Clarendon Building. He had taken two dignified Georgian façades left from Hart Hall and linked them with an entrance worthy of Vanbrugh, with a flourish of Venetian windows. The inside of this block,

Jacobean medievalism: Exeter Hall

facing what is called Old Buildings Quad, is adorned with an Oxford original, a spiral staircase borrowed from the French Renaissance Château de Blois. It is extraordinary.

Equally extraordinary is the Bridge of Sighs. This was not erected until 1914, to enable undergraduates to get from the old quad to Hertford's only bathrooms in the new building to the north. Here Jackson decided that the best answer to a 20th-century need lay with the 15th century. As Pevsner remarked, Jackson was an architect 'who knew no fear'. The whole composition is a most charming contribution to the story of English Picturesque, in this case in a style sometimes termed 'Anglo-Jackson'.

JESUS COLLEGE *

Turl Street
Jacobean college with decorative gables

The college was traditionally Welsh. Although founded under Elizabeth I by Hugh Price, it did not start building until 1617. It was Protestant but Anglican Church of Wales. It had no truck with the Oxford Movement. Half its members were Welsh well into the 20th century, with fellowships for Welsh speakers. In her satirical novel, *The Matter of Wales*, Jan Morris had a victorious Hitler appoint the Principal of Jesus King of Wales.

Jesus is a classic instance of Jacobean Oxford choosing 'any style provided it is Tudor-Gothic'. The corner block between Turl Street and Market Street dates from the 16th century but the remainder of the two main quads were built in the 17th century as and when funds sufficed. They have the familiar Oxford Tudor windows and decorative Dutch gables, crowding the skyline like Welsh dragons' teeth and lightened by exuberant flower boxes.

The hall has 17th-century panelling and a screen with more Welsh dragons. A keen eye can detect dragons even in the fine stucco work. One of the college's three portraits of Elizabeth I hangs over the high table. Jesus library is a delight, with its 17th-century bookcases intact.

KEBLE COLLEGE *

Parks Road
Butterfield's magnum opus with sumptuous
chapel

Is Keble lovely or is it not? For at least a century after its completion, Keble was seen as the
epitome of High-Church Victorianism and/or
muscular Christian evangelism. It was widely
detested as such. How fashion changes.

Keble was founded in 1868, two years after
the death of John Keble, founder of the Oxford
Movement. It was endowed from public
subscription, for poor students entering the
priesthood, the first new foundation at Oxford
since Wadham in the early 17th century.
The commission to design it went to William
Butterfield, architect of All Saint's, Margaret
Street in London and 'archbishop' of Oxford
Tractarianism. His first Oxford work was
the modest Balliol Chapel. At Keble, public
subscription was enhanced by money for
the chapel, library and hall from the Bristol
guano tycoon, William Gibbs (*see* Tyntesfield/
Somerset). Butterfield had money and to spare.

The college is unlike any other, spacious,
generous and as grand as Gothic could be. It
is formed of two asymmetrical quads, conventional only in having chapel, hall, library
and residential ranges. The rooms were off
corridors rather than staircases, cheaper and
considered more conducive to college life.
Keble undergraduates were assumed to be too
poor to need servants.

Butterfield seemed unmoved by Oxford's
traditional Tudor-Gothic or by its sandy limestone. He employed patterned polychrome
brick to lozenge-patterned walls below restless
gables and turrets. No façade is the same. At
Keble, the eye never rests.

Over all towers the chapel, much the biggest
in Oxford. It towers as does an abbey church
over its cloisters. The whole composition of
Keble was intended to point to its chapel, and
through it to God. Its height is given added

Hertford: 20th-century Renaissance

thrust by the quad outside having a sunken
lawn and by the nave window sills lying above
the quad roofline.

Keble Chapel is Italian Gothic. Its interior
height is emphasized by the elevation of the
windows above mural-covered walls and by a
stupendous high altar. In a side chapel hangs
Holman Hunt's *The Light of the World*. Hunt
was so furious at the college charging visitors –
the porter adding that '*The Light of the World*
cannot be seen on Sundays' – that he painted a
copy for St Paul's Cathedral in London.

The hall and library are as remarkable as the
chapel. Reached by a staircase worthy of an
Arthurian film, the two vast chambers are
wonders of Victorian design. High Gothic
windows light stencilled ceilings and dark
panelled walls. The exterior brick and stonework needs regular cleaning. Keble red-and-
white is exhilarating. Keble maroon-and-black
is grim.

LINCOLN COLLEGE *

Turl Street
Surviving medieval quad with Jacobean chapel

Early medieval Oxford was in the Diocese of
Lincoln. In 1427, a college was founded by
Richard Fleming, eager to counter the reform-
ing influence of the Lollards, Wyclif and others
to whom the Church seemed vulnerable.
Oxford was always a bastion of tradition. For
good measure, Fleming exhumed Wyclif's
body and burned it. He desired to protect the
Papacy against 'the swinish snouts who presumed to feed upon its precious pearls'. It is
ironic that Lincoln educated John Wesley, a
son of an orthodox Lincolnshire parson but
later scourge of the Anglican church.

Lincoln is a small college on a confined
site. The Front Quad retains the character of a
15th-century town house, with hall facing the
gatehouse. It is one of my favourite Oxford
quads, the Victorian refacing of the ranges
concealed by a mass of creeper and window
boxes, the latter regarded as the best in
Oxford. Old architecture makes its peace with
nature. The hall roof is original. Outside is a

copy of the Lincoln Imp, a carving on the roof of Lincoln cathedral.

The Jacobean period also saw a new chapel built (after 1608), still Gothic but with superb Renaissance woodwork of cedar, and a barrel vault with decorative motifs. The window glass is painted by Bernard van Linge's studio at its most artistic.

MAGDALEN COLLEGE ****

High Street
Medieval tower and cloister, Georgian range in deer park

The tower of Magdalen has defined the city and the University since the Middle Ages. The spread of quadrangles and cloisters between the High and the River Cherwell, backed by an ornamental deer park, epitomizes gracious academic living. Magdalen seems detached from the bustle of Oxford, like an aloof stately home.

The college was the last of the great medieval trio of foundations, after New College and All Souls. Its progenitor was William Waynflete, Bishop of Winchester and Lord Chancellor of England, one of those bishop-statesmen who flourished in pre-Reformation England. He founded his college in 1458 on the site of a hospital for travellers outside the east gate of the city. It was endowed with manors and suppressed priories. Waynflete also founded a grammar school as part of the college.

Magdalen was Oxford's last great project before the Reformation. Its architect was William Orchard, master of late Perpendicular. By 1481 work was sufficiently advanced to receive Edward IV. Erasmus stayed here twenty years later. With space at its disposal, the college never had to rebuild Orchard's work and, as a result, by the 1970s the stone was crumbling to dust. It had to be replaced in its entirety, leading sceptics to reclassify the college façade as *c*1980. The rebuilding, including replica gargoyles, was immaculate.

Magdalen's bell-tower dominates all, rising direct from the street in four stages and

culminating in a chamber of ten bells. From the roof, choristers welcome the dawn on May Day. Entrance to the college is through a tiny door in a gatehouse, as if this were still a medieval hospital. This part of the frontage dates from *c*1300.

In the front quad is a fragment of Waynflete's old grammar school, facing the magnificent west front of the chapel, with the Founder's Tower acting as ceremonial entrance to the cloister. This is a splendid space, recently repaved and floodlit, the bosses under the tower brilliantly recoloured. The chapel is T-shaped, refurnished in the early 19th century and now hung with the college's great treasure, a contemporary copy of Leonardo's *Last Supper* fresco in Milan.

Beyond lies the Great Quadrangle. Its cloisters do not project into the square but are built into the ground floor of the ranges, with hall, chapel and various towers rising on two sides. This is a supreme work of late-Gothic architecture, with a steep roof and bold battlements. The mythical beasts that 'support' the buttresses form a brilliant gallery of medieval carving.

The hall is original. Renaissance panels depicting Mary Magdalene flank the dais end. The college Fellows process into dinner through a side door across the leads of the cloister roof. To perform this feat on a dark autumn night, past windows flickering with candles, is to enjoy a rare reminder of ancient Oxford.

Beyond are the gardens and the Grove, in which sit the Georgian New Buildings. These were designed in 1733 and stretch over 27 bays, seeming to float through the trees on a ground floor loggia. Miles Jebb describes it happily as 'an innocent relic of the Age of Reason placed at a respectful distance from the central glories of the college'. Deer nose at ground floor windows while undergraduates lounge against the loggia walls.

After the dreadful Waynflete Building, erected next to Magdalen Bridge in the 1960s, the college redeemed itself thirty years later with a new lecture theatre and residential block to the north-west by Demetri Porphyrios. The style is part classical, part deferential neo-Tudor, Oxford architecture reinventing its old style with panache.

MERTON COLLEGE ***

Merton Street
Oxford's earliest buildings and first Renaissance quad

Merton can claim to be the oldest proper college in Oxford or Cambridge. It was pre-eminent from its foundation in 1274 until the arrival of Wykeham's New College over a century later. Walter de Merton rose to be Lord Chancellor. Eager for his many nephews to attend Oxford, he founded a college to house them. The college produced four Archbishops of Canterbury in the succeeding century. For seven centuries, the college bell was rung at 10.30 am every Friday, the time of Walter's accidental drowning in the Medway.

The old gatehouse on Merton Street gives onto a courtyard with the hall opposite. This was the first college building to be constructed for teaching and dining. Although totally rebuilt by Sir Gilbert Scott in the 1870s, it retains its medieval door, coated in swirling ironwork.

The chapel dates from 1290 and has fine Decorated tracery. It was intended to have a nave running across the site of the present Corpus Christi. This was not built, but in 1448 a tower was added, with majestic crossing arches. Its haunting bell sequence chiming the hours is based on Gregorian plainchant.

In 1304 came the two residential ranges attached to the rear of the chapel, now called Mob Quad. Its rooms were originally shared, unheated and had no window glazing. The quad was completed, with its library and treasury, by the 1370s. It has a steep Gothic roof and turret in the north-east corner. The library retains an original stall, with chains for books. Rooms next door are preserved as a memorial to the college's most celebrated Victorian, Max Beerbohm, author of *Zuleika Dobson*, a satire on the impact of women on the all-male University.

The Elizabethan Warden, Henry Savile, had been tutor to the Queen and was a progressive educationist. He founded professorships in mathematics and astronomy and planned Merton's Fellows' Quadrangle next to the hall. The entrance to this quad, the Fitzjames Gateway of 1500, was intended to house queens of England should they visit the university. It is a work of great nobility, with a lierne vault adorned with the signs of the zodiac and other late-Gothic carvings.

The new quad was built in 1610 with, on its far side, a bold Renaissance frontispiece in the form of a 'tower of the orders'. This is a somewhat clumsy precursor of the frontispieces that were later to adorn many college quadrangles, such as William Laud's at St John's. Savile is commemorated in a chapel memorial, attended by Renaissance heroes, Ptolemy, Euclid, Tacitus and others.

NEW COLLEGE ***

New College Lane
Medieval foundation, with quad, cloister and city wall

No part of Oxford retains the atmosphere of a medieval *quartier* as does Queen's Lane. High walls flank narrow alleys between old gardens. Over these walls loom stables, smallholdings, secret groves and even farm buildings. Opposite the entrance to New College is a medieval barn. The walls are black and unrestored. This was the defensive architecture of England during the Peasants' Revolt.

New College was founded and built in 1379 by William of Wykeham, son of a Wiltshire peasant and proof that birth was no bar to advancement in pre-Reformation England. As Bishop of Winchester and Chancellor of England, Wykeham sought merit in foundations at Winchester and Oxford, intended for poorer scholars. His 'new' college of seventy fellows housed more than all other Oxford colleges combined. The quad was four times the size of Merton's Mob Quad.

New College was intended as a communal entity in the manner of a monastic house. The area was spacious, land in this part of Oxford being cheap after the Black Death. The Warden's Barn for tithes was built, linked by a bridge (as today) over the lane. The college entrance is at the end of a narrow cul-de-sac beneath a small gatehouse, with statues of the founder and the Virgin Mary in niches over the door.

Inside, lodgings flanked three sides of the 14th-century Great Quad, with chapel and hall filling the fourth side. The quad today is altered from Wykeham's time only by the addition in 1670 of an extra storey, rather spoiling the proportion. The sashes and battlements give it a Gothick appearance.

New College chapel with its soaring antechapel fills the north-west angle of the quad with a forest of tracery, buttresses and pinnacles. The interior was heavily restored by Sir Gilbert Scott in 1877–81, including a new east reredos like that at All Souls. The choir misericords and medieval glass survive, plus other glass with designs by Reynolds in the west window. Near it stands Epstein's disturbing statue of Lazarus, *Ecce Homo* (1951). To the west of the chapel and in place of a nave is a secret cloister with bell tower. This is a lovely Oxford backwater, a haven little used except for college plays in summer.

The hall is reached by a spectacular staircase with stone lierne vault. The interior was re-roofed by Scott and the panelling is 16th century. Beyond the hall are fragments of the old city wall.

A separate passage leads from the Great Quad into the Garden Quad. This was created in the 1680s by a local architect, William Bird, as rooms for gentlemen-commoners. It is a mildly Baroque composition, the façades stepped outwards towards the garden like the backdrop to a rustic theatre. The elevations are full of teasing conceits. The three narrow windows on the inner range become three wide ones on the outer.

A viewing mount was erected in the gardens in 1594, later completed with steps and gazebo. It has now become a wilderness, though bold Fellows occasionally propose to restore its formality.

NUFFIELD COLLEGE *

New Road
Modern college in fake Cotswold style

Nuffield requires a sense of humour. The college was founded in 1937 by William Morris, Lord Nuffield, creator of the car empire that arose at Cowley east of the city (Nuffield, above). Eager to beautify the city's west approach, he bought the old canal basin near the station and proposed a graduate college dedicated to engineering and accountancy be built on the site.

The university old guard was horrified. Nuffield was duly persuaded by the Vice-Chancellor, A. D. Lindsay, to widen his vision to embrace the social sciences generally, but further argument now surrounded the design of the college.

The university selected as architect the little-known Austen Harrison, who had worked mostly in the Mediterranean. His original design was for a Levantine college with flat roofs, blank exteriors and no spire. Morris was a generous man but old-fashioned and precise in the object of his benefaction. He wanted a 'traditional design' and refused otherwise to give a penny.

Compromise was achieved only after the Second World War when Harrison conceded pitched roofs, tiles, gables and dormers, all in Cotswold stone. He even added a 'dreaming spire', which Morris insisted be the highest in Oxford. Two quads are linked by a flight of steps, with pools, almost puddles, in their centres, relics of Harrison's 'Mediterranean'. The hall lies at the head of the main axis, emphasized with a Tudor oriel window. The hall has concrete arches and a red roof.

The tower is at best ungainly. It is used to house the library and rises without modulation to a weak spire. Pevsner claimed that it had a touch of Lutyens and 'will, I prophesy, one day be loved'. I doubt it. Vegetation is its best hope, as for the rest of Nuffield. Cotswold revival should be an affectionate style, but is not here. A small chapel in the roof has abstract stained glass by John Piper and Patrick Reyntiens.

ORIEL COLLEGE **

Oriel Square
Jacobean rebuild of medieval foundation,
Wyatt library

The college is named after the oriel window that adorns its façade. It was founded in the early 14th century, in honour of Edward II, a king who might qualify as the first of Oriel's many lost causes. Once the staunchest defenders of the Stuart ascendancy, it was a cradle of Anglo-Catholicism in the 19th century and the last college to admit women, in 1984.

The college grew by acquiring a series of old residential halls between Merton Street and the High. In 1619 it did a clean sweep, rebuilding them all by 1642. The Royalist style employed the customary Oxford gables with Renaissance touches.

This is best exemplified by the spectacular composition of the hall and chapel, directly facing the entrance. Six large traceried windows fill the façade, culminating in two Tudor-style bay windows. The central porch, reached up a splendid sweep of steps, announces that Charles I was reigning at the time it was built. The whole is anachronistically surmounted by a classical gable. The symmetry of the range conceals a traditional medieval plan. The hall is off-centre behind the porch and has a screens passage. It has the last hammerbeam roof to be built in Oxford.

Oriel's Back Quad is a place of trees and creeper, setting for James Wyatt's fine library façade of 1789. Here Wyatt is in classical mode. He built it above a 'common room' in the space below, the first such room in Oxford. It was here that the Anglo-Catholic Oxford Movement took root, with John Henry Newman, John Keble, Edward Pusey and Richard Froude. Oriel also saw the early application of the tutorial system, one-to-one supervision of undergraduate work.

To the north lies St Mary's Quad, relic of St Mary's Hall added to the college in 1902. It is a picturesque jumble of buildings, dominated by Basil Champneys' 1908 Rhodes Building,

a throwback to the style of the Front Quad, complete with a Dutch Renaissance gatehouse on the High. This is no longer used.

PEMBROKE COLLEGE *

St Aldate's Street
Jacobean quad, Victorian hall, Kempe chapel

Pembroke is the unknown college. Tucked away behind St Aldate's church, it can seem little more than a supplicant outside the gates of Christ Church opposite. It was founded in 1624 with funds provided by an Oxfordshire maltster and a Shropshire clergyman. At Pembroke, named after the university chancellor of the day, these funds never seemed sufficient. The college's most distinctive alumnus was Dr Johnson, but he left after a year.

Pembroke has a pleasant Old Quad, of intimate and unadorned 17th-century ranges, refaced by the Victorians. Beyond, a passage leads the noble Chapel Quad. This is dominated by a Victorian Gothic hall of 1846 by John Hayward, lofty with a hammerbeam roof and reached up a long flight of steps. To the south, after a break for a garden, is the chapel. The classical exterior is by the Oxford Georgian builder, William Townesend. The interior was completely redecorated in 1884 by C. E. Kempe and is one of his most dazzling works, in High Renaissance style and with a glorious painted ceiling. It alone is worth visiting Pembroke to see.

THE QUEEN'S COLLEGE **

High Street
Georgian façade in French style, 17th-century library

Queen's is the centrepiece of the view up the High towards St Mary's. So stately is its appearance that few realize how alien is its form, that of a French *cour d'honneur*. Such is Oxford's diversity that it seems perfectly in place.

The first queen was Philippa, wife of Edward III, and succeeding queens consort have been *ex officio* patrons. The early college offered places for scholars from Cumberland specifically and from other northern counties, a tradition that lasted until stopped by political correctness at the end of the 20th century. The college was much given to medieval ceremony, with costumes for Fellows and choristers, a trumpet for dinner and a horn loving-cup. The original college was housed in a warren of medieval inns and halls at the junction of the High and Queen's Lane. At the end of the 17th century, a bequest from Sir Joseph Williamson enabled a complete rebuilding, assisted by Wren and enhanced by the later patronage of Queen Caroline, wife of George III. Her statue occupies the cupola on the High.

Queen's is the finest classical building in Oxford. The Front Quad, begun in 1709, was said to have been inspired by Hawksmoor but designed by the amateur Oxford architect, George Clarke of All Souls, and by the builder, William Townesend. The inspiration was allegedly the Palais de Luxembourg in Paris. The concept of an open screen to enclose a front courtyard is indeed Parisian, though one which Hawksmoor employed shortly afterwards in his new quad at All Souls. Despite its alien style and aloof façade, the screen and indeed the whole façade contrive to elevate the character of this superb street.

The Front Quad was completed by 1734. The central block is severely classical, with a portico and cupola echoing that of the loggia arcades beneath. The hall has a lofty classical interior with sweeping barrel vault and high windows. The chapel is likewise classical with plasterwork worthy of a City of London church. The ceiling roundel is by Sir James Thornhill, no less.

Townesend seems to have been left to complete the North Quad himself. Its east range conceals an earlier range by Wren, now visible only from Queen's Lane outside. Opposite is the magnificent library designed in 1692 by one of Oxford's many architectural dons, Dean Henry Aldrich of Christ Church's Peckwater Quad. The loggia below was once open, as at Wren's Trinity Library in Cambridge. Above runs a serene 11-bay façade worthy of an Austrian palace, its pediment surmounted by what looks like an imperial eagle.

The library interior is as much banqueting hall as library. High windows illuminate swirling Rococo plasterwork in the ceiling panels, by Thomas Roberts, an outstanding local craftsman responsible for the ceilings at Rousham. The bookcases are open and spacious, beautifully crafted, a contrast with the cramped stacks of their Jacobean precursors. They speak of the world of Wren, Newton and Locke, defying the introverted closets of the medieval schoolmen.

ST CATHERINE'S COLLEGE
*

Manor Road
Immaculate Modernist import from Scandinavia

As 20th-century Oxford architecture, St Catherine's is everything Nuffield is not. After Nuffield we need a pint of beer. After St Catherine's we need a sauna. Nuffield's patron sought consolation in the past, and failed to find it. St Catherine's was meant to evoke a socialist academic utopia. It was the creation of its first Master, Lord Bullock, yet it could hardly be farther removed from the personality of this down-to-earth, bangers-and-mash character. For some reason Bullock thought being modern meant Scandinavian.

St Catherine's Society had been formed in 1868 for poor students unable to afford the cost of college membership. It became a full college in 1962 and needed a proper building. Bullock went on a tour to find an architect appropriate for his vision. He decided on the Dane, Arne Jacobsen, 'from the moment I walked into [his] Munkegaards School' near Copenhagen. The plan is ruthlessly geometric. It pays no respect to the curve of the adjacent Cherwell River, or to any curve at all. The only curved thing is the bicycle shed which greets visitors at the entrance, and a fine bronze by Hepworth.

The most pertinent comment on St Catherine's is that nobody has ever imitated it. Usually photographed through a thick

Cherwell mist, its parallelograms disappear to infinity. Its harsh concrete and steel have not softened with age. The rooms are as hard inside as outside, divorced from the world behind sheets of water and glass. Jacobsen designed everything, even the spoons. It seems an offence to move so much as an armchair from its dominant right angle. This is truly the architect as dictator.

St Catherine's minimalist asceticism engendered much debate. The critic, Reyner Banham, called it the 'best motel in Oxford'. Pevsner, the college's most enthusiastic celebrant, remarked that if young people did not like the college 'that may be an argument against them rather than the college'. He felt it embodied architectural discipline against youthful 'self-permissiveness'. That says it all.

ST EDMUND HALL *

Queen's Lane
College in miniature with library in Norman church

This tiny, charming college must be inhabited by Hobbits. It was the last surviving non-collegiate academic hall in Oxford. Most were merged with colleges in the 19th century, St Edmund's joining with neighbouring Queen's. It finally won independent collegiate status in 1957, keeping hall in its title in deference to history. Its nickname is Teddy Hall.

The college is essentially one quad with modern insertions behind. An unobtrusive entrance to the street leads to a tiny picturesque courtyard with a disused well in the centre and a robinia tree. The hall is next to the entrance, the size of a modest dining room.

At the far side of the quad is the old library, an eccentric essay in Oxford Baroque, designed by a local mason in 1682. A quaint Ionic portico rises two storeys to a pediment containing a small bell. The columns appear to be an afterthought, given how they crowd out the windows. A lesser pediment over the door rests on piles of books. Beneath the library is a lobby to the equally small chapel, a charm-

ing 17th-century chamber with windows by Burne-Jones and a pretty Flemish triptych.

The rest of Front Quad is 20th-century reproduction Tudor. Through an arch to the north is a path across the churchyard of the former Norman church of St Peter-in-the-East, now the library. The whole group is a delicious backwater in the heart of Oxford.

Less happy are the new buildings which were crammed beyond the Front Quad in 1968, by the local firm of Kenneth Stevens. Walls are of stone and shuttered concrete. The upper storeys attempt to repeat the gables and chimneys of the Front Quad, flanking them with a lift tower in concrete.

ST JOHN'S COLLEGE **

St Giles
Canterbury Quad with Carolean frontispieces

Just when Oxford seems to dissolve into suburb up the wide thoroughfare of St Giles, St John's appears, spread comfortably along its right-hand flank.

The medieval Front Quad was mostly built by Archbishop Chichele in 1437, as a Cistercian college dedicated to St Bernard, whose statue guards the gatehouse. The college was unfinished at the Dissolution and was refounded by Thomas White during the Marian Counter-Reformation in 1555. A City merchant, White was Roman Catholic and required his college 'to strengthen the orthodox faith'. He dedicated it to St John as patron of tailors and endowed it with extensive land north of the city. This land has been the basis of the college's wealth.

On the gatehouse is a fine Eric Gill statue of St John the Baptist. The Front Quad embraces the hall, chapel and President's lodgings, all dating from White's refoundation. None is special, although the Buttery is said to be a survival of the old Cistercian buildings. The hall screen is by James Gibbs. William Townesend's massive hall fireplace generated so much

Overleaf: St John's Canterbury Quad

heat – I recall as an undergraduate at the college – that nobody could sit near it.

St John's glory is Canterbury Quad. White's Fellows were to study theology to counter Lutheran and Calvinist heresy and the college remained a bastion of the Stuart Counter-Reformation. William Laud was President from 1611 to 1621 and later Archbishop to Charles I. He built this quadrangle in 1631. His entertainment of the King here in 1636 was said to have cost as much as the quad itself. Laud adapted the old medieval library, but built new ranges to the east and west, crowning them with Renaissance frontispieces dedicated to the King and his queen, Henrietta Maria.

These frontispieces are among the jewels of Oxford. They address each other across the grass, man and wife in dignified conversation. The classical orders are simple, two tiers, one Doric the other Ionic, but the bases are elongated, adorned with cartouches and drapes. The niche statues are by the French sculptor, Le Sueur, also responsible for the equestrian statue of Charles I in London's Trafalgar Square.

The two ranges are set on classical loggias, but above them the Middle Ages survive in the form of rude battlements and grotesque corbel heads. The old religion needed the last architectural word.

The library is Elizabethan, L-shaped round the corner of the quad. It still has its ancient cases, shelves and seats, some looking out over the college's fine gardens. The North Quad contains the controversial 'beehives' by the Architects' Co-Partnership in 1958. These curious rooms were among the earliest Modernist buildings in Oxford, deliberately eschewing the prevailing Oxford stone. They have not worn well.

To the north of the old college is the Thomas White Quadrangle by Arups in 1975, its Brutalist concrete offset by white stone turrets containing staircases. Beyond is an excellent work of the 1990s, the Garden Quad by Richard MacCormac, Oxford's most successful variation on a quadrangle theme. Staircase pavilions, classical in form but not in detail, are set round a Piranesian well. This is brilliantly lit at night, and by day offers a Mediterranean play of light and darkness on its colonnades.

TRINITY COLLEGE **

Broad Street
'Wren' chapel and garden quad

Trinity is oddly unobtrusive. It was founded in 1555, the same year as St John's, on the site of an existing Benedictine hall called Durham College. Its founder was Sir Thomas Pope, Henry VIII's Treasurer, and linked to Magdalene College, Cambridge. Like Magdalene, it became fashionable among the lesser county aristocracy. During the Civil War it was captured by Colonel Ireton, himself of Trinity, surely the only man to have literally taken his old college by storm.

The college is best known for its gates on Broad Street, designed in 1737 and a more stylish face to the world than Oxford's usual wall of Cotswold stone. A range of quaint 17th-century cottages forms the actually entrance. They were saved from demolition in the 19th century by a letter from William Morris to the *Daily News*. Inside the front garden and partly masked by cedars and catalpas are two Victorian ranges of 1883, by T. G. Jackson in a laboured neo-Dutch style. Behind them is the modern Cumberbatch Quad, a terrible mess.

The true entrance to the college is beneath its chapel tower. The architect is unknown, although the ubiquitous Sir Christopher Wren is thought to have approved the design. Dating from 1691, it was the first Oxford chapel in the classical style (yet a quarter-century after Wren's Pembroke Chapel in Cambridge). Four arched windows with Corinthian pilasters are offset by a fine tower topped by statues of Geometry, Medicine, Astronomy and Theology. Inside is the finest Baroque reredos in Oxford. The swags are possibly by Grinling Gibbons, set in a wonderful array of woodwork and plasterwork.

Beyond lies Durham Quad, the east range dating from the old Durham College of c1417. To the left is the Jacobean hall of 1618, still with a medieval bay window, redecorated in the 18th century. The Garden Quad to the north completes the sequence. Two sides of this quad were by Wren in 1665, but his work was altered to conform to a Georgian wing added in 1802. Here again we see Oxford's genius for three-sided courtyards facing gardens or country.

The garden was originally a formal parterre culminating in more fine gates onto Park Road. This was destroyed by the Victorian craze for naturalism. It should be restored.

UNIVERSITY COLLEGE *

High Street
Uniformly Tudor Gothic quads, Shelley memorial

University College is an architectural curiosity. It was formed by William of Durham to support a dozen scholars in 1249. Its fortunes waxed and waned (mostly waned) until, like many colleges, it found the energy to redevelop its mixed bag of properties on the High in the early 17th century. Later John Radcliffe, physician to William III, endowed the completion of the work, adding University College to his benefactions to the Camera and the Infirmary.

Two quads form the core of the college, their outer walls backing onto the High. The Front Quad was begun in 1634, in the Anglo-Dutch style. Hall and chapel are back-to-back along the south side of the quad. After many vicissitudes, the hall saw its hammerbeam roof reinstated facsimile in 1904. The second quad of 1719, on Radcliffe's express wishes, imitated the style of the first. This hardly made for innovation, qualifying as Gothic revival revival. There is even fan-vaulting under the gatehouse. Radcliffe appears in a niche, with his doctor's emblems of rod and snake.

In the chapel is a memorial by Flaxman depicting the naturalist, Sir William Jones, taking notes from Red Indians. More extraordinary is the Shelley Memorial in its own mausoleum. This flamboyant undergraduate was expelled for atheism and indiscipline in 1811, yet is commemorated in a quasi-religious shrine. The memorial was designed by Basil Champneys in 1892. The sculpture by Onslow Ford is of a naked youth lying on a slab supported by the mourning Muse of Poetry. It is a surreal Oxford relic.

WADHAM COLLEGE *

Parks Road
Neo-medieval quad with Modernist additions

My first experience of Wadham was as a schoolboy applying for entrance. I was put in a freezing attic with a damp bed up a winding staircase. The building, which backed onto Blackwell Street, might well have been condemned as uninhabitable. Mercifully, it has since become one of the college's most harmonious new quads, an informal urban space behind the houses of the old street.

The college was not medieval. It was founded in the academically fertile reign of James I by the widow of a Somerset man, Nicholas Wadham. She never visited Oxford, but presided over its creation from her West Country home. Wadham was another Oxford patron to regard the medieval plan and the Tudor-Gothic style as the only one appropriate for a seat of academic learning. The college was built between 1610 and 1613, with nothing added until the late 20th century.

The Front Quad is of three storeys, each side symmetrical, with chapel and hall filling the far range. Between them is a frontispiece, a 'tower of the orders' as at Merton, with James I and the Wadhams filling the niches. The hall is original, with high hammerbeam roof and openwork pendants. At the time of its construction, there was even an open central hearth, not replaced until 1826. This was surely carrying medievalism to extremes. The smoke louvre in the roof survives.

Wadham shared that fate of many Oxford colleges, with new buildings of the 1970s and 80s partly redeemed by later work of the 1990s. The old gardens now contain a library in incongruous black glass and shuttered concrete by Gillespie, Kidd and Coia. A new quad has been formed next to it from a group of

1950s buildings. Overlooking them is a work by the best of Oxford's recent architects, Richard MacCormac. The Bowra Building comprises a series of staircases and oriel windows leading off an internal street. This is picturesquely aligned to the tower of New College. The materials are properly Oxonian, mostly stone, and each element of the design has its own personality, a doorway, step or vista.

WORCESTER COLLEGE **

Beaumont Street
Hawksmoor in a medieval setting, Burges chapel

Worcester is a college out on a limb. It sits at the end of Beaumont Street on the site of a former Benedictine foundation of 1283 called Gloucester College. The site was acquired by Sir Thomas White, founder of St John's, under Mary I and renamed Gloucester Hall. It languished for two centuries but was refounded in 1714 under the endowment of Sir Thomas Cookes, whose Worcestershire estates led to the change in name.

The new Worcester was an event in Oxford architectural circles. Many offered plans, but the assiduous Hawksmoor appears to have won, collaborating with the All Souls amateur, George Clarke. Their intention was for an H-shaped, classical building facing open country beyond. Money was short and only one range on the far side was completed, producing the picturesquely lop-sided Main Quad of today. A range of 15th-century buildings from the old Gloucester College was left standing, with a medieval yard behind them.

The main façade of Worcester towards Beaumont Street is the front of the H, containing the hall and chapel, both culminating in bold Venetian windows. From the quad, Hawksmoor's block is a serene composition with deep eaves, large windows and shadows in the loggia beneath. The hall was decorated by James Wyatt in the 1780s. His decoration of the chapel was swept aside by William Burges in 1864. The High Victorian Burges called Wyatt's work the 'vilest Renaissance of George III's time'. His replacement is astonishing, a riot of birds, animals, mosaics and wall paintings by Henry Holiday, Oxford's best Victorian interior.

The arches of the loggia are repeated blind on the residential north side of the quad. This range culminates in the Provost's Lodgings of 1773, a handsome Palladian house, designed by Henry Keene. Its garden front rises three storeys above a basement, with a fine double staircase down to the lawn. The stone is a golden Cotswold.

The old medieval range crouches on the south side of the quad, as if cowering before the impending demolition. It is not a complete range, like Merton's Mob Quad, but a row of distinct houses, known as *camerae*, each one for scholars sponsored by a different monastery and with the relevant monastic emblem above its door. Behind the range is the tiny Pump Quad, fashioned from two more *camerae*. Here one can see the old chimney flue of the medieval kitchen.

The south side of Worcester contains some of Oxford's worst modern buildings and one of its best. The latter is on the far side of the lake, another work by the ubiquitous Richard MacCormac, built in 1984. It is like a Frank Lloyd Wright set in a Japanese water garden, yet with an Oxford urbanity. No two rooms are the same.

Shropshire

Shropshire is big, wild country. Although it tails into the Midlands to the east and Cheshire to the north, it has areas as remote as any in England. Shrewsbury and Ludlow were guardians of the northern Marches against the Welsh. The Normans gave the land to the Montgomery and Mortimer clans, and the early architecture is similar to that of the northern Border country.

The great castle at Ludlow is still in good repair, surrounded by an exquisite town. Fortified manors of the 13th century survive at Acton Burnell and Stokesay. Elizabethan vernacular survives at Wilderhope, Jacobean at Benthall and Boscobel, where still stands an offspring of King Charles's oak. Many of these houses were strongly Catholic and Royalist, demonstrated in plaster-work motifs, priest's holes and an absence of 18th-century alteration.

Georgian Shropshire produced two masterpieces, Francis Smith's Mawley and the cold grandeur of Attingham. Hawkstone is an eclectic house of the period, in a glorious Picturesque landscape. William Chambers is represented diminuendo at Walcot and John Nash fortissimo in his Gothick interior at Longner. Shropshire mostly slept through the 19th century, but the Darby diaspora from Coalbrookdale contributed Norman Shaw's Adcote.

Acton Burnell *
Adcote **
Attingham ***
Benthall ***
Boscobel **
Clun:
   Trinity Hospital *
Detton **
Dudmaston **
Hawkstone ***

Ironbridge:
   Rosehill House **
Longner Hall ***
Loton **
Ludlow:
   Castle *
   Castle Lodge *
   Dinham House *
   Feathers Hotel *
Mawley ***

Moreton Corbet *
Morville Hall **
Rowton Castle *
Shipton **
Stokesay Castle ***
Upton Cressett **
Walcot Hall **
Wellington:
   Sunnycroft **
Wilderhope Manor **

ACTON BURNELL *

Acton Burnell, 7m NE of Church Stretton
Remains of 13th-century fortified manor (EH)

Robert Burnell was Bishop of Bath and Wells and Edward I's Lord Chancellor. A power in 13th-century England, he built the great palace at Wells and in 1284 was granted permission to crenellate the family home in Shropshire. A year earlier, King Edward had held a parliament on this spot, the first at which 'the Commons' were represented. The meeting was reputedly in the great barn, whose ruin lies a small distance from the castle. It surely merits some celebration.

The 'castle' is a fortified house in a charming grove of yews overlooking adjacent Acton Burnell Hall (now a college). The old house passed to the Dukes of Norfolk in the 16th century and was partly dismantled in the 17th. It was used as a picturesque folly for the Hall and a pyramid roof was added to one of the turrets to act as a dovecote.

Acton Burnell is a rare mansion of the 13th century, distinguished for keeping all its walls intact. It clearly developed as a residence rather than as a defensive castle, strange in a part of England by no means safe from attack (from the Welsh). It has no keep, gatehouse or moat, nor is it planned round a secure courtyard. The house is of three storeys with corner towers, in red sandstone. The interior comprised a large hall and solar to one side and three storeys with smaller rooms to the other. There were no fireplaces. The house must have seemed outdated, smoky and uncomfortable by the 16th century.

ADCOTE **

Little Ness, 7m NW of Shrewsbury
Norman Shaw neo-Tudor and Art Nouveau house (P-R)

There is something about stone walls, lofty turrets, battlements and long drives that appeals to the parents of teenage girls. Perhaps it is the hint of prison. In reality, Adcote is one of Richard Norman Shaw's most comfortable Tudor houses. Chimneys and gables rise over the trees of an extensive park. Close to, it displays a free-handed quirkiness that inspired the young Edwin Lutyens. It is indeed now a girls' school.

The house was built in 1879 for Rebecca Darby of Coalbrookdale. By then the great Shropshire ironworks was in decline and, like most English industrial families, members had diversified into art, antiques and land. The Darbys filled Adcote with their collection, later moving it to Dudmaston (below). Its place was taken by school impedimenta. Rebecca Darby's garden has been faithfully maintained.

The interior is the sort of neo-Tudor that no Tudor would recognize. The entrance hall leads upwards to the Great Hall past giant fireplaces and heavy detailing. The Great Hall is Adcote's centrepiece, a huge chamber with sweeping stone arches beneath a wooden roof. A tall bay window looks over the garden. There is a screen and a minstrels' gallery, in which are excellent Art Nouveau panels of tooled and gilded Spanish leather. Behind the gallery is what appears to be the exterior of a Tudor house. It is hard to believe that this was ever a living room.

The library has a plaster ceiling and de Morgan tiles round the fireplace. The inglenook in the former dining room is similarly decorated, with Pre-Raphaelite windows on either side. It is sad to see a house to which furniture and art were considered integral now denuded of them. Perhaps Dudmaston can one day surrender some of its loot.

ATTINGHAM PARK ***

4m E of Shrewsbury
Georgian mansion with classical interiors and pictures (NT)

Attingham is one of those pointlessly large houses built by English gentlemen in the 18th century, with more taste than soul. Noel Hill was great-grandson of Sir Rowland Hill of Hawkstone, Lord Mayor of London. Each generation of Hills veered between business talent and debauchery, the house always in the balance.

Noel Hill was an MP, cultivated and with a wealthy wife. He was given the lesser family seat of Tern Hall in 1768 and four years later began a new house directly in front of it, of a size commensurate with his political status. He called it Attingham by latinizing the name of the local village, Atcham. Later ennobled as Lord Berwick, he asked his Cambridge tutor for a motto and was sent some Terence: 'Let wealth be his who knows its use'. The message was wasted on his heirs.

Noel died at forty-three in 1789. His eldest son, Thomas, set off on a Grand Tour and spent his fortune on pictures. He inserted the present gallery, designed by John Nash, but after marriage to a seventeen-year-old courtesan and further extravagance he went bankrupt. A sale of the entire contents duly took place in 1827.

Thomas Berwick's brother now came to the rescue. He contrived to restock the house with objects acquired during an equally extravagant posting as a diplomat in Italy, but died soon afterwards. Yet another brother now succeeded to the title and estate, a parson with a speech impediment. Not to be outdone by his siblings, he 'swallowed more wine than any man in the county'. He was one of the few Berwicks to produce a son, whom he detested. That son, Richard Noel-Hill, saved Attingham. He cleared the estate of debt, invented a rifle, played the flute, repaired the house and founded the famous Attingham herd of Hereford cattle.

The house enjoyed a burst of social activity in the 1920s under the 8th Lord Berwick and his half-Italian wife, Teresa. An art-lover, she named their calves Picasso, Matisse and Gauguin. But that was the end of the Hills at Attingham. Negotiations between them and James Lees-Milne for the National Trust in 1937 are vividly recalled in his diary. They were conducted standing up 'in the ravishingly beautiful yet slightly distressed apartment'. Lady Berwick would admit only to the estate being 'embarrassed'.

The house was built for show rather than comfort. The architect was George Steuart, a follower of James Wyatt, and this is his only surviving country house. It is just two rooms deep, like a stage set to be seen across the park from the Shrewsbury road. The façade is uncomfortably tall, almost barracks-like, the portico columns painfully thin. The interior is in the French style, one side for Lord Berwick and the other for his wife.

The hall is classical with scagliola columns and pilasters, the walls with grisaille panels by an Irishman, Robert Fagan. Mercury, god of travellers, and Minerva, goddess of the hearth, look faintly surreal. The stone floor has recently been protected with a linen 'floor-cloth', more enjoyable than the customary black-and-white chequerboard. The 'female' side of the house starts with the drawing room, serenely classical in pale green and gold, its Italian furniture upholstered by the last Lady Berwick. Round the fireplace are three masterpieces by Angelica Kauffmann.

The Sultana Room is where ladies would take tea, with much red silk and a long banquette or *sultane* in an alcove. A musical box depicts a monkey conducting a harp, a charming piece. Beyond are an ante-room and a circular boudoir. The latter was decorated by Kauffmann on a theme of love, since the 2nd Lord Berwick had married against the family's wishes. The motifs are Adamish and of great delicacy.

Nash's picture gallery was designed in 1805. It has red walls and huge console tables with Sicilian jasper tops. The pictures have been assembled from those sold in 1827 and re-acquired later. They are hung in tiers after the custom of the time. None is of distinction, but some have endearing fake monograms of Leonardo, Guercino and Raphael.

The male wing is approached backwards, from intimacy to grandeur. Lord Berwick's Octagon and ante-room contain political pottery. Then comes the inner library, dark red with what remains of the Berwick book collection. The masculine dining room balances the feminine drawing room. It is deep maroon with white plasterwork, its Axminster carpet like the roof of a splendid tent.

Downstairs are the servants' quarters, silver room and kitchens, all spacious, spotless and rather frigid. The deer park was designed by Repton and carries the road over a classical bridge from which the distant façade is seen at its best.

BENTHALL HALL ***

Broseley, 3m NE of Much Wenlock
Elizabethan house by Ironbridge Gorge (NT)

Benthall was one of a chain of Royalist houses located round Shrewsbury during the Civil War. Their Jacobean character was preserved from alteration by recusant poverty. One Anfrid de Benetala lived here in 1100 and there have been Benetalas, now Benthalls, here ever since.

The Elizabethan William Benthall appears to have begun the present house. His descendants sold it in 1844 but returned as tenants and bought the property back in 1934, passing ownership to the National Trust in 1958 with continued occupation. The present Benthall is 29th in line. On such rocks are many English houses founded.

The house has no great park or noble setting. It is tucked onto a plateau on the west side of Ironbridge Gorge, sheltered from Telford New Town. To sit in its garden on a warm afternoon is to imagine that the industrial revolution, born in the vicinity, was a mere whim of history.

Benthall is Elizabethan with amendments. The façade is dated to the 1580s, with little of the Renaissance finery of Moreton Corbet (below), twenty miles away. Four central gables with two canted bay windows are balanced by a projecting solar wing and two large chimneys. The porch carries the marks of the quincunx or five holy wounds, believed to indicate Catholic occupancy and a coded welcome to priests. Hence the line in the folksong, 'Five for the symbols at your door'.

The downstairs rooms are unspectacular. The screens passage has gone and the fireplace in the hall is Jacobean, crowned with an overmantel of the 1630s. It celebrates the marriage at that time of a Benthall to a Cassy, represented by a leopard and a wyvern respectively. The refectory table is one of the few pieces of original furniture in the house.

The pride of Benthall is its staircase. This is of 1618, rising two storeys and bursting with Jacobean vigour. The strapwork balustrade depicts more leopards and wyverns and even a crowned lion, another Benthall device. The newel posts are monstrous things, possibly with Victorian additions.

The drawing room upstairs has a plasterwork ceiling rich with arabesques, animals and birds, a virtual menagerie. The overmantel again celebrates the Benthall and Cassy alliance, here depicted in rollicking Artisan Mannerism.

Directly above the porch is a priest's closet, like that at Moseley Old Hall (Staffs), here converted into an oratory. It appears to have a false floor for the hiding of religious vessels. This would have been a good vantage point from which to watch for the arrival of friend or foe when caution was a matter of life and death.

BOSCOBEL HOUSE **

5m N of Albrighton
Charles II's refuge after Worcester (EH)

The story of Charles II's flight after his defeat at Worcester in 1651 is an epic of English history. With Cromwell's army in pursuit, the twenty-one-year-old King's bid to evade capture was now desperate. With a small group of retainers, he rode north past Wolverhampton but the towns were hostile and search parties everywhere. His need of friendly quarters was acute.

He headed for the houses of the Royalist Cotton family at Boscobel and adjacent White Ladies. Accompanied by their servants, the Penderel brothers, the King made an abortive ride towards Wales. Two days later, he returned to Boscobel and spent a night in the safety of an oak tree in its grounds. The royal oak has been celebrated ever since.

After another two days, shorn and in

servant's clothes, the King left for Moseley (Staffs) and escaped to Bristol and France. The Penderels receive a pension in thanks to this day.

Boscobel house became a farm, but was acquired by Walter Evans in 1812 for its Royalist associations. He restored it in a picturesque Jacobean style, painting over the render to look like timbering. It was opened to the public and became a place of Victorian homage to the King. The 'royal' oak was torn to pieces by souvenir hunters but the present tree is believed to be its sapling. In 1954 the house passed to the government and was returned by English Heritage to its 19th-century state.

Boscobel is displayed as a farmyard, complete with geese. Along one side is a 16th-century range (now an exhibition), with the main house at right angles. This seems to have been a hunting lodge built by the Giffards of Chillington (Staffs). It is now a white-painted 19th-century re-creation of how Evans thought it might have appeared in 1851.

Carolean relic at Boscobel

A visit to the house is blighted by a guided tour, allegedly demanded by health-and-safety after a visitor twisted an ankle on a priest's hole. Entry is through the farmyard, now with a collection of implements, into what would have been the Tudor hall. The parlour is dark and welcoming, with portraits of both Charles and Cromwell, which is broadminded. Above the mantelpiece are scenes of Charles's escape. The 'board' table is said to be one at which Charles dined. A large German dresser portrays a pub crawl.

Beyond is a small oratory. This is a Victorian fiction illustrating the Catholic devotion of the Cotton family. Here, as elsewhere, the plaster walls have been grained to imitate Jacobean panelling. Upstairs, a single chamber has been divided into two, one as the Squire's Room with a supposed priest's hole, the other a furnished bedroom. It is near impossible to tell what is original and what a hagiographical reconstruction.

The attic is genuinely Jacobean, with the hiding place in which it is thought the King slept after his uncomfortable night in the tree. (All this Charles II later recounted to Samuel Pepys.) The wall has painted fragments. From here is a fine view down into the knot garden below.

CLUN: TRINITY HOSPITAL *

Craven Arms Road
Quadrangle of shepherds' almshouses (P-R)

This must be the most isolated of the properties belonging to Henry Howard, Jacobean Earl of Northampton. He founded almshouses in honour of his various manorial lordships. They were dedicated to the Holy Trinity at Greenwich in London and Castle Rising in Norfolk. Clun was founded in 1618 specifically for poor shepherds from the surrounding hills.

The inmates wore black serge capes and lived in large dormitories open to the roof. These ran along each side of a simple one-storey quadrangle. It was spartan accommodation for those well used to it. The south range has a more prominent façade, with Jacobean stepped gables to an upper storey. At one side is a refectory, with an original table and some odds and ends of furniture, including a lady's modesty bath. A chapel was added in 1837.

The place remained in this form until a dearth of candidates in 1920 forced a change of accommodation and the dormitories were converted into small flats for couples. Little else has changed. Weekly worship is still held in the chapel, although the nightly curfew has been relaxed.

A recent warden, Brian Corley, has built a pergola, a pond and a fountain. In summer, they are glorious with rose and honeysuckle. Art has also appeared, with a statue of two former inmates by Jemma Pearson. One was a local butcher; the other, 'Joe the Bear', was said to have wrestled a bear at Knighton fair.

DETTON HALL **

Neen Savage, 1m N of Cleobury Mortimer
Tudor fragment, much amended and restored (P-R)

We pass down a muddy lane far from the main road assuming incorrect directions. Round a bend through a farm suddenly rise three storeys of stone wall, timber and plaster. The tiled and gabled roofs are said to have twenty-five different planes. Nothing about Detton is straightforward, and not much is straight. But what was a derelict farmhouse riddled with damp, rot and deathwatch beetle is now a model of careful restoration.

Detton is a work of personal dedication by a tenant farmer, now owner, Eric Ratcliff and his wife, in residence since 1952. He is clearly a masterbuilder and craftsman. The house, he says, as the flour-dusted Mrs Ratcliff bakes pies for visitors, is 'a wife killer'. It is a view to which many 'house' wives would assent.

The house is believed to date in part from the 14th century. Owned by a family called Detton, it passed through such splendidly English names as Cresswell, Botfield and Moses Cadwallader. The main house dates from the late 16th century, apparently a much altered and extended cross-wing of a now vanished hall. The two main rooms are in what must have been a later Jacobean kitchen. The present sitting room has a huge fireplace with the present kitchen beyond. To the rear of the former is an old staircase, a solid oak structure with massive plain strapwork balustrade. Its walls include oversailed floors from an exterior wall of the old cross-wing.

From here on nothing is simple. The rooms of the cross-wing are those of a handsome house, not farm, panelled and plastered. One has a carved internal porch. Beams start out of odd corners. Chimneys descend into cavities. No sooner has one worked out that this must be an early roof or a later extension than something literally hits one on the head to suggest otherwise. The attic is a delight. A rear staircase rises into the sky to a random belvedere. Detton is a house of surprise and pleasure.

DUDMASTON **

Quatt, 4m SE of Bridgnorth
18th-century house in Picturesque landscape
(NT)

The heroine of Dudmaston is the widow of Sir Thomas Wolryche, who rebuilt it in 1695. She had to watch as their wastrel son squandered the family fortune, before mercifully drowning in the River Severn after a drinking bout in 1723. She and her brother then had to piece the estate back together again. They did so in some style. They continued the medieval tradition of hospitality at the hall 'board' well into the 18th century. Tenants, farmers, visitors or friends were welcome to the table at one o'clock each day. Anyone who came late had to eat with the servants, but no one was refused food.

The house was in continuous family ownership from the 12th century to the 20th. The Wolryches acquired the property in 1403 by marriage to a local family who had been granted the property by Henry I. The house passed to the Whitmores and Laings, both merging their names with Wolrych as part of the inheritance. The house endured difficult 19th and 20th centuries, each generation seeming to rescue it from the depredations of the last. But the post-war ownership of the Laboucheres, she descended from the Coalbrookdale Darbys, was happy. It brought the Darby art and porcelain from Adcote (above) to be added to the Laboucheres' own collection, all bequeathed to the National Trust in 1978.

Dudmaston occupies a steep slope over the valley of the Severn. The exterior is believed to have been an early work by the Smiths of Warwick but is of little distinction. The entrance is into a dark panelled hall with formal pilasters and a portrait of Jack the Fool, who was employed in the 18th-century house, as well as many Wolryches. Beyond is the Regency library created from two of the Smith rooms and fitted with bookcases modelled on

Rustic Jacobean charity at Clun

those at Weston (Staffs), earlier home of a Wolrych Whitmore wife. The room displays two fine Dutch flower paintings by Jan van Os and van Huysum. These sit alongside works by Augustus John and Modigliani.

The remainder of the rooms, other than those still occupied by the family, are devoted to pictures, rendering the house more a gallery than a residence. There are works by Nicholson, Moore, Hepworth and Chadwick, and modern Spanish paintings acquired by the Laboucheres during diplomatic service in Madrid.

Terraced lawns drop steeply to the Dingle and Big Pool. The National Trust is restoring the former to the Picturesque style of the late 18th century.

HAWKSTONE ***

4m E of Wem
Georgian seat of the Hill family in romantic park (P-R)

Hawkstone was the seat of the Hills of Shropshire since the Middle Ages. Most of the family ran to ruin in the 19th century (Attingham, above) and the house and its ornamental estate were divided, decayed, sold and resold. Yet both are now safe. Since 1926, the house has been home to the Roman Catholic Order of Redemptorists, readily accessible by appointment. I am told that surviving Hills return occasionally to wander through their ancestral halls. The estate is part golf course, part a Picturesque landscape open separate and at some distance from the house.

Hawkstone was a William-and-Mary mansion to which Palladian quadrants, wings and a saloon were added in the 1720s. A later Hill landscaped the remarkable crags and ravines which erupt from the rolling terrain immediately behind the house. Dr Johnson considered the place 'magnificent compared with the rank of its owner'.

The next Hill to extend the house, one of many Sir Rowlands, decided in 1826 to call in Lewis Wyatt who, like most architects, recommended a complete rebuilding. Instead,

in 1832, came more wings and an ostentatious ballroom and winter garden. Inevitably, this extravagance was to be the ruin of Hawkstone. Within two generations, the family was bankrupt and the house, parks and contents were sold.

The house today shimmers in red brick with creamy dressings, as new as a dolls' house. The main block is clearly original, with corner pavilions and stuccoed central section. The hall inside was subdivided by Wyatt. The saloon beyond is attributed to Henry Flitcroft in the 1740s and is a superb room, with a dark stucco and gold-leaf ceiling above ornamental picture surrounds. On the walls are portraits of William and Mary, hardly Redemptorist icons. Beyond is a small library donated by Bishop Moriarty, whose old books add greatly to the atmosphere of the house.

Wyatt's ballroom would be a shock in any demure English house, let alone a Catholic seminary. It is in the most florid Louis XIV style, with Hill heraldry picked out in heavy gilded Rococo plasterwork. This was clearly the path to bankruptcy. Beyond is Wyatt's delightful indoor conservatory or winter garden, fully restocked with plants.

It leads to a graceful double staircase curving up to a room that has seen many uses. It was a library, then a Methodist chapel (a Hill was a lay preacher), then a billiard room, then a Catholic chapel with a swimming pool below. It retains the chapel apse, with much alabaster, and an overmantel tapestry depicting the Cromwellians sacking Basing House in Hampshire. Although institutionalized, the house has been well conserved.

The park, grottoes and follies of Hawkstone were designed by the Hills as the embodiment of the English Picturesque, reacting against the more natural landscapes of Capability Brown and Repton. The champion of the Picturesque, Richard Payne Knight, lived near Hawkstone and attacked the 'dull, vapid, smooth and tranquil scene' of Brown's style. The park today has a separate entrance.

Hawkstone: the Rococo ballroom

IRONBRIDGE: ROSEHILL HOUSE **

Coalbrookdale, 3m S of Telford
Home of the iron-founders, re-created from 1850 (M)

Ironbridge was and still is a landscape of charcoal furnaces and hand forges, of inclined planes, tramways and canals. A museum of the early Industrial Revolution is spread along the sides of a gorge, reflecting industry before the age of mass production. The Quaker Darbys established their ironworks here at the start of the 18th century and ran Coalbrookdale into Victoria's reign, when South Wales and the North of England stole Shropshire's industrial crown.

Abraham Darby I built his house, Dale House, on the hillside overlooking the gorge in 1715 but he did not live long enough to occupy it. Next door, his clerk and son-in-law, Richard Ford, built Rosehill House in 1738. Four generations of the family lived in these houses, until smoke drove some of them into the surrounding countryside (*see* Adcote and Dudmaston).

The buildings are typical of the 'big house on the hill' that overlooked many early industrial settlements. Richard Darby's daughter, Rebecca, lived in Rosehill until her death in 1908. The house was tenanted until 1951, and became a hotel until passing to the Ironbridge Trust in 1975. (Dale House next door is still used for meetings by local Quakers and as a study centre.)

Dale and Rosehill from outside might be two great-aunts with different experiences of life. The former is in a severe redbrick, the latter more raffish, limewashed with rusticated quoins and a pedimented door. The main rooms of Rosehill have been restored to their state in 1850 and look conventionally prosperous. Downstairs is the dining room, the table laid with artificial food. Wine was served, despite this being a Quaker house. On the wall is a picture of a limekiln, to remind visitors of the source of this wealth.

Opposite is Darby's study, well displayed with stacks of papers, wills, indentures and

company books. The fireplaces are Coalbrookdale castings. The family was not shy in commissioning portraits of themselves, examples
hanging everywhere in the house. Upstairs,
conservation puts the visitor behind white
railings in each room – as if one were watching a different Derby. In the parlour, the ladies
talked and sewed, their faces protected from
the heat by movable fire screens. The bedroom
includes an iron bedstead and local Coalport
porcelain. To the rear is a museum of Quakerism in the area. Even at the height of their
prosperity, the two houses shared just four
servants.

LONGNER HALL ***

5m SE of Shrewsbury
Nash house with Gothick plasterwork in
Repton landscape (P-R)

Longner has been home to Burtons 'since time
out of mind'. The estate is next to the nobler
Attingham along the bank of the Severn. The
Hills of Attingham may have been grander but
they are long gone. The Burtons of Longner
are still here.

When Repton came to advise the family on
a new seat in 1803, he sought to dissuade them
from rebuilding their old house. He said that
people associated 'new money with gauche
houses'. He advised the Burtons to stick to the
antique and, presumably, let him spend the
money on landscape. Unpersuaded, the family
at the same time summoned John Nash, who
blithely offered to work 'in any style, Grecian,
Swiss, any kind of Gothic'. They chose the last.
Nash's Longner Hall is his most bravura work
in the Gothick manner.

Most of the old house was demolished
in 1803, leaving only the offices, stables and
service wing round what is now a delightful inner yard. Even this Nash gothicized,
with an entrance beneath a pretty clock-
tower. The interior is an exhibition of Gothick.
Most extraordinary is the staircase hall. A fan-
vaulted ceiling drips with giant pendants like
the interior of a limestone cave. The eye is
led up the staircase, which divides and returns

to a semi-circular landing. Here the fan vault
erupts into one of the most assured examples
of the style. The stair is lit by a large stained-
glass window, depicting Edward IV and two
Burtons in attendance. One, in civilian clothes,
was Edward Burton, who is said to have 'died
of joy' on hearing of the death of the Catholic
Queen Mary in 1558.

The library has more fan-vaulting, with
pendants of continued richness, the plaster
painted to look like wood. The bookcases, too,
are Gothick. A portrait on glass of Elizabeth I
(or of 'another Elizabethan woman') is built
into the overmantel. The room is pleasantly
crowded not just with books but also with
taxidermy of birds, rabbits and an albino pole-
cat. The dining room is almost entirely
Victorian, of 1868 and dark. The heraldic
window glass shows families that married into
the Burton line. In the yard is a game larder
dating from 1842.

LOTON PARK **

Alberbury, 9m W of Shrewsbury
Ancestral property of Leightons, private
theatre (P-R)

Everything about Loton is eccentric – house,
history and owner. The last, Sir Michael Leighton, declares his Saxon ancestry and proudly
points to three medieval Welsh princesses in
the family tree. They threw dice in Ludlow
Castle to divide up their inheritance.

The Leighton name is one of the oldest in
Shropshire, reaching back to Tihel de Lathune
in the early 12th century. By 1312 Leightons
were local MPs, and continued to be so in every
century until the 20th. The present Sir Michael
is understandably immersed in his genealogy,
reeling off a head-spinning list of manors,
quarterings and connections. To listen to him
is to sense the ancestors on the walls, the paintings of old houses, the crests and coats of arms
swirling out of the pages of *Debrett*.

The house at Loton sits beneath Breidden

Nash in Gothick mode at Longner

Hill, its park stretching down to the banks of the Severn. The whole of the valley to Oswestry might be its domain. The 17th-century façade of red brick and stone is flanked by stables to the left and a Victorian theatre wing to the right. In front is a large *cour d'honneur* in the shape of a horseshoe. The house is clearer from behind. The central seven bays are late 17th century, flanked by bays of 1720 by Smith of Warwick. This forms an impressive face to the valley below, and all the better for not looking over-restored.

The interiors of Loton are hard to date since much was clearly restored in the 18th and 19th centuries. The downstairs rooms have excellent panelling, mostly in pine, with bold fluted pilasters. Portraits of Leightons and their relatives hang heavy and splendid from the walls. In one room is a fine Rococo fireplace by the Shrewsbury designer, T. F. Pritchard.

A total contrast is the theatre wing added in 1873 by a Lady Leighton with a taste for the stage. This is a substantial hall, with dais at one end and gallery at the other. It has been decked with magnificent antlers, all from the estate, and the present baronet's collection of china birds of prey. The house is set in a magnificent park, including the ruins of Alberbury Castle.

LUDLOW CASTLE *

Castle Square
Mortimer stronghold, base of Marcher lords (M)

Ludlow was built as a Norman bastion in 1086 against the Welsh and became the seat of the great Mortimer clan, Earls of March. After the Wars of the Roses, the castle passed to the Crown and was headquarters of the powerful Council of the Marches. It is strongly sited above the confluence of the Teme and Corve rivers. Although the town was Royalist in the Civil War, the castle was surrendered and spared demolition. It was bought by the Earls of Powis in 1811, to protect it as a ruin, and the family maintain it to this day.

Ludlow Castle is shielded from the market place by the wall of its outer bailey, now a garden. The oval inner bailey lies beyond. It was once reached through a gate in the actual keep; this was blocked up in the 12th century when a small entrance was pushed through the wall to the right. The use of a keep as a gatehouse was unusual as it left defenders immediately vulnerable should an attacker break through the door. Here it contains the old Norman hall, long since divided. Below the keep lies a small inner yard with a well, forming the defensive heart of the castle.

The remainder of the inner bailey displays the later residential buildings of the Marcher lords. Against the far wall is a Great Hall with its solar at one end and Great Chamber and Tudor lodgings at the other. The Powis owners have been freer than English Heritage in putting some atmosphere back into these rooms, including reinserting floors.

I would go further. Ludlow is the carcass of a truly splendid medieval palace. With modern scholarship and craftsmanship, it could be rebuilt and refurnished. England is short of great medieval castle/palaces reinstated to something like their original form. This is due largely to conservation ideology. We still happily reinstate Tudor and later buildings. If we can recreate Hampton Court and Uppark, why not Ludlow?

Against the south wall of the inner bailey are the 16th-century judges' lodgings. These were built towards the end of Ludlow's career as an administrative capital and are now a gaunt gabled ruin. The view from the castle over the valley below is magnificent.

LUDLOW: CASTLE LODGE *

Castle Square
Former guild house, linenfold panelling (P)

The richest of medieval guilds in Ludlow were the Palmers. They had, supposedly, made the pilgrimage to Jerusalem and won the right to carry the 'palm' along the Via Dolorosa. They were the jet-set of their day and the most exclusive club in the town. A chapel in the town's church contains the magnificent Palmers' window.

The house ostentatiously set on the corner of Castle Square is believed to have been occupied, if not built, by the Palmers. It later fell on hard times, becoming a school, hotel and finally a candidate for demolition. The property was rescued by a private owner in 1990 and has been expertly restored. The chief feature of the house is the surviving Elizabethan panelling in almost all the rooms.

The ground floor appears to be 14th century, with timbered Tudor upper storeys. The entrance hall and parlour have linenfold and ornamental plaster ceilings. Overmantels display carved heads in relief. Upstairs, a Great Chamber looks out over the market place. Again, it has linenfold panelling and a carved frieze. The top floor has yet more timbering and panelling, including a painted main beam over the stairs and some revealed lath and plaster. The future ownership of this remarkable medieval house was in doubt at the time of writing.

LUDLOW: DINHAM HOUSE *

Dinham
Georgian town house with panelled interiors (P)

When I visited Dinham on a warm summer day the rooms were roasting hot. The building was partly a showroom for wood-burning stoves and staff were feeding a dozen grates as the sun blazed through the windows. The adjacent castle walls smiled down in amazement. The house is currently also in use as a furniture shop, craft centre and museum.

Dinham had been acquired by Richard Knight, a local ironmaster, as a town house for his ambitious son. The latter became a lawyer, married into the local gentry and extended the house in 1748. The Knights moved to Croft Castle (Herefs) and Dinham was their 'place in town'. By the end of the century they had sold it to the Earl of Powis, owner of the castle. During this period, in 1811, Lucien Bonaparte, brother of the emperor, was held here in open confinement.

The house was and is a large mansion of five bays with wings, much the largest in Ludlow. The interior appears to survive from an earlier plan. The door gives onto the side of the hall, with offices to the right and parlour to the rear, a pre-Georgian pattern. The extensions at either end provided generous dining and drawing rooms and a large kitchen.

Some of the rooms have been restored and refurnished, retaining the spacious feel of a comfortable provincial town house, a form now rare. The staircase is wide. Dinham still has its plaster ceilings and panelled rooms and a sweep of garden down towards the river.

LUDLOW: FEATHERS HOTEL *

Bull Ring
Richly carved façade of famous inn (H)

The Feathers has one of the most ostentatious half-timbered façades in England. The property was acquired by a Welsh lawyer named Rees Jones who had a successful practice at Ludlow's Council of the Marches, the High Court for the region. In 1619, he rebuilt the existing house in what must have seemed an old-fashioned style, timbered Midlands black-and-white.

The house was soon being rented to important visitors to the town. It became an inn in 1670, with a cockpit and stabling for 100 horses. It was scene of many celebrated Ludlow incidents, including allegedly the highest bribe (yet) of a single voter, in the 1839 election, of £300.

Apart from a 19th-century balcony, the front is a masterpiece of Jacobean design. First and second storeys are jettied over the street, their oriel windows heavily leaded and the walls with quatrefoil studding. The interior rooms remain original in their proportions. Their beams and plasterwork are darkened with age, smoke and the murky conversation of litigants and travellers. The principal room upstairs has a plasterwork ceiling, a swirling burst of roses, flowers and foliage. Welsh lawyers were, and still are, men of means.

MAWLEY HALL ***

1½m SE of Cleobury Mortimer
Smith of Warwick house, plasterwork and marquetry (P)

Running the length of the great staircase at Mawley is a handrail in the form of a wavy serpent. It typifies the inspiration of this sensational early Georgian interior. Nothing seems to have been too daring or too exotic for the itinerant Italian plasterers who decorated English houses in the reigns of the first two Georges. They seemed able to turn their hands to whatever classical motif was suggested to them by the architect or client.

In 1728, Francis Smith of Warwick was commissioned by Sir Edward Blount to create a stately mansion in a no less stately park. The resulting house passed through many vicissitudes until acquired in the 1960s by the Galliers-Pratt family, who live there today. Mawley is one of the few houses of this period in full family occupation, which is the more precious.

The entrance hall is all in white. Every inch seems to have been planned by Smith in tandem with his craftsmen, in this case probably Francesco Vassalli. We sense a single creative mind, from the starburst of trophies over the fireplace to the animal capitals on the screen columns and the near-Rococo ceilings. Each door frame is a temple doorway. This is not pattern-book classicism but free-thinking artists at work. What fun they must have had.

Between the dazzling entrance hall and the staircase hall are three rusticated arches. The staircase plasterwork is more restrained. The serpent handrail looks extraordinary. I have seen this motif elsewhere only in the church at Old Warden in Bedfordshire, but that was imported from the Continent. The upstairs screen on the landing echoes that below, with niches containing busts of Roman emperors. The formal promenade of the house appears to embrace the landing, but only one of the bedrooms is granted plasterwork worthy of the corridor outside and the halls beneath.

Four of the downstairs reception rooms are on display. The Oak Drawing Room is panelled, with heavy fluted pilasters and a chimneypiece in the style of Grinling Gibbons. The apsed dining room is by T. F. Pritchard in a version of the Adam style, a discreet interpolation later in the 18th century. A challenge to the hall is presented by the Marquetry Room. Every inch of its walls and floor is covered in wood *tarsia* of superb craftsmanship. Not a cornice or pilaster is without inlay. Oak, elm, yew, ebony, even ivory, are pressed into service. The doorway back into the hall is a masterpiece of carpentry, ranking among my great doors of England.

MORETON CORBET CASTLE *

Moreton Corbet, 7m NE of Shrewsbury
Romantic ruin of Elizabethan mansion (EH)

I came across Moreton Corbet from a distance over the meadows at sunset. I should have been on horseback, trotting towards lit windows, huge fires, tapestries and tankards of ale. What shone through its windows was only the sun but the sun had a magic effect, bringing to life the crumbling Renaissance frontispiece and ruined walls.

An old keep and medieval enclosure survive behind the façade of the house begun by Sir Andrew Corbet in 1579. Corbets had lived here since the 13th century. To Pevsner it was 'amongst the most impressive and consistent designs' of its date in the country. Yet no sooner was it completed than the Civil War devastated it. The castle changed hands four times during the fighting round Shrewsbury. By the 18th century the Corbets had moved out and by 1790 the house was stripped and partly demolished.

What stands today is picturesque. The main Elizabethan range has corner pavilions with classical ornament not simply attached to a medieval façade but integral to the design. Tuscan orders on the ground floor rise to Ionic ones above, crowned by ogival gables. It is sad that the Victorians were not here to restore it, before a later age demanded it be preserved in its present ruined state. To add insult to injury, the Ministry of Defence has left a mess of derelict aircraft hangars across the field from the main façade. If ever a shell needed the cloak of ivy and shrubbery, it is Moreton. The place is embarrassingly nude.

MORVILLE HALL **

2½m W of Bridgnorth
Elizabethan house behind Georgian façade (NT)

Morville Hall sits by the main Bridgnorth road beneath a steep backdrop of the Severn escarpment. The building is apparently a Palladian house with quadrants and wings, yet closer inspection reveals that this was tacked onto an earlier building. An Elizabethan mansion keeps bursting through, its staircase turrets still evident in the angles of the present façade.

The old house was built by a local MP, Roger Smyth, on the ruins of an old priory. His descendants, the Weavers, georgianized the exterior in 1748 but presumably ran out of money. Two side pavilions were added and rudimentary Doric pilasters were attached to the wings. A few stone balls were placed on walls. Further alterations were made and then removed, until we now have a bizarre version of 'failed' Palladian.

The interior is mostly from the Elizabethan house. The entrance hall runs to the left of the porch. The parlour, now dining room, is to the right. Morville has been a model of serendipitous rescue. It is owned by the National Trust, whose tenants, Dr and Mrs Douglas, answered an advertisement for the empty property, moved in and furnished it over the course of the 1990s. They have filled it with their own collection, acquiring pieces appropriate to the period of each room.

Two drawing rooms beyond the hall have fine views across the garden to the near hills. The most remarkable survival is the ceiling in a former grand bedroom, now the kitchen. Ornate Elizabethan plasterwork has recusant symbols similar to those found at neighbour-

ing Upton Cressett and Wilderhope, clearly by the same group of craftsmen. Morville has no grand staircase, access to the upper floors being by two Elizabethan spiral stairs. This intimacy continues in the upstairs bedrooms, furnished with robust Jacobean beds.

Mrs Douglas is reinstating the old garden single-handed, including a box parterre and rose garden. An early canal and possibly an old banqueting house have emerged from the grounds, which give gently onto the meadows. A small vineyard lurks behind a yew hedge.

ROWTON CASTLE *

Rowton, 8m W of Shrewsbury
Romantic victorianized castle on Welsh border (H)

What looks like a castle in vivid red sandstone sits behind a huge cedar tree on the main Welshpool to Shrewsbury road. At first sight, the place looks unreal and certainly not old. Yet Rowton was a castle destroyed by the Welsh in 1234 and often rebuilt. By 1482, the Lyster family were in residence, and stayed until 1884. The house was eventually sold to a blind school in 1941, and became a hotel in 1989.

The deeds to the house, and most of its history, were lost in the Second World War. The footings of the round tower and adjacent courtyard look medieval, even Norman. The brick and roof dormers to the rear are 17th century, but the house is essentially a creation of the 19th-century Picturesque movement. In 1824, the last Lyster married Lady Charlotte Ashley-Cooper, at which stage he rebuilt the house in Shropshire pink brick and stone. The castellation of the round and square towers also dates from this time.

The hotel contains a number of handsome Georgian function rooms. Some of these have been decorated by a Sheffield artist, Jaci Vianna, on a theme of monkeys. Those in the Georgian Room are anthropomorphic, those in the lounge Rococo. The cedar in front of the building is claimed to be the oldest and biggest in Europe.

Lady Charlotte's brother was the philanthropist Earl of Shaftesbury. This led to the many hostels for the homeless in London being named Rowton Houses.

SHIPTON HALL **

Shipton, 8m NE of Craven Arms
Corvedale manor with Rococo interiors (P)

Shipton Hall is a house of the sort that stitched together the landscape of England for 300 years. It is an Elizabethan manor of 1587, overlooking the glorious sweep of upper Corvedale, one of Shropshire's secret valleys. The building is of grey local stone that might have been hacked into shape by an estate mason on the spot. The façade has two wings flanking the old hall, but with a tower over an unusual sideways entrance. This is unlikely to have been a stair turret and was probably a belvedere, of the sort much in fashion at the time.

Shipton is of note for its decoration for the Mytton family by the Shrewsbury architect, T. F. Pritchard, in the 1760s. What is probably his hall comes as a shock after the Elizabethan domesticity of the exterior. Four grand pedimented doorways grace each corner of the room, with a Rococo foliage composition over the fireplace, portraying the double-headed eagle from the Mytton coat of arms. Pritchard also contributed the delicate mantelpiece in the sitting room.

Pritchard's best work at Shipton is his staircase. This has an intricate ceiling in the same Gothick style as he employed at Croft Castle (Herefs). Pritchard at Shipton seems to have been wholly eclectic. After classical hall and Gothick stair, his library overmantel is best described as neo-Mannerist. A flourish of pilasters culminates in a goddess with a basket of fruit for a headdress. Old bookcases are filled with a rare Georgian gentleman's library, still intact.

In one of the bedrooms, Queen Elizabeth is said, most definitely, to have slept when

Jacobean gatehouse at Stokesay

lost between Shrewsbury and Ludlow. She left a talisman as proof. In another room, a Mytton girl was locked away in 1792 for trying to elope with an unsuitable lover, engraving her remorse on the window pane. Unlike a similar victim of parental displeasure at Hellens (Herefs), she finally won her father's agreement to the match.

STOKESAY CASTLE ***

7m NW of Ludlow
Complete 13th-century fortified manor (EH)

On my drives to Wales as a boy, Stokesay marked what seemed the last outpost of English civilization. Behind lay the lanes and teashops of Ludlow. Ahead lay a Wales of tortuous roads and driving rain. Stokesay always seemed beset by weather, enveloped by storm clouds or picked out by sun above a valley mist. With its stone tower and half-timbered gatehouse, it embodies the watchful security of the fortified manor.

The house is a castle only in name. It was a manor owned after the Conquest by the Montgomerys. The first recorded tenants appear to have built a small keep with adjacent hall. In 1281, the property passed to a wool merchant named Lawrence, as a country house outside his base at Ludlow. He acquired a country estate of 200 acres and erected what for its day was an impressive manor, with crenellated tower and walls round an inner bailey. His family occupied Stokesay until 1598.

The house passed to the Cravens, who built the quaint gatehouse about 1620 and gave the 'castle' its only taste of military action. It was half-heartedly defended against a Parliamentary force in 1645 but ceded without a shot being fired. The curtain wall was duly demolished and by 1706 the enclave was in use as farm buildings. This doubtless saved it. The castle was 'talent spotted' by the redoubtable Mrs Stackhouse Acton in 1850 and sold to the Allcroft family in 1869, who stabilized the decay. It was eventually repaired under the aegis of the Society for the Preservation of Ancient Buildings and opened to the public in 1908.

What survives is an excellent example of a fortified manor in its original form and setting, comparable with Aydon (Northumbs). The breezy Jacobean gatehouse is a gem, eulogized by Alec Clifton-Taylor for its 'lozenges in the gable, diamonds on the first storey and pilasters at the doorway, the infill a lovely yellow ochre'. It leads into a modest courtyard surrounded by rebuilt curtain walls. None of this would have given much trouble to an attacker.

Ahead lies the hall, a remarkable survival lit by three large Gothic windows. Stairs lead to the solar block of private apartments. The roof is supported on curved crucks. There is no chimney but an open hearth on the floor, from which smoke would have risen to the rafters. Servants would have slept on the floor.

On either side of the hall are Lawrence's private chambers. To the right is the 13th-century tower with a suite of rooms, one of which contains an early fireplace. To the left is the solar and beyond it Lawrence's south tower of c1290. Unlike most 'castles', almost all we see was apparently built in one programme.

The solar was altered in the 17th century, the main room having rich oak panelling and a carved overmantel. The buildings are roofed and stand ready for refurnishing, when English Heritage can summon up the courage to defy its archaeologists. The guide suggests that the old Ludlow road once ran on the far west side of the castle. From there, the walls would have seemed almost symmetrical, an effect only noticeable from the meadow behind. Properly restored, both Ludlow and Stokesay castles could recreate a sense of medieval England more evocative than anywhere in England.

UPTON CRESSETT **

4m W of Bridgnorth
Romantic Tudor house in wooded landscape
(P-R)

Upton Cressett was, in 1970, an ancient deserted settlement buried in the wooded hills of the Marches. It was then that William and Biddy Cash made their way up a long lane west of the River Severn at Bridgnorth and found a semi-derelict gatehouse and a range of Tudor buildings. With a budget of '£100 per room' they set about restoration, now complete. The place is still isolated, almost two miles from the main road but, after thirty years, the house and outbuildings are back in habitation. A lost hamlet is found.

The manor was held by the Cressett family from the Conquest to the 20th century. The present hall is earlier than the rest of the complex. Apart from the gatehouse, the courtyard has gone, to be replaced by a medieval garden planted by Mrs Cash. The gatehouse is an Elizabethan gem, with oak spiral stairs, small corner turrets and a central gable. Its upper rooms have plasterwork that includes Catholic sacred hearts and other recusant symbols (also to be seen at Morville and Wilderhope).

The main house is not easy to read. Its hall is 14th century with an inserted upper storey concealing its roof timbers. The 16th century added parlours and side chambers, including a newel staircase and two gigantic chimneys with twisted stacks. These are the most prominent features of the exterior. The Tudors loved their chimneys. The panelling was mostly stolen when the house was empty and the Cashes have had to replace it. The rooms now contain Jacobean furniture and paintings appropriate to the house's Royalist past.

The kitchen fireplace is one of the largest I know, 13 ft across and more appropriate to the hall of a medieval palace. There is said to be a secret passage from the parlour to the distant chapel. Medieval numbers are still visible on the roof beams and braces of the bedroom above the hall.

WALCOT HALL **

3½m SE of Bishop's Castle
Chambers house for Clive of India (P-R)

What on earth possessed Clive of India, on returning from Madras, to select this wild spot as the place for a country villa? He already had a house in Berkeley Square and was building a palace at Claremont in Surrey. The answer is that every Englishman needs roots, especially if he means to go into politics. Shropshire was Clive's ancestral home. It was here that he established his political base after making his name and fortune in India, and in this county that he eventually became lord lieutenant. He bought land at Walcot and in 1763 commissioned Sir William Chambers to design him a house on the hill.

The house continued in Clive family ownership, later as Earls of Powis, until 1933. It was then sold, gutted and much altered. It is now occupied by the Parish family, although the stables and portions of the house are sublet.

Even today this seems outlandish England, between the Long Mynd and the Forest of Clun. The house is reached along a long drive over a causeway between two lakes. The building of blood-red brick sits on a plateau with, behind it, an arboretum continuing up the hillside. For Chambers, it is a modest work, an eleven-bay box with a small Doric portico. Alterations were introduced after 1933, including a higher pedimental feature to relieve the external monotony and an opening out of the warren of Georgian rooms round the entrance hall.

The interior now spreads out from a huge central staircase, 50 ft long, and a landing so spacious a Jeep could drive up and down it. Stairs and landing are lit by a large bow window that looks out onto a courtyard below, with a detached ballroom beyond. The window floods the house with light.

I know of few houses where the presence of the occupants is so pervasive. The rooms are of limited architectural interest. The drawing room has a fine plaster ceiling and the former music room has Chinese hand-painted wall-hangings, similar to those in Powis Castle over the border in Wales. This is overwhelmed by the clutter of the Parish family. They appear to be the most creative magpies. Bolts of material drape over the staircase. Papers, pictures, fabrics, toys, memorabilia are strewn hither and thither. The boot room is so full of boots, shoes, Wellingtons, coats and sticks that one would need a machete to find

anything. In such houses the visitor feels like a voyeur.

It is hugely enjoyable. Walcot is clearly a going concern. Chambers' ballroom, still used as such, is a surprise in so isolated a spot. Allegedly, it was built to house a giant Indian carpet, now at Powis. In the arboretum is reputedly the largest Douglas fir in England.

WELLINGTON: SUNNYCROFT **

200 Holyhead Road
Edwardian villa in suburb, needlework collection (NT)

Sunnycroft is for addicts. The house is a detached suburban villa of 1899, lived in by the same family until 1997 when it was bequeathed intact to the National Trust by Joan Lander. It is poorly signed through a housing estate from a car park. Timed tours take a mind-bending one hour and ten minutes, for what is a relatively unspectacular house. This is not recommended for children.

Yet the house is one of a fast disappearing genre. Sunnycroft belonged to a prosperous wine and spirit merchant at the turn of the 20th century. It was mostly built by the Slaneys and sold to a brother-in-law, John Lander, in 1912. He was a solicitor and his son ran a local engineering firm. They lived at Sunnycroft with bourgeois punctiliousness, though little grandeur. There were three live-in staff. The most imposing feature of the house is the avenue of Wellingtonias flanking the front drive, now grown to a preposterous height.

The exterior of Sunnycroft is redbrick and gabled of two storeys, with veranda and greenhouse. The grandest feature of the interior is a generous staircase, heavily Edwardian. The reception rooms almost qualify as pokey. We do not know the name of the architect, presumably a local speculative builder. The contents are drawn from catalogues and pattern books. Their charm lies in their completeness *in situ* and the regime of domestic decorum they reflect.

The entrance hall contains pictures of Lander ancestors. The billiard room is decorated with hunting and battle scenes. In the dining room is a minor delight, *The Card Players* by the Victorian artist, Alfred Gilbert. Joan Lander was the last family occupant of the house, unmarried and a noted teacher at the Royal School of Needlework. Her speciality was work in metal thread, much prized for ecclesiastical garments, and she was selected to work on Elizabeth II's coronation gown. The garden and conservatory are as Joan left them, an oasis in the adjacent sprawl of Telford New Town. The Lander Daimler is still in the garage.

WILDERHOPE MANOR **

6m E of Church Stretton
Unaltered Elizabethan manor house (NT-R)

A muscular Elizabethan house stands on Wenlock Edge gazing over Corvedale. It is unaltered outside and in. Although the house was begun *c*1584, such contemporaries as Hardwick Hall (Derbys) and Longleat (Wilts) are as stylistically distant as Palladio's Venice. These are the raw Marches. Houses had to be big and strong. The present occupants, youth hostellers, arrive in kind, tramping through the great door to warm themselves by a log fire.

The house was built by the Smallman family. A Royalist Major Smallman escaped from the house during the Civil War by leaping his horse off the side of Wenlock Edge and surviving by landing in a bush – the horse died. The house later passed to the Lutwyches, became a farm and then fell into dereliction, which preserved it from alteration. In 1935 the Cadbury Trust bought it as a Youth Hostel.

Wilderhope looks magnificent from the valley. Four large gabled wings dominate the front. Behind these is the Great Hall, with a three-storey porch. The Hall's bay window rises through three storeys. To one side is a parlour, to the other the kitchen wing. Wilderhope retains mullioned windows, chimneys and roofs unchanged from the time of its construction.

The interior has been stripped of original furnishings, yet the skeleton is of noble proportions. The Great Hall with its dominant window still has a longbow rack over the fireplace. Other rooms have their original ceilings, the best being in the parlour. The motifs are similar throughout, strips of ribbing containing the Smallman monogram, with Tudor roses and the 'heart of Jesus' emblem. Similar recusant plasterwork is seen at neighbouring Morville and Upton Cressett.

To the rear, the house has an original solid wood spiral staircase and impressive three-storey garderobe which youth hostellers are discouraged from using. The attic rooms have spectacular roof beams. The only thing spoiling this place is the crudest fire regulations I have ever seen. Ancient beams, floorboards and plasterwork are desecrated with fire-doors, glass partitions and garish signs. Wilderhope survived four previous centuries without such vandalism.

Somerset with Bristol

Somerset brings the great limestone scar of the Cotswolds down across the Mendips to the marshy Levels beyond Glastonbury. It goes on to embrace the Vale of Taunton and the Quantock Hills, producing combes of delightful intimacy. Here are found some of south-west England's most favoured houses. Manors from the 15th century to the early 17th conducted a Renaissance of their own in halls, chimneypieces, stained glass and plasterwork. Somerset is blessed with England's finest stone: creamy round Bath, a golden biscuit colour round Ham, and deep red across the Vale of Taunton.

The earliest domestic works were modest, to be seen in such ecclesiastical properties as Muchelney, Cleeve and Martock. They became more substantial as the 16th century progressed. Cothay, Lytes Cary, Clevedon and Gaulden are late-medieval houses, typical of many built by merchant owners rich on Tudor prosperity. In the reign of Elizabeth the houses became even grander, at Barrington and Montacute. Red Lodge in Bristol reflects the great wealth of that city in Elizabethan times.

The county is relatively weak in houses of the Restoration and Georgian eras, except for the spectacular City of Bath. The latter is unique in England in town houses open to the public, from the splendour of the Royal Crescent to the modest Herschel House. In the 19th century, Salvin restored the picturesque castle/house at Dunster, while vast sums were later lavished by the Gibbs family on their mansion of Tyntesfield outside Bristol. Somerset looked after its past. The Edwardian manorialists descended enthusiastically on Barrington, Dillington and, most sensitively, on lovely Cothay.

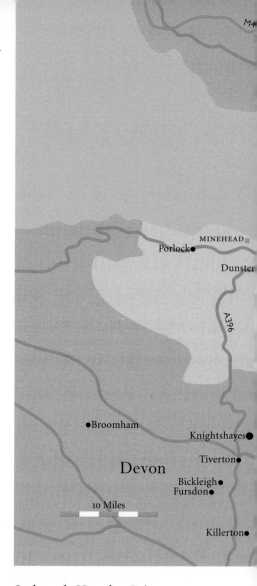

Bristol *see* page 683

Iron Acton
Gloucestershire
M5
M4
M32
Dyrham
A420
Clevedon   Tyntesfield
BRISTOL
A4
Corsham
Gatcombe Court
A370
Beckford's Tower   Great Chalfield
A38
BATH
Claverton
Holt
Westwood
A368   A37
A36
A39
Norton St Philip
Ston Easton
Beckington
Somerset
A371
A39   A37
A361
Wells
Longleat
Fairfield
Dodington
Wiltshire
eeve Abbey   Nether Stowey
Glastonbury
Stourhead
A39
A358   M5   A372
Gaulden Manor
A37   A371
Hestercombe
Lytes Cary
TAUNTON   Muchelney Abbey
A303
Cothay   M5
Sandford Orcas
Martock   Compton House
Barrington   Stoke-sub-Hamdon   Sherborne
Dillington   Montacute
A303   A30
Fiddleford
Cricket St Thomas
Dorset
Forde
Minterne
Higher Melcombe
HONITON   Mapperton

BARRINGTON COURT **

Barrington, 4m NE of Ilminster
Great Elizabethan house, now showroom
(NT)

Many owners destroy houses. Some houses destroy owners. Barrington is one, a monument to Elizabethan *folie de grandeur*. The Earl of Bridgwater spent ten years in the 1550s trying to complete Barrington, and failed. On his death, it is said that there was not even the 'means to buy fire or candles or to bury him'.

Modern house owners at the mercy of innovative architects may feel the same. The work was finished by a London merchant, William Clifton, and the house then passed through various hands to the Strode family, who added the 1674 stable block next door.

Nor was that the end of Barrington's travails. It suffered death by a dozen ownerships. By the end of the 19th century, it was little more than a barn, its fittings gone and its windows bricked up. Such a place naturally caught the attention of the eager founders of the National Trust and was bought before the days of caution, and the requirement that all acquisitions should be properly endowed. For years afterwards the cry of 'Remember Barrington' struck terror into the Trust's treasurers and committees.

Then, in 1920, a literal 'sugar-daddy' appeared. The sugar baron, Colonel Arthur Lyle, leased the house and completed its full restoration. Lyle reclothed its stripped rooms with his collection of historic woodwork. He sent boxes of soil to the elderly, almost blind Gertrude Jekyll, who was able to suggest what would grow by merely crumbling the soil in her fingers.

Lyle employed the architect J. E. Forbes to restore Barrington and also its old stables, now Strode House next door (below). He built estate houses in the Arts and Crafts style, producing a medievalist's garden city of cottages, farmhouses and stables spaciously planned and decorated with heraldic beasts. Barrington was occupied by Lyle's son until 1978 and in 1986 sublet by the third Lyle generation to Stuart Interiors as a design and antiques showroom. The house was saved, but not its atmosphere. The interior might be a National Trust supermarket. The furniture is admirable and everywhere, but every piece has its price attached.

The exterior is a Tudor E-plan in Ham stone, its south front crowned by a forest of gables, finials and twisted chimneys. The reverse front is almost as fine but its symmetry is broken by large chimney flues. Downstairs, the Great Hall and parlours are decorated with Lyle's imported collection of linenfold and lozenge panelling. The spiral oak stairs are modern but finely executed in the prevailing Jacobean style.

Upstairs, the Grand Chamber has a restored fireplace and overmantel with extensive surviving paintwork. This is not for sale. The four-poster goes for £18,000 and the Elizabethan table for £4,500. Strangest feature is the top floor, a gallery with corridors into the gables covering the entire roof area and completely empty apart from imported panelling. It is like a hotel with no guests. Surely more could be made of this great house.

BARRINGTON: STRODE HOUSE *

1920s Jacobean revival house, Jekyll garden
(NT)

J. E. Forbes converted the 1674 stables of Barrington Court as a residence for the Lyles while working on the house next door. In doing so he created a Jacobean revival house in its own right, one that must have seemed the more comfortable by far. While Barrington Court sits in lonely commercial splendour, Strode House is busy and friendly.

The redbrick building sits round an arched courtyard that once comprised the stables of the big house. A steep pitched roof is surmounted by neo-Jacobean chimneys. Inside, the courtyard space is well handled, the roof sweeping down past large dormers in the Lutyens style. The interior has an Arts and Crafts staircase which appears to rise in waves rather than steps. The building now contains a National Trust shop but the old morning room with rich dark panelling survives as a dining room. It was imported from a house in the City of London in the early 20th century and is of the finest quality. The carving of the cornice and doorcases is exceptional late 17th-century work.

Outside are classic Jekyll gardens, semi-formal outdoor 'rooms'. The White Garden is said to be a precursor of the one at Sissinghurst. A faun dances in ecstasy against a backdrop of an old farm wall with oval windows.

BATH: 1 ROYAL CRESCENT **

Bath
Restoration of grand Bath town house (M)

The Royal Crescent is one of the finest sweeps of town architecture in Europe. It forms the climax to a sequence of 18th-century streets,

Below stairs in Bath's Royal Crescent

lanes and vistas rising up the hillside from the medieval city core. Bath was the product of the most frivolous commercial development, thrown up in a hurry to meet an obsession of the Georgian leisured classes for quack remedies. It was the Marbella of its day. Fashion proved customarily fickle and within half a century Bath's heyday had passed. By the 1830s, sea bathing at Brighton was dominating the hypochondria market.

The city was promoted by four men of rare enterprise. Richard Beau Nash became the town's Master of Ceremonies in 1705 and for forty years enforced rules by which new money could commune with old. Ralph Allen was the businessman who financed the building of terrace upon stately terrace with material from his local stone quarries, watching it all from his palace at Prior Park (below). His architects were the two John Woods, father and son. The marriage of these talents was astonishing. As Bath's historian David Gadd puts it, 'here familiarity breeds only delight'.

The thirty houses of the Royal Crescent are articulated by a continuous row of 114 Ionic columns. The elder John Wood visualized it in the 1750s and the younger designed and executed it from 1767. No. 1 was the show house and the first to be built. Tenants at £140 per annum arrived the following year, soon to include the Duke of York. When Bath's decline set in, No. 1 became a girls' school in the 1840s and went on to suffer the general decay of the early 20th century. Not until 1968 was it acquired by a benefactor and given to the Bath Preservation Trust, which now runs it.

The house exterior is old-fashioned for its period, with no trace of the surface decoration then being used by the Adam brothers in London. A simple five-bay façade has a strong cornice and balustrade, designed to show the world that this was the best address in town. At the time it would have looked out over fields and grazing cattle.

The interior is simple in plan, intended for temporary rent not extended residence. Despite the Bath diktat that gentlemen should not entertain in rented property but attend the Assembly Rooms, this house was clearly built for entertainment. It has a dining room and study or smoking room on the ground floor, and a withdrawing room for ladies and a principal bedroom on the first floor. Bedrooms for servants and others are upstairs, kitchens and services are in the basement.

Each room has been furnished in contemporary style. The paintings throughout are of the period and admirably chosen. The dining room is laid for dessert, with pineapples and port. The study has contemporary copies of *The Times*, gambling chips and clay pipes on the card table. The upstairs drawing room is laid for tea and biscuits. Its contents include two lovely Chelsea candlesticks and a William Hoare painting of *A Market Woman Asleep at her Fruit Stall*. The principal bedroom was as much for morning *levée* as for sleeping. On the dressing table is a holder for face patches.

The most memorable room at No. 1 is the kitchen. Despite its pristine state, it is full of incident. Every inch is covered in Georgian cookery paraphernalia, including wax food. The only thing missing is a real dog being chased round the spit treadmill by a live coal – hence the phrase 'dog tired'. On the table is a lengthy account of such cruelty to animals. There is also a candle that can be 'burned at both ends'.

BATH: 16 ROYAL CRESCENT *

Bath
Renaissance of largest Crescent town house
(H)

At No. 16 Royal Crescent, Bath's elegance can be lived as well as seen, albeit at a price. In 1997, the central house of the Crescent was acquired by the Cliveden Hotel group and incorporated with No. 15 next door. The house was singled out by John Wood only to the extent of pairing its columns.

The result is a *tour de force* of historic building restoration. From the front, the hotel is unadvertised. Access requires braving a courteous but awesome doorman and at least the price of a drink or cup of tea. The bedrooms are not accessible, except by glimpses from outside. They are sumptuously 'themed' to reflect famous occupants. The entrance hall and staircase have black-and-white tiles and the downstairs sitting room is beautifully restored, with a Gainsborough Dupont of George III.

The rear gardens, bought from neighbouring houses and thus more extensive than the frontage, are a surprise. The rear walls of the Crescent houses are of scruffy undressed stone, yet the façades of the old coach houses at the bottom of the gardens form a splendid Palladian group, designed to be seen from the rear windows of the Crescent. They are virtually a stage set – the Villa, the Pavilion, the Dower House and the Bath House – used variously as tea-rooms and gyms. This is Bath as Beverley Hills. Beau Nash would have cheered.

BATH: CROWE HALL *

Widcombe Hill
Neo-Georgian mansion in ancient garden
(P-R)

When Crowe Hall was gutted by fire in 1926, all Bath is said to have come to watch. Only the portico and hall were left standing, with two flanking rooms. To add to the excitement, the decapitated body of the cook was found among the ashes.

The pleasant villa sits amid an enjoyable garden across the combe from Prior Park. It dates from the 1770s and was owned by a family of bankers, the Tugwells, throughout the 19th century. They added bow windows and a baronial hall, rebuilding the interior after the 1926 fire. When the house was acquired by Sir Sydney Barratt, father of the present owner, in 1961, he ripped out anything Victorian that remained. He had an aversion to the period and the style, asserting that 'art stopped short on the death of King William IV in 1837'. Baronial fireplaces went to Texas and the panelling anywhere. The interior was recreated in its original 18th-century form, with furniture and pictures to match.

When asked if the house is Georgian, the present owner replies, 'Yes, but the George is George V.' The result today is a stately Bath residence with the furnishings and pictures typical of English genteel taste in the second half of the 20th century. Nothing is spectacular, all is decorous

The gardens cover ten acres of preciously preserved combe hillside. They begin above the house with an arboretum and meadow, sweeping round to the Hercules Garden. Here a mosaic under the pond has wisely replaced a statue stolen from above it.

BATH: HERSCHEL HOUSE **

19 New King Street
Terrace home of great astronomer (M)

William Herschel emigrated to Bath from Hanover in 1766 with his eighteen-year-old sister, Caroline. They sought work as musicians in the newly fashionable town. He became organist at the Octagon Chapel, earning money so as to pursue his other enthusiasm, astronomy. The two pursuits were in constant conflict, with William rushing home from conducting a concert in order to scan the heavens with his new lenses. Caroline, whose devotion to her brother was absolute, would read him novels as he worked and place food in his mouth so as not to slow his movement. She later became an astronomer in her own right.

The Herschels moved to New King Street in 1780 but stayed there only two years. He was offered a stipend (and later a knighthood) by George III. They were able to take a bigger house near Slough, where William made ever bigger telescopes. But it was in Bath in 1781 that he discovered the planet Uranus and in the basement that he manufactured his early lenses. The house today is valuable less for its astronomy than as an example of how lesser mortals lived in Georgian Bath.

The house could hardly be simpler. On the ground floor is a reception room and dining room, the latter with a Rowlandson drawing of an astronomer. The first floor comprises a drawing room and music room, filled with musical instruments of the sort that the Herschels would have played. There are also displays of early scientific instruments. In the basement is the kitchen, still with its old stove, and behind it in place of a pantry is the work-shop. Here are the furnace, bellows and lathe where William ground his lenses and turned his telescopes.

The garden has been replanted as in the 18th century, with cypresses, herb garden and a quince orchard. It was from a platform here that Herschel noted Uranus. Never can the contrast of ancient and modern science be so vivid as in the field of astronomy. This is Bath's forerunner of a NASA space station.

BATH: PRIOR PARK *

Ralph Allen Drive
Landscaped setting for Allen's mansion (NT-G)

Prior Park was 'a noble seat which sees all Bath and which was built for all Bath to see'. It was designed by John Wood senior as a country seat for the Cornish entrepreneur and philan-thropist, Ralph Allen. The house dominates the hill south of the city, where Allen also had a town house. It sits at the top of the steep defile of Combe Down running down to the River Avon. Allen wished to keep an eye on the booming spa opposite.

Allen began the house in 1734 in part as an advertisement for his Bath stone. He had just failed to win the contract for the Greenwich Hospital, which had gone to Portland, and was determined to recover from the loss. He was indefatigable. Allen started the first postal system so that those taking the waters could keep in touch with home. He pioneered the Avon Canal and built tracks to transport the stone that he loved and wanted the world to use.

Wood's mansion was, to Pevsner, 'in the Grand Manner, the most ambitious and the most complete re-creation of Palladio's villas on English soil'. Yet no dynasty was founded

to maintain it. The house became a Catholic school in the 19th century and saw extensive building at each end of its curved colonnade. The west end is dominated by J. J. Scoles's 1844 chapel, built in a less relaxed classical style.

The school is private except for open days and the interior is of little interest, having been often gutted by fire. The façade can be appreciated and the grounds are in the care of the National Trust, with magnificent views over the city. They are being restored to their original form which was by Allen's friend, Alexander Pope. Here he fulfilled his maxim of landscape design, 'let Nature never be forgot . . . consult the Genius of the Place'. Yet Pope's contribution, largely the Wilderness immedi-ately beneath the entrance, was formal and contrived. It is the marriage of his work and that of Capability Brown in the 1760s that makes Prior Park so remarkable.

The walk runs anti-clockwise round the park, starting with Pope's Wilderness and Sham Bridge, then crossing the central vista beneath the school. The view both up and down the combe is spectacular. Up lies the house against the sky, set above flights of steps adorned with twisted urns. Down lies Capa-bility Brown's park. It is not so much a sweep as a swoop of green, cascading between thick groves of ornamental trees to two lakes at the bottom.

Crossing one of these lakes is the Palladian Bridge, copied by Richard Jones from Pal-ladio's bridge at Bassano. It is one of three such copies in Britain, the others being at Wilton (Wilts) and Stowe (Bucks), each a beautiful example of landscape architecture. The bridge shimmers white above a spring mist or radiates gold on a summer evening.

BECKFORD'S TOWER *

Lansdown Road, 2m NW of Bath
Romantic's folly with belvedere outside Bath (M)

William Beckford, Regency antiquarian, col-lector and romantic, was obsessed with towers. On his grand estate at Fonthill in Wiltshire,

Prior Park's Palladian Bridge

'England's wealthiest son' commissioned James Wyatt to erect the tallest Gothic tower in England. As he cried 'higher, higher', the masons continued until the stupendous edifice had risen 260 ft. Beckford's financial worries led him to sell Fonthill and much of his collection and in 1823 he moved to Bath. He was not a moment too soon. Two years later, the Fonthill tower collapsed and destroyed the house.

In Bath he soon dreamed of a new tower on the hills north of the city to which he could retreat, to read and dream. In 1826, he began work to designs by Henry Goodridge, based on the defensive *torre* of medieval Italy. The tower was to have his mausoleum, library and sanctuary below and a belvedere on top. No sooner was it finished than old Beckford took hold and cried 'higher!' yet again. An exquisite Athenian lantern, covered in gold leaf, was duly added to the top.

After Beckford's death, the tower had a chequered history, mostly as chapel to the adjacent Lansdown cemetery. In 1995 urgent repairs were necessary to prevent collapse and a local trust raised money to save and restore the structure. It is now in part a Landmark Trust holiday let and in part a museum. Beckford's Scarlet Drawing Room and vestibule on the ground floor are restored, the former with deep red and blue walls and hangings, and a painted ceiling in the style of an Italian villa.

Upstairs, a cantilevered spiral stair climbs past the museum rooms to the belvedere, looking out over the Bath downs and north-west to Wales. This has been immaculately reinstated as in Beckford's day, with long curtains and window stools with, outside, a gilded balustrade. The curtains were intended to be thrown aside in a theatrical gesture to reveal the view to guests. The central column has more steps up to the lantern.

BECKINGTON: OLD MANSE *

Beckington, 2m N of Frome
Tudor house behind Jacobean façade (P-R)

Some houses defy description. The Old Manse in Beckington is a late Elizabethan town house of which Somerset must once have possessed thousands, and now has almost none. What elsewhere would have been of wood and plaster is here of stone. Parts are claimed to go back to 1480, but the three-gabled façade is of c1620. The entrance shows signs of having once been wide enough for packhorses, suggesting a merchant's house.

The interior is privately tenanted and wonderfully chaotic. I admire anyone who admits the public to his private house, but there are times when one feels like a voyeur. Amid the clutter are the remains of a fine Jacobean house. The staircase, dividing left and right, has two sets of carved balusters.

The one-time Great Chamber was given a ceiling with strapwork and what appears to be an original Tudor fireplace. Other rooms have mysterious bulges, dips and fragments of plaster moulding. The whole place seems to await a house detective.

The attic, still divided up into tiny rooms as it would have been for most of its life, has a confusion of roof beams darting in all directions.

CLAVERTON MANOR *

2m SE of Bath
Regency mansion converted for Americana
(M)

Claverton now houses the American Museum and its interior has been wholly converted to that purpose. It was built by Sir Jeffry Wyatville in 1820 for John Vivian in a severely classical style. The entrance is to the courtyard at the back, while two large Regency bow windows face the view on the other side. The façade to the garden is refined Palladian. This was the most elegant period of Georgian architecture, if a little dull.

The museum was opened in 1961 by two American enthusiasts for Anglo-American cultural relations, Dallas Pratt and John Judkyn. All of the rooms have been transported from America, yet this fact is often hard to believe, given the stylistic proximity of the two sides of the Atlantic in the 18th and 19th centuries.

The Jacobean Keeping Room, the Lee Room, the Deming Parlor and Conkey's Tavern might all be from southern England. Only the portraiture is clearly 'colonial'. The most evidently American rooms are the Shaker and Mexican Indian ones. The New Orleans Bedroom, heavily classical in style, is betrayed only by its mosquito net.

The grounds are outstanding, with a colonial herb garden and a section copied from Mount Vernon outside Washington. The original had itself been planted with seeds (and even a gardener) sent from Bath. It has thus come home.

CLEEVE ABBEY *

3m SW of Watchet
Restored monastic ruin, painted chamber
(EH)

Cleeve Abbey sits in a valley below the Quantocks in traditional Cistercian isolation. The abbey was prosperous before the Dissolution, after which its church was demolished. Some residential buildings survived round the old cloister. Used as a residence, Cleeve became a collection of farm buildings in the 18th century and by the 19th was owned by the Luttrells of Dunster.

The enterprising Luttrells appreciated the tourist potential of Cleeve's ruins, not least to bring customers to their Taunton–Minehead railway. The farmer's daughter, Cleeva Clapp, named after the abbey, acted as guide for a shilling a head (a large sum in those days). Her stories of her private night-time 'communings' with the ghosts of monks became hugely popular. The sale of the Luttrell estate in 1949 brought Cleeve to the Ministry of Works, now English Heritage.

The Ministry turned what had been a romantic ruin into what at first looks like a lawn catalogue. Trees, shrubs, creeper and weeds were removed. Aggressive new roofs and floors were inserted, walls turned a dazzling white and stonework scrubbed. Cleeve might come from a build-your-own-abbey kit. Any patina of age was lost.

Entry is through an outstanding medieval gatehouse at some distance from the site. Ahead is the old farmhouse, divided into cottages during the Luttrell ownership. It was once occupied by a Captain Angelo of the Indian Army, who grew giant Himalayan tomatoes here. The two surviving ranges of the monastery lie behind, the abbot's lodgings, refectory and dormitory.

The refectory is a fine relic of domestic monastery architecture. It has a Perpendicular wooden roof and panel tracery in large windows. The roof has angel corbels and excellent wood bosses. Adjacent are assumed to be the prior's chambers, including a room with painted walls. A large mural depicts a man crossing a bridge surrounded by emblems of the Passion.

At a right angle to the refectory is the most impressive dormitory, in which some three dozen monks would have slept. A door at the far end led to the night stairs into the church. The roof is post-Reformation. Beneath the dormitory are the living and working rooms of the monastery. These include the chapter house and the warming room, where a fire was kept lit throughout the winter. There are Early English windows at one end.

All the rooms are unfurnished. If the English Heritage ideologues can give us, at considerable expense, their idea of a medieval roof, floor and door, not to mention signs galore, why not put in medieval furniture and fittings?

CLEVEDON COURT **

Clevedon
Medieval house with private chapel (NT)

Clevedon Court sits on a series of terraces on the edge of the downs west of Bristol. The scene, wrote John Betjeman, is 'like the background of a Flemish stained-glass window. The Bristol Channel is a bronze shield streaked with sunlight.' Since 1709 it has been the home of the Elton family, one-time wealthy Bristol merchants, now tenants of the National Trust.

The Eltons have been baronets, radical MPs, poets, firemen and potters. Tennyson, Thackeray and John Betjeman were visitors to the house and mentioned it in their writings. Vividly coloured Elton Ware has been sold at Tiffanys. The house contains an Elton collection of glass walking sticks, birds and pipes, as well as prints of bridges and piers. It is a memorial to all these family activities.

Although Clevedon is noisily close to the M5, the main façade retains its ancient dignity. The entrance is a two-storey porch with the Great Hall to its left and a bold chapel window where the dais bay would normally be. To the right lies a curious structure, a semi-detached hall lying at an angle to the main house. This appears to be an earlier hall or barn, backed by a 13th-century defensive pele tower.

This combination of pele and hall is usual in the much-raided Border country of the North but not in peaceful Somerset. Such a tower is remarkable attached to any house in southern England. It is of four storeys with immensely thick walls and slit windows, apparently mid-13th century in origin. Perhaps the early residents considered themselves too close to Wales. The hall is a museum room, filled with Elton Ware.

The main house, built in 1320 by Sir John de Clevedon, thus appears to have been planned at an angle to an older one, perhaps to face out towards the moor or perhaps to orient his chapel. The latter has bold reticulated tracery in both front and east windows which are incongruously big, as if the mason could only do them church-sized. The solar wing was gutted by fire in 1882, rebuilt and then half demolished in the 20th century. Its side façade was competently reconstructed in a neo-Jacobean style.

The interior was much altered by the Eltons in the 18th century. The medieval screens passage remains, with an impressive row of arches to the service rooms to the right. The Great Hall is now Georgian, with a minstrels' gallery, a Gothic arch to the chapel alcove and, as a surprise, an Elizabethan Mannerist doorway imported from elsewhere. The room is forested with tall-backed Stuart chairs. Portraits of Eltons gaze down from the walls.

The staircase landing is hung with prints of engineering projects and a Tillemans of Clevedon prior to its Georgian alteration. The upstairs rooms are post-fire replacements, except for the chapel. This is a lovely chamber with space only for the family and priest. The tracery is overpowering, enhanced by Clayton & Bell glass which, on a sunny day, fills it with a kaleidoscope of colour.

COTHAY MANOR ****

4m NW of Wellington
Edwardian restoration of medieval manor (P)

In the grounds of Cothay Manor are avenues down which medieval ladies would exercise their unicorns. Since these beasts, as we know, were visible only to virgins, it was never easy to police this facility. The house was built in the 1480s, 'modern' enough to avoid Tudor alteration yet now incomparably antique. The site was that of a 12th-century hall house, and the owners were the Blewitt family. It was transferred to the Every family a century later and remained an obscure farmhouse until 1925, when it met its saint.

Colonel Reggie Cooper was a bachelor diplomat in the *Country Life* circle of Edward Hudson and Christopher Hussey. Cooper had been at the Istanbul embassy in 1914 with Harold Nicolson (of Sissinghurst/Kent) and Gerald Wellesley (of Stratfield Saye/Hants), all friends of Hussey. In the distant south, they dreamed of English manors, of old stone, rich wood, grey-green tapestries and flickering candles. Cooper had already restored Cold Ashton north of Bath in such a spirit. To Hussey, he was little short of a genius, for whose 'lightness of healing touch . . . no praise is too high'. Cooper lived at Cothay for eleven years. It is now owned by the Robb family.

The house sits beyond its own fish pond, lost in the meadows and woods of the Vale of Taunton. Few houses in England remain so evocatively medieval in appearance. The plan comprises gatehouse, courtyard, porch leading into screens passage and Great Hall. At the dais end are a parlour and solar; at the service end is a gallery with upper guest room and small chapel. Some new panelling was inserted at the end of the Elizabethan period, when a small Renaissance dining room was constructed. Otherwise nothing has been altered, apart from a few rooms in a wing added by Cooper for his own use. The group is in a restful pink-brown stone, with steep tiled roofs and original fenestration. Even the gatehouse door is medieval.

The Great Hall has a tall arch-braced roof with minstrels' gallery. On a wall is an indistinct painting of Reynard the Fox. The parlour is panelled in oak stained to look like walnut, above which is a painted frieze. The original spiral staircase leads up to the solar, open to another fine arch-braced roof. A small window looks onto the hall. A charming feature of this room is its decoration by the daughter of the present owner, Arabella Robb, in a style wholly sympathetic to its past. Her design is of plants with stalks and tendrils roaming free, even covering the radiator. Here are cornflowers, carrots, sweet peas, tulips, pears, quinces – exactly what the Middle Ages would have done with this space. This is a magic room, somehow medieval and of today at the same time.

Below one end of the solar and next to the parlour is the old undercroft, now a library. Mrs Robb has decorated this in deep red. With its thick beams covering ceiling and walls, it is a chamber of medieval intimacy. Across the hall is the Everys' later dining room. The ceilings are here plastered with vines. The chimneypiece is wood, carved with caryatids of the four Virtues, first glimmerings of the Elizabethan Renaissance. The curtains are modern but based on medieval designs.

Cothay has not finished with us. At the service end of the hall off the gallery and over the porch is a small oratory. This has a squint from the adjacent bedroom. The gallery may have been where the servants gathered to hear mass in the oratory. The priest's chamber next door is known as the Gold Room. It has a 15th-century fresco of the Madonna and Child,

Cothay: medieval treasure house

badly restored and now hanging away from its wall. More paintings decorate the guest bedroom next door. One, very primitive, is of the Virgin, possibly at the Annunciation. Another appears to be of a Blewitt. Round the frieze is a scroll, its lettering lost. These are surviving medieval interiors of incomparable value.

Even when the house is not open, the garden may be accessible. It is divided by deep yew walls into private rooms of its own. Its dark green recesses reflect the medievalism of the house. Mrs Robb created the avenues for the aforementioned unicorns.

CRICKET ST THOMAS: CRICKET HOUSE *

Cricket St Thomas, 4m E of Chard
Soane house in wildlife park (H)

Cricket House is set in a landscape of great loveliness. The drive from the main road leads through trees to curve in front of the house. The land beyond slopes down to a series of lakes before rising again to a distant bank of woods. It is best in the gloaming of a summer evening.

The house was altered for Lord Bridport, previously Admiral Hood, by Sir John Soane in 1786 and 1801. It remained in the family until 1897 when it was sold to the chocolate manufacturer, Francis Fry. A wildlife park was developed on the estate in the 1960s and the house passed in 1998 to Warner Holidays, controversial saviours of many English country houses. The exterior lies low and dignified, in warm Ham stone with a Tuscan porch. Some care has been taken to conceal the ugliness of the hotel beyond, but not enough inside.

How much of Soane's interior survives is hard to discern. Drawings in the Soane archive show a library that bears little relationship to the present one. The staircase, the most remarkable feature of the house, is undeniably Soanian, if not by Soane. It sweeps upwards from the hall before dividing and returning on itself to an upper landing. Most of the principal reception rooms seem unaltered and the

house has retained some of its dignity. On the walls is a fine collection of French prints.

DILLINGTON HOUSE *

1m N of Ilminster
Victorianized Elizabethan mansion (P-R)

The house is a miniature Barrington Court, but while the latter sits isolated amid open lawns, Dillington is tucked into the hills, closely attended by gardens. Faced with Ham stone, its façade glows in the sun, patched with green and white lichen. Since 1949, the house has been a Somerset County Council study centre, open on occasions and visible from the drive and park.

The house is a traditional mid-16th-century E-plan, the conversion of an earlier hall house. The owner was John Bonvile. The house later passed to the Georgian prime minister, Lord North, and was remodelled by Sir James Pennethorne in neo-Gothic in 1838. Pennethorne was Nash's assistant, academic rather than inspired, who went on to design the Italianate west wing of Somerset House in London. He gave Dillington its present symmetrical appearance. As so often with the Elizabethan revival, it is hard to tell restored from new but this façade is a beautifully modulated work, with porch, wings, gables and chimney in perfect balance. It seems a timeless style, forever English.

The interior is institutional but has panelling similar to that at Barrington. It is said to have been removed from that house, which subsequently had to import some more of its own. The screen opposite the kitchen appears old, but is it original? The rest of the house is Jacobethan.

DODINGTON HALL *

Dodington, 10m W of Bridgwater
Manor house with unusual roof (P)

How have these places survived? The manor house lies on a rise at a distance from the main road, to form a picturesque group with church, barn and farm buildings. All remain intact, looking out across the fields towards the Severn Estuary and the distant coast of Wales.

The manor of the Dodington family now belongs to Lady Gass of Fairfield (below) and is tenanted. It is divided into two houses on either side of the screens passage. The left-hand one is a Victorian re-creation. The right-hand one comprises the old Great Hall, apparently Elizabethan, with bay window and solar wing, occupied by an enthusiast for its architecture. The entrance porch has a shell shrine in its wall.

The hall still has its minstrels' gallery and is open to the roof. This displays an extraordinary pattern of scissor wind-braces, while the main beams are cut wavy rather than straight. They rest on angel corbels. It is all restless and decorative, sign of someone having both money and a sense of style. Equally extraordinary is the fireplace. This is of 1581, in an Elizabethan Mannerist style. It is decorated with negroes, Aztec warriors and primitive figurines with prominent genitalia, demonstrating a fascination with the New World typical of the late 16th century.

The arch to the bay window appears Norman, while the window chamber itself has a massively beamed roof. These features cannot be in their original positions. The parlour is again handsomely decorated, with close-laid beams and a 17th-century frieze. The plaster everywhere makes copious use of the Dodington arms of three bugle horns.

DUNSTER CASTLE ***

Dunster
Medieval castle with Jacobean interiors (NT)

Dunster is a dream of Camelot. Few castles have a finer aspect. The view from the coast road shows the battlements prominent against the backdrop of Exmoor. A watch tower guards the settlement from neighbouring Conyger Hill. Beneath lies the picturesque village high street.

The castle hill – or tor – was chosen by the Norman lords of Devon, the Mohuns, for their stronghold. It was sold in 1376 to the Luttrells, who held it against all-comers except Cromwell. A Luttrell built the mighty gatehouse, another commissioned William Arnold to expand an earlier house within the walls in 1617. Another refurnished it after slighting in the Civil War and another commissioned Anthony Salvin in 1868 to 'refortify' the castle that we see today. Dunster is like Arundel (Sussex), Belvoir (Leics) and Windsor (Berks), essentially a Victorian ideal of what a great medieval palace should be. The castle was only conquered by the taxman in 1976, passing to the National Trust with the family as tenants.

The military prowess of the site is immediately apparent in the steep climb up to the entrance. This has too much distressing tarmac. The north façade is by Salvin, embracing medieval, 17th-century and Victorian elements. The red Somerset sandstone is combined with honeyed limestone to create a pleasing variety of tones. This mix is more pronounced above the terrace to the rear, where walls that would once have seemed unassailable are now picturesque.

The building has two halls, an outer one created by Salvin and an inner one dating from the Elizabethan house. The outer hall is Jacobean revival, taking the place of the former parlour and filling the width of the castle. It is hung with family portraits. The inner hall has a Salvin fireplace and the iconographical Luttrell portrait of 1550. This extraordinary picture shows Sir John Luttrell, Elizabethan commander in Scotland, rising from the waves, encumbered with allegory. Peace caresses his fist and Venus calms War, while girls hold money bags to indicate the ransom that was needed to rescue him. This is a contemporary copy of the original in the Courtauld Gallery in London.

Beyond the inner hall is the dining room with a fine 1680s ceiling of deeply undercut plasterwork and dark panelling. Of the same period is the Restoration staircase. It displays acanthus decoration running riot over ceiling and balustrade panels alike. Each balustrade is carved from planks of elm, nine inches thick. Hounds dart between the leaves in pursuit of the fox, while Luttrell military trophies adorn the gallery above.

The staircase leads into the much-altered morning room and a sequence of Salvin bedrooms. The downstairs at Dunster was planned for the men, the upstairs for women. The principal bathroom of the 1880s was reputedly the first in Somerset – and the only one in the house. The gallery is notable for its embossed leather wall panels depicting Antony and Cleopatra. These are French or Flemish, of the mid-17th century. Antony is said to look suspiciously like Louis XIII while Cleopatra on her horse appears bemused. The scenes are formal and stylized, especially the deaths of the two heroes.

The King Charles Room was supposedly used by the king as a young prince during his visit to drum up support in the West Country during the Civil War. Its fine overmantel portrays the Judgement of Paris of 1620. Downstairs, the billiard room and library, both by Salvin, complete the male domains. He also built a completely new tower on the site of a former chapel. The view from here out towards the Bristol Channel is spectacular.

The outside terrace that runs across the south front enjoys the same view. The garden steps down the side of the tor in paths lined with shrubs of tropical fecundity. These slopes are sheltered from the north and east winds and bathe only in Channel breezes. Dunster seems to ride on a wave of perpetual greenery.

FAIRFIELD **

Stogursey, 10m NW of Bridgwater
Elizabethan mansion with Georgian additions (P)

Fairfield needs a saint as owner and fortunately has one. Large, rambling and with rooms galore, it has lived as many lives as it has seen changes in its family name. The house has remained in the same line of descent since the Middle Ages, variously as Verneys, Palmers, Aclands, Acland-Hoods and the Gass family.

The present incumbent, Lady Elizabeth Acland Hood Gass, has both restored the house and revealed much of its past in her uncovering of its walls.

The entrance façade to the drive is restrained and apparently Georgian. This is merely a side elevation of an Elizabethan E-plan mansion, immediately visible round the corner. Here is a most enjoyable façade, with three-storey porch and canted windows to its wings. The date over the porch is 1589. But this is not all. Round another corner are found the remains of an even earlier medieval house fashioned into the left-hand wing of the E-plan. Its traces are visible in the walls. Fairfield has thus had three distinct façades demonstrating various stages of its history, medieval, Elizabethan and Georgian.

The interior of the house was georgianized in appearance, if not in plan. The faded walls of the Great Hall are hung with ancestors, apparently in chronological order. The old parlour beyond formed the Georgian entrance hall. The dining room displays various portraits of nautical Hoods, one of whom sailed round the world with Captain Cook in 1772 at the age of fourteen.

An earlier ancestor, Thomas Palmer, sailed with Drake and Hawkins. He produced a son, William, who 'being a person of great learning chose always to live in London'. Early monarchs were keen to keep aristocrats and landed gentry away from the temptations of the capital and remain looking after their country estates. Palmer was duly fined £1000 by the Star Chamber of Charles I for having been so disobedient to the King's demand 'requiring all persons of estate to reside and keep hospitality at their houses'.

GATCOMBE COURT **

W of Long Ashton, 5m SW of Bristol
Ancient manor with Roman well (P-R)

'Do you speak house?' I was once asked when visiting an old building, as if such concepts could only be discussed in a private language. Gatcombe Court is such a place. Nothing is regular, nothing of the same period, yet every-thing pleasing. Owned by the Clarke family, the house is too small to be regularly open, yet the brochure offers appointments, 'hospitality and cost to be cheerfully agreed'. They are best made during the rose season, a Gatcombe speciality.

The house was built in the Middle Ages on the remains of a Roman settlement, evident in a huge rampart in the grounds. This is claimed to be wider than Hadrian's Wall. There is also a floodlit Roman well outside the kitchen. The oldest part of the house survives from the 13th century. To this was added a solar and possibly a Great Chamber above the hall. The left side of the façade has two gables and dates from an extensive rebuilding in 1683. There is a fine staircase inside of this period, rising from basement to attic.

Gatcombe was tenanted until the 1920s and has been steadily restored ever since. Bricked-up windows have emerged under restoration and the outside displays 16th- and 17th-century fenestration. The interior is that of a com-fortable family home, its walls a museum of architectural clutter. There is an intriguing lintel, a re-sited chimneypiece, a medieval arch and a series of strange wall holes. The Clarkes have filled every inch with family memorabilia, fusing house and family in a single personality worth a hundred museums.

From the windows can be seen a voluptuous yew hedge and Queen Anne gates – and the illustrious roses.

GAULDEN MANOR **

Tolland, 9m NW of Taunton
Medieval house with 17th-century
plasterwork (P)

From a lane beneath overhanging beeches a track turns into an old courtyard. On the right is a jumble of medieval buildings that have long made their peace with nature. The house lies ahead, guarded by a two-storey porch and old casement windows. Gaulden Manor goes back to the 12th century, when it passed to the Priory of Taunton.

After the Dissolution Gaulden's owners and tenants came and went. It may have offered refuge to the Roman Catholic Bishop of Exeter, James Turberville, after his release from the Tower in 1563. The Wolcott family bought the house in 1618. They then emigrated to America, thus assuring the house a flock of transatlantic adherents, including a Society of the Descendants of Henry Wolcott. In 1639 the Turbervilles returned and gave the hall its astonishing plasterwork. Since then the house has been a farm, occupied since 1966 by Mr and Mrs James Starkie.

Gaulden is a classic Somerset manor. Dogs yap, fires burn and books tumble from shelves. Mrs Starkie has long been a mistress of the art of paint, rightly divining that the way to enliven a medieval interior is with bright colours, not whitewash. If only the National Trust had her courage. Thus the entrance passage is green. The old kitchen, now dining room, is red. Its fireplace still has alcoves for bread and salt and a herringbone fire-back.

Across the screens passage is the hall, in vivid blue, a room that may once have been a kitchen. Yet it has a ceiling worthy of a great house, its plasterwork dated to the 1640s. This ceiling dominates what is a modestly propor-tioned chamber. It has a giant central pendant and roundels on either side. One is of the Last Trump, an angel summoning a skeleton, and the other of King David's harp. Round the frieze, some of it like dripping icing sugar, are biblical themes alleged to relate to the saintly life of the episcopal Turberville. The ceil-ing continues into an alcove known as the chapel, clearly of the same period. The ceiling would seem an act of homage to the ancestral bishop.

A surprisingly spacious double flight of stairs, with crimson William Morris wallpaper, leads to the landing and the Turberville bed-room. This has more fine plasterwork over the fireplace from the same hand as downstairs. Everywhere in the house are old prints and pictures of horses and families. In the garden is a medieval stewpond. The old house can be seen from every angle, sprouting from its enveloping greenery.

GLASTONBURY: ABBOT'S KITCHEN *

Magdalene Street
Kitchen surviving from Abbot's house (M)

Modern Glastonbury is one of the oddest places in England. It is part market town and part fantasy capital of Avalonia. In the latter role it is the pilgrimage centre for Holy Grail searchers, druids, Arthurians, mystics, hippies and drop-outs.

The bush in the churchyard allegedly sprouted from the Crown of Thorns brought by Joseph of Arimathaea. On the great tor, visible across the Somerset Levels for miles round, any legend you care to name is buried. The main street is filled with the odours of herbs, spices and incense. Goodness knows what the monks would have made of this.

I expect the answer is that, as today, what would have been made is money. Glastonbury was founded on an island in the Somerset Levels by Saxon missionaries in the 8th century. Rebuilt by the Normans it became one of the wealthiest foundations in England. Of its monastic splendour little remains but what does remain is outstanding, the gatehouse and one of the best-known works of domestic architecture in England, the Glastonbury Abbot's Kitchen in all its medieval splendour.

How the kitchen survived is something of a mystery, since such structures were usually used as quarries after the Dissolution. It probably became a barn. The building is intact, dating from the mid-14th century, four-square in plan, comparable only with the kitchens at Stanton Harcourt (Oxon) and Berkeley Castle (Gloucs).

Each corner contained a fireplace, turned by the masons to architectural effect by making the upper section octagonal, with two tiers of lantern. The smoke would have escaped through corner chimneys, other fumes through the lanterns.

The exterior is ornamented, with Gothic windows above the doorway. The lanterns are treated as if they were the turrets of a church, with three sloping roofs interspersed with battlemented panels and windows. This is a beautiful structure, evidence of the prosperity of the house to which it was attached.

HESTERCOMBE HOUSE *

2m NE of Taunton
Victorian house, garden by Lutyens and Jekyll (P-G)

Hestercombe House is no obvious beauty. I was shown round by a custodian who wished it gone. Yet the building is focus of a superb landscape and if its present occupants, the Somerset Fire Brigade (and its chief officer), move out, a more dignified use may be found for it.

The house was that of the Warre family from the 14th century to the end of the 19th (as Warre Bampfyldes). They built the Queen Anne house that lies hidden within the present pile and began landscaping the grounds in the 18th century.

In 1873 the house was bought by Viscount Portman, owner of much of Marylebone and father of the builder of Bryanston (Dorset). His grandson, Edward Portman, in 1904 commissioned Edwin Lutyens and Gertrude Jekyll to produce a dramatic garden landscape on the terraces below the house and up the slopes of the Quantocks behind.

The interior is institutional. Apart from a fine hall and staircase the chief interest is said to be the Chief Fireman's bathroom. The exterior is at best eccentric. The symmetry of the old house was thrown off balance by the erection of a crude Victorian tower to its left. The side front onto the garden has lost all coherence and is just a sequence of bays with a jumble of pediments, windows and recesses in soft pink stone.

The gardens are sensational. The landscape garden runs uphill of the house; this was first designed by Coplestone Warre Bampfylde who inherited in 1750. The garden below the house is by Lutyens and Jekyll, with architecture here in the ascendant. Lutyens's Orangery in Ham stone is a most accomplished work of 'Wrenaissance'.

LYTES CARY **

4m NE of Ilchester
Medieval and Tudor manor house (NT)

The composition of Lytes Cary is delightfully eccentric. The core of the building is a Great Hall with parlours, chapel and Great Chamber to the left of the porch. In front is a garden party of squat yews, like ladies-in-waiting in farthingales. To the right looms a Georgian extension, wholly out of place, an uninvited guest at this medieval occasion.

The original hall house was built by Thomas Lyte in the 1450s and 'modernized' by John Lyte in the 1530s. His son in turn, Henry, was a noted Elizabethan botanist who developed the garden and filled the house with family heraldry. Lytes Cary was a farm until acquired by Sir Walter Jenner, brother of William Jenner of Avebury (Wilts), in 1907. Like Reggie Cooper at Cothay and others of the *Country Life* circle, he was an enthusiast for manorial architecture and restored and passed the house to the National Trust in 1949.

The Great Hall is open to the roof, its wind-braces handsomely cusped. An unusual Gothic arch embraces a small dining area, fashioned in the 1530s from the former dais window bay. One can imagine the family tucked behind the screen while the servants went about their business in the Great Hall outside. Adjacent to it is the 14th-century chapel, showing the close fusion of domestic and religious life in a pre-Reformation manor.

The family rooms added as a rear wing in the 1500s are intact. From the garden they look like a miniature Elizabethan mansion in themselves. A two-storey bay of Elizabethan windows in the centre of the façade lights the Great Parlour and the Great Chamber above. The interiors are deliciously dark and ancient, with windows giving glimpses of the gardens below. The Jenners filled them with furniture chosen not as contemporary with the house but as suitable to its scale and style, a subtle distinction.

The Great Parlour has a mirror framed in early embroidery, known as stumpwork. The Little Parlour, where Lyte worked on his herbals, has a pretty 18th-century niche with a *trompe-l'œil* shell backing. The Tudor ceiling of the Great Chamber upstairs is decorated with lozenges and the arms of Henry VIII. Dated 1533, it is said to be among the earliest examples of this style in a private house. The door retains its draught-excluding porch, with linenfold panelling.

Relics of the herbal and horticultural endeavours of Henry Lyte are on display. His Tudor garden disappeared and the Jenners restored the grounds on Gertrude Jekyll lines. But one bed is now planted with Lyte's herbs and a copy of his *Niewe Herball* can be seen in the hall.

MARTOCK: TREASURER'S HOUSE *

Martock
Medieval group in shadow of church (EH)

The medieval Treasurer of Wells Cathedral was also rector of Martock. He needed a house in which to live when in town and an office in which to collect tithes and do business. Both survive directly opposite Martock church.

The Great Hall has a high timbered roof and ochre walls the colour of powdered Ham stone. This is clearly a noble room, but the absence of a fireplace suggests it was for business purposes. The 14th-century windows have double arches (or rere-arches) and seats fashioned in their sills as if large numbers of people were expected. On the walls are brackets for oil lights.

Adjacent to this hall is what would have been the old residential hall and solar, since divided both horizontally and vertically. Upstairs are fragments of a 13th-century structure, including a wall painting of the Crucifixion.

To the back is the old kitchen. This has a gigantic fireplace made of two slabs of Ham stone, each 6 ft long. Here I learned the derivation of 'curfew', the call each evening for fires to be covered (*couvez les feux*) to reduce the risk of night-time conflagration.

MONTACUTE HOUSE ✳✳✳✳

Montacute, 4m W of Yeovil
Elizabethan house, refurnished and with
Jacobean garden (NT)

Montacute House came to be regarded as
the epitome of grand Elizabethan architecture.
Its Ham stone is so richly yellow-red as to look
as if made of warm embers. The style lacks the
originality of Longleat (Wilts) or Hardwick
Hall (Derbys), nor has it the pomp of the
Jacobean prodigy houses. Montacute rather
displays the rich and comfortable final era
of Good Queen Bess. This hugely appealed to
the Victorians. Montacute was a house much
copied during the time of the Jacobethan
revival.

The house was built, probably by William
Arnold, for a lawyer, Sir Edward Phelips, at the
end of the 16th century. Speaker of the House
of Commons and Prosecutor of Guy Fawkes,
Phelips was also organizer of the spectacular
1612 wedding of the 'Winter Queen' (*see* Ash-
down/Oxon). The same family occupied the
house into the 20th century.

In 1915 the house was rented by Lord
Curzon, former Viceroy of India and obsessive
restorer of English houses (including Bodiam/
Sussex, Tattershall/Lincs and his own
Kedleston/Derbys). After the death of his first
wife, he briefly shared Montacute with his mistress, Elinor Glyn, and then (to Glyn's fury)
with his second wife. Despite being only a tenant, Curzon spent lavishly on the 'preservation
of a lovely thing for the nation'. He stripped
the walls of inappropriate paint, rush-matted
the floors, rehung the fabrics and filled the
house with Tudor furniture.

Following Curzon's death in 1925, the
Phelips family decided in 1931 to sell Montacute for scrap. It mercifully escaped this fate
under a second benefactor, Ernest Cook,
grandson of Thomas. He had made a fortune
from the sale of the family travel agency to
Wagons Lits, and used the proceeds to buy and

Montacute: late-Elizabethan Renaissance

give to the National Trust not just Montacute
but other properties as well (including Buscot
Park/Oxon). The Trust has since struggled to
refurnish the house with donated textiles and
tapestries, and paintings from the National
Portrait Gallery.

No house in Somerset has a finer approach,
down a sweeping avenue from the road. The
rear façade, however, is not original but a
stroke of antiquarian genius of the 1780s.
Edward Phelips utilized stonework from an
earlier period, from Clifton Maybank near
Yeovil, to give himself a new entry to what was
the rear of the building. It was this imported
façade that so attracted the Victorians. Dating
from the mid-16th century, it is of a delicate
beauty that contrasts with the rather ponderous Elizabethan towers on either side.

The present visitors' entrance is on the far
side, facing the garden. This is a magnificent
cliff of Elizabethan architecture. A court of
pavilions, walls and strapwork frames the steps
rising to the main door. Statues of 'worthies'
look down from above. The door leads into the
screens passage, with the dining room to the
left and the Great Hall to the right. The former
was converted in the 18th century from the
old buttery and has an eccentric fireplace
assembled in the 1780s. It is filled with Tudor
portraits. Here hangs a masterpiece of French
Gothic art, the Tournai *millefleurs* tapestry
of 1477, depicting a knight on horseback in a
glorious field of flowers.

The Great Hall is not big. By the late 16th
century such rooms were losing their communal significance. However, at the far end is
a Montacute curio. A frieze shows a man
caught drinking when supposedly minding a
baby, and being paraded round town tied to
a pole as punishment. Why this scene, known
as the Stang Ride, should adorn the main
reception room is a mystery.

Montacute is a big house. The remaining
rooms on the ground floor are the parlour and
drawing room, much altered but carefully
restored. In the drawing room is a hunting
portrait by Daniel Gardner and paintings by
Reynolds and Gainsborough. Here too is a
pair of fierce Chinese 'Dogs of Fo'. The stairs

lead to Lord Curzon's bedroom where, in the words of the poem, he presumably 'sinned with Elinor Glyn'. He certainly installed a fine Edwardian bath.

The library was formerly the Great Chamber, a room full of light looking down on the north garden with its yews like guardsmen standing to attention. The room has its original plasterwork frieze and chimneypiece, the latter flanked by classical columns embracing an elaborate heraldic panel. The niches on either side were once filled with nudes, sadly not replaced after their removal by prudish Victorians. The windows carry heraldic glass of the marital activities of the Phelipses. Despite their fine house, from the 17th century to the 20th they lived and died plain Mr.

The Crimson Bedroom has an exquisite frieze but looks strangely naked without its tapestries beneath. Its bed posts are like tree trunks. The second floor is dominated by a Long Gallery, reputedly the longest in England. This has been much altered and displays a set of early portraits from the National Portrait Gallery. The low-light controls entirely wreck the spirit of this gallery, which should be flooded with sun and give views out over the surrounding countryside. Such conservation is a sort of visual vandalism.

MUCHELNEY ABBEY **

Muchelney, 2m S of Langport
Surviving abbot's lodgings (EH)

Muchelney Abbey was Glastonbury's poorer sister. The Benedictine abbey church has all but vanished, but the abbot's lodgings, which became farmhouses on the Dissolution, are virtually intact and most rare. They include parlours, kitchens and living rooms. At the end of the Middle Ages, a church inspector remarked that the monks lived too well and 'ate in private'. The rooms date from the early years of the 16th century, the last flowering of monastic building.

The lodgings stand tall and bold beyond the displayed footings of the ruined abbey church.

They form one side of the old cloister, located at the end of the vanished refectory. To the left of the entrance are two kitchens on either side of a large double fireplace. The steward's range lies beyond. The principal rooms are the downstairs ante-room and the upstairs abbot's parlour, with private closets above the cloister walk. These splendid rooms suggest a lifestyle quite distinct from that of the monks, of whom there were just eleven here at the Dissolution.

The cloister walk is a beautiful relic of the monastery arcade, with high arches and Gothic vaults broken off where a ceiling was inserted. The abbot's parlour is reached up a generous flight of stairs. Its overmantel is decorated with quatrefoils and vine leaves and rises to two carved lions. Pevsner extols this as 'one of the most sumptuous pre-Reformation fireplaces in the country'. The benches are backed by linenfold. Three adjacent rooms, perhaps bedrooms, have their original roofs, one with remains of wall-paintings.

MUCHELNEY: PRIEST'S HOUSE *

Muchelney, 2m S of Langport
Medieval cottage with upper chambers intact
(NT)

This is a chocolate-box cottage. An order to build a priest's house at Muchelney was issued from Wells in 1308. A single span of thatched roof rises above a medieval door with a two-tier hall window to one side. The plan was of the customary hall with upstairs solar at one end and kitchens at the other. The only later alterations were a fireplace and an additional room over the hall. The house was occupied by a priest into the 19th century and was saved from demolition in 1901 by the intervention of Thomas Hardy, Bernard Shaw and William Morris's widow. It is now owned by the National Trust and tenanted.

The house is a gem of medieval architecture. Everything seems original. An old door leads into a screens passage, still of blackened oak.

Into this was at some point let a giant slab of Ham stone to support a new fireplace and chimney. This may have been inserted here rather than against an outside wall for extra warmth.

Beyond is the priest's study, with a medieval window and his bedroom above. The main chamber over the hall reveals its old roof beams and part of the hall window rising into its wall-space. Some of the woodwork, including the steep staircase, is not original but the work of Ernest Barnsley of the Cotswold group of architect craftsmen. It is most appropriate.

NETHER STOWEY: COLERIDGE COTTAGE *

Nether Stowey, 7m W of Bridgwater
House where 'Kubla Khan' was written (NT)

No Xanadu this. The picture village of Nether Stowey is placid, just a few houses and the Ancient Mariner pub. Opposite the pub stands the house where Samuel Taylor Coleridge lived for three years with his young wife, Sara, and their son, Hartley. Its appearance is appropriately ascetic.

This is how Coleridge wanted it. The year was 1797 and a publishing venture in London had failed. Coleridge's friend, Thomas Poole, lived in Nether Stowey and Coleridge, close to destitution, insisted on coming down as a neighbour. He wanted no servants, no preaching, one pig and a vegetable garden. He called it his 'dear gutter' and settled down to write poems. He also found 'a large number of very pretty young women in Stowey all musical; I am an immense favourite for I pun, conundrumise, listen and dance'.

The years at Nether Stowey were among Coleridge's most productive. He was visited by his literary friends, including many whose revolutionary attire and demeanour alarmed the locals (and Poole). Here too came the notorious 'person from Porlock', to interrupt the opium-induced reverie of Kubla Khan. The three years at Nether Stowey yielded 'The Rime of the Ancient Mariner', 'Frost at Midnight' and Coleridge's contribution to the *Lyrical Ballads*.

The cottage would have been thatched at the time, but was reroofed in the 19th century. Only the four front rooms on the ground and upper floors are original. They have been converted into a museum of pictures, manuscripts and memorabilia. This includes a lock of Coleridge's hair, sword and magnificent Boulle ink stand, the latter a particular treasure.

The place is admirably fusty. The custodian, resplendent with a mariner-like white beard, winds up an ancient clock and sells Coleridgiana. It is notoriously hard to bring a writer's house to life. But at least a poet can be read. Here a more vivid touch to Coleridge might perhaps be to have readings from a tape of 'The Ancient Mariner' rather than display one page of an early edition.

NORTON ST PHILIP: THE GEORGE *

Norton St Philip, 7m S of Bath
Fine medieval hostelry (H)

Here is a rare survivor of medieval hospitality, a true caravanserai. The Carthusian monks of Hinton Priory are said to have established both a lodging house for travellers and a market for their produce. It is today a busy inn with three bars, dining rooms and eight medieval bedrooms to the rear with ancient furniture.

The façade, dominating the centre of the village, is impressive. The ground floor is of stone. The upper floors are black-and-white, jettied and with three idiosyncratic oriel windows. Even more impressive is the rear elevation, three stone storeys surrounding a courtyard. Here the outhouses have Collyweston tiles. An octagonal stair turret leads to a timbered gallery serving the upstairs rooms.

Given the fate of most hotels fashioned from ancient houses, the interiors at the George have fared well. Stalls and partitions are still in place. Fires burn in the grates. The Charter-house Bar is a medieval hall with beamed ceiling and fireplace. The Monmouth Bar is buried below, with low beams and flagstone floors, named after the rebel commander vanquished at Sedgemoor nearby. It was the last battle fought on English soil, in 1685 (with due respect to various urban 'riots'). The hapless Duke of Monmouth, illegitimate son of Charles II and Protestant pretender to the throne, is said to have rested in this house.

The George is described by Clifton-Taylor as among 'the finest and most venerable of English hostelries'. If ever there was a true 'public house', this is it.

PORLOCK: DOVERY MANOR *

Porlock, 6m W of Minehead
Exmoor village manor with spectacular window (M)

Dovery, or Doverhay, is a medieval house sitting at the head of a picture village beneath a notoriously steep hill leading down from Exmoor. The manor is an L-shaped building comprising entrance hall, solar wing and later addition on the other side. The exterior is most remarkable for its picturesque setting under the slope of the hill, and for the unusually grand hall window facing the street. The interior is splendidly atmospheric.

The window is a square composition, with ogees in the lower tier and curious broken ogees in the upper one. The whole work is beautiful, exuding modest opulence. One would love to know from what pattern book or recollection the local mason who built it derived his inspiration.

The interior was much restored by the Victorians but still has its original room layouts. There is a gigantic fireplace in the hall, as if vying with the window for ostentation, and two further chambers upstairs with plaster ceilings and fireplaces. They are filled with local museum paraphernalia. Like many such places, the whole is more than the sum of its parts.

STOKE-SUB-HAMDON PRIORY *

Stoke-sub-Hamdon, 2m SE of Martock
Hall house with farm building (NT)

Stoke is for stone. Here 'sub Hamdon' has long been quarried, in my view, the finest limestone in England, the glory of Montacute and houses and churches throughout Somerset and Dorset. It has found a thousand metaphors. Ham is biscuit and honey, liquid gold at dawn and blood red at dusk. Examine it under a magnifying glass and you will find its kaleidoscope reflecting a myriad shells and crystals.

How lucky therefore to find the old priory farm still standing in North Street, a chantry foundation of the Provost of Beauchamp. It backs onto the street and fronts onto a yard behind. A porch, screens passage and hall survive and are open to the public. Round it are grouped medieval farm buildings, all in the famous stone.

There is little special to see, just an original hooded doorway and a chapel overlooking the road. The two-storey solar wing also survives. The hall is open to the roof and has a big Tudor window and balcony.

STON EASTON **

7m N of Shepton Mallet
Georgian mansion with saloon plasterwork (H)

Ston Easton is a grand house of the 1740s yet has no known architect. It was built for the Hippisley family, who acquired the estate at the Dissolution and retained it until 1956. The house was then acquired and restored by the Rees-Moggs before being sold in 1982 and becoming a hotel.

The façade is curious. The central part is of three recessed bays with projecting wings and appears Queen Anne. These wings are then flanked by further wings in a later, Palladian, style. It is all most handsome but a little cold. The reception rooms are conventionally Georgian, with the exception of the ground-floor saloon. This is said to have been decorated by the younger John Wood of Bath in 1769, although it looks twenty years earlier. A giant roundel carries a relief of Jupiter's eagle in the centre. Pedimented niches at either end contain busts. Panels have *trompe-l'œil* grisailles. Most splendid is the doorway from the hall, a Corinthian composition worthy of a London palace.

The dining room, now in bright yellow, displays Chippendale furniture, not all of it original, and family portraits. It is dominated by a painting of house servants in 1770, a poignant tribute to 'below stairs'. The housekeeper in the group is said to have murdered the stillroom maid for kissing the bailiff. Of the other rooms, the library has a classical overmantel framing a picture of the Roman Forum. The house has a rare surviving print room, with 18th-century prints stuck to the walls as decoration.

The park at Ston Easton was laid out, reputedly, by Humphry Repton, and restored by Penelope Hobhouse. It runs down to a stream in a dell below the rear terrace.

TYNTESFIELD ***

Wraxall, 2m NE of Nailsea
Gothic extravaganza with contents intact (NT)

Unknown Tyntesfield burst onto the map after Lord Wraxall died and left his estate not to his son but to be divided equally between nineteen relatives, Continental fashion. In 2002, the executors concluded that a sale of the entire house and contents was the only option and the National Trust had to gird its loins for battle. It won with Lottery help, and the house was opened to the public in 2003, with admirable dispatch.

The house was re-built from 1863 onwards for the guano tycoon, Anthony Gibbs. A devout Anglo-Catholic, he would walk each day from his London house in Hyde Park to London Docks to inspect the latest shipment of seabird droppings which would be converted into fertilizer. He and his son, William, were to make a phenomenal £100,000 a year in profit. They spent most of it on their house at Tyntesfield, on Keble College, Oxford, and on evangelical churches in the Tractarian cause. At the house they built the largest private-house chapel in England, proclaiming God's glory, a presence amid all this dung and money.

The house emerges from a fold in the Mendip foothills overlooking its own valley. Ramparts of rhododendron and azalea part to offer glimpses of Gothic grey. Turrets, pinnacles and gables loom through trees. Lichen clings to rust-stained windows. The house exterior is of the sort that Thomas Warton described in his lines, 'Lead me, Queen Sublime, to solemn glooms/ Congenial with my soul; to cheerless shades,/ To ruin'd seats, to twilight cells and bowers.'

The building was remodelled from an 1813 house by John Norton in 1863, with additions by Henry Woodyer in 1885 and the magnificent chapel by Sir Arthur Blomfield. Its plan is relatively symmetrical, although not its exterior appearance. This is in the most romantic Gothic style. It survives as built, except for the loss of a once soaring tower over the entrance porch.

The entrance faces the drive, but the main rooms face south over the park. The façades all have Gothic windows, Tudor oriels, chimneys and attic dormers. The building material is grey and even on the sunniest day the effect is severe.

This is not true of the interior. Here Norton and Woodyer designed suites of richly ornamented chambers, employing the leading craftsmen of the day. Star was the firm of J. G. Crace, master of Longleat (Wilts) and Knightshayes (Devon). Tyntesfield retains these interiors intact, including furniture, fabrics and household contents.

Each room is different. The library, filling the wing flanking the courtyard, is open to its roof and is heavy with a splendid Crace-designed carpet. The dining room has a bay devoted to Indian design by Woodyer, its frieze decorated with animals. The staircase hall has a balcony on three sides above bold Gothic arches, overseen by portraits of William

Tyntesfield: billiard room

Gibbs and his wife, Matilda. They peopled the hall with busts of Anglo-Catholic divines. The drawing room beyond has a barrel vault, silk wall-hangings and ivory inlaid doors.

Everywhere the craftsmanship is of the first quality. Lord Wraxall's study is decorated with a frieze of fruit and Jacobean scrollwork even on the window shutters. A gigantic moose's head gazes down on the billiard room which has a heated table and electric scoring board. The Tyntesfield estate maps wallpaper a passage. In a rear courtyard are Gothic kennels, as though awaiting the return of their mastiffs.

The house, on my first visit, was a true time warp. It had not been weeded of junk and seemed like a great aristocratic house down on its luck and awaiting bailiffs. Shelves creaked with crockery. Leather books were stacked against walls. Curtains drooped lusciously over furniture. The upstairs rooms were as if guests had just fled in despair, with a telephone receiver hanging from the wall. Everywhere were prints of Gothic churches and religious art. This is a culture not of our time, but I wonder if 'salvation' can really save it.

WELLS: BISHOP'S PALACE

**

Market Place
Walled and moated residence (P)

There are finer palaces in England but few have settings more picturesque than the home of the Bishop of Bath and Wells. It was intended as a fortress to protect the bishop from the townspeople, an English Albi. It is now a gentle harmony of stone, water and trees.

Even when the precinct is closed, the walk round the moat and the view through its gatehouse are a delight. I once sat on the bank and watched an iridescent kingfisher at work. It darted among the mute swans which are trained to pull a bell rope below a window for their daily feed.

The palace is not what it was. The Great Hall of Bishop Burnell, now a ruin, must have been a gigantic 13th-century chamber. A century later a dispute between Bishop Ralph and the townspeople led to the building of the wall and moat round an enclave covering 13 acres. Had this been left to evolve undisturbed, it would now be a precious medieval survival. Instead it has been gradually cleared and landscaped to form a decorous park, where the Palace Croquet Club meets in summer.

The chapel and ruins of the hall stand to the right of the palace itself. This was drastically altered by the architect, Benjamin Ferrey, in 1846. His ecclesiastical contacts far outstripped his ability. How much he ruined is unclear, for his new façades and interiors are neither Gothick nor robust medieval. The style reflects the 'muscular Christianity' of an English public school.

Inside there is still much worth seeing. The hall is part of the old undercroft, with bold rib-vaulting and a spectacular medieval fireplace. Upstairs, Ferrey designed the Long Gallery and a panelled room, the windows with trefoil or sometimes quinquefoil arches. What appear to be Purbeck marble columns are, in fact, enamelled iron. The wallpaper in the Long Gallery forms a splendid backdrop to a collection of episcopal portraits.

Bristol

Blaise House *   Kings Weston **
The Georgian House *   Red Lodge **

BLAISE HOUSE *

Henbury, 4m NW of the city centre
Rebuilt manor in Repton landscape (M)

The village of Henbury is sandwiched between central Bristol and the commercial horrors of Cribbs Causeway. Lost and unsignposted in its midst is Blaise Castle, a fragmentary survival of the Picturesque creation of Humphry Repton and John Nash.

Blaise was a magnet for Bristol visitors in the mid-18th century, when the estate was bought by a sugar merchant, Thomas Farr. He built a fake castle from which he, his guests and tourists could watch merchantmen coming up the river from Avonmouth. The view must have been superb. Farr went bankrupt and the property eventually passed to another tycoon, John Harford, a Quaker and Merchant Venturer.

Harford became instantly unpopular. He restricted access to what had come to be regarded as a public park. He closed footpaths, chopped down trees and demanded back keys which local people had used to reach the castle. He also demolished the old manor and built a square house to express 'substance, directness,

dignity and security'. Harford sounds a miserable character.

However, Harford had even more Picturesque ambitions than Farr. He engaged Repton to redesign an entrance away from disagreeable Henbury, and to open up a new view of the Bristol Channel and Wales. Repton's work at Blaise was among his most successful. He was delighted that almost all his effects were achieved 'by the axe', rather than new planting. He used the new drive to the house as an opportunity to give visitors a constantly changing view. 'Where man resides,' he wrote of Blaise, 'nature must be conquered by art.' He later gave way to his partner and eventual rival, John Nash, who designed the eccentric hamlet, built as almshouses in 1810.

Harford's house was typical of the period, solid, simple and unexciting. His son, also John, extended it with the architect, Charles Cockerell, in 1832 to incorporate a picture gallery. His descendants sold the estate to Bristol Corporation to save it from development in 1926. Blaise Hamlet passed to the National Trust in 1943. The park is now open and, on a fine day, the castle still offers a view towards Wales.

The house interior is grand but of little interest, being now a museum of Bristol life, which tends to mean Bristol objects. The blandness of the display has its own appeal. One room is entirely of washing equipment. Another is entirely of lights and another is a school where 'real' Victorian lessons are held. The best room is the old picture gallery, which has pictures from the Corporation's fine collection of mostly Victorian works.

THE GEORGIAN HOUSE *

7 Great George Street
Family town house of sugar merchant (M)

The Georgian House is a simple terraced house just three bays wide, similar to hundreds in the Clifton area of Bristol. It was built for an 18th-

Wells's Bishop's Palace: crowned head

century Bristol merchant, John Pinney, in 1788 on his return from making a sugar fortune in Nevis in the West Indies. He died in 1818, worth the equivalent today of £17m. He was a slave owner and the house contains a didactic exhibition of the West Indian slave trade on the top floor. It was bought by Canon Thorold Cole in 1905, who gave it to the City in 1937.

The house reflects the speculative architecture of this part of Bristol, developed by the Georgian Paty family. The ground floor has been altered to open up the study inside the front door, somewhat spoiling the intimacy of the hall. The room has fine bookcases with broken pediment tops.

On the first floor is the main drawing room. It is laid for tea, beneath Nicholas Pocock's grand picture of the island of Nevis seen from St Kitts. Next door is the library with a magnificent bookcase of Cuban mahogany. Wavy tracery is set into its glass doors. The bedroom above has a portrait of John Pinney in a colourful waistcoat.

The basement appears to retain its original fittings, including those of the laundry. At the bottom of the stairs is a stone cold-water plunge-bath, which Mr Pinney used as a reminder of his apprentice days in London.

KINGS WESTON **

Shirehampton, 3m NW of Bristol
Vanbrugh villa on terrace over Avonmouth (P)

The terrace in front of Kings Weston must have enjoyed one of the great views of England. Below it lay the mouth of the River Avon, through which passed each day a glittering fleet on its way to Bristol, laden with the wealth of the known world. Beyond was the Bristol Channel and Wales. Today, the vista is equally spectacular, but in its ugliness. From horizon to horizon is a sprawl of warehouses, oil depots, car dumps and the M5.

Nor has this majestic house been better treated. It was commissioned in 1710 for Edward Southwell, Clerk to the Privy Council and Secretary of State for Ireland. The architect was none other than Sir John Vanbrugh. He never saw it completed, building continuing for most of the succeeding decade. The house was sold by the Southwells in 1822 to the builders of Avonmouth docks, the Miles family, who sold it in turn in 1937 to the Bristol Municipal Charities. Disaster ensued. The house became a barracks, a school of architecture, then a police training college until, in 1995, Bristol Corporation left it empty to be vandalized. In 2000 it was bought by a valiant private entrepreneur, John Hardy.

The exterior remains glorious, although the grounds are sadly run-down. The main front to the garden has a pilastered portico above which rises an astonishing coronet of chimneys. These are set on an arched arcade running round all four sides of the inner roof, so the chimneys appear to decorate the view of the house from each angle. The chimney pots are paired, offsetting the corner urns. Vanbrugh built this in wood beforehand to see how it would look. It has a wholly theatrical effect and is great fun.

The interior ground floor is accessible and mostly institutional. It is no less dramatic for that. The entrance hall is on a Vanbrughian scale, although altered by Robert Mylne in 1764. An immensely tall space has three decks of portraits in fitted plaster frames, all by 'school of' Kneller and Lely. The second hall behind is equally exhilarating. It is entirely filled by a freestanding 'hanging' staircase rising the full height of the house. On the walls are painted niches and statues. The saloon and other reception rooms have had their plasterwork restored.

RED LODGE **

Park Row
16th-century house with oak interiors (M)

The desecration of Bristol by its post-war council has outstripped anything inflicted by Hitler's bombs. Park Row is no exception.

What should be a stately progress along the contour overlooking the centre is a straggle of unkempt public buildings and multi-storey car parks. Yet in its midst sits a jewel. Red Lodge was built by Sir John Younge c1590 as an outpost of his principal mansion lower down the hill where he entertained Elizabeth I on a visit in 1574. If this smaller house is any guide, the big one must have been truly magnificent.

Red Lodge is a fine example of an Elizabethan town house, indicating the wealth and style of Bristol's merchant class. While the exterior has no pretensions, the oak-panelled rooms have some of the best fittings of their period. The Great Oak Room upstairs is the main reception room. It is hard to exaggerate the splendour of this chamber, a match for similar work in the City of London lost in the Great Fire. Decoration is concentrated in the ceiling, chimneypiece and carved wooden porch.

The room's internal draught porch, a fitting all but vanished from most English houses, here serves as a ceremonial foyer. A visitor would have stood momentarily under its arch, crowned by a Renaissance canopy with entablature rising double the height of the arch. It is covered in relief carvings, including of Red Indians. The room's classical chimneypiece of stone is no less ornate, its coat of arms puffing out its chest in pride. Local Friends of Red Lodge have supplied some furniture and fabrics. The room is at its best when sun streams through its windows and brings its oak to life.

The other rooms are more conventional. The Small Oak Room next door leads into a bedroom, with good reproduction bedhangings. The remainder of Red Lodge was much altered in the 18th century. The house contains a scattering of pictures and furniture from Bristol's municipal collection.

The garden has been laid out as a 16th-century knot garden, using plants known to have been common at that time. It is a lovely parterre, kept in good repair. It is a pity about the surroundings.

Red Lodge's draught porch, detail

Staffordshire

Staffordshire has two industrial areas, the Black Country of the West Midlands and the Potteries around Stoke. Both are bleak. But the county has dramatic corners. The spectacular valley of the River Churnet penetrates the Peak District, part of which is inside the county. Lichfield and Stafford are uncommonly attractive towns. If much of Staffordshire is indeed dreary, the more precious are its many gems.

Buried in a suburb of West Bromwich is a surprising survival, the medieval and moated Old Manor House. Ford Green Hall is an outstanding Elizabethan work lost in outer Stoke. Moseley Old Hall offers a delicious reminder of mid-17th-century comfort, sheltering by the M54. The county's finest mansion, Weston Park, was one of the few English houses designed by a woman, Lady Wilbraham.

Staffordshire shone under the Georgians. Soane gave Chillington one of his most splendid halls. Shugborough is the masterpiece of Samuel Wyatt. For architectural landscapes, Staffordshire can hardly be rivalled, with Capability Brown and James Paine at Chillington and Weston, 'Athenian' Stuart at Shugborough, and all and sundry at Alton Towers. The last is one of the most romantic 'ghost' houses in England, built by A. W. N. Pugin for the Earl of Shrewsbury and crying out for rescue from its theme park. The 19th century was crowned by Wightwick, epitome of an erudite Arts and Crafts residence.

Alton Castle *
Alton Towers **
Barlaston **
Castern *
Chillington ***
Clifton Hall *
Ford Green Hall **
Hoar Cross *
Izaak Walton's Cottage *
Kinver Rock Houses *

Lichfield:
  Erasmus Darwin
    House *
  Johnson's Birthplace *
  Moseley Old Hall ***
Sandon Hall **
Shugborough ***
Sinai Park *
Stafford:
  High House **

Tamworth Castle **
Trentham *
West Bromwich:
  Oak House **
  Old Manor House **
Weston Park ***
Whitmore **
Wightwick ****
Wolverhampton:
  Bantock House *

Peover Hall●

●Capesthorne

MACCLESFIELD BUXTON

Gawsworth●

Chatsworth●

Cheshire

Haddon●

Little Moreton●

Rode Hall●

A34

A53

A515

Crewe Hall●

A500

A53

Castern●

Tissington●

A523

Ford Green●

A520

Derbyshire

A51

Highfields

STOKE-ON-TRENT

A52

Alton●

Whitmore●

Trentham●

A520

A50

A52

A53

Barlaston●

Kedleston●

Staffordshire

Sudbury●

M6

Sandon●

A518

A515

Izaak Walton's Cottage●

A34

A519

BURTON UPON TRENT

STAFFORD●

Shugborough●

Hoar Cross●

Sinai Park●

A513

A51

Shropshire

A518

A38

Catton Hall●

A41

Clifton Hall●

A5

Weston Park●

Boscobel●

Lichfield●

TELFORD

M54

Chillington●

A5

Ironbridge

Moseley●

A34

Tamworth●

Benthall

A449

M42

Wightwick●

WOLVERHAMPTON●

Middleton●

A5

A454

A41

Morville●

A4123

Upton Cressett●

A38

West Bromwich●

A449

A491

Dudmaston●

A458

M5

M6

BIRMINGHAM●

Kinver●

A45

Warwickshire

A38

10 Miles

Hagley●

M42

Worcestershire

ALTON CASTLE *

Alton, 4m E of Cheadle
Fantasy castle on bluff above ravine (P-R)

The Earls of Shrewsbury were England's answer to Ludwig of Bavaria, creating their castles above the ravine of the River Churnet. Alton Towers, designed by the young A. W. N. Pugin, was intended as the 16th Earl's family home. The purpose of this second house a mile down the valley, also by Pugin, changed during construction. It looks as if it were designed for a Wagnerian princess, seized with a fit of piety.

The castle is a Rhineland Gothic fantasy of towers, turrets and steep roofs. It soars on a rock across the ravine separating it from the Hospital of St John. This is a Catholic school, house and almshouse, part of the same settlement.

The exterior to the courtyard is that of an L-shaped crenellated mansion, but with tower and the chapel piled up behind, as if to stop it sliding downhill. The chapel roof is in vivid yellow and green tiles. The polygonal apse dominates the skyline from the valley.

The castle is now a Catholic youth centre and a polite request is needed to gain entry, although the outside is impressive enough. The principal room is the chapel. This is an extension of the central hall, a bizarre arrangement for any home. The hall is Puginian, brightly painted and rising past a gallery to a lantern. It serves as a foyer to the chapel, the whole interior being emphatically ecclesiastical. It really should be more accessible.

ALTON TOWERS **

N of Alton, 5m E of Cheadle
Ruin of Gothic palace lost amid theme park (P)

Where to begin? Alton Towers is today a ruin, a grotesque and melancholic Castle Grim and backdrop to a shamelessly inappropriate theme park and funfair. The creeper-encrusted walls of the old house gaze down at the plastic boats on the lake, across which are a fake

village street, fast-food outlets and roller-coasters. 'I don't go near the place, it's spooky,' said the ticket lady when I asked if the ruin was accessible. Yet spookiness is the saving grace of Alton, defying the surrounding vulgarity. This is truly a place of Goths. The great-aunt from Transylvania may be a corpse but her eyes are still open. She will be there still when the rest has vanished.

Alton Towers was built for two Talbots, both Earls of Shrewsbury, from 1810 onwards. The bulk of the house was begun for the 15th Earl to designs possibly by James Wyatt and others. A series of architects laid out the gardens along the contours of the Churnet valley, filling them with exotic structures. At this stage, all was normal Regency Picturesque. The 16th Earl succeeded in 1827 and moved up a gear. In 1837 he imported the toast of the Victorian Catholic aristocracy, the twenty-five-year-old Augustus Welby Pugin, and proceeded to transform his uncle's house. Like Scarisbrick (Lancs) and Carlton Towers (Yorks, N), Alton was to be the embodiment of Catholic Romanticism.

The house is the more impressive the nearer one gets. It is accessible to the public visiting the theme park, and refreshingly empty. The roof has been restored and stairs give access to upper floors. Of Pugin's own interiors, the Great Banqueting Hall, forming the spine of the house, and the chapel interior survive. The former has two magnificent Gothic fireplaces. Hardman glass survives in the bay window. The chapel has also been restored, with modern stained glass. Otherwise one can walk along passages and enter the shells of the drawing room, gallery and music room. Remains of the walls survive in the library and in an alcove called the Poets' Corner. Stripped brick vaults echo with the ghosts of medieval entertainment.

The theme park owners are trying slowly to restore more of the rooms. The upper rooms are accessible and give splendid views over what was once the park. To the rear is a wide grassy courtyard with ruined domestic offices. This place needs only a modern Pugin and a modern Shrewsbury.

BARLASTON HALL **

Barlaston, 3m N of Stone
Potteries villa by Sir Robert Taylor (P)

The house sits lonely on a hillside overlooking the River Trent. Its proximity to the Wedgwood works suggests the residence of a Potteries magnate but this is not so. It was completed in 1756 for a Leek lawyer, Thomas Mills, on marrying a local heiress, Ester Bagnall, in 1742.

Mills's architect was almost certainly Robert Taylor, recently returned from the Grand Tour. The style is that of a Palladian villa and must have seemed tall and sophisticated in a landscape of Jacobean manors and scruffy industrial workings. It seems no less sophisticated today.

From the outside, the house is unusually plain. The plan is cruciform, of four large reception rooms set round a central staircase hall, rising the full three floors of the house. The rooms are occupied privately by the Hall family and are still being restored.

The rescue of Barlaston in the 1970s was a *cause célèbre* of the lobbying group, SAVE Britain's Heritage. The house had been stripped even of its fireplaces by the Coal Board, whose subsidence had apparently doomed it to collapse. It was bought from the original owners, Messrs Wedgwood, for £1. Coal Board compensation paid for a lengthy programme of restoration.

Chief discovery was Taylor's elaborate Rococo plasterwork. His motif of octagonal lozenge shapes is everywhere. They appear in window frames, panelling, plasterwork, even bookcases. In the course of salvage, other rich Baroque and Rococo designs have emerged, product of Taylor's Italian studies. In the dining room, the picture frames, roundels and overmantel are all of Rococo design. The saloon is lit by a large sweeping bow and has a plasterwork frieze.

The library bow window has roundels of Shakespeare and, now, of John Betjeman, hero of the conservation movement to which we owe the survival of this house.

CASTERN HALL *

2m N of Ilam, 4m NW of Ashbourne
Ancient panelled hall lost in Peak (P-R)

The village of Ilam is the most picturesque in the Staffordshire Peak area. Its old hall is now a Youth Hostel, but a road up the isolated valley beyond reveals an apparition. Round a fold in the moors is a stylish 18th-century façade that might be in the centre of Derby. In front are a wall, posts and steps hinting at a long-lost courtyard. Behind is a rough-and-tumble farmyard.

The house is that of the Hurt family and its hindquarters show it to be of some antiquity. Massive rubble walls conceal a maze of blocked doors, windows, arches and odd angles. The front is Queen Anne in style though Georgian in date, 1730. The front door is a lovely composition, rusticated with a pedimented window above.

The house inside is still being restored. The hall has a fine stone fireplace with a vaguely Baroque curve to its mantelpiece. The Oak Room has imported panelling of c1610. With each phase of repair, a new discovery is made. This a house whose past is still in its future.

CHILLINGTON HALL ***

3m N of Codsall
Mansion by Soane in park by Brown and Paine (P)

There have been Giffards at Chillington since 1178. The present incumbent is a policeman, indeed the Chief Constable of Staffordshire, and his Texan wife. The house has been restored and the Giffards are now at work on the majestic 1,000-acre park. This seems in revolt. Its unruly trees and grass seem to be marching up to the foot of Soane's portico and challenging the family to return Chillington to Nature.

The Giffards were Midlands recusants who paid dearly for their faith. They arrived with William the Conqueror, served Henry VIII and turned spy on Mary Queen of Scots.

Ardent Catholics, they joined the Penderels of neighbouring Boscobel (Salop) in helping Charles II escape after Worcester. The family still act as trustees of the Penderel Pension, paid by Charles as a reward.

Giffards never gained national fame or nobility, preferring the quiet virtues of estate management. Their one celebrity came from an incident in the 16th century when a Giffard shot a panther that had escaped from his menagerie and was about to savage a mother and child. The panther was immortalized as the family crest in 1513, a bearded archer being added ten years later. The family motto is 'Take breath and pull strong'.

The house is approached along a mile of drive, magnificently landscaped by Capability Brown. Landscape buildings are by James Paine and others. Although sliced by the M54 and the Shropshire Union Canal, this wild park contrasts with the manicured landscape, also by Brown and Paine, at neighbouring Weston. A Grecian temple, possibly by Robert Adam, faces the lake, along with assorted temples, bridges, cottages, terraces and urns. All this is in process of repair.

The Giffards rebuilt their old Tudor courtyard house in two bursts of energy in the 18th century. The first is attributed to Francis Smith of Warwick but was probably by the local architect, Richard Trubshaw. The second was by the young Sir John Soane, who contributed the portico in 1786. Soane's architecture is not always loveable and his east wing, naked amid lawn and gravel, does not smile. Trubshaw's south front, built in 1724, is less austere, of red-brick with stone dressings. Soane had intended a complete rebuild, but was obliged to keep this wing. The poor join can be seen at the attic storey.

Soane's interiors are spectacular. The entrance hall with Ionic columns is as he designed it, in bright turquoise. The vivid colours displayed throughout Chillington, much to its advantage, are claimed to be original. The Soane front comprises a drawing room and

Soanian elegance at Chillington

dining room. The drawing room mirror is Soanian, crowned with the Giffard panther's head. The dining room contains two magnificent paintings by Batoni.

Behind the hall, Soane intended a family chapel where had been the Tudor Great Hall. Instead he created a saloon. This is the most exciting space in the house, reminiscent of Soane's lost chambers at the Bank of England in London. Wide Soanian arches support an elliptical cove to a lantern, which floods the room with light. The walls are again turquoise. The fireplace is a brutal neo-Tudor confection out of place in this room. It depicts, yet again, Giffard shooting the panther.

Beyond is the 1720s staircase hall and everything that Soane is not, sensuous and decoratively fussy. The stair treads are adorned with panthers. The wall panels contain busts and plasterwork in the style of Artari and Vassalli. The effect is overwhelmed by a 19th-century window depicting the heraldry of recusants who married Giffards. The morning room contains a stucco ceiling of swirling panels and a roundel of the Goddess of Architecture.

CLIFTON HALL *

Clifton Campville, 9m S of Burton upon Trent
Restored fragment of Smith house (P-R)

The chief exhibit in Richard Blount's house is his collection of before-and-after photographs. He and his wife are two of the country house saints who devote themselves to bringing hope to hopeless houses. Blount was defeated by Sinai (below) and is rescuing Staunton Harold (Leics). Clifton is his own. It was designed by Francis Smith of Warwick for the Pye family in 1705. The great house was intended to fill the centre of the composition, with wings for the stables and kitchens. The main house was never built, only the wings. In c1720 one of these was altered to make a family house. The empty site in the middle is a walled garden, enclosed grass and a lonely cedar.

The two identical wing-houses were farm buildings, roofless and derelict when Blount took them in hand in 1996. Vegetation had enveloped the walls. Tractors sat where shelter survived. Both wings have now been restored, one as the Blounts' home. They stand overlooking a field outside Clifton Campville. The material is pink brick with nip-and-tuck mortaring. So robust are the Midlands stone dressings as to have needed almost no repair.

Two magnificent doorways face each other across the court, with scrolly Baroque pediments embracing the Pye coat of arms. The windows have glazing bars and handmade glass, giving a lovely reflecting sheen to the façades. On one front English Heritage insisted that Victorian sash windows be kept as 'part of the building's history', stupidly spoiling Smith's symmetry. I suppose the formerly collapsed roof was also history.

There is not much to see inside. This is essentially a family home. The original kitchen retains its massive fireplace and storage cupboards. A fine oak floor has been reinstated on the ground floor. Every part of the interior is flooded with light from the 48 windows. Clifton shows that no historic building is beyond redemption. Blount has an imitation Knyff drawing of Clifton as it would have been if completed. In a way it has been.

FORD GREEN HALL **

Smallthorne, 2m N of Stoke-on-Trent
Jacobean yeoman's house in Stoke suburb (M)

A certain desperation surrounds the few historic houses of the Potteries. Stoke is uncompromisingly dreary and Ford Green Hall is its oasis. Such houses seem relics of an alien civilization left stranded in a desert of roads, car dealers, factories, warehouses and interminable dingy terraces. This is industrial England on whose works Shelley might have invited us to look and despair.

Ford Green House is an excellent black-and-white, half-timbered building set in a valley between two Potteries' suburbs. The house was built in 1624 for a yeoman farmer, Hugh Ford. A new wing was added in 1734. The house continued in the Ford family into the 19th century, when it decayed until rescued after the Second World War. It is now a local museum.

The exterior has close-studded timberwork. There are lozenge panels and, over the porch, remarkable timbering imitating a staircase balustrade. Such work indicates both wealth and decorative flair. The porch carries the inscription of its maker, 'Ralph. Sutton. Carpenter'. The interior is conventionally medieval. The parlour, main hall and kitchen have contemporary furniture. The kitchen pets look lifelike.

The staircase walls retain rough timbering with adze marks to hold a plaster coating. Of the upstairs rooms the most charming is the study over the porch, furnished for late-night letter-writing. The best bedroom has a fine chest and a four-poster bed. The latter is left unmade, a stylistic quirk now considered obligatory by politically correct custodians.

HOAR CROSS HALL *

Hoar Cross, 7m W of Burton on Trent
Ghost of Ingram mansion with Bodley interiors (H)

The Victorian, Hugo Francis Meynell Ingram, was a hunting addict. His ancestor founded the Quorn Hunt and he himself died young in the field in 1871. His wife, Emily, daughter of Lord Halifax, commissioned G. F. Bodley to design the splendid memorial church near the new house, into which she and her husband had not yet moved. She occupied the 70 rooms as a childless widow. The couple had already inherited Temple Newsam (Yorks, W) from her father and were victorianizing its interior at vast expense. At Hoar Cross, they were starting from scratch. It was and is a gigantic pile, now a hotel and health centre.

The architect was Henry Clutton and the style is a dutiful neo-Jacobean. The severity is relieved by the three canted bays to the garden terrace, further softened by copious creeper. The entrance front echoes Halifax's Temple Newsam, with 48 chimneys and turrets crowned with cupolas. The chief exterior virtue of Hoar Cross is the magnificent garden laid out by Lady Emily along lines suggested by Francis Bacon in the 17th century and now admirably restored.

The interiors of Hoar Cross are lifted by the presence of G. F. Bodley, architect also of the house's chapel. The plasterwork ceilings are mostly by him, with wallpapers by his friend, William Morris. They are excellent. The library walls are of 'Spanish leather'. On the ceiling, each plasterwork petal and leaf has been picked out in coloured paint, as have the roses in the Long Gallery. The dining room pendants are in similarly virulent colours.

The hotel uses a photographic technique for its 'paintings'. I prefer the signed photos of visiting celebrities. Departing visitors are warned by a notice, 'Paradise is just behind you'.

IZAAK WALTON'S COTTAGE *

Shallowford, 3m E of Eccleshall
Farmhouse cottage, angling museum (M)

Walton never lived in this cottage. He was a Stafford man who became a prosperous merchant in the City of London. As a Royalist during the Commonwealth he found it politic to leave the City and go fishing. Rather than write on so dangerous a topic as biography or theology, he decided to write a book about angling. The masterpiece, *The Compleat Angler*, has not been out of print to this day.

Walton bought Shallowford Farm in 1655 and donated its revenues to the poor of Stafford, adding money for them to have coal at 'the hardest and most pinching time of winter'. The cottage was eventually sold in 1920 and opened by a charitable trust in 1924 as a small museum to Walton and to fishing. Although sandwiched between the main line railway and overbearing farm buildings, the timbered and thatched cottage, with its herb garden, is charming.

Inside, the downstairs parlour is furnished in 17th-century style. Izaak sits in wax surrounded by his fishing equipment. Upstairs is a museum of angling history and a small

library. Everywhere are rods, lines, flies and stuffed fish, with copies of *The Compleat Angler* helpfully left open for visitors to read. The museum has a complete run of reels, from the 18th century to today.

KINVER ROCK HOUSES *

Kinver, 4m W of Stourbridge
Rock houses embedded in sandstone cliff (NT)

The English have neither the inclination nor the geology to boast many troglodytes. But there are some rudimentary rock houses in Nottingham (Notts) and Knaresborough (Yorks, N). The best are carved into an outcrop of vivid red sandstone overlooking the village of Kinver. The rock is known as Holy Austin after a hermit who was reputed to have lived on or in it. The earliest historical reference is by an 18th-century traveller caught in a storm on Kinver Edge. He hurried down the 'tremendous steep slope to some smoke I saw issue from a romantic rock near the foot'. It was occupied by 'a clean and decent family'.

By 1861 there were eleven families living in the excavated rocks, over forty people on three separate levels. The top level included a three gabled brick house extension. Small gardens spread down the slopes towards the wood. Numbers declined with the closure of the local ironworks and by the Second World War there were just two families here, one in the proper house, the other in the entire lower level. The caves had internal and outside wells and were supplied with gas. They suffered from damp and still gather mould.

Today the gabled house has been rebuilt and is private. Most of the old dwellings have suffered from vandalism and collapse, a terrible comment on the local authority. But the three lower houses were restored by the National Trust in 1997 and two are now open to the public, although one is given over to Trust self-promotion and 'interpretive display', a curse of these small properties.

The other house, of just two rooms, has been re-created as it was when occupied by Mr and Mrs Fletcher in the early 20th century. A fire burns cheerily in the stove. The table is laid for tea. The walls have been sealed, as far as they can be, with limewash that allegedly had to be purchased from America.

LICHFIELD: ERASMUS DARWIN HOUSE *

Beacon Street
Town house of scientist near cathedral close (M)

Darwin was the supreme scientific innovator of his age. He expounded the theory of the survival of the fittest, of biological variation and of evolution. He wrote extensively, was influential and widely celebrated. To his contemporaries, the name of Darwin was everywhere synonymous with science. This Darwin was not Charles but his grandfather, Erasmus. Wandering through this shrine to the great man, one starts to wonder just how much credit Charles deserved. At very least, Darwin junior's *Beagle* discoveries were exercises in testing his grandfather's theories.

Darwin was an 18th-century polymath. After studying medicine in Edinburgh, he arrived in Lichfield in 1725 and became a successful doctor. He was a giant of a man, overweight and afflicted with smallpox scars. Everything fascinated him, from zoology to engineering. He was a prominent member of the Lunar Society of Birmingham and friend of Wedgwood, Arkwright, Watt, Priestley and Boulton (*see* Birmingham: Soho House/Warks). He invented a speaking machine, a potato plough, a steam carriage, an artificial bird and a copying machine so accurate that copy and original could not be told apart.

Darwin was also a writer and a poet. He expressed the 'loves of the plants' with erotic accounts of stamens and pistils. His poem 'The Botanic Garden' caused a sensation. His theory of evolution was also set out as a poem, 'The Temple of Nature'. He even foretold Birmingham's motor age: 'Soon shall they arm, Unconquer'd Steam afar,/ Drag the slow barge or

drive the rapid car.' His reputation collapsed abruptly during the Napoleonic wars. The heroes fighting the barbaric French did not like being told they were descended from apes.

It was in the 1760s that Darwin and his first wife, Polly Howard, transformed the old medieval house near the cathedral. They added a new front of reception rooms, with four handsome Venetian windows. The interior has been badly mauled by health-and-safety fanatics and is afflicted with museumitis, including costly audio-visual kit, stripping some rooms of their 18th-century atmosphere. But Darwin's personality dominates all. He fills the house and is present in two of the rooms in waxwork. From the rear windows is a glorious view towards the close and the west front of England's loveliest small cathedral.

LICHFIELD: JOHNSON'S BIRTHPLACE *

Breadmarket Street
Writer's childhood home, now a shrine (M)

Dr Johnson loved two things, company and books. 'Sir,' he said, 'I am obliged to any man who visits me.' As for books, what better than to enter the house where he was born and find oneself in a second-hand bookshop, which is what it was in his day. Michael Johnson, his father, was a man of books.

The house was built in 1707, a handsome structure with columns on the ground floor, tall rooms and two further storeys with attic above. It passed through various hands and was opened by the local council as a museum in 1901. It now houses memorabilia not located in Johnson's own house in Gough Square (London, C). There is a fine collection of prints and drawings and, in an upstairs study, a library with all his works.

That said, the museum is heavily didactic. Each room traces a different stage in Johnson's life, some as tableaux, some as wall placards. On the ground floor, behind the bookshop, is Michael Johnson in his bookbindery. In those days a bookseller was everything – publisher, printer, binder and salesman. He was businessman and craftsman. We see him here as craftsman.

In the basement in the re-created kitchen is a delightful surprise, an effigy of the nine-year-old Johnson reading *Hamlet*. It is said that when he reached the ghost scene in the play, 'he suddenly hurried upstairs to the street that he might see people about him'. This was the time when, deep in his books, he refused to help his sick father by attending his bookstall at neighbouring Uttoxeter market. The incident so weighed on his conscience that, fifty years later, he went to the same market and stood silent in the rain as an act of filial penance.

The upper rooms, in one of which Samuel was born, are mostly galleries of pictures, bindings and memorabilia. Johnson's true memorial is the books that fill the place. 'You can never be wise,' he said, 'unless you love reading.'

MOSELEY OLD HALL ***

4m N of Wolverhampton
Reclad hall house with Royalist associations (NT)

Moseley presents an image of a desperate and bedraggled Charles II, aged just twenty-one, arriving with a few friends at the back door in the early hours of 8 September 1651. His army had been annihilated at the Battle of Worcester.

The owner of the house, Thomas Whitgreave, was a known Catholic, and he and his priest, Father Huddleston, hid the young man from Parliamentary troops combing the area. Two days later, Whitgreave watched him depart, disguised as a servant, heading not for London and the throne but for Bristol and escape to France. Every moment of the incident was recounted by the King to Samuel Pepys and confirmed by Whitgreave. On Charles's Restoration nine years later, Whitgreave was given a pension of £200 a year and dubbed 'the Preserver'.

Whitgreaves lived at Moseley until 1820. The old house was then encased in Victorian brick, which saved it from collapse but spoiled its black-and-white exterior. It passed to the National Trust in 1962. The subsequent refurbishing of Moseley is one of the Trust's most successful exercises, giving it the warm embrace of Jacobean domesticity. A fire burns in the hall grate, herbs hang from rafters, dogs roam and Catholics pray.

Entrance is through the back door, claimed as the one on which King Charles knocked that famous night. The brewhouse is furnished as a kitchen. So immaculately displayed are the contents – herbs, peppers, spices, dried fruits – as to serve for a Dutch still life. The hall and parlour are cosy and filled with panelling, dark floorboards and old portraits and pewter.

Upstairs is the bed in which Charles slept. It was sold to Wightwick Manor in 1913 but sent back by the owners on Moseley's restoration. In the floor of the garderobe is the trapdoor of the hiding place in which Charles was hidden. He declared it 'the best place I was ever in'.

A corridor outside is hung with pictures and prints of Charles's escape. Mr Whitgreave's room is a panelled parlour filled with 17th-century furniture and much scrollwork and barley-sugar legs. It gives onto the intimate study from which Whitgreave is said to have watched Charles's supporters straggle down the lane for their long and dangerous walk back to Scotland.

The attic contains a small oratory chapel, with barrel-vaulted ceiling and star painting on its small celure. The chapel was used for services until a century ago. The priest's bedroom is next door and the roof contains many priest's holes. Upstairs at Moseley is a wonderfully secret place.

The garden reflects the same 17th-century intimacy as the interior. The National Trust has sought to re-create the topiary work, paths, alleys and knot gardens of the period. Flowers are self-consciously English. Trees are cherry, quince, mulberry and medlar. The sense of seclusion is marred only by the

passing M54. Perhaps one day we can devise quieter engines and quieter tarmac.

SANDON HALL **

Sandon, 5½m NE of Stafford
Neo-Jacobean mansion by William Burn (P-R)

Such are the demands of country-house economics that Sandon must call its attractions 'exclusive' and its dining room 'a setting for prestige dinner parties'. There is force in the exclusive. To gain entry I had to brave a fierce blue tit guarding its young nesting in the mouthpiece of the entrance security telephone. Lord Harrowby defends his territory in style.

The house is grey, stern and Victorian, as rebuilt after a fire by William Burn in 1852. Burn was master of Jacobean Revival and Sandon is a virtuoso display. Giant banks of rhododendrons and azaleas line the drive from the main road. Cedars rise in a glorious crescendo.

The entrance façade is a symmetrical E-plan with central *porte-cochère* crowned by turrets. Windows have fiddly strapwork and quoins are like leather straps. The interior is virile neo-Jacobean, recalling Burn's work at Harlaxton (Lincs). Most magnificent is the hall, divided by two screens of columns, the walls scarlet and the panelling dark wood. At the end is a fine staircase rising and returning in two flights to the landing. It seems designed for a cavalier to come galloping down the hall and sweep a damsel off her feet. Angelica Kauffmann depicts three Harrowby girls as *The Three Graces*.

The state rooms are heavy. Burn's giant pendants drip like stalactites over the guests below. Learning does not sit light on the library, weighed down with books and busts. The drawing room has hand-painted Chinese wallpaper, clearly older than the house. A magnificent conservatory was added in 1864. It too is bombproof Victorian.

Moseley: Charles's Catholic refuge

SHUGBOROUGH ***

4m NW of Rugeley
Seat of Admiral Anson's brother with classical interiors (NT)

Some houses start with a place, others with a person. Shugborough starts with two brothers, Thomas Anson who inherited the house in 1720, and his younger brother, George, who became England's most celebrated 18th-century admiral. George sailed round the world for four years, during which he captured a Spanish galleon out of Acapulco, the *Nuestra Señora de Covadonga*, which carried £400,000 in gold, a stupendous sum. These English sea captains were little short of privateers. Anson's share of the money paid for his brother's rebuilding of Shugborough.

Thomas's first task was the garden, intended to rival that of Stowe (Bucks). He commissioned James 'Athenian' Stuart to dot the park with classical monuments, including a triumphal arch, Doric temple and Tower of the Winds. In among them wandered Corsican goats. Poussin was to be reincarnated in the glades of Staffordshire on the profits of Spanish gold.

As for the house, Thomas Anson added wings to the old William-and-Mary building, and filled it with excellent plasterwork by Vassalli. This 1740s house was converted by a great-nephew, Viscount Anson, between 1790 and 1806, to designs by Samuel Wyatt, brother of James.

Wyatt turned a lively vertical house into a severe horizontal one, early Georgian into late Georgian. A colonnade united the central block with one pavilion with domed bow windows on either side. (The domed bow is a Samuel signature.) The outside he covered in grey dressed slate, a smart but cold material even when polished to look like the finest ashlar.

There is nothing cold about the interior. The Anson family is now represented by the flamboyant photographer, Lord Lichfield, who lives in part of the house. The rest is run by Staffordshire County Council in collaboration with the

National Trust. Lord Lichfield's personality is present throughout. His celebrity photographs enliven every shelf and table top.

The rooms contrast classical severity with flashes of Baroque ostentation. The first rooms on the ground floor display Greek and Roman antiquities. The north wing ends in the dining room, with a fitted set of paintings of Roman ruins by Nicholas Dall. The chimneypiece has a picture of the Admiral in most unnautical robes. The enormous Red Drawing Room is Samuel Wyatt's most accomplished work, of 1794 in the Adam style.

Wyatt built the great saloon to receive the Prince Regent, who never came. Next door, a billiard room includes a Rococo ceiling brought from the old Chinese House in the grounds. It is a charming confection of oriental motifs in Italian settings. Also here is a set

Shugborough: late-Georgian sobriety

of Chinese porcelain given to Anson in thanks for his sailors extinguishing a fire during a visit to Canton.

The last, and most intimate, of the public rooms is the library. This is in two parts, divided by a Soanian arch with columns and niches, penetrating the wall of the original house. Although formal in architecture, the two rooms are pleasantly cluttered with books, magazines and photographs of the Royal Family. Mirrors make it look as if the books go on for ever.

Lichfield family rooms beyond are sometimes open to the public. This is a well-presented house, despite the perils inherent in co-management.

SINAI PARK *

2m W of Burton upon Trent
Semi-derelict hall house under restoration
(P-R)

Restoration is hardly the word for what Kate Newton is doing to this romantic ruin on a wild bluff overlooking Burton upon Trent. Drivers on the A38 see a gaunt skeleton on the horizon, of a roof collapsed in what seems a derelict farm. Close to, we can discern a medieval E-plan coming back to life, with help from copious grants and total dedication.

The house was an outpost of a Burton monastery of *c*1500. It passed to the Paget family at the Dissolution, who added a central hall range to create the present house. This became a farmhouse but was wrecked by the RAF, worst of the Services in abusing houses during the Second World War. Salvaged as six cottages, the house was then used as a barn. The local authority took no action to stop it collapsing, until eventually the great oak beams of the roof fell and ruined the interior wall-paintings. The place was, and still is, dangerous. Only its isolated location can have saved it from the bulldozer.

Miss Newton acquired Sinai in 1994 and she and her partner have rebuilt and occupied one wing, with meticulous conservation of surviving details, including fragments of the wall-paintings. The new oak staircase is by Venables of Stafford. The rest remains to be done when funds permit. The house is dry-moated, with a small 18th-century bridge. These buildings need saints and Sinai is lucky to have found one.

STAFFORD: ANCIENT HIGH HOUSE **

Greengate Street
Rich merchant's house of 16th century (M)

Elizabethan town houses were the skyscrapers of their age. Crammed onto a prominent central site, what is claimed as the 'largest timber-framed town house in England' glows with pride in the middle of Stafford. Less excusable is the desecration of the place by health-and-safety officials. They have taken a building that has resisted fire for four centuries and inserted a fire-door exhibition centre.

The building is positioned on a street corner. The close-studding of its timbers, the plethora of windows and the prominent chimney stacks all indicate wealth as well as strength. A Richard Sneyd lived here in the 17th century. The house was rebuilt in 1595 and the present rooms illustrate their occupancy over subsequent centuries. The staircase turret to the rear, rising three storeys, is a splendid timber structure.

The rooms are municipal-historical. The Civil War room was used to house Royalist prisoners 'of the better sort'. Others were tossed into the town gaol. Prince Rupert's dog is portrayed in wax. The Stuart bedroom has a fine Adam and Eve bed-head. There is a Victorian sitting room and an Edwardian office. The upper storeys turn to social history. The shop has real rather than wax fruit 'on sale'. There is a herb garden at the back.

TAMWORTH CASTLE **

The Holloway
Norman castle transformed (M)

The castle of the Marmions of Tamworth has failed to keep all enemies at bay. It is besieged on one side by tower blocks and on the other by shedlands. Even inside I fear that on a hot day it might become a pool of wax.

Yet this is a magnificent place. The castle passed from the medieval Marmions through the Ferrers in the 15th century to the Townshends in the 18th. In 1897, the Marquis Townshend sold it to the council for £3,000. The castle is a Norman motte-and-bailey, with a herringbone fragment of original wall surviving under the approach. The plan is of a shell keep, with fortified chambers tightly grouped round an inner courtyard.

The interior is medieval on the ground floor, with state rooms on the first and domestic

rooms on the second. Under the tower is a dungeon (with wax prisoner). The banqueting hall, with a 15th-century roof, is reached through a fine Renaissance doorway. The state rooms are formed from an earlier Long Gallery. A Jacobean gentleman rests on a sumptuous bed, entertained by a taped lutenist. Beyond is the dining room with florid overmantel. This, with other 17th-century features, was brought from Chislehurst in Kent during the castle's 19th-century 'jacobeanization'. The tablecloth appears in disarray and the bread looks admirably fresh.

The top floor rooms display the castle's last period of occupation under Townshend's tenants, the Cooke family, in the 1880s. We see the Cooke bedrooms, nursery, bathroom and the endearing clutter of a large Victorian family. Annie Cooke's room has a quilted counterpane and is enhanced by an effigy of her reading a book. The Cookes lived comfortably in their castle, proving that ancient structures can be well adapted to modern use.

A haunted bedroom has an actress on video warning a waxen Lord Marmion to 'repent of your evil act', followed by a terrible wailing. This is surely meant for the local planning officer.

TRENTHAM PARK *

2m S of Stoke-on-Trent
Ghost of great Victorian mansion (M)

Here in the suburbs of Stoke could be a set for the surrealist cult film *Last Year in Marienbad*. A roundabout on the A34 advertises Trentham Park Gardens, a tatty 1960s conference centre attended by cafés and a car boot sale. Huts and prefabs abound. This might be former Eastern Europe.

Be not deterred. Buy a ticket from an ice cream stall and follow directions over a bridge and through the bushes. Beyond lies a ghost. Even Pevsner had to abandon a strict rule 'not to describe buildings that have been demol-

Tamworth: Marmions at table

ished' to conjure up the pleasure dome of Trentham. It was designed by Sir Charles Barry for the 2nd Duke of Sutherland in 1833. The house had belonged in 1540 to James Leveson, one of the Duke's ancestors; it was rebuilt by Smith of Warwick and Henry Holland before the arrival of Barry.

For the 2nd Duke, Barry built an Italianate palace as spectacular as anything in the country, comparable with the similar Italianate house the same pair were creating at Cliveden (Bucks). The Duchess had rightly rejected the original designer, Edward Blore, as 'that cheap architect'. Trentham was to cost £123,000. Almost everything was destroyed in 1912, when industrial pollution of the river forced the abandonment of the house. The site passed to a property company.

Remaining at present is the entrance colonnade and *porte-cochère*. A panel carries the Duke's coat of arms, a glimpse of former splendour. Behind is a lawn where the house lay, with the remains of the stables and clocktower. A notice in front announces 'the largest formal garden in England', the work of William Nesfield. Here yew and box stand silent witness to the passing greatness of the place, as they do at Witley Court (Worcs). The terracing has been repaired and glides down to the edge of the restored lake.

All this forms the setting for a new hotel planned on the site of the old mansion. At the time of writing, a developer promises a building with 'the scale' of Barry's. If he can find an architect fit for the task, well and good, but why not rebuild Barry? The present dereliction is a blot on the face of Staffordshire.

WEST BROMWICH: OAK HOUSE **

Cambridge Road
Jacobean black-and-white mansion (M)

West Bromwich needs all the historic buildings it can find. This one languishes in all its glory, a Cinderella amid the most depressing industrial squalor, even for the Black Country. I could find no trace of a sign anywhere near.

The black-and-white Midlands manor is dated c1600, despite the 1488 on a drainpipe. Pictures of the house before its restoration as a museum in 1898 show it as now, dominated by three wide gables and a fourth, close-studded, over the porch. More remarkable are the four colossal chimney stacks accompanying the black-and-white belvedere on the roof. This must have been intended as a look-out, a form much favoured by late-Elizabethan builders.

The interior is of a familiar plan, although the old screens passage has fallen foul of museumitis and the hall has had its ceiling removed. This is apparently to allow a view up to the look-out, which is pointless. The service wing is to the left, the parlour and solar to the right. These are excellently restored, panelled and with old beams and furniture of the period. In the dining room is a Tudor oak chair with carved back and sides. A 17th-century morning room has panelling with shelves, a dresser and a writing desk.

Upstairs is a warren of small bedrooms with four-posters and old flooring. One of the beds has original 17th-century needlework hangings, simple but charming. This is a delightful house, but does anyone know it is there? There was no guidebook on my visit.

WEST BROMWICH: OLD MANOR HOUSE **

Hall Green Road
Complete medieval manor rediscovered (H)

'Button-bustin' Feasting and Merriment' is the promise that greets visitors to this astonishing place. I would add, 'eye-poppin''. No sooner have the suburbs of the West Midlands anaesthetized the senses than round an anonymous bend is an apparition. A derelict 'old hall' surrounded by later clutter came on the market in 1950 and the local council found they had on their hands a 13th-century moated manor, complete with hall, courtyard, solar and chapel wing. They spent months trying to demolish it and then gave up. In 1957 a narrow majority

decision was taken to restore it, with James A. Roberts as architect. The building was then rented to Ansell's Brewery as a pub.

The house has all the gaudiness of a Midlands eaterie. Muzak shrieks, fruit machines clatter, bars are crowded and 'merriment' utters from private rooms decked with medieval shields and banners. An armoured knight on a horse guards the buffet at the dais end of the hall. Yet there is nothing phoney about this building. It is the real McCoy. The moat has been dug out and filled with water. Unused corners, such as the medieval chapel, have been used for small displays of artefacts found on the site.

The courtyard is entered through an Elizabethan gatehouse. A tiny medieval courtyard lies inside with the entrance to the Great Hall ahead. This is open to the roof, a structure of c1290 supported on two massive cruck beams with rare double braces. All suggest a wealthy owner, believed to be William de Marnham, lord of the local manor in the 14th century. A pretty wooden screen with two ogee arches leads to the old service quarters (now another bar).

At the other end of the hall is a bay window alcove, and an excellent swooping canopy of honour above the now vanished dais. Behind this is the solar wing, with a Great Chamber almost as splendid as the hall. It has another open roof, its panels and frieze liberally stencilled and painted with medieval motifs and banners. A family gallery overlooks the two-storey chapel below. As far as I could see all this is original and admirably restored. I cannot object to these ancient halls re-employed as a raucous place of entertainment. That is what they always were.

WESTON PARK ***

Weston-under-Lizard, 7m E of Telford
17th-century mansion in Capability Brown landscape (P)

Weston Park is a splendid boast. It promises that 'royalty, politics, drama and tragedy' are part of its history. The facilities assure

Gobelins resplendent at Weston

'confidentiality and security'. Bill Clinton and Tony Blair had just signed the visitor book on my visit. A rock concert was departing the 1,000-acre park, to be followed by a country fair. The rooks in the surrounding woods mingled with the whistle of a miniature steam engine.

Given the pomp of its interior, the house is lucky to retain a jolly 17th-century outside. The house was built in 1671 by Lady Wilbraham, who possessed a heavily annotated 1663 edition of Palladio's *First Book of Architecture* and appears to have designed Weston herself. Unless we include Bess of Hardwick, she is possibly England's first woman architect. She placed bold segmental pediments on the south front wings. Her daughter and heir married into the Bridgeman family, later Earls of Bradford. It was this family that put the house

into a charitable trust in 1981. The Earl of Bradford lives locally.

The entrance to the house was moved to the east front in 1865. It now goes into the former library, a fine chamber of classical columns and friezes. Weston has a superb picture collection, here devoted to horses. A 19th-century Earl of Bradford was Master of the Horse to Queen Victoria. Beyond is the small breakfast room housing a set of Tudor and later portraits, including a Holbein.

At the heart of Elizabeth Wilbraham's house was an open courtyard, enclosed by the Victorians and refashioned as a hall and billiard room. These are now spaces for the display of pictures, sculptures and Chinese porcelain, including paintings by Bassano and Salvator Rosa. Weston also has a large collection of over 1,100 letters from Disraeli to the then Countess of Bradford, as well as a yellow parrot which he sent her. It was thought to be male, but laid 23 eggs and then dropped dead.

The main reception rooms are so heavily redecorated as to seem more 20th century than historic. The dining room is a shock. Scaled for giants, it was created in the 1860s by combining two rooms on the ground floor and more on the floor above. The new doorcases are thus higher than the old ones. Much of the opulent detail is the work of the 6th Earl's wife in the 1960s, including the hanging of rich pink wallpaper. The room is dominated by the pictures of Lely, Kneller, Dahl and a number of van Dycks. Most splendid is the portrait of Sir Thomas Killigrew, creator of the Theatre Royal and the first manager to put women on the stage. Weston should be a feminist shrine.

The present library is a mid-Victorian creation in classical style, with rich wood panelling and deep sofas. Fake books covering the doors include nine volumes of *The American Peerage*. To one side is a superb Indian lacquer screen bordered with Chinese characters promising long life. The room has two rare portraits by Constable and others by Reynolds, Hoppner and Hayter. Their colouring is as rich as the decoration.

The drawing room is emphatically 'a ladies' room'. It is by James Paine, who may have been responsible for much of the mid-Georgian work both indoors and outdoors at Weston. The main portrait here is a Lely of Lady Wilbraham, looking most determined. An Anglo-Indian cabinet is faced in tooled ivory, decorated with charming oriental street scenes. The tapestry room is exquisite. Designed by Boucher for Gobelins, the tapestries of 1766 frame scenes by Watteau, Rubens and others. Birds take flight across a rich rose-tinted background. The furniture shrinks away in deference.

Weston has a large and formal set of stables and farm buildings built by Sir Henry Bridgeman, an enthusiast for 18th-century rural 'improvement'. The landscape, by Brown, is still contained within a five-mile perimeter wall. Paine designed most of the Palladian landscape features, a bridge, obelisk, tower and summer house. Not far from the entrance stands his Orangery and linked Temple of Diana, a lovely folly.

WHITMORE HALL **

Whitmore, 4m SW of Newcastle-under-Lyme
Tudor and Restoration family house (P)

The hall stands delightfully positioned, enclosing the end of a long lime avenue from the parish church. At first sight, it seems conventionally William-and-Mary, with tall windows and steep pitched roof. Closer inspection reveals a rougher past, that of the Restoration and earlier. The windows are not the same. Huge chimneys poke rudely from behind a parapet. The Victorian porch looks tipsy. The Mainwarings, as politicians, soldiers, sailors or farmers in the Australian outback, claim to be celebrated for their drinking.

Whitmore defies historians. It has been in single family ownership since the Norman Conquest and the present Mainwarings have every intention of keeping it that way, 'planning authority and government' willing. The house was a medieval timbered E-plan encased in brick in 1676, and then given an 18th-century front and entrance hall. By this device, many an ancient English house was inexpensively transformed from medieval to 'modern'.

The rooms are light and bright, as of a comfortable Georgian house. Yet each springs a surprise. The guide, Mrs Cavenagh-Mainwaring, reveals lost Tudor walls, patches of lath and plaster, paperwork friezes and, under a table, a peacock found dead in the cellar. Fireplaces are lined with beautiful Minton tiles from the Potteries. The dining room with its ferocious family portraits looks like a warning against the demon drink.

Below the house by the stream are Elizabethan stables containing early 17th-century horse boxes. These are remarkable examples of equestrian architecture, though the form was common at the time. Each stall is arched and separated by a Doric column. They are earlier than those at another Mainwaring house at Peover (Cheshire) of 1654. A number of horses perished here in a fire in the 18th century and no horse since has ever been induced to remain in the building overnight. Its survival is the more remarkable.

WIGHTWICK MANOR ****

Wightwick, 3m W of Wolverhampton
Arts and Crafts survival, original paintings
(NT)

Wightwick is a Pre-Raphaelite banquet. Only a snooty Metropolitan would wonder at such a place existing in the provinces. There is nothing comparable in London, not even Leighton House (London, C). Here are the Pre-Raphaelites, William Morris and the Arts and Crafts movement immaculately displayed. Wightwick (pronounced Wittick) embodies the Victorian medieval revival.

Theodore Mander was a Wolverhampton paint and varnish manufacturer who married an American, suitably named Flora Paint. Mander was a follower of John Ruskin and Morris. He bought the Wightwick estate in 1887 and began six years of intense building and patronage, continued by his son, Sir Geoffrey Mander MP, and his wife, Rosalie Grylls. They amassed a collection of Pre-Raphaelite art when it was unfashionable and cheap. The house went to the National Trust in 1937 but their daughter still lives upstairs. She writes fiercely of the Manders as parents who 'discarded people but not things', of 'emotional scars . . . and painful memories'. The house was heated only when occasionally opened to the public. It was mostly freezing.

Wightwick was built in the Tudor style in two stages, six years apart. The earlier west wing is half-timbered with a brick ground floor. The more overtly antique east wing is in a timber-framed Cheshire style. Both are by Edward Ould, creator of 'Ould English'. He claimed that no other style would 'continue to live on terms of such good fellowship with other materials'. Our age of tawdry concrete and glass has proved him right.

Inside, the wallpapers, wall-hangings, fabrics and furniture are almost all by the William Morris Partnership, and are of great richness. Much of the stained glass is by Charles Kempe, signed with his wheatsheaf badge. De Morgan supplied tiles for the fireplaces and inglenooks. The latest electricity and central heating were installed. Walls are hung with paintings by Millais, Burne-Jones, Rossetti, Madox Brown, Watts, Ruskin and Leighton. Books on the shelves are bound by Morris's Kelmscott Press.

The older wing includes the drawing room with its Arts and Crafts furniture. Here is the celebrated portrait of Janey Morris with flowing red hair, begun by Rossetti but completed by Madox Brown. It hangs above a fine walnut-and-rosewood piano. The hall is lit with opaque glass in which are set Kempe's Virtues. The panelled library opposite, heavy with Hansards, also has Pre-Raphaelite glass.

The newer wing is more spectacular. It begins with the parlour, in effect a Great Hall. This revival of a medieval form was well described by Henry James in *The Other House*: 'Bright, large and high, richly decorated and freely used, full of corners and communications, it evidently played equally the part of a place of reunion and a place of transit.' The inglenook is a room in itself. Kempe decorated the ceiling and frieze panels with exotic animals in a forest. The walls are enlivened by Mander's noble quotations. The room radiates colour, not least from Watts' portrait of Jane Hughes and Burne-Jones's medievalist icon, *Love Amongst the Ruins*, under the gallery. This is one of the finest rooms of late-Victorian England.

The rest of the wing is heavily neo-Jacobean. The billiard room has Morris Pimpernel wallpaper. Delft and Spode fill the dining room. The Pomegranate Passage is hung with a Burne-Jones tapestry of *The Mill*. Each of the visitors' bedrooms is designed to a decorative theme: Honeysuckle, Indian Bird, Acanthus and Daisy.

The Oak Room, with its linked dressing room and writing room, forms a perfect guest suite. The folding bed, contained within an ornamental cupboard, belonged to Swinburne. It opens to reveal not just a bed but a complete alcove, panelled, carved and painted. The ensemble cost £6.25 in 1939. Today it must be priceless. Beyond are two delightful nurseries, day and night, with toys and dolls of all periods. Downstairs is a Turkish bath.

The garden is by Thomas Mawson, adapted

by Geoffrey Mander. Such a layout, said Mawson, should become 'freer' the further it progressed from the walls of the house, as if nature were to be allowed slowly to take over from architecture. There is a plethora of topiary. On the lower lawn, the yews lead away from the house like a regiment of Cheddar cheeses.

WOLVERHAMPTON: BANTOCK HOUSE *

Finchfield Road
Mayor's house restored to Arts and Crafts period (M)

Modern Wolverhampton may be a monument to the Unknown Traffic Manager, but the old town enjoyed men of a more subtle aesthetic. The Bantock family, father Thomas and son Baldwin, were mayors of Wolverhampton at the turn of the 20th century. They created the painted ware for which their town was famous. Like the Manders of Wightwick, they were patrons of the Arts and Crafts movement. In 1938, with confidence collapsing across wealthy England, they gave up and donated their suburban home to the town for a museum. The downstairs has been restored as it would have been during family use.

Although the exterior is Georgian, the interior is mostly late Victorian. The entrance through the conservatory is into a dark panelled hall, decorated in the Arts and Crafts style. There are chairs of the period and a fine brass fireguard. Two Burne-Jones designs hang on the walls, facing a bold Art Nouveau lectern. The door hinges are beautifully crafted.

Facing the main entrance are portraits of the Bantocks in their mayoral robes, next to two incongruous suits of armour. To the left is the Home Room, decorated in William Morris style and with a japanned screen. This ancient lacquer technique was adapted by Wolverhampton craftsmen to fuse paint with tinplate, the source of the town's wealth – and of Bantock's.

To the right is the Garden Room. Desks and books are still in place, together with beautiful chinaware and fireplace tiles. Wolverhampton manufacturers were men of taste. Through the bay windows we can see the Bantocks' treasured gardens. These have been retained as a compromise between conservation and municipalization, with the latter currently in the ascendant.

Suffolk

Suffolk is a civilized county. It has no peaks or torrents, nor even a rocky coast. It absorbed the Saxon invasion and grew rich on cloth in the Middle Ages. The county then declined and is remarkably short of Georgian and later buildings.

Of early architecture there are only fragments, such as Norman Moyse's Hall in Bury St Edmunds and the castles of Orford and Framlingham. In the Tudor era it was, above all, a county of brick, as in the great gatehouse at Hengrave and the moated walls of Helmingham. Melford Hall and Kentwell are substantial Elizabethan survivors. More modest, although more complete, from this period are the old hall houses at Otley and Lavenham Little Hall. Christchurch in Ipswich, is an ostentatious Jacobean merchant's mansion.

The Georgians in Suffolk are more demure. Euston Hall is only a shadow of its former self, but redeemed by its splendid Stuart portraits. Glemham has been well preserved from this period. The Bury St Edmunds town house of the Herveys, Earls of Bristol, is restored as a museum. But nothing in the county equals the Bristols' country home at Ickworth, one of the most extravagant displays of Grand Tour opulence in England. The Victorians reverted to the Jacobean era for Somerleyton on its sandy knoll outside Lowestoft.

Bury St Edmunds:
  Manor House **
  Moyse's Hall *
Euston **
Framlingham Castle *
Glemham Hall **
Haughley *
Helmingham *
Hengrave Hall **
Hintlesham Hall **

Ickworth ***
Ipswich:
  Christchurch ***
Lavenham: Little Hall **
Long Melford:
  Kentwell ***
  Melford Hall **
Orford Castle **
Otley ***
Shrubland Park **

Somerleyton ***
South Elmham Hall *
Sudbury:
  Gainsborough's House *
West Stow *
Wingfield Old College ***
Woodbridge:
  Seckford Hall **

BURY ST EDMUNDS: MANOR HOUSE **

Honey Hill
Bury town house of the Ickworth Herveys (M)

The Manor House at Bury was built in 1736 by the Herveys, Earls of Bristol. While their country seat was Ickworth, the Manor House was to be their 'place in town', indicating the importance of local civic life even to the grandest of landed aristocrats. The architect was a local man, James Burrough, and the house was so well furnished that a signed list of contents had to be handed from generation to generation, since Lady Hervey regarded the house and its contents as heirlooms. In addition, each inheritor had to include her maiden name, Felton, in theirs.

Civic status did not last for ever for the Herveys. They sold the house to the 1st Lord Moyne, who was assassinated by the Stern Gang in Jerusalem in 1944. Soon afterwards the house was bought as council offices. Not until 1993 was it restored as a museum.

The exterior is that of a handsome early Georgian mansion, in redbrick with stone quoins and window dressings. The most spectacular space inside is the entrance hall, dominated by a classical fireplace with a three-arched screen to the stairs and, on the other side, an enfilade of rooms. Architecture is at the service of show. The walls are yellow, the plasterwork in rich metropolitan taste. The principal rooms, the dining room, library and ballroom upstairs, all retain their decoration. This is clearly a nobleman's house in town.

If such houses must be museums, they should be done the Bury way. Donations of pictures, furniture, costumes and clocks are scattered through the rooms, making them seem busy and used. The museum contains a glorious Tissot portrait of Sydney Milner-Gibson but has slightly too many glass cases.

BURY ST EDMUNDS: MOYSE'S HALL *

Market Square
Norman merchant's house within later shell (M)

The hall faces the market square behind a Victorian flint façade. This appears to be a retooling of a Norman original and constitutes a rare survivor of a 12th-century domestic building in an English town – and on a surprisingly large scale. The assumption that such houses were occupied by Jews is based only on their being costly. In the early Middle Ages, only Jews could lend money and thus became the new urban rich. There is no documentary evidence that this house belonged to Jews, and Moses was a common Suffolk name.

What survives is a 19th-century reworking of a Norman house above an original undercroft. The vaults to the latter are extremely simple, suggesting that they were for storage. Upstairs is the old hall and solar. The latter is well preserved, albeit with a Tudor fireplace and windows. An old photograph of the room, taken when used as a private house in the 19th century, shows it as a dark and mysterious chamber. The doorway next to the fireplace is clearly Norman.

The museum displays that stock-in-trade of town museums these days, instruments of incarceration, torture and death.

EUSTON HALL **

Euston, 3m S of Thetford
Restoration mansion with ducal collection (P)

The Earl of Arlington was a loyal Secretary of State to Charles II. As evidence of his fidelity, the King suggested that Arlington might wed his only daughter, the five-year-old Isabella, to the King's nine-year-old illegitimate son, Henry *fils-roi*, by his mistress Barbara Villiers. Arlington, presumably unnerved by the suggestion, remarked that he had hoped his daughter would marry a duke. The genial monarch obliged, making the young couple

Duke and Duchess of Grafton. The Duke of Grafton resides at Euston to this day. The eponymous station is on what was the Fitzroy estate in north London.

The house built for Arlington in 1666 was three-sided with balconies and domes at its corners. In the 1750s the house was palladianized by William Kent's assistant, Matthew Brettingham. He removed the French domes and substituted small pyramids in the style of Holkham (Norfolk). Only the Restoration stables remained untouched. The old house was gutted by fire in 1902 and rebuilt by the then Duke as what the present one calls 'a barracks'. This in turn was demolished in 1950, except for the only Brettingham range to survive the fire.

Today, there is a modest house of the sort that owners term 'manageable'. It is redbrick with two of Brettingham's corner turrets. The effect, however, is remarkably grand. The sweeping drive, arch and forecourt present the existing façade as a stage-set. The nine even bays are 'stretched' by their wide spacing and by the two low towers peeping behind.

With the interiors much restored, the appeal of the house lies in the Grafton portrait collection and the 17th-century gardens, laid out mostly by John Evelyn. There is a mill and folly by Kent set in grounds completed by Capability Brown.

Most of the pictures were collected by Lord Arlington, including many from the Royal Collection acquired after their sale by Cromwell. The outer hall contains copies of van Dycks and a painting of Barbara Villiers, whose beauty was fount of the family's fortune. She is seen as 'penitent Magdalen'. In the Small Dining Room are a fine Stubbs and a picture of the old house before Brettingham's changes.

The main family pictures are in the Grand Dining Room. The first Duke of Grafton grew up to be an admiral, dying for William of Orange when fighting against his natural uncle, James II. His wife and son are depicted in angelic poses by Kneller. Upstairs a room named The Square displays more van Dycks and Lelys, blazing amid crimson walls and carpets.

FRAMLINGHAM CASTLE *

Framlingham
Late Norman castle with intact curtain wall
(EH)

Framlingham was owned by the Norman Bigod family and built *c*1190. It is most unusual. There is no evidence of a keep, as at neighbouring Orford, only a massive curtain wall, into which are set roughly equal mural towers. These were purely defensive, still square in the early Norman style. Their picturesque chimneys are a Tudor addition. Domestic buildings would have been built inside the curtain.

Framlingham belonged to the Bigods until surrendered to the king in 1307, after a member of the dynasty had denied his feudal duty to fight for Edward I on foreign soil. His excuse was that the duty only applied if fighting alongside his monarch. The castle was later granted by the king to the Mowbray Howard family, whose magnificent tombs fill the local church. With the (temporary) fall of the Catholic Howards in the 16th century, the castle passed to the Crown and was given by Edward VI to his sister Mary. It was here that she was declared Queen in 1553. It later returned to the Howards. The castle was no longer of military significance, which may explain its survival unslighted in the Civil War.

From the outside, the castle looks remarkably intact. Its thirteen towers are linked by a rampart walk which can be perambulated. This is an exhilarating experience, offering views over the defensive ditch below and the surrounding countryside, including Framlingham School on an opposite slope. One tower crowns the entrance, another forms part of an early hall. Traces of Norman chimneys can be seen at the bottom of the Tudor ones. The towers were mini-bastions with internal drawbridges, and defensible even should an enemy succeed in penetrating the court or scaling the parapet.

Stuart stateliness: Euston Hall

The only structures to survive within the castle are relics of England's early welfare state. A long flint range of 1729 contained the old poor-house. It is flanked by two wings, that on the right remaining from the late Norman hall. On the left is a 1664 house of brick, the former workhouse.

GLEMHAM HALL **

Little Glemham, 7m NE of Woodbridge
Georgianized house restored with Yale fortune (P)

The story of Glemham is hard to discern since all local records were destroyed by a parish clerk 'in a fit of insanity'. It is known that the de Glemham family sold the big house outside Little Glemham to Dudley North in 1708. North was married to the daughter of the Madras Governor and tycoon, the American-born Elihu Yale. He poured most of his wealth into his new college in New England, but whatever was not spent on Yale was spent on Glemham. The Norths rebuilt the entire front of the house in 1712 and their descendants remained here until 1923. It then passed to the brewing Cobbolds, who live here still.

The interior belies the exterior. This is a big-boned but friendly house from whose main rooms the family has not retreated into domestic apartments. The Cobbolds have contrived to fill Glemham with life. The Great Hall is on the site of the Elizabethan original, to the right of the entrance. The screen has become just four Corinthian columns and the hall turns at the old dais end into a magnificent staircase. The pine panelling was painted and then stripped in 1937. (Fashion is now for repainting.) In the middle of the hall is a table commissioned by the present Cobbold to celebrate the Millennium, with a time capsule in the middle.

The downstairs reception rooms are all Georgian. Pictures of the family include a lovely Gainsborough of two ladies in a landscape. The house is rich in oriental porcelain and lacquerwork. The stairs are impressively generous, with twisted triple balusters and high windows. Glemham is a house full of light. Above the hall is the old ballroom, now a bedroom with a chintz four-poster.

Beyond the main rooms there seems an infinity of bedrooms. To the rear, corridors change from Georgian to Jacobean, roofs rise and fall, ceilings fight back damp, family paraphernalia litters the floor. One room is still set aside for the emptying of chamber pots. Two dead pheasants hang in the dining room – or did on my visit.

HAUGHLEY PARK *

Haughley, 4m NW of Stowmarket
Jacobean house restored after fire (P)

A traffic jam of cars was leaving Haughley at the time of my visit. They were from a chicken-processing factory apparently on the same site. The house of Haughley appears sublimely indifferent to its noxious factory extension, amid gravel drives, dells, lakes and formal lawns. The two parts of the estate are shielded from each other by trees, although the factory offices are now located in the south wing of the house.

Haughley was built by the Sulyards in 1620 in a grand Jacobean style. The old Elizabethan E-plan is formal, the windows bays and door pediments classical. The exterior is mostly of local brick, with stepped gables, big chimneys and ornamental finials to the gables.

The house was partly rebuilt in the 19th century when a fire in the north wing led the new owner, the Crawford family, to build a castellated Georgian north front. The house passed through many vicissitudes before being given to London Zoo as a safari park in 1956. The estate was then acquired by the Williams family for a food factory. Yet no sooner was the factory built than the house again caught fire. Its rebuilding was completed in 1964.

Given this chequered history, the house is remarkably worthwhile. The reinstatement of the Jacobean and Georgian interiors has been sympathetic. The old staircase has been carefully reproduced. The unburned spiral stair

and the panelled Justice Room survive, as do many excellent paintings. In a small gallery is one of just six contemporary copies of the only known portrait of Richard III. The original is now lost.

HELMINGHAM HALL *

Helmingham, 10m E of Stowmarket
Moated manor set in fine garden (P-G)

This is Suffolk's most celebrated moated manor. Although not normally open to the public, it is visible from all angles from the superb surrounding gardens. The house is that of the Tollemache family, once of Ham House (London, W) and Peckforton (Cheshire). It is a rare survivor of that most romantic of English buildings, with walls of red brick rising from water, clothed in rambling roses.

Helmingham's moat is 60 ft wide and a formidable barrier. The two drawbridges are still raised every night. In addition to the moat, a secondary set of waterworks protects the walled garden, a rare feature (*see* Birtsmorton/Worcs).

The Tudor ranges are set round an enclosed courtyard, reached through a gateway across one of the drawbridges. From the moat, it appears as a complete four-sided mansion, mostly in diapered red brick with parapet and stone dressings. Despite appearances, this is not as the Tudors left it. The main entrance façade is an 1800s brick recladding by John Nash of old timbered walls. He also added the battlements and renewed most of the windows.

Much of the exterior was again remodelled in 1841, at the height of the Jacobean revival. This is reflected in the even gables and heavily mullioned Victorian bay and oriel windows overlooking the water. Yet there is no harm done. The forest of chimneys and pinnacles radiates Suffolk warmth across water, grass and rose beds. This is a happy place, an English water palace floating on its lake.

Jacobethan idyll: Helmingham Hall

HENGRAVE HALL **

3m NW of Bury St Edmunds
Tudor magnate's house with ornate gateway
(P)

The Kytsons were no fools. Thomas Kytson, an upwardly mobile cloth merchant, built his house and magnificent gatehouse in 1525. The family remained Catholic through the Reformation yet Thomas was sufficiently careful to entertain and be knighted by Elizabeth I. This followed a pledge by him to change allegiance and worship, briefly it turned out, in the Protestant faith.

In the 17th century Hengrave passed to the Gage family and was lent by them to a group of nuns from Bruges during the French Revolution. They were led by Sister Mary More, last descendant of Sir Thomas More. The house was extensively altered by the Victorian, Sir John Wood, but reverted to convent use in 1952 and became a religious retreat-house in 1974.

The gatehouse at Hengrave is one of the glories of Tudor design. It declares the voluptuousness of High Gothic on the threshold of the English Renaissance. Two tapering towers flank the doorway. In the middle is a billowing 'trefoil' oriel window carrying the Kytson and royal coats of arms. The lights rise in three convex bays to battlements, scale-coated finials and gables. Beneath is a Renaissance moulding with cavorting cherubs and naked putti, all celebrating the Kytson emblem of three trout. The colours at Hengrave have been meticulously researched and convey the richness with which Tudor architecture was adorned, both inside and out.

The exterior is in a most unusual material for its time, yellow brick apparently chosen to merge with stone brought from farther afield. Beyond the gatehouse is a complete courtyard, of two storeys except on the far side, where the Great Hall rises the full height of the court. The three sides are united not by collegiate staircases but by a corridor joining the rooms, one of the first uses of a corridor in this fashion.

Most of the accessible rooms were heavily restored, if not created, by Wood at the end of the 19th century. The chapel contains the house's treasure, a set of Flemish glass, apparently in mint condition, depicting the Bible story of the Creation and the Life of Christ. It is believed to date from 1526 and is as fine as any glass in such English churches as Fairford in Gloucestershire or St Neot's in Cornwall. At the back of the chapel is a small gallery with fretwork screens.

The hall is magnificent but mostly Victorian. The hammerbeam roof is of painted plaster, but the fan vault in the bay window appears original.

HINTLESHAM HALL **

Hintlesham, 4m E of Hadleigh
Georgian mansion, 17th-century ceiling (H)

I first visited Hintlesham when Robert Carrier was pioneering the concept of the country house restaurant. He bought what was a destitute mansion, refurbished it and served, according to an old *Good Food Guide*, 'sautéd foie gras with pools of buttery Sauternes sauce'. Dress codes were enforced.

Since then, the place has twice changed hands and added leisure clubs and treatment centres, much as the Victorian houses added bachelors' and servants' wings. With cocktails on the lawn before dinner and a walk in the herb garden after, the illusion is of an interwar house party. Non-resident visitors can look round for the price of a drink.

Tudor Hintlesham was home of the Timperley family from the 15th to the 18th century. Their family ties to the Howards kept them loyal to the Catholic faith, and resulting fines and ostracism prevented much change to their old home. The symmetrical Georgian façade conceals an earlier E-plan mansion, its brick walls and chimneys visible at the rear. The house passed from the Timperleys to the Powys family in 1720. The

Gothic greets Renaissance at Hengrave

inside of the E-plan was filled by the present colonnade and Palladian frontispiece.

The interior of Hintlesham is respectful of its past, despite the hotel atmosphere in the public rooms. (Deep sofas and *Country Life* are no substitute for country house clutter.) Behind the central entrance colonnade is the old Great Hall, now saloon, still rising two storeys but georgianized and with a huge classical doorcase at one end. There are two fine oak staircases. The drawing room on the first floor has a Timperley ceiling, which Pevsner eulogized as 'among of the best of the late-17th century anywhere in East Anglia'. The plasterwork, an oval with rectangular panels at each end, is undercut into a froth of foliage.

ICKWORTH ***

Horringer, 2m SW of Bury St Edmunds
Home of Earl-Bishop and monument to Grand Tour (NT)

The Herveys appear to have been genetically eccentric. It was widely said that there were 'men, women and Herveys'. The family were distinguished courtiers under the Tudors. They advanced under the Whig ascendancy, were satirized by Pope, painted by Hogarth, and were spendthrift, arrogant and art-loving by turn. Then, in 1779, the Earldom of Bristol and the Ickworth estate passed to Frederick, brother of the 3rd Earl of Bristol. After trying the law he had settled on the church, having secured the lucrative Bishopric of Derry. Hervey duly diverted diocesan rents to his own purse and took off to the Continent. Accompanied by a retinue, he travelled in a splendid coach, conferring the name of Bristol on hotels that took his fancy, a name that many proudly retain to this day.

The Earl-Bishop decided to rebuild Ickworth as a grand oval building in which he would live, with wings to house his collection of Roman antiquities. The amassed collection was still in Rome when Napoleon's troops arrived in 1798, and was confiscated and sold at auction by the French. Hervey spent the rest

of his life trying to recover his possessions, but failed. He died miserably by a roadside in Italy in 1803, a local farmer having refused to allow a Protestant bishop to expire on his property. The Ickworth rotunda was only half built and the rest of the house was a shell.

Bristol's successor, the 5th Earl, found himself with a title, the walls of Ickworth and just £1,000 a year. Yet he restored the family finances, was elevated from Earl to Marquess and in 1821 restarted work on the house. He even found the money to stock it with pictures. His grandson in turn created the Pompeiian Room as a sort of shrine to his ancestor. The house passed to the National Trust in lieu of death duties in 1956, although the then 7th Marquess sold his remaining lease to the Trust for £100,000 in 1998, shortly before his premature death from drugs. A luxury hotel has been established in his wing.

Ickworth's rotunda emerges along the drive through the deer park, framed by massive cedars and firs. The render is a cold grey. Designed by an Italian, Mario Asprucci, in 1794, it might be a Russian palace outside St Petersburg. Immediately beneath the drum is a frieze of panels depicting scenes from the early Olympic Games and from Homer, in deep relief. The interiors are in keeping with the Roman exterior. The columns in the entrance hall frame grand Hervey portraits above a John Flaxman sculpture group, *The Fury of Athamas*. It was bought for the then stupendous sum of £600. It too was confiscated by Napoleon but re-bought in Paris in the 1820s. This hall is no place for a cosy chat.

The main reception rooms fit to the plan of the rotunda. The ground floor ceilings were high, required by the Earl-Bishop since his 'lungs played more freely . . . in lofty rooms than in low ones'. The dining room has Rococo pier-glasses from Italy and a picture by Romney of the true hero of Ickworth, the 1st Marquess who completed it. The library, with huge curtained windows looking out over the park, is semi-circular in shape. Here are the finest surviving pictures, including a Velasquez of Prince Carlos and West's *Death of General Wolfe*.

The drawing room was remodelled by the Edwardian, Arthur Blomfield, and contains two fine Portuguese pier-glasses in heavy gilt Rococo. On the walls are Herveys by Gainsborough. The wing corridors are interrupted by two rooms, the smoking room to the east, with Hogarth's *Hervey Conversation Piece*, and the Pompeiian Room to the west. The latter is the prize of Ickworth. Although not executed until 1879 by J. G. Crace, it is based on the Villa Negroni in Rome, discovered during one of the Earl-Bishop's visits. The room is a final homage to this outrageous, eccentric and finally tragic figure.

IPSWICH: CHRISTCHURCH MANSION ***

Christchurch Park
Elizabethan manor, with Gainsboroughs and Constables (M)

Go to Christchurch for Gainsborough and Constable, but go also for the miniature Hawstead Panels acquired in 1924 from Bury St Edmunds. They were painted sometime after 1610 by an amateur artist, a Lady Drury, to comfort herself during her husband's absences at Court. Her motto was, 'Never less a lonely lady than when a lady alone'. Each panel depicts a moral tale from contemporary literature, many of the meanings now lost. The Porch Chamber in which these panels hang is an exquisite boudoir, decorative and moving in a corner of this busy house.

Christchurch shows what can be done with old buildings in council ownership, where there is a will and a budget. The house overlooks a park near the centre of the town. It was originally built on a former monastic site by Edmund Withypool, the son of a London merchant-tailor, c1548. The old E-plan house was substantially improved after the Devereux family, Viscounts Hereford, inherited it in 1645 and gave it a fine flourish of East Anglian Dutch gables.

The windows, some Elizabethan, some 18th century, are symmetrical, although the Great Hall is in the original position to one side. The house passed to the Fonnereau family in the 18th century and was sold as a building site in 1894. At that awesome moment, an enlightened member of the purchasing syndicate relented and gave the house to the council on condition that it and its grounds be kept intact.

Christchurch has exceptionally rich interiors. The Great Hall is a Restoration refashioning of the Tudor original, with an arcaded minstrels' gallery. In the 1920s another hall was erected behind it, taken from a demolished Elizabethan house elsewhere in the town. It is wonderful room, a hymn to polished oak in beams, floorboards, linenfold panelling and rich furniture. The Eldred Overmantel celebrates a local navigator, a virtuoso display of 16th-century carving.

The right-hand wing of the house retains its 17th-century appearance downstairs, but upstairs is redecorated in Georgian style to display works by Gainsborough. These are shown not as in a gallery but in furnished domestic rooms. To the rear is the state bedroom, added by the Fonnereau family, Gainsborough's early patrons. A Georgian bed sits expectantly behind a Rococo screen, with Chinese lacquer cabinets and costumes.

To the rear, the house degenerates into a museum. Rooms display the relics of lost local houses. The re-created Victorian rooms are the best. The service rooms include the Christchurch estate office with two huge guns and a giant rent desk.

Also on display are paintings and ceramics by local artists, hung alongside not just Constable and Gainsborough but Crome, Cotman, Munnings and Wilson Steer.

LAVENHAM: LITTLE HALL **

Market Place
Medieval hall house restored and refurnished in 20th century (P)

Lavenham has one of the most extensive group of medieval buildings in England. Most would have been modest hall houses of clothiers and related tradesmen. Rubble walls would have been reinforced with timber under thatched roofs. The prosperity of the wool trade in the 15th century brought brick chimneys and tiled roofs, with solar chambers extending into rear plots. The decline in East Anglian broadcloth manufacture in the 17th century left Lavenham a backwater, preserving it for all time, and thus enabling its current revival as a popular tourist destination.

Dating from the 1390s, Little Hall is of this pattern. The house was owned in the Middle Ages by the Causton family, clothiers and later farmers, butchers and schoolmasters. The house became multi-occupied – it had twenty inhabitants in 1851 – until rescued in 1924 by two enthusiasts, the Gayer-Anderson brothers. They were twins, both soldiers, with a shared interest in Egyptology, art and collecting. They gave their house to the Suffolk Preservation Trust.

The house looks out on the Market Place with an off-centre door and a tall mullioned hall window. Beyond is a jettied solar wing. The interior was restored and richly furnished by the Gayer-Andersons in Edwardian manorial style, as opposed to English Heritage hall houses which tend to be archaeological and spartan.

What would have been a two-storey hall is divided by a massive-beamed floor into the dining room below and dormitory above. The former has a fine oak dresser made by one of the brothers in 1905. The windows contain a mix of 17th-century Flemish and modern stained glass.

The remaining rooms are dedicated to the Gayer-Anderson collection. The library and a panelled room are heavy with books and works of arts, including paintings by the brothers. In the back room are Persian lacquerwork panels and ancient Egyptian doors, a cosmopolitanism that would have appealed to medieval Lavenham.

The upstairs dormitory is so-called for the evacuees and art students who used the building during and after the Second World War. The windows retain their slots for shutters, before the advent of glass.

LONG MELFORD: KENTWELL HALL ***

1m N of Long Melford
Tudor mansion set amid re-created medieval estate (P)

If anyone asks how an old house can survive into the 21st century, I reply, the Kentwell way. When I first visited the house in the 1970s, Patrick and Judith Phillips were on their knees trying to repair the floor of what they hoped to make a family home. Since then the place has gone to their heads. Eschewing grant, they have created two distinct entities. One is a mildly eccentric historic house with 'no grand family connections or collections', moated and of Tudor origin. The other is a so-called 're-creation' of how the settlement might have seemed at the end of the Middle Ages. Kentwell's medieval events are so authentic that participants whose costumes betray even a sign of machine-stitching are turned away.

The house is approached down a mile-long avenue from Long Melford. In that church is the chantry of the wool-rich Cloptons, builders of Kentwell in the 1540s and 50s. The house passed through many hands until a fire in 1826 gutted the centre block. The businessman owner, Robert Hart Logan, recruited Thomas Hopper to restore it.

Neglect followed until the arrival of the Phillipses in 1971. The resulting improvements have been prodigious and not to every taste. Most remarkable is the work in the grounds, reinstating the moat house, ice house, dovecote, walls, barns, cottages, byres and brewhouse, all to working order.

Most of the public rooms are Hopper recreations in the Tudor/Gothic style. He used cheap plaster stained and moulded to look like oak. The dining room is garish, the Great Hall a pastiche, with paintings of the Phillipses in medieval dress. They have given Hopper's drawing room a new ceiling by a local artist, Paul Dufficey, 'after Brueghel'. The frieze is of

Kentwell: Tudor vernacular survival

children's games. The billiard room contains Clopton heraldic glass similar to that in the church.

The upstairs bedrooms are a blend of Tudor, Hopper and Phillips. The state dressing room has become a bathroom, Roman style, with a bath which was found in the woods. The murals are again by Dufficey. The house publishes a regular update on existing and forthcoming changes. 'Most stately homes have had their development stopped at some time in the past,' says Phillips, 'but not so Kentwell.'

LONG MELFORD:
MELFORD HALL **

Long Melford
Tudor house with seafaring relics (NT)

William Cordell was an Elizabethan lawyer who rose to be Speaker of the Commons and Master of the Rolls. He married a cousin of the wealthy Cloptons of Kentwell and began his new house of Melford Hall in the 1550s. In 1578 he welcomed Elizabeth I to Suffolk with an event of legendary extravagance. There were 200 young gentlemen in white velvet and 300 'of the graver sort' in black, plus 1,500 serving men on horseback. All had to be fed and entertained. Cordell's feasting, said a contemporary, 'did light such a candle to the rest of the shire that they were glad bountifully and frankly to follow the same example'. They must have cursed Cordell his expense.

The house passed through many hands before being bought in 1786 by the current occupiers, the Hyde Parkers, a family of admirals and clergymen. One gave the order at Copenhagen to which Nelson turned his famous blind eye. The family reconstructed the interior in 1813 under Thomas Hopper. The house was nearly wrecked while under military occupation during the Second World War, when the north wing was gutted by fire. The family moved into the south wing, leaving the rest to the National Trust.

Melford Hall declares itself with a bold wall and charming pavilion peering over the adjacent green. The latter has an octagonal banqueting room with sixteen pinnacles on its roof, a gesture of ostentation boasting to the road outside. The house itself is an architectural oddity. The west front to the green presents a forest of towers and cupolas, in the manner of Blickling (Norfolk). This is not the entrance, although it may have been to an earlier monastic house on the site. The entrance is in a U-shaped court facing out into the park. The porch is Tudor Renaissance, with fluted pilasters, a beautifully delicate work.

The interiors of Melford are mildly disappointing. The middle section had the stuffing knocked out of it by Hopper's alterations in 1813. This turned the Great Hall and screens passage into a lobby for the grand but rather institutional staircase, leading the eye upstairs as if to a *piano nobile* that is not there. The hall is filled with family portraits and has highbacked Carolean chairs. The house retains its estate map of 1580, on which local people can identify their cottages.

Of the accessible rooms the library is the best, inserted by Hopper in a severely classical style with columns of scagliola rising above Grecian couches. Over the fireplace is a Romney of the most celebrated of the naval Hyde Parkers, the 5th Baronet. He ran away from school, joined the merchant navy, sailed round the world with Anson and rose to the rank of admiral. When offered a peerage by George III he refused it on the grounds that he would rather the King paid attention to the state of the navy. He 'wanted none of your Majesty's titles'. He was hugely popular with his men, but died in a shipwreck.

The upstairs rooms are enlivened by various items of captured loot, much of it from the *Santissima Trinidad*, seized by Hyde Parker in 1762 off Manila. It carried gifts from the Emperor of China to the King of Spain. Beatrix Potter was a Hyde Parker cousin and stayed here with her travelling menagerie of hedgehogs, rabbits and other creatures, sustenance to her imagination.

Norman domesticity at Orford

ORFORD CASTLE **

Orford, 11m E of Woodbridge
Norman keep overlooking coast (EH)

The village straggles inland of a silted-up harbour. Bungalows have been located with the tactical ugliness beloved of East Anglian planners. Only the mighty church saves the place from banality and the castle. The latter has lost its bailey and curtain wall in a tumble of mounds, but it has its keep, one of the best preserved in England.

The castle exterior, especially its location, is sensational, visible from across the marshes in all directions. Any walk along this part of the Suffolk coast is made under its distant stare. The sea may have retreated from Orford – so much for global warming – but Orford can see the sea from Aldeburgh to Bawdsey. On the shingle spit opposite are the fascinating remains of the army camp where radar was first tested in 1935, now National Trust.

The castle was built for Henry II in 1165 and was an early, perhaps the first, instance of a polygonal rather than square keep. This was intended to reduce the risk of undermining by sappers and was reinforced by three external towers. The stone is a beautiful white septaria, for some reason patched with ugly sandstone. The entrance porch with chapel above is so restored as to look new. The castle became militarily obsolete and by the 14th century was let in perpetuity to the Earls of Suffolk. It is now owned by English Heritage.

The inside retains the old three-storey form, with halls one above the other. One was for soldiers and ordinary mortals, the top one was for the constable or visiting dignitaries. The turrets are big enough to contain private rooms and closets of their own. Legend has it that in Norman times a 'wild man' covered in hair was dragged from the sea by a fisherman and held in Orford dungeon. Despite being liberally tortured, he refused to communicate with his captors 'like a Christian', and eventually escaped back to the sea and was never seen again. The castle rooms have been restored in English Heritage primary school style.

OTLEY HALL ***

1m N of Otley, 9m E of Needham Market
Elizabethan house with possible early theatre (P)

Otley is an immaculate Tudor house with no edge untrimmed and no dust on any shelf. A cobweb would be an arachnoid impertinence. The house was acquired in 1997 by Nicholas Hagger, whose books and poems promoting his 'unified theory of history and religion' fill the place.

Heavy emphasis is laid in the guidebook on a link between the name of an early owner, Gosnold, and the Jamestown settlement in America. Yet Jamestown's founder, Bartholomew Gosnold, never lived in the house and the thesis that the USA was 'founded' at Otley is fanciful.

Instead we should be content with a superb example of 16th-century Suffolk architecture. The house is not easy to read at first sight. The entrance beyond a small duck pond presents a jumble of Tudor walling, with a chimney flue, gables and leaded casement windows.

The entrance has, since 1911, been into what was the stair turret. This leads into a passage with the Great Hall to the left. The original entrance was on the far side, with the frame of the old screens passage now a feature of the hall interior. The floor is stone-flagged and real foliage drips from the screen.

The adjacent parlour is lit by a large mullioned and transomed window inserted at the end of the 16th century. Its linenfold panelling is so ornate that legend attributes it to Wolsey's Hampton Court (London, W). It is possible that when Wolsey handed Hampton Court to Henry VIII he removed some of the panelling, intending it for his new school at Ipswich but storing it at Otley which he then also owned. He died before the school could be completed. The panels fill the room with warmth, enhanced by a brick fireplace and rush matting.

Brick triumphant: Otley Hall

In 1588 Robert Gosnold appears to have built a 'playhouse' wing facing onto what would have been a former courtyard. The jettied façade of this wing still has four wooden columns, as if flanking an outside stage or at least a loggia behind one. Inside this wing is a banqueting room, its panelling with lovely Renaissance decoration. The moat and H-shaped stewpond have also been reinstated.

SHRUBLAND PARK **

5m N of Ipswich
Italianate villa with Tivoli terraces (P-R)

The celebrated health clinic can be visited either for expensive treatment or by discreet appointment. It lies on a bluff overlooking a park on the outskirts of Ipswich. The drive winds past trees that seem themselves to be on a diet. Even the sheep in the park are lithe and trim.

The house is to outward appearances a Victorian villa by Sir Charles Barry. A tower pins the composition to the hill while ornamental terraces and patios lead down to grottos and temples. The core of the house is a Georgian mansion by James Paine, built in the 1770s for a prosperous clergyman, John Bacon. Paine's work survives in the conventional plasterwork in the main reception rooms. In the 1830s the house passed to the Middleton family, who commissioned J. P. Gandy-Deering to italianize it. He produced the exotic Orangery, situated below the so-called 'light diet' dining room with, on my visit, a bleak sideboard of melon slices.

In 1848 Barry arrived and the present Shrubland emerged. It is an echo of Osborne on the Isle of Wight (Hants). Barry never lost his sense of theatre. The entrance porch is heavily rusticated with galleries (now gyms) on either side and a long rising staircase to the main hall ahead. A tower was added and the gardens given their Italianate sequence of steps, balustrades and urns. They are said to be modelled on Tivoli. Palm trees, cedars and oaks cannot relieve the noise of the all-too adjacent A14.

SOMERLEYTON HALL ***

Somerleyton, 5m NW of Lowestoft
Victorian extravaganza with maze (P)

This marvellous house is at the back of beyond. The estate was acquired in 1843 by Sir Morton Peto, railway magnate, builder and property entrepreneur. He was a devout Baptist and at one time reputedly the 'largest employer of labour in the world'. The house was a Jacobean work on a sandy bluff above a wide sweep of the River Waveney near Lowestoft. Peto transformed it out of recognition, although still in the Jacobean style. His architect was John Thomas, protégé of Charles Barry. Peto went bankrupt shortly afterwards and had to sell his 'earthly paradise'. The house passed to the Crossleys of Halifax, whose fortunes were more securely founded on carpets. The same family own the house to this day.

Somerleyton presents an enjoyably busy front to the drive and a more sedate one to the gardens behind. The entrance is flanked by a courtyard with grand stables with cupola to the right and an Italianate tower to the left. The entrance itself is concealed behind a Baroque screen linking the two wings of the house and embracing a grandiloquent entrance.

The door leads into a dark foyer, a Victorian valhalla. This has a stained glass dome and heavy coffered ceiling. Two huge bears greet visitors on either side of a poignant statue of a Crossley boy in rustic garb. It might be the entrance to a London club. Beyond, things calm down. The staircase hall is a generous space, a tiger skin casually draped over the balusters. Above are Somerleyton portraits and coronation robes.

The reception rooms include some surviving from the original house. The Oak Room has magnificent oak panelling and, round the fireplace, swags and vegetation reputedly from the hand of Grinling Gibbons. Here too is a silver and gilt mirror acquired by Peto from Stowe (Bucks), and originally in the Doge's Palace in Venice. The library was formed in the

Somerleyton: railway Italianate

20th century from the lower half of the old banqueting hall, when more bedrooms were needed upstairs. Beyond is a dining room in Adam style. It contains a superb Ferdinand Bol portrait of Rembrandt and Saskia and a number of seascapes by the master of the genre, Clarkson Stanfield. Of him, it was said that his pictures were so realistic they made viewers seasick.

Somerleyton has lost its once spectacular winter garden, but has an ornamental maze with paths wide enough to wander in without getting lost.

SOUTH ELMHAM HALL *

South Elmham St Cross, 6m SW of Bungay
Relic of medieval hall inside farmhouse (P-R)

This is the 'Saints' country along the Suffolk–Norfolk border, one of those notorious regions of England where it is said law and order are in abeyance. Paganism allegedly lingered here long after its disappearance elsewhere, hence the need for so many villages named after saints. Certainly South Elmham has the remains of Suffolk's only recorded minster, normally a sign of missionary zeal.

The house looks like a conventional Victorian villa. A brick ground floor has a plastered upper story and deep gabled cross-wing. Yet the house behind is full of antique features. It was built for the bishops of Norwich *c*1270 and, after the Dissolution, possibly served as a hunting box. It has the customary form of an upstairs hall for eating and for watching the chase from windows or a balcony.

Inside the front door are medieval chamfered arches, with further arches upstairs. These appear to be part of an original hall. The walls of one corridor are decorated with medieval floral paintings believed to be 13th century, comparable with work at Norwich Cathedral. At the end is the old solar with more such paintings and a 16th-century fireplace.

The house lies within a medieval moat with ruins of a reputed chapel in the grounds. An air of ancient mystery hangs about this isolated place.

SUDBURY:
GAINSBOROUGH'S HOUSE
*

46 Gainsborough Street
Artist's birthplace with many of his works (M)

Gainsborough's father was a dealer and weaver of worsted who went bankrupt and found work as the town's postmaster. He lived in some comfort at what was 46 Sepulchre Street, where young Gainsborough was born in 1727 and now has his shrine. The boy played truant from the local school to sketch in the surrounding fields and by fourteen was training in London under Francis Hayman. He returned to Sudbury in the early years of his marriage but stayed only three years, moving to Bath in 1759 and then to London in 1774.

Although the façade is of *c*1720, the building is formed of two linked houses that appear to predate 1500. Glimpses of this antiquity appear here and there, as in the early beams in the ground floor parlour. Wattle and daub can be seen in a room upstairs. At the back is old Gainsborough's weaving room, with big windows to provide the workers with light.

The garden has a mulberry tree planted in 1610, under which the young master is assumed to have sketched. The interior is mostly a museum, claiming the largest single collection of Gainsboroughs anywhere, mostly early and lesser works of great charm. It seems far removed from the grand salons and galleries in which his paintings normally hang.

WEST STOW: SAXON
VILLAGE *

6m NW of Bury St Edmunds
Reconstruction of Saxon village (M)

West Stow is England's most extensive ex-cavated Saxon settlement. First unearthed in the 1960s, some 50 structures have been discov-ered. Since then digging has proceeded slowly with finds displayed in the adjacent museum. It features Saxon garments, fabric and 'fashion'.

The hut interiors lack some of the imaginative zeal of Ryedale (Yorks, N) or Mountfitchet Castle (Essex). Money seems to have been spent on the visitor centre and museum. But this was a true village and authenticity com-pensates for the paucity of the on-site display.

The village was probably Stowa, on the edge of the deserted East Anglian Brecklands. The poverty of the sandy soil made it reputedly the least populated area of the southern half of England. Rows of pines frame the village site, which is itself isolated in woods north-west of Bury St Edmunds.

The houses themselves are primitive. One is of timber and daub, with wattle frames giving protection to the window openings. Others are of split timber logs dressed with adzes. The roofs are thatched and the floors are planks raised above pits as a protection against damp. Central hearths are sometimes lit, filling the rafters with smoke. Some huts have beds and tables with earthenware and simple decoration. Everything looks a little too archaeological, including Anselm, the Saxon pig.

WINGFIELD OLD COLLEGE
***

Wingfield, 8m E of Diss
Medieval collegiate range behind Georgian façade (PR)

Wingfield is a study in medieval upward mobility. John of Wingfield fought along-side the Black Prince in the 14th century. He captured and ransomed a rich Frenchman and was able, on his premature death in 1361, to endow his old manor as a college of priests to pray for his soul. The college flour-ished but was dissolved at the Reformation and reverted to domestic use. An 18th-century owner, Squire Buck, added a new façade.

Isolated amid fields, Wingfield appears as a low, whitewashed Georgian façade, like an early American farmstead. A wide pediment covers five central bays including a handsome doorway. The wings are asymmetrical, with many windows blank.

Inside are two sides of the old medieval college round what is left of a quadrangle. The extent of the remains was revealed through the efforts of the present owners, the Chance family. Every inch of Wingfield's interior is intriguing. Two rooms either side of the entrance are georgianized and comfortable. The floor here was lowered in the 18th century to give the ground floor rooms more headroom. Behind is the former enclosed cloister or pentice, which runs across the end of the Great Hall.

This hall is an aisled structure of *c*1300, that is of the earliest Wingfield manor. It is short but high, with an oriel window. Above are mostly original roof timbers, including a huge tie beam and a crownpost. This has the appearance of charcoal, blackened and burnt by sparks from an open fire below. Against the far wall is a screen with carved relief portraits. The kitchen beyond has medieval mullioned windows buried behind the fake windows of the Georgian façade, here shown to be only a few inches deep.

This is a truly historic house, its skeleton a maze of medieval woodwork. The upper floors, presumably old dormitories, were roughly converted into bedrooms after the Dissolution and retain their Tudor proportions behind Squire Buck's new façade. The end room has a side window looking out onto the churchyard. The hall is used for concerts and festivals, decorated with carpets and kelims, rendering it as colourful as in its heyday.

WOODBRIDGE: SECKFORD HALL **

1m W of Woodbridge
Tudor brick mansion with exquisite hall screen (H)

The old hall makes an immediate impact over the crest of a slope from the Woodbridge bypass. The façade of red brick rises to a rhythmic sequence of six stepped gables dancing attendance on a two-storey porch. The house is now a hotel.

The symmetry soon dissolves on closer inspection. The former hall is to the left of the entrance, with a two-storey window indicating the dais end. Still, with its creeper and with the right-hand wing rebuilt after dereliction, Seckford is a formidable display of Suffolk brickwork. The chimneys have tiny onion domes.

The Seckford family were prominent 16th-century lawyers. Elizabeth I is said to have held one of her peripatetic courts here. In the 18th century, the house was sold and degenerated into use as a farm, until rescued in the 1920s by one of that valiant band of manorial enthusiasts, a Colonel Woodley. He gave way in 1940 to Sir Ralph Harwood who converted the place to its present use as a hotel. A large amount of woodwork was imported from elsewhere, with satisfying effect.

The entrance leads into the Great Hall, sheltered by a screen brought from a West Country church, with fine Perpendicular tracery. The beams overhead are decorated with grapes and the doors have exquisite panelling, part Gothic, part with portrait medallions of great delicacy. These came from Polesden Lacey (Surrey) which, I imagine, could ill spare them.

The dining room and bar have more beams and panelling. I am told that one of the hotel beds is so big that it must have been built *in situ* and is therefore the one 'in which Elizabeth must have slept'. There is a thesis to be written on these beds of Good Queen Bess.

A pleasant courtyard lies to the rear with a fountain and lake in the distance. In front of the house by the road is an eccentric summer house known as the Hunting Lodge. Four storeys rise to a stepped gable, a romantic conceit above a maze of brick walls round the garden.

Surrey

Until the coming of the railway, the chalk soil and heavily wooded North Downs of Surrey proved a major barrier to development south from London. Other than along the Wey Valley to the west, this was the poorest of the Home Counties. There were few big estates, only thick beech, oak and chestnut woods and even thicker clay. Today, the Downs form the county's one haven of calm, an often secret landscape with sudden views south towards the Weald.

The Guildford corridor saw the Bishops of Winchester build Farnham Castle, with keep, tower and fine interiors. The Molyneuxs' Loseley is a substantial Elizabethan mansion, believed to contain woodwork from vanished Nonsuch, and still in a substantial park. The county can also boast a Palladian epic at Leoni's Clandon. A modest set of Adam interiors has been revived at Hatchlands.

Of a later date is Mrs Greville's treasure trove of art on the sandy ridges south of the Downs at Polesden Lacey, while a similar collector's house survives at picturesque Titsey. Connoisseurs of eccentric Victoriana cannot miss the Royal Holloway College above Egham.

Clandon ✶✶✶
Claremont ✶
Farnham Castle ✶✶
Godalming: Red House ✶
Great Fosters ✶✶

Guildford:
  Abbot's Hospital ✶
  Guildford House ✶
Hatchlands ✶✶✶
Loseley ✶✶✶

Nonsuch ✶✶
Polesden Lacey ✶✶✶
Royal Holloway
  College ✶✶
Titsey ✶✶

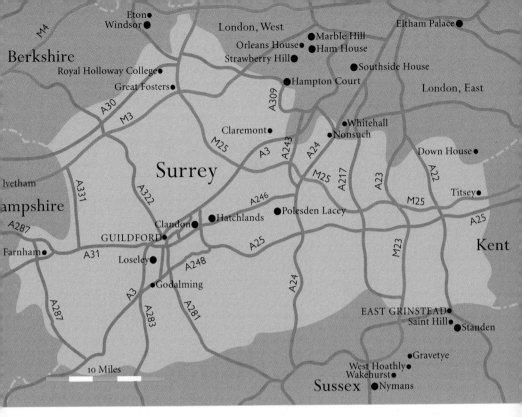

CLANDON PARK ***

3m E of Guildford
Palladian mansion of Onslows with porcelain collection (NT)

Onslows were lawyers. Three rose to be Speakers of the House of Commons, the first being 'Black Onslow' in the reign of Elizabeth I. The family acquired the Clandon estate in 1641 and continued in the style of their profession, steering a course between Royalty and Revolution, corruption and integrity, high office and high dudgeon. Onslows regarded the Lord Lieutenancy of Surrey as a hereditary right. In 1813, eight Onslows were county JPs. The family built a new mansion at Clandon *c*1731. The house experienced the familiar saga of brilliance, decline, ruin and rescue. In 1956 the family passed the house to the National Trust whilst continuing to live in a house in the park.

Clandon is indeed a lawyer of a house, formal to the world behind a Victorian porch, but with a certain pompous jollity in private. The designer was the Venetian, Giacomo Leoni, builder of Lyme Park (Cheshire). His client, the 2nd Baron Onslow, had profited hugely from his marriage to a Jamaica heiress, Elizabeth Knight. She was said to be so miserable that her ghost still haunts the house. I once visited Clandon with its windows still shuttered. The parade of gloomy rooms overseen by portraits of dark, domineering Onslows was a good place for such a ghost.

The house includes one of the great rooms of early Georgian England, the Marble Hall. Unlike the house of Onslow's rival, Walpole's Houghton (Norfolk), Clandon permits access directly into the Great Hall. The effect is sensational. White and dazzling, the walls rise through two storeys of orders past balconies to a spectacular ceiling. This might be an Italian *cortile* with the mythical gods romping across the *trompe-l'œil* sky above. The stuccoists, Giuseppe Artari and Giovanni Bagutti, have here bettered their ceiling at Houghton. Putti and slaves are in deep relief, their legs and

arms hanging free yet foreshortened as they spill over the coving into space. The chimney-piece is by Rysbrack. The room is further enlivened by two pictures of an ostrich and a cassowary, by Francis Barlow.

The rooms at Clandon are heavily classical, so much as to be almost relentless. They are relieved by the light touch of Artari and Bagutti, notably the ceilings of the Palladian Room and the saloon. Relief is also supplied by Clandon's other treasure, the collection of furniture and porcelain gathered between the wars by Mrs David Gubbay and donated to the National Trust. It was allocated to Clandon to replace much that had been sold, an admirable partnership.

While the Gubbay furniture seems to merge into the background of the rooms, the porcelain is a different matter. It includes some fifty Chinese birds, which seem to flutter from every mantelpiece. They are everywhere, perching on top of cabinets and side tables and darting among the Meissen, Sèvres and Bow. They bring colour when it is needed and delicacy when the ponderous Onslows seem overpowering.

Of the individual reception rooms, the Hunting Room contains a set of Soho tapestries to designs by Wootton. The Speakers' Room is dedicated to the three Onslows who attained that office. The Stone Staircase is hung with paintings of racehorses by Ferneley.

CLAREMONT *

Portsmouth Road, Esher
Clive of India mansion by Holland (P-R)

Catch Claremont in a good light and it might still be shimmering in a landscape in India. It was built for Lord Clive on his return from India, to complement his sumptuous house in Berkeley Square. The site looks out over Surrey towards London and had been chosen by Vanbrugh for a country house of his own. It was bought by Clive in 1769 and Capability

Simplicity in stucco: Clandon hall

Brown was asked to design a new house and landscape. Brown designed the exterior but employed his son-in-law, Henry Holland, on the interiors. Holland in turn collaborated with the young John Soane. The mansion dominates a sweeping park. Vanbrugh is recalled only by a belvedere on an adjacent knoll.

The house is now a Christian Science girls' school. As John Julius Norwich wrote, we can only feel for the 'schoolgirls who, on the first evening of their first term, climb the twenty-two steps to that gigantic portico'. The house is a box of white brick with stone dressings. The front portico is of four giant Corinthian columns, the back has pilasters. The coat of arms includes an elephant and a griffin. While the front steps are straight, those behind are beautifully curved.

Here Clive can have imagined himself still a proconsul, ruling Esher as if it were Madras. The house was advanced. The basement was designed to ensure that servants did not suffer damp. Clive insisted on such features as water closets, a separate kitchen block and a vaulted bathroom big enough for swimming. He committed suicide in 1774 before he was able to enjoy any of this.

The interior is very much a school, but this in no way detracts from its majesty. The entrance hall is an oval of red scagliola columns inside a rectangle, a design for which Soane was later to claim credit. The ceiling is reflected in the pattern of the marble floor. On the walls are reliefs of Victory apparently resting on her laurels and surrounded by trophies.

The former reception rooms were decorated by Holland, with fine ceilings and Adamish motifs on the doors and cornices. Some of the designs he went on to use at Berrington (Herefs) on a more intimate scale. In 1816, Claremont was acquired by the government for the Prince Regent's daughter and her husband, the future King of the Belgians. The young Victoria often stayed in the house and worshipped in the private pew that Vanbrugh designed in Esher church.

The grounds of Claremont were laid out by Vanbrugh, Bridgeman, Kent and Brown and belong to the National Trust. They are an attraction now separate from the house.

FARNHAM CASTLE **

Castle Hill
Keep and former house of Bishops of Winchester (P)

The castle sits high on its bluff over the town as if Surrey were the Dordogne. It belonged to the Bishops of Winchester, a stopping place on the way to and from London and close to the Pilgrims' Way. The keep dates from the 12th century, as does the triangular bailey immediately below it, with curtain wall immediately beneath. The keep (owned by English Heritage) is merely a bastion, offering a good view of the North Downs. The bailey embraces a remarkable range of old buildings, now an international business college.

The plan of the domestic quarters can be seen from the inner courtyard. A Great Hall faced the entrance, with the old chapel to its right and kitchens behind. Farther round are Tudor guest rooms behind timbered walls. The bishop's lodgings were to the left. The whole castle was badly mauled in the Civil War, but rebuilt after the Restoration by Bishop George Morley, to whom we owe most of the present residence.

His hall is a large Carolean chamber rising two storeys and with balconies on two sides. Its fireplace is truly episcopal, flanked by giant consoles instead of pilasters. The balcony and upper rooms are reached by a magnificent staircase, showing a mastery of architectural space. The fruit-covered newel posts were reputedly by Grinling Gibbons, as are the swags and drops of Morley's upstairs chapel. The remaining rooms are institutional. The drawing room is said to have a fine scissor-beam roof hidden above its ceiling.

On the other side of the hall is some surviving medieval work. Fox's Tower, built by Bishop Waynflete in the 1470s, dominates the town below. Beyond are Norman kitchens with a large fireplace. Next to them is a Norman chapel, still consecrated for services.

GODALMING: RED HOUSE *

Frith Hill Road
Lutyens house on edge of ravine (P-R)

This eccentric house is strictly for Lutyens' addicts. The architect designed it when he was just twenty-eight and on the brink of celebrity. It clings to the edge of a precipice, as might an early work by Frank Lloyd Wright. Round it slope the remains of Gertrude Jekyll's attempt at mountain gardening. The house was built for a master at nearby Charterhouse, W. H. Evans, in 1897. The fall of land appealed to the theatrical in Lutyens.

The house is modestly neo-Georgian to the road above, marked only by massive Lutyens chimneys. From here it might be a two-storey town house. The more remarkable elevation is overlooking the valley below, a bold wall of plain brick with canted bays and casement windows. It harks back to Hardwick Hall (Derbys) and forward to Lutyens's Castle Drogo (Devon).

Inside, the spaces are dictated not by a hall but by a wide spiral staircase, running up the core of the house, much of which is below the level of the entrance. The treads are wide and shallow, to accommodate the disablement of the original owner. The staircase is now the best thing left of the interior, apart from two Lutyens fireplaces with niches.

The current owner is struggling to bring the rooms back to their original appearance. He has a long way to go. Jekyll's garden seems beyond recall.

GREAT FOSTERS **

Stroude, 1m NE of Virginia Water
Tudor house with Jacobean interiors and stairs (H)

Great Fosters dates from the 1550s and was reputedly used by Elizabeth I as a hunting lodge. Its most intriguing occupant was Sir John Chapman, a progressive doctor who was said to have treated George III for his madness in Windsor. Rumour, though not record, even has the King being brought to Great Fosters in person for treatment. The house was modernized by the up-market country house architect, W. H. Romaine-Walker, after 1918. It is a rare and surprisingly little-known Elizabethan house so close to London.

Since 1930, the Sutcliffe family have run Great Fosters as a discreet hotel, convenient for Ascot. It hosted the Ascot Ball in 1931, with royalty present. The appearance is still that of a private house at which guests would arrive only if invited. There is a wicket gate in the front door.

The main entrance carries the date of 1598, but the hall beams are older. The Jacobean fireplace must have contributed to the thick yellow patina on the plaster ceiling. The original staircase survives behind the hall in a rear turret. The stair baluster is heavy and crude, with a giant newel post rising to the ceiling. This contrasts with the staircase's later and more delicate wall panelling.

The old drawing room, now the (Flemish) Tapestry Room, has a Jacobean chimneypiece depicting the story of Genesis. The Anne Boleyn Room retains its original ceiling. It is decorated with emblems of the queen, whether in her honour or because of a claimed link with the house is unknown. The garden dates from the 1918 redesign and includes fine topiary, a knot garden and an early swimming pool with 'listed' bathing boxes. The tithe barn is extraordinarily old, and is dated 1390; it was moved here from Ewell.

GUILDFORD: ABBOT'S HOSPITAL *

High Street
Jacobean almshouses with gatehouse (P-R)

The grandest building in Guildford High Street is not a town hall, church or hotel. It is an old people's home, or rather the gatehouse of the Hospital of the Blessed Trinity. Access is by friendly appointment, through a gigantic door panelled with heraldry and topped by a wooden Gothic fan light.

George Abbot was a Guildford man who rose from humble origins to be Archbishop of Canterbury in the troubled early 17th century. His brothers became Bishop of Salisbury and Lord Mayor of London, sign of the upward mobility of late-Tudor England. In 1619 Abbot founded an almshouse in the town 'out of my love to the place of my birth'. It opened in 1622, housing twelve brothers and eight sisters. They had to be resident in the town, over 60 and of good character. There are twenty-four inmates today.

The gatehouse is that of a traditional Jacobean building, strongly built as if for defence. The main reception rooms are above the entrance, in a century-old fashion familiar from Layer Marney (Essex) and Oxburgh Hall (Norfolk). The quadrangle has two storeys with an attic, all redbrick, and might be the court of a Cambridge college. The whole building seems a deliberate anachronism, as if so elevated a purpose demanded a medieval form.

The communal interiors can be visited. The Common Hall is beautifully panelled and furnished with old settles, simple but comfortable. The Guesten Hall has a Jacobean overmantel with grotesque carvings and portraits of donors. Doors and hinges are superbly crafted.

GUILDFORD: GUILDFORD HOUSE *

155 High Street
17th-century townhouse with original plasterwork (M)

Despite the ugliness of Guildford below the hill, the old High Street displays the best of Surrey townscape. Its jolliest building is this Restoration town house. Although the ground floor was long ago converted to a shopfront, the upper storeys are a spirited work of 1660. The house was built by a lawyer, John Child, and later sold to a mayor of Guildford, John Martyr. It became the local museum in the 1950s.

The façade above the ground floor might be

termed 'Inigo Jones provincial'. The façade is almost all window, with the upper floors jettied over the pavement. Yet the casements are divided by four bold pilasters rising to an overhanging entablature, the middle two bays slightly projected, a most inventive composition. A 17th-century balcony overlooks the street from above the front door. The rear is equally enjoyable, tile hung and with a pretty oriel window.

The interior is mostly spoilt by museum use, the walls frigidly white with little feeling of the old house. But the staircase survives, a generous structure with original pattern of acanthus leaves for its balustrade. The newel posts carry urns of flowers. The Powell Room on the first floor has an original plaster ceiling of circles and ovals divided by ornamented beams. The survival of the casement windows and their old handles is particularly happy.

HATCHLANDS PARK ***

East Clandon, 4m E of Guildford
Adam house with Old Masters and keyboard instruments (NT)

Hatchlands is a jewel in the National Trust crown. This is due to its having the collector, Alec Cobbe, as its tenant and giving him freedom to furnish an empty house to his own, sometimes controversial, taste. A shell left to the Trust in 1945 by the architect, H. S. Goodhart-Rendel, is now filled with pictures, furniture and historic keyboard instruments. Some were moved from Cobbe's family house outside Dublin. His particular delight is to wander the rooms with visitors, stopping at an instrument and playing snatches of music.

The house, begun in the 1750s by a sea captain, Admiral Boscawen, was built like Anson's Shugborough (Staffs) on the spoils of Georgian piracy. He commissioned Stiff Leadbetter to design the unexciting exterior and the young Robert Adam, then just back from Italy, on the far more exciting interior. Repton arrived later to lay out the park. Like the adjacent Clandon, Hatchlands retains open Surrey countryside within its borders.

Adam reigns supreme, but it is an unfamiliar, youthful Adam. The date is 1758–9 and the classical detail is relatively heavy, closer to the earlier Georgian of Leoni at Clandon. In addition, the Adam work was so battered after the war that Cobbe, himself a painter, has reinstated much of it to his own researched designs. The library has an Adam ceiling and cornice, with roundels by Cobbe 'after' Angelica Kauffmann.

The adjacent saloon is hung with red silk beneath a spectacular Adam ceiling of swirling acanthus. The frieze, celebrating Boscawen's maritime career, is of dolphins, similar to those on Adam's Admiralty Screen in Whitehall. The fireplace, flanked by two giant caryatids, was carved by Rysbrack. This saloon is the principal exhibition room, hung with Old Masters from the Cobbe collection and dominated by a Guercino. These are interspersed with family portraits, Cobbe claiming descent from both Cromwell and Charles II through the Duchess of Cleveland. The room could be in a Venetian palazzo.

Apart from pictures, the rooms are crammed with keyboard instruments. Everywhere are pianos, some fifty slotted into every alcove and corner. Each has a story and a personality of its own. There are pianos owned by Beethoven, by Marie Antoinette, by the Medici and one played by Mozart. Each seems eager to vanish beneath the clutter, as if to avoid another Cobbe performance. This is erudite clutter, in blessed contrast to customary National Trust tidiness. Music and books are stacked on chairs and side tables. The artful mind cannot be neat.

The staircase hall soars the full height of the house, making it seem higher than it is. It was embellished c1800, probably by Bonomi. An alcove below contains Mahler's piano. Beyond is the Edwardian music room, added by Sir Reginald Blomfield. It offers eight more pianos, including ones played by Liszt and Chopin and that on which Elgar composed the Enigma Variations.

To receive a queen: Loseley

In the dining room, a sideboard lid opens to reveal yet another piano. This is a house as it should be, occupied, loved and nudged this way and that by its inhabitant – and to hell with the owner.

LOSELEY PARK ✱✱✱

2m SW of Guildford
Elizabethan family house, Nonsuch panelling (P)

Loseley was one of the earliest houses to open to the public after the war. Its motto claims, 'I am closed to envy but open always to a friend.' The owners, Mr and Mrs More-Molyneux, recall that the place was transformed overnight from somewhere 'grubby, geriatric, unkempt, into a beautiful creature, friendly, steeped in peace, that people loved to visit'. Owners were as pleased as was the public.

Loseley was built by an Elizabethan courtier, Sir William More, who added to an earlier house in 1562. It was intended, like so many mansions at the time, to entertain the Queen on her progress round the country, yet in the hope that she would not bring bankruptcy in her train. She visited Loseley in 1570 and the house survived. A More heiress married Sir Thomas Molyneux and inherited the house in 1689. The house has been owned by More-Molyneuxs ever since.

This is now a house, a home and very much a business. All seem in good health. As in Elizabethan days, the family are preoccupied with hospitality. The house is set in a spacious park, home to the celebrated Loseley herd of dairy cattle and the resulting dairy products.

The exterior appears at first glance a typical Tudor E-plan, of white stone rubble. It is asymmetrical, with windows still reflecting the internal plan in the medieval style. The entrance bay is off-centre and narrow. The Great Hall has a wide bay window.

Inside, this a magnificent room. The panelling was allegedly imported from the demolished Nonsuch Palace, an attribution based on emblems of Henry VIII and Katherine Parr.

The painted canvas panels in the gallery are from Henry's banqueting tents, of high quality and great rarity. The designs are Italian, remarkable for their date in England. The screen doors below have elaborate *trompe-l'œil* marquetry.

Beyond the Great Hall is the library, a rich chamber with pilastered bookcases and a cornice carrying the maxim, 'I soothe troubled minds and while away the centuries'. Over the eccentric mantelpiece, which seems a Victorian amalgam, is a panel commemorating the coveted visit by Elizabeth I.

An even more elaborate ceiling with pendants graces the remarkable drawing room, apparently inserted for a visit from James I. Its mantelpiece is carved from a single block of chalk, a mass of swirling scrollwork inside a classical frame, guarded by caryatids and monsters. The Mannerist style is wayward and enjoyable. So too is the huge Mannerist mullion to the window, ending in a giant claw. It must be something that a Tudor mason saw in an Italian pattern book.

Upstairs three bedrooms are displayed, all with geometrical ribbed ceilings and stately panelling. Two contain spectacular 17th-century Oudenarde tapestries. One set depicts a hunt at night and is said to come to life if lit with a red light after dark.

NONSUCH MANSION HOUSE ✱✱

Cheam Road, Ewell
Wyatville house near site of Nonsuch Palace (P-R)

The demolition of Henry VIII's palace of Nonsuch, or 'Nonpareil', was one of the catastrophes of English architecture. Towards the end of his life and as its crowning glory, Henry brought artists and craftsmen from all over Europe to demonstrate Tudor England's Renaissance prowess. What had begun as a royal hunting lodge emerged as an English Fontainebleau.

The palace was so famous that it was depicted throughout the land on so-called

'Nonsuch' chests. After Henry's death, Elizabeth visited the house but it was eventually given to the grandson of the Duchess of Cleveland. He could not afford it and demolition began in the 1680s. Only a few outbuildings survived.

Nonsuch Park, which straddles the London boundary at Cheam, is picturesque. Fragments of Elizabethan wall abound. Fine oak avenues have been planted and the undulating terrain retains a sense of its hunting past. The old quarry has been converted into a dell. The site of the palace, in the south-west corner of the park, was inexcusably covered after excavation in 1959. The adjacent Cherry Orchard farm survives.

One outbuilding to the north-east of the house was said to have belonged to a palace official with the title of 'the Sergeant of the Sauces'. This passed in 1799 to Samuel Farmer of Cheshire. He commissioned a new building on the site in the Tudor Gothic style from Sir Jeffry Wyatville; it was begun in 1802. Whether Wyatville sought to imitate the original façade of Nonsuch can only be a matter of conjecture.

Nonsuch Mansion House has its own garden, parterre and copse of trees and is a substantial Gothic building. It passed from the Farmers, who rose to be Lords Lieutenant of Surrey, to the local council in 1937 and has been well restored.

Wyatville's house survives virtually unaltered. The exterior has tall Gothick windows, turrets and a battlemented roof. Gothick woodwork and plasterwork are intact in the main reception rooms, including doors and window shutters. The interiors have been restored to their original colours. Many are similar to Wyatville's later work at Windsor Castle.

Thus the entrance hall is dark brown, with shields picked out in the frieze. The library and drawing room run together from front to back, with ceilings of unusual richness. Niches for pier-glasses are uniformly Gothic. The windows have Victorian stained glass depicting Henry VIII and Elizabeth I, and a Tudor rose decorates the dining room ceiling. Such echoes of Nonsuch are repeated throughout

the house, interspersed with the Farmer coat of arms.

The Friends of Nonsuch battled in 1992 to prevent the house and park becoming a golf club. They are restoring the Georgian service wing, which survives from a precursor of the Wyatville house, reinstating the scullery, game store, kitchens and laundry. On display is a set of Nonsuch glass, including a 'parakeet' work of stained glass painted by Margaret Pearson in 1776.

POLESDEN LACEY ***

4m NW of Dorking
Edwardian interiors, Greville picture collection (NT)

The defining event in the history of Polesden Lacey was its purchase by Mr and Mrs Ronald Greville in 1906. Mrs Greville, heiress to the Scottish McEwen's brewery fortune, converted the house into a place of lavish and apparently majestic entertainment.

She was a social monster: 'better a beeress than a peeress,' she said. To Balfour, her acerbic wit was 'honeyed poison'. To Cecil Beaton she was a 'galumphing, greedy, snobbish old toad'. She went to the Nuremberg rally and supported the fascists as 'better than the bolshies'. Yet she was hugely hospitable and her food and wine were superb. Kings and prime ministers found themselves swept into her circle. Edward VII, an expert at being entertained, described her 'gift for hospitality' as amounting to 'positive genius'. On her death in 1942, Mrs Greville left the house, park and art collection to the nation.

The house had previously been occupied until his death in 1816 by the playwright Richard Brinsley Sheridan. It was then largely demolished and rebuilt by Thomas Cubitt, builder of Belgravia. The 1821 exterior is that of a neo-classical seaside villa, well set on the edge of a steep slope and park. Surrey is a place of many secrets.

On buying the house, Mrs Greville employed the Ritz architects, Mewès and Davis, to convert the interiors for entertainment. Her

husband, a self-effacing Tory MP, died within two years of their taking up residence, but this only increased his wife's social activity, both here and at her house in Charles Street, Mayfair. She revelled in her ability to attract nobility to her table and once boasted that three kings had sat on her bed at her morning *levée*. The late Queen Mother began her honeymoon at Polesden in 1923.

The house carries its opulence with an intimacy rare in Edwardian interiors. The central hall is spacious, adorned with a magnificent reredos from Wren's church of St Matthew's, Friday Street in the City. The dining room is hung with British portraits by Lawrence, Reynolds and Raeburn. In this room occurred the most celebrated Greville anecdote. Alarmed at the state of her butler, she passed him a note telling him he was drunk and should leave at once. The butler duly passed the note to the principal guest, the Tory grandee Sir Austen Chamberlain. The under-butler was an overt Communist.

The barrel-vaulted corridor is a Jacobean import. With plaster scrollwork, dark panelling and red carpet, it is a perfect setting for works by de Hooch, Teniers, Cuyp and van Goyen. Indeed Polesden houses one of the Trust's finest if little known collections. At the end of the corridor is a portrait by Carolus-Duran of a more than life-size Mrs Greville, looking improbably demure at the time of her marriage.

The library is kept full of flowers from the garden. Beyond is Mrs Greville's study, with her collection of Meissen and a Fürstenberg tea-caddy decorated with oriental scenes. The saloon was Mewès and Davis at their most Ritzy: 'fit to entertain maharajahs in' was the instruction. To Beverley Nichols, from a later and no less snobbish generation, it was 'over-gilt, over-velveted, over-mirrored like an extremely expensive bordel'. The National Trust plans to permit billiards in the billiard room, a good innovation. Next they should permit cigars in the smoking room.

Polesden Lacey: Mrs Greville presiding

ROYAL HOLLOWAY COLLEGE **

1m S of Egham
Gigantic fake Loire château, Victorian pictures (P-R)

Like it or loathe it, the Royal Holloway is a phenomenon without equal. To some it suggests a creation of the cartoonist, Charles Addams. From a distance, including from the M25, the place shimmers above the tree-line like a lost temple in the Cambodian jungle.

The college was built by Thomas Holloway with the millions made from 'Holloway's Patent Pills' in the 1870s. He was an epic Victorian entrepreneur/philanthropist, his wife a passionate believer in women's education. Holloway created what must have been the largest single building in England and filled it with young ladies and with art. Apart from the addition of some male students, it remains true to his principles to this day.

The building was erected in just eight years from 1879. Holloway's template was the Château de Chambord on the Loire. His architect, W. H. Crossland, was sent for two years to study the château before beginning work. The result is a variation on a French Renaissance theme, a monumental house blown up by three, four, five times the normal size round two spacious courtyards, yet its scale is not relentless or even institutional. Crossland achieved a careful sense of proportion and covered it in a wealth of ornamental detail. Like Sir Gilbert Scott's St Pancras Chambers, this is a Victorian building that can handle its size. I am not sure we can.

The building is near impossible to describe in detail. Three gatehouses penetrate the two courtyards, as in St John's College, Cambridge. The exterior is adorned with projecting turrets every few bays, rising to towers (or *tourelles*). These are interspersed with chimneys adorned with segmental pediments and a parade of dormers. The courtyards carry Renaissance frontispieces left and right, with colonnades along the main façades. The central lanterns are elaborate coronets, the middle one with giant crocodiles climbing up its buttresses. In one court is a statue of Queen Victoria, in the other Holloway and his wife, portrayed as assisting the cause of education.

The interiors are by contrast dull, although the chapel has a magnificent Renaissance roof. The figures in its frieze are in deep relief, as if about to pounce on the girls below. In the Picture Gallery is Holloway's collection of Victorian art. This includes such celebrated works as Frith's *Paddington Station* and Luke Fildes' *Applicants for Admission to a Casual Ward*.

TITSEY PLACE **

Titsey, 2m N of Oxted
Regency house overlooking North Downs
estate (P)

Five miles south of Croydon, London runs into the rolling foothills of the North Downs. Suburb retreats and thickly wooded slopes lead towards the steep southern escarpment, with views over the Weald. Hidden along this escarpment is the old Leveson Gower estate. For a brief moment, we might be in Gloucestershire.

Titsey was one of the many properties of the Elizabethan Gresham family, City merchants and builders of Osterley (London, W). The line descended through daughters to the Leveson Gowers (pronounced Looson Gores). By the 20th century they found themselves with three bachelor brothers and, in 1992, no heirs. The estate, one of the largest in Surrey, passed to a trust in the care of David Innes, godson of one

of the brothers. He occupies the house and opens it and its grounds to the public.

After a drive across sweeping grassland, past cedars and Wellingtonias, the house presents a pale face to the world. It was the work in 1826 of James Wyatt's assistant, William Atkinson, in neo-Tudor with grey render. The exterior encases a Georgian predecessor, built by Sir John Gresham in 1775, and this in turn encases a Tudor original round what is now a servants' hall. This is a house of many boxes.

The character of Titsey largely rests with the genealogy-obsessed Squire Granville Leveson Gower. Between 1860 and 1895, he built cottages, lodges and a church on the estate and planted half a million trees. He added a large battlemented tower to the north side of the house, destroying the symmetry of Atkinson's Regency façade. The inside he filled with Leveson Gower portraits, coats of arms and antiques. Excellent panelling was imported from elsewhere. One such piece is the 1646 chimney surround in the drawing room.

The rather ordinary interior is redeemed by the care of the restoration to Squire Granville's period. Thus Atkinson's staircase landing is lit by a skylight crowded with heraldic glass. The boudoir, over the Victorian dining room below, contains a collection of 16th- and 17th-century panelling, gathered by the Squire. It is offset by a fireplace surrounded with Delftware tiles. The dining room has four lovely Canalettos of Venice and the Old Dining Room a portrait of the last Leveson Gower brothers, by the wildlife artist, David Shepherd.

Sussex

Sussex rivals Kent for outstanding houses in the south of England. It was once a landscape of woods and upland moors. Its oaks were so plentiful they were dubbed the 'Sussex weed'. After the Norman conquest, its valleys became populated with the citadels of the Normans and those fearful of their successors, the French, often built with stone shipped over from Caen. There are early medieval castles at Pevensey and Bodiam. Early monastic activity is recalled at Battle Abbey and St Mary's Hospital in Chichester. Herstmonceux is one of the oldest brick mansions in England, and is externally still one of the most impressive.

Of the Elizabethan and Jacobean era Parham is, after Knole, the finest example in the south of England. Sussex stepped up a grade in the late 17th century, with the Duke of Somerset's palace at Petworth and the less pretentious Uppark, now a controversial example of a complete modern reconstructed interior. Georgian Sussex added the splendours of Goodwood. Of the Regency period, nowhere in England is the equal of Brighton Pavilion and the creamy town houses of Hove. Arundel Castle is one of the finest neo-Gothic fantasies of the Victorian age.

Sussex, like most of southern England, was colonized by enthusiasts for manorial Tudor in the 19th and 20th centuries. Their leader was William Morris's friend, Philip Webb, at Standen. Among writers, Kipling found peace at Bateman's, Henry James at Rye and the Bloomsbury Set at Charleston and Rodmell.

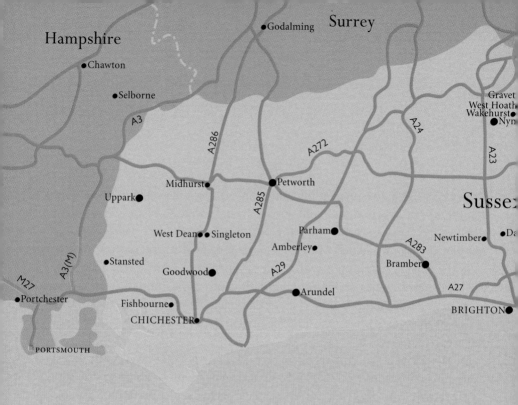

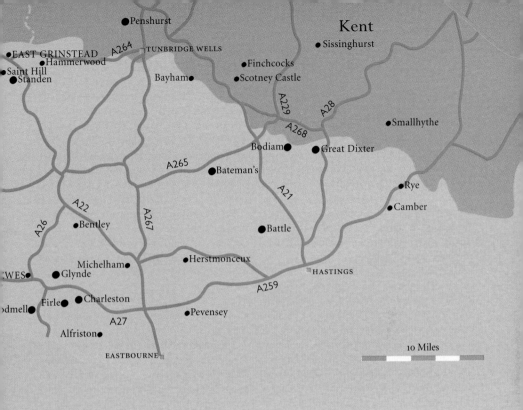

ALFRISTON: CLERGY HOUSE **

The Tye, Alfriston
Medieval house in picture village (NT)

The drive to Alfriston over the Downs from Seaford is one of the most spectacular on the south coast. From the strip development of the Sussex shore, the contours open out to reveal wild vistas which, on a misty day, seem like moonscape, a treeless topography of convex curves. I have felt more lost on these hills than anywhere on the Pennines or Dartmoor.

The road drops down into the picturesque village of Alfriston. Tile-hung and weather-boarded houses cluster round the green. Next to the church is the old Clergy House, the first building to be taken into custodianship by the National Trust, in 1896. I first visited the house as a student when it was tenanted by two elderly schoolmistresses, who showed off its cluttered rooms with pride. It is now an empty visitor attraction, littered with Trust publicity leaflets.

The structure is that of a rectangular box with a hipped thatch roof, exposed beams and jettied end. As one looks at it from the green, one sees the central hall and, to the left, the old parlour and solar. The timbers are widely spaced with diagonal braces. The far end was rebuilt in the 16th century, at the time when English houses were acquiring fireplaces and privacy.

The hall is set between solar and service wings, typical of yeoman houses of the 15th and 16th centuries. The interior has been restored by the National Trust to a pristine simplicity it never knew when occupied.

AMBERLEY CASTLE **

Amberley, 2m SW of Storrington
Fortified manor within curtain wall (H)

Amberley stands proud above water meadows where the River Arun forces its way through a dramatic gap in the Downs. The castle's curtain wall looks particularly imposing from across the valley, with the old village clustered beside it. The area was so prone to flooding that Amberley women were said to be born with webbed feet.

This was never a true castle but a fortified manor of the Bishops of Chichester, built against French raiders during the 'great crenellation' of the late 14th century. The then bishop erected a twin-towered gatehouse and extended the manorial buildings round the Great Hall within. The property passed to the Crown and fell into ruin, before being acquired by the medievalist Duke of Norfolk in 1893. By then the Great Hall and much of the old manor had collapsed, and a private residence was created from the fragments. These have been turned into a picturesque and comfortable hotel nestling within the old walls.

The interior of the castle is reached through the gateway with raised portcullis. White doves shelter in a Gothic window. The lower court is filled with ornamental yew trees round which lie the ruins of the guest lodgings and soldiers' quarters. The Great Hall has gone but its kitchen range now offers a terrace in the outer wall, with views over the valley and a well-preserved garderobe to its left.

What survive of the manor house are the undercroft of the old solar and the smaller hall, possibly for servants, flanking the upper court. These buildings have mostly Gothic windows and doorways but an elaborate Norman arch survives in the small hall. In this range are some 16th-century panels of heroines of antiquity. The Victorian reception rooms are cosy and the staircase modest, a pleasant facsimile of Elizabethan Sussex.

ARUNDEL CASTLE ****

Arundel
Seat of Dukes of Norfolk, largely Victorian reconstruction (P)

Arundel is Victorian, and magnificently so. It was rebuilt round its ancestral keep not once but twice in the 19th century alone. But the house is no castellated folly. Its rooms are bravura Victorian revival, gigantic and, in some cases, virtually unusable. Round them are spread majestic gardens and miles of open downland.

The castle was founded in 1067 for Roger de Montgomery, one of the Conqueror's most loyal barons. By 1232 it was in the hands of the FitzAlans, passing to an heiress of the Howards in 1580. They hold it to this day. That the Howards, now Dukes of Norfolk, have for centuries been both senior court office-holders and devout Roman Catholics is a testament to a sort of English tolerance (most of the time).

Until the 19th century few Howards regarded Arundel as their premier seat, preferring Worksop in Nottinghamshire, Deepdene in Surrey and Norfolk House in London. It was the Regency Picturesque movement that led the 10th Duke to sell his leases in London's Strand to finance the rebuilding of Arundel.

The work was begun by his son who decided to be his own architect. By the time of his death in 1815, much of the old castle had been reconstructed. However, the devout 15th Duke, builder of Arundel Cathedral next door, pulled down much of what the 11th Duke had erected and again rebuilt it. This work was completed in the 1890s with the aid of the Catholic architect, Charles Buckler.

Visitors enter what survives of the medieval castle, principally the keep. This is chiefly of interest for the view it offers out to sea. There follows the stone hall and armoury, which includes a spectacular two-edged English longsword and a Chinese execution blade. Of the 15th Duke's Victorian rooms, the largest is the Barons' Hall, replacing not just the medieval hall but also its Regency successor.

The theme for the decoration was the barons who drew up the Magna Carta, while the giant hammerbeam roof is said to have been inspired by Westminster Hall and Penshurst (Kent). The pictures, vast portraits and historical landscapes, seem postage stamps in this space. There is nothing medieval about the furniture, which includes a Rococo sleigh and a sedan chair.

The picture gallery is lined with Howard portraits commissioned in periodic bursts of family pride. Facing the stairs is an exquisite depiction of the 16th-century Earl of Surrey in a setting said to be designed by Inigo Jones. A soldier poet, he is credited with bringing the sonnet form to England.

The dining room, incorporating part of the shell of the 12th-century chapel, is an original design of Buckler's and must be the most graceful Early Gothic refectory in the country. Lancets and foliated capitals look down on diminutive diners far below. The relics of Mary Queen of Scots are displayed in a case, including the rosary carried by her at her execution. Here too is the quill pen with which George IV signed the Catholic Emancipation Bill of 1829.

The Grand Staircase is lit by tall lancet arches of grey stone and hung with Gobelins tapestries. It leads to stone-vaulted corridors and mostly Gothic bedrooms. These rooms might be thought unsuited to slumber, but Arundel, like Eastnor (Herefs), has risen to the challenge and overcome it, largely by the bold use of colour.

The York Bedroom has brilliant crimson hangings. The Victoria Suite has bed, portrait and furniture commissioned for a visit by the young queen in 1846, she having given the Norfolks a considerate two years' advance warning. The Small Drawing Room has triumphed over its heavy proportions with warm carpet and furniture and the dramatic lighting of a set of Canalettos. The main drawing room next door is even more virile, dominated by the Norfolks' heraldic devices prominent over the fireplace. The window arches are giant trefoils and the walls carry magnificent portraits by Mytens and van Dyck, Reynolds and Gainsborough.

The ante-library and library remain from the Regency rooms designed by the 11th Duke and are delightful spaces. The former is filled with lacquer furniture, and is set beneath a van Dyck of the 17th-century 'Collector' Earl and his wife, here advertising their sponsorship of an expedition to Madagascar.

The library itself is collegiate in atmosphere, grand but not pompous. The style is Gothick

of *c*1800, the shafts and ribbing slender and the vaulting in a rich mahogany. The lanterns are Brighton Pavilion Chinese, the later chimney-pieces deeply coved with Gothic arches. The library has 10,000 books, including a large collection on Catholic history. It is one of the most spectacular in England, a room to make one want to read.

BATEMAN'S ✱✱✱✱

½m SW of Burwash, 6m E of Heathfield
Home of Rudyard Kipling, rooms as he left them (NT)

Every inch of Bateman's is Rudyard Kipling. Every tree, lake, creeper, stone, panel and fire-iron seems to carry his stamp. He found the house when he was in his late thirties and it remained his and his wife Carrie's home all their lives. Like its owner, it contrives to be English yet exotic, childish yet elderly. It is hung about with the innocent fantasies of much of Kipling's writing, and with the intro-spective sadness of his old age. This is a house of ghosts.

Bateman's was bought in 1902 at the height of the writer's wealth and fame. He had just experienced four unhappy years in America, from which he escaped after a court case involving his wife's unstable brother. He was distraught from the death of his adored daughter, Josephine, at the age of just seven. Kipling still seemed the vagrant son of an art teacher in India.

At Bateman's, he felt he had found home. He wrote to a friend: 'It is made up of trees, and green fields and mud and the gentry, and at last I am one of the gentry.' He craved privacy and had refused a knighthood. He also craved the settled status of a returning imperialist. Adam Nicolson, historian of Bateman's, writes that if Sussex 'lacked the sheer extent of empire, it more than made up for it in the depth of its history . . . and the things that were underneath'.

Arundel's ducal Gothic

Isolated in the valley of the River Dudwell, the house was probably built by a Sussex ironmaster and has the date 1634 over the door. The rudiments of an E-plan suggest an earlier original. The Kiplings carved their initials on the door post as if to stamp it with their presence.

The interior is dark and Jacobean, as Kipling and Carrie liked it and left it. This is no place for the light of day, more for the darker memories of the night. Bateman's is not a shrine, except insofar as Kipling's life was that, and contains much of the light-hearted oddness of *The Just So Stories*, *Puck of Pook's Hill* and *The Jungle Book*. 'The worst of the place,' said Kipling, 'is that it will not let us use modern furniture.' That did not stop him import-ing Indian rugs and oriental miniatures. His library bookplate was an elephant. Bateman's is the Empire exotic rather than political.

In the old hall is the large fireplace in which Kipling burned his personal papers so that 'no one's going to make a monkey out of me after I die'. The parlour was the family sitting room, again dark, where guests awaited dinner while they heard the great man pacing up and down in his study overhead. The room has a case of Kipling's 'household gods' and a Tiffany lamp. The dining room is sumptuous, hung with Venetian 'Cordoba' leather acquired by Carrie on the Isle of Wight. The ever-formal Kiplings always dressed for dinner even if alone.

The upstairs study is the heart and head of the house. Here Kipling wrote as he hummed and smoked, sometimes pacing, sometimes stretched out on the day-bed. He worked messily, a mess which the ever-tidy National Trust refuses to re-create, thus arbitrarily denying this room its most obvious authority. He called his desk his dunghill. Ink spattered papers, the table and Kipling himself. When clad in white in the tropics, this inkiness nick-named him the Dalmatian. He hated the type-writer since 'the beastly thing simply won't spell'. It was used by his secretary. As for books, this was a working library. They were the tools of his trade and he accepted that his treatment of them was 'barbarian'.

Beyond a small exhibition room is the

bedroom, always kept the most private in the house and, as Nicolson says, 'a shrine to nurtured grief'. The death of the Kiplings' son, John, in the Great War left them numb with misery. Their surviving daughter, Elsie, always suffered from her parents' love for her vanished siblings. The room contains portraits of the children.

The garden at Bateman's was as important to Kipling as the house, especially to his sense of childhood delight. Laid out with his £7,700 Nobel Prize for Literature in 1907, he designed both the formal and informal parts, and fashioned the wildness of Pook's Hill. He drew up a medieval charter giving his children 'rights' to the river. A mill was built in an old mill house, which still works, albeit with an auxiliary engine. The Kipling Rolls Royce remains in the garage.

BATTLE ABBEY ***

High Street
Abbey remains near site of Battle of Hastings (EH)

The origins of the abbey need no introduction. The Battle of Hastings was the last successful military invasion of Britain, its outcome decided by superior Norman cavalry and archers. The site is for all to see, although argument continues between those who would like the field to be clear and those who, for some odd reason, prefer it hidden by trees and undergrowth. The battle is thus incapable of re-enactment.

The Abbey was founded by William the Conqueror in thanks for his victory and in penance for the spilled blood. The altar of the abbey was to be on the spot where Harold died. This was structurally inconvenient for the Benedictine monks, but they had no option. The abbey was duly consecrated in 1094. It prospered and was still a rich enough prize at the Dissolution to pass to Henry VIII's Master of Horse, Sir Anthony Browne. He demolished the church, cloister and chapter house and remodelled the rest as a country house.

This house saw mixed fortunes until it was occupied by the Duke and Duchess of Cleveland from 1857 to 1901. They converted and extended the west range of the Tudor house, which was later let to a school (as it remains). The Clevelands also restored the surviving fragments of the monastery, which include a complete set of monastic chambers, beautifully vaulted; these may be visited.

A magnificent gatehouse guards the entrance from the town square. Dated 1338, it is one of the finest in England surviving from the 14th century, with blind arcading and high octagonal turrets. The gatehouse was originally fortified against French raids, ironic given its heritage. In the chamber upstairs is a reconstructed medieval fireplace.

Across the courtyard lies the west range of the old abbey. The Great Hall, now part of the school, is open during summer holidays. Visitors to the battle site and ruins pass along the wall to the right, where the terrace walk goes under the hugely buttressed walls of the monastic guest house. This had to be built against the ridge of the hill where the battle was fought. The storehouse vaults are accessible – large, damp, gloomy chambers.

Farther along the terrace are the dormitory and the latrine. The latter's arches carrying first-floor seats are fascinating to children. The dormitory includes a novices' vaulted chamber, one of the most impressive 13th-century residential rooms anywhere in England. It retains a glorious forest of columns and ribbed vaults, its windows deep-set and narrow. The walls are of rough Caen stone. Beyond is the equally fine Common Room, again Early Gothic with lancet windows and carved corbel heads. The rest of the ruins are unroofed but give a good indication of the scale of this great monastic house.

BAYHAM OLD ABBEY *

5m SE of Tunbridge Wells
Gothick villa in monastery ruin (EH)

In 1714, Sir John Pratt, Chief Justice of the King's Bench, acquired the old monastic ruins of Bayham Abbey as an investment. They were the finest such relics in Sussex. His agent made them less so by unroofing them to render them more picturesque. His grandson then built a small villa next door in the Gothick style, much admired by Horace Walpole in 1752. At the end of the 18th century the house was extended by the 2nd Lord Camden, with help from Humphry Repton, whose advice to remove the villa to a distant hill and thus a better view was ignored.

In 1869 another Lord Camden, now a marquess, did as Repton had recommended and built on the hill not a villa but a vast pile by David Brandon. Today's combination of distant mansion, villa, ruin, chapel and park forms a fine composition. The ruins are extensive, if somewhat artfully arranged, and do indeed form a picturesque backdrop to the villa which is now known as the Dower House.

This is in process of restoration to its early 19th century form. On my last visit, only two rooms, the old library and drawing room on either side of the front door, were open. Both have pretty Gothick doors, fireplaces and window frames. They look out on the same scene that so charmed Walpole.

BENTLEY HOUSE **

Halland, 6m NE of Lewes
Raymond Erith conversion of Sussex farmhouse (P)

Gerald Askew bought the old farm at Bentley in 1937. It was a brick house with four bedrooms. After the war, he and his wife wanted something larger and in 1959 wrote to the neo-classical architect, Raymond Erith, asking for help. Erith was then working on the renovation of Downing Street.

Erith rejected the idea of new ranges round a courtyard, Sussex fashion. Instead he offered an elongated façade in a French manner, looking almost like a set of almshouses. It took the Askews a decade to agree. They had amassed a collection of wildfowl paintings which needed wall space. This collection now forms the core of a park that embraces the house, a wildfowl reserve, a motor museum and a large shop.

Country Life wrote in 1984 that the house has 'a certain Gallic quality blown into Sussex from across the Channel'. The simple farmhouse, with a small Baroque doorway, is surmounted in the middle bays by four dormer windows. The façade then spreads left and right beneath a heavy cornice line to flanking Palladian pavilions. Each has a grand Venetian window. The house is inhabited by Mr Askew's widow and is held in trust by the local council.

The entrance is at one end. This is a pity since visitors begin not with the intimacy of the original Sussex farmhouse but with a spacious saloon, the Bird Room, in one of the wings. The fireplace is derived from Palladio's Villa Maser. The central table rests on cast-iron swans from Belgium, and the walls are hung with Philip Rickman's bird paintings. A far door reveals Erith's *coup de théâtre*, the enfilade running the entire length of the façade.

Erith's achievement is to make this enfilade seem not as one long passage but a series of surprises. The dining room has low beams and old painted furniture. The hall is graced with silk curtains and bird pictures by Peter Scott. The morning room is Regency in style, its topographical pictures including Devis drawings of Rome. At the end is the other pavilion, the Chinese Room with 18th-century wallpaper, green and rich.

BODIAM CASTLE ***

Bodiam, 3m SE of Hawkhurst
Romantic moated castle rescued by Curzon (NT)

The year was 1916. The former Viceroy of India, Lord Curzon, had lost his first wife and was pondering a second marriage to a young American, Grace Hinds, after his dalliance with the actress, Elinor Glyn. Grace recalled being collected by Curzon with his chauffeur and driven down to Bodiam village. 'Suddenly he told the chauffeur to stop and we got out.

Overleaf: Bodiam's elfin magic

Turning to me, he said, "Now give me your hand, and climb up this bank with your eyes closed, and don't open them until I tell you." He helped me up the bank and then said, "Now, look!" I have that picture in my heart for all time ... I dared not take my eyes off it, for fear that when I looked again it would have disappeared in a mist or a cloud – it could only be a fairy castle.' Curzon proposed to Grace, she accepted and he bought Bodiam.

The castle is England's most promiscuous ruin. It was built in 1385 by Sir Edward Dalyngrigge, a gentleman who had done well from the French wars and wished to protect himself from retaliation. The location was mildly strategic, at the navigable head of the River Rother, though Dalyngrigge seems unlikely to have built Bodiam for defence. The interior plan is that of a noble house and the sequence of surrounding ponds suggests an eye for setting and noble approach as much as utility. But the defences were awesome, with a wide moat to impede sapping and two bridges and gates, each with the latest in 14th-century fortification.

When Curzon came upon Bodiam it was derelict and overgrown. In the 18th century, a farmer had built a small cottage inside the walls and used the courtyard for vegetables. The castle was much painted and photographed by lovers of the Picturesque, but in the 1820s it was in danger of being demolished for its stone. As at Montacute (Somerset) and Tattershall (Lincs), Curzon proved himself a true conservationist. He bought the castle and restored fallen stones to its walls and towers. The moat was drained and excavated, with cannon balls retrieved from the mud. The crenellation was entirely renewed, as was the causeway. He left Bodiam to the National Trust on his death in 1925.

The gatehouse has gun ports, machicolations and murder holes for pouring arrows and boiling oil through from above. There are portcullises galore. The chapel still has its Early Gothic lancets. The footings of the hall, kitchens and other chambers can be seen in the over-cropped grass. A well in the south-west tower has been reopened and floors replaced in other towers, enabling visitors to climb to the battlements.

The experience of Bodiam is essentially scenic. The castle is chiefly a work of 20th-century conservation, a magic stage set, an artifice of stone set in a silver lake. In the right light, with the sun low on its walls or the mist rising from its moat, it is a place of elfin magic.

BRAMBER: ST MARY'S ✱✱✱

Bramber, ½m E of Steyning
Monastic inn with Tudor rooms, *trompe-l'œil* panels (P)

St Mary's is a shrine to medieval Sussex. It lies at the heart of the old village by the river, overlooked by a ruined castle. The roof is of Horsham stone, the walls close-studded and the gardens warm, English and enveloping. Set round four sides of a central courtyard, this was a monastic hostel for passing pilgrims. Only the east range survives in the original form. What was an external gallery is now embedded in an upstairs passage.

The house enjoyed a brief period of ostentation at the end of the 19th century, when it was converted as a centre for entertainment by Algernon Bourke, son of the Earl of Mayo and proprietor of White's Club in London. His wife's name was Gwendolen. Oscar Wilde borrowed their names for *The Importance of Being Earnest*. The house was ravaged by wartime requisition and had constantly to fight off collapse or demolition. It was finally rescued in 1984 by the Thorogood and Linton families, who rode to its rescue and created the St Mary's Trust. Having restored the house, they are embarked on an ambitious programme to resurrect the Tudor gardens.

The downstairs borders on the twee. The old Warden's Room or parlour would once have comprised two monks' cells. It has simple oak panelling and a deep inglenook, the latter with a pot crane. The much-converted hall has an Elizabethan overmantel.

Bramber: the Painted Room

The real fun of the house begins on the 17th-century stairs. These rise to what would have been the gallery of the inner courtyard. Six doors open off it to the former dorters. These were later fashioned into bedrooms, of which the 17th-century Painted Room is the most remarkable. Its panels have 16th-century *trompe-l'œil* perspectives of arcades, some of them with landscapes or battles in the distance. This chamber is a gem of English design, enhanced by contemporary furniture.

The King's Room is more conventional, with wattle and daub walls and heavy beams. The library beyond has a fireplace surrounded by a truncated classical order. The doors are reputedly from Spanish galleons. The room houses Mr Thorogood's exhaustive collection of works by and on Thomas Hood. To the rear of the house the Bourkes created a pretty octagon and Gothick music room. The former, decorated in Pre-Raphaelite style, is used as a museum of Wildeana. The place is eccentric and delightful.

BRIGHTON:
13 BRUNSWICK SQUARE *
Hove
Town house in seafront square (P-R)

Brunswick Square is Brighton's answer to Bath, albeit over the border in Hove. The plan supplied to the Brunswick Estate in 1823–5 by Amon Wilds and C. A. Busby is one of England's most accomplished town designs. As at Bath, the intention was commercial, to build houses for letting to prosperous summer visitors. The craze for sea-bathing, under the rubric 'Dr Brighton', was given added impetus by the patronage of the Prince Regent in the 1790s. Since every visitor wanted a sea view, the town grew rapidly east and west along the coast. Unlike at Bath, the popularity lasted.

The plan of the Hove development was simple. It took its cue from London's Regent's Park, then also under construction. Two long terraces faced the sea, flanking a deep three-sided square rising up the slope inland. From its apex a further street disappeared to the horizon. The buildings had classical façades coated in foaming cream stucco. The enclosed lawns were dotted with wild broom.

The seafront terraces are conventional, almost a copy of those round Regent's Park. The square is different. Each house is bow-fronted with Ionic columns, yielding an undulating façade. This rhythmic effect is occasionally broken by a different form, at one point a strange wedding cake of columns. Houses have their original railings and some still have sliding blinds to shield ladies from the sun.

No. 13 is a relatively modest work, with pilasters rather than columns. It was acquired by a group of enthusiasts, known as the Regency Town House, for restoration to its original state. At the time of writing, work had a long way to progress, but a visit includes an adjacent basement to display 'below stairs' conditions in these houses, complete with game larders and wine cellars. This should soon be a spectacular addition to the Hove scene.

BRIGHTON: THE PAVILION
*****
The Steine
Prince Regent's Oriental palace (M)

When Brighton Pavilion was attacked by an arsonist in 1975, I remember thinking that such a fate was inevitable. There were too many dragons vomiting fire, too many clashing reds and golds, too much foliage, too many kitchens, too much heat and not enough cool.

The Prince Regent first visited Brighton in 1783 at the age of twenty-one. Eager to escape the stifling court of his father, George III, he stayed with his disreputable uncle, the Duke of Cumberland. The Prince, said a contemporary, was of 'as ripe an age as could be desired for ruin; in three short years he was ruined'. He installed his lady friend, Mrs

Brighton's Regency oriental

Fitzherbert (whom he secretly married in 1785), in a house on The Steine and had Henry Holland convert a 'modest farmhouse' next door as his villa. The villa was fitted out with chinoiserie. A huge stable block in a rather ponderous 'Hindoo' style was then added to the rear. In 1815, with the Prince now the Regent, his partner in matters amorous and architectural, John Nash, produced a design to turn the villa into a palace. They converted the interior into a phantasmagoria.

The plan is still Holland's, that of a modest villa, composed of a central saloon with flanking reception rooms, linked by a rear corridor. But by the time Nash had finished, this had erupted with minarets, turrets, onion domes, fretted screens and cusped arches. The inspiration was in part the similar nabob villa of Sezincote (Gloucs), which the Prince had visited in 1812. Though the style was called Hindoo, it is more Mohammedan Indian, with Perpendicular Gothic frills. Above all, it is witty and light-hearted. Contemporaries were derisive. William Cobbett's recipe was 'take considerable number of bulbs of the crown imperial, the narcissus, the hyacinth, the tulip, the crocus. Let the leaves of each sprout to about an inch and . . . that's a Kremlin'.

I know of few buildings which, by day or night, are such a joy to contemplate. The Pavilion is a monument to the frivolous in kingship. The Prince ascended the throne as George IV in 1820, but after the Pavilion's completion in 1823, he hardly used it, paying his last visit in 1827. It is as if, like Henry V, he told his subjects to 'presume not that I am the thing I was'. Queen Victoria used the Pavilion for a time but, on building Osborne, she decided to sell it to Brighton & Hove Council, whose custodianship since has been immaculate.

The interior, mostly decorated in 1815–23, is a near-indecipherable mix of Chinese, Indian, Rococo and Regency. The decorator/designers were Frederick Crace and Robert Jones, with much help from the Prince. The entrance hall has a clerestory of dragons on stained glass. The Long Gallery runs down the rear spine of the house, decorated like a japanned jewel

case. Bamboos adorn the wallpaper and bells hang from the cornices. The lighting is by lanterns, while serpents and dragons keep watch from on high. The furniture is mostly bamboo. Mirrors give an illusion of infinite space.

The banqueting room is Jones's masterpiece, completed early in the conversion. The Prince once staged a dinner here of sixty dishes. The table setting is of silver gilt, but all eyes turn upwards to the ceiling. Here an astonishing burst of giant palm leaves against a deep blue sky reveals a huge dragon holding the chandelier, itself composed of lesser dragons spewing light. In the arches and spandrels of the ceiling are masonic motifs, reflecting the Prince's interest in Freemasonry. Beyond the banqueting room and almost as splendid is the Great Kitchen, its roof supported by cast-iron palm trees.

Back through the banqueting room to the gallery and the central saloon are decorations more conventionally Chinese in style. The gallery pillars are iron palm trees, round which are placed Regency giltwood chairs and sofas made to commemorate Lord Nelson. In the saloon, the mirror frames might be those of an extravagant head-dress. The ceiling is painted to look like sky. Beneath a huge panel of Chinese wallpaper is an exquisite mirrored cabinet with ormolu decoration. But this is no more than an overture to the adjacent spectacle of the music room.

The music room balanced the banqueting room at the far end of the house and was Crace's answer to Jones's work. It is a dazzling composition. The walls are decorated with Chinese landscapes in gold on a red background. Above, voluptuous curtains rise to a roof that might be the lair of a flying dragon. Its giant chandelier drips like a lotus flower in a sea of gold. The panels are of blue, turquoise, green and scarlet, outlined everywhere in gold. No sooner had the room been restored after the 1975 fire than a hurricane dislodged one of the minarets and sent it smashing through the ceiling. These dragons never sleep.

The rest of the Pavilion is comparatively austere, which means merely ravishing. The upstairs bedrooms are mostly chinoiserie. On a landing hangs Rex Whistler's mildly obscene satire of *The Prince Regent Awakening the Spirit of Brighton*. Queen Victoria's apartments are charmingly 'un-Victorian', even her water closet being 'willow pattern'. Throughout the domestic rooms, oriental scenes are set against hand-painted wallpapers and silk bed hangings.

The galleries are decorated in a trellis of cut-out papers to imitate bamboo. Not an inch is left untouched by art, with none of the 20th century's chromatic timidity. Brighton is a celebration of the sense of sight.

BRIGHTON: PRESTON MANOR **

Preston Drove, 2m N of Brighton
Edwardian house, from grand drawing room to servants' hall (M)

Preston Manor was long occupied by the Stanfords, developers of Grand Avenue, Hove, and the richest family in Sussex. Stanfords owned it into the 20th century under the aegis of Ellen Bennett-Stanford. Her only son and heir, John, lived at Pythouse (Wilts) and was as irascible as she was extravagant. They became deeply estranged and she determined that he should not inherit the house. Over years of feuding, the vast Stanford estate, with property across southern England, was dissipated on high living and lawyers' fees. Preston was left to Brighton & Hove Council on Ellen's death in 1932, and thus was it saved for posterity. When John died his obituary suggested tactfully that 'some never understood him . . . he was born 300 years too late'.

The house today is outwardly that of a Regency villa, with shuttered windows and rendered walls. Inside, it has been preserved as the residence of wealthy gentry at the turn of the 20th century, immaculate and rather dull. Preston is the antithesis of the Pavilion. It embodies Brighton as an antique dealers' Mecca. Given what is known of the lifestyle of Ellen Bennett-Stanford and her son, some sense of high living and family turbulence

would have been welcome. There is none here.

The hall forms the core of the house, with access directly into the garden beyond. It is filled with the family's exquisite 17th- and 18th-century furniture, including marquetry cabinets. A small Poussin hangs above one of the fireplaces. To the left of the hall is the Macquoid Room, installed in 1939. It is used to display majolica and panelling veneered in Australian black bean wood, giving the room a tropical warmth.

The Cleves Room is chiefly notable for its leather wall-hangings, gilt embossed and with patterns like Rorschach tests. It was here that the Stanfords held a séance in 1896 to discover and then exorcize the house ghost. The guidebook quotes the housekeeper in Dickens's *Bleak House* who 'regards a ghost as one of the privileges of the upper classes; a genteel distinction, to which the common people have no claim'.

The drawing room is notable for two fine classical doorcases of 1924, and for 19th-century landscapes. The dining room, added in 1905, is dominated by a case filled with 'probably the world's largest collection of Buddhist Chinese lions', 124 of them. The upstairs bedrooms include a ghost in the form of 'a hand without an arm moving up and down the post of the four-poster'. More evocative are the staff rooms, also fully furnished but with bare boards and cracked ceilings. The basement kitchen range is crowned with the motto, 'Waste not, Want not': a cheeky remark given the habits of the owners.

CAMBER CASTLE *

1m S of Rye
Henrician fort isolated on dunes (EH)

Of all the South Coast fortresses ordered by Henry VIII to defend England against the French, Camber is my favourite. No road leads to it, and it must be reached by a mile-long walk over the sands from Rye. Like Deal (Kent) and Portland (Dorset), this was essentially a platform for the mounting of cannons. The design is a set of clover leaves providing firing platforms, rather than a defensive fortress intended to hold territory.

Camber was begun in 1539 round an earlier tower. Its plan is complex but simple in appearance. This is actually a 12-sided building with lobes for bastions. Only Deal is bigger in overall size. The exterior is of stone and the inner walls brick-faced. The central tower has Tudor roses carved on its walls. While the main fortifications were demolished in 1642, Camber remains a warren of tunnels and firing positions, more so than its over-restored sisters.

At its peak of activity in 1542, Camber had a garrison of forty-two. They must have lived bleak and isolated lives, sleeping and eating in these stone chambers in conditions little improved from medieval barracks. Eventually the river silted up and both Camber and any plausible threat receded into history. Camber became what it remains, a romantic ruin.

CHARLESTON ****

6m SE of Lewes
Bloomsbury Set's country cottage (P)

Charleston was the Bloomsbury Set *sur l'herbe*. Its story is incomprehensible without the so-called family tree in the guidebook. This records not the ancestry of a great family but the informal relations, mostly sexual, of members of the Bloomsbury Set during the first half of the 20th century. Luckily, it is in full colour: yellow for heterosexual link, blue for homosexual and mauve for 'close friendship but unrelated'. Those who find all this tedious should stay away.

In 1916 two artists, Vanessa Bell and her lover Duncan Grant, moved their summer home to the old Charleston farmhouse. They brought with them Vanessa's semi-estranged husband, Clive, and their children. They also brought Duncan's close friend, David Garnett. Vanessa's sister, Virginia Woolf, rented a house nearby and would shortly buy Monk's House (below). Maynard Keynes moved to neighbouring Tilton. Others such as T. S. Eliot,

Lytton Strachey, Roger Fry and Dora Carrington came and went. Vanessa Bell and Grant died in the 1960s. Their daughter, Angelica, lived at Charleston until 1980, a trust having been formed to preserve the house as it was.

Few houses so completely express the taste of their owners. Charleston is far from the later Edwardian style of neo-Queen Anne or neo-Jacobean. It is little closer to the Arts and Crafts Movement or inter-war Art Deco. It is better regarded as wholly idiosyncratic. We must imagine Bells and Grants wandering round in smocks, perpetually dabbing paint on walls, cupboards, doors, chairs, anything that caught their eye. 'It's mine,' they would say, 'and I'll treat it as I like.' The young Quentin Bell recalled that, 'Ours was an elastic home: it never broke.' The remark was stylistic as well as matrimonial.

As such, the house lacks the spontaneity of being still in use. It is immaculately preserved. But the lie of a brush on a palette, the tilt of a book on a shelf, the level of whisky in a bottle all seem the product of some curatorial debate. Charleston is best seen as a brilliant display of the art of Bell and Grant. Their whimsical English picturesque inspired the inter-war Omega workshop and perfectly suited the decoration of a simple farmhouse. Charleston makes us want to look afresh at our own homes, wondering how a touch of the paintbrush might bring them more to life.

Clive Bell's study has its fireplace, chair fabric, door panels and table all decorated by Vanessa or Duncan, the work of the two being near indistinguishable. The dining room is a *tour de force*, with black stencilled wallpaper and a large portrait of Lytton Strachey on the wall. The group liked copying Old Masters, here with a copy of Piero della Francesca's *Duke of Urbino*. Omega pottery fills the kitchen.

In the bathroom, even the sides of the bath are painted. Clive's bedroom has *trompe-l'œil* on its walls by Vanessa. Maynard Keynes, who kept a room at Charleston for many

Charleston: Bloomsbury sur l'herbe

years, contributed to its upkeep and was therefore awarded the best furniture, including
Duncan's 'Morpheus' bed-head.

Duncan's bedroom has the most complete
decorative scheme in the house, every inch
painted and with silhouettes of his family.
Vanessa's bedroom has a 'Picasso' by Grant.
The garden room served as the living room, its
paintings, screens and fabrics more carefully
contrived as an overall scheme. It was here that
Eliot read *The Waste Land* aloud and Blooms-
buryites summoned up the courage to tell their
children who were their real parents.

The studio is left as it was when brushes
were finally laid to rest in the 1970s. Paintings
stand on easels. Coffee mugs and memos fill
the mantelpiece. The stove awaits lighting.
With upstairs corridors and junk-filled attics,
this is a place from which ghosts refuse to
depart.

CHICHESTER: PALLANT HOUSE **

9 North Pallant
18th-century town house as art gallery (M)

The Pallants are Chichester's most stately
grouping, an enclave of 18th-century façades
ideal for movie-making. The setting is formal
yet not overbearing. Pallant House sits in the
centre, built in 1712 for a leading local wine
merchant, Henry Peckham. It is sometimes
known as the Dodo House because of the
ostriches, the Peckham crest, on the gatepiers.

The exterior is ostentatious Queen Anne
rather than restrained Georgian. It has a projecting centre bay, exceptionally tall windows
(six panes by three), ornamental railings and
steps up to a Corinthian pilastered doorway.
The brickwork is extraordinary. The window headstones are 'gathered' like cloth and
given carved emblems. The interior continues
this pomp. The front hall, staircase, landing
and upstairs ante-room comprise one-third
the floor area of the house. The staircase is a
superb work with tread-ends carved into
acanthus leaves and twisted balusters.

Since the conversion of the house to a
gallery, much care has gone into restoring
the panelling and furnishings, each room
reflecting a different period in its history. The
downstairs drawing room is William IV and
the dining room George I. The upstairs landing is a beautiful set piece, a carved screen
dividing the landing from a parlour with
three great windows. This must have been an
impressive reception space, with views over
fields to the rear and over the newly handsome
Chichester in front.

The Pallant's pictures are mostly 20th-
century British school, with Piper, Nash and
Moore among more modern works. The
Georgian garden has been restored.

CHICHESTER: ST MARY'S HOSPITAL **

St Martin's Square
Medieval hospital built as nave of church
(P-R)

Visitors to this building witness a vision from a
dream. In the aisles of an ordinary Gothic
church are elderly people cooking at stoves in
open-plan kitchens, while televisions chatter
away in rooms behind them. This place is said
to be unique in England, a medieval almshouse in what appears to be the nave of a
church, with its chapel in a chancel at the far
end.

St Mary's dates from the tradition of the
monastic infirmary, where sick or dying monks
could witness the ceremony of the Mass from
their beds. St Mary's was created c1229 on the
site of an earlier nunnery. The hospital is
hidden behind a later range on St Martin's
Square. This includes a gatehouse and custodian's flat. Beyond is the Victorian flint façade
of what appears an ordinary church, the roof of
which sweeps down to just 7 ft off the ground.
What is immediately noticeable is that this roof
has rows of chimneys.

The interior is open to the rafters. At the
chancel end is a chapel with Decorated Gothic
windows and a merman misericord. The aisled

nave is not a church at all, but was once an open space with its aisles divided into cubicles. In the 1680s these cubicles were converted into seven separate apartments, each with its own fireplace. These are now miniature flats. (The eighth is a bathroom.) Their kitchens are in front, flanking the central aisle and semi-public. This means that residents can converse when cooking, before retreating to their private quarters to eat. It seems an ideal pattern of semi-private communal living.

A charity board indicates the complex entitlements of the dozen inmates, including ten shillings each two years 'in lieu of a new gown'. The surrounding gardens are blissfully quiet.

DANNY **

1m S of Hurstpierpoint
Elizabethan mansion converted in 18th century (P-R)

'It is like living in a place of one's own in olden times, with lots of relatives you do not have to meet.' Thus said one resident of the historic houses taken on by the Country Houses Association after 1956 for conversion into residential flats. Here the genteel elderly are able to live in a great house, renting private apartments yet sharing the cost of the reception rooms and servants. The result has not only been enjoyed by thousands but has saved and restored nine distressed mansions, including Aynhoe (Northants), Gosfield (Essex), Flete (Devon), Pythouse (Wilts) and Swallowfield (Berks). Danny is the jewel in this crown.

The house sits between Hurstpierpoint and Wolstonbury Hill beneath a dramatic outcrop of the South Downs. The drive into the park is an uplifting relief from the suburban estates which now surround almost every Sussex village. The land itself seems to relax.

The house is massively Elizabethan in front and impressively eclectic behind. The property was bought by George Goring in 1582 and remodelled over the next ten years. He fashioned the cheerful E-shaped east front and erected massive Great Hall windows. These

rise two storeys without ornament and with the thinnest of mullions. They are balanced by three tiers of windows on the other side of the porch. With its redbrick walls, broad gables and spacious fenestration, Danny can be seen as the last throw of 16th-century medievalism before the Jacobean era.

The house was sold in 1652 to the Parliamentarian Courthope family, by whom it passed by the female line to the Campions. It was the Campions who converted the interior and remodelled the mildly classical south front in 1728. The house was used by Lloyd George in the Great War and saw occasional meetings of the War Cabinet, largely because the Prime Minister's aide, Lord Riddell, took a liking to the place. The Campions owned Danny until 1984 when they sold to the CHA, sadly disposing of the contents separately.

The interior mostly reflects the early-Georgian refashioning. The Great Hall remains two storeys high but has a false ceiling. At each end is a screen partition of two classical arches, white beneath bright crimson walls. Heraldic Campion glass fills the upper windows. The former service wing is now apartments but the southern family wing retains its 18th-century layout.

In its middle is a superb staircase, rising on shallow flights in a sweeping curve to the landing. The billiard room is still in use. The drawing room appears to have an Elizabethan ribbed ceiling, with a late portrait of Charles I over the mantelpiece. In the library is a curious display of ancient shoes. Most of the portraits are of Campions, repurchased by the CHA to make good the losses of previous sales.

EAST GRINSTEAD:
SACKVILLE COLLEGE *

High Street
Almshouses with Jacobean rooms and chapel (P-R)

Those who grieve for the welfare state might consider its forerunner. Sackville College graces the upper slopes of East Grinstead, set round a central court on the pattern of Abbot's Hospital in Guildford (Surrey). Its lemon sandstone, gabled centrepiece and old flagstones are a happy retreat from the town's bustle yet are not isolated from it. I know of no modern old people's home to equal the charm of these ancient places.

The 'college' was founded in 1609 by Robert Sackville of Knole, the 2nd Earl of Dorset, but he died seventeen days after making his will. His son Richard is described in the guide as 'more inclined to spend his money on fine clothes, gaming, tilting and women than upon charitable undertakings imposed on him by a dead hand'. He did indeed build the college but his widow, the redoubtable Lady Anne Clifford, and her family spent forty years in court trying to deny the place funds. They eventually lost. Richard himself is depicted, a resplendent dandy, in a portrait by Larkin in Kenwood House (London, W). The hall range includes the warden's lodgings, with balancing windows on either side of a central pedimented porch. It is crowned by a pretty bell and two Sackville leopards rampant in the coat of arms.

The interior of the hall has a small hammerbeam roof with lozenge-panelled screen and fireplace. There is an original refectory table with, at one end, a chair of 1659 said to have been used by Charles II (which must have applied to half the chairs in England). The Common Room fills the centre of another range, with portraits of the founders and wardens. There is excellent linenfold panelling in the main entrance porch. The chapel is Victorian. Sackville College continues to offer a home to fifteen pensioners with roots in the town and of slender means.

FIRLE PLACE ****

West Firle, 4m SE of Lewes
Downs house with Rococo plasterwork and fine pictures (P)

Firle proudly overlooks its flint village beneath the giant folds of the South Downs. The Gage family, now Irish viscounts, arrived here in the 1530s during the redistribution of English property after the Dissolution. They have been here ever since. Despite being beneficiaries of the Reformation, the Gages were Catholics, to be later fined, imprisoned and impoverished. In 1713 Sir William Gage inherited the house, renounced Catholicism and duly became rich. He added piecemeal to Firle's buildings and wholescale to its art. Firle has a rewarding picture collection, of the sort that makes English house visiting such a delight.

This house is on Tudor foundations, concealed by landscape rather than raised up by it. The exterior is mostly Queen Anne at least in style, with hipped roofs and a jumble of friendly façades clad in creeper. The creamy stone building material is believed to have been reused from the earlier Tudor house, itself salvaged from the medieval Lewes monastery. Access to the Great Hall is in the old style, from an inner courtyard, itself a lovely space shaded by fig trees.

The Great Hall is white, georgianized and strangely grand for so domestic a house. It has the customary armour and the antlers of the 'extinct Irish elk', without which few English houses seem complete. It also displays two lovely pietra dura table tops. Dominating the hall is a van Dyck, a flamboyant Jacobean composition that seems a million miles from rustic Firle.

The downstairs drawing room is a dazzling array of 'Ionian white and gold'. It is divided into three sections by two screens of columns; the fireplace is from a design by William Kent. Gainsborough and Reynolds perform in classical frames, as if the sitters had posed in the same Chinese Chippendale chairs that are scattered about the room. The Little Hall, containing the Great Staircase, is another bright confection of white and pale blue plasterwork. Here the 18th century pays homage to the 16th, for the staircase is dominated by a framed portrait of Sir John Gage, Tudor builder of Firle, in his Garter robes.

The upstairs drawing room has more Rococo plasterwork. Here are lesser Italian

Founder's honour: Firle staircase

masters but greater pieces of furniture, including two Chippendale cabinets filled with Sèvres. These marquetry works, known as the Panshanger cabinets, relate to commodes made by Chippendale to Adam designs now at Renishaw (Derbys) and Harewood (Yorks, W). The Victorian ante-room beyond has walls of Chinese porcelain plates, alarmingly like targets in a shooting gallery. The room was created by a Victorian daughter-in-law of the family, Sophia Knightley, whose wistful portrait by Thorburn stands on the table. The room is filled with Gage mementoes.

The Long Gallery, decorated in yellow and white, fills the first floor of the Palladian east wing. Firle benefited from the acquisition of four art collections belonging to relatives, one from the shocking demolition of Panshanger House in Hertfordshire in 1953 and another from the stripping of Taplow Court (Bucks). The gallery is, as the guide notes, 'densely hung'. Works include a Reynolds of the Lamb children, their young faces filled with boisterous Georgian confidence. Others are by Hoppner, Mengs, Lawrence, Zoffany and, over the fireplace, a magnificent Teniers of *The Wine Harvest*.

The small dining room downstairs is a jewel, its Dutch landscapes dominated by a superb de Koninck. In the billiard room, medieval panels look across at Pannini views of Rome. The present Lord Gage is himself an artist and a pleasant aroma of oil paint hangs over parts of the house.

FISHBOURNE ROMAN PALACE *

Fishbourne, 2m W of Chichester
Roman villa with Cupid mosaic (M)

The discovery of extensive Roman remains near Chichester in 1960 caused great excitement. What was at first thought to be a conventional villa has been revealed as a palace of up to 100 rooms. It may have been that of Cogidubnus, head of a local tribe of ancient Britons regarded as allies of the Romans. The palace was burned at the end of the 3rd century after two centuries of existence. Much of it is beneath the A27, too important a thoroughfare to be disturbed by history, but what is revealed qualifies Fishbourne as the largest domestic building from Roman Britain.

Beyond that I find there is little to say. These heavily manhandled sites are anaesthetized and devoid of atmosphere (*see* Lullingstone/ Kent). It is as if an actor were asleep and we had to read his lines from a book. The mosaic floors have had tiny walls erected round them amid sand and gravel, like a rock garden. The site is interlaced with ramps and walkways and a giant shed has been erected over the top. The shed is approached across a car park, past toilets, shops, administration buildings and tended grass verges. It might be a local government office.

The palace was clearly stupendous, the area four times as big as what has so far been uncovered. One sees just the north wing, the rooms set round a courtyard. The mosaics take pride of place, the finest set *in situ* in England. They include depictions of geometric shapes, architectural features and, most famous of all, the *Cupid on a Dolphin* mosaic.

This depicts the god surrounded by urns, dragons and vine leaves, a loveable, much reproduced composition. A model shows how the villa/palace would have appeared when built. Build it again.

GLYNDE PLACE ***

Glynde, 3m E of Lewes
Elizabethan house with panelled gallery (P)

Two Welsh wyverns guard the gates to Glynde, or at least guard the drive that runs down its flank. It is as if the house's 18th-century owner, Bishop Trevor of Durham, were ashamed of not having a proper entrance, and hoped that these magnificent gates would do. Trevors had inherited the house through marriage to

Episcopal wyverns at Glynde

the Morleys, the house having been built in 1569 by an ironmaster named William Morley. Bishop Trevor was responsible for the alterations to Durham and Auckland Castles (Durham) and reorganized the entrance to Glynde. This chiefly meant moving the entrance from its old-fashioned and more secure location within the courtyard to the outside of the front facing the garden. His descendants, the Brands, Viscounts Hampden, live here to this day.

Glynde's exterior is curious. The old Elizabethan gatehouse still stands on the west side of the house, roughly symmetrical with three beefy flint gables and two equally massive chimneys sandwiched between them. This still offers a route to the Great Hall beyond, though Trevor's formal entrance remains on the far side.

The interior of this hall is very much Trevor, that is cold and Georgian. Pillared screens were inserted at each end, relieved only by two Tudor bay windows containing Flemish Biblical roundels. Two splendid Ramsays, of George III and Queen Caroline, grace the walls. In the Speaker's Room are memorabilia of the most distinguished Brand, Victorian Speaker of the House of Commons. He was celebrated for presiding over the Parnell filibusters, one lasting 41 hours, in 1881. The Yellow Drawing Room has modern hand-stencilled wallpaper. Over the fireplace is a Grand Tour Brand in an unusually ornate frame. A Brueghel of the Nativity has surrounding cameos by other painters.

The staircase survives from a late 17th-century alteration to the house. It is a generous space with a fireplace on the landing. The upstairs gallery is Glynde's showpiece. Its dark panelling, contemporary with the staircase, includes woodcarving in the style of Gibbons. Everything, fireplace, picture frames and door surrounds, has received the carver's attention. The portraits are by Lely and landscapes by Guardi and Canaletto. From the windows are superb views over the Downs. The dining room is bravely decorated in brown wallpaper, a challenge to a magnificent set of Snyders still-lifes.

GOODWOOD HOUSE ★★★★

3½m N of Chichester
Regency palace by Wyatt and others (P)

Goodwood is a thoroughly modern historic home. The Dukes of Richmond and Gordon have taken the house and estate in hand and decided to make it work for a living. In my view they have been allowed to go too far. At times, Goodwood is like a suburban country club leased to a global corporation. The house is surrounded by a clutter of race course, golf course, airfield and speedway, anything that meets the love of speed of the Duke's heir, the Earl of March. That a gigantic grandstand, visible from the Isle of Wight, can have been permitted on the crest of the South Downs is outrageous.

That does not detract from a fascinating house. The first building on the site was erected by the Jacobean Earl of Northumberland as a hunting lodge. This was bought by the Duke of Richmond in 1697 for the same purpose. The lodge was given wings in the 18th century and dramatically extended in 1800–06 by James Wyatt, aided by John Nash. These additional ranges were for the 3rd Duke's picture collection, salvaged from the fire which engulfed Richmond House in Whitehall in 1791. The present building, in grey stone and flint, is on an eccentric plan, forming three sides of a notional octagon. It is still essentially a villa, two-storey and low-slung, with picturesque domed towers at the 'hinges' of the wings.

The rear entrance is to the Long Hall of the old Jacobean house. It contains two spectacular Canalettos of the Thames from old Richmond House and Stubbs's magnificent *Lion and Lioness*. Behind the hall is a room designed by Wyatt for a set of Gobelins tapestries acquired by the 3rd Duke while ambassador to France in 1765. The ceiling shows Wyatt at his most exquisite, in soft greens and golds. This room claims to have seen more

Napoleonic Egyptian at Goodwood

Privy Council meetings than any other private house in England, due to its proximity to Goodwood races. The fireplace by John Bacon is unusual, of two figures 'unveiling' the fire within.

The music room, which brings us to the Wyatt wings, is daringly painted in a dark claret and includes William Kent's fireplace from Richmond House. The front hall contains a set of Stubbs paintings, made during the young artist's nine-month stay at Goodwood in 1759. It was a visit almost as productive as Turner's to Petworth.

The Egyptian Dining Room next to the hall at first offers a delightful conundrum. It might be dated 1800, 1920 or even 1990, if not 1000BC. It was, in fact, designed by Wyatt in 1802, when Napoleon's Nile campaign of 1798 was flooding Europe with Egyptian finds. Everything, fireplaces, doorcases, frieze, statuary, supposedly evokes the age of Cleopatra. The furniture is of mahogany and ebony. The room 'vanished' under Victorian alteration, but has been brilliantly restored and lit. It is unique in England.

Goodwood's colour schemes are as wild as its planning, and more successful. The Yellow Drawing Room seems designed to shock. The yellows of the drapes clash fiercely with gilt frames and defy the skin tones of the portraits by Romney, Ramsay and Mengs. The ballroom beyond is also hung with family portraits, including Lelys and van Dycks on rich flock wallpaper.

GRAVETYE MANOR **

3m SW of East Grinstead
Elizabethan house, William Robinson garden (H)

Gravetye is every foreigner's dream of an English manor. The house sits in a secluded valley along an unobtrusive drive from the main road. Even in the gravel forecourt there is nothing to indicate that this is no longer a private house but a luxury hotel. Gabled walls are hung with ivy, vine, clematis, rose, anything that can get a hold. A small notice asks drivers not to spray the verges with exhaust.

Gravetye was built in 1598 for a local iron-master, Richard Infield, but its most celebrated owner was the father of traditional English gardening, William Robinson. He bought Gravetye and its large estate of 1,000 acres in 1884 and held it until his death in 1935. Here he set out his creed, that an English garden should enhance and not compete with nature. A long wall downhill to the lake (an old hammer pond) guards a herbaceous border of perennials. Beyond is a meadow of wild flowers.

The tiny lawn is a mere interruption of the casual terrain of lupins, foxgloves, hollyhocks, lavender and roses everywhere. Up the side of the hill, the flowers appear to take on a life of their own, nature only partly tamed. Towards the end of his life, Robinson would simply scatter seeds from his wheelchair.

The house is substantial, of two storeys plus an attic, its roofline forested with brick chimneys and gabled dormers with finials. The interior rooms have been much altered, although without losing their Elizabethan intimacy. All have retained, or had restored, heavy plaster ceilings with much scrolling and strapwork. Whenever he could, Robinson repanelled them in wood from the estate, in the traditional manner. The main sitting room has pilasters and cartouches round the fireplace. The ceilings are smoke-yellowed.

GREAT DIXTER ***

Northiam
Lutyens's reinstatement of Wealden hall in classic garden (P)

Great Dixter is a jolly English house surrounded, embraced, disciplined, almost embarrassed by its garden. It is Falstaff about to be put in the laundry basket. Nor does the metaphor end there. The gardens are those of the horticulturalist, Christopher Lloyd, whose lady admirers fuss round the flowerbeds as if they owned them. They declare the roses on

Great Dixter: Tudor art and Sussex nature

form or the exotics 'over the top'. This is a deeply serious enterprise.

The garden was laid out early in the last century round what had been an old farm by Lloyd's Mancunian father, Nathaniel, in collaboration with Sir Edwin Lutyens. They planted the famous topiary yews which divide the garden's 'rooms'. Every part of the old farm was put to use. Lutyens restored the chicken house as a loggia and the cattle troughs as planting boxes. Grass is allowed to run to meadow, with an effusion of wild flowers.

The house itself is partly a masterpiece of Lutyens the miniaturist. The core is a mid-15th-century hall house, with kitchen, parlour and solar. To the back of this, in 1910, Lutyens and Lloyd attached another old hall bought for £75 from a contractor in Benenden. This supplied a bedroom with service rooms in between. The interior of Great Dixter is thus wholly Tudor, yet its sweeping roofs, soaring chimneys and profusion of dormers have the unmistakable touch of Lutyens.

The Great Hall has a massive timber frame. The customary features are retained, or restored, including hammerbeams, curved braces and original doors to the parlour and solar. The parlour is cosy; a large chair by the fireplace was embroidered by Nathaniel Lloyd's wife, Daisy. The stairs to the solar are by Lutyens, as is the squint down into the Great Hall. Lloyd was a man of art as well as commerce. He designed a number of internal furnishings, including the lamp standards in the solar.

The imported hall to the rear, now known as the Yeoman's Hall, is more modest, although panelled and with a Lutyens fireplace. There is a billiard room below. But all eyes lead to the garden.

HAMMERWOOD PARK **

3½m E of East Grinstead
Greek revival emerging from dereliction (P)

Hammerwood is a rare early work of the English Greek revival. It dates from the turn of the 19th century, a time when radicals were tiring of Adam and Wyatt and turning to 'democratic' Greece, the style of revolutionary France and America. A few English examples survive, at Belsay Hall (Northumb), The Grange (Hants) and Downing College (Cambs).

Hammerwood was earlier than these, designed by Benjamin Latrobe in 1792. Inheriting property in Pennsylvania, Latrobe emigrated to America in 1795, where his Greek enthusiasm appealed to Thomas Jefferson. He became Surveyor of Public Buildings in 1803 and was party to the design of both the White House and the Capitol. The American republic came to regard the most rigid classicism as the only style appropriate for democracy, justice and national ceremony.

The commission came from an Essex man, John Sperling, who wished to convert the existing house to become a Greek feature on a hill over a narrow valley. Sperling did not enjoy Hammerwood for long, and the property changed hands continually into the 20th century. The house nearly failed to survive occupation by the pop group, Led Zeppelin, in the 1970s and was bought by the present owner, David Pinnegar, in 1982. Mr Pinnegar is one of those eccentrics without whom half the houses in England would have vanished. He conducts tours while leaping about in a garrulous Dionysian whirl. Hammerwood appears constantly on the brink of apotheosis.

The new façade was designed to look its best from across the valley. It is composed of a central portico, joined to Doric pavilions on either wing. The columns are stumpy and fluted only at the top, showing 'primeval force' (Pevsner). The façade uses different coloured stones to heighten the scale and dramatic effect.

The interior is a work of painstaking restoration by Mr and Mrs Pinnegar. Most of the rooms are now usable and open to view. The central drawing room has remarkable wall mirrors. Set at varying angles, they reflect each other and the valley outside. The doors of the library are said to have sixteen successive layers of paint exposed. In the old kitchen is a miniature copy of the Parthenon frieze obtained from Charterhouse School. The dining room alone remains derelict, but while walls are still stripped to brickwork and much of the ceiling is on the floor, the table is laid immaculately for dinner.

The Victorian architect, S. S. Teulon, may have worked at Hammerwood and installed some of the neo-Jacobean ceilings and the staircase. The Pinnegars' contribution to the Millennium was a gentle *trompe-l'œil* mural filling the staircase hall. It is by two young Frenchmen, Jean-Louis Grand and Guillaume Avonture. They have made the hall a sunny, pillared cortile filled with birds, insects and children, all in soft unassertive shades.

HERSTMONCEUX CASTLE
**

4m E of Hailsham
Exterior of medieval moated palace (P-R)

Herstmonceux is outwardly among the most spectacular of English moated castles. A drive leaves the main road and passes the domes of the former Royal Greenwich Observatory. It rounds a hill, falls into a valley and suddenly reveals a confection of gold-red English brick. Towers, turrets, chimneys, slits and oriels are reflected in a wide moat. Flags flutter from the battlements and ducks fuss under the bridges. Herstmonceux is all of a piece.

The castle was begun in 1441 – long before such upstarts as Hampton Court (London, W) – and ranks with Caister and Oxburgh (Norfolk) among the earliest brick mansions in England. The builder was Sir Roger Fiennes, Henry VI's Treasurer, a hugely profitable job. Although ostensibly a castle, its military defences are insignificant. Neither the gun ports nor the arrow slits properly cover the approaches, while artillery could demolish the walls in an instant. The house was sold in 1708 and by 1776 was derelict. Its contents and fittings were dispersed and the building left to ruin.

Like Bodiam, Herstmonceux became a picturesque resort, and was even the venue for a Victorian tearoom. Henry James with Edith Wharton would visit it 'by motor' from his home in Rye.

A series of attempted restorations began in 1911, successively by the Lowther, Lawson and Latham families. The courtyard was cleared of rubble and undergrowth, and given new ranges of fake medieval buildings. These included a Great Hall, chapel and the staircase from the demolished palace of Theobalds in Hertfordshire. Sir Paul Latham, an MP who owned the house in the 1930s, installed another staircase from Wheatley outside Doncaster. This was supposedly by Grinling Gibbons. After the war the effort proved too much and the castle was again sold, this time to the Royal Greenwich Observatory. That use lapsed in 1989 when light pollution spreading across southern England rendered the telescopes of little use.

Herstmonceux was at serious risk of becoming a housing estate but it was bought in 1993 by a Canadian engineering tycoon, Alfred Bader, and given to his home university in Kingston, Ontario. It is now, in the jargon of the day, an 'educational and conference facility'. The interior is institutional. The chapel is a lecture theatre and the hall a canteen. The staircases can be seen on application. Better to sit on the banks of the moat and enjoy the exterior. This is for real.

LEWES: ANNE OF CLEVES HOUSE ******

52 Southover High Street
Hall house with furnishings (M)

This medieval house has little to do with Anne of Cleves. She was granted it as part of her divorce settlement from Henry VIII, but is not known to have visited the place. It was owned or tenanted by a succession of Sussex yeomen, with wonderfully Shakespearean names such as Stempe, Saxpes, Towers, Dunk and Verrall. They might be waiting to be 'pricked' by Falstaff. It was Verrall who gave the house to the Sussex Archaeological Society in 1923 for a museum.

The house is of a standard Wealden pattern, although much altered. There is a porch onto the main road, with a pretty room above it. Tile-hung jettied chambers adorn both ends, the more important one with a cross gable.

Inside, the ground floor has suffered a bad attack of museumitis. The hall had a large fireplace inserted by the Elizabethans, blocking the old entrance and screens passage but leaving a fine five-light window onto the street. This hall rises the full height of the building and well evokes a prosperous town house of the 1500s.

The building is filled with an array of old Sussex paraphernalia, including tilting pots known as Sussex pigs. At one end upstairs is a Tudor bedroom, with original windows and a Flemish four-poster bed. Behind is a small Soho tapestry room sheltering four early 18th-century chinoiserie works by John Vanderbank.

The largely reconstructed rear wing of the house is a museum displaying carvings salvaged from the old Lewes Priory. There is also a spectacular collection of Wealden iron firebacks.

LEWES CASTLE *

High Street
Town castle with Downland view (M)

Lewes Castle is a bold structure, not isolated on some distant hill but built on two mounds immediately behind the High Street. The builder in *c*1100 was a Norman grandee, William de Warenne, Earl of Surrey. The castle was besieged by Simon de Montfort in 1264, when the defeat of Henry III's garrison presaged the establishment of the first English parliament. It is as well for British liberty that the castle was vulnerable.

The substantial keep is reached not through the barbican which straddles a cul de sac but through gardens rising out of what was the

Wealden vernacular in Lewes

moat. So overbuilt is this area that the outer bailey is no longer recognizable except as the town bowling green. Apart from the barbican, the keep survives, with polygonal angle towers to give archers a better range of fire.

The western of these towers was prettified with Gothick windows in the 19th century. The other tower offers a superb view over the Ouse Valley to the South Downs and the sea. It is a remarkably serene vista, were it not for the deplorable County Council offices beneath. They must surely be demolished. Even Lewes Gaol is more handsome.

MICHELHAM PRIORY **

2m W of Hailsham
Fragmentary Tudor conversion of priory (M)

Medieval Michelham Priory was sold at the Dissolution to John Foote, who demolished much of it and made the rest into a gentleman's residence. The house passed through numerous hands, including the Sackvilles', only to decay in the 19th century and require desperate rescue in the 20th.

This came from the Beresford-Wright family. They restored the building and offered it to the National Trust, who declined it. The Priory was saved by the Sussex Archaeological Society in 1959 with an endowment from Lord Inchcape.

While the parkland, farm, watermill and outbuildings offer an admirable rural exhibition, the house itself is more picturesque than absorbing. The Priory lies beyond a fine gatehouse of 1388, across a moat dug not just round the Priory but round the entire settlement, a protection against French raids. The surviving buildings are of all periods, from the 14th century through to 20th-century neo-Tudor. They offer an attractive façade to the moat on the far side.

The interior comprises a 13th-century Prior's Chamber and the rebuilt Tudor wing beyond. Entry is through the undercroft of the former, with a bold central pier and vault. The hall leads to the old kitchens on the left and Tudor rooms on the right, built after

1587. On the ground floor, the latter house a collection of Jacobean and Georgian furniture and tapestry. A small child's room upstairs is a charming backwater, filled with 18th-century toys and furniture.

The most evocative room is the oldest, the Prior's Chamber. Although ceiling and floor are Victorian, a realistic 'prior' is working at his desk and appropriate music is playing in the background. It brings the room half to life, but half is better than none. In the grounds is a splendid 16th-century barn.

MIDHURST: COWDRAY HOUSE *

½m NE of Midhurst
Romantic ruin in park (P)

The ruins of old Cowdray House are so substantial and parts so capable of restoration that I cannot omit them, even though they are currently fenced off with barbed wire for health-and-safety reasons.

The site is at the end of a causeway across a water meadow outside Midhurst. Nearby is an octagonal house, a cricket field, stream, woods and meadows open to the South Downs. The ruins seem empty and lost, as if awaiting the arrival of a Shakespeare troupe in the forecourt.

The house was occupied by various favourites of Henry VIII, among whom was Sir Anthony Browne, last Viscount Montague, who later entertained Elizabeth I here. It was gutted by fire in 1793, leaving only the original walls standing. Their form is traditional, with the gatehouse range facing the road, an inner courtyard behind and then the east range with a Great Hall. The porch has a fan vault and the façade is decorated with Renaissance ornament.

At the time of writing, the house appears to be returning to a Victorian state of ivy-clad ruination. It offers a romantic contrast to the sterilized properties of English Heritage. I would either leave it as it is and let people wander closer to its walls, or rebuild it for someone to use properly.

NEWTIMBER PLACE *

Newtimber, 4½m S of Hurstpierpoint
Moated manor with classical murals (P-R)

Newtimber Place once nestled amid trees near the road to Brighton. It now nestles amid the roar of the 'upgraded' A23. As a result, it is even more secluded. The moat remains, generously wide and with no fewer than three bridges. The house's Tudor origins are visible at the back, where the walls drop directly into the water. The main front is William-and-Mary, with nine bays of Sussex flint with brick window surrounds. The façade is superbly offset by a giant cedar.

The house belonged to Earl Buxton, Liberal Chief Whip to Gladstone and Governor-General of South Africa. It remains in the family. The interior is that of a comfortable manorial dwelling, but with one exceptional feature. The front hall appears to be from the Elizabethan house, remodelled when the new front was built in the 1700s.

This is filled with neo-classical murals believed to date from the end of the 18th century and subject of much scholarly speculation. They are copies of plates from William Hamilton's book on Neapolitan antiquities, and were possibly executed by Biagio Rebecca or J.F. Rigaud. With matching furniture, they form a magnificent *coup de théâtre*, as if the Elgin Marbles had turned up in a Sussex farmhouse.

The dining room has a set of excellent Chinese wallpapers. Other rooms contain memorabilia of Buxton activities in Liberal and imperial politics.

NYMANS ***

Handcross, 6m NW of Haywards Heath
Relic of fake medieval manor in spectacular garden (NT)

There are two Nymans. The first is the ghost of a mansion originally adapted by a German stockbroker, Ludwig Messel, in the late 19th century. It was not at all to the liking of his son, Leonard Messel, and daughter-in-law, Maud. In 1923, they commissioned Walter Tapper to pull it down and rebuild it as an oversized medieval manor, a place of great halls, gothic windows, sweeping gables and moulded ceilings. *Country Life* described it as a 'glorious pastiche' so good that future antiquaries might well be deceived by it. Nymans 'expressed in every corner the cult of the manor house in its last, but not least glorious, phase'. The porch was modelled on Great Chalfield (Wilts).

This building went up in flames in 1947, tragically consuming the Messels' large library of antique botanical books. The heartbroken Messels abandoned the house but not the garden, which continued to express the ambitions of their father, Ludwig, to outdo his horticultural neighbours, the Loders at Leonardslee and William Robinson at Gravetye. The Messels' daughter, the Countess of Rosse, later recolonized the surviving ground floor rooms, which she called 'my potting shed'. These are now open to the public.

The Rosse rooms are modest, as if a Tudor custodian were squatting in the ruins of a pre-Reformation abbey. They are furnished with antique tapestries, doors, fireplaces, carpets and furniture mostly brought from elsewhere. There are candles in mirror sconces and flame-stitch on the chairs. An early television has been decorated by Leonard Messel's designer son, Oliver, as if it were a theatre proscenium. In the library, writing implements lie on the table and a drinks tray beckons from a window. It is most peaceful.

The second Nymans is the garden. One arrives at a cottagey visitor centre and makes one's way through a wall of holly and yew as if into a secret wilderness. Gradually trees and shrubs give way to more orderly paths. The vegetation slowly becomes architectural. To the left rise the huge gables of the old ruined house, forming a stark stage set.

Nymans is one of England's most crafted 'house-scapes'. The burnt walls are now cliffs of vegetation. The battered giant is hugged by magnolia, clematis, wisteria and what is claimed as the biggest rambling rose anywhere.

What fire leaves, nature claims. Nymans is England's Ankor.

PARHAM HOUSE *****

1m W of Storrington
Elizabethan house barely altered, with collection of rare embroidery (P)

Whenever my mother was finding life a strain, she would drive over from her house in Brighton to Parham. There she would walk the contours of its grounds and wander in the soft light of its halls. She loved the calm of the place. Never did English building so capture this spirit than in the last glorious years of the reign of Good Queen Bess.

Parham was begun by Thomas Palmer in 1577, the first stone being laid by his two-year-old heir. It was sold to the Bysshopp family (later Zouche) in 1601, by whom it was held until sold to the Pearsons of Cowdray in 1922. Clive Pearson and his successors have restored and enriched its architecture, pictures and park ever since. The family also amassed the finest collection of historic needlework outside London.

The house is approached across a deer park. This park, rising towards the Downs, is refreshingly bare of trees and thus crucial to the setting. The house is best first seen from the south, facing the garden, where the formal Elizabethan E-plan can be appreciated and the plan falls into place. Entry is past the much-altered east wing and then through 18th-century outbuildings, which gives visitors a confusing first impression.

Parham's interiors are mostly of the late 16th and early 17th centuries, the cusp of the Elizabethan and Jacobean eras. At the top of the entrance is the Great Hall, successor to Penshurst in the canon of late-medieval spaces. The ceiling has heavy pendants and the windows are walls of glass from floor to ceiling. This was the new architecture of light, of sun streaming onto oak and bringing heraldry and portraits to life. The portraits include the celebrated image of the doomed Henry, Prince of Wales in 1611, pursued by winged Time. The

guidebook dramatically compares the picture before and after cleaning.

The adjacent parlour was restored by the Pearsons in keeping with the original style. The ceiling had previous been removed and the room merged with the Great Chamber above. This ceiling has been reinserted. The saloon is quite different, a work of 1790 by the Zouches, and Georgian in both style and contents. It has a delightful set of portraits of John Fawcett, manager of Covent Garden Theatre, and his family.

The Great Chamber above is the first room in which the Pearson embroidery comes into its own. The great bed is hung in flame-stitch of the most elaborate pattern, framing earlier 16th-century bedcovers. The neo-Elizabethan overmantel is modern, portraying the house, the Pearsons and, for good measure, Elizabeth I. The West Room is ablaze with flame-stitch, some of the earliest known in England. In the ante-room is a superb Coromandel cabinet standing on a 17th-century *gros point* carpet. Round it are walls of Hungarian needlework.

The Green Room is dedicated to the 18th-century spirit of discovery and the career of Sir Joseph Banks, explorer and President of the Royal Society. The room is dominated by Reynolds's *Portrait of Omai*, the first Polynesian to visit Europe. He returned with Captain Cook's second expedition and was feted by London society. He is portrayed here by Reynolds (one of two versions) as a classical dignitary, only his lack of shoes indicating the 'Noble Savage'. The room contains globes, prints of yachts and two Stubbs paintings of a kangaroo and a dingo.

Passing upstairs to the second floor, we reach the final glory of Parham, the Long Gallery. This stretches the length of the south front looking out over the sweep of the Downs. It was primarily a place of exercise, and was even used to drill the Parham Yeomanry during the Napoleonic emergency. The roof is ceiled with canvas panels painted with Tudor foliage (by Oliver Messel). The vista from end to end is superb, like that of a great church, its transept windows sending shafts of light across the floor.

In the gallery's alcoves and siderooms are displays of more embroidery from across the world, including a Mexican *rebozo* or shawl. Here too are a Roman cistern found on the estate in 1943, a Morris desk, some Staffordshire jugs and embroidered Stuart 'stumpwork'. Nothing at Parham is superfluous, nothing unloved. It is a house of magic.

PETWORTH: COTTAGE MUSEUM **

346 High Street
Seamstress's cottage 1910 style (M)

In 1996 the tenancy ended on a small cottage belonging to the Petworth Estate. The house was in a terrace occupied from 1901 to 1930 by Mrs Cummings, a seamstress at the big house. Rather than re-let it, Lord and Lady Egremont decided to convert it into a small museum, that of a genteel estate worker in the year 1910. Mrs Cummings had been married to an Irish sergeant major who had served in the Crimea and India but proved an unreliable worker at Petworth. He appears to have been thrown out of the matrimonial house by Mrs Cummings.

The cottage sits close to the centre of the town in a row that must date back to the 17th century. An alley leads to an old flower garden, where there is still the privy with a side arch for the removal of night soil. By the back door is a meat safe and piece of seaweed. The scullery contains its old copper boiler. The parlour has a 'Petworth range' for both cooking and heating, as installed in all estate cottages. This is kept lit. A copy of the *News of the World* is dated 1910.

Upstairs is Mrs Cummings' sewing room, with the lady herself at her treadle machine. Her bedroom is furnished with dresses, improving books (on the virtues of marriage) and hats. Mrs Cummings had been trained in Dublin as a milliner. At the top of the house is a tiny attic where three daughters slept

Not-so-happy royal families at Parham

in cramped conditions. The house does not pretend to depict poverty. The Cummingses, when still together, were comparatively well-paid workers. It is an immaculate portrayal of working-class life in a settled small town before the Great War.

PETWORTH HOUSE ****

Petworth
Aristocratic palace with Grand Tour pictures and Turners (NT)

Wander round the little town of Petworth and an uneasy, unseen presence is felt. Brooding over its back streets is a mighty stone wall into which is set a forbidding classical gate, like something the Gonzagas would have built in Mantua. Petworth was once the southern domain of the mighty Percys, Earls of Northumberland, and the place cannot quite escape their hauteur. When James Lees-Milne was negotiating the transfer of the house to the National Trust and hoped for a bite to eat, he was sent by the owner, Lord Leconfield, to a local snack bar and told to 'put yours down to me' (it was closed). His lordship added, with a stern look at the Lees-Milne suit, 'I'd sack your man if I were you'.

Petworth is a connoisseur's house. It contains the National Trust's finest collection of art, including works shared with the Wyndham family, who still occupy part of the house. The building may turn its back on the town but from the park to the north-west it is glorious, spreading languidly along the contour, the embodiment of aristocratic elegance. In the setting sun, nature and architecture melt into Turner's swirls of yellows, golds and reds.

The house was a seat of the Percys from the 12th century, but passed by marriage to the 6th Duke of Somerset in 1682. This led to a rebuilding of the house in what is regarded as a French style. The west front of Petworth is a long, monotonous façade devoid of real architectural emphasis, somewhat similar to the French-influenced Boughton (Northants). The front shelters an enfilade of state rooms. Somerset, known as 'the Proud Duke', had

amassed a large collection of paintings and sculpture and needed a place of splendour in which to house them.

The house then passed to the Wyndham family (later Egremont and Leconfield), who added a second great collection of paintings over the course of the 18th century. The 3rd Earl of Egremont extended the North Gallery and in 1827 invited Turner to celebrate the house and its surroundings in paint, which he continued to do over the following decade. What the 3rd Earl left on his death in 1837 is essentially what we see today. The Victorians were kind to Petworth, the 20th century even more so, but what the public sees remains essentially a museum.

The interior is at first a curious arrangement. The original entrance was from the garden side but this was reordered in the 18th century when Capability Brown landscaped the estate and created the deer park. As a result, there are now two entrances, two Great Halls and two grand staircases on the east side of the house.

Most of the ground floor rooms are arranged for the hanging of pictures. These are the traditional mixture of family portraits and Old Master landscapes. Thus in the Somerset Room we find Bosch, Cuyp and Hobbema alongside Claude and Lely. The Square Dining Room contains large canvases by Reynolds and van Dyck, guarded by stamped mohair curtains and pelmets in the style of Gibbons.

The Marble Hall, the 17th-century entrance on the west front, has a stone floor and classical statuary. The Beauty Room next door refers to the Dahl portraits of Queen Anne's court ladies. Their lower quarters are bizarrely rolled up within their frames to allow the hanging beneath them of pictures celebrating Wellington's victories over Napoleon. The Grand Staircase is part of the 17th-century house. Its murals by Laguerre depict the myth of Pandora and *The Triumph of the Duchess of Somerset*, painted at the same time as his great mural at Blenheim.

Petworth: ducal signature

The Little Dining Room on the other side of the Marble Hall has an extraordinarily rich cornice and is filled with van Dycks. It is an appetizer for the magnificent Carved Room beyond. This is Petworth's jewel, with Grinling Gibbons's frames rivalled by those of his contemporary, John Selden, and the 19th-century Jonathan Ritson. After much debate, the original 18th-century picture hang has been restored, with the van Dycks hung above the Petworth Turners. Henry VIII stands impressive guard over the fireplace. This is one of England's great chambers, the more enjoyable for drawing inspiration from artists of such differing periods and styles.

Beyond the Carved Room, Petworth rests on its laurels. The North Gallery contains the pictures and statuary for which there is no room elsewhere. It is an admirable example of Grand Tour taste in exhibition. Each of the works cries, 'Look at me.'

PEVENSEY CASTLE *

Pevensey, 3m NE of Eastbourne
Roman and Norman castle, 20th-century refortification (EH)

Pevensey is drowned in history. Here one can still envisage Romans landing and building their castle. Here William the Conqueror landed and rebuilt it. The Tudors refortified it and the 20th century hid military pillboxes within its remains. The Pevensey Levels west of Hastings, low and accessible to the valleys between the North and South Downs, have always seemed a good place from which to invade England.

Pevensey is still remarkably isolated. The Roman outer bailey is large, now an open park surrounded by massive walls. The inner bailey is reached by a bridge over a dry moat. Inside is a smaller courtyard surrounded by semicircular towers and the remains of the original medieval keep.

The chief interest of Pevensey is its conversion as a defensive post in the Second World War, Pevensey being an obvious landing place for German tanks. The pillboxes look little different from their medieval forerunners, with much the same purpose, except that a machine gun needed a horizontal field of fire and an arrow slit a vertical one.

The other towers were converted for use as a barracks, one of the few such conversions to nod in the direction of history. The purpose was to fool German spies into thinking this was still nothing but an old fort. The interior of the north tower is still recognizably medieval, but had the Germans landed and discovered the British army using a historic building as a fort, they would doubtless have treated every such building as a legitimate target.

RODMELL: MONK'S HOUSE ***

4m NW of Newhaven
Bloomsbury weekend cottage, intact (NT)

In 1919 the Woolfs, Virginia and Leonard, bid £700 for Monk's House at auction and bought it. The house, she announced (at the age of thirty-seven), 'will be our address for ever and ever'. It was. The place was initially miserable, the kitchen flooding on their first day. But literary success brought creature comforts to Monk's House and the couple were happy. Virginia walked the Downs and recited her sentences out loud. In the evening they listened to records. Here they read and wrote, and read and wrote.

Virginia Woolf died in 1941, a year after their London property had been bombed. Their books had already been moved to Rodmell. Monk's House now became Leonard's home until his death in 1969, when it passed to the National Trust. Although the library was sold, it has been replenished with appropriate volumes and this and the other rooms are among the National Trust's most sensitive restorations. While neighbouring Charleston is a place of ghosts, here one feels the Woolfs have just popped out for a walk.

The cottage is that of two intellectuals who liked comfort without ostentation. The exterior is clapboarded and slate roofed, 'an unpretentious house', Virginia called it. Inside, it was colourfully decorated by her and filled with simple furniture. There are cottagey surprises, such as the painted chairs and tiled table by Duncan Grant and Vanessa Bell, or the needlepoint firescreen by Grant's mother. She also stitched the canvas frame to the hall mirror.

The main room downstairs was 'knocked-through' in true second-home style to give a sitting room-cum-hall. The room is left as was, with an old *Spectator* in the wastepaper basket and a letter from the 'Free Albania' committee on the desk. Next door is the dining room with an English primitive picture of the Glazebrook family over the fire. This had come with the house and Virginia loved its oddity.

Outside is a 1929 extension, built as Virginia's workroom then bedroom. 'Everything must be absolutely what I am used to,' she wrote. 'I find that a sunny house is incredibly cheering.' As I left, the custodian offered me some windfall apples 'from Virginia's tree'.

RYE: LAMB HOUSE **

West Street
Home of Henry James (NT)

I have a peculiar affection for Lamb House. It was here, by the kindness of the custodians, that my wife and I spent the first night of our honeymoon. We arrived late from London with a great moon low over Romney Marsh, and were guided upstairs to the attic by candles left out for us. To shelter under this roof and descend to breakfast under the famous mulberry tree was truly to feel the Jamesian spirit of the place.

To Henry James, Lamb House was more than a spirit. It was a passion. 'The essential amiability of Lamb House only deepens with experience,' he wrote. On a visit to America he swore he would 'give the whole bristling State of Connecticut' for that 'old battered purple wall of the poor little Lamb House garden'. He had seen the house in 1896 and had 'made sheep's eyes at it, the more so that it is called

Lamb House'. Within a year he was renting it and two years later bought it for £2,000, occupying it until his death in 1916.

It was here that Edith Wharton would visit him with such delight, to spend 'some of my richest hours'. She would arrive to a familiar ritual of 'cries of mock humility at the undeserved honour of my visit'. Arm in arm, James and Wharton would then walk through the morning room and, so she recalled, 'out on to the thin worn turf of the garden, with its ancient mulberry tree, its unkempt flower-borders, the gables of Watchbell Street peeping like village gossips over the creeper-clad walls, and the scent of roses spiced with a strong smell of the sea'.

The house had been built for the Lamb family, brewers and hereditary mayors of Rye in the 18th century. James Lamb rebuilt what had been an older house on the brewery site in 1722. The style is conventional early Georgian. The façade to the street is just four bays wide with a carved canopy over the front door and aprons below the first floor windows. Fire insurance plaques are still in place. A former banqueting hall, later a chapel, once stood in the garden and this became James's garden room where he worked in summer. It was destroyed by a bomb in 1940 and with it most of James's library.

The house remains not just as James left it but as Lamb left it. Though unspectacular, the Georgian interior is intact. Downstairs are two panelled rooms, the Green or so-called Telephone Room, after an instrument James adored, and a morning room looking onto the garden. They form a small museum of James memorabilia, letters and pictures. The morning room contains James's massive French writing desk. There is a painting of the young James in a beard, by Burne-Jones, and a signed copy of the celebrated 1913 Sargent portrait now in the National Portrait Gallery.

Upstairs is a panelled bedroom in which George I spent his first three nights on British soil on arriving from Hanover in 1726. The ship bringing him to his coronation foundered in a storm on Camber Sands and Lamb, as mayor, gave him shelter. It was hardly convenient, since Lamb's wife was in labour and gave birth during the brief stay. The child was named George and the King was his godfather.

The garden is surprisingly large, a full acre in the centre of the town. A painful hole is where the Garden Room stood, sadly not rebuilt as hoped when the house passed to the National Trust in 1950. Later tenants included the writers A. C. and E. F. Benson and then Rumer Godden. But the place will always be James's.

SAINT HILL MANOR **

Saint Hill, 2m SE of East Grinstead
Georgian villa with 'monkey' murals (P)

Many will find incongruous the use of a Georgian villa as shrine to a 20th-century religious oddball, but Saint Hill also belonged to an Edwardian archaeologist, Edgar Marsh Crookshank, an American ambassador and the Maharajah of Jaipur. The bizarre relics of L. Ron Hubbard and his still-active Church of Scientology are just another chapter in the story of an English house. Hubbard certainly looked after the place.

The drive down to the entrance passes the modern buildings of the college, castellated and of local sandstone. Saint Hill itself is below, in a private valley. The house was built in 1792 but was comprehensively extended by Crookshank in the Edwardian period. Rather spoiling the original composition, he raised the wings by a storey, level with the centre block. He put the entrance at the back, under a superb cedar tree, and built a long loggia overlooking the garden. The terrace below contains 100 different varieties of rose.

The interior of Saint Hill is mostly Edwardian. Black marble columns in the entrance hall were introduced in the 1940s by the Maharajah, giving it a touch of New Delhi. To him we also owe the servants' bells in the passage, with such labels as 'Prince Bubbles', 'Prince Pat' and 'Her Highness's Sitting Room'.

One of Crookshank's wings contains Saint

Hill's most treasured work, the Monkey Room. The room was converted into a cinema during the occupancy of the American ambassador's wife, Mrs Drexel Biddle, in 1945–7. She wanted a 'talking point' while guests waited for the show and had the walls entirely covered in a mural of monkeys disporting themselves in a Mediterranean resort.

The painting, on strips of canvas, is by Churchill's nephew, John Spencer Churchill. Painted in 1945, it depicts 145 monkeys of twenty carefully studied species. Many of the faces satirized leading figures of the day. A Capuchin monkey at an easel is said to be Uncle Winston. Holes for the film projectors can be seen in the mural.

At the other end of the house is the Crookshanks' winter garden, handsomely restored as a dining room. Also on view are Hubbard's library, containing his 530 books and 3,000 recorded lectures, and his study. The latter is not to be missed. It has an Arabic door and fireplace, apparently a Crookshank import, with 12th-century Indian tiles. More prominent are Hubbard's three organ consoles, on which he composed his hymns. His photographic image peers down from every wall and shelf. The house is beautifully panelled throughout.

SINGLETON: WEALD AND DOWNLAND OPEN AIR MUSEUM

S of Singleton, 5m S of Midhurst

This is England's most extensive collection of relocated historic buildings. The Singleton valley opens out into a small village round a lake below. Isolated farmhouses have been relocated along the edge of the Downs, much as they would have been in this district prior to the 18th-century enclosures.

The houses may seem like retired carthorses, left to graze in this sheltered valley, but England is the most denuded country in Europe of examples of its early architecture. These structures, mostly medieval, are desperately rare, and hard to see and study other than in collections such as here and at Ryedale (Yorks, N). All the Singleton houses are authentic and each illustrates a different style of domestic building. I mention only the more prominent.

SINGLETON: BAYLEAF FARMSTEAD **

originally at Chiddingstone, Kent

Bayleaf is a prosperous farmhouse of the Wealden type, substantial buildings found across south-east England. They are characterized by a high central hall with two-storey wings under a continuous thatched roof. The wings are normally jettied out. This was not to provide more space in the upstairs rooms but to rest the upper walls on the ends of the floor beams away from the lower walls and thus stop them bowing in the middle.

The familiar 'black-and-white half-timbered' look was a later affectation, the wood originally being covered in protective limewash or painted red, as are such exposed woodframe houses in France. Here the brick chimney, widely introduced in the 16th century, has not been inserted. The exterior appearance of these houses greatly appealed to suburban developers and chocolate box manufacturers.

The interior displays the classic features of the hall house, furnished contemporary with its construction in the 15th century. The hall still has a central fire and family high table at the far end from the screens passage. It rises to the roof, black with soot, supported on two massive arch braces. Behind the table is an upstairs solar with parlour below. At the other end is the buttery, pantry and servants' quarters. The furniture and cooking utensils are conjectural but add atmosphere, as does the primitive garderobe.

Outside the museum is a primitive garden and other features of a farmhouse of the period. I assume the rain-soaked schoolchildren packing the place on my visit replicate crowded tenants seeking shelter from a marauder.

SINGLETON: BOARHUNT HALL *

originally at Boarhunt, Hampshire

This simple house dates from the early 15th century. It is still medieval in plan. More interesting, it is a rare example of base-cruck structure, two large cruck posts rising directly from the ground. They do not support the roof apex but rather a cross-beam, enabling the roof to rise higher than their length.

The house had been covered in brick, and a chimney and dormer inserted, but its structural interest was thought to merit its reinstatement in the form suggested by its original timbers. These are still coated in medieval soot. Thatch was put back on its roof. The interior is now empty, revealing the cruck construction and simple partitions.

The house sits aloof from most of the museum buildings, just beneath the tree line on the valley slope. From West Dean Park opposite, it looks as a house on this spot might always have looked when this landscape was far more populated than it is now.

SINGLETON: HANGLETON COTTAGE *

originally at Hangleton, W of Worthing

This is the earliest structure in the museum and, in its clearing in the woods, one of the most evocative. It dates from the 13th century and was reconstructed from excavated evidence in the village of Hangleton, a village lost in the Black Death. It is the simplest possible dwelling, standard throughout England for over a thousand years. I have seen its like from the Amazon to the Himalayas. Here, the sole architectural distinction is the use of flint for walls. These flints are gathered and held together with lime daub, as in early churches.

The roof is supported on poles and covered with straw, with vents at each end to let out smoke from the fire. There is evidence that some such huts would also have used tiles, wooden shingles or turf for the roof. The open central hearth has been reconstructed from tiles laid on edge. There is a simple oven in the inner room. A tiny window admits a limited amount of light. These must have been miserable places in the rain.

SINGLETON: LONGPORT HOUSE *

originally at Newington, Kent

In 1992, the sprawling Eurotunnel terminal pushed its boundary fence ever closer to the walls of Longport, outside the village of Newington near Folkestone. The building, dating from the 1550s and later clad in brick, became a besieged and pathetic sight. The terminal authority demanded the site for a police station. While the old building was being demolished it was found to be an earlier building moved once before. It is now the museum's formal entrance.

Longport's story is complex. The left wing was the solar of a 16th-century hall house. The centre was another 16th-century building brought from elsewhere in the 17th century. Over the course of time, the timber-framed walls were encased in brick for added strength and warmth. Each brick was numbered and reused here. My chief quarrel with Longport is the removal of the Jacobean fireplace 'to ease visitor flow'. This is the triumph of commerce and regulation over authenticity that these museums should avoid.

SINGLETON: NORTH CRAY HOUSE *

originally at Bexley

The London Borough of Bexley decided in 1968 to wipe from the map one of its few scenic attractions to make a slightly wider road. It has been re-erected here in what approximates to its original position, in the middle of the 'village'. The house is a full medieval hall

house, subsequently divided into a grocer's shop and two small cottages. It has been reconstructed in its 15th-century form, with the later additions of a fireplace, smoke bay and chimney.

The house is one of the best at the museum in which to study this modernization, so widespread in the course of the 16th century. The hall is in the centre, with storerooms to one end and 'best room' or solar at the other. The most interesting development is in the middle, where the fireplace was inserted. The screens passage was formed behind it to create a smoke bay upstairs, in which meat would be hung for curing. Even smoke was too precious to be allowed to escape unused. Many of the beams at North Cray were found to be painted red. The custom died out but can be seen on protected portions of wood in this example.

SINGLETON: PENDEAN FARMHOUSE *

originally at Midhurst

Sometime in the late 16th century, when Bramante and Palladio were refashioning the Renaissance houses of Italy, a lesser revolution was occurring in northern Europe. Primitive hall houses were giving way to recognizably modern residences. The chief innovations were of lighting and heating, with windows glazed and interiors warmed by an internal fireplace, flue and chimneystack of brick.

One such house was Pendean, a yeoman's farm in Midhurst, casually demolished to allow a company to quarry sand from beneath it. It had retained even its original fenestration, although with glass in place of wood slats. It is essentially a house of downstairs and upstairs rooms built round a large chimney. This gave back-to-back inglenooks, one with ovens for cooking, the other to warm the parlour. A third fireplace warmed an upstairs bedroom. Another flue exists for drying clothes and perhaps curing meat. The upper storey is still unceiled and used wattle-and-daub for its partitions.

SINGLETON: POPLAR COTTAGE *

originally at Washington, N of Worthing

This is an odd structure, of unknown age but believed to date from the mid-17th century. It appears to have been a 'waste' building, or squatter's house, built on the edge of common land in the village of Washington. The occupant would have been a landless labourer or village craftsman, perhaps with rights of pasturage on the common.

By this date, such houses normally had chimneys but this house has a large hearth against the outer wall of its hall. Its smoke rose not to a chimney but to be gathered in a smoke bay or void both to heat the upper floor and to cure meat. The occupants must themselves have become 'smoked' over the years. At the time of its demolition, it still looked much as it had in early photographs which makes its removal from its original site all the more shocking.

As reconstructed, it has had its attic dormers removed and later tiles replaced by thatch. The service room downstairs has been fitted as a primitive kitchen and live demonstrators slave to prepare food in something like original conditions.

On display is a charming Victorian photograph of the cottage's occupants sitting by the door, a picture of respectability.

SINGLETON: WALDERTON HOUSE *

originally at Walderton, SW of Singleton

The dismantling and reconstruction of the Walderton House in 1982 was considered significant enough to be the subject of a BBC-TV documentary. Outwardly a 17th-century flint-clad house, it had been adapted from a medieval hall house, illustrating the steady transition of English domestic building from one era to another. It shows chimneys inserted into screens passages, floors built across open halls, wattle-and-daub walls clad in brick and flint. The 20th century swept away most such structures, cosy and easily adaptable though they were.

The Walderton house has been reconstructed to illustrate these transitions. The old hall shows the blackened timbers, sculleries and baking oven of the medieval house. The interior rooms have been reinstated to their 17th-century furnishings, based on the inventory of the occupier at the time, a man with the Shakespearean name of John Catchlove. That these houses survive the battering of relentless school parties is a testimony to their engineering.

SINGLETON: WHITAKER'S COTTAGES *

originally at Ashstead, Surrey

Anyone questioning the need for a 'house museum' need only look at photographs of Whitaker's Cottages where they once stood, on a site in Ashstead abutting the Epsom–Leatherhead railway track. They were built for rent in the 1860s by a local man, and named after the previous owner of the land, Richard Whitaker. In 1987, the charming pair was demolished to make way for a housing estate, its developer unable to tolerate such diversity of character on his estate and its planners clearly pusillanimous.

The semi-detached cottages are tiny, just 12ft wide and 20ft long. A report to the Board of Agriculture in 1796 was that 'twelve feet is a width sufficient for a dwelling that is deemed to be a cottage; if it be wider it approaches too near to what I would call a house for a superior tradesman'.

The cottages are two rooms up and down, with one fireplace each for heating and cooking. The front room downstairs is for living and eating, the rear for storing and preparing food. The two upstairs rooms are bedrooms. The house is timber framed, clad in wood and painted. Sections of wall inside have been left unceiled to show its construction.

SINGLETON: WINKHURST HOUSE *

originally at Chiddingstone, Kent

Winkhurst is a medieval hall house whose removal from Chiddingstone was necessitated by the need for a new reservoir. It was the museum's first building, arriving in 1969. The 16th-century house is of just two bays, one open to the roof, the other with a floor inserted to provide an upstairs sleeping chamber. The hall timbers are blackened with soot from what would have been an open central fire. The walls have their timbers widely spaced, indicating the relative poverty of the building – 'close-studding' being a sign of prosperity since wooden beams were very expensive. The panels are filled with wattle-and-daub. The windows are the original size and would not have been glazed.

Winkhurst stands tall and handsome under its crown-post roof, the classic English medieval house.

STANDEN ***

2m S of East Grinstead
Arts and Crafts work by Philip Webb, Morris furnishings (NT)

Standen is the final masterpiece of the Arts and Crafts architect, Philip Webb. It was designed in 1891 for a rich solicitor, James Beale. As an act of medieval homage, Webb insisted on retaining the original farmhouse, Holly-bush, on the site. This tile-hung cottage is the theme to which the big house of Standen is a set of architectural variations.

The originality of Standen is hard to enjoy because it was so imitated and debased by suburban imitators. Here is the template for a thousand 'Stockbroker Tudor' mansions of the mid-20th century. Nor has the National Trust brought it to life. Visitors are forced to enter through the billiard room and see the hall twice, confusing the plan.

Webb was determined to use local materials and to allow plan to follow function. The exterior is an extraordinary mix: the entrance Queen Anne, the garden front gabled, the farm court Elizabethan. Everywhere is stone, pebbledash, brick and weatherboarding, punctuated by Webb's beloved dormers and tall chimneys.

Inside, much of Webb's work was considered too dark by the Beales and briskly repainted white. The billiard room is white, making the heavy ceilings faintly hospital-like. The furniture, however, is superb. Throughout the house, fabrics, wallpaper and tiles are mostly from the Morris firm. Cabinets are by Ashbee and ceramics by de Morgan. The conservatory is filled with bougainvillea, oleander and plumbago.

The drawing room is most emphatically Webb, with bold geometrical panelling, rich wallpapers and hangings, and quiet corners flooded with light. Beside the fireplace are Morris 'Tulip and Rose' curtains. The cushions were embroidered by ladies of the family using Morris patterns. In the staircase hall is a painting of Mrs Beale at work on such a cushion, by William Nicholson.

The stairs are jolly with 'Bachelor's Button' wallpaper, offering a fine backdrop to Pre-Raphaelite paintings and ceramics, including Ford Madox Brown's *Baptism of King Edwin*. Most of the bedrooms are still in the process of restoration, chiefly showcases for more Morris fabrics. The place aches for a family in residence.

The sublime garden looks out over a reservoir to the Medway Valley and Ashdown Forest. The terracing is informal and thick with rhododendrons and azaleas.

STANSTED PARK **

4m NE of Havant
Edwardian mansion with Gothick chapel (P)

Stansted across its park appears to be a comfortable Restoration pile, sister perhaps of neighbouring Uppark. Yet the house is Edwardian. The former, much-altered building was gutted by fire in 1900 and reproduced roughly in replica by Sir Reginald Blomfield in

1903. While rebuilt Uppark is still regarded as 17th century, rebuilt Stansted is emphatically 20th. The house was acquired by the Ponsonby family, Earls of Bessborough, in 1924 after the loss of their house in Ireland to a mob. Since the death of the 10th Earl in 1993, the house has been run by a trust.

The exterior is Blomfield at his most respectful of Wren. The redbrick walls and white cupola woodwork might indeed be of the 1690s. Only close to are the edges harder and the façades clearly modern. The interior proportions are Edwardian and severe.

The library has been left as it was on the 10th Earl's death, on the instructions of his wife. Even the desk clutter is as it was. The music room beyond has portraits of 20th-century Bessboroughs, including the late Earl with his wife with their pet parrot. The Earl's enthusiasm for birds produced a wonderful display of Dutch ornithological paintings in the staircase hall. The staircase carries two of the great Brussels tapestries celebrating Marlborough's Blenheim campaign, the others being at Blenheim (Oxon) itself.

The dining room has Georgian portraits of the 2nd Earl and his wife by the French artist, Jean-Etienne Liotard. More Liotards adorn the neo-Georgian Blue Drawing Room, designed not by Blomfield but by his contemporary, H. S. Goodhart-Rendel (who refashioned a delightful Downland church at neighbouring Idsworth). The house has an extensive 'below stairs' display in the basement.

Stansted was occupied in the 19th century by Lewis Way, committed to a scheme for converting the Jews to Christianity. To this end he built a lovely chapel in Regency Gothick style some way from the house. Its chancel is a blaze of colour, beneath a window depicting Solomon's Temple and the Ark of the Covenant, an aid to the fusion of Christians and Jews. It was redecorated in the 1920s by Goodhart-Rendel.

The chapel is now the centrepiece of a remarkable group of walled gardens, some of great antiquity. Defoe on a visit to Stansted in 1724 claimed that its mile-long beech avenue could offer a view of 'the town and harbour of Portsmouth and the ships at Spithead'.

UPPARK ****

5m SE of Petersfield
Post-fire replica of Restoration mansion (NT)

On 30 August 1989, disaster struck. A workman's torch set light to the roof of 17th-century Uppark and by nightfall the entire house was engulfed in flames. The first floor was a complete loss and only heroic action by staff and firemen saved 90 per cent of the ground floor's contents. By morning the house was a total ruin.

The National Trust's reinstatement of Uppark was controversial. Should it be restored as was, or 'as found', with a 20th-century interior constructed inside the burnt-out shell? If restored as was, what was 'was' – the 17th- or 18th-century phases of its creation? In my view the right decision was made. Uppark had often been repaired and updated and now it was simply updated to its state on the day before the fire. But if such a drastic restoration could be tolerated here, why not in so many other houses likewise ruined by fire or age such as Seaton Delaval/Northumbs?

Uppark is a beautiful example of the most satisfying era of English house, that of the late Stuarts from Charles I through the reign of Queen Anne. The exterior is immaculate when seen from the garden. Nine bays of lofty windows, dressed in stone on redbrick, rise to a hipped roof on deep eaves. In front is a bold doorcase above spreading steps, granting this style the mildest application of the word Baroque.

The house was built c1690, probably by William Talman, and left unaltered until bought by Sir Matthew Fetherstonhaugh, a Northumbrian coal and wine shipper, in 1747. An assiduous Grand Tourist, Sir Matthew transformed the house into a gallery of art, sculpture and plasterwork. He commissioned not one but eight paintings, including two portraits of himself by Pompeo Batoni, and acquired French and Dutch masters and copies of Canalettos. James Paine arrived in the 1750s to update the interior, supplying a new saloon and set of ceilings.

Sir Matthew's son, Sir Harry, kept the house in style, briefly installing the fifteen-year-old Emma Hamilton (as she later became) as his mistress. He was persuaded to offer the house to the Duke of Wellington as the nation's gift after Waterloo, but he priced it at a phenomenal £90,000. The Duke declared that, having crossed the Alps once, he could not climb the hill from neighbouring Harting. In 1825, at the age of seventy, Sir Harry married his twenty-year-old dairy maid, Mary. She not only kept him happy until his death but guarded the ''ouse as Sir 'Arry 'ad it' until her own death half a century later in 1874. It was then protected by Sir Harry's daughter Agnes and Mary's sister, Frances. H. G. Wells's mother was their housekeeper.

In the 20th century, Uppark passed by bequest to the Turnour and then Meade families. Each double-barrelled their names to imply continuity and each stuck to a policy of non-alteration. In the 1930s, a programme of conservation was undertaken, the fabrics being laboriously repaired rather than replaced: Uppark under Lady Meade-Fetherstonhaugh became a byword for immaculate needlework. The house passed to the National Trust in 1954 with members of the family still in residence. They now live on the estate.

The formal rooms are arranged round a central stairwell. To the left is the dining room, created in neo-classical style by Repton in 1812. It was reputedly on this table that the future Emma Hamilton danced naked during dinner (for this compulsion, *see also* Brocket Hall/Herts). In Paine's Little Parlour, the old ladies Frances and Agnes would sit of an afternoon, pursuing what Wells called 'their shrunken routine, reading and slumbering and caressing their two pet dogs'. Two of the curtains are original.

The saloon was fashioned by Paine from the old entrance hall and contains two magnificent Batonis, of Meekness and Purity of Heart. The room is a most accomplished restoration. The plasterwork ceiling is Adamish Rococo,

Uppark's serpent scorched by fire

the doorcases delicately Roman. For some reason, a writhing limewood snake has been left by one of the doors with its back and head new but the rest still blackened by fire. Throughout the house, the visitor is similarly teased by what is new and what original. This detracts from the craftsmanship of the new and should have been left to the museum (in the grounds).

The Red Drawing Room was a wall-paperer's delight after the fire. Fragments were revealed from previous hangings and debate raged over which to replace with what. The old Axminster carpet has been reinstalled, parts reknotted, parts left burnt, conservation gone pedantic. The staircase, like the roof, was entirely rebuilt, its plasterwork incorporating 'free work' left to the plasterers' own imagination in the 18th-century custom. On one of the chimneys a mason carved his mark, 'Margaret Thatcher resigned as I was making this'.

Uppark has a complete set of servants' quarters below stairs, mirroring the plan of the rooms above.

WAKEHURST PLACE *

4m N of Haywards Heath
Manor house amid Kew Gardens arboretum
(NT)

Wakehurst gardens and Millennium Seed Bank are heavy-duty horticulture. At their heart lies what is left of a great Elizabethan mansion, built in 1590 by the Culpeper family, Wealden ironmasters and later celebrated botanists. The house once ran round four sides of a courtyard, but is now a dignified E-plan, reached from the main gardens past three magnificent Wellingtonias.

The façade is most enjoyable. It is symmetrical and of two storeys with an attic, demonstrating the coming of age of the big Elizabethan house in the late 16th century, after the demise of the medieval Great Hall. The porch is framed by a classical frontispiece and the roofline is entertained with gables, volutes and finials.

The inside is disappointing. The interiors

were much altered by the Marchioness of Downshire in 1869. A spacious staircase with gigantic pendants was reordered and a small chapel added, its windows designed by C. E. Kempe. There are some good ribbed ceilings and a jolly, if crude, Jacobean fireplace in the library. The house was acquired in 1935 by the 'Fifty Shilling Tailor', Sir Henry Price, who handed the entire property to the National Trust in 1963. The former hall with Gothick ceiling is a shop. Apart from a bleak scatter of Georgian chairs and tables, the rooms are *en garde* against the next school party.

WEST DEAN **

5m N of Chichester
Eccentric house of Surrealist patron (P-R)

In the Great Hall at West Dean hang not the customary armour and heraldry but the relics of the Siege of Khartoum. Woven into the carpet of a spiral stair are the footprints of a ballet dancer who once climbed them with wet feet. In an upstairs bedroom rises a giant serpent with a lamp emerging from its mouth. West Dean is England's most Surrealist house.

That is not how it looks outside. West Dean was a Gothic house of 1804 by James Wyatt. It was then refashioned in the 1890s by William James, ambitious son of an American tycoon, with the help of the firm of Sir Ernest George and Peto. His work was 'surrealized' by his son, the eccentric Edward James, in the 1930s. Edward was briefly and disastrously married to the dancer Tilly Losch, whose footprints are immortalized on the stairs. He later retreated to the similarly surreal Monkton House in the woods behind.

The house interior is extraordinary, the style being that of George and Peto in their 'South Kensington' mode. The hall has fierce Elizabethan strapwork above the fireplace. Its woodwork, like that of the adjacent grand staircase, is vaguely after Grinling Gibbons. Pictures by Beechey and Batoni jostle with 1930s portraits of James's friends. The dining room carpet was designed by Rex Whistler.

The house is a private college of art, craft and design. A tapestry for the House of Commons was being made in an outhouse on my last visit. The outlook across the park and valley towards the Singleton cottages and the Downs is glorious.

WEST HOATHLY: THE PRIEST HOUSE *

West Hoathly, 7m N of Haywards Heath
Medieval cottage in ancient garden (M)

West Hoathly is a Sussex village tableau with the Priest House at centre stage. It is a simple black-and-ochre cottage with Horsham stone tiles, seemingly afloat on a cascade of garden flowers. There is no known connection with any priest although this may have been a church property. The house is believed to be early 15th century, much rebuilt in the Elizabethan period when fireplaces were inserted. It was divided, fell to ruin but was bought in 1905 and turned into a museum.

Like all medieval cottages, the Priest House takes some minutes to 'read'. The original door into what would have been the screens passage can be seen in the wall immediately to the left of the present one. The building of a 16th-century chimney blocked this entrance, depriving the hall of its screen in favour of a proper fire and a 'central heating' system for the whole house. At the same time, an upper floor was inserted into the hall.

None of this matters much. The house is simply an atmospheric old building, a place of huge beams with wattle-and-daub partitions covered in cream limewash. The brick floor of the kitchen is littered with iron utensils. The parlour is laid with pewter. Other contents are gathered from what would appear to be every local attic, some of it too genteel for a cottage of this period. There is a lantern clock and an early piano. Upstairs is embroidery, old dolls, early photographs and Sussex men's smocks. Satirists suggest that wealthy Londoners buying second homes in these parts should have to wear such smocks when going about the village at weekends, for the benefit of tourists.

Warwickshire

Warwickshire sits astride the centre of England and has played host to many of its great events. Despite its recent industrial character, it remains blessed with remarkable houses. Two grand historic castles, Warwick and Kenilworth, lie within its borders, the former well restored and displayed.

The Elizabethan era is magnificently on show at Aston Hall in Birmingham, at Charlecote and moated Baddesley Clinton. No less impressive are the restored houses linked with Shakespeare in Stratford. It is the 18th century, however, that Warwickshire shows in abundance. Smith of Warwick created Stoneleigh, and Gibbs and James Wyatt the great interiors of Ragley. The Italian plasterers were busy also at Ragley and in the remarkable hall and octagon at Honington. The Gothick movement was never more extrovert than in the fan vaults of Arbury, celebrated by George Eliot.

The Victorians were more unobtrusive, with polychrome Ettington the most notable work of Gothic revival. The Elizabethan revival was active at Charlecote and the manorial revival at Packwood. Upton offers an excellent example of modern arts patronage.

Arbury ★★★★
Baddesley Clinton ★★★
Birmingham:
  Aston Hall ★★★
  Blakesley Hall ★★
  Selly Manor ★★
  Soho House ★★
Charlecote ★★★
Combe Abbey ★★
Coughton ★★★
Ettington Park ★★
Farnborough ★★

Honington ★★★
Kenilworth Castle ★★
Middleton ★
Packwood ★★★
Ragley ★★★★
Stoneleigh ★★★
Stratford:
  Anne Hathaway's
   Cottage ★★★
  Shakespeare's
   Birthplace ★★
  Hall's Croft ★★

Stratford:
  Mary Arden's
   House ★
  Nash's House ★
Upton ★★
Warwick:
  The Castle ★★★★
  Lord Leycester
   Hospital ★★

ARBURY HALL ****

3m SW of Nuneaton
Elizabethan house with Gothick interiors (P)

Arbury's interior decoration is England's out-standing evocation of 18th-century Gothick. George Eliot, whose father was agent to the Arbury estate, later described its decoration as 'petrified lacework'. She spoke of the house (Cheverel Manor in *Scenes of Clerical Life*) as 'growing from ugliness into beauty'. It sur-passed even its progenitor, Horace Walpole's Strawberry Hill (London, W). The house was and is the seat of the Newdigates, Viscounts Daventry.

Sir Roger Newdigate was a Georgian anti-quarian and scholar. Like Walpole, he assem-bled a group of enthusiasts to advise him on the new Gothick style and proceeded, over fifty years, to transform his Elizabethan house outside Nuneaton accordingly. He died at the age of eighty-seven with the house unfinished. His 'committee of taste' embraced the Mid-lands Gothicist Sanderson Miller, with Henry Keene, Henry Couchman and a changing group of craftsmen and stuccoists.

Work on the interiors at Arbury began in 1750. Their essence is lightness, not the levity or frivolity often associated with the Gothick, but serious-minded lightness. Each of the principal reception rooms was redecorated in turn, mostly in variations on the Tudor fan vault. Since the Elizabethan structure remained, the vaults were entirely cosmetic.

Each room is a feast of decorative art. The brilliance of the stucco work is so delicate as never to be overpowering. It could not be further from the later Gothic revival of the Regency, of Nash, the Wyatts and Salvin, nor from the high seriousness of Pugin and the Victorian Goths. The style is well described by its historian, Terence Davis, as a branch of Rococo.

The exterior of Arbury is dull, an Eliza-bethan building uniformly medievalized. The entrance hall leads into a Gothic cloister built into the central courtyard of the old house, its atmosphere monastic. A modest but graceful staircase sweeps upwards in a vanishing curve.

The principal rooms begin with the chapel, not Gothic but 17th-century classical and thickly decorated with cherubs, swags and drops. That is the last we see of Rome at Arbury. From now on, it is the fan vault that wholly obsessed Newdigate. Four of these devices decorate the School Room, set round an ogival chimneypiece. The tempo quickens in the Little Sitting Room, with a panelled ceil-ing and receding window opening. This room is hung with 17th-century Newdigates.

With the saloon, the fan vaults mature, fluttering and dipping like the farthingales of ladies at a grand opera. The central panel is a burst of Gothick panelling, with a central pendant at the end of which hangs a chan-delier. The window opening is framed by a rim of delicious fretwork. These foaming waves of stucco are the masterpiece of Henry Couch-man. Above the fireplace is a Reynolds of John the Baptist.

The drawing room is a wilder variant on the Gothick theme. The ceiling here is not fan-vaulted, except in the bow window, but barrel-vaulted. Yet the vault is entirely covered in Gothick panels that seem to ebb and flower as the eye travels their length. The extraordinary fireplace canopy, of ogival cinquefoils, is based on a tomb in Westminster Abbey.

The climax of Sir Roger Newdigate's handi-work is reached in the dining room. It is built inside the old Great Hall, the height allowing the fans to erupt from wall piers and spread over the ceiling in broad sweeps of plaster. Subsidiary fans decorate the small aisle. The walls are lined with canopied niches and statues. Two putti kiss over the fireplace. A magnificent portrait of Elizabeth I, appropri-ately holding a fan, adorns one wall.

The Elizabethan Long Gallery, with con-temporary pictures and furniture, is some-thing of a relief after this excitement; it is filled with Elizabethan furniture. The Dutch-gabled stables outside were reputedly designed by Christopher Wren, apparently for the price of a candlestick. Arbury is the more precious for being located in the dreariest of Nuneaton suburbs.

BADDESLEY CLINTON ***

Baddesley Clinton, 8m NW of Warwick
Moated manor revived by Victorians (NT)

At the heart of Baddesley Clinton lies the beautiful image of Rebecca Dulcibella Orpen. Born in 1830 and living in County Cork with her aunt, Lady Chatterton, she captivated all and sundry. It is said that when the wealthy young Edward Dering came to ask permission to marry her from her fifty-three-year-old aunt, the partly-deaf spinster misunderstood. She told the world that Dering had asked for her own hand and she had accepted. Dering was too much a gentleman to withdraw. They both became romantic novelists.

Events now turned to Baddesley. In 1867, the pre-empted Rebecca married its owner Marmion Ferrers, the 'pleasantest and most genial old squire' in Warwickshire. When he caught an old lady stealing wood from his forest, he merely offered to carry it home for her. He would challenge poachers to boxing matches. Within two years of her marriage to Marmion, Rebecca had invited the Derings to share Baddesley with them. Soon Edward Dering was paying off mortgages and meeting expenses on the house.

The two couples, devoutly Catholic and immersed in the mid-Victorian artistic revival, became the Baddesley 'Quartet'. The house became a centre of literary and religious activity. It might have been a stage set for Gilbert and Sullivan's *Patience*. A painting of Dering has him looking like William Morris dressed as Oscar Wilde.

As a happy ending, when Lady Chatterton and Marmion Ferrers both died, Rebecca and Dering were at last married. She lived at Baddesley until her death in 1923, visitors noting a decrepit retainer still dressed in black with epaulettes. There were no children. Much of the furniture was sold to Baron Ash at Packwood (below). Ferrers relatives struggled to keep the house going but eventually an endowment was found (ironically from the Baron Ash family) to give it to the National Trust in 1980.

The moated manor defies the enveloping villas of Birmingham's 'Marbella belt', in what claims to be a relic of the vanished Forest of Arden. Its charm lies first in its approach. An open drive through meadows reveals a simple 15th-century gatehouse, amended in the Jacobean period. It faces a bridge over a moat, a mix of stone, timber and romance. On the gatehouse wall hangs a monstrous processional sword. The inner courtyard has lost its old Great Hall, demolished to leave a gap with a view over the moat. The new hall is to the left. The half-timbered range directly ahead is a Victorian service wing.

The interiors must be seen as manifestation of late-Victorian medieval revival, largely under Rebecca's influence. The new Great Hall is a lovely room, dominated by a stone overmantel encrusted with heraldic devices to the glory of the Ferrers. A fire burns in the grate. The pictures (most by Rebecca) depict the Quartet in various artistic poses. Rebecca's self-portrait hangs in the drawing room, painted in 1885, the year of her eventual marriage to Dering, but when still in mourning for Marmion. Both the dining and drawing rooms are warm and cosy. I am told that the sherry in the decanters is real but not for paying visitors (or Trust members) to drink. So for whom? For the staff?

Upstairs we pass through the rather denuded Ferrers and Blue Bedrooms with views out over the 'Forest of Arden'. Next door is the sacristy (with priest's hole) for the adjacent chapel. This is a panelled room converted from a former chamber in 1875. The reredos paintings are by various members of the Quartet and a fireplace stands ready to warm the worshippers.

The Great Parlour and the library were created by a 17th-century Ferrers known as 'the Antiquary' and his son. The parlour has a high Jacobean window beneath a barrel-vaulted ceiling. The furniture in the library is more Georgian, its books artfully scattered on the tables. The floor stain in front of the fire is said to date from the murder of a priest by a pre-Ferrers occupant, a badge of martyrdom on the old house.

BIRMINGHAM: ASTON HALL ***

Trinity Road, 2m NE of city centre
Jacobean mansion complete with furnishings
(M)

Aston Hall stands brave in a depressed quarter of Birmingham, its park and surrounding streets almost exclusively patronized by the city's Asian population. As a result, it can seem like a forgotten imperial palace in the suburbs of Lucknow or Calcutta. The great house in darkened brick and stone overlooks the old Birmingham–Lichfield road. Gloomy rooms and brooding corridors seem to gasp out their protest at the enveloping sprawl. There are plans for its renaissance. May they come quickly.

The Jacobean house was built by a grandee, Sir Thomas Holte, whose family had done well from the Dissolution of the Monasteries and who purchased himself a baronetcy from James I. He needed a house to match. Aston was one of the last so-called prodigy houses of the Jacobean age, designed to plans by John Thorpe and completed in the 1630s. The house was later rented by James Watt, son of the engineer, and after much argument acquired by Birmingham Corporation in 1864 as a museum, the first in what was to become a fine tradition of urban house rescue by civic authorities.

The view from the east is of a characteristic Jacobean façade, two storeys with an attic crowned with turrets, chimneys and gables. The other façades are more idiosyncratic. The south front has a long loggia, the west a splendid array of windows. Like Montacute (Somerset), Aston was to be much imitated by Victorian revivalists.

The interiors are remarkable in quantity and quality. The Great Hall took its present symmetrical form late in the 17th century, when the screens passage was removed and its arches used for the doorways to the surrounding rooms. The fireplace with a scrollwork overmantel is where the screen once was. This reordering of the hall is flamboyant and must

look wonderful when Aston is decked out for 'Jacobean evenings'.

The Great Parlour beyond is panelled from floor to ceiling and contains 17th-century furniture and a tapestry from Chastleton (Oxon). On the first floor is the formal suite of state rooms. These begin with the Great Dining Room directly above the Great Parlour, its frieze crowded with mythical incident. The furniture is Chippendale.

The lovely King Charles Room was used by the King for one night before the Battle of Edgehill, hospitality that was to cost Holte a three-day siege and a fine of £2,000. The Green Drawing Room beyond has fierce wallpaper, carefully copied from an 18th-century original, and another of the Jacobean fireplaces that are the pride of Aston.

The Long Gallery is the most magnificent room in the house. The strapwork ceiling is in place and the oak-timbered floor might be the deck of a galleon. The French tapestries are after that familiar 17th-century model, paintings by Raphael.

Aston continues with a wing used by the family in the 18th century, including the Chinese Room with japanned furniture and the Best Bedchamber now containing a state bed acquired by Aston in 1934. Former servants' quarters in the attic storey are open to the public, as is a charming small nursery with antique dolls. Back stairs lead down to the kitchen and servants' hall.

BIRMINGHAM: BLAKESLEY HALL **

Blakesley Road, Yardley
Restored Elizabethan manor, reproduction
wall-hangings (M)

Richard Smalbroke dealt successfully in ironware, textiles and spices in the High Street at Digbeth, now a suburb of Birmingham. He inherited the Yardley estate from his father in 1575. The property passed out of his name shortly after his death but he is recalled in the city's ring road, the Smallbroke Queensway.

He is also recalled in the house that he built at Yardley, Blakesley Hall.

Today the hall falls into the category of 'houses in most unexpected places'. We drive for ages through suburban Birmingham. Suddenly round a bend is a fine Elizabethan mansion in full black-and-white strip. The façade is a delight: a Great Hall with a gabled room over the porch and another over the dais alcove. To the left is a long, jettied and gabled Great Chamber wing. The half-timbering is close-studded below and diagonal on the first floor, a confident and jolly composition.

The inside has been well restored. The old table in the Great Hall, sold by the last private owner in 1932, was recovered through an advertisement in 1976. Good for Birmingham. The Great Parlour is dominated by a set of reproduction wall-hangings on canvas. Canvas hangings with dyed paintings on them were poor men's tapestries. As Falstaff patronizingly told Mistress Quickly, 'this waterwork is worth a thousand of these fly-bitten tapestries'.

Very few survive, as they soon fell to pieces. These paintings, from the Bible story of Joseph and his Brothers, are by David Cuppnal and can be compared with rare originals at Owlpen (Gloucs). They are a good example of bold reinstatement.

More hangings are in the Little Parlour behind, now a dining room, where loose blue and red drapes were used to conceal damp walls. At the top of the stairs is more decoration, here original, in the Painted Chamber. It has been meticulously uncovered on the plaster and timberwork but is, I fear, dull and archaeological compared to the new work. This was never great art and could surely be touched up to convey the original blazing colours.

These are being reproduced in the wall-hangings of the bedroom at the rear, again a bold decorative project. The house is full of bulging walls, creaking floors, kitchens, dairy and pantry with hanging rabbits, all most atmospheric.

Aston's relocated screen arch

BIRMINGHAM: SELLY MANOR **

Maple Road, Bournville, 4m S of Birmingham city centre
Medieval house rebuilt in model village (M)

Bournville was a planned garden suburb. Its creators were the Quaker Cadburys who had moved their old chocolate works from the centre of Birmingham to a hygienic and comfortable site in the countryside in 1879. The suburb, begun in 1893, was purely residential, a living community independent of the factory and not exclusively for Cadbury workers. The architect appointed in 1894 was Alexander Harvey, in close consultation with George Cadbury, who was also a keen gardener. Bournville preceded such better-known model settlements as Port Sunlight in Cheshire and Hampstead Garden Suburb in north London.

The dominant style was neo-Tudor, though neo-rustic might be a better term. In its midst was positioned a 'real' Tudor house, moved stick by stick from neighbouring Bournbrook. Cadbury re-erected it in 1912 as a central feature, surrounding it with a church, institute, meeting house and shops. With interest in medieval revivalism now booming, the Cadburys researched what had degenerated into a tumbledown row of workers' cottages, restoring the structure to full manorial glory.

The house is a fine example of a medieval hall house given a fireplace and bedrooms in the course of the 16th century. The original hall was in the centre of the building, its screens passage replaced by a chimneystack and its plaster walls replaced by brick. One wing formed the kitchen and the other, grander, wing the parlour and solar above. The latter was given its own outside staircase entrance, a rare feature.

The interior is remarkable, not just for the purity of its restoration but for the furnishings. They include a Nonsuch chest (*see* Nonsuch, Surrey), a mantrap and crossbows adapted for firing bolts or balls. The Tudor and Jacobean vernacular pieces, gathered by an active local trust, are one of the best collections of early furniture in the Midlands.

BIRMINGHAM: SOHO HOUSE **

Soho Avenue, Handsworth, 2m NW of Birmingham city centre
Manufacturer's late Georgian house with inventions (M)

Matthew Boulton was one of the true fathers of Birmingham's wealth. He was an 18th-century inventor and entrepreneur, still with the outlook of an enlightened Georgian im-prover rather than a Victorian capitalist. His Soho Manufactory was a workshop with many small processes and trade outlets under one roof. These were not located far from the proprietor's mansion so as to avoid pollution in the understandable 19th-century custom. They were next door across the lawn. Today, at half its original size, Soho House might be a comfortable vicarage, were it not for the numerous 'mod cons' designed by Boulton and his friends.

Soho House was built over two and a half centuries ago, and is now adjacent to a mu-seum devoted to the birth of Birmingham industry. The surrounding community is more completely Asian and West Indian than any in Britain, and the building is in the shadow of a large Hindu temple. The museum is a good one and the house, though over-municipalized, has been well restored.

Boulton built the house in the 1760s and remodelled it with the help of Samuel and James Wyatt in the 1790s. The style is reminis-cent of John Soane. The façade is a simple Georgian box, its entrance front decorated with four pilasters and a hipped roof. The walls are covered in rendered slate tiles. In the small garden is a thatched hermitage.

The interior comprises a suite of rooms whose formal staircase was never completed. The diminutive entrance hall, with a screen of alabaster columns, is the one touch of grand-ness. There is a lobby with a 'Bramah' water

closet. Like the steam-heated water supply and central heating released from holes in the stairs, these devices put Boulton's house in the van of convenience.

The hall leads into the dining room. This was the meeting place for Boulton's Lunar Society, a group of Midlands scientists and engineers who discussed inventions and new products (*see* Erasmus Darwin House, Lich-field/Staffs) and took forward the region's industrial revolution. The thin glazing bars on two of the windows are of 'eldorado' alloy, developed by one of the members, James Keir. The room has a gently groined ceiling and marbled pilasters. The calico curtains copy the pattern of this marbling. The Gothick dining chairs are by Gillow.

Downstairs are the breakfast room, drawing room and study, furnished with pieces by James Newton in the early 19th century. In the drawing room, Newton designed the base for one of Boulton's magnificent sidereal clocks. Here too are busts of Boulton by Flaxman and of James Watt by Chantrey.

The study contains various inventions, such as a letter-copying machine and a baro-meter. Beyond is a fossilry, displaying various specimens of interest to the Lunar Society. This was truly an age when invention and develop-ment marched hand-in-hand with commerce and nodded occasionally in the direction of art.

Upstairs are mostly bedrooms, well fur-nished but suffering from acute museumitis.

CHARLECOTE PARK ***

Charlecote, 4m E of Stratford
19th-century reinstatement of Elizabethan mansion (NT)

Charlecote marks the point where southern England emphatically becomes Midlands. This is Henry James's 'midmost England, unmiti-gated England'. When he visited Charlecote, he viewed its 'venerable verdure' as being 'like backward years receding to the age of Eliza-beth'. It was and is the house of the Lucys.

There have been Lucys at Charlecote since

the 13th century. It was a Lucy who completed the new house in 1558, receiving Queen Elizabeth here in 1572. Young Shakespeare is said to have been caught poaching in the park, taking revenge on the relevant Lucy by making him Justice Shallow in the *Merry Wives of Windsor*. He complains to Falstaff that his friends 'have beaten my men, killed my deer and broke open my lodge'. The authenticity of this tale is debated in the guidebook.

Shakespeare's Charlecote is now no more than a ghost inside the house which was refitted and extended by George Hammond Lucy and his wife over the four decades following 1823. His decorator was the antiquarian glass-maker, Thomas Willement. Lucy spent £3,400 at the great sale of William Beckford's Fonthill Abbey (*see* Beckford's Tower/ Somerset) in 1823. His purchases included a pietra dura table in the hall and later the ebony state bed.

At this time, Lucy also added a complete new west front beyond the hall, facing the River Avon. Willement produced ceilings and wallpapers, carpets, chair covers and bookcases. Charlecote is a supreme example of the Elizabethan revival.

From the mid-19th century, the house suffered a long decline. Lucy children were teased at Eton for their girlish surname and, when victims of the agricultural depression, sold paintings to pay bills. Heiresses forced reluctant husbands to call themselves Lucy to live there.

Finally the National Trust was summoned by the irascible Sir Henry Fairfax-Lucy, a man who left his children so hungry they had to escape to the local village to beg food. He knew he had come to an end, but his dealings over the house's transfer with James Lees-Milne were so appalling that when he died in 1944 in the course of them, 'nobody seemed to regret it very much'. His son had already been sent to Kenya as a punishment. This son now returned and tried to summon the servants by clapping. Soon there was none left.

At first, the National Trust doubted whether so completely victorianized a house merited its attention. But Charlecote is Charlecote. Across England, almost all Elizabethan houses are Victorian houses, and many Victorian houses are Elizabethan. The rest is archaeology. Charlecote still shimmers from a distance down its long avenue of limes, like the backdrop to a Shakespearean history play. In front is its jewel, the little Renaissance gatehouse doubling as a banqueting house and foil for the great façade beyond.

The interior is an excellent study in early-Victorian taste. The Great Hall is reached past the morning room, redecorated in dark brown, blue and gold. In the hall is the Fonthill table and an alabaster vase with carved doves from Italy. Family portraits crowd the walls. The dining room and library were built and furnished entirely in the reign of William IV, with Willement wallpaper and armorial glass. In the former room is that pride of every Victorian dining room, a massive sideboard carved in 1858 by Willcox of Warwick. It was, to Lees-Milne, a 'monster of inelegance, and ghastly curiosity of mid-Victorian joinery'.

Over the mantelpiece in the billiard room is a magnificent Batoni of the 18th-century George Lucy. The drawing room contains more pietra dura, ebony and a cabinet made for Beckford and acquired at the Fonthill sale. Upstairs are two guest bedrooms and a dressing room refurnished as in an inventory of 1891. The Ebony Bedroom, with its romantic view over the courtyard to the gatehouse, has a Beckford bed once slept in by Nelson and Lady Hamilton, albeit at Fonthill. It was made from a 17th-century East Indies settee.

The service wing and stables contains the scullery, kitchen, brewhouse, tackroom and travelling coach. These are displayed with typical National Trust meticulousness. In the park, Capability Brown has been allowed to survive, his landscape marrying house to river. The deer park still has the animals which Shakespeare may or may not have poached, and the Jacob sheep introduced by the Georgian Thomas Lucy in 1756.

The present Sir Edmund Fairfax-Lucy, the artist, lives in a wing and has designed the new forecourt garden.

COMBE ABBEY **

3m E of Coventry
Norman abbey and Restoration mansion,
now fantasy hotel (H)

This is *Gormenghast* extravaganza. Arriving at
what is now a hotel, visitors are greeted by
plainsong chant and two giant pulpits, Bibles
open at the ready. Icons and suits of armour
jostle for space on the walls. Telephone boxes
are converted from old confessional booths.
Gift display cases are High Gothic caskets.
Books are left lying everywhere. Somewhere
an organ plays. Everything is dark, including
the brows of the staff. An internal portcullis conceals the quay of an underground
moat.

The old abbey was a Cistercian foundation
which passed to Lord Harington at the Dissolution, then in 1622 to the Craven family.
They retained it until 1923, when it was sold to
a local builder and eventually to Coventry
Council. It is now a 'No Ordinary Hotel', in
the same group (and madcap style) as the Earl
of Scarborough's Lumley Castle (Durham).

The relics of the monastery are still visible
in the cloister plan of the U-shaped forecourt
and the red sandstone arches of the old chapter house. The cloister windows remain with,
above them, Elizabethan windows and a
variety of gables. All this was intended to turn
an old monastery into a Jacobean gentleman's
residence.

Onto this was later tacked a handsome
range to the west, with large reception rooms
and pedimented windows. This was designed
in 1682 by the Restoration architect, William
Winde, who probably also built Ashdown
(Oxon) for Lord Craven and the first Buckingham House (later Palace) in London.

The house survived in this form until 1862
when the then Earl of Craven commissioned
W. E. Nesfield to adapt it as a large Victorian mansion and the family's principal seat.
It became a rambling palace surrounded by
a moat and ornamental gardens. Most of
Nesfield's work was later demolished and the
Wilde wing mutilated, to be supplemented in
the 1990s by today's beefy, neo-Norman hotel
extension.

The present interior, much of it original, is
monstrously ill-used but can only be accepted
on its own terms. The entrance, remarked
Country Life recently, 'could easily lull the
visitor into an expectation of quiet good
taste'. Not the inside. Apart from the already
described entrance lobby and hall, the main
reception rooms are more respectful of their
17th-century antecedents, perhaps by virtue of
heritage listing.

The north saloon has a huge Wrennish fireplace and plaster ceiling. The Walnut Room is
rich in panelling. In a passage I tripped over a
medieval bishop lying silent in prayer. Yet
Combe seems to us as Strawberry Hill (London, W) or Cardiff Castle probably did to their
contemporaries. Taste takes time to adjust – at
Combe, I imagine, quite a long time.

COUGHTON COURT ***

2m N of Alcester
Tudor house of recusant Throckmortons
(NT)

Coughton is about Catholics. Of the Throckmortons of Coughton, it has been written that
'The family's strict adherence to the Catholic
faith and their continued confrontation with
authority seems to have condemned them
to a less significant place in history than their
abilities would otherwise have earned them.'

Why some English families stayed Catholic
and aloof from the mainstream of English
Reformation, even to the point of treason, has
puzzled historians. The medieval Throckmortons were wealthy Tudor courtiers, like
thousands of others, but they opposed Henry
VIII's divorces in the 1530s and since then have
'never capitulated'.

Throckmortons became a clan. They inter-
married with other Catholics, maintained
close links with the Continent and supplied
monks and nuns to their Church. They were

The Old Religion: Gothic Coughton

also implicated in various plots to usurp the English throne, from the Throckmorton Plot to the Gunpowder Plot. Treason, goes the saying, may be a matter of dates, but these Midlands rebels lived dangerously. As for Coughton (pronounced 'coaton') and the family's manor at Harvington (Worcs), recusancy proved a great conservationist. The chief change at Coughton, its Georgian gothicization, was probably carried out by the architect, John Carter, known as 'antiquity's most resolute friend'. The Gothic style was always associated, sometimes vaguely, with the Old Religion.

Coughton gatehouse is a typical Henrician tower. The former carriageway through its centre is now an entrance hall, fan-vaulted in the 1780s. This cold, stone chamber is relieved by such country house paraphernalia as antlers, an armorial screen, pewter and funny hats. Next door is a Georgian staircase lined with family portraits, many with grim faces seemingly set on martyrdom.

The domestic rooms are of a mix of periods and styles. The drawing room was allegedly the place where Lady Digby and her Jesuit friends sat eagerly awaiting news of the Gunpowder Plot. The turret windows next to the oriel carry the arms of the Catesby and Tresham families, both plotters. Over the fireplace is a portrait of the 18th-century Sir Robert Throckmorton, looking like a Bourbon courtier. It is by Nicolas de Largillière, who also painted the family nun.

The Little Drawing Room is beautifully adorned with sets of Worcester and Coalport china. Also displayed is a Mass cabinet, a travelling container for the Host. Its door reveals a stage set with mirrors, an exquisite work of kingwood veneer from the West Indies. From here, we climb to the tower room, dedicated to the Throckmortons' pedigree, and offering a view of the rear of the house, with its timbered Tudor wings extending into the fine garden.

The dining room, with 16th-century panelling, was formerly the Tudor Great Chamber. The room contains an old abbey dole gate and an armorial panel over the fireplace. Other curios include a chair made from 'the wood of the bed on which Richard III slept before Bosworth', and a cup from the wood of a tree 'under which Shakespeare once sat' in Stratford. The Tapestry Dressing Room is dominated by an entire wall depicting the *Rape of the Sabine Women*, an uncomfortable scene with which to fall asleep. More restful is the best set of gouaches by Ducros (1748–1810) to be seen in England: shipyard scenes and pavilions set deep in woods.

The house now becomes even more emphatically Catholic. The Tribune contains such relics as the supposed chemise in which Mary Queen of Scots was beheaded, and in which her dog was found whimpering hours after her death. Here is Catherine of Aragon's cope and an alabaster relief of the Nativity. Beyond is the saloon, formed in 1910 from the 17th-century chapel and reached down the fine carved staircase brought from Harvington.

Here we can see the coat made in 1811 for a wager that it was impossible to make Sir John Throckmorton a coat from two live sheep between sunrise and sunset. The wool was cut, spun, spooled, warped, loomed, woven, burred, milled, rowed, dyed, dried, sheered, pressed and tailored in 13 hours 20 minutes – and the wager won.

The new garden at Coughton 'sympathetically echoes the Tudor architecture of the house'. The River Arrow has been diverted into pools and lakes, watering a delightful bog garden.

ETTINGTON PARK **

Newbold on Stour, 6m SE of Stratford-upon-Avon
Gothic Mansion in polychrome stone and sculpture (H)

This Victorian Gothic confection is located on a platform overlooking the River Stour. It has suffered for much of its life for being 'over-the-top'. Like many such houses, it had a tragic 20th century, being hospital, school, hotel and disco, until wrecked by fire in 1980. It has since been well restored as a hotel, glorying in the dubious accolade of being England's 'most haunted'.

The house belonged to the eccentric Victorian Evelyn Philip Shirley, descendant of the 1st Earl Ferrers. It was on the site of a village that the family had owned since before the Norman Conquest, but had since removed. The family were devout Catholics. The 4th Earl Ferrers was the last aristocrat to be hanged, at Tyburn in 1760, for murdering a rent collector. He claimed a peer's silk rope. Evelyn Shirley was the local MP, but he immersed himself in genealogy, archaeology and architecture, appearing as Ardenne in Disraeli's *Lothair*, 'a man of ancient pedigree himself, who knew everyone else's'.

In 1858 Shirley commissioned the architect T. F. Pritchard to redesign his house in Ruskinian Early Gothic. The walls were embellished throughout with friezes of his family's history. The exterior is a mass of mid-Victorian stone polychromy, known as 'streaky bacon style' but here well controlled and delicate. It honours Ruskin's belief in sculptural detail, to 'point a moral or adorn a tale'. Ettington is Victorian architecture at its most ideological. The combination of polychrome brick and extensive sculptural decoration is matched only by Teulon's Elvetham (Hants).

The entrance has a *porte-cochère* fronting a Gothic screen. Behind rise three gables flanked by one square and one rounded tower, with wings thrusting forward on either side. The windows are pointed or flat-headed. The right-hand tower turns the corner to the garden front where it confronts an even more splendid tower festooned with monarchs and gargoyles.

Here everything is balanced yet never symmetrical, each Gothic feature striving to outdo its neighbour. Panels depict Shirleys in numerous gallant and pious exploits, including killing Saracens in the Holy Land.

The interior is more heavy-handed. The modest entrance hall is blessed with a large Elizabethan fireplace with logs blazing beneath the arms of the Shirleys. The library contains Gothic bookcases and a Decorated Gothic fireplace.

FARNBOROUGH HALL **

Farnborough, 6m N of Banbury
Grand Tour house with Rococo rooms (NT)

William Holbech went on the Grand Tour in the 1720s and returned with Canalettos, Panninis and a large collection of Roman busts. He promptly refashioned along classical lines the house his family had built in the 1690s. He also refashioned its park to replicate a landscape in the Roman *campagna*.

The house sits secluded in a dell, russet-walled, with bold classical windows and parapet. A handsome terrace walk stretches nearly a mile to the distant hills, Warwickshire as a plausible version of Italy, at least in a dry summer. The scene is dotted with temples, a pavilion and an obelisk. Although owned by the National Trust, the house is still occupied by the Holbech family.

The redesigned house was almost certainly by William Jones, surveyor to the East India Company (Honington, below), although the family vigorously maintain that Sanderson Miller was the architect. The rooms were decorated with Rococo plasterwork by William Perritt in the 1740s. The stucco is as rich as that at Ragley and some may be attributed to the great Italian stuccoist, Francesco Vassalli. The contrast at Farnborough is startling between the rugged classical exterior of ochre ironstone and the warm, delicate interior.

The entrance hall, staircase and two rooms are open to the public. The hall is chiefly remarkable for the brackets and niches designed to carry the Roman busts. These are of emperors and noble ladies, forming one of the largest such collections remaining in their designed setting. The ceiling has panels with Rococo designs.

The Georgian dining room beyond was built into what had been originally the rear courtyard of the earlier house. The plasterwork is outstanding, not only on the ceiling but also round the panels framing Holbech's copied Canalettos and Panninis (the originals were sold in 1929). The dining table is surrounded by 'splat-backed' chairs, intended for removing boots. They are remarkably comfortable.

The staircase hall has more Rococo plasterwork and busts in niches. Here the ceiling oval is earlier, dating from the William-and-Mary period, with garlands of fruit and foliage, almost vulgar against the adjacent Rococo. The stair treads are shallow, as was the custom c1700. There is also fine plasterwork in the Oval Pavilion, reached by a long trek up the Terrace Walk.

HONINGTON HALL ***

Honington, 1½m N of Shipston on Stour
Restoration mansion, Rococo interiors (P)

'I have lost my balls again', was the regular cry of one of the 20th-century owners of Honington, Sir Charles Wiggin, to the local police as vandals tipped his bridge ornaments once again into the River Stour. It enlivened an otherwise dull beat. The old man was struggling to maintain this jewel of a house and vandals were the last thing he needed. His balls are still with us and his family live in the house to this day.

Honington lies in a lost landscape where the Cotswolds peter out yet the Midlands has yet to begin. Here England momentarily loses a sense of direction. The park has a charming gatehouse in the village in the style of Wren. The house itself sits at the end of a graceful drive, redbrick with white eaves and a hipped roof. It is a picture of quiet dignity.

The house was built by a London lawyer, Henry Parker, who married into the Hyde family and became MP for Evesham. The date is c1682 and the architect unknown. The house was sold in 1737 to Joseph Townsend who, in the 1740s and 50s, embellished it with curved screens and reordered and decorated the interior. He arranged twelve Roman emperors on the façades, like the busts at Farnborough (above). The architect, who also worked at Farnborough, was probably William Jones.

The 1750s were a period of innovation in English interiors, notably in the Midlands. The hall at Honington is sensational. Townsend created a screen between it and a new stairwell beyond, forming a sort of *porte-cochère* to the octagonal saloon beyond. The ingenuity is reminiscent of Mawley Hall (Salop) or John Chute's work at The Vyne (Hants), an amateur conversant with architectural language and able to instruct his craftsmen with assurance. The craftsman here was probably Charles Stanley, although William Perritt and Thomas Roberts of Oxford are also mentioned.

The hall is yellow but almost every inch is coated in foaming white Rococo. Over the fireplace an ornamented panel contains not a painting but a bas relief. The ceiling roundel is a giant starburst. The stairwell drips with plaster foliage as if still wet from the rain.

To the left of the hall is the Oak Room, now the Wiggin family sitting room. The original 17th-century panelling has been retained but with a Georgian doorcase of sumptuous grandeur. Two reclining cherubs rest on its pediment while winged sphinxes (possibly later additions) sit over its lintel. This door is fit for an emperor.

The pink-walled boudoir leads into the octagonal saloon, executed in 1751. It is hard to overstate the beauty of the Honington Octagon. Classical doorways crowned with cherubs are set against blue wall panels. These are interspersed with swirling Rococo pier-glasses and plaster swags and festoons, depicting the seasons, Aesop's fables, the elements and cornucopia.

Above, a coffered semi-dome rises to a painting of Acis and Galatea by Luca Giordano. Each of the rosettes in the coffers is a different design. Three of the eight walls are windows, giving views over the valley outside. Sacheverell Sitwell, encountering this room for the first time, rated it with the great palaces at Holkham and Houghton (Norfolk).

The design of the Octagon and other alterations are attributed to an amateur architect, John Freeman of Henley, whose estimate stipulated £100 'for a little carving, gilding and embellisment for the ladies'.

English Rococo at Honington

KENILWORTH CASTLE **

Kenilworth
Ruins of great medieval fortress (EH)

There are those who regard Kenilworth as the definitive English castle. It shares with Rochester (Kent) the distinction of having suffered a real medieval siege in the 13th century. But its glory lies in its occupancy by Robert Dudley, Earl of Leicester, and his nineteen-day entertainment of his adored Elizabeth I in 1575. The event was immortalized by Walter Scott in *Kenilworth* and made this a place of huge Victorian appeal. The castle has never lacked for romance, except perhaps now.

The Norman keep was held in 1266 by rebel supporters of Simon de Montfort against Henry III. The resulting assault lasted nine months. Siege engines came from Nottingham, boats to cross the moat were summoned from Cheshire and arrows from the Forest of Dean. Every stratagem of war was employed, from excommunication to the plague. At Kenilworth's eventual surrender, the defenders were allowed to walk free.

The castle was later turned into a palace by John of Gaunt and embellished by Dudley to receive the Queen. The castle never recovered from his downfall and was slighted in the Civil War. In 1937 it was bought as a ruin by John Siddeley, Lord Kenilworth, and is now cared for by English Heritage. The great defensive mere, or lake, has been drained and the ruins tamed with lawns.

The approach to the castle is over what would have been the causeway. The outer walls are intact and the keep of the old castle retains its original proportions. Round it are ranged the ruins of Gaunt's palace, including the vast Great Hall with Gothic doorway and bay window. To the left of the inner enclosure is the three-storey block built by Leicester for Elizabeth. The windows are large, the rooms spacious.

In the outer court opposite is Leicester's new gatehouse, still intact but closed to visitors. Its entry is a pretty classical portal

decorated with Tudor roses and containing a curiously ribbed arch. It contributes a dash of Renaissance charm in this awesome medieval place.

MIDDLETON HALL *

Middleton, 4m S of Tamworth
Medieval farm buildings round courtyard (P)

The country between Birmingham and Tamworth is much abused. Poor Middleton Hall is a victim of this, despite efforts being made to rescue it. The house was home in the 17th century to the naturalist Sir Francis Willoughby, a founder of the Royal Society. More remarkable today is the group of medieval farm buildings round a courtyard to the rear, dating from the 13th to the 16th centuries.

The house itself has a plain 18th-century façade to the garden. Behind is the former Elizabethan Great Hall, georgianized and with a theatrical staircase rising to a balcony between incongruous fluted columns. Poor copies of ancestral pictures gaze down from the walls. Embroidery panels upstairs depict the history of Sutton Coldfield.

The buildings round the courtyard behind were being restored at the time of writing. One dates from the late 13th century and includes a manorial undercroft and evidence of stone mullioned windows. There is an upstairs solar. Next door is a fine timber-framed building, presumably Tudor, and next to it another with oversailed upper floor. They should form an exciting group when fully reinstated.

PACKWOOD HOUSE ***

9m NW of Warwick
Tudor yeoman's house re-created (NT)

The yew garden at Packwood is a horticultural Karnak. The columns of the Egyptian temple of Amun are said to come alive at dusk with the spirits that inhabit them. The same goes for these mighty yews. They are called the Sermon on the Mount, listeners attending the distant preacher, nodding, muttering and growing increasingly excited in the wind. Packwood in the Civil War harboured both Cavaliers and Roundheads. These can only have been Roundheads.

The house is now a monument to the 20th-century manorial revival. It had belonged to the Fetherston family from the 15th to the 19th centuries. Charles Fetherston, inheriting in 1815, insisted that everything he ate, drank, used and wore be grown on his land and made within his walls, even his shoes. This early sustainability did not last. The house fell to ruin and was eventually bought by a Midlands industrialist, Alfred Ash, in 1905. His son, Baron Ash, made its restoration his life's work. Everything we see of the interior was inserted in the 1920s and 1930s, garnered from decaying houses across Britain. The connoisseurship was immaculate.

Baron Ash (a name not a title) was of a generation which disliked Georgian and abominated Victorian. His antiquarianism was aesthetic. There is nothing proletarian about Packwood's Tudor, and none of the political correctness of Ruskin or Morris. Ash was obsessively neat. He hated a book incorrectly set on a table. His clothes were always pressed, proving to James Lees-Milne 'that he was not really a countryman'. A guest arriving a minute late for an appointment or even a meal was sent away. As for the galvanized iron foundries that were the source of his family's wealth, they were never, ever to be mentioned under his roof.

So what are we to make of Ash's creation, a home or a museum? It was undoubtedly his home, but that of a man so fastidious that only a museum would do for a home. Since National Trust conservationists are Baron Ash reincarnated, perhaps we cannot complain. None of them can tolerate a cobweb. Yet Ash's motto was the admirable, 'Not for us but for everyone'.

The public road to Packwood turns through gateposts and appears to be a private drive. To the left are the billowing rollers of the yew garden. Beyond is the rich façade of the house, a series of Elizabethan gables and chimneys, much restored.

Two words sum up the interior, wood and tapestry. Wood came from the adjacent Forest of Arden. Tapestries came from anywhere Ash could find them, notably superb Brussels works acquired from neighbouring Baddesley Clinton. Entrance is to the screens passage, leading to the hall which has a floor laid in chevron pattern. This was acquired from Lymore Park in Montgomeryshire, where it had subsided into the basement during a dance. The Powis family subsequently threw it out in embarrassment.

From the hall Ash led a gallery to an outlying barn, which he reconstituted as a second, more formal Great Hall. He acquired an enormous table from Baddesley, more tapestries and a fireplace from Stratford 'in front of which Shakespeare may have sat'. Hatchments and banners from his proud term of office as High Sheriff of Warwickshire adorn the roof. A stone staircase leads to the bedrooms, beautifully furnished and named after distinguished visitors.

Queen Mary's Room, with a child's setting of table and chairs, was 'at her disposal' during a brief visit in 1927. Queen Margaret's Room is named after a bed in which she may have slept (somewhere else). Ireton's Room, with its solid Parliamentary four-poster, was allegedly occupied by the colonel before the Battle of Edgehill in 1642.

The downstairs drawing room, study and dining room are those of the original house, albeit swamped by imports. The pictures are not distinguished, being chosen rather to fit in than impress, an admirable aim. The dining room has flame-stitch hangings and Flemish window roundels.

The garden at Packwood was described by Geoffrey Jellicoe as having 'worldliness combined with a curious vague, indefinable mysticism'. The layout is Jacobean, an orderly sequence of Fountain Court, sunken garden and wilderness beyond, all overlooked by gazebos. Beyond is the ever-stern Sermon on the Mount. The yews rise up the hillside towards the mysterious mound where stands a single mighty yew, the master, preacher and monitor of the foibles below.

RAGLEY HALL ****

1m SW of Alcester
Gibbs Great Hall and Wyatt interiors vividly
restored (P)

Ragley is the home of the Marquess of Hertford
and he does not mind who knows it. Like
Beaulieu (Hants) and Woburn (Beds), this is a
country house which sells itself on dynasty,
here that of the Seymours. Big houses in
modern England have learnt to survive either
on bureaucracy or on egotism. I prefer egotism. The modern family mural that adorns the
south staircase hall is an astonishing assertion
of 20th-century heredity.

This is the more remarkable since, in 1930,
there were plans to reduce Ragley to a villa and
in 1951 the family's trustees proposed to
demolish it altogether. The determination of
the then twenty-one-year-old 8th Marquess to
save it was assisted by quantities of public
money. 'A house is a life sentence,' he said in
a phrase echoed by many a house owner. He
served it until he died in 1997, a sentence to be
continued by his son.

Ragley has a conventional exterior but
sensational interior. It was first designed by
Wren's associate, Robert Hooke, in 1680 but
not completed until the mid-18th century
under James Gibbs and James Wyatt. To
Gibbs, we owe the Great Hall, and to his Italian
craftsmen, especially the Artari brothers, the
astonishing plasterwork in the main reception rooms. Wyatt later added the central
portico and flowing front stairs, a touch of
late-Georgian Baroque.

Entry into the house is under the portico,
directly into the two-storey Great Hall.
The impact is immediate. Ragley's pink and
white hall is the nearest an English grand
chamber came to architectural, rather than
decorative, Rococo. Fluted pilasters rise to an
upper storey of blind arcading, swags, busts
and urns. The ceiling medallion is of Minerva
holding a spear. French windows allow light to
stream in from the portico. The whole is
boldly coloured pink, warmed by a carpeted
floor. The plasterwork was not begun until

1756, so Gibbs would never have seen his
design realized.

The main reception rooms are each an essay
in paint and plaster. The music room is in
varieties of blue, again with Gibbs plasterwork. The breakfast room is in orange with a
Rococo overmantel. The dining room goes for
a vivid yellow. Everywhere the colours are
made to talk.

The wall panels are designed to frame portraits by Hoppner and others. Only in the
north staircase hall does boldness get the better
of common sense. A shocking gash of blue and
yellow by the modern artist, Ceri Richards,
diminishes the wallpaper round it and jars
with the architecture.

The decorative features introduced by
Wyatt in the 1780s are less extrovert, closer to
the delicacy associated with Wyatt's rival,
Robert Adam. The crimson damask of the
Red Saloon, with a beautiful painted ceiling,
is based on the original colour. The Green
Drawing Room is hung with Seymour por-
traits by Reynolds, and two exquisite Chinese
Chippendale mirrors.

The great south staircase hall, filled with
the famed *trompe-l'œil* mural by Graham Rust,
was executed between 1969 and 1983. It depicts
the then Hertford family in modern dress
but in a scene after the manner of Thornhill.
Although controversial, the Baroque design
fits into its Georgian setting, responding to
the off-white shades of the doors and balusters. Not everything works, notably the
kitsch ceiling roundel of *The Temptation*, but
the composition is complete and executed
with panache.

The Victorian Hertfords neglected Ragley
and spent their money accumulating one
of England's greatest art collections. This was
passed not to the house but to Richard
Wallace, illegitimate son of the 4th Marquess,
who lived in Paris. Wallace left it, with his
London house in Manchester Square, as the
Wallace Collection.

As a result, Ragley's pictures are disappoint-
ingly poor. With hundreds of paintings in
store, I cannot believe the Wallace could not
loan some works.

STONELEIGH ABBEY ***

2m E of Kenilworth
Restored Smith of Warwick masterpiece in
Repton landscape (P)

Stoneleigh is a triumph of 18th-century building and landscaping, and of valiant 20th-
century rescue. The seat of the Leigh family
since 1561 seemed doomed after a fire in 1960.
It might have become a golf club, offices or a
ruin. Now controversially restored, it is regain-
ing some of its former splendour. The family
set up a preservation trust and have returned
to live in part of the house.

The original abbey was founded by the
Cistercians in 1154. Fragments of this period
survive round the rear courtyard and in a fine
early 14th-century gatehouse, a rare example of
this form not in ruins. It guards the entrance
to the drive beneath a giant cedar, the tree so
tilted as if about to blow away at any moment.

The main west wing dominates the scene. It
is a rectangular box begun by Francis Smith of
Warwick in 1720 for the 3rd Lord Leigh after
his return from the Grand Tour. This box
stimulated Jane Austen to her description of
Sotherton in *Mansfield Park*. In 1809, Humphry Repton produced a Red Book for the
landscape, including the diversion of the River
Avon to form a lake to reflect the great west
façade. John Rennie built a classical bridge
over it five years later. Gothic Revival stables
and a riding school were added shortly afterwards. Stoneleigh was a complete aristocratic
encampment.

The fire in 1960 destroyed the upper part
of Smith's wing, leaving it derelict for over
twenty years. Today, a scheme suggested by
the last-resort saviour of many country houses,
Kit Martin, has turned most of the house
into apartments. The state rooms have been
reinstated and are accessible, although their
commercial use appears to demand fitted
cream carpets, a dire anachronism which is at
least reversible.

More controversial was the trustees' decision to patch rather than restore completely
Smith's 15-bay façade. The result is plain ugly.

Smith's vertical emphasis of rhythmic pilasters
seems to have contracted a skin disease, the
most virulent case of 20th-century 'conserve as
found' I have encountered. It may work for
a jumbled medieval façade, but devastates a
classical design that depends on precision of
detail and surface and the casting of shadow.
One day, the unrestored stones will presumably need replacing, so Stoneleigh will be
forever faced with chequerboard.

The interior was, at the time of my visit, still
searching for personality beyond that of corporate hospitality. The staircase hall is superb,
rising to a balcony and Venetian arch. Its walls
are adorned with panels, trophies and hunting
scenes beneath a ceiling rich in swags and
shells. The balusters are composed of three
different designs to each tread, twisted, spiral
and classical.

Of the other rooms, the grandest is the 1765
saloon. It is surrounded with free-standing
and attached columns in scagliola. The plasterwork, especially the oval ceiling panel and
doorways, is of the highest quality. Reliefs
depict the Labours of Hercules. On the wall
is a portrait of Helene Leigh, 'buccaneer'
American wife of the 3rd Lord Leigh (of the
second creation), whose money helped save
Stoneleigh during a previous crisis at the turn
of the 20th century.

Of the other rooms, the drawing room
is wood-panelled and has the Leigh unicorn
even on its light switches. The library has been
refurnished with Georgian tapestry chairs by
William Gomm, rightly returned to the house
by the government after being surrendered by
the Leighs in lieu of tax. There is a Georgian
chapel with a plaster ceiling. The detached
Gothic stables have been beautifully restored;
the 1820s stalls are in their original state, sadly
without horses.

The old house looks out once more over
Repton's lake and park of 1808. He explicitly
sought 'the graceful and picturesque combina-
tions which we admire in the works of the best
painters such as Poussin and Claude Lorraine
and the scenery of the graceful Watteau'.
Mansion and lake cast echoes at each other,
especially on the riverside terrace.

STRATFORD-UPON-AVON: ANNE HATHAWAY'S COTTAGE ✳✳✳

Shottery, 1m W of Stratford
Cottage of Shakespeare's wife (M)

This is the most famous cottage in England, if not in the world. Anne Hathaway was Shakespeare's wife. The image of her birthplace has sheltered a million chocolates and taxed a million jigsaw-puzzlers. Never was so small a spot so desirable to world tourism. Yet visit it off season and you may still have it to yourself. Anne Hathaway's Cottage is a masterpiece of unobtrusive fame.

Will and Anne married when he was eighteen and she an 'old maid' of twenty-six. Hathaways continued to live in the house for another three centuries. Celebrity came early. Tennyson and Dickens were enthusiastic visitors and Mary Baker, occupant of the cottage for much of the 19th century, was a practised guide. The Shakespeare Birthplace Trust acquired it in 1892.

Even without these associations, the cottage would be a pretty place. A thick bonnet of thatch slopes low over timbered walls and small windows. Roses and shrubs crowd close, while a herb garden and orchard grace the distance. This is the England of which expatriates dream and which many recreated in suburban repose.

The smaller half of the cottage is very old, probably 15th century, while the higher extension at the rear is of the 17th century. The rooms are intended by the Birthplace Trust to convey the appearance of the cottage at the time of its purchase at the end of the 19th century. There is little sign of museumitis, not much bardolatry and many charming relics of the cottage's past, including early photographs.

There are flagstones in the hall and game hanging in the larder. Upstairs is a series of bedrooms with old rope beds, origin of the night-time bidding to 'sleep tight'. On show is a beautifully carved crib and a chair made of straw. If these rooms were so well furnished, the Hathaways must have been prosperous. Between the old and new parts are exposed cruck beams and wattle-and-daub infill.

Despite the care shown with the cottage itself, I counted no fewer than four shops carefully inserted in the outbuildings. Opposite is the small pond in which, of course, Ophelia drowned.

STRATFORD-UPON-AVON: SHAKESPEARE'S BIRTHPLACE ✳✳

Henley Street
Shakespeare's family home (M)

We may scoff at the scale of the Shakespeare industry, but what is Stratford to do? Block the roads, put guards at the gates, and sell timed tickets on the M40? The town has been a tourist magnet since the 18th century and much has indeed become tacky and commercialized. Yet for all the hordes, Stratford has at least guarded its shrines. The Shakespeare Birthplace Trust, set up in 1847, owns five properties in and round the town. Their quest for authenticity is not easy but almost everywhere is tasteful and sincere.

Shakespeare was born, educated and married amid the Elizabethan Midlands bourgeoisie. To their houses he returned in middle age and lived there for the last six years of his life until his death aged fifty-two in 1616. The houses are best visited in mid-winter, although they are never allowed to become overcrowded since all are small, domestic residences. Adapt them for crowds, and they would collapse.

The Birthplace itself stands somewhat uncomfortably on Henley Street. Entry is through a modern visitors' centre which has displays that would be inappropriate in the house itself, such as the Bard's study and school desk. The original house is reached across a garden planted with herbs and flowers

Fame well-tended: Hathaway's Cottage

mentioned in the plays. The house remained in Shakespeare descent to the 19th century, when it passed to the Trust. Sadly, the houses on either side were demolished lest they ever catch fire and destroy the main house. They should be rebuilt facsimile.

Shakespeare's father, John, was a glover and clothier. In the rear parlour is a spinning wheel and much cloth. Next door is the family hall, combining as kitchen and dining room with the table laid for a meal. Beyond is John Shakespeare's workroom, complete with dressed animal skins. The plays are full of references to the skinner's trade.

The upstairs bedrooms are charmingly furnished with objects and fabrics from 16th-century originals. Here is the holy of holies, Shakespeare's birth-room, called in a Victorian advertisement 'the truly heart-stirring relic of England's immortal bard'. Here is a crib and baby clothes. A small exhibition describes the story of the house as a visitor attraction, with no celebrity omitted.

STRATFORD-UPON-AVON: HALL'S CROFT **

Old Town
House of Shakespeare's son-in-law (M)

John Hall married Shakespeare's eldest daughter, Susanna, and appears to have built and occupied this house in 1613. Three years later he moved to Shakespeare's own house at New Place, now destroyed. Hall's Croft is an example of a town house to which Shakespeare might have aspired as a boy, and to which he returned at the end of his life. Hall was a physician and wealthy. His work is well documented and the house is an early museum of 'general practice'. Almost all the furniture is of the period.

In the downstairs parlour hangs a Dutch painting by Claeissins of a 16th-century family saying grace before a meal, the boys to one side, the girls to the other. On the table is a large haunch of beef, symbol of prosperity. Also in the room is a peculiar luxury, a beautifully turned child's high chair. Next to the parlour is Hall's consulting room, with Dutch paintings of apothecaries. The wall cupboard and work table display jars, pestles and mortars and other medical equipment. Everything looks painful.

Upstairs the rooms are mostly arranged for sleeping. One contains a lavatory stool with hinged lid. Even the servant's bedroom, on the same floor, is well appointed. The garden supplied the raw material for many of Hall's more complex herbal concoctions; a doctor had also to be a botanist. It has been beautifully restored, with an arbour and herbaceous border as well as herb garden. Shakespeare was intrigued by medical science. Theses have been written on the medicine in his plays, assumed to derive from his friendship with Hall.

STRATFORD-UPON-AVON: MARY ARDEN'S HOUSE *

Wilmcote, 4m NW of Stratford
Farm home of Shakespeare's mother (M)

We have Shakespeare's birthplace, his wife's house, his daughter's house and his granddaughter's house. Here, we even have his mother's family house, a substantial farm owned by the Arden family in the village of Wilmcote, north of the town. Recent research suggests that Glebe Farm, across a small meadow, may be the Arden house rather than the present building. The Shakespeare Birthplace Trust owns that as well. The holdings illustrate Shakespeare's rural roots alongside his upbringing as a tradesman's son. Mary Arden's House has been restored in Trust style, as picturesque as Anne Hathaway's Cottage. This is the Shakespeare of *As You Like It* and the Forest of Arden.

The first shock on passing the ticket desk is to encounter two live rams in a pen. This remains a farm. There are carts, calves, hayricks, a cider press and a dovecot, all listed in the will of Mary's father, Robert Arden. So too were the contents of the farmhouse, down to the pots, pans and furniture. They have been meticulously reinstated. The only anachronism in the living area is a Victorian mousetrap. The upstairs sleeping quarters were inserted at a later date into what had been a large open hall. The resulting attic beams offer a risk of banged heads.

In the Great Barn outside are further displays of Elizabethan and farmyard crafts. There is a working forge and falconry. Glebe Farm has now been restored and opened, and includes a late-Victorian laundry. It is all well done, the only omission being any dust, dirt or scruffiness. Perhaps they will come with time.

STRATFORD-UPON-AVON: NASH'S HOUSE *

Chapel Street
Elizabethan house, Shakespearean garden (M)

Shakespeare would recognize Stratford's Chapel Street and Church Street. A Gothic church tower acts as the focus of a series of jettied upper storeys and timbered façades. On one side are the buildings of the Bard's old school. Beyond is the house occupied by Thomas Nash, who married Shakespeare's granddaughter (*see* Northampton: Abington/Northants). It is next to the site of New Place, where Shakespeare himself had a house for the last eighteen years of his life and where he died in 1616. The demolition and replacement of New Place in 1702, when its historic importance was already known, was a tragedy. The replacement was destroyed in 1759. We can only wander in the garden that marks its site.

New Place would have been similar to Nash's House. It is the most museum-like of the five Shakespeare houses, with pictures and furnishings of the period. On the ground floor, the hall, parlour and kitchen are emphatically Dutch, reflecting close links between Britain and Holland at the turn of the 17th century. Porcelain and Flemish pictures line the walls. In the hall is a 'cupboard of boxes', a large 16th-century dresser. The kitchen is dis-

played as in the 19th century, reflecting the time when this part of the house was extended. (I note that museums require authenticity except when someone decides otherwise.)

The rooms upstairs contain a museum of Stratford history, including the first Shakespeare festival organized in the town by the actor David Garrick, in 1769. Outside, the knot garden is based on Elizabethan books and features plants mentioned in Shakespeare's plays. Beyond a pergola on the site of Shakespeare's old house is the Great Garden, flanked by an extraordinary yew hedge fronting the road. It is a series of trees shaped like gun batteries, with box hedges behind as ammunition. Who, other than tourists, is the enemy?

UPTON HOUSE **

7m NW of Banbury
Inter-war house rebuilt for art collection (NT)

The first Viscount Bearsted was the son of an East End importer of decorative sea shells. He founded an oil company, which he named after his father's passion. His son in turn acquired an estate in Warwickshire and extended it in 1927 by buying a William-and-Mary hunting box at Upton.

Bearsted devoted himself not only to chairing his father's company but to amassing a huge art collection. Desperate to avoid death duties and the consequent break up of his collection, he gave it to the National Trust in 1948, heavily endowed. The condition was that his descendants be granted a perpetual tenancy. Samuels lived in the house until 1988 and the family still owns most of the estate, where they have a new house.

Upton is visited to see its paintings, porcelain and gardens, not architecture. Its 1920s interior is of the sort favoured by the international super-rich. Even the National Trust guidebook awards it 'the impersonality of a hotel or a liner'. Most of the rooms constitute a furnished art gallery, attended by a well-meaning but bossy staff. The pictures are unlabelled (as if in a private house) but numbered at random and not listed in numerical order in the catalogue, rendering it near unusable. Any attempt to retrace one's steps to see a missed painting is stopped by guards.

Yet the Upton collection is a model of personal connoisseurship, one of those miniature 'national galleries' which abound in English houses. The entrance hall is hung with four Brussels tapestries. The first of the display rooms, the dining room, contains three Stubbs masterpieces, *The Haymakers*, *The Labourers* and *The Reapers*, majestic tributes to the dignity of work. The Long Gallery contains Dutch masters, including some charming Jan Steens. Cases of porcelain are predominantly of Chelsea.

The Picture Room gathers together historical English portraits by Reynolds and Raeburn and a Romney of William Beckford. Here hang two Hogarths for his print series of *The Four Times of Day*. The separate Picture Gallery, converted from a new squash court in the 1930s, displays works by Memling, van der Weyden, El Greco, Tintoretto and Hieronymous Bosch, the more enjoyable for being little known.

The gardens at Upton are, for Warwickshire, unusual. The lawn stretching away from the south front falls to what looks like a ha-ha, with a sheep-clad hillside in the distance. On closer inspection, it is not a ha-ha but a deep ravine. Terraces and herbaceous borders, avenues and ponds stretch over a mile into the distance. The National Trust's new restaurant in a handsome neo-classical style by Jeffrey Haworth is boldly sited as a garden feature.

WARWICK CASTLE ✶✶✶✶

Warwick
Grand castle with interiors recreating medieval, 17th-century and Edwardian eras
(P)

Everything about Warwick is spectacular – the setting, the old town, the church, the high street and, above all, the castle. The last has seen every touch, turn and treachery of English history. When the hereditary custodians,

the Brooke family, mercifully sold the place to Madame Tussaud's in 1978 and vanished overseas, the place at last came into its own.

Visiting Warwick Castle is a major (and costly) undertaking. Tussaud's run it as a business. They get no grant and give no quarter to critics of theme-park presentation. The castle is displayed round three periods, the Middle Ages, a 17th-century palace of state and a Victorian aristocratic residence. All are excellently done and Warwick is a delight to visit. It is a model of how hundreds of similar houses must adapt when they are no longer residences but must attract the public as customers rather than supplicants. If a house cannot be a home, at least let it pack a punch as Warwick does.

The original castle of William the Conqueror survives on a mound behind the existing one. The surrounding bailey was progressively fortified in the 12th and 13th centuries. But it was the arrival of the Beauchamps in 1268 that produced the present romantic composition, of towers, halls and curtain walls. The Beauchamps, first alone and then through marriage to the Nevilles, embodied the might of baronial England. They fought, schemed, married, built and fought again. Then they built some more.

The last of the line, the 'Kingmaker' Richard Neville, deposed two kings during the Wars of the Roses before falling to the Yorkists at the Battle of Barnet in 1471. After his death, the castle was seized and held by the Crown, until James I awarded it to the Fulke Grevilles, later Barons Brooke; they regained the title of Earls of Warwick in the 18th century.

The castle's outer wall shuts it away from the town along its entire length. Once inside the grounds, however, we see the work of centuries. Most magnificent is the view from the River Avon below, of the main façade and Caesar's Tower. Here Warwick is presented as a textbook of military-cum-residential architecture, on a par with Windsor (Berks), Arundel (Sussex) and Raby (Durham). While

Tudor charity: Lord Leycester Hospital

it is hard to tell medieval from Victorian restoration, I am inclined to answer, so what? From the 14th century to the 19th the English have regarded castellation as the true sign of ancestral dignity.

The interior is approached through the inner bailey. The castle today presents itself in three distinct guises. First, we see it enmeshed in the Wars of the Roses on the eve of battle. The torture chamber and dungeon of death or glory are accompanied with armouries, smithies, stables and fond farewells. These are the best tableau recreations of medieval England that I know. Elsewhere in the bailey are lesser keeps, turrets, ramparts and a haunted tower. The last is furnished in the Jacobean style of its restorer, Sir Fulke Greville, who was killed in an argument over money with a servant. In his room is a magnificent Jacobean bed. His ghost is said still to haunt the tower.

The residential castle begins with the chapel and state dining room. In the latter hangs one of five van Dyck depictions of Charles I on a horse. The Great Hall contains a mass of armour, beams and bears. Here too is the celebrated Kenilworth Buffet, covered in Victorian carving depicting Elizabeth I's arrival in splendour at Kenilworth Castle to be entertained by her admirer, Dudley.

There follows a sumptuous suite of Stuart and Georgian reception rooms, named Red, Cedar and Green. Queen Anne's bedroom was furnished for a visit in 1704 which never occurred. She was dreadful at keeping these dates. The tapestries depict royal gardens; their colours were fixed with urine, a workman being paid to drink quantities of beer to maintain supplies.

Finally comes Warwick's tableau of an Edwardian 'royal weekend party', based on a genuine 1898 guest list. Guests preparing for dinner included the Prince of Wales, Lord Curzon, the Dukes of Devonshire and Marlborough, Randolph Churchill and their ladies. The characters are depicted in Tussaud's finest wax, gossiping, dressing, singing, smoking and having their hair prepared for dinner. A maid even fills a bath (with real water). This is done with admirable realism, as close to life as artifice allows. If wax we must have, let it be Tussaud's wax.

WARWICK: THE LORD LEYCESTER HOSPITAL **

High Street
Surviving medieval guild premises (M)

The Lord Leycester Hospital lies over the West Gate into Warwick beneath the outer walls of the castle. It was home to the pre-Reformation United Guilds of Warwick, a group of societies which worshipped in the old chantry chapel of St James above the gate and met in buildings flanking the street. After the Dissolution, Robert Dudley, Earl of Leicester, sought a home for his pensioner soldiers and their wives, and acquired the guild premises. In 1571 they were assigned to a Master and twelve resident Brethren.

Thus they have remained ever since, with only a mild adjustment to the governance and a reduction from twelve brethren to eight. They support themselves by keeping the place in order and selling tickets to tourists. They must worship every day in the chapel, where each has a stall.

The ensemble is picturesque and often in use as a film set. The courtyard is surrounded by the old guild hall, the Great Hall, the kitchen and the Master's house. The last is a colourful Victorian veneer on what was an unstable timbered wall, now painted to look original. The heraldic emblems are added for antique effect: the Bear and Ragged Staff is the emblem of Dudley and the Porcupine of his descendants, the Sidneys. The Great Hall dates from the 1380s, with a magnificent queen-post roof. The plastic chairs are a pity.

The hall in which the guilds met is later, c1450, but smaller and more barnlike, with collar-beams and plaster walls. It forms part of a regimental museum. Back in the courtyard is the brethren's kitchen where the inmates ate collectively until given self-contained flats in the 1960s. The room is now a cafeteria where tourists eat under the motto 'droit et loyal'.

Wiltshire

Wiltshire's landscape can lay claim to the oldest settlements in England. Apart from the temples at Stonehenge and Avebury, little of this survives. But we sense it on the Marlborough Downs and the majestic curves of Salisbury Plain, the largest untilled chalk downland in Britain. Later in history, the county was one of the richest in medieval England. A contemporary said its wild uplands 'could sustain an infinity of sheep' and its wooded valleys offer fast flowing water for its cloth mills. Scratch the history of any Wiltshire manor and you find cloth. In the 15th and 16th centuries, the flanks of the Cotswolds rolled bales of wool into the watermills of the Wiltshire valleys. Until the 17th century it was the most industrialized part of England, dominated after the Dissolution by three grandees, Herbert of Wilton, Thynne of Longleat and Sharington of Lacock.

Of early Wiltshire, we still have the manors. Those of Avebury, Great Chalfield, Norrington and Westwood are classics from the 15th and 16th centuries. Their intensive rescue in the Edwardian era was one of the unsung triumphs of the early conservation movement. They are surpassed by two of the most impressive Elizabethan houses in England, the 'reversible façades' of Littlecote and a supreme work of the early English Renaissance, Longleat. Robert Smythson, who worked on Longleat, may also have designed the handsome front of Corsham.

Wilton remains the best surviving work attributable at least in part to Inigo Jones, with its Single and Double Cube Rooms now splendidly restored. From the late 17th century are the gracious mansions round Salisbury Close, notably Mompesson and Malmesbury Houses. Palladian Georgian is represented by the Hoares' Stourhead and by the sad Bolingbroke house at Lydiard. Late-Georgian classicism is present at Pythouse and Philipps House.

The county was not a centre of Victorian activity, with the exception of Crace's interiors at Longleat, but the Edwardians did more than restore old manors. At Hamptworth they showed they could refresh Jacobethan with the finest amateur craftsmanship.

Gloucestershire

Bibury

Oxfordshire

Woodchester

Kelmscott

Berkeley   Owlpen   Rodmarton   Buscot Old Parsonage

Chavenage   Buscot Park

CIRENCESTER

M5

Newark

Westonbirt

A419

A361

Lydiard   SWINDON   Ashdown

M4   A429

A350

Berkshir

Dyrham   A420

A4361

CHIPPENHAM

A346

Corsham   Bowood   A4   Littlecote   Welfor

Lacock   Avebury   Froxfield

MARLBOROUGH

A350   A361

BATH   Great Chalfield   A342

Claverton

Holt   A342   DEVIZES

Westwood   A361

Norton St Philip   A342

A36   A338

Beckington   ANDOVER

Somerset   Wiltshire

A362   A360

Longleat   Hampshire

A350   A36   A30

Stourhead   A303   Houghton

Philipps House   Little Clarendon

Pythouse   Wilton   SALISBURY   Mottisfont

Old Wardour   A30   A354   A36

Norrington Manor   Romsey

Breamore   Hamptworth

M27

Chettle

Fiddleford   Dorset

10 Miles

Avebury ******
Bowood ******
Corsham ******
Froxfield:
    Somerset Hospital *****
Great Chalfield
    Manor *******
Hamptworth ******
Holt:
    The Courts *****
Lacock ********

Little Clarendon *****
Littlecote *******
Longleat ********
Lydiard *******
Marlborough:
    Merchant's
    House ******
Norrington Manor ******
Old Wardour Castle ******
Philipps House *****
Pythouse ******

Salisbury:
    The King's House *****
    Malmesbury
        House *******
    Mompesson House ******
    The Wardrobe *****
Stourhead *******
Swindon:
    Railway Cottage *****
Westwood *******
Wilton *********

AVEBURY MANOR ******

Avebury, 6m W of Marlborough
Elizabethan manor amid the stones (NT)

I prefer Avebury to Stonehenge. Its stone circles and avenues are scattered round the old village, looming beside the road and behind back gardens. They are like Don Giovanni's Commendatore, the past eager to grasp us in a clammy hand. The early Christians founded a monastery outside the circle to avoid (or appease) its pagan demons. This may have formed the basis of the present manor.

Avebury was bought in 1547 by William Sharington of neighbouring Lacock, possibly on the profits of clipping the coinage at the Bristol Mint, a serious crime for which he narrowly escaped execution. The manor was later a farmhouse, until being restored in 1902 by Leopold and Nora Jenner. They made Avebury a model of vernacular restoration. Hudson remarked on its 'true note of homeliness … with enough variety of style and character to give a sense of continuous habitation'.

After 1935, the house frequently changed hands. It was left empty for years although various commercial uses were planned. It was acquired by the National Trust in 1991 and refurnished by tenants, but lacks the character of its more celebrated contemporaries. A lecture tour of just the five rooms on view is compulsory, where none is needed.

The entrance leads into a screens passage with a library to the left and hall to the right. The latter, lit by large Elizabethan windows, was modernized in the early 18th century with classical doors and panelling. It is rather bleak. The two best rooms are upstairs, the Tudor Bedroom and the Great Chamber above the hall. The overmantel in the former is c1600, its scrollwork and arcaded panel complementing a curvilinear ceiling. In the Great Chamber the embroidery of the bed covers was by Mrs Jenner, whose ubiquitous needlework is outstanding.

The best feature of Avebury is its garden, with a circular yew border. This was laid out by the Jenners in the style of Gertrude Jekyll, strongly architectural and well maintained.

BOWOOD HOUSE ******

4m SE of Chippenham
Fragment of Adam house with gallery (P)

When the 8th Marquess of Lansdowne retired from Bowood to Perthshire in 1972, he warned his son that 'you may find maintaining the house and estate quite a challenge'. It was a challenge he had considerably eased in 1955 by flattening Henry Keene and Robert Adam's so-called Big House and retreating into the Little House, a rear extension at the back.

Lansdowne had inherited Bowood from a

cousin who had died in the Second World War, but even in the 1950s the demolition was controversial. The family's Lansdowne House in Berkeley Square had been demolished before the war. To demolish two great houses inside a generation was going too far. Adam's Bowood dining room is now bizarrely suspended halfway up Lloyd's of London in Leadenhall Street.

The Marquess's son, the Earl of Shelburne, converted the fragmentary remains of the property into a country estate run as a business concern. He lives in the Little House and has redecorated Adam's Diocletian Orangery and screen as an art gallery and museum. The screen was designed to conceal the service courtyards, and now supplies an architectural backdrop to the formal gardens.

The Orangery is open to the public. Its gallery is filled with Old Masters and historical and contemporary works. In the middle is a chapel, erected in the 19th century by C. R. Cockerell. The reredos frames a central Madonna, adapted from an organ case reputedly by William Kent.

At one end of the Orangery is Cockerell's neo-classic library, converted from a surviving Adam room. It is a virtuoso chamber, warmly decorated with ceiling medallions of classical writers and fine Wedgwood urns on the bookcases. The Orangery's other end leads through Adam doors, rescued from the Big House, into a tapestry gallery hung with sculptures.

The former stables have been converted into an exhibition wing. This contains a reproduction Georgian room with effigies, costumes and original pictures and furniture. Upstairs is the Bowood collection of watercolours, with works by Turner, Varley, Lear and Bonington.

CORSHAM COURT **

Corsham
Tudor mansion with Grand Tour collection
(P)

Corsham Court lies in one of the prettiest villages in Wiltshire, glimpsed from afar across a vista of parkland. Owned by one family, the Methuens, since the 18th century, it is guarded by a skirting of parish church, voluptuous yews and 16th-century riding school. Its Elizabethan walls have received the attention of Robert Smythson (possibly), Henry Keene, Capability Brown, Humphry Repton, John Nash and Thomas Bellamy yet the original character of the house has somehow survived. It is filled with a prodigious collection of Grand Tour art.

The house was begun by an Elizabethan merchant, Thomas Smythe, in 1582 with sufficient echoes of Longleat to suggest the hand of Robert Smythson. In 1745, the property was bought by Paul Methuen, descendant of a Bradford-on-Avon clothier. He had Capability Brown extend the building to display his collection of Italian and Dutch paintings. In the 1840s, these were augmented by the Sanford bequest of Old Masters after the marriage of another Paul Methuen to Anna Sanford in 1844. This required a Victorian north front by Bellamy, a copy of the Elizabethan south front.

The interiors are a little cold, as if the main rooms had been turned over to a museum and the family fled (which is not true). Display cases and neon lights deprive the rooms of domesticity. Visiting Corsham is like visiting an elderly great-aunt, albeit a magnificent one.

The state rooms are now filled with the paintings and furniture of a Georgian man of taste. The picture gallery contains van Dyck's *Betrayal of Christ* and in the Cabinet Room is a Filippo Lippi Annunciation. The Octagon Room, albeit no longer so shaped, contains a beautiful Michelangelo of a sleeping Cupid and two superb Rococo mirrors. There are also works by Claude, del Sarto and Guercino. The corridors and halls are lined with display cases of porcelain.

Corsham has fine grounds and an arboretum. Apart from the yews to the west and a lake to the east, the drooping arms of an oriental plane on the lawn are 240ft in perimeter. Beyond is Capability Brown's Cold Bath House of 1761, a charming Gothick conceit and a handsome landscape.

Corsham: the garden front

FROXFIELD: SOMERSET HOSPITAL *

Froxfield, 4m W of Hungerford
Extensive almshouse with Gothick chapel (P)

This is one of the largest and grandest of 17th-century almshouses. The founder was the Duchess of Somerset in 1694. The ranges are set round a long rectangular garden with a smart Regency Gothic chapel in the middle, far more generous than the customary pokey quadrangle. The hospital sits on the A4, the former Great West Road, and is an enticing a place to end one's days as I can imagine.

The building is clearly of two periods. The early ranges are to the right of the entrance gate with stone-mullioned windows. The range to the left has identical roofs and dormers but the windows are no longer stone but wood. This later work is dated 1775, by when the original design must have seemed exceptionally old-fashioned. The chapel, dated 1813, in the courtyard is delightful. It has bold pinnacles and a whimsical panel of crocketed gables on the side facing the entrance.

The hospital was intended to serve the needs of twenty retired clergy and thirty lay widows. It still does.

GREAT CHALFIELD MANOR ***

Great Chalfield, 3m SW of Melksham
Ancient manor with restored wings (NT)

Great Chalfield has long been a front runner in the 'best medieval manor' stakes. It sits in a Wiltshire countryside as yet unpolluted by development. There is a moat, gatehouse and barn to guard its beauty and an adjacent church to guard its soul. Such houses have at some time needed a kindly restorer. Great Chalfield's was Robert Fuller, a local businessman who bought it in 1878 and began restoration in 1905.

The house was built c1470 on the profit of wool, that of Thomas Tropnell, clothier and lawyer. The layout was traditional, a hall house with a courtyard to the rear. What was novel was that the services and kitchens were pushed to the back. The front thus has not one but two 'family' wings either end of the Hall, both gabled and with elegant Perpendicular oriels. One gable is crowned with an armed soldier, the other with a dog and monkey.

By the 19th century, the solar wing was derelict and the Great Hall was divided into farm workers' quarters. Fuller set about rescuing the place. He had the Corsham architect, Harold Brakspear, completely rebuild the solar wing, which gives visitors the familiar West Country problem of disentangling Edwardian work from medieval. The house passed to the National Trust as an early gift in 1943, but with the Fuller family, now the Floyds, in continued residence. On my last visit, the rooms were very much occupied, the Great Hall recovering from a teenage party.

This Great Hall still rises the full height of the building. Its interior is of the original proportions, but has been edwardianized, with a new minstrels' gallery above a reproduction screen. High on the solar wall are grimacing viewing masks, peepholes through which ladies might have watched what was happening below.

To the right of the entrance is Tropnell's dining room, with an Elizabethan plaster ceiling and panelling. On the wall is a mural painting, believed to be of Tropnell himself. The figure is shown with five fingers plus a thumb, considered to be a sign of covetousness. If it is indeed Tropnell, this is the earliest picture of a Member of Parliament in England. Above the dining room is a bedroom with an ante-room over the porch; this contains a concealed bath tub. In the bedroom window are depicted two birds advising, 'Love God, drede shame, desire worship and kepe thy name.' Name was synonym for everything from reputation to boy heirs.

At the other end of the Great Hall is the solar, as rebuilt in the 1900s. The upper chamber is a re-creation of the original, Brakspear being meticulous in his archaeology. The semi-circular oriel window, copied from Victorian drawings, is a conceit of fan vaults

and pendants. It offers a view over the front courtyard and little church belfry, a placid English scene.

South of the house, beyond the footings of the old quadrangle, the land falls away towards former stew ponds. The roses are undiluted by hybrids, as English as the house itself.

HAMPTWORTH LODGE **

Hamptworth, 11m SE of Salisbury
Jacobean revival house with homemade furniture (P-R)

In 1910, the wealthy Edwardian eccentric, Harold Moffatt, bought Hamptworth Lodge, took one look at it and cried, 'Thank God, dry rot!' He demolished the place and, with the architect, Guy Dawber, built a new Jacobethan mansion. It had all modern conveniences and a spacious internal layout.

Moffatt made almost all the interior carpentry and furniture himself. Although he also rebuilt Goodrich Court in Herefordshire, Hamptworth was his masterpiece. As the classicists had striven to recreate Palladio at Chiswick (London, W), so Moffatt strove to recreate the Middle Ages. Hamptworth must be England's most remarkable display of amateur cabinet-making, if amateur is the word.

The exterior displays a fanatical revivalism. The walls are timber-framed. Some windows have stone mullions, some wood. Gables sweep down on all sides, with large chimneys rising above them. Entry is into a screens passage with a staircase hall and gallery. This forms the heart of the house. Two downstairs drawing rooms, one for men, one for women, are entirely neo-Tudor. The furniture is either 'period' or Moffatt reproduction.

The dining room table and sideboard are by Moffatt, as are the oak chairs with strapwork. So too are the dressers, one of them inlaid with mother-of-pearl. Some of the bedroom ceilings are barrel-vaulted, others have complex Jacobean plasterwork. The largest room in the house is the Great Hall with an unusual roof construction. It houses a Willis organ and has a wooden screen, again by Moffatt.

Many rooms display 'apprentice pieces', miniatures made by young carpenters as advertisements. They were favourites in Moffatt's collection. The house is now owned by Moffatt's descendants, the Andersons, who are admirably respectful of his work.

HOLT: THE COURTS *

2m SE of Melksham
Secret garden by Georgian clothier's house
(NT-G)

The Courts is a gem of a house. Its National Trust tenant from 1943 to 1990 was Moyra Goff, spinster daughter of the former owner. She adored the garden, planted its arboretum and raced her magnificent AC Cobra sports car up and down the street outside until she was well over eighty. Locals swore that she deliberately increased the speed commensurate with her age.

The house is small and the garden disproportionately large. Only the garden is at present open to the public, but the house façade is so integral to it as to make them seem one and the same creation. A small gateway leads from the main street into a short avenue of pleached limes. This is closed at the far end by the house's classical façade in warm Bath stone.

The Courts was built by a Quaker clothier in c1720 on the site of the old village court. He used the stream that flows through the garden to power a small mill, and to dye the finished cloth. The mill stream ran where the main lawn is now. He built onto his house a Georgian façade fit for a gentleman. This is a delight, appearing rather as a façade with a house attached to the back.

The style is anything but Quaker. It might rather be termed Clothier's Baroque, with similar flourishes to those found on the chest tombs round the parish church of Painswick in Gloucestershire. The doorway has Tuscan columns and a curved broken pediment. The window pediment above has scrolls, flanked by more windows with broken pediments. It is all topped off with a bold gable. Pevsner

called it all the product of 'a vulgar mind', art historian's snobbery.

The garden layout was started by Sir George Hastings after 1900, but within nine years he had sold the property to two ladies, Miss Barclay and Miss Trim, and then to Major Goff and his wife, Lady Cecilie. It was they who perfected the garden we see today, Lady Cecilie mapping the enclosed flower gardens. Her philosophy was that a garden should be a thing of mystery and not be seen entirely from one viewpoint. The Yew Walk has a topiary of dancing bears.

LACOCK ABBEY ****

Lacock, 3m N of Melksham
Renaissance and Gothick conversion of ancient abbey (NT)

One gloomy winter afternoon during the Second World War, James Lees-Milne arrived at Lacock to negotiate its transfer to the National Trust. He found himself trapped. The spinster owner, Matilda Talbot, was maintaining her tradition of a regular *thé dansant* in the Great Hall. 'Where she collected her young ladies from, it is hard to say,' Lees-Milne recalled. 'All were exceedingly plain and utterly speechless. To an ancient gramophone which required winding every two minutes, we danced the Roger de Coverley while the fog swirled against the Gothick windows . . .'

The music was a lament for the decline of the English house. Not since the 1539 Dissolution of the old nunnery had Lacock's fate seemed so hopeless as in the 1940s. Yet Lacock is with us still, complete with its estate and picture village. Talbots are in part occupation. This lovely house is secure once more.

With the closure of the monastery, Lacock passed to William Sharington, a rogue best known for debasing the coinage in the Bristol Mint and narrowly escaping execution. But he respected medieval architecture and was eager to convert rather than demolish his acquisition. Unlike most Tudor occupiers of monastic remains, he kept the conventual buildings in place, retaining the intimate, claustral atmosphere. Sharington's tower at Lacock of *c*1550 is a superb example of Tudor Renaissance, as is his tomb in the parish church.

Sharington was succeeded by his brother, whose daughter, Olive, fell in love with a Talbot from Shrewsbury, a descendant of the abbey's original founder. Defying her father's opposition, she is said to have leaped from the abbey roof into her lover's arms, saved from injury by her voluminous petticoats acting as a parachute. To this Lacock invention, a later Talbot, the Victorian William Henry Fox, added that of calotype photography. Grainy relics of his work can be seen throughout the house.

In 1753, John Ivory Talbot decided to gothicize Sharington's house, with the help of Sanderson Miller. It was one of the earliest instances of Georgian Gothick, and executed with panache. The old Great Hall was converted into a chamber just three bays wide, with a flowing double flight of steps leading up to the front door. Cupolas and a decorative parapet adorn the façade. The interior of the hall is a Sanderson masterpiece, as if Robert Adam had been asked to decorate a French museum of the Middle Ages. Talbot had the arms of his friends emblazoned in the ceiling, to share in the glory of his creation. On the north wall is a scapegoat, with a lump of sugar kept on its nose for almost a century, said to bring luck.

Lacock from this point on should be seen as two houses, one on the ground floor and formed of the former nunnery cloister, the other Tudor above. The upper residential floor contains the Sharington rooms, including the Brown Gallery, Stone Gallery, domestic apartments and South Gallery. The lower floor comprises the rooms of the convent, which Sharington left in place, but are now empty. They are a rare survival of a complete monastic set. These two layers are two unrelated houses, yet both pay obeisance to the building's history.

The galleries are filled with Talbot impedimenta, some valuable, most merely quaint. In the Brown Gallery are medieval carvings from

the old abbey and a portrait of Matilda Talbot, the last owner. The Stone Gallery was fashioned by Sharington from the old convent dormitory. It is like a medievalist's attic, a jumble of ancient stained glass, moose horns, funeral helms, a rocking horse and a fine set of Flemish shell-backed chairs. Portraits of the Gothick Talbot and his wife are by Dahl.

A group of 18th-century rooms forms the junction of the Stone Gallery and South Gallery. In one is displayed a copy of the Magna Carta, the only one still legible, which was presented in 1946 by the Talbots to the British Museum. Such copies were sent to every county by Henry III and this alone survived. Sharington's octagonal tower contains his Strong Room with, in its centre, the carved stone Lacock Table, an outstanding work of 16th-century English Renaissance. It rests on a classical capital surrounded by four satyrs on pedestals. Its carver was reputedly John Chapman.

The long South Gallery was much altered by Fox Talbot in the 19th century. It contains portraits of Sharington and other family members. Here too is the window that appeared in Fox Talbot's first-ever photograph in 1835, a dim outline of light on a dark chemical plate, wonderfully atmospheric. The photograph is on display.

The delight of Lacock is to wander from these busy, cluttered rooms downstairs to the serenely ascetic nunnery chambers. It is easy to see what fascinated owners, from the Elizabethans to the Victorians, with the medieval style. Here are fine vaulted rooms, with traceried windows and wall-paintings. Thanks to Sharington we have a memorial to what might have survived all over England, had it not been for the Dissolution.

The south cloister walk is worthy of a cathedral, with superb vault bosses. In the days of the nunnery, these were mostly service rooms for the living quarters above. They include the chaplain's room, sacristy, chapter house, warming room and rere-dorter. North of the main block is Sharington's stable courtyard, a charmingly unaltered work of the 16th century.

LITTLE CLARENDON *

Dinton, 6m W of Wilton
Daffodil breeder's medieval house (NT)

Little Clarendon needs a lit fire, a boiling kettle, a cat and an old lady. The house was a cottage and farmhouse from the 15th century, but was bought and restored in 1901 by the Reverend George Engleheart. His daughter, Catherine, recalled it as being in a 'dreadful state . . . divided up between two families in a warren of passages and rooms like biscuit tins . . . ceilings set to hide the old beams, and half the mullioned windows were built up'.

Within a year, Engleheart had returned the house to its medieval form and planted a charming cottage garden round it. He was an ardent breeder of daffodils, an obsession which 'drew him further away from clerical life'. His daffodils won him a medal from the Royal Horticultural Society, and still fill the garden in spring.

The house is in its 17th-century form. The two-storey porch gives onto what would have been the hall, with a medieval fireplace and low beams. To one side is the drawing room with vernacular furniture and more beams. The parlour or solar wing to the right is of three storeys with mullioned windows. The interior is furnished as the Englehearts left it, but the National Trust has scrubbed it within an inch of its life. All it needs is some rough edges.

LITTLECOTE ***

3m NW of Hungerford
Medieval and Elizabethan mansion,
Cromwellian chapel (H)

The great medieval house of Littlecote belonged to the Darrell family until it fell into the hands of 'Wild Darrell'. A bullying, lawless local grandee, he found himself accused of infanticide, and gave the house as a bribe to a lawyer cousin, Sir John Popham, later Lord Chief Justice. Darrell died falling from a horse in 1589. It was Popham who built the main late-Elizabethan façade of c1600, but he left the earlier Darrell house to the rear as an architectural Siamese twin. This gives Littlecote an extraordinary back-to-front appearance.

Pophams held the house into the 20th century when it passed to the Wills family. Then in 1985 and amid much controversy, it passed to the tycoon, Peter de Savary, who briefly turned it into a Cromwellian theme park. This did not last but the Littlecote collection of 17th-century weapons was sold to the Royal Armouries Museum. The house went to Warner Hotels, who are now trying to retrieve some of the armour.

Warners have saved many houses and gardens from a worse fate. Life has been breathed into once deserted interiors, which are more accessible than conversions into apartments. But 'mid-market hotel', as their literature claims, means what it says. Furniture and fittings tend to be institutional and all sense of original family occupation is lost. Littlecote needs to recapture its soul.

The front and rear are completely distinct. Popham's front is redbrick and E-plan, symmetrical and with tall windows on either side of the entrance. It is unadorned and dull, like a Victorian reproduction. The rear is fascinating. It is not one façade but two lying side by side – owners of Littlecote could not bear to demolish anything. On the right is the earliest, medieval, house of the Darrells, an old-fashioned hall with gabled cross-wings. On the left of this, added by the father of 'Wild Darrell' in the 1530s, is an E-plan extension primarily housing an early Long Gallery. Much restored by later generations of Pophams, it has a hexagonal bay window as frontispiece and walls of flint.

The interior is similarly divided between the Popham rooms at the front and a warren of medieval chambers behind. Popham's Great Hall has a fine Jacobean screen and plaster ceiling with pendants. The windows contain Continental stained glass and a love-knot of Henry VIII and Jane Seymour, who reputedly courted in this house (as in many others). The staircase was erected in the 19th century, when the kitchens were moved to a side wing. The drawing rooms are large and plain, although one has chinoiserie panels.

The rooms of the older house behind are exceptional. The Tudor chambers surviving from the Darrell house have been well conserved. They are entered from the library and begin with the Dutch Parlour. This enchanting room is entirely covered in panels painted by imprisoned Dutch seamen in the 1660s. They include scenes from *Don Quixote* and other Spanish legends and form a composition unlike any room in England.

A series of allegedly haunted rooms leads to a chapel, converted from the medieval hall. This survives as an unaltered Puritan preaching box, furnished in oak with pews, galleries and a pulpit where the altar would have been. The thin-seated pews were said to be designed so that any sleeper would 'drop off' them, hence the phrase. An oak staircase leads to Darrell's Long Gallery. This is again of oak, panelled and with thin pilasters. It carries a magnificent plaster frieze and a selection of Popham portraits.

Such was the Tudor revivalism of later Pophams that Littlecote never succumbed to naturalistic landscaping in the era of Capability Brown. Despite the depredations of the 20th century, both de Savary and the present owners have beautifully restored the herbaceous borders and walled gardens. We await the return of the old house.

LONGLEAT ★★★★

4m W of Warminster
Elizabethan mansion with Victorian interiors (P)

There is no finer sight in England than Longleat from the heights of Cranborne Chase on a late-autumn afternoon. The sun slants across the countryside. Animals, tame and wild, roam the park. The old house stands with the light full on its face, illuminating its walls with a golden flame. Architecture and nature are in total harmony.

Longleat was one of the great prodigy houses of the Elizabethan era, ranking with Wollaton (Notts) and Hardwick Hall (Derbys). The property was acquired by Sir John Thynne, later Steward to the Protector Somerset, in 1541. As befitted a servant of Edward VI, he was a zealous Protestant whom the Catholic Mary I ordered to 'remain in his own country' during her reign. After a fire in 1567, Thynne, by now an Elizabethan courtier, decided to rebuild Longleat. It was known as 'the first well-built house in England', its design evolving swiftly during its construction from gabled Tudor mansion to the epitome of an English Renaissance palace.

Longleat drew inspiration from the pre-eminent building of the age, old Somerset House in London, for which Thynne had been responsible to his patron, Somerset. Of this period only the exterior, the Great Hall and a number of chimneypieces survive. The interior was completely remodelled by Sir Jeffry Wyatville in 1806–13 and redecorated by J. G. Crace in the 1870s.

Yet, while Crace's interiors at Longleat are effusively Victorian, they match as well as any revivalist house of the period the ostentation of the 16th-century exterior. Thynnes occupy the house to this day, with increasing eccentricity. In 1949, it was the first house to open commercially to the public, introducing 'the lions of Longleat'. The exotic paintings and other manifestations of the bohemian lifestyle of the present Marquess of Bath add greatly to its appeal.

Seen close to, the outside of Longleat is a severe façade of classical pilasters rising three storeys to the flat roof. The latter is astonishing, a crowded forest of domes, banqueting pavilions, ornamented chimneys, finials and scrollwork. Thynne's guests were expected to climb up after dinner and promenade and play games among these devices, high above the woods spread out below them. It might all be a stage-set for *A Midsummer Night's Dream*.

Given the ruthlessness with which the 19th century treated Longleat, the survival untouched of the Great Hall illustrates the sanctity that attached to these shrines of ancestral history. The Hall is still set off-centre, reached by a screens passage. The ceiling bears the arms of Thynnes down the centuries and is supported by ten giant hammerbeams. The chimneypiece is original as are the panelling and minstrels' gallery. Even the original oak table remains, overlooked by the antlers of an Irish elk, now an extinct species whose remains were much beloved of Great Hall decorators everywhere.

From here on, the house is mostly of the 19th century. Modernization was carried out by the 2nd Marquess in the 1800s and his grandson in the 1870s. The first sought corridors and a grand staircase, to bring warmth and privacy to the rooms and ease of access for servants. The second wished to bring to his house the colour and romanticism of Italy. Seven of the main reception rooms are by Crace and are his masterpiece. Their only equal for Victorian Italianate is the grand suite at Alnwick (Northumbs).

The reception rooms on the ground floor are mostly libraries, seven in all. The house claims 40,000 books, the finest collection in Europe in private hands. The Red Library is Crace at his most vivid, with deeply embossed wall-coverings and gilded ceiling. No less extravagant is the breakfast room, with a superb Lawrence of the 1st Marquess and a Watts of the 4th Marchioness. Crace's ceiling to the dining room is more astonishing still, based on one in the Ducal Palace in Venice. Everywhere are Thynne portraits of all periods, including modern ones, often startlingly juxtaposed.

The rear corridors and stairs are decorated by the present Marquess. They include stained glass from the old chapel, modern paintings of his 'Wessex School' and an exhibition of the ravages of the voracious deathwatch beetle at Longleat. On the first floor are Crace's three great state rooms. His ceiling in the state dining room frames paintings by the school of Titian. A van Dyck depicts Isabella Rich, wife of Sir James Thynne in the reign of Charles I, who danced naked across old London Bridge. The room contains two exquisite Flemish ebony cabinets.

The saloon is formed from the old gallery, its ceiling based on the Palazzo Massimo in Rome and its fireplace based on one in the Doge's Palace. Flemish tapestries clothe the walls and Boulle furniture the floors. The drawing room ceiling takes us to the library of St Mark's Cathedral in Venice. Everything in this room is by Crace, apart from the Old Masters and furniture. His virtuosity as a 'revivalist' is as accomplished as that of William Kent for the Palladians. Yet who knows anything of Crace?

Longleat now rambles on with a life of its own. A corridor is decked with family dresses and cabinets of Sèvres and Dresden. The Chinese Bedroom has handpainted wallpaper. In the old music room can be found a Terborch portrait; in the Prince of Wales's Bedroom two superb Ruisdaels. The circuit is completed by Wyatville's Grand Staircase, a theatrical promenade hung with flamboyant Snyders pictures and some of the finest hunting works of the under-appreciated John Wootton.

The best-known paintings at Longleat are the murals by the present 7th Marquess. These were begun in 1964, ten years after the aristocratic hippy took up residence in the west wing. They are now said to cover a third of the house interiors. They are presented as 'keyhole glimpses into my psyche', and include pictures of the Marquess's various 'wifelets' and the 'Kama Sutra Mural'. Mosaics on psychedelic themes are being prepared by the Marquess's nephew, Alexander Thynne. Some of this comes with a taste warning, but in years to come the murals will doubtless be seen as important works of late 20th-century art.

Longleat once lay at the centre of an extensive web of formal parterres. These were swept away in the 18th century by Capability Brown and Repton, but have in part been restored. A huge maze, reputedly the largest anywhere, has been built and others are promised. The astonishing Safari Park, which rescued Longleat's finances in the 1950s, is well screened from view. The Elizabethans would have found nothing strange in elephants, giraffes, lions and monkeys gliding and prancing past their façades. Longleat was always the architecture of the exotic.

LYDIARD HOUSE ***

Lydiard Tregoze, 4m W of centre of Swindon
Palladian box with Georgian decoration (M)

In 1873, the 5th Viscount Bolingbroke (and 6th Viscount St John) demanded that the loud hooter on the Great Western Railway's Swindon factory be silenced. Used to summon workers from nearby villages, the hooter woke him at 5.15 every morning. Since the workers lost pay if they were a minute late, the hooter was a local necessity and a petition of 4,339 names was raised to keep it. It was silenced on his lordship's request, with the help of a doctor witness. The nation rose in ridicule and the railway installed another hooter with a different note. His lordship was humiliated. It blew its last in 1986.

This was not the first reverse suffered by the St John family. They inherited Lydiard House from the Beauchamps, whose old hall can still be seen in traces to the rear of the present house. Active in the Civil War, a St John saw three of his sons die for the King while two triumphed with Cromwell. A later St John rose to political prominence, and in 1712 was ennobled under the old family title of Bolingbroke.

Money was always short and the house which Bolingbroke rebuilt in 1743 was always in debt. By the 20th century, the family had retreated before advancing decay. When Lydiard was requisitioned in 1940, it was declared unfit even for military habitation. The family sold it to Swindon Corporation for £4,500. The interior was restored and it is now an excellent museum.

Lydiard was possibly designed by Roger Morris in the 1740s, the main façade in the style of Inigo Jones. A Palladian box is elaborated by a pedimented central bay and corner pavilions with pyramid roofs. The main rooms retain their Georgian decoration, with rich stucco ceilings. The council has struggled to acquire and reinstate the original St John pictures and furnishings, and even dares a wax effigy of 'Hooter' St John at his desk in the library. A concession to showmanship is the numerous teddy bears strewn about the rooms for children to count.

The dining room is laid for dessert, with what remains of the St Johns' own tea and coffee service. The drawing room still has its 18th-century damask flock wallpaper, and the ceiling is a copy of Inigo Jones's ceiling from the Queen's House, Greenwich (London, E). An oddity is the state bedroom. This was previously the ballroom and part of its ceiling is delightfully Rococo. The picture frames, painted grey, are said to derive from the colour used by the St Johns when told they could not afford regilding.

The gem of the house is a 17th-century Huguenot painted window in the boudoir, made of quarries depicting rural and mythical scenes. Here too are pictures by an 18th-century Lady Diana Spencer, wife of the 2nd Viscount, whose speciality was cupids and the like. Her own portrait hangs here and she is strikingly similar to her relation.

MARLBOROUGH: MERCHANT'S HOUSE **

132 High Street
Intact Cromwellian town house, painted interiors (M)

In April 1653, a Marlborough tanner who had 'professed himself to be Christ' found his house consumed by fire. A strong wind carried the flames throughout the town, destroying 250 properties. In the recent Civil War, Marlborough had supported Cromwell, who duly organized a national collection to help in rebuilding. This took place swiftly. Within a year John Evelyn could declare the place 'now new built'.

There are few buildings intact from this period. One is the Merchant's House on the north side of the High Street. The building is timber-framed and tile-hung, with three bold gables surmounting its third storey. It was a

'Hooter' St John in Lydiard's library

branch of W. H. Smith until acquired in 1991 by the council and given to a trust. This is seeking to restore the interiors to their 1650s state, evidence for which miraculously remains in all eighteen rooms that will one day be on display.

The house belonged to a silk merchant, Thomas Bayly, and includes to its rear an extraordinary dining room. This was painted with vertical stripes to look like coloured silk wall-hangings, decoration which was admirably restored before English Heritage began meddling. The beefy, 17th-century staircase has carved balusters, matched by the same balusters painted on the walls. On the top flight are Italian cedar panels on built-in cupboards.

The first floor is one large panelled room with a bay window looking out over the market place. In its window pane is a stained-glass sundial, with a fly in its central panel, a play on the phrase, 'time flies'. The wide beamed floor is deliciously undulating, like the contours of a Wiltshire Down. The room cries out for furniture of the period.

The house is in severe danger of becoming a monument to conservationist pedantry. The trust battles against bureaucrats whose job seems to be to hinder not help those struggling to preserve old buildings. Original windows discovered in later walls cannot be restored and are absurdly represented by paint. The staircase murals have been restored only as fragments to give 'an impression' of the original and are so absurd as to be surreal. Some paintwork over fireplaces and round cornices has been reinstated, some has been 'conserved as found'. Grants are offered for education officers and project managers, not carpenters or painters. It is all mad.

This house, properly furnished and with its decoration reinstated, would be a superb example of a mid-17th century town house, to rank with the Red Lodge in Bristol (Somerset) or Restoration House in Rochester (Kent). This will never happen while its custodians are crippled by red tape and London faddishness. Marlborough should revive the spirit of Cromwell.

NORRINGTON MANOR **

near Alvediston, 12m SW of Wilton
Medieval farmhouse with undercroft and solar (P-R)

The old manor of Norrington lies secluded high on Cranborne Chase. It is invisible from a distance, nor can it see any other house. Here in deepest Wiltshire a medieval hall was built by the Gawen family in 1377, passing to the Wyndhams in 1658. A wing was added and the house bought by the Sykes family, its present owners, in 1952.

The first glimpse over the hill is a delight. Gothic windows mark the hall, with a medieval porch to the right and later wings projecting on both sides. The façade is pleasantly clothed in greenery. The porch contains a Gothic vault of tierceron ribs and a boss of a monster with its mouth open, a sophisticated carving.

The interior has been much altered. The screens passage has become an entrance hall and the hall a comfortable sitting room. Most interesting is the now derelict solar wing. This has been left agricultural, with an undercroft as richly vaulted as the porch. This could have been a chapel, storeroom or manorial treasury. There is a fragment of a Tudor stair tower outside. Above is the old parlour, with a large fireplace and windows, still displaying the dereliction that afflicted many English manors before 20th-century gentrification.

The other wing of the house, which would have contained the manorial offices, was rebuilt in the 17th century as the private house. The Sykes family, soldiers and farmers, take a lively interest in local history.

OLD WARDOUR CASTLE **

12m SW of Wilton
Ruin of medieval and Elizabethan mansion (EH)

Where would they be, these great fortified houses of England, had there been no Civil War? It led to the 'slighting' or destruction of hundreds of them. Yet without that war, some far worse cataclysm might have engulfed their custodians. France and Germany kept their châteaux and schlossen but later revolutions and wars left few in as good a state as those that survived in England.

Old Wardour is buried in the tumbling hills of Cranborne Chase. It looks across the valley to 18th-century New Wardour, now a monument to the stability that created the English Picturesque. The castle was built as a 'fortified residence' by Lord Lovel at the end of the 14th century, during the brief but dazzling reign of Richard II. At the time, courtiers' residences were harking back to a more chivalrous and romantic past.

The castle's plan was hexagonal, a shape derived from Burgundian castles of the Duc de Berry. It had a central Great Hall with symmetrical wings set at uniform angles, a form unusual in England at this early date. Overlooked by a hillside and composed entirely of vulnerable angles and walls, it was for show and not for war.

In 1547 the house was sold to a Cornish grandee, Sir Thomas Arundell, whose son Matthew reordered it, possibly with help from Robert Smythson in the 1570s. Matthew enlarged the windows and inserted the larger chambers needed for Elizabethan entertainment. The Arundells were Catholics and the house was besieged in the Civil War and bravely defended by Lady Blanche Arundell and her household, many of them women. Like Lady Bankes's defence of Corfe Castle (Dorset), such female heroism became the stuff of Royalist legend. One side of the castle collapsed through sapping during the siege.

The family moved to Breamore (Hants), not returning to a smaller house in the grounds until the 18th century. In 1769 the 8th Lord Arundell commissioned James Paine to build him a new house two miles away across a lake. The old castle formed the focal point in early landscaping by Capability Brown. The paying public were admitted as early as 1830. This view survives today. New Wardour is now a private residence, after half a century as Cranborne Chase, a girls' boarding school.

A surprising amount of the entrance front and outer walls of the castle survives. A corner turret, a fine Renaissance doorway and assorted fireplaces and tower rooms may all be admired. In the garden the 1773 Banqueting House is intact and used as a 'Victorian' tea-room. A grotto and fake stone circle complete the setting for what amounted to a true Georgian theme park.

PHILIPPS HOUSE *

Dinton, 6m W of Wilton
Regency classicism in sylvan landscape (NT)

Philipps House does not get a good press. Its own National Trust guidebook uses such words as 'uninspired … austere and unadorned', yet the drive across the estate is magnificent and the sight of the house in the distance is most picturesque. It was built in 1813 for the local squire, William Wyndham, by Sir Jeffry Wyatville. The house was sold to Bertram Philipps in 1917, from whom it passed to the Trust in 1943, becoming a YWCA hostel. The house is now privately tenanted, the main reception rooms being open to the public.

Philipps House is Wyatville at his most Soanian and severe. The exterior is a rectangular stone box, adorned with a simple Ionic portico. No vegetation is permitted to soften the exterior. Inside, the hall frieze offers a brief flourish of shells and cornucopia. Decorative exhaustion then sets in. The staircase hall demonstrates Wyatville's strongest suit, a flair for large spaces.

The whole house is arranged round this staircase. Its cold stone is almost surreal, with galleries hidden behind columned screens. The stair treads are thin and the space heated by vents from a basement furnace. This was so effective that a 19th-century Wyndham could write to her son that 'it is like living in the South of France and much more agreeable to me than a winter in Italy'.

Of the remaining rooms there is little to be said. The library has fine mahogany bookcases but little effort has been made by the

National Trust or its tenants to bring things to life. Regency classicism is a style that requires opulence in its fittings.

PYTHOUSE **

4m NE of Shaftesbury
Family mansion in Regency Greek style (P-R)

Pythouse stands proud over its park against a hillside of trees, as in a romantic Regency print. It was designed in 1805 by the immensely tall 'Long John' Bennett, who married an heiress and stood for Parliament on a radical platform of Catholic emancipation, press freedom and franchise reform. He was not a tactful man and his enthusiasm for agricultural reform had his new threshing machines smashed by a mob. Bennett had at one point to be rescued from his own tenants by the Yeomanry.

As a true radical, Bennett designed his house as a temple, in the Greek style adopted as 'democratic' by the American and French revolutions. The style of Pythouse is reflected in Belsay (Northumbs) and Hammerwood (Sussex).

Encasing an earlier Georgian house, Bennett added three rooms to the front behind a new portico and constructed two recessed porticos on the side elevations. For an amateur this is a most accomplished work. The neighbouring Philipps House, designed a decade later by Wyatville, is uncannily similar in outward appearance. The severity of the portico is softened by its attraction to multi-coloured lichen.

The interior is mostly as Bennett left it when he died in 1852. The hall has a frieze and door-cases decorated with Greek motifs. Both main reception rooms are adorned with imported Italian fireplaces, somewhat diluting the Grecian effect. The staircase is odd, continuing straight as an arrow from the entrance hall, then suddenly dividing into two and vanishing.

The house remained in the Bennett family until 1958, after which it passed to the Country Houses Association, who have restored it admirably. The family, now Rumbolds, still live on the estate. One of the tenants has made himself an authority on the house's history.

SALISBURY: KING'S HOUSE *

65 The Close
Medieval mansion with Jacobean plasterwork (M)

The ghost of a grey lady is said to haunt the north staircase of the King's House. The same ghost should haunt a house in Des Moines, Iowa, home of the Weeks family, cosmeticians.

The Weekses visited the King's House in 1922 and so liked it that they decided to recreate it, to the inch, as their American home. They spent $1,500,000 stripping this and other Salisbury houses of panelling and antiques, which their owners were happy to sell. The Des Moines facsimile is now a museum. So is the King's House. I imagine I would prefer Iowa's. What a poor comment this is on English civic pride.

This was one of the finest medieval palaces in The Close, belonging to the abbots of Sherborne. Their signature, Ham stone, can be seen on the façade. Seized by the Crown (hence the name) on the Dissolution, it was leased to secular tenants until 1851, when it became a training college for schoolmistresses.

This closed in 1978 and, like the nearby Wardrobe, use as a museum became the house's salvation. No attempt has been made to retain the different character of the rooms. To see any traces of the old house, one must peer behind display cases and boards.

Yet the house is still magnificent. The exterior is richly medieval. A porch with a fan vault is to the left of the two-gabled Great Hall. A large solar and parlour wing stands to the right. The chief surviving features date from the Jacobean period. There is an original staircase with, upstairs, geometrical ceiling plasterwork and a good frieze in the Abbot's Chamber. One of the motifs is a Red Indian chief beneath a pilgrim's scallop shell. I wonder how many Cree Indians made it to Santiago de Compostela.

SALISBURY: MALMESBURY HOUSE ***

15 The Close
William-and-Mary mansion, Gothick
interiors (P)

Malmesbury House is picture-book William-and-Mary. Hidden down an alley in the north-east corner of The Close, it was built by a member of the Harris family as an extension to a former canonry. In 1698 James Harris commissioned Wren's assistant, Alexander Fort, to extend the previous 17th-century building with a seven-bay façade overlooking a private garden. The exterior is an exquisite composition, of silvery-white stone beneath a hat of jutting eaves and a single, assertive dormer. The effect is almost Chinese. Two stone pipers play on either side of the door.

Harris's son, also James, had a house in Twickenham near Horace Walpole's Strawberry Hill (London, W). Mesmerized by Walpole's stylistic eclecticism, Harris redecorated some of his interiors in the same Gothick style. The family later became Earls of Malmesbury and their Salisbury house languished, until bought in 1968 by a Conservative MP, John Cordle. His restoration has been exemplary.

The Georgian redecoration is immediately apparent in the spacious entrance hall, furnished with Napoleonic chairs upholstered with lions, each with an individual expression. The walls are a soft Wedgwood blue with plasterwork rising up the spacious staircase, with shallow 'Queen Anne' treads. The dining room has a mildly Rococo ceiling on a terracotta background. It is hung with paintings of Cordle ancestors.

Upstairs, a bedroom is named after Charles II who stayed here when escaping the plague in 1665. He is said to have looked down on St John Street from the rear oriel window and been appalled at the poverty below. The admirable monarch called for his horse and rode through the town to boost morale. Over the fireplace is a rare Georgian display stand, decorative shelves designed to hold precious objects. Opposite is Handel's Room, used by the composer when performing in the former chapel next door. The ceiling contains the Harris family emblem of hedgehogs, a play on the French for hedgehog, *hérisson*, the nearest they could get to 'Harris and Son'.

The prize of Malmesbury House is the library, directly above the drawing room. This is one of the most delightful Gothick rooms I know. The plasterwork is like icing sugar, teased and moulded into ogees and crockets on every surface. The plaster is white, then gilded and set on pastel backgrounds. The ogee is repeated in arches, bookcases and the Rococo chimneypiece. The handling of the window alcove, with ribbed and crocketed vaulting, is supreme. The guide dates this work to 1740, but this is ten years before Walpole began Strawberry Hill. It must be later.

At the end of the lawn, next to a truly monumental hedge, is a pretty classical Orangery. In its pediment is said to be a secret chamber for hiding Royalists.

SALISBURY: MOMPESSON HOUSE **

The Close
Baroque town house with 18th-century
interiors (NT)

The smartest of the houses round the Close was built in 1701 for Charles Mompesson, lawyer and local MP. It was tenanted by the Townsend family until 1939 when the last representative, Barbara Townsend, died at the age of ninety-six. She was a celebrated figure in The Close, with her sketching equipment, large hats and gigantic shawls. The house served briefly as the residence of the bishop, but passed in 1952 to the National Trust. It is beautifully presented but lacks the glamour and domesticity of its rival, Malmesbury House. It needs another Miss Townsend.

The façade to The Close is that of a handsome town mansion at the turn of the 18th century. Its designer may be the same as that of the exterior of Malmesbury House, although here in more elegant, even ornamental, vein. Mompesson has a more Baroque frontispiece, with a broken pediment over the door and dentilated eaves. It now boasts a splendid magnolia.

The rooms are conventionally Georgian, dating from the 1740s. The entrance hall was described in 1913 as 'a great clutter of chairs, tables, coat stands, rugs and shawls, with pot plants massed in the corners . . . the walls hung with pictures from cornice to dado'. This is sadly no more. A bold arch with floral spandrels gives onto the house's best feature, the staircase hall. The large stucco panels seem to demand large paintings. In the ceiling is a depiction of King Midas with ass's ears. The staircase, wide as at Malmesbury, has spiral balusters.

Of the downstairs rooms, the best is the drawing room, with an elaborate ceiling and overmantel. The dining room table is Hepplewhite, the china Sèvres, and the drinking glasses 18th-century. Upstairs is the elegant Green Room, hung with black-and-white portrait prints. Outside it is a display of Miss Townsend's watercolours.

SALISBURY:
THE WARDROBE *

58 The Close
Georgian Rococo in medieval mansion (M)

Too few of the houses round The Close are accessible to the public. What was the bishop's storehouse was disused on Pevsner's visit in 1975 and was then all but gutted for a regimental museum. Its modern display cases and institutional seats diminish its character as a historic building – though not totally.

The Wardrobe's façade is enticing. The central hall range, dating in part from 1254, was rebuilt in the 15th century. To this were added prominent gabled wings. A small entrance arcade leads into the ground floor, with a large Tudor window lighting the main room above. Much of this was altered in 1633 and then victorianized.

The most diverting feature of the interior is a reordering that must have taken place in the mid-18th century, presumably to upgrade the building as a residence. Handsome fireplaces were inserted, for instance in the rear saloon. Unusual *papier mâché* Rococo decoration was then applied to ceilings and walls. This is of a simple design, as if run up quickly by the plasterer's mate, but is rich and enjoyable, especially on the staircase. Behind the house is a peaceful garden with a fine copper beech.

STOURHEAD ***

Stourton, 3m NW of Mere
Early Palladian mansion with Regency library (NT)

Sir Henry Hoare, owner of Stourhead in the 1940s, had a difficult war. Finding his staff establishment depleted by conscription, he bombarded the War Office with letters. He demanded that the authorities at least supply him with the 'bare minimum' necessities of life – a cook, a butler, a maid and anyone 'properly qualified to polish silver vases with peacock feathers'. He was quite happy to accept evacuees provided they were qualified. Surely Whitehall should put its shoulder to the wheel? Did it not realize 'there is a war on'?

The house was built in 1720–24 for another Henry Hoare, a banker, at a time when English Baroque was giving way to English Palladian. The architect was Colen Campbell, doyen of the Palladians. Campbell had just designed Burlington House in London's Piccadilly and Wanstead in Essex for another banker, Richard Child. Hoare's son was 'Henry the Magnificent', banker to the Burlington set. He was a Medician figure, filling the house with works by Poussin, Mengs and Rysbrack. Extended by Colt Hoare in the 1790s, Stourhead was then mercifully left alone until transferred to the National Trust in 1946.

The house today looks warm and Italianate in a summer sun. Campbell's entrance portico (not built until 1838) is a serene essay in Palladian proportion. Steps lead up from each side, flanked by large eagles, the Hoare emblem, drinking from the stone basins. The façade would have the charm of Chiswick (London, W) were it not flanked, and inevitably weakened, by wings erected at the end of the 18th century.

The interiors of the central block were lost in a fire in 1902 but were restored facsimile. They can seem cold and forbidding. Hoares still live on the estate and tenant part of the house, but the place badly needs a Marquess of Bath (Longleat, above). The entrance hall is a handsome cube, reconstructed after the fire with broken pediments above the doorcases and fireplace. It is hung from floor to ceiling with Hoare portraits arranged, according to Colt Hoare in the early 19th century, to 'remind us of the genealogy of our families and recall to our minds the hospitality of its former inhabitants'. The finest work is an equestrian portrait of Henry the Magnificent, jointly by Michael Dahl and John Wootton.

The Regency library wing was designed by Colt Hoare himself and is one of the finest of its date (1792) in England. It has a dramatic barrel vault running the length of the room and is decorated with paintings of classical scenes. The bookcases are recessed into the olive green walls. The furniture includes a magnificent desk made, apparently on the spot, by the younger Thomas Chippendale, its pilasters portraying philosophers.

The Little Dining Room has a white Corinthian screen above red walls and carpet and is still used by the family. Behind the hall is the saloon. This was intended as a chapel but was soon pressed into service for 'county balls, theatricals, concerts and other entertainments . . . essential to all country houses of consequence'. After the 1902 fire, it was refashioned as an Edwardian drawing room, marked by heavy picture frames and ferns. When the National Trust restored it, the red wallpaper shocked the decorator, John Fowler, who told James Lees-Milne that it looked like a 'Bewlay-House pipe shop'. That, came the reply, was precisely the intention.

The Italian Room was once the state bedroom, the pretty Gothick bed alcove now filled with copies of Old Masters. The Cabinet and picture gallery are used to display the Hoares' principal pictures and furniture. The cabinet in the first room is an exquisite work of 17th-century Italian craftsmanship, covered in pietra dura and used to house precious gems and cameos. These rooms are hung with English landscapes and Old Masters, among them Poussin's *The Choice of Hercules*. Carlo Maratta's colloquy of *The Marchese Pallavicini and the Artist* embodies the Georgian ideal of the cultivated country gentleman.

The garden at Stourhead is a masterpiece of English landscape, casual yet contrived, natural yet architectural. In autumn, when the leaves are turning, the different shades of red and green round the serpentine lake are sublime. Henry Hoare began laying out the gardens with the help of Henry Flitcroft in the 1740s. He immediately opened it to the public and found it a sensational success, so much so that he had to build a hotel for visitors. A magazine declared, 'Prepare the mind for something grand and new/ For Paradise soon opens to the view!'

SWINDON: RAILWAY COTTAGE *

Access via Steam Exhibition
Ghost of God's Wonderful Railway (M)

When the great railway works at Swindon closed in the 1980s, it left the largest area of covered factory in Europe. The government duly demolished it, leaving some 'historic' walls as memorials. A railway museum now makes some effort to compensate, as does the walk through the old workers' tunnel to the model village. This remarkably intact estate was designed by Sir Matthew Digby Wyatt in the 1850s, for workers on the Great Western Railway, built by Brunel.

The village is a neighbourhood of pale stone cottages laid out on a grid, with school, chapel and institute. They still have the decorum of Georgian town planning. For train drivers and other skilled workers and supervisors, the cottages were substantial. They were handsome terraces, with small front gardens and rear access along alleys. One has been preserved in its original state, the others are occupied.

The cottage is extraordinarily evocative. The ground floor has parlour, dining room and kitchen, furnished with the usual Victorian household objects. The floors are covered in lino and rag rugs. The tables are littered with oil lamps, a Bible, Staffordshire pottery.

WESTWOOD MANOR ***

Westwood, 2m SW of Bradford-on-Avon
Medieval manor with Jacobean
embellishments (NT)

Westwood is one of the manor houses that caught the eye of Edward Hudson of *Country Life* and his conservationists in the early years of the 20th century. Without their dedication, the West Country would be poorer by far. At the time, these houses may have seemed no different from thousands of run-down farms across England. Hudson made their renaissance a scholarly crusade.

Westwood belonged to a family of clothiers, the Hortons then Farewells, into the 18th century, when cloth gave way to agriculture as source of local wealth. The house became a farm. In 1911 it was acquired by a retired diplomat and Fellow of the Society of Antiquaries, Edgar Lister. He filled the house with panelling and internal porches, rescued from demolitions elsewhere. Tudor and Jacobean furniture came too and the floors were covered with oriental carpets. Lister left the house to the National Trust in 1956.

The house forms a picturesque group near Bradford-on-Avon, sandwiched between a medieval barn and a church. It is medieval in form, the exterior of stone and render, L-shaped with an original stair turret in the angle of the L. The old house had been comprehensively refurbished by John Farewell at the start of the 17th century, and it is this period that dominates the interior. Farewell inserted a Great Parlour above the old hall.

A porch leads into the modest hall on the left, while on the right are two charming small rooms where once would have been kitchens.

The name of the rear King's Room probably refers to its use for a manorial court. It has extensive Jacobean plasterwork on the ceiling and, round the fireplace, Red Indians, totem poles and a two-tailed mermaid, fashionable Jacobean emblems. In addition, Lister imported wall panelling painted with the kings and queens of England. The day-bed is covered in flame-stitch, executed by Lister himself, a skilled needleworker.

Lister was an enthusiast for early keyboard music and turned the Great Parlour into the present music room. Its coved plaster ceiling is covered in huge acanthus fronds. His furniture is dark and polished, its upholstery embroidered by himself. The west wing contains the old dining room and, upstairs, the Panelled Room and Oriel Room. These have been immaculately restored. Much of the panelling and the rare internal draught porches were acquired from a house in Bristol.

WILTON HOUSE *****

Wilton
Palladian palace with Inigo Jones and Wyatt
interiors (P)

Wilton is one of the great houses of England. The old nunnery was granted to a Welshman, William Herbert, by Henry VIII in 1544 on Herbert's marriage to Catherine Parr's sister. Herbert thus became, briefly, the King's brother-in-law. The house came with a huge estate of 46,000 acres and, eventually, the Earldom of Pembroke. Herberts were to be powers in the land and patrons of the arts. The 2nd Earl sponsored Shakespeare, while his wife, Mary Sidney, scholar and adored sister of the dazzling Sir Philip, was 'the greatest patroness of wit and learning of any lady in her time'. She was also an early breeder of horses. It was her second son, the 4th Earl, who employed John Webb in 1647 to implement plans for rebuilding the earlier house, first prepared by his mentor, Inigo Jones. The family founded the Wilton carpet factory, were prominent in the Burlington circle in the 18th century and supported Florence Nightingale in the 19th. The house has been well restored. Rooms have taped music, adding to their enjoyment; modern sculptures dot the gardens.

Visitors are greeted with a trumpet blast worthy of Blenheim. In 1801, James Wyatt moved Sir William Chambers's triumphal arch from a distant hill and placed it bang in front of the courtyard. It brings the house towards the town and gives the approach to Wilton a taste of imperial France. Despite that, the house exterior is unpompous. It is square built, like Lacock and Syon (London, W), on the nunnery remains. The south front facing the lake is by Inigo Jones and his pupil John Webb in 1648. Each corner is crowned with a small gabled pavilion which seems not to know which way to face.

The character of much of Wilton's interior is due to James Wyatt. Entry to the house is into Wyatt's Gothic north front, presided over by a statue of Shakespeare copied from William Kent's in Westminster Abbey. Steps lead up to the cloisters, inserted by Wyatt in honour of Wilton's monastic past. Courtyard windows flood its galleries with light. Wyatt thus offers a delicate Gothic hors d'oeuvre to the Italianate splendours ahead. Two smoking rooms survive from the earlier house, with simple classical fireplaces. The Large Smoking Room contains Chippendale's Violin Bookcase, so-called for the carved instruments above the central Rococo roundel, an exquisite work. The Little Ante-Room contains some of Wilton's finest small pictures, by Teniers, Poussin and van Goyen.

Wilton's tempo quickens with the six great state rooms of the Jones/Webb front. Here Jones sought his celebrated contrast: 'Outwardly every wise man carries a gravity, yet inwardly has his imagination set on fire and sometimes licentiously flies out.' Wilton is as good as his word. In these voluptuously decorated rooms, white plaster is encrusted with gold decoration. Bold red walls and pink carpets offer a backdrop to glorious paintings.

The Corner Room has Prince Rupert by Honthorst in pride of place over the mantelpiece, surrounded with works by Claude, Rubens, del Sarto and Hals. The Colonnade Room was converted for a visit of George III and has a phenomenal French Rococo ceiling of the 1730s by Andien de Clermont. Here hangs a serene Reynolds of Elizabeth Spencer. In the Great Ante-Room is a portrait of Rembrandt's mother and a gentle depiction of the hapless Edward VI by Holbein.

Now comes the explosion. Jones's Double Cube Room is English architecture shaking off medieval inhibition and joining the European mainstream. The chamber is 6oft by 3oft. The overmantel is flanked by garlanded pendants, as are the great doors. The coving, painted in the 1650s by Edward Pierce, depicts urns, fruit and cherubs. In the ceiling are set three Baroque paintings. The fastidious Sacheverell Sitwell found not all about this room to his taste. 'The carving heavy and not equal to the best Italian work,' he said, but accepted that this may be inevitable in a room of this grandeur.

The room was designed by Jones to take the van Dyck paintings that fill the wall panels. The largest is a stunning work of the 4th Earl and his family, arrayed in a variety of flamboyant poses like models on a catwalk. They seem about to step out of the frame and parade across the carpet below. The room is furnished mostly by Kent and Chippendale.

It is regrettable that, on the tour, the visitor reaches the Single Cube Room after the Double Cube, the opposite being Jones's intention. The result is slight anticlimax. The decorative scheme is the same, with white painted panelling enriched with gold leaf. The coving is less aggressively decorated, more classical and harmonious.

The Upper Cloisters offer yet more of Wilton's art collection, including two Brueghels and Samuel Scott's views of London, including of Jones's first Covent Garden development. The windows look down on a new knot garden. In the grounds, the Palladian bridge by Roger Morris has been restored and continues to preside quietly over lake, house and grounds alike.

Overleaf: Wilton's Double Cube Room

Worcestershire

Worcestershire is a predominantly lowland county, watered by the rivers Severn, Avon and Teme. It mixes a rich, dark limestone with half-timbering and is celebrated for its apple orchards and dairy herds. The southern reaches touch the Cotswolds round Broadway, with villages of intense if mannered charm. The north round Redditch and Hagley is invaded by the awesome spread of the West Midlands. Here the chief crop is suburbs.

Of the Middle Ages are Worcester's beautifully restored Greyfriars and Commandery, and a superb Great Hall at Little Malvern. This part of the West Midlands in the 16th and 17th centuries was a hotbed of recusancy. The Pakingtons' house at Harvington claims the most priest's holes in England. William-and-Mary Hanbury contains Thornhill's superb painted staircase, as good as his work at Greenwich. The Lyttletons built a Palladian celebration of the Grand Tour at Hagley, complete with excellent Rococo plasterwork.

Birmingham money spread down into Worcestershire at Witley Court, where the Earls of Dudley built (and then lost) one of the greatest palaces of its day in England. At Château Impney, a local tycoon created a Loire fantasy for his French wife. At Madresfield, the Lygon family rolled all ages and tastes, including early 20th century, into a single majestic fantasy of Old England.

Avoncroft:
  Bromsgrove House *
  Yardley Prefab **
Birtsmorton **
Broadway:
  Lygon Arms **
Broadway Tower *
Croome *

Droitwich:
  Château Impney *
  Evesham Almonry *
Hagley ****
Hanbury ***
Hartlebury **
Harvington ****
Little Malvern Court *

Lower Broadheath:
  Elgar's Birthplace *
Madresfield ****
Witley Court **
Worcester:
  Commandery **
  Greyfriars **

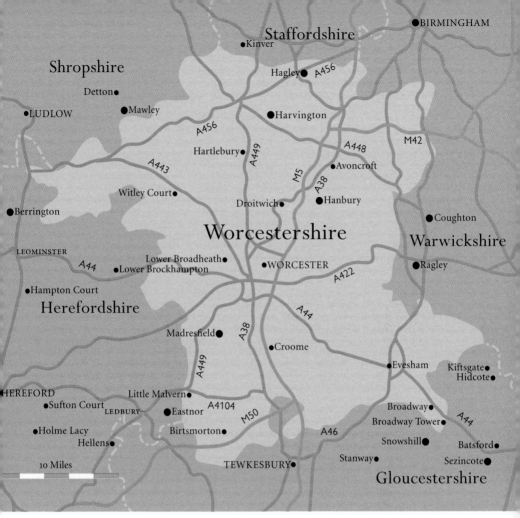

AVONCROFT MUSEUM

2m S of Bromsgrove

Since 1967, Avoncroft has been rescuing old buildings otherwise doomed to destruction. Most are vernacular, of the sort that have been demolished in their thousands over the past half-century. These structures are far more vulnerable and are now even rarer than grand historic buildings. That Bromsgrove could not retain its fine merchant's house is as shameful as that Yardley could not keep one example of its post-war 'prefab' architecture. Thanks to Avoncroft both survive. One day perhaps these buildings might return (like those at Singleton/Sussex) to their places of origin.

AVONCROFT: BROMSGROVE MERCHANT'S HOUSE *

originally in Station Street, Bromsgrove

The building was located on the corner of Station Street and Worcester Road, forming a significant feature of a much battered Midlands town. Nowhere else in Western Europe would a town destroy such a relic of its past. The threatened demolition for road widening led to its being dismantled and re-erected as the first of Avoncroft's structures in 1967.

The house is a fine example of a late 15th-century town building. It was known to have been occupied by a family of dyers, the Lylleys, in the 1550s. The house had survived on a busy town road, its quality concealed by dilapidation. The plan is of a traditional hall house with screens passage, hall and a cross-wing of parlour and jettied solar above. The frame is of pegged oak with wattle-and-daub panels. All the roof construction is visible. Windows have been returned to rough wooden mullions and no glass.

This and other houses at Avoncroft can be rendered almost impenetrable with smoke. The reason is that they are displayed with an element present in every medieval house yet rare in modern reincarnations, fire. Visitors to poor neighbourhoods of India or Africa will know what this means. Living rooms were designed round the source of heat, which in turn dictated the allocation of space. No medieval hall would have been without a fire, first in the central hearth and later in a fireplace.

The Bromsgrove house had a chimney but this was a Tudor insert and has been replaced by the original louvred vent over a lit hearth. Smoke oozes from the windows and doorway and makes visitors' eyes sting. Excellent.

Less admirable is the emptiness of most of the rooms, in deference to modern archaeological correctness which holds that building fabric can be reinstated but not contents. On my visit, there was a battered rope-bed and suitably verminous covering, but not much else.

AVONCROFT: YARDLEY PREFAB **

originally in Moat Lane, Yardley

The Yardley Prefab was first 'moved' from its factory to its original site in Moat Lane in 1946. It was moved again in 1981 to its present setting. The first residents, Mr and Mrs Stokes, attended its re-erection.

The fiasco of post-war prefabrication is told under the Chiltern Museum (Bucks). Prefabs were made by the central government in disused bomber factories from 2,500 numbered parts. They turned out to cost three times more than conventional brick houses in the private sector. The houses also proved near impossible to ventilate. Yet they were the pride and joy of the Ministry of Works. The Arcon Mark V was exhibited at the Tate Gallery at the time. The Tate should have it back as a work of art.

The house is now a period piece. It is built on a concrete base with a steel frame and walls of corrugated asbestos cement. Doors and windows are steel, the paintwork green and cream. The plan is for two bedrooms, sitting room and kitchen, round a core service unit containing electricity, hot water, heating and refrigerator. The houses were, in themselves, cosy cottages. They were demolished in favour of even more expensive blocks of flats, which have proved unpopular with their tenants and are now being demolished in favour of brick-built cottages.

The prefab at Avoncroft is furnished in the style of the period. Everything is of the 1940s, including the attendant who wears a wrap-around apron and hair tied up in a bun. There is Utility furniture, Daz, Swan Vestas, a bakelite wireless and battered linoleum. The bedroom is suitably untidy. That said, the house is not far removed from much working-class housing of today.

BIRTSMORTON COURT **

Birtsmorton, 6m SW of Upton upon Severn
Moated manor with 15th-century chamber (P-R)

This fortified manor was salvaged by an Edwardian enthusiast, Francis Bradley-Birt, in 1911 and substantially rebuilt before the existence of historic building controls. The result is delightful but confusing. We see not one but two moats and a wonderfully picturesque roofscape. The house comprises a medieval gatehouse, inner courtyard and hall, now surrounded by a Georgian range, a Tudor banqueting hall and a 'medieval' east wing erected in the 1920s.

Bradley-Birt's grandson, an Indian civil

servant, left Birtsmorton 'to the nation' unendowed in 1963. Like many such gifts, the nation was not sure what to do with it and sold it to the present owners, the Dawes family. They honour the legacy by opening by appointment. They have planted an enchanting all-white garden, with a modern Art Nouveau gate leading to the surrounding meadow.

The core of the house was built in 1424 by a Cornish family with the curious name of Nanfan. The principal interior room is still the medieval Great Hall, with massive wall-posts embedded in the plasterwork. Like most of the house, this was remodelled in the Elizabethan period, with new ceiling and fireplace. The screen, now of Georgian columns, carries panels of colourful Nanfan heraldry. The parlour, known as the Council Chamber, has Elizabethan carving of a lion's head frieze and brightly painted overmantel. Upstairs, 16th-century wall-paintings have been revealed.

The banqueting hall appears to have taken over from the Great Hall as chief reception room. It is two storeys high, with timbered walls and a ceiling boldly plastered in pink. Variously a barn, cheese factory and local school, it is now once again used for banqueting.

BROADWAY: LYGON ARMS **

High Street
Medieval house with Jacobean interiors (H)

One of the best Cotswold manors is now preserved and accessible as a hotel. For all its tourist celebrity, Broadway remains architecturally intact, its warm limestone walls nestling under the escarpment. The Lygon Arms was once the White Hart, mentioned in parish records as early as 1532. Its origins, as manor or farmhouse, are unclear although fragments of a 14th-century house are visible inside. The 16th-century building was given a new Jacobean front in 1620 by the Trevis family. The house was sufficiently substantial to claim both Cromwell and Charles I as visitors during the Civil War.

The front to the street is the ideal of a rich Cotswold house. It is of four storeys, two of them with dormer windows within the roof space. A magnificent wisteria holds the composition together. The interior is not overwhelmed by its status as a luxury hotel. To the left and right are panelled Jacobean rooms with deep fireplaces, old salt cupboards, iron tongs and appropriate pictures.

There appear to be earlier medieval walls to the rear, but the former coachyard has been swamped by infilling. One of the bedrooms is nominated the Great Chamber. Another, with a plasterwork ceiling, is named after Cromwell and another after the King. The hotel was acquired by one of Wellington's generals, General Lygon, in about 1815. His butler become manager and changed its name to that of his employer's family.

The Lygon Arms was bought by the Russell family at the turn of the 20th century. They added a 'new' Great Hall, designed by C. E. Bateman in neo-Jacobean style. It has a splendid barrel vault ceiling, a 17th-century minstrels' gallery and painted coats of arms on the walls.

BROADWAY TOWER *

3½m SE of Broadway
Georgian folly on Cotswold peak (M)

The tower occupies a commanding view from the escarpment of the Cotswolds above Broadway village. It was built in 1799 as a folly by the 6th Earl of Coventry, to be used as a signalling point to his seat at Croome Court, 18 miles to the north. The designer was James Wyatt, who also did work at Croome, and this constitutes his medieval whimsy. The adjacent Springhill estate was a subsidiary Coventry seat, used to get away from the bustle of Croome which, as James Lees-Milne put it, 'was No. 1, Worcestershire'. The hillside was later planted with clumps of trees to represent the location of British divisions at Waterloo.

Broadway Tower was soon sold to a local landowner, Sir Thomas Phillipps, a Regency antiquarian whose bold dream was to own a copy of every book in the world. In 1822 he established a printing press here to publish some of his manuscript collection, making it a place of pilgrimage for bibliophiles and, later, for Pre-Raphaelites and Cotswold Arts and Crafts enthusiasts. William Morris and Burne-Jones both stayed in the Tower. Morris's daughter recalled the place as 'absurd – the men had to bathe on the roof when the wind didn't blow the soap away'. Yet she added, 'how the clean aromatic wind blew the aches out of our tired bodies and how good it all was'.

The building is hexagonal with circular turrets on three of its points. The style was described as Norman, with a base 'battered' outwards to resist undermining. The interior has four storeys of comfortable rooms, the second storey being the principal one. This has handsome Georgian windows giving onto balconies, with neo-Norman stone balustrades. The building was occupied until 1972 by tenants of the adjacent farm. They appear to have cooked with bottled gas and lit the rooms with oil lamps.

Now a museum of the Pre-Raphaelites and the Cotswolds, the tower is heavy with display boards and videos. For many years it housed waxworks showing 'the quality' upstairs and servants downstairs. The faces were all similar. The top offers superb views over the Avon and Severn valleys.

CROOME COURT *

5m NW of Upton upon Severn
House and early landscape by Capability Brown (NT-G)

The house is the focus of what was one of the great landscaped parks in England. It was commissioned by the 6th Earl of Coventry in 1750 from the young Lancelot 'Capability' Brown after the latter's departure from Stowe. Brown drained the Earl's land and re-designed the exterior of the house, which was given interiors by Robert Adam. The form was of a simple Palladian villa looking out across its estate to the Malvern Hills.

The story of the house is sad. Its exterior, in durable Bath stone, has a pedimented façade and corner towers. A graceful two-armed staircase rises to the *piano nobile*. The interior has lost its once superb Adam furnishings, although the finest room (the Tapestry Room) can be studied in the Metropolitan Museum in New York, where these things are more valued than in the old country.

The virtue of the house today lies in its setting. Brown had to engage in a huge amount of earth moving and drainage in the 1750s to create an undulating Worcestershire topography without unduly interfering with the Earl's farm. A serpentine Croome 'River' was created and woods planted to vary the line of view. A sinuous walk 'used light and shade to stimulate visitors' emotions', with clumps of deciduous and evergreen shrubs to offer 'cool, sequestered retreats'. It is hard for us to appreciate how revolutionary this must have seemed to an England accustomed to straight avenues and formal parterres.

Brown included the architecture beloved of the earlier Palladians. Robert Adam designed a Temple or Greenhouse and an exquisite Island Pavilion. James Wyatt supplied the Dry Arch bridge. All this is now being restored under the aegis of the National Trust. More distant features were a Panorama Tower towards Severn Stoke and the Broadway Tower (above) on the Cotswolds.

The house is best appreciated from the lookout point in front of the Gothick church, itself one of the 6th Earl's park ornaments. I first stood here when the house was a school and cricket was being played on the lawn in front of the portico. It was an idyllic English scene.

DROITWICH: CHÂTEAU IMPNEY *

1m NE of Droitwich
Tycoon's Loire château for French wife (H)

John Corbett, the son of a Victorian bargee, rose to become king of the Midlands' salt industry. He met his French wife in Paris, where she was a 'beautiful governess', and together they visited the châteaux of the Loire. He decided to make her a present of one of them. Corbett summoned an architect named Tronquois from Paris and told him to run up something similar. Château Impney, then known as Impney Park, was built in 1869.

At the time, there was nothing in this style in England, French being as unpopular for house exteriors as it was popular for interiors. The Rothschilds had yet to create Waddesdon (Bucks). The Royal Holloway College (Surrey) was still ten years off. The nearest parallel was the Bowes Museum (Durham), coincidentally designed in the same year by another tycoon eager to please a French wife.

Three thousand men are said to have worked to create the house and park, an astonishing army. The house is in the style of Louis XIII, with a steeply pitched roof and heavy Mannerist details, an architecture later much favoured by the Hammer House of Horror. The building has recently been made less horrific by cleaning and restoration, its exterior now jolly with redbrick and cream stone dressings. The dormer windows and chimneys are a mad effusion, apparently unrelated to anything behind. Some of the gables are like Siamese head-dresses.

That is about it. The entrance has been spoiled by a hotel company. What should be 'over-the-top' French aristocratic is 'under-the-top' Midlands commercial. A fine staircase survives inside and displays stained glass in honour of Chaucer, Shakespeare and Spencer. A picturesque park was laid out round a stream, the Salwarpe, with an ornamental bridge, lofty hedges and dark evergreen glades.

EVESHAM ALMONRY *

Abbey Gate
Relic of monastic hostel (M)

Almonries were normally located outside monastic gatehouses. Their job was to process the flow of poor and sick seeking help within, a medieval social services department. Most vanished at the Dissolution and Evesham's is a rare survivor. It is filled with relics of its time

as a house, shop and workshop, before becoming the town museum in 1957. The contents seem like the sweepings of every attic in Evesham, enjoyably tossed about the rooms in roughly generic order.

Parts of the building, including the hall undercroft, are said to date from 1400. The timbered and gabled upper storeys appear later, in the 16th and 17th centuries. The interior is best enjoyed as a creaking warren of rooms and passages, thick with objects. The downstairs Abbey Room, presumably the almoner's parlour, has a fine Gothic fireplace with overmantel of *c*1500. It contains the bishop's *cathedra* from the abbey, a 14th-century chair.

A passage leads along the undercroft of the former hall. It is cluttered with the tools of Evesham trades, including specialist equipment for digging asparagus. The former kitchens are decked out with civic regalia. The upstairs rooms, carved from the old hall and solar chambers, are more like a museum. The de Montfort Room has good panelling.

HAGLEY HALL ****

Hagley
Palladian mansion with restored Rococo interiors (P)

Hagley has survived extravagance, poverty, fire, divorce, age and the encroaching Midlands. The present owner, Viscount Cobham, bewails his woes in the guidebook, spattered with such words as 'soul-searching . . . survival . . . not easy . . . struggle . . . work'. A picture appears to show him writing out another cheque to keep the place afloat. He looks like a man regretting the wild oats sowed three centuries back on the Grand Tour.

The house was the creation of his ancestor, the 1st Lord Lyttleton, in the 1750s. Sanderson Miller is believed to have suggested a design in the new Strawberry Hill Gothick, but Lyttleton decided on a conservative Palladian. The exterior is a dull quadrilateral with prominent corner pavilions and pyramid roofs, Inigo Jones style. The architect's original estimate

was £12,000 but the eventual cost was £34,000. Nothing changes. The grounds were landscaped with follies and a church. On a visit in 1753, Horace Walpole declared that 'I wore out my eyes with gazing, my feet with climbing and my tongue and vocabulary with commending'. The money had been well spent.

Hagley is handsomely set against its hillside. The entrance to the *piano nobile* is reached up a double flight of steps, offering a fine view of the Lyttletons' beloved cricket matches, played on the lawn in front. The interior is a monument to the taste of the 18th-century Grand Tourist, the rooms planned to display a classical collection. A fire in 1925 destroyed the library and many of the contents, but the house has been restored largely as built. While the exterior is severe, the interior contains some of the most effusive Rococo decoration in England, mostly by the Italian, Francesco Vassalli.

The entrance hall is Italianate and no place for scruffy cricketers. Its plasterwork is by Vassalli in yellow and white, the stone chimneypiece flanked by Herculean figures. To the left of the hall are the informal family rooms. The library has a bust of Alexander Pope over the mantelpiece and busts of other great writers adorning the bookcases. Contents include a complete set of Wisden's *Cricket Almanac*.

Beyond the adjacent boudoir, filled with Lyttleton portraits, is the house's chief oddity, a neo-Jacobean library. Its walls are lined with woodwork salvaged from a former house on the site. Here hangs an anonymous Dutch painting, *The Misers*, against which the reckless 2nd Lord Lyttleton reputedly wagered Hagley – and won.

Beyond are Vassalli's masterpieces, the state rooms. The dining room (the old saloon) has plasterwork displaying the same naturalistic freedom that Grinling Gibbons executed in limewood. White ribbons, fronds and rustic trophies cascade down pale yellow walls. The ceiling is an exquisite swirl. Portraits of Lyttletons by Wilson, Ramsay, West and Batoni gaze

Hagley: art and nature combined

down in approval. In the adjacent drawing room, Rococo spreads beyond the ceiling and pier-glasses to embrace the Soho tapestries covering the walls. Their patterns are reflected in the embroidery of the sofas and chairs. This is a glorious chamber.

The gallery is remarkable chiefly for having survived its use by generations of Lyttletons for indoor cricket practice. The Rococo Ho-Ho birds on the ceiling and the fireplace pagodas had to dodge hurtling balls. The room is no longer so abused. Even shuttlecock would seem an impertinence. The sequence ends with the Crimson Drawing Room, boasting fine pier-glasses and a large Mortlake tapestry. Hagley is worth his lordship's struggle.

HANBURY HALL ***

3m E of Droitwich
Vernon seat with Thornhill ceilings (NT)

All was well in the Vernon household until 1776, when the heiress to the Hanbury estate, Emma Vernon, was married by an ambitious mother to Henry Cecil, future Earl of Exeter. The Vernons, rich lawyers, had acquired Hanbury in 1631. In the 1690s, the house was expensively rebuilt by Thomas Vernon, but by the 1770s there was no male heir and a general feeling that a title was needed. Hence the Cecil match.

It proved a disaster. The couple spent every penny they had and Emma 'took to Norris's drops and Madeira'. Husband and wife then completely disappeared, separately. Emma had eloped with the Hanbury curate, Will Sneyd, settling in Lisbon. Henry Cecil had adopted the name of John Jones and took up with Sally Hoggins, daughter of a Shropshire farmer, who forced 'Jones' into a shotgun (and bigamous) marriage when she became pregnant. Cecil frantically gained a secret divorce from Emma via the House of Lords and, with Sally still in ignorance of his identity, took her to the family seat at Burghley (Hunts). When the girl alighted from the carriage and heard the staff addressing her as 'your ladyship', she collapsed with shock. She never recovered, but lived on at Burghley as the 'cottage countess' after her husband's early death.

Fate now took a hand. The Hanbury curate died of consumption in Lisbon. Emma duly returned home and married an upstanding citizen of Droitwich, John Phillips. Mr and Mrs Phillips returned to Hanbury, and lived there 'quietly and charitably' ever after. The house remained in Vernon hands and passed to the National Trust in 1953, although it remained occupied by Sir George Vernon's estranged wife, Doris Lady Vernon, for another ten years. Lady Vernon lived as a recluse with her cats, entertaining nobody but the local bishop, provided he brought his own sandwiches. The house was so poorly endowed that it was for a while tenanted and is currently used for the milder sort of corporate functions.

The house appearance is classic William-and-Mary, with red brick, white woodwork, pitched roof and dormer windows. Prominent wings flank a recessed central entrance beneath a deep pediment. Above rises a jaunty cupola, like a Dutch gallant with a weak chin. Apart from some Gothick decoration upstairs, the interior is mostly unaltered since Emma Vernon's day.

Hanbury's forte is its hall and staircase. The hall is a dark-panelled chamber with arched doorcases and a ceiling painted to look like stone. But this is little more than an ante-room for the staircase filling its west end. Here we are suddenly transported to Wren's Greenwich Hospital (London, E). The walls are covered with murals by Sir James Thornhill, who was working at Greenwich at the time, c1710. The side panels are the story of Achilles, set in trompe-l'œil architectural frames.

The downstairs rooms are of a conventional late 17th-century house, adapted in the 18th. The drawing room is Georgian in style, but the dining room still has its original ceiling with more paintings by Thornhill. The dining room fireplace surround has outstanding Rococo work, complete with Ho-Ho birds. The upstairs rooms are furnished with four-posters, porcelain and paintings. Most remarkable are the corridors, flanked by wild Baroque doorcases and Gothick wallpaper. The doors might be from a temple of fun. The best of the bedrooms is the Hercules Room, so named after the fireplace statue in its dressing room.

From these rooms can be seen the garden parterre, restored to its 18th-century pattern and flanked by a long gallery in a detached building. So unusual is the latter that historians have wondered if it survives from an earlier house on the site. Hanbury has a fine orangery, that of Kensington Palace in miniature.

HARTLEBURY CASTLE **

Hartlebury, 2m E of Stourport-on-Severn
Bishop's palace with Rococo plasterwork (P)

The house is the country residence of the Bishops of Worcester, once epicentre of county society. A medieval house was much altered in the 17th and 18th centuries to produce the present episcopal mansion. The exterior is in red sandstone, long, low and gothicized, with Y-tracery in its windows. At each end is a four-bay Georgian wing. Above the hall is a charming cupola. Somehow all this escaped Victorian alteration.

The state rooms are reached through the servants' wing and what is now the county museum. They are graceful but hardly merit the stipulated hour-and-a-half visit. The Great Hall, still open to the roof, was divided in the 18th century into the present hall and saloon. At one end is a theatrical staircase leading to an upper chamber.

The saloon is a surprising flourish of Rococo *papier mâché*, mostly framing pictures or medallions but some applied to the open walls, as if for the sheer thrill of decoration. Episcopal portraits fill both rooms.

To the rear of the hall was a cloister, above which an 18th-century bishop, Bishop Hurd, installed a private library. It is said that he so loved Hartlebury as to have turned down Canterbury to stay here. Two Ionic screens divide the room, with its bookcases built into the walls to take the weight of books. Many of these come from the collection of Alexander Pope.

HARVINGTON HALL ****

3m SE of Kidderminster
Moated Tudor mansion with priest's holes
and wall-paintings (P)

Harvington is a shrine to West Midlands
Catholic recusancy. It survives virtually unaltered from the Elizabethan era, and conveys
the intensity of the religious conflicts of
the time. It boasts more priest's holes than
any house in England. Four of these are attributed to one carpenter, Nicholas Owen, who
merits the title of purveyor of priests' holes
to the Jesuit Superior, Henry Garnet, during
the reign of the hated Protestant Elizabeth I.

Owen created a network of 'safe houses'
in the Midlands. Their chief refuge was the
now demolished Hindlip outside Worcester,
where Owen himself hid after the Gunpowder
Plot. The authorities knew he was inside
but could not find him. He was eventually
starved out, tortured and killed. That plot was
no joke.

Harvington, owned by the Pakington family
from 1529, is also a monument to recusancy
intermarriage. The Pakingtons were linked to
such great Catholic families as the Dacres,
Sacheverells, Yateses and Throckmortons. In
the 18th century, one such liaison joined
Harvington to the Throckmorton family seat
at Coughton (Warwicks). In 1910, this sadly led
to the removal of its great staircase and much
of its panelling to that property. Harvington
became a Catholic girls' school but fell into
dereliction, ivy-clad and intensely picturesque.
It was bought by a benefactor in 1923 and given
to the Roman Catholic Archdiocese of Birmingham for restoration. When the ivy was removed from the central hall it was found, like
the trees at Ankor, to have been holding up the
roof, which promptly collapsed.

The house today is antique in every sense.
The visitor is greeted not by some grand park
but by a medieval clutter of outer courtyard
and old malthouse. Beyond is a moat and random series of façades, dominated by a Tudor
tower of red brick with stone-mullioned windows. On the left over the moat is the old
Great Hall, its parlour or audience room now a
restaurant roofed in extraordinary gnarled
beams. The kitchens are full of smoky smells
and pottery dredged from the moat.

The important family chambers are on the
first floor, while beyond lies a maze of bedrooms, passages and priest's holes. The withdrawing room has a barrel ceiling and dark
floors. Six mahogany chairs are set round
a Queen Anne table, as if in preparation
for a Jacobite conspiracy. The Great Chamber next door, with reproduction Elizabethan
panelling, is gloriously light. Over the
chimneypiece is inscribed the noble motto,
'What was ancient and abandoned, you shall
rebuild'. Beyond is the Mermaid Passage,
named after its Renaissance arabesque graffiti
painted by Flemish artists in the late 16th
century. On the floor immediately above are
murals of the Nine Worthies, different in style
although possibly contemporary.

Off the staircase between the two is Harvington's *coup de théâtre*, 'Dr Dodd's secret
library', which is the most cunning priest's
hole anywhere. A vertical timber, apparently
structural, swings out to reveal a small cavity
behind. It cannot have been comfortable but
was surely foolproof. More such holes abound
in the attic. Differing levels and wall thicknesses could hide a seminary of priests. The
Marble Room looks as if a monk has been
disturbed while writing and has vanished into
the wall. He has, since even the fireplace is a
fake, concealing another hole. An axonometric
drawing shows the location of the various
hides, at least of those so far discovered.

The house now becomes a warren of simply
furnished rooms. The attic chapel, as permitted after the Toleration Acts of the 1680s, is
legal but not ostentatious and might be easily
converted into a sitting room. Next to the
nursery is another chapel, possibly an earlier
and more secret one. It has gruesome drops of
white and red blood for wall covering. The
staircase is a 1930s copy of the original now
at Coughton.

At the top of the back stairs is Lady Yates's
bedroom, formerly the Tudor 'best room'. It is
dark-panelled with an ornate overmantel and

garderobe. The pretty bed-hangings are reproduction 17th century. This was the teacher's
room when the house was a Catholic school. It
must have been alternately picturesque and
bleakly cold.

LITTLE MALVERN COURT
*

Little Malvern, 3m S of Great Malvern
Great Hall with Flemish altarpiece (P-R)

Church and court sit well on the slopes of the
Malvern Hills, with the remains of an old priory between them. All around are rich gardens.
The house is private, still owned by descendants of the Russells, recusants to whom it had
been given by Mary I. Of the present house,
part is medieval, part Elizabethan and part
Victorian, a picturesque composition.

Only the old Great Hall of the Benedictine
priory is available to view. It has a spectacular
roof, freed of a later ceiling. It dates from
the 14th century and is of five bays, with
cusped wind-braces and most sympathetically
restored. A romanticized painting of Thomas
Wentworth, 1st Earl of Strafford, on his way to
the scaffold in 1641, adorns one end of the hall.
The other end has a 15th-century altarpiece
from Antwerp, an exquisitely carved treasure.
It is a delight to find such works displayed to
the public in a private house and not stored in
a museum.

A spiral stair leads to what would once have
been a secret chapel above the ceiling level
of the old hall. This has been restored as a
memorial to Worcestershire recusancy.

LOWER BROADHEATH:
ELGAR'S BIRTHPLACE *

Lower Broadheath, 3m W of Worcester
Composer's shrine in country cottage (M)

Edward Elgar's father was a piano tuner with
a small shop in neighbouring Worcester. He

'Dr Dodd's priest's hole', Harvington

maintained the piano at Witley Court (below)
on which visiting royalty played, and could
therefore advertise himself as 'by appointment
to royalty'. The Elgars lived in a small country
cottage which, when they moved out, was
taken by a labourer named Davies. The composer was born here in 1857.

Elgar became something of a snob and was
openly ashamed of being born 'into trade'. Yet
he was deeply attached to this simple house.
His first piece, written at the age of ten, had
been titled 'Humoreske, a Tune from Broadheath' and the place became the focus of his
later nostalgia for an idyll of old England. Later
in life, he would regularly have his chauffeur
take him on drives through the Worcestershire and Herefordshire countryside, carefully
passing Broadheath as they went.

When he was made a baronet, Elgar added
'of Broadheath' to his title, despite baronetcies
not normally adopting seats. He lived in over
twenty-five houses but told his daughter he
wanted his memorial here. The cottage was
acquired by Worcestershire Council at the
prompting of the daughter, and turned into a
museum in 1939. It is now run by the Elgar
Foundation.

The cottage is a simple redbrick structure
with four rooms downstairs and three upstairs.
A porch with scalloped bargeboards gives onto
a pretty garden with roses and forget-me-
nots. In the garden is the summer house from
Elgar's last home. With his desk, it is the only
furniture directly associated with the composer. Next door to the cottage is a small coach
house and stable where Elgar's father kept a
pony and trap.

The interior is furnished not as it would
have been when Elgar was born but to accommodate memorabilia of his life, his love of
Worcestershire and his hobbies, including racing, golf, cycling and travel. He would often
cycle fifty miles a day. The custodian will play a
CD of any requested Elgar work while visitors
go round, an admirable custom rare in English
houses.

Next door is a large Elgar Centre, its design
and atmosphere completely at odds with the
rustic simplicity of the house.

MADRESFIELD COURT ****

Madresfield, 2m NE of Great Malvern
Victorian re-creation of Tudor moated manor
(P-R)

Madresfield is the classic house-lover's house. It sits in the lee of the Malvern Hills, Tudor in appearance, gabled, moated and enfolded in herbaceous borders and yew parterres. A dreamy mist seems to envelop it in all weathers. The house has never known anything so vulgar as a sale, passing down the Lygon family, Earls Beauchamp, since the Middle Ages. It is now occupied by the niece of the last Earl, Lady Morrison.

As with so many Tudor houses, Madresfield is mostly a Victorian fantasy, the work of Philip Hardwick in 1865. His client was the Anglo-Catholic 6th Earl Beauchamp, a Puseyite and co-founder of Keble College, Oxford. His alterations were completed by his son, the 7th Earl, an enthusiastic patron of the Arts and Crafts movement. He was sent out as Governor of New South Wales at the age of twenty-seven, one of the more bizarre cases of imperial patronage (satirized in Hilaire Belloc's *Lord Lundy*). He was later Liberal Leader in the House of Lords and a craftsman who embroidered the house's many flame-stitch chairs. In later life, the Earl was a friend of Evelyn Waugh, and Madresfield is often suggested (among others) as a model for Brideshead.

The appeal of the house is not so much architectural as what architecture could evoke. Here it evokes two strands of late-Victorian taste, Anglo-Catholic medievalism and Arts and Crafts vernacular. With a family rich enough to buy whatever they wanted, Madresfield is to the 19th century what the Grand Tour mansions were to the 18th. The whole is far greater than the sum of its parts.

The original Tudor house had the normal plan of a moated manor. There was a gatehouse leading to an inner courtyard on the far side of which would have been the Great Hall. A solar wing and long gallery were on one side and domestic offices on the other. All this

survives in spirit. But Hardwick added new rooms inside the courtyard, crowding it with a gallery, cloister and a tower with spire. A second large hall was constructed with a new staircase and wing of reception rooms. The result is a house that seems to yearn after grandeur yet mercifully fails to achieve it.

Each room in Madresfield is completely different, and thus the more memorable. The library was decorated not by Hardwick but by C. R. Ashbee of the Cotswold Guild of Handicraft. The door panels and bookcase ends are remarkable works of English Art Nouveau, depicting the various paths to wisdom. An appropriate library motto declares simply, 'Thou Shalt Not Steal'. It is a narrow, dark gallery of a room, crammed with books, where the mere act of subsiding into a chair seems to impart wisdom.

The Arts and Crafts theme is continued in the adjacent chapel, created by the wife of the 7th Earl as a present to her husband. Murals are everywhere, including depictions of the couple's children. Every inch of wall, ceiling and woodwork is painted in the manner of a medieval church. Most of this is by Henry Payne, of the Birmingham School of Arts and Crafts, yet it has none of the solemnity of the Pre-Raphaelites, suggesting rather the picturesque tradition of Edwardian book illustration. (It is described almost exactly in *Brideshead Revisited*.)

The Long Gallery survives from the pre-Victorian house. Overhead is a neo-Jacobean ceiling and to one side a Jacobean chimney-piece. The room is full of Beauchamp acquisitions, here mostly 17th-century and Arts and Crafts furniture and porcelain. Parallel to this gallery is another one inserted into the old courtyard by Hardwick, named the 'So What Room'.

Beyond is the Victorian staircase hall formed from the solar wing of the old house. It is a grand reception room, rising to the roof and lit by three crystal domes. Round it on three sides is a balcony with twisted glass

Plutocratic ghosts: Witley's Poseidon fountain

balusters. Pictures cover every inch of the walls, their hang based on a painting of the family gathered here for a birthday in 1924. They look like a cast line-up for a Noël Coward play. Here are Meissen birds, English and German silver, Cromwellian snuffboxes and an apothecary's chest. The place is overflowing.

In comparison, the saloon and drawing room in the Victorian extension, the one bright blue, the other green, seem demure. They were designed to reflect the taste and collecting zeal of the French wife of the 1st Earl. They contain Boulle furniture, Limoges enamels, Sèvres porcelain, more snuffboxes and family portraits by Wright, Romney and Reynolds. A jade hookah, belonging to Tipoo Sultan, arrived from the Fonthill sale in 1823 (*see* p.665). The curtains are said to have been stitched by Queen Anne and the Duchess of Marlborough, presumably before their falling out (*see* Blenheim/Oxon).

The former Great Hall is now the dining room, refashioned by Hardwick with a hammerbeam roof, Jacobean chimneypiece and minstrels' gallery. Tudor portraits include Elizabeth I with a sieve, bizarre symbol of her virginity. She gazes across a polished table at sets of dragoon banners and Australian boomerangs. The courtyard outside is overlooked by open balconies and a tall timbered range with *sgraffito* plasterwork. We might be in the yard of a Burgundian *hôtel*. The pavement pattern is a maze.

WITLEY COURT **

Great Witley, 9m NW of Worcester
Ruin of Victorian palace, restored fountains
(EH)

Witley is the ruin of one of the most palatial private residences in England. It is a place of ghosts. But with its gardens and fountains restored, the ghosts can at least be enjoyed. The house was bought by a family of Midlands ironfounders and nailmakers, the Foleys, in 1655. In the 1730s, they extended the house and removed the village more than a mile away to Great Witley. The village church was rebuilt *in situ* to designs by James Gibbs, compelling the villagers to walk back to the house to worship. The sumptuous church is in use to this day.

The Foleys finally succumbed to extravagance and debt. Thomas Foley was so fat he was known as 'Lord Balloon'. He had John Nash add the fine porticos to Witley that survive to this day. The Foleys were succeeded at Witley by a new generation of industrialists. The Dudleys were rich on iron, coal and quarrying and by 1860 had risen to the rank of Earl. The 1st Earl proceeded to expand the old 17th-century house into a stupendous mansion, designed by Samuel Daukes. Victorian photographs show sprawling Italianate halls and ballrooms, heavy with chandeliers, palm trees and embroidered chairs. The Earl and Countess's private suite in the east range was of legendary richness, filled with gold leaf and antique furniture. The house was a popular resort of the then Prince of Wales, who bagged over 1,000 Witley pheasants.

Yet even the Dudleys found themselves hard-pressed. After the Great War they could no longer afford two huge houses. They kept Himley in Staffordshire. Witley was sold in 1920 and in 1937 a severe fire left it a ruin. It was then sold for scrap, a devastating fall from grace in a matter of years. The house was not demolished but wrecked by salvage contractors and vandals. The empty walls were stabilized by the government in 1972 and are in the care of English Heritage.

The gardens were laid out by William Nesfield, and formed one of his grandest projects. Terraces, parterres, gravel avenues and box-bordered flower beds spread across the landscape as if for a Carlsbad spa. A balustraded wall protected the garden from an 800-acre deer park. A complex series of pipes took water from the pools up to a reservoir in the park and then down to the gigantic Poseidon and Flora fountains.

The former is reputedly one of the largest sculpted monoliths in Europe, bigger even than the Trevi in Rome. Bing Crosby tried to buy it for his Hollywood home. When working, it made a noise 'like a mighty steam engine'. It has now been restored and has a cascade of 30 arched jets around a central plume of 100 ft. The rainbows are said to be sensational.

WORCESTER:
THE COMMANDERY **

Sidbury
Hall house with painted room (M)

This early Tudor hall house served as a soldiers' billet after the Battle of Worcester in 1651 and has never looked back. On my visit, it had plausibly recreated the scene. Live soldiers lay snoring on straw in the hall. Troopers were swearing and falling into line on the lawn. Ladies were sorting herbs and gossiping in upstairs rooms. Muskets were everywhere. The building is clearly a 'living' museum. My only regret is that some iconoclast was not allowed to drive a few pikes through the display cases and put a musket ball into the nearest health-and-safety inspector. They come close to wrecking the place.

The building lies along the old canal, presenting a timbered end wall to the main road. It was once the hospital of St Wulstan, founded in 1085, whose governors called themselves commanders. The house is H-shaped with later extensions. At its core is a Great Hall of real splendour.

The roof is of ornamented tie-beam trusses. Below are a screen and screens passage adorned with twisted balusters. The dais end has a coved canopy and the bay window has pretty stained glass panes. The furniture of a military barracks makes a refreshing change from the usual Jacobean oak.

The rest of the Commandery is a Civil War museum. Some original rooms remain, including a remarkable chamber apparently from the medieval hospital, with murals of c1500. They display Death and Redemption, the martyrdom of Becket and the disembowelling of St Erasmus, popular medieval horror stories. The panelled and furnished rooms in the solar wing are used for re-enactments.

WORCESTER:
THE GREYFRIARS **

New Street
Rich town house restored and refurnished (NT)

Worcester city council struggled for seven years to demolish The Greyfriars before admitting defeat in 1943 and leaving its rescue to the local archaeological society. An indication of the council's preferred architecture can be seen up the street, a concrete multi-storey car park. Medieval New Street and its environs were and could still be a miniature York – and booming with visitors – were it not for its council. The authority's wreckage of this fine old city has continued until recently.

The Greyfriars is a 15th-century merchant's town house, near the site of an old monastery of that name. The ruined building was taken on in 1949 by a brother and sister, Matley and Elsie Moore, who lived in it and devoted the rest of their lives to its restoration. Old tenements were cleared from the rear and a garden laid out. Miss Moore was a fine needlewoman, filling the house with hangings and tapestries. Buildings opposite were acquired and this part of the street preserved. The group was passed to the National Trust in 1966, including a lovely secluded rear garden.

The exterior of The Greyfriars is that of a large English town house of c1480, black-and-white with a long jettied upper storey and two gabled cross-wings. Entry is as it always was through an arch into the courtyard, where visitors could be inspected and the dirt and smell of the street left outside.

The one solecism within is the creation of a 'great hall' out of the two downstairs rooms where none existed before. Such houses on the ground floor would have had an inner and an outer chamber, principally for the conduct of business. The original arrangement is evident in the placing of the fireplace at one side. The present hall is filled with furniture, rugs and tapestries acquired by the Moores in the style of the house. Here are two tapestries, a Mortlake and a Flemish. Mr Moore produced a screen from fragments of leather wall-hangings found elsewhere in Worcester. Over the fireplace is a beautiful embroidery of flowers by Miss Moore.

Behind the hall is a little dining room, decorated with yellow Georgian panelling by the Moores in deference to their few pieces of 18th-century furniture. The panels contain rare 18th-century wallpapers. The staircase is Jacobean, rising between what would have been two separate Tudor ranges. The three upstairs rooms are a bedroom, parlour and library, all floored and panelled in dark elm and oak, and richly furnished. The Moores lived in these rooms and they still reflect a sense of occupancy.

In the bedroom is a hanging of 17th-century crewel-work almost filling one wall. The parlour has a frieze of Welsh dragons, a popular subject given the proximity to Wales. The library comprises a collection of antiquarian books collected by the Moores. On the wall are paintings by Thomas Shotter Boys of the street outside in the mid-19th century. Each room has a grandfather clock, many of them made in Worcester.

Yorkshire, East Riding

The East Riding of Yorkshire, once briefly Humberside, is the Cinderella of the North. The county lies where the flatlands of eastern England peter out north of the Humber, yet as soon as the landscape finds contours and character, it leaves East Riding behind.

In houses, as in churches, the East Riding makes up in quality what it lacks in quantity. The county is almost without houses of the medieval or early Tudor periods, apart from a fragment at Burton Agnes Manor. Yet it has two masterpieces from the Elizabethan-Jacobean watershed, Burton Constable and Robert Smythson's Burton Agnes Hall. The latter ranks among the finest, and best presented, houses in England.

The county's chief city, Hull, is now a gap-toothed wasteland, but it retains an enclave of mercantile houses of the 17th and 18th centuries, well represented by Wilberforce House, with its eccentric Jacobean façade, and the remarkable staircase of the Maister House. Sledmere, after its fire, is a fine restoration, from Joseph Rose's plasterwork to Francis Johnson's library.

Burton Agnes:
  Hall *****
  Manor House *

Burton Constable ****
Hull:
  Maister House *

Hull:
  Wilberforce House **
Sewerby *
Sledmere ***

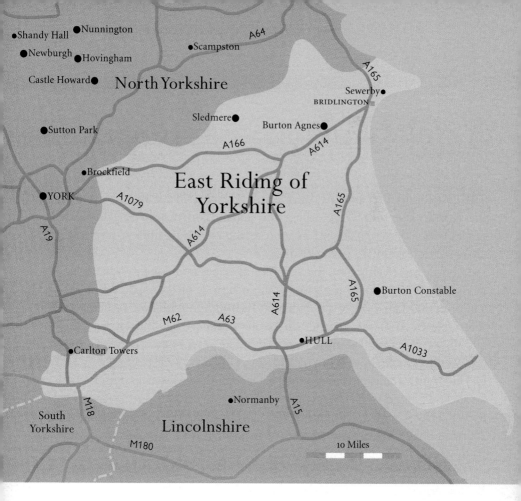

BURTON AGNES HALL *****

Burton Agnes, 7m SW of Bridlington
Late-Elizabethan house by Smythson (P)

I first saw Burton Agnes with a low evening sun warming its brick crevices and deepening the shadows of the yews across the lawn. It is the perfect English house, embodying the climax of the first great age of domestic architecture, Elizabethan, at the hand of Robert Smythson, its finest exponent. The house was begun in 1601 by Sir Henry Griffith, descendant of the Norman owner of the estate, Roger de Stuteville. It has been held in line of descent by Griffiths, Boyntons and Cunliffe-Listers ever since, now as a trust.

The house has no great park but is reached up steps direct from the village. The entrance is through a three-storey gatehouse of 1610. This is of pink bricks and has domed turrets. Renaissance features include arched niches on the ground floor and a stone frontispiece flanked by caryatids. The front courtyard is now a lawn populated by clipped topiary yews. The façade is a typical Smythson stage-set, a sequence of projecting and receding bays, some squared, some bowed. There is no obvious door, the entrance being tucked in beside one of the bays, yet with a frontispiece of its own. This is in the same manner as at Chastleton (Oxon), suggesting some Smythson link with the latter house – or at least an enthusiastic imitator.

The Great Hall is without parallel of any

Burton Agnes: the honeysuckle ceiling

house of this period. Where the Italians played with space, the English played with ornament. The screen and chimneypiece at Burton Agnes fight each other to a draw. The former rises the full height of the entrance wall. Three tiers of tableaux form a gallery of sculpted figures. Set in an architectural frame, they are a Jacobean Elgin Marbles. The chimneypiece replies in alabaster, Wise and Foolish Virgins supporting a celebration of the Griffith, then Boynton, line of owners. It is flanked by large portraits of 18th-century Griffith Boyntons.

The doorway to the inner hall is a work of art in itself. Here stands a Nonsuch chest, its decoration recalling Henry VIII's lost palace in Surrey, and a Gheeraerts painting of the three daughters of the original house. The drawing room beyond is a glowing chamber, ranking in spectacle with the hall. It is covered in panelling with painted arches and stumpy pilasters.

The house now changes key to Georgian. In the 18th-century Chinese Room, cool walls frame lacquer panels depicting Chinese festivals. The dining room is enlivened by a fireplace brought down from the Long Gallery and is hung with landscapes by Marlow and Gainsborough and portraits by Reynolds and Cotes.

The staircase is a funnel of grandeur. Wide, shallow treads seem compressed into a central well, as if a farthingale were trying to negotiate a corkscrew. The craftsman has carried the flights upwards using a group of four newel posts on small arches. The big first floor drawing room, panelled c1700, is light and classical, its furniture copied from Kent, Adam and Chippendale. French Post-Impressionists hang on the walls. Burton Agnes never ceases to surprise.

The state bedrooms are predictably sumptuous. The King's Room has exquisite panelling and scrollwork on the bed-head, the centre of which is covered in original sky-blue damask. The Queen's Room has a plasterwork ceiling of honeysuckle so deeply sculpted it seems ready to creep down the walls and wind itself round the furniture. It was once haunted by a daughter of the house who, on her deathbed, demanded her head be buried within its walls. It was not, and she duly wandered the place so determinedly that she had to be exhumed and accorded her wish.

The crowning glory of Burton Agnes is the Long Gallery, running the entire length of the top floor. This is no Elizabethan attic but a true gallery, again similar to that at Chastleton. The room was later divided and most of the ceiling lost. The barrel vault was restored and replicated by Francis Johnson first in 1951 and the remainder in 1974. Its peach-coloured walls with white pilasters are hung with works by Courbet, Cézanne, Corot, Boudin, Gauguin, Matisse, Renoir, Rouault and Pissarro.

This splendid collection was mostly gathered by Marcus Wickham-Boynton, who died in 1989. Burton Agnes still has an 'artist in residence', resident in what is already a work of art.

BURTON AGNES MANOR HOUSE *

Burton Agnes, 7m SW of Bridlington
Norman hall in medieval grouping (EH)

Sitting outside the formal walls of Burton Agnes Hall, the manor house pre-dates that house by four centuries. The outside is of brick and with 18th-century windows, but this is a façade. The building was the Great Hall of the original Griffith manor, and was built by the present family's predecessor, Roger de Stuteville, in about 1173. Presumably respect for ancestors protected it down the years; it is now guarded by English Heritage. Even its conversion for use as a Georgian laundry was deferential.

The entrance leads into the undercroft. This is exceptionally grand and well preserved. The massive piers have waterleaf capitals and the vaults are heavily ribbed. Upstairs is the hall itself, much altered but still with an appropriate sense of majesty. The roof has a kingpost and dates from the 15th century. Original fragments can be detected in the walling and a small slit window survives, lighting the staircase. I overheard a tourist who had just visited the big house next door saying, 'I prefer this one: I know what I could do with it.'

BURTON CONSTABLE HALL
****

8m NE of Hull
Elizabethan mansion converted into Grand Tour treasure trove (P)

Burton Constable invites comparison with its near namesake, Burton Agnes. It is contemporary but in every way different. Both were Elizabethan creations by old Yorkshire families whose descendants still occupy them. Burton Constable, though the bigger, was not big enough for the 18th-century William Constable, whose character and taste dominate the house. He expanded and georgianized the interior, making it unmanageable for the 21st century. The house now has an air of mild desperation. Where Burton Agnes Hall is compact and intimate, Burton Constable seems lonely and lost in the open fields of Holderness.

Constables still live in one wing. The rest is run by a trust and, greatly to its credit, by the City of Leeds which owns the contents of the main part of the house. Work needs doing, although much of the charm lies in how much is still undone. This is one of the few large houses whose nether regions remain undiscovered and uncatalogued. Even my guide seemed lost among unlit storerooms, passages, basements and turrets. This is a place of secrets and hermits. Long may it remain so.

Sir John Constable, of Norman descent, built a new front onto his Burton property in the 1560s, forming an Elizabethan façade with a central bay window and side entrance to a screens passage. William Constable's 18th-century alterations left little of this work untouched. He installed the present central door and frontispiece, rising to the Constable coat of arms on the roof. The resulting façade seems rather flat. The front door leads directly into the Great Hall, bringing with it wind and

rain and demonstrating the virtues of screens passages. The Hall of 1763 is by Timothy Lightoler, deeply coved with mini-vaults above a heavy cornice. It is a remarkable example of a Jacobean revival interior, well before its time.

William Constable was a man of divided loyalties. He was reputedly sorry to part with the Elizabethan Great Hall and screen, in which he liked to dine, medieval fashion, with his wife and thirty-four servants, his 'family' as he called them. Yet he was also an assiduous Grand Tourist and longed for a house that reflected the new Augustan taste. Demosthenes and Hercules flank the fireplace, Marcus Aurelius and Sappho are on the mantelshelf. The Constable arms on the chimneypiece are attended by boughs of imitation oak and laurel. Huge family portraits stare down from the walls, including one of William and his wife in ancient Roman garb. This was truly a man torn between past and future.

William apparently rejected plans for an adjacent dining room by Robert Adam in favour of one by Lightoler. Here the Middle Ages altogether vanish. Three giant medallions decorate the walls, one showing the Three Graces dancing before Pan, another Bacchus and Ariadne. William, in a fervour of indecision about whom to prefer, employed different craftsmen on each feature of the room. The ceiling, copied from Italy, is by Joseph Cortese. Attention was paid to every detail, from the grapes on the overmantel to the crests on the wine glasses. Nothing was less 'provincial' than the taste of these Yorkshire grandees.

The Grand Staircase occupies a large volume in the centre of the house. Pevsner regarded it as 'uneventful' but he did not see the fierce yellow paint applied to it in 1972. This outdazzles even the heavy-duty pictures intended to fill the open wallspace. Coriolanus's mother glares across the emptiness at Constable forebears, the Astons.

The staircase balcony leads into the Long Gallery, which runs the length of the rear elevation. This is in the form of a richly panelled library, with ceiling of roundels and pendants, again Jacobean revival. It has a charming Georgian fireplace with flanking columns garlanded with flowers growing from pots. Embroidered samplers and 17th-century chairs mix with Nanking vases and early portraits.

We now see another side to William Constable. He was not just a Grand Tourist but a scientist and collector. Closets and 'cabinets of curiosities' follow one after another, filled with a phenomenal variety of objects – guns, fossils, shells and scientific instruments. These include an early electricity machine, a condenser and a table pump. Georgian science laboratory co-existed with drawing room. Burton Constable is the best example of an Enlightened gentleman's collection.

The bedrooms are also Georgian. The Gold Bedroom has a Rococo four-poster and exotically framed mirrors. A suite of state rooms was converted from the old Tudor Great Chamber and from what may have started as a pele tower buried in the later building. The conversion demonstrates Lightoler at his most inventive.

Burton Constable now delightfully loses control. Rooms fall out of each other apparently at random. On the ground floor is a Catholic chapel, in the richest of Italianate decoration of 1844 and still in use. The adjacent silk-hung ballroom was designed in 1775 by James Wyatt and furnished by Chippendale. The door handles are of Worcester porcelain.

Three more drawing rooms follow, by which stage the visitor's head is whirling. In the Chippendale Room is a mechanical orange tree with singing birds. The Chinese Room has wallpaper as good as any I know, each wall a sweeping composition of birds fluttering across leaves and flowers. The room is littered with oriental figures and the chandelier is a Chinese lantern. There are dragons everywhere. This is a miniature Brighton Pavilion of the North.

Despite evidence of the presence of some London craftsmen, most of Burton Constable was by workers from Hull and Doncaster. It demonstrates not just the taste of one country gentleman in the Georgian era but the quality of work generally present in the North of England at the time.

HULL: MAISTER HOUSE *

160 High Street
Georgian merchant's house (NT)

The Maister family were prosperous Hull merchants with a business and house in the High Street. One April night in 1743 a fire consumed the building, killing Henry Maister's wife, daughter and two servants. He himself survived another eighteen months but his brother took charge of the rebuilding. The exterior was severe and Palladian. The interior, or at least one feature of it, was astonishing. The staircase of the Maister House is virtuoso plasterwork. Although the building is used as offices, it is owned by the National Trust and the stairwell is accessible to view.

Work on the staircase involved consultation with none other than Lord Burlington. Why he should have concerned himself with a merchant's house in Hull is unclear, except that he had property in the East Riding and would have known many local citizens.

The ground floor would have been occupied by business, so a grand entrance to the family chambers above was important. The stairs, which rise the full height of the interior, were decorated by a local stuccoist, Joseph Page, with a wrought-iron balustrade by Robert Bakewell of Derby.

Page's stucco work is superb. Swags, busts, statue niches and medallions adorn the walls. The first-floor landing has palatial doors and swirling Rococo decoration in the ceiling panels. Roses fill the undersides of the top gallery, above which rises a Rococo ceiling to the top-lit lantern. It is as rich as could be, buried within a Hull office block.

HULL: WILBERFORCE HOUSE **

25 High Street
Artisan Mannerist house (M)

Oh, to have known Hull in the 17th century! Grand merchants' houses backed onto gardens and staithes, at the end of which ships from across the North Sea and Baltic dropped anchor. Every house was a family home, a business and a travel agency in one. The nearest extant example I have found is at Old Cochin in Kerala, India, but Hull was grander.

One such house would have been the home of a Baltic trader, Robert Wilberforce. His son William, born here in 1759, was to be the great slave-trade abolitionist. The house was designed almost a century earlier by William Catlyn, a Hull bricklayer of ability and learning, who also designed neighbouring Crowle House. He crammed his learning into the façade. The mid-17th century style was known as Artisan Mannerist, emanating in part from the Netherlands.

The frontage to the High Street is of nine bays, which is very wide. The façade is entirely of brick with fake rustication and pilasters on the first floor. Most odd is the frontispiece over the door. This rises three storeys with no parapet or gable but flanking pilasters, with each rusticated panel adorned with a 'jewel'. Pedimental niches flank the doorway arch.

Although the interior of the house is now the Wilberforce Museum, many original features survive. The drawing room downstairs was refashioned in the 18th century with Ionic pilasters and a Rococo ceiling. The fine staircase with Rococo plasterwork is spoiled with over-clever painting. The medallions are bright blue and the Wilberforce eagle black. On the first floor, the Banqueting Room has excellent panelling, especially round the fireplace, and a treasure chest. Most of the other rooms suffer from museumitis and political correctness. Hull citizens apparently still need telling that slavery was not a good idea.

SEWERBY HALL *

Sewerby, 2m NE of Bridlington
Georgian house on bluff (M)

Sewerby Hall was the seat of the Greame family from 1694. They were local land agents but pretended descent from the Scots Grahams, Dukes of Montrose. A Victorian Greame,

called 'Yarborough', so preferred his Christian name as to change his surname, becoming Yarborough Yarborough.

Those days are past. Few houses are sadder than those overlain with an alternative use for which they were not designed. Sewerby was sold to the local council in the 1930s and has become a museum, looking out to sea from a stately terrace and weeping for its past. Its magnificent garden is defaced by health-and-safety cages which protect the public from the municipal llamas.

The house remains a fine one, built in the early 18th century and covered in cream render with stone window dressings. The corner bows were added in 1808. The interior rooms not filled with museum cases have good panelling and plasterwork. Fluted pilasters flank the arch from the hall to the cantilevered staircase. The best room is the early Georgian Oak Room. It retains dark panelling and a shell-headed niche, decoration repeated in the bedroom above.

Sewerby has been refurnished and an effort made to recapture some of its past charm. One room is dedicated to Amy Johnson, the early aviator. Yarborough's Victorian gardens are exotic, including one of the oldest monkey puzzle trees in England.

SLEDMERE HOUSE ***

Sledmere, 8m NW of Driffield
Restored Georgian house, re-created Joseph Rose interiors (P)

Sledmere is a Yorkshire Lanhydrock (Cornwall), a house destroyed by fire (in 1911) and reinstated to the enhanced standards of Edwardian country-house living. Here the reproduction is Georgian rather than Jacobean. The house was the seat of the Sykes family of Hull, grandees of the East Riding. It was begun in the mid-18th century but mostly designed, largely by Sir Christopher Sykes, in the 1780s. His passion for tripartite windows, each set within an arch, lends the place a noble eccentricity. The outstanding plasterwork was by Joseph Rose. Even if the post-fire interiors seem indisputably 20th century, the reproduction of Rose's work is a wonder of conservation. So too are the post-war amendments by Francis Johnson. Sledmere is, in truth, a 'Georgian' house designed over three centuries.

The small entrance hall is adorned with weapons, trophies and a rusticated fireplace. A statue of Laocoon was relieved of pomposity (on my visit) by a bowler hat. Beyond is the central hall, created by Walter Brierley after the 1911 fire, as the spine and chief adornment of Sledmere. It runs across almost the entire building. Scagliola columns the colour of amber divide the hall into bays adorned with Adamish swags and scrolls on soft green walls. The stairs that form the climax are Baroque in effect. They narrow past large urns before dividing in front of a copy of the Apollo Belvedere and turning back to the landing. This is a splendid space, the more dramatic when an organ under the stairs is playing full blast during public visits. Music is a feature of Sledmere.

The reception rooms downstairs are lavishly decorated. The relief plasterwork in the music room is after Adam. In front of another organ is an exquisite Chinese enamel table. The drawing room is a celebration of Joseph Rose.

His ceiling in the Adam style depicts 'Greek religious rites' amid a familiar decoration of shells, anthemion and laurel. The walls are hung with Sykes portraits, including one of Sir Tatton Sykes on horseback, the embodiment of a great Victorian 'improver'. The boudoir has scarlet damask walls with another Adam-style ceiling and marquetry chests. The dining room is in blue and gold with a Romney of Sir Christopher Sykes, builder of the house, an English country gentleman and his wife.

The glory of Sledmere is upstairs: Sir Christopher's great library was restored to Rose's original designs and colours by Francis Johnson in 1979–81. As a work of architectural reinstatement, it ranks with that of Uppark (Sussex). The ceiling is arched and vaulted in the richest of Roman motifs, gold and blue on a cream background. A marquetry floor repeats the old carpet, lost in the fire. The original book collection included a Gutenberg Bible. Mercifully it had been sold before the fire and is now in New York's Metropolitan Museum.

On the way out, visitors can see the Turkish Room, copied from a sultan's apartment in Istanbul. It is a dazzling display of blue tiles. The park is by Capability Brown.

Yorkshire, North
with York

North Yorkshire is one of England's loveliest counties and most richly endowed with houses. The uplands of the Dales and the North York Moors long attracted both castles and monasteries. The Vales of York and Pickering were relatively free of recusancy poverty and saw large Georgian houses set amid grand sporting estates. In the 1970s, boundary changes embracing parts of the West Riding added to its wealth.

Great keeps survive at Helmsley, Middleham and Richmond. There are rare medieval courtyard castles at Bolton and Skipton, and incomparable relics of monastic domestic architecture at Fountains and Rievaulx. Markenfield is a picturesque fortified manor house.

The Tudors left less in Yorkshire than in Lancashire, or perhaps their descendants replaced more. The long gallery at Newburgh is derelict and the tower at Ripley a fragment. Only Smythson's Fountains Hall is a remarkable Elizabethan work, and it was not built until the Queen was dead.

Yorkshire comes into its own with the advent of English Baroque, with Vanbrugh's majestic palace for the Earl of Carlisle at Castle Howard, and the lesser house that it inspired at Duncombe. Both lent themselves to great landscape architecture. The Palladians contributed eccentric Hovingham and Robert Adam produced at Newby Hall one of his best rooms in England.

The county is also a place of gems: the Grand Tour hall at Beningbrough, Nicholas Stone's chimneypiece at Newburgh, and the tortoiseshell tea-room at Sutton. James Herriot's house in Thirsk is one of the best renderings of a 1950s interior England.

Aske Hall ＊＊
Barden Tower ＊
Beningbrough ＊＊＊＊
Bolton Castle ＊＊＊
Brockfield ＊
Broughton ＊＊＊
Carlton Towers ＊＊
Castle Howard ＊＊＊＊＊
Constable Burton ＊
Crathorne ＊
Duncombe ＊＊＊
Fountains:
　　Abbey ＊＊
　　Hall ＊＊
Hazlewood ＊＊
Helmsley Castle ＊
Hovingham ＊＊＊
Kiplin ＊＊
Kirkleatham:
　　Turner's Hospital ＊
Knaresborough:
　　House in the Rock ＊
Markenfield ＊＊＊
Marmion Tower ＊
Middleham ＊
Moulton ＊
Mount Grace ＊
Newburgh Priory ＊＊＊
Newby Hall ＊＊＊＊
Norton Conyers ＊＊＊
Nunnington ＊＊＊
Ormesby ＊＊
Richmond Castle ＊
Rievaulx:
　　Abbey ＊＊
　　Ionic Temple ＊
Ripley ＊＊＊
Ripon:
　　House of Correction ＊

Ripon:
　　Union Workhouse ＊
Ryedale Museum:
　　Crofter's Cottage ＊
　　Harome Cottage ＊
　　Manor House ＊
　　Stang End ＊

Scampston ＊＊
Settle:
　　The Folly ＊
Shandy Hall ＊＊
Sion Hill ＊＊
Skipton ＊＊＊
Stockeld ＊＊

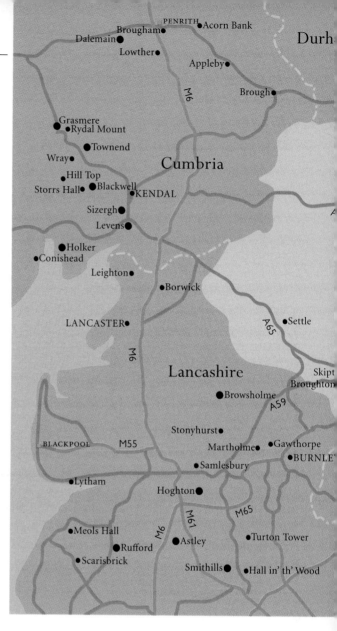

ASKE HALL **

2m N of Richmond
Aristocratic mansion in ornamental park
(P-R)

The seat of the Marquesses of Zetland broods on its hillside outside Richmond, pondering a future of corporate activity and rural enterprise. Can an old lady dabble in such things and keep her dignity? The house seen from the main road is magnificently framed by trees. It was much reduced in the 1960s by the neo-classicist, Claud Phillimore, who refaced the main façade in stone. The entrance was placed at the back, in a quiet courtyard behind the wall of a 15th-century pele tower, a rare survival in Yorkshire.

The principal reception rooms flank the main hall behind the portico. They are mostly devoted to the Zetland picture collection. In the hall, dark Stuart courtiers gaze out from beetle brows. The marble fireplace is a relic from the sadly demolished Clumber Park in Nottinghamshire. Richard Wilson landscapes illuminate the saloon. The drawing room, possibly by Carr of York, has a Zoffany of the same room showing a row of bronze statues on the mantelpiece, which the present family has enterprisingly tried to reassemble after an earlier sale. All these rooms have fine views down to the lake.

The approach to the house is past gargantuan Victorian stables more magnificent than the house itself. In the grounds at Aske is a fragment of Richmond Castle, demolished and rebuilt as a folly called Oliver's Ducket.

BARDEN TOWER *

5m NE of Skipton
Picturesque pele tower in Wharfe valley (P)

The ruin of Barden Tower stands in the valley of the Wharfe above Bolton Abbey, where the gorge broadens onto the moor. It was one of many Pennine houses that Lady Anne Clifford took in hand during her sovereignty of the North (*see* Appleby/Cumbria). The tower had been a feudal base for resisting Scottish raids down Wharfedale. In the 14th century it passed to the Cliffords of Skipton. Henry Clifford had been sent to live with shepherds as a youth, to protect him from the Wars of the Roses. Known as the 'Shepherd Lord', he resided at the pele tower of Barden under Henry VII, regarding it as safer than his place at Skipton.

Clifford rebuilt Barden but it was his descendant, Lady Anne, who restored what had become a ruin. Although her ownership was contested by Lady Burlington of adjacent Bolton Abbey, Anne brooked no opposition. She restored every property she claimed, journeying between them in a litter. She added chapels and almshouses where she could. After her death in 1676, Barden reverted to the Burlington family, through whom it descended to the Dukes of Devonshire, who own it still.

Lady Anne is probably responsible for the fine arched entrance to Barden and the flanking windows with Jacobean tracery. The main façade is symmetrical, with tower wings rising four storeys. The domestic rooms are on one side and services on the other. Although now roofless, the walls are intact and form an impressive example of the domestic buildings that Lady Anne sought to maintain, with appropriate ritual, against the Cromwellian revolution.

To the south of the house, a 17th-century chapel and priest's house form a picturesque foreground to the sombre ruin next door.

BENINGBROUGH HALL ****

Beningbrough, 8m NW of York
Grand Tour house with NPG pictures (NT)

The young John Bourchier returned home from the Grand Tour in Italy in 1706 and married his wealthy childhood sweetheart, Mary Bellwood. Their new house at Beningbrough was designed by a local man, William Thornton. It was to be based on Bourchier's researches in Rome, with occasional flourishes

Regal slumber: Beningbrough's state bed

of Borromini and Bernini on the entrance front. The house descended through Earles and Dawnays before being acquired by Lord Chesterfield in 1917. It passed to the National Trust in 1957.

The façades are in red brick and look back to the 17th century rather than forward to the Palladians. The entrance leads directly into the hall, a huge chamber which defies the simplicity of the exterior. Giant pilasters soar two storeys to groined vaults. They pass balconied openings from the staircases, in the manner of Vanbrugh. Knellers look down with satisfaction from the walls.

The plan is old-fashioned, with state bedrooms on the ground floor, still with their closets. The resulting enfilade of panelled rooms is more Dutch than Italian in style. Decoration is wood rather than plaster and the walls carry tapestries, china and miniatures. The prize of Beningbrough is Lord Chesterfield's state bed. Brought by him from Holme Lacy (Herefs), it is French in style and heavy with red damask.

The adjacent dining room is hung with Kneller's portraits of members of the Kit-Cat Club, borrowed from the National Portrait Gallery. This group of Whig literati pledged themselves to maintain the Protestant succession when it was considered at risk under Queen Anne. The faces are so stylized as to reveal little individual personality.

The drawing room has woodcarving worthy of Grinling Gibbons and the enfilade is completed by a dressing room and closet, the latter with parts of a Chinese screen set into the panelling, matching the Chinese lacquerwork furniture. On every wall there seems to be Kneller, as if he worked exclusively for this one house.

The climb to the saloon reveals glimpses of the upper level of the hall through openings and balconies. On the first floor, corridors penetrate the house from end to end. The saloon is light yet grand, with Bourchier more in Italian mode. Pilasters are gilded and ceilings coffered. In the attic are more paintings lent to the house by the National Portrait Gallery, an admirable practice.

BOLTON CASTLE ***

Castle Bolton, 5m W of Leyburn
Keep-castle overlooking Wensleydale (P)

Bolton is a 14th-century fortress palace. Held by descendants of the 12th-century Scropes, it is everything English Heritage castles are not allowed to be. It is damp, smelly, rambling, romantic and faintly desperate. The stones do not speak for themselves but are helped in the task. A waxen Mary Queen of Scots sits huddling with her retinue in a cold bedchamber. A priest mumbles his vespers in a dripping chapel. A horse tries to grind corn on a threshing floor and I distinctly heard a man groaning in the dungeon.

The castle was built and crenellated in 1379 by the 1st Baron, Richard Scrope, and completed by his son, William. The latter went on to acquire the Kingdom of the Isle of Man and serve as Treasurer to Richard II. For this, he was beheaded without trial, first of a series of mishaps to befall the Scropes. The line survived through illegitimate heirs. The castle incarcerated Mary, Queen of Scots in 1568, on her way to Fotheringay, but was slighted by Cromwell after declaring for the King in the Civil War. In 1653, a Scrope daughter married a Powlett, who became Duke of Bolton and moved from the Castle into Bolton Hall. Orde-Powlett descendants continue as owners and custodians.

Restoration of the old castle began in the 1990s and continues today. Unlike Skipton's informal range of buildings round a courtyard, Bolton is a single rectangular fortress, one of the finest to survive in this form in the country, with square corner towers five storeys high. To Pevsner, Bolton represented a 'balance between the claims of defence, domestic complexity and comfort, and an aesthetically considered orderliness'.

The castle looks out onto Wensleydale as if still its overlord. The entrance, in summer, is through the double gatehouse, a narrow

Lordly Bolton in Wensleydale

passage where arrows, pitch, boiling oil and other missiles could be rained down on attackers. Inside, the courtyard is cobbled, the massive walls and towers looming on all sides. The ground floor chambers were for stabling, storage and food preparation. All are in good repair.

Though the outer walls and lower floors survive, only the south-west tower remains complete to its roof. The west range of the castle and the tower rooms are well restored, the latter with solar and two floors of bedchambers above. The nursery room retains its original ceiling. The interiors are roughly furnished as they might have been during Mary, Queen of Scots' stay. We can see where water jugs would have rested by latrines, where fires would have burned and salt kept dry.

The grander rooms are along the west range, essentially the private apartments leading at right angles to the now ruined Great Hall. These comprise the Guest Hall on the first floor and the Great Chamber above. Valiant efforts have been made to find carpets, tapestries, arms and banners to bring these rooms to life. It might be better to concentrate on recreating just one. A human bone was recently found still manacled to a rock in the dungeon.

BROCKFIELD HALL *

Warthill, 5m NE of York
Regency house with spectacular staircase (P-R)

The guide to Brockfield Hall states, 'Since 1951 this has been the happy family home of Lord and Lady Martin Fitzalan Howard. He is brother of the late Duke of Norfolk and son of Baroness Beaumont of Carlton Towers. There are interesting portraits of her old Roman Catholic family, the Stapletons.'

His lordship, who conducts tours of the house, goes further. His father's family, the mighty Howards, were 'not important' in the county, he says emphatically. His mother's family, the Stapletons, were. He inherited the Stapleton portraits, but has had to buy Howard ones at auction.

The house is restrained and domestic, indeed it might be a country rectory. The design was by Peter Atkinson of York in 1804. The chief feature is the entrance hall and staircase. Their curved walls fill the heart of the house, the stairs circling upwards to a balcony whose Venetian window towers over the front door. It is as if his lordship were expected to depart through this window by levitation.

The other reception rooms have dignified Regency interiors. The oval drawing room has a caryatid fireplace surround and delicate plaster ceiling. A case contains a collection of unusual glass walking sticks.

BROUGHTON HALL ***

Broughton, 3m W of Skipton
Georgian house with Italianate grounds and private chapel (P)

The Tempests were staunch recusants who can trace their line back to the 12th century. They show no sign of dying out. The younger generation draw cartoons for *Country Life* and run an enterprise consultancy in the basement. The stables are the Broughton Hall Business Park with a dozen company name-plates on the gatepost.

The Georgian house of c1750 has been much extended. William Atkinson added wings in 1810. George Webster of Kendal added a clock-tower to the stables and a monumental *porte-cochère* to the main front in 1839. The effect is in keeping with the Italianate gardens to the left and behind. Broughton has panache.

The interior turns on a handsome central hall with scagliola columns. This leads straight through the house to a 1850s conservatory beyond, forming a happy vista to W. A. Nesfield's Italianate gardens climbing the hillside at the back. The conservatory wall has a mural of various past Tempest homes, including one in Africa.

The reception rooms are by William Atkinson, Regency and enjoyably ponderous. The Red Drawing Room has an Egyptian fireplace and is hung with copies of Old Masters once in the family's possession, a relief from the relentless portraiture that dominates so many lesser English houses. The library seems entombed in leather, with a ceiling of oak leaves and posies.

The house is very much occupied and the Gothick private chapel very much worshipped in. Its Edwardian stencil work recalls that at Madresfield (Worcs). Tradentine Mass is held here four times a week, as it has since time immemorial.

CARLTON TOWERS **

Carlton, 6m S of Selby
Victorian Gothic extravaganza (P-R)

From a distance, we see only the black towers and turrets of a fantastic architectural joke. The Manor of Carlton was owned by Stapletons since the Norman Conquest. They were grand-daughters of Bess of Hardwick and, as Catholic Beaumonts, founded Beaumont College.

In 1869, the young Henry Stapleton, Lord Beaumont, renounced his father's conversion to Anglicanism, reverted to Catholicism and decided to rebuild the family home in an effusive neo-medieval style. No sooner was this under way than Beaumont left to fight variously for the Spanish pretender, Don Carlos, and in the Franco-Prussian and Zulu wars. He returned, became a Kensington property speculator and died a ruined man.

Beaumont's architect at Carlton was Edward Pugin, son of Augustus Welby, who had worked on a similarly eccentric project at Catholic Scarisbrick (Lancs). According to Mark Girouard, Edward had 'an uncontrollable temper, a passion for rows and litigation and a complete lack of prudence ... In his buildings as in his quarrels, he never knew when to stop.' The original house was 17th century, extended in the 18th and 19th centuries. Pugin coated this with Gothic embellishments. After his early death in 1875, the interior was fitted out for Beaumont by another Catholic architect, J. F. Bentley, designer of Westminster Cathedral.

The exterior is L-shaped and embattled. Pugin intended a third range, a 'Hall of the Barons', which was never built. He covered most of the exterior in dun-coloured cement, much blackened and scored to look like stone. He added three truly ugly towers and a massive entrance dominating the angle of the L-shape. The doorway is festooned with Gothic ornament derived from the Low Countries, its steps guarded by heraldic beasts holding flags. The left-hand wing has been allowed to acquire modest creeper.

The interior is astonishing. The entrance hall rises past more heraldry to the main hall, or Armoury. This is beamed and painted in over-the-top Gothic motifs. Steps to the right continue up to Bentley's state apartments. The main chamber is the Venetian Drawing Room. Its Gothic chimneypiece is enriched with Stapleton heraldry and its walls are of plaster, stamped and gilded to look like Spanish leather. The black panelling carries scenes from *The Merchant of Venice*.

The two rooms beyond are its equal in scale if not in splendour, linked by beautifully crafted Gothic doors. Visitors should arrive mounted and in armour.

CASTLE HOWARD *****

5m SW of Malton
Vanbrugh's Baroque palace (P)

Horace Walpole exclaimed, 'Nobody had informed me that I should at one view see a palace, a town, a fortified city, temples on high places, woods worthy of being each a metropolis of the Druids ... and a mausoleum that would tempt one to be buried alive.' The North will never be dull as long as it has Castle Howard. This is not a castle but the true palace of an aristocrat.

The house crowns a spur of the North York Moors. I have seen its limestone glowing in the spring sunshine across fields of daffodils. I have also seen it on a winter dawn, its mane thick with snow, growling defiance at a world that has often told it to lie down and die. Howards built this great house. Howards

Yorkshire palatial: Castle Howard's garden front

restored it after a terrible fire, and Howards live there today.

Castle Howard was built by the 3rd Earl of Carlisle, politician and man of culture. He preferred the latter pursuit. It was as a member of the Whig Kit-Cat Club (Beningbrough, above) that he met the young playwright, John Vanbrugh, and told him of his desire for a grand house on his Yorkshire estate. The initial approach appears to have been made in 1699.

Far from any centre of fashion or taste, this would be a castle of delight to draw his friends to what must have seemed an inaccessible wilderness. Carlisle did not like plans previously prepared by William Talman, architect of Chatsworth. Although Vanbrugh had never built a house, he set to work in 1700 with his assistant, Nicholas Hawksmoor. Carlisle resigned all public offices and devoted the rest of his life to the house, which was only half completed on his death in 1738.

What many regarded as disaster ensued. The earl's son-in-law, the Burlingtonian architect, Sir Thomas Robinson (*see* Rokeby/ Durham), tore up Vanbrugh's Baroque design for completing the west wing and, in the 1750s, began a rectangular west block. He seemed eager to demolish what Vanbrugh had created in what he saw as an old-fashioned style. This new Palladian west wing was not finished until 1811 and the result is a clear imbalance. Even today this so embarrasses the Howards that no picture of the West Wing appears in the guide-book. Worse was to follow. In 1940 a terrible fire broke out in the south-east wing, destroying twenty of the Vanbrugh rooms and the central dome. It took the late Lord Howard the rest of the 20th century to restore the dome. Some rooms remain derelict.

Castle Howard is regarded, with Blenheim, as a masterpiece of English Baroque. Yet it was a house rooted in the Palladian tradition. Vanbrugh's plan, of a central block with colonnades and wings, was that of a Palladian villa, its rooms along one floor rather than stacked vertically. Yet outside and inside, the house has spacial and decorative movement, planes advancing and receding in Baroque fashion.

The house is entered through Robinson's Georgian wing, with portraits of Howards galore and with two suites of 18th-century bedrooms, each with a magnificent bed. The one in the Castle Howard Bedroom is by John Linnell, sitting well amid the Marco Ricci landscapes on the wall. The bed in Lady Georgiana's Bedroom is extraordinary, like a French chevalier with his legs in the air.

Classical busts brought back from many a Grand Tour line the Antique Passage, like a guard of honour, to the Great Hall. This is the heart of the house, rising 70 ft to the dome. Vanbrugh here plays virtuoso stage designer, with four massive arches rising past balconies to the rotunda and cupola. Spaces recede from these balconies to meet hidden arches beyond. Pellegrini's murals were of *The Four Elements*, repainted after the 1940 fire by a Canadian, Scott Medd. They depict the fall of Apollo's son, a play on Carlisle's political fortunes. A fire burns below in a stupendous Baroque fireplace. This is one of England's grandest rooms.

The remaining interiors of Castle Howard are diminuendo. The Garden Hall was restored by the late Lord Howard with money from the filming here of *Brideshead Revisited*. It is in 'the spirit of Vanbrugh', with large capriccios of the house by Felix Kelly. The rooms to the left of the Garden Hall contain an exhibition on the house's restoration.

The reception rooms to the right survived the fire and contain the family's art collection. This includes works by Reynolds, Gainsborough and, in the Orleans Room, Canaletto, Rubens, Claude Lorraine and Holbein. The final Museum Room is filled with 19th-century paintings by Watts and Leighton, and by the 9th Earl, artist, Liberal and enthusiast for the later Pre-Raphaelites.

The corner here turns into the Georgian wing. Robinson's Long Gallery was decorated in 1811 and is punctuated by a central dome. Here hang more Howards and Italian landscapes by Pannini. The tour ends with the 18th-century private chapel, still in use. This was boldly redecorated at the end of the 19th century with embroidery by Morris, windows by Burne-Jones and murals to designs by C. E. Kempe. In the lobby outside is a delightful small museum of curiosities, such as a stuffed monkey, an ornamental wheelbarrow, a bleeding bowl and many commemorative trowels and spades.

The grounds at Castle Howard are as celebrated as the house. To the east lies the famous Ray Wood with its unique collection of rare trees and shrubs. Vistas are dotted with Vanbrughian towers, obelisks and pyramids, including his Temple of the Four Winds, and Hawksmoor's Mausoleum, the finest in England and a palace in itself.

CONSTABLE BURTON HALL *

3m E of Leyburn
Gardens set round Carr of York house (P-G)

The drive from the road is through open farmland and into dense ornamental woods. Two magnificent cedars part and reveal a villa that might be in the Italian Veneto. A double flight of stairs rises from the forecourt to the entrance, recessed behind four columns and a portico. There is a single, wide bay on either side. This is not a big house and it is almost as pure in its Palladianism as if by Inigo Jones.

Constable Burton – not to be confused with Burton Constable (Yorks, E) – was designed by Carr of York for Sir Marmaduke Wyvill, c1762. It is said that Wyvill went on the Grand Tour leaving strict instructions for Carr to repair his old house, not build a new one. Like many an architect, Carr appears to have 'misunderstood'. He was presumably forgiven and Wyvills occupy the house to this day.

Although the building is not open to visitors, they can perambulate the splendid exterior from the surrounding gardens. Parking is in front of the house and there is no sense of exclusion. The grounds embrace an extensive collection of maple and conifer along terraces flanking the slope down to a river. The finest view of the house is from across the park. It is attended by a magnificent copper beech, standing like a rich uncle, noticeable yet never out of place.

CRATHORNE HALL *

Crathorne, 2m S of Yarm
Bravura Edwardian country house (H)

The house cuts a dash on a bluff over the River
Leven, south of Middlesbrough. It was one of
the last grand houses of the Edwardian era,
built for the cotton tycoon, Lionel Dugdale,
between 1903 and 1906. The architect was the
Queen Anne revivalist, Sir Ernest George.
There were 115 rooms, including 41 bedrooms,
and the Dugdales had a staff of 26 indoor
servants.

Dugdale's ambitious wife ensured that her
daughter became a countess and her son,
James, became the local MP, marrying the elegant Nancy Tennant. On Lionel's death in
1941, James Dugdale turned Crathorne Hall
into a centre of political entertainment. His
ministerial career ended with the Crichel
Down affair in 1954. (He is forever remembered as the last politician to accept personal
responsibility for a mistake made by his civil
servant.)

After Dugdale's death in 1977, the house
became a hotel. The younger members of the
family sent it off with a huge Edwardian Ball,
saying goodbye to the place 'in a blaze of light'.

The entrance façade is Vanbrugh-revival,
the porch rusticated and with a segmental
roof. Massive neo-Jacobean towers fill the two
angles of the courtyard. The garden front is
again after Vanbrugh, with a lofty armorial
pediment supported by an Ionic colonnade. A
wrought-iron balcony adorns the first floor.
The whole composition looks confidently over
the valley, as if Dugdales and houses like this
were forever. England in the 1900s had not a
care in the world.

The interior is well mannered. The vestibule, with a barrel vault, acts as corridor to the
main reception rooms. The central drawing
room has Dugdale heraldry over the fireplace
and pilastered doorways. The walls have
thankfully retained their family portraits, including some by Nancy Dugdale herself. In the
dining room is a superb landscape by Miles
Birkett Foster.

DUNCOMBE PARK ***

Helmsley
Baroque mansion with post-fire Victorian
interiors (P)

The landscape of Rievaulx, Helmsley and
Duncombe is among the most celebrated in
England. Abbey, castle and great house once
stood separate, but were brought together in
the 18th century by Duncombe money and the
collective genius of English architecture.

Sir Charles Duncombe was a Restoration
banker, tax collector and reputedly the richest
commoner in England. He bought the entire
Helmsley estate in 1689, shortly before being
committed briefly to the Tower of London
for fraud. After his death in 1711, his niece's
husband, Thomas Browne, adopted his wife's
name and commissioned a grand house in the
rolling landscape behind Rievaulx. The builder
was William Wakefield but the inspirer, it is
thought, was Vanbrugh, then working at Castle
Howard. The palatial west front is undeniably
Vanbrughian, as is the robust portico on the
east front. The west is now the entrance,
reached up a flight of steps from the courtyard.
The flanking service wings are later, by Sir
Charles Barry.

The interior was destroyed by fire in 1879.
Thomas Duncombe's descendant, the Earl of
Feversham, rebuilt it in 1895, employing
William Young, architect of town halls and of
country houses that look like town halls. Only
the main hall reappeared as it had been. The
rest was replaced in the French Empire style.
The hall rises the full height of the house, its
bare stone walls punctuated by openings and
adorned with classical medallions. Two gigantic fireplaces are surmounted by urns in
niches. It is strongly reminiscent of the hall at
Castle Howard.

The rebuilt saloon was draped in the
heaviest of Continental furnishings, thick
with palms and aspidistras. The effect, says
the admirable guidebook, was to create 'for the
humble Earl and Countess of Feversham the
agreeable illusion that they were Louis XVI
and Marie Antoinette on vacation in Hawaii'.

The pillars and oak panels with gilded swags seem more an assembly room in the style of Wren than a saloon.

The room leads into the more intimate withdrawing room. A picture by Andrea Soldi depicts the Georgian, Charles Duncombe, as a boy holding a pheasant. Legend relates that he overheard a village girl singing, 'What e'er may come, what e'er may fall,/ I will be mistress of Duncombe Hall.' He fell in love with her on the spot and married her. The ever-lively guidebook suggests the scene would now have to take place in 'some kind of out-of-town shopping precinct'.

The dining room contains flamboyant portraits of Feversham girls in their Victorian prime by Edward Hughes. Hermione, Duchess of Leinster, was considered 'the most beautiful woman in England' by that connoisseur of these matters, Edward VII. Other rooms on show include the library and upstairs bedrooms.

There could have been no better era in which to restore a great house than the late 19th century. Art was confident and craftsmanship meticulous. The teak windows at Duncombe have never needed replacing, despite the house's sixty years as a girls' school after the Great War. The present Lord Feversham has restored the house as his family home.

FOUNTAINS ABBEY **

Studley Royal, 3m SW of Ripon
Surviving ruins of great monastery (NT)

Which to prefer, Fountains or Rievaulx? I am marginally for Rievaulx, although on a misty autumn day the majestic outline of Fountains Abbey with its defiant tower, erected on the brink of the Dissolution, is hard to beat. Thirteen monks arrived in 1132 from the Benedictine St Mary's, York, switching their loyalty to the new Cistercian order. Their inspirer was Geoffrey of Clairvaux, expert in monastic foundation. He had already begun Rievaulx two years earlier. Despite the wildness of the place, the new community was to extend its domain over a hundred square miles of

Yorkshire, prospering here for four centuries.

The ruins of Fountains are among the most complete of any English monastery, largely because of their remoteness. They are now a World Heritage site and owned by the National Trust. Most of the residential ranges can still be discerned either on the ground or in standing walls. Of these, the finest is the ruined dormitory, 300 ft long, with its storeroom beneath. The western prospect of this range, dating from the late 12th century, was to Pevsner 'one of the most impressive experiences of monastic architecture in England . . . a world of exacting order unmatched in the secular world'.

The building stretched unbroken from the west end of the church to the River Skell. The inside of the storeroom is no less impressive, a long double nave of rib-vaults in bare stone, ascetic in the extreme. Of the other ranges, only the refectory walls survive, but the adjacent warming room is complete, with its vaulted roof and large fireplace. From here stairs lead up to windows, fireplaces and walls, all paying obedience to the great church next door.

These places are no more than stage-sets of a vanished lifestyle and a vanished supremacy. I did once glimpse how they might have been, in the strongly monastic Himalayan kingdom of Bhutan. The answer is noisy, dirty, introverted and obsessively conservative. But they enjoyed an astonishing longevity and left the most impressive early medieval architecture in England.

FOUNTAINS HALL **

Studley Royal, 3m SW of Ripon
Late Smythson mansion (NT)

In order to reach Fountains Hall, the Fountains Abbey visitor centre, which might be in a zoo, must first be breached. There follows a walk across the rolling acres of the Abbey estate to Skelldale. Here is a cluster of buildings by an old bridge where, behind warm stone walls and yew hedges, lies Fountains Hall, still heartbreakingly empty.

The hall was built in 1611 by Sir Stephen Proctor, son of a lead and coal magnate. Proctor was a fierce Calvinist and hunter-down of recusants. In this role he was created 'Collector of Fines on Penal Statutes', his qualifications being of an 'unscrupulous and unsqueamish' temperament. He was hated locally and two attempts were made on his life. He robustly adopted as his motto, 'Finding nothing, I will earn everything'. He built him-self a new house in the grounds of Fountains Abbey to designs ascribed to the elderly Robert Smythson. By 1620 Proctor had vanished, whether killed or bankrupted, nobody knows.

The Aislabie family acquired the Fountains Estate in 1767, their main house already being at Studley Royal. Fountains Hall was allowed to fall into disuse. It was restored by the Vyner family in the 1930s and was even considered as a Yorkshire seat for the then Duke of York, later George VI. The house became a school before being acquired by the local council in 1966. It passed to the National Trust in 1983 but only the hall and ground floor are open to the public at present.

The front to the formal garden is Smythson at his most complex and mature. The garden is entered by a pretty gateway through magnifi-cent yews that accentuate the towers of the house against the green hillside behind. The façade is a series of projecting and receding planes with castellated flanking bays and wide windows.

The central bay is sensational. As at Hard-wick (Derbys), everything is an expanse of glass, including the bow window lighting the Great Chamber. Yet there is something eccen-tric about this house. The two sides do not quite balance, as if a wayward local mason were determined to medievalize Smythson's plan.

The frontispiece is crowded with Renais-sance statuary and heraldry. The door is up hidden steps, sideways on to the front, and gives into a screens passage and asymmetrical Great Hall. The rooms inside are empty, except for display boards. Upstairs, the Great Cham-ber contains a superb ceiling and Renais-sance overmantel depicting the Judgment of Solomon.

HAZLEWOOD CASTLE **

3m SW of Tadcaster
Restored medieval castle with Carr of York interiors (H)

If Hazlewood is the future for many English houses, it will not be dull. The castle is now a Carmelite monastic retreat, teamed with a cookery school, luxury hotel and conference centre. The reception boasts 'a distinctly different lifestyle experience'. My guide broke off to carry a guest's case upstairs.

This was the ancestral home of the Vavasour family, who survived the Wars of the Roses, recusancy, Popish plotting and the Civil War, but could not survive 20th-century financial ineptitude. The old house was sold in 1908. A succession of later owners were sympathetic to its architecture and, luckily, to its religion. The house passed to the Carmelites in 1967 and is now in excellent condition.

The main façade is a Georgian refacing of a medieval Great Hall, probably attached to a pele tower at the rear. Today, the present Hall is classical, reached by a wide flight of steps and Doric doorway. It is supremely stylish. The conversion was reputedly by Carr of York. There are green walls flanked with columns on all four sides, rising to coved arches beneath a bold Jacobean ceiling. In each arch is a roundel displaying the Vavasour arms. The windows are big and flood the room with light. A fragment of medieval wall survives in one bay.

Behind this Hall is the present hotel en-trance, known as the Flemish Hall. This was created in the 1960s and lined with 17th-century Flemish panelling from a Carmelite church in Ghent. The panels depict the lives of saints and are of high quality. In the centre of the wall facing the entrance is the famous Jezebel fireplace brought from Heath Old Hall when it was demolished in 1961. Lucky Hazlewood.

Next door is a small rotunda, again attrib-uted to Carr of York, as are the dining room and staircase. Behind the rotunda is a library in the base of the old pele, with an amusing fake door. Of the smaller reception rooms, the finest is the Victoria Room with 'metallic' wall-paper and a curious hooded fireplace, again installed in the 1960s. The castle was a mater-nity hospital during the war and this was the delivery ward. Many local women were called Hazel in its honour.

The adjacent 13th-century chapel was redec-orated in the Carr style in about 1770 and is still in use for Catholic worship.

HELMSLEY CASTLE *

Helmsley
Castle with remains of Elizabethan mansion (EH)

The castle was begun by the Norman magnate, Walter l'Espec, Lord of Helmsley, to guard the River Rye. Its massive bastions gaze across the acres of Duncombe Park towards the great house and the terraces above Rievaulx. The keep can be seen for miles around. Espec is said to have built the first fortification at the same time as he invited the Cistercians to found Rievaulx Abbey in 1132. The earliest buildings are attributed to the de Roos family, from the end of the 12th century. The family held the castle until 1508.

An impressive double ditch surrounds the site, forming a deep slope on which children are still allowed to play (pending the arrival of the health-and-safety spoilsports). The curtain wall is entered by a strong barbican, parts of which have been allowed to retain their creeper. Inside the bailey is the D-shaped keep, neatly sliced in half by the Roundheads after a prolonged siege in 1644. It retains a vaulted ground floor and relics of upper chambers are visible in the wall.

More remarkable is the survival of a late Elizabethan house on the opposite side of the bailey. This appears to be the solar tower of a ruined Great Hall. It has four storeys and contains Tudor windows and fireplaces. Next to it is a more ordinary Elizabethan house. This has a ground floor chamber with tim-bered partitions. Upstairs are two rooms with panelling and decorative plasterwork. This was the distant predecessor of Duncombe Park.

HOVINGHAM HALL ***

Hovingham, 8m W of Malton
Palladian stables with house attached (P)

If Caligula could make his horse a consul, the Worsleys could make their stables a home. Hovingham is as odd as any house in England. It sits, French style, in the centre of its village rather than at a distance outside it. More eccentric, its entrance is (or was) through a riding school leading to a dismounting hall. Horses were to be stabled on either side, where normally would have been the 'rustic' family rooms beneath the state rooms above. Family and guests were to be housed in wings.

The creator of the house was Thomas Worsley, amateur architect and professional horseman. He had studied these vocations in Switzerland and, having inherited from his father in 1750, determined to put both to good use at Hovingham. Although he held the sinecure of Surveyor-General at the Office of Works from 1760, and thus had access to London craftsmen, he drew up his own plans for his new house.

His model was Palladio's proposed 'recon-struction' of a Roman house, with courtyards, atrium and rectangular vestibules. He built the riding school and central stable block but had added only one residential wing when building ceased. He then found stables were not ideal so near a house – they smelled – and moved them back into the courtyard. The result was a hopeless mess.

Today, Worsley's obsession with horses – he also ran a stud farm – is everywhere on display. The disused Riding School remains the pride of the place in the middle of the composition. Each end has a Tuscan screen and loggia, from one of which guests could watch horses per-forming without standing in a muddy court-yard. Beyond would normally have been the house entrance and hall, but instead there is the paved Samson Hall, supposedly for dis-mounting, modelled on a Roman loggia with groin vaults. On either side are the intended horse boxes. These are now vestibules, one with a fine array of tapestries.

The rooms above the Samson Hall include reception rooms and a ballroom. The ballroom has grisaille murals by Sebastiano Ricci and Cipriani. Next door is a pretty Ionic Room, its walls crowded with pictures hung in the Georgian manner. Hovingham's collection includes works by van Dyck, Poussin and Boucher, which might sink without trace in a large museum yet are a delight to find scattered round a family house.

These rooms are necessarily removed from the family quarters, always in the side wing. The former state bedroom has become the dining room, hung with Worsleys from the 18th to the 20th centuries. The fireplaces and capitals are of excellent workmanship, allegedly from Worsley's London craftsmen.

On the lawn outside is one of the oldest family cricket pitches in England. The view up the valley embraces the remains of a classical landscape with a fine Palladian bridge.

KIPLIN HALL **

Kiplin, 5m E of Catterick
Victorianized Jacobean mansion (P)

The redoubtable Bridget Talbot died in 1971. A socialist, Red Cross volunteer and fierce defender of Kiplin, she set up a charitable trust to preserve the old house after her death. With insufficient endowment, this could be achieved only by the drastic measure of digging up its park as a gravel quarry. Today, the quarry has gone, replaced by a graceful lake, with a folly on an island and fishermen on the bank. The National Trust refused the house as too 'Victorian' and the Kiplin Hall Trust, the gravel exhausted, struggles on as best it can.

George Calvert, 1st Lord Baltimore, and founder of Maryland in America, built Kiplin between 1622 and 1625. It is nearly a square, with projecting towers and cupolas not on each corner but in the middle of each side. This verticality happily left the main chambers filled with light from two sides, and the central space free of staircases. The façades are of redbrick with diaper patterning, the entrance flanked by handsome paired columns. The

symmetry of the 'box' is spoilt only by a large library of 1818 built to one side.

The interiors and much of the exterior brickwork are Victorian. A Kiplin heiress married John Carpenter, the 4th Earl Tyrconnel, in 1817. Having no heir, she fastened on a young naval cousin, a member of the Catholic Talbot family, as inheritor of the estate. Her will required him both to become a Protestant and to marry one, a pledge subject to a seven-yearly investigation by a team of Anglican clergymen. He should also change his name from Talbot to Carpenter. All this he did. He rose to the rank of admiral and his memorabilia fill some of the rooms. Eden Nesfield was brought in to modernize the house and build the fine stables.

In the library is a school of van Dyck of Charles II. Paintings in the dining room are by G. F. Watts and Angelica Kauffmann. The staircase inserted in the 18th century leads to a pleasant series of domestic rooms upstairs, including a sitting room filled with watercolours by another Talbot relative, Lady Waterford. A Long Gallery looks out over the restored park. Many of the rooms are still in process of restoration and refurnishing.

KIRKLEATHAM: TURNER'S HOSPITAL *

Kirkleatham, 2m S of Redcar
Survivor of Restoration philanthropy (P-R)

Sir William Turner was the Lord Mayor of London charged with rebuilding the City after the Great Fire. He was also a Yorkshireman. He died in 1692 and his family's house has been demolished. Other buildings survive. The church and Turner mausoleum, by James Gibbs, defied the wreckers. The Free School, erected in 1708 after Turner's death, is a magnificent two-storey structure with a giant pedimented central door. And there are the almshouses.

Although a man of standing in London,

'Maryland' Jacobean: Kiplin Hall

Turner acknowledged his duties to his home village. The hospital he founded in 1676 was mostly rebuilt by his descendant, Cholmley Turner, in 1742. The present almshouses are among the finest of the period in England. They do not display the usual cottage quadrangle but comprise three ranges around an open courtyard. Pride of place goes to the tower above the chapel, with schoolrooms arranged to its left and right. The courtyard is flanked by two wings, for twelve men and twelve women each, of brick with stone dressings. Each culminates in a substantial house for the master and mistress respectively. Stone statues of an old man and an old woman adorn these houses, possibly carved by Scheemakers. The courtyard is open to the road, with ornamental railings and gates.

The chapel is a Baroque gem. The central tower rises over the porch. Inside is a square interior with Ionic columns worthy of a Wren church in the City. At the west end, a gallery rises up steps to a magnificent doorway, above which presides a bust in honour of the donor, a dramatic touch. The carvings are 'after Gibbons' and the doors Rococo. Nothing was too good for the people of Kirkleatham in those days.

KNARESBOROUGH: HOUSE IN THE ROCK *

Knaresborough
Georgian folly set into cliff face (P)

In 1774 a linen weaver called Thomas Hill built himself a house in a cleft in the rock overlooking Knaresborough gorge and the River Nidd. Here he lived with his wife and six children, in four rooms stacked on top of each other. His descendants owned the house until 1916, castellating it and renaming it Fort Montague. It was bequeathed to Ampleforth Abbey, owner of the adjacent chapel, and opened as a curiosity and tea-room. The house was sold in 2000 and was being restored for reopening at the time of writing.

The house's location is superb, with a picturesque drama more common to the river gorges of France than England. Next door is the Shrine of Our Lady of the Crag. This tiny chapel was hewn from the rock in 1409 as thank offering for a local boy who was saved from death in a rockfall by an apparition of the Virgin Mary. It has been a place of pilgrimage, on and off, ever since.

MARKENFIELD HALL ***

3m SW of Ripon
14th-century moated farmstead (P)

The small settlement sits alone in fields south of Ripon, looking much as it did when built in the 14th century. While most such fortified farms were extensively altered in the 16th century and later, Markenfield is mostly medieval. It has been beautifully restored and its chapel reconsecrated. From the roof of the solar is an uninterrupted rural view.

The builder was John of Markenfield, Chancellor to the hapless Edward II. The house needed to be fortified to protect him from his (or the King's) local enemies, licence being duly granted in 1310. The family was devoutly Catholic and were leaders of the anti-Protestant Rising of the North from Ripon. They lost the house in the process. In the 17th century, Markenfield passed to the Grantleys of nearby Grantley Hall, who occupy it to this day in the name of Curteis.

The house is like an apparition across the fields. Two farm buildings flank a track over a wide moat to an imposing stone wall. Here a two-storey Tudor gatehouse guards the entrance to the inner courtyard. The old house is in the right-hand corner, at an angle to the Great Hall directly ahead. This hall is on the first floor, with kitchens and storage underneath. The ghost of an old outside doorway can be seen in its wall. Its windows have 14th-century tracery.

The Great Hall interior has lost most of

Knaresborough: Shrine of Our Lady of the Crag

its medieval features. The roof is 18th century and the staircase from the undercroft below is Victorian. The adjacent restored chapel has one of the loveliest small piscinas that I have seen in any church. It is proudly multi-denominational, a recent service being attended by one Catholic, one Anglican and one Methodist. Bedrooms and sitting rooms have been fitted into the chapel tower and the medieval chambers below. Old rib-vaults have been restored. Furniture is being assembled. Markenfield is a rare treasure in the hands of dedicated custodians.

MARMION TOWER *

West Tanfield, 6m NW of Ripon
Medieval tower with oriel window (EH)

The tower lies sandwiched down a lane between a wild garden running down to the River Ure and St Nicholas Church in West Tanfield. The church was built curiously close to the walls of the old castle, although it may have been the other way round. A door in the church is dated c1200. Either way, the setting is picturesque.

The building was erected as a gateway to the castle in the late 14th century and is clearly decorative rather than defensive. Now accessible and in the care of English Heritage, it is of three storeys. There is a fine fireplace on the ground floor. Stairs built into the corner masonry lead to the roof and look-out. A projecting latrine faces the river while a pretty oriel window floods light into the first floor chamber.

Here a Juliet might listen to her Romeo singing in the lane below. It is a magical spot.

MIDDLEHAM CASTLE *

Middleham
Extensive ruins of Richard III's northern fortress (EH)

The small town of Middleham guards the approach to Coverdale. While racehorses stalk through the main street on their way to the gallops, the great fortress in which Richard III spent his youth still broods over its south flank. Although a ruin, it is a most evocative medieval structure. To stand on the platform of Middleham keep and look into its cavernous Great Hall is to gaze into a dark corner of history.

The castle was built by Alan, post-Conquest Lord of Richmond, to assert his authority over the Dales. The present keep was constructed a century later in the 1170s, and is among the most massive of its period. A suite of chambers is divided between Great Hall and Great Chamber, with associated kitchens and ante-rooms.

Another century later, the castle passed to the Nevills, who built an outer curtain wall and developed the space inside it. The castle was Richard III's northern headquarters and was duly seized by Henry VII after Bosworth. It never recovered its former glory.

Although unroofed, Middleham has a mighty presence, its silhouette largely intact. The gatehouse leads into the outer courtyard, surrounded by the remains of the late medieval settlement. In the centre rises the vast keep, with stairs leading down to kitchens and up to a view of the Great Hall. From the roof is a superb view over the castle to Wensleydale. The hoofbeats of history still echo round these walls.

MOULTON HALL *

Moulton, 2m SE of Scotch Corner
Dutch gabled house with florid staircase
(NT-R)

Two houses loom over the little village of Moulton. Both were built in the 1660s, both in an archaic Jacobean style. The private manor is the more conservative, U-plan with gabled wings and small pediments over the windows. Moulton Hall beyond, owned by the National Trust, is the more remarkable. Three flowing Dutch gables peer above a high yew hedge, odd features to find in the Yorkshire countryside. The gables are similar to those applied to Kew Palace (London, W) in the

1630s. Perhaps these took their cue from those at Norton Conyers (below).

The façade of the house is a delight. The first-floor windows have alternately triangular and segmental hoods. The round windows are off-centre to the gables, as if the mason were unsure of his instructions.

The chief feature of the interior is the staircase, a remarkable construction of 'yeoman's Baroque' built to the rear of the house. It rises in eight flights to fill the entire three storeys of the building. There are finials and pendants in the style of the mid-17th century, the panels a complex work of carving, rich in acanthus leaves. One of the lower panels has the coat of arms of the Peake family, curiously framed by a monstrous open mouth, with nostrils and eyes above it and the lower lips closed by a rope. The symbolism of these torments is obscure.

MOUNT GRACE PRIORY: CELL EIGHT *

7m NE of Northallerton
Monk's cell of Carthusian monastery (EH)

The Carthusians first came to England in 1178, invited by Henry II in penance for the death of Becket, but they expanded rapidly after the Black Death in 1348. The London Charterhouse was founded in 1371 and Mount Grace on the isolated slopes of the Cleveland Hills in 1398.

Dissolved at the Reformation and ruined, the site would be nothing but rubble were it not for the rebuilding of the guests' quarters as a mansion in the 17th century. This was extended and a single cell of the old monastic quarters was restored in 1901. The cell dated from the early years of the 16th century, just before the Dissolution.

The Carthusians were unlike other monks. A closed and solitary order, they lived, worked, prayed and slept in isolation in little cottages round a big central courtyard. This offered security and access for servants. Monks saw each other only for church services. Lay workers brought them food, leaving it in L-shaped cupboards so each could not see the other. This method was also used to collect the product of their labours, for monks spent most of their time earning their keep. This might be copying, book-making, weaving and tailoring. Each monk worked completely alone and the design of the cells prevented any communication.

The two-storey cell is remarkable for its self-sufficiency and comfort. At the rear is a small garden for the growing of herbs and vegetables, as well as a privy with running water. On the ground floor are the living room with fireplace, bedroom and a charming private cloister. Above is the workroom, equipped with a weaving loom. Appropriate furniture has been recreated, herbs grow in the rear garden.

The place is peaceful and moving. I can see why monastic life is enjoying a revival. The adjacent 17th-century mansion is now in part a museum.

NEWBURGH PRIORY ***

7m SW of Helmsley
Tudor and Jacobean mansion with Georgian additions (P)

Newburgh is part ruin, part home, part 'ongoing project'. The old Augustinian priory lay in a lovely fold in the hills, passing at the Dissolution to the Bellasis family, briefly Earls of Fauconberg. Their descendants hold it to this day under the name of Wombwell. They are struggling to rescue parts of the house that were damaged in a severe fire in 1947, caused by that most incendiary of tenants, a girls' school. The Wombwells need all the help they can get.

The house, inside and outside, is hard to read. Medieval, Tudor, Jacobean and 18th century jostle each other, while floor levels seem to dart in all directions. A medieval entrance, darkly panelled, leads up to rooms once used by the manorial courts. These include the Black Gallery and the Justice Room, gaily painted in blue. Both are hung with early Bellasis and Wombwell portraits.

One Bellasis was killed in a duel, after which his wife was courted and offered marriage by the future James II. As a desperate reward from the Royal Family for agreeing to revoke the contract, she was given a barony in her own right.

The house is full of surprises. A cosy study is furnished in memory of the 4th Wombwell baronet, who survived the Charge of the Light Brigade despite having had two horses killed under him. Up a warren of stairs, past doors and thick walls is 'Cromwell's Tomb', by tradition never to be opened. His body was reputedly brought here, possibly minus his head, by his third daughter Mary, Lady Fauconberg. Even a visiting Prince of Wales, later Edward VII, could not induce an estate worker to open it.

Large gondola lanterns lend an exotic touch to the main staircase which contains a display of portraits and china. The passage beneath is panelled by estate carpenters with delightful depictions of local landscapes. The Great Hall, now the dining room, has portraits of Mary Cromwell and Lord Fauconberg gazing down on it.

The prize of this room, perhaps of the house, is a Renaissance overmantel depicting Mars and Diana on pedestals between pillars. They look at each other across a semi-recumbent Venus, evincing a *Country Life* eulogy that there was 'nothing comparable with this in contemporary English sculpture'. The carver is believed to be Nicholas Stone.

The grand rooms added to the side of the old house in the 1760s were gutted by fire in 1947. There has never been the money to restore them. They present a tragic spectacle of missing floors, blackened beams and fluted pilasters floating in space.

Beneath them survives an indication of their lost glory: the Small Drawing Room has a superb plasterwork ceiling by Joseph Cortese and paintings of a stag hunt by Snyders. The Large Drawing Room, also with Cortese work, has two magnificent Rococo mirrors. Everywhere are family portraits. Everywhere are ghosts. Much of Newburgh's charm lies in its incompleteness.

NEWBY HALL ****

3m SE of Ripon
William-and-Mary house refashioned by Carr and Adam (P)

If Castle Howard is the crown of the North, Newby is a jewel. The estate lies at the foot of the Dales on the banks of the River Ure. The house was completed for Sir Edward Blackett in 1693, redbrick, stone-quoined and with projecting corner pavilions. It was sold in 1748 to William Weddell, a wealthy dilettante. He transformed it in the 1760s with the help of John Carr and then of Robert Adam. This is Adam at his most light-hearted and enjoyable, an architectural cabinet in which to display Newby's treasures.

In the Regency, the house passed to Weddell's cousin, Thomas Robinson, Lord Grantham and later Earl de Grey. No sooner did he consider alterations to Newby than he inherited Wrest Park (Beds) and turned his attention there, which was as well for Newby. The house passed eventually to relatives of the Marquesses of Northampton, the Comptons, by whom it is owned to this day. This family continuity is the strength of the house. One elderly attendant told me she had been at her post for fifty years, having 'lived' at Newby for almost ninety.

The blue entrance hall is an Adam feast of Roman motifs, in white on sky-blue with a patterned stone floor. This is an introduction to the bold colour schemes introduced by the present Mrs Compton throughout the house. The hall is furnished with tables by Chippendale and an organ case by 'Athenian' Stuart. The boldly decorated Red Passage leads to the drawing room, a perfect late-Georgian chamber flooded with light from the garden. Here hangs a superb Thomas Lawrence of Lady Theodosia Vyner. The yellow dining room is a variation on a theme of Chippendale, with his tables, side-tables and chairs beneath family portraits by Mytens and van Loo.

Grand Tour statuary at Newby

Stairs lead upstairs to the house's eccentric Victorian Wing past the 'Chamber Pot' Room, an art form giving full licence to the potter's sense of humour. This wing is a complete contrast to the rest of the house, a dark masculine retreat for those who found Adam and Chippendale too effete. It is a world of guns, racing trophies, hunting bags and dark, smoky recesses. The raised alcove in the billiards room might be an opium den. Here too is a shrine to Mary Vyner's son, killed in 1870 by Greek brigands when his demanded ransom failed to arrive in time. The money was instead devoted to building Burges's magnificent memorial church in the park, surrounded by weeping beeches.

The Motto Bedroom is decorated with French sayings on walls, doors, bath, even water jug. The bedroom sequence includes a Print Bathroom and bedroom, and a Circular Room with ceiling panels from Herculaneum, copied by Weddell's wife. The landing has serene Adam pier-glasses and elongated Ionic pillars and arches. Nothing at Newby is overstated, everything exquisite.

The acanthus-decorated stairs lead down to the Tapestry Room, designed by Adam around a set of Rococo tapestries from Gobelins. The contrast between the geometric ceiling and the floral abundance of the tapestries adds to the glory of this room. Adam's work is a frame for tapestries which are themselves frames for their central roundels of the Loves of the Gods. The whole world is a frame. Even the backs of the Chippendale chairs are frames for tapestry flowers.

The library is by Adam, assisted by Angelica Kauffmann and Antonio Zucchi for the paintings and the younger Joseph Rose for the stucco. The room has apses at each end, with Corinthian screens and ceiling roundels. It is more successful than Adam's library at Kenwood for being clearly true to its purpose. A tweed jacket hangs on a chair. There is wastepaper in the basket and books on the table.

Weddell's Grand Tour statue gallery fills one of the 18th-century wings. Again by Adam, it is a series of immaculate Roman chambers. Plasterwork fills each niche. Statues are not scattered everywhere but correspond with the architecture. Nothing looks cold. The table tops have scagliola flowers and birds. The family in 2002 sold the most important of the statues to pay for the upkeep of the house.

The gardens at Newby are a sequence of interlocking rectangles. Designed by successive generations of Comptons, they are outlined in varieties of evergreen, spreading on either side of an axis from the house to the river.

NORTON CONYERS ***

4m N of Ripon
Antiquated 17th-century house (P)

There have been Grahams at Norton Conyers since the 17th century, but they seem to cling on by their fingertips. The family has yet to recover from a Victorian 7th Baronet and his fondness for 'fast women and slow horses'. The present Lady Graham calls him 'Number Seven' and blames him for every ill to have afflicted the house. Few places in this book seem so delightfully faded. Norton is a true period piece. Here we are more likely to be garrotted by a cobweb than fleeced by a corporate hostess.

The character of Norton Conyers lies chiefly in its hinterland, in dusty back kitchens and corridors, in the lack of heating and the paucity of plumbing, and in romantic attics, many of them not open to normal public view. The attics run the length of the roof space and deserve a tour in their own right. They are packed with the detritus of centuries, prints stacked against rafters, pictures without number, steamer trunks with exotic labels, shelves of dusty books, boxes, cases, chests, cabinets . . .

One gable room supposedly incarcerated the Mad Woman of the family, of whom Charlotte Brontë heard tell when she visited Norton Conyers in 1839 as a governess. The house is thus assumed to be the basis for Rochester's Thornfield Hall in *Jane Eyre*, and the Mad Woman to be Mrs Rochester. The gable room still has a rocking chair and hip-bath.

The house is outwardly early 17th century,

Dutch gables at Norton Conyers

with render covering old brickwork. The core is earlier, a 16th-century hall house, traces of which can be seen at the rear. The exterior is dominated by four large Dutch gables, topping all three main façades, behind which run the celebrated attics. The classical doorway in the middle of the west façade leads into one side of the old Great Hall, clearly not the original arrangement.

The Hall, like most of the house, is a study in faded browns and yellows. Grahams of all ages and reputations gaze down from the walls. Above the old refectory table (with marks for shove ha'penny) is a huge painting of the Quorn Hunt by Ferneley. It was won by the then baronet by lot between those depicted. Opposite is Sir Richard Graham, who fought for the King at Marston Moor and whose horse returned home with him wounded in the saddle. The horse is said to have galloped into the Hall and then tried to carry Sir Richard upstairs to bed, its scorched hoofprint still visible on one of the landings. This staircase was built onto the back of the Hall, presumably in the early 17th century.

The adjacent parlour is now a sitting room and library. In one of these rooms the 4th Baronet died horribly in 1755. He was supposedly poisoned by a cup of tea prepared for his mistress/housekeeper by disgruntled kitchen staff, which he drank by mistake. The upstairs rooms are used to display family costumes.

The Georgian dining room contains family portraits by Romney and Batoni. The plasterwork is liberally covered in wings, the family's crest awarded to an early Graham for his speed in carrying royal dispatches home from Spain. The stables and gardens at Norton Conyers continue in the style of the house, atmospheric and down at heel. In the walled garden is an astonishing eruption of peonies.

NUNNINGTON HALL ***

Nunnington, 4m SE of Helmsley
French front added to Jacobean house (NT)

Nunnington was briefly the home of Dr Robert Huicke, celebrated as the bold doctor who had to tell Elizabeth I that she would never have children. He became the patron saint of bad news.

Nunnington is utterly tranquil, set at the foot of an incline on the banks of the River Rye, here little more than a stream. The place seems lost between the Vale of York and Pickering. It was never grand enough for its titular owners to occupy and was usually rented. The owners were Grahams, Viscounts Preston, until the 19th century and then a Liverpool family, the Rutsons, who did not use it until the 1920s. It passed to the National Trust in the 1950s. The last Rutson heiress married a big game hunter named Fife, whose trophies adorn the Stone Hall. Fifes still live on the estate. The attic is used for a collection of miniature objects, firmly described as 'not dolls' houses'.

The history of Nunnington is in its walls. The earliest house is visible to the side, where a jumble of chimneys and gables rises above the entrance to the old Stone Hall. Quite different is the south front facing the garden. It was added by Lord Preston in the 1680s, probably on his return from a brief stay as Charles II's ambassador to France and before his imprisonment as confidant of James II. Work on Nunnington appears to have ceased in 1688.

No one returned from the Paris of Louis XIV untouched by building mania. While the Duke of Montagu sought a Versailles at Boughton (Northants), the French influence at Nunnington was confined to a pretty ironwork balcony over the front door and the rusticated walls and gate piers. Conservative England remained in the wide gabled wings and heavy chimneys.

The interiors retain their 17th-century character. The Stone Hall was converted into a kitchen when the new hall was added on the south side. The dining room begins the

Preston range, with original panelling painted turquoise. On the walls are mezzotints of Reynolds portraits. The 'new' Oak Hall fills the centre of the range, its panelling stripped in the 1920s. A French chimneypiece is another ghost of Preston's Paris years. A screen of three arches leads to a wide staircase with shallow treads, hung with French tapestries.

The upstairs drawing room was once Preston's Great Chamber, since divided into two. The rest of this floor is for wandering. Nunnington's charm lies in spotting the joins between the periods of its history. Beams start out of plasterwork. Finely-turned staircases appear and disappear.

Upstairs is a glorious display of miniature carpentry, pottery and needlework. Much of it needs a magnifying glass.

ORMESBY HALL **

Ormesby, 3m SE of Middlesbrough
18th-century house with modern paintings (NT)

The Pennymans' Ormesby estate was all but destroyed by 'the wicked Sir James' in the 1770s. Inheriting the house built by his uncle in the 1740s, he became an MP, mayor of Beverley, racing fanatic and gambler. He had Carr of York design lavish stables at Ormesby, and died bankrupt in 1808.

Somehow the family rescued the estate. His descendants lived in the house, with increasing forbearance, until 1983. The last occupant, Ruth Pennyman, staged Shakespeare in the stables and offered rehearsal space for Joan Littlewood's theatre troupe. Ormesby passed to the National Trust in 1961.

The house adorns an otherwise bleak corner of Teeside. It is reached across a park thankfully freed of the noisy sprawl of Middlesbrough, and stands four square and rather forbidding, its stone yellow-green with lichen. The chief feature of the hall and reception rooms is the remarkable plasterwork commissioned by Lady Pennyman (Sir James's aunt) in the 1740s. Scallops and woodcarving surround pictures recently collected by the last Mrs Pennyman, including modern and abstract works.

The dining room has the finest ceiling in the house, a *trompe-l'œil* work of the 1770s. The pictures are mostly copies, of the sort often made when the originals have been sold to make ends meet. They are preferable to none. The Den beyond contains a rare collection of estate maps on rollers.

Ormesby's upstairs gallery is formed from what is, in essence, a landing and a corridor running across the centre of the house. The doors to the bedrooms are each decorated with different grades of ornament, depending on the importance of the room. This subtle architectural class distinction embellishes the most notable space in the house.

RICHMOND CASTLE *

Richmond
Norman keep with detention cells (EH)

Richmond's huge walls of masonry, dating from the Norman Conquest, tower over a wooded bend in the River Swale. This is the site of the Great Hall of the Earls of Richmond. The D-shaped courtyard beyond was large enough to protect all the townspeople in time of attack. At the town side of this courtyard rises the Norman keep, in remarkably good repair. Outside is the market place, commerce and castle in happy proximity.

Although the Great Hall, known as Scolland's Hall after Earl Alan's steward, is a walled ruin, the tower keep survives, a fine remnant of Norman military architecture dating from the mid-12th century. Walls are still square and of great thickness. The plan is simple. A ground floor for storage and a well are accessible only from above. The next floor contains a large chamber probably used by soldiers. Above that is the principal chamber of the castle constable. Stairs and smaller chambers are built into the width of the walls.

The roof walk offers fine views over Swaledale. The castle was used as an army barracks in the 19th century, most of the buildings having since been removed. A series of deten-

tion cells survive. They housed conscientious objectors during the Great War when death sentences were commuted to hard labour. The cells still have graffiti by these prisoners, testament to one of the British Army's less edifying episodes.

RIEVAULX ABBEY **

Rievaulx, 2m NW of Helmsley
Picturesque Cistercian ruin (EH)

Rievaulx is the best surviving relic of the Cistercian colonization of North Yorkshire in the 12th century. Its surrounding hills and glades came to embody the subsequent cult of English Picturesque. The founder in 1132 (two years before the start of Fountains) was William, secretary to the order's presiding genius, St Bernard of Clairvaux. He was invited here by Walter l'Espec, Lord of Helmsley, who shared Henry I's religious zeal. The Rievaulx community rapidly expanded, embracing 640 monks and lay-brothers at its peak.

The ruins are those of a monastery in the Early Gothic style. Rievaulx church saw one of the first pointed arches in England, the masons presumably imported from Burgundy. The residential quarters are as fine as those of Fountains, but more complex. Nothing like it in its full glory can have been seen in Northern Europe since Roman times, certainly nothing in Yorkshire. To the Saxon and Viking inhabitants, this building on the wooded banks of the River Rye must have seemed utterly awe-inspiring.

The refectory survives complete, almost to roof height. Six lavers or washing places flank its north door. Early English windows are interspersed with blind arcading, decorated with shafts. Here the monks ate in silence, listening to readings from the pulpit. Less complete but still impressive is the dormitory.

Next to it are the ruins of the abbot's house, converted by Abbot Burton into reputedly one of the largest such residences in England. It included a Long Gallery and the usual private chambers of a Tudor dignitary. A late Gothic window survives with, above it, a relief of the

Annunciation in alabaster. The old Infirmary Cloister was converted into the Abbot's private garden. These quarters were still being built at great expense during Rievaulx's final decline.

RIEVAULX: IONIC TEMPLE

*

Rievaulx, 2m NW of Helmsley
Banqueting hall in Picturesque landscape
(NT)

The Picturesque quality of the Rievaulx Terraces has long been regarded as supreme in England. Thomas Duncombe of Duncombe Park treated the Abbey ruins as the most 'Heaven-sent' of landscape features. They were a foil for his classical mansion, located a mile distant in a secluded valley of the River Rye. Here in 1758 Duncombe laid out a terrace with a temple at either end. Between them runs a serpentine alley from which sudden views were cut through the trees to the ruins below. One temple was circular and Doric, a rotunda, the other rectangular, Ionic.

The Ionic Temple is a banqueting house. The interior is one large room, immaculately designed in the style of William Kent and well restored by the National Trust. It has a deeply coved ceiling based on one in the Palazzo Farnese in Rome. The coving copies Farnese motifs by Annibale Carracci. The ceiling above is by Giovanni Borgnis, a copy of a Guido Reni at the Casino Rospigliosi. Italy has come to Yorkshire in style, architecture massaged into landscape. A broken pediment crowns the marble fireplace. There are two grand Kentian settees in heavy giltwood, and the table is laid out for dinner.

RIPLEY CASTLE ***

Ripley, 3½m N of Harrogate
Tudor tower house with Georgian mansion attached (P)

In 1355 Thomas Ingilby was lucky enough to rescue Edward III from a menacing boar. He was knighted and richly rewarded. Twenty-six generations of Inglebys have occupied this site ever since. Their boar's head device is everywhere, in the village, church and inn. Ingilby history drips from every wall and gazes from every portrait. The guidebook to the castle is 32 pages long, 22 of them devoted to the doings of the family. They clearly mean to stay.

The castle's most striking aspect is from across the lake, on which it appears to float like a magic tableau. The approach from the village is more severe. The walls are intact and the 1450s gatehouse impressive. On its inner side is where Cromwell's troops executed Royalist soldiers after Marston Moor, the stones still pitted with their shot. Across the court are two ranges, the Old Tower of 1555 and the main house rebuilt in the 1780s by William Belwood, a protégé of Robert Adam. The castle is today run as part residence, part business, curiously described by the owner as a 'coral reef'. On my last visit, it was crowded with Peugeot salesmen and driving simulators. Good luck to them.

Over a door in the entrance hall is a picture of Edward III and above it the head of the celebrated boar, source of the family's blessings. The Georgian dining room recalls the many Ingilbys who have served their nation in war and on film and television. Ripley's credits must be the longest of any English house, from 'Jane Eyre' to 'Frankenstein'; the current Lady Ingilby has appeared on television with 'handy hints' on how to clean chandeliers with a hose.

The 16th-century Old Tower contains three chambers, one on each floor. The library, sadly short of books, is dark with rich panelling and old portraits. Despite siding with Edward III against the boar, the Ingilbys were otherwise on the 'wrong' side of history. Devout Catholics, they were implicated in the Gunpowder Plot and joined Prince Rupert's army during the Civil War, a daughter enlisting as 'Trooper Jane'. They lost their fortune and almost their lives. They sided with James II and had to flee the country in 1688.

The upper landing is lit by a fine Venetian

Ripley's glory reflected

window filled with armorial stained glass, depicting sixteen generations of Ingilbys. The Tower Room is panelled from floor to plasterwork ceiling, with emblems celebrating James I's procession from Scotland in 1603, when he seems to have stopped at every house in the North. The room was especially decorated for his stay.

At the top of the Old Tower is the Knight's Chamber, with original oak ceiling and a collection of ancient armour and weapons, including Cromwellian boots and shoes. The room carries the arms of Queen Mary and King Philip, rare in English houses given the brevity (and unpopularity) of their joint reign. The room contains some of the finest pictures in the house, including one of Elizabeth I. She, at least, ensured glory for one family member, the Blessed Francis Ingilby, whom she martyred in 1586. He was beatified in 1987. Although no longer Catholic, the family went to Rome for the ceremony.

RIPON: HOUSE OF CORRECTION *

St Marygate
Surviving Georgian cell block (M)

The town of Ripon has what it calls a 'Law and Order Trail'. This includes a lock-up, police cells, courthouse, debtors prison, house of correction and workhouse, all from the 19th century or earlier. Nothing is too grim for modern tourism. The original 17th-century house of correction was for the 'correction of vagabonds and sturdy beggars', but the severity of the punishment, including whipping and hard labour, was clearly no deterrent (or correction) since the magistrates constantly needed more room. A new prison block was built in 1816 and remained in use into the 1950s.

Here the prisoners lived two to a cell, men and women segregated, with eight cells in all. Food was carefully regulated, as was the hard labour on a treadmill in the yard, yet the parish authorities ensured that prisoners worshipped daily and were taught to read if illiterate. They rarely spent more than short periods incarcerated. Only one person in fifty years was known to have died in the prison.

The cells are now used mostly for an exhibition of Ripon policing, including displays of whipping and flogging and the history of handcuffs. But one cell is furnished as it was in the 1860s, with simple plank, mug, plate and Bible, and a prisoner in uniform. He also has a punishment 'crank', whereby he had to turn a handle connected to a rod in sand outside the wall. Screw adjustments made this labour harder or easier, giving rise to the term 'screw' for warder.

RIPON: UNION WORKHOUSE *

Allhallowgate
Rare surviving Poor House (M)

'Hush-a-bye baby, on a tree top,/ When you grow old, your wages will stop,/ When you have spent the little you made,/ First to the poorhouse and then to the grave.' Thus ran the rhyme that greeted new inmates to the workhouse. In 1832, the Ripon institution had thirty-three of all ages and genders. An inspection led to reform and expansion.

A new workhouse was built in 1855, with master and matron, treasurer and doctor. There were eventually separate wards and exercise areas for men and women, a vegetable garden, infirmary and even nursery. Everything, including the daily diet, was prescribed by the Board of Guardians. This was not so much a mini-welfare state as a civic kibbutz. At Christmas there was a special dinner and the mayoress sang to the inmates, accompanied by the vicar on the piano.

The Ripon Workhouse is one of the few such residential compounds to survive (*see* Southwell/Notts). The master's house and main wards have been converted for use by the local social services department. The 1877 vagrants' wing remains in its original form and

Carbolic charity: Ripon Workhouse

is open as a museum. This is where those 'of no fixed abode' would be rounded up, washed, given an evening meal and a task to earn their keep – and told to leave the next morning.

Visitors are greeted with the smell of carbolic soap from the adjacent decontamination bathhouse. Next door is the eating room with a list of prescribed ingredients and a stove. Inmates could insist on a proper diet. Beyond are the 14 night cells. The exercise yard outside has its spikes pointing inwards to prevent escape before the required regime had been completed. With the advent of the welfare state, the poorhouse cells were briefly converted into 'rooms', with flowers, curtains and open doors.

RYEDALE FOLK MUSEUM

Hutton-le-Hole, 8m NW of Pickering

This museum contains some of England's best vernacular buildings. The houses are not left empty but are imaginatively furnished and benefit from being set behind the village in a field leading up onto the open moor as if a street. All are original cottages, although the Crofter's Cottage is re-created from fragments.

RYEDALE: CROFTER'S COTTAGE *

I did not know there were English crofts. This is a re-creation of the museum's poorest habitation. It is a single chamber, as existed from the 13th century to the end of the Middle Ages. Two beds occupy one end, a fireplace the middle and animals the other. The fire is kept burning. Smoke fills the roof. The shack contains the tools and utensils of the period, pots and sacks hanging from the rafters. The place needs animals and smells.

The beds are remarkably warm and comfortable, according to the custodian who has slept on one. The hardness of country life is often stressed by historians and archaeologists. It is refreshing to see that make-do-and-

mend could also yield a convenient and self-sufficient home in which misery was not necessarily dominant.

RYEDALE: HAROME COTTAGE *

originally at Harome, SE of Helmsley

This cottage came from Harome in the 1970s and has been restored to its condition as at the end of the 19th century. The structure is cruck and very old. It still has 'opposing doors' at the kitchen end so a through draft could blow away the chaff when the floor was being used for threshing. The house is stone-built with a steep, thatched roof. The windows have Yorkshire sashes which slide sideways.

Inside are now three rooms, the kitchen, with a range of dried fruit and herbs, a downstairs bedroom and a sitting room. There are more bedrooms upstairs, privacy being the chief 19th-century innovation for the poor. The house is fully furnished and a fire burns in the range. It seems a pity nobody lives here. The cottage has its own garden, planted with lavender, columbine, leopard's-bane, Jacob's ladder and primula.

RYEDALE: MANOR HOUSE *

originally at Harome, SE of Helmsley

This is a grander affair, also brought from Harome. Formerly called Harome Hall, it was on the Helmsley estate of the Duncombes, Earls of Feversham, where surely it could have been retained. The structure is again cruck-framed, but the crucks are massive and repeated, with tie-beams to support the roof and stone walls. In its early medieval form, it would have offered a large communal chamber, the lord and his servants sleeping and eating together.

By the 16th century, one end had been partitioned with timbers, wattle and daub. The hall would later have had a complete upper floor inserted. This has been removed, leaving only the lord's upper chamber or solar at one end as his private room, with wood block stairs up to it. The house is used for exhibitions, depriving it of much of its character.

RYEDALE: STANG END CRUCK HOUSE *
originally at Danby, 14m W of Whitby

So picturesque are these early structures that it is hard to imagine, let alone recreate, the poverty they concealed. This house is a 15th-century cottage from Danby on the North York Moors, moved here in 1967. The construction is a simple cruck on stone footings, with a steep roof thatched with heather. Before partitioning, it would have been just one room, which the family shared with their cattle when the latter needed shelter. Later it was partitioned and, later still, given an upper floor for bedrooms and storage. The upper floor has been removed.

The house is thus presented in its intermediate, partitioned form. There is a living room at one end with a salt-and-spice box and a rare witch-post to ward off evil. The centre space is taken up with a milk-and-cheese house, for the making of Danby cheese. At the far end is a rough bedroom with a spinning wheel. The house is furnished on the basis of an old inventory.

SCAMPSTON HALL **
Scampston, 5m NE of Malton
Regency mansion with Leverton interiors (P-R)

Never judge a house by its face. Scampston from the main road is forbidding, a well-proportioned Regency villa rendered the colour of gunmetal. Who, having pondered stucco or limewash, could have chosen grey? Yet Scampston is grey and means to stay that way.

Grey the interiors are not. The house was remodelled in 1800 for the St Quintin family by the London architect Thomas Leverton

(designer of Bedford Square). The plan is ingenious, with two fronts, an entrance and a longer façade to the garden. Both are enlivened by large bow windows. The house is surrounded by a formal parterre, the eye gliding easily into the park and to a graceful Palladian bridge over the lake.

The entrance is into a stone hall warmed by pale salmon walls and a battery of family portraits. To one side is a sitting room, with small landscapes by Samuel Scott. There is also a picture of an open book, the only case I know of painting thus deferring to literature. On the other side of the hall is the drawing room, turning the house along the garden axis. This was redecorated in the 1860s and retains carpets, curtains and wallpaper sparkling with mica from that period. On the wall is a Gainsborough landscape.

The library is the best room at Scampston. Marbled pilasters and attached columns frame the bow window, while the bookshelves are recessed into the walls under Soanian arches. The pictures, mostly by Gainsborough, are particularly well placed in the bow. Beyond is the dining room which, like the drawing room, is of exceptional width for a small private house. It is heavier in style and hung with an array of St Quintin baronets.

The staircase hall is Leverton at his best. As in his Bedford Square town houses (and as with Robert Adam), he had a talent for creating splendour in confined spaces. The St Quintin family continue to occupy Scampston under the name of Legard. Its reclamation is largely the effort of the present Lady Legard, a historic buildings enthusiast, in the 1990s.

SETTLE: THE FOLLY *
High Street
Town house with extraordinary fenestration (P)

English architecture in the 17th century was rarely dull. In 1679 a wealthy Settle merchant named Richard Preston built himself a town house overlooking the market place. We assume he told his builder to give him big rooms, large fireplaces and a grand staircase, with some novelties so as not to look old-fashioned. Preston soon sold the house to a man named Dawson, whose descendants owned it for three centuries. By the 18th century it was no longer a house but a commercial building, divided into two. The Dawson family sold it in 1980 and the main portion has been opened as a rather bleak museum.

Most remarkable is the exterior, covered in Jacobean motifs of the sort a local builder might have in his pattern book. The doorway is clearly a figment of his imagination. Two Gothicky arches beneath a squared hood are framed by two columns that are more Burmese than British, with mini-stupas on top. To the right are the mullioned windows of the old Great Hall. These continue across the recessed central bay of the house and round the projecting bay to the right. This handling of windows round a corner is more Bauhaus than 17th century, although it is reminiscent of Astley Hall (Lancs). What is surprising is that the mullions can carry the weight of the walls and roof above. Similar fenestration adorns the upper two floors.

Inside, the fireplaces are huge, as are the rooms themselves. The hall fireplace takes up almost the whole of one side, while the back wall is composed mostly of the stairwell. The staircase has twisted balusters and strange pilasters on the newel posts. It rises two storeys with generous treads, the sort of staircase normal in a grand house with space to spare. The rooms desperately need matting, tapestries and furniture, and why not a shop on the ground floor? The name of the house is obscure, probably because a good use could never be found for it.

SHANDY HALL **

Coxwold, 6m SE of Helmsley
Final home and shrine of Laurence Sterne (P)

Laurence Sterne was an impecunious vicar who earned fame and fortune with the publication of his comic novel, *Tristram Shandy*, in 1760. In that year, he acquired the living of Coxwold where he lived until his death in 1768. Although a modest cottage, it was immediately dubbed Shandy Hall. Here Sterne continued to write and, after being abandoned by his wife, to recover from falling in love with the twenty-three-year-old Eliza Draper.

After Sterne's death, Shandy Hall became a farmhouse. It was near derelict when a trust was established in 1967 to restore it as a shrine to the writer and as a home for the honorary curators, the Monkmans, who still occupy it. The house is a brick-covered cottage, guarded by holly trees. Gabled cross-wings on either side of the old hall are flanked in turn by a massive kitchen chimney to the right and by Sterne's Georgian extension to the left. In the little garden is Sterne's summer house or 'sweet pavilion'.

The inside is cosy. The parlour/kitchen has a 17th-century range and decorated bread oven door. The beamed study contains a library of Sterniana, evocative of a literary clergyman. The dining room is on the site of what would have been the Great Hall, oak-panelled and painted, with Shandy prints and pictures on the walls. Most enjoyable is Sterne's sitting room. It is the nearest the place comes to grandeur. He called it one of the 'elegant touches to my Shandy Castle'.

SION HILL HALL **

Kirby Wiske, 4m NW of Thirsk
Edwardian mansion with antiques collection (P)

Sion Hill is a monument to the antique collector as addict. A century of assiduous buying and selling has shown that a good eye and a keen ear for a bargain can amass in a few decades what it would take a public museum centuries to acquire. The present incumbent, Michael Mallaby, inherited Sion Hill from Herbert Mawer, a Yorkshire businessman who had bought it in 1962 and filled it with antiques. These were mostly of French furniture and china. Eager to keep the house and collection together as a memorial to his endeavour, Mawer put them into a trust, with

Mr Mallaby in occupation and in charge. He was permitted to sell so as to buy.

The house was built in 1913 by Walter Brierley of York for Percy Stancliffe, on the ruins of a decayed Georgian mansion belonging to the Lascelles family. Brierley was dubbed the 'Lutyens of the North'. His low spreading manor house is in that architect's style, red-brick of two storeys with steep hipped roofs and tall assertive chimneys. The house is fine, even if the details lack the flair and humour of the master.

The reception rooms are laid out along a spinal corridor the length of the ground and first floors. These corridors are modulated by keystoned arches and warmed by the dark reds and blues with which Mr Mallaby has decorated them. The rooms follow a formal sequence of breakfast room, dining room, drawing room and library. The style is rich and crowded, sometimes Curzon Street Baroque, sometimes antique dealer's Louis XVI. Surfaces are so crowded that there is scarcely room to place a champagne cooler or copy of *Country Life*.

Yet no inch is without thought or interest. A honey pot is in the form of a bee. A gin decanter is in the form of a pig. At every turn is a case of Meissen, a shelf of Crown Derby, a cabinet of Sèvres. Mr Mallaby is a clock specialist and the house is alive with ticking and chiming. The old kitchen has been re-stored with much burnished copper and is in regular use as a dining room.

SKIPTON CASTLE ***

Skipton
Clifford stronghold with medieval inner court (P)

Skipton's Market Place leads joyfully uphill to Skipton Castle. The pink-and-black gate-house bursts with medieval self-confidence. The outer bailey is picturesque rather than forbidding, a good place for a picnic, but the seven towers of the inner castle are daunting. Two of them glare down on the sole entrance below, like thuggish bouncers challenging any attempt

on the door. On the far side, the walls drop to the ravine of the Eller Beck.

The entrance itself is oddly delicate. Its oriel window was apparently the 17th-century insertion of Anne Clifford (*see* Appleby/Cumbria), whose family had held Skipton since 1310. She assiduously restored and fenestrated the castles in her custodianship, in defiance of her foe, Oliver Cromwell. Inside is the delightful medieval Conduit Court, surrounded by walls, towers, windows and doors. It is a miniature version of the old court at Berkeley (Gloucs). An ancient yew planted by Lady Anne presides over its centre. Steps rise to the Great Hall.

The undoubted magic of Conduit Court partly evaporates as we explore the interior. Although intact and roofed, the rooms are all bare, scraped, scrubbed and restored. Beams are exposed everywhere and walls covered in whitewash. This smacks of English Heritage corporate identity, odd since the house is privately owned. There is no distinction between any of the chambers and little indication of their use. Most are empty.

On the ground floor are former cellars, ancient cobbled guardrooms and worn steps to fighting platforms and dungeons. The first floor includes the Great Hall, kitchens, bed-chambers and an impressive watchtower. In the East Tower is a Shell Room with tableaux showing the deities of Fire, Air, Water and Earth, ascribed to Isaac de Caux.

The best way to appreciate Skipton is to choose a day with few crowds and wander the rooms and battlements at random, leaving the imagination to do the work. The view from any of the chambers down onto the courtyard on a sunny day is blissful. Surely something can give these stones some life.

STOCKELD PARK **

2m NW of Wetherby
Paine house with Baroque exterior (P-R)

This house does not wear its heart on its sleeve. It is reached across an extensive park outside Wetherby. The old part of the house is in a pink-grey ashlar, with millstone grit for the

Victorian extension. The façade is unwelcoming, a heavy porch having been added in 1885.

Yet the main part of the house, by James Paine in 1758, hugely excited Pevsner as a work of what he called the Vanbrughian revival. The rooms received external expression, not concealed within a formal Palladian box. Wings are thrust forward from the central hall, with pediments and arched bays of their own. This is truly a ghost of Seaton Delaval (Northumbs).

The chief interest of the interior is the staircase, to which the word Baroque can again be applied. It is reached from Paine's entrance hall, with fine plasterwork round the doors. The staircase rises three storeys, the height of the house. It is cantilevered within an oblong volume, every feature of which reflects curvature. The architect is conductor of the interior, with doors and windows his orchestra. Each floor has semi-circular niches, within which are two curved doorways apiece. Seen from below, this creates a superb sense of mystery.

The other rooms have been much altered, although the dining room is still evidently Paine's, curved at each end. The house's owners, the Grant family, have recently redecorated the reception rooms in bold colours, a practice that seems appropriate where Georgian interiors are in need of a lift.

SUTTON PARK ***

Sutton-on-the-Forest, 8m N of York
Small Georgian house with Cortese plasterwork (P)

The Sheffield family goes in the male line back to the 13th century. Variously Earls of Mulgrave and Dukes of Buckingham, they are now back to baronets. In 1963, the family decided to vacate their seat at Normanby (Lincs) and buy the smaller Sutton Park. It is a charming small Georgian house with none of the aloofness of Regency architecture. Sutton was also blessed by the stucco work of Joseph Cortese.

The exterior is plain, of c1745, with a single wide pediment embracing the entire five-bay façade. This is offset by flanking wings and, on the garden front, a bold frontispiece with a French window. The interiors are exquisite. The entrance hall is screened from the stairs by Corinthian columns beneath a Rococo ceiling by Cortese. This runs continuously from the door across the hall and up the stairs. The composition is enhanced by pale yellow walls and a stone floor. Waves and fronds billow from the depths of Cortese's imagination.

Sutton's reception rooms have benefited from imports from other houses, each with a distinct personality. The library has another Cortese ceiling, if anything finer than that in the hall. It is like a basket of flowers tied up with endless ribbons. The morning room has pine panelling worthy of a palace. It was made by Henry Flitcroft for a house in Leeds. Fluted pilasters run from floor to cornice line. The panels between them seem designed to frame the pictures they contain. One is a fine Holbein copy.

The Tea Room walls are painted in imitation tortoiseshell and have a display of Japanese porcelain while the adjacent Porcelain Room has Meissen and Chelsea. The Chinese Drawing Room, on a grander scale than the others, loses the visitor in a delicate oriental forest of Chinese wallpaper. Here is a Smirke fireplace from Normanby, a walnut bureau from old Buckingham House in London (also a one-time Sheffield property) and a dazzling Rococo mirror, complete with Ho-Ho bird.

The dining room was restored after the Second World War by Francis Johnson and is one of his happiest works. The leather screen came from an Armada ship.

SWINTON PARK **

Swinton, 6m S of Bedale
Aristocratic Victorian mansion (H)

When I first visited Swinton on a dark winter evening in the early 1970s, it seemed the sort of place in which the Victorians imprisoned their daughters for safe keeping before marriage. The elderly Earl of Swinton was being perambulated by his butler up and down gaunt corridors. Guests arriving, as I was, for occasional conferences in the house, would inhabit vast, cold reception rooms.

The original house was built in the 1690s but was never left in peace. It was altered by Carr of York in 1764 and further enlarged at the end of the 18th century and the beginning of the 19th. It was further extended by the 19th-century Lord Masham, described by John Cornforth as a 'gigantic Victorian of fantastic energy and compelling vigour'. Swinton is of Disraelian gloom and grandeur, castellated, mildly romantic, and now a luxury hotel.

The house is on rising ground on the outskirts of the village. A drive through fine gates and lodges reveals a large tower set over the entrance, with an L-shaped building beyond. The story of Swinton is of the progressive 'fortification' of both house and owner. The first gothicizing was by Robert Lugar in 1821, working for William Danby. Lord Masham bought the house in 1882 and added storeys, wings, billiard room and library. He also raised the height of the tower; it looks like a fat man bursting out of his coat.

The hotel has retained the Victorian interiors, even at some expense of cosiness. The dining room has been restored, with gilded ceiling and heavy curtains. Family portraits and books still grace walls and bookshelves. The drawing room has a grand fireplace and bow window, possibly designed by James Wyatt. In an eccentric bar are comforting copies of the *Yorkshire Archaeological Journal*.

THIRSK: JAMES HERRIOT'S HOUSE **

23 Kirkgate
Television vet's house and dispensary (M)

The 'World of James Herriot' comes in three parts. First is the original home of the local Thirsk vet. Second is a television studio recreating the same house to the rear, as used in the series, 'All Creatures Great and Small'. Third is a museum of veterinary science. Only the first concerns us here, although the others are first class of their kind.

James Herriot was the pen name of Alf Wight, a real vet. He moved to Thirsk in 1940 and joined the practice of Donald Sinclair, publishing his first volume of popular memoirs in 1970. He continued in practice until his death in 1995. The house in which he lived and worked is Georgian, but the interiors have been restored to their 1950s appearance. This has been done with scholarship and wit. Wight was an enthusiast for clutter.

Downstairs, the dining room doubled as the office. There is also a sitting room, breakfast room, surgery and kitchen. Wight, in a cardigan, is depicted in effigy in the sitting room, but with his back to the door. Toys cover the floor, comics are everywhere and George Formby whines on the radio. The only living thing is a budgerigar. The dining room has a typewriter, copies of *The Lady* and *Tailwagger* and books from the Boots Circulation Library. An early black-and-white programme is playing on the television set.

Most extraordinary is the kitchen, portrayed at the moment of a Yorkshire tea. I have never seen artificial bacon and sausages look so real. The Herriot museum shows wax and plaster admirably employed to bring the past alive. The key is to do it well.

WHITBY: BANQUETING HOUSE *

Whitby Abbey, on coast E of town
Fantastical façade, modernized (EH)

After the Dissolution of the Monasteries, Whitby Abbey on its cliff overlooking the town was acquired by the Cholmley family. They used the abbot's lodgings as a house and, in 1672, added a new banqueting house next door. This was clearly built for splendour rather than comfort and was rarely used. The building decayed and soon became derelict. No one who visited it on a bleak windy evening could doubt its inspiration as the English landfall of Bram Stoker's Count Dracula.

The massive façade is of 11 bays, with a fine Mannerist frontispiece flanked by columns and topped by an open pediment with garland. It was among the most ambitious such buildings in England at the time. Even ruined, the bricked-up windows had the silent assertiveness of their age. They marked the passage of time, while Whitby went about its business in the valley below.

They still do, but oh dear. I am in favour of reinstatement and admire the confidence with which Victorians went about rebuilding what were otherwise meaningless ruins. But English Heritage's 2002 work at Whitby is not reinstatement but a folly at the expense of a fine old building. The new Whitby visitor centre suggests a modern architect with no respect for the atmosphere and character of antiquity.

The windows have been replaced with cold plate glass. The walls have been stripped and scrubbed. The architects were clearly obsessed with imposing their favoured concrete, glass and steel, wholly alien materials, wherever they could. Ruining Whitby must have cost a fortune. To rub salt in the wounds, an actor dressed as 'Sir Hugh Cholmley' greets visitors to what is neither ancient nor modern. It is a warning of the fate which state ownership holds in store for all old buildings.

York

The City of York has England's finest concentration of historic buildings outside Oxford and Cambridge. It is also still blessed with medieval street alignments. Medieval hall houses include the Merchant Adventurers' Hall, the King's Manor and St William's College. Both Jorvik and the Castle Museum have excellent 'living displays'. Fairfax House is pre-eminent among Georgian town houses. At the Treasurer's House, history is brought full circle in an immaculate late-Victorian revival.

Bar Convent Museum *
Barley Hall *
Clifford's Tower *
Fairfax House ****
Jorvik **

The King's Manor **
Mansion House **
Merchant Adventurers' Hall ***
Middlethorpe Hall **

St William's College **
Treasurer's House ***
York Castle Museum *

BAR CONVENT MUSEUM *
Blossom Street
Conversion of Georgian convent school (P)

A reorganization of secondary schools in York in 1982 did away with the old Bar Convent School. It had been founded in 1686 by the 'Jesuitesses', an order of nuns of the Institute of the Blessed Virgin Mary. They were dedicated to what was almost unknown at the time, exclusively female education. The convent was much favoured by St Michael, whose sudden appearance miraculously saved it from destruction by an anti-Catholic mob in 1696.

The convent and school were rebuilt in 1787 as a pedimented Georgian town house, its chapel discreetly hidden across a small courtyard within. An adjacent extension, more ostentatious with larger windows and pilasters, was added in 1844.

Reorganization led the school to amalgamate with other Catholic schools at the rear of the site. The main buildings were converted for use as a museum, conference centre and 'bed & breakfast' for visiting groups. The convent still houses 10 active nuns and 10 retired. On the ground floor is the handsomely furnished Great Parlour where guests are greeted beneath portraits of benefactors and Superiors of the Order.

The Victorian extensions led to the courtyard being glazed, thus forming a charming winter garden. The bright floor tiles are from Coalbrookdale. Upstairs rooms offer a museum of the history of Christianity in York. Sometimes accessible are the library, with books on Catholic history, and the chapel, a rotunda supported by fluted Ionic columns, recently restored to its original Georgian appearance.

BARLEY HALL *

Coffee Yard, off Stonegate
Reconstruction of medieval hall house (M)

In the 1980s, archaeologists seeking a Roman house beneath a plumber's workshop hit the footings of the hall house of a former Lord Mayor of c1400. They stopped there and decided to reconstruct it.

The floor tiles and some of the timbers are original. The rest is a replica designed by the York Archaeological Trust, named after its founder, Maurice Barley. Given the opposition of most archaeologists to such reconstruction, the Trust and the York planning authority deserve all praise.

The site is a godsend to hard-pressed tour guides. It comprises a hall and two-storey solar range, thought to have belonged to Nostell Priory. The Great Hall is visible from a glass screens passage formed from what is a public alleyway. It is of two bays with roof trusses, balcony and lord's platform. The chamber is well crowded with new medieval furniture.

Having gone this far, I cannot see why the Trust does not go two steps further and recreate some of the mess, dirt, colour and rats of a medieval hall. They should take a leaf from the Jorvik book. Barley looks too much like a medieval kit.

CLIFFORD'S TOWER *

Tower Street
Keep of medieval castle (EH)

The tower is the keep of York's medieval castle. It sits atop its grassy motte within the old city walls, wholly dominating what is now York Castle Museum at its foot. The round bastions have subsided slightly, giving the walls an alarming outward tilt, but the building is intact and offers a fine view of the city from above.

The castle was built after the Norman Conquest and was an important fortress. The present keep was erected in 1244, by which time the old Norman square shape was outdated and round was 'in'. The quatrefoil plan is unique in England, supposedly based on the Château d'Étampes outside Paris. It was designed to give defenders the widest range of fire from the windows. The Clifford family were hereditary constables of York Castle. Locals nicknamed it the mince pie.

The entrance gateway, up 55 steep steps, is Jacobean and dated 1642, the last time the keep was garrisoned during the Civil War. Then in 1684 a spectacular fire destroyed most of the interior and left it a picturesque folly. The interior would have had two floors, supported by a massive central pier, the foot of which remains. There is a Gothic chapel above the gatehouse. The tower is a jolly place spoilt only by laboured English Heritage marketing.

FAIRFAX HOUSE ****

27 Castlegate
Georgian nobleman's restored town house (M)

Those who lament the loss of so many fine English town houses can take comfort from Fairfax House. All but a ruin in the 1920s, the building was used variously as a dance hall and a foyer and cloakroom to an adjacent cinema. It is now again among the finest Georgian survivals in England. Begun c1745 and fitted out for Viscount Fairfax c1755–62, it was created

from the wealth of land and restored from the wealth of chocolate. The interior is the masterpiece of Carr of York, but it is also a masterpiece of restoration by Francis Johnson for the York Civic Trust in 1982–4. The rooms hold the Noel Terry collection of furniture, clocks and porcelain. They seem cold, watched over by spectral attendants, but that is a small price to pay for a feast.

The façade onto Castlegate is of five bays with a central pediment, the doorcase a handsome Doric. The interior of the ground floor survived years of abuse when there was a public dance hall and leaking lavatories above. Almost all the stucco is contemporary with the house and is English Rococo. The furniture is Georgian. The hall and staircase are a crescendo of Joseph Cortese's plasterwork, creating a maximum of impact inside a minimum of space. The stair rises to a Venetian window crowned with the Fairfax arms, returning to a landing flanked by magnificent Corinthian doorcases. Walls and ceiling are encrusted with Cortese's stuccowork. Palms and swags support busts of Newton and Shakespeare. The deeply coved ceiling is militaristic, with weapons, trophies, flags and putti holding a light for the 'true religion', Fairfax being a Roman Catholic.

Two superb rooms grace the first floor, the drawing room and the saloon. The drawing room ceiling has fronds embracing a depiction of Friendship. The walls are hung with green damask. The saloon plasterwork is the finest in the house. The foliage seems in perpetual motion, swirling across the ceiling towards a frieze of lions and leaves.

The Viscount's bedroom across the passage was rescued from use as a cinema lavatory. The bed is a four-poster designed by Francis Johnson himself. On it is laid a fine silk dressing-gown with velvet cuffs, together with a rosary and book of poems. Fairfax's daughter Anne's bedroom has vivid wallpaper in what is known as a Mock India pattern. A painting over the fireplace depicts her as a shepherdess.

Rococo Shakespeare in Fairfax House

The kitchen downstairs shows preparation for the Viscount's dinner on 15 April 1763. He ate well. The present entrance to Fairfax House is through an adjacent building. This is a pity since it denies proper access through the front door.

JORVIK VIKING CENTRE: THE LEATHERWORKER'S HOUSE **

Coppergate
Re-creation of Viking street (M)

Archaeologists excavating what is now the Coppergate Shopping Centre in the early 1980s suddenly found themselves walking down what appeared to be a Viking street. It ran along the old bank of the River Ouse. They discovered not only a wealth of material but also wooden beams of original houses. The street was preserved beneath the modern building and the houses were carefully reconstructed *in situ*. Some new properties were added to create at least part of an authentic Viking settlement. York was a Norse-speaking city of 10,000 people in AD975, less than a century before the Norman Conquest. The site is hugely popular.

Visitors are conveyed down the street in open cars on an overhead track. Countryside has been painted in the distance. Two-storey houses of wood flank a street populated with animated figures, workers, merchants and fishwives, all chatting in Old Norse. A man sits on a primitive toilet.

At a point in the tour, the car swivels round and goes inside the biggest of the reconstituted houses, that of a leatherworker. In the car, the visitor rises from cellar to first floor, seeing storage casks in the former, and women and children working the leather above. Skins hang to dry inside the roof. Next door a man turns wooden cups on a small lathe, hence the 'cuppergate' or street of the makers of cups.

Jorvik is a good example of confident reconstruction of the past – by a private company – of a sort that public authorities seem unable to do. And it stinks – as old streets did.

THE KING'S MANOR **

Behind Museum St
Abbey relics now housing modern university
(P-R)

St Mary's Benedictine abbey was the wealthiest monastic house in the north of England. Such was its prosperity and prominence that monks dissatisfied by its luxury deserted in 1132, joined the Cistercian Order and founded Fountains and Rievaulx abbeys to the north. We therefore have much for which to be thankful to the monks of St Mary's.

The present manorial buildings were the abbot's lodgings, seized by the Crown at the Dissolution to become the headquarters of the powerful Council of the North and residence of its President. It was here that the monarchs would stay on visits to the city.

The manor has re-established a sort of monastic heritage as York University. Next door are the old abbey ruins, where the York Mystery plays are still performed. While alteration has left few interiors of special merit, the ensemble is picturesque and not unlike an Oxford college.

The manor is round two courtyards, its pleasure derived from their various façades. Sixteenth- and early 17th-century frontispieces frame each doorway, often in crumbling form. Most of the ranges house the university's architecture and archaeology departments. For some reason, 'advanced architecture' is in a medieval block, medieval architecture in a modern one.

Entry is by the Postern Gate. The original block is a U-shaped medieval house of the late 15th century. This has a superb Jacobean doorway with pilasters, coat of arms and a high pediment. Passing into the courtyard, we see ranges, steps, windows and doors of all periods, built as and when required and to no overall plan. Since most of the interiors were sanitized when the university arrived in the early 1960s, a dreadful architectural era, there is little of interest inside. On the left is an old Hall, now a refectory, while on the right is the Council Chamber.

MANSION HOUSE **

St Helen's Square
Georgian mayor's residence (P-R)

York is rightly proud of its Mansion House, claiming it as the only one in England in which the mayor actually lives during his or her year of office. (This is, however, true of London's Mansion House.) It is accessible on request. The city's ancient Guildhall lies behind. The house was completed in 1729, possibly by a local man, William Etty. The façade is simple, of stuccoed brick with colourful decoration and is very much the centre of attention in St Helen's Square.

To the left of the entrance hall is a dining room running from front to back of the building, filled with one giant table. The ceiling looks like stucco but is wallpaper. The climax of the house is the progress to the main state room above. Arch, stairs and landings are crowded with gilded stucco.

The stairwell is dominated by a portrait of York's most controversial son, the 'railway king', George Hudson. He built the line from York to London and lived in the largest house in Belgravia, now the French Embassy. He went bankrupt, was accused of embezzlement and disgraced. The burghers of York scratched the name from his portrait, but could not bring themselves to take down the picture. (Doncaster Mansion House is shocked that York should decorate its stairs with such a man.)

At the top of the stairs is the small Yellow Drawing Room with a fireplace brought from Robert Adam's Adelphi Terrace in London. Its frieze has been reset upside down. The state room is the main ceremonial chamber: it overlooks the square and embodies the pomp and autonomy of a great civic corporation. Corinthian pilasters and green and gilt panelling rise to a coved ceiling. At each end are large fireplaces topped by the coats of arms of the Crown and the City of York. Large portraits of kings and mayors hang above, arranged such that the dignity of the one does not detract from the majesty of the other.

MERCHANT ADVENTURERS' HALL ***

Fossgate
Complete surviving group of medieval guild hall and rooms (P)

Do not approach the building from Piccadilly, with its ugly shopping centre and naked gardens. From that angle, it looks suburban, even mock-Tudor. Approach instead from Fossgate, through a Tudor arch set beneath a coat of arms. Entry is into a 15th-century courtyard overhung by gables and old brick-work. The space is enclosed and intimate, with carved lintels and leaded windows, flagstones on the ground and antiquity in the air.

Merchant Adventurers' Hall is the finest medieval survivor in York; indeed, it claims to be the most complete group of guild buildings in Europe. The guilds were religious and charitable fraternities, many of which evolved into commercial oligopolies controlling apprenticeship and trade. They were the backbone of civil society in pre-Reformation England. In the City of London, they became liveried companies, most of their halls burned in the Great Fire. In York a number survive in their medieval form, still with domestic premises attached.

The Merchant Adventurers' Hall was dedicated to any who 'adventures his own money in overseas trade'. It consists of one great chamber dating from the mid-14th century, with two 'naves' divided by oak crown-posts. The roof is exposed, its curved trusses forming a textbook of medieval carpentry. The sash windows are Georgian insertions. The painted governor's dais came from the old Assize Court.

Beneath the hall is its most evocative relic. The posts of the undercroft are massive and distorted, as if buckling under the weight of money above. This was a hospice for the poor and infirm members, in use from 1373 until 1900. Here lived adventurers whose 'boats had not come home'. Niches in the walls were for them to keep their modest belongings. To one side is a remarkable four-sided fireplace, which must have suffused the room with heat. It gave all inmates 'a place by the fire'. The room contains a display of copies of medieval guild banners that would once have been paraded through the streets (as today in Siena).

Overlooking the courtyard is a series of Tudor service rooms, offering privacy to the Governor and his court. Three ante-rooms precede admission to the governor's presence. Most are filled with company memorabilia and portraits.

MIDDLETHORPE HALL **

Bishopthorpe Road
Ironmaster's mansion with panelled interiors (H)

Middlethorpe is a handsome William-and-Mary mansion standing in its own grounds opposite York Racecourse. ''Tis a very pretty place,' said Lady Mary Wortley Montagu in 1713, and it still is. The house was built for Thomas Barlow, son of a family of iron-masters, cutlers and Quakers of Sheffield and Leeds, one of many rich young men of the 18th century who began what Giles Worsley calls the 'slow drift from industry to gentry that was the characteristic of descendants of the post-Restoration ironmasters'. It has been true of the rich throughout English history.

Thomas Barlow acquired 'arms' as a knight but did not feel secure enough to set up as a gentleman near Sheffield, instead acquiring the manor of Middlethorpe in 1698. By 1702, he had built himself a new house 'in the Italian mode' and ten years later took himself and his son on a Grand Tour. When they reached France he promptly died. His son sold his manufacturing interests and invested in land.

The house remained unaltered but increasingly derelict over its life. Like many large houses, it sought a future as a school, as flats, even as Brummels Nightclub 'where the age of Regency elegance lives on'. Not until the 1980s did the York sprawl loom on the horizon and bring Middlethorpe and its proximity to the racecourse to the attention of the hotel industry. This proved its salvation. Its rescuer and

owner is Historic House Hotels (*see* Hartwell/ Bucks).

The interior has been immaculately restored, with little atmosphere of a hotel. Beyond the entrance hall with fine doorcases is the stair hall facing the garden. A bright enfilade of reception rooms runs along the garden front. The stairs have thickly carved treads and balusters and rest on a fine Corinthian column. The walls are hung with old family portraits, albeit of poor quality. To the right of the hall is a small panelled library with Piranesi prints. Beyond is the old ballroom, now the drawing room.

On the left of the hall is the Oak Room, with Ionic pilasters and panelling that breaks forward in Baroque fashion round the fireplace. Single-storey wings give the house a graceful profile to the gardens.

ST WILLIAM'S COLLEGE **

Minster Yard
Conversion of medieval priests' college (P)

The present buildings were erected in the 1450s as accommodation for priests at the Minster. The arrangement would have been collegiate, with staircases and rooms off them. A large hall was positioned in the north range, facing the entrance across the courtyard. The building was sold at the Dissolution and occupied by the Earl of Carlisle while he was building Castle Howard. It was reacquired by the Minster in 1902 and converted as a conference centre.

Had it not been for the heavy-handedness of the conversion by the architect, Temple Moore, medieval St William's might outshine the Merchant Adventurers' Hall. Moore refashioned the street façade in conventional neo-Tudor, with an orderly roof and shop windows along a stone-built ground floor. Inside, he rebuilt the screens passage and Great Hall as an entrance hall with, behind it, a two-storeyed structure. The upper part of this hall

York: Merchant Adventurers' Hall

is now the Maclagan Hall, with some original roof timbering. The frontispiece is 17th century.

The best feature of the college is the quiet courtyard where visitors can refresh themselves after the exertions of visiting the Minster next door.

TREASURER'S HOUSE ***

Minster Yard
Edwardian restoration of Jacobean house (NT)

Many historic buildings are museums trying to look like homes. The Treasurer's House was a home trying to look like a museum. The treasurer was that of the medieval Minster, an office of great wealth and little work, abolished at the Reformation. 'The Treasure having been confiscated, there is no further need of a Treasurer,' said a contemporary record. The house became the archbishop's residence but was then successively demolished, rebuilt, altered, sold, divided and left to decay. What we see today is the creation of one man, Frank Green, who seized the ghosts of its past and refashioned them after his own educated imagination.

Green was a scion of upwardly mobile Wakefield entrepreneurs. Fastidious, effete, unmarried and a great connoisseur, he cuts a fine figure alongside his father dressed in hunting clothes in a photograph in the guidebook. He bought the Treasurer's House in 1897 and worked with Temple Moore to strip away its Victorian accretions and reinstate what he took to be the 17th-century original. Rooms were carefully designed to reproduce periods appropriate to his art and antiques. Christopher Hussey of *Country Life* was an admirer of Green, regarding his furniture as 'one of the finest collections in England'. He gave the house intact to the National Trust in 1930.

By then Green was completely eccentric. He slept each night in fresh Jaeger sheets, having them laundered in London and sent up by train. He was fanatically tidy, creeping downstairs at night to the kitchen to check that the

cutlery lay in proper rows in the drawers. Workmen had to wear slippers indoors. Yet his attention to decorative detail, including fabric and wallpaper, created a remarkable work of Edwardian revival. Lady Diana Cooper encountered him as a girl on his antique-hunting expeditions. 'We thought him sound as a bell,' she recalled, 'until one day he admitted to veering towards Victorian taste. We stopped our ears.'

Each of the rooms seems to hang on a single work. The entrance hall has arabesque wall paintings copied from a house in King's Lynn. The West Sitting Room, fashioned from a larger room, has a voluptuous Baroque chimneypiece. The hall was entirely Green's creation, based on the conjectured location of a medieval hall. Beyond is the Blue Drawing Room, with panelling from floor to ceiling, its details picked out in bronze.

The William-and-Mary staircase is papered in green and leads to Green's sumptuous bedrooms. Each drips with canopies, drapes and panelling. The Queen's and Princess Victoria's Rooms recall a much-prized royal visit in 1900. The King's Room veers towards the absurd: a gigantic bed, reputedly from Houghton House in Norfolk, has been crammed into a simple 16th-century chamber with stencilled walls. It is like squeezing a cardinal's retinue into a Quaker meeting house.

The loveliest room is the dining room. This has an 18th-century fireplace and overmantel framing a Flemish landscape. In the plaster ceiling, a central oval incorporates what appear to be earlier cross-beams. The kitchen has been 'Trustified', but we can still imagine the old man running his finger along a shelf to check for dust and complaining of an out-of-place three-pronged fork.

YORK CASTLE MUSEUM: DEBTORS' PRISON *

Tower Street
Surviving cells of old city prison (M)

York's Castle Museum has the finest 'historic lifestyle' display in England. It embraces the history of the North from cottage hearth and chocolate factory to fine Jacobean and Georgian interiors. There are sounds and smells as well as sights. Over it hangs a pall, that it occupies the old city jail and makes no attempt to hide the fact. Here people lived and died in misery. A graffiti notes: 'This Prison is a House of Care, a Grave for Man Alive,/ A Touch Stone to Try a Friend, No Place for Man to Thrive.'

The centre block was built in 1701 in the style of Vanbrugh and was for debtors. They were allowed more salubrious quarters and could work to pay off their debt. From the outside, it might be a palace were it not for the grilles on the ground floor windows and the absence of a door. Carr of York later built a wing for female prisoners and various exercise yards to the rear. Two old York streets have been reconstructed in these yards, Kirkgate and Half Moon Court.

The surviving rooms of the old jail are in the basement of the Debtors' Prison. These are the cells for those who had committed serious crimes and were awaiting sentence of death or deportation. There were 200 of these cells in the early 19th century. They are well displayed, without the ghoulishness considered obligatory in prison museums elsewhere. The condemned cell has a charcoal stove, fire and bed. It is where Dick Turpin, the celebrated highwayman, supposedly spent his last night before being hanged in 1739.

Antiquarian piety: Treasurer's House

Yorkshire, South

South Yorkshire was carved in the 1970s from parts of the West and East Ridings and has since relapsed into the Sheffield–Doncaster conurbation. It is not England's happiest landscape, yet it boasts one of England's most intact Norman keeps at Conisbrough. Outside Barnsley, two early 18th-century palaces can be seen at Wentworth Woodhouse and Wentworth Castle, where Rockinghams and Straffords vied for architectural glory. Both await full accessibility. The Georgian Mansion House at Doncaster is a civic gem, while Victorian sobriety is displayed at 19th-century Brodsworth.

Brodsworth **
Cannon Hall *
Conisbrough *
Doncaster:
  Cusworth Park **
  Mansion House **

Sheffield:
  Bishops' House *
Wentworth Castle **
Wentworth
    Woodhouse *

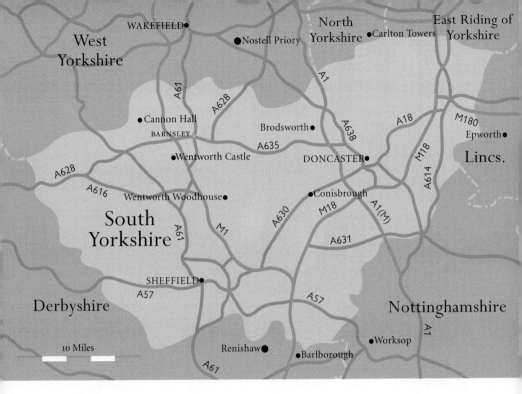

BRODSWORTH HALL **

Brodsworth, 6m NW of Doncaster
Victorian Italianate mansion (EH)

The story of this house starts with a court case. The grandson of a Huguenot refugee and banker, Théophile Thellusson, died in 1797 and willed that his fortune be left to accumulate during the lifetimes of all his surviving male descendants. Only when his great-grandson had died could his money pass to his sons' lineal descendants. Should none exist, it was to be used to pay off the National Debt. This was considered so unfair, and potentially de-stabilizing to the national economy, that it was bitterly contested. Such wills were made illegal by Act of Parliament in 1800.

By the time the inheritance fell due, in 1856, lawyers had taken most of it, but enough survived for Charles Thellusson, a yachting enthusiast with six children, to demolish and rebuild the family home at Brodsworth. The new house was inherited by each of his four sons in turn, all dying childless. It then passed to a daughter, Constance. I first visited the house in 1989 when her granddaughter, Pamela Williams, and her husband were vainly trying to keep out rain and damp while living in one room round an oil heater. It was a desperate sight. The National Trust was uninterested and she finally pleaded with English Heritage to help. The house was reopened in 1995.

Brodsworth was completed in 1863. It is long, low and Italianate, and hugely improved by stone cleaning. It looks like a mansion in London's Kensington Palace Gardens. The entrance front boasts a fine *porte-cochère*. Two projecting bays and copious urns on a balustraded roof enliven the symmetrical garden façade. Whereas earlier country houses have a parade of reception rooms for entertaining, Brodsworth's rooms are more attuned to middle-class domesticity. This is borne out by the names of the rooms: morning room, smoking room and library. Servants are not banished to an attic but given respectable quarters behind a baize door in a wing of their own. The rooms are spacious without being extravagant. Show is confined chiefly to the hall and staircase. The architect was the

little-known Philip Wilkinson, while an unknown Italian, Chevalier Casentini, contributed to the garden buildings.

The furnishings were almost all from the London firm of Lapworths and survive virtually intact: painted walls, stained glass, silk curtains and Axminster carpets. In the hall is Thellusson's collection of Italian marble sculptures, mostly sentimental Victorian works such as Pietro Magni's *Swinging Girl*. Other than a family Lawrence in the dining room and some equestrian pictures in the billiard room, the paintings are not distinguished but admirably complement the decoration. Bedrooms and lesser rooms are enjoyably furnished with the paraphernalia of the time. The fully equipped kitchen and pantries display life 'below stairs'.

The original park has been curtailed, but the formal gardens, Quarry Garden and Target Range (for archery) survive and are maintained with 1860s vigour and smartness.

CANNON HALL *

Cawthorne, 4m W of Barnsley
Home of Spencers with interiors by Carr of York (M)

Cannon Hall is Barnsley's lung, if not its heart. The house dominates a long, landscaped slope and is now a museum and art gallery. It was built by the local Spencer family in the 18th century on the wealth of iron. Wealth led to art and the Spencer-Stanhopes became members of the Pre-Raphaelite circle. The walls of the house display their paintings and works from the National Loans Collection Trust.

The core of the house is c1700 but the entrance and much of the interior were altered and decorated by Carr of York in the 1760s. This was to display Grand Tour treasures brought back by the bachelor dilettante, John Spencer. The adjacent Oak Room appears to survive from the earlier house, the panelling over its fireplace dated 1697.

Brodsworth: time-warp kitchen

The south front rooms are mostly by Carr. The dining room has an excellent Rococo ceiling depicting musical instruments. The Georgian sideboard is designed to conceal its mundane purpose of knife storage. The urns on either side of the fireplace conceal basins for washing glasses.

The library displays the taste of a provincial gentleman of the Regency era. Plasterwork depicts hunting and country pursuits. Books indicate classical taste and a love of nature. The bookcases are original, bar one which came from the old *Times* offices in Printing House Square. In the Ballroom is a large chimneypiece from Florence, decorated with the Spencer and related coats of arms. The Red Damask Room contains Spencer-Stanhope portraits, including Pre-Raphaelite works, covering seven generations of the family. This theme is repeated in photographs in the corridors.

CONISBROUGH CASTLE *

Conisbrough
Norman keep with interior and defences intact (EH)

Forget dreary South Yorkshire for a moment and concentrate on Conisbrough keep on its hill overlooking the River Don. 'In the beauty of its geometrical simplicity,' wrote Pevsner, it is 'unsurpassed in England'. The keep survives almost intact, a monument to medieval might. It inspired Walter Scott's castle of the Saxon kings in *Ivanhoe*, drawing Victorian tourists en masse, and is still managed by the Ivanhoe Trust of behalf of English Heritage.

Conisbrough is pure Norman. It was built in c1180 apparently to his own design by Hamelin Plantagenet, son of Geoffrey of Anjou. The plan is found elsewhere only in Plantagenet's castle at Mortemer in Normandy. The form is of a single round keep on a large mound, with clinging buttresses battered outwards at their bases to resist sapping.

The first-floor entrance is reached along a causeway, lethally exposed from above. The lower storeys can be reached only by a ladder. There are no windows on the first floor, which was for storage. The lord's chamber was on the second floor, later supplanted by a Great Hall located elsewhere in the surrounding, mostly vanished, bailey.

This room has a large fireplace with a giant hood. Above is the solar with a small chapel contained within one of the buttresses. The keep retains its staircases, garderobes and alcoves, remarkable in a building of this age. It is otherwise empty.

The interiors are displayed for primary school children. On the ground floor a tape recording recites over and again that 'the walls of the castle have ears'. From the roof is a view over the few remaining trees of the Don Valley.

DONCASTER: CUSWORTH PARK **

2m W of Doncaster
Merchant's house with plasterwork by Joseph Rose (M)

The house was built for William Wrightson in 1740 in fine parkland on a hill overlooking Doncaster. The architect was a local man, George Platt, but the ubiquitous James Paine (also working on the town's Mansion House) soon took over. The entrance forecourt displays a comfortable Georgian mansion in crumbling stone, enclosed by service wings. The garden front looks out over the Don Valley, which must once have been a splendid view. The house is owned by the local council and is desperately in need of full restoration. A fine house is struggling to get out.

Few rooms are free of museumitis, yet behind the stands and display cases can be detected fine plasterwork by Adam's stuccoist, Joseph Rose. The small library is a delight, with Gothick bookcases set into the walls. It is the only instance I know of bookshelves continuing low over a fireplace, with no care for the fate of the precious leather.

Cusworth's treasure is its chapel, again with plasterwork by Rose. It might be the private oratory of a Roman cardinal, which may have been Wrightson's intention. There is a classical screen to the apse and the walls are being stripped to reveal religious murals that appear to fill the room, some by Francis Hayman. These at least are now being restored. More should surely follow.

DONCASTER: MANSION HOUSE **

High Street
Georgian townhouse by Paine with grand ballroom (P-R)

Doncaster Mansion House is one of only three in England of this splendour (with York and the City of London) still equipped for mayoral residence. It was commissioned from James Paine in 1744 and stands prominent on a bend in the High Street. It is like a Georgian buck lost in a suburban supermarket. How much civic pride Doncaster must once have boasted, and how little it displays today, a place of ring roads and cheap stores, and even Cusworth (above) unrestored.

The house is a brash townhouse of three grand bays, designed when Paine was working on Cusworth Park. The façade has a rusticated ground floor, attached columns and three large windows to the first-floor ballroom. The doorway is deeply recessed, as if welcoming visitors into a masonic temple. The entrance hall is all red carpet and green scagliola. The stair rises dramatically to a Venetian window, doubling back on itself, its handrail adorned with acanthus balusters.

The ballroom is magnificent for what was then a small town. A punctilious official told me that it cost £4,523.4s.6d when built. Joseph Rose was commissioned to do the Rococo plasterwork. It has been repainted fiercely by Crown Paints, apparently true to the original colours. Doors and doorcases, inside and outside the ballroom, are beautifully made. To each side, again through fine doors, are the mayoress's withdrawing room and the grand saloon. Would that civic pride in England might one day be permitted to repeat such glory elsewhere.

SHEFFIELD: BISHOPS' HOUSE *

Meersbrook Park, 2m S of Sheffield
Medieval farmhouse surviving in suburban park (M)

Sheffield has little of architectural note. Nowhere has been so harshly treated by de-industrialization and has so little to show for its 20th-century urban renewal. Bishops' House is the best bet in a small park, Meersbrook, in the village of Norton on the southern outskirts.

The house is a timber-framed structure, hardly large enough to be considered manorial. It dates from the 15th century when it was a farmhouse owned by the Blythe family, ancestors of a Bishop Blythe after whose job it is named. A council parks employee lived here until it was restored as a museum.

The exterior is jolly enough, with black-and-white timbering above a rough stone ground floor. Most of the windows look original, with some projecting oriels. The plan is L-shaped, with a central hall and parlour and upstairs chambers in the cross-wing. Although the core of the house is Tudor, the domestic wing was extended in the 17th century.

The former Great Parlour is laid out as a dining room with period furniture and pewter. The Hall is bare, with some revealed fragments of ornamental panelling. Upstairs is more interesting. There are two crude but attractive plaster overmantels, one with fruit trees growing inside Renaissance arches, the other with two ferocious dogs and a winged head of a man. These date from the mid-17th century when William Blythe was a Parliamentary army officer. The vast floorboards are only half dressed, their bark still showing in the cracks.

WENTWORTH CASTLE **

3½m SW of Barnsley
Façade of northern Baroque palace (P-G)

The castle is a palatial house built in 1670 and extended by the Wentworths in the 18th century. It is now a college. Most of the rooms have been institutionalized and their fireplaces removed, sold and dispersed, but the fine gardens are accessible and discreet glimpses may be had of the interior by appointment. The three main façades are magnificent.

The original house is the modest seven-bay front facing north towards the entrance drive. There is a scrolly pediment over the main porch and a Restoration staircase inside, rightly described by Pevsner as 'thickly and juicily carved'. Round the corner to the left and overlooking the valley to the east is an architectural trumpet blast. This façade was erected c1710–20 by Thomas Wentworth, later Earl of Strafford. He should not be confused with his earlier namesake at neighbouring Wentworth Woodhouse, which this house was meant to rival. Our Wentworth, Lord Raby at the time, was ambassador in Berlin and returned with a design by Jean de Bodt, architect of the Arsenal at Potsdam, for a house in the Franco-Prussian manner. Lord Montagu had likewise built at Boughton (Northants).

The façade is of extraordinary grandeur, a far cry from the timid Yorkshire Baroque of, for instance, Newby or Beningbrough. Two storeys of black-ochre stone rise to an attic buried beneath a parapet. The windows are elaborately pedimented. The centre has three big arched windows on the first floor. These are divided by pilasters and crowned with a mass of foliage and heraldry. The composition is unmistakably by a continental.

Nor is this all. The far frontage onto the garden is later, of the early 1760s and in a purer Palladian style. It is of rusticated stone, with a central portico, and with Venetian windows in the end pavilions. Inside, the grand east range has a first-floor long gallery of stupendous proportions, apparently completed by James Gibbs. It is closed to public view, perhaps to conceal its misuse. That a building should be so treated in the cause of education is wrong.

The grounds of Wentworth Castle are of Burlingtonian stateliness. They include a folly castle (Stainborough Castle), an obelisk, a rotunda and the customary temples. Beside the entrance from the main road is an open-sided market cross. The last stands on 16 columns with drum bases like a Roman temple, sadly purposeless. It was allegedly designed by Horace Walpole, presumably as an antiquarian folly.

WENTWORTH WOODHOUSE *

Wentworth, 5m NW of Rotherham
Façade of great house in park (P-G)

Wentworth is one of the most splendid houses-in-a-landscape in England. It claims the longest continuous façade in the country, of 600 ft. Its closure to public access behind security fences is a crying shame. John Carr's massive stables are locked, occupied on my visit by mangy pheasants pecking at barbed wire. Behind more wire is an encampment of Georgian outhouses and a derelict 1960s teacher training college. I include the house because its exterior is fully visible from the TransPennine Way, passing directly in front, and in the hope of better things to come. Even today, Wentworth Woodhouse cuts a dash in an oasis between the outskirts of Sheffield, Rotherham and Barnsley.

The original house was built by Thomas Wentworth, 1st Earl of Strafford, in the 1630s. He was executed by the Parliamentarians in 1641. This house was transformed in the 1720s by another Thomas Wentworth, later Marquis of Rockingham, in the Baroque style. Fluted pilasters flank decorated windows with a giant cartouche overhead.

In 1734, with this transformation just complete, plans for a completely new east range, back-to-back with the old, were shown to Lord Burlington's Committee of Taste by Henry 'Burlington Harry' Flitcroft. The design was similar to Colen Campbell's vanished Wanstead but grander by far. This was to be the biggest house in England and probably still is. The front is nineteen bays long, with a double flight of steps in the middle, rising to an entrance portico. Wings seem to flow without ceasing from either side, each section a house in itself. These wings end in corner pavilions with cupolas added by Carr of York in the 1780s.

Behind this front are rooms designed by Flitcroft and filled by Rockingham and his successors over the years with an epic collection of art. Wentworth Woodhouse ranked with Harewood and Castle Howard among the great mansions of the North. When Arthur Mee visited it in the 1940s, he saw it as 'standing astonishing witness to the commonplace grandeur of the 18th century'.

The house displayed portraits of kings, queens, Straffords and Rockinghams by van Dyck, Lely and Reynolds. There was a painting by Stubbs of the celebrated horse, *Whistlejacket*, and Hogarth's Rockingham family group. Even the austere Pevsner called this a house of 'quite exceptional value . . . from the Viennese or Venetian gaiety . . . to the Palladian purity . . . not easily matched anywhere in England'.

The house is still the property of the Fitzwilliam-Wentworth Estate, may God rest its soul. The contents are dispersed, although some are retained by the family elsewhere. The building is let to a retired architect from London who, I am told, means well.

Yorkshire, West

The West Riding of Yorkshire, now shorn of South Yorkshire, is a fine rolling landscape 'where only man is vile'. The concentrated Victorian mill towns, with their tall chimneys and Florentine municipal buildings, have mostly, and sadly, been replaced by tower blocks and estates, showing no respect for the contours that defined the earlier settlements.

The Middle Ages left a few fragments of military and ecclesiastical architecture, notably the Cistercian Kirkstall Abbey. A good pele survives, astonishingly, within Bolling Hall in Bradford and an unexpected medieval house is emerging at Longley in Huddersfield. The Jacobean era is well represented, with fine yeomen's houses at Oakwell, Shibden and East Riddlesden. Towering over the county is the Ingrams' Temple Newsam, restored to its old glory by the City of Leeds.

The West Riding has less to show for the 18th century, but Harewood and Nostell are splendour enough, with Adam at his most prolific in both houses and Capability Brown at his most spectacular.

Bradford:
  Bolling Hall **
Bramham **
Gomersal:
  Oakwell **
  Red House *
Halifax:
  Holdsworth House *
  Shibden Hall ***

Harewood *****
Haworth:
  Bronte Parsonage *
Huddersfield:
  Longley Old Hall **
Keighley:
  Cliffe Castle *
  East Riddlesden ***

Leeds:
  Kirkstall Abbey *
Lotherton Hall **
Nostell Priory ****
Temple Newsam ***
Wakefield:
  Clarke Hall *

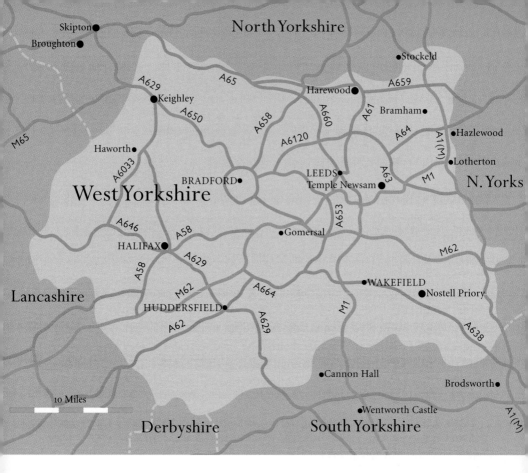

BRADFORD: BOLLING HALL **

Bowling Hall Road, 1½m S of centre of Bradford
Jacobean house built round pele tower with
Carr of York interiors (M)

Black the landscape, black the Hall and, on a
rainy March day, black the effort of trying to
find this dignified old Yorkshire lady in the
suburbs of Bradford. Bolling Hall looks
indestructible.

The house was founded by the Bollings in
the Middle Ages, from which survives a large
pele tower. This is a formidable thing to find
in deeply urban Yorkshire. It passed to the
Tempests of Broughton, who added a hall to
the tower, and then to Saviles, Lindleys and
Woods. The last employed Carr of York in 1779
to redesign the east wing. Surrounded by min-
eral workings, the house declined until taken

over by the council in 1912. From the garden
to the south, there is a magnificent view of
the pele, Hall, Georgian wing and balancing
tower.

The entrance is under the pele tower, with
an impressive medieval kitchen. The hall,
known in these parts as the housebody, was
altered internally in the 18th century, with
an unusual balcony linking the tower to the
east wing. The massive window contains 17th-
century heraldic glass depicting the Bolling
and Tempest families. Carr's rooms in the
east wing, ornate and rather cold, are used
to display Bradford's admirable collection of
18th-century furniture.

Upstairs are two Carr rooms. One contains
a great treasure, a Chippendale couch bed in
red damask made for Harewood and acquired
by Bradford in 1976, much to its credit. At
the back is a room dedicated to a famous son
of Bradford, Frederick Delius. It includes his

piano and Yorkshire furniture in the Art Nouveau style. Beyond the Hall is the Ghost Room, alive with wood carving and a geometrical plaster frieze. The pele tower contains a mid-1400s chamber with painted hangings in place of tapestries, a rarity (*see* Birmingham: Blakesley Hall/Warwicks).

BRAMHAM PARK **

6m S of Wetherby
Queen Anne mansion with rare garden (P-R)

Bramham is a rare example of Baroque landscape principles applied to a domestic English house. The languid approach from the main road gradually forms into a magnificent composition of courtyard, house and grounds. On all sides are the intersecting vistas beloved of the early Georgians aping Le Notre, and detested by the later ones. Somehow these formal ponds, cascades, obelisks and temples survived the clean sweep of Capability Brown and the Romantics elsewhere.

The house was built *c*1705–10 by Robert Benson, Lord Bingley, in a style that barely hints at Baroque. The main block is flanked by service wings round a central courtyard rising up the slope. Only the curving coach ramp and steps to the front door yield much sense of theatre. The central doorway misses a grander storey above. The steps to the garden entrance behind are more successful, a scene of swaying architectural motion.

Bramham was mostly gutted in a fire of 1828 and left derelict for eighty years. In 1906, a Bingley descendant, George Richard Lane Fox, commissioned Detmar Blow to restore the old house. Blow left battered stone walls in the entrance hall, as savaged by the fire, a picturesque touch. Richness is confined to the 17th-century chandelier and huge pictures by Kneller and Reynolds. The Long Gallery is neo-Queen Anne, hung with family portraits. Centrepiece of the room is a newly acquired Louis XV bureau with beautiful swirling inlay.

The appointments system is eccentric. I was refused pre-arranged admission as the hall was in use for yoga.

GOMERSAL: OAKWELL HALL **

Birstall, 1m NW of Gomersal
Elizabethan house with *trompe-l'œil* panelling (M)

Charlotte Brontë used Elizabethan Oakwell as the model for Fieldhead in *Shirley*. She called it, 'neither grand nor comfortable; within as without it was antique, rambling and incommodious'. An Edwardian tenant was a Batley lawyer, George Maggs, who forestalled a plan to ship the hall to America, where such buildings are more valued. In 1928, it was handed instead to the local council.

So many Yorkshire yeomen's houses have vanished that the survival of any one is a miracle. Oakwell sits back from the road, with space enough to distance itself from the Batley to Bradford sprawl. The core of the house is late 16th century but the fine panelling, ceilings and fireplaces are 17th.

The house's first remarkable feature is its façade. Close-mullioned windows fill the entire front wall of the Hall, with wide sweeping gables on the wings on either side. Inside, the Hall has original Doric columns to its screen and the stairs have openwork dog-gates. The Great Parlour is richly decorated, with crude caryatids flanking the window bays and panelling painted in *trompe-l'œil*, known as scumbling. Most of the designs are abstract, but over the mantelpiece they include delightful landscapes.

The Great Parlour Chamber above has a large Elizabethan bed and a garderobe. The remaining rooms have been appropriately furnished, many with old chests. A bed exhorts its occupant to 'Drede God, Love God, Prayes God'. The Painted Chamber to the rear of the house has similar scumbling to the Parlour downstairs, grained to look like walnut. This is a great rarity since most oak panelling was later stripped to reveal its grain, a habit recently extended to pine. The bed in the New Parlour Chamber has massive turned posts on square plinths, like thick Jacobean calves stuck in monstrous shoes.

In the roof space above the kitchen is a rare Kitchen Chamber. Here food would hang and servants sleep, warmed from the fires below.

GOMERSAL: RED HOUSE *

Gomersal
Georgian cloth merchant's house (M)

This is a cloth merchant's house of the 'middling' sort. It was built by and for the Taylor family in the 1660s and owned by them until 1920. In the 1830s, one of Joshua Taylor's six children, Mary, became a close friend of Charlotte Brontë from Haworth. Brontë featured the family and house in her novel, *Shirley*, as she did Oakwell above. It is from this association that the building draws much of its celebrity.

The house sits by the main road, and is called Red for the unusual colour of its brick construction. The outside is Georgian, as is much of the interior, although the latter suffers severely from museumitis. The rooms are all pretty-genteel. The Hall is painted to look like stone, the pine wood grained to resemble mahogany and the arches 'marbled'. Stained-glass heads of Milton and Shakespeare adorn the dining room. It is as described by Brontë, 'no splendour but taste everywhere'.

Waxwork figures portray the Taylors at work and play. The women paint watercolours, the children are tutored. Other tableaux show the servants in the kitchens, well equipped with original implements.

HALIFAX: HOLDSWORTH HOUSE *

2m N of Halifax
Jacobean house with eccentric windows (H)

The setting of Holdsworth House must once have been sublime, in its private cleft in the moors. It now stands in a grimy valley, full of the scars and shedlands north of Halifax. But the exterior is a fine display of Yorkshire Jacobean, built c1598 and extended in the early 17th century. The porch is dated 1633. The

formal entrance is through noble gateposts into a knot garden. An original gazebo is in one corner and muscular stone walls flank the sides.

The main façade is extraordinary, crowded with thick-mullioned windows. This is well-set, virile Yorkshire. The porch has to its right two gabled bays, one with a cross of St John indicating past Crusader activity on some-one's part. The lower hall window has eleven lights, asymmetrically arranged. The left wing has a two-tier window composition, again with a wide gable. It is all most assertive. Older byres and barns extend behind.

The interior is much altered but contains Jacobean furnishings, beams and fireplaces. The house was acquired by the Pearson family in 1963 and turned into a country club for dining and gambling. In 1964 it achieved immortality as the venue for John Lennon's twenty-fourth birthday party. Guests can still sleep in beds in which the Beatles are alleged to have slept that night, forced to sleep two to a room. The hotel literature boasts also that 'Jayne Mansfield and Sir Alec Douglas-Home slept here'. The mind boggles.

HALIFAX: SHIBDEN HALL ***

1m NE of Halifax
Medieval hall house restored in 19th century (M)

The doyenne of Shibden was Anne Lister (1791–1840), a lesbian who left a coded journal detailing every aspect of a propertied lady's life in late-Georgian Yorkshire. Many entries run to 2,000 words a day. It was Anne who restored the house in Jacobethan style in the 1830s. She reopened the Hall to the roof and installed new beams and a neo-Gothic tower.

Shibden today is a superb medieval hall house, periodically updated but with its character intact. It sits on a lonely hill outside Halifax, amid a pleasant garden but sur-rounded by a desecrated landscape. It was built in the mid-15th century and bought in 1612 by the coal-rich Listers, who handed it to Halifax Council in 1933.

While the exterior is of blackened sandstone, the inside is a glorious mass of dark oak. The entrance is into a screens passage, off which a study takes the place of the old buttery. This has been recreated as a den of walnut furniture, leather books, old guns and smoking equipment. It lacks only smells. The Hall, a Yorkshire housebody, is lit by a twenty-light Elizabethan window, filled with family heraldry. A portrait of Anne Lister peers down from the walls. In the middle of the Hall is a fine 1590s dining table.

Beyond the Hall is the Savile drawing room, with an early English piano made by Pohlmann in 1769. The staircase, with a view from the gallery into the Hall below, was installed by Anne as part of her restoration. The Red Room is so-called for the Tudor frieze and contains a chunky four-poster with canopy. The guidebook claims that the purpose of the canopy was to protect the sleeper from falling spiders and bird droppings, which is new to me. An early powder closet guards the entrance to the Victorian library tower.

Other rooms include the tiny bedchamber in which Anne herself slept, constantly complaining to the staff that it was either too hot or too cold.

HAREWOOD HOUSE *****

Harewood, 8m N of Leeds
Adam palace altered by Barry, Old Master collection (P)

Harewood is a place of dazzlement, a St Petersburg palace on a Yorkshire ridge. It affirms 18th-century taste, 19th-century wealth and 20th-century ingenuity, privately owned and superbly presented.

Edwin Lascelles inherited the estate which his father acquired in 1738 and, on the advice of Lord Leicester of Holkham, commissioned John Carr of York to design him a new mansion. At the same time, he turned to the thirty-three-year-old Robert Adam in 1758 for the interiors, although work on them did not begin until 1765. While the exterior was mostly Carr, the interiors were to be Adam's biggest single commission, albeit one wracked by arguments over cost and delay. Lascelles was not an easy man. Adam brought to the task his preferred team of Joseph Rose and William Collins for the plasterwork, Angelica Kauffmann, Antonio Zucchi and Biagio Rebecca for the decorative paintings. Furniture was to be exclusively by Chippendale and landscaping by Capability Brown. Harewood is a monument to them all.

Only a Victorian would have dared tamper with such work. But such was Lady Louisa Harewood, who summoned Sir Charles Barry in 1843 to add new attics and upset the delicate balance of Carr's exterior. Barry italianized the terrace façade to the rear and tampered with at least three of Adam's glorious rooms.

Harewood could take it. Entry is direct into Adam's Hall, its pillars and frieze recently painted in a colour rare in classical architecture, chocolate. In the middle is an acquisition by the present Lord Harewood, a giant Epstein of Adam. The statue was rescued from a Blackpool fun fair, to which 20th-century ridicule had consigned it. This primitive figure gazing up at his namesake's delicate ceiling might depict Beauty and the Beast. Gestures such as this, a rhythm of old and new throughout the house, give Harewood its character.

Adam's main reception rooms are charmingly interspersed with small galleries. The Old Library has one of his most serene ceilings, divided geometrically into panels filled with anthemion and other motifs, in greens and blues. Blank arches are filled with paintings or plasterwork of mythical scenes. Smaller rooms follow, including an apsidal chamber decorated by Sir Herbert Baker in 'Adam Revival' style. Closets have been converted into galleries for watercolours and modern art. Here are 20th-century works from Munnings to Piper.

Grandeur returns with Princess Mary's Sitting Room. The ceilings are now a bolder

Overleaf: Harewood's terrace front

Adam, with fans containing classical plaster reliefs. The room's three Adam-Chippendale masterpieces, a secretaire and two commodes, were to Sacheverell Sitwell 'among the greatest work of English craftsmanship' (although he said there was a better one at Renishaw/Derbys). Their decorative reliefs are of exquisite inlay. The Spanish Library displays the heavier hand of Barry. Solid bookcases now contrast with a lighthearted ceiling. In the New Library, really a saloon, we are back to Adam, the ceiling rising above a glorious coving of urn motifs dancing the length of the room.

Two further reception rooms, the Yellow and Cinnamon Drawing Rooms, show Adam at his most inventive. His ability to get teams of craftsmen to execute meticulous designs, while other clients were baying at his door, was astonishing. The Yellow Drawing Room has a Reynolds reflected in a Chippendale Rococo mirror and Chippendale furniture. The ceiling pattern is matched in the carpet. The Cinnamon Room contains portraits by Reynolds and Gainsborough.

The climax is yet to come. The Gallery at Harewood has an Adam ceiling but the walls and windows are by Barry. The walls are hung with one of the best private art collections in England. Old Masters by Bellini, Cima, Titian, Veronese and El Greco share pride of place with the view over the terrace to Capability Brown's landscape beyond.

The dining room and music room bring us back to the Hall. Almost as an afterthought, Adam leaves us with his music room, to some the most serene chamber in the house. Walls, ceiling and carpet all act as a frame for Reynolds' masterpiece, *Mrs Hale and her Children*.

HAWORTH: BRONTE PARSONAGE *

Haworth
Shrine to the writing sisters on moor's edge
(M)

England's most famous parsonage is now a shrine to the Brontë sisters, climax of the 'Haworth Experience'. The setting is remarkable. A village clings to the steep hillside outside Keighley. The shops are almost all dedicated to souvenirs. Visitors troop in their thousands up the hill towards the church. Some at least push further into the parsonage that inspired so much literary output.

Patrick Brontë came to Haworth in 1820 with his wife and six children. Two died, as did the wife, but Brontë outlived them all. Even before Charlotte, Emily and Anne had died, they were famous and Haworth was a place of pilgrimage. It is to this period, the 1850s, that the Brontë Society has restored the parsonage rooms.

The survival of the environs of the house is miraculous, with churchyard in front and open moor behind. On all but the sunniest of days this can seem a sombre spot. The interiors are those of a modest house of the late 18th century, with Georgian furniture and delicate fabrics and prints. Only in the dining room, where the girls did most of their writing, can we sense the industry of the place. The room contains the sofa on which Emily died.

Upstairs is all shrine. On the landing is a copy of the brother, Branwell Brontë's, celebrated portrait of the three girls. Patrick's bedroom is as he left it. Charlotte's own room is crowded with display cases, including one containing her tiny shoes. It is worthy, but does not come alive.

HUDDERSFIELD: LONGLEY OLD HALL **

Longley, 1½m SE of Huddersfield
Medieval house revealed inside Victorian shell
(P-R)

Longley is hidden away from central Huddersfield, through a characterless housing estate and down a cul-de-sac behind a row of cottages. A stone gable comes into view. The scene is unprepossessing. Yet the house has recently proved an architectural goldmine.

The Old Hall was owned by a prominent Huddersfield family, the Ramsdens, who in 1976 sold what they thought was a Jacobean house which had been much restored in